Few things free you to live your life more fully like a mobile phone.

Of course, a mobile is only as good as the network it's connected to. The better the network – the more freedom you'll enjoy. Connect to Cellnet and you'll have access to the most advanced range of business features and personal communications options available.

On Cellnet, for example, you can use your mobile to keep in touch while travelling abroad in 21 countries – with more to follow.

In the UK, you can use your mobile virtually anywhere.

What's more, with Cellnet Call Saver you can enjoy low cost flat rate local calls wherever in the UK you happen to be.

During the coming year, we shall be introducing many more innovative network features to help you make more of your mobile phone.

With all the mobile communications services you're ever likely to need, and simplified tariff selection, Cellnet makes it easier to enjoy the advantages – and the freedom – of owning a mobile phone.

In this guide, you'll find an introduction to Cellnet's tariffs and services. If you'd like further information contact your Service Provider or Dealer – or call...

0800 214000

Egon Ronay's Guides
35 Tadema Road
London SW10 0PZ

Consultant **Egon Ronay**
Editorial Director **Andrew Eliel**
Publishing Director **Angela Nicholson**
Sales & Marketing Director **Stephen Prendergast**

Chairman **Roy Ackerman**
Leading Guides Ltd
Part of the Richbell Group of Companies

Designed and typeset in Great Britain by Paul Fry, Bookman Projects Ltd.

First published 1995 by Bookman Projects Ltd
Floor 22
1 Canada Square
Canary Wharf
London E14 5AP

All restaurant and hotel inspections are anonymous and carried out by Egon Ronay's Guides' team of professional inspectors. Inspectors may reveal their identities at hotels in order to check all the rooms and other facilities. The Guide is independent in its editorial selection and does not accept advertising, payment or hospitality from listed establishments.

Egon Ronay's Guides Awards

Some of the winners are pictured here. Full details will be found on the pages indicated.

20 Cliveden
Hotel of the Year

22 The Seafood Restaurant, Padstow
Restaurant of the Year

24 Glyn Stevens
Chef of the Year

FULL CONTENTS, Page 4

EGON
RONAY'S
GUIDES

1996 AWARDS

CONTENTS

Welcome to the Egon Ronay's Cellnet Guide 1996 Hotels and Restaurants.

Recognised as the authoritative guide to hotels and restaurants throughout the UK, it offers impartial advice and information on a wide ranging selection of establishments to suit all tastes and pockets.

Just as the guide offers the customer a choice, so Cellnet shares the same values of putting its customers first and providing the products and services they want. We are dedicated to giving the best value and service, and as the UK cellular market continues to expand, we are continually upgrading and increasing the quantity and quality of our systems.

With over two million customers on our analogue service we are now concentrating on developing our digital service. The key benefits of digital are superb call quality, enhanced call security and the facility to use your mobile phone to make and take calls whilst travelling outside the UK.

Together, Cellnet and Egon Ronay's Hotel and Restaurant Guide are a winning combination for the business traveller, and I hope you will make the most of both of them.

Steve Rowley
General Manager, Cellnet

Monitoring the Cellnet network.

Cellnet's advanced mobile communications system is controlled from the Network Management Centre.

From here, Cellnet engineers keep a watchful eye over the entire network ensuring that potential problems are identified and rectified long before they can effect our service to customers.

NATIONAL COVERAGE

To make the most of your mobile phone, you need Cellnet, the network that offers truly national UK coverage – and links to the world beyond.

After all, if you can't use your mobile wherever life takes you – why have one at all?

COVERING 98% OFTHE

Cellnet is part of BT – the most advanced company in the telecommunications industry.

Since 1985, over £700 million has already been spent in developing our national network. By 1998, up to £700 million more will have been invested in sophisticated enhancements to Cellnet's digital service and expanding network coverage still further.

UK POPULATION

Today, Cellnet is one of the largest networks of its kind in the world, covering more than 98% of the UK population.

THE NET THAT SETS YOU FREE

for further information call
0800 214000

WHICH TARIFF?

Choosing the right tariff – the best combination of affordability and network features – is important if you're to get the best value from your mobile phone.

With Cellnet, choosing a tariff couldn't be simpler.

To identify the service best suited to your needs, all you have to do is decide how many calls you're likely to make.

It's as easy as ABC.

THE NET THAT SETS YOU FREE

 cellnet

for further information call
0800 214000

FREQUENT
CALLER PLUS

FOR CUSTOMERS MAKING OVER 30 MINUTES
OF CALLS A WEEK.

REGULAR
CALLER PLUS

BETWEEN 8 AND 30 MINUTES PER WEEK.

OCCASIONAL
CALLER

UP TO 7 MINUTES PER WEEK.

A, B or C. Choosing Cellnet,
is that easy.

Introduction
by Andrew Eliel
Restaurant trends

As predicted, the change from formal and expensive eating out has taken place, with free-and-easy and mid-price restaurants/brasseries/cafés now jostling those restaurants that aspired to great culinary heights in the mid-80s. Granted all the temples of gastronomy are still around (see our starred restaurant list), but today's emphasis is on good-quality cooking where an establishment can achieve a high turnover, keeping prices down. Restaurants are getting larger (is this the era of the 'super' restaurant?) – witness new 200/300-seaters such as Heathcote's Brasserie in Preston, The People's Palace and Belgo Centraal in London, with three more about to be launched Condou/Loubet's L'Odéon, Oliver Peyton's Coast and Sir Terence Conran's 700-seater Mezzo) as this Guide is published, and others in the pipeline. London already has several cavernous Chinese restaurants, Quaglino's, Planet Hollywood, the Hard Rock Café (the last two in our Just A Bite Guide) and the Atlantic Bar & Grill, so it begs the question who's going to fill all the seats.

Food trends

This year the vogue is for Caesar salad, risotto, salsa, scallops, pithiviers, cheap cuts of meat, confit de canard, offal, red mullet, tuna (in all forms), lemon grass sprouting out of control and tiramisu. And if these similarly-priced eateries are all going to serve the same dishes, how does the public decide which to choose? The answer is probably by theme, whether it be rock and pop, cinema, fashion or sport. Inevitably, gimmickry will replace quality; no longer will customers actually care or notice what they're eating, it will be the buzz and ambience that dictate where to go and, providing that the value-for-money and service are up to the mark, who's to say that the public should not vote with their feet? No restaurant has the divine right to expect custom, and by the same token no restaurant should assume entry in our Guides just because they're busy and successful. As ever, recognition by us is achieved on merit, with consistency an all-important factor. The catering and leisure industries are almost at one – for the most part nowadays we go out for a meal to spend time with family and friends (witness the massive expansion of family-friendly pub chains); sometimes on business; but how often on the spur of the moment when we're hungry?

Hotel restaurants

One place you would probably pass by is the hotel restaurant, and in most cases you would be right to do so (we recommend restaurants in less than 25% of our listed hotels). As it is, the public still feel slightly intimidated entering a hotel, so why is it that, in general, their restaurants/dining-rooms are so mediocre or downright shameful? While the decor and comfort levels are usually OK, and large kitchen brigades are in situ, the food served is more often than not simply awful and the staff, though abundant, are all too often unfriendly and robotic. Menus are either fashionable and beyond the ability of the kitchen or they are presented in dinosaur fashion, offering dishes of mouthwatering attraction such as soup of the day (often not known, slink off to the kitchen and ask), melon, Dover sole (probably frozen, over-baked and over-priced) and crème brulée from the trolley that's been sitting around too long. Here are just three examples from top London hotels (though we could have illustrated the point with dozens and dozens of inspectors' reports from around the country): "Attractive dining-room with intimate atmosphere. Gained good publicity from its opening launch, so much going for it. Unfortunately the chef can't cook (grey and ammonia-smelling sea bass served with limp and tired vegetables) and service is very slack, surprising since the manager came from an established and well-respected restaurant". Or, how about this: "Menu and food little changed from what is perhaps a foreigner's view of British cooking. No non-resident customers among the gathered throng of nine (including me) assembled in the large 60-seater dining-room". But perhaps worst of all: "Expensively-printed menus with blank spaces to fill in prices, so the kitchen is not governed by what's seasonally fresh and available from the markets. No table d'hote menus. Some skill and effort goes into lavish presentation (silver domes), but absolutely none into the cooking, which was so lacklustre and dull that even the waiters have become accustomed not to bother to ask if 'everything was alright' while clearing away practically untouched dishes".

Hotel prices

A major innovation over the last few years has been the burgeoning development of inexpensive chain hotels providing modest and practical accommodation built to a formula. Often called lodges, they are mostly situated at motorway service areas or on major roads and, though the facilities are quite basic, they offer a competitive alternative to often over-priced, middle-range hotels. Service is virtually non-existent, but then it leaves a lot to be desired at many hotels charging two or three times the price for a room. How often are you escorted to your room or have your bags carried? When was the last occasion that room service breakfast was delivered on time, or you didn't have to serve yourself a buffet breakfast in the dining-room/restaurant? Always be suspicious of the words "for your convenience" – inevitably this means a (non) service that it is for a hotel's convenience, not yours! Why shouldn't we expect high standards of quality and service at the lower end of the market? The hospitality industry is, after all, a service industry.

The reality is that hotel prices have hardly risen in the last two or three years, though they are beginning to creep higher, and if the advent of these lodges keeps all prices down, we really should not complain. Nearly every hotel offers some sort of deal, especially at weekends, so it always pays to ask and avoid paying the standard (or rack) rate, but don't get taken in by seemingly good-value half-board terms where you are obliged to eat in a mediocre restaurant. Rather than relying on incoming tourists, hoteliers should concentrate on attracting the home market by charging more realistic prices – the customers are there, with increased leisure time, get them in (and serve them good food), or else they will continue to holiday abroad at half the cost.

Wine list mark-ups must come down

Not being a major wine producer, this country is not obliged to promote its own product and as a result our restaurateurs have developed probably the most diverse wine lists in the world. With so many specialist retailers and knowledgeable wine merchants to advise them, they also have access to the best wines, historically from France, increasingly from the New World.

See over

Around a thousand lists pass through our hands every year, so we are in a perfect position to comment on trends, quality and prices, the latter causing us most concern, since the restaurant customer is paying far too much for the product, whether it's a *premier grand cru* or a humbler house wine. Mark-ups must come down. When you see the same wine of the same vintage with a £600 price differential between two restaurants, someone's pulling a fast one!

Of course, there are exceptions, not least the wine lists prepared by John Hoskins MW for his own group of East Anglian establishments and the Arcadian Hotels group. These lists, worthy recipients of our Cellar(s) of the Year award, adopt a sensible pricing policy: the more expensive wines attract a lower percentage mark-up, with fair mark-ups on cheaper wines, not to mention plenty of half bottles, good bin ends and a dozen or so available by the glass. Wine lists should be balanced both in depth and in price, certainly equating to the prices charged for food, so if you're paying, say, £40 for two for a meal, a really good bottle of wine should cost no more than half that sum. Similarly, why are we paying so much for champagne in restaurants? *Grandes marques* that will cost you between £15 and £20 in an off-licence or supermarket are rarely priced at less than double – consider anything under £30 on a list as an absolute bargain. Accepting that a certain profit margin has to be made, sometimes the justification for a high mark-up is that the diner is buying not just a bottle but the restaurant's expertise in selecting, storing etc. How then do you explain the even greedier mark-ups on bottled water? What expertise is on tap there?

Chef of the Year

For several years we have been running our Chef of the Year competition (see pages 24-27) in association with the Meat & Livestock Commission. Their aim is to promote British meat, since quality of produce is one the first requirements of good dishes in a restaurant, allied to talent in the kitchen. Around the UK chefs are chosen to represent their regions by our own team of inspectors, based on their first-hand knowledge of the restaurants they have visited. This year, and in future years, we invite the previous year's runner-up to participate, the winner to assist in the judging, alongside Catey Hillier, Editor of *Chef* in the Caterer & Hotelkeeper magazine, Derek Andrews of MLC and me.

And finally . . .

Egon Ronay's Guides lead the way, and are delighted to be linked with these like-minded companies: our title sponsor Cellnet, National Britannia, Ilchester Cheese and the Scotch Beef Club, launched by the Scotch Quality Beef and Lamb Association to promote awareness of the special qualities of Scotch beef. Scotland is justifiably proud of the reputation of its beef industry and only the finest, genuine Scotch beef is served in Scotch Beef Club member establishments. Originally started in Italy, the Scotch Beef Club has grown rapidly in key European countries. Look out for the Black Bull symbol which identifies members of the Scotch Beef Club recommended by this Guide. This year we are pleased to welcome Wines of Italy, whose superb wines have always featured prominently on the best wine lists, and this trend is set to grow as awareness of the D.O.C and D.O.C.G. classification systems increases among consumers. We also lead the way to Ireland, and have, since 1994, annually produced Egon Ronay's *Jameson* Guide Ireland, so the Republic of Ireland no longer appears in this Guide, though Northern Ireland, being part of the United Kingdom, remains.

We welcome bona fide letters of praise and complaint, but urge you to complain to us only as a last resort, always reminding you to take up your complaint with the management at the time, not with us several weeks or months later.

Let's hope you receive more satisfaction than one of our readers, the recipient of probably the most arrogant reply we've seen this year. Having spent £1,000 for three persons over three days, and following a legitimate complaint about the quality of food served over Christmas, he received a letter from the hotel manager, containing the following sentence: "we did have problems in the kitchen during Christmas, in the sense that we were unable to employ a head chef and our sous chef was off sick following a motor accident. However, we did have a full complement of staff in the kitchen, as we utilised the services of a chef agency. You will appreciate that the head chef and the sous chef are the two key members of staff in a kitchen and the fact that they had not previously worked together, we do believe that possibly the food was not up to our usual standard". And, the compensation offered? "When you, or any other members of your party, return to our hotel we will arrange for a bottle of champagne to be placed in your room, with our compliments". (Editor's note – would you go back?). Not unreasonably, our reader felt this offer of compensation somewhat derisory, and said so, and he received this response: "I am most surprised at your displeasure on my offer of a complimentary bottle of champagne to be placed in your bedroom, to you, or any other members of your party, on your return to our hotel". The hotel manager ended the letter thus: "Bearing in mind that throughout your stay, with a party of seven people, you had cause for complaint for three meals, I find your comment that our offer of a complimentary bottle of champagne, which retails at £20 per bottle, to you, or any other members of your party, on your return to our hotel is derisory, to be offensive. If, when you have a packet of crisps and you find a 'rotten' crisp in there, do you then expect the crisp manufacturer to send you a box of crisps?"

EGON
RONAY'S
GUIDES
1996

How to Use This Guide

As well as our recommended establishments this Guide includes many interesting features and useful quick reference lists and tables designed to help you select the hotel or restaurant that best suits your requirements. Detailed maps and lists of hotels and restaurants by county, with key statistics, prices and features, will allow you to see at a glance what is available in the area where you intend to stay. Conference and banqueting capacities are included – a boon to organisers of business meetings or functions; sports facilities are also highlighted. For details of all listings consult the contents pages.

Order of Entries

London appears first, in alphabetical order by **establishment name**. Entries outside London are in alphabetical order by **location** within divisions of England, Scotland, Wales, Channel Islands, Isle of Man and Northern Ireland. See contents page for specific page numbers, and the index for individual entries.

Map References

Map references alongside each hotel or restaurant entry are to the map section at the back of the book. Use the map section in conjunction with the county lists to select establishments in areas you wish to visit.

Hotels

Hotel entries are identified by the letter '**H**'. The Percentage shown on a hotel entry is an individual rating arrived at after careful testing, inspection and calculation according to our unique grading system. Hotels that achieve a grading of 80% or over are classified as De Luxe and are listed separately on page 19.

We assess hotels on 23 factors, which include the quality of service and the public rooms – their cleanliness, comfort, state of repair and general impression. Bedrooms are looked at for size, comfort, cleanliness and decor. The exterior of the building, efficiency of reception, conduct and appearance of the staff, room service and leisure facilities are among other factors. The percentage is arrived at by comparing the total marks given for the 23 factors with the maximum the hotel could have achieved.

The size of a hotel and the prices charged are not considered in the grading, but the food is, and if we recommend meals in a hotel a separate entry is made for its restaurant. Only hotels where we recommend the restaurant food are categorised as '**HR**'. There is thus a very important distinction between '**H**' and '**HR**' entries.

'**B**' is the letter used for hotels (mainly in London), offering fairly basic facilities at generally budget prices. These hotels are ungraded. The category of chain hotels, built and run to a formula and offering cheap, practical accommodation and not much else, is denoted by the letter '**L**'. These lodges (ungraded) are not included in the gazetteer section of the Guide, but their locations and other details will be found in the county lists at the back of the book.

Certain other hotels are ungraded. These include private house hotels ('**PH**'), which are often de luxe 'bed and breakfast' hotels offering comfortable, often luxurious accommodation and personal service, but do not have a public restaurant or public rooms – although some have a drawing room. Also ungraded are hotels undergoing major construction or refurbishment programmes at the time of research, and those which opened too late for the fullest inspection.

Inns, identified by the letter '**I**', are also ungraded, being distinguished from hotels proper by their more modest nature, usually with respect to the day rooms. For our purposes an inn is normally either a pub with hotel-style accommodation or a small hotel with a bar and the atmosphere of a pub.

Prices

These are based on current high-season rates at the time of going to press and include VAT (also service if applicable), for a *double room for two occupants with private bath and cooked breakfast.*

Bargain breaks. Almost all hotels now offer bargain breaks of some kind. Specific details regarding the availability and price of such breaks should be checked with individual establishments. In addition to bargain breaks many hotels continue to offer price reductions more or less across the board. Phone the hotels in the area you're visiting and see what they have to offer. Don't be swayed by half-board terms offered in hotels where we don't recommend the restaurant.

Wheelchair access.Consult the round-up section at the back of this Guide for hotels with facilities for disabled guests.

Restaurants

Restaurants are identified by the letter '**R**'. We award one to three stars (★ ★★ ★★★) for excellence of cooking. One star represents cooking much above average, two outstanding cooking, and three the best in the land.

↑ beside stars indicates a restaurant at the top of its star range.

↑ by itself indicates a restaurant approaching star status.

The symbol '**RR**' denotes a restaurant with rooms, a category based on restaurants avec chambres in France. Food is the main attraction, but overnight accommodation is also available. Details of these establishments may be found within the County Listings at the back of the Guide.

We only include restaurants where the cooking comes up to our minimum standards, however attractive the place may be in other respects. We take into account how well the restaurant achieves what it sets out to do, reflected in the menu, decor, prices, publicity, atmosphere – factors that add up to some sort of expectation.

Symbols

Crowns are awarded to restaurants offering a degree of traditional luxury 👑 or some striking modern features 👑. They have nothing to do with the quality of the cooking.

   This symbol represents a wine list that is outstanding.

   Signifies a wine list featuring a wide choice of (good-quality) New World wines.

   Signifies a restaurant serving a selection of good-quality wines by the glass.

   Signifies a restaurant serving a good choice of Italian wines (sponsored by Wines of Italy).

   Signifies a restaurant serving notable desserts.

   Signifies a restaurant serving good British cheeses (sponsored by the Ilchester Cheese Company Ltd).

   Signifies that Sunday lunch (often including a traditional roast) is offered in a recommended restaurant.

   Signifies a restaurant offering a separate vegetarian menu, or a reasonable choice of vegetarian main courses.

   Indicates that the establishment is a member of the Scotch Beef Club.

Restaurant prices, correct at the time of going to press, are for a three-course meal for two including one of the least expensive bottles of wine, coffee, service and VAT. The total is generally rounded up to the nearest £5.

Set-price menus. Prices quoted will often not include coffee or service and usually exclude wine. They are not necessarily of three courses. Where two prices are given thus – £14.50/£17.75 – it indicates that there is a 2 or 3-course option; prices given thus – £17.95 & £24.95 – indicates that there are two different set-price menus. A great number of restaurants now only offer a set-price menu (although this will usually include a choice).

Starred Restaurants

London ★★★

Chez Nico at Ninety Park Lane **W1**
Le Gavroche **W1**
Restaurant Marco Pierre White **SW1**
Les Saveurs **W1**
La Tante Claire **SW3**

England ★★★

Bray-on-Thames The Waterside Inn
Great Milton Le Manoir aux
    Quat'Saisons
Shinfield L'Ortolan

Scotland ★★★

Ullapool Altnaharrie Inn

London ★★

Inter-Continental London **W1** †

Alastair Little **W1**
Aubergine **SW10**
The Capital **SW3**
The Connaught **W1**
Dorchester: Terrace Restaurant **W1**
Four Seasons Hotel: Four Seasons
    Restaurant **W1**
Pied à Terre **W1**

England ★★

Baslow Fischer's Baslow Hall
Dartmouth Carved Angel
Hambleton Hambleton Hall
Longridge Paul Heathcote's
    Restaurant
Ridgeway Old Vicarage
Winteringham Winteringham
    Fields

London ★

The Halkin **SW1** †
Hilaire **SW7** †
Nico Central **W1** †
The Square **SW1** †

London ★ (continued)

Al San Vincenzo **W2**
Bibendum **SW3**
Bistrot Bruno **W1**
Blakes Hotel **SW7**
Bombay Brasserie **SW7**
Café Royal Grill Room **W1**
Chinon **W14**
Clarke's **W8**
Fung Shing **WC2**
The Halcyon **W11**
The Ivy **WC2**
Kensington Place **W8**
The Lanesborough **SW1**
Le Meridien: Oak Room **W1**
Ming **W1**
Museum Street Café **WC1**
Neal Street Restaurant **WC2**
Panda Si Chuen **W1**
The Savoy: Grill Room **WC2**
The Savoy: River Restaurant **WC2**
Simply Nico **SW1**
Le Suquet **SW3**
Tatsuso **EC2**

England ★

Bath Royal Crescent Hotel †
Gillingham Stock Hill House †
Grasmere Michael's Nook †
Ludlow Merchant House †
Newcastle-u-Tyne 21 Queen Street †
Padstow The Seafood Restaurant †
Staddlebridge McCoy's †
Taunton Castle Hotel †
Waterhouses Old Beams †

Bradford Restaurant 19
Bristol Restaurant Lettonie
Brockenhurst Le Poussin
Bury Normandie Hotel & Restaurant
Chagford Gidleigh Park
Cheltenham Le Champignon
    Sauvage
Chester Chester Grosvenor
Great Gonerby Harry's Place
Grimston Congham Hall

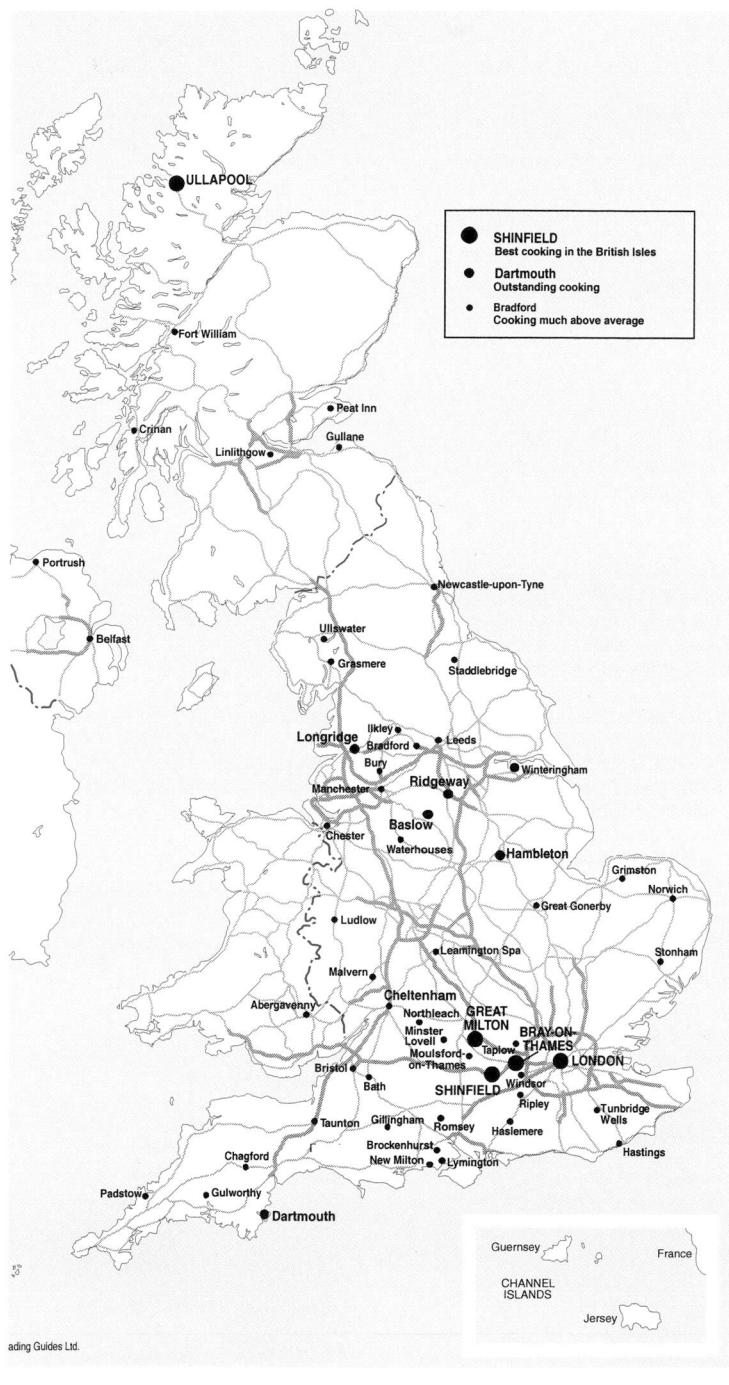

ULLAPOOL

SHINFIELD
Best cooking in the British Isles

Dartmouth
Outstanding cooking

Bradford
Cooking much above average

Fort William

Peat Inn

Crinan
Linlithgow
Gullane

Portrush

Belfast
Newcastle-upon-Tyne

Ullswater

Grasmere
Staddlebridge

Ilkley
Longridge   Bradford   Leeds
Bury   Winteringham
Manchester   Ridgeway

Chester   Baslow
Waterhouses   Hambleton

Grimston
Norwich

Ludlow   Great Gonerby
Stonham

Malvern   Leamington Spa

Abergavenny   Cheltenham
Northleach   GREAT
Minster   MILTON   BRAY-ON-
Lovell   Taplow   THAMES
Bristol   Moulsford-   LONDON
on-Thames
Bath   SHINFIELD   Windsor
Taunton   Gillingham   Ripley   Tunbridge
Romsey   Haslemere   Wells
Chagford   Brockenhurst,   Hastings
New Milton   Lymington
Padstow   Gulworthy
Dartmouth

Guernsey   France

CHANNEL
ISLANDS   Jersey

ading Guides Ltd.

Starred Restaurants (cont)

Gulworthy The Horn of Plenty
Haslemere Fleur de Sel
Hastings Roser's Restaurant
Ilkley Box Tree
Leamington Spa Mallory Court
Leeds Pool Court at 42
Lymington Gordleton Mill
Malvern Croque-en-Bouche
Manchester Yang Sing
Minster Lovell Lovells at Windrush
    Farm
Moulsford-on-Thames Beetle &
    Wedge
New Milton Chewton Glen
Northleach Old Woolhouse
Norwich Adlard's
Ripley Michels'
Romsey Old Manor House
Stonham Mr Underhill's
Taplow Cliveden: Waldo's
    Restaurant
Tunbridge Wells Thackeray's House
Ullswater Sharrow Bay

Scotland ★

Peat Inn The Peat Inn †

Crinan Crinan Hotel
Fort William Inverlochy Castle
Gullane La Potinière
Linlithgow Champany Inn

Wales ★

Abergavenny Walnut Tree Inn

N Ireland ★

Belfast Roscoff
Portrush Ramore

London †

L'Accento Italiano **W2**
Albero & Grana **SW3**
Avenue West Eleven **W11**
Bistrot 190 **SW7**
Le Caprice **SW1**
Chez Max **SW10**
Chutney Mary **SW10**
Del Buongustaio **SW15**
dell'Ugo **W1**
Dorchester: Oriental Room **W1**

Downstairs at 190 **SW7**
The Eagle **EC1**
L'Escargot **W1**
Euphorium **N1**
Fulham Road **SW3**
Greenhouse **W1**
Hyatt Carlton Tower: Chelsea Room
    SW1
Langan's Brasserie **W1**
Launceston Place **W8**
Mijanou **SW1**
192 **W11**
Le Pont de la Tour **SE1**
The Ritz **W1**
Shampan **E1**
Soho Soho **W1**
Turner's **SW3**

England †

Aston Clinton The Bell Inn
Bath Bath Spa Hotel
Bath Hole in the Wall
Brimfield Poppies Restaurant
Christchurch Splinters
Goring-on-Thames The Leatherne
    Bottel
Hunstrete Hunstrete House
Keyston Pheasant Inn
Langho Northcote Manor
Leeds Brasserie Forty Four
Melbourn Pink Geranium
Moulsford-on-Thames Beetle
    & Wedge: The Boathouse
New Barnet Mims Restaurant
Nottingham Sonny's
Oxford Restaurant Elizabeth
Ponteland Café 21
Ston Easton Ston Easton Park
Torquay Table Restaurant
Turners Hill Alexander House

Scotland †

Aberfoyle Braeval
Dunkeld Kinnaird
Edinburgh The Atrium
Edinburgh The Balmoral Hotel
Glasgow Puppet Theatre

Channel Islands †

Gorey Jersey Pottery Garden

N Ireland †

Bangor Shanks
Helen's Bay Deanes on the Square

De Luxe Hotels

London

91%	The Connaught **W1**
	The Dorchester **W1**
	The Savoy **WC2**
89%	The Berkeley **SW1**
	Four Seasons Hotel **W1**
	The Lanesborough **SW1**
88%	Claridge's **W1**
87%	Hyatt Carlton Tower **SW1**
	The Regent London **NW1**
86%	Conrad International London **SW10**
	47 Park Street **W1**
	The Halkin **SW1**
	The Ritz **W1**
85%	The Capital **SW3**
84%	Churchill Inter-Continental Hotel **W1**
	Inter-Continental London **W1**
	Le Meridien **W1**
83%	Grosvenor House **W1**
	The Waldorf **WC2**
82%	Blakes Hotel **SW7**
	Hyde Park Hotel **SW1**
81%	The Athenaeum **W1**
	The Goring **SW1**
	Howard Hotel **WC2**
	May Fair Inter-Continental **W1**
80%	Dukes Hotel **SW1**

England

92%	**Taplow** Cliveden
89%	**New Milton** Chewton Glen
88%	**Ston Easton** Ston Easton Park
87%	**Bath** Bath Spa Hotel
	Stapleford Stapleford Park
86%	**Aylesbury** Hartwell House
	Great Milton Le Manoir aux Quat'Saisons
85%	**Thundridge** Hanbury Manor
84%	**Bath** Royal Crescent Hotel
	Chester Chester Grosvenor
	East Grinstead Gravetye Manor
	Hambleton Hambleton Hall

83%	**Colerne** Lucknam Park
	Torquay Imperial Hotel
	Woolton Hill Hollington House Hotel
82%	**Chagford** Gidleigh Park
	Hintlesham Hintlesham Hall
	Ullswater Sharrow Bay
81%	**Amberley** Amberley Castle
	Ashford Eastwell Manor
80%	**Broadway** Lygon Arms
	Buckland Buckland Manor
	Castle Combe Manor House
	Cheltenham The Greenway
	Leamington Spa Mallory Court
	Lower Slaughter Lower Slaughter Manor
	Nantwich Rookery Hall
	Sutton Coldfield New Hall
	Thornbury Thornbury Castle

Scotland

90%	**Fort William** Inverlochy Castle
86%	**Auchterarder** Gleneagles Hotel
84%	**Turnberry** Turnberry Hotel
83%	**Edinburgh** The Balmoral Hotel
82%	**Dunblane** Cromlix House
	Glasgow One Devonshire Gardens
	St Andrews St Andrews Old Course Hotel
81%	**Alexandria** Cameron House
	Dunkeld Kinnaird

Wales

81%	**Llyswen** Llangoed Hall

Channel Islands

80%	**St Saviour** Longueville Manor

Awards

Hotel of the Year

Cliveden
Taplow, Berkshire

O ne of the great country houses of England and in a most glorious setting, Cliveden became a hotel in 1986, since when it has proved beyond doubt that it's one of the finest, if not *the* finest, in the country. Combining a long and colourful history with up-to-date facilities and technology, the hotel offers the ultimate experience in luxury, with service that is both formal and courteous, entirely in keeping with the surroundings. Observe the magnificent Great Hall, the

superb 18th-century French Dining Room, the Nancy Astor bedroom which overlooks the Parterre, and the luxurious Pavilion Leisure complex, just some examples of a unique building meticulously restored and brilliantly converted to its present role.

CONGRATULATIONS TO THE RESTAURANT OF THE YEAR 1996

Awards

PAST WINNERS				
	1995	**The Halkin** London	**1990**	**Gidleigh Park** Chagford
	1994	**One Devonshire Gardens** Glasgow	**1989**	**The Savoy** London
	1993	**The Chester Grosvenor** Chester	**1988**	**Park Hotel** Kenmare
	1992	**The Dorchester** London	**1990**	**Homewood Park** Freshford
	1991	**Longueville Manor** St Saviour		

EGON RONAY'S GUIDES

Awards

Restaurant of the Year

The Seafood Restaurant
Padstow, Cornwall

Childhood memories brought Rick Stein back to Cornwall twenty years ago to open what has become Britain's most successful seafood restaurant. His parents retired here and his dad bought a lobster boat, so he has long been aware of the value of freshness, be it turbot or sea bass, the humbler mackerel, plaice and cod, or mussels and langoustines. The fishermen who land at Padstow deliver straight to the restaurant's kitchen, so you are assured of the freshest of catches. The style of cooking is basically natural, bringing out the full flavours of

the ingredients – a platter of steaming shellfish or, say, grilled plaice with a *beurre blanc*. The restaurant itself is relaxed, informal, cheerful, with charming staff and the added attraction of ten bedrooms overlooking the harbour.

CONGRATULATIONS TO THE
HOTEL OF THE YEAR 1996

Awards

PAST WINNERS				
	1995	**Fischer's Baslow Hall** Baslow	1991	**L'Ortolan** Shinfield
	1994	**Le Soufflé, Inter- Continental Hotel** London	1990	**Waterside Inn** Bray-on-Thames
			1989	**L'Arlequin** London
	1993	**The Carved Angel** Dartmouth	1988	**Morels** Haslemere
	1992	**Bibendum** London	1987	**Walnut Tree Inn** Abergavenny

EGON RONAY'S GUIDES

THE NET THAT SETS YOU FREE

The Recipe FOR SUCCESS

British meat continues to provide modern, creative and above all enjoyable recipes for our leading chefs and their customers.

The trend towards healthy eating has also highlighted the nutritional benefits of British meat, for example, lean, trimmed pork has less fat than plain cottage cheese. Red meat also contains many important vitamins and minerals and can play an important role in a healthy, balanced diet.

Derek Andrews
Catering Development
and Promotions Manager

Eating out is a special occasion whether it's a birthday, anniversary or a romantic valentines dinner for two. Enjoy British meat, your favourite 'Recipe for Love'.

Take six chefs, representing six outstanding restaurants known to the Guide for their consistency and high standards, ask them to

prepare a three course meal of their choice, with a main dish using British meat and leave it to four independent judges to decide on the winning menu.

Among the factors considered were menu balance, creativity, technical ability, quality of ingredients and, of course, flavours, taste and presentation. The overall standard was naturally impressive but a winner there had to be, and surprisingly perhaps, it was the youngest and probably least experienced who deservedly carried off the first prize: Glyn Stevens of Atrium Restaurant in Edinburgh. Congratulations to Glyn and to all the chefs who took part.

EGON RONAY'S GUIDES **and** BRITISH MEAT

PRESENT

The NINETEEN NINETY SIX

CHEF *of the* YEAR

COMPETITION

Glyn Stevens

*Atrium
Cambridge Street
Edinburgh*

David Everitt-Matthias

*Le Champignon-
Sauvage
Suffolk Road
Cheltenham*

Jean-Christophe Novelli

*Four Seasons
Restaurant
Hamilton Place
Park Lane
Mayfair*

Ian Watson

*Garden Room
Restaurant
St Tudno Hotel
The Promenade
Llandudno*

Peter Gorton

*The Horn
of Plenty
Gulworthy
Tavistock*

Simon Gueller

*Miller's,
The Bistro
1 Montpelier
Mews
Harrogate*

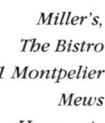

BRITISH
MEAT

The Recipe FOR PORK

Second placed chef David Everitt-Matthias produced an innovative and flavoursome main course of **Pavé of Wiltshire pork wrapped in caramelised onions with a Choucroute of beetroot.**

This was preceded by David's Charlotte of Cornish crab.

Warm pistachio tart, followed and was particularly well received by the judging panel.

Ian Watson achieved a creditable runner-up position with a second interesting and tasty British pork dish.

British pork and smoked bacon faggot cooked in a sweet Hereford cider sauce.

BRITISH
MEAT
Pork

The Recipe FOR LAMB

Peter Gorton and Simon Gueller both demonstrated their skills by preparing menus featuring the quality and versatility of British lamb.

Simon's **Cutlets of British lamb with roast sweetbreads, artichokes and parsley purée** was highly regarded.

Peter's **Roast best end of British lamb with a brioche herb crust on aubergine galette with candied shallot and garlic in a Madeira sauce** also scored well.
The three runners-up were awarded £500 of travel vouchers as runners-up.

BRITISH
MEAT
Lamb

The *Recipe* FOR *Beef*

This year's winner and **1996 Egon Ronay British Meat Chef of the Year** is Glyn Stevens. Glyn's combination of starter, British beef main course and dessert was a perfect balance of simplicity, quality and blend of flavours. £4,000 of travel vouchers and the coveted title are Glyn's to enjoy.

WINNER

Starter:
Grilled sea bass fillet with crab, salsa, couscous and frisée salad.

Main Course:
British beef fillet, lentils, peas and artichokes with provalone crumble.

Dessert:
Tart of blueberries with watermelon sorbet.

BRITISH MEAT

Beef

The *Recipe* FOR *Veal*

Jean-Christophe Novelli is regarded by many as one of London's finest chefs. In preparing British veal Jean-Christophe had a challenging task which was approached with his usual enthusiasm and creativity. **Roast fillet of British veal served with marrow bone, thin crispy carlos potatoes and baby turnips with red wine sauce was the excellent result.** Jean-Christophe's dessert was also highly regarded giving an overall third place.

PREVIOUS WINNERS

1992 - Marco Pierre White
1993 - Shaun Hill
1994 - Paul Heathcote
1995 - Nigel Haworth

BRITISH MEAT

Veal

Awards

Cellar(s) of the Year

John Hoskins MW
Huntsbridge Group

The award this year goes not to one wine list, but to several, in fact to the work of an individual: John Hoskins MW, who compiles the lists for his own Huntsbridge group, consisting of the Old Bridge at Huntingdon, The Pheasant at Keyston and Three Horseshoes at Madingley, as well as acting as a consultant to the Arcadian International Group of hotels and his uncle's George of Stamford. Indeed, The Old

Bridge at Huntingdon received our Cellar of the Year award in 1989, and it's encouraging to note that the quality of wines has been maintained and built upon in the ensuing years. John's lists are not necessarily long, usually numbering around a hundred or so bins, but they are always well balanced, offering a mixture of young and vintage wines from most wine-growing regions, a cross-section of established growers, names and lesser-known labels. Tasting notes are sensibly concise and informative, and, most importantly, wines are always keenly priced. Furthermore, there are plenty of half bottles and wines by the glass, but above all there is choice, so you can push the boat out and order a 1986 Le Montrachet from Jacques Gagnard (only one barrel a year is made) at £98, or spend a mere £1.85 on a glass of Shiraz-Cabernet/Sémillon-Chardonnay Aussie Kirkton Vale. So, experiment and enjoy!

Congratulations
from

Awards

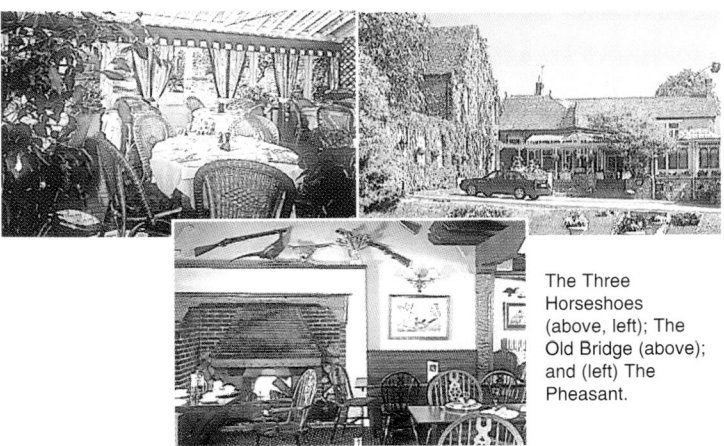

The Three Horseshoes (above, left); The Old Bridge (above); and (left) The Pheasant.

PAST WINNERS

1995	**The Manor** Chadlington		**1990**	**La Potinière** Gullane
1994	**Gravetye Manor** East Grinstead		**1989**	**Old Bridge Hotel** Huntingdon
1993	**Croque-en-Bouche** Malvern		**1988**	**Champany Inn** Linlithgow
1992	**The Cross** Kingussie		**1987**	**Au Jardin des Gourmets** London
1991	**White Horse Inn** Chilgrove			

Regional Winners pages 30-31

Awards

Cellar of the Year
Regional Winners

London
Fifth Floor at Harvey Nichols
London, SW1

A marvellously comprehensive wine list, the house selection (little list) alone numbers some fifty wines including own labels (eg Bourgogne Blanc Reserve Harvey Nichols £14.50), the majority under £20. The big list contains many great names from most regions.

Home Counties
Pink Geranium
Melbourn, Hertfordshire

France, with Leflaive dominant among the white burgundies (eg a 1992 Montagny 1er Cru at £20), is listed by region, whereas the New World is presented by grape variety, including the excellent 1992 Hamilton Russell Pinot Noir from South Africa at a not unreasonable £16.

South of England
Hotel du Vin & Bistro
Winchester, Hampshire

With such a name it's hardly surprising that the list here is a fine one, the work of joint-proprietor Gerard Basset, who has won a clutch of wine awards over the years. In addition to the cellar list (notable for lots of pudding wines), there's a daily selection of wines to match the menu, though is £6.50 for a glass of champagne in a bistro not just a weeny bit steep?

West Country
Riverside
Helford, Cornwall

A thoughtfully and expertly compiled list that represents very good examples from most regions, including an outstanding selection of half bottles. Champagne at a very reasonable £25, a 1991 Chablis Grand Cru Les Clos at just over £30 and 1988 Chateauneuf du Pape Clos des Papes offer excellent value.

Awards

Midlands/Heart of England
Old Vicarage
Worfield, Shropshire
An unpretentious yet impressive list of around two hundred bins (excluding some 100 half bottles) – large for a hotel of this size – demonstrating a good balance between Europe and the New World. Fair prices, for example a 1991 Condrieu from Georges Vernay at £32.50.

East of England
Adlard's
Norwich, Norfolk
This is a list to be proud of and rather bucks the system by placing French wines last, encouraging a dip elsewhere - perhaps among New World wines? Half bottles, including many fine growers, are also prominently and clearly presented. Good prices - a 1985 Louis Roederer Cristal champagne at £75 is hardly marked-up at all.

North of England
Sous le Nez en Ville
Leeds, West Yorkshire
A smashing and decently priced list (Krug champagnes are almost, but not quite, given away!) with both Spain and Italy showing well in Europe, and the New World well represented. Hard to decide what to choose – all pockets are catered for: a William Fèvre 1992 Chablis under £15, a 1986 Chablis Grand Cru Blanchots at £30.

Scotland
The Peat Inn
Peat Inn, Fife
The list is presented in an easy format with guidance notes on regions and occasionally on an individual wine. David Wilson is a wine enthusiast, which is reflected in the choices available, so it's well worth seeking advice if you can't make up your mind. Quite fair mark-ups encourage experiment.

Wales
Fairyhill
Reynoldston, West Glamorgan
A 1985 Louis Roederer Cristal champagne here is 50p cheaper than in Norwich (see above), setting the tone for this hotel's wine pricing policy – excellent value! A really well-balanced list, with even their own principality featured, also offers monthly recommendations, as well as a good choice under £15.

Awards

Dessert (s) of the Year

David Everitt-Matthias
Le Champignon Sauvage
Cheltenham, Gloucestershire

Refreshingly, and how important it is for a meal to end triumphantly, leaving you with abiding memories, the desserts here taste as good as they look. While they are artistically presented, they are by no means 'fussy' but all the better for it – what you see is what you get, a combination of contrasting ingredients (some quite unusual), flavours,

textures and colours. David has only a very small team in the kitchen, and it's important for his young chefs that his skills encompass all areas, so that they can learn and observe; many have already profited and gone on to become successful in their own kitchens – it is absolutely true that success breeds success.

Congratulations from

Awards

Left, Croustillant of mango with lime leaf and lemon grass cream with spiced red wine syrup.

Below, Hot pistachio tart with roasted strawberries and orange and liquorice sorbet.

Facing page:
Warm carrot cake with caramelised carrot sauce and crystallised carrot.

PAST WINNERS		
	1995	**Phil Vickery** The Castle, Taunton
	1994	**John Burton-Race** L'Ortolan, Shinfield
	1993	**Jean-Christophe Novelli** Le Provence, Lymington
	1992	**Roger Pizey** Harveys, London

Awards

British Cheeseboard of the Year

Harveys Restaurant
Bristol, Avon

The name of Harveys is perhaps best known for its association with the sherry, port and wine trade, but the restaurant also offers fine food, and chef Ramon Farthing sets great store by his excellent cheeseboard, which offers daily some dozen varieties of British farmhouse cheeses (many local). Typical examples are a particularly rich baby Stilton from Colston Bassett; the Scottish Shere, a raw cow's milk cheese with a washed rind, and an Isle of Avalon, a creamy unpasteurised cow's milk cheese with a wine-washed rind. The last two are both matured by James Aldridge in Sussex. Mary Holbrook, from nearby Timsbury, provides the Tymsboro' ash pyramid, an unpasteurised and creamy goat's milk cheese, while traditionalists will appreciate Montgomery's Cheddar, matured for well over a year, and made from unpasteurised milk from their own herd of Friesian/Holstein cows in North Cadbury, Somerset. Lovers of smoky cheeses will enjoy Chris Duckett's smoked Wedmore, also from Somerset, made from unpasteurised cow's milk, centred with chives and oak-smoked by James Aldridge (again!)

Congratulations
from

Ilchester

Awards

PAST WINNERS	1995	**Poppies Restaurant** Brimfield
	1994	**The Lygon Arms** Broadway
	1993	**Old Vicarage** Witherslack

Regional Winners page 36

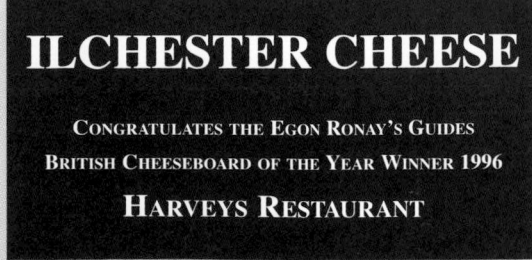

Awards

British Cheeseboard of the Year
Regional Winners

London – Grill Room The Dorchester London, W1

There's usually a choice of two dozen cheeses, some familiar, others less so, on the trolley, indeed the four-course evening menu features a cheese course. Choose perhaps the Camembert-style Bonchester made with the cream from Jersey cows on the Curtis farm in the Borders region, or the Gospel Green from Surrey, a full-flavoured creamy Cheddar/Cheshire type.

Home Counties – Sully's County Hotel Canterbury, Kent

Regularly appearing on the cheeseboard are Tornegus, a Caerphilly made in Surrey, soaked in Kentish wine; blues from Dunsyre in Lanarkshire and Harbourne, the latter unusually made from goat's milk; Olde York, a soft, unpasteurised cheese with added herb flavours, and an extra-mature 18-month-old Cheddar from Times Past Dairy in Bridgwater.

South of England – The Hungry Monk Jevington, East Sussex

Cornish Yarg, Shropshire Blue, Bonchester, oak-smoked Cheddar and Kevin Blunt's local Golden Cross (unpasteurised and creamy goat's cheese) are regularly available. Less well-known are an English-made parmesan-style Avanti and Flower-Marie, a soft white ewe's milk cheese also made by Kevin Blunt.

West Country – Priory Hotel Wareham, Dorset

Alongside, say, a mature farmhouse Cheddar, some unfamiliar names here: Belstone, a smooth unpasteurised cow's milk cheese in a natural rind from Devon; Tala, made from unpasteurised ewe's milk; Quantock Blue, a powerful soft cheese from ewe's milk.

East of England – Rumbles Cottage Felsted, Essex

Typical cheeses featured include several blues: Blue Vinney (unpasteurised cow's milk), or Beenleigh Blue from Ticklemore in Devon (available August-January, as the ewes are milked only from March-July) and Ticklemore itself, an unpasteurised goat's cheese.

Midlands/Heart of England – Bridge End Hayfield, Derbyshire

Hand-made cheeses from small farms: Jocelyn Townsend's Vulscombe from Devon, an unrenneted fresh and creamy curd cheese; Malvern from Nick Hodgetts, a slightly salted, pasteurised ewe's milk cheese; 12-month-old Somerset Cheddar.

North of England – Linthwaite House Bowness, Cumbria

A huge selection offered here: Beamish from Co Durham, a hard cow's milk cheese made in the museum (open to the public); Caprini's goat's cheese from Sussex; Mull of Kintyre Cheddar, surrounded by black wax; Cotherstone, from the Yorkshire Dales, made from full-fat unpasteurised cow's milk.

Scotland – Arisaig House Arisaig, Highland

Naturally, Scottish cheeses are to the fore here – Crottin (soft goat's cheese); Belle d'Ecosse or Bonchester White from the Curtis family's Jersey cows who also produce the Teviotdale, a full-fat hard cheese; Brodick Blue from the Isle of Arran, a blue-veined, unpasteurised ewe's milk cheese, and the Lanark Blue, made with the milk from a single flock of ewes.

Wales – Tyddyn Llan Llandrillo, Clwyd

Mainly Welsh cheeses, usually a selection of half a dozen or so: Pencarreg (full-fat soft pasteurised), Teifi (a slightly oaky Gouda-type cheese that's rich and creamy), St David (semi-soft, full-bodied), Caws Cenarth (a moist and almost creamy Caerphilly) and from just across the border Appleby's Cheshire.

Distinctive and delicious...
definitively Ilchester

Great British Cheeses

ILCHESTER CHEESE CO LTD
Ilchester, Somerset BA22 8LJ
Telephone: 01935 840531 Telex: 46639 Fax: 01935 841223

Awards

Host of the Year

Antonio Carluccio
Neal Street Restaurant, London

He's passionate about them and an acknowledged expert on them: mushrooms certainly play a major part in Antonio's life. At his longstanding Covent Garden restaurant they make regular appearances on the menu, perhaps in the guise of a wild mushroom soup or mixed sauté of funghi of the day. But there's more to the man than just mushrooms! He's an accomplished cook, a wonderful story-teller, engaging, generous, in short an Italian with a zest for life and boundless enthusiasm. Customers, whether in the restaurant or the shop next door, are treated as friends – and not surprisingly he has a host of them!

Congratulations
to Egon Ronay's Guides Host of the Year 1996
Antonio Carluccio

Awards

PAST WINNERS		
	1995	**Richard & Kate Smith** Beetle & Wedge, Moulsford
	1994	**Francis Coulson & Brian Sack** Sharrow Bay, Ullswater
	1993	**Peter & Nita Hauser** Stock Hill House, Gillingham
	1992	**Katherine & Frank Rendle** Woodhayes, Whimple

ROMBOUTS

is a well-established brand name within the fresh-ground coffee market. In 1996 it celebrates 100 years of providing its customers with both quality coffees and excellent service. ROMBOUTS, originators of the one-cup filter, has also developed a range of coffees suitable for all types of coffee-making equipment, including filter coffee machines and cafetières.

Awards

Newcomer of the Year

Hotel du Vin & Bistro
Winchester, Hampshire

The combined talents of Robin Hutson and Gerard Basset have reaped immediate rewards with the successful opening of their centrally located hotel. Robin's management experience and Gerard's wine knowledge have created a hotel of considerable charm, demonstrating

that it is possible to provide quality accommodation and food at a realistic price. Privately-run hotels such as this, and a handful of others around the country, surely point the way to the future, by offering a creative and competitive alternative to the chain product. There is no substitute for excellence – here you are looked after with just the right amount of deference in a relaxing and very civilised atmosphere.

Congratulations from

EGON
RONAY'S
GUIDES
1996

Awards

Awards

Kitchen of the Year

Winteringham Fields
Winteringham, Humberside

Germain Schwab's new kitchens are proving as popular a draw as his enticing menus – every night customers ask to be taken on guided tours! The new areas consist of main kitchen, pastry kitchen, cold starters section and dish wash area, all connected by an intercom system. All sections (each with its own sink and lever taps) have independent fridges for meat, fish, dairy, cheese and desserts, and there's a large walk-in cold store for general use. All the equipment in the main kitchen is stainless steel with a mains gas Bonnet stove the centrepiece. Walls are cladded from floor to ceiling, floors are covered by non-slip quarry tiles, windows PVC double-glazed with internal fly-screens. There are two separate ventilation systems; one over the charcoal grill and salamander, the other over the stove. The pastry kitchen, some ten feet away from the main kitchen, uses an induction method of cooking, has a convection oven, bench fridge with cool top and an upright freezer. The total cost was well into six figures, but the investment has already paid rich dividends, and will doubtless continue to do so.

Awards

PAST WINNER	
1995	**Cliveden**
	Taplow

NATIONAL BRITANNIA

**CONGRATULATES THE EGON RONAY'S GUIDES
KITCHEN OF THE YEAR WINNER 1996,**

WINTERINGHAM FIELDS

In good
health and.......

The Britannia Food Safety & Hygiene Award

Valid for one year, the Britannia Food Safety & Hygiene Award demonstrates and acknowledges high standards of food safety and hygiene (the award certificate may be removed should standards fall below the level required).

1995 Britannia Food Safety & Hygiene Award holders include:-

Alexandra Hotel, Pound Street, Lyme Regis
The Ancient Raj, 9 The Parade, Frimley
Cafe Rouge, Canary Wharf, London, E14
Claygate Tandoori, The Parade, Claygate, Surrey
Cliveden, Taplow, Berkshire
Corkers Restaurant & Cafe Bar, 1 High Street, Poole, Dorset
Cornish Arms, Pendoggett, Port Isaac, Cornwall
Derwentwater Hotel, Portinscale, Keswick, Cumbria
The Dorchester Hotel, Park Lane, London, W1A
Dumbleton Hall, Evesham, Worcestershire
Brighton Hydro Hotel, 465 South Promenade, Blackpool
Ednam House Hotel, Bridge Street, Kelso, Roxburghshire
Fairwater Head Hotel, Hawkeschurch, Axminster, Devon
Farleyer House Hotel, Aberfeldy, Perthshire
Friars Carse, Auldgirth, Dumfries
The Gonville Hotel, Gonville Place, Cambridge
Hook Tandoori, 1 Fairholme Parade, Hook, Basingstoke
The Knife & Cleaver, The Grove, Houghton Conquest, Bedford
Mr Kuet Chinese Takeaway, 3 Fairmead Road, Saltash, Cornwall
La Capannina, 24 Romilly Street, London, W1
Lloyds of London, 1 Lime Street, London, EC3M
Langstone Cliff Hotel, Dawlish Warren, Devon
Lucullus Seafood Restaurant, 48 Knightsbridge, London, SW1
MEPC (UK) Ltd, 12 St James's Square, London, SW1Y
Oatlands Park Hotel, Oatlands Drive, Weybridge
Old Watch Restaurant, 14 The Square, St Mawes, Cornwall
Nobody Inn, Doddiscombsleigh, Exeter, Devon
Poissonnerie De L'Avenue, 52 Sloane Avenue, London, SW3
Saqui Tandoori, 317 Richmond Road, Kingston-upon-Thames
Serena Restaurant, 12 St Peters Street, Huddersfield
Splinters, 12 Church Street, Christchurch, Dorset
Tontine Hotel, 6 Ardgowan Square, Greenock
Whatley Manor Hotel, Easton Grey, Malmesbury, Wiltshire
Waterhead Hotel, Coniston, Cumbria

...in safe hands

Environmental Hygiene and Safety Services
available from National Britannia

Food Safety

Response*line*
The National Britannia Environmental Information Service

Training

Pest Prevention

Fly Control

Bird Proofing

Health and Safety

Consultancy and Inspection

Water Tank Maintenance

NATIONAL
BRITANNIA

**Environmental Hygiene
and Safety Specialists**

For further information, contact
Caroline Owen on 01222 852000

Specially Selected Scotch Beef

The True Taste Of Quality

Scotland's world-wide reputation for producing prime beef cattle owes much to nature. Favoured with the ideal stock-rearing conditions of a temperate climate, an abundance of grass and pure water, and vast tracts of unspoiled countryside, generations of Scottish farmers have used their skills to produce beef for the discerning tables of the world.

300 Years Of Tradition And Development

As far back as the 17th century, the beef from Scottish cattle was in demand, and each year tens of thousands were exported
- on foot - to eager English markets.
A century later agricultural improvements enabled whole herds to be fed through the winters, and attention was then turned to improving native cattle breeds. The result, by the early 19th century, was beef breeds which were to become renowned throughout the world.
Until the 19th century Scotch beef cattle continued to be walked to markets in the south, but the introduction of steam navigation, then railways, brought the cattle droving tradition of generations to an end. Prime Scotch beef could now travel to London in peak condition, and the modern meat industry began.
Now, one hundred years on, fleets of refrigerated vehicles daily transport Specially Selected Scotch Beef to markets throughout the UK and continental Europe.

REPUTATION FOR EXCELLENCE

Like other products with a reputation for excellence - such as vintage red wine and famous malt whiskies - it takes time and skill to produce Specially Selected Scotch Beef. Generations of experience in cattle rearing, backed by the quality assurance schemes of today, means that Specially Selected Scotch Beef is produced to the highest farming standards throughout. The Scotch meat  industry has its own expertise, and Specially Selected Scotch Beef is matured in the traditional, time-honoured way to maximise the flavour and tenderness for which it is world renowned.

EUROPEAN QUALITY BEEF

The EC recognises the contribution of the Scottish meat industry in setting standards of quality. The use of the European Quality Beef logo signifies that strict EC standards for quality control and product traceability from farm to consumer have been adhered to - further enhancing the reputation of Specially Selected Scotch Beef for consistent product quality.

A WHOLE NEW EATING EXPERIENCE

Specially Selected Scotch Beef is recognised as a popular choice for caterers around the world and many top class restaurants have enhanced their reputations with the quality of the Scotch beef they serve.

For the true taste of quality and a whole new eating experience, discover the flavour and tenderness of Specially Selected Scotch Beef at one of the many Scotch Beef Club restaurants, highlighted throughout this Guide.

This advertorial is partially funded by the EC.

WELCOME TO THE SCOTCH BEEF CLUB

An elite club with over 600 members throughout the UK and continental Europe - each one a distinguished restaurant with an international reputation for excellence.

This Guide, recognised for the quality of its listed establishments and an indispensable aid to the discerning diner, features many of the Scotch Beef Club members.

Chefs demand exacting standards of quality in the beef they buy. Scotch Beef Club members purchase not only one of the world's finest meat products, but a true taste of quality.

This, together with their culinary expertise produces Specially Selected Scotch Beef dishes that enhance their international reputations and confirms their listing in the Guide.

D.S. Cameron

"At Turnberry we cater for the most discerning of both national and international clientele, and are proud to feature the finest of Scotch beef throughout the hotel's three restaurants. The Scotch Beef Club ensures that the highest standards are constantly maintained and protected for the future. Turnberry Hotel is proud to be a founder member of this prestigious Club".

**D.S. Cameron,
Executive Chef de Cuisine,
Turnberry Hotel.**

Look for the Black Bull symbol to identify members of the Scotch Beef Club.

So whether you favour a succulent steak, a tender roast or a more exotic international recipe, visit a Scotch Beef Club member and experience the flavour and tenderness of Specially Selected Scotch Beef for yourself.

The Scotch Beef Club operates in Belgium, France, Germany, Great Britain, Holland, Italy and Spain - and each member restaurant is identified by a distinctive door sticker or plaque.

For a full list of all Scotch Beef Club members, please contact the Scotch Quality Beef and Lamb Association on

0131•333 5335

or write to: **Scotch Quality Beef and Lamb Association, Rural Centre, West Mains, Ingliston, Newbridge, Midlothian EH28 8NZ, Scotland.**

ONE SIGN YOU SHOULD LOOK OUT FOR IN
1996

There's no better accompaniment to a good meal than a glass or two of fine Italian wine. But how can you find a restaurant that's certain to have a superior selection of Italian wines?

Easy. Look for this sticker in the restaurant's window. It means that an inspector from "Egon Ronay's Cellnet Guide 1996 Hotels & Restaurants" will have assessed the wine list and will have been sufficiently impressed with both the quality and selection of Italian wines to have awarded this prestigious mark of quality.

It's your guarantee of fine wine — and a sign which really is worth seeking out.

VINO

THE QUALITY OF LIFE.

EGON RONAY'S
CELLNET GUIDE 1996
HOTELS & RESTAURANTS
19
96
SUPERIOR
ITALIAN WINE LIST
EGON
RONAY'S
GUIDES

Your **Guarantee** of
Quality and **Independence**

- Establishment inspections are anonymous
- Inspections are undertaken by qualified Egon Ronay's Guides inspectors
- The Guides are completely independent in their editorial selection
- The Guides do not accept advertising, hospitality or payment from listed establishments

Titles planned for 1996 include

Hotels & Restaurants ● Pubs & Inns ● Europe
Ireland ● Just A Bite
And Children Come Too ● Paris
Oriental Restaurants

Gourmet Crossword Competition, 1995

There was a strong entry for the £2,500 *Egon Ronay's Cellnet Guide 1995* Competition. The winning prize included a Motorola GSM pocket phone, plus free connection to Cellnet's *Primetime Plus* service, a year's free rental plus £250-worth of free calls. From Martell, the winner also received an all-expenses-paid two-night trip for two to the Chateau de Chanteloup, including a tour of the production facilities and a cognac tasting. Our winner was:

Neville Benke, of Thames Ditton, Surrey.

Congratulations!

The solution was:

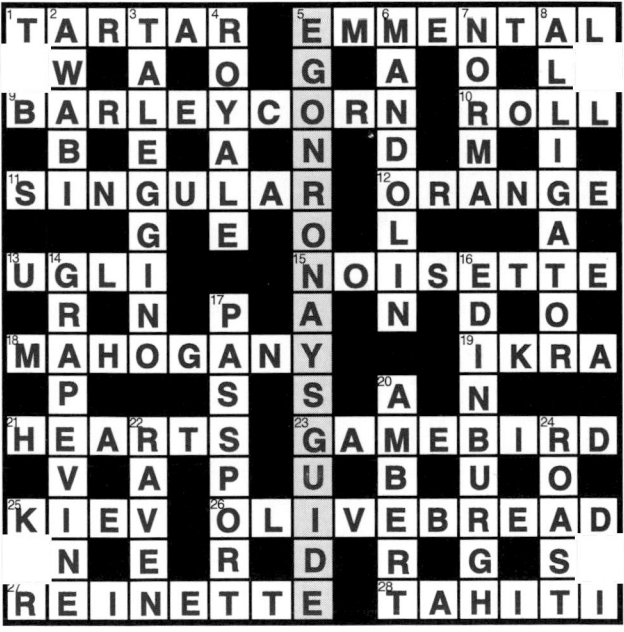

CELLNET

BUSINESS INFORMATION

MOBILE DATA

WHEN IT'S NEEDED

COMMUNICATIONS

WHEREVER IT'S NEEDED

Providing the fastest direct link between people in the field and head office – between their lap-top terminals and your host computer or desktop PCs – Cellnet offers an unrivalled mobile data service.

Data can be sent or received reliably and securely while you're on the move, and transmitted continuously for as long as needed.

Sending data over Cellnet Digital has many advantages:

- enhanced data integrity
- complete protection from electronic eavesdropping
- international data transmission while travelling abroad
- access to UK digital information networks

Cellnet. Your best choice – now and for the future

Whether you are seeking to secure a competitive advantage today, or to protect your investment in mobile communications in the years ahead, you'll find Cellnet unrivalled in its commitment to the continuous development of advanced, reliable and cost effective business services.

THE NET THAT SETS YOU FREE

for further information call
0800 214000

MANAGING

MORE EFFICIENTLY

YOUR COMPANY

MORE COST-EFFECTIVELY

MOBILES

MORE EASILY

Ensuring that the mobile phone's potential for enhanced efficiency and personal productivity is fully realised, that costs are controlled, and that the purchasing power of telecoms budgets is maximised, are key imperatives.

To assist Comms Managers in these tasks, Cellnet is continuously developing more cost-effective links between the network and its corporate customers (by avoiding the need to use public networks and offering highly competitive business rates).

We're working on faster direct links between your people in the field and head office, too. And introducing ever more sophisticated techniques and powerful tools for managing and monitoring your mobiles.

With Cellnet's help, your organisation can not only contain the cost of mobile business communications but also maximise its telecomms budget – cutting airtime spend by up to 40% – and thereby, perhaps extending the service (and hence productivity gains) to other members of the workforce.

THE NET THAT SETS YOU FREE

for further information call

0800 214000

THE REVOLUTIONARY WAY

CELLNET

TO ACCESS INFORMATION

TEL-ME

WHILE YOU'RE ON THE MOVE

Focused on the particular needs of mobile business users, Cellnet Tel-Me offers easy, speedy and affordable access to a wealth of information – via a laptop computer – enabling you to:

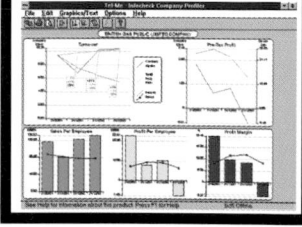

- pin point potential customers – by listing target companies by trade or location, and supplying full address details.

- run a company check – by initiating credit searches, giving you access to a company's balance sheets, profit and cost performance and other key information.

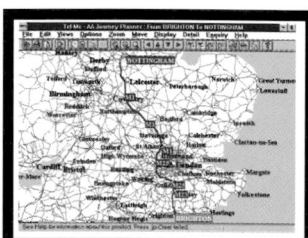

- plan a journey – by recommending the best routes and providing a map of your journey.

- check the latest news – by scanning the last 30 day's coverage on any particular subject.

- check the weather – by accessing forecasts for the UK and continental Europe.

- send E-mail anywhere in the world – by providing FREE, unlimited access to Internet E-mail.

Accurate and up-to-the minute, Cellnet Tel-Me draws on the powerful databases of some of the UK's most respected organisations. Each database is a useful source of information on a specialised topic – together they form a unique and powerful business tool that promises enormous benefits for Cellnet customers.

THE NET THAT SETS YOU FREE

for further information call
0800 214000

CELLNET MOBILE DATA

With 2-way data flow, fax, and sophisticated on-line

SO EASY

business information services, Cellnet sets the

SO FAST

pace for mobile data communications, providing

SO AFFORDABLE

real application solutions to specific business needs.

THE NET THAT SETS YOU FREE

for further information call

0800 214000

London

W2   Abbey Court   £138

Tel 0171-221 7518 Fax 0171-792 0858   Map 18 A3   **PH**
20 Pembridge Gardens W2 4DU

Usefully located near Kensington Gardens and not far from Notting Hill Gate, the Abbey Court is an elegant Victorian five-storey building, maintained to the high standards you would expect of a townhouse hotel. Within the 22 bedrooms there is a range from single or double through to de luxe or four-poster; all are well fitted out with antiques as well as modern electrical gadgets. Italian marble bathrooms have decent showers, whirlpool baths and heated towel rails. Instead of an in-house restaurant there's a 24hr room service of hot and cold dishes, and an honesty bar operates in the conservatory. Friendly service; no children under 12, no dogs. *Rooms 22. Access, Amex, Diners, Visa.*

W2   L'Accento Italiano   ↑   £55

Tel & Fax 0171-243 2201   Map 18 A3   **R**
16 Garway Road W2 4NH

The decor may be minimalist, but the food certainly is not – satisfying and decent-size portions of modern rustic North Italian cooking, commencing with a variety of breads served with superior virgin olive oil and starters such as pizzetta with bacon and goat's cheese, saffron risotto with Italian sausages or a spicy salad of grilled squid and radicchio. All starters are available as main courses for a £1.50 supplement. Main courses in their own right could include sea bass baked in a foil parcel Genoa-style, osso buco, roast breast of chicken stuffed with leeks and sun-dried tomatoes, and roast saddle of lamb with a sweet red wine sauce and juniper berries. Tiramisu tops the pudding list, which also contains ice creams, chestnut and chocolate roulade, and sweet ravioli stuffed with ewe's milk cheese. Besides the à la carte selection there's a good-value set menu lunchtime and evenings. The rear conservatory area features a sliding roof for alfresco eating. The restaurant is located just a few steps off Westbourne Grove. *Seats 65. Private Room 25. L 12-3 D 6.30-11.30. Closed Bank Holidays. Set meals £10.50. Access, Visa.*

W12   Adam's Café   £30

Tel 0181-743 0572   Map 17 A4   **R**
77 Askew Road W12

English café by day, Tunisian restaurant by night. Popular starters are chorba (a hearty lamb soup) and the filo pastry brik filled with an egg, tuna, vegetables or seafood. Speciality main courses are of course couscous, with either lamb, or vegetables, or both together plus beef meatballs. There are also grilled mullet, king prawns, and spicy merguez and, to finish, pastries, sorbets or a hot lemon pancake. Wines from Tunisia and Morocco accompany the robust food. *Seats 60. Parties 36. Private Room 24. D only 7-11. Closed Bank Holidays. No credit cards.*

SW7   Adelphi Hotel   62%   £112

Tel 0171-373 7177 Fax 0171-373 7720   Map 19 A5   **H**
127 Cromwell Road SW7 4DT

White-painted period-style hotel on a busy corner of Cromwell Road, with its main entrance in Courtfield Gardens. All bedrooms have en-suite facilities, most with both tubs and showers. Comfortable Executive bedrooms are on the top two floors. Standard rooms are more modestly furnished, but all rooms have TV and other amenities. Comfortable public rooms. No restaurant. Conference suite holds up to 80. *Rooms 68. Access, Amex, Diners, Visa.*

WC2   Ajimura   £60

Tel 0171-240 0178 Fax 0171-497 2240   Map 21 B1   **R**
51 Shelton Street WC2H 9HE

Sushi, sashimi, tempura and teriyaki are the specialities at a popular Japanese restaurant which sticks mainly to familiar dishes with a healthy slant. It opened in 1972, which makes it the longest established Japanese restaurant in Britain. Pre-theatre dinner (from £13) served Mon-Fri, 6-7.30. Regular customers have their own chopsticks! *Seats 58. Private Room 20. L 12-3 D 6-11. Closed L Sat (all Easter Sat), all Sun, Bank Holidays. Set L from £8.50 Set D £19.50 & £35. Access, Amex, Diners, Visa.*

W8   Al Basha   £70

Tel 0171-938 1794 Fax 0171-937 3405   Map 19 A4   **R**
Troy Court 222 Kensington High Street W8 5RG

Lebanese restaurant with the accent on comfort and good service. The outdoor seating area has now been covered with a glass conservatory extension. Meze is a house speciality. 15% service charge is added to all bills. *Seats 140. Private Room 65. Meals 12-11.55. Set meal £14. Access, Amex, Diners, Visa.*

SW1   Al Bustan   £60

Tel 0171-235 8277   Map 19 C4   **R**
27 Motcomb Street Belgravia SW1X 8JU

One of the prettiest and best of London's Lebanese restaurants. A generous plateful of salad items is as crisp and fresh as the summery decor. A robust selection of hot and cold hors d'oeuvre accounts for more than half the menu: moutabbal (baked aubergines blended with sesame oil and lemon juice), batarik (fish roe, olive oil and garlic), kalawi (fried lamb's kidney's), makanek (Lebanese mini-sausages), jawaneh (grilled chicken wings topped with garlic sauce). Main courses mostly come from the charcoal grill, though there are four options using raw lamb. Sweet Lebanese pastries, seasonal fresh fruits and *oum ali* – a Middle Eastern bread-and-butter pudding. *Seats 70. Private Room 10. Meals noon-11pm. Closed 25 & 26 Dec, 1 Jan. Access, Amex, Diners, Visa.*

W1   Al Hamra   £55

Tel 0171-493 1954   Map 18 C3   **R**
31 Shepherd Market W1Y 7RJ

In the heart of Shepherd Market, this is one of London's best-known and most popular Lebanese restaurants, with close-set tables and outside eating for 20 in fine weather. Munch on crunchy salad, olives and bread while awaiting your meal – typically a selection of hot and cold hors d'oeuvre, something from the charcoal grill and, if you're still not replete, a honey-sticky sweet or two. *Seats 75. Meals 12-12. Closed 25 Dec & 1 Jan. Access, Amex, Diners, Visa.*

W2   Al San Vincenzo   ★   £80

Tel 0171-262 9623   Map 18 B2   **R**
30 Connaught Street W2 2AF

A modest, almost stark, seven-table restaurant close to Marble Arch, with red and orange candy-striped loose-covered chairs providing almost the only decorative colour – it's Vincenzo Borgonzolo's food that takes centre stage, along with service from Elaine and Angela. Vincenzo, born in Naples, works almost singlehandedly in the downstairs kitchen, producing Southern Italian dishes with a difference. Traditional bourgeois dishes are subtly modernised using top-quality ingredients, although this is not a restaurant to follow the latest fads and trends. Interesting starters are typified by snails and cannellini beans in a slightly spicy sauce, carpaccio of tuna or smoked sturgeon, or gnocchi with caviar, chives and nutmeg. Half a dozen or so main courses might include roast grey-legged partridge with broccoli, octopus and potato stew, zampone, cotechino e lenticchie (pig's trotters, pork sausage and lentils), and a daily fresh fish dish such as pan-fried fillets of red mullet spread with a thin layer of smooth basil pesto and surrounded by pine kernels cooked in olive oil with the carefully pounded livers – a brilliant touch. Desserts include Vincenzo's unmissably delicious panettone bread pudding – slices of panettone dribbled with Cinzano bianco, before being baked with a sauce of mascarpone, eggs, vin Santo, cinnamon and orange juice – the result is a rich, moist, creamy creation; and the equally amazing melanzane alla ciocollata – slices of aubergine dipped in dark chocolate. Superb organic Italian farmhouse cheeses – a glass of sweet aleatico di Puglia is recommended to complement them. The carefully chosen wines are exclusively Italian – one can commence a meal with a glass of sparkling dry prosecco (with cassis, peach, pear or apricot for the house aperitif), moving on through a dozen or so reasonably priced whites or reds. *Seats 22. Parties 4. L 12.30-2 D 7-10.15. Closed L Sat, all Sun, 1 week Christmas. Access, Visa.*

Set menu prices may not always include service or wine.

W1   Alastair Little   ★ ★   £85

Tel 0171-734 5183   Map 21 A2   **R**
49 Frith Street Soho W1V 5TE

Foremost among Soho's eating places for its exceptional cuisine, the restaurant has
a decor that leaves some cold, because of its stark modernity. The rows of tiny strip lights
that decorate the ceiling illuminate a room whose pale walls are hung with abstract
contemporary artwork. Tables and designer chairs are jet-black in contrast. The simplicity
of the decor is a perfect foil for a style of cooking which gives the impression of being
uncomplicated. Alastair Little's skills are in the assembly of top-rate ingredients into dishes
with an often surprising complexity of well-married flavours and textures. Changing daily
and continually evolving, the menus include starters such as a small, thin and very crisp
pizza topped with slivers of mozzarella, with rocket and potato, houmus with a goat's
cheese salad and flat breads or tagliatelle with morels, asparagus and peas. To follow,
baked sea bass with a parsley salad and roast tomato sauce dribbled with olive oil,
tournedos with a superb pesto on a nicely browned polenta base or a plump chicken
breast stuffed with herbs under the skin and accompanied by a rich, creamy morel sauce.
As a finale there's a creamy crème brulée, a very rich chocolate marquise with a ginger
sauce or a superb rhubarb trifle studded with crunchy pistachios. Downstairs there's a bar
where a simple £12.50 lunchtime-only fixed-price menu operates. Fair prices on a wine
list that covers both Old World and New. *Seats 38. Parties 8. Private Room 16. L 12-3
D 6-11.30. Closed L Sat, all Sun, Christmas & Bank Holidays. Set L £12.50 (basement only)
& £25. Access, Amex, Visa.*

EC1   Alba   £60

Tel 0171-588 1798   Map 16 D3   **R**
107 Whitecross Street EC1Y 8JD

Northern Italian is the cooking style at this friendly place close to the Barbican centre.
Spinach frittata with tuna cream filling, Parma ham with mango and a salad of 'interesting
wild lettuces with quail's eggs and anchovies' are among the antipasti choices. The menu
continues with soup, pasta and a choice of about half a dozen meat and three fish main
courses, typified by swordfish steak with sun-dried tomatoes and capers, *bollito misto
piemontese* and quail in brandy sauce with polenta. Desserts from the trolley, Italian
cheeses served with pears. Coffee served with Cantucci biscuits. *Seats 40. L 12-3 D 6-11.
Closed Sat, Sun, Bank Holidays, 1 week Christmas. Access, Amex, Diners, Visa.*

SW3   Albero & Grana   ↑   £70

Tel 0171-225 1048   Fax 0171-581 3259   Map 19 B5   **R**
Chelsea Cloisters 89 Sloane Avenue SW3 3DX

Spanish food both traditional and contemporary is served in this stylish and fashionable
restaurant designed by Jose Antonio Garcia. An undulating back wall has the Seville sand
colour of the bullring, another wall is of glass bricks and the ceiling is tented with striped
cotton ticking. The short evening menu (in Spanish and English) proposes beautifully
prepared dishes such as melon and lobster gazpacho, eel and salmon terrine, crab with an
aubergine gratin, duck served with pears marinated in port and suckling pig Segovian-
style. Don't miss the super desserts – perhaps nougat ice cream on a chocolate sauce or
caramelised pastry horn filled with honey ice cream and fruits. A loud and busy bar at the
front serves traditional tapas lunchtime and evening (from 6pm). The wine list sticks to
Spanish wines and sherries, both groups expertly annotated. *Seats 150. L 12.30-3
D 7 (tapas from 6)-11. Closed L Sun, some Bank Holidays. Access, Amex, Diners, Visa.*

WC2   Alfred   £60

Tel 0171-240 2566   Map 21 B1   **R**
245 Shaftesbury Avenue WC2H 8EH

At the Eastern end of Shaftesbury Avenue, Alfred is done out as a 90s version of
a workman's café with bright yellow formica-topped tables and a very simple decor

including high-gloss blue walls with an aubergine-coloured dado. The food is modish, with a strong British accent. Dishes include cullen skink, Glamorgan patties, cod and herb fish cakes, stuffed chicken with a vegetable and dumpling broth and rabbit in a beer and sage sauce with roast bacon, onion and mushrooms. Cooking is quite enjoyable though some flavours are ill-balanced, as in a lavender custard reminiscent of something from a perfume bottle. Excellent range of British ales and wines. *Seats 67. L 12-3.45 D 6-11.45. Closed Sun, Bank Holidays. Set L £11.95/£15.90. Access, Amex, Diners, Visa.*

W11   L'Altro   £60

Tel 0171-792 1066   Map 16 B3   **R**
210 Kensington Park Road W11

A glass front encloses a stylish recreation of a very Italianate courtyard complete with authentic wall lamps and trompe l'oeil stone walls and classical statues. L'Altro specialises in seafood prepared simply in the modern Italian manner. The evening menu, which changes weekly, offers a choice of four antipasti, four pasta and about ten main courses. Typical dishes run from clams and mussels with tomato and garlic to spinach and parmesan ravioli, sea bass baked with herbs, lobster and crab risotto with asparagus tips and best end of lamb with potato and porcini mushrooms. The antipasti bar provides about 20 well-priced options for lighter lunchtime eating. *Seats 43. Parties 20. L 12.30-3 D 7.30-11. Closed D Sun, Bank Holidays, Christmas, Easter. Access, Amex, Diners, Visa.*

N1   Anna's Place   £50

Tel 0171-249 9379   Map 16 D2   **R**
90 Mildmay Park Newington Green N1 4PR

Anna Hegarty has been running her restaurant for nearly twenty years now, and its popularity seems undiminished. Until dark, when the table candles add an air of romanticism, the atmosphere resembles a cosy tea room, with tightly packed tables, framed prints and green hanging plants. The menu relies on perennial Swedish favourites supplemented by verbal renditions, from enthusiastic staff, of the daily specials. Thus, good gravlax and excellent marinated herrings may be followed by biff Strindberg (diced marinated beef in a mustard sauce with pickled cucumber) or pork loin with celeriac fritters. Short list of desserts includes excellent home-made ices. *Seats 42. Parties 12. L 12.15-2.15 D 7.15-10.30. Closed Sun, Mon, Easter, Aug, Christmas & New Year. No credit cards.*

W8   Apollo Hotel   £73

Tel 0171-835 1133 Fax 0171-370 4853   Map 19 A5   **B**
18-22 Lexham Gardens Kensington W8 5JE

Long-established bed and breakfast hotel, in a quiet position just off Cromwell Road. Modestly furnished bedrooms all have TVs, direct-dial phones and en-suite bathrooms – some with tubs, but mainly with modern walk-in showers. A few triple-bedded rooms. One child up to 12 can stay free in parents' room. Small conference room seating 20. No dogs. *Rooms 50. Access, Amex, Diners, Visa.*

W8   Arcadia   NEW   £65

Tel 0171-937 4294 Fax 0171-937 4393   Map 19 A4   **R**
Kensington Court 35 Kensington High Street W8 5EB

All change here, except that the new owners have retained the restaurant's name. On two floors, the existing decor has had an almost Parisian touch added, though the most dominating feature is Sally and Stanley, colourful and sometimes squawking macaws that preside atop the stairs. The menu is French, at times classical and traditional, with starters such as salade niçoise and crab-filled pastry cases with a brandy and lobster sauce. For a main course, the tournedos Rossini is correctly served and, unusually these days, tongue is available – try it with caper sauce. Excellent frites accompany; desserts include trifle, crème brulée and caramelised fruit salad; in fact several dishes throughout the menu here are 'caramelised'! Sensible wine list with most bottles under £20, house champagnes just over. *Seats 80. Private Room 16. L 12-2.30 D 7-11.30. Closed L Sun. Access, Amex, Visa.*

W1   Arirang Korean Restaurant   £50

Tel 0171-437 6633   Map 18 D2   **R**
31 Poland Street W1V 3DB

Comfortable Korean restaurant on two floors just off Oxford Street, with friendly staff to guide the uninitiated through the menu. The full range of traditional dishes is offered: start perhaps with sesame-flavoured bracken stalks, one of the many soups or preserved cabbage pickle, follow with shrimps in a hot and spicy sauce, delicious vermicelli with mixed vegetables or bulgogi – thinly sliced marinated beef, which has practically become the national dish. There are also tofu options and a good selection of fish. Set meals are available for two or more people. Weekends are busy, and service can seem pushy in its desire to process more customers. *Seats 80. Private Room 30. L 12-3 D 6-11. Closed L Bank Holidays, all Sun, 25 & 26 Dec. Set meals from £19.50. Access, Amex, Diners, Visa.*

W1   Arisugawa   £60

Tel 0171-636 8913 Fax 0171-323 4237   Map 18 D2   **R**
27 Percy Street W1P 9FF

The first choice of many Japanese diners, this smart modern restaurant in a basement has a menu of more than usual interest. The à la carte selection contains many unfamiliar dishes (fried sliced burdock roots, boiled black seaweed, grilled ox tongue), while the set menus are a better bet for the less adventurous. Teppan cuisine is offered in the ground-floor room, traditional Japanese in the basement. *Seats 120. Private Room 30. L 12.30-2.30 D 6-10. Closed L Sat, all Sun, Bank Holidays, Christmas/New Year. Set L from £7 Set D from £25. Access, Amex, Diners, Visa.*

W8   The Ark   £45

Tel 0171-229 4024   Map 18 A3   **R**
122 Palace Gardens Terrace Notting Hill Gate W8 4RT

A popular neighbourhood restaurant, narrow and built of wood, and some may say, ark-shaped. There's a shortish menu of well-known dishes beginning with moules marinière, eggs benedict and stuffed grilled mushrooms. To follow there's rack of lamb with herbs, baked skate with black olives and capers and half a roast Gressingham duck with caramelised parsnips. Subtle modern influences are creeping in but this is essentially traditional bourgeois cooking. Chocolate pot and crème brulée are the favourite desserts. Go early in the evening, or book. *Seats 75. Private Room 25. L 12-3 D 6.30-11. Closed L Sat & Bank Holidays, all Sun, 4 days Easter, 4 days Christmas. Set L £7.95. Access, Amex, Diners, Visa.*

N8   Les Associés   £60

Tel 0181-348 8944   Map 16 C1   **R**
172 Park Road Crouch End N8 8GT

Small, cosy restaurant serving enjoyably prepared, marginally modernised bourgeois French cooking from a short, interesting menu. Marinated salmon with preserved vegetables, turbot millefeuille with spinach, pork fillets with apple in cinnamon sauce and fillet of beef in shellfish sauce show the style. *Seats 38. Parties 20. L 12.30-2 D 7.30-10. Closed L Sat, all Sun & Mon, 1 week Christmas, 1 week Easter, 2 weeks Aug. Access, Visa.*

SW7   Aster House   £94

Tel 0171-581 5888 Fax 0171-584 4925   Map 19 B5   **H**
3 Sumner Place South Kensington SW7 3EE

Quiet and comfortable bed and breakfast hotel in an elegant terrace, handy for the Kensington museums and shopping trips to Knightsbridge. Bedrooms, ranging from small singles to a four-poster studio suite, have plush carpet and good-quality soft furnishings. All have private bath/shower, TVs, direct-dial phones, fridges and mini-safes. No cooked breakfast, so the room price is for the health-conscious buffet breakfast, served in a delightful first-floor conservatory. No smoking. Unlicensed. No children under 12. No dogs. Minimum booking for two nights, with full payment (most unusually) expected in advance to "discourage insincere reservations". *Rooms 14. Garden. Access, Visa.*

Set menu prices may not always include service or wine.

NW1   Asuka   £70

Tel 0171-486 5026   Map 18 C2   **R**
209a Baker Street NW1 6AB

In an arcade at the northern end of Baker Street, Asuka is also the name of a traditional
Japanese feast of soup, seven dishes and fruit. That's at the top of the price range, but
there's plenty more to choose from, notably the speciality 'saucepan dishes' prepared at
the table. These include udon suki, home-made wheat noodles with seafood, meat or
duck and vegetables in a thick broth. There's also a large selection on display on the sushi
trolley. *Seats 40. L 12-2.30 D 6-10.30. Closed L Sat, all Sun, Bank Holidays.
Set L from £12.50 Set D from £23.90. Access, Amex, Diners, Visa.*

W1   Atelier   ★   NEW   £70

Tel 0171-287 2057   Map 18 D3   **R**
41 Beak Street W1R 3LE

Originally there were artisans' workshops here, hence the name. It was also once home
to Canaletto. While the exterior retains some of the original character the interior has
been completely updated, creating a stylish and very attractive restaurant decorated in
warm, summery colours. Walls have a terracotta hue and down one side runs a series of
large plain, curved, canvas screens. Place settings include very colourful handmade plates
featuring quite life-like fruit and vegetables. Stephen Bulmer, the chef, and partner
Joanna Shannon have both gained experience with Raymond Blanc at Great Milton and
bring their resulting expertise to this new West Soho venture. The short menu features
a selection of truly delicious and very well-prepared dishes. The cooking style is simple
with the emphasis on clear, well-defined flavours. Begin with a splendid plump and
tender quail boudin served on a bed of spinach with a pea purée and delicate marjoram
jus, chilled gazpacho with orange and thyme breadsticks or warm spinach mousse with
white anchovies, tomato and parsley. For a main course there could be pan-fried tuna
served on smooth saffron mash with a topping of pistou and a sauce of red peppers and
coriander – a wonderful combination of Mediterranean flavours. Other choices are
a salad of duck confit, duck ham and crispy skin, apple and celeriac with a walnut
dressing, roasted lamb chump with basil-flavoured mashed potato, tomato fondue and
rosemary jus and pan-fried monkfish with mussels, fresh linguine and a tarragon and
mustard seed sauce. Only three desserts but they are not to be missed, particularly the
exceptionally brilliant warm chocolate torte accompanied by a cherry compote subtly
flavoured with cinnamon and kirsch and served with a nugget of chantilly cream. The set
meals are very well balanced, no choice at lunch and two dishes per course for dinner.
*Seats 45. Parties 20. Private Room 16. L 12-2.30 D 6-10.45. Closed L Sat, all Sun, 2 weeks
Jan, 2 weeks Aug. Set L & D from £14.50. Access, Amex, Diners, Visa.*

**Consult the blue pages for summary tables and lists of
recommended establishments.**

W1   The Athenaeum   81%   £246

Tel 0171-499 3464 Fax 0171-493 1860   Map 18 C3   **H**
116 Piccadilly W1V 0BJ

The new owners of this luxurious hotel overlooking Green Park have recently completed
a major renovation, and no effort has been spared. Peter Inston's clever design includes
new skylight windows in the restaurant, and the skilful use of colourful plants, which
together give a feeling of space and light in the smallish lounge. Bedrooms combine
discreet touch-button technology (with bedside controls for everything from the air-
conditioning, to the do not disturb sign) with comfort and style. In the marble
bathrooms, heated wall-sized mirrors, excellent showers over the tubs, and even
a Roberts portable radio, continue the attention to detail and comfort. Comprehensive
24hr room and full valet service are available. A choice of four meeting rooms caters for
gatherings of up to 44 people. The basement, formerly accountants' offices, has been
converted into a top-class gym with sauna and large spa pool – for the use of guests only.
There are also 33 equally luxurious apartments, with their own entrances in Down Street,
where full modern kitchens might tempt one to employ one's own skills! Valet parking.
No dogs. *Rooms 124. Gym, sauna, spa bath, steam room, beauty salon, lounge service
(24 hrs). Access, Amex, Diners, Visa.*

W8   Atlas Hotel   £73

Tel 0171-835 1155 Fax 0171-370 4853   Map 19 A5   **B**
24-30 Lexham Gardens Kensington W8 5JE

Neighbour of the Apollo Hotel in the same ownership. Light, airy residents' bar and lounge, overlooking a patio garden. Modestly furnished rooms have recently been refurbished; all have TVs, direct-dial phones and en-suite bathrooms – some with tubs, but mainly with modern walk-in showers. A few triple-bedded rooms, and one four bedded. One child up to 12 can stay free in parents' room. No dogs. *Rooms 50. Access, Amex, Diners, Visa.*

Consult the blue pages for summary tables and lists of recommended establishments.

SW1   The Atrium   NEW   £60

Tel 0171-233 0032 Fax 0171-233 0010   Map 17 C4   **R**
4 Millbank London SW1P 3JA

Housed in a posh building (revolving door, marble entrance hall, security desk) that contains the Westminster TV studios, part of the the informal restaurant is indeed located in an atrium, though the room inside is much cosier with light wood panelling, a Welsh dresser and walls adorned with signed childhood photographs of mostly young stage and film stars. Antony Worrall Thompson is the consultant chef here (though the actual cooking is done by David Greenhaulgh) and his culinary stamp is evident on the menu that will please MPs particularly, since many of the dishes will remind them of Public School food, albeit rather better cooked. A division bell sounds when it's time to return to The House. There are daily pot and roast dishes (eg Monday: fish pie, Wednesday: baked honey-roasted ham, Friday: cod, chips and mushy peas) alongside, say, tomato and basil soup; hot asparagus with hollandaise; pan-fried duck breast with roast beetroot, bubble and squeak, and gooseberry compote; and salmon and cod fish cake with parsley sauce and spinach. Comfort puddings such as tipsy trifle, lemon meringue pie and Spotted Dick will send Members back to vote in good order. The wine list is short and sensibly priced. Staff are rather stiff and would benefit from an occasional smile. *Seats 155. Parties 14. Private Room 22. L 12-3.30 D 6.30- 11. Set L £15.95/£18.95 Set D 10/£15.95/£18.95. Closed L Sat & all Sun, Bank Holidays, 1 week Christmas. Access, Amex, Diners, Visa.*

NW8   Au Bois St Jean   £70

Tel 0171-722 0400 Fax 0171-586 0410   Map 18 B1   **R**
122 St John's Wood High Street NW8 7SG

A basement restaurant with lots of wood, where dishes have a Mediterranean feel: starters include moules marinière, duck breast and pleurotte mushroom salad and aubergine and courgette terrine with a leek sauce. There are fish dishes such as succulent salmon fillet baked in pastry with a creamy dill sauce or sautéed fillet of John Dory with a garlic-flavoured potato purée and fennel sauce, while meat dishes feature roast rack of lamb with Provençal herbs and garlic butter or spiced chicken breast served with a wild mushroom sauce. On Sundays and Mondays there is a 10% discount on the restaurant menu for cash and cheques only. A pianist tinkles away in the evenings and staff are amiable and on the ball. The bistro on the ground floor is also open for lunch and offers an inexpensive menu of similar style to the restaurant. *Seats 60. Parties 25. Private Room 60. D only 7-11.30. Closed 3 days Christmas, 2 days Easter. Set D £18.50/£23.50. Access, Amex, Diners, Visa.*

W1   Au Jardin des Gourmets   £75

Tel 0171-437 1816 Fax 0171-437 0043   Map 21 A2   **R**
5 Greek Street Soho W1V 5LA

Set squarely in Soho's culinary revival area, this long-established restaurant operates as two distinct dining-rooms. At street level, the salle à manger: dark red walls, big Chinese-style mirrors and close-set tables fill the room. Brasserie-style dishes predominate here – mackerel rillettes, asparagus risotto with Bayonne ham, roast rack of lamb with Provençal herbs, or perhaps traditional bourride antiboise. The two-course set menu offers good value with 2 or 3 choices per course. Upstairs is a comfortable and more formal setting, with a more elaborate and expansive menu. Venison medallions with juniper berries and a compote of sweet and sour red onions, breast of corn-fed chicken with girolles, port and cream and poached salmon with beetroot and a raspberry vinegar dressing are typical choices. Prices on the wine list are pushed up by the addition of a 15% service charge. The list is resplendent with French burgundies and clarets, but light elsewhere. *Seats 150. Parties 10. Private Rooms 50. L 12.15-2.30 D 6-11.15. Closed L Sat, all Sun, D Bank Holidays. Set meals £10.95 & £24.50. Access, Amex, Diners, Visa.*

Set menu prices may not always include service or wine.

SW10   Aubergine   ★★   £90

Tel 0171-352 3449 Fax 0171-351 1770   Map 19 B6   **R**
11 Park Walk SW10 0AJ

Chef-patron Gordon Ramsay's smart, yellow-themed restaurant goes from strength to strength, so much so that booking days if not weeks in advance is often necessary. The influence of one of his mentors, Marco Pierre White, is now less apparent, but that of Guy Savoy is visible in the delicious cappuccino soups sometimes appearing as amuse-gucule and sometimes as starters. The menus are written in a confusing mixture of English/French and some mid-channel patois; starters might include mosaique of rabbit with cabbage and ceps, salad of roasted langoustines with candied aubergine or an excellent terrine of foie gras and confit canard. Follow perhaps with pot-au-feu of Bresse pigeon with choux farci; caramelised calf's sweetbreads, etuvée of carrots jus sauternes with curry; or blanquette of turbot with ravioli of oyster and cucumber. Fish, in particular, is expertly handled, as was demonstrated at a recent lunch which included a wonderful selection of six varieties of the freshest morsels on a base of choucroute with a light coriander jus, the whole topped with a julienne of carrots whose flavour was so intense one imagines they came straight from a garden at the back! A splendid selection of French cheeses is offered, all in perfect condition. Desserts now scale the same heights, in both taste and display; and petits fours show the confectioner's art to the full. Service, under the charming direction of Jean-Claude Breton, is possibly too earnest for some. A no-choice "Menu Prestige" is also offered for dinner, 6 courses for £44 – showing just what the kitchen can do. Fame has brought an increase in prices, but no more than the food deserves; but at lunchtime a short, daily-changing set menu is offered in addition to the main carte. At £19.50 for 3 courses and no skimping of standards this must be one of London's best bargains. An improved wine list, albeit denuded of any notes, and without sparkling wines, just champagne (quite steeply priced, except for a couple or non-vintage lesser *marques*). *Seats 40. Parties 10. L 12.15-2.30 D 7-11. Closed L Sat, all Sun, Bank Holidays, first 2 weeks August, 23 Dec-1 Jan. Set L £19.50 Set D £34/£44. Access, Amex, Diners, Visa.*

NW8   L'Aventure   £65

Tel 0171-624 6232   Map 16 B3   **R**
3 Blenheim Terrace NW8 0EH

Owner Catherine Parisot's personality is stamped all over this delightful little French restaurant with a terrace for summer eating. In a friendly, intimate atmosphere a short, appealing daily-changing menu offers classical French cooking such as *parfait de champignons sauvages, turbot roti à l'huile de homard, blanquette de veau à l'ancienne,* and *confit de canard,* with puddings like tarte fine au citron and ile flottante. *Seats 45. L 12.30-2.30 D 7.30-11. Closed L Sat, 1 week Christmas, 4 days Easter. Set L £18.50 Set D £25. Access, Amex, Diners, Visa.*

We welcome bona fide complaints and recommendations on the tear-out pages at the back of the book for readers' comments. They are followed up by our professional team.

W11   Avenue West Eleven   †   £65

Tel 0171-221 8144   Map 18A3   **R**
157 Notting Hill Gate W11 3LF

Philip McMullen, the owner, designed the innovative and strikingly original Moroccan
theme of his newest restaurant and Mark Hill contributed the very abstract wall
sculptures. Tables, set on a dark stone-tiled floor, have unusual and characterful appliquéd
coarse sacking and brown paper coverings while in the basement, the bar with its deep
blue-painted walls and colourful furnishings, has an intimate Mediterranean ambience.
Lunch comprises a two or three course fixed-price menu while dinner is à la carte. The
cooking is now by Mark Broadbent and is extremely good, featuring dishes which are
a blend of carefully assembled flavours and textures. Changing daily, the choice could
begin with Cornish crab, baby spinach, guacamole and almond aïoli, cep and potato
broth or a very fresh-tasting confit of yellow-fin tuna niçoise. Main dishes range from
griddled calf's liver with melted onions and mostarda di Cremona, saffron risotto with
fava beans, purple basil and parmesan and fillet of black bream with couscous and
chermoula (a North African version of gremolata) to a zarzuela of hake, salt cod, bream,
mussels and chorizo and stuffed saddle of lamb with apricots, rosemary and garlic.
Wonderful desserts like chocolate pie with crème fraiche, *crostata di limone* and summer
fruits in champagne with fromage frais add the finishing touches to a very memorable
meal with staff on their toes and helping things along splendidly. *Seats 56. Parties 12.
Private Room 14. L 12.30-2.30 D 7-11.15 (10.30 Sun). Closed L Sat, all Bank Holidays,
4 days Christmas. Access, Amex, Diners, Visa.*

W1   Baboon   £70

Tel 0171-224 2992   Map 18 C2   **R**
Jasons Court 76 Wigmore Street W1 9DE

Tucked away in an alley between Wigmore Street and Marylebone Lane, this basement
dining-room is worth seeking out. Chef John Armstrong refreshingly flies in the face of
fashion by sticking mainly to the British cooking of the 70s and 80s, so denying new-
wave Mediterranean influences and the olive oil brigade. Offerings might include soufflé
of goat's cheese with rocket, lamb and wild mushroom sausage with a warm potato salad
or a perfectly judged terrine of lobster and sweetbreads to begin, with perhaps rabbit and
grain mustard stew with celeriac mash, a pot-roast of chicken and crab or fillets of sea
bass and pike with a tarragon and fennel fondue to follow. Finish with traditional puds,
the excellent British farmhouse cheese, or the unusual four-cheese Welsh rarebit.
A pianist performs every evening and heightens the romantic atmosphere. *Seats 65.
Parties 16. Private Room 16. L 12-3 D 6-11. Set L £10/£12.50 D £15/£17. Closed L Sat,
all Sun, 3 days Christmas, all Bank Holidays. Access, Amex, Diners, Visa.*

W1   Bahn Thai   £60

Tel 0171-437 8504   Fax 0171-439 0340   Map 21 A2   **R**
21a Frith Street Soho W1V 5TS

Kensington was the original (1981) location of Bahn Thai, and in its Soho premises the
aim is unchanged – to prepare and present authentic Thai cooking. The menu has plenty
of guidance notes on ordering a Thai meal (including heat warnings against the more
fiercely spiced items), making this a useful place to go for those new to the cuisine. For
those already familiar with the genre, though, there are equally enticing choices, some
not often found on Thai menus, like wild boar, venison, calf's liver and mussels steamed,
shelled and cooked in a batter pancake with bean sprouts, as well as the less surprising
chicken, prawns, scallops and beef. *Seats 120. Private Room 25. L 12-2.45 (Sun 12.30-2.30)
D 6-11.15 (Sun 6.30-10.30). Closed Bank Holidays. Access, Amex, Diners,Visa.*

W12   Balzac Bistro Restaurant   £50

Tel 0181-743 5370   Map 17 B4   **R**
4 Wood Lane Shepherds Bush W12 7DT

Classic French bistro cooking at a long-popular restaurant just up from bustling
Shepherds Bush Green. The decor includes many French knick-knacks, café parasols at
some of the tables and signed photographs of visiting stars (the BBC studios are just up

the road). *Seats 75. Parties 40. Private Room 60. L 12-2.30 D 7-11. Closed L Sat, all Sun, some Bank Holidays, 10 days after Christmas. Set L & D £9.90/£13.90/£15.90. Access, Amex, Diners, Visa.*

SW7   Bangkok   £40

Tel 0171-584 8529   Fax 0171-823 7883   Map 19 B5   **R**
9 Bute Street South Kensington SW7 3EY

A long-established Thai restaurant, the Bangkok is sparsely appointed and has been run by the same family since its opening in 1967. The short menu includes beef and pork satay, minced beef omelette, fried prawns, spare ribs, beef and chicken curry and Thai rice noodles. *Seats 60. Parties 12. Private Room 20. L 12.15-2.15 D 7-11.15. Closed Sun, Bank Holidays, Christmas. Set L from £6.50. Access, Visa.*

SW13   Bangkok Garden   £35

Tel 0181-392 9158   Map 17 A5   **R**
8 Rocks Lane Barnes SW13 0DB

50-seater Thai restaurant in shades of brown and tan behind a huge plate-glass window. The menu, printed on strips of bamboo, offers a fair cross-section of Thai cuisine plus guidance notes on eating Thai food. Now only open in the evening. *Seats 50. D only 6-11. Set D £14.95 (min 2). Access, Amex, Visa.*

SW15   Bangkok Symphonie   £35

Tel 0181-789 4304   Map 17 B5   **R**
141 Upper Richmond Road Putney SW15 2TX

Spot the red and gold exterior of a delightful Thai restaurant where the South Circular meets Putney High Street. Inside, charming staff serve a good selection of their native cuisine to the gentle accompaniment of classical music. The menu is full of musical references, with the customer designated as the conductor. *Seats 45. L 12-3 D 6-11. Closed L Sat. Set L £5.95 Set D £9.95. Access, Amex, Diners, Visa.*

SE3   Bardon Lodge   56%   £84

Tel 0181-853 4051   Fax 0181-858 7387   Map 17 D5   **H**
15 Stratheden Road Blackheath SE3 7TH

Just off the A2 and conveniently close to the A102(M), the hotel, which has easy access on to Blackheath Common, also offers cosy, homely comforts. Rooms are neatly maintained and all are double-glazed. There's also a quite separate annexe across on another road; here there's only limited service and guests have to return to the main building for the bar and breakfast. *Rooms 60. Garden. Access, Amex, Diners, Visa.*

SW3   Basil Street Hotel   71%   £200

Tel 0171-581 3311 Fax 0171-581 3693   Map 19 C4   **H**
Basil Street Knightsbridge SW3 1AH

An Edwardian English atmosphere pervades a privately-owned hotel 'just 191 steps' from Harrods (and almost the same from Harvey Nichols!). Public areas have a country house feel, from the antique-lined corridor leading to the dining room to the spacious lounge in sunny yellow with rug-covered polished parquet floor. Well-kept bedrooms are of a good size, usually with a sitting area, traditionally furnished and decorated with understated good taste; most have equally roomy private bathrooms. Family accommodation can cater for up to two adults and three children in two rooms, sharing one bathroom; alternatively, children under 16 may share their parents' room free. Old-fashioned standards of courteous and obliging service include shoe cleaning, servicing of rooms in the evenings and 24hr room service. The Parrot Club is a unique ladies-only retreat, ideal for lunch or tea. 24hr NCP car park within 100 yds. Banqueting/conferences for 65/75. *Rooms 93. Access, Amex, Diners, Visa.*

We welcome bona fide complaints and recommendations on the
tear-out pages at the back of the book for readers' comments.
They are followed up by our professional team.

SW3   The Beaufort   £163

Tel 0171-584 5252 Fax 0171-589 2834   Map 19 C4   **PH**
33 Beaufort Gardens Knightsbridge SW3 1PP

In a quiet, tree-lined cul-de-sac 200 yards from Harrods, this elegant town house offers
personal service and almost uninterrupted tranquillity. Guests are greeted with
a complimentary glass of champagne and a genuine welcome reminiscent of a bygone era.
A relaxing drawing room, with deep sofas, is the only public room. Air-conditioned
bedrooms range from two singles with shower/WC only to a small suite. All are
individually decorated in pastel colours and deep-carpeted. Fresh flowers abound, and the
hotel boasts an excellent collection of English floral water-colours. Continental breakfast
is served only in the bedrooms; this includes home-made jams and home-baked croissants
and rolls. One night's non-refundable deposit is required for all first-time reservations.
Membership of a local health club is included. No tipping expected. No dogs. *Rooms 28.*
Access, Amex, Diners, Visa.

NW1   Belgo Noord   £50

Tel 0171-267 0718   Map 16 C3   **R**
72 Chalk Farm Road NW1 8AN

With the opening of Belgo Centraal, the Chalk Farm original has added Noord to its
name. This remarkable restaurant was inspired by the idea of a contemporary monastic
refectory, and its design has many unique features, including a high-tech wheel and
pulley system for the stairs and huge chrome pipes for the heating and air systems. The
restaurant area itself has concrete walls inlaid with Rabelais-inspired names of obscure
fish, and the tables are refectory style, topped with ash. Waiters are dressed in monks'
habits, a practical garb for serving the hefty portions of mussels that are the most popular
order. They come ten ways, usually with frites and mayonnaise, and often washed down
with Belgian beer – they stock dozens of varieties, some smooth and smoky, others bitter
and spicy, some flavoured wtih fruit, a few as strong as wine. Alternatives to mussels
include ham-wrapped chicken with béchamel sauce, wild boar sausages, guinea fowl,
lobster and *carbonnade flamande*. Start with asparagus, cheese or shrimp croquettes or
a salad, and try a schnapps with your desserts. There are several set menus, including beat
the clock, available from 6 till 8. Arrive at 6.30 and you pay £6.30 for one of three
special meals, saving up to £5. A big hit from the moment it opened, this is a place for
tucking into simple, sustaining food, for drinking beer and talking – and not in
a whisper! Bookings are taken up to two weeks in advance with tables allocated for two
hours maximum. 15% service charge is added to bills. *Seats 125. Parties 10.*
Closed 25 & 26 Dec. L 12-3 D 6-11.30 (Sat 12-11.30, Sun 12-10.30). Set L from £5
(Mon-Fri, main dish & lager) Set D £10. Access, Amex, Diners, Visa.
Also at:
WC2 Belgo Centraal 50 Earlham Street Covent Garden WC2 Tel 0171 813 2233   Map 21 B2

SE1   Bengal Clipper   £70

Tel 0171-357 9001 Fax 0171-357 9002   Map 17 D4   **R**
Cardamom Building Shad Thames Butler's Wharf SE1

Up-market Indian restaurant within the new development at Tower Bridge. The theme
of the area's origins (spice warehouses for the East India Company) works well, the
restaurant's interior being designed to mimic an old tea clipper. The menu is extensive
and highlights Bengali and Goan specialities. Start with a giant Bay of Bengal prawn,
minced, wrapped in a spicy poppadum then deep fried, and move on to saffron lamb in
a creamy sauce with lemon rice and a side dish of spinach with aniseed and garlic.
Friendly service. *Seats 170. Parties 35. L 12-3 D 6-11. Closed 25 & 26 Dec.*
Set L £12.95/£15.50/£18.50 Set D £18.50. Access, Amex, Diners, Visa.

We publish annually, so make sure you use the current edition.
— It's well worth it!

NW3   Benihana   £75

Tel 0171-586 9508 Fax 0171-586 6740   Map 16 B3   **R**
100 Avenue Road Swiss Cottage NW3 3HF

Part of a world-wide group with branches from Beverly Hills to Tokyo, London's first Benihana is a typically lively establishment in a bright basement ambience next to the Hampstead Theatre and Swiss Cottage underground. Teppanyaki griddle cooking is the speciality, and the chefs working at their hibachi tables are great entertainment. Steak and lobster are the main attractions, and the entrées, served with multifarious accompaniments, include Rocky's Choice (chicken teriyaki, hibachi steak with mushrooms), Seafood Combination (cold water lobster tail, king prawns, scallops and calamari) and tuna steak with chopped ginger. Great-value weekday lunches and a Sunday lunch with children's entertainment. New sushi menu. Short wine list, but sake and a vast choice of cocktails. *Seats 112. Parties 10. Private Room 8. L 12.30-3 D 6.30-12. Closed L Mon, 25 Dec. Set L from £8.45 (Sun £13.95) Set D from £13.95. Access, Amex, Diners, Visa.*

Consult the blue pages for summary tables and lists of
recommended establishments.

SW3   Benihana   £75

Tel 0171-376 7799   Map 19 C5   **R**
77 Kings Road Chelsea SW3 4NX

A plate glass door simply inscribed with the restaurant's name is all that is visible from the exterior while inside a wide staircase rounds a corner presenting a stunningly original and very striking ultra-modern decor. A long gallery leads to a sweeping bifurcated staircase, one side leading down to the spacious tent-ceilinged bar, the other to a sea of white pebbles crossed by 'stepping stones' of black iron to reach the dining area of gleaming hibachi tables. These accommodate up to eight diners, who are treated to the dexterity of the chef preparing the food on the teppanyaki grill. The menu runs from sashimi, tempura and rock oyster cocktail to entrées offering various combinations of steak, chicken and seafood served with onion soup, ginger-dressed salad, prawns, beans, courgettes, hibachi vegetables, rice and green tea. New sake list and sushi menu. *Seats 140. Parties 8. Private Room 12. L 12.30-3 D 6.30-11. Set L £8.90. Access, Amex, Diners, Visa.*

W1   Bentinck House Hotel   £80

Tel 0171-935 9141 Fax 0171-224 5903   Map 18 C2   **B**
20 Bentinck Street W1M 5RL

Large, comfortable bedrooms (three family rooms, 9 rooms en suite) in a small hotel behind Oxford Street. *Rooms 20. Access, Amex, Diners, Visa.*

Set menu prices may not always include service or wine.

W1   Bentley's   £80

Tel 0171-287 5025 Fax 0171-287 2972   Map 18 D3   **R**
11 Swallow Street W1R 7HD

This club-like first-floor dining-room has been specialising in fish since its inception in 1916. While keeping abreast of fashion, it has resisted the temptation to cook multi-coloured tropical breeds, and remained faithful to native products – sometimes presented with modern disguises. Oysters, Scottish smoked salmon, caviar, tempura crab claws with black bean sauce and shellfish bisque are among a wide choice of starters, while main courses run from plaice and chips to scallops provençale, bouillabaisse-style fish stew and roast monkfish in Parma ham with sage polenta. On the ground floor the Oyster Bar offers a shorter menu. *Seats 90. Private Room 14. L 12-2.30 D 6-11.30 Oyster Bar Meals 12-11.30. Closed all Sun, Bank Holidays, 3 days Christmas. Set L & D £16.50/£19.50. Access, Amex, Diners, Visa.*

SW1   The Berkeley   89%   £332

Tel 0171-235 6000 Fax 0171-235 4330   Map 19 C4   **HR**
Wilton Place Knightsbridge SW1X 7RL

Located in a relatively quiet residential part of Knightsbridge, the hotel dates from the early 70s, is built of Portland stone, and has a very solid and somewhat unprepossessing exterior. A newly installed management team has brought with them very subtle refinements to the interior which bears the hallmarks of a hotel 'de grand luxe'. Panelling by Lutyens and a collection of glittering chandeliers are features and outstanding flower arrangements and highly polished marbles of different hues create an impressive entrance. The split-level, relatively dark intimacy of the Perroquet Bar offers an alternative meeting-place to the more formal and traditional lounge with its splendid olive-green leather winged armchairs and others in a fashionable dark bamboo style. The design of each new refurbishment of the bedrooms, usually in small groups, is undertaken by a top designer and this is very evident from the classical, sumptuous decor that breathes style and good taste. There are three presidential suites, one with its own conservatory, and 21 further spacious suites. Even the standard bedrooms are beautifully appointed, differing only from superior rooms in being marginally smaller. Most rooms have a separate dressing room adjacent to the immaculate Italianate marble bathrooms, which feature a wealth of pampering extras including complimentary towelling slippers. Modern comforts like extensive satellite television coverage, video recorders and fax points are common to all as are wall safes. There are valet buttons by beds and baths which are answered promptly, typifying service of an exemplary very high standard. On the top floor is a superb leisure complex with a swimming pool that in summer can slide its roof back. *Rooms 160. Indoor swimming pool, gym, sauna, solarium, beauty & hair salon, valeting, cinema, coffee shop (9am-9.30pm Mon-Sat). Access, Amex, Diners, Visa.*

Restaurant   £115

A collection of medieval portraits set in antiqued mirror surrounds (themselves forming part of ornately carved lined-oak panelling) creates, together with beautifully appointed, well-spaced tables and elaborate flower arrangements, an air of great sophistication which is also reflected in John Williams' classical menus. Subtle innovation, with modern, carefully thought-out concepts, results in dishes that are exciting for both presentation and taste. To begin, the choice could be between a raviolo of soft egg yolk served with a truffled leek fondue, a terrine of goose foie gras marinated in white port or a salad of scallops with gazpacho vinaigrette. There is no shortage of choice and fish dishes include a fillet of John Dory with Swiss chard and a mustard sauce, and roast turbot with shellfish in a light butter sauce. Meat and game include excellent grills and roasts as well as lamb noisette with baked tomato and a basil fondue, braised duck magret with spiced apple and a pepper sauce and a fillet of veal with morels and a mustard and leek sauce. Well-made desserts from the trolley vie with such delights as a hot rum and candied ginger soufflé, chocolate millefeuille with tiramisu and a praline sauce and poached pear sablé accompanied by an Amaretto and rosemary ice cream. A very fine wine list features some of the best names around. Not much under £20, but, commendably, several decent wines are available by the glass. *Seats 65. Parties 14. Private Rooms 14/34. L 12.30-2.30 D 6.30-10.45. Closed Sat. Set L £24.50/£27.50 Set D £24/£27.*

W1   Berkshire Hotel   72%   £231

Tel 0171-629 7474 Fax 0171-629 8156   Map 18 C2   **HR**
350 Oxford Street W1N 0BY

Occupying its own small triangular block on the north side of Oxford Street, almost facing the top of New Bond Street, the Berkshire possesses comfortable though not extensive public rooms, with a chintzy, panelled drawing room and the intimate Ascot Bar. Bedrooms, including two floors designated non-smoking, are attractively appointed, much use being made of rich, colourful fabrics and darkwood furniture. Executive rooms are bigger and have more accessories; suites have whirlpool baths. Children up to 8 stay free in parents' room. 24hr room service. Owners Edwardian Hotels aim for a country-house welcome and an Edwardian feel here. Valet parking to NCP Welbeck Street. *Rooms 147. Access, Amex, Diners, Visa.*

Ascot's Restaurant   £75

A country club feel pervades this first-floor dining-room with its deep carpet, panelled walls and racing prints. James Chapman's imaginative menus offer a balance of modern and traditional styles; perhaps Perthshire smoked salmon with buckwheat pancakes, duck and pigeon terrine with kumquat marmalade or wild mushroom mousse with goose livers and Malmsey sauce to start; then calf's liver and bacon with a citrus sauce, casserole of rabbit with baby vegetables or loin of lamb with aubergines and a rosemary and garlic sauce as main courses. Great care is taken in choosing ingredients and in the quality of saucing. Desserts maintain this high standard with lemon tart, chocolate indulgence or various ices all presented like works of art. Service is under the skilful direction of Nabil Chakoui. *Seats 38. L 12.30-2.30 D 5.30-10.30. Closed L Sat & Sun. Set L & D £17.50/£23.50.*

W1 The Berners Hotel	73%	£162

Tel 0171-636 1629 Fax 0171-580 3972   Map 18 D2   **H**
10 Berners Street W1A 3BE

Built in 1835, the Berners was a very grand private residence before becoming a hotel around the turn of the century. A polite "good morning sir" from the liveried doorman sets the tone for notably smart and helpful staff as one enters into the spectacular entrance hall/lounge with its marble column topped by gilt Corinthian capitals, elaborately draped windows, trompe l'oeil murals and ornate ceiling high above. The equally grand, and if anything more ornate, former ballroom houses both restaurant and smart cocktail bar – no draught beer, they specialise in cocktails and champagne. Bedrooms are comfortable and stylish, the 14 Executive rooms being the most spacious, although the 1970s bathrooms, while still perfectly serviceable, look a little dated. All have at least two telephones (one in the bathroom) with many a third at the desk, and multi-channel, multi-language TVs. 24hr room service offers a choice of hot dishes throughout the night. Children up to 12 stay free in parents' room. No dogs. The hotel has no parking of its own. *Rooms 226. Access, Amex, Diners, Visa.*

WC2 Bertorelli's		£60

Tel 0171-836 3969 Fax 0181-836 1868   Map 21 B2   **R**
44a Floral Street Covent Garden WC2E 9DA

Modern Italian cooking by Maddalena Bonino at a famous address opposite the stage door of the Royal Opera House. There's a very fashionable ring and an excellent taste to such dishes as pasta ribbons with a spicy chicken liver and tomato sauce, baked smoked haddock fillet on spinach and lemon rice with a spicy prawn butter, and wild boar sausages on a sauté of savoy cabbage and roasted red onion with a balsamic vinegar and black cherry sauce. A £1.50 cover charge gets you grissini and Italian breads, olive oil, gherkins and olives. There's an associated café/wine bar in the basement. You do not always find a good Italian wine list in an Italian restaurant – here you do! Few half bottles maybe, but plenty available by the glass. Free parking in the Drury Lane NCP for customers dining in the restaurant after 6pm. *Seats 100. Parties 30. L 12-3 D 5.30-11.30. Closed Sun, 26 Dec. Access, Amex, Diners, Visa.*

WC2 Bhatti		£50

Tel 0171-831 01817 Fax 0171-831 4249   Map 21 B2   **R**
37 Great Queen Street WC2B 5AA

Popular, long-established and civilised Indian restaurant in a 17th-century building just off Drury Lane. A fairly familiar range of chicken, lamb and prawn dishes is joined by quail and pomfret fish – both cooked in the clay oven. Chicken tikka masala and lamb pasanda are among the 'chef's recommendations'. *Seats 90. Parties 8. Private Room 40. L 12-2.45 D 5.30-11.30 (Thu-Sat to 11.45). Set meals from £7.95. Closed 25 & 26 Dec. Access, Amex, Diners, Visa.*

Many hotels offer reduced rates for weekend or out-of-season bookings. Always ask about special deals.

SW3   Bibendum   ★   £120

Tel 0171-581 5817 Fax 0171-823 7925   Map 19 B5   **R**
Michelin House 81 Fulham Road SW3 6RD

Still one of the most fashionable restaurants in town – making booking pretty much essential – where chef Matthew Harris has taken over at the helm in the kitchen, having been Simon Hopkinson's right-hand man for several years. The dining-room is located on the first floor (there is a lift) of the famous Michelin building, so Bibendum (the Michelin tyre man) is evident throughout, appearing on the plates, sitting on the ashtrays and featuring in a couple of huge stained-glass windows; even the wine decanters and flower vases reflect his corpulent frame. A novel feature is that chairs have loose linen covers with a different colour for each season. The menu (à la carte at night; fixed-price at lunchtime, though with some water, a glass of wine, coffee and service you should add at least a tenner to the price) is a mixture of French, modern European and classic bistro dishes, perhaps a lunch of warm salad of *andouillette au canard,* perfectly poached egg, crispy lardons and a subtle mustard dressing, well-cooked poached skate with tomato vinaigrette and basil, pear and ginger sorbet, the latter nudely presented – just three scoops with no accompaniment whatsoever. In the evening you'll encounter more luxurious dishes: ballotine of fresh foie gras, roast *poulet de Bresse* with tarragon (for two), *tarte fine aux pommes,* served with vanilla ice cream. Good coffee comes with giant chocolate truffles. With the service charge reduced to 12½ per cent, the very fine wine list is in effect even better value than previously. While the list is seriously French, it is not to the exclusion of wines from elsewhere, which are equally well represented. There's quality throughout – no inferior drinking here! Service is not always as well ordered as the cooking. *Seats 72. Parties 8. L 12.30-2.30 (Sat & Sun to 3) D 7-11.30 (Sun to 10.30). Closed 4 days Christmas, Easter Monday. Set L £27. Access, Amex, Diners, Visa.*

SW3   Bibendum Oyster Bar   £70

Tel 0171-581 5817 Fax 0171-823 7925   Map 19 B5   **R**
Michelin House 81 Fulham Road SW3 6RD

At the front and on the ground floor (below its big sister) of the wonderfully exuberant and stylish Michelin building, the Oyster Bar serves an all-day menu majoring on splendid seafood. Nothing is more splendid than the plateau de fruits de mer, including crab, langoustines, oysters, clams, prawns, crevettes grises, winkles and whelks. Also on the list are excellent salads (grilled duck breast with Cumberland sauce, orange and watercress, loin of lamb with grilled leeks and rocket salad). Take-away shellfish service from the little lorry outside. *Seats 44. Parties 18. Meals 12-10.30pm (Sun 12-3 & 7-10). Access, Amex, Visa.*

NW1   Big Night Out   £55

Tel 0171-586 5768 Fax 0171-482 4176   Map 16 C3   **R**
148 Regents Park Road NW1 8XN

Up the spiral staircase is a small, dark, cosy dining room while on the ground floor the available area is larger and brighter, its walls hung with huge multiple canvases of modern art inspired by Michelangelo. The menu is in two parts with a two- or three-course set price option as well as a short, varied à la carte. The cooking style is up-to-date, with well-thought-out, innovative combinations. Typical starters are confit of duck leg with a potato and rosemary cake, red mullet soup with coriander and garlic toast and a brill and crab tartlet with a truffle and lemon grass dressing. Main courses include roast rump of lamb with gratin potatoes and grilled asparagus, wild duck and sage sausages with parsley chips and red cabbage, and baked sea bass in a paper parcel with clams, thyme and saffron potatoes. Sticky toffee pudding, chocolate truffon and rhubarb crumble are among the desserts. Sunday brunch price includes an alcoholic drink. *Seats 65. Parties 8. Private Room 30. L 12-3 D 7-11. Closed L Mon, D Sun, 25 Dec, 1 Jan. Set L £5.50 (Sun £10). Access, Amex, Visa.*

Set menu prices may not always include service or wine.

W1   Bistrot Bruno   ★   £70

Tel 0171-734 4545 Fax 0171-287 1027   Map 21 A2   **R**
63 Frith Street Soho W1V 5TA

Bruno Loubet's is still the dominant influence here though he also keeps a watch on the café next door. In September 1995, after we went to press, L'Odeon was due to open at 65 Regent Street, a major event on the London restaurant scene. In the meantime the Bistrot continues, a simple restaurant furnished in a modern style that reflects the warm, sunny aspects of the cooking which has its heart in Loubet's home territory, South-West France. Seemingly simple dishes have that rare quality of combining lightness with a complex and beautifully synthesised marriage of flavours. Seared tuna appears with grilled squid, a rocket salad of marinated white anchovy fillets with a mix of finely diced peppers (with the subtlest hint of chili) and a balsamic vinegar dressing. Thinly-sliced cold roast lamb with grilled aubergine, feta and aïoli; smoked mackerel rillettes and jellied oysters with creamed horseradish; wild mushroom fricassee on a round of toasted brioche with a poached egg and truffle oil and snail cromesquis on a tomato relish and green oil are other examples of the magic that emanates from these kitchens as starters. The main courses offer equal inventiveness based on classic French country cooking. A quite substantial middle cut of steamed sea bass comes with a pot au feu of spring vegetables accompanied by a delicious garlicky rouille. The selection might also include roast breast of duck with a sweet wine sauce and very thick pea 'pancake', roast neck of lamb provençale and veal breast with butternut pumpkin risotto. There is satisfaction in every mouthful. Desserts aren't quite in the same league though they are not without appeal. A puff pastry case with a pear in vanilla fudge, brioche-and-butter pudding and marinated strawberries with green peppercorn ice cream feature, as well as a most enjoyably chocolatey chocolate tartelette, cooked to order, and served with a coffee cream. Splendidly relaxed and informal service complement the restaurant's generally laid-back atmosphere. Café Bruno next door offers a short selection of inexpensive light meals prepared with the same meticulous attention to flavour and texture. *Seats 40. Parties 12. L 12.15-2.30 D 6.15-11.30. Closed L Sat, all Sun, Bank Holidays, 1 week Xmas. Access, Amex, Diners, Visa.*

We welcome bona fide complaints and recommendations on the tear-out pages at the back of the book for readers' comments. They are followed up by our professional team.

SW7   Bistrot 190   ↑   £50

Tel 0171-581 5666 Fax 0171-581 8172   Map 19 B4   **R**
190 Queen's Gate SW7 5EU

Long opening hours, a flexible menu and the watchful eye of Antony Worrall Thompson ensure continued success for the ground floor bistro part of the operation at 190 Queen's Gate (see also Downstairs at 190) and the Gore Hotel. The lively atmosphere and friendly service add to the appeal, already considerable because of the food. Try a salad of hot oysters with crabmeat gratin, crispy bacon and frisée, or goat's cheese and wild mushroom rösti to start, then chargrilled chicken with polenta mash, spicy lentils and deep-fried celeriac or Creole blackened tuna with three salsas and new potato salad. Finish with baked pumpkin and cognac cheesecake or lemon and lime tart with blackberry coulis. Both a Sunday brunch and a fixed-price menu (with a traditional roast) are offered. All the wines on the shortish, frequently changing wine list are available by bottle or two-glass pichets; over a dozen unusual bottled beers. *Seats 55. Parties 10. Private Room 25. Meals 7am-12.30am (Sun to 11.30pm). Set Sun L £12.95. Closed 3 days Christmas. Access, Amex, Diners, Visa.*

SW3   Blair House Hotel   £90

Tel 0171-581 2323 Fax 0171-823 7752   Map 19 C5   **B**
34 Draycott Place SW3 2SA

Well-equipped bed and breakfast hotel conveniently located near Sloane Square with quiet bedrooms at the back. Lift to all rooms. *Rooms 16. Access, Amex, Diners, Visa.*

SW7   Blakes Hotel   82%   £268

Tel 0171-370 6701 Fax 0171-373 0442   Map 19 B5   **HR**
33 Roland Gardens SW7 3PF

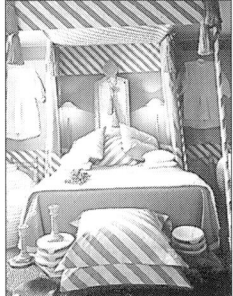

In converting a row of Victorian town houses over the last ten or so years, designer Anouska Hempel has created a small luxury hotel unlike any other; it's a dramatic, almost fantastic exercise in personalised opulence and elegance using the finest craftsmen and the choicest raw materials. The small foyer/lounge area is papered black yet warmed by the browns of polished natural wood and bamboo with leather seating piled high with plumped-up cushions. The overall effect is Oriental, a theme carried through to the Chinese Room that leads off the smart basement restaurant where an intimate bar is also to be found. Bedrooms vary widely in decor – from the extravagance of one containing the Empress Josephine's day bed to the clever simplicity of an all-white room with white-painted floorboards and trompe l'oeil wall paintings. The more expensive rooms are singular in design with masses of heavily swagged drapes in unusual fabrics and polished wood floors; furnished with antiques, objets d'art and a profusion of framed prints along with delicate Venetian glassware. Mostly beautiful bathrooms with marble surrounds, though standard rooms have small modern white-tiled ones. In the oldest part, the rooms, some on the small side, have clothed walls, carpets, bedding, draped curtains, upholstery, even the woodwork all in an absolutely identical shade of flannel grey. On the lower floors there are lighter rooms with a monochrome decor, black-and-white tartans against plain white backgrounds. The newest of all the bedrooms has a stunning Middle Eastern influence. Breakfasts can be English, Continental or Kyoto Country. Room service can provide sandwiches, salads, pastries and refreshments round the clock. The room rate quoted is for one of the smaller doubles. Large doubles and suites range upwards from £333. An unusual and exotic hotel with friendly and helpful staff. *Rooms 51. Access, Amex, Diners, Visa.*

Blakes Restaurant   £150

The restaurant is every bit as original as the rest of the hotel, with elegant black-and-white furniture and framed Thai warrior costumes and jewellery. Plate-glass screens divide some of the tables in what is a small, discreet and elegantly contemporary room. In this unique setting Neville Campbell presents a range of dishes for which the word 'eclectic' could have been invented, a cuisine which unites East and West in eye-catching harmony. From the Orient come prawn toast wrapped in bean curd with chili sauce and chicken tikka with cucumber mint and chili raita; from nearer home soufflé suissesse, inkfish risotto and baked sea bass with crispy fennel skin. Chicken Fabergé, filled with lobster and ginger, is a Hempel-inspired creation of chicken and lobster moulded into the shape of a large egg, tied with a ribbon of nori seaweed to look like a Fabergé egg and served with a basil sauce. The short and expensive wine list is too insignificant for serious comment. Drinks and coffee may be served in the Chinese Room or bar. *Seats 35. Parties 14. Private Room 20. L 12.30-3 D 7.30-11.30. Closed L 25, 26 Dec.*

E1   Bloom's   £40

Tel 0171-247 6001   Map 16 D3   **R**
90 Whitechapel High Street E1 7RA

Long-established, world-famous fine kosher restaurant, where a rabbi and a religious supervisor are always in attendance. As well as salt beef (hot or cold) there are other favourites such as gefilte fish, chopped herring, heimishe barley soup, gedempte meatballs, sweet and sour cabbage, beetroot salad and potato latkas. Finish with an excellent apple strudel. Quick service from wise-cracking, long-serving staff. The restaurant has its own parking. *Seats 144. Meals 11.30-9.30 (Fri to 2.30pm). Closed D Fri, all Sat, Jewish Holidays. Christmas. Access, Amex, Diners, Visa.*
Also at:
NW11 130 Golders Green Road NW11 8HB Tel 0181-455 1338   Map 16 B1
Open till 2am Sun-Thur (Sat to 4am). Closed D Fri, L Sat, Jewish Holidays.

SW6   Blue Elephant   £70

Tel 0171-385 6595 Fax 0171-386 7665   Map 19 A6   **R**
4-6 Fulham Broadway SW6 1AA

Verdant decor incorporating a waterfall, a bridge over a stream and a veritable jungle of greenery – an exotic setting in which to enjoy luxurious, MSG-free Thai cooking. The Royal Thai banquet menu is still one of the most popular ways of dining – it includes at least six starters and six main courses, so everyone gets plenty of taste sensations. Hot dishes are indicated by little red elephants (up to three) on the menu. Separate vegetarian menu £18.50. Other Blue Elephants are in Paris, Brussels and Copenhagen. *Seats 250. Parties 30. Private Room 100. L 12-2.30 D 7-12.30 (Sun to 10.30). Closed L Sat, 24-27 Dec, 1 Jan. Set L & D £25/£28 (Sun buffet L £14.50, special price for children). Access, Amex, Diners, Visa.*

SE1   Blue Print Café   £60

Tel 0171-378 7031 Fax 0171-378 6540   Map 17 D4   **R**
Design Museum Shad Thames Butlers Wharf SE1 2YD

Flashes of red, yellow and blue add colour to a bright, stylish restaurant on the first floor of the Design Museum with views overlooking the Thames. Chef Lucy Crabb changes her menu daily, providing dishes in the modern fashion with influences from Europe and further afield. Speciality dishes include hot spiced mussels with coconut and coriander; pan-fried John Dory with clams and white wine sauce; roast duck breast with port, prune and blood orange sauce; and vanilla cheesecake with bananas and maple syrup. Summer eating on the outside balcony tables has the added benefit of wonderful views of Tower Bridge. Put your car in the park on the riverfront at the end of Curlew Street. *Seats 86. Parties 15. L 12-3 (Sun to 3.30) D 6-11. Closed D Sun, 4 days at Christmas. Access, Amex, Diners, Visa.*

SW7   Bombay Brasserie   ★   £70

Tel 0171-370 4040 Fax 0171 835 1669   Map 19 B5   **R**
Courtfield Close Courtfield Road SW7 4UH

The most glamorous Indian restaurant in town, and a hit since opening its doors in 1982. The handsome room, with its Raj pictures and paddle fans, is from a time past, evoking a grand hotel of a century ago. Entrance is to a roomy bar area where mango Bellini is a popular cocktail. One part of the restaurant proper is a large and flowery conservatory, which despite its lack of views manages to convey a garden feel. The kitchen garners its recipes from Northern and Western regions of the sub-continent and numbers Goan, tandoori and vegetarian dishes among its specialities. Some of the best dishes are Bombay seaside snacks (*sev batata puri*), *papri ma gosht* – a Parsee dish of lamb and flat bean stew with herbs and garlic, Goan fish curry, chicken biryani and lobster *hara masala* (pan-fried and flavoured with fresh green herbs). Meat and vegetarian thali provide tasting portions of many dishes. Lunchtime buffet. Evening pianist. *Seats 175. Parties 20. Private Room 100. L 12.30-3 D 7.30-12 (Sun to 11.30). Closed 25 & 26 Dec. Set buffet from £14.95. Access, Diners, Visa.*

SW6   Bonjour Vietnam   £45

Tel 0171-385 7603 Fax 0171 610 2423   Map 19 A6   **R**
593 Fulham Road SW6 5UA

The decor is 1950s in style, the cooking South East Asian with dishes from Malaysia – satays, mixed seafood croquette; Thailand – tom yum spicy beef, cuttlefish cakes; Vietnam – spring roll wrapped in lettuce, baked squid in garlic butter sauce; Japan – crispy aubergine in batter, mushrooms in butter; and the various regions of China – crispy aromatic duck, sweet and sour fish fillet, sautéed beef in honey sauce. What is really unusual though is the format with none of the dishes individually priced (apart from the few desserts) but a fixed price per head for dinner bringing as many dishes as you like from the menu. At lunchtime a lower price lets you choose three starters, two main courses and one noodle or rice dish from a rather shorter version of the carte. This format might change. One of the Zen group of restaurants. *Seats 100. Private Room 25. L 12-3 D 6-11.30. Closed 2/3 days Christmas. Set L £8.80 Set D £14.80. Access, Amex, Diners, Visa.*

WC1   The Bonnington in Bloomsbury   62%   £100

Tel 0171-242 2828   Fax 0171-831 9170   Map 16 C3   **H**
92 Southampton Row Bloomsbury WC1B 4BH

During 80 years of the same family ownership this hotel has kept bang up to date. It is conveniently located for the British Museum and the shops of Oxford Street. Beyond the spacious foyer and lounge are a comfortable pine-clad bar, with a buffet serving salads and pub style food; and the airy Waterfall restaurant/breakfast room, complete with a genuine waterfall. Comfortable if modestly furnished bedrooms (over 50% of which are designated non-smoking) are all en suite, with tub and overhead shower. Under-14s share parents' room free. Four rooms are equipped for disabled guests. Air-conditioned facilities for up to 250 delegates. *Rooms 215. Access, Amex, Diners, Visa.*

SW7   La Bouchée   £50

Tel 0171-589 1929   Fax 0171-584 8625   Map 19 B5   **R**
56 Old Brompton Road South Kensington SW7 3DY

Bustling and very French, this brasserie on ground and basement floors has been feeding francophiles of South Kensington for four years. As well as standard bistro offerings – snails in garlic butter, warm goat's cheese salad and steak frites, there are always more elaborate dishes, not often found in this price range – perhaps steamed clams with white wine and shallots, globe artichoke vinaigrette and Irish oysters (at only £4.95 for six!) then maybe John Dory with a gazpacho sauce, confit of rabbit with celeriac mash and excellent ox tongue with sauce piquante as main courses. A short, carefully chosen wine list contains bargains such as a single domaine Viognier at £11 and Guigal's Cotes-du-Rhone at £10.50. Candle-lit tables are closely packed, and service can be stretched; but this is still a place for fun eating! A few pavement tables are perfect for people-watching in fine weather – if you can put up with the traffic. Sunday roast. *Seats 85. Meals 9am-11pm (Sun 9.30am-10.30pm). Set L & D (until 8pm) £4.95 & £9.95. Closed 25 & 26 Dec, 1 Jan. Access, Visa.*

W8   Boyd's   £70

Tel 0171-727 5452   Fax 0171-221 0615   Map 18 A3   **R**
135 Kensington Church Street W8 7LP

Intimate and comfortable, this glass-roofed restaurant is now well established on the London eating scene. Boyd Gilmour's cooking draws heavily on French tradition, with carefully reduced sauces, and makes only a passing nod at the olive oil and parmesan-shaving school of modern fashion. So perhaps onion soup with gruyère croutons, sautéed foie gras with girolles or an excellent lobster ravioli with tarragon and saffron to begin; roast chicken with goat's cheese and a Chardonnay sauce, a cep risotto or rack of lamb (again with wild mushrooms) to follow. Much care is taken over the display of all dishes, but the general timing and taste combinations are not always so successful; an excellent Madeira sauce accompanied overcooked saddle of venison and oversweet fried onions. A short table d'hote is offered at lunchtime, in addition to the carte, with two choices at each stage. *Seats 40. L 12.30-2.30 D 7-11. Closed Sun, 2 weeks Christmas, Bank Holidays. Set L £14. Access, Amex, Diners, Visa.*

W6   The Brackenbury   £55

Tel 0181-748 0107   Map 17 A4   **R**
129-131 Brackenbury Road W6 0BQ

The Brackenbury is not only one of West London's best-patronised neighbourhood restaurants, but from the day it opened in 1991 it has made many ripples extending far beyond its expected hinterland. The reason is clear – a winning mix of good, easy-to-enjoy food, very reasonable prices and a friendly, bustling atmosphere helped along by cheerful, hardworking staff. Moreover, almost all the wines on the broadly-based list are available by the glass (more than 20). The place used to be a wine bar, and a bar area still remains; the eating areas are utilitarian yet welcoming. Adam Robinson cooks a short menu that changes at each session and demonstrates the quality and accessibility of modern British cooking. The plate of savouries which heads the menu offers generous nibbles (often of what is to be found down the list) to accompany drinks and not necessarily to replace starters such as cullen skink, eggs poached in red wine, crostini of lamb's brains with salsa verde or stir-fried squid, spaghetti, parsley and garlic. Main courses are typified by steamed fillet of brill with spinach and hollandaise sauce, lamb stew with flageolet beans, confit of duck with celeriac gratin, and roast rib of beef, chips and béarnaise (for two). Good cheeses, and some tempting desserts – hot spiced pears with saffron ice cream and madeleines, banana Yorkshire pudding with vanilla ice and hot chocolate sauce. *Seats 55. Parties 8. L 12.30-2.45 D 7-10.45. Closed L Mon & Sat, D Sun, Bank Holidays, 1 week Christmas. Access, Amex, Diners, Visa.*

SW14   Le Braconnier   £60
Tel 0181-878 2853   Map 17 A5   **R**
467 Upper Richmond Road West East Sheen SW14 7PU

A splendid little restaurant offering a fixed-price-only menu of French regional dishes. Start, perhaps, with moules gratinées, pigeon and duck breast with lentils or celeriac soup and proceed to cod bordelaise, cassoulet (a speciality) or entrecote steak marchand de vin. They now offer a main course of 6 or more mini-dishes all on one platter. Half a dozen half bottles on a wine list which features a bargain house champagne (specially imported). *Seats 30. L Sun Nov-Mar 12.30-2.30 D 7-10.30. Closed D Sun, all Mon, Bank Holidays, 1 week Christmas. Set L £15.50 Set D £16.50. Access, Amex, Visa.*

NW3   Bradleys   £65
Tel 0171-722 3457   Map 16 B3   **R**
25 Winchester Road NW3 3NR

Simon Bradley's restaurant has been a neighbourhood secret for far too long – hidden in a residential street behind Swiss Cottage underground station. The clever trompe l'oeil on the walls gives diners the impression of sitting in a converted book or antique shop. Bare floorboards and bentwood chairs complete the stage. Bradley's cooking is confident and with a strong piscine emphasis, cooked with a light touch: to start, mussel chowder with corn griddle cakes; half a dozen Cuan oysters or rocket salad with peppered trout, anchovies and parmesan; followed perhaps by escalope of salmon with Niçoise vegetables and salsa rossa; soy-fried Dover sole with shredded vegetables and ginger or some delicious scallops with squid, black risotto and saffron sauce. Equal care is taken with vegetables: one visit brought crisp French beans, chargrilled celeriac and superb cauliflower beignets with sour cream and chives – and a vegetarian main course of chargrilled vegetables with mushroom and tarragon stew and tomato-roasted haricot beans. Carnivores are not forgotten: offerings might include Cajun beef fillet with smoked shallots, potato shavings and tomato chili chutney or calf's liver with herb mash and pear fritters. Leave room for the tempting desserts – a baked apple sorbet with cinnamon banana and apple tequila fritters still lingers in the memory. The completely New World wine list is carefully chosen and has modest mark-ups. *Seats 45. Parties 8. L 12.30-2.30 D 6.30-10. Set Sun L £12/£15. Closed 1 week Christmas, Bank Holidays. Access, Visa.*

SW3   La Brasserie   £60
Tel 0171-581 3089 Fax 0171-823 8553   Map 19 B5   **R**
272 Brompton Road SW3 2AW

A *true* and versatile brasserie, open all day, every day except Christmas Day. Breakfast can be anything from a croissant to kippers, French toast to bacon and eggs. *Le petit menu* proposes two dozen dishes, from ham omelette or salade niçoise to quiche, tortellini and steak frites. The main menu of brasserie classics (onion soup, terrine, boudin noir aux deux pommes, coq au vin, pork with calvados, sole meunière) is supplemented by blackboard specials such as skate with black butter or an excellent couscous. Standards are being admirably maintained, and with the easy-going atmosphere and the reasonable prices, it is rightly at the top of many people's list of favourite places. *Seats 130. Parties 20. Meals 8am-midnight (Sun 10am-11.30pm). Closed 25 Dec. Access, Amex, Diners, Visa.*

W10   Brasserie du Marché aux Puces   £50

Tel 0181-968 5828   Map 16 B3   **R**
349 Portobello Road W10 5SA

Very much a locals' restaurant at the out-of-town end of Portobello Road. It's not particularly smart, with old vinyl tiles on the floor, a motley collection of tables that have lost most of their polish, an old mahogany bar counter and large windows with curtain poles loosely draped with muslin. It's coffee and croissants (and a cooked breakfast if you ask) till midday, when the main menu comes on stream. Dishes are listed in ascending order of price but with no distinction between starters and main dishes thus encouraging all appetites and pockets. Tagliatelle with pesto and plum tomatoes, asparagus hollandaise (the spears grilled, unusually, and with a good sauce but served on top of a rather unnecessary salad), smoked haddock and rocket salad, lamb shank with couscous, chicken curry with rice and plantain, and grey mullet with tropical fruit salsa show the style. A useful restaurant to know of if in the area but perhaps not justifying an expedition. *Seats 40. Parties 14. Private Room 25. Open 10am-11pm. Closed Sat, Sun & 5 days Christmas. Access, Amex, Visa.*

SW3   Brasserie St Quentin   £55

Tel 0171-581 5131 Fax 0171-584 6064   Map 19 B4   **R**
243 Brompton Road Knightsbridge SW3 2EP

Refubished in January 1995, the elegant and civilised Brasserie St Quentin is even more lively and sparkling, and is invariably busy every day of the year. Nigel Davis is now thoroughly at home, and from his cooking you wouldn't know that he's not French born and bred. The range of starters extends from soupe à l'oignon, escargots, rillettes and oysters to the robust assiette landaise – a plate of duck confit, foie gras and smoked goose breast. Scallops, sole and sea bass are regular features on the fish menu. Toulouse sausages, veal chop, rack of lamb and cassoulet on the meat. Finish with a delectable tarte au citron (well known to patrons of this group's traiteur outlet at Brompton Cross) or pavé de chocolat amer. The concise wine list is, of course, French. *Seats 80. Private Room 25. L 12-3 (Sun to 3.30) D 7-11.30 (Sun 6.30-11). Set L & D £9. Access, Amex, Diners, Visa.*

> Set menu prices may not always include service or wine.

W1   Britannia Intercontinental Hotel   77%   £226

Tel 0171-629 9400 Fax 0171-629 7736   Map 18 C3   **H**
Grosvenor Square W1A 3AN

Behind the grand, colonnaded frontage of three Georgian houses overlooking the Mayfair square is an appropriately elegant interior. The luxurious, chandeliered lobby sets the civilised tone, which the cocktail lounge and bar follow. The latter has live piano music every evening. The Waterloo Despatch bar is in pub style serving traditional ales. The Japanese Shogun restaurant (see separate entry) is also on the premises. Air-conditioned bedrooms range from standards (decent size, with reproduction furniture) to de luxe, each with a desk, seating area and bar, and the top-of-the-range suites, which offer many extras and luxury touches. One floor of rooms (60) is designated non-smoking. A business centre supports the conference facilities (max 110 delegates). No dogs. *Rooms 318. Gym, solarium, hair salon, news kiosk, florist, valeting, shopping arcade. Access, Amex, Diners, Visa.*

E14   Britannia International Hotel   68%   £125

Tel 0171-712 0100 Fax 0171-712 0099   Map 17 D4   **H**
Marsh Wall E14 9SJ

Blending in with the surrounding modern architecture the tall International stands just off West Ferry Road almost in the shadow of the Canary Wharf Tower which faces it across part of the former West India and Millwall Docks. Public rooms make full and good use of the waterside location and the views become panoramic from the bedrooms. No fewer than 15 conference and banqueting rooms for up to 600 delegates. The hotel is colourfully decorated throughout and features numerous large Chinese artefacts. There's limited underground parking. *Rooms 442. Indoor swimming pool, gym, sauna, steam room, solarium, beauty & hair salon. Access, Amex, Diners, Visa.*

W1   Brown's Hotel   76%   £256

Tel 0171-493 6020 Fax 0171-493 9381   Map 18 D3   **HR**
Albermarle Street W1A 4SW

Among the most English of London's grand hotels, Brown's was opened by a retired gentleman's gentleman in the year Queen Victoria came to the throne. Queen Victoria herself was a frequent visitor, Napoleon the Third stayed here and Theodore Roosevelt was married from the hotel. Mellow oak panelling and period moulded ceilings are hallmarks of the day rooms along with fresh flowers and smart, helpful staff. The lounge with chintzy wing-armchairs is the venue for their renowned afternoon teas while the clubby bar is named after St George, who is depicted in a stained glass window. Upstairs the bedrooms, which vary from spacious standard rooms to full suites with various categories in between including four new four-poster rooms, have all benefited from total refurbishment over the last couple of years, very much in English country house style with floral fabrics, antique (or reproduction) furniture (TVs and mini-bars are discreetly tucked away in nice veneered cabinets), good armchairs, little crystal chandeliers or gilt light fittings and splendid new marble bathrooms with deluge showers over the bath tubs, enveloping bathrobes and Floris toiletries. All rooms are now air-conditioned, although in some cases it's with portable units. Levels of service are high with beds turned down at night, 24hr room menu, valeting and concierge service. Valet parking (£30 per 24 hours). No dogs. Forte Hotels. *Rooms 116. Access, Amex, Diners, Visa.*

Restaurant   £95

Aidan McCormack has brought a lighter and more modern touch to dishes served here, in contrast to the polished and rather quaint service. Alongside the à la carte menu, there's a frequently-changing table d'hote offered at both lunch and dinner – typical examples being rillettes of rabbit and hazelnuts with roasted langoustines, seared halibut with a herb jus and medallions of beef with wild mushrooms and a seed mustard sauce. Traditional dishes such as Dover sole, a trolley roast and sausages with creamed potato and onion gravy are also popular. The wine list is expensive, with a glass of house wine an iniquitous £5.90 excluding service. *Seats 35. Parties 14. Private Room 8. L 12.30-2.30 D 6-10 (Sun 6.30-9.30). Closed L Sat. Set L £21.50/£24.50 Set D £29.*

EC1   Bubb's   £75

Tel 0171-236 2435   Map 20 B1   **R**
329 Central Markets EC1A 9NB

A little corner of France at the junction of Snow Hill and Farringdon Street. Though it's more or less part of Smithfield market, Bubb's is an excellent place for fish as well as meat. The fish choice changes according to what's best on the day, so you might find grilled sardines, poached salmon or halibut with sauce dieppoise. On the meat front come escalope of veal with lime, duck à l'orange, lamb cutlets with herbs and beef fillet with mushrooms and béarnaise sauce. *Seats 75. Parties 18. Private Room 25. L 12-2.30 D by arrangement only. Closed Sat, Sun & all Bank Holidays. Access, Amex, Diners, Visa.*

SW11   Buchan's   £59

Tel 0171-228 0888 Fax 0171-924 1718   Map 19 B6   **R**
62 Battersea Bridge Road SW11 3AG

200 yards south of Battersea Bridge, Buchan's announces itself with a bright blue double-shop frontage. Inside, the area is divided between front bar and restaurant behind. The style is French/Scottish, with a good choice of bar snacks (from moules frites to venison liver paté with whisky) complementing the fortnightly-changing restaurant menu. The latter might feature quails stuffed with pheasant, Scottish steaks flambéed in whisky and salmon in pastry with a fennel sauce alongside haggis with neeps and tatties and traditional Scottish fare. Well-risen hot soufflés are something of a speciality, apple pie and apricot steamed pudding both with crème anglaise are also among the puddings, or perhaps Scottish cheeses or Gaelic coffee take your fancy. Sunday lunches offer good value. A few tables are set outside on the pavement in good weather. *Seats 70. Parties 50. Private Room 50. L 12-2.45 D 6-10.45 (Sun 7-10.30). Closed 25 & 26 Dec. Set L (Sun) £8.50/£10.50. Access, Amex, Diners, Visa.*

SE1   Butlers Wharf Chop-house   £80

Tel 0171-403 3403 Fax 0171-403 3414   Map 17 D4   **R**
Butlers Wharf Building 36E Shad Thames SE1 2YE

This representative of Sir Terence Conran's string of restaurants, also benefitting from a superb riverside location close to Tower Bridge, offers predominantly British cooking, often using less common ingredients such as Lincolnshire chine or kipper paste. The bar offers a range of light dishes (sandwiches and cheeses, fish, pies and grills), and this is also where you'll find the afternoon tea and weekend brunch menus, the latter of which kicks off with a head-blowing pint of Theakston's best. The restaurant is particularly busy at lunchtimes and deservedly so – enjoy duck salad with celeriac, orange, celery and walnuts; or mussel, saffron and leek soup; or breaded lamb's sweetbreads with bacon and almonds. Main courses range from plaice and chips with tartare sauce to venison chops with cranberries, or roast veal kidney with bubble and squeak, black pudding and mustard sauce. Toothsome puds like Cathbridge burnt cream, Eccles cakes with vanilla ice cream and raspberry and peach gratin tempt even the most strong-willed. There's something rather comforting about serving wines by the jug, as they do here, as well as several by the glass. Overall, it's a splendid wine list, with helpful notes, though on the whole not cheap, especially when a further 12½ per cent service will be added. *Seats 115 (rest) 40 (bar). Parties 12. L 12-3 (Sat & Sun bar from 11.30) D 6-11 Jun-Sept 12-11. Set L £22.75 (weekends: bar brunch £13.50/£15.75). Closed L Sat (Rest), D Sun (all), 1 Jan. Access, Amex, Diners, Visa.*

W8   Byblos   £40

Tel 0171-603 4422   Map 19 A4   **R**
262 Kensington High Street W8 6ND

A dark, intimate restaurant filled with Middle Eastern artefacts. The Lebanese food is simple and authentic: hot and cold hors d'oeuvre, charcoal-grilled kebabs, couscous for two or more. For the best value try meat and chicken or vegetarian mezze. *Seats 45. Parties 22. Meals 11.45am-11.45pm. Closed 5 days Christmas. Set L £7.35 Set D £9.85 & £14.65. Access, Amex, Diners, Visa.*

SW1   Cadogan Hotel   74%   £170

Tel 0171-235 7141 Fax 0171-245 0994   Map 19 C4   **HR**
75 Sloane Street SW1X 9SG

Lillie Langtry lived here in the 1890s in a house which later became part of the hotel, and it was in the hotel that Oscar Wilde was arrested and taken to Reading Gaol. Management pay great attention to offering a personal welcome and service and panelled drawing room and elegant restaurant are part of its traditional old-fashioned charm. Double bedrooms are large and attractively arranged, and amenities include colour TV, trouser press, mini-bar, hairdryer and safe. Bathrooms are beautifully done out with blue Portuguese tiles. Enquire about the hotel's special rates during the summer, at weekends and during major London shows. Banqueting/conference facilities for 32/50. No dogs. *Rooms 64. Garden, tennis. Closed 24-29 Dec. Access, Amex, Diners, Visa.*

Restaurant   £55

A large portrait of Lillie Langtry keeps careful watch over the excesses of the guests in this airy and comfortable dining room. Graham Thompson's short table d'hote menus, though mainly traditional, keep a finger on the pulse of modern trends. Thus starters might include vegetable soup, a warm salad of chicory with scallops and pesto, or ravioli of duck confit with buttered cabbage; follow with fillet of cod with grain mustard sauce, roast monkfish with herb risotto and baby fennel or breast of guinea fowl with wild mushrooms and spinach (perfectly cooked and served with an unctuous veal reduction). Regular lunch dishes for each day of the week (Monday – steak and kidney pudding, Tuesday – roast poussin) provide a safe bet for the less adventurous. Hot soufflés are a dessert speciality. Concise wine list with inexpensive house selection. Two halves of Krug champagne, Grand Cuvée are cheaper than a bottle. The 2-course set lunch includes a glass of house wine, while 3 courses includes half a bottle. *Seats 32. L 12-2 D 5.30-10. Closed L Sat. Set L £11.90/£16.90 Set Sun L £17.90 Set D £21.90.*

SW1   Café Fish   £55

Tel 0171-930 3999 Fax 0171-839 4880   Map 21 A3   **R**
39 Panton Street off Haymarket SW1Y 4EA

Part of the Chez Gérard group, an informal café-restaurant in theatreland. The menu is more or less all fish and seafood. Specialities include plateau de fruits de mer (oysters, crab. prawns, mussels, langoustines, clams etc.), coquilles St Jacques, kedgeree and mixed seafood casserole. Downstairs is a bustling wine bar open from 11.30am to 11pm Mon-Sat (closed Sun) and serving a simpler selection plus steak and club sandwiches. *Seats 94. L 12-3 D 5.45-11.30. Closed L Sat, all Sun, 25 & 26 Dec. Access, Amex, Diners, Visa.*

SW7   Café Lazeez   £60

Tel 0171-581 9993   Map 19 B5   **R**
93 Old Brompton Road South Kensington SW7 3LD

A minimalist brasserie/restaurant on two floors next to Christie's South Kensington auction rooms. The cooking of Indian-inspired dishes is as unlikely as the starkly modern setting. Separate brasserie and restaurant menus offer a mix of traditional and 'evolved' dishes – from chicken karahi and lamb korma to more unusual ingredients such as mallard, tuna and salmon. Sunday brings a fixed-price buffet menu (£8.95). Omar Kayyam Indian champagne (the 'house bubbly') is also sold by the glass. *Seats 130. Private Room 60. Meals 11am-12.30am (Sun 11am-10.30pm). Closed 25 Dec. Access, Amex, Diners, Visa.*

EC1   Café du Marché   £55

Tel 0171-608 1609   Map 16 D3   **R**
22 Charterhouse Square Charterhouse Mews EC1M 6AH

Tucked away in a mews between Smithfield Market and the Barbican, this former meat warehouse has the feel of a converted country barn, with a lively ambience, increased by a good pianist at night. The short wine list is perhaps a little disappointing, but the fixed-price menu of mostly French regional cooking, with half a dozen choices at each course, has plenty to recommend it. Several dishes of the day, in addition to the likes of tuna risotto or an authentic fish soup with all (rather too many in fact) the trimmings, followed by, say, turbot provençale, calf's liver or steamed baby clams with the ubiquitous crème brulée, strawberry mousse and pear tart (excellent with cinnamon ice cream). *Seats 100. Parties 10. Private Room 65. L 12-2.30 D 6-10. Closed L Sat, all Sun, Bank Holidays, 1 week Christmas. Set L & D £19.75. Access, Visa.*

W1   Café Royal Grill Room   ★   £135

Tel 0171-439 9090   Map 18 D3   **R**
68 Regent Street W1R 6EL

The jewel in the crown of the Café Royal complex is the Grill Room, splendidly decorated in grand baroque style, with ornate mirrors, murals and ceiling paintings. Herbert Berger is the chef and he has introduced a touch of sophisticated modernity to a varied classical French menu. Begin with terrine of foie gras with celeriac, truffles and parsley oil, hot duck confit with apples, salad leaves and walnut oil or open ravioli of langoustines with a light tarragon butter sauce. Pot-au-feu of turbot and baby clams with grain mustard and horseradish or medallions of veal with saffron risotto, spinach, vegetable confit and basil might follow. Desserts are as interesting and complex as the preceding courses, for example, caramelised pastry leaves with marinated berries, sorbet and raspberry coulis. Service is formal, and well orchestrated by maitre d' David Arcusi. Definitely a place for the special occasion. Jackets and ties are required for gentlemen. A grand wine list to complement the surroundings here, though with quite excessive mark-ups in some areas! Plenty of choice, offering the best value, outside France. In the ground-floor, also rather grand, the Brasserie, with an all-day menu, offers simpler fare à la carte or fixed-price. *Seats 45. Parties 14. Private Room 50. L 12-2.30 D 6-10.45. Closed L Sat, all Sun, Bank Holidays (except L 25 Dec). Set L £24 Set D £39. Access, Amex, Diners, Visa.*

NW3   Caffè Graffiti   £60

Tel 0171-431 7579   Map 16 B2   **R**
71 Hampstead High Street NW3 1QP

A former coffee shop transformed into a charming little restaurant with pavement tables
for summer dining. The food is Mediterranean in style beginning with delicious country
bread served with a garlic and herb-flavoured Tuscan oil or an excellent black and green
olive tapénade. Typical dishes are warm goat's cheese salad with raspberry vinaigrette,
fresh mussels with pesto and garlic croutons, breast of chicken stuffed with mozzarella,
basil and sun-dried tomatoes and confit of duck on a bed of green lentils and coriander
garnished with deep-fried celeriac. There are good vegetarian options, too, and enjoyable
sweets such as honey and fromage frais tart or mixed fruit zabaglione. Overall, a simple,
friendly local restaurant serving very acceptable food. *Seats 45. Parties 20. L 12-3 (Sat till
4) D 6.30-11 (Sun Meals 12-9). Closed 25 Dec. Access, Visa.*

NW1   Camden Brasserie and Underground Café   £55

Tel 0171-482 2114   Map 16 C3   **R**
214-216 Camden High Street NW1

A winning formula ensures the continued success and very deserved popularity of this
restaurant, which has recently undergone a subtle change. The Underground Café which
occupies the next door basement now offers the same menu as the ground-floor brasserie.
The menu features more choice, with modern Mediterranean cooking very much in
evidence and the food is, as always, excellent. Begin perhaps with grilled merguez served
with a coriander and cumin yoghurt, duck liver terrine with plum chutney, chickpea
pancakes with caponata or a salad of baby spinach with goat's cheese and toasted almonds
(also available as a main course). To follow maybe braised shank of lamb with garlic
potato mash, grilled salmon with sorrel – or from the charcoal grill – corn-fed chicken
with rosemary, lamb fillet with roast peppers or entrecote béarnaise. To accompany the
grills are some of the best pommes frites in the country. Good espresso coffee and
attentive, amiable staff. *Seats 100. Parties 20. Private Room 60. L 12-3 D 6-11.30 (Sun 12-4,
6-10.30) Closed 25 & 26 Dec, 1 Jan. Access, Visa.*

SW19   Cannizaro House   76%   £160

Tel 0181-879 1464   Fax 0181-879 7338   Map 17 B6   **HR**
West Side Wimbledon Common SW19 4UF

On the edge of Wimbledon Common,
a Georgian mansion where the tone is
set by stately lawned gardens and the
bay-windowed drawing room, which
boasts giant flower arrangements, antique
furniture, oil paintings and sumptuous
seating. Similar elegance is to be found in
the Queen Elizabeth room, with cream,
pale green and pink colour scheme,
crystal chandelier, draped curtains and
ornate gilt mirror. The bedrooms, each
with its own character, are superbly
appointed, with top-quality reproduction
furniture and bathrooms featuring marble fittings, radio/TV speakers, phones and
bathrobes. New-wing rooms are smaller, their views inferior. Reduced rates at weekends;
higher rates during the All England Lawn Tennis Championships at the end of June.
No children under 8. Conference/banqueting facilities for 45/80. Thistle & Mount
Charlotte Hotels. *Rooms 46. Garden. Access, Amex, Diners, Visa.*

Restaurant   £95

Staff in morning suits provide correct, formal service that fits perfectly into the Georgian
dining-room with its central chandelier and tall windows looking out over a terrace to
the common beyond. The menu states that for customers too a dress code (jacket and tie
for gentlemen) "will be strictly observed". Cooking is also very correct with no short

cuts used in Stephen Wilson's kitchen to produce a menu which combines the straightforward – smoked salmon, salade niçoise and grilled Dover sole – with some modish offerings like a steamed red mullet with stir-fried bean shoots, spring onions and ginger, noisettes of lamb en crépinette on a beetroot, carrot and potato galette and several interesting vegetarian dishes. Flambé dishes too. The wine list promises more than it delivers. No children under 8 years. *Seats 36. Parties 10. Private Room 24. L 12-2.30 (Sun 12.30-2) D 7-10.30 (Sun to 10). Set L & D £21.55 (£25.95 Fri & Sat) Sun L £16.50.*

SW10   The Canteen   £75

Tel 0171-351 7330 Fax 0171-351 6189   Map 19 B6   **R**
Harbour Yard Chelsea Harbour SW10 0XD

Some changes here with a new head chef, Tim Powell, succeeding the previous incumbents. Decor has a bold 'suit of cards' theme with huge flower arrangements and generally well-spaced tables. Book in advance for a table with a marina view. The choice on the menu is extensive, with more than a dozen each of both starters and main dishes, many of which also appear at Marco Pierre White's The Restaurant, though here they are tempered down, still retaining the essential elements of quality but delighting the pocket as well as the palate. Begin with a wonderful creamy mussel soup with saffron; vichyssoise of smoked haddock and chives; risotto of scallops; terrine of sweetbreads, chicken and foie gras with sauce gribiche; or carpaccio of tuna with salad of herbs. Main dishes include salmon with savoy cabbage and white truffle oil; roast sea bass with pommes boulangère, aubergine caviar and sauce antiboise; roast quails with Ventreche ham, braised cabbage, brioche dumpling and thyme jus; and escalope of calf's liver with Alsace bacon, pommes purée, braised cos lettuce and sauce diable. Superb puds include beautifully risen soufflés as well as a classic lemon tart and outstanding tarte tatin of pears. Wines are sensibly priced, with over 20 bottles at £20 or less; a list of fine wines is also available on request. *Seats 135. Parties 12. L 12-3 (Sun 12.30-3.30) D 6.30-12 (Sun 7-11). Access, Amex, Visa.*

SE1   Cantina del Ponte   £65

Tel 0171-403 5403 Fax 0171-403 0267   Map 17 D4   **R**
Butlers Wharf Building 36C Shad Thames SE1 2YE

The opportunity for fine weather alfresco dining on a terrace overlooking the Thames is a major feature in this light, airy restaurant, next to *Pont de la Tour* in Sir Terence Conran's Gastrodrome. Inside, a sunny Mediterranean ambience also reflects the inspiration of the cooking. Try tomato mousse with pesto and mozzarella; calamari, blackeye bean and spinach salad; or risotto croquettes with sautéed chicken livers and Madeira to start, then fillet of red mullet in red wine sauce or paillard of venison with chicory and mustard fruits for main course. Good pizzas, too. Desserts like pear and chestnut cake with pear sorbet, or poppy seed parfait with poached dates in rum complete the meal. Concise, mostly Italian wine list. *Seats 95. Parties 20. L 12-3 D 6-11. Closed D Sun, Good Friday, 4 days Christmas. Access, Amex, Diners, Visa.*

SW3   The Capital   85%   £257

Tel 0171-589 5171 Fax 0171-225 0011   Map 19 C4   **HR**
Basil Street SW3 1AT

Just fifty yards from Harrods in fashionable Knightsbridge, Margaret and David Levin's very stylish hotel is grand in every sense, yet small by London standards. You are assured of a warm greeting on arrival in the redesigned front hall, which sets the elegant standard throughout the handsomely furnished building. Changes, some imperceptible, take place continuously – this year the recarpeting of the sixth floor and redecoration of the second and third floor bedrooms. Additionally, a new floor-service area has further improved room service (24hrs). Margaret's hand is evident in individually-designed bedrooms that are models of good taste with custom-built furniture, fine fabrics and excellent lighting controlled from the bedside. Each bedroom is equipped with adjustable air-conditioning, mini-bar and satellite TV, with further amenities (eg safe, guest umbrella) in the de luxe rooms. Extra personal touches are evident as well, such as the daily replenishment of fresh fruit, invariably just one variety in season. Bathrooms are exquisite (suites have a separate cloakroom) with luxurious bathrobes and best-quality toiletries, while housekeeping is exemplary, naturally including the turn-down of beds (note the comfortable mattresses

See over

and real bed linen) in the evening. In fact, all the staff are thoroughly professional and courteous. Two first-floor private rooms can provide banqueting for 24 guests and conferences for 30. Own parking for 16 cars. *Rooms 48. Access, Amex, Diners, Visa.*

Restaurant £120

Newly designed by Margaret Levin, the restaurant is now both more spacious and comfortable. It's also a showpiece for David Linley's craftsmanship – note the wooden shutters and framed mirrors with créations tournées displayed on brackets at either end of the room. The space has been created by the reconstruction of the hotel's facade, in essence pushing it out to the street. Still visible however are the chefs in the kitchen with Philip Britten at the helm, and what has also not changed is the quality of the cooking and service (which now includes the distaff side), both hallmarks of The Capital's style. Excellently prepared and presented dishes can be described as modern British, albeit French-inspired, typically langoustine risotto, honey-roasted Barbary duck long-cooked in a slow oven, and a trilogy of chocolate desserts. There are various menus, thankfully written in sensible English – at lunch a fixed-price menu, preceded by an amuse gueule, say a mini-brochette of seared/grilled tuna, followed by perhaps a terrine of poulet de Bresse, steamed salmon with leeks, and a rice pudding. Alongside the à la carte, there's a six-course fish menu (four plus two desserts), which might include a consommé of scallops and beetroot with crème fraiche, fresh spinach pasta and warm marinated salmon, and baked sea bass with braised fennel. Finish with a vanilla parfait and caramel syrup, a pear tarte tatin and cinnamon ice cream, or British cheeses served with pecan bread and grapes, culminating in super coffee accompanied by a variety of petits fours. The wines from David Levin's own vineyards are outrageously priced! Seriously, the list here is serious indeed, with fabulous clarets and decent burgundies, and a good-value house selection. Prices include service. *Seats 40. Parties 8. Private Room 24. L 12-2.30 D 7-11.15. Set L £22.50/£25 Set D £35/£40 (6 courses).*

SW1   Le Caprice   £70

Tel 0171-629 2239 Fax 0171-493 9040   Map 18 D3   **R**
Arlington House Arlington Street SW1A 1RT

After almost 15 years, Chris Corbin's and Jermy King's cool and fashionable restaurant is still one of *the* places in town. Decorated in black and white, with a collection of classic David Bailey photographs on the walls, the stylish room is the perfect backdrop in which to enjoy the cooking, which mixes trendy and traditional, with seared scallops, Alsace bacon and sorrel, Mexican griddled chicken salad and Scandinavian iced berries with white chocolate sauce sharing the list with eggs benedict, steak tartare, and tournedos Rossini. Sunday brunch is launched with pitchers of Bucks Fizz or Bloody Mary. Booking essential. *Seats 70. Parties 8. L 12-3 (Sun to 3.30) D 6-12. Closed Christmas-New Year. Access, Amex, Diners, Visa.*

W1   Caravan Serai   £45

Tel 0171-935 1208 Fax 0171-431 4969   Map 18 C2   **R**
50 Paddington Street W1M 3RQ

Caravan Serai is a cheerful, relaxed place with bright Afghan decor and artefacts and authentic Afghan cooking that puts the emphasis more on subtle spices than fiery chili, reminiscent of both Arab and Indian cuisine. Among the house recommendations are the national dish ashak – pasta filled with leeks served with minced lamb and yoghurt (there's also a vegetarian version); poorshuda – stuffed poussin; and shahi korma – king prawns cooked in delicate spices. *Seats 55. Private Room 16. L 12-3 D 6-11.30 (Sun to 10.30). Closed 25 & 26 Dec. Set L £9.95. Access, Amex, Diners, Visa.*

We publish annually, so make sure you use the current edition
— It's well worth it!

N1   Casale Franco   £60

Tel 0171-226 8994 Fax 0171-359 5569   Map 16 C3   **R**
134 Upper Street Islington N1 1PQ

The illuminated chevron sign of a Citroën garage locates the cul de sac on Upper Street which opens out into a courtyard with outside tables. The restaurant has a truly authentic rustic decor with rough redbrick walls and a concrete floor. It's a popular place, especially in the evening, so arrive early to avoid the queues. The food is fairly classic Italian, the staple being pasta with grilled meats, fish and particularly good pizzas. Wild boar and venison also make seasonal appearances. *Seats 140. Parties 25. Private Room 35. L Fri-Sun 12.30-2.30 D 6.30-11.30 (Sun to 11pm). Closed L Tue-Thu, all Mon, 1 week end Aug, 1 week Christmas. Access, Visa.*

Set menu prices may not always include service or wine.

SW10   Chapter 11   £50

Tel 0171-351 1683 Fax 0171-376 5083   Map 19 B5   **R**
47 Hollywood Road Fulham SW10

Just off Fulham Road, opposite the new Chelsea & Westminster Hospital, John Brinkley's informal, busy brasserie serves a menu that mixes traditional and modern elements: Caesar salad, seared squid with rocket and ginger, fish cakes with parsley sauce, grilled calf's liver with caramelised apple, haricots verts and mashed potato. They now have a full cocktail bar with a happy hour till 8. Bar snacks are also available. In summer tables (seating 35) are set out in the back garden. Hollywood Road is 'no entry' from its north end. *Seats 60. Parties 12. Private Room 40. D only 7-11.30. Closed Sun, Bank Holidays. Access, Amex, Visa.*

SW3   Charco's   £65

Tel 0171-584 0765   Map 19 C5   **R**
1 Bray Place SW3 3LL

Just off Kings Road and not far from Sloane Square, Charco's is making a name for itself as a serious eating place as well as a popular and fashionable wine bar. Chef Jon Bentham, whose pedigree includes spells with Stephen Bull and John Burton-Race (L'Ortolan at Shinfield), presents an appealing menu which shows a style and inventiveness that's very much his own. Cured salmon with potatoes, capers and mint, twice-cooked crab soufflé and pressed oxtail terrine with curried mango chutney are typical starters, while a choice of half a dozen or so main courses might include feuilleté of scallops with coriander and steamed cucumber, roast calf's liver with sweet wine and pink grapefruit, and braised lamb with balsamic vinegar, glazed turnips and herb butter. Intriguing combinations continue right through the menu with desserts such as lemon and almond tart with lavender ice cream or baked white chocolate and caramel cheesecake. Shortish but good wine list, with many available by the glass. *Seats 70. L 12-2.30 D 6.30-10.30. Closed Sun. Access, Amex, Visa.*

NW3   Charles Bernard Hotel   60%   £65

Tel 0171-794 0101 Fax 0171-794 0100   Map 16 B2   **H**
5 Frognal, Hampstead NW3 6AL

Quiet 70s hotel, conveniently situated just off Finchley Road, ideal for business travellers. Open-plan public rooms are light and airy. Small, modestly furnished bedrooms have satellite TV, trouser press, hairdryer and tea/coffee-making facilities. All have en-suite bathrooms with tub and shower attachment. No dogs. Small private car park. *Rooms 57. Access, Amex, Diners, Visa.*

W5   Charlotte's Place   £50

Tel 0181-567 7541 Fax 0181-567 0346   Map 17 A4   **R**
16 St Matthew's Road Ealing W5 3JT

Intimate little bistro/restaurant on the edge of Ealing Common (easy parking) serving unpretentious, mainly English fare from haddock smokie pie and garlicky stuffed mushrooms to salmon with hollandaise sauce, lamb cutlets and a salad of warm duck breast. Beef Wellington is a speciality. *Seats 40. Private Room 20. L 12.30-2 D 7.30-10. Closed L Sat, all Sun, Christmas-New Year. Set L £12.50/£14.50. Access, Amex, Diners, Visa.*

SW1   The Chelsea   61%   £200

Tel 0171-235 4377   Fax 0171-235 3705   Map 19 C4   **H**
17-25 Sloane Street Knightsbridge SW1X 9NU

Modern hotel close to Knightsbridge underground station, Hyde Park and the temptations of Harrods. The open-plan public rooms are under a glass-roofed atrium, which features an art deco polished steel spiral staircase. Bedrooms, though compact, are equipped with all modern accessories; all have en-suite bathrooms, with marble-clad walls and tubs with overhead showers. 24hr room service. A certain amount of refurbishment is required to maintain the high standard of the amenities, which the new owners hace indicated will be done later this year. Three bedrooms have been designated for non-smokers. Children up to 14 stay free in parents' room. NCP parking. *Rooms 225. Hairdressing, lounge (8am-midnight). Access, Amex, Diners, Visa.*

NW1   Cheng-Du   £60

Tel 0171-485 8058   Map 16 C3   **R**
9 Parkway Camden Town NW1 7PG

Friendly Szechuan restaurant at the lower end of Parkway. Among the dishes on offer are crispy beef shreds with chili and carrots, sautéed fresh squid in a Szechuan hot bean sauce and scrambled egg Fu-Yung with fresh salmon and Chinese chives. *Seats 70. L 12-2.30 D 6.30-11.30. Set D £17.20. Closed 24-26 Dec. Access, Amex, Visa.*

W1   Chesterfield Hotel   74%   £210

Tel 0171-491 2622   Fax 0171-491 4793   Map 18 C3   **H**
35 Charles Street Mayfair W1X 8LX

Just off Berkeley Square, this hotel is named after the third Earl of Chesterfield, a renowned Mayfairite of the 18th century. It is very English in feel, and guests are welcomed by a splendid marble floor with Persian carpets, masses of flowers and a picture of the Earl himself. A comfortable club-style bar, with deep green walls and leather easy chairs, where a pianist plays on weekday evenings, is a useful place to meet before dinner (disappointing on our last visit, but we're led to believe that improvements have since been made) in either the restaurant or the plant-filled conservatory. There are five floors of bedrooms, all recently refurbished in an elegant and luxurious style and equipped with TVs with satellite (including CNN), direct-dial phones and 24hr room serivce. The en-suite bathrooms have deep tubs with hand-held showers, good-quality toiletries, bathrobes and hairdryers. There are nine air-conditioned suites, some with their own dining/conference facilities; these have comprehensively stocked mini-bars. Comfortable, air-conditioned conference space for up to 110. No dogs. Guests have free use of the nearby Lansdowne Club. *Rooms 110. Access, Amex, Diners, Visa.*

SW17   Chez Bruce   NEW   £55

Tel 0181-672 0114   Fax 0181-767 6648   Map 17 C6   **R**
2 Bellevue Road SW17 7EG

Bruce Poole's new restaurant on the site of the erstwhile Harveys, made famous by Marco Pierre White, sensibly makes no attempt to emulate its illustrious predecessor. Poole's menus are more reminiscent of mentors Marc and Max Renzland (see *Chez Max*), for whom he was head chef. Thus there is a firm French accent on the cooking, although the menus are written in a confusing mixture of French and English. A recent list offered *soupe garbure, jambon persillé, moules normande* and *tarte à l'oignon* among the starters followed by *petit salé* with creamed flageolet beans, *daube de boeuf* and roast cod with spinach and olive oil mash amongst main-course choices from the good-value set menu. Although an enthusiastic charcutier, Poole's *jambon persillé* was so packed with jambon that the delicious garlicky flavour in the jelly remained elusive (a sampler plate of his charcuterie is available on the evening menu (£3 supplement) and can include chicken liver parfait, pork rillettes, rabbit ballotine, *fromage de tete* – and is accompanied by onion marmalade and delicious rémoulade). *Soupe garbure* is correct as is the daube of beef, though the latter lacked the lip-sticking quality so beloved of the daube aficionado. Traditional desserts might include tarte tatin (made with unannounced pears on one visit), crème brulée and an excellent lemon tart. The dining-room is decorated in a faux-rustic style which lacks conviction. The kitchen too needs to forsake this early nervousness and knock out the 'on yer bike' flavours for which he justly earned his reputation at Hampton Wick and Fulham. *Seats 65. L 12-2 D 7-10.30. Closed L Mon & Sat, D Sun, Bank Holidays, 1 week Christmas. Access, Amex, Diners, Visa.*

N4   Chez Liline   £45

Tel 0171-263 6550   Map 16 C2   **R**
101 Stroud Green Road Finsbury Park N4 3PX

Mauritian restaurant with a long, exclusively fishy menu that could include bourgeois, perroquet (parrot fish), sea bream and sole. Assiette Créole is a selection of tropical fish with tomatoes, herbs and chili. Lobsters and prawns are other specialities. A family business with a happy atmosphere. *Seats 44. Set L & D £10/£11.75. L 12.30-2.30 D 6.30-10.30. Closed Sun & Bank Holidays. Access, Amex, Visa.*

SW10   Chez Max   £80

Tel 0171-835 0874   Map 19 A5   **R**
168 Ifield Road SW10 9AF

Approached by a wide spiral staircase, the Renzlands' cosy basement dining-room provides the second of their restaurants (see *Le Petit Max* in Hampton Wick) and is soon to be joined by a third in Covent Garden. Menus from the restaurants of the great and the good adorn the peppermint walls, while bare wooden tables and a small roofed courtyard set the scene for some of London's finest francophile fare. Start with first-rate imam bayeldi, millefeuille of duck cassoulet with red cabbage or an assiette of the house terrines (ox tongue with leek, duck confit with foie gras and *jambon persillé* on one visit); follow with *pot au feu* of guinea fowl, roast sea bass with baked Provençal vegetables or the tenderest rack of lamb with a herb crust and sauce diable. Ingredients are chosen with great care, from the calamata olives and Charentais butter to the free-range chicken and guinea fowl. Only two cheeses are offered, but in perfect condition. Finish perhaps with an authentic crème brulée or petit pot au chocolat. There is a short, well-chosen wine list, though guests can still bring their own, but with a hefty corkage charge of £7.50. Service is relaxed and can belie the seriousness of this kitchen. *Seats 60. Private Room 10. L 12.30-2.30 D 7-11. Closed L Mon & Sat, all Sun, Bank Holidays, 1 week Christmas, 1 week Easter, 2 weeks summer. Set L £15/£17.50 Set D £25.50/£29. Access, Visa.*

W11   Chez Moi   £85

Tel 0171-603 8267   Map 17 B4   **R**
1 Addison Avenue Holland Park W11 4QS

The enduring partnership of chef Richard Walton and co-owner Colin Smith reaches its 28th anniversary this year. In a world of changing food fads and fancies the restaurant gallantly soldiers on producing a selection of superior classical dishes, though the menu does feature a few ethnic dishes by way of contrast. Flavours are distinct and saucing is a strong point, so results on the plate are very enjoyable. Quail's eggs with smoked salmon in a pastry case with sauce mousseline, classic Polish beetroot soup with soured cream, dill and delicious spicy turnovers or seared marinated scallops with a Japanese roll could precede goujons of John Dory with tartare sauce, rack of lamb with garlic and mint, or tournedos of beef with béarnaise sauce. An aromatic lamb couscous with spicy harissa and Thai-style chicken breast are interesting alternatives before some fine desserts. There is an intimacy to the very plush décor that makes the restaurant ideal for romantic dinners. Plenty of good drinking under £20. *Seats 45. Parties 16. L 12.30-2 D 7-11. Closed L Sat, all Sun, Bank Holidays. Set L £14. Access, Amex, Diners, Visa.*

W1   Chez Nico at Ninety Park Lane   ★★★   £150

Tel 0171-409 1290 Fax 0171-355 4877   Map 18 C3   **R**
90 Park Lane London W1A 3AA

The setting is an opulent dining room elegantly appointed with honey-coloured panelling and brightened by mirrors and discreet lighting. Menus are written in refreshingly straightforward English with no florid descriptions and the choice is long, with over 10 dishes at each stage. Sensational signature dishes remain, as in a warm salad of foie gras on toasted brioche with caramelised orange – a glorious combination of flavour and texture, though Nico's highly individual style of creativity continues to evolve. Dishes are constantly being reworked, often simplifying but also subtly refining them; but invention never takes a back seat. Delights such as a rosette of grilled scallops with baby spinach leaves, crispy salmon with ginger and teriyaki sauce and a salad of crisp guinea fowl with French beans in truffle oil and truffles are among the starters. The choice of fish main

See over

courses might include John Dory with a sweet and sour Oriental sauce and brill or turbot with a potato crust, while meat and offal dishes range from honey-roasted Bresse pigeon with cabbage and foie gras to saddle of lamb with a herb crust and fillet of Scotch beef with truffles, celeriac purée and foie gras. Sauces are simply sensational – glossy veal reductions that simply burst with flavour; there are no corners cut in these kitchens. A magnificent climax to a truly unforgettable meal is the grand plate of assorted mini-desserts (£6 supplement) – a tasting of many of the desserts, which include a slice of chocolate tart with pistachio ice cream, praline ice cream with glazed fruit and apricot sauce, lemon tart with cassis sorbet and cassis sauce and iced nougat with caramelised nuts. The thin apple tart with caramel sauce and vanilla ice cream is worth the advertised 20-minute wait – after all, a meal here is not one to be hurried. Consistency is of supreme importance in a restaurant that heads the Premier Division and Nico's watchful eye ensures that all is just as it should be. Around a couple of dozen wines are priced under £30, otherwise most wines on the very fine list are steeply marked up. *Seats 70. Parties 10. Private Room 20. L 12-2 D 7-11. Closed L Sat, all Sun, 4 days Easter, L Bank Holiday Mondays, 10 days Christmas/New Year. Set L £29 Set D £48 (2 courses)/£57. Access, Amex, Diners, Visa.*

W1   Chiang Mai   £40

Tel 0171-437 7444   Map 21 A2   **R**
48 Frith Street Soho W1V 5TE

Vatcharin Bhumichitr, author of *The Taste of Thailand* and *Thai Vegetarian Cooking*, runs this Thai restaurant just by Ronnie Scott's jazz club. The menu runs from satay, tempura and soups to hot and sour salads flavoured with lemon and chili and good-value, one-dish rice and noodle dishes. Vegetarians are well catered for. *Seats 75. Private Room 22. L 12-3 D 6-11 (Sun till 10.30). Closed L Sun, all Bank Holidays. Access, Amex, Visa.*
Also at:
W4 99 Chiswick High Road W4 Tel 0181 995 5774   Map 17 A4
Thai Bistro

WC1   Chiaroscuro   NEW   £65

Tel 0171-636 2731 Fax 0171-580 9160   Map 21 B1   **R**
Townhouse 24 Coptic Street WC1A 1NT

The chiaroscuro effect refers mainly to the decor with its contrasting bold hues. The restaurant comprises a longish, fairly narrow room, tables arranged down one wall with a classically-themed bas-relief frieze running its entire length. At the far end, a small rectangular area is dominated by an enlarged print of a painting by the 17th-century Renaissance artist, Guido Reni. The menu features a short, select choice of modern interpretations of Italian and Provençal dishes. Delicious warm herb rolls accompany a thick, well-flavoured fennel and lemon-thyme soup, a simple pan-fried artichoke galette with a herb aïoli or a saffron risotto with caper relish. Most of the the starters are also available as main-course portions too. The main courses proper include rare grilled tuna with a celeriac fritter and tomato concassé, roast chicken with borlotti beans, bacon and a hint of chili and grilled lamb cutlets with roast tomato and a rosemary pesto. A near perfect individual summer pudding or rich chocolate terrine with vanilla crème anglaise rounds off a very enjoyable meal.The evening set meals are available between 6 and 8pm and after 10.30 only. Accompanied children under 10 years eat free for Sunday Brunch. *Seats 59. Parties 12. Private Room 14. L 12-3.30 D 6-11.45. Closed L Sat, D Sun, some Bank Holidays. Set L & D £10. Access, Amex, Visa.*

WC2   China City   £55

Tel 0171-734 3388 Fax 0171-734 3833   Map 21 A2   **R**
White Bear Yard 25a Lisle Street WC2H 7BA

This surprisingly spacious and comfortable restaurant in the heart of Chinatown offers a lengthy carte, with a bemusing selection of carefully prepared, though fairly standard, Chinese fare. As well as traditional favourites like pancake rolls, Peking duck and lemon chicken, an unusual salad of crispy chicken with jelly fish and stir-fried beef in satay sauce (both coconut and chili featured here) provide a refreshing change. A strong seafood selection includes lobster, crab, squid and abalone, all on offer for fair prices and each cooked in several different ways. Numerous set meals are available, for a minimum of two (from £8 per head). Service is helpful and friendly. *Seats 500. Meals 12-11.45. Closed Christmas Day. Access, Amex, Diners, Visa.*

NW1   China Jazz   £70

Tel 0171-482 3940   Map 16 C3   **R**
29-31 Parkway Camden Town NW1 7PN

Jazz (live every evening, late at weekends) accompanies fairly expensive Chinese food cooked without additives, preservatives or artificial colouring. *Seats 110. Parties 90. L 12-2.30 D 6.30-11.30 (Fri & Sat till 1am Sun meals 1-10.30). Closed L Sat. Access, Amex, Visa.*

W14   Chinon   ★   £55

Tel 0171-602 5968   Map 17 B4   **R**
25 Richmond Way Shepherds Bush W14 0AS

An excellent and individualistic Shepherds Bush address, where Jonathon Hayes sets great store by the quality of his raw materials. That quality is enhanced by his own skill, application and inventiveness. Flavours and texture combinations are particularly successful as shown by crab ravioli with a light butter sauce, tempura of crevettes with leeks, sautéed squid with pesto, pesto mash and roasted red pepper, breast of duck with swede purée and a dome of vegetables and fillet of venison with savoy cabbage and fondant potato (vegetables are very much an integral part of each dish, and not merely a garnish). Desserts keep up the fine work, with ice cream and sorbets something of a speciality. *Seats 50. L 12.30-2 D 6.30-10.30. Closed Sun, few days Christmas & Easter (ring for details). Access, Amex, Visa.*

W6   The Chiswick   NEW   £55

Tel 0181-994 6887   Map 17 A4   **R**
131 Chiswick High Road W6

In the same ownership as The Brackenbury, and every bit as popular, The Chiswick is situated on Chiswick High Road nearly opposite Turnham Green Terrace. Decor and appointments are quite simple: lavender grey and cream walls, wood-block tables, 60s-looking pressed-wood chairs offering reasonable comfort, no tablecloths but proper linen napkins. Cooking is modern British with mainly Mediterranean influences: spiced aubergine salad, fishy hors d'oeuvre (gravad lax with dill sauce, mussels, anchovies on a cucumber salad), excellent marinated fillet of beef with rocket, truffle oil and parmesan, hake with tomato, saffron and capers, calf's kidneys with lentils, bacon and mustard, roast chicken leg with rösti and cep sauce. Apricot tart, chocolate mousse terrine and orange granita are typical desserts. Pavement tables in summer. Like The Brackenbury, this is very much a place for chatting as well as eating, and since the ceiling is rather low the noise level can be rather high. *Seats 70. Parties 14. L 12.30-2.45 D 7-11.30. Set L & D £8.50. Closed L Sat, D Sun, 25 Dec-1 Jan (phone to check Christmas closures). Access, Amex, Visa.*

W4   Christian's   £60

Tel 0181-995 0382 Fax 0181-995 0208   Map 17 A5   **R**
Station Parade Burlington Lane Chiswick W4 3HD

A smart striped awning on the outside and an equally elegant interior with Regency striped sage green walls hung with a collection of contemporary art is Christian Gustin's domain. He surveys all from a pristine, white-tiled, raised, open-plan kitchen at the rear. Menus change daily and consist of a short but varied selection of modernised bourgeois classics prepared with considered regard to flavours and textures. Soufflés are a speciality and can appear beautifully risen, moist and featherlight, flavoured with a subtle blend of English cheeses to begin or as a hot chocolate soufflé for dessert. Other choices could be a bowl of tomato soup and salsa, pressed belly of pork with a herb vinaigrette, steamed cod with fennel and capers, or grilled leg of lamb with mint. The plate of desserts is a very tempting finale. Service is relaxed and friendly. Annual and public holiday closures are when Christian "feels like it". No children under 7 "unless well behaved". *Seats 42. L (Tue-Fri) 12-2.30 D 7-10.30. Closed L Sat, all Sun & Mon. Access, Amex, Visa.*

Set menu prices may not always include service or wine.

WC2   Christopher's American Grill   £80

Tel 0171-240 4222   Fax 0171-240 3357   Map 20 A2   **R**
18 Wellington Street Covent Garden WC2E 7DD

A grand Victorian building which in 1863 became the first licensed casino in London.
Today, a sweeping stone staircase leads past reception (reservations are a must) up to
a lofty, tall-windowed dining room resplendent in its stylishly ultra-modern interpretation
of neo-classical decor. This is one of London's foremost centres of American food, with
steaks (imported from the USA) and 3lb Maine lobsters among the specialities. America
and the Med meet throughout the menu with the likes of smoked tomato soup, clam
chowder, Caesar salad, swordfish with Provençal mussels, burgers and New York strip
steak. A pre-theatre menu is available between 6 and 7 (three courses £15). The bar-café
with a separate menu that includes salads and sandwiches as well as many of the Grill's
dishes. Sunday brunch is served in the café between 12 and 3.30. Plenty of choice on the
wine list, from both Old and New Worlds. A dozen champagnes. *Seats 100. Parties 8.*
Private Room 32. L 12-2 D 6-11.30. Closed D Sun, Bank Holidays, 1 week Christmas.
Access, Amex, Diners, Visa.

W1   Chuen Cheng Ku   £35

Tel 0171-734 3281   Fax 0171-434 0533   Map 21 A2   **R**
17 Wardour Street W1V 3HD

Huge and popular Chinese restaurant in the heart of London's chinatown serving an
extensive range of Cantonese dishes. Dim sum are especially popular, and are served from
11am to 5.45pm daily – you make your choice visually from the trolleys that trundle
around the room, rather than from a menu. This lists the house specialities as well as
traditional favourites. *Seats 450. Private Room 180. Meals 12-11.45pm (Sun to 11). Closed*
25 & 26 Dec. Set meals from £9. Access, Amex, Diners, Visa.

W1   Churchill Inter-Continental   84%   £282

Tel 0171-486 5800   Fax 0171-486 1255   Map 18 C2   **HR**
30 Portman Square W1A 4ZX

Overlooking Portman Square, the hotel
opened in 1970. It was acquired and
extensively refurbished by the Inter-
Continental group in 1994 and now
offers public areas which are very grand
indeed with plenty of shiny marble
floors, columns, together with crystal
chandeliers and particularly comfortable
seating in the Terrace Lounge (a
favourite spot for afternoon tea that
includes fruit cake made to an authentic
recipe from a member of Winston
Churchill's household). The bar, on the
other hand, has a more club-like atmosphere, a theme repeated on the eighth floor,
which is designated the 'Club' floor: 55 bedrooms, including own check-in, secretary,
lounge, complimentary Continental breakfast, valet service and free use of boardroom –
well worth the additional charge of £25. In fact, business people are really well catered
for here – there's a fully-staffed business centre that includes the hire of mobile phones;
the 39 suites, with a walk-in shower as well as tub in the bathrooms, have a fax machine,
a music centre and VCR (all rooms are equipped with fax/modem points and hi-tech
TVs that allow you not only to receive incoming messages but also to read your up-to-
date bill); a multi-media personal computer is also available in the rooms. The good-
sized, air-conditioned and immaculately kept bedrooms are splendidly furnished in
country-house style with a variety of overseas touches, and the super bathrooms reflect
the exemplary standards of housekeeping and service found throughout the hotel, under
the direction of General Manager Christopher Cowdray. Comprehensive 24hr room
service (plus mini-bars in all rooms) and all-day snacks served in the lounge area. Fine
banqueting (240) and conference (350) facilities in a number of meeting rooms. Children
up to the age of 12 free in their parents' room. Underground NCP parking. No dogs.
Rooms 448. Garden (Portman Square with tennis), business centre, beauty & hair salons,
theatre desk, news kiosk, shop, coffee shop (8am-midnight). Access, Amex, Diners, Visa.

Clementine's
£80

A spacious and stylish dining room housing an extensive collection of contemporary British art, with a marble floor, inlaid in parts with herring-bone oak, mirrored columns, shuttered windows, pretty dried flower arrangements, and a long, panelled bar down one side of the room (its focus being the Cruvinet machine offering generous 6oz measures of fine wines by the glass). The menu has a distinct Mediterranean slant and chef Idris Caldora cooks with a sure and lightish touch, his dishes having strong and aromatic flavours. Supplementing the seasonally-changing à la carte are daily-changing market specialities, perhaps whole duck terrine with a rocket salad, egg and spinach ravioli gratinated with parmesan among the starters, some having two prices, the second as a main-course options. Main courses could include steamed sea bass with spring vegetables in a herb jus, baked cod with a pesto crust in a ragout of butter beans, pancetta and wild mushrooms and roast fillet of beef with artichokes, sausage, potato and tomato. For dessert, look no further than a chocolate tart with a white chocolate ice cream or a fresh fruit crepe omelette. Staff, dressed in boldly striped waistcoats, go about their business efficiently. A very sensible wine list that is fairly priced and clearly, very cleverly compiled. **Seats** *108. Parties 24. L 12.30-3 D 6-11. Closed L Sat. Set L £19.50 Set D £21.50.*

SW10   Chutney Mary   ↑   £60

Tel 0171-351 3113 Fax 0171-351 7694   Map 19 B6   **R**
535 Kings Road SW10 0SZ

Almost on the corner of Kings Road and Lots Road, Chutney Mary has made a niche for itself as 'the world's first Anglo-Indian restaurant'. Behind a nondescript modern facade, it's a roomy, attractive place with Raj pictures on pale walls, mirrored alcoves and a jungly glazed conservatory. The menu is like no other, with dishes from all over India based on recipes of the Memsahibs: calamari stir-fried with Kerala spices, crispy salmon samosas from Bombay, a salad of cashew-encrusted goat's cheese, masala roast lamb. Two of the most popular specialities are Country Captain – chicken breast braised with red chilis, almonds, raisins and spices, served with lemon rice; and scallop kedgeree served with dal. There's plenty of choice for vegetarians, a selection of desserts and regular food festivals. Sunday sees a grand buffet lunch. The colonial-style Verandah Bar at street level serves drinks, snacks and light meals, plus the restaurant menu in the evening. The name Chutney Mary was used by conservative Indians to describe an Indian woman who adopted English garb and manners. **Seats** *130. Parties 20. L 12.30-2.30 (Sun to 3) D 7-11.30 (Sun to 10.30). Closed D 25 Dec & all 26 Dec. Set L from £10 (Sun £13.95) Set D (after 10) £10/£12.95. Access, Amex, Diners, Visa.*

W14   Cibo   £70

Tel 0171-371 6271 Fax 0171-602 1371   Map 17 B4   **R**
3 Russell Gardens W14 8EZ

Popular neighbourhood restaurant, comfortable, lively and welcoming. Bold pictures line the walls and the regional Italian carte offers a profusion of contemporary dishes, with a strong emphasis on seafood, as in grilled squid with chili peppers, spaghetti with lobster, whole sea bass baked or grilled with fresh herbs and the favourite selection of grilled fish and shellfish, seafood and lobster. Starters include a splendid assortment of cured meats, and there are some unusual pasta dishes – try agnolotti with apple in a venison ragu or tagliolini with scallops and saffron. On the meat front come baked rack of lamb with broad beans and pan-fried calf's liver and sweetbreads with sautéed aubergines, zucchini and peppers. End with a classic tiramisu or panna cotta. The wine list is awash with some very fine wines at prices to suit all pockets. **Seats** *50. Parties 18. L 12-3 D 7-11. Closed D Sun. Set L £12.50. Access, Amex, Diners, Visa.*

Many hotels offer reduced rates for weekend or out-of-season bookings. Always ask about special deals.

| W1 | Claridge's | 88% | £316 |

Tel 0171-629 8860 Fax 0171-499 2210   Map 18 C3   **HR**
Brook Street Mayfair W1A 2JQ

A new management team, led by the redoubtable François Touzin, has replaced the long-serving Ronald Jones OBE and Michael Bentley at this, one of the world's great hotels. Established almost 100 years ago, Claridge's is synonymous with classic elegance, grace and dignity, which characterise every aspect. From the imposing front entrance to its numerous magnificent suites, the calm and tranquillity of the past blends perfectly with modern comforts. The Front Hall with a wide, sweeping staircase has a black and white marble floor, polished to a mirror-like shine. There is no bar proper but footmen in scarlet breeches, white hose and gold-braided tail coats are constantly on hand, while in the background the lilting strains of a Hungarian quartet can be heard both at lunchtime and in the evening. The Reading Room, a softly-lit lounge, is dominated by a portrait of Mrs William Claridge, the hotel's founder, under whose watchful eye sedate afternoon teas are served. A significant part of the hotel was added in 1932 to include the ballroom and many of the bedrooms. These are all furnished and decorated in a distinctive art deco style, each retaining irreplaceable original furnishings and fittings. The remaining bedrooms contrast in being more traditional in character and ambience featuring fine plaster mouldings and beautiful period furniture. Modern influences include satellite TVs, dual telephone lines and fax sockets, but thankfully little else has changed over the years. Bathrooms are marble-clad and boast probably the best showers in London with sunflower-size shower heads, many also with additional shoulder showers. Standards of service are exemplary with room buttons to summon maid, valet or floor waiter. For room service breakfast there is no menu but a waiter will discuss all individual requirements. Gentlemen have the use of the adjoining Bath and Racquets Club while ladies can visit the Berkeley Health Club roof-top swimming pool and gymnasium. Guests with a recognised golf handicap may play complimentary golf at Wentworth; similarly, tennis facilities are provided for guests at the Vanderbilt Club. Function rooms are luxurious – from the elegant Orangery and Drawing Room right up to the Ballroom Suite catering for up to 220 seated guests. No dogs. **Rooms** 190. *Valeting, ladies & gents hairdressers, travel & theatre desk. Access, Amex, Diners, Visa.*

Restaurant   £130

A splendid dining room designed in 1926 by Basil Ionides. It encapsulates the art deco style perfectly while a Christopher Ironside mirrored mural, a more recent addition, further enhances the opulence of the setting. Marjan Lesnik, maitre chef des cuisines, offers a suitably classical, enjoyable French menu with an emphasis on more modern interpretation and presentation. The three-course set menus represent good value with dishes like scallop and rosemary risotto with balsamic sauce, tournedos of beef with seared oyster mushrooms and sauce Chambertin and to finish crème brulée with wild strawberries or a choice of desserts from a trolley. From the à la carte come dishes such as foie gras terrine with truffle and Sauternes jelly, glazed poached egg with wild mushrooms and basil, grilled wild salmon with fennel and roast Tuscan pigeon with creamed Savoy cabbage and oregano sauce. Vegetables are straightforward and simple. Sweets are served from a beautifully presented trolley. Surprisingly perhaps, there are only two Grand Cru red burgundies on the wine list (nothing from Vosne-Romanée or Romanée-Conti), otherwise there's an excellent choice from around the world. The list is easy to use with the least expensive wines in each category first. Service, under Daniel Azoulai, runs as smoothly as the trolley. Dinner dances are now held on Friday and Saturday nights. **Seats** 120. *Parties 12. L 12.30-3 D 7-11.15 (Fri, Sat to 11). Closed L Sat. Set L from £24 (Sun £28) Set D £32 (£35 dinner dance).*

Set menu prices may not always include service or wine.

The Causerie   £85

⚜ ♟ 🌿 🍸 🗋

The fixed-price (including a drink) lunchtime smörgåsbord is the main attraction here. Simple pre-and post-theatre suppers are served from 5.30-7.30 and 10.15-11. A la carte is also offered at both lunch and dinner; this might cover a range from Cajun risotto with prawns and lobster bisque to roast game in season, Claridge's hot chicken pie, and rack of lamb with aromatic vegetable crust. *Seats 45. Parties 8. L 12-3 D 5.30-11. Closed L Sat, all Sun. Set L & D £17.50.*

W8 Clarke's	★	£90

Tel 0171-221 9225 Fax 0171-229 4564   Map 18 A3   **R**
124 Kensington Church Street W8 4BH

🗋 ♟ 🌿 🍸 🗋

Sally Clarke and Elizabeth Payne put the emphasis on tip-top produce and generally uncomplicated, accessible and highly skilled cooking with Mediterranean and Californian influences. Almost uniquely in London there is no choice on the four-course evening menu (though the menu changes daily and never repeats itself). The chargrill produces most of the main courses, typified by chump chop of spring lamb grilled with thyme leaf glaze and a fritter of field mushrooms; corn-fed chicken with lemon and spinach, a potato pancake and parchment-baked mushrooms; and fillet of tuna with tartare sauce, leek fritters, grilled aubergine and red pepper. Starters are fresh, perky and absolutely delicious: salad of various leaves with salted anchovy, fennel, artichoke and parmesan toasts, three-bean salad with prosciutto, black olive, parsley and red onion dressing, warm sea kale with smoked haddock in a light saffron sauce. Superb British cheeses precede a dessert such as poached pear and prunes with blood orange and almonds or port cream pot with fresh fruits and biscotti. The dinner price includes the four courses, coffee, truffles and service. Lunch is in similar style but offers a choice of three dishes per course. Not a huge wine list, but there's quality throughout with California wines (the only New World representation) very much to the fore. The ground-floor room is non-smoking. *Seats 90. Parties 12. L 12.30-2 D 7-10. Closed Sat & Sun, Bank Holidays, 2 weeks August, 10 days Christmas. Set L £22/£26 Set D £37. Access, Visa.*

Many hotels offer reduced rates for weekend or out-of-season bookings. Always ask about special deals.

W1 The Clifton-Ford	73%	£210

Tel 0171-486 6600 Fax 0171-486 7492   Map 18 C2   **H**
47 Welbeck Street W1M 8DN

Enjoying a quiet location, this 60s-built hotel is nonetheless handy for Oxford Street and the West End. Spacious public rooms include a marble-floored lobby inset with Persian-style carpets, a civilised lounge area with numerous cosy corners and an intimate dark-panelled bar. Bedrooms vary from small to large, the latter including four penthouse suites (three with private balconies) and studio rooms. Rooms are colour-coded to facilitate rebooking: yellows, for example, are Executive singles having three telephone lines, one with computer modem, good work space and video playback machines. All rooms have multi-channel TVs and many have air-conditioning. Marble features in good bathrooms that all offer towelling robes and large bath sheets. Good facilities for small to medium conferences. Private parking for 30 cars – book in advance, £14 for 24 hours. Round-the-clock room service includes a hot "dish of the night". *Rooms 200. Access, Amex, Diners, Visa.*

NW3 Clive Hotel	60%	£73

Tel 0171-586 2233 Fax 0171-586 1659   Map 16 C3   **H**
Primrose Hill Road NW3 3NA

Modern hotel, part of the Hilton Group, close to Primrose Hill Park and within easy reach of the West End. Modestly furnished bedrooms all have TVs and in-house movie facilities plus tea/coffee-making equipment. Children up to 12 stay free in their parents' room, and there are a few inter-connecting rooms suitable for families. Small free car park. Versatile conference facilities for up to 350. *Rooms 96. Access, Amex, Diners, Visa.*

SW1   Collin House   £60

Tel & Fax 0171-730 8031   Map 19 C5   **B**
104 Ebury Street SW1W 9QD

Town house bed-and-breakfast hotel, owned by Dafydd and Beryl Thomas since 1982 and handy for Victoria railway and coach stations. Simply furnished but comfortable bedrooms, half with their own shower and WC. No TVs or phones. They are particularly proud of their cooked breakfasts. No dogs. *Rooms 13. Closed 10 days Christmas. No credit cards.*

W9   Colonnade Hotel   63%   £90

Tel 0171-286 1052 Fax 0171-286 1057   Map 18 A2   **H**
2 Warrington Crescent Maida Vale W9 1ER

In the heart of residential Little Venice, the Victorian Grade-II listed building stands across from Warwick Avenue Underground station. Owned and personally run for almost half a century by the Richards family, the hotel maintains an attractive, homely and friendly environment. First-floor rooms are the biggest, but all are of quite good size and are kept in good decorative order with smart bathrooms. Top of the range are suites and rooms with four-posters. *Rooms 48. Access, Amex, Diners, Visa.*

W2   Columbia Hotel   £60

Tel 0171-402 0021 Fax 0171-706 4691   Map 18 B3   **B**
95 Lancaster Gate W2 3NS

Repeat visits by contented guests are the secret of success at this privately owned Victorian hotel. With an elegant entrance in Lancaster Gate, the comfortable public rooms overlook Hyde Park. Modestly furnished bedrooms (some with park views) vary in size, but all have en-suite facilities (with tub and shower), TV, mini-safe and direct-dial phone. A few inter-connecting and four-bedded rooms are ideal for families. Cots are available for £6 per night. No room service. Small free car park. Well-decorated function rooms have a maximum capacity of 200 for theatre-style conferences. *Rooms 103. Access, Amex, Visa.*

SW5   Concord Hotel   £60

Tel 0171-370 4151 Fax 0171-244 9091   Map 19 A5   **B**
155 Cromwell Road SW5 0TQ

On the main road to Heathrow and points west, this bed-and-breakfast hotel is also handy for Earls Court, Olympia and the museums of South Kensington. Simply furnished bedrooms, some en suite with shower, include a few family-sized rooms. Unlicensed. *Rooms 40. Access, Amex, Visa.*

W1   Concorde Hotel   £87

Tel 0171-402 6169 Fax 0171-724 1184   Map 18 C2   **B**
50 Great Cumberland Place Marble Arch W1H 7FD

Next door to the Bryanston Court Hotel and under the same ownership, the Concorde offers cheaper accommodation with colour TV, tea/coffee facilities, hairdryer, new bathrooms and a friendly welcome from the Theodore family, here since 1967. Children up to 10 can stay free in their parents' room. Furnished apartments also available. *Rooms 27. Access, Amex, Diners, Visa.*

W1   The Connaught   91%   £320

Tel 0171-499 7070 Fax 0171-495 3262   Map 18 C3   **HR**
Carlos Place W1Y 6AL

Built towards the end of the 19th century, the hotel is as distinguished today as it was then, an elegant country house in the heart of Mayfair. It is neither glamorous nor fashionable, but therein lie its endearing qualities, a tranquil haven of old-fashioned, dignified standards and traditions, offering unrivalled privacy and hospitality. It is formal, its staff, many of whom have seen a lifetime's service, smartly attired and courteous at all times. Business meetings in the public areas are frowned upon, yet technology is in place if required; the elegant day rooms, retaining original features such as marble fireplaces, oak panelling and ornate plasterwork, are handsomely and comfortably furnished with antiques, paintings and fine rugs. Almost all the luxurious bedrooms (note the first-rate linen bedding), including the 24 suites, each with an antique chinoiserie cocktail cabinet, are now fully air-conditioned. Decorated in rich chintzes and pastel shades, they are individually and tastefully furnished in an English country style, free of clutter, though everything is available on request, which will be remembered the next time you stay. Bathrooms are fitted out in precious marble and provide luxurious bathrobes and top-quality toiletries, and, as throughout the hotel, benefit from exemplary housekeeping. No dogs. *Rooms 90. Access, Amex, Diners, Visa.*

Restaurant & Grill Room   £160

Whether you eat in the handsome mahogany-panelled restaurant or the smaller Georgian-style Grill, both air-conditioned, there is no difference between the menus, all prepared by one kitchen brigade under the guidance of long-serving (over twenty years) chef Michel Bourdin, one of the finest interpreters of classical French and English cooking, with an increasingly light touch. Unashamedly old-fashioned dishes, complementing the style and character of the hotel, include some specialities which should be ordered in advance, say, mousse de homard Neptune or filet d'Angus farci en croute strasbourgeoise. Regular English luncheon dishes do not change from day to day – Monday sees steak, kidney and mushroom pie, Wednesday roast sirloin of beef and Yorkshire pudding, Friday oxtail or salmon, and this emphasis on English dishes is carried through to the table d'hote dinner menu, finishing with the likes of savoury Scotch Woodcock or sherry trifle and bread-and-butter pudding. On the other hand, you can pretend you're in France by choosing homard et langoustines grillés aux herbes, galette Connaught aux 'diamants noirs', salade Aphrodite, ending with a marquise au chocolat et Cointreau or crème brulée aux baies rouges. Alternatively, the cheese trolley features many that are British farmhouse. Note that the French dishes are not translated on the menus, though they will be carefully explained by the staff, who work under a strict regime of authority under the excellent Monsieur Chevallier. Steep prices (with an additional 15% service charge which is added to bills) on the wine list that now includes Australia, New Zealand and California under New World wines, though South Africa appears elsewhere! Guests are requested not to smoke. No children under 6.
Seats Restaurant 75. Grill Room 35. Parties 10. Private Room 22. L 12.30-2.30 D 6.30 (Grill from 6)-10.30 (Grill till 10.45). Set L £25 (£30 Sun) Set D (Grill only) £35. Grill Room closed L Sat & Sun, Bank Holidays.

SW10	Conrad International London	86%	£285

Tel 0171-823 3000 Fax 0171-351 6525   Map 19 B6   **HR**
Chelsea Harbour SW10 OXG

Were it not for the uncertainty of the British climate the all-suite Conrad, with its glass-balconied, gleaming white-stoned exterior overlooking an exclusive marina, could well be mistaken for being in some sunny Mediterranean spot. The setting has the further advantage of being blissfully quiet. Designed by David Hicks, the tastefully furnished, double-glazed, air-conditioned suites offer every modern comfort: twin wardrobes, three telephones with two lines, multi-channel TV with video, mini-bar and many extras, such as fresh fruit, flowers, books and magazines, suit-carriers and even an umbrella. In the luxurious marble bathrooms you'll find a walk-in shower as well as a large tub, twin washbasins, bidet, separate loo (some suites also have a guest loo), bathrobes and quality toiletries. There's a cool and relaxing feel in the spacious marble-floored public areas, where uniformed and smartly-dressed staff are always on hand to offer a high standard of service, including valet parking. Drake's Bar, with its windy terrace, is a relaxing spot in which to enjoy a light snack, especially during the Wimbledon fortnight in front of a large TV screen. There's a free car service to Knightsbridge. Conference/banqueting facilities for up to 200. *Rooms 160.*
Terrace, indoor swimming pool, sauna, solarium, steam room, gym, beauty & hair salon, kiosk. Access, Amex, Diners, Visa.

See over

Brasserie £85

A plush dining-room with a pleasant outlook; a brasserie it is not! But, Peter Brennan's à la carte menu, supplemented by set menus both at lunchtime and in the evenings, features exciting modern dishes such as langoustine and smoked salmon salad with plum dressing, roasted pheasant breast with pumpkin, onion confit and port sauce, and hot pear and blueberry streussel. From the grill you could choose simple Dover sole or rack of lamb. Though there are tasting notes alongside each wine, the thin list is rather disappointing for a hotel of this class, though wines of the week and several available by the glass offer good value. *Seats 45 (+40 on terrace). Parties 16. L 12.30-3 D 6-10.30. Set L £17/£19 (Sun champagne brunch £31.50) Set D £22.50/£24.50.*

W8   Copthorne Tara   69%   £148

Tel 0171-937 7211   Fax 0171-937 7100   Map 19 A4   **H**
Scarsdale Place Kensington W8 5SR

A modern 12-storey hotel close enough to Kensington High Street to be convenient for the shops but far enough away to be free of the bustle and the traffic. Thoughtfully furnished rooms, ranging from 'Classic' singles to suites, include non-smoking rooms and facilities for disabled guests, all with efficient air-conditioning and electronic controls on lighting and other facilities. Convivial day rooms include the newly opened Dublin Bar. There's a purpose-built conference and banqueting centre catering for up to 500. 90 parking spaces − £10 for 24 hours. *Rooms 825. Café. Access, Amex, Diners, Visa.*

W8   Costa's Grill   £25

Tel 0171-229 3794   Map 18 A3   **R**
12-14 Hillgate Street Notting Hill Gate W8 7SR

Remember when Greek holidays really were cheap? Relive those memories at Costa's, where hefty portions of grills and baked dishes are still served at rock bottom prices. Only fresh fish from the charcoal grill is likely to make a dent in your drachmae − again, just like over there. Outside eating area. Almost next door is Costa's fish and chip shop. *Seats 50. Parties 25. L 12.30-2.30 D 5-10.30. Closed Sun, Bank Holidays, Sep. No credit cards.*

W2   Craven Gardens Hotel   £66

Tel 0171-262 3167   Fax 0171-262 2083   Map 18 B3   **B**
16 Leinster Terrace W2 3ES

Comfortable bed-and-breakfast hotel in a residential street just off Bayswater Road, handy for Hyde Park and the West End. Refurbished bedrooms now all offer TV, tea/coffee-making facilities, direct-dial phone and en-suite bathrooms (only a few with tubs). Children under 7 can stay free in parents' room. No room service. No dogs. *Rooms 43. Access, Amex, Diners, Visa.*

SW14   Crowthers   £65

Tel 0181-876 6372   Map 17 A5   **R**
481 Upper Richmond Road West Sheen SW14 7PU

Philip and Shirley Crowther have been at their cosy little neighbourhood restaurant since 1982, serving well-balanced, fixed-price menus of good British produce in French style (matched by the traditional French country decor). Start with the day's soup − perhaps cream of sweet potato and garlic − or filo pastry parcels of mushrooms, peppers and herbs, and move on to Barbary duck with caramelised apples and dry cider sauce or sautéed calf's liver with melted onions, sage and mashed potatoes. Grilled fruits with kirsch sabayon and mango sorbet make a splendid dessert. *Seats 32. L 12-2 D 7-10. Closed L Sat, all Sun (but open Mothering Sunday & Easter Sunday) & Mon, Bank Holidays, 2 weeks Aug, 1 week Christmas. Set L £16/£18.50 Set D £17.50/£21.50. Access, Visa.*

NW3   Cucina   £65

Tel 0171-435 7814   Map 16 B2   **R**
45a South End Road NW3 2QB

This useful neighbourhood restaurant tucked away behind an estate agent offers a market-governed eclectic menu. It might include mussels with coconut milk, kaffir and coriander; warm grilled squid with aïoli, or black bean cakes with guacamole as starters; chargrilled rib of beef, wild mushroom stroganoff or cornfed chicken with grilled radicchio to follow. Basics are skilfully bought – bread, olive oil and pancetta, for example. The menu relies heavily on the chargrill, cleverly enlivened by unusual ingredients: Mahi fish from the Indian ocean or grouper from the Mediterranean. More elaborate dishes have been less successful. Interesting wine list with modest mark-ups. Seats 65. L 12-2.30 D 7-10.30 (Fri & Sat till 11). Set D £11.95. Closed L Sat, D Sun, 3 days Christmas, some Bank Holidays.

W1   Cumberland Hotel   69%   £155

Tel 0171-262 1234 Fax 0171-724 4621   Map 18 C3   **H**
Marble Arch W1A 4RF

London's second largest hotel is at the Marble Arch end of Oxford Street, overlooking Speaker's Corner. An impressive octagonal central lobby has bright red columns, white marble and a large floral display as its focal point. From here the restaurants (including Mon Japanese – see separate entry) and a café radiate. Three bars and a shopping arcade add an international air to the public areas. Bedrooms spread over eight floors are spacious, well maintained and attractive, with a good range of amenities. A variety of conference and banqueting suites caters for 500+. Children under 16 free in their parents' room. NCP next door. *Rooms 900. News kiosk, theatre ticket agency, hair salon, coffee shop (6.30am-midnight). Access, Amex, Diners, Visa.*

SW15   Dan Dan   £50

Tel 0181-780 1953   Map 17 B5   **R**
333 Putney Bridge Road SW15

Just off the bridge end of Putney High Street, an unpretentious Japanese restaurant offering good-value lunches based around one main dish (plus miso soup, appetiser and fresh fruit) and a wider choice of Japanese classics in the evening. Good fresh sushi and kaiseki dinners with hors d'oeuvre chosen from a trolley. *Seats 60. Parties 40. Private Room 24. L 12-2.30 D 6.30-10. Closed L Sat & Sun, all Mon, 10 days Aug. Set L £7/£10.50 Set D from £19/£23. Access, Amex, Visa.*

SW3   Dan's   £75

Tel 0171-352 2718 Fax 0171-352 3265   Map 19 B5   **R**
119 Sydney Street Chelsea SW3 6NR

Stripped pine floors, peach walls and some very English pictures combine to give Dan's its informal "Chelsea goes to Sussex" feel and in summer the large garden is a real bonus. A smiling patron warmly greets from behind the small bar and the dining room is a flurry of, mostly French, efficiency. A short à la carte menu is supplemented by daily specials (including game in season) or a set two- or three-course deal. While the dishes are attractively displayed, and saucing is generally good, details and the inaccurate timing of some dishes can disappoint. The wine list, often with interesting bin ends, concentrates mainly on France. *Seats 52. Private Rooms 12 & 35. L 12.30-2.15 D 7.30-10.30. Closed L Sat, all Sun (but open L Sun in Summer), Bank Holidays, 1 week Christmas. Set L £13.50. Access, Amex, Visa.*

NW1   Daphne   £45

Tel 0171-267 7322   Map 16 C3   **R**
83 Bayham Street Camden Town NW1

In a part of town where Greek restaurants abound, Daphne has the edge over most of them. Its menu of traditional favourites is given a boost by numerous daily specials with an emphasis on fish: bream marinated and charcoal-grilled, monkfish souvlaki, fish meze served as a 3-course meal – cold dips and numerous fish dishes including calamari, baby cuttlefish, giant prawns and monkfish. There's also a generous choice for meat-eaters, plus ample vegetable dishes. The restaurant extends over two floors, with a fair-weather roof terrace seating 25. *Seats 85. Parties 30. L 12-2.30 D 6-11.30. Closed Sun, 25 & 26 Dec, 1 Jan. Meze (min 2) £8.75. Access, Visa.*

Set menu prices may not always include service or wine.

SW3   Daphne's   £85

Tel 0171-589 4257 Fax 0171-581 2232   Map 19 B5   **R**
112 Draycott Avenue SW3 3AE

Perennially fashionable restaurant equally popular with both the international 'jet-set' and those on the London scene, particularly women (there are few offices in the area but plenty of expensive shops), who appreciate the healthy Mediterranean-style cooking. The menu is divided into various sections with Starters – crudités with three salsas, beef carpaccio with rucola and parmesan shavings, hot foie gras with polenta, lentils and balsamic plum sauce; Salads – Caesar, lobster with saffron dressing, spinach with avocado and crispy bacon; Pasta & Risotto – anolini with zucchini and zucchini flower, lobster ravioli, risotto milanese; Fish – poached salmon with spring vegetables, Dover sole grilled or meunière; Roasts & Grills – roast breast of chicken with forest mushrooms, grilled calf's liver with caramelised onion, pancetta and sage, costoletta milanese; and Side Orders like artichoke mash, zucchini fritters and grilled vegetables. Puddings might include a good caramelised lemon tart, fresh fruit and berries, and tiramisu. There's a wonderful selection of Italian breads but the butter, put out on the tables ahead of time, was almost liquid one lunchtime last summer – despite the air-conditioning. Over half the wines on the list are priced under £20, which isn't bad for one of the trendiest spots in town! Decor features burnt orange stucco-effect walls; dining areas at the rear of the restaurant have glass roofs. Booking advisable. *Seats 120. L 12-3 (Sun to 4) D 7-11.30 (Sun to 10.30). Closed 1 week Christmas. Access, Amex, Diners, Visa.*

SW6   De Cecco   £40

Tel 0171-736 1145   Map 17 B5   **R**
189 New Kings Road Parsons Green London SW6 4SW

Booking is advisable at this bright, bubbly place, which has a loyal following. The food features the best elements of both traditional regional Italian cooking as well as some more modern influences. Thus spaghetti carbonara and veal escalopes milanese sit happily alongside ravioli filled with smoked salmon and spaghetti with lobster. Be sure to take note of the day's specials as these can be exceptionally good. No young children after 7pm on Saturdays. *Seats 68. Parties 12. L 12.30-2.45 D 7-10.45. Closed Sun, Bank Holidays, 2 weeks August, 1 week Christmas. Access, Visa.*

W1   Defune   £80

Tel 0171-935 8311 Fax 0171-487 3762   Map 18 C2   **R**
61 Blandford Street W1H 3AJ

Book to be sure of a table, as this is a popular (and very small) Japanese restaurant. Otherwise you can sit at the counter and see your sushi and sashimi being prepared. The à la carte spans a fairly familiar Japanese range, from soups and noodle dishes to barbecued beef, pork and fish, and specialities such as shabu-shabu and yosenabe. *Seats 15. Parties 15. L 12-2.30 D 6-10.30. Closed Sun, Bank Holidays, 1 week Christmas. Set L from £12.50. Access, Amex, Diners, Visa.*

SW15   Del Buongustaio   ↑   £60

Tel 0181-780 9361   Map 17 B5   **R**
283 Putney Bridge Road London SW15 2PT

Simple but imaginative decor in soft shades of sand and terracotta with colourful Faenza ceramics sets the tone for a relaxing meal in this cheerful country Italian restaurant ('osteria con cucina'). The emphasis is on a slightly updated version of classic Northern Italian cooking, notable for wholesome ingredients and forthright flavours. Piatto pizzicarello is an interesting, plated assortment of savouries to commence a meal, which you could follow with sformatino di broccoli (broccoli, parmesan and egg pudding with pistachio and tomato sauce), plaice salad in a marjoram dressing or spaghetti with scallops, mussels and courgettes. Roast stuffed goat with roast Mediterranean vegetables, cuttlefish risotto and garlic-sauced steak are typical main courses. Deep pockets are not necessarily required for good drinking here, with just Australia featuring alongside Italy. House wine is also served in jugs. Fresh cheeses are imported directly from Naples. Two-course lunches offer excellent value. Sundays see a degustazione menu (three to five courses). Seats 60. Parties 8. L 12-3 (Sun 12.30-3.30) D 6.30-11.30 (Sun to 10.30). Closed L Sat, 10 days Christmas/New Year. Set L £9.50 (Sun £14.50/£17.50) Set D £19.50. Access, Amex, Visa.

W1   dell'Ugo   ⬆   £40

Tel 0171-734 8300 Fax 0171-734 8784   Map 21 A2   **R**
56 Frith Street Soho W1V 5TA
🍷

Antony Worrall Thompson's immensely popular, multi-storey Soho restaurant provides something for everyone on a lengthy menu which is full of clever ideas, most of which work well. The style is 'rustic Mediterranean' and covers a wide range, from bruschetta, crostini, chargrilled polenta with garlic field mushrooms, and spaghetti with artichokes, prosciutto and peas to chargrilled mackerel with shredded courgette and parmesan and haddock brandade crostini; pot roast pig with garlic, bay and thyme with mash and roast vegetables; duck confit with caraway cabbage, lentils and chorizo or slow cooked lamb shank with borlotti beans, garlic rosemary and mash – the list is endlessly enticing. Other dishes are homespun favourites with contemporary tuning – even the potatoes are cleverly offered as a side order of garlic potatoes, mash, chips or frites! Although essentially fairly simple in concept and preparation, the emphasis on strong, fresh flavours wins through in dishes that draw inspiration from around the globe, examples being: mussels with ginger, chili and garlic in a coriander and lentil broth; pan-fried calf's liver and bacon with colcannon cake and shallot jus; Tunisian orange cake with Greek honey and yoghurt. The ground floor café/bar offers an equally enticing 'from tapas to meze' menu – delicious light snacks including risotto croquettes with chargrilled corn relish, deep-fried stuffed olives and spicy lamb meatballs with yoghurt and mint. A constantly-changing wine list is laid out by price and offers affordable prices, with over a dozen wines by the glass. Finish with Italian coffees or 'hippy teas'. The first-floor bistro opens from 7pm and continues to 12.30am, whereas the second-floor restaurant opens from 5.30pm and closes at 11pm; no bookings are taken in the café. *Seats 180. Private Room 14. L 12-3 (not Sat), D 5.30-12.30 (ground-floor café 11am-12.30am inc Sat). Closed Sun & Bank Holidays. Access, Amex, Diners, Visa.*

NW8   Don Pepe   £50

Tel 0171-262 3834 Fax 0171-724 8305   Map 18 B2   **R**
99 Frampton Street St John's Wood NW8 8NA

London's first tapas bar when it opened 20 years ago, Don Pepe has survived and thrived. Besides the tapas there's a full restaurant menu including Spanish classics such as gazpacho, Asturian-style bean stew, lubina a la sal (sea bass cooked in salt) merluza a la gallega, zarzuela and paella. *Seats 50. Private Room 20. L 12-2.30 D 7-11.30. Closed D Sun, 24 & 25 Dec, 1 Jan. Set L & D £13.95 (Set Sun L £13.50 includes wine). Access, Amex, Diners, Visa.*

W1   The Dorchester   91%   £298

Tel 0171-629 8888 Fax 0171-409 0114   Map 18 C3   **HR**
Park Lane W1A 2HJ

Since opening its doors in 1931, the Dorchester has been among the world's top hotels, renowned for its enviable standards of service, comfort and cooking. The grand oval foyer, with its rug-strewn black-and-white marble floor, bustles with the comings and goings of smartly attired porters, page boys and guests. The splendid, long Promenade, complete with enormous floral display at one end and rows of faux-marble columns with ornate gilt capitals, is very much the heart of the hotel and a wonderful place to take traditional English afternoon tea. Another focal point is the bar (see entry below). Bedrooms have an essentially English style with fine fabrics varying from striking floral prints and delicate damasks to heavy tapestries; the bed linen is, of course, real linen. All rooms are triple-glazed and have white Italian marble bathrooms with bidets and hand showers in addition to powerful showers over the bathtubs; many even have separate shower cubicles and twin washbasins, while most have

See over

natural light. Four superb roof garden suites, all restored to their original splendour, put the icing on the cake. Standards of service throughout the public areas are superlative and are matched on the bedroom floors following the implementation of the call button system for valet, maid and waiter room service (the hotel boasts an amazing ratio of three staff to each room). Breakfasts, as one can expect from a hotel with such an outstanding culinary history, are first-rate, covering English (a superior fry-up, poached haddock, grilled kippers, coddled egg with smoked salmon or chives), Continental (excellent baking includes croissants and apple scones) and low-fat and low-cholesterol options; served from 7am (7.30am Sun) in the Grill Room. Among the many elegant public rooms, opulent banqueting and conference facilities (for up to 550) feature over 1500 square metres of gold leaf gilding and are among London's finest. The Dorchester Spa offers thermal therapy as well as the more usual relaxations. *Rooms 247. Gym, sauna, steam room, spa bath, solarium, beauty & hair salon, shopping gallery. Access, Amex, Diners, Visa.*

Terrace Restaurant £120

Here, in an elegant setting off the fabled Promenade, can be found a showcase for Willi Elsener's talents. The restaurant is open only on Friday and Saturday for dinner and it is essential to book in order to ensure a table in a room that is decorated with great style: there are mirrored columns, Chinese-inspired painted wall panels, a central gazebo where four couples can dine in relative seclusion, and a band which strikes up from mid-evening till late (around 1am), the singer inviting diners to face the music and dance. The menu offers a fixed-price meal of either three or four courses. The choice is of imaginative, modern, sophisticated dishes. There is also a very extensive vegetarian menu, its dishes a very creditable and worthwhile alternative, and a result of increased demand. The orthodox menu begins with a super appetiser and might continue with carpaccio of scampi marinated in an orange vinaigrette, or a light guinea fowl timbale with morel mushrooms in a cream sauce. A granité follows and for a main dish the choice could be a beautifully fresh roasted centre cut of turbot, Oriental style, a trio of veal – the fillet, sweetbreads and liver served with a simple jus – or roast breast of chicken with a lemon grass-flavoured sauce. Examples of the desserts are brought to the table, making them irresistible. Service is superbly professional. There's a sommelier's selection and bin ends, both well worth·perusing, in addition to the well-rounded list of wines from around the world. Most of the better known names are represented, prices are predictably on the high side. No children under 12. *Seats 81. Parties 14. D only 7-11.30. Closed Sun-Thurs, Aug. Set D £38/£42.*

Grill Room £130

Largely unchanged since the hotel first opened in 1931; although the decor is grand Spanish, the menu is firmly and splendidly English. Tables are widely spaced, which is just as well given the numerous trolleys that bring not just the traditional roast rib of beef and Yorkshire pudding and the side of smoked salmon – to be sliced at the table – but also the dish of the day (Monday's boiled silverside and caraway dumplings, Friday's Cornish fisherman's pie), the wide range of breads, salads, good desserts and the notably wide selection of British cheeses. The à la carte extends to just about every corner of the British Isles from Glamorgan sausages and cock-a-leekie soup to glazed South Coast scallops and prawns with a delicate mustard sauce. See Terrace Restaurant for the wine comment. *Seats 84. Parties 12. L 12.30-2.30 D 6-11 (Sun & Bank Holidays 7-10.30). Set L £24.50 Set D £32.*

Oriental Room £120

London's most elegant and exclusive Chinese restaurant and almost certainly the most expensive, too. The mainly Cantonese menu features many luxurious items. Super dim sum are available at lunchtime and specialities from the carte include Peking duck, beef with lemon grass and steamed sea bass in black bean sauce. No monosodium glutamate is used in any of the dishes. Staff are smart, charming and knowledgable under a suave and accomplished manager. No children under 12. Lovely private rooms (Indian-themed, Chinese, Thai). See Terrace Restaurant for the wine comment. *Seats 51. Parties 16. Private Rooms 6/10/14. L 12-2.30 D 7-11. Closed L Sat, all Sun, Aug. Set L £22.50/£24.50 Set D from £32.*

Dorchester Bar   £70

👑 🍷 ⬤ 🍓

Beautiful Delft-tiled panels alternating with mirrors in a carved, light-oak framework take the eye in this brightly lit, split-level bar. A baby grand piano covered in mirror mosaics, crisply-clothed tables, comfortable banquettes and light tan leather chairs complete a most elegant setting in which to enjoy excellent modern Italian cooking. A selection of antipasti (available only at lunchtime) is spread out next to the entrance. Other choices could be panzerotti filled with four cheeses and served with minted fresh tomatoes, tagliatelle with Beluga caviar, monkfish with a wild fennel sauce and veal cutlet with wild mushrooms. Delicious sweets too such as Amaretto parfait with prickly pear sauce or ice cream bombe round off an enjoyable experience. Service is first-class. Several well-chosen though pricey wines available by the glass. Booking is advisable. *Seats 80. Parties 8. Meals 12-11.45 (Sun 12-2.30 7-10).*

W4   La Dordogne   £55

Tel 0181-747 1836 Fax 0181-994 9144   Map 17 A4   **R**
5 Devonshire Road Chiswick W4 2EU

This comfortable bistro exudes an air of French sophistication, with crisp white napery and dark green walls festooned with pictures. The menu is based on dishes of the region in the name, so duck features heavily and in many guises: cured, smoked and its foie gras as starters, or sliced breast as a main course. A good selection of seafood is listed: four ways with lobster, turbot with champagne or monkfish with port and bacon on a recent visit. There is a choice of French or Irish rock oysters and natives when in season. Desserts are skilfully prepared, and the assiette gourmande (a mere £4.50) is an excellent introduction – especially when accompanied by a glass of Clos Guirouilh (sweet Jurançon). Service is efficient. Seats 80. Private Room 20/30. L 12-2.30 D 7-11. Closed L Sat & Sun, Bank Holidays. Access, Amex, Diners, Visa.

We welcome bona fide complaints and recommendations on the tear-out pages at the back of the book for reader's comments. They are followed up by our professional team.

NW1   Dorset Square Hotel   74%   £150

Tel 0171-723 7874 Fax 0171-724 3328   Map 18 C2   **HR**
39 Dorset Square Marylebone NW1 6QN

An elegant house amid the white Georgian facades of a garden square just north of Marylebone Road, with Regent's Park a short walk away. Within, there's an attractive combination of hand-painted woodwork, gilt-framed paintings, tapestry cushions and antique furniture giving a warm, refined atmosphere to the public rooms on the ground floor. The guest lounge is furnished with colourful armchairs, a 19th-century rolltop desk and an antique cabinet which holds an honesty bar. Each bedroom has its own personality, artistically blending patterns and materials. Most rooms are air-conditioned, and all have satellite TV, books and magazines. Marble and mahogany bathrooms enjoy natural daylight. Careful thinking has gone into every detail, making it very much an individual home from home. A chauffeur-driven Bentley Continental is available by prior arrangement. *Rooms 37. Garden. Access, Amex, Visa.*

The Potting Shed   £65

Cricket memorabilia and a wall of unglazed flower pots serve both to justify the name of this basement dining room and to evoke the days when the MCC played in the square outside. Trevor Baines' short, monthly-changing menus are bang up to date, however, and might offer Caesar salad or potted chicken livers with pistachios and olive bread followed by baked sea bream with a lemon grass sauce or breast of chicken with a red pepper and truffle oil sauce. Sandwiches and a one course 'club menu' are available at the bar. *Seats 30. L 12-2.30 D 6-10. Closed L Sun, all Sat. Set meals (Mon-Fri) £11.95.*

SW7   Downstairs at 190   ↑   £60

Tel 0171-581 5666 Fax 0171-581 8172   Map 19 B4   **R**
190 Queen's Gate SW7 5EU

Underneath *Bistrot 190* (qv), a busy brasserie-style restaurant under the watchful eye of roving chef Antony Worrall Thompson. Seafood dominates the menu, with just a few choices for carnivores. Mussels and clams are steamed in five different ways (lemon grass, ginger and minted peanut sauce for the Thai taste), and the chargrill is put to good use for the daily-changing selection of market-fresh fish and shellfish; a variety of accompaniments is offered, including perhaps orange lentils, aubergine and cabbage, or leeks, polenta and truffled vinaigrette. Fishcakes are served in small or large portions in three always-interesting versions; among recent choices were salmon on leaf spinach with sorrel sauce, and crab and corn on wilted greens with poached eggs and hollandaise. Fish and chips is a permanent favourite, the fish deep-fried in beer batter, the chips chunky, the peas mushy and the sauce tartary. Vegetarian options; 'traditional' or 'alternative' appetisers; half a dozen puddings; farmhouse cheeses with walnut pickle. The wine list is serious indeed, one for the connoisseur! Every month there are some 30 selected wines to choose from, not necessarily inexpensive, but to suit all pockets. As for the rest of the list, it's thoroughly comprehensive, with wines from around the world, and contains knowledgeable tasting notes where necessary, with quite fair prices throughout. *Seats 70. Parties 10. Private Room 28. D only 7-12. Closed Sun, Bank Holidays, 1 week Christmas. Access, Amex, Diners, Visa.*

W1   Dragon Inn   £30

Tel 0171-494 0870   Map 21 A2   **R**
12 Gerrard Street Soho W1

Hugely popular Chinese restaurant offering Cantonese and Peking cooking in an unsophisticated but friendly atmosphere. Dim sum are served from 11 till 5. *Seats 120. Parties 12. Meals 12-11.45. Closed 25-26 Dec & from 8pm 24 Dec. Access, Amex, Visa.*

W1   Dragon's Nest   £45

Tel 0171-437 3119   Map 21 A2   **R**
58 Shaftesbury Avenue W1V 7DE

There is a comfortable, old-fashioned air here, much as a Chinese hotel dining room might have been in the 1930s. The cooking is Cantonese and Szechuan in origin, favourites being sweet and sour prawns, Szechuan crispy duck and beef with oyster sauce, which vie with the more unusual, perhaps tripe with preserved vegetables – all cooked with above-average care. A word of warning – the dried peppers mentioned in some dishes are chilis, not the sweet variety, and definitely to be approached with caution! Useful for pre-and post-theatre dining. *Seats 130. Parties 40. Private Room 60. L 12-3 D 5-11.30. Closed 24-26 Dec. Set meals from £9. Access, Amex, Diners, Visa.*

SW3   The Draycott   £176

Tel 0171-730 6466 Fax 0171-730 0236   Map 19 C4   **PH**
24-26 Cadogan Gardens SW3 2RP

Formed from a pair of redbrick Victorian town houses this is one of the most charming hotels in London, due in no small measure to the fact that it does not feel like a hotel at all but much more like staying as a house guest at a private residence. It's easy to miss the little brass name plate by the entrance but a large union flag hanging above will help to find it. Ring the door bell to gain admittance to the yellow drag-painted entrance hall, beyond which a civilised drawing room, with views of (and access to) the peaceful Cadogan Gardens, is the focus of the dayrooms. At the foot of the stairs are two great stone vases filled with apples, to which guests are encouraged to help themselves. Antique-furnished bedrooms vary from very small singles to spacious Junior Suites, all individually decorated in country house style with pictures, objets d'art and fresh or dried flower arrangements giving the homely touch while satellite TVs, video players, mini-bars and air-conditioning (portable units on request) provide the modern comforts. Good bathrooms, all with showers over the bathtubs, are provided with bathrobes and quality toiletries. Rooms are properly serviced in the evening and 24-hour room service compensates for the lack of a restaurant. Children stay free in parents' room and nanny services are available. Guests have free membership of a nearby health centre and the Vanderbilt tennis club. No dogs. No parking. *Rooms 25. Access, Amex, Diners, Visa.*

SW1   Dukes Hotel   80%   £213

Tel 0171-491 4840 Fax 0171-493 1264   Map 18 D3   **H**
35 St James's Place SW1A 1NY

Now under the same ownership as the Egerton House and Franklin hotels, this redbrick building, which originally opened as a hotel in 1908, is hidden down a quiet cul-de-sac off St James's Street. The new owners have restored the public rooms to their original splendour: reception lobby, drawing room and splendid cocktail bar have comfortable period furnishings, historical pictures and prints and other objets d'art. Comfortable bedrooms, are individually decorated; modern amenities are not forgotten with satellite TV (including CNN), mini-bars and complimentary mineral water. A luxurious penthouse has views over Green Park and access to a large rooftop terrace. Comfortable meeting rooms in the basement provide conference or banqueting facilities for up to 70 delegates. Air-conditioning is installed in the meeting rooms, restaurant (not open to the public), penthouse floor and bedrooms in the extension. No dogs. *Rooms 64. Terrace. Access, Amex, Diners, Visa.*

SW1   Durley House   £260

Tel 0171-235 5537 Fax 0171-259 6977   Map 19 C5   **PH**
115 Sloane Street SW1X 9PJ

Close to fashionable shopping and Sloane Square, this comfortable hotel is composed entirely of spacious one- and two-bedroom suites. From the moment of entering, an air of quiet luxury prevails. Deep carpets, original paintings, carved wooden mantels, luxurious soft furnishings and a profusion of flowers fill the rooms. Suites, all with king-size beds, have a separate sitting-room and modern kitchen. Each is individually designed and furnished, one with a grand piano (whose quality satisfies visiting concert pianists!) and all with tastefully chosen antiques. All bedrooms face the rear, away from any traffic noise. The modern world is not neglected however: two TVs with satellite (including CNN), two telephone lines and a fax machine are provided in all rooms. There is no restaurant, but each sitting room has a polished mahogany dining table, and 24hr room service allows one to entertain in privacy – this renders the kitchen (complete with its comprehensively stocked mini-bar) comparatively irrelevant. A comfortable ground-floor drawing-room, with an honesty bar, is ideal for meeting friends. Guests have the use of private tennis courts in Cadogan Park. Under the same ownership as Dorset Square and Pelham Hotels. *Rooms 11. Access, Amex, Visa.*

W1   Durrants Hotel   65%   £106

Tel 0171-935 8131 Fax 0171-487 3510   Map 18 C2   **H**
George Street W1H 6BJ

Close to the Wallace Collection and Oxford Street, Durrants comprises four adjoining houses dating back more than 200 years. Its appeal is traditional and club-like with wood panelling in the foyer, an intimate bar, authentic smoking room and cosy, but not large, bedrooms, ten of which are not en suite. Marble bathrooms have quality fittings. No dogs. *Rooms 96. Access, Amex, Visa.*

EC1   The Eagle   ↑   £40

Tel 0171-837 1353   Map 16 C3   **R**
159 Farringdon Road EC1R 3AL

♉

Sounds like a pub, feels like a pub, tastes sensational! No bookings taken but persevere, share a table, order your food at the top of your voice and enjoy the robust Mediterranean dishes, cooked by David Eyre in an open-plan kitchen. Options are marked up on a blackboard, about eight or ten, changing at least daily. Popular demand keeps one stalwart, the marinated rump-steak sandwich, bifeana, as a permanent fixture. Other choices might include fettuccine with ricotta, peas, bacon and basil; Andalucian chick pea and mussel soup; grilled swordfish steak with potato salad; and stuffed leg of lamb with olives, rosemary and lemon. Great food, good prices, a splendid buzz and an excellent range of wines by the glass. *Seats 55. L 12.30-2.30 D 6.30-10.30. Closed Sat, Sun, Bank Holidays, 2/3 weeks Christmas. No credit cards.*

SW1   Ebury Wine Bar   £40

Tel 0171-730 5447 Fax 0171-823 6053   Map 19 C4   **R**
139 Ebury Street Victoria SW1 9QU

The Ebury is one of London's original wine bars, having been established in 1959, and it enjoys a strong regular customer base. The food is modern European, and chargrills are a speciality. Naturally, there's an excellent range of wines by the glass. *Seats 80. Parties 16. L 12-2.45 D 6-10.30 (Sun 7-10) Open for drinks 11-11 (Sun 12-2 & 7-10.30). Set D £18.*

W1   Efes Kebab House   £40

Tel 0171-636 1953 Fax 0171-323 5082   Map 18 D2   **R**
80 Great Titchfield Street W1N 5FD

Khazim and Ibrahim opened their Turkish restaurant in 1974 and it's remained popular since. Lamb and chicken kebabs are the principal attraction, preceded by a wide selection of hors d'oeuvre including carrots with yoghurt, stuffed vine leaves, aubergines and peppers, chicken with a walnut sauce, and cream cheese salad. Turkish sweets from a trolley (try sutlu borek – cream custard and almonds in pastry). Efes II, which features belly dancing seven nights a week, is not far away at 175 Great Portland Street W1 Tel 0171-436 0600. *Seats 50. Meals 12-11.30. Closed Sun. Set meals from £15. Access, Amex, Diners, Visa.*

Set menu prices may not always include service or wine.

SW3   Egerton House   £184

Tel 0171-589 2412 Fax 0171-584 6540   Map 19 B4   **PH**
17-19 Egerton Terrace Knightsbridge SW3 2BX

Hidden away down a side street not far from Harrods, this handsome redbrick town house gives no clue to the haven within. Bedrooms, with deep carpets, are tastefully decorated with carefully chosen antiques and original paintings. Modern necessities are not forgotten, with satellite TV, air-conditioning and 24hr room service offered. Some of the bedrooms have four-posters and the majority overlook the gardens. Bathrobes and high-quality toiletries are provided in the marble-clad bathrooms, all of which have a shower over the bathtub. Downstairs, a comfortable drawing-room and study with honesty bar add to the relaxed air. Flowers and other decorative items abound, making this a real home from home. Excellent breakfasts are served in the rooms or in the bright basement breakfast room. No dogs. *Rooms 30. Access, Amex, Diners, Visa.*

SW6   El Metro   £45

Tel 0171-384 1264 Fax 0171-736 5292   Map 19 A6   **R**
10-12 Effie Road Fulham Broadway SW6 1AA

Café-brasserie and tapas bar in a side street opposite Fulham Broadway underground station. Breakfasts, burgers, sandwiches, pasta, steaks, tapas, paella. *Seats 60. Parties 20. Meals 9am-midnight. Closed 25 & 26 Dec. Access, Amex, Diners, Visa.*

W1   Elena's L'Etoile   £80

Tel 0171-636 7189 Fax 0171-637 0122   Map 18 D2   **R**
30 Charlotte Street W1P 1HJ

Elena Salvoni, the doyenne of London's greeters, now lends her name to the former L'Etoile where she reigns as maitre d' surrounded by celebrity photographs which crowd the yellow ochre walls. The interior has been revamped but retains some original features such as the etched glass screen at the rear. The menu still lists a range of bourgeois classics albeit with a more modern slant. Typical dishes include breast and confit of duck with braised red cabbage, beef in red wine with puréed potatoes, salmon and leek fishcakes and tarte tatin. *Seats 80. Parties 18. Private Room 26. L 12.30-2.30 D 6-midnight. Closed L Sat, all Sun, Bank Holidays. Set L & D £14.50. Access, Amex, Diners, Visa.*

Many hotels offer reduced rates for weekend or out-of-season bookings. Always ask about special deals.

SW1   Elizabeth Hotel   £70

Tel 0171-828 6812   Map 19 D5   **B**
37 Eccleston Square SW1V 1PB

Georgian town house bed-and-breakfast hotel, quietly situated in a garden square.
Modestly furnished bedrooms range from singles to family size; all have tea/coffee-
making facilities, all but three have TVs and most bathrooms have tubs and showers.
Public rooms display an impressive collection of old prints and photographs relating to
the area. Local, covered, car parking at very competitive rates (by arrangement). No dogs.
Rooms 40. No credit cards.

SW7   Embassy House Hotel   61%   £105

Tel 0171-584 7222 Fax 0171-589 3910   Map 19 B4   **H**
31 Queen's Gate SW7 5JA

Victorian terraced hotel near Hyde Park, the Royal Albert Hall and the Kensington
Museums. Modestly furnished bedrooms all have TVs, direct-dial phones and en-suite
bathrooms (most with tubs and showers). Doubles have good workspace. Children under
12 can stay free in their parents' room, and over 12s pay 50% of adult rate. 15 bedrooms
are reserved for non-smokers. No dogs. Jarvis. *Rooms 69. Access, Amex, Diners, Visa.*

WC2   Emerald Garden   £45

Tel 0171-437 5042   Map 21 A2   **R**
8 Little Newport Street Soho WC2H 7JJ

A popular Chinatown restaurant with bright, cheerful decor throughout its three floors.
The menu is Cantonese but with a few other regional specialities such as Szechuan squid
with chili in a salt crust, the squid deliciously dry and almost crispy, with fresh baked
garlic flakes and spring onion adding extra pungency. The selection of seafood is
extensive and familiar favourites such as king prawns in a black bean sauce or beef in
oyster sauce are prepared with good attention to detail. *Seats 68. Parties 12. Private Room
30. Meals 12-12 (Fri & Sat to 3am). Closed 25 & 26 Dec. Set L £3/£5. Set D from £7
(min 2 persons). No credit cards.*

SW3   English Garden   £75

Tel 0171-584 7272 Fax 0171-581 2848   Map 19 C5   **R**
10 Lincoln Street off Kings Road SW3 2TS

Modern English cooking in a stylishly converted Chelsea town house with a Gothic
conservatory. Dishes include starters such as skewered scallops with mint hollandaise, leek
and goat's cheese tart and saddle of hare and raisin salad. Main courses include grilled
fillet of beef with celeriac purée, steamed guinea fowl breast with peppercorn sauce and
roast rack of lamb with roasted garlic. Puddings are typified by a lemon curd bread-and-
butter pudding, poached peppered pears in sloe gin syrup and apple and cinnamon tart.
*Seats 55. Parties 20. Private Room 32. L 12.30-2.30 (Sun & Bank Holidays till 2)
D 7.30-11.30 (Sun & Bank Holidays 7-10). Closed 25 & 26 Dec. Set L £14.75 (Sun £18.75).
Access, Amex, Diners, Visa.*

SW3   English House   £75

Tel 0171-584 3002 Fax 0171-581 2848   Map 19 C5   **R**
3 Milner Street Chelsea SW3 2QA

English cooking in a homely Victorian setting off Draycott Avenue. Potted cheese,
chicken liver paté or smoked mackerel with apple and potato are typical starters (on
a spring menu – the choice changes seasonally), followed by boned guinea fowl on a bed
of savoy cabbage and caraway cream sauce, grilled fillet of beef with a celeriac pancake
and port sauce or chicken, leek and lemon pie. Mostly French wines on a quite
comprehensive list. *Seats 30. Parties 8. Private Room 20. L 12.30-2.30 (Sun & Bank
Holidays till 2) D 7.30-11.30 (Sun & Bank Holidays 7-10). Closed D 25 Dec, all 26 Dec.
Set L £14.75 Set D £19.75. Access, Amex, Diners, Visa.*

SW15   Enoteca   £45

Tel 0181-785 4449   Map 17 B5   **R**
28 Putney High Street SW15 1SQ

On a corner site just south of Putney Bridge, Enoteca offers modern Italian cooking at very reasonable prices in a friendly, relaxed atmosphere. The short, interesting menu is strong on pasta (tagliatelle with tomato and basil, ravioli with oyster mushrooms and a mascarpone and sour ricotta sauce) and main courses could include poached halibut with parsley, garlic, shredded vegetables and spinach galette, roast guinea fowl with savoy cabbage and bacon and breast of duck with herbs and honeyed roast vegetables. Fixed-price lunches Mon-Fri. Tasting notes for all the wines (Italian only). Practically no half bottles available. *Seats 40. Private Room 45. L 12.30-2.30 D 7-11. Closed Sun, 1 week Christmas. Set L £6.50/£9.50. Access, Amex, Diners, Visa.*

SW3   The Enterprise   £55

Tel 0171-584 3148   Fax 0171-584 1060   Map 19 C4   **R**
35 Walton Street SW3

A charming converted pub, tastefully refurbished, with a restaurant and American bar. It's a pleasant retreat for lunch, dinner or a drink. The modern menu offers the likes of smoked trout with fresh horseradish, baby new potato skins with caviar and sour cream, warm crab tart with hollandaise, hot goat's cheese salad with pecans, home-made salmon fishcakes with tomato rémoulade, french fries and salad and blackboard specials. Cooking is unpretentious and plates are put together with care. 25 seats outside in good weather. Cheques not accepted. *Seats 35. Parties 12. L 12-2.30 D 7.30-10.30 (Sun till 10). Closed 25-28 Dec, 1 Jan. Access, Amex, Visa.*

We publish annually, so make sure you use the current edition.
– It's well worth it!

W1   L'Escargot   ↑   £100

Tel 0171-437 6828   Fax 0171-437 0790   Map 21 A2   **R**
48 Greek Street Soho W1V 5LQ

Originally the town house of the Duke of Portland, L'Escargot has been one of Soho's leading restaurants since 1927. Refurbished and revitalised in 1993, it now offers a choice of dining with a ground floor Brasserie – bustling waiters in floor-length aprons, colourfully upholstered chairs, red banquettes – and First Floor Dining Room, the latter more peaceful and exclusive with cream-painted panelled walls. Both feature a changing exhibition of contemporary art, mostly abstract, courtesy of a local gallery. The cooking, now solely in the charge of Garry Hollihead, is Provençal/Mediterranean in style with the Brasserie menu (not really brasserie in format as there is a fixed price for each course, the same menu lunch and dinner but with a higher price for main dishes at night) offering starters like gazpacho andalouse with a crostini of Provençal vegetables, roast goat's cheese à la niçoise, and Mediterranean fish soup with rouille and gruyère before mains such as braised cod with mushroom juice, broad beans and chives; warmed tuna carpaccio with horseradish and soya dressing; roast duck breast on a gratin of turnips and osso buco of lamb with milanese rice. Familiar desserts such as tarte au chocolat, sable à la fraise, and tarte tatin. Upstairs the short fixed-price menu (priced for two or three courses) is more sophisticated – roast foie gras with mango and ginger (the amount of ginger nicely judged, a most successful dish), beignet of langoustine with soy dressing, roast duck with endive and a parsley jus, sea bream with lemon and fennel, hot raspberry soufflé, baked fruit en papillote. There's also a no-choice set dinner menu (for two) that for an extra £2.50 includes a cheese course, coffee and petits fours (the latter an extra £4 otherwise, but the petits fours are exceedingly good). The First Floor Dining Room is closed on Mondays and during August and at night opens one hour later and takes last orders a quarter of an hour earlier than in the brasserie. Ask about the special combined theatre ticket-dinner offers that are often available. The thoroughbred wine list is easy to use, with least expensive wines first. The top names naturally attract top prices, but there are several decent bottles under £20. Italy and the New World are particularly well represented. *Seats 85 (Brasserie) 38 (Restaurant). Parties 20. Private Rooms 12/60. L 12-2.15 D 6-11.15. Set L £17/£21.50 (Brasserie), £21.50/£25 (Restaurant) Set D £21.50/£25 (Brasserie), £27/£34 & £36.50 (Restaurant). Closed L Sat, all Sun, 24-26 Dec, 1 Jan. Access, Amex, Diners, Visa.*

W8   L'Escargot Doré   £85

Tel & Fax 0171-937 8508   Map 19 A4   **R**
2 Thackeray Street Kensington W8 5ET

A cool basement retreat on hot summer days and suitable for intimate candle-lit dinners. The menu covers a range from warm spinach mousse with a fresh parmesan sauce, duck foie gras and soup with monkfish, salmon and prawns to crab-sauced scallops, corn-fed chicken with a shallot glaze and filet mignon with a sauce of forest mushrooms. Lighter snacks are available in La Petite Brasserie, a small bar-brasserie area at street level. *Seats 50. Parties 20. L 12-2.30 D 6.30-11.30. Closed Sun, Bank Holidays, last 2 weeks Aug. Set L £13.50/£15.50. Access, Amex, Diners, Visa.*

Many hotels offer reduced rates for weekend or out-of-season bookings. Always ask about special deals.

W1   Est   £40

Tel 0171-437 0666   Map 21 A2   **R**
54 Frith Street Soho W1V 5TE

A buzzy Soho media restaurant with large windows looking on to Frith Street. The menu is very much in the modern Mediterranean mode, with simple, full-flavoured dishes such as calamari with chili salsa, Caesar salad, risotto of the day, lamb shank and chicken breast with slow-roasted tomato, aubergine and pine nuts. *Seats 40. Parties 26. L 12-3 D 6-11 (Fri & Sat to 11.30). Closed L Sat, all Sun, Bank Holidays. Access, Amex, Diners, Visa.*

SW7   The Establishment   NEW   £50

Tel 0171-589 7969 Fax 0171-589 9996   Map 19 B4   **R**
1 Gloucester Road SW7 4PP

Bustling and trendy brasserie/bar, mainly set in an airy basement, but with a galleried dining area above. The menu has been cleverly composed of the most popular bistro dishes around town. So expect fish soup with rouille, grilled goat's cheese salad or potato skins with sour cream and mock caviar to start; various grills, steaks, lamb, tuna or roast duck (all offered with good sauces) to follow. Bangers and mash, fish cakes and a daily-changing pasta dish are other options. An impressive choice of champagnes is available. Service is friendly and slick. *Seats 62. L 12.30-2.30 D 7.30-11. Closed L Mon, all 25 Dec & 1 Jan. Set L £10 Set D £15. Access, Visa.*

WC2   L'Estaminet   £60

Tel 0171-379 1432   Map 21 B2   **R**
14 Garrick Street WC2E 9BJ

An attractive French brasserie on the fringe of Covent Garden (off Floral Street). The short, largely traditional menu runs from onion or fish soup, moules marinière and herring salad to Dover sole, duck confit with lentils, poulet basquaise and speciality grilled meats. La Tartine wine bar is downstairs, open for wine, beer and quick bites. *Seats 60. Private Room 20. L 12-2.30 D 5.45-11.15. Closed Sun, Bank Holidays. Access, Amex, Visa.*

We welcome bona fide complaints and recommendations on the tear-out pages at the back of the book for reader's comments. They are followed up by our professional team.

N1   Euphorium   ↑   NEW   £70

Tel 0171-704 6909   Map 16 C3   **R**
203 Upper Street N1 1RD

Islington's newest venture has an eyecatching decor featuring artwork by Nadia Turin.
Rough cream plaster walls are decorated with giant pictures of potatoes. Quite tightly
packed on to the brown granite tile-floored room is a mix of square and round zinc-
topped tables with lemon-yellow chairs. Jeremy Lee, formerly Alastair Little's head chef,
offers a short, fortnightly-changing menu that combines simplicity with innovation.
Begin with a soup of parsley and fennel, terrine of chicken livers, new season's garlic with
bruschetta of goat's cheese and tapénade or a wonderfully creamy risotto of morels, peas
and broad beans. To follow choose between skate and spring onion with chili, ginger and
coriander; rabbit with sage, button onions and crispy bacon; fillet of beef with shallots,
red wine and herbs or a meaty portion of roast black leg chicken breast with salsify and
a tarragon cream sauce. For dessert there's steamed raisin pudding with custard, poached
pear and ginger bavarois and 'wee' cakes (little ginger sponge cakes) or rhubarb compote
with an orange mascarpone sabayon. For lunch 2- or 3-course menus only are offered.
The food is similar to the dinner carte but is a little lighter. A short wine list of one
champagne and fine reds and whites, all carefully chosen, is offered. There's a lively,
informal atmosphere and booking is very advisable. *Seats 40. Parties 8. Private Room
12. L 12.30-2.30 (Sun till 3) D 7-11. Set L £13.50/£16.50. Closed Bank Holidays & 1 week
Easter. Access, Amex, Diners, Visa.*

WC1   Euston Plaza Hotel   66%   £148

Tel 0171-383 4105 Fax 0171-383 4106   Map 18 D1   **H**
7 Upper Woburn Place WC1H 0HT

Across Marylebone Road from the main line station, the hotel boasts a smart, modern
decor. The lobby has polished cream marble floors which continue into the cool,
spacious bar. The Victorian-style plant-filled conservatory serves as a wine bar complete
with dripping candles on the white marble tables. Fully air-conditioned bedrooms have
smart lightwood furniture and a good range of amenities. Children up to 12 stay free in
parents' room. The health club is a useful feature, with gym equipment ranged around
a raised jacuzzi in the centre of an airy room. *Rooms 150. Gym, sauna, steam room, spa
bath, solarium. Access, Amex, Diners, Visa.*

E8   Faulkners   £30

Tel 0171-254 6152 Fax 0171-249 5661   Map 16 D2   **R**
424 Kingsland Road E8 4AA

Very popular fish 'n' chip restaurant offering huge portions of fresh fish from Billingsgate
(except fish soup which comes from France). Older favourites like jellied eels and
rollmops rub shoulders with prime halibut, sole, salmon, plaice, skate, haddock and
prawns. Ice creams or apple pie to finish. *Seats 160. L 12-2 (Fri from 11.30) D 5-10
(Fri from 4.45, Sat 11.30-10, Sun 12-9). Closed Bank Holidays, 2 weeks Christmas.
No credit cards.*

SW3   The Fenja   £154

Tel 0171-589 7333 Fax 0171-581 4958   Map 19 C5   **PH**
69 Cadogan Gardens SW3 2RB

A handsome private residence turned into a home-from-home hotel of town house
character with bedrooms each named after a notable writer or painter who lived nearby
(Turner, Swinburne, Rossetti). Antiques, fresh flowers, marble busts and English prints
and paintings of the 18th and 19th centuries are features, and both towels and bedding
are of high quality. Breakfast (cooked to order until 2pm for late risers!) and light meals
from room service (no restaurant); drinks on a tray in the room or in the cosy drawing
room with an open fire. Guests have access to Cadogan Gardens. No dogs. *Rooms 12.
Garden. Access, Amex, Diners, Visa.*

Set menu prices may not always include service or wine.

SW1   Fifth Floor Restaurant at Harvey Nichols   £80

Tel 0171-235 5250 Fax 0171-235 5020   Map 19 C4   **R**
Knightsbridge SW1

When the store is closed the fifth-floor restaurant, café and bar are reached by an express lift from either Sloane Street or Seville Street. The restaurant menus (fixed price at lunchtime, fixed and à la carte in the evening) are as fashionable as any in town: zampone fritters, winter salad and mustard dressing; aubergine and pimento roulade with herbed goat's cheese; saffron risotto with melted taleggio; acorn-fed black pig ham with capers and quince cheese and the delicious platter of six native oysters served with hot, grilled spicy sausages. Main dishes are equally imaginative and include fillet of sea bass with tomato mash, wild mushrooms and saffron meat juices; pan-fried scallops with bordelaise sauce and shredded duck confit; boudin blanc with a mustard and Madeira sauce and prune and bacon rolls; pan-fried veal sweetbreads with onion purée and gremolata. Excellent separate vegetarian menu. Plenty of desserts – each with a dessert wine suggestion. While the food is good, the wine list is in a class apart. Unless you really want to push the boat our, look no further than the house selection, which alone would be the envy of many restaurants. So much choice, so much good drinking – difficult to make a selection, so seek advice, which is readily available. London regional winner Cellar of the Year. **Seats** 110. Parties 6. L 12-3 (Sat to 3.30) D 6.30-11.30. Set L & D £17.50/£21.50. Closed Sun, D Bank Holidays, 25 & 26 Dec. Access, Amex, Diners, Visa.

We publish annually, so make sure you use the current edition.
— It's well worth it!

N8   Florians   £50

Tel 0181-348 8348   Map 16 C1   **R**
4 Topsfield Parade Middle Lane Crouch End N8 8RP

Busy and loud premises with a wine bar at the front. Simple, unfussy Italian food is prepared in the modern, lighter manner, exemplified by pappardelle of chestnuts with mushroom sauce and ricotta, breast of duck with a honey and pomegranate sauce and Italian sausages braised with white cabbage. There's also a bar menu. **Seats** 70. Parties 8. L 12-3 D 7-11 (Sun to 10.30). Closed Christmas holidays. Set L & D £5.95 (bar only). Access, Visa.

SW10   Formula Veneta   £50

Tel 0171-352 7612 Fax 0181-295 1503   Map 19 B6   **R**
14 Hollywood Road SW10

Northern Italian specialities in a bright and summery setting. There's a lengthy menu of mostly modern dishes including risotto with radicchio, deep-fried squid with fennel seeds, fillets of sole with a lime sauce and breast of duck with aubergine. **Seats** 55. Parties 30. Private Room 30. L 12.30-2.30 D 7-11.15. Set L £9.95 (Sun £12.95). Closed D Sun, Bank Holidays. Access, Amex, Diners, Visa.

WC1   Forte Crest Bloomsbury   65%   £147

Tel 0171-837 1200 Fax 0171-837 5374   Map 18 D1   **H**
Coram Street WC1N 1HT

A large, modern, purpose-built hotel located in a largely residential part of Bloomsbury a short walk from the British Museum. It was designed and equipped with the business person very much in mind, and there are conference and banqueting facilities for up to 700 and the normal Crest conveniences. Bright, marble bathrooms and even Lady Crest rooms. 40 family rooms with both a double and single bed. Half the bedrooms are designated non-smoking. NCP adjacent. No dogs. **Rooms** 284. Brasserie (7am-11pm). Access, Amex, Diners, Visa.

SW1   Forte Crest Cavendish   71%   £176

Tel 0171-930 2111   Fax 0171-839 2125   Map 18 D3   **H**
81 Jermyn Street SW1Y 6JF

Built in the site of the original Cavendish, where Rosa Lewis entertained royalty in the early 1900s, this hotel is now geared to the international businessman. Her spirit lives on, however, in the comfortable club-like Sub Rosa cocktail bar and in the life-size portraits dominating the stair-well. The hotel has 14 floors of comfortable bedrooms. The top floor, comprising air-conditioned suites with sitting areas and spa baths, is not serviced by a lift but benefits from this extra privacy and an impressive view. Bedrooms are tastefully decorated and designed with communication in mind, all having satellite TV, voice mail, computer modems, two direct-dial phone points and good work-space. Creature comforts include mini-bars, armchairs and marble-floored en-suite bathrooms. Millers lounge is open 24 hours a day for light refreshments. Children up to 14 can stay free in parents' rooms. 50% of bedrooms are reserved for non-smokers. Banqueting and conference facilities for 80/100. 80-space basement car park. 24hr room and valet service and a fully staffed business centre open round the clock. *Rooms 255. Access, Amex, Diners, Visa.*

W1   Forte Crest Regents Park   64%   £125

Tel 0171-388 2300   Fax 0171-387 2806   Map 18 D2   **H**
Carburton Street W1P 8EE

Over half the bedrooms are reserved for non-smokers at this purpose-built '70s hotel; and within that there are seveal categories or styles of room. Business and leisure visitors are thus accommodated with equal ease, and children up to 16 stay free in parents' room. A new conference centre is scheduled for spring '96. No dogs. *Rooms 317. Coffee shop (6.30am-11pm, from 7am Sun) Access, Amex, Diners, Visa.*

NW3   Forte Posthouse   65%   £75

Tel 0171-794 8121   Fax 0171-435 5586   Map 16 B2   **H**
215 Haverstock Hill NW3 4RB

Close to Belsize Park Underground station and a short walk from Hampstead Heath. Top-floor bedrooms offer splendid views; 30 Executive rooms are equipped with various extras, including mini-bars and stereo in the bathrooms. Half the bedrooms are designated non-smoking. Children up to 14 stay free in parents' room. Ample free parking. Brasserie with outdoor seating. *Rooms 140. Access, Amex, Diners, Visa.*

W1   47 Park Street   86%   £310

Tel 0171-491 7282   Fax 0171-491 7281   Map 18 C3   **H**
47 Park Street Mayfair W1Y 4EB

The 52 suites in this gracious Edwardian town-house include kitchen facilities, but their use in many cases will probably be limited. For this most English of establishments is French owned and French designed and downstairs happens to be *Le Gavroche* (qv) which beckons as a venue or can provide the ultimate in 24hr room service. Superlatives flow thick and fast – sumptuous, elegant, tasteful – in describing the suites of rooms themselves (generously proportioned, perfectly equipped) or the standards of maintenance (impeccable). There's a concierge round the clock, a business centre (during normal office hours), leisure facilities adjacent, and the epitome of banqueting/conference facilities for 20/30. It's very probably one of the most expensive places to stay in London, but it's certainly one of the very, very best. *Rooms 52. Hotel limousine, valeting (8am-5pm), baby-sitting, hairdressing, shopping service. Access, Amex, Diners, Visa.*

SW7   Forum Hotel   62%   £157

Tel 0171-370 5757   Fax 0171-373 1448   Map 19 B5   **H**
97 Cromwell Road SW7 4DN

A vast, functional hotel ideally located for those coming in from Heathrow with easy connections to the Airbus and Underground. Bedrooms are small but contain all the expected amenities, including satellite TV and a mini-bar; 60 rooms are designated non-smoking. Families are well catered for: children up to 14 are free in parents' room. Two bedrooms are equipped for the disabled. Room service is available 24hrs a day and there's a fitness suite. Underground parking for 80 cars (£12 for 24 hours). *Rooms 911. Keep-fit equipment. Access, Amex, Diners, Visa.*

W2   Four Seasons   £50

Tel 0171-229 4320   Map 18 A3   **R**
84 Queensway W2 3RL

A decent Chinese restaurant, one of several in cosmopolitan Queensway. Service is friendly and attentive, and the predominantly Cantonese menu runs the gamut of familiar dishes. There's a tempting display of cooked meats in the window, and chef's specialities include shredded beef with crispy rice noodles, stuffed bean curd in a hotpot and fried prawn cake with vegetables. Sizzling dishes are also popular. *Seats 70. Parties 12. Meals 12-11.30. Closed 25 & 26 Dec. Set D from £10.50. Access, Amex, Visa.*

W1   Four Seasons Hotel   89%   £331

Tel 0171-499 0888 Fax 0171-493 1895   Map 19 C4   **HR**
Hamilton Place Park Lane Mayfair W1A 1AZ

A small garden of sycamore trees at the front slightly obscures this hotel from the bustle of Park Lane and though several storeys high it is somewhat overlooked by its neighbours. Inside, the modernity of the exterior gives way to a stylish elegance firmly rooted in classic good taste. The lobby walls are clad in rich mahogany with a huge Venetian chandelier suspended from the ceiling, while underfoot is a floor of polished light brown and other matching coloured marbles. The lounge, as well as being a place to meet and relax, is also where all-day light meals and superb afternoon teas are served in gracious, supremely civilised surroundings with colourful, springy carpets and, as elsewhere in the public areas, Grecian-style urns of exquisite flowers in grandiose arrangements. Equally grand is the wide bifurcated staircase which leads to the bars, restaurants and banqueting rooms. Among the finest of the splendid bedrooms are the 11 Conservatory rooms which are especially bright and airy. There are 26 suites, including five grand apartment suites. The suites have CD players but all rooms have stereo televisions, video players and satellite broadcasts in six languages as well as a Reuters and an in-house channel, the latter showing first releases on video. There's also a library of 200 feature films available for guests' use. Not only are the rooms beautifully decorated in soft hues with fine furniture (some with marble tops), spacious, well-equipped, but the beds too are extremely comfortable – queen-size in single rooms and king-size or twin in double. Bathrooms in fine cream marble live up to expectations with every facility provided including bidets (not in single rooms), fine toiletries and ample thick towels. The Conservatory fitness club on the second floor is for the exclusive use of residents and is an up-to-date, light room with a comprehensive selection of the latest exercise equipment each with individual TV monitors and headphones. The hotel has fine banqueting suites including the magnificent Pine Room with its ornate 18th-century panelling. Breakfasts are, as one would expect, superb, not only for choice – a lengthy à la carte is supplemented by four set-price breakfasts including Japanese and healthy options – but also for quality. Staff are on the whole excellent, providing efficient, discreet and smiling service. Underground garage and valet parking. *Rooms 227. Garden, gym, florist, news kiosk, valeting, coffee shop (9am-1am). Access, Amex, Diners, Visa.*

Four Seasons Restaurant   ★ ★   £120

Jean-Christophe Novelli is probably one of the country's most ambitious and innovative chefs. He is certainly the most artistic, and his creations, always visually stunning, are the flamboyant manifestation of a sharp eye for detail and the infinite patience required to execute the elaborately constructed and sometimes quite radical combinations. The menu comprises an extensive choice of dishes whose ingredients are in quite complex but well-thought-out and perfectly balanced compositions. Novelli's influences are those of Provence and the South West tempered with a few subtle flavours from further afield – notably the Orient. Dinner could begin with a tiny coffee cup of creamy sun-dried tomato soup and move on to an hors-d'oeuvre such as a skewer of mackerel and scallops, by themselves an unusual marriage, but whose accompaniments are also quite extraordinary. Having been marinated with orange zest and roast cardamon they are grilled on a lemon grass skewer and surrounded with a beetroot oil escabèche. The result

See over

is amazingly good. A slice of terrine composed of the ingredients of a traditional South Western cassoulet makes a rich and very satisfying starter too. Fish main dishes include a millefeuille of pan-fried Dover sole fillets interleaved with crisp paper-thin slices of aubergine and courgette with sun-dried tomato, anchovy and pistou creating the taste of sunshine so typical of the food here. Meat dishes include some much-favoured offal dishes as well as the more conventional cuts. Roast fillet of beef is served on a piece of baked marrow-bone, surmounted by a crown of ultra-thin, crisp rounds of potato and a deep-fried bay leaf, a rich red wine sauce surrounding the meat. The cheese trolley features a small but superb collection of some of the best from Britain and France. Filip Tibos, the patissier, uses his considerable skills to produce desserts that are a fitting complement to Novelli's food. A tiramisu of the lightest creams comes on a fine pastry gondola on a rippled Kahlua sea. Other choices could be a banana tatin with rum and raisin ice cream and a caramel sauce or hot chocolate mould with a melted chocolate centre and white chocolate ice cream. Service is very much of the old school – which does have its charms. House wines (with tasting notes) apart, the list is on the expensive side though prices are inclusive of service and VAT. Comprehensive choice, good balance. The room, florally decorated in shades of charcoal and pink, has a discreet elegance and is on the first floor of the hotel. The main aspect is out over a small tree-filled garden whose summertime leaves screen diners from the hustle of Park Lane. Novelli was a finalist in our Chef of the Year competition (see Awards pages). *Seats 50. Parties 8. L 12.30-3 D 7-10.30.Set L £14.50/£25 (Sun £28) Set D £45.*

Lanes Restaurant   £80

A stylish and smartly decorated restaurant; although windowless, the room has a splendidly light and contemporary decor and features a central buffet with wonderful displays throughout the day. Executive chef Eric Deblonde offers a choice of fixed-price three-course lunch menus all including wine. Dinner menus are well laid out and simply priced: your pick of the buffet as first or main course, ditto for pasta, grills, or other main courses like pan-fried spiced cod with squid and saffron-mashed potatoes, salmon escalope with a Sauternes and mango sauce and osso buco with tomato and orange, served with rice. Lanes' Alternative Cuisine offers light and vegetarian options. Superb breakfasts cover every almost choice from healthy to self-indulgent, from British to Japanese. The wine list attracts the same prices as in the main restaurant, but there's a shorter list; house wines have tasting notes. One half of the restaurant is reserved for non-smokers. *Seats 75. Parties 10. L 12-3 D 6-11 (Sun 6.30-10.30pm). Set L from £22.75 Set D £25.*

SW3   Foxtrot Oscar   £50

Tel 0171-352 7179 Fax 0171-331 1667 **(call first)**   Map 19 C5   **R**
79 Royal Hospital Road Chelsea SW3 4HN

Long-fashionable neighbourhood Chelsea restaurant serving a large variety of familiar dishes from an international repertoire: eggs Benedict, herring roes, steaks and salads. The cocktail list runs to more than two dozen. A fun place – be sure to book. *Seats 50. Parties 20. Private Room 35. L 12.30-2.30 (Sat & Sun to 3.30) D 7.30-11.30 (Sun to 10.30). Closed Aug Bank Holiday and 4 days Christmas. Access, Amex, Visa.*

We welcome bona fide complaints and recommendations on the tear-out pages at the back of the book for reader's comments. They are followed up by our professional team.

SW3   Franklin Hotel   £170

Tel 0171-584 5533 Fax 0171-584 5449   Map 19 B4   **PH**
28 Egerton Gardens London SW3 2DB

This comparatively recent addition to the London hotel scene is usefully located near Harrods and the Victoria & Albert museum, an elegant setting for its equally elegant clientele. Luxuriously equipped and serviced, bedrooms and public rooms combine antique furniture with impressive modern amenities, including air-conditioning. The 24hr room service menu is complemented by a list of local restaurants recommended by the hotel. *Rooms 40. Garden. Access, Amex, Diners, Visa.*

N1   Frederick's   £65

Tel 0171-359 2888 Fax 0171-359 5173   Map 16 D3   **R**
Camden Passage Islington N1 8EG

Smart conservatory restaurant, established in 1969, offering mostly 'safe' dishes from the
French/English/European repertoire on regularly-changing menus (note that menu prices
include service): crab and avocado salad with lobster mousse and saffron sauce, grilled
asparagus with parmesan, sole meunière, seared tuna and couscous, guinea fowl with lentils
and wild mushrooms, pan-fried beef fillet with polenta and salsa verde. By any standards,
London's especially, prices on the wine list are very reasonable. Latour, Duboeuf,
Trimbach and Jaboulet appear frequently on a fine list that shows great enterprise. Wine is
treated very seriously here, with five monthly tastings. The garden patio opens for outdoor
eating in summer, seating 36. Some keen prices on the decent wine list. Special children's
Saturday lunch (£5.95). *Seats 130. Parties 20. Private Room 30. L 12-2.30 D 6-11.30.
Closed Sun, Bank Holidays. Set L £10.50 Set D £16.50. Access, Amex, Diners, Visa.*

W1   French House Dining Room   £50

Tel 0171-437 2477   Map 21 A2   **R**
49 Dean Street Soho W1V 5HL

Small, unpretentious dining room – paper squares on the tables, chunky white crockery,
one mirrored wall, the others and the ceiling in mottled red – above the last of Soho's
Bohemian pubs. Cooking is hearty and straightforward in style without frills but not
without interest. Starters like sweet potato soup, kidneys and beetroot on toast, or
steamed mussels in crab broth might be followed by boiled ham, vegetable (a single large
carrot) and unpeeled buttery new potatoes and parsley sauce; lamb's tongue, chick peas
and spring greens and baked cod with potatoes and saffron. Finish with Welsh rarebit,
steamed plum pudding, chocolate cake or cheese, perhaps red Cheshire and Milleen. The
short menu changes twice daily. *Seats 30. L 12.30-3 D 6.30-11.30. Closed Sun, Bank
Holidays & 10 days Christmas. Access, Amex, Diners, Visa.*

W1   Fuji   £70

Tel 0171-734 0957 Fax 0171-409 3259   Map 18 D3   **R**
36 Brewer Street W1R 3HD

Well-prepared selection of Japanese standards (yakitori, sushi, sashimi and tempura) served
by charming waitresses. You cook some dishes at your table (after instruction!): these
include shabu-shabu (beef simmered in a boiling broth) and sukiyaki. There's a separate
noodle menu. Japanese tea is served free with all meals. *Seats 50. L 12-2.30 D 5.30-10.45.
Closed L Sun. Set L from £9.50 Set D from £17. Access, Amex, Diners, Visa.*

SW3   Fulham Road   ↑   £80

Tel 0171-351 7823   Map 19 B5   **R**
257 Fulham Road SW3 6HY

Modern British cooking by Richard Corrigan in a comfortable fashionable restaurant
whose decor includes elephant-motif banquettes. Big flavours are the order of the day,
and meat dishes, including game and offal, are particularly good: terrine of foie gras and
pheasant with celeriac and Madeira jelly: feuilleté of veal kidneys, sweetbreads and black
pudding with sage and grain mustard; roast rump of lamb with white bean casserole.
Seafood dishes are equally interesting and also feature intense flavours, as shown by grilled
fillets of Dover sole with parmesan cheese shavings and salsa verde, or roast scallops with
salt cod cream, sweet peppers and pancetta. Vegetables, also excellent, could include
Jerusalem artichokes with lemon cream, spinach with pine nuts and colcannon or blue
cheese potato gratin. Desserts continue the good work, and there's a good British cheese
platter. The wine list is similar to but more comprehensive than those in Stephen Bull's
other restaurants, though prices are on the whole higher. It's a good list, with plenty of
variety. *Seats 80. Parties 8. Private Room 12. L 12.15-2.15 D 7-11. Set L £18/£21 (Sun £23).
Closed Bank Holidays, 1 week Christmas. Access, Amex, Visa.*

Set menu prices may not always include service or wine.

WC2   Fung Shing   ★   £52

Tel 0171-437 1539 Fax 0170-734 0284   Map 21 A2   **R**
15 Lisle Street Soho WC2 7BE

One of London's very best Chinese restaurants, in a street of them. Dishes on the long Cantonese-themed menu read fairly similarly to their Chinatown neighbours, but what arrives on the plate is, quite simply, better – probably because the chef has been here since 1984, when it opened. Steamed scallops with garlic, deep-fried oysters in batter, soft-shell crab with chili and salt, superb crispy aromatic duck, barbecued pork, sizzling beef fillet, and other dishes using abalone, carp, crab, eel, lobster and prawns are among a selection which includes both familiar favourites and dishes to tempt the adventurous (chicken with preserved clam sauce, crispy fried intestine, double-boiled fluffy supreme shark's fin). Booking is almost essential. *Seats 85. Private Room 30. Meals 12-11.15. Closed 24-26 Dec. Set meals from £11. Access, Amex, Diners, Visa.*

W1   Le Gavroche   ★★★   £160

Tel 0171-408 0881 Fax 0171-491 4387   Map 18 C3   **R**
43 Upper Brook Street Mayfair W1Y 1PF

In a restaurant long considered by others as the benchmark for quality and standards, head chef Michel Roux (jr only because he shares his forename with his uncle) continues to perform in top gear. Of course, his father Albert is still involved, but the style of cooking is very much Michel's, which he delightfully describes as "traditionally French with a Roux touch". However, Albert's signature dishes, such as soufflé suissesse, l'assiette du boucher and omelette Rothschild, which have played such a large part in the restaurant's success over the years, remain. The dining-room, orchestrated by manager Silvano Giraldin, so instrumental himself in the restaurant's achievements, is situated on the lower ground floor, reached via the street-level reception area where you can peruse the menus while nibbling exquisite canapés. On the lunch menu, a real bargain considering it includes service and a half bottle of excellent wine per person, there are three choices within each course, perhaps, respectively, soufflé de homard parfumé à l'armagnac, mignonette de boeuf gratinée aux poivres and plateau de fromages (these from Maitre Jacques Vernier in Paris). Alternatively, you can select from the à la carte menu, Michel's fixed-price menu, the six-course menu exceptionnel, for an entire table only, and additional daily-changing dishes, typical examples being charlotte d'asperge et crabe en salade, ragout de langoustines et pied de cochon à la graine de moutarde, canon d'agneau et ragout de morilles, ending with a petite assiette du chef, a tasting of several desserts. As you can see, everything is very French, though each dish is meticulously explained if required. The cooking is top notch, precise, imaginative and correct in all aspects; presentation is stunning. Service, like a well-oiled motor, purrs along, the staff almost unnoticeably at your side whenever appropriate. All the trappings of a luxury restaurant are there as well, from fine table settings and comfortable, elegant seating to well-baked bread and little stands of petits fours, almost a dessert in themselves, that accompany coffee. Evian mineral water is free. California (plus three from Spain) apart, the wine list is (fabulously) French. Expensive it may be, but the quality more than makes up for this fact, and remember that prices are inclusive of service. Minimum evening charge £50. *Seats 60. Parties 10. Private Room 20. L 12-2 D 7-11. Closed Sat & Sun, Bank Holidays, 10 days at Christmas/New Year. Set L £37/£75 (six courses) Set D £55/£75. Access, Amex, Diners, Visa.*

W1   Gay Hussar   £60

Tel 0171-437 0973 Fax 0171-437 4631   Map 21 A2   **R**
2 Greek Street Soho W1V 6NB

Chef Laszlo Holecz has cooked at this Soho institution for 20 years. HIs endearingly successful and unchanging menu offers hearty portions of traditional Hungarian food. Specialities include chilled wild cherry soup, smoked breast of goose with scholet (beans and barley), stuffed cabbage, poppy seed strudel and sweet cheese pancakes. A recent meal of fish salad, roast duck with red cabbage and apple sauce, ending with home-made Liptoi cream cheese could not be faulted, nor the service under the guidance of manageress Bela Molnar. "Jól enni, jól inni, jól élni." *Seats 60. Parties 12. Private Rooms 12/22. L 12.30-2.30 D 5.30-10.45. Closed Sun, Bank Holidays. Set L £16. Access, Amex, Diners, Visa.*

W8   Geales   £30

Tel 0171-727 7969 Fax 0171-229 8632   Map 18 A3   **R**
2 Farmer Street W8 7SN

A family business established in 1919, Geales remains one of London's favourite fish restaurants. Their formula does not vary: the fish cooked in beef dripping, the chips in vegetable fat. Specialities include cod, haddock, skate, plaice, lemon sole, salmon and salmon fish cakes. Nearly always busy, and no bookings, but you can wait for a table upstairs with a drink. Pavement tables in summer. *Seats 100. Private Room (L only) 35. L 12-3 D 6-11. Closed Sun & Mon, 2 weeks Jul, 2 weeks Christmas. Access, Visa.*

SW3   La Giara   NEW   £70

Tel 0171-591 0210   Map 19 B4   **R**
6 Yeoman's Row Knightsbridge SW3

A bright, lively and very congenial Sicilian restaurant which has quickly won friends with its excellent cooking. Flavours are fresh, clear and sunny in dishes like pappardelle with tomato, pesto, tuna and chili; swordfish steak with olives and tomato sauce; sardines stuffed with soft breadcrumbs and herbs; and terrific meatballs sautéed with peppers or grilled in lemon leaves. Risotto with wild fennel and prawns is another fine dish, and the five or so pasta dishes can be ordered as either starter or main course. *Seats 40. Parties 10. L 12-3 D 6-11.15. Set L £10.50. Access, Amex, Visa.*

SW7   Gilbert's   £55

Tel 0171-589 8947   Map 19 B5   **R**
2 Exhibition Road South Kensington SW7 2HF

At the bottom end of Exhibition Road near South Kensington Underground Station, Gilbert's is by far the cosiest and snuggest of all the restaurants in this area, with dark terracotta walls, gilt-framed mirrors, tiny tables and cane chairs. The atmosphere is very civilised, very English and just slightly middle-aged. The cooking is mainly French-inspired, light and quite refined, with some subtle hints of the East, and the menus (fixed-price only) offer a choice of five dishes at each stage. These dishes are 'safe' but never dull, as shown by a fine, light hot blue cheese and walnut tart, chicken liver parfait, asparagus with orange mousseline, tenderly pink rack of lamb with thyme jus and brochette of king prawns and bacon. Desserts include some splendid English favourites – chocolate tipsy cake, Mrs Beeton's lemon tart – and coffee is served with home-made fudge. There's an interesting wine list that breaks the mould, with wines presented mostly by grape variety. The tasting notes are very reasonable and the choice comprehensive, with wines from around the world, and featured wines of the month. Enterprising owner Julia Chalkley organises a food and wine club whose activities include special theme dinners. *Seats 30. L 12-2 D 6-10 (from 5.30 during the season). Closed L Sat, all Sun, Bank Holiday Mon, 1 week Christmas, 5 days Easter. Set L £12.50/£16.50 Set D £17/£21. Access, Amex, Diners, Visa.*

EC1   Ginnan   £50

Tel 0171-278 0008   Map 16 C3   **R**
1/2 Rosebery Court Rosebery Avenue EC1R 5HP

Opposite Mount Pleasant, this is a well-run modern Japanese restaurant where the emphasis is on fresh produce throughout an extensive menu. Besides the more familiar choice there are many unusual dishes: most parts of the chicken appear among the kushiyaki (charcoal-grilled on a skewer), there's oxtail boiled with garlic, salmon dipped in sea salt and grilled, and rice and bitter melon wrapped in seaweed. *Seats 72. Parties 20. L 12-2.30 D 6-10.30 (Sat 5-10). Closed L Sat, all Sun, Bank Holidays, 11 days at Christmas/New Year, 1 week Aug. Access, Amex, Diners, Visa.*

WC2   Giovanni's   £65

Tel 0171-240 2877   Map 21 B2   **R**
10 Goodwin's Court 55 St Martin's Lane WC2AN 4LL

Theatregoers and business people are among those attracted to Giovanni Colla's long-established Italian restaurant in a little passage off St Martin's Lane. The menu is familiar Wian, with variations on pasta, meat, poultry and fish dishes. *Seats 40. Parties 10. L 12-3, D 6-11.30. Closed L Sat, all Sun, 25 Dec, 1 Jan. Access, Amex, Diners, Visa.*

SW7   The Gloucester   75%   £221

Tel 0171-373 6030 Fax 0171-373 0409   Map 19 B5   **HR**
4 Harrington Gardens South Kensington SW7 4LH

One of the largest hotels and, for its size, probably the best in the area, spick and span throughout with a splendid, very spacious marble-floored foyer lined with beautiful modern wood panelling. Large jazzy carpets with ample, comfortable seating, equally colourful in turquoise, gold and beige, occupy the centre. Humphreys, an elegant and sophisticated location for a drink, has voluptuous drapes in old gold with exciting splashes of colour provided by the vibrant, watered turquoise upholstery on a few of the chairs. Bedrooms include two club floors on the 6th and 8th. They share an exclusive and comfortable lounge on the 6th where complimentary cocktails are served in the evening together with Continental breakfast and further pampering extras. The bedrooms are all bright and spacious, club rooms having fine yew furniture, fax terminals and two incoming phone lines as well as safes and two relaxing armchairs. In all rooms double beds are king-size while single beds are 4ft wide. Bathrooms are splendid, fitted with brown marble and having excellent shower heads. There are conference and banqueting facilities (max 400) and a 24hr business centre. *Rooms 548. News kiosk, coffee shop (6.30am-11.30pm). Access, Amex, Diners, Visa.*

South West 7   £60

South West 7 is a spacious, comfortable, well-appointed room with plenty of staff and an automatic grand piano that knows everything in the repertoire of light standards. The menus show a Cal/Med influence with such dishes as peppered seared salmon with sesame noodles, lemon and soy; lasagne of roasted Mediterranean vegetables with garlic and herb cream cheese; and rosemary-seared breast of chicken with linguini, arugula and melted tomato. Also more mainstream British dishes – braised beef with vegetables and dumplings, lamb cutlets, Dover sole, steaks. Decent cooking, attractive presentation, affable service. The other eating outlet is Bugis Street Café, with the feel and flavour of Singapore. *Seats 156. Meals 12-10.45. Set L £8.95/£11.95 (Sun £17.95).*

SW10   Il Goloso   £50

Tel 0171-352 9827   Map 19 B5   **R**
204 Fulham Road SW10 9PJ

Civilised little Italian restaurant with French windows that open out onto an outside area (albeit on busy Fulham Road). Cooking is traditional, with a notably light touch, and among the dishes to note are San Daniele ham, mussels in a gentle Provençal sauce and calf's liver veneziana served with either potatoes or polenta. *Seats 50. Parties 20. L 12.15-2.30 D 6.15-11.45. Closed Sun, some Bank Holidays, 1 week Christmas, 1 week Easter. Set L £5.95 Set D £9.95. Access, Amex, Diners, Visa.*

WC1   Gonbei   £45

Tel 0171-278 0619   Map 16 C3   **R**
151 Kings Cross Road WC1X 9BN

Popular Japanese restaurant with a shortish à la carte offering excellent sashimi and deep-fried dishes plus several set dinner menus. *Seats 34. Parties 8. Private Room 20. D only 6-10.30 (Sat to 10). Closed Sun, Bank Holidays. Set D £15/£20. Access, Diners, Visa.*

SW3   Good Earth   £65

Tel 0171-584 3658 Fax 0171-823 8769   Map 19 B4   **R**
233 Brompton Road SW3 2EP

Comfortable, elegant, smartly staffed, with consistently capable cooking: the usual
attributes of a superior non-Soho Chinese restaurant. This one (and its stablemates in Mill
Hill and Esher) has two floors of main dining space, plus a large bar with stools. The
menu, while not of epic Chinatown proportions, nonetheless offers a more-than-
generous variety of dishes from the general repertoire of Chinese favourites. The kitchen
is very reliable, and among the chef's specialities are Szechuan prawns, lemon chicken,
crispy lamb and an extensive vegetarian choice. *Seats 145. Private Room 36. Meals
12-11.15. Closed 24-27 Dec. Set L £9.95 Set D £17.95. Access, Amex, Diners, Visa.*
Also at:
NW7 143 The Broadway Mill Hill NW7 Tel 0181-959 7011 Map 16 A1
Seats 90. Open 12-2.15 & 6-11.15.

W1   Gopal's of Soho   £50

Tel 0171-434 0840 Fax 0171-434 1621   Map 21 A2   **R**
12 Bateman Street W1V 5TD

Booking is essential at this comfortable Indian restaurant where chef-owner Gopal Pittal
offers regional dishes from the sub-continent not often seen in this country, so don't
expect all the familiar favourites. However, the culinary tour of India provided by the
menu is a lesson in itself. Start with patta kebab from Hyderabad, minced lamb with
herbs steamed in a colocassia leaf; Mangalorean crab – crabmeat flaked with coconut and
spices – or kofta Benarasi – delicious vegetable dumplings. Maybe follow with
Mangalorean mutton curry, Goan chicken curry or one of the good-value mixed Thali
(either vegetarian or meat). For dessert don't miss the excellent kulfi (Indian ice cream),
here flavoured with pistachio and almonds. Service can become rushed and dry up on
necessary advice as the dining-room fills. *Seats 50. Private Room 30. L 12-2.45 D 6-11.30
(Sun to 11). Closed 25 & 26 Dec. Access, Amex, Visa.*

SW7   The Gore   65%   £166

Tel 0171-584 6601 Fax 0171-589 8127   Map 19 B4   **H**
189 Queen's Gate SW7 5EX

Near the Royal Albert Hall and Hyde Park, the Gore is a hotel of pleasantly mellow
character, established a little more than 100 years ago. The striking bar-lounge has dark
green walls and comfortably arranged sofas. Best bedrooms are elegant and well appointed,
with small sitting areas; among them is the fine Tudor room, dark and atmospheric. The
hotel houses the successful Bistrot 190 and Downstairs at 190, both masterminded by
Antony Worrall Thompson. Guests enjoy concessionary rates at the Imperial College
gym. *Rooms 54. Closed 25 & 26 Dec. Access, Amex, Diners, Visa.*

SW1   The Goring   81%   £179

Tel 0171-396 9000 Fax 0171-834 4393   Map 19 D4   **HR**
17 Beeston Place Grosvenor Gardens Victoria SW1W 0JW

Family owned and run since 1910, culminating in March
1995 in a lavish 85th birthday party, this stylish hotel
benefits also from meticulous attention to detail (repaid by
the loyalty of its clientele) and an ongoing programme of
refurbishment (this year the bar area) and improvements.
At the helm are George Goring himself and Director
William Cowpe, one or both of whom personally greet
guests at lunchtime, an example of the high standards of
service exemplified by all the staff. Elegance and
immaculate housekeeping ensure that any visitor here feels
special, no matter how long or short the sojourn. Polished
marble floors and chandeliers in the entrance set the style,
which is maintained throughout, especially in the
handsome air-conditioned bedrooms, some with balconies
overlooking the garden, that have modernised bathrooms
offering splendid fittings, fine toiletries and good towels. The bedrooms, properly serviced in
the evenings, are watched over by the hotel's trademark wooden ducks, and though they have
a habit of disappearing, a proliferation of sheep from Devon seem to have taken up residence!

See over

24hr room service. Conference/banqueting for 50/70. Children up to 14 stay free in parents' room. Covered parking for seven cars (£15 per day). *Rooms 78. Valeting. Amex, Acess, Diners, Visa.*

Restaurant   £95

A change of emphasis here in the refurbished dining room (pianist at dinner) with chef John Elliott's traditional English dishes now appearing on fixed-price menus, with daily changing lunch dishes of the day. Don't be misled into fearing heavy cooking – his touch is light and he keeps abreast of fashion, though still in evidence, however, are the trolleys offering hors d'oeuvre, a roast, and desserts. Choose perhaps between a leek and Stilton tart, a salad of chargrilled tuna with quail's eggs and cherry tomatoes, or salmon fishcakes with sorrel sauce; wing of skate with nut butter, a classic grilled calf's liver and bacon with mashed potatoes, or roast best end of lamb with herbs. Finish with a definitive crème brulée or prune and armagnac parfait. Alongside the extensive French selection on the excellent wine list, Germany and the New World get a look in. Super list, sensible prices. check George Goring's wine suggestions that appear next to the day's dishes, what's available by the glass and whether a bin ends list is in operation. *Seats 70. Parties 10. Private Room 12. L 12.30-2.30 D 6-10. Set L £17.50/£21 Set D £26.*

W1	Grafton Hotel	63%	£160

Tel 0171-388 4131 Fax 0171-387 7394   Map 18 D1   **H**
130 Tottenham Court Road W1P 9HP

Edwardian Hotels own the Grafton, whose own Edwardian origins are still in evidence though the bedrooms are modern. Two floors out of five are non-smoking. There are six family rooms (children under 12 stay free in parents' room). The hotel's location at the northern end of Tottenham Court Road makes it convenient for the British Museum and Regent's Park. NCP round the corner. *Rooms 324. Access, Amex, Diners, Visa.*

SW4	Grafton Français		£65

Tel 0171-627 1048   Map 17 C5   **R**
45 Old Town Clapham Common SW4 0JL

Traditional French cooking in Clapham's oldest building, dating from the 17th century. Typical dishes on the menu include poached eggs on a bed of spinach with basil sauce, duck terrine or mussels in the half-shell sautéed in garlic butter to begin. To follow there's a choice of some eight main dishes including roast fillet of pork with a sage sauce, lamb fillet with braised leeks in puff pastry with a Madeira sauce, breast of duck with a calvados sauce or salmon with a mixed herb sauce. To finish there's lemon brulée, armagnac parfait and an unusual raspberry mousse with a hint of tarragon. A dozen or so interesting clarets and burgundies on the wine list, which is arranged by grape variety. *Seats 76. Private Rooms 33. L 12-3 D 7.30-11.30. Closed L Sat, all Sun, last 3 weeks Aug, 10 days Christmas. Set L £12.50 Set D £14.95. Access, Amex, Diners, Visa.*

W1	Grahame's Seafare		£45

Tel 0171-437 3788   Map 18 D2   **R**
38 Poland Street W1V 3DA

Fish coated in matzo meal and deep-fried or else grilled, steamed or poached in milk and butter in spick-and-span premises just off Oxford Street. Gefilte fish, chopped herring, egg and onion, potato latkes, new green cucumbers also on the menu. Poland Street car park is 100m away; special rates after 6.30pm. *Seats 86. L 12-2.45 D 5.30-9 (Fri & Sat to 8). Closed Sun, Bank Holidays, Jewish New Year. Access, Amex, Diners, Visa.*

N1	Granita		£50

Tel 0171-226 3222   Map 16 C3   **R**
127 Upper Street Islington N1 1QP

Is this London's most minimalist eating places in terms of both decor and menu? Behind a stark plate-glass and concrete frontage, the room is light, bright and airy, with pale wooden floors, the simplest of tables and chairs, a zinc bar and very little in the way of decor. With a menu of just four starters, a pasta and four mains, one cheese and five desserts, there's no excuse for the chef not to get it right. The style is New Med with a nod to California. Lunch is of two or three courses with a choice of perhaps crispy fried calamari with anchovy mayonnaise, aubergine ravioli with roasted garlic, oregano, basil, tomato sauce and parmesan followed by salmon or chicken (both chargrilled) then desserts (caramel rice pudding with plum compote, milk chocolate malt ice cream with fudge sauce). There's plenty of variety on the plate, though portions are on the small side – a marinated chump of lamb, chargrilled, comes with flageolet bean purée, lemon, olive oil and grilled baby leeks, while breast of Barbary duck, pan-roasted, is served with savoy cabbage, crushed buttered new potatoes and duck gravy. *Seats 60. L 12.30-2.30 D 6.30-10.30 (Sun to 10). Closed L Tue, all Mon, Bank Holidays, 10 days Christmas, 5 days Easter, 2 weeks August. Set L £11.50/£13.50. Access, Visa.*

NW1 Great Nepalese	£30

Tel 0171-388 6737   Map 18 D1   **R**
48 Eversholt Street NW1 1DA

Pork, duck and fish are added to a large variety of more familiar Indian dishes in a durable restaurant near Euston station. Specialities include *masco-bara* (black lentil pancakes with a curry sauce or with meat), *haku choyala* (barbecued diced mutton with hot spices, garlic and ginger), *mamocha* (steamed meat or vegetarian pastries) and Nepalese mixed grill of chicken, mutton and prawns served with salad and roti bread. *Seats 48. Parties 34. L 12-2.30 (Sun to 2.15) D 6-11.30 (Sun to 11.15). Closed 25 & 26 Dec. Set L & D £10.95. Access, Amex, Diners, Visa.*

N1 Great Northern Hotel	60%	£99

Tel 0171-837 5454 Fax 0171-278 5270   Map 16 C3   **H**
Kings Cross N1 9AN

The Great Northern, opened in 1854 as London's first purpose-built hotel, is a convenient pausing point for travellers and meeting point for businessmen; it's between St Pancras and Kings Cross BR stations and within walking distance of Euston. Accommodation is comfortable rather than stylish and includes family rooms, all but a few with en-suite facilities; under-14s share parents' room free. All have satellite TV. Function facilities for 100 in 11 meeting rooms. Private parking limited to 13 spaces. No dogs. *Rooms 89. Closed 25 & 26 Dec. Access, Amex, Diners, Visa.*

We welcome bona fide complaints and recommendations on the tear-out pages at the back of the book for readers' comments. They are followed up by our professional team.

NW8 Greek Valley	£40

Tel 0171-624 3217   Map 16 B3   **R**
130 Boundary Road NW8 0RH

Effie Bosnic creates something of a party atmosphere in her popular Greek restaurant, while husband Peter satisfies the inner man with some very good cooking. Familiar dishes like taramasalata, kleftiko and moussaka share the menu with some less universal choices such as grilled flat mushrooms in garlic butter, stuffed cabbage (seasonal and delicious) or prawns baked in tomato sauce with feta cheese. Home-made spicy sausages are particularly good, and special traditional dishes are served at Easter (Greek Easter is not necessarily at the same time as British). Note that Greek Valley is open only in the evening; the lunchtime business is handled by their Café along the road. *Seats 62. Private Room 30. D only 6-12. Closed Sun. Set D £7.95. Access, Visa.*

NW3 Green Boat	£45

Tel 0171-722 8474   Map 16 B3   **R**
7 New College Parade Finchley Road NW3 5EP

The former Mr Ke has been transformed into a restaurant offering a good choice of well-prepared Vietnamese items. The latter include an unusual 'all beef' menu as well as prawns with a spicy lemon grass sauce, crispy sliced lamb belly with a chili and sour sauce and stir-fried chicken with a satay sauce. Friendly, helpful staff. *Seats 50. Parties 12. L 12-2.30 D 6-11.30. Closed Mon (except Bank Holidays), 25 & 26 Dec. Access, Amex, Diners, Visa.*

NW3   Green Cottage   £40

Tel 0171-722 5305   Map 16 B2   **R**
9 New College Parade Finchley Road NW3 5EP

A Cantonese restaurant that is one of the most popular Chinese restaurants of the half
dozen in the area. Old favourites like roasted duck and pork, barbecued spare ribs,
steamed fish and stir-fried everything are all on offer, while the adventurous should try
soyed mixed meats (barbecued liver, gizzard, squid and duck wings). Unusual vegetarian
Zhai duckling is formed from layers of deep-fried soy bean sheets. *Seats 95. Meals 12-
11.15. Closed 25-26 Dec. Set D from £11.50 (min 2). Access, Amex, Visa.*

W1   Green Park Hotel   67%   £164

Tel 0171-629 7522 Fax 0171-491 8971   Map 18 C3   **H**
Half Moon Street Mayfair W1Y 8BP

Away from the bustle of Piccadily, a terrace of attractive Georgian town houses has been
converted into a comfortable hotel. Air-conditioned public rooms are attractively
decorated, and furnishings include soft sofas and reproduction antiques. There are several
meeting rooms and a smart cocktail bar (the Half Moon) with intimate alcoves. Standard
bedrooms vary in size and are modestly furnished; but all have TVs, direct-dial phones,
tea/coffee-making facilities and en-suite bathrooms (a few with showers only). The top
floor has recently been refurbished; some rooms are classed as de luxe, with large beds
and more lavish fittings, including marble-floored bathrooms with bidets and spa baths.
One spacious top-floor suite is very popular for business meetings. Children up to 14 stay
free in parents' room. No dogs. *Rooms 161. Access, Amex, Diners, Visa.*

SW11   The Green Room   £50

Tel 0171-223 4618   Map 17 C5   **R**
62 Lavender Hill SW11 5RQ

At the Queenstown Road end of Lavender Hill, an organically and ecologically sound
restaurant that's comfortable and unpretentious. The menu reflects the influences of many
cuisines, and vegetarians are particularly well catered for, with a dozen starters and nearly
as many main courses. Non-vegetarian choices run from cheese, tomato and prawn
pancakes to Chinese chicken, pepper-crusted monkfish and chargrilled steak. Also main-
course pasta and salads, with sorbets, pancakes and fruit slices to finish. The policy is that
all foodstuffs are organically and ecologically sound. *Seats 40. D only 7-11.15. Closed 25
& 26 Dec. Access, Amex, Diners, Visa.*

SW1   Green's Restaurant & Oyster Bar   £75

Tel 0171-930 4566 Fax 0171-491 7463   Map 18 D3   **R**
36 Duke Street St James's SW1Y 6DF

Traditional British cooking in a traditional British setting. Booking is advisable to get
a table in one of the small dining rooms but there are also seats around the bar. Native
oysters naturally head the menu, and other classics include potted shrimps, crab and
lobster, crab and lobster, salmon fishcakes with tomato sauce, bangers and mash, liver and
bacon, mixed grill and cold meats. A second menu is more modern in style, offering the
likes of grilled marinated vegetables with olives, herbs and mozzarella, roast skate with
Pommery mustard crust and caper butter sauce, or noisettes of lamb with baked
aubergines, pesto and coriander jus. Ice creams, sorbets, bread-and-butter pudding, rice
pudding and caramel, baked Cox's apple with honey and sultanas. cheeses from Paxton
and Whitfield. There are some good ideas on the wine list, not least bracketing several
wines under one price banner. Note also the sections for house wines and wines of the
month, both featuring well-chosen wines, mostly French but some from the New World.
*Seats 65. Parties 10. Private Room 44. L 11.30-3 (Sun 12-2.30) D 5.30-11. Closed D Sun.
Set Sun L £16.50/£20. Access, Amex, Diners, Visa.*

Many hotels offer reduced rates for weekend or out-of-season
bookings. Always ask about special deals.

W1   Greenhouse   ↑   £80

Tel 0171-499 3331   Map 18 C3   **R**
27a Hays Mews Mayfair W1X 7RJ

In a quiet mews behind the hurly-burly of Park Lane there's a real gem. Gary Rhodes (he of the cook books, TV series and boundless enthusiasm) has been influential in both creating and serving up culinary trends in recent years. A firm believer in all things British, he takes the best ingredients, adds a dash of the best of the rest of the world, and there you are: grilled mackerel on warm potato and anchovy salad, spinach gnocchi with tomato dressing, breast of duck with neeps and tatties, pan-fried halibut with noodles in cream sauce with crispy Bayonne ham, chocolate tart with glazed clementines, hot apple fritters with vanilla ice cream and apricot sauce. Whatever you choose you can be sure of good food, served up with plenty of motherly advice from the friendly staff, though service can sometimes suffer when under pressure. There's a concise list of about 20 wines. Sunday lunch (£18.50 for 3 courses) is a high spot. Booking essential. *Seats 90. Parties 12. L 12-2.30 (Sun 12.30 to 3) D 7-11 (Sun 7-10). Closed L Sat, Bank Holidays, 1 week Christmas. Set Sun L £18.50. Access, Amex, Diners, Visa.*

W1   alistair Greig's Grill   £90

Tel 0171-629 5613 Fax 0171-495 0411   Map 18 C3   **R**
26 Bruton Place Mayfair W1X 7AA

Prime Scotch steaks and grills have been the speciality here since its doors opened in 1954; all are simply grilled with a traditional accompaniment of grilled tomato, button mushrooms and watercress. Behind the those doors there's red plush and old-fashioned civility. Set lunch includes a glass of wine. *Seats 60. Parties 30. L 12.30-2.30 D 6.30-11. Closed L Sat, all Sun, 25 & 26 Dec, 1 Jan. Set L £19.50. Access, Amex, Diners, Visa.*

SW1   The Grenadier   £65

Tel 0171-235 3074   Map 19 C4   **R**
18 Wilton Row Belgravia SW1 7NR

Secreted down a quiet mews near Belgrave Square, a small, but striking and very typical London pub whose dark, candle-lit restaurant offers good traditional English fare: eggs benedict, smoked haddock, smoked salmon, beef Wellington (a speciality) and lamb noisettes with garlic and sage crust show the style. *Seats 28. Parties 8. L 12-2 D 6-10 (Sun from 7). Closed D 24 & 31 Dec, all 25 & 26 Dec & 1 Jan. Access, Amex, Visa.*

SW3   Grill St Quentin   £55

Tel 0171-581 8377 Fax 0171-584 6064   Map 19 B4   **R**
3 Yeoman's Row Knightsbridge SW3 2AL

A cool, stylish basement restaurant with the look and feel of a Parisian brasserie. French staff of youth and charm provide semi-formal service, and the whole place invites relaxation over a leisurely meal. Charcoal-grilled meats and fish served with splendid little chips as well as excellent shellfish are the mainstay of the menu, supported by plats cuisinés such as coq au vin, choucroute and canard aux olives. Also excellent patisserie from Spécialités St Quentin. *Seats 140. Parties 25. L 12-3 (Sun to 3.30) D 6.30-11.30 (Sun to 11). Set L & D £9. Access, Amex, Diners, Visa.*

W1   Grosvenor House   83%   £272

Tel 0171-499 6363 Fax 0171-493 3341   Map 18 C3   **H**
90 Park Lane W1A 3AA

Overlooking Hyde Park, Grosvenor House was built on the original site of the Earl of Grosvenor's 18th-century home. The facade, designed by Sir Edward Lutyens, has been a famous London landmark since its completion in 1929 and after major modernisation Forte's flagship offers superb overnight accommodation and some of London's most popular function rooms. The splendid, unpillared Great Room banqueting hall (originally an ice rink in the days of society galas) has a capacity of 2400 for banquets and is where the annual Antiques Fair is held in June. Various smaller private dining and conference

See over

suites (from 4 to 100+) at 86 Park Lane mean that the hotel is always busy with functions of every kind. The lavish interior includes a vast lounge and intimate bar; there are three restaurants, including *Chez Nico at 90 Park Lane* (qv) arguably London's finest top-flight restaurant. A wood-panelled Library is an ideal spot to while away an hour or two. All the bedrooms are large, light and airy, with a separate lobby and air-conditioning; even 'single' rooms have double beds. Solid furniture and soft colours please the eye and the bathrooms are splendid, with marble floors and excellent toiletries; many enjoy natural light. The seventh floor is the Crown Club, with separate express check-in and a small lounge and boardroom for Executive guests only; rates include breakfast, mini-bar, room-service dinner and valet pressing. Sovereign Suites are top of the range with private bars, hi-fi, video and compact disc libraries, private telephone and fax lines, and limousine service to and from the airport. 140 luxury service apartments, with a separate entrance, also offer spacious accommodation and use of the extensive facilities in the Health Club, where a 65ft swimming pool takes centre stage. Round-the-clock room service. Private garaging nearby (£27.50 for 24 hours), with valet parking. No dogs. The former Pavilion Restaurant was due to open as a rotisserie (under Nico's direction) after we went to press. Forte Exclusive. *Rooms 454. Indoor swimming pool, gym, sauna, solarium, beauty & hair salon, valeting, coffee shop (7am-2am), shops (china, jewellers, perfumery, fashion). Access, Amex, Diners, Visa.*

SW1   Grosvenor Thistle Hotel   62%   £143

Tel 0171-834 9494 Fax 0171-630 1978   Map 19 D4   **H**
101 Buckingham Palace Road SW1W 0SJ

Built in the mid-19th century, the Grosvenor Thistle retains many of its handsome Victorian features, notably the splendid galleried foyer with pillars reaching up to its glass dome. The club-like Harvard Bar is a favoured meeting place for travellers, as the hotel has direct access from Victoria railway station. Modestly furnished rooms are of a good size, with desk-space, tea/coffee-making facilities, trouser presses, hairdryers and en-suite bathrooms. Spacious luxury rooms have more comfortable furnishings, queen-sized beds with canopies and a sitting area. There are six suites with marble-clad bathrooms, bidets, tubs with separate showers, and smart toiletries. Air-conditioned banqueting/conference facilities for 110/200. Children up to 12 stay free in parents' room. Over a third of rooms are reserved for non-smokers. 24hr lounge and room service. NCP car park nearby. No dogs. *Rooms 366. 24hr coffee lounge. Access, Amex, Diners, Visa.*

NW6   Gung-Ho   £50

Tel 0171-794 1444   Map 16 B2   **R**
330-332 West End Lane Finchley NW6 1LN

Stylish Chinese restaurant located on the northern extremity of West End Lane. The decor is a fashionable mix of ochre red and dark blue with direct spotlights on the table centre to highlight the food. The menu offers the usual Szechuan dishes plus "special selections" such as crispy Mongolian lamb with iceberg lettuce, scrambled egg fu yung with fresh salmon and Chinese chives, and steamed chicken with red dates, black fungi and golden lilies. Also yin and yang feasts for a minimum of two. *Seats 105. Parties 14. L 12-2.30 D 6.30-11.30. Closed 3 days Christmas. Set D from £18.50. Access, Visa.*

W11   The Halcyon   79%   £235

Tel 0171-727 7288 Fax 0171-229 8516   Map 17 B4   **HR**
81 Holland Park W11 3RZ

A splendid, large town house occupying a corner site on Holland Park Avenue. The hotel benefits from spacious and elegant, well-proportioned rooms that retain much of their original Victorian architectural character and include a welcoming reception area-cum-lounge furnished in a fashionable period style with additional homeliness and warmth promoted by an open fireplace and grandfather clock. The bar is below stairs and has an air of intimacy and a collection of outstanding fruit vodkas. Bedrooms, even more magnificent after recent redecoration, include light, airy suites, one with its own tropical-style conservatory. Quality furniture and fabrics, together with fine antiques, feature throughout, with even the more modest single bedrooms possessing individual charm and character. Bathrooms, in marble, are kept in pristine order and several boast spa baths. All the usual amenities such as satellite TV and full 24hr room service are offered and guests have temporary membership of the Vanderbilt tennis club nearby. Valet service, chauffeur service. No dogs. *Rooms 43. Access, Amex, Diners, Visa.*

The Room at the Halcyon   ★   £90

With its own entrance on Holland Park Avenue, the restaurant is situated on the hotel's lower ground floor, and offers the opportunity for alfresco dining at eight tables under smart canvas parasols on a patio. The shades of cream and the studiedly arranged contemporary artwork and mirrors on the walls provide an unpretentiously elegant setting for the talents of chef Martin Hadden, whose dishes show a great deal of precision and no little imagination, influenced perhaps by his mentor Nico Ladenis. Fish and shellfish are a particular strength, as shown by grilled fillet of Cornish mullet with black olives, cherry tomatoes, basil and a piquant tomato sauce, pan-fried langoustines with celeriac purée and truffle, or steamed fillet of Cornish sea bass with a glazed dill sauce, scallop mousse and confit fennel. Meat dishes are no less enticing, and desserts could include warm plum tart with cardamom ice cream or a plate of four different chocolate creations. Alternatives to the à la carte selection include a two-course lunch menu, a vegetarian menu, and set dinners (three-course or six-course dégustation). Sunday brunch à la carte. An easy-to-use (least expensive first) and manageable wine list has some twenty wines under £20. No smoking. The restaurant has a separate telephone number: 0171-221 5411. *Seats 50. Parties 8. Set L £18 Set D £26/£32. L 12-2.30 (Sun to 4pm) D 7-10.30 (Fri/Sat to 11, Sun to 10). Closed L Sat.*

W2	Halepi	£50

Tel 0171-262 1070 Fax 0171-229 1343   Map 18 B3   **R**
18 Leinster Terrace Bayswater W2 3ET

Regulars have been returning for the Greek food and the convivial atmosphere since opening day in 1966. All the familiar favourites are on the menu – moussaka, stuffed vine leaves, afelia, sausages and dips – along with charcoal-grilled meat and fish (sea bass a speciality), giant prawns, oven-baked baby lamb and roast beef. As we went to press a 200-seat sister restaurant had just opened in St Johns Wood. *Seats 68. Meals 11.30am-12.30am. Closed 25 & 26 Dec. Access, Amex, Diners, Visa.*

Many hotels offer reduced rates for weekend or out-of-season bookings. Always ask about special deals.

SW1	The Halkin	86%	£262

Tel 0171-333 1000 Fax 0171-333 1100   Map 19 C4   **HR**
5 Halkin Street Belgravia SW1X 7DJ

Secreted away down a quiet street close to Hyde Park Corner, the Halkin possesses all the style and elegance expected of a top-class modern hotel. The advanced Italian design that manifests itself throughout is a model of cool sophistication. The bright, spacious lobby features highly polished granite and marble floors with a few richly coloured leather armchairs creating an informal lounge area to one side. A screen separates the rear of this lounge from a small, intimate bar. Bedrooms are furnished to an exactingly high standard, each with its own sitting area. Decor is uncluttered and ultra-modern with mahogany, cherry or rosewood much in evidence together with thick plate glass and gleaming mirrors. Individual heating and air-conditioning controls as well as two line phones, fax machines, wall-safes and mini-bars are standard. All lights are on dimmer switches and the eleven suites have a VCR and CD player. Comfortable beds, either king- or queen-size, are fitted with Egyptian cotton sheets and goosedown pillows and complement the really splendid all-marble bathrooms, all except eight of which have separate walk-in showers; costly toiletries, slippers and ample thick towels are some of the cosseting touches provided. For the inveterate businessman there's an FT room on the second floor and it is appropriately equipped with a pink phone and numerous current financial journals. Staff are superb – professional, discreet and unfailingly helpful, everything you would wish from a hotel of this class. *Rooms 41. Access, Amex, Diners, Visa.*

Restaurant   ★ †   £100

A strikingly modern restaurant with arched windows overlooking a floodlit garden. The arches are mirrored on the opposite wall by semi-circular paintings in a 17th-century

See over

style of well-known Italian wine producing estates. Decor is simple and classical with a highly polished granite and marble floor, pink marble dado and tables with crisp white linen and gleaming silverware. At night white candles flicker in double glass candlesticks adding, together with fresh flowers, a soft, romantic touch. Stefano Cavallini, seemingly more confident now that he is no longer under the influence of Gualtiero Marchesi back in Milan, presents an Italian menu of four courses with a complimentary appetiser to begin with. Pasta dishes to follow could be an unusual version of a Romagnan dish – *ferrara garganelli*, hand-made macaroni with broccoli and red mullet. Fish and meat dishes offer equally exciting eating, for instance, roasted langoustines served with lentils, white beans and pearl barley; pan-fried sea bass with courgette flowers, broccoli tortellini and a red pepper sauce; breast of chicken stuffed with foie gras, celeriac purée and served with a warm tomato and black truffle sauce; roasted aubergine, tomato and courgettes with thyme, glazed sweetbreads and toasted hazelnuts. An amaretto cream caramel with whisky sauce, a wonderfully rich tiramisu (is there better in London?) or delicious chocolate heart with raspberry coulis could precede superb coffee and delicious petits fours. While acknowledging that this is an Italian restaurant and that there is a superb selection of Italian wines to accompany the dishes, why is France the only other country represented on the list? Polished service from smartly attired staff. *Seats 45.*
Private Room 26. L 12.30-2.30 D 7.30-10.30 (Sun from 7). Closed L Sat & Sun, 25 & 26 Dec. Set L £18/£24.

WC2 Hampshire Hotel	78%	£248

Tel 0171-839 9399 Fax 0171-930 8122   Map 21 A3   **HR**
31 Leicester Square WC2 7LH

A Radisson Edwardian hotel in the very heart of London, with instant access to theatres, shops and major tourist sights. Low-ceilinged public rooms have an elaborate decor with a strong Oriental theme through hand-woven Thai carpets and Chinese furnishings. Although not to scale with the bedrooms, the small lounge with cosy sofas and fireplace, the wood-panelled bar and elegant restaurant have the comforting feel of a private club. Oscars Café is open from 8am to 11pm in summer, noon to 6pm at other times. Bedrooms vary in size, the most agreeable ones being the suites with large tinted picture windows overlooking Leicester Square. Decor is rather busy with chintzy flowery fabrics done in shades of pink or blue. Bathrooms, all in Italian marble and mahogany finish, are well appointed. The Penthouse suite, which can accommodate up to 80, has a fine view over Trafalgar Square and Westminster. *Rooms 124. Access, Amex, Diners, Visa.*

Celebrities Restaurant   £75

Intimate dining-room with comfortable seating and a new terrace for use in the summer. Cooking is of English and international influence: grilled meats, lobster with cognac and marsala sauce and wild rice, venison cutlets with spatzli. Vegetarian main courses available. *Seats 55. Parties 50. L 12.30-2.30 D 6-11. Set L £15/£19.50 Set D £16 (pre-theatre), /£20 & £27.50.*

W1 Harbour City	£40

Tel & Fax 0171-439 7859   Map 21 A2   **R**
46 Gerrard Street Soho W1

Set on three floors, this restaurant is extremely busy with a largely Chinese clientele. Unlike most of its competitors in the street, staff take good care of their customers, advising on the menu or recommending dishes. Dim sum (served until 4.45pm) are selected from an extensive menu (of nearly 90 items) rather than from a trolley and are among the best in London, most being prepared to order and include some more exotic choices. The main menu is extensive including Cantonese hot pots, sizzling hot pot platter dishes, Szechuan set dinners, special seafood dinners, and mini-banquets for parties of eight or more. Cooking is assured and authentic. *Seats 180. Parties 14. Private Room 80. Meals noon-11.15. Closed 24 & 25 Dec. Set meals from £10.50/£18.50. Access, Amex, Diners, Visa.*

W1   Hardy's   £50
Tel 0171-935 5929   Map 18 C2   R
53 Dorset Street off Baker Street W1

Lively bistro with tables on the pavement in fine weather. The short, straightforward menu changes every couple of months or so and is augmented by daily blackboard specials. Typical dishes might include gravad lax, steamed mussels, cannelloni with spinach and ricotta and a tomato and chili sauce, liver and bacon with mash, steak and frites, sea bass and salmon fishcakes. *Seats 80. Parties 20. L 12.30-3 D 5.30-10.30. Closed Sat, Sun & Bank Holidays. Access, Amex, Visa.*

SW7   Harrington Hall   72%   £142
Tel 0171-396 9696 Fax 0171-396 9090   Map 19 A5   H
5-25 Harrington Gardens South Kensington SW7 4JW

An elegant, privately-owned hotel behind a handsome period facade. The open-plan public rooms are airy and comfortable. Large bedrooms offer extensive amenities: discreet door bells, spy-eyes, message telephone as well as the usual mini-bar, trouser press and tea/coffee facilities. Bathrooms are more basic. There is a small fitness centre and sauna. Stylish conference facilities (the largest suite accommodates 100+) and a business centre. *Rooms 200. Gym, sauna. Access, Amex, Diners, Visa.*

NW7   Hee's   £50
Tel 0181-959 7109   Map 16 A1   R
27 The Broadway Mill Hill NW7 3DA

Enormous Chinese characters are simple but effective wall decorations in a popular restaurant serving well-prepared dishes originating in Peking and Szechuan. Starters such as bang bang chicken are big on flavour as are steamed scallops with garlic and spring onion. Main dishes include good deep-fried shredded beef with chili, and king prawns, quite carefully deveined, sizzling in a black bean sauce or with sweet and sour sauce. Red bean paste pancakes make a fitting end to an enjoyable meal served by pleasant, courteous staff. *Seats 100. Parties 15. Private Room 40. L 12-2.30 D 6-11.15. Closed 25 & 26 Dec. Access, Amex, Diners, Visa.*

NW4   Hendon Hall   62%   £107
Tel 0181-203 3341 Fax 0181-203 9709   Map 16 B1   H
Ashley Lane NW4 1HF

The country house feel of this impressive Georgian building is lent romance by the knowledge that it was once the home of actor-manager David Garrick. Approached through an arched gateway and set in spacious grounds, the hotel offers peaceful seclusion while maintaining close access to the M1 and A1 road systems. Comfortable but modestly furnished bedrooms are linked by a warren of corridors. En-suite bathrooms have tubs with overhead showers (except for three single rooms); and 12 rooms are reserved for non-smokers. 24hr room service. Children up to 5 can stay free in parents' room. No dogs. Free parking for 70 cars. Thistle & Mount Charlotte. *Rooms 50. Garden. Access, Amex, Diners, Visa.*

SW7   Hilaire   ★ ↑   £85
Tel 0171-584 8993   Map 19 B5   R
68 Old Brompton Road South Kensington SW7 3LQ

Bryan Webb's imaginative style encompasses a range of dishes from both far and near but his fondness for British (especially Welsh) and Mediterranean foods remains paramount. His menus are very well researched and feature some unusual and successful combinations. Starters include a curried aubergine and crab soup, saffron risotto with pesto and deep-fried oysters with onion rings and a Thai dip. Main courses could be roast cod with haricot beans, radicchio and lemon vinaigrette, sea bass 'beurre blanc' with laverbread, oxtail faggot with mashed potato and red wine sauce or roast calf's sweetbreads with a potato and olive cake and lemon cream sauce. Desserts such as ricotta cheesecake, almond tart with crème fraiche, apple and quince parfait with prunes and chocolate brownies with vanilla ice cream and fudge sauce make a fitting finale. For dinner there's also a simple two-course set supper menu available before 7.30pm and after

See over

10. There's also a good vegetarian menu offering baked aubergine with pesto and buffalo mozzarella, and Piedmontese peppers among the starters and wild mushrooms and truffle risotto, baked artichoke with twice-baked goat's cheese soufflé and ragout of baby vegetables with a chervil butter sauce as main courses. The selection of cheeses from Neal's Yard, all British farmhouse, is superb. The wine list, bold in all aspects, is presented by style. Prices are fair, the choice is interesting, and tasting notes are short and to the point. *Seats 60. Private Room 30. L 12.15-2.30 D 6.30-11.30. Closed L Sat, all Sun, Bank Holidays. Set L £16.50 Set D £16.50/£32.50. Access, Amex, Diners, Visa.*

NW8   Hilton International Regent's Park   73%   £150

Tel 0171-722 7722 Fax 0171-483 2408   Map 18 B1   **H**
18 Lodge Road St John's Wood NW8 7JT

Not far from London Zoo and overlooking the nursery end of Lord's cricket ground, this Hilton International numbers free parking (for 70) and 24hr room service (offering Japanese and Arabic specialities) among its facilities. There's a spacious and comfortable lounge bar, a well-equipped business centre and several conference suites, named after cricketers or their paraphernalia, and catering for up to 150 delegates. Bedrooms, some with balconies, include Executive rooms and three-bedded rooms for family occupation. High-pressure showers are a good feature. There's even Japanese satellite TV. No dogs. See separate entry for the Kashinoki Japanese restaurant. *Rooms 377. Hair salon, coffee shop (7am-2am), kiosk. Access, Amex, Diners, Visa.*

W11   Hiroko   £80

Tel 0171-603 5003   Map 17 B4   **R**
179 Holland Park Avenue Shepherds Bush W11 4UL

On the ground floor of the London Kensington Hotel, the restaurant has two entrances – one from the street and one from the hotel lobby. Smartly decorated but in a minimalist Japanese fashion it has a very traditional menu featuring a wide choice of set lunch options and a good à la carte sushi selection. The sukiyaki and shabu-shabu are firm favourites here. *Seats 72. Parties 15. L 12-2.30 D 6-10.30. Set L & D from £15. Closed Mon. Access, Amex, Diners, Visa.*

W1   Ho-Ho   £60

Tel 0171-493 1228 Fax 0171-408 0862   Map 18 D3   **R**
29 Maddox Street W1 9LD

The bare floorboards are in contrast to the smartly decorated walls and spruce, well-dressed tables of this Chinese restaurant specialising in good interpretations of inter-regional cuisine. The menu includes a selection of classical dishes from Szechuan as well as specialities from the Malaysian peninsula. The grilled dumplings are superb, as is mee goreng – stir-fried Malaysian noodles. *Seats 80. Parties 10. Private Room 40. L 12-3 D 6-11. Set L from £10 Set D £17.85. Closed L Sat, all Sun & Bank Holidays. Access, Amex, Diners, Visa.*

N1   Hodja Nasreddin   £25

Tel 0171-226 7757   Map 16 D2   **R**
53 Newington Green Road N1

Turkish eating in friendly, homely surroundings. Highlights include houmus, mixed meze (6 dishes, minimum 2 people), spicy sausages and succulent kebabs. House specialities are sote (small pieces of lamb with herbs, mushrooms, tomatoes and onions) and Hodja's Special featuring a selection of their best meat dishes. Seats 48. Parties 26. Private Room 30. Meals noon-3am. Closed 25 Dec. Access, Amex, Visa.

SW5   Hogarth Hotel   62%   £92

Tel 0171-370 6831 Fax 0171-373 6179   Map 19 A5   **H**
Hogarth Road Earls Court SW5 0QQ

This modern hotel located in a quiet stretch of Hogarth Road is handy for Earls Court exhibitions. Modestly furnished bedrooms all have TVs with satellite channels, tea/coffee making facilities, trouser press, hairdryer and work space; many of the en-suite bathrooms need refurbishing; those on the top floor have been completed, and progress with the rest is promised. Children under 12 stay free in their parents' room. Secure underground parking (£10 per night). Marston Garden Court Hotels. *Rooms 86. Access, Amex, Diners, Visa.*

NW2   Holiday Inn Garden Court   60%   £92

Tel 0181-455 4777 Fax 0181-455 4660   Map 16 A2   **H**
Tilling Road Brent Cross NW2 3DS

A tall, modern, purpose-built hotel just off the roundabout at the foot of the M1. Bedrooms are bright and smart; rebranding from Garden Court has brought expanded room service and some Executive rooms designed for the business traveller. Children up to 12 stay free in parents' room. Ample free parking. *Rooms 153. Access, Amex, Diners, Visa.*

W1   Holiday Inn Garden Court   56%   £148

Tel 0171-935 4442 Fax 0171-487 3782   Map 18 D2   **H**
57 Welbeck Street W1M 8HJ

A modernised hotel in a quiet location, just north of the Oxford Street big stores. There is no room service and breakfast is from a hot and cold buffet. *Rooms 138. Access, Amex, Diners, Visa.*

SW7   Holiday Inn Kensington   68%   £187

Tel 0171-373 2222 Fax 0171-373 0559   Map 19 B5   **H**
100 Cromwell Road SW7 4ER

Stylishly modern hotel, behind an Edwardian facade, close to Gloucester Road Underground station. Public rooms are polished and spacious and, in common with the rest of the hotel, air-conditioned. Bedrooms are all comfortably furnished and have TVs with satellite channels, trouser presses, tea/coffee-making facilities and double or triple glazing. A £25 supplement affords membership of the Executive club and a range of extras, from bathrobe and slippers to complimentary orange juice and mineral water and an evening turndown service. There are also 19 Duplex suites on two floors connected by a spiral staircase, these; are ideal for families and include a sofa bed and two TVs to avoid arguments! Plenty of rooms for non-smokers (on the 1st or 4th floor). Under-19s can stay free in parents' room. 24hr room service. No dogs. Small private car park (£15 for 24 hours). *Rooms 162. Garden, keep-fit equipment, sauna, spa bath, steam room, lounge bar (6.30am-1am). Access, Amex, Diners, Visa.*

WC1   Holiday Inn Kings Cross/Bloomsbury   68%   £165

Tel 0171-833 3900 Fax 0171-917 6163   Map 16 C3   **H**
1 Kings Cross Road WC1X 9HX

Useful modern hotel, just a stone's throw from Kings Cross, St Pancras and Euston stations. The spacious public rooms include Charings cocktail bar and a comfortably furnished lounge. Bedrooms include the Holiday Inn hallmarks such as large beds (doubles – even in single rooms), TV with in-house movies, direct-dial phone, hairdryer, trouser press, good work space and en-suite bathroom (with tub and overhead shower). Mini-bars are installed but stocked only on request. Executive rooms are similar, but with upgraded furnishings, complimentary soft drinks/mineral water and a basket of fresh fruit. There are ramps for disabled guests – wide lifts and purpose-built bedrooms. Almost 50% of bedrooms are for non-smokers. The excellent basement leisure facilities are free to guests. Banqueting/conference facilities for 180/250. 24hr room and lounge service. Children under 12 stay free in parents' room. The whole hotel is air-conditioned, with individual controls in bedrooms. *Rooms 405. Indoor swimming pool, gym, squash, sauna, spa bath, steam room, solarium, beauty & hair salon, news kiosk. Access, Amex, Diners, Visa.*

W1   Holiday Inn Mayfair   72%   £172

Tel 0171-493 8282 Fax 0171-629 2827   Map 18 D3   **H**
3 Berkeley Street W1X 6NE

A few steps from Bond Street, Green Park and the Royal Academy with a bar, lounge and restaurant that merge one into the other and gain an elegant air from the moulded ceiling and glittering chandeliers. Good-size bedrooms (24hr room service) offer luxuriously large beds and all the expected accessories including air-conditioning and mini-bars. Executive rooms are even more generously proportioned and have fax machines and spa baths. Children up to 19 stay free in parents' room. Conference/banqueting for 70/50. No dogs. *Rooms 185. Coffee lounge (11am-11pm). Access, Amex, Diners, Visa.*

WC2   Hong Kong   £40

Tel 0171-287 0324   Map 21 A2   **R**
6 Lisle Street Leicester Square WC2

A cavernous setting serving a daytime selection of dim sum popular with snackers and a Cantonese menu of proverbial favourites like sculptured squid and prawn balls, fried noodles with roast pork, sizzling platters and hot-pots (including exceptional braised lamb with dried bean curd). The more adventurous might choose crispy pig's intestines, fried fillet of eel, fried oyster with scrambled egg or even stir-fried carp with superior soup. Finish with a fruit fritter or tapioca cream. *Seats 200. Parties 18. Meals 12-11.30. Closed 25 & 26 Dec. Set D from £8.50 (min two people). Access, Amex, Visa.*

EC1   The Hope & Sir Loin   £40

Tel 0171-253 8525   Map 16 C3   **R**
94 Cowcross Street Smithfield EC1M 6BH

Vast breakfasts start the day in the dining-room above a traditional Smithfield pub, the largest involving egg, bacon, sausage, black pudding, kidneys, liver, baked beans, tomatoes, mushrooms and toast. Grills and roasts are the lunchtime specialities, plus the likes of deep-fried scampi, veal in cream and mushrooms and steak & kidney pie. *Seats 32. Parties 16. Private Room 20. Meals 7.15am-9.30am & noon-2pm. Closed Sat, Sun, Bank Holidays, 25 Dec-5 Jan. Access, Amex, Visa.*

W2   Hospitality Inn Bayswater   62%   £113

Tel 0171-262 4461 Fax 0171-706 4560   Map 18 A3   **H**
104 Bayswater Road W2 3HL

Immediately opposite Hyde Park and a short walk from Notting Hill Gate, this modern hotel with its entrance in Porchester Terrace offers comfortable accommodation that is also within easy reach of Oxford Street and the West End. Double-glazed bedrooms have TV, hairdryer and individually controlled air-conditioning. En-suite bathrooms have tubs with overhead showers. Front rooms on the upper floors have splendid views over the park. Children up to 13 stay free in parents' room. 24hr room service. Free underground parking. *Rooms 175. Access, Amex, Diners, Visa.*

W1   Hospitality Inn Piccadilly   62%   £139

Tel 0171-930 4033 Fax 0171-925 2586   Map 21 A3   **H**
39 Coventry Street W1V 8EL

Behind the grand Victorian facade of this centrally located hotel (main entrance in Whitcomb Street) there's a commendably high level of peace and comfort. Bedrooms are modestly furnished, but all boast en-suite bathrooms with tubs and overhead showers. Good work space, tea/coffee-making facilities, trouser presses and direct-dial phones. Bedrooms at the rear are particularly quiet. 24hr room service. No dogs. *Rooms 92. Access, Amex, Diners, Visa.*

EC3   The Hospitality Suite   £75

Tel 0171-617 5042 Fax 0171-617 5050   Map 20 D2   **R**
London Underwriting Centre, 3 Minster Court Mincing Lane EC3R 7DD

♛

Advance booking and the names of all guests is a prerequisite at this smart new colony in the Roux empire, all part of the strict security measures at the impressive Minster Court complex. This is all worthwhile, however, as you will be lunching in a room with one of the best views in London including the Tower of London and its bridge. The short table d'hote menu changes daily, and is classically French. Start with lobster bisque with crab and coriander fritters or terrine of duck with pear chutney. Roast guinea fowl breast with lentils and foie gras, fillet of sea bass with a saffron butter sauce or pan-fried pork fillet with caramelised apples might follow. Desserts could include a pithiviers of apricots and pear custard or iced lemon parfait with a warm cherry compote. Service is professional and formal. The short wine list is restrained in its mark-ups for a restaurant of this standard: Georges Duboeuf house wine is £8.75, for example. *Seats 30. L only 12-2.30. Closed Sat, Sun, Bank Holidays, 1 week Christmas. Set L £29.50. Access, Amex, Diners, Visa.*

SW3   L'Hotel   £145

Tel 0171-589 6286 Fax 0171-225 0011   Map 19 C4   **HR**
28 Basil Street Knightsbridge SW3 1AT

Just a stone's throw from Harrods, this comfortable little *pension* is under the same ownership as the Capital Hotel next door. Individually designed bedrooms are comfortable and tastefully decorated in a French country style, with deep carpets and solid pine furniture. All have TVs, direct-dial phones, comprehensively stocked mini-bars and en-suite facilities with deep tubs and hand-held showers. No room service apart from breakfast, which can be taken in the bedroom or Le Metro restaurant below. Free cots. No dogs. *Rooms 12. Access, Amex, Diners, Visa.*

Le Metro   £40

An ultra-modern basement wine bar/brasserie beneath the hotel, where Philip Britten's team produces a lively menu at reasonable prices. Inspiration is English and French, and specialities include spinach fettuccine, braised ham hock with potato dumplings and lentils, and apricot mousse. Also open for breakfast and afternoon teas. Nearly all the wines on the list are available by the generous glass. Fair prices, excellent selection. *Seats 40. Parties 8. L 12-2.30 D 6-11.15 Closed Sun & Bank Holidays.*

E1   The Hothouse   £50

Tel 0171-488 4797 Fax 0171-488 9500   Map 17 D4   **R**
78 Wapping Lane E1 9NF

Heavy wooden beams and bare brick walls with American Indian decorations are features of this 200-year-old former spice warehouse constructed on two floors. On the ground floor there's a short modern menu ranging from smoked bacon and lentil broth, Thai steamed mussels, risotto alla milanese and seafood fishcake to roast salmon with Piemontese pepper and rouille, choucroute alsacienne and confit of duck with bok choy and soy sesame lemon dressing. There's live jazz on Wednesday and Friday evenings. *Seats 150. Parties 20. Private Room 45. L 12-3.30 D 6-11. Closed Bank Holidays. Set L & D £12.50 (Sun £10) Access, Amex, Visa.*

WC2   The Howard   81%   £267

Tel 0171-836 3555 Fax 0171-379 4547   Map 20 A2   **HR**
Temple Place Strand WC2R 2PR

Overlooking the Thames, the modern exterior of the Howard is in complete contrast to the opulent interior. This is very much a hotel in the grand tradition. Reception staff and porterage are first-rate, well able to handle the demands of visitors from all over the world. Public areas are dominated by the fine decorations, Adam-style friezes, chandeliers and Italian marble pillars of the foyer-lounge, which typifies the ornate tone throughout. The Temple Bar has views over the tiered garden and leads through into the Quai d'Or restaurant; both are pretty in pink with ruched window drapes, plush green chairs and intricate ceilings. Bedrooms are mainly twin-bedded and classically furnished with French marquetry pieces and have modern comforts such as air-conditioning, individual heating control and multiple phones, plus superb marbled bathrooms. Best rooms have small terraces with panoramic views over the River Thames – from St Paul's to Westminster. 24hr 'à la carte' room service is offered, and a special Japanese breakfast (among others) is served either in the restaurant or in your room. Function rooms cater for up to 150. No dogs. *Rooms 137. 24hr lobby service, valeting. Access, Amex, Diners, Visa.*

Le Quai d'Or   £100

The domed ceiling and renaissance decor make a splendid setting for French cuisine in a very correct mould. Dressed Cornish crab, salmon mousse in aspic or *crepes florentine* could precede a plain roast, a grill or something a little more elaborate like *filet de barbue dieppoise, coeur de filet en feuilletage* (beef fillet with duxelles and goose liver paté baked in puff pastry and served with a Madeira and truffle sauce). At lunchtime a silver trolley carries the dish of the day – rib of beef on Wednesday, stuffed salmon on Friday, coq au vin on Saturday. Classic desserts and savouries. The wine list is somewhat pedestrian for a hotel of this class. *Seats 95. Parties 25. L 12.30-3 D 6.30-11 (Sun till 10.30). Set L £25.*

W2   Hsing   £50

Tel 0171-402 0904   Map 18 B1   **R**
451 Edgware Road W2 1TH

Metal, wood, water, fire and earth: Hsing represents the five elements on which the restaurant decor and philosophy are based. The interesting Chinese menu puts an emphasis on fish: special crispy fish with vegetables or sweet and sour sauce or Hsing special feast of braised shark fin or abalone. Meat dishes include a delicious, crispy, fragrant and aromatic lamb and vegetarians are not forgotten. *Seats 60. Parties 14. L 12-3 D 6-11.30. Closed Sun, 3 days Christmas. Access, Amex, Diners, Visa.*

NW1   Hudson's   £65

Tel 0171-935 3130   Map 18 C1   **R**
221b Baker Street NW1 6XE

A Victorian-style dining room on the ground floor of the Sherlock Holmes museum. Named after Holmes' housekeeper, the restaurant offers a short carte of quite traditional English dishes given a modern treatment. Starters range from West Sussex churdles with mushroom relish – sautéed chicken livers with apples and herbs and Old English saffron mussels with white wine and cream to deep-fried cheese croquettes with apple chutney. Main dishes include tender lamb wrapped in mint and prune stuffing, baked in crisp pastry and served with a port and redcurrant sauce and Professor Moriarty's chicken pie – with a good lightly curried filling. To finish there are simple sweets like hot chocolate and walnut sponge with butterscotch sauce or fruit compote with honey ice cream. Delightful service by waitresses in Victorian uniforms. *Seats 45. Parties 25. L 12-2.30 (Sun to 3) D 6-10.30 (Sun 7-10). Closed D Bank Holidays, all 24 & 25 Dec. Set L & D £16.50. Access, Amex, Diners, Visa.*

SW1   Hunan   £50

Tel 0171-730 5712   Map 19 C5   **R**
51 Pimlico Road Belgravia SW1W 8NE

Small Chinese restaurant where the chef-owner prepares Hunan specialities. The atmosphere is quiet and homely with classical music in the background and very attentive service. Many customers, including regulars, opt for the special 'leave-it-to-us feast', which can be adapted to individual preferences. *Seats 50. L 12-3 D 6-11.30 (Sun 7-11). Closed L Sun, 4 days Christmas, Bank Holidays. Access, Amex, Visa.*

SW1   Hyatt Carlton Tower   87%   £295

Tel 0171-235 1234   Fax 0171-245 6570   Map 19 C4   **HR**
2 Cadogan Place Knightsbridge SW1X 9PY

Towering high above Cadogan Gardens, this most opulent of London's smart hotels features the fashionable Chinoiserie (all-day snacks and afternoon tea served 3-5.30pm) on the ground floor, where enormous flower arrangements burst out of colourful Chinese glazed pots, creating an air of elegance which is continued throughout the hotel. The most sought-after bedrooms are those with balconies overlooking the verdant splendour of the square below. There are also balconies on those bedrooms looking out west over Sloane Street and Knightsbridge. The 16 bedroom floors include 62 enormous suites and an 18th-floor (the top) Presidential suite which enjoys both splendid views and high levels of security. Standard rooms are both spacious and well appointed. King-size beds are a feature of the majority. Decor throughout is a timeless pale cream and beige with elegant furniture to match. The style is typified by the brass carriage clock placed on every desk, and the comfortable armchairs. All rooms have full air-conditioning and there are wall safes for valuables and umbrellas in the wardrobes for rainy days. Bathrooms in marble have fine toiletries as well as thick towels, bathrobes and scales. Excellent standards of

housekeeping include a twice-daily maid service with evening turn down. The Peak
Health Club is a bright, spacious and airy, state-of-the-art 9th-floor rendezvous for
fitness fanatics; there's a Club Room for post-exertion wind-down and a separate work-
out studio with sprung floor; the tennis court is in Cadogan Square.
Banqueting/conference facilities for 300/250. One child up to 18 may stay free in
his/her parents' room. Covered parking (£20 overnight). No dogs. *Rooms 224. Gym,
work-out studio, sauna, steam room, solarium, beauty & hair salon, valeting,
Chinoiserie (7am-11pm), news kiosk. Access, Amex, Diners, Visa.*

Chelsea Room 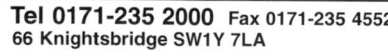 £115

Overlooking Cadogan Gardens, under
a curving glass conservatory roof, the Chelsea Room is a sumptuous restaurant. There's
a bright and open feel to the whole of the dining room, which is elegantly decorated
with pickled wood panelling. In the evening, soft lights and piano music complete the
picture. Long-serving chef Bernard Gaume's menu offers French classics with a modern
touch. Start, perhaps, with dariole de foie gras chaude aux morilles or a fresh vegetable
soup with Dublin Bay prawns, lobster, garlic and basil, following with straightforward
grills (steak, lamb cutlets, veal, liver, sole, turbot),
a choice of three vegetarian options or the likes of sautéed scallops with shredded
celeriac and mustard, fillets of duck with citrus fruit segments and green peppercorns, or
whole sole baked with a saffron and almond crust, served on a tomato coulis. Salad of
langoustines, foie gras aux raisins and petits filets de boeuf are considered specialities
along with a hot passion fruit soufflé. Grand prices on a pretty classical, mostly French
wine list, though the New World section is both imaginative and better priced.
*Seats 63. Parties 30. Private Room 35. L 12.30-2.45 D 7-11.15 (Sun to 10.30).
Set L £22.50 Set D £29.50.*

Rib Room £110

An elegantly appointed, split-level room with rich mahogany panelling and a discreet,
clubby ambience. A very traditional and classic carte offers simple, well-prepared dishes,
the speciality being roast ribs of Aberdeen Angus beef served with crisp Yorkshire
puddings and jacket potato with sour cream. Lunchtime daily specials include steak and
kidney pie on Tuesday and cod dugléré on Friday. Service is very, very civilised but can
still get you in and out in an hour if you're in a hurry. Private boardroom-style dining
room for 16. Seats 84. Parties 10. L 12.30-2.45 D 6.30-11.15 (Sun 7-10.15).
Closed 1-3 Jan. Set L £22.50 Set D £29.50.

| SW1 | Hyde Park Hotel | 82% | £306 |

Tel 0171-235 2000 Fax 0171-235 4552   Map 19 C4   **H**
66 Knightsbridge SW1Y 7LA

Once an exclusive gentleman's club, this imposing neo-
gothic Victorian hotel enjoys an unrivalled position in the
heart of Knightsbridge. On entering the magnificent foyer
with its marble floor and Corinthian columns, one
encounters a world of crystal chandeliers and luxury –
cocooned from the pressures of city life. The sumptuously
furnished public rooms have been rearranged this year to
include a club-like piano bar. The lounge, with its elegant
plaster-moulded ceiling, comfortable armchairs and tasteful
furnishings, has views overlooking Hyde Park and Rotten
Row. Air-conditioned bedrooms are individually
decorated with good-quality matching fabrics, traditional
polished wood furniture and comfortable armchairs and
sofas. The business traveller is not neglected, with voice
mail, a computer modem and bedroom fax facilities
available. Marble bathrooms have bidets, telephones and loudspeaker extensions. Service
is good, with a full valet service on offer. 19 elegant suites all overlook the park, those on
the first floor having private patios. Up to 250 can be accommodated theatre-style in four
splendid function suites. Valet parking. A canny Forte coup here is teaming up with
Marco Pierre White whose Restaurant has a canopied entrance from the street (see entry
under "M"). Forte Exclusive. *Rooms 185. Mini-gym. Access, Amex, Diners, Visa.*

W1   Ikeda   £110

Tel 0171-629 2730 Fax 0171-628 6982   Map 18 C3   **R**
30 Brook Street Mayfair W1Y 1AG

Traditional Japanese cooking by Mr Ikeda in a quiet, civilised little West End restaurant, just off New Bond Street and a few steps from Claridge's. A place at the bar gets you a ringside seat to the sushi show, while the tables are all close enough to the kitchen to make you feel part of the action. The daily-changing chef's specials are the choice of many. *Seats 30. Private Room 8. L 12.30-2.30 D 6.30-10.30 (Sat 6-10). Closed L Sat, all Sun, Bank Holidays. Set L from £14 Set D from £33. Access, Amex, Diners, Visa.*

W1   Ikkyu   £50

Tel 0171-436 6169   Map 18 D2   **R**
67a Tottenham Court Road W1P 9PA

Busy basement Japanese restaurant by Goodge Street Underground station offering fine home-style cooking (robatayaki) on a long and varied menu with short, to-the-point descriptions: cold tofu, fried chicken, grilled tentacles. Good-value lunchtime menus include grilled fish set, sushi set and ramen noodles. Finish off with fresh fruit. New branch at 7 Newport Place WC1, Tel 0171 439 3554. *Seats 45. L 12.30-2.30 D 6-10.30, Closed L Sun, D Bank Holiday Mon, all Sat, 10 days Christmas. Access, Amex, Diners, Visa.*

EC3   Imperial City   £55

Tel 0171-626 3437 Fax 0171-338 0125   Map 20 C2   **R**
Royal Exchange Cornhill EC3V 3LL

A busy and popular Chinese restaurant in the brick-lined vaults beneath the Royal Exchange. The menu, compiled with the help of Ken Hom, is short and succinct, featuring a mix of regional Chinese dishes with fairly conservative spicing. Steamed salmon with black bean sauce, Cantonese pressed duck, 'Lion Head' meatball casserole, crispy lacquered quail and firecracker sweet wontons are typical dishes. Decor is bright and colourful, service friendly and as quick as required. *Seats 180. Private Room 16. Meals 11.30am-8.30pm. Closed Sat, Sun, Bank Holidays & 24 Dec. Set meals from £14.90. Access, Amex, Diners, Visa.*

SW1   L'Incontro   £100

Tel 0171-730 3663 Fax 0171-730 5062   Map 19 C5   **R**
87 Pimlico Road SW1W 8PH

A stylishly modern, up-market Italian restaurant whose exterior is adorned by flowers in huge terracotta pots. A one-dish lunch (choice of four dishes) supplements the two- or three-course menu and à la carte, while in the evening the choice is only à la carte. Specialities in young Venetian chef Nicola Celmanti's repertoire include baccalà with polenta, cuttlefish in ink sauce, fresh pasta and poached sea bass in a balsamic vinegar sauce. The Piano Bar is a popular venue for private parties. Alongside a splendid list (naturally) of Italian wines, there are a few French bottles. *Seats 55. Parties 20. Private Room 35. L 12.30-2.30 D 7-11.30 (Sun to 10.30). Closed L Sat & Sun, 25 & 26 Dec. Set L £13.50/£16.80. Access, Amex, Diners, Visa.*

W1   Hotel Inter-Continental London   84%   £277

Tel 0171-409 3131 Fax 0171-409 7460   Map 19 C4   **HR**
1 Hamilton Place Hyde Park Corner W1V 1QY

Always popular with Americans both on business and on holiday, the hotel, located at Hyde Park Corner, has a vast, elegant foyer with highly polished, coloured marble floors leading to a stylish lounge well provided with supremely comfortable seating. It's also a fine conference and banqueting venue (up to 1000/850) and the fully equipped business centre has four private meeting rooms. There's also a purpose-built Video Conferencing Suite. Bedrooms, though not particularly large, are sleek and airy with seating areas, air-conditioning, double-glazing and mini-bars; bathrooms provide quality towelling and good toiletries. Rooms extend over eight floors, and those at the top enjoy fine views. The hotel offers a luxury airport service – the chauffeur will telephone ahead to advise reception of your arrival ensuring minimum delay when checking-in. There's underground parking for 100 cars. *Rooms 460. Gym, sauna, spa bath, solarium, beauty salon, coffee shop (7am-11pm). Access, Amex, Diners, Visa.*

Le Soufflé Restaurant

  £150

One of the most discreet and least known of London's top dining rooms, Le Soufflé has stylishly modern decor with a memory of 'Grand Hotel' style maintained by formally attired staff who provide exemplary old-fashioned standards of service. Hailed as a maestro by his peers, Peter Kromberg, the restaurant's chef-patron, keeps a low profile, avoiding publicity. He prefers to maintain a true hands-on approach in his kitchens, overseeing a dedicated and skilled team producing extraordinary food both for the restaurant and for the splendid banquets that are held in the hotel's function suites. As one would expect from the restaurant's name, soufflés both savoury and sweet are a feature of the menus. The carte has among its many delicious starters a soufflé of langoustines and fresh dill with a salad of spinach and scallops, a truffle and goose foie gras soufflé with lamb's lettuce and a rich truffle and foie gras sauce as well as tender Scottish lobster with asparagus, chives and ravioli of lobster and a risotto of cep mushrooms, asparagus and rocket. Main dishes follow in the same highly innovative and very accomplished style including a fillet of sole filled with lobster with a caviar and chive champagne sauce and fillets of venison wrapped in smoked bacon in a cherry sauce garnished with pommes dauphin and Belgian endive. In making a decision full consideration should be given to the superlative *Le choix du Chef* menu which comprises seven outstanding, well-balanced courses. You must look carefully for value-for-money wines on the list here, many falling under the sommelier's suggestions. However, it is a good list, though the word 'fine' is somewhat overused. Gentlemen are requested to wear jacket and tie. *Seats 80. Parties 12. L 12.30-3 D 7-10.30. Closed L Sat, D Sun, all Mon, August, 2 weeks Christmas. Set L £27.50 (Sun £28) Set D £37.50/£43.*

W1   Interlude de Chavot   NEW   £80

Tel 0171-637 0222 Fax 0171-637 0224   Map 18 D2   R
5 Charlotte Street W1P 1HD

Elaine Emmanuel has been joined by restaurateur/entrepreneur Marco Pierre White and chef Eric Crouillere-Chavot (hence the restaurant's new name) as owners at what used to be Walsh's. The menu is distinctly French, and Marco's guiding influence can be observed in well-tried and trusted dishes, such as foie gras and chicken liver parfait with toasted brioche, ox cheek braised in red wine, and the ubiquitous lemon tart. Eric cooks with a light touch and flourish, notably in a quail pithiviers with a port and sherry reduction, brill in a mustard grain sauce with fresh pasta, and a quite marvellous chocolate soufflé to finish. Service is accomplished; the wine list, though heavily weighted towards France, does include several New World bottles at reasonable prices. *Seats 54. Parties 10. Private Room 25. L 12-2.30 D 7-10.30. Closed Sat L, all Sun, Bank Holidays. Set L £24.50 Set D £26.50. Access, Amex, Diners, Visa.*

SW1   Isohama   £60

Tel 0171-834 2145 Fax 0171-233 7743   Map 19 D4   R
312 Vauxhall Bridge Road Victoria SW1V 1AA

Whitewashed walls, bare darkwood tables and purple velvet chairs add up to a simply decorated little restaurant just a few steps from Victoria station. Japanese dishes both familiar and less so make up an interesting menu which staff will happily explain to you. Good cooking, unfussy presentation, simpler fare at lunchtime, when there's a good-value set meal. *Seats 30. L 12-2.30 D 5-10.30. Set L from £6.50 Set D from £25. Access, Amex, Diners, Visa.*

Set menu prices may not always include service or wine.

N16   Istanbul Iskembecisi   £30

Tel 0171-254 7291 Fax 0171-881 3741   Map 16 D2   **R**
9 Stoke Newington Road N16 8BH

The smartest Turkish restaurant in the area. Pale pink walls, chandeliers and ornate gilt framed pictures contrast with the taped Turkish music playing in the background. The menu of authentic, simple fare includes tripe soup, boiled sheep's head soup, whole roast lamb's head (boneless) and skewered intestines – dishes popular with a clientele of largely Turkish émigrés. The rest of the menu is rather more familiar, with kebabs and grills as the centrepiece, a wide choice of mezze to start, and sweets such as pastry with mixed nuts and syrup, or dried mixed fruit pudding. Staff are helpful and friendly. Live music Monday to Thursday. *Seats 74. Parties 30. Meals 5pm-5am (Sun 2pm-5am). Closed 25 Dec, 1 Jan. Access, Amex, Visa.*

WC2   The Ivy   ★   £70

Tel 0171-836 4751 Fax 0171-497 3644   Map 21 B2   **R**
1 West Street WC2H 9NE

A favourite with theater-goers, just like the old Ivy, this stable-companion of Le Caprice features mirrored wood panelling, stained–glass diamond lattice windows and some particularly handsome works of art. The menu is modern European, with international influences. Some dishes are long-time favourites – salmon fish cakes, eggs Benedict, corned beef hash, fried eggs with crispy Alsace bacon – while others show more innovative touches, among them tortellini of ricotta with artichokes and rosemary, or roasted Rosevale potatoes with duck livers, garlic and pancetta. Desserts are especially enticing – try Italian blood orange and marmalade tart, iced Scandinavian berries with white chocolate sauce or sliced persimmons with coconut and lime sorbet. Very practical list with most wines under £20. *Seats 100. Parties 8. Private Room 60. L 12-3 D 6-12. Closed 1 Jan. Set L Sat £14.50. Access, Amex, Diners, Visa.*

N5   Iznik   £45

Tel 0171-354 5697   Map 16 D2   **R**
19 Highbury Park N5 1OJ

During the day this is a British and Turkish café but come the dusk it is transformed into a restaurant serving some of the finest Turkish food in North London. The ceiling sparkles with numerous tiny candle lamps and midnight-blue shaded spot lamps. Walls are of white-painted bricks and also have little candle wall lights as well as a host of Turkish artefacts. The tables, with their richly coloured cotton coverings and brass–encased lights, add to the very homely, informal and friendly atmosphere. The menu is extensive and includes a good selection of vegetarian dishes. There are some unusual offerings too, among them exceptional courgette and feta cheese fritters accompanied by kisir, a relish of cracked wheat, parsley, spring onion, lemon juice, tomato and chili. Hunkâr begendi is a dish of very tender lamb cubes served in a creamy aubergine sauce with delicious nutty rice. Sweets too are not run-of-the-mill: bramble mousse, perhaps not one of Turkey's better known dishes, is a creamy confection of blackberries and black cherries. *Seats 54. Parties 20. D only 6.30-11 (Sat & Sun 7-12). Closed 4 days Christmas. No credit cards.*

W1   Jade Garden   £35

Tel 0171-437 5065   Map 21 A2   **R**
15 Wardour Street Soho W1V 3HA

A superb selection of well-prepared dim sum is the daytime highlight here. They are served through till 5pm with weekends and Sundays, in particular, being especially busy days. The lengthy menu also features sections for prawns, eel, oysters, abalone, a dozen ways with pork, sizzling dishes and noodles (fried or in soup). The cooking is mainly Cantonese, but one of the set menus features Peking cuisine. *Seats 150. Parties 15. Meals 12-11.30 (Sun till 10.30). Closed 25 & 26 Dec. Set meals from £9.50. Access, Amex, Visa.*

Consult the blue pages for summary tables and lists of recommended establishments.

EC1   Japanese Canteen   NEW   £25

Tel 0171-833 3222   Map 16 D3   **R**
394 St John Street EC1

The former Crown & Woolpack is now but a shadow of what it used to be. The exterior walls remain but the insides have been stripped to create a Japanese restaurant with a very spartan decor. All there is now are plain white walls, wooden refectory tables, bench seating, tiny paper napkins and brown paper place mats with the menu printed on them. The choice is a simple one with a handful of starters such as raw salmon rolls, yakitori and vegetable dumplings. The remainder consists of a choice of bento boxes – complete meals in a box. These are accompanied by miso soup and comprise salmon teriyaki, griddled chicken with miso and ginger, vegetable and prawn tempura and pork tonkatsu (fried in breadcrumbs). Other choices could be ramen or udon noodle soup (ramen are finer). These come in huge, well-filled bowls with poached salmon, seafood or sliced roast pork. There's sashimi too as well as sushi. Drinks are limited to green tea, coke, Japanese beer, a glass of house white or red and house champagne. *Seats 120. Parties 8. Private Room 40. L 12-2.30 D 6-11. Closed 25 & 26 Dec. No credit cards.*

We welcome bona fide complaints and recommendations on the tear-out pages at the back of the book for readers' comments. They are followed up by our professional team.

W2   Jarvis London Embassy   68%   £138

Tel 0171-229 1212   Fax 0171-229 2623   Map 18 A3   **H**
150 Bayswater Road W2 4RT

Modern accommodation overlooking Kensington Gardens, appealing to both business and tourist visitors. Children up to 15 stay free in parents' room. 35 of the rooms are designated non-smoking. 24hr room service. There are several conference and banqueting rooms. Own car park (£5 for 24 hours) *Rooms 193. Access, Amex, Diners, Visa.*

W10   Jimmy Beez   £60

Tel 0181-964 9100   Map 16 B3   **R**
303 Portobello Road W10 5TD

Manhattan's Greenwich Village restaurants provided the inspiration for this very friendly, laid-back restaurant where fashion appears on the plate as well as in the clientele's garb, which tends to be designer distressed. Lunch and brunch (the latter available from 11am to 6pm at weekends) are very informal affairs with menus of light meals including eggs royale with smoked salmon and steak sandwich on rye with guacamole and salsa. In the evening the choice consists of starters such as Peking duck salad with chili and coriander leaves. Main dishes include Pacific seaweed pasta with squid and scallops, grilled salmon fillet with basil and grilled lamb steak with a Malaysian peanut and curry sauce. Banoffi pie is a favourite, and rich, ending. *Seats 55. Parties 20. Private Room 25. Meals 12-11 (Sat 11-11). Closed 1 week Christmas. Access, Amex, Visa.*

Set menu prices may not always include service or wine.

NW3   Jinkichi   £60

Tel 0171-794 6158   Map 16 B2   **R**
73 Heath Street Hampstead NW3 6UG

A Japanese restaurant which can get noisy and crowded, particularly towards the weekends and at peak meal times. Very much a local place with a simple, unfussy decor and ambience. Bar stools surround a central counter, off the right of which a chef cooks selections of the thirty different yakitori dishes available – from crispy salmon skin and chicken morsels to gigantic prawns – all carefully prepared. Other familiar choices include sushi, tempura and shabu-shabu. *Seats 42. Parties 15. L (Sat & Sun only) 12-2.30 D (Wed-Mon only) 6-11.30 (Sun to 10.30). Closed 4 days Christmas, 3 days Easter. Access, Amex, Diners, Visa.*

WC2   Joe Allen   £40

Tel 0171-836 0651 Fax 0171-497 2148   Map 20 A2   **R**
13 Exeter Street WC2E 7DT

Still trendy and relatively inexpensive, not much changes at this basement American restaurant, which hardly advertises itself – only a small plaque on a redbrick wall marks its entrance. Black bean soup, eggs Benedict, tiger shrimp risotto, grilled corn-fed chicken with caponata and braised brown rice, and meatloaf with toasted mashed potatoes and gravy show the straightforward style. Tables are usually turned over twice in the evenings, the second sitting after theatres turn out. *Seats 180. Parties 8. Meals Noon-12.45am (Sun to 11.45pm). Closed 24 & 25 Dec. No credit cards.*

SW3   Joe's Café   £70

Tel 0171-225 2217   Map 19 B5   **R**
126 Draycott Avenue SW3 3AH

Stylish, split-level brasserie-restaurant with an oyster and black decor offering a fashionable modern menu for its fashion-conscious patrons. Dishes reflect a wide range of cuisines, none with café origins. Vegetable broth with borlotti beans, tomato and thyme toasts; salmon and crab salad with avocado, cucumber and dill dressing; grilled tuna with tomato salsa, roasted chilis and couscous; and roast lamb with wilted escarole, roast garlic and basil butter are typical choices, with poached pears and figs in red wine with fromage frais and chilled lemon cheesecake among the desserts. Special Sunday brunch menu. 15% service charge. *Seats 80. L 12-3 D 7-11. Closed D Sun, 25 & 26 Dec. Access, Amex, Diners, Visa.*

WC2   Joy King Lau   £50

Tel 0171-437 1132 Fax 0171-437 2629   Map 21 A2   **R**
3 Leicester Street WC2

The decor is modern, done in claret and blue tones with an intimate, relatively quiet atmosphere. The menu offers well-executed familiar dishes like Peking duck or beef in black bean sauce, along with more unusual duck webs with sea cucumber, fried pig intestine and braised fish lips. There is a large selection of fish and shellfish on the extensive menu. Dim sum, served until 5pm, are among the very best in London. *Seats 200. Parties 12. Private Room 60. Meals noon-11.30pm (Sun 11-10.30). Closed 24 & 25 Dec. Set meals from £8 (min 2 people). Access, Amex, Diners, Visa.*

W11   Julie's   £70

Tel 0171-229 8331 Fax 0171-229 4050   Map 17 B4   **R**
135 Portland Road Holland Park W11 4LW

A Holland Park institution, comprising restaurant and (at 137) a splendid wine bar. The succession of dining rooms each has a unique atmosphere, from the flowery champagne bar to a Gothic alcove and even a smart white theme conservatory. The menu takes its influences from near and far: sardine, ginger and lime paté with orange salad; wild mushroom timbales with beetroot and butter parmesan sauce; roast duck with tawny port, peach sauce and winter berries; calf's liver with leeks, red pepper marmalade and polenta; steak and kidney pie; chocolate and kahlua torte; two berry sorbet. A good selection of English cheeses can be enjoyed with a glass of wine or port. There's little over £20 on the mostly French wine list. Traditional Sunday lunch. *Seats 120. Parties 26. Private Room 32. L 12.30-2.45 (Sun 12.30-3) D 7.30-10.45. Closed Easter Bank Holidays, 1 week Christmas. Set L & D from £11.95. Access, Amex, Diners, Visa.*

SW7   Jurys Kensington Hotel   64%   £125

Tel 0171-589 6300 Fax 0171-581 1492   Map 19 B5   **H**
109 Queen's Gate SW7 5LR

Seven elegant and carefully converted townhouses constitute a hotel situated at the corner of Old Brompton Road and Queen's Gate – it is the first venture in London of this Irish hotel group. Open-plan public rooms are comfortable and clad in bright, almost garish curtains and soft furnishings. A pianist or harpist plays in the lively bar area every evening. Spacious, but modestly furnished bedrooms are in the process of being refurbished. All have TVs (many on the small side, but all with CNN), direct-dial phones, tea/coffee-making facilities, hairdryers and en-suite bathrooms (all with tubs and overhead showers). Children up to 12 stay free in parents' room. Friendly service. No dogs. *Rooms 172. Access, Amex, Diners, Visa.*

NW4   Kaifeng   £80

Tel 0181-203 7888 Fax 0181-203 8263   Map 16 A1   **R**
51 Church Road Hendon NW4 4DU

A smart and expensive restaurant serving an unlikely sounding match of food – Kosher and Chinese. Careful if unadventurous cooking matches the plush, elegant surroundings. Some dishes traditionally associated with pork are here made with lamb and the result of this replacement is not always successful. Service is quite formal and rather serious. *Seats 70. L 12.30-2 D 6-10.30. Closed Fri (& Sat April-Sept), all Jewish religious holidays. Set L £9.95 (Sun buffet £13.95) Set D £19.95/£24.95. Access, Amex, Visa.*

W2   Kalamaras   £40

Tel 0171-727 9122   Map 18 A3   **R**
76-78 Inverness Mews Bayswater W2 3JQ

Owner-manager-head chef Stelios Platonos has been at the helm for almost 30 years at one of the best and busiest of London's Greek restaurants. The menu ranges far beyond the usual choice, and the more unfamiliar items include *tsirosalata* (small fillets of dried fish served with wine vinegar), *varkoula* (baked courgettes topped with fresh salmon and béchamel sauce) and *bouyatsa* (a speciality sweet made with eggs, semolina and cinnamon served hot). Fish specials (they vary with the market) are always worth trying, so too the spinach and spring onion filo triangles *(spanakotyropites)* and the casseroled lamb *(arnaki lemonato me spanaki)*. There's a list of 20 Greek wines. The restaurant is located at the end of a mews running parallel to Queensway. Kalamaras Micro, an unlicensed sibling, is at no. 66. *Seats 88. Private Room 30. D only 6-12. Closed Sun, Bank Holidays. Set D £15.50. Access, Amex, Diners, Visa.*

SW10   Kartouche   £60

Tel 0171-823 3515 Fax 0171-823 3991   Map 19 B5   **R**
329 Fulham Road SW10 9QL

Crowd control is a problem in very few restaurants, but Kartouche has been used to queues from the moment it opened. There's no booking in the evening, so a bar downstairs operates as a waiting place for the constant stream of customers who want to join in the fun. This really is one of the buzziest, noisiest places in town, and the decibel level soars off the meter by about 9 each evening. The food sometimes seems less important than the partying, but it's certainly very acceptable, from the bread, olives, houmus and roast garlic to enjoy with an aperitif to the salads, ribs, burgers and daily roast. Other choices, many with Mediterranean or Far Eastern influences, could include warm crab tart, chargrilled vegetable bruschetta, babaganoush with cucumber yoghurt, teriyaki scallops, baked cod with roasted fennel and pepper salsa, venison sausages and sautéed calf's liver with spring greens and redcurrants. To finish, perhaps apple brulée, chocolate tart or nougat and peanut spring roll with ice cream. The wine list is presented in price order, which makes it easy to choose a price but difficult to pinpoint a wine. *Seats 78. Parties 10. L 12-3 (Sat/Sun till 3.30) D 6-midnight (Sun till 11). Access, Amex, Visa.*

NW8   Kashi-Noki   £70

Tel 0171-586 0911   Map 18 B1   **R**
18 Lodge Road NW8 7JT

Access to this ground floor restaurant across the road from the nursery end of Lord's cricket ground is either from the street or from the lobby of the Hilton International, Regents Park. Very simply decorated in blond woods, it has quite friendly staff and a very classical Japanese menu. A long list of sushi comes either as two pieces of just fish and vinegared rice or as six pieces if the fish and rice are rolled in seaweed. Less fish is used in the latter and they are more substantial. *Seats 42. Parties 10. L 11-2.15 D 5.30 10. Set D £30. Closed Mon, 25 & 26 Dec & 1-3 Jan. Access, Amex, Diners, Visa.*

W1   Kaspia   £70

Tel 0171-493 2612 Fax 0171-408 1627   Map 18 C3   **R**
18/18a Bruton Place Mayfair W1X 7AH

The London offshoot of the renowned Paris caviar shop and restaurant is tucked away discreetly off Berkeley Square. It's a comfortable, well-appointed place, with lightwood panelling, sea-blue tablecloths, Russian pictures and plates on display and Russian bassi profundi gently exercising their tonsils on the sound system. If the order is for caviar all round the bill here will naturally be hefty, but elsewhere on the menu prices are reasonable, particularly for the splendid smoked fish salad – a very generous plateful of smoked salmon, trout, eel, sturgeon and cod roe. Other specialities include oysters, gull's eggs, paté de foie gras, fish cake with lobster sauce, steak tartare and gravad lax. *Seats 60. Parties 20. Private Room 16. L 12-3 D 7-11.30. Set L & D from £27. Closed Sun, also Sat in Aug, Bank Holidays. Access, Amex, Diners, Visa.*

W1   Kaya   £70

Tel 0171-437 6630 Fax 0171-439 7269   Map 21 A2   **R**
22 Dean Street Soho W1V 5AL

Korean food, not as varied as Chinese nor as "pretty" as Japanese, finds a friendly home in Soho. Some items, including modoum gui (assorted seafood and vegetables), dak (chicken fillet), ojingo (squid) and sokum gui (sirloin steak with spring onions) are prepared at the table. 15 % service charge. *Seats 70. Private Room 40. L 12-2.45 D 6-10.45. Closed L Sun, all 25 Dec & 1 Jan. Set L & D £38 & £45. Access, Amex, Diners, Visa.*

SW1   Ken Lo's Memories of China   £75

Tel 0171-730 7734 Fax 0171-730 2992   Map 19 C4   **R**
67 Ebury Street SW1W 0NZ

The large, airy, modern dining room is painted white and decorated with subtle displays of Chinese lettering, almost reminiscent of graffiti. The tables are cleverly separated by Chinese wooden screens, giving a semblance of privacy. The carte is well planned, and not overlong by Chinese standards. Bang bang chicken, five-spice spare ribs or siu mai (meat-stuffed dumplings) could be followed by steamed sea bass, crispy soft-shell crab, or perhaps one of the many iron-plate sizzlers. New Zealand mussels combine well with black bean and chili sauce, which cleverly exaggerates the flavour of the sea. Peking quick-fried lamb with garlic and spring onions is another success. Specialities are marked on the menu with an asterisk, and make choosing easier. The set menus take you on a gastronomic tour of China, and offer the best choice for two or more people. Don't leave your order too late if you'd like a hot dessert, as the kitchen can close early, leaving you with ice cream or nothing. Cheaper eating is available at the Chelsea branch (qv). *Seats 120. Private Room 20. L 12-2.30 D 7-11.15 (Sun till 10.30). Closed L Sun, Bank Holidays, few days at Christmas. Set L from £15.25 Set D from £23.50. Access, Amex, Diners, Visa.*

SW10   Ken Lo's Memories of China   £60

Tel 0171-352 4953 Fax 0171-351 2096   Map 19 B6   **R**
Harbour Yard Chelsea Harbour SW10 0QJ

The Chelsea Harbour branch of Ken Lo's Ebury Street original caters for all pockets and purses by offering various à la carte and set menus. Best value is undoubtedly provided by the bar snack menu (12-2.30 Mon-Fri) with main courses priced under £3.50. The favourite way to start is with a selection of excellent fried dim sum. The main menu ranges far and wide, with Cantonese lobster and steamed sea bass at the luxury end. Popular main courses include quick-fried beef in oyster sauce with mangetout, spiced pork with shredded vegetables and Peking egg-battered garlic and ginger sliced chicken. *Seats 175. Private Room 60. L 12.30-2.30 D 7-10.45 (Sun to 10). Closed 25 & 26 Dec, 1 Jan. Set L £13.50/£15.30 Set D £26/£29.60. Access, Amex, Diners, Visa.*

WC1   Kenilworth Hotel   63%   £172

Tel 0171-637 3477 Fax 0171-631 3133   Map 21 B1   **H**
97 Great Russell Street WC1B 3LB

A handsome redbrick building near the British Museum. The foyer gives a good impression, decorated in warm colours, with plenty of seating. There are seven conference rooms, with a capacity of 150 in the largest. Smart bedrooms are quite pretty in floral pinks and green, and some top-floor rooms have four-posters. All are double-glazed, with two armchairs and a desk. In the bedrooms are plenty of shelves and good towels and toiletries. Children free in parents' room up to age 10. No dogs. A Radisson Edwardian Hotel. *Rooms 187. Access, Amex, Diners, Visa.*

NW1   Kennedy Hotel   63%   £106

Tel 0171-387 4400 Fax 0171-387 5122   Map 18 D1   **H**
Cardington Street Euston NW1 2LP

Conveniently situated by Euston main-line station, a modern hotel with simply decorated rooms. It's also close to Drummond Street, where there's a fine choice of Indian restaurants. Conference facilities for up to 100, banqueting for 60. Children up to 14 share parents' room free. Small underground car park (£5 overnight, £10 for 24 hours). Thistle & Mount Charlotte. *Rooms 360. News kiosk (7am-9pm). Access, Amex, Diners, Visa.*

W8   Kensington Close Hotel   59%   £135

Tel 0171-937 8170 Fax 0171-937 8289   Map 19 A4   **H**
Wrights Lane Kensington W8 5SP

A minute's walk from the shops of High Street Kensington, the hotel boasts fine leisure/keep-fit facilities and its own underground car park (£16 for 24 hours). Top of the bedroom range are the Executives, which all have sitting areas. There are 15 function and meeting rooms, and a staffed business centre. Children up to 16 share parents' room free. Forte. *Rooms 530. Garden, gym, squash, sauna, solarium, beauty salon, news kiosk. Access, Amex, Diners, Visa.*

SW5   Kensington Court Hotel   £75

Tel 0171-370 5151 Fax 0171-370 3499   Map 19 A5   **B**
33 Nevern Place Earls Court SW5 9NP

A modern block in the heart of Earls Court. All bedrooms are double or triple bedded and have simple en-suite facilities. No dogs. *Rooms 35. Access, Amex, Diners, Visa.*

SW7   Kensington Manor   £94

Tel 0171-370 7516 Fax 0171-373 3163   Map 19 A4   **PH**
8 Emperor's Gate South Kensington SW7 4HH

Small bed-and-breakfast hotel in a late-Victorian building just moments from Gloucester Road Underground station (cross Cromwell Road into Grenville Place, which leads to Emperor's Gate) and handy for the South Kensington museums. 24hr private bar. Extensive buffet breakfast. No dogs. *Rooms 14. Access, Amex, Diners, Visa.*

W8   Kensington Palace Thistle   62%   £127

Tel 0171-937 8121 Fax 0171-937 2816   Map 19 A4   **H**
De Vere Gardens Kensington W8 5AF

Just across the road from Kensington Gardens and convenient for the Albert Hall, this hotel offers modestly furnished but well-equipped and generously proportioned bedrooms. Many rooms are interconnecting and thus ideal for families. Over 50% of bedrooms are reserved for non-smokers. Although bedrooms have easy chairs, lounge space is limited for the size of the hotel. Air-conditioned conference facilities for up to 180 delegates. Children under 15 stay free in parents' room. Buffet-style breakfast only. No dogs. *Rooms 299. News kiosk, coffee shop (7am-11.30pm). Access, Amex, Diners, Visa.*

W8   Kensington Park Thistle Hotel   67%   £165

Tel 0171-937 8080 Fax 0171-937 7616   Map 19 A4   **H**
16-32 De Vere Gardens W8 5AG

Quiet, comfortable and fairly roomy hotel opposite Kensington Gardens and just off Kensington High Street. Though lacking the facilities of many big hotels, it has two eating outlets, the Carrington Grill and Moniques Brasserie. 100 of the bedrooms are designated non-smoking. No dogs. *Rooms 332. Access, Amex, Diners, Visa.*

**Consult the blue pages for summary tables and lists of
recommended establishments.**

W8   Kensington Place   ★   £70

Tel 0171-727 3184 Fax 0171-229 2025   Map 18 A3   **R**
201-207 Kensington Church Street W8 7LX

Since day one, back in 1987, Nick Smallwood's and Simon Slater's restaurant has been one of London's culinary hot spots, a hive of animation behind its long windowed frontage. Rowley Leigh's menus are nothing if not approachable, written in clear, straightforward English, and his cooking is similarly honest and frill-free. Everything is good, and many dishes are outstanding, notably specialities such as chicken and goat's cheese mousse with olives, griddled scallops, griddled foie gras with sweetcorn pancake, grilled sole fillets with lentils and salsa verde, and civet of wild duck with mushrooms and bacon. Noisy, buzzing with lively conversation, KP grants no great concessions to comfort or ornamentation; at the entrance is a small, glitzy bar, at the other end of the long room a vast mural depicting an alfresco eating scene in gay pastel shades. Wines from around the world, and several dessert wines by the glass to accompany anything from coffee and mascarpone semifreddo to tarte tatin, rhubarb fool and baked tamarillos with vanilla ice cream. *Seats 140. Parties 26. L 12-3 (Sat & Sun to 3.30) D 6.30-11.45 (Sun to 10.15). Closed 24-26 Dec & 1 Jan. Set L £13.50. Access, Visa.*

We welcome bona fide complaints and recommendations on the
tear-out pages at the back of the book for readers' comments.
They are followed up by our professional team.

SW7   Khan's of Kensington   £45

Tel 0171-584 4114 Fax 0171-581 2900   Map 19 B5   **R**
3 Harrington Road South Kensington SW7 3ES

Just a few steps from South Kensington station. Light green is the main colour of the stylish modern decor, and the greens and pinks of the chairs are taken up in the waiters' waistcoats. Tiny lights are hung from tramline wires, and a silk banana plant stands in one corner. Downstairs is a colonial-style lounge bar. The menu includes classic Indian dishes as well as a few less familiar dishes such as fish goawala – pomfret fish cooked in a sauce of roasted coriander seeds – and a south Indian delicacy of nariyal gosht – lamb cooked in coconut and mild spices and tinda (pumpkin) cooked with fresh herbs and spices – a Punjabi recipe. Besides the à la carte there are meat and vegetarian set menus for one, a set lunch (Mon-Fri) and a Sunday lunchtime buffet (till 3.30). Above-average standards of cooking and service. *Seats 60. Private Room 25. L 12-2.30 D 5.30-11.30. Closed 25 & 26 Dec. Set L from £7.50 Set D from £12 (vegetarian) & £15. Access, Amex, Diners, Visa.*

SW3   Khun Akorn   £65

Tel 0171-225 2688 Fax 0171-225 2680   Map 19 B4   **R**
136 Brompton Road Knightsbridge SW3 1HY

Owned by the Imperial Hotel in Bangkok, with a sister branch in Paris, an up-market Thai restaurant spread across three split levels. Decor features traditional carvings and plants abound; a snake-shaped bar curves its way through the centre of the restaurant. The menu lists well-known Thai specialities ('weeping tiger' steak with chili sauce) and doesn't venture much into originality. Tongsai platter for 2 is a popular appetiser. Cooking is reliable and prices substantial, except for a bargain lunch menu. *Seats 70. L 12-3 D 6.30-11. Closed 25 Dec. Set L £12.50 Set D £17.50. Access, Amex, Diners, Visa.*

SW7   Khyber Pass   £30

Tel 0171-589 7311   Map 19 B5   **R**
21 Bute Street South Kensington SW7 3EY

Popular little Indian restaurant established well over 20 years ago and still attracting a loyal local following with its reliable run-of-the-mill cooking. Curries climb all the way up to the blistering Bangalore phal. *Seats 32. L 12-2.45 D 6-11.30. Closed 25 & 26 Dec. Access, Amex, Diners, Visa.*

SW10   Kingdom   £50

Tel 0171-352 0206   Map 19 B6
457 Fulham Road SW10 9UZ

A quiet, civilised restaurant with a menu of Chinese dishes both familiar and a little out of the ordinary. A hot buffet is served lunch and evening. *Seats 80. Private Room 25. L 12-2.30 D 6-11.30. Closed 24-26 Dec. Set L £5.50 Set D from £8.50 (min 2). Access, Amex, Diners, Visa.*

SW1   Knightsbridge Green Hotel   £129

Tel 0171-584 6274 Fax 0171-225 1635   Map 19 C4
159 Knightsbridge SW1P 7PD

A family-run private hotel in the very heart of Knightsbridge offering comfortable, spotlessly-kept accommodation with double-glazing and the usual conveniences – except, that is, for a restaurant or bar, as the hotel is unlicensed; however, this is hardly an inconvenience given the superb location. Breakfast (English or Continental) is served in the bedrooms from 7.30am (8am Sun and Bank Hols) to 10 and tea/coffee and cakes are available all day long in the Club Room. Refurbishment to 4th-floor rooms includes air-conditioning and marble bathrooms. No dogs. *Rooms 25. Access, Amex, Visa.*

SW1   Kundan   £60

Tel 0171-834 3434 Fax 0171-834 3211   Map 19 D5
3 Horseferry Road Westminster SW1P 2AN

A division bell summons MPs from this comfortable and roomy basement restaurant, interrupting a meal based on the rich cuisine of northern India. Chef Mohammed Aziz Khan counts prawns and quail among his specialities, barbecued in the tandoor or featuring in carefully prepared curries. Others are chicken and lamb johl fraizee, lamb's brains and karahi kabab sarhadi – diced chicken grilled with spices, chopped tomatoes and green peppers, served sizzling in its iron pot. Note, too, the excellent vegetable kebabs and the dal of the day. *Seats 117. Parties 12. Private Room 40. L 12-3 D 7-12. Closed Sun, Bank Holidays. Set L £15 Set D £18. Access, Amex, Diners, Visa.*

SW1   Kura   £90

Tel 0171-581 1820 Fax 0181-458 4601   Map 19 C4
304 Park Close SW1X 7PQ

A delightful, friendly little Japanese restaurant tucked away between Knightsbridge and Hyde Park. Bare wooden tables are separated by screens, there's ethnic piped music and plenty of Japanese families enjoying the atmosphere. Lunchtime offers the better bargains here, with a good selection of one-course meals. Dinner is more elaborate, including several set meals consisting of many courses. Assorted sashimi (sliced raw fish) and other Japanese delicacies are always available. Advisable to book, as space is at a premium. *Seats 25. L 12-2.30 D 6-10.30. Closed L Sun, all Sat, 1 week Aug, 3 days New Year. Set L from £9.50 Set D from £20. Access, Amex, Diners, Visa.*

W1   Lal Qila   £40

Tel 0171-387 4570 Fax 0171-387 5332   Map 18 D2   R
117 Tottenham Court Road W1P 9HN

Lal Qila, meaning red fort, is a long-standing restaurant, and a seminal influence of North Indian cuisine in Britain. The traditional food produced here, shami kebab, roghan josh, murg makhani and the like, are all as they should be. A few Indian desserts follow, for the sweet tooth – ras malai, gulab jamun (fried balls of flour and yoghurt, soaked in syrup), or perhaps the cooling effect of kulfi. Sunday buffet lunch and dinner £9.95. *Seats 64. L 12-3 D 6-11.30. Closed 25 & 26 Dec. Access, Amex, Diners, Visa.*

NW1   The Landmark London

See under The Regent London

Set menu prices may not always include service or wine.

SW1   The Lanesborough   89%   £334

Tel 0171-259 5599 Fax 0171-259 5606   Map 19 C4   **HR**
1 Lanesborough Place Hyde Park Corner SW1X 7TA

Enjoying a splendidly prominent position on Hyde Park Corner, the hotel's classical Regency facade is complemented by an impressively elegant interior where original Regency designs and neo-Georgian furnishings are combined to magnificent effect. Enormous and exotic flower arrangements abound, reflected in the highly polished coloured marble floors adding opulence to the already stylish decor. The hotel's bar – The Library – has rich mahogany panelling inset with bookshelves which, along with leather-upholstered seating, creates a deeply civilised effect. Next door is The Withdrawing Room, a sumptuously elegant room with a striking old-gold colour scheme. Public rooms have many quiet corners and a general level of intimacy that one might more usually associate with country house hotels in rural England. Very effective triple soundproofed glazing throughout the hotel ensures that outside noises appear as no more than a very distant murmur. On arrival, guests are issued with their own personalised stationery and business cards, while each of the 95 bedrooms (which include 46 suites) has two direct-access telephone lines as well as a fax line (their system allows for 1000 numbers with 200 reserved permanently for repeat guests). Security, too, is given a very high priority with 35 surveillance cameras, window sensors and alarms that include a sophisticated door-key system; briefcase-sized safes are also provided. Upon being shown to their rooms, guests are introduced to a butler who, in terms of service and information, is their only point of contact; all the butlers have been trained in the traditional manner and will unpack, pack, iron, and even run baths as required. Bedrooms are equipped to a high-tech standard as well as having exquisite decor, with comfort being paramount. Each has a VCR, CD and tape decks – all fully remote and secreted in attractive pieces of furniture, together with the TVs. Bathrooms are lined with white marble and have every conceivable amenity including, in most, steam showers and spa baths. Exercise equipment can be placed in the rooms at no extra charge and there's free membership of a local health club. Valet parking for the basement car park. *Seats 95. Car hire desk, coffee shop (7am-midnight). Access, Amex, Diners, Visa.*

The Conservatory   ★   £90

The elegantly flamboyant decor of the restaurant contains ornate Victorian Gothic-style cloisters with beautiful and exotic chinoiserie all under a lofty glass canopy. Paul Gayler's menu offers a multitude of choices combining elements of lightness, sophistication and price. His innovative skills are demonstrated in such appetisers as a tart of caramelised chicory with Cornish scallops, risotto of cepes, chicken livers and Madeira and lettuce spring rolls with crab, soy and ginger. Main dishes too are outstanding with feuilleté of beef and veal kidney with cumin-braised carrots, gigot of lamb 'osso buco' with parsnip purée and roast red bream with tarragon and artichoke barigoule being typical. He continues to espouse vegetarianism with a short but imaginative selection and desserts finish off the meal on a suitably high note, his cappucino brulée bring a perfect example of his ability and art. The steep prices on the admittedly fine wine list do not encourage experimentation. *Seats 106. Parties 16. L 12.30-2.30 (Sun brunch 11-3) D 7-12. Set L £22.50 (Sun brunch £24.50 children under 12 £16) Set D £28.50.*

W1   Langan's Bistro   £65

Tel 0171-935 4531   Map 18 C2   **R**
26 Devonshire Street W1N 1RJ

A popular bistro next to its big brother Odin's just off Marylebone High Street. The short menu (fixed-price 2 or 3 courses and coffee) is English by inspiration: salmon and broccoli mousse, game paté and Cumberland sauce, roast vegetable kebab with wild rice, sausages and mash with a white onion sauce, pan-fried lamb's kidneys with red onion marmalade, rhubarb crumble and custard, Mrs Langan's chocolate pudding. *Seats 34.*

Parties 8. L 12.30-2.30 D 7-11.30. Set L & D £15.95/£17.95. Closed L Sat, all Sun, Bank Holidays, Easter weekend, Christmas. Access, Amex, Diners, Visa.

W1	Langan's Brasserie	↑	£85

Tel 0171-491 8822 Map 18 D3 **R**
Stratton Street W1X 5FD

The legendary Langan's Brasserie, on two floors just off Piccadilly, remains one of London's most glamorous eating places. The long menu features around 80 dishes, from seafood salad, venison terrine and carpaccio with parmesan shavings to cold meats and coleslaw, braised knuckle of gammon with butter beans, grilled king prawns with pesto and a glazed vegetable and pasta bake. The mix covers both traditional English and French – spinach soufflé served with an anchovy sauce is the speciality on the ground floor, carré d'agneau roti aux herbes de Provence upstairs. Among the 25 or so desserts you might find apple strudel, blueberry tart, crepes des Alpes, and profiteroles with chocolate sauce. Traditionalists could be well pleased with a meal of cod and chips or bangers and mash with white onion sauce followed by rice pudding or trifle, washed down, of course, with a favourite champagne. The ground floor is always bustling (see and be seen!), while upstairs the Venetian room has its own quieter charm. *Seats 220. Parties 12. L 12.15-3 D 7-11.45 (Sat 8-12.45). Closed L Sat, all Sun, Bank Holidays, Easter weekend, Christmas. Access, Amex, Diners, Visa.*

W1	The Langham Hilton	75%	£240

Tel 0171-636 1000 Fax 0171-436 1346 Map 18 D2 **H**
Portland Place W1N 4JA

The epitome of Victorian high style when built in 1865, the Langham retained its fashionable status until 1940, when war damage caused its closure. Fifty years later it was lavishly restored to its original splendour. It stands across the road from a temple of the 30s – the BBC's Broadcasting House. Smart doormen in Tsarist uniforms set the tone for the stylish interior, which has been transformed into a sophisticated modern hotel retaining many of the original features. The Grand Entrance Hall with polished marble, Oriental rug-strewn floors and thick Portland stone pillars leads to a light yet fairly intimate Palm Court, where afternoon tea is served (to the accompaniment of a pianist) and food is available all day and all night. The Chukka Bar is very much in the gentleman's club tradition with polo memorabilia decorating the walls. Bedrooms, furnished in solid, traditional style, have all the expected extras but the suites, of which there are 50, also have video recorders and hi-fi units. Two rooms offer facilities for disabled guests. Bathrooms throughout are in white marble and, while all have good showers, only some have bidets. There are conference rooms for up to 320, banqueting to 240, and a well-equipped Health Club. No dogs. *Seats 379. Gym, steam room, sauna, sun beds, beauty & hair salon. Access, Amex, Diners, Visa.*

W8	Launceston Place	↑	£65

Tel 0171-937 6912 Fax 0171-938 2412 Map 19 A4 **H**
1a Launceston Place Kensington W8 5RL

A quieter, more comfortable and more stylish elder sister to Kensington Place, just off the tourist track and a must for many loyal locals. Cathy Gradwell's menus are an agreeable mix of traditional British (perhaps the majority) and more modern elements. Pea and ham soup, brawn with pickled walnuts and poached smoked haddock with parsley sauce represent the 'safe' side, while for the slightly more adventurous are stir-fried squid with lemon, garlic, ginger and coriander or pan-fried calf's liver with cotechino, lentils and salsa verde. Round things off in style with a blood orange sorbet, apple fritters with armagnac anglaise or rhubarb and raisin bread-and-butter pudding. Sunday lunch is a particularly jolly occasion here, and the menu offers late risers the appealing opportunity to catch up on breakfast with a starter such as kippers with lemon and herb butter and move straight on to a roast, sautéed calf's liver or grilled brill and scallops. A late supper (10pm-11.30pm), comprises a dozen dishes in the price range £3.50-£8.50 with no no mimimum charge. A short wine list without frills; mostly French, a little from the New World. *Seats 80. Private Rooms 12/30. L 12.30-2.30 (Sun to 3) D 7-11.30. Closed L Sat, D Sun, Bank Holidays. Set L & Set D (7pm-8pm) £13.50/£16.50. Access, Amex, Visa.*

NW2   Laurent   £40

Tel 0171-794 3603   Map 16 B2   **R**
428 Finchley Road NW2 2HY

Little changes at Laurent Farrugia's has run his couscous restaurant. This excellent North African dish of steamed semolina grain comes in various forms: vegetarian with basic vegetables, complet with added lamb and merguez, royal boosted to festive proportions by lamb chop and brochette; chicken; and fish (halibut steak). The only starter is brique à l'oeuf, a deep-fried thin pastry parcel with a soft egg inside – fun but tricky to eat. North African wines stand up well to the hearty food. The restaurant is situated by the junction with Cricklewood Lane. *Seats 36. Parties 12. L 12-2 D 6-11. Closed Sun, Bank Holidays, 1st 3 weeks Aug. Access, Amex, Visa.*

W11   Leith's   £115

Tel 0171-229 4481   Map 18 A3   **R**
92 Kensington Park Road W11 2PN

A stylish and thoroughly modern interior now greets diners at Prue Leith's renowned and long-established restaurant. Bright, modern artwork and simple yet effective flower arrangments serve to bring colour to an otherwise uncluttered setting where Alex Floyd continues to produce innovative dishes which have a mainly British pedigree. To begin: a selection of hors d'oeuvre, now plated since the trolley has been discontinued, and a few other starters on the carte such as langoustine and crab salad and ravioli of foie gras and veal tongue in a light Scotch broth. Main dishes are like the rest, very carefully assembled, each a well-balanced synthesis of flavours as in pan-fried fillet of sea bass with a scallop and courgette galette and tomato and basil oil, best end of lamb with a grain mustard and herb crust and tarragon jus or feuilleté of roast pigeon with swede purée, wild mushrooms, braised cabbage and thyme. A superb selection of new British cheeses is available to follow and finally some unmissable desserts such as chocolate and chestnut soufflé with white chocolate ice cream or prune and marzipan parfait with bitter orange sauce. Vegetarians have the rare opportunity of enjoying food from their own well-thought-out and carefully constructed menu. The wine list is one of pure quality everywhere you look. For the most part prices are not unreasonable, though if you're prepared to spend, the bottles are there for you to choose from! Nick Tarayan prefaces each section with helpful tasting notes – note the Spanish section, which includes some cavas, an alternative to champagne. *Seats 70. Parties 16. Private Room 40. L 12.15-2.15. D 7-11.30. Closed L Sat & Mon, all Sun. 2 weeks Aug, 2 weeks from Dec 24. Set L £16.50/£19.50. Set D £26.50/£36. Access, Amex, Diners, Visa.*

NW1   Lemonia   £40

Tel 0171-586 7454 Fax 0171-483 2630   Map 16 B3   **R**
89 Regent's Park Road NW1 8UY

Roomy though this splendid Greek restaurant certainly is, it's still full to bursting at peak evening times. What's more, the atmosphere is invariably lively and everyone always seems to be having fun. Outside and in there's a Mediterranean air, with lots of light and masses of hanging flower baskets. Specialities include baby squid, chicken shashlik, kleftiko, keftedes and the meze selection at £10.50, which should satisfy even the biggest appetite. Look, too, for the special three-course lunch (Mon-Fri) and daily specials that supplement the regular menu. Limani, opposite at 154, is in the same ownership. *Seats 140. Parties 14. Private Room 40. L 12-3 D 6-11.30. Set L (not Sun) £7.95. Closed L Sat, D Sun, 25 & 26 Dec, 1 Jan. Access, Visa.*

W1   The Lexington   £65

Tel 0171-434 3401 Fax 0171-287 2997   Map 18 D2   **R**
45 Lexington Street W1R 3LG

The dining-room has a stark modern feel – bare wooden tables, turquoise walls and contemporary artwork – and serves a short carte with a fashionable Mediterranean flavour. Maybe merguez sausage with couscous or mussels in white wine to start; saffron risotto, rump of lamb with aubergine and red onion or grilled chicken with chicory and grain mustard dressing to follow. Good-value set menu is available in the evening. *Seats 45. Private Room 20. L 12-3 D 6-11.30. Closed L Sat, all Sun, Bank Holidays, 10 days Christmas. Set D £10. Access, Amex, Diners, Visa.*

W1   Lido   £40

Tel 0171-437 4431   Map 21 A2   **R**
41 Gerrard Street Soho W1V 7LP

A maze of sparsely decorated rooms behind darkened glass in the middle of Chinatown's main street. Long hours attract night owls, who flock here to eat from a wide-ranging menu that's particularly strong on seafood, with sections for crab and lobster, scallops and squid, prawns, eel and abalone. For parties on Fridays and Saturdays there's a minimum charge of £15 a head. *Seats 140. Parties 50. Meals 11.30am-4am. Closed 25 Dec. Set D £10.50 (min 2). Access, Amex, Diners, Visa.*

W1   Lindsay House   £80

Tel 0171-439 0450   Fax 0171-581 2848   Map 21 A2   **R**
21 Romilly Street Soho W1V 5TG

A touch of country-house elegance in a Soho town house, where guests ring the bell to gain admittance and take a drink in the comfortable lounge. The menus are modern beginning with chicken and quail terrine with apple and pear chutney, grilled goat's cheese salad and pan-fried foie gras with rösti potatoes and a Madeira sauce. To follow: roast breast of duckling with ginger and armagnac, grilled fillet of beef or fillets of Dover sole with a crab and herb mousse. Chocolate nut pudding with hot chocolate sauce or lemon tart makes an excellent finale. A few non-French wines appear on the list; the "we recommend" section offers particularly good value. *Seats 30. Parties 10. Private Room 36. L 12.30-2.30 (Sun & Bank Holidays till 2) D 6-12 (Sun & Bank Holidays 7-10). Closed 25 & 26 Dec. Set L £10/£14.75 (Sun £16.75). Access, Amex, Diners, Visa.*

Set menu prices may not always include service or wine.

W1   Lok Ho Fook   £35

Tel 0171-437 2001   Map 21 A2   **R**
4 Gerrard Street Soho W1V 7LP

The menu at this simply appointed Chinatown restaurant covers Cantonese, Peking and Szechuan dishes, from a choice of 16 soups to sea-spice braised egg-plant, fried squid cake with minced meat, belly pork and yam hot pot, to braised carp with ginger and spring onion, and all the usual favourites. There's also a pictorially descriptive dim sum menu for daytime eaters (noon until 6pm). *Seats 100. Private Room 150. Meals 12-11.30. Closed 25 & 26 Dec. Set meals from £7.50 (min 2). Access, Amex, Diners, Visa.*

W1   London Chinatown   £50

Tel 0171-437 3186   Fax 0171-437 0336   Map 21 A2   **R**
27 Gerrard Street Soho W1V 7LP

At the Wardour Street end of Gerrard Street in the teeming heart of London's Chinatown, this aptly named restaurant is one of the friendliest in the area. 'Locals' and visitors interdine on a fine selection of Cantonese and Peking-style food; aromatic crispy duck with pancakes is a favourite here, as in many similar establishments, and the dim sum, served until early evening, are particularly good. *Seats 150. Private Room 70. Meals 12-11.30 (Sun 11-11). Closed 25 & 26 Dec. Set D from £6.95. Access, Amex, Visa.*

W1   London Hilton on Park Lane   75%   £250

Tel 0171-493 8000   Fax 0171-493 4957   Map 18 C3   **HR**
22 Park Lane W1Y 4BE

London's first skyscraper hotel, now more than 30 years old, enjoys panoramic views of London from its prime Park Lane location. A few easy chairs and settees on a carpeted island, amidst a sea of marble in the spacious lobby, are the only lounge seating although the Victorian-themed St George's Bar offers comfortable leather tub chairs. Other public areas include an all-day brasserie, Trader Vic's Polynesian-styled restaurant in the basement and the cocktail bar with the main restaurant on the 28th floor. The refurbished Grand Ballroom can accommodate up to 1200 delegates/banqueters, and there are a dozen smaller rooms for functions/meetings plus a business centre. Standardised bedrooms are of a reasonable size, with polished mahogany furniture which

See over

neatly hides the multi-channel TV, and the convenience of telephones at both desk and bedside in addition to an extension in the marble bathroom. De luxe and Executive rooms are the same size as the others, though bathrooms are larger, but have newer lightwood furniture and more stylish soft furnishings. The latter also enjoy the privilege of a special room with complimentary Continental breakfast, traditional afternoon tea, drinks, use of small meeting room, free local phone calls (from the lounge) and separate check-in and out. There are over 50 full suites, some luxurious, others in similar style to the standard rooms. Beds are turned down on request and there is an extensive 24hr room service menu. Car parking £26 for 24 hours. Small dogs only. *Rooms 448. Keep-fit equipment, beauty & hair salon, brasserie (7am-12.45am, Fri & Sat to 1.45am), theatre desk. Access, Amex, Diners, Visa.*

Windows £125

Comfortably perched on top of the hotel, and enjoying spectacular views on three sides, sits this aptly named restaurant. Jacques Rolancy's cooking is rich and in the French classical mould, with maybe potage of Brittany clams topped with a sea urchin meringue, goose liver with muscat grapes and raisins or more simply a baby spinach and roquette salad to begin; scallops with a pearl barley risotto, fillet of lamb roasted in a parsley and truffle crust or roast partridge with green cabbage to follow. Desserts are a strong point and all the food is beautifully presented, but demands on the pocket far exceed those commanded for this level of cooking – so insist on a window table and perhaps justify the prices! Set menu prices include house wine, and offer the best value. The wine list is far from cheap, with champagne starting at over £40 a bottle! There's a sommelier's suggestion (some of which appear on the regular list), though whether the wines listed are seriously suggested is difficult to judge, especially with some priced at £250! A strict dress code operates; jacket and tie for men and definitely no jeans. Cheaper Park Brasserie on the ground floor. *Seats 104. Parties 10. L 12.30-2.30 D 7-11.30 (Fri & Sat till 12.30). Set L & D from £30.95. Closed L Sat & D Sun.*

W11	London Kensington Hilton	67%	£165

Tel 0171-603 3355 Fax 0171-603 4326 Map 17 B4 **H**
179-199 Holland Park Avenue W11 4UL

Formerly the Hilton International Kensington, this is a large, busy, modern hotel next to Shepherds Bush roundabout. The Executive Floor has superior bedrooms and business facilities. The Crescent lounge is open for snacks 24 hours every day of the week. Banqueting and conference amenities for up to 300. Children up to 12 free in parents' room. Covered parking beneath the hotel. See separate entry for Hiroko Japanese restaurant. *Seats 603. Hair & beauty salon, news kiosk. Access, Amex, Diners, Visa.*

W1	London Marriott	77%	£266

Tel 0171-493 1232 Fax 0171-491 3201 Map 18 C3 **H**
Grosvenor Square W1A 4AW

A redbrick Georgian facade heralds the prime Mayfair location of this modern hotel (entrance in Duke Street). Public areas include a small foyer with sofas set in mirrored alcoves, a lounge and a panelled bar. Bedrooms are big, well designed and comfortable, with large double beds, armchairs and plenty of modern desk furniture. Greens and pinks predominate among the fairly sober soft furnishings. Each bedroom has its own air-conditioning. Superior Executive rooms and suites enjoy their own lounge and complimentary happy hour cocktails and Continental breakfast. Bathrooms are on the small side, but are comprehensively kitted out. Children up to 12 stay free in parents' room. No dogs. Conference/banqueting facilities for 900/500. Considerable tariff reductions are sometimes available with advance booking. *Rooms 223. Gym, valeting, flower shop, lounge service (10.30am-1am). Access, Amex, Diners, Visa.*

W2   London Metropole Hotel   69%   £194

Tel 0171-402 4141 Fax 0171-402 4111   Map 18 B2   **H**
Edgware Road W2 1JU

The newest part hosts impressive conference facilities (up to 1300 delegates), an open-plan marble lobby and lounge, a well-fitted leisure centre, two restaurants and the most recent bedrooms. There are 541 Executive rooms, 175 Crown rooms and 26 suites. Crown bedrooms and suites are attractively shaped and furnished: seating areas, mini-bars and complimentary newspapers are features. 250 rooms are designated non-smoking. *Seats 742. Indoor swimming pool, keep-fit equipment, sauna, spa bath, solarium, kiosk, bar (meals available 24 hours a day). Access, Amex, Diners, Visa.*

W1   London Mews Hilton on Park Lane   68%   £207

Tel 0171-493 7222 Fax 0171-629 9423   Map 18 C3   **H**
2 Stanhope Row Park Lane W1Y 7HE

This delightful club-like hotel is tucked away behind Park Lane and offers rare seclusion in a busy part of London. Generally compact bedrooms are immaculately furnished, as is the rest of the hotel; double-glazed and air-conditioned they offer all mod cons. Light meals can be ordered here, or the various dining-rooms at the *London Hilton on Park Lane* are available to guests, as are its gym and other facilities. State-of-the-art conference rooms for up to 55 delegates. Limited private parking. *Rooms 72. Access, Amex, Diners, Visa.*

W14   London Olympia Hilton   66%   £149

Tel 0171-603 3333 Fax 0171-603 4846   Map 17 B4   **H**
380 Kensington High Street W14 8NL

Close to the Olympia exhibition halls, and equipped to serve the professional businessman – a staffed business centre is open between Monday and Friday 8am-6pm. Modestly furnished bedrooms have most amenities including good work space and state-of-the-art TVs with video systems with touch-button display of billing and conference messaging. Bathrooms are en suite and the Plaza suites have queen-sized beds, better furnishings and upgraded toiletries as well as a complimentary newspaper, fruit and chocolates. Banqueting/conference facilities for 350/500. Children up to 14 stay free in parents' room. NCP parking available beneath the hotel. *Rooms 405. Access, Amex, Diners, Visa.*

SW5   Lou Pescadou   £50

Tel 0171-370 1057 Fax 0171-244 7545   Map 19 A5   **R**
241 Old Brompton Road Earls Court SW5 9HP

An unmistakably French (with native waiters) seafood restaurant serving oysters, mussels (marinière and stuffed), fish soup and daily specials such as bream with beurre blanc, lemon sole meunière and red mullet with pipérade or an excellent brandade de morue. The Plateau Pescadou (oysters, clams, langoustines) is a popular dish, and others are omelettes, pasta, pizza and pissaladière; steaks and seasonal venison for the red-blooded. An £9 three-course lunch menu provides outstanding value for money – one of London's very best restaurant bargains. Lou Pescadou is just by the junction with Earls Court Road. "An optional 15% service charge will be added to your bill." *Seats 69. Private Room 40. L 12-3 D 7-12. Set L £9. Closed Sun in Jul & Aug. Access, Amex, Diners, Visa.*

SW1   The Lowndes   76%   £242

Tel 0171-823 1234 Fax 0171-235 1154   Map 19 C4   **H**
Lowndes Street Belgravia SW1X 9ES

The Lowndes is the smaller, more intimate sister hotel to the *Hyatt Carlton Tower* in the neighbouring square (where guests may use the Peak Health Club and charge restaurant meals to their room here). Public rooms are limited to a small limed-oak panelled lounge area partly open to the lobby and Brasserie 21, open for breakfast, lunch and dinner, and also operating as a bar for cocktails or pre-dinner drinks, with pavement tables in summer. Bedrooms are appealing, with good-quality darkwood furniture, chintzy floral curtains and more masculine check-patterned bedcovers over duvets. All are air-conditioned, but controllably so (and the windows open), and have smart, marble bathrooms with good towelling. Each room has remote-control satellite TV, trouser press, hairdryer and safety deposit box. There are five splendidly-appointed suites. Beds are turned down in the evening, and there's 24hr room service. Two floors of rooms are designated non-smoking. No dogs. *Rooms 78. Access, Amex, Diners, Visa.*

EC3   Luc's Restaurant & Brasserie   £50

Tel 0171-621 0666   Fax 0171-336 7315   Map 20 D2   **R**
17-22 Leadenhall Market EC3V 1LR

Well located in the very centre of Leadenhall Market, this busy French brasserie is open Monday to Friday for lunch (dinner by arrangement for large parties only). Food is well prepared and deftly served, from fish soup with rouille and croutons, vegetable pancakes and chicken liver paté (served warm with brandy sauce) to grilled prawns, monkfish in a lettuce leaf with vermouth sauce, and grilled steaks served with béarnaise sauce. Classic desserts include profiteroles and crepes Suzette. *Seats 140. L only 11.30-3. Closed Sat, Sun, Bank Holidays, 5 days Christmas. Access, Amex, Diners, Visa.*

SE19   Luigi's   £65

Tel 0181-670 1843   Map 17 D6   **R**
129 Gipsy Hill SE19 1QS

The standard of cooking here remains reliable and consistent. The long-standing menu offers daily specials to supplement the choice of Italian classics. There are fairly few pasta dishes (linguine marinara, home-made cannelloni and vegetarian quattro stagione are favourites available as either starter or main course) but a decent choice of antipasti, meat and poultry (and a much enhanced fish section) all in generally familiar preparations. Between Tooting and Eltham. *Seats 65. Private Room 25. L 12-3 D 6.30-10.30. Closed Bank Holidays. Access, Amex, Diners, Visa.*

WC2   Magno's Brasserie   £70

Tel 0171-836 6077   Fax 0171-379 6184   Map 21 B2   **R**
65a Long Acre Covent Garden WC2E 9JH

Bustling, Parisian-style brasserie offering good food served by jovial French waiters in relaxing surroundings. Langoustine croquettes with leeks, potato galette with smoked haddock or pan-fried foie gras with green pea purée to start could be followed perhaps by a selection of pasta or breast of chicken with ginger, spring onion and shiitake mushrooms or grilled fillet and sausage of venison with apple compote and port sauce. Sweets could include creamed rice pudding with caramelised orange, lemon and pink grapefruit and dark and white chocolate mousse with a praline sauce. Good-value set menus and blackboard specials. A useful place for a pre-or post-theatre meal. *Seats 60. L 12-2.30 D 5.30-11.30. Closed L Sat, all Sun, Bank Holidays, 4 days Christmas. Set L & D £13.50/£16.50. Access, Amex, Diners, Visa.*

SW7   Majlis   £35

Tel 0171-584 3476   Map 19 B4   **R**
32 Gloucester Road SW7 4RB

Same connections as *Memories of India* (a few doors away) and *Khan's of Kensington*, with a menu based around lamb, chicken and prawns (plus a fair vegetarian choice). Specialities include chicken jalfrezi and king prawn masala. A la carte, or set menus for one upwards. *Seats 32. L 12-2.30 D 6-12. Closed 25 & 26 Dec. Set meals from £14.50. Access, Amex, Diners, Visa.*

W8   Malabar   £40

Tel 0171-727 8800   Map 18 A3   **R**
27 Uxbridge Street Notting Hill W8 7TQ

Indian restaurant behind the Coronet cinema, with a look and style all its own. The look is Mediterranean (an Italian restaurant was on the site previously) but the home-style cooking features not only familiar dishes but some rarely seen elsewhere. Among the latter are chili bhutta (sweetcorn with green chili and green peppers), prawn philouries (shelled prawns deep-fried in potato flour), long chicken (cooked with cloves and ginger) and kayla foogath (sliced banana cooked with ginger and spices). Sunday buffet lunch £6.95. Menu prices all include service. *Seats 56. Parties 16. Private Room 20. L 12-2.45 D 6-11.15. Closed last week Aug, 4 days Christmas. Access, Visa.*

SW6 · Mamta £30

Tel 0171-736 5914
692 Fulham Road London SW6 5SA

Map 17 B5   **R**

At the Parsons Green end of Fulham Road, a small restaurant with something of a spartan air created by quarry-tiled floor and mushroom-coloured walls hung with earthy-coloured Indian art. "Pure Indian food" from a partnership of chef's has an ethereal quality – the cooking of vegetables and exotic spices creating a myriad of stunning flavours and textures completely obviating the need for meat. The selection of dishes is long and, considering only vegetables are used, surprisingly varied. Traditional Indian set meals represent excellent value. All the food is served on and eaten off polished stainless-steel platters with helpful and amiable service making the experience a highly enjoyable one. *Seats 40. Parties 20. L 12.30-2.30 D 6-10.30. Closed L Mon & Tue, all 25, 26 & 31 Dec. Set L £4.95. Access, Amex, Diners, Visa.*

W2   Mandarin Kitchen £50

Tel 0171-727 9012
14 Queensway W2 3RX

Map 18 A3   **R**

A spacious restaurant with quaint 70s' decor. The speciality is seafood with lobsters heading the list and crabs and king prawns also prominent. Quiet at lunchtimes but booking advisable in the evenings, when it's at its best. *Seats 110. Parties 15. Meals 12-11.30. Closed 3 days Christmas. Set meals from £8.90. Access, Amex, Diners, Visa.*

W1   Mandeville Hotel 62% £135

Tel 0171-935 5599 Fax 0171-935 9588
Mandeville Place W1M 6BE

Map 18 C2   **H**

Just north of Oxford Street, a practical hotel with an all-day coffee shop, two bars and a late night bar-lounge. 24hr room service. Children up to 12 stay free in parents' room. New features include ladies rooms with spy holes and safety chains. No dogs. *Seats 165. Coffee shop (12-10.30). Access, Amex, Diners, Visa.*

EC1   Mange-2 £70

Tel 0171-250 0035 Fax 0171-780 2202
2-3 Cowcross Street EC1M 6DR

Map 16 D3   **R**

A stone's throw from Smithfield market, a restaurant whose very modern decor is matched by Dominique Theval's up-to-date cooking, which produces a well-conceived selection including mussels cooked in wine, garlic, tomato and basil, and rockfish soup with saffron among the starters. Follow with roast monkfish with tapénade, red wine and broad beans, roast pheasant with grapes, armagnac and celeriac purée or French duck breast roasted with garlic, confit of turnips, cider and honey. Simple desserts could include a thin-crust apple tart with caramel and brandy sauce or passion fruit charlotte. A short brasserie-type menu is available throughout the day. A jazzy duo plays in the evenings. Not that many wines to choose from, but those that there are have been well selected and offer good value. *Seats 80. Private Room 25. L 12-2.30 D 6.30-10.30. Closed L Sat, all Sun, Bank Holidays, 1 week Christmas. Set D £15.85. Access, Amex, Diners, Visa.*

W11   Manzara £25

Tel 0171-727 3062
24 Pembridge Road Notting Hill Gate London W11 3HL

Map 18 A3   **R**

In the window is a mouthwatering array of home-baked pastries, beyond it a smart modern restaurant serving Turkish dishes. The house speciality is a selection of hot and cold hors d'oeuvre. Main courses – cooked in foil, casseroled or charcoal grilled – are served with pommes noisettes or Basmati rice. *Seats 40. Parties 20. Meals 8am-11.30pm (Sun to 10.30). Access, Amex, Diners, Visa.*

Consult the blue pages for summary tables and lists of recommended establishments.

WC2   Manzi's   £70

Tel 0171-734 0224   Fax 0171-437 4864   Map 21 A2   **R**
1 Leicester Street WC2H 7BL

The Manzi family came here in 1928 and down the years this has become one of London's best known and best loved seafood restaurants. The ground-floor room and the quieter upstairs Cabin Room have similar menus, mainly traditional in their range, from rollmop herrings, deep-fried crab claws, jellied or stewed eels and calamares to moules marinière, scallops, trout and sole, the latter a speciality, served grilled, meunière or Colbert on the bone, or filleted with a variety of sauces. (The restaurant has 15 basic letting bedrooms.) *Seats 110. Parties 50. L 12-2.45 D 5.30-11.45 (Sun till 10.30).* *Closed L Sun & 25 & 26 Dec. Access, Amex, Diners, Visa.*

Set menu prices may not always include service or wine.

W1   Marble Arch Marriott   68%   £189

Tel 0171-723 1277   Fax 0171-402 0666   Map 18 C2   **H**
134 George Street W1H 6DN

Major pluses at the Marble Arch Marriott include an underground car park (70 cars), health and leisure facilities and a location handy for West End shopping and some of the major tourist sights. Darkwood clubby decor gives an elegant feel throughout. The Executive bedrooms are the most comfortable, though rooms in general are of a good size, and many are ideal for families. *Rooms 239. Indoor swimming pool, keep-fit equipment, sauna, spa bath, solarium, gift shop, coffee shop (7am-10.30pm). Access, Amex, Diners, Visa.*

SW1   Restaurant Marco Pierre White   ★★★   £175

Tel 0171-259 5380   Fax 0171-235 4552   Map 19 C4   **R**
66 Knightsbridge London SW1Y 7LA

♔ 🍾 🍷 🦐 🍓

Marco Pierre White's fuller figure looms larger than ever and his influence is expanding further to encompass some of London's premier and most modish establishments. A true genius, this Cantona of the kitchen is obsessed with his art and can always call upon a fresh flow of inspiration. He creates new dishes with the meticulousness of a scientist often working far into the night. The end results he presents in a stylish and elegant dining room beneath the Hyde Park Hotel. On offer is a fixed-price three-course menu which features a mouthwatering selection of starters followed by an almost too lengthy choice of exquisite main dishes and, finally, desserts which are so good that one is seriously tempted to order more than one. Begin with grilled scallops, which have a hint of curry and are accompanied by a confit of garlic and wonderful Sauternes jus, salad of lobster with tomato confit, vichyssoise of oysters with caviar chantilly or a galette of foie gras with elderberries. Fish is a forte – roast fillet of sea bass with olives, artichokes barigoule and tomato butter, tranche of salt cod with a thyme crust, young spinach and sabayon of grain mustard are typical. Meat dishes include braised pig's trotter 'Pierre Koffmann' with potato purée and morel essence; fillet of lamb with olives, a millefeuille of aubergine, couscous and the roasting juices with rosemary; and roast Bresse pigeon with ventreche, garlic ravioli, braised cabbage, fondant potatoes and thyme jus. Thierry Busset produces sybaritic confections such as a stunning tarte tatin of pears, omelette Rothschild and hot raspberry soufflé. Roger Pizey, the creator of 1992 Dessert of the Year, has moved to The Criterion, a Piccadilly restaurant now in Marco's constellation, due to open as we went to press. The wine list is impressive, with carefully chosen wines from around the world. At first sight it seems expensive, but prices are inclusive and at around £30 per bottle you can drink very well. Spend more and you can drink exceptionally well – the food certainly deserves it! *Seats 50. Parties 12. L 12-2.30 D 7-11. Closed L Sat, all Sun, Bank Holidays, first 2 weeks in Aug, 2 weeks Christmas. Set L £29.50 Set D £70. Access, Visa.*

WC1   The Marlborough   70%   £167

Tel 0171-636 5601 Fax 0171-636 0532   Map 21 B1   **H**
9-14 Bloomsbury Street WC1B 3QD

This comfortable hotel has a truly Edwardian feel, from the elegant lobby to the giant bowl of pot pourri in the reception desk. Handy for New Oxford Street and the British

Museum, it nevertheless manages to retain a country house feel. Two discreet alcoves house leather-clad desks with telephones for private business. Lounge space is limited to the Brasserie Bar, which although comfortable, lacks chairs which encourage "that fall asleep feeling". Spacious, comfortable bedrooms (including two floors reserved for non-smokers), are due to be further improved in 1995. Air-conditioned conference facilities are housed in the basement, and have been completely refurbished. Four bedrooms are specially equipped for disabled guests. Children up to 10 stay free in parents' room. No dogs. *Rooms 169. Access, Amex, Diners, Visa.*

W2	Maroush	£70

Tel 0171-723 0773   Map 18 C3   **R**
21 Edgware Road W2

One of London's most luxurious Lebanese restaurants, serving a standard range of above-average hot and cold starters (at least 40 in all) and mainly charcoal-grilled main courses of lamb and chicken. Houmus, quail and stuffed lamb are among the specialities, along with grills and a few fish dishes. Cover charge £1.50 lunchtime, £5 in the evening up to 10pm. Minimum charge £48 after 10pm. Background music in the daytime, live at night. No cheques. *Seats 90. Parties 20. Meals noon-1am. Access, Amex, Diners, Visa.*
Also at:
SW3 Maroush II 38 Beauchamp Place SW3. Tel 0171-581 5434. Map 18 C3
Open till 5am.
W1 Maroush III 62 Seymour Street W1. Tel 0171-724 5024.   Map 19 C4
Last orders 12.30am. Closed 25 Dec.

Many hotels offer reduced rates for weekend or out-of-season bookings. Always ask about special deals.

W11	Mas Café	£45

Tel 0171-243 0969   Map 18 A2   **R**
6 All Saints Road W11 1HH

There's something of a workman's café atmosphere here if you take into account the rather basic, plain, wooden furniture. The walls, however, hung with huge abstract artwork, and painted in bold, earthy colours, add an element of modernity, offsetting, to a degree, the plebeian character of the tables and chairs. The menu is certainly bang up to date, featuring a choice of modish dishes in the form of a short selection of starters and mains all very competently prepared and highly enjoyable. Fresh asparagus with grated parmesan on a garlic buttered crouton and a balsamic vinegar dressing, tiger prawns with sea salt and chili or chicken liver crostini are among the starters. To follow, there's salmon with sauce vierge, lemon sole with lemon sauce and olive oil and roast poussin with Dijon mustard. Simple but good desserts to finish. Service is easily as laid-back as the mostly young, arty clientele. *Seat 60. Parties 20. L 11-5 D 7-11.30. Closed L Mon-Fri, all Bank Holidays. Access, Visa.*

W1	Masako	£100

Tel 0171-935 1579   Map 18 C2   **R**
6 St Christopher's Place W1M 5HB

Just off Oxford Street (almost opposite the top of South Molton Street, by Bond Street tube station), a delightful Japanese restaurant with friendly, attentive staff and traditional decor of black lacquered tables, open screens and red plush chairs. A fine selection of set meals provides good value, using quality ingredients and showing delicacy in preparation. The set lunch menus include an appetiser, soy bean soup, something grilled or boiled, a main course, rice, pickles and dessert. *Seats 43. Parties 20. Private Room 16. L 12-2.30 D 6-10. Closed Sun, Bank Holidays. Set L from £20 Set D from £35.*
Access, Amex, Diners, Visa.

We welcome bona fide complaints and recommendations on the tear-out pages at the back of the book for readers' comments. They are followed up by our professional team.

W1   May Fair Inter-Continental   81%   £258

Tel 0171-629 7777   Fax 0171-629 1459   Map 18 C3   **HR**
Stratton Street W1A 2AN

A surprisingly intimate hotel, despite its large number of bedrooms, 50 of which are suites (with fax machines), including the refurbished May Fair, Maharajah, Monte Carlo and Penthouse (£1,200 plus for these), the last with two bedrooms, large lounge, dining area, small roof garden and private lift from the street. There's a tranquil atmosphere in the public areas, especially in the lounge, where a harpist plays each afternoon while tea is served. The clubby May Fair bar, with its red leather seating, is a popular rendezvous, while the smaller Chateau cocktail bar (open to 2am with live piano music) which adjoins the restaurant has a whole wall displaying signed photos of showbiz personalities who have either stayed at the hotel or performed at the theatre (seating 290 for conferences, with optional writing tables for each delegate) next door. The spacious air-conditioned bedrooms (almost a quarter non-smoking), now provide voicemail, and many have seating areas. They are decorated in two different styles, English or French; the former with green leather armchairs and traditional darkwood furniture, the latter with softer and more contemporary decor. Splendid bathrooms, some with separate walk-in shower as well as bath tub, offer the usual luxury toiletries, generous-sized towels and bathrobes. The extensive round-the-clock room service can provide hot meals at all hours, just one example of the dedicated service you'll encounter from all the staff, ably led by general manager Dagmar Woodward. The business centre, from where you can hire a wide range of equipment, is fully staffed during the day, and the hotel benefits greatly from its luxurious basement health club with swimming pool – a rarity in the West End. Children up to 14 stay free in parents' room (some adjoining). Several meeting rooms with the Crystal Ballroom accommodating up to 320 for banquets. No dogs.
Rooms 287. *Indoor swimming pool, sauna, solarium, keep-fit equipment, beauty & hair salons, news kiosk, valeting. Access, Amex, Diners, Visa.*

The Chateau   £80

👑 ✦ 🍷 ✦ 📱

Executive head chef Michael Coaker's cooking is on the whole contemporary British, while the smart setting is more Italian in style. Around three times a year the restaurant holds a promotion (asparagus in June), otherwise choose from the one-page carte, which includes the chef's daily-changing fixed-price lunch and dinner menus and some dozen choices of first and main courses, such as fillet of red mullet with spinach or fish cakes with Pommery mustard sauce to start with, followed by breast of duck with shallot lyonnaise and bubble and squeak or grilled lamb cutlets with kidney. Good cheeses from the trolley and desserts, perhaps strawberry shortcake with mascarpone cream or hazelnut and vanilla parfait with caramel sauce, end a meal in style. Decent coffee, petits fours, and a fine, not over-long French-only wine list with some fair prices (*marque* champagne £25) and quality wines by the glass. There's a 'special' menu at £25 which includes house wine, and the Sunday jazz brunch buffet includes either a Bucks Fizz or a Bloody Mary. Jolly service with the effervescent Richard Briggs leading from the front. **Seats** 65. L 12.30-2.30 D 7.30-10.30 Closed L Sat. Set L £22.50 (Sun £20/£23) Set D £29.50 (5 courses).

Café   £55

✦

Brasserie-style in yellow and blue, this is a pleasant spot for a light lunch or pre-theatre dinner. Pop in for a quick snack of, say, croque-monsieur with French fries or grilled pepper and couscous salad with lemon dressing, or linger a little longer over a more substantial main course such as beef casserole with mushrooms and herb mash. Fixed-price daily menu also available. **Seats** 75. **Parties** 20. L 12-3 D 5.30-10.30. Set L & D £10/£14.

Set menu prices may not always include service or wine.

SW7   Memories of India   £40

Tel 0171-589 6450   Fax 0171-584 4438   Map 19 B4   **R**
18 Gloucester Road SW7 4RB

The shiny menu complete with illustrations shows you exactly what to expect at this neighbourhood Indian restaurant, and reality, with ceiling fans and rattan chairs, lives up to the expectations. There is the usual range of tandoori and karahi dishes plus set meals. Specialities include chingri jhol (Bengal-style prawns), chicken jhal frazi and karahi gosht (lamb cooked in spices and served in an iron pot). *Seats 75. Private Room 30. L 12-2.30 D 5.30-11.30. Closed 25 Dec. Set L from £6.95 Set D £14.50. Access, Amex, Diners, Visa.*

W1   Le Meridien   84%   £271

Tel 0171-734 8000   Fax 0171-437 3574   Map 18 D3   **HR**
Piccadilly W1V 0BH

One of the most centrally located London hotels, and without doubt one of the very best, and a haven of peace and style in the bustle of Piccadilly. A harpist plays under the chandeliers in the grand Lounge during afternoon tea, while a pianist tinkles away in the Burlington bar (open to 1am except Sundays) which evokes the aura of a gentleman's club with its baize-green decor. Bedroom decor is tasteful, with style and quality in equal evidence: pink and turquoise are dominant colours, with flowery quilted bedspreads and reproduction pieces featuring; the marbled bathrooms are nothing short of immaculate; bathrobes are, of course, provided. 4th-floor rooms are reserved for non-smokers. Under-12s stay free in parents' room. Afternoon tea is served in the elegant Tea Lounge (3-6pm). Impeccable service. Membership of Champneys health-club downstairs is free to guests – the fun-dungeon is a real plus point. Conference and banqueting facilities for 250. No dogs. *Seats 266. Indoor swimming pool, plunge pools, Turkish baths & sauna, spa bath, solarium, gym & dance studio, squash, snooker, beauty & hair salons, news kiosk & gift shop, coffee shop (7am-11.30pm). Access, Amex, Diners, Visa.*

Oak Room Restaurant   £135

A grand restaurant of majestic proportions and among London's most elegant, with walls panelled in limed oak inlaid with enormous mirrors and surmounted by festoons of classically-inspired gilt mouldings. From the ornate plaster hang six huge crystal chandeliers, added decoration is also provided by large Chinese vases bursting with exceptional flower arrangements. Dominique Zunda took over as executive chef just as we went to press, replacing the talented Alain Marechal, who has returned to the South of France. His collaboration with consultant chef Michel Lorrain of La Cote St-Jacques at Joigny resulted in cooking of the highest order. We hope the new incumbent will prove as successful. In the meantime Michel Lorrain continues to create the restaurant menus, visiting the kitchens periodically to oversee and implement new menus. On offer is a carte of superb sophistication which is supplemented by a stunningly good menu gourmand of seven perfectly balanced and remarkably light courses. Among the starters from the dinner menu are a chef's tasting of goose and duck foie gras, poached oysters wrapped in spinach leaves with shellfish and served with a horseradish and watercress cream sauce and a dish of scrambled eggs with truffles, kidneys and sweetbreads in a veal jus. Main dishes range from pan-fried scallops with parsley ravioli and a mushroom jus to veal cutlet and sautéed endives in a sauce infused with coffee, pan-fried lamb fillet with a truffle risotto and roasted lobster in a pecan and pistachio sauce with a sweetcorn galette. Splendid desserts round off a marvellous experience. An undeniably fine wine list (mostly French) though prices are a bit steep. Good to see that both Australia and New Zealand have joined California in the New World section. Service is by a skilled team headed by the affable maitre d', Jean Quero. *Seats 45. Parties 8. L 12-2 D 7-10.30. Closed L Sat, all Sun, Bank Holidays, 3 weeks Aug, 1 week Jan. Set L £24.50 Set D £28/£46.*

Terrace Garden Restaurant   £65

Two floors up, overlooking busy Piccadilly, is the lovely, leafy, split-level conservatory-style restaurant, the front, lower section of which is reserved for non-smokers. Served from breakfast until dinner, dishes range from potted chicken liver parfait with a port jelly and toasted brioche, ricotta and tomato ravioli and a club sandwich to breast of Barbary duck in an armagnac sauce and pan-fried fillet of beef stuffed with croutons and herbs in a light cream sauce. Fine wines by the glass from a Cruvinet machine. *Seats 120. Parties 30. Meals 7am-11.30pm. Set meals from £18.50 Sun brunch £23 (under-12s half-price). Closed Bank Holidays.*

W1   Merryfield House   £50

Tel 0171-935 8326   Map 18 C2   **B**
42 York Street W1H 1FN

Family-run bed-and-breakfast hotel, handy for Oxford Street and the West End. Small, simply furnished bedrooms, with comfortable fold-away beds, all have en-suite bathrooms with tubs. Remote-control TV and hairdryers provided. Telephone and coffee-making facilities on each landing. Full English breakfast is served between 7.30 and 9 in bedrooms only. Unlicensed. No dogs. *Rooms 8. Closed Feb. No credit cards.*

EC1   Le Mesurier   £65

Tel 0171-251 8117   Fax 0171-608 3504   Map 16 D3   **R**
113 Old Street EC1V 9JR

Competent cooking in a small, intimate and individualistic restaurant offering a concise menu with some interesting choices at each course. Try spinach soufflé with anchovy sauce, chicken with sherry vinegar and tarragon, and lemon and chocolate tart to finish. *Seats 20. Parties 25. L only 12-3 (open evenings by arrangement for party bookings). Closed Sat & Sun, Bank Holidays, 1 week Christmas, 2 weeks Aug. Access, Amex, Diners, Visa.*

SW1   Mijanou   ↑   £95

Tel 0171-730 4099   Fax 0171-823 6402   Map 19 C5   **R**
143 Ebury Street SW1W 9QN

Ring the bell to gain entry to this comfortable little restaurant on two floors of a private house. Sonia Blech and her team produce French-inspired seasonal dishes, little touched by passing fashion, from a summer menu (all priced at £9) which might include a light terrine of red mullet, avocado and fennel with pesto vinaigrette; asparagus in puff pastry with a goat's cheese and orange sauce or a delicious oxtail, foie gras and duck terrine – this studded with a tiny mirepoix of crisp vegetables and served with an excellent onion marmalade. Main courses (all priced at £16) continue the style, maybe best end of lamb with grilled Provençal vegetables, grilled grey dorade with consommé and vegetables or wild boar noisettes with a ragout of Toulouse sausages. Winter food tends to be more warming and substantial. Excellent desserts can be spoilt by being flooded with cream, so beware! Neville Blech runs the front of house charmingly and also maintains one of London's more interesting wine lists. It's fairly priced and comes in two sections: a conventional layout at the back, by style and to match dishes on the menu at the front. Bear in mind that the owners also run a retail wine shop (from where many of these wines come), so the choice here is diverse, interesting and expertly annotated. In the summer the courtyard at the back is an idyllic place to eat. The ground floor is reserved for non-smokers. *Seats 28. Private Room 24. L 12-2 D 7-10. Closed Sat & Sun, Bank Holidays, last 3 weeks Aug, 2 weeks Christmas, 10 days Easter. Set L £12/£15 Set D (dégustation) £38.50. Access, Amex, Diners, Visa.*

W8   The Milestone   78%   £275

Tel 0171-917 1000   Fax 0171-917 1010   Map 19 A4   **HR**
1-2 Kensington Court W8 5DL

A Victorian mansion opposite Kensington Gardens, totally transformed a few years ago into a hotel of considerable style and class, with many restored original features. Bedrooms, individually decorated to high standards, offer modern comforts of air-conditioning, two telephone lines, private fax machines, satellite TV and VCR. Suites have been cleverly designed, creating mezzanine levels in the 24-foot-high rooms which overlook the Park. Most of the suites have antiques and four-posters. 24hr room service includes a creative menu for breakfast. Nothing here is left to chance, from the complimentary basket of fruit on arrival to valet parking (charged at meter rate) and the house doctor. *Room 57. Gym, sauna, spa bath, solarium, lounge (24hrs). Access, Amex, Diners, Visa.*

Restaurant   £80

The cosy panelled dining room maintains the overall high standard of the hotel, yet remains its best-kept secret. Chef Cara Baird likes definite flavours and her dishes are fine examples of this no-nonsense approach. Starters might include couscous with wild mushrooms, gorgonzola and tomatoes, cream of chicken soup with black pudding and chorizo sausage or a red mullet terrine with roasted peppers, set in an aspic of delicious concentration. Lamb with baby leeks and ginger, roast lobster with rosemary, squid ink pasta and a port sauce and the tenderest venison (perfectly cooked) with a potato and mushroom fricassee are typical main courses. Desserts too, show skill and balance. This then is serious food deserving a larger audience. An additional table d'hote menu, in a lighter style, is available for lunch. *Seats 30. Private Room 6. L 12.30-3 D 7-11. Set L £13. Closed L Sat, all Sun. Access, Amex, Diners, Visa.*

Set menu prices may not always include service or wine.

SW1   Mimmo d'Ischia   £90

Tel 0171-730 5406 Fax 0171-730 9439   Map 19 C5   **R**
61 Elizabeth Street Eaton Square SW1

Sound, straightforward Italian cooking – but at a serious price – in a durable and fashionable restaurant whose walls are adorned with signed photographs of celebrity visitors. Among the specialities are mixed pasta, sea bass, osso buco and spare ribs. *Seats 70. Parties 12. Private Room 40. L 12-2.30 D 7-11.30. Closed Sun, Bank Holidays. Access, Amex, Diners, Visa.*

W1   Ming   ★   £55

Tel 0171-734 2721   Fax 0171-435 0812   Map 21 A2   **R**
35 Greek Street Soho W1V 5LN

Ming's menus are particularly interesting, based on Northern Chinese cuisine and specialising in prawns, duck and lamb. Chef Jack recently spent a few weeks in Taiwan and returned with new ideas from his mum: crispy fish rolls, braised crab meat balls and garoupa steak in light soya or hot sauce. Changing specials include steamed eel in black bean sauce with tangerine peel, chicken fried with almond flakes and served with an orange sauce and – a favourite winter dish – braised duck and aubergine hot-pot. From the à la carte selection come stir-fried lean pork with onion pancakes, crab with ginger and spring onion and an 18th-century lamb dish from Emperor Qian Long's chef. The Ming bowl menu offers dishes which are complete meals in themselves: among these are steamed or grilled mantou – a home-made bread served with shredded duck or chopped pork, as well as rice dishes such as chopped beef, lettuce and egg rice and noodle dishes like hot and spicy Szechuan noodle soup. Friendly staff are another plus at one of London's best Chinese restaurants. Tables are set on the pavement in very good weather. A carefully chosen wine list includes a good choice of champagnes and New World wines recommended for certain dishes. *Seats 70. Meals 12-11.45 (Bank Holidays from 5pm). Closed Sun (open Chinese New Year), 25 & 26 Dec. Set L from £10 Set D from £12. Access, Amex, Diners, Visa.*

WC2   Mr Kong   £45

Tel 0171-437 7341   Map 21 A2   **R**
21 Lisle Street Soho WC2 7BE

This is one of the best of the 80 or so Chinese restaurants crammed into the area. The extensive à la carte menu, specialising in Cantonese dishes from the East River, includes all the traditional favourites, and other delicious temptations such as satay eel, spicy salted squid or paper-wrapped chili spare ribs; plus parts of the body not suitable for the squeamish, all at bargain prices. A selection of braised 'pot dishes' is particularly mouthwatering. Food arrives with remarkable speed, but there is no pressure to leave, even when the queue stretches down the road. There are no puddings. Service is orchestrated by Edwin Chau. The restaurant is on three floors – choose a table on the ground floor if possible. Minimum charge of £7 after 5pm. Good-value set meals are for two or more diners only. *Seats 115. Meals noon-2am. Set L & D from £8.60. Closed 4 days Christmas. Access, Amex, Diners, Visa.*

We publish annually, so make sure you use the current edition.
— It's well worth it!

SW5   Mr Wing   £65

Tel 0171-370 4450   Map 19 A5   **R**
242-244 Old Brompton Road Earls Court SW5 0DE

Many restaurants use flowers and plants in their decor, but beside Mr Wing they have the look of a desert, or at best arid scrubland. Ground floor and basement are almost a jungle of tropical greenery, virtually obliterating other decorative features like the fish tank and the paintings. Prices are on the high side, but the food is acceptable and it's quite fun to be there. Try shredded chicken or pork in lettuce wrapping, spare ribs, grilled or steamed dumplings, squid with peppercorn salt, sole in wine sauce, sizzling steak, quick-fried lamb with spring onions, fried bean curd with mixed meats and vegetables. Red bean paste pancakes make a good ending – if you've still got room! The restaurant is near the junction of Old Brompton Road and Earls Court Road. *Seats 120. Parties 25. Private Room 10. Meals 12.30-midnight. Closed 4 days Christmas. Set D £25. Access, Amex, Diners, Visa.*

W6   Mr Wong Wonderful House   £40

Tel 0181-748 6887   Map 17 A4   **R**
313 King Street Hammersmith W6

One of the friendliest Chinese restaurants in London, decorated in gentle eau-de-nil with Mr Wong leading a team of helpful staff. The food, based on Peking and Singapore cuisine, includes a good selection of daytime dim sum (note, no cheung fun on Mondays). Plenty of sizzling dishes, and bean curd for vegetarians. *Seat 200. Parties 25. Private Room 100. L 12-3 D 6-midnight (Sat & Sun noon-midnight). Closed 25 & 26 Dec. Set meals from £13.50. Access, Amex, Diners, Visa.*

SW1   Mitsukoshi   £100

Tel 0171-839 6714   Fax 0171-839 1167   Map 18 D3   **R**
Dorland House 14-20 Lower Regent Street SW1Y 4PH

In the basement of a Japanese department store, this is a roomy, comfortable restaurant making stylish use of frosted glass panelling. You can choose from the à la carte selection or plump for one of the many set meals. These range from a fairly simple hana – appetiser, tempura, grilled fish, rice, miso soup and pickles – through shabushabu (beef slices and vegetables boiled and served with lemon–soya and sesame–soya sauces, prepared at table) to sushi, sukiyaki and the ten-course kaiseki feasts served in the private rooms. *Seats 56. Parties 12. Private Room 24. L 12-2 D 6-9.30. Closed Sun, Bank Holiday Mondays, 10 days Christmas. Set L from £15 Set D from £18. Access, Amex, Diners, Visa.*

EC4   Miyama   £80

Tel 0171-489 1937   Fax 0171-236 0325   Map 20 B2   **R**
17 Godliman Street EC4V 5BD

A stylish operation offering immaculately produced Japanese food in crisp, business-like surroundings: a sushi bar upstairs and tables downstairs. The main menu covers the usual range, from salmon or turbot grilled with salt and bean curd boiled, deep-fried or cold with bonito to sashimi, soups, tempura and teriyaki. Interesting set menus both lunchtime and evening. 15% service charge. Entrance is in Knightrider Street. *Seat 85. L 12-2.30 D 6-9.30. Closed D Sat, all Sun. Set L from £18 Set D £32/£40. Access, Amex, Diners, Visa.*

W1   Miyama   £75

Tel 0171-499 2443   Fax 0171-493 1573   Map 18 C3   **R**
38 Clarges Street W1Y 7PJ

The West End version of the City branch, stylish and modern, with opaque screens for privacy. Cooking is of a high standard, flavours delicate and refined. Set lunches offer the best value (raw fish, grilled fish, tempura, beef or chicken teriyaki, pork ginger or pork deep-fried). The rest of the menu spans the expected range, from appetizers like yaki tori (skewered chicken) to rice and noodle dishes, nabemono specialities and teppan yaki meals prepared at the table. Excellent service (for which 15% is added). Between Piccadilly and Curzon Street. *Seats 67. Parties 30. Private Room 16. L 12-2.30 D 6-10.30. Closed L Sat, Sun and Bank Holidays, all 25, 26 Dec & 1 Jan. Set L £12-£18 Set D £32-£40. Access, Amex, Diners, Visa.*

need new #

WC2   Moat House   65%   £150

Tel 0171-836 6666 Fax **0171-831 1548**   Map 21 B1   **H**
10 Drury Lane Covent Garden WC2B 5RE

High-rise hotel handy for Covent Garden and many West End theatres. Maudie's Bar is
a good spot to unwind with a drink and smile at the Osbert Lancaster cartoons. Children
up to 12 stay free in parents' room; family-sized rooms available. Conference and
banqueting facilities for up to 100. Covered parking (£15 a day). Developments in hand
as we went to press included ongoing bedroom refurbishment and the creation of 11
additional bedrooms from two function rooms. New staffed business centre. *Rooms 153.
Gym, solarium. Access, Amex, Diners, Visa.*

N1   Mojees   £45

Tel 0171-226 0307   Map 16 D3   **R**
87 Noel Road Islington N1 8HD

Open only at weekends (apart from party bookings at other times), Mojees is located
down a quiet Islington road above the Island Queen pub. The room is lofty, painted
plain white, with a few leafy plants and discreet ceiling spot lamps creating a charmingly
informal ambience. Diners are presented with a menu of English inspiration with
international influences. Just the main courses are printed, with an explanation that they
help themselves to a buffet of hot and cold starters in the lobby just outside the dining
room. Gnocchi with spinach and cottage cheese in a cheese sauce, supreme of chicken
filled with a julienne of leeks, carrots and celeriac, and lamb shank Greek-style are typical
main choices. There is no restriction whatsoever on the amount you can eat – every dish
on the menu is included for the £15.95 charge, if you have the appetite. *Seats 45.
Parties 30. L Sun only from 1pm D Fri & Sat only 7.30-9.30. Closed all Mon-Thu, D Sun,
Bank Holiday weekends, all Aug, 2 weeks Christmas. Set D £15.95. Access, Amex, Visa.*

W6   Los Molinos   £35

Tel 0171-603 2229   Map 17 B4   **R**
127 Shepherds Bush Road W6 7LP

A popular pine-furnished restaurant by Brook Green, serving a wide variety of tapas,
almost all available in two sizes. Marinated anchovies, sole fillets stuffed with scallops,
salted cod with mustard and coriander, battered squid, crab-stuffed mushrooms and garlic
prawns are just a few from the fish section, while on the meat side of the menu are
fabada asturiana (a stew of chorizo, black pudding and white beans), veal scallops with
sun-dried tomatoes, cured mountain ham, kidneys in sherry, coriander lamb croquettes
and rabbit casserole with wild herbs. There's also an excellent vegetarian choice. *Seats 80.
Parties 45. Private Room 45. L 12-2.30 D 6-11. Closed L Sat, all Sun, Bank Holidays, 1 week
Christmas. Access, Amex, Diners, Visa.*

W5   Momo   £50

Tel 0181-997 0206   Map 17 A4   **R**
14 Queens Parade North Ealing W5 3HU

Cosy Japanese restaurant just off Hanger Lane (by North Ealing Underground). One-dish
lunches served with rice and miso soup offer particularly good value; the extensive menu
in the evenings includes the likes of assorted sashimi, sukiyaki and beef with teriyaki
sauce. *Seats 30. L 12-2.30 D 6-10. Closed Sun, Bank Holidays, 1 week Aug, 10 days
Christmas. Set L from £7. Set D from £23.50. Access, Amex, Diners, Visa.*

W1   Mon   £70

Tel 0171-262 6528 Fax **0171-706 2531**   Map 18 C3   **R**
Cumberland Hotel Marble Arch London W1A 3RF

On the ground floor of the Cumberland Hotel, Mon has all the usual trappings of a smart
modern Japanese restaurant. The dining area is divided by low wooden screens with
private rooms also available. The menu offers a wide selection of very carefully prepared
traditional Japanese dishes with lunchtime and pre-theatre offering the best bargains.
Service is friendly and helpful. *Seats 96. Parties 8. Private Room 28. L 12-2 D 5.50-11.15.
Closed Christmas/New Year. Set L & pre-theatre D from £13.95. Access, Amex, Diners, Visa.*

WC2   Mon Plaisir   £50

Tel 0171-836 7243 Fax 0171-379 0121   Map 21 B2   **R**
21 Monmouth Street WC2H 9DD

There are daily specials according to market availability but otherwise it's a reassuring case of *plus ça change* at Mon Plaisir, the original of Alain Lhermitte's small group of restaurants. Regulars go back for rillettes, onion soup, *St Pierre à la niçoise*, steak tartare, entrecote béarnaise, profiteroles and crème brulée. Set menus at lunch and pre-theatre times (6-7.15pm). *Seats 95. Parties 20. Private Room 30. L 12-2.15 D 5.50-11.15. Closed L Sat, all Sun, Bank Holidays, 1 week Christmas-New Year. Set L and early D £13.95. Access, Amex, Diners, Visa.*

SW3   Monkeys   £80

Tel 0171-352 4711   Map 19 B5   **R**
1 Cale Street Chelsea Green SW3 3QT

A neighbourhood restaurant, in the true sense, where customers are welcomed as friends into the wood-panelled dining room. There is a feeling of a private party amid the profusion of fresh flowers and blue linen. Game features strongly in season, and other favourites are home-potted shrimps, hot foie gras salad, foie gras terrine, poached salmon hollandaise and stuffed sea bass with red pepper sauce. Popular, too, are the plats du jour – salmon fishcakes on Monday, braised oxtail and dumplings on Wednesday. Excellent French cheeses, carefully kept. Hand-written list of mostly French wines, several under £20. *Seats 40. Parties 8. Private Room 10. L 12.30-2.30 D 7.30-11. Closed Sat & Sun, Bank Holidays, 2 weeks Easter, 3 weeks Aug. Set L £15/£22.50 Set D £22.50/£35. Access, Visa.*

WC1   The Montague   64%   £135

Tel 0171-637 1001   Fax 0171-637 2506   Map 18 D2   **H**
12-20 Montague Street Bloomsbury WC1B 5BJ

Nine Georgian town houses make up the Montague Park, which stands in the heart of Bloomsbury right by the British Museum. Public rooms (reception and lounge recently redesigned) are spacious and comfortable: the bar has a small terrace looking out on to private gardens and the basement breakfast room has a bright conservatory roof. Bedrooms are small but well equipped, with satellite TV, trouser press, hairdryer and tea/coffee facilities. Sparkling clean bathrooms are well appointed. Conferences for up to 120. The hotel's new restaurant, Bistro Bistrot, is open for lunch and dinner except Saturday and Sunday. Children up to 12 stay free in parents' room. *Seats 109. Access, Amex, Diners, Visa.*

W1   The Montcalm   76%   £234

Tel 0171-402 4288   Fax 0171-724 9180   Map 18 C2   **HR**
Great Cumberland Place W1A 2LF

Named after an 18th-century general the Marquis de Montcalm, the hotel stands in a residential crescent near Marble Arch and Oxford Street. The smart entrance and foyer set the tone for public areas which are more akin to a private club than a hotel; this is best illustrated in the cosy bar which has deep green walls, distinctive wood panelling, an open fire, a mahogany bookcase and a collection of comfortable leather chairs and upholstered sofas. Light meals are served here from 11am to 11pm. Though several of the air-conditioned bedrooms are on the small side, they are finely decorated and furnished; among the suites are the honeymoon suite with half-tester, heated waterbed – is it the only one in a London hotel? – and bathroom jacuzzi, two penthouse suites (with sauna) and twelve unusual duplex suites with entrances on two floors and a spiral staircase in between. In the bathrooms there are bathrobes, a bidet and good toiletries, as well as a telephone extension, while the bedrooms have mini-bars and safes in addition to the usual facilities. A nice touch is the subdued lighting underneath the bedside table, so you don't have to switch on a light in the middle of the night if you need to get out of bed in darkness. First-class service, and a Japanese breakfast among the morning options. For business, there are private rooms and an air-conditioned suite which can accommodate up to 80 for meetings. Children up to 12 stay free in parents' room. 24hr room service. No dogs. *Rooms 116. Access, Amex, Diners, Visa.*

Crescent Restaurant £80

♗ ♓ ◫

The air-conditioned room is dominated by a large mural of a country landscape and garden painted by Lincoln Seligman. Chef Gary Robinson's style leans towards modern British cooking with the set lunches (one, two or three courses) including unlimited house wine or mineral water. The fixed-price dinner menu also includes a half bottle of house wine, but if you prefer to choose from the wine list a £5 reduction per person is made off the price (£19.50 becomes £14.50). Typical of the interesting dishes are garlic mushrooms gratinated with smoked cheese and granary breadcrumbs; tiger prawns flambéed with brandy, ginger and garlic; collops of monkfish cooked tempura-style accompanied by a lime dill butter sauce; roast breast of duck on a black pudding with a port wine sauce; and pan-fried minute steak with a green peppercorn sauce. The £43 speciality five-course dinner menu includes a glass of wine to accompany four of the courses. Hors d'oeuvre buffet, dessert trolley, decent cheeses and coffee. Commendably, there are four *marque* champagnes under £30, as well as several good wines under £20. New World thinly represented. **Seats** 60. *Parties 12. L 12.30-2.30 D 6-10. Closed L Sat, all Sun. Set L £14.50/£17.50/£19.50 Set D £19.50 & £43 (set meal prices include wine).*

W2	Mornington Hotel	63%	£89

Tel 0171-262 7361 Fax 0171-706 1028   Map 18 B3   **H**
12 Lancaster Gate W2 3LG

In a residential area just north of Hyde Park, the Swedish-owned Mornington (spot the Swedish flag over the entrance) scores on housekeeping and efficiency. There's a fresh, bright look to the place, both in the day rooms (panelled foyer-lounge, library bar) and in the bedrooms. Rates include a Swedish buffet breakfast. Children up to 12 stay free in parents' room. There's a new, small conference room (up to 18 theatre-style). **Seats** 68. *Sauna. Access, Amex, Diners, Visa.*

EC2	Moshi Moshi Sushi	NEW	£20

Tel 0171-247 3227   Map 20 D1   **R**
Unit 24 Liverpool Street Station EC2

Cocooned from the din and chill of the great railway station below by a clear perspex enclosure, the bar sits atop Platform I behind a food and wine shop. Serving an excellent range of well-made sushi with jars of pickled ginger at intervals, the place's unique feature is the continuously moving belt which winds its way round the central counter. The chefs put plates of sushi on it as the need arises and diners pick them off. Prices are based on the colour or pattern of the plate. Miso soup and drinks are ordered from one of the waitresses. There's a £10 minimum charge for credit cards. **Seats** 60. *Sushi 11.30am-8.45pm. Closed Sat, Sun, Bank Holidays & 1 week Christmas. Access, Visa.*

W1	Mostyn Hotel	62%	£124

Tel 0171-935 2361 Fax 0171-487 2759   Map 18 C2   **H**
Bryanston Street W1H 8DE

Tucked away quietly behind Marble Arch, the 18th-century building was originally the home of Lady Black, a lady-in-waiting to the Court of George II. Inside, period detail blends with up-to-date amenities, but the most impressive features – a Georgian staircase, Adam carved ceilings and fire surrounds – are in the conference areas, where various rooms cater for up to 130 for banquets and 60 for conferences. Public rooms include the colonial-style Tea Planter restaurant (where breakfast is served) with its own street entrance. Bedrooms come in various sizes. The top (4th) floor is designated non-smoking. *Rooms 122. Access, Amex, Diners, Visa.*

SW1	Motcomb's		£60

Tel 0171-235 9170 Fax 0171-245 6351   Map 19 C4   **R**
26 Motcomb Street Belgravia SW1X 8JU

♗ ◉

Old-established basement restaurant beneath a wine bar. An international menu provides plenty of choice, including oysters, Caesar salad, chicken and mushroom pancakes, lobster thermidor, fishcakes, smoked haddock with poached egg and sea bass with mint vinaigrette. Rack of lamb, chateaubriand béarnaise and seasonal partridge and pheasant are among the meaty options. **Seats** 70. *Private Room 22. L 12-3 D 7-11.45. Closed D Sun, all Bank Holidays. Set L from £11.75/£14.75. Access, Amex, Diners, Visa.*

WC2   Mountbatten Hotel   70%   £207

Tel 0171-836 4300   Fax 0171-240 3540   Map 21 B2   **HR**
20 Monmouth Street Covent Garden WC2H 9HD

On the edge of Covent Garden and thus an ideal stop-over for theatre-goers, the hotel is themed around the late Lord Louis, with a glass case of memorabilia in the lobby and portraits, photographs and relevant bric-à-brac scattered about the public rooms. The marble-floored reception is elegant and the comfortable Polo Bar a good meeting place. Bedrooms vary in size (some very small singles) but are all comfortably furnished and include all modern necessities (TV, mini-bar, trouser press etc.) and an evening turn-down service. En-suite bathrooms are marble clad, with robes and tubs with overhead showers. The Mountbatten theme continues in the spacious suites, most of which have spa baths. Smart conferences facilities include the ground-floor Broadlands Suite (modelled on the drawing room of the Hampshire family home). Plans are afoot to open a basement cabaret bar. Children under 14 stay free in parents' room. Radisson Edwardian Hotels. *Rooms 127. Access, Amex, Diners, Visa.*

Ad Lib Restaurant   £55

Relaunched restaurant (previously L'Amiral), with its own entrance in Mercer Street, now catering for the hungry diners of theatre-land in considerable comfort. The menu offers simple modern favourites, all cooked and presented with enthusiasm by Keith Walker and his kitchen team. Begin perhaps with half a dozen Rossmore oysters, Caesar salad or a skilfully-made duck and venison terrine with green peppercorns. Follow with cod fishcakes and parsley sauce, sirloin steak with shallot sauce or salmon in puff pastry with spinach mousse. No short cuts are taken with the saucing and vegetables show equal care. Finish with treacle tart and custard, profiteroles with chocolate sauce or the well-kept British and Irish cheeses. *Seats 75. Parties 12. L 12.30-2.30 D 5.30-11.30. Closed L Sat & Sun. Set L & D £15.50. Access, Amex, Diners, Visa.*

W1   Le Muscadet   £60

Tel 0171-935 2883   Map 18 C2   **R**
25 Paddington Street Marylebone W1M 3RF

Classic French bistro dishes are listed on the handwritten menu at this popular little spot. Typical items include quail's egg salad, lobster terrine with a prawn sauce, salmon with hollandaise, breast of chicken with a champagne sauce, medallions of veal with cep mushrooms and peppered fillet of Scotch beef. *Seats 35. L 12.30-2.30 D 7.30-10.30 (Sat to 10). Closed L Sat, all Sun, Bank Holidays, 3 weeks Aug. Access, Visa.*

WC1   Museum Street Café   ★   £55

Tel 0171-405 3211   Map 21 B1   **R**
47 Museum Street Bloomsbury WC1A 1LY

A café by name but the atmosphere, albeit informal with its bright white walls and simple, dark furniture, is much more that of a restaurant. The choice is a short one but is imaginative and eclectic with inspiration for dishes depending on the availability of the fine ingredients that are essential to this simple, unfussy, contemporary style of cooking. Neal's Yard Dairy, Monmouth Coffee Company and Frances Smith (organic salad grower) are among the suppliers. Much use is made of the chargrill and this is Mark Nathan's domain, while Gail Koerber's task is preparing the breads, starters and desserts. What comes from the kitchen continues to captivate the palate with its delicacy and subtlety. Lentil, chestnut and red wine soup or a salad with bresaola, parmesan, roasted fennel and grilled courgette could be your starter choice, followed by lamb with tapénade, salmon with soy, ginger and coriander, or calf's liver with grilled sweet red onions. Desserts are every bit as appealing as the rest – try olive oil and Sauternes cake with blood oranges and crème fraiche. No smoking. *Seats 37. L 12.30-2.30 D 6.30-9.30. Closed Sat & Sun. Set L £12/£15 Set D £17/£21. Access, Visa.*

**We publish annually, so make sure you use the current edition.
— It's well worth it!**

SE1   Mutiara   £25

Tel 0171-277 0425   Map 17 D4   **R**
14 Walworth Road Elephant & Castle SE1 1HY

Indonesian/Malaysian restaurant whose decor is highlighted by large paintings and an enormous vase of exotic leaves. Try classics like satay, prawn fritters, sesame chicken and beef slices with five spices, served by charming, helpful staff. Plenty for vegetarians. *Seats 70. L 12-2.30 D 6-11. Closed L Sat, all Sun, Bank Holidays. Access, Amex, Visa.*

W1   Nakamura   £50

Tel & Fax 0171-935 2931   Map 18 C2   **R**
31 Marylebone Lane W1M 5FH

A sushi bar is at street level, and a narrow stairway spirals down to the sparsely appointed main restaurant. Food takes centre stage with preparation and presentation both receiving detailed attention; specialities include sushi, sashimi, tempura and – prepared at table – sukiyaki and kamo nabe (duck and vegetables in steaming hot broth). *Seats 33. Parties 15. Private Room 6. L 12-2.30 D 6-10.30 (Sun to 10). Closed Sat, 10 days Aug, 4 days Christmas. Set L from £9.50 Set D from £25.90. Access, Amex, Diners, Visa.*

We welcome bona fide complaints and recommendations on the tear-out pages at the back of the book for readers' comments. They are followed up by our professional team.

N1   Nam Bistro   £45

Tel 0171-354 0851   Map 16 D3   **R**
326 Upper Street Islington N1 2XQ

An agreeable family-run restaurant on two floors with a simple, clean, modern line in decor. The Vietnamese dishes on offer are of the homely variety, simple, straightforward and highly enjoyable, and worth the wait. Fresh herbs and clear spicing ensure that the food is very flavoursome, though without some of the fieriness associated with food from its close neighbour, Thailand. There are many Chinese influences, too. For those unfamiliar with cooking from this country, advice is willingly given. *Seats 80. L 12-3 D 6-11. Closed Mon, 25 & 26 Dec. Access, Amex, Diners, Visa.*

E1   Namaste   £35

Tel 0171-488 9242 Fax 0171-488 9339   Map 20 D1   **R**
16 Prescot Street E1 8AZ

A change of venue, albeit only a block away, to a more spacious Indian restaurant with access for the disabled. Chef patron Cyrus Todiwala serves a range of excellent dishes that includes some rarities, particularly on the weekly speciality menu. *Galinha cafreal* is a Goan version of a Portuguese dish – chicken tikka marinated in puréed mint, coriander, green chilis, garam masala and lemon juice. *Vagyo chem ambotik* is king prawns cooked in a hot and sour curry. *Jungli soocar ka achar sailana* is diced haunch of wild boar cooked with crisp browned onions, cane molasses, garlic and cloves flavoured with nigella. Non- smoking section *Seats 125. Parties 45. Private Room 40. L 12-3 D 6-11 (Sat 7-10). Closed L Sat, all Sun, Bank Holidays & Christmas week. Access, Amex, Diners, Visa.*

W6   Nanking   £60

Tel 0181-748 7604   Map 17 A4
332 King Street Hammersmith W6

In a street bursting with ethnic restaurants Nanking is one of the smartest, and quite intimate in atmosphere. Decor is cool, staff admirably helpful and friendly. The menu has plenty of interest, especially in the 'special selection' section, where you'll find sizzle-grilled sesame steak with teriyaki sauce, veal slices in a lemon and lime sauce, double-sautéed string beans with crushed dry shrimps and 'mou shee' crab meat with iceberg lettuce. *Seats 95. Private Room 60. L 12-2.30 D 6.30-11.30. Set meals from £17.20. Access, Amex, Visa.*

WC2   Neal Street Restaurant   ★   £100

Tel 0171-836 8368   Fax 0171-497 1361   Map 21 B2   **R**
26 Neal Street Covent Garden WC2H 9PS

Mushroom fan and media personality Antonio Carluccio runs one of the capital's most successful restaurants, and in Englishman Nick Melmoth-Coombs he has a head chef very much in sympathy with Italian cuisine. Wild mushrooms and truffles hold a prominent place throughout his menu. Wild mushroom soup, truffled endive salad and baked eggs with truffles are typical starters, along with seafood or vegetable antipasto. Of the pasta dishes, the fresh tagliolini with creamy truffle sauce (the parmesan is already included) is stunning, while other choices could be black angel hair with seafood and bottarga or pappardelle with funghi. Piemontese bollito misto is a great favourite and is carved at the table; equally appealing is baked schiaccata (paper-thin slices of beef with truffle cheese). Fish-lovers might choose Dover sole grilled or meunière, grilled monkfish with globe and Jerusalem artichoke sauce or fritto of scallops and prawns with seaweed and lime. Sweets include a marvellous Barolo-poached pear with creamy, golden vanilla ice cream or the definitive Sicilian cassatina. Alongside the excellent Italian selection there are some wines from other areas, but its best to stay native to complement the food. 15% service charge is automatically added to all bills. Skilful, friendly service. *Seats 60. Parties 12. Private Room 24. L 12.30-2.30 D 7.30-11. Closed Sun, Bank Holidays, 1 week Christmas/New Year. Access, Amex, Diners, Visa.*

> Set menu prices may not always include service or wine.

W1   New Fook Lam Moon   £50

Tel 0171-734 7615   Map 21 A2   **R**
10 Gerrard Street Soho W1

A simply furnished restaurant in Soho's Chinatown where meats hang invitingly in the window. Fast service from a long list of sound Cantonese cooking. Good choice of one-pot, porridge and noodles in soup dishes – spare ribs with sauce, duck with yam and minced meat with noodles are typical. Order barbecue suckling pig in advance. *Seats 80. Meals 12-11.30 (Sun to 10.30). Closed 25 Dec. Set meals from £11. Access, Amex, Diners, Visa.*

W2   New Kam Tong   £35

Tel 0171-229 6065   Map 18 A3   **R**
59 Queensway W2 4QH

Other Queensway restaurants come and go, but New Kam Tong has been around longer than most. The menu is predominantly Cantonese, with a huge choice, from deep-fried stuffed crab claws and 17 soups to dozens of ways with chicken, beef, prawns and pork, plus oodles of noodles and braised, roast or aromatic crispy duck. Daytime dim sum. Almost next to Bayswater Underground station. *Seats 130. Meals 12-11.15. Set meals from £9.80. Amex.*

W1   New Loon Fung   £60

Tel 0171-437 6232   Fax 0171-437 3540   Map 21 A2   **R**
42 Gerrard Street Soho W1V 7LP

A fairly steep, wide, mirror-lined staircase makes an impressive entrance into a first-floor, split-level restaurant located above a Chinese supermarket. The menu must rank as one of the longest in Chinatown, with 250+ dishes on offer. While a long menu often means the quality of the cooking suffers, such is not the case here. This is not a restaurant to come for a quick, inexpensive meal but one where good ingredients are combined to produce beautifully cooked dishes that are full of flavour and interest. The mainly Cantonese menu has some Peking and Szechuan dishes, too. Set dinners are available in either Szechuan or Cantonese style, the former being much spicier. Steamed scallops come with a separate chili and spring onion dressing, crispy shredded lamb and Peking duck are offered as starters while Szechuan spicy prawns and sliced fish in crisp batter with a sweetcorn sauce are typical of an extensive seafood selection. To finish there are simple sweets and orange segments to cleanse the palate. *Seats 400. Parties 10. Private Room 30. Meals 11.30-11.30 (Fri & Sat to midnight). Closed 2-3 days Christmas. Set meals from £9 (min 2). Access, Amex, Diners, Visa.*

W1   New World   £35

Tel 0171-434 2508   Map 21 A2   **R**
1 Gerrard Place Soho W1V 7LL

Join several hundred others and enjoy a meal in one of Soho's most typical and traditional Chinese restaurants. The menu is suitably vast, starting from daytime dim sum and ranging through seafood and vegetarian specials, popular provincial dishes and chef's specialities. *Seats 600. Private Room 200. Meals 11am-11.45pm (Fri & Sat to 12.15am, Sun 11-11). Closed 25 & 26 Dec. Set meals from £7.20. Access, Amex, Diners, Visa.*

SW4   Newton's   £55

Tel 0181-673 0977   Map 17 C6   **R**
33 Abbeville Road Clapham Common South Side SW4 9LA

♟ ❦ ⊘

A popular neighbourhood brasserie in two separate rooms, one of which is non-smoking. The menu is worldly ("modern British/European with a touch of Thai") with an eclectic mix of dishes that range from carpaccio of vegetables, salt cod beignets and a salad of salted walnuts and anchovies to osso buco with deep-fried chili polenta, smoked haddock fish cakes with a light curry sauce and chicken breast with orange and Madeira sauce. Half-pounder hamburger and Thai curries are specialities. The Sunday brunch menu includes a traditional roast and papers on the bar. Children are especially encouraged on Saturdays (12.30-5.30) with a special menu to colour, a clown and a Club menu for mums and dads. Outside eating (30 seats) on an enclosed roadside terrace in good weather. *Seats 70. Parties 30. L 12.30-2.30 (Sat till 4) D 7-11.30 (Sun meals 12.30-11). Closed 25-27 Dec, 3 days Easter. Set L £6.95 (Sun £9.95) Set D £11.95. Access, Amex, Visa.*

W1   Nico Central   ★ ↑   £60

Tel 0171-436 8846 Fax 0171-355 4877   Map 18 D2   **R**
35 Great Portland Street W1N 5DD

▰ ❦

A stone's throw from Oxford Circus in the West End's garment district this is one of Nico Ladenis' three starred establishments in the capital. In accordance, the decor is elegantly stylish, yet the place has an agreeable informality and the food is, quite simply, brilliant. An art deco-style roof light and a mirrored dado strip together with large Picasso and Juan Gris prints are indicative of the fashionable aspects of the L-shaped room. The menu, fixed-price for both lunch and dinner, offers a selection of dishes that bear Nico's hallmarks of exceptionally well-prepared, classically-based creations. Starters include a splendid raviolo stuffed to overflowing with fresh crab and smothered in a well-made tartare sauce, an individual Roquefort soufflé set on a salad with slivers of pear poached in red wine and crisp roasted walnuts and a chicken and foie gras sausage accompanied by caramelised onions. Main courses feature an outstanding roast duck – pink, yet meltingly tender, accompanied by sweet potato croquettes and an orange sauce; braised knuckle of veal with roasted carrots, baked fillet of brill with croutons and Provençal vegetables and a 'noisette' of ox tongue braised in Madeira with spinach and beetroot. Dishes are served with lovely chips and even better puréed potatoes with olive oil. To finish, desserts such as hot ginger and walnut sponge with whisky ice cream, lemon tart and chocolate marquise with an orange crème anglaise round off the perfect occasion. The set meal prices are inclusive of service. An excellent and sensibly priced wine list has several wines that will cost you half as much again at Nico's posh place on Park Lane. Lots under £20. *Seats 55. Private Room 10. L 12-2 D 7-11. Closed L Sat, all Sun, Bank Holiday Mons, 4 days Easter, 10 days Christmas. Set L £20/£23.50 Set D £22. Access, Amex, Diners, Visa.*

We welcome bona fide complaints and recommendations on the tear-out pages at the back of the book for reader's comments. They are followed up by our professional team.

W1   Nicole's   NEW   £75

Tel 0171-499 8408 Fax 0171-499 7522   Map 18 D3   **R**
158 New Bond Street W1Y 9AP

The basement of Nicole Farhi, the currently very fashionable designer clothes shop, has been transformed into a smart, bright restaurant with stark white walls hung with arty monochrome framed photographs of actors. At lunchtime, the quite closely spaced tables quickly become filled with the Bond Street beau monde. The short simple menu offers a selection of voguish dishes which are light and fresh. Begin with the risotto of the day, which could be fennel. Seared beef fillet with pecorino and grilled marinated vegetable salad are other choices. For a main course there could be grilled tuna with deep-fried beans and anchovy mayonnaise, baked cod with crab and parsley butter sauce and for meat – pan-fried duck breast with watercress and pear salad, grilled calf's liver with thyme and olive oil mash. Desserts include a delicious zuccotto with creamy chocolate sauce, lemon sponge pudding with lime syllabub or a summer fruit tartlet. The bar has seats along the counter as well as on a few tables for a lighter menu including marinated lamb with pitta bread and a chick pea salad. Breakfast is served in the restaurant from 10 till 11am (11.30 Sat). *Seats 70. Parties 20. L 12-3.30 D 6.30-11. Closed D Sat, all Sun, 24-26 Dec. Access, Amex, Diners, Visa.*

SW10   Nikita's   £70

Tel 0171-352 6326 Fax 0181-993 3680   Map 19 A6   **R**
65 Ifield Road Fulham SW10 9AU

For more than 20 years diners have come to this snug red-and-gold basement restaurant to dive into the fast-flowing waters of the River Vodka and tuck into hearty Russian food. Speciality dishes include blinis, smoked fish, shashlik and goluptzi (parcels of cabbage filled with lamb, herbs and dried fruits, braised with cream). Snuggest areas are two cosy, curtained alcoves, each seating six. *Seats 38. Private Room 12. L by arrangement only D 7.30-11.30. Closed Sun, 3 weeks Aug. Set D from £18.50. Access, Amex, Visa.*

W1   Ninjin   £60

Tel 0171-388 4657   Map 18 C2   **R**
244 Great Portland St W1N 5HF

A modestly appointed Japanese restaurant beneath its own food shop, Ninjin is in the same group as Ginnan, Masako, Hiroko and Kashinoki. Set lunches (£10.50-£20) include appetiser, miso soup, rice, pickles and fresh fruit plus one of a dozen main dishes, from fried bean curd and deep-fried oysters to Scotch salmon, raw fish fillets and beef grilled with teriyaki sauce. Also sukiyaki, shabu shabu and bento lunches. Dinner brings more elaborate set meals plus an à la carte menu featuring kushiyaki (skewered dishes) as a speciality. *Seats 54. Parties 20. L 12-2 D 6-10. Closed Sun and Bank Holidays. Set L from £10.50 Set D from £26. Access, Amex, Diners, Visa.*

NW1   Nontas   £30

Tel 0171-387 4579 Fax 0171-383 0355   Map 16 C3   **R**
14 Camden High Street London NW1 0JH

A bustling, neighbourhood Greek Cypriot restaurant which also offers overnight accommodation. The menu covers a familiar range, including the ever-popular meze for two or more (£8.75 per person) and charcoal-grilled prawns, rump steak, quails and lamb cutlets. Look out for fresh fish specialties. The separate Ouzerie area serves snacks, teas and coffee from 8.30am to 11.30pm. *Seats 50. Parties 24. L 12-2.45 D 6-11.30. Closed Sun, Bank Holidays and for 1 day at Christmas, New Year and Easter. Set meals meze from £8.75. Access, Amex, Diners, Visa.*

SW5   Noor Jahan   £40

Tel 0171-373 6522   Map 19 B5   **R**
2a Bina Gardens off Old Brompton Road SW5

Popular and durable Indian restaurant with a straight-down-the-line menu: various styles and heat levels of lamb, chicken and prawn dishes. Tandoori specialities. Swift, friendly service. *Seat 60. Parties 25. L 12-2.45 D 6-11.45. Closed 25 & 26 Dec. Access, Amex, Diners, Visa.*

SW7   Norfolk Hotel   64%   £167

Tel 0171-344 9955 Fax 0171-581 1874   Map 19 B5   **H**
2 Harrington Road South Kensington SW7 3ER

The splendid original staircase helps preserve the Victorian air of the Norfolk which was purpose built in 1888. The high-ceilinged bedrooms, some with original moulded plasterwork, are nicely proportioned and (though modestly furnished) have up-to-date amenities. Front-facing bedrooms on the top two floors have small balconies. Studio rooms boast sitting areas and sofa beds. All rooms have en suite bathrooms (a few singles have showers only); refurbishment, however, is still needed in some. Not much public space is designated for relaxation, except the in-house pub or the cosy basement wine bar/bistro. Children up to 12 stay free in parents' room. No dogs. County Hotels. *Rooms 96. Gym, sauna. Access, Amex, Diners, Visa.*

SW6   Nosh Brothers   £65

Tel & Fax 0171-736 7311   Map 17 B5   **R**
773 Fulham Road SW6 5HA

Good neighbourhood ground-floor and basement restaurant serving a daily-changing menu of well-cooked, brasserie-style food. Decor is on the designer-scruffy side, and the lights get dimmer as the place comes to life after about 9.30. Vichyssoise or ceviche of monkfish might be followed by skate with something or steak and chips. Chargrilled meats are a speciality. Short, but well-balanced wine list which travels the world. Laid-back, friendly and occasionally quirky service. Booking advisable. *Seats 60. Private Room 55. D only 7.30-11. Closed Sun, Bank Holidays & Christmas week. Access, Amex, Diners, Visa.*

W6   Novotel   64%   £116

Tel 0181-741 1555 Fax 0181-741 2120   Map 17 B4   **H**
1 Shortlands Hammersmith W6 8DR

Large modern hotel, alongside (though not accessible from) Hammersmith flyover. The open-plan public areas (which can become overcrowded) include an in-house pub – The Frog & Bulldog – and an all-day restaurant. Most of the modestly-furnished bedrooms have been refurbished to a comfortable standard; work on those remaining should be completed by the time this guide goes to press. All have satellite TV, direct-dial phone, mini-bar and en-suite bathrooms with tub and shower. Extensive conference facilities range from small suites on the second floor to a ground-floor hall seating 900 delegates. Bedrooms on two floors are reserved for non-smokers. Children up to 16 stay free in parents' room. *Rooms 635. Access, Amex, Diners, Visa.*

SW7   Number Sixteen   £130

Tel 0171-589 5232 Fax 0171-584 8615   Map 19 B5   **PH**
16 Sumner Place South Kensington SW7 3EG

In a terrace of white-painted early-Victorian houses, this bijou residence offers style, seclusion and efficient service (telephone messages get through). There's a comfortable informality about the drawing room, and the conservatory opens on to a walled garden. Drinks are taken from an honour bar in the library or from mini-bars in the bedrooms, which are smartly furnished with a combination of antiques and traditional pieces. A tea and coffee service is available throughout the day. Rate includes Continental breakfast in rooms. No children under 12. No dogs. *Rooms 36. Garden. Access, Amex, Diners, Visa.*

W1   Nusa Dua   £35

Tel & Fax 0171-437 3559   Map 18 D2   **R**
11-12 Dean Street Soho W1V 5AH

Indonesian food is a delightful mixture of tastes and aromas involving sweet, pungent, hot and spicy. Chicken, beef, prawn and beancurd satays, whole fish cooked in banana leaves, lamb chops with chili and sweet soya sauce, and mixed vegetables cooked in tamarind soup are just a few of the 70+ dishes on offer. The restaurant is on two levels, lighter at street level, more intimate below. Set meals provide good value, ranging from low-priced lunches to a rijsstafel (rice table) banquet. *Seats 65. L 12-2.30 D 6.30-11.30. Closed L Sat & Sun, 25 & 26 Dec. Set L from £4.95 Set D £13/£15. Access, Amex, Visa.*

W1   O'Conor Don–Ard-Rí Dining Room   NEW   £50

Tel 0171-935 9311   Map 18 C2   **R**
88 Marylebone Lane W1

On the first floor of a traditional Irish pub, a spacious dining room is augmenting the already popular trend of the pub-restaurant. The enthusiasm of the kitchen is noticeable throughout, from the home-made soda bread to the carefully chosen Irish cheeses. A short, weekly-changing, table d'hote menu offers three or four choices at each stage: perhaps hot buttered Donegal oysters; a soup of celery, Cashel Blue and walnuts or stuffed lamb's heart with excellent red cabbage, followed by sea trout with champ and snow peas, terrific Irish stew with pearl barley or roast stuffed suckling pig with spiced apple and a celeriac purée. Traditional desserts might include treacle tart with clotted cream, or baked apple with fresh custard. Charming, friendly service. *Seats 45. L 12-2.30 D 6-9.30. Closed L Sat, all Sun, Bank Holidays & 1 week Christmas. Set L £15 Set D £18. Access, Visa.*

NW1   Odette's   £65

Tel 0171-586 5486   Map 16 C3   **R**
130 Regents Park Road Primrose Hill NW1 8XL

Close to Primrose Hill, amid the bustle of Regents Park Road. The small main dining room is attractively decorated in green with gilded mirrors of all sizes covering the walls. At the back, a charming balcony room overlooks a conservatory. The handwritten menu, which changes daily, offers a mix of modern English and eclectic dishes: roasted tomato soup with basil croutons; red mullet and blood orange terrine in seaweed jelly; crab, avocado and apple filo wafer; roasted suckling pig with roasted potatoes and plum sauce; scallop and salmon cannelloni with parsley sauce. Desserts, no less interesting, are typified by fresh cheese mousse with cranberries and pine nut shortbread, white chocolate and muesli ice cream and blood orange and stem ginger jelly with saffron custard. Specialist Spanish cheeses. There's a wine bar in the basement (additionally open lunchtime Sat & Sun) where simpler dishes and a set lunch are also offered. The wine list, laid out by style, is easy to use, with the least expensive wines first. Many are under £20, some well under, and with helpful tasting notes accompanying, this is an enterprising and imaginative list. *Seats 60. Parties 30. Private Room 8. L 12.30-2.30 D 7-11. Closed L Sat, all Sun, 10 days Christmas. Set L £10. Access, Amex, Diners, Visa.*

W1   Odin's   £65

Tel 0171-935 7296   Map 18 C2   **R**
27 Devonshire Street W1N 1RJ

Traditionally appointed, almost club-like premises with a wealth of artwork on the walls, some of it (along with the menu) depicting founder Peter Langan. Dishes are a mix of familiar British and French classics. Starters include a fish soup with croutons and rouille, venison terrine with Cumberland sauce, home-made pork and sage sausages with herb mashed potatoes and hot salmon mousse in filo pastry with a shellfish sauce. Main dishes follow in much the same style, for example, roast duck with sage and onion stuffing and apple sauce, braised rabbit with grain mustard and fresh pasta, and pan-fried skate wing with tomato and ginger. Homely desserts include date and ginger pudding, almond slice with custard and creamed rice pudding. *Seats 60. Parties 10. L 12.30-2.30 D 7-11.30. Closed Sat, Sun, Bank Holidays. Set L & D £20.95/£22.95. Access, Amex, Diners, Visa.*

SW7   Ognisko Polskie   £55

Tel 0171-589 4635   Fax 0171-581 8416   Map 19 B4   **R**
55 Exhibition Road SW7 2PG

Gold is the dominant colour in the slightly faded grandeur of a hotel-style dining room in the Polish Hearth Club. Staff and most of the guests are Polish, and the walls are hung with portraits of notable Poles past and present. The menu is Polish plus Continental, portions more than robust, flavours bold but not without subtlety. Beetroot soup – a sparkling, brilliantly fresh-tasting consommé, comes with a herby veal sausage roll;

buckwheat blinis are topped with smoked salmon, cream and Sevruga caviar; ham knuckle, falling off the bone and beautifully succulent, is teamed with a splendid mustard sauce; cheesecake is a traditional baked version with sultanas. The main–course set lunch and dinner menu offers remarkable value. **Seats** 70. *Private Rooms 150/30. L 12.30-3 D 6.30-11. Closed Bank Holidays, 2/3 days Easter, 4 days Christmas. Set L & D from £7.50. Access, Amex, Diners, Visa.*

SW17   Oh'Boy Thai Restaurant   £40

Tel 0181-947 9760   Fax 0181-879 7867   Map 17 B6   **R**
843 Garratt Lane SW17 0PG

A neighbourhood Thai restaurant whose menu delivers authentic tastes and good–value Royal Thai set meals. Among the most popular dishes are seafood soup (for 2), minced pork and prawns in pastry cups, Thai beef salad, roast duck curry and Emerald chicken (fried spicy chicken with onion, chili and fresh basil leaves). **Seats** 45. *Parties 12. Private Room 15. D only 7-11. Set D £9.50/£15.50. Access, Amex, Diners, Visa.*

SW1   Olivo   £55

Tel 0171-730 2505   Map 19 C5   **R**
21 Eccleston Street SW1W 9LX

Modern Italian cooking with an emphasis on Sardinian dishes is offered at this friendly and relaxed restaurant in the heart of Victoria. Shorter menus at lunchtime, and a longer *carta* in the evening, with some dishes common to both. Try mallordeus sardi (pasta twists with sausages and tomato sauce), calf's liver with balsamic vinegar and peppers, chargrilled tuna with rocket, and beef escalope with a juniper berry sauce. Caprino, a soft Sardinian goat's cheese, is an alternative to desserts. **Seats** 43. *Parties 6. L 12-2.30 D 7-11. Closed L Sat, all Sun, Bank Holidays, 1 week end Aug. Set L £13.50/£15.50. Access, Amex, Visa.*

W11   192   ↑   £75

Tel 0171-229 0482   Map 16 B3   **R**
192 Kensington Park Road W11 2JF

Long popular with a young, cosmopolitan local crowd, 192 has, for the last couple of years, enjoyed even greater sucess with the skills of young Albert Clarke showing in every dish. His menus are modern European, unashamedly fashionable and changing on a daily basis. Caesar salad has become a great favourite, and among the 30 or so dishes offered on a typical day you might find roasted vegetables with gorgonzola, pan-fried scallops with spicy cabbage and soy butter, terrine of chicken, pancetta, asparagus and morels, herb-crusted skate with tomato sauce, calf's liver with beetroot, bacon and wild garlic, and roasted duck breast with pumpkin, ginger and coriander. Vegetables are as carefully cooked as everything else, and you mustn't miss one of the desserts – perhaps chocolate fudge cake with crème fraiche or apple and pear crumble with custard. There's a clever and sensibly priced wine list with a huge array (around 40 wines) on offer by the glass. Drink champagne between 5.30 and 7.30, when it's under £20 a bottle. You don't even have to stay for dinner, though we suggest you do! **Seats** 100. *Parties 8. L 12.30-3 (Sun to 3.30) D 7-11.30 (Sun to 11). Set L £9.50 (Sun £12.50). Access, Amex, Diners, Visa.*

SW5   Hotel 167   £75

Tel 0171-373 0672 Fax 0171-373 3360   Map 19 B5   **B**
167 Old Brompton Road SW5 0AN

A Victorian private house where each room has its own character, many of them with art deco inspiration. Big original modern pictures abound, but some period features also survive, including the black-and-white mosaic in the hall. Bedrooms are centrally heated and double glazed. Continental breakfast only. Unlicensed. No dogs. The hotel is located on the corner of Cresswell Gardens. **Rooms** 19. *Access, Amex, Diners, Visa.*

Consult the blue pages for summary tables and lists of recommended establishments.

W11   Orsino   £60

Tel 0171-221 3299   Map 17 B4   **R**
119 Portland Road London W11 4LN

A popular West London restaurant in the same stable as Orso and Joe Allen. The menu is laid out in similar style to Orso, with a similar regional modern Italian slant. The place differs in being smaller and instead of being in a basement it occupies the ground and first floor of an unusual wedge-shaped building. Black and white prints of old Italian scenes are hung on the rough pink walls while tables and chairs are in a multitude of Mediterranean hues. Parma ham with pears, calamari with tomato and red pepper sauce, splendid little pizzas and flat pasta with peas, asparagus and artichokes precede mainly grilled main courses. To finish there are cheeses, ices, always a mousse and the superb Tuscan speciality, Vin Santo (dessert wine) with dried almond biscuits. Booking is essential. *Seats 106. Parties 8. Private Room 32. Meals 12-10.45 (Sun to 9.45). Closed 25 Dec. Set L (till 6.30) £11.50/£13.50. No credit cards.*

WC2   Orso   £65

Tel 0171-240 5269   Fax 0171-497 2148   Map 20 A2   **R**
27 Wellington Street Covent Garden WC2E 7DA

A fashionable basement restaurant in Covent Garden whose walls are hung with arty black and white photographs. The menu is of Italian inspiration, with a contemporary slant. Chicken, white bean and spinach soup; grilled asparagus with salami and gorgonzola; super little pizzas with anchovies, black olives, onion and mozzarella; thin pasta with prawn, white wine, garlic, tomato and chili; and risotto with Fontina and escarole show the style. Chocolate cake with coffee zabaglione tempts among the desserts. *Seats 100. Parties 10. Meals 12-12. Closed 24 & 25 Dec. No credit cards.*

SW11   Osteria Antica Bologna   £45

Tel 0171-978 4771   Map 17 C6   **R**
23 Northcote Road SW11 1NG

Italian cooking – as different from a local trattoria as one can imagine – at kind prices in friendly, unpretentious surroundings that feature wood-covered walls and matching pottery jugs and vases. That's the Osteria formula, and it works extremely well. The menu is long and enticing, offering a range from all parts of Italy: assaggi dell'osteria (Bolognese tasting portions – the Italian version of tapas) are a fun way to start a meal, or can be combined into an excellent light meal. These range from olives stuffed with mortadella sausage and fried to grilled smoked cheese and radicchio, boiled octopus with rocket, olive oil and chilis, and Swiss chard leaves stuffed with millet, ricotta and thyme in a basil and tomato sauce. Other sections on the enticing menu are devoted to salads, pasta, middle dishes (capretto alle mandorle is a speciality – goat cooked with rich tomato and almond pesto) and desserts. Good-value Italian wines – hardly a bottle over £20. Special Easter menus. Free parking in side streets. In the same ownership as Del Buongustaio. *Seats 75. Parties 30. Meals 12-11 (Fri, Sat to 11.30, Sun 12.30-10.30). Set L (not Sun) £7.50. Closed 10 days Christmas/New Year. Access, Amex, Visa.*

NW1   Otafuku   £60

Tel 0171-482 2036   Map 16 C3   **R**
75 Parkway Camden Town NW1

Decor is simple and completely unpretentious with polished wooden tables and bentwood and rattan chairs. The menu is a comprehensive selection of familiar Japanese dishes with the emphasis on sashimi and sushi – there's a 30% discount on the latter on Tuesdays, Thursdays and Saturdays. Otafuku is the name of a celebrated Japanese lady. *Seats 40. D only 6.30-10.30. Closed Sun, Bank Holidays. Access, Amex, Diners, Visa.*

Set menu prices may not always include service or wine.

SW1   Overtons at St James's   £80

Tel 0171-839 3774 Fax 0171-839 4330   Map 18 D3   **R**
St James Street SW1A 1EF

Diners enter a club-like atmosphere, with pine panelling, framed prints and a long bar
which has its own menu. The main dining room beyond is arranged under a huge
skylight; blue and gold are the featured colours, incorporated in the carpet, chair seats and
pictures and shellfish motifs are cleverly woven into the carpet and cut into the glass
panels which divide traditional and modern. Nigel Davies' menu includes some
contemporary trends with the likes of seared scallops with a confit of plum tomatoes and
fennel or poached brill with a truffled bouillon of vegetables. Ragout of sole, scallops and
crayfish with saffron noodles and a crab and ginger sauce is considered a speciality, so too
chargrilled venison with a lentil and wild mushroom galette and a Cahors wine jus. Daily
specials (boiled gammon and parsley sauce on Tuesday, smoked haddock fishcakes on
Friday) and crème brulée or comforting nursery puddings such as steamed chocolate
sponge. The wine list (mostly French) is short in extent but long in quality. Some 20
bottles around £15. *Seats 52. Parties 8. Private Room 20. L 12.30-2.45 D 6.30-10.45.
Closed Sat, Sun, Bank Holidays, 10 days Christmas. Access, Amex, Diners, Visa.*

SW18   Le P'tit Normand   £50

Tel 0181-871 0233   Map 17 B6   **R**
185 Merton Road Southfields SW18 5EF

Cheerful *restaurant du quartier* with mock-rustic decor and good honest cooking in
traditional French regional style by chef-patron Philippe Herrard. The choice is quite
simple and straightforward, as shown by *moules marinière, magret de canard Vallée
d'Auge, pot-au-feu,* navarin of lamb and *boeuf bourguignon. Seats 35. Parties 20. Private
Rooms 15/25. L 12-1.30 D 7-10.30. Closed L Sat. Set L £9.95 (Sun £11.95). Access, Amex,
Diners, Visa.*

**We publish annually, so make sure you use the current edition
— it's well worth it!**

W8   La Paesana   £40

Tel 0171-229 4332   Map 18 A3   **R**
30 Uxbridge Street Notting Hill W8 7TA

Standard Italian fare in a lively Notting Hill restaurant behind the Coronet cinema. All
the antipasti and pastas are available as either starters or main courses. Spaghetti with
seafood cooked in a paper bag, home-made lasagne and various ways with veal (alla cindy
is with wine sauce and orange segments). The ground floor has been converted into
a wine bar. *Seats 60. Parties 20. Private Room 30. L 12-2.45 D 6.30-11.45. Closed Sun.
Access, Amex, Diners, Visa.*

WC2   Le Palais du Jardin   £60

Tel 0171-379 5353   Fax 0171-379 1846   Map 21 B2   **R**
136 Long Acre London WC2E 9AD

Changes in the cooking at this popular brasserie/oyster bar have increased its appeal if
futile attempts to get a table on a summer evening are anything to go by. Lighter dishes
have replaced the cuisine grand'mére style and might now include timbale de poissons,
terrine of confit of duck or moules marinière to start. Fillet of beef with béarnaise sauce,
loin of lamb in a herb crust or a much-enjoyed fricassee of chicken and lobster with
a coriander jus as main courses. An excellent range of fruits de mer remains a serious
bargain, eg £4.50 for half a dozen oysters! A list of simple puddings is headed by an
assiette gourmande, which includes both a mini-chocolate soufflé and a tarte tatin.
Booking is necessary at peak times, but an extension to the dining-room is nearing
completion as we go to press. *Seats 220. Parties 35. Private Room 22. Meals 12-12 (Sun to
10.50). Closed 25 & 26 Dec. Access, Amex, Diners, Visa.*

W1   Panda Si Chuen   ★   £50

Tel 0171-437 2069   Map 21 A2   **R**
56 Old Compton Street W1V 5PA

Just outside the traditional heart of Chinatown, Panda Si Chuen is one of London's best
Chinese restaurants. The cooking of Szechuan province is renowned for its generally
spicy nature and here it has reached an exalted level which produces dishes of often
exquisite flavour. Grilled dumplings to begin burst with succulent meats and juices while
Szechuan tea-smoked duck (a speciality) is imbued with a distinct and delicious flavour
reminiscent of Lapsang Souchong. Deep-fried oysters are large, with a moist, plump
inside and crisp outside, kung-po chicken has the fieriness of chili and the sweet
crunchiness of cashew nuts. Among the 'variety meats dishes' section are shredded pork
with eggplant in sea-spiced sauce, home-style double-cooked pork and fried beef with
seasonal vegetables. Staff are helpful, polite and friendly. *Seats 63. Parties 18. Private
Room 13. Meals 12-11.30. Closed Sun, Bank Holidays. Access, Amex, Diners, Visa.*

W1   The Park Lane Hotel   77%   £249

Tel 0171-499 6321   Fax 0171-499 1965   Map 18 C3   **H**
Piccadilly W1Y 8BX

Built in 1927, the hotel has some
distinctive art deco features, although
the feel throughout the public rooms
and bedrooms is very traditional. The
Palm Court Lounge, where afternoon
teas and 24hr snacks are served, is
brightened by a magnificent vaulted
ceiling with arched art deco stained
glass. Standard bedrooms are of a good
size but tend to look out on the dark
inside courtyard. All rooms have
double-glazing, multi-channel TV,
mini-bars and bathrobes. The best
rooms are 53 suites (half of which are
air-conditioned) looking out either on to the central court or Green Park and benefiting
from private sitting-rooms and more luxurious bathrooms. 24hr room service. Large-scale
banqueting suites (including an art deco ballroom) for up to 600; conference facilities for
up to 500. Private parking for 180 cars is provided in a covered garage opposite the main
entrance. *Rooms 307. Gym, sun beds, beauty & hair salons, brasserie noon-11pm, business
centre, news/kiosk, shop, garage. Access, Amex, Diners, Visa.*

W2   Parkwood Hotel   £55

Tel 0171-402 2241   Fax 0171-402 1574   Map 18 C3   **B**
4 Stanhope Place W2 2HB

Bed and breakfast town house in a quiet position handy for Oxford Street and the West
End. Reception doubles up as a small lounge which is suitable for meeting friends.
Modestly furnished bedrooms vary in size, a few being very small. Private bathrooms all
have tubs, mostly with hand-held shower attachments. Four rooms on the top floor share
a bathroom. All rooms have TVs and hairdryers. The hotel is particularly proud of its
breakfasts, which are served in a cosy, well-decorated basement. Unlicensed. No dogs.
Rooms 18. Access, Visa.

N1   Pasha   £35

Tel 0171-226 1454   Fax 0171-359 1127   Map 16 D3   **R**
301 Upper Street N1 2 TU

A Turkish restaurant with a bright, attractive decor and friendly staff. The menu offers
carefully cooked dishes with a good selection of vegetarian starter options, multiple meze
dishes and value-for-money set menus. *Seats 80. Parties 20. L 12-3 D 6-12. Closed 25
& 26 Dec, 1 Jan. Set L £5.95/£9.95/£14.95 Set D £5.95 (before 8pm)/£9.95/£14.95.
Access, Amex, Visa.*

Set menu prices may not always include service or wine.

EC1   The Peasant   £50

Tel 0171-336 7726   Map 16 D3   **R**
240 St John Street EC1V 4PH

The setting is a converted Victorian gin palace dating from 1890. Food is very much its raison d'etre nowadays and booking is essential. The decor has been revamped but is still quite basic with plain wooden tables, darkwood bench seating and a mix of old-fashioned dining chairs. John Pountney is the chef here now and very good he is too. The menu has lost some of its Italian influences, a more varied selection has been introduced. The food still comes with excellent crusty rustic bread with extra virgin olive oil dip and many of the dishes are served in huge china bowls. Starters could be vine tomato, Jersey royal and rosemary soup; fried halloumi with a lemon and onion relish; Thai pork meatballs with a peanut and coriander sauce and fried polenta with marinated aubergines, mushrooms, olives and artichokes. For a main course the choice ranges from grilled skewers of monkfish with vine leaves and tabouleh to calf's liver with potatoes, artichokes and a lime and mint butter; skewered lamb with a vine tomato, cos, feta and mint salad and spaghettini with anchovies, tomato, chili and black olives. Equally desirable and well made are the desserts, which include lemon tart, water melon and passion fruit with Greek yoghurt, dark chocolate honey terrine with strawberry coulis and vanilla and caramel ice cream with biscotti. Also on offer is a prime British cheese served with oatcakes and celery. They offer a short, carefully chosen wine list and real ales. *Seats 80. Parties 30. L 12.30-2.30 D 6.30-11. Closed L Sat, all Sun & Bank Holidays, 10 days Christmas. Access, Amex, Visa.*

SW7   Pelham Hotel   76%   £194

Tel 0171-589 8288   Fax 0171-584 8444   Map 19 B5   **HR**
15 Cromwell Place South Kensington SW7 2LA

Close to the South Kensington museums and Knightsbridge Kit and Tim Kemp's hotel has a smart, white-painted porticoed exterior. Inside they have created the ambiance of a charming and very elegant English country house with public rooms that are furnished with great thought to design and comfort. The drawing room has 18th century pine panelling together with a crystal chandelier, oil paintings, elaborate flower arrangements and fine furniture. There's also a smoking room done out as a Victorian-style snuggery, its mahogany panelling providing it with a club-like atmosphere. Bedrooms are splendid – a blend of beautiful chintzes, antiques and fine ornaments creating a very superior home from home. Practicalities are not forgotten, either, with all rooms having a useful second telephone by the desk and full air-conditioning. Rooms facing South Kensington tube and the traffic are obviously noisier than those at the rear. Excellent bathrooms. Under the same ownership as Durley House and Dorset Square hotels (see entries). Valet service and 24hr room service. Guests have free use of the garden and outdoor swimming pool of the hotel's administrative building opposite. *Rooms 41. Access, Amex, Visa.*

Kemps   £50

Pleasant basement restaurant and bar, with wooden floor, panelling, yellow and blue square motif fabrics, and lots of attractive pictures. The food is tasty and simple, being both contemporary and good value, with wines equally fairly priced. Starters feature fresh mussels with tagliatelle cooked in saffron wine, chicken livers layered with crisp potato, mushrooms and pistachio nuts and a salad of crab claws with a poached egg and dandelion leaves. Follow with baked cod fillet topped with an olive crust served with capered mash potato and saffron roast duckling with root vegetables and fried leaves, roast pork with red cabbage and lemon thyme or, for vegetarians, ravioli of spinach and ricotta with tomato and basil cream. For dessert the choice could be an orange and walnut tartlet with custard, or deep-fried pineapple with home-made pineapple ice cream. Fresh baguette bread, sliced on arrival, is served with unsalted butter. Also open for breakfast and afternoon tea. *Seats 30. Parties 15. L 12-2.30 D 6-10.30. Closed L Sun & Bank Holidays, all Sat, 25 & 26 Dec. Set L £8.95/£12.40 Set D £17.50.*

W2   Pembridge Court Hotel   66%   £115

Tel 0171-229 9977   Fax 0171-727 4982   Map 18 A3   **H**
34 Pembridge Gardens Notting Hill W2 4DX

An elegant 19th-century town house away from the bustle of Notting Hill Gate and close to Portobello market. Victorian bric-a-brac tastefully decorates both public rooms and bedrooms. Manageress Valerie Gilliat pampers her guests, generating an atmosphere of home from home. Bedrooms, all tastefully furnished, range from small singles with showers to the spacious and luxurious air-conditioned Holland Park Room. Modern amenities are not neglected with all bedrooms having TV and direct-dial phones. Children up to 10 stay free in parents' room. Good breakfasts. The two private parking places must be reserved. *Rooms 20. Access, Amex, Diners, Visa.*

SE1   People's Palace   NEW   £70

Tel 0171-928 9999   Fax 0171-928 2355   Map 20 A3   **R**
Level 3 Royal Festival Hall South Bank SE1 8XX

A long, high-ceilinged room with an expansive window frontage on level 3 within the Royal Festival Hall is the new venture of restaurateur David Levin, his son Joseph and chef Gary Rhodes, who actually cooks on site several days a week. On offer is a concise, weekly-changing à la carte and a two- or three-course set menu, all served on their own personalised plates. The starters range from potato, smoked bacon and parsley soup and potted salmon with garlic toasts to a delicious flaky smoked haddock fishcake on a light tomato and herb concassé. Main courses offer an open roast beef salad sandwich (three thick slices of rare beef on a bed of watercress), baked salmon and new potatoes mashed with sour cream on a bed of puréed spinach and an accordingly-priced vegetarian main choice of gruyère, leek and onion flan. The puddings are worth saving room for: steamed raspberry jam sponge was light and served with real custard, apple and almond tart came encased in buttery pastry with clotted cream, and there is always a cheese of the day. Everything on the wine list is available by the glass, carafe or bottle, thus they offer over 80 wines by the glass. *Seats 180. Parties 16. L 12-3 D 5.30-11. Set L & D £10.50/£13.50. Closed 25 Dec. Access, Amex, Diners, Visa.*

SW7   Periquito Queen's Gate   £73

Tel 0171-370 6111   Fax 0171-370 0932   Map 19 B5   **B**
68-69 Queen's Gate SW7 5JT

Standing on the corner of Cromwell Road and Queen's Gate, the hotel is characterised by a bright and colourful decor. Some bedrooms are smallish but all are attractively decorated, and eight of the small singles have been knocked into four twins. First-floor rooms are non-smoking. *Rooms 61. Access, Amex, Diners, Visa.*

NW5   Le Petit Prince   £30

Tel 0171-267 0752   Map 16 C2   **R**
5 Holmes Road Kentish Town NW5 3AA

Decor is inspired by St Exupéry's Le Petit Prince and the atmosphere is often fittingly exuberant. Couscous is the main offering (meat, chicken, fish or vegetarian), along with salady starters, and fried plantain with peanut sauce. The mixed platter is a selection of starters also available as a main course. Drink Algerian red wine or Normandy cider. Theatre evenings 7-9 Sun-Wed. *Seats 60. Private Room 30. L 12-3 D 7-12. Closed L Sun, 1 week Christmas. No credit cards.*

W8   Phoenicia   £60

Tel 0171-937 0120   Fax 0171-937 7668   Map 19 A4   **R**
11-13 Abingdon Road Kensington W8 6AH

A relaxed and civilised, family-run Lebanese restaurant just off Kensington High Street. Hot and cold hors d'oeuvre, from several ways with aubergine, stuffed vine leaves, goat's cheese in thyme and smoked cod's roe to grilled quails and spicy sausage, precede charcoal-grilled main courses, with delicious home-made sweets to finish. Besides the à la carte there are several set menus, including vegetarian options, and a good-value lunchtime buffet available Monday to Saturday 12.15-2.30 (30 dishes, eat as much as you like). Chateau Musar and the Lebanese national drink arak go down well with this excellent food. *Seats 100. Private Room 50. Meals 12-11.45 (Buffet L 12.15-2.30). Closed 24 & 25 Dec. Set L £9.95 Set D £15.30 to £28.30. Access, Amex, Diners, Visa.*

SW11   Phuket   £60

Tel 0171-223 5924   Map 17 C5   **R**
246 Battersea Park Road SW11 3BP

A local Thai restaurant which has established itself as a favourite with the residents of
Battersea and Clapham. Clever use of mirrors opens up a rather long and narrow room.
The Eastern feel is preserved with tall tropical plants and slow-spinning ceiling fans. Start
with prawns in a blanket, a house speciality, or one of the many tom yum soups. Follow
with crispy pomfret with mild chilis or a mushroom sauce or a yum salad. Various red
and green curries are offered – and their heats can be adjusted on request. The difficult
task of balancing strong Thai flavours is achieved with precision and care. *Seats 60.*
D only 6-11.30. Closed 4 days Christmas. Set D £12.50. Access, Amex, Visa.

W1   Pied à Terre   ★★   £110

Tel 0171-636 1178   Map 18 D2   **R**
34 Charlotte Street W1P 1HJ

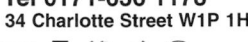

Richard Neat is not yet 30, but he has
a wealth of experience that includes spells
with Joël Robuchon, Raymond Blanc and
Marco Pierre White. His cooking is
among the most original and exciting in
London, full of confidence and technically
superb. Snails with morels, girolles,
asparagus and garlic purée, deep-fried crab
with smoked salmon sauce and roasted
scallops with Jerusalem artichokes are
terrific starters, heralding even greater
pleasures among the main events: John
Dory fillets and galette potatoes with peas
in a foie gras sauce has already become a classic, and there are some fine offal dishes – veal
sweetbreads and kidneys with roasted parsips; trotter and pig's head with celeriac purée
– along with seasonal game and always vegetarian options. The sweets are every bit as
good as the rest, whether a simple grapefruit parfait or a luscious dark bitter chocolate pavé
with a coffee and black cherry sorbet. There's a limited selection of wines under £20 on
the list, which leans heavily towards France, though the New World does feature, so too
the odd red from Italy and Spain. Surprisingly perhaps there are 15 house wines, as well
as 15 "bottles of the best" which the French describe as *derrière les fagots*. The room is
cool and modern, its walls hung with Pop Art prints by Warhol and Lichtenstein. Service
by partner David Moore and his young team is knowledgeable and stylish. *Seats 36.*
Parties 10. Private Room 12. L 12.15-2.15 D 7-10.30. Closed L Sat, all Sun, Bank Holidays,
last 2 weeks Aug, last week Dec, first week Jan. Set L from £16.50 Set D from £33. Access,
Amex, Diners, Visa.

SW3   Poissonnerie de l'Avenue   £95

Tel 0171-589 2457   Fax 0171-581 3360   Map 19 B5   **R**
82 Sloane Avenue SW3 3DZ

This wood-panelled restaurant has now been feeding the fish-eaters of South Kensington
for 30 years and has recently acquired a modern, lighter look. Expert handling of good
ingredients produces traditional dishes and also some more contemporary offerings: crab
in pastry on a bed of spinach, deep-fried devilled anchovies, salmon fishcakes, turbot
braised with a delicious white wine sauce or grilled with hollandaise. Friendly, attentive
service. *Seats 100. Parties 10. Private Room 22. L 12-3 D 7-11.30. Closed Sun, Bank*
Holidays, 10 days Christmas. Set L £16.50. Access, Amex, Diners, Visa.

Consult the blue pages for summary tables and lists of
recommended establishments.

SW1   Pomegranates   £80

Tel 0171-828 6560   Fax 0171-828 2037   Map 19 D5   **R**
94 Grosvenor Road Pimlico SW1V 3LE

Patrick Gwynn-Jones, for more than 20 years the amiable chef-patron of this popular basement restaurant by Dolphin Square and the Thames, presents menus of literally world-wide inspiration. Gravad lax, Danish pickled herrings, Welsh salt duck, braised oxtail and mash, Mauritian chili prawns and West Indian curried goat are among the specialities, and many diners don't even try to resist the home-made honey and cognac ice cream. *Seats 50. Parties 14. Private Room 12. L 12.30-2.15 D 7-11.15. Closed L Sat, all Sun, Bank Holidays. Set L £9.95/£12.95 Set D £13.95/£16.95. Access, Amex, Diners, Visa.*

W11   La Pomme d'Amour   £50

Tel 0171-229 8532   Map 17 B4   **R**
128 Holland Park Avenue W11 4VE

Good-value neighbourhood restaurant with an airy conservatory and a classic French menu. To begin perhaps soupe de poissons, mousse of sole with chives or a Provençal vegetable terrine. Salmon with béarnaise sauce, roast venison with beetroot sauce and a perfectly-cooked breast of duck with an orange and ginger sauce are possible main courses. Simple desserts are presented with equal care. Accurate cooking, but flavours lack that extra sense of adventure. Mostly French wines, with many bottles under £20. *Seats 62. Private Room 40. L 12.30-2.30 D 7-10.45. Closed L Sat, all Sun, Bank Holidays, 3 days Christmas. Set L £10.75 Set D £14.50/£16.75. Access, Amex, Diners, Visa.*

SE1   Le Pont de la Tour   ↑   £95

Tel 0171-403 8403   Fax 0171-403 0267   Map 17 D4   **R**
Butlers Wharf Building 36D Shad Thames Butlers Wharf SE1

Part of Sir Terence Conran's 'Gastrodrome' in a beautiful setting on the south bank of the Thames right by Tower Bridge and overlooking St Katharine's Dock across the water. In fine weather the large canopied terrace allows for alfresco dining with a very Continental air. Lunch is fixed-price with half a dozen or so starters and main dishes whilst in the evening a slightly more extensive à la carte applies, plus a pre- and post-theatre menu at £19.50 for three courses. Dishes are, as befits the cool, stylish elegance of the setting, very fashionable, with strong Mediterranean influences. Twice-cooked cheese soufflé with mustard and chives or wild mushroom tart with rocket and parmesan could precede sauté of scallops with grilled plum tomatoes and gremolata, grilled duck breast with confit of red cabbage or persillade of calf's liver with peppercorn sauce. Vegetables and potatoes are priced separately. Desserts are superb – steamed ginger sponge pudding or a stunning blueberry and vanilla millefeuille. An exceptional wine list with exceptional names at exceptional prices, though to be fair, there is plenty of choice under £20 as well – those on the house selection are accompanied by tasting notes. If you like what you drink here, all wines are available for sale and delivery at retail prices. Excellent espresso and chocolate coffee beans round off a splendid meal served by on-the-ball staff. In addition to the main restaurant there is a less formal bar and grill open noon to midnight every day; plateau de fruits de mer is the speciality there. Brunches on Saturday (in the bar) and Sunday are very popular. Park at the end of Curlew Street on the riverfront. *Seats 105. Parties 9. Private Room 22. L 12-3 D 6-11.30. Closed L Sat, Good Friday & 5 days Christmas. Set L £26.50. Access, Amex, Diners, Visa.*

W2   Poons   £55

Tel 0171-792 2884   Map 18 A3   **R**
Unit 205 Whiteleys Queensway W2 4YN

A Chinese restaurant in the third-floor food court, with cool, black and white decor. There's a long and varied main menu, and a large range of dim sum, including steamed buns, pot rice and noodle dishes, is served between noon and 4pm (4.45 weekends). *Seats 100. Meals 12-11 (Sun to 10.45). Closed a few days at Christmas. Set meals from £15 for 2. Access, Amex, Diners, Visa.*

WC1   Poons   £55

Tel 0171-580 1188   Map 18 D1   **R**
50 Woburn Place Russell Square WC1H 0JZ

One of the larger of the Poon family's restaurants. This one has well-spaced tables and a decor that owes much to the 70s. The cuisine is mostly that of Canton and Peking. The menu selection is mainly familiar though there are one or two unusual items such as wind-dried duck, chicken pieces sandwiched with melon, steamed scallops topped with minced prawns and sea bass steamed with preserved mandarin peel. Roast suckling pig is one dish that needs to be ordered in advance. *Seats 100. L 12-3 D 5.30-11.30 Closed 4 days Christmas. Set meals from £9. Access, Amex, Diners, Visa.*

WC2   Poons   £30

Tel 0171-437 1528   Map 21 A2   **R**
4 Leicester Street WC2H 7BL

Unsophisticated, wholesome, mainly Cantonese food served swiftly in simple surroundings spread over three floors. Wind-dried meats and steamed chicken with Chinese sausage are specialities. Original rice hot pot and noodle soup dishes make for inexpensive eating out. *Seats 110. Parties 12. Meals 12-11.30. Closed a few days at Christmas. Set meals from £13 for 2. Access, Amex, Visa.*

Consult the blue pages for summary tables and lists of recommended establishments.

WC2   Poons   £30

Tel 0171-437 4549   Map 21 A2   **R**
27 Lisle Street WC2H 7BA

The decor at William Poons's expanded café plays third fiddle to the food and the rock-bottom prices. Barbecued and wind-dried food is the speciality, covering duck, pork, sausages and bacon, and there's a big choice of composite rice and noodle dishes. *Seats 50. Private Room 25. Meals 12-11.30. Closed 4 days Christmas. No credit cards.*

EC3   Poons in the City   £50

Tel 0171-626 0126   Fax 0171-626 0526   Map 20 D2   **R**
Minster Pavement 2 Minster Court Mincing Lane EC3R 7PP

Ⅴ

An excellent Chinese restaurant in the Poons group, located below the stunning neo-gothic Minster Court, and offering classic Cantonese cooking in spacious, elegant surroundings. Crispy squid, scallops or soft-shell crab, chicken or beef satay and Poons' renowned wind-dried bacon are among the starters, while main courses include some notable duck dishes – Cantonese roast, fillet in plum sauce, tropical (with ginger and pineapple), Kung Po in a hot, spicy sauce, crispy aromatic and the three-course Kam Ling special (crispy skin with pancakes, soup, stir-fried meat). Also plenty of bean curd and vegetable dishes, plus dim sum, and a pavement menu in summer. At lunchtime half the restaurant is given over to a 'fast food' menu. *Seats 200. Parties 12. Private Room 60. Meals 11.30am-10.30pm. Closed Sat, Sun & 24-27 Dec. Set L from £6.20 (fast food) Set D £20.80. Access, Amex, Diners, Visa.*

W11   Portobello Hotel   60%   £120

Tel 0171-727 2777   Fax 0171-792 9641   Map 18 A3   **H**
22 Stanley Gardens Notting Hill W11 2NG

Two six-floor houses in an 1850 terrace near Portobello antiques market converted into a unique hotel decorated in an eclectic mix of styles. There are singles, doubles, twins and suites, plus some compact cabins. The 24hr bar/restaurant in the basement caters admirably for those guests with nocturnal life styles. Guests have membership of a nearby health club (daily fee). *Rooms 24. Access, Amex, Diners, Visa.*

Set menu prices may not always include service or wine.

SW1   La Poule au Pot   £55

Tel 0171-730 7763   Fax 0171-259 9651   Map 19 C5   **R**
231 Ebury Street Victoria SW1W 8UT

In a suitably rustic setting the restaurant specialises in good grandmère-style cooking. The menu offers a familiar choice, with starters such as cheese or onion quiche, fish mousse, French onion soup and snails in garlic butter. For a main course there's skate in black butter, salmon with sorrel or hollandaise, guinea fowl with apples and calvados, leg of lamb with flageolets, goose cassoulet and of course poule au pot. A menu of enjoyable French classics served with charm. *Seats 72. Parties 12. L 12.30-2.30 D 7-11.15 (Sun to 10.30). Closed 24-26 Dec, 1 Jan. Set L £12.95 (Sat £10.95 for 2 courses). Access, Amex, Diners, Visa.*

Set menu prices may not always include service or wine.

WC1   President Hotel   £68

Tel 0171-837 8844   Fax 0171-837 4653   Map 18 D2   **B**
Russell Square Bloomsbury WC1N 1DB

Close to the British Museum, this large hotel on the corner of Guilford Street and Russell Square opened in 1962. It caters mainly for tour parties and delegates – whose conferences take place at neighbouring sister hotels. All bedrooms have en-suite bathrooms with tubs and showers over, also TVs, direct-dial phones, trouser presses and tea and coffee-making facilities. Underground (pay) car park. *Rooms 447. Coffee shop (10am-2am). Access, Amex, Diners, Visa.*

SW5   La Primula   £55

Tel 0171-370 5958   Map 19 A5   **R**
12 Kenway Road SW5 ORR

In a part of the world filled mainly with fast-food and take-away restaurants, La Primula is a notable exception. Straight-down-the-line Italian cooking is the order of the day, and there's a friendly feel about the cream-coloured, print-hung room with seat-height mirrors that let you see yourself to infinity. Try pasta with spinach and ricotta cheese, risotto with mushroom sauce, liver veneziana, beef carpaccio, and chicken with cream and tarragon sauce. *Seats 40. Parties 30. Private Room 30. L 12-2 D 6-11. Set L £8.50/£14.50 Set D £14.50. Closed L Sat & Sun, a few days Easter, Christmas. Access, Amex, Visa.*

SW7   Pun   £50

Tel 0171-225 1609   Fax 0171-584 0320   Map 19 B5   **R**
53 Old Brompton Road South Kensington SW7 3JS

More comfortable, more Westernised and more expensive than its Soho compatriots, Danny Pun's restaurant is also a much friendlier place than some of those. The food's pretty good, too, and from a reasonably wide-ranging menu you could choose Peking ravioli in hot red pepper sauce, stuffed crab claws, sea bass soup with coriander, prawns done one of a dozen ways, lemon chicken or baked pork ribs with Szechuan peppercorn salt. Steamed fish and crispy duck are specialities. *Seats 70. Parties 20. Private Room 28. L 12-2.45 D 6-11.30 Meals Sat & Sun 12-11.30. Closed 25 & 26 Dec. Set L & D £13.80 & £18. Access, Amex, Diners, Visa.*

NW3   Qinggis   £55

Tel 0171-586 4251   Map 16 C2   **R**
30 Englands Lane Belsize Park NW3 4UE

Of the two floors that comprise this Chinese restaurant, the basement is the larger and busier, with views up to street level for tables at the front. The menu is a round-up of familiar Chinese regional dishes and a feature is the selection of seafood ranging from baked crabs and lobsters to various ways with Dover sole. *Seats 75. Parties 20. Private Room 15. L 12-2.30 D 6-11.15. Closed 25-26 Dec. Set meals from £14.90. Access, Amex, Visa.*

SW1   Quaglino's   £70

Tel 0171-930 6767   Fax 0171-836 2866   Map 18 D3   **R**
16 Bury Street St James's SW1Y 6AL

Three years into its renaissance, Sir Terence Conran's Quaglino's is still one of London's
most fashionable dining destinations. After entering through a distinctive glass frontage on
Bury Street (just south of Jermyn Street), you descend down a curving stone staircase to
a gallery level where there's an informal antipasti bar area (no bookings, live music Fri
& Sat nights) serving snacks all day and a private room to one side. This private dining
room overlooks the cavernous dining area one floor below, whose ceiling is cleverly lit
by a computer-controlled mock skylighting system three floors above. With such an
enormous dining area (over 300 seats), the volume of diners' incessant chatter often rises
to an ear-tiring level – the only serious criticism that one can level at the place (but the
owners can hardly be held responsible for the decibel level!). High columns within the
dining area are indiviudally painted and the central dividing structure always features
a glorious floral display. In contrast, at the other end of the room, is an equally sensational
display of shellfish on a mirrored crustacean altar (try the dressed crab with mirin and
soy). Chef Martin Webb and his team cope admirably with the demanding hordes,
serving up both traditional and more modern, adventurous dishes. A prix-fixe menu at
lunch and pre-theatre (5.30-6.30) might offer spinach and parmesan tart followed by
shoulder of pork with crackling and apple sauce or grilled skate with sauce gribiche.
A recent à la carte encompassed bresaola with poached egg and mustard, caviar with
crème fraiche and melba toast, grilled bream with fennel confit, carpaccio of beef, spiced
lamb with roast onions, and prune parfait, crème brulée, or orange tart to finish.
A shortish (though not short on quality) and inexpensive list here, with several wines
available by the glass or by the pot. *Seats 338, Bar 90. Parties 10. Private Room 40. L 12-3
D 5.30-12 (Fri, Sat to 1am, Sun to 11). Closed 3 days Christmas. Set L & pre-theatre
D £12.95. Access, Amex, Diners, Visa.*

EC1   Quality Chop House   £45

Tel 0171-837 5093   Map 16 C3   **R**
94 Farringdon Road EC1R 3EA

Chef-proprietor Charles Fontaine reopened a Victorian chop house in 1990 with the aim
of providing straightforward, no-nonsense food in friendly, informal surroundings. Much
of the original atmosphere survives, and period features include the high-backed
mahogany booths and the embossed wallpaper. Value for money is a watchword
throughout the menu, which combines traditional English food (egg, bacon and chips,
corned beef hash, lamb chop, grilled spring chicken) with dishes of a wider provenance
such as fish soup and rouille, Caesar salad, bang bang chicken, and Toulouse sausages with
mash and onion gravy. A number of dishes are available as starter or main course. Jugs of
Bloody Mary and Bucks Fizz head the Sunday brunch menu. *Seats 48. Parties 6. L 12-3
(Sun till 4) D 6.30-11.30 (Sun from 7). Closed L Sat, L Bank Holidays, 24 Dec-3 Jan.
No credit cards.*

NW2   Quincy's   £60

Tel 0171-794 8499   Map 16 B2   **R**
675 Finchley Road NW2 2JP

A gem of a local restaurant with a friendly, homely ambience. The shortish menu changes
monthly and features imaginative, well-prepared dishes that are not too complex. Begin
with leek ravioli in mustard broth, smoked haddock mousse or cheddar cheese soufflé
with a roast onion salad and continue with mushroom stroganoff with saffron risotto,
beef fillet with a horseradish crust and Madeira sauce or lamb with mint couscous and
sun-dried tomato butter. *Seats 30. Parties 8. Private Room 14. D only 7-11. Closed Sun
& Mon, 1 week Christmas. Set D £25. Access, Amex, Visa.*

Many hotels offer reduced rates for weekend or out-of-season
bookings. Always ask about special deals.

W1   Radisson SAS Portman Hotel   77%   £225

Tel 0171-208 6000   Fax 0171-208 6001   Map 18 C2   **H**
22 Portman Square W1H 9FL

Comfortable modern hotel within easy reach of Oxford Street and the West End. An open-plan ground floor includes a plush, club-style restaurant with an international menu. The recently refurbished bedrooms have been decorated on four distinct themes – British, Oriental, Scandinavian or "classic", though they all offer modern amenities with satellite (in seven languages) TV including an automatic billing system. Business rooms are larger and provide work space, complimentary tea and coffee, plus an evening turn-down service. Tiled, en-suite bathrooms include power showers over the baths. The first floor is dedicated to a series of plush conference and banqueting suites (380/420). The intimate library suite is particularly popular for business lunches. 24hr room service. Underground NCP car park with direct access to the hotel. A check-in service is provided for SAS or British Midland passengers. *Rooms 272. Coffee shop (11am-11pm). Access, Amex, Diners, Visa.*

SW7   Radisson Vanderbilt   62%   £139

Tel 0171-589 2424   Fax 0171-225 2293   Map 19 B5   **H**
68-86 Cromwell Road London SW7 5BT

A Grade II listed building comprising ten linked town houses on busy Cromwell Road houses Radisson Edwardian's Vanderbilt, with its classical early Victorian frontage. Inside, the period atmosphere is retained with frescoed ceilings (notably in the Georgian Bar) and heavy floral drapes. *Rooms include some Executive singles. Rooms 223. Access, Amex, Diners, Visa.*

NW11   Raffles Place   £50

Tel 0181-458 9273   Map 16 B2   **R**
634 Finchley Road Golders Green NW11 7RR

Colourful, abstract artwork now decorates the walls of this smart little restaurant (previously called Tiger Under the Table) in a parade of shops in the centre of Golders Green. Recently revamped, it also now features a new menu. The style remains Singaporean but the food is now even more enjoyable than it was previously. Dishes are lightly cooked and have a freshness attributable to the use of good-quality herbs and spices. Begin with *teochew* crispy rolls – minced prawn, pork and chestnut in a thin, crispy soya bean crepe, spare ribs or soft-shell crabs in spicy sea-salt and chili pepper and follow with wok-grilled red snapper with a chili and shrimp paste sauce, or *nonya* beef tempra (thin slices of fillet steak stir-fried with lime juice, lemon grass, chili and onions). Crispy Oriental duck comes with either a plum sauce or a really delicious orange sauce laced with Shao Shing wine. Accompaniments are good too, particularly *chye tow kway* – a savoury radish cake, fried with pickled turnip, eggs, garlic and chili. Very friendly, helpful service. *Seats 70. Parties 25. L 12-3 D 6-11.15. Closed 25 & 26 Dec. Access, Amex, Diners, Visa.*

W1   Ragam   £35

Tel 0171-636 9098   Map 18 D2   **R**
57 Cleveland Street Fitzrovia W1P 5PQ

Popular little South Indian restaurant specialising in Kerala vegetarian cooking making good use of rice and lentil flour, green chilis, semolina, yoghurt, coconut, curry leaves and tamarind juice. It's not exclusively vegetarian by any means, and besides speciality dishes such as *adai* (mixed lentil pancake), *avial* (mixed vegetables cooked with coconut and yoghurt) and *rasam* (hot pepper soup with tomato and tamarind juice) there are plenty of chicken, meat and seafood dishes. *Seats 36. Private Room 16. L 12-3 D 6-11.15 (Fri till 11.45, Sun till 11). Closed 25 & 26 Dec. Access, Amex, Diners, Visa.*

W12   Rajput   £35

Tel 0181-740 9036   Map 17 A4   **R**
144 Goldhawk Road Shepherds Bush W12 8HH

Friendly North Indian restaurant whose straightforward menu includes as specialities chicken tikka masala, king prawn patia, and a selection of muglai dishes. The Sunday buffet is very reasonably priced at £6.95. *Seats 50. Parties 20. L 12-2.30 D 6-12. Closed 25 Dec. Access, Amex, Diners, Visa.*

N3   Rani   £40

Tel & Fax 0181-349 4386   Map 16 B1   **R**
7 Long Lane Finchley Central N3 2PR

Five minutes walk from Finchley Central station, Rani is one of London's top Indian vegetarian restaurants – a clean and sparkling family-run diner with a wide frontage and a fine repertoire of Gujerati home cooking. Full use is made of grain flours and various dal combined with fresh, exotic vegetables and delicate spicing and no eggs, fish, meat or animal fats are allowed on the premises. The range is impressive, and the full menu is available Tues-Sun evenings; a buffet operates Monday evening and Sunday lunchtime. Among the many specialities are black lentil fritters with a yoghurt dipping sauce, stuffed parathas, banana methi (bananas, fenugreek leaves, tomatoes) and stuffed aubergine and potato curry. Super chutneys. Prices are extremely reasonable and service is by professional, young and motivated staff. A new Rani (open all day) at 3 Hill Street, Richmond, Surrey Tel 0181-332 2322, opened after we went to press. *Seats 90. D 6-10.30. Opening hours might vary – check before setting out. Closed 25 Dec. Set D from £13. Access, Visa.*

SW11   Ransome's Dock   £65

Tel 0171-223 1611   Fax 0171-924 2614   Map 19 B6   **R**
35 Parkgate Road Battersea SW11 4NP

Martin Lam changes the menu monthly at his comfortable waterside restaurant, where the terrace provides a quiet haven for alfresco eating. The short menu is Mediterranean in flavour, and always supplemented by daily specials. Celeriac rémoulade with Norfolk smoked eel, mushroom and Madeira soup or a plate of Spanish charcuterie could be followed by calf's liver with winter cabbage, grilled duck breast with blood orange sauce or spinach, aubergine and feta cheese filo. Ingredients are painstakingly chosen, even down to the delicious vine tomatoes used for salads and coulis. Except for fizz and the house selection, wines are presented by style and more or less in price order, offering quite a lot under £20. Friendly and informed service. *Seats 65. Parties 20. Meals 12-11 (Sat to midnight). Closed D Sun, 1 week Christmas. Set L £11.50 (not Sat or Sun). Access, Amex, Diners, Visa.*

N16   Rasa   £40

Tel 0171-249 0344   Map 16 D2   **R**
55 Stoke Newington Church Street N16 0AR

Shiny brass chandeliers combined with an attractive cinnamon and cream decor create a welcoming ambience for a short menu of well-prepared vegetarian dishes, most of which originate from the South Indian states of Kerala, Tamil Nadu and Southern Andra Pradesh, and which are characterised by subtle spicing and deliciously creamy sauces. Several dishes on the new menu are 'village specialities' appearing in London for the first time. Friendly service. No smoking. *Seats 42. Parties 20. L 12-2.30 D 6-12. Closed 25 & 26 Dec. Access, Visa.*

W1   Rasa Sayang   £40

Tel 0171-734 8720   Fax 0171-734 0933   Map 21 A2   **R**
10 Frith Street Soho W1V 5TZ

Singaporean/Malaysian and South-East Asian food (prepared without using MSG) served in congenial surroundings. Set meals provide a good introduction to an interesting cuisine that includes traditional dishes like nasi goreng (fried rice with egg, shrimps, chicken and peas), fish ball soup, beef rendang (in a thick, spicy coconut gravy) and gado gado (Indonesian salad with peanut sauce). Serve-yourself lunchtime buffet (£6.50) *Seats 180. L 12-2.45 D 6-11.30 (Fri till 12.30am, Sat meals 1pm-12.30am, Sun meals 12-10.30). Closed 25 & 26 Dec. Access, Amex, Diners, Visa.*
Also at:
W2 38 Queensway Bayswater W2 Tel 0171-229 8417 Fax 0171 229 9900
60 seats. Open Noon-11.15 (Sun till 11). Closed 25 Dec.   Map 18 A3

W1   Rathbone Hotel   69%   £162

Tel 0171-636 2001   Fax 0171-636 3882   Map 18 D2   **H**
30 Rathbone Street W1P 2LB

An intimate hotel near Oxford Street. Crystal chandeliers, Italian marble and objets d'art adorn the limited public areas. The stylishness is matched in carefully modelled bedrooms (all fully air-conditioned), where smoked-glass mirrors add depth and boldly patterned curtains enrich the colour. Brightly lit, marbled bathrooms all have powerful showers. Executive rooms and suites feature whirlpool baths. Half the bedrooms are designated non-smoking. Not a hotel for children. No dogs. *The Royal Terrace Hotel* in Edinburgh is a sister establishment. *Rooms 72. Access, Amex, Diners, Visa.*

NW1   Ravi Shankar   £25

Tel 0171-388 6458   Fax 0171-388 2494   Map 18 D1   **R**
133-135 Drummond Street Euston NW1 2HL

South Indian vegetarian cooking at basement prices in a friendly restaurant with wooden flooring, hand-painted murals and air-conditioning. The house speciality is Shankar Thali, a complete set meal, while individual orders include wholewheat breads, dosas from Madras and snacks from Bombay. *Seats 60. Private Room 20. Meals 12-10.45. Set meals from £4.95. Access, Visa.*
Also at:
EC1 422 St John Street EC1 Tel 0171-833 5849   Map 16 D3
L 12-2.30 D 6-10.30 (Fri & Sat till 11).

W1   La Reash   £35

Tel 0171-439 1063   Map 21 A2   **R**
23 Greek Street Soho W1V 5LG

In the heart of Soho, at the junction of Old Compton Street and Greek Street, La Reash specialises in Lebanese and Moroccan cuisine. Meat or vegetarian mazah (a selection of hot and cold starters) represents the former, couscous and tagines the latter. There's a cheap set-lunch menu which changes every week. Tapas bar beneath the main restaurant. *Seats 100. Meals 12-12. Closed 25 Dec. Set L £6.95. Access, Amex, Visa.*

Many hotels offer reduced rates for weekend or out-of-season bookings. Always ask about special deals.

W1   Red Fort   £70

Tel 0171-437 2115   Fax 0171-434 0721   Map 21 A2   **R**
77 Dean Street Soho W1V 5HA

Opened in 1983 by Amin Ali, the stylish Red Fort takes its name from the red sandstone fort built by Emperor Shah Jahan on the banks of the River Jamuna in Delhi. Tandoori food is a popular choice (lamb, chicken, prawns, salmon, pomfret) and other specialities include venison, *murgh jaipuri* (chicken with whole spices and red chilis) and *safed maas* (lamb cooked to a white finish using cream, yoghurt and almond paste). The restaurant is on two floors: street-level fronted by a bar area with seats, and a more intimate, low-lit basement. *Seats 130. Parties 12. Private Room 60. L 12.15-2.45 D 6-11.30. Buffet L £12.50. Access, Amex, Diners, Visa.*

SW7   Regency Hotel   69%   £166

Tel 0171-370 4595   Fax 0171-370 5555   Map 19 B5   **H**
100 Queen's Gate SW7 5AG

Privately owned hotel at the junction with Old Brompton Road, near the South Kensington museums and Knightsbridge shopping. Beyond the marble foyer the Terrace (more marble, and natural light) is open day and night, and there's a cocktail bar and several conference/banqueting rooms (maximum capacity 100/180). Bedrooms are all double-glazed; top of the range are junior suites or duplexes with jacuzzis. Children up to 6 share their parents' room at no charge. Full 24hr room service (including a night chef) and an on-site health club are among the bonuses. No dogs. *Rooms 210. Gym, sauna, spa bath, steam room, sun beds. Access, Amex, Diners, Visa.*

NW1   The Regent London   87%   £245

Tel 0171-631 8000   Fax 0171-631 8080   Map 18 B2   **HR**
222 Marylebone Road NW1 6JQ

New owners took over in August 1995 and changed the name to *The Landmark London*. An impressive piece of Grade II-listed Victorian Gothic architecture restored handsomely to its former glory, it is now a luxurious hotel with a relaxed and informal atmosphere. A glass-canopied entrance leads into a spacious lobby with a polished, pale cream stone floor from which a series of steps leads up to the Winter Garden (informal snacks all day), in an impressive eight-floor-high, glass-covered atrium. On a mezzanine gallery there's a gazebo with additional, quieter lounge space overlooking the floor below; 60ft coconut palms rise to the occasion. The strains of a pianist and voices sound hushed amid the cathedral-like acoustics. The hotel has six floors of smart bedrooms, all large and well appointed. Junior suites have beautiful black marble-topped executive desks and an armoir that houses the room bar and satellite TV. There are three phone lines to each room plus a data line for PCs and fax. Bathrooms are as splendid as the bedrooms; lined with white marble, most have separate shower cubicles, but only the top suites have bidets. Thick towelling bathrobes, scales, wall safes and even umbrellas are among a host of thoughtful touches provided to pamper guests. Top of the range of the bedrooms are the sixth-floor Penthouse suite and the fifth-floor Presidential suite, the latter featuring two bedrooms, a private dining-room and even a grand piano. Families are extremely well catered for (as one would hope for at this level); almost every family accoutrement can be provided; children up to 14 may share their parents' room at no charge. Service from young, enthusiastic staff can be one of the hotel's biggest assets – from 24hr room service, picnic baskets in summer and 4-hour rush dry-cleaning service to an evening turn-down and an overnight shoe shine (with footwear returned wrapped in tissue). A basement health club is a further asset and impressive function rooms hold up to 360; the Tower Suite on the fifth floor is next to the Penthouse suite and has a lovely double-storey-high glass ceiling plus facilities for up to 20 boardroom-style. Limited underground car parking. Business centre with Reuters information. Superb choice for breakfast.
Rooms 309. Indoor swimming pool, spa bath, gym, sauna, steam room, beauty & hair salon, shop. Access, Amex, Diners, Visa.

Dining Room   £95

Three enormous and magnificent crystal and silver chandeliers dominate the very elegant and beautifully proportioned room, although the lighting level is little higher than a romantic level at dinner. The menu encompasses a mix of mostly modern Italian dishes together with simple French classics. Italian wines are prominent on a list presented by style. Many bottles priced under £20. New chef Roger Peters took over as we went to press. *Seats 100. Parties 14. L 12-3 D 7-11. Closed L Sat. Set L £21.50 (Sun £29) Set D £29.*

NW3   Regent's Park Marriott   73%   £169

Tel 0171-722 7711   Fax 0171-586 5822   Map 16 B3   **H**
128 King Henry's Road Swiss Cottage NW3 3ST

A modern hotel with a lot to offer: good-sized rooms with large beds, desks, breakfast tables and easy chairs; 24hr room service; 100 free car spaces; facilities for up to 400 conference delegates; a large indoor swimming pool. The foyer features marble flooring, pale-wood panelling (also in the bar lounge) and an enormous vase of flowers. Two children can stay free in parents' room. Five minutes' walk from Swiss Cottage Underground. *Rooms 303. Garden, indoor swimming pool, gym, sauna, solarium, beauty and hair salon, massage, shop. Access, Amex, Diners, Visa.*

Set menu prices may not always include service or wine.

SW7   Rembrandt Hotel   70%   £155

Tel 0171-589 8100   Fax 0171-225 3363   Map 19 B4   **H**
11 Thurloe Place South Kensington SW7 2RS

The location of this Sarova group hotel is excellent, being close to the heart of
Knightsbridge as well as directly opposite the Victoria & Albert Museum. Public rooms
include a spacious lobby with glittering crystal pendant lighting. Double doors lead into
a quiet, traditional oak dado-panelled lounge with classical columns and an open
fireplace. Bedrooms are light, decorated in soft pastels and are spacious. Executive rooms
are larger and also have settees, air-conditioning and push-button controls for lights. Also
the majority of their bathrooms have spa baths with bidets and beautiful polished granite
floors. Standard bathrooms can be compact but all have good shower roses. Aquilla is the
hotel's splendid health complex in the basement. Children up to 13 stay free in parents'
room. No dogs. *Rooms 195. Indoor swimming pool, gym, sauna, spa bath, solarium, beauty
salon. Access, Amex, Diners, Visa.*

SW6   La Réserve   62%   £90

Tel 0171-385 8561   Fax 0171-385 7662   Map 19 A6   **H**
422-428 Fulham Road Fulham Broadway SW6 1DU

Contemporary small hotel whose bedrooms (some small road-facing singles; rear rooms
look on to Chelsea football ground) feature modern art and modern technology. Bar and
lounge have comfortable modern leather sofas. *Rooms 40. Closed 1 week Christmas.
Access, Amex, Diners, Visa*

Set menu prices may not always include service or wine.

W1   The Ritz   86%   £249

Tel 0171-493 8181   Fax 0171-493 2687   Map 18 D3   **HR**
150 Piccadilly W1V 9DG

The Ritz was opened in 1906 by César Ritz, whose intention was to create "the most
fashionable hotel in the most fashionable city in the world". With a prime position in
Piccadilly next to Green Park, the Ritz is certainly one of London's most famous
landmarks, and continues to maintain its position in the capital's top hotel league.
Standards of comfort and housekeeping are enviably high and service is generally
everything one might expect from "one of London's smaller hotels" – of the 130
bedrooms, 14 are suites. The "Belle Epoque" feel to the generously proportioned
bedrooms is enhanced by delicate pastels and gold leaf, marble fireplaces, Louis XVI
furnishings and lavishly equipped marble bathrooms, all with bath and shower; almost
incongruously, but welcomed by guests from all around the world, satellite TV is offered.
Suites feature elegant lounges, a hallway, personal bar and writing desk; some are air-
conditioned. Afternoon tea at the Ritz is part of our heritage and the Palm Court is one
of London's most elegant teatime settings. The rest of the hotel is equally grand: the Long
Gallery, the sumptuously beautiful restaurant and the private salons. Children up to 12
stay free in parents' room. Conference/banqueting for up to 60. Charged parking.
No dogs. Part of the Mandarin Oriental Group. *Rooms 130. Garden, valeting, dinner
dance (Fri & Sat). Access, Amex, Diners, Visa.*

Louis XVI Restaurant   £120

A grandiose dining room of perfect proportions, elegantly furnished in pink,
harmoniously matching the marble decor. A giant trompe l'oeil ceiling, from which
hangs a carousel of gilded chandeliers, highlights the room. The Italian garden and terrace
for alfresco dining are no less sumptuous. Staff are helpful and attentive, giving tempting
descriptions of chef David Nicholls' menus which mix ancient and modern dishes.
Lunchtime daily specials see a roast on the trolley (except on Fridays when there's salmon
in puff pastry with lobster and scallops) and other specialities – from steak and kidney pie
(Thursday) to osso buco with risotto milanese (Monday). Table d'hote menus are offered
at both lunch and dinner, alongside the lengthy à la cartes. Crab and lobster Antoinette,
oysters glazed in champagne with cucumber and caviar, fillet of Dover sole Ritz and sea
bass are considered specialities, while crown of asparagus with lobster and truffles, grilled
Dover sole, fillet of Aberdeen Angus beef with béarnaise sauce and Peach Ritz are also
popular. Pre-and post-theatre menus. (6-6.45 & 10.30-11.15: £30) and also Friday (high

season) and Saturday dinner-dances (in the Palm Court from 10pm to 1am). Perhaps surprisingly, children are welcome for Sunday lunch, when high-chairs are available and special consideration accorded – they can choose from a special children's menu (even including potato 'casings' and pizza!) or join their parents in roast Scottish prime rib of beef served with Yorkshire pudding. *Seats 100. Parties 26. Private Room 48. L 12.30-2.30 D 6.30-11.15. Set L £29 Set D from £46.50.*

SW13   Riva   £75

Tel 0181-748 0434   Map 17 A5   **R**
169 Church Road Barnes SW13 9HR

Andrea Riva's sparsely decorated modern restaurant offers food notable for honest, robust flavours. Many of chef Francesco Zanchetta's regularly changing dishes are seldom seen elsewhere: smoked goose prosciutto with chicory, nuts and truffle oil; tagliatelle with duck, cinnamon and onions; pan-roasted cod fillet on a bed of Swiss chard 'au gratin' with a pink peppercorn sauce; roast lamb with a mustard-mint sauce, pecorino, herbs and barley pancakes. Choose between modern dishes, such as grilled vegetables and brodetto (fish soup) or grilled chicken breast marinated in thyme and balsamic vinegar with oven-dried tomatoes and roast garlic, or more classical offerings – calf's liver with sage, breaded veal cutlet with matchstick potatoes. A menu that constantly strives for subtle innovation, and an Italian wine list that is equally appealing. There's a splendid selection of grappa plus good strong espresso. *Seats 50. L 12-2.30 D 7-11 (Sat to 11.30). Closed L Sat, Christmas, Easter, 2 weeks Aug. Access, Visa.*

W6   River Café   £80

Tel 0171-381 8824   Fax 0171-381 6217   Map 17 B5   **R**
Thames Wharf Studios Rainville Road Hammersmith W6 9HA

Were it not for the inconsistencies and coolness of the British climate, this restaurant, whose west-facing all-glass outer wall takes full advantage of the afternoon and evening sun, would not be out of place alongside the Arno or Tiber instead of the Thames. Ruth Rogers and Rose Gray began the operation in 1987 and were forerunners in the renaissance of new-wave Italian cuisine in this country. They introduced the concept of simple rusticity in keeping with the origins of real Italian food. All this accounts for the continued immense popularity of this riverside restaurant. Tantalising menus whose dishes are a well-orchestrated fusion of the true flavours of middle and northern Italy feature on a daily-changing basis. Starters could be chargrilled scallops with fried aubergines marinated in red wine vinegar with chili and mint, buffalo mozzarella crostini with sun-dried tomatoes and anchovies, and pasta rolls filled with spinach, ricotta and parmesan, served with sage butter. Main dishes are mostly chargrilled and could include sea bass fillet with salsa verde and fennel, seared wild salmon with Roman-style artichokes, lentils and chopped black olives and mint and leg of lamb with potato and red onion roasted with balsamic vinegar and thyme. Desserts include the ever popular chocolate nemesis, a slice of tangy lemon tart or hazelnut and ricotta cake or there's a selection of good Italian cheeses including an unusual combination of pecorino served with broad beans. Champagne apart, it's an all-Italian wine list with plenty of bottles under £20. *Seats 100. Parties 10. L 12.30-2.30 D 7.30-9.30. Closed D Sun, 10 days Christmas, 4 days Easter, Bank Holidays. Access, Visa.*

W2   Romantica Taverna   £40

Tel 0171-727 7112   Map 18 A3   **R**
10 Moscow Road Bayswater W2 4BT

Enjoyable, straightforward Greek fare in a long-established restaurant just off Queensway. Meze for two is the speciality of the house, along with classic dolmades, afelia, kleftiko and moussaka. Some good fish dishes, too. *Seats 90. Private Room 50. Meals 12-12. Closed 3 days Christmas, Good Friday. Access, Amex, Diners, Visa.*

Consult the blue pages for summary tables and lists of recommended establishments.

W12   The Rotisserie   £40

Tel 0181-743 3028   Fax 0181-743 6627   Map 17 B4   **R**
56 Uxbridge Road Shepherds Bush W12 8LP

Friendly and informal eating place next to Shepherds Bush Central Line Underground station. Pride of place in the large room goes to the charcoal grill/rotisserie, where the main courses are prepared: corn-fed chicken, paper-wrapped salmon, Toulouse sausages, Barbary duck, calf's liver, rack of lamb, venison, tiger prawns and the very popular Aberdeen Angus steaks. *Seats 90. Parties 40. L 12-3 D 6.30-11. Closed L Sat, all Sun. Access, Amex, Visa.*

SW15   Royal China   £60

Tel 0181-788 0907   Map 17 B5   **R**
3 Chelverton Road Putney SW15 1RN

Entering the heavy wooden doors, the impression is of being inside a black lacquer box, with flights of golden birds decorating the walls. This is a smart restaurant, with almost a nightclub atmosphere. Yellow linen on the tables, fresh flowers in wicker baskets and polished, helpful service add to the elegant feel. The menu is large, both physically and in terms of choice, with 12 types of fish alone. Peking duck comes as two separate courses. The set dinners provide the best value, and offer either four or five generous courses, though the choices may be conservative. Like most Chinese restaurants the set dinners are not available to lone diners. Good house wine on an interesting, short wine list. *Seats 70. L 12-4 D 6.30-11. Set D £20/£26 (for 2+). Access, Amex, Diners, Visa.*

W2   Royal China   £50

Tel 0171-221 2535   Map 18 A3   **R**
13 Queensway Bayswater W2 4QJ

A high-class Chinese restaurant with striking decor of black lacquered walls, gold and silver inlaid murals and spotlights. The style is Cantonese, with seafood and dim sum among the specialities, the latter (a particularly long and interesting selection) served until 5pm. Favourites include seafood hot pot, steamed minced pork with salted egg and sautéed beef steak with lemon grass. Fresh lobster is prepared in six different ways (hot and spicy salts, mandarin sauce, steamed naturally, ginger and spring onion, yellow bean sauce, black bean sauce) and other items at the luxury end include poached king clams, abalone and steamed or pan-fried sea bass and Dover sole. *Seats 100. Parties 14. Private Room 15. Meals 12-11.15. Set meals from £20. Closed 23-25 Dec. Access, Amex, Diners, Visa.*

SW1   Royal Court Hotel   63%   £154

Tel 0171-730 9191   Fax 0171-824 8381   Map 19 C5   **H**
Sloane Square Chelsea SW1W 8EG

Facing Sloane Square, the hotel is near to both Knightsbridge and Kings Road. An elegant collection of theatrical prints, reflecting the Royal Court Theatre almost next door features throughout. The decent public areas are rather let down by the double-glazed bedrooms, which though comfortable enough (single rooms are small) with modern amenities, would benefit from refurbishment and better housekeeping, bathrooms especially. The third floor is reserved for non-smokers. Children up to 15 stay free in parents' room. Three exclusive parking spaces (£20 for 24 hours). Conference/banqueting facilities for 40. 24hr room service. *Rooms 102. Access, Amex, Diners, Visa.*

W8   Royal Garden Hotel

Tel 0171-937 8000   Fax 0171-938 4532   Map 19 A4   **H**
Kensington High Street W8 4PT

The hotel is due to open in February 1996 after a major structural and decorative refurbishment. The building, which stands at the south-western corner of Kensington Gardens, has a brand new exterior while internally 190 of the bedrooms and the public rooms have been completely remodelled. The remaining 250 rooms have been redecorated, with brand new bathrooms installed.

SW1   Royal Horseguards Thistle   71%   £146

Tel 0171-839 3400   Fax 0171-925 2263   Map 18 D3   **H**
2 Whitehall Court SW1A 2EJ

An imposing Portland stone pile, backing on to the Thames Embankment, that could easily be mistaken for one of the surrounding Ministries. The foyer, with its marble floor and elegant crystal chandeliers, is dominated by a Wedgwood-style, plaster-moulded ceiling; this and the comfortable lounge, with its country house feel, set the tone for the rest of the hotel. There is an in-house pub, the 2A Bar, a terrace coffee shop (open all day for snacks and light meals) and the clublike Granby restaurant with a division bell to alert MPs. Bedrooms range from a single above Whitehall Court to spacious air-conditioned Executive rooms with private balconies overlooking the Thames. All have en-suite bathrooms and the expected modern amenities. 24hr room service. Breakfast is buffet-style only. Impressive conference rooms cater for up to 300 delegates. Children up to 12 stay free in parents' room. No dogs. *Rooms 377. Coffee shop (11am-10.45pm). Access, Amex, Diners, Visa.*

Set menu prices may not always include service or wine.

W2   Royal Lancaster Hotel   £191

Tel 0171-262 6737   Fax 0171-724 3191   Map 18 B3   **H**
Lancaster Terrace Lancaster Gate W2 2TY

High-rise hotel overlooking Hyde Park at Lancaster Gate (Lancaster Gate Underground station is directly under the hotel) on the northern edge of the park. It's Thai-owned (there's a sister hotel in Bangkok) and the summer of 1995 saw work begin on a major refurbishment and remodelling of the extensive public areas (hence we leave the hotel ungraded this year). Of the bedrooms – which, apart from 20 or so studio rooms and 15 full suites, are not very spacious – five floors had been refurbished with lightwood furniture, pleasant colour schemes and new bathrooms boasting telephones and TV speaker extensions. All rooms have air-conditioning, double-glazing, satellite TV and mini-bars and room safes are being added as refurbishment continues. 24hr room service. Children up to 12 stay free in parents' room. No dogs. Banqueting and conference facilities for up to 1500. Parking for 100 cars (£15 per 24 hours for residents). *Rooms 418. Hairdressing, news kiosk, car hire desk, garage. Access, Amex, Diners, Visa.*

WC2   Royal Trafalgar Thistle   65%   £151

Tel 0171-930 4477   Fax 0171-925 2149   Map 21 A3   **H**
Whitcomb Street WC2 7HG

Discreetly located behind the National Gallery, the Royal Trafalgar has the double advantage of a quiet setting and one that is enviably central. Some of the rooms (a third non-smoking) are quite small, but all offer the standard range of amenities – remote-control TV, in-house movies, trouser press, hairdryer. *Rooms 108. Access, Amex, Diners, Visa.*

SW1   Royal Westminster Thistle   71%   £151

Tel 0171-834 1821   Fax 0171-828 8933   Map 19 D4   **H**
Buckingham Palace Road Victoria SW1W 0QT

Two-storey modern hotel close to Buckingham Palace and Victoria Station. Best of the public areas is the Royal lounge, with its Chinese artefacts, a stylish venue for afternoon tea. The air-conditioned bedrooms are spacious and comfortable with queen-sized beds, en-suite bathrooms and most modern amenities, including extra sofa beds in some rooms and an evening turn-down service. The enthusiastic management team provides a friendly service making this a pleasant place to stay. 24hr room service. Banqueting/conference facilities for up to 150/180. Children up to 16 stay free in parents' room, or qualify for a 25% discount in rooms of their own – so half term can be busy! *Rooms 134. Café (7am-11pm), bureau de change. Access, Amex, Diners, Visa.*

We welcome bona fide complaints and recommendations on the tear-out pages at the back of the book for readers' comments. They are followed up by our professional team.

SE1   RSJ   £65

Tel 0171-928 4554   Map 20 B3   **R**
13a Coin Street Waterloo SE1 8YQ

🍶 🍷

Modern British cooking with French influences in a very friendly and relaxing restaurant
that's a favourite spot before or after a play or concert at the South Bank. There's
a choice of fixed-price or à la carte menu, with typical dishes running from spring
vegetable soup with chervil and warm salad of confit of rabbit with Puy lentils, pancetta
and balsamic dressing to roast monkfish with peas, broad beans, new potatoes lyonnaise
and thyme jus, calf's liver with bacon, garlic mash, spinach and red wine shallot sauce,
and to finish double chocolate cake or apple and calvados clafoutis with honey and
almonds. Unbelievably kind prices mark out the wine list, which for the most part
features a quite magnificent selection from the Loire. This has to be the collection of all
collections, with many wines otherwise unseen in this country. There's a small selection
of wines from Australia and other parts of France, and, quirkily, a 1985 Bollinger Grande
Anneé champagne, under £40 mind, appears under 'other sparkling wines' – wonderful!
*Seats 90. Parties 10. Private Room 22. L 12-2 D 6-11. Closed L Sat, all Sun, Bank Holidays.
Set L & D £15.95. Access, Amex, Visa.*

SW1   Rubens Hotel   66%   £149

Tel 0171-834 6600   Fax 0171-828 5401   Map 19 D4   **H**
Buckingham Palace Road SW1W 0PS

Opened at the turn of the century, the Rubens stands in a prime position facing the
Royal Mews behind Buckingham Palace; it's also conveniently close to Victoria Station
(2 minutes walk) and Westminster. Comfortable day rooms in country house style
include a library lounge and a cocktail bar with resident pianist. Well-appointed
bedrooms (just one suite) offer the usual extras. Children up to 16 stay free in parents'
room. Five conference suites cater for up to 75 delegates. No dogs. Sarova Hotels.
Rooms 180. Access, Amex, Diners, Visa.

WC2   Rules   £60

Tel 0171-836 5314   Fax 0171-497 1081   Map 21 B2   **R**
35 Maiden Lane Covent Garden WC2E 7LB

🍴

Tradition rules in one of London's oldest eating places (but your order gets keyed into
pocket computers). Oysters, game both furred and feathered, wild salmon, Aberdeen
Angus beef, steak and kidney pies/puddings and Spotted Dick are among the specialities.
*Seats 140. Parties 10. Private Room 48. Meals 12-11.30 (Sun to 10.30). Set L £12.95.
Closed 4 days Christmas. Access, Amex, Visa.*

WC1   Hotel Russell   68%   £146

Tel 0171-837 6470   Fax 0171-837 2857   Map 18 D2   **H**
Russell Square WC1B 5BE

Extravagant, late-Victorian, red stone hotel dominating one side of Russell Square. The
entrance hall is appropriately grand with acres of marble, ornate plasterwork and a huge
chandelier. There is no lounge as such, just a few sofas in odd corners of the lobby, but
one of the two panelled bars is very comfortable and clubby with lots of button-back
leather seating and tartan covered wing armchairs. Bedrooms, which are currently
benefiting from a refurbishment programme, vary somewhat in shape, size and furniture –
some is built-in and some have traditional freestanding pieces – but all are equally well
appointed. For a relatively small premises the 25 Executive rooms on the top floor share
a lounge (with complementing Continental breakfast), their own check-out desk and get
mini-bars and bathrobes as extras in the rooms. 24hr room service. Children up to 16
stay free in parents' room. No dogs. The hotel has no parking of its own but there are
a couple of public car parks nearby. Banqueting facilities for 300, conferences for up to
400. No dogs. Forte. *Rooms 328. Access, Amex, Diners, Visa.*

Set menu prices may not always include service or wine.

W14   Russell Bistro   £50

Tel 0171-603 7645   Map 17 B4   **R**
10 Russell Gardens W14 8EZ

A bustling dining-room and popular local haunt (until recently Olivers). Wooden tables with bentwood chairs, abundant green plants and bare brick walls form a backdrop for the classic French bistro menu. Moules marinière, squid provençale or home-made soup for starters; chicken with tarragon sauce, grilled lemon sole or various steaks to follow. There is a set menu with dishes taken from the carte, and traditional Sunday lunch. Children's portions. *Seats 80. Meals noon-11.30pm (Sun till 10.30). Closed 25 Dec. Set L £9.50 Set Sun L £13.50. Access, Visa.*

SW3   S & P   £40

Tel 0171-351 5692   Map 19 B5   **R**
181 Fulham Road SW3 6NJ

Thai restaurant on the corner of Sydney Street and Fulham Road. The menu has all the usual piquant Thai dishes, including specialities of spicy prawn soup, deep-fried fish in a tamarind sauce and stir-fried duck fillet in a red curry sauce. Well-priced set lunch and Executive set lunch menus. *Seats 60. Private Room 20. L 12-2.30 D 6.30-11. Set L £7.95/£9.95 Set D £18.50/£22.50. Closed 25 & 26 Dec, 1 Jan. Access, Amex, Diners, Visa.*
Also at:
SW3 S & P Patara 9 Beauchamp Place SW3 1NQ Tel 0171-581 8820 Map 19 C4

NW10   Sabras   £25

Tel 0181-459 0340   Map 16 A2   **R**
263 High Road Willesden NW10 2RX

Opened in 1973, Sabras maintains its reputation for excellent vegetarian cooking from Bombay, Gujarat and South India. Many of the ingredients are not seen in many London establishments – violet Indian yam, cluster beans, split pigeon peas, unripe bananas. Value for money is exceptional. *Seats 32. D only 6.30-10.30. Closed Mon. No credit cards.*

W1   Saga   £85

Tel 0171-408 2236   Map 18 C3   **R**
43 South Molton Street W1Y 1HB

High-class Japanese cooking in both the main eating area and the sushi bar. The sushi choice is particularly good, so too the table-prepared specialities sukiyaki, shabu-shabu and udonsuki (Japanese noodles, chicken, fish and vegetables cooked in broth and served with mooli and spring onion). *Seats 100. Parties 16. Private Room 10. L 12.30-2.30 D 6.30-10. Set L from £6.50 Set D from £37. Access, Amex, Diners, Visa.*

W1   St George's Hotel   67%   £166

Tel 0171-580 0111   Fax 0171-436 7997   Map 18 D2   **HR**
Langham Place W1N 8QS

The continued refurbishment of bedrooms and the smartening-up of the lobby have enhanced this centrally located hotel next door to the BBC at the top end of Upper Regent Street. Choose between Standard and Executive rooms, the latter offering complimentary newspaper and express breakfast. The top floor has spectacular views of London's skyline. Children under 15 stay free in parents' room. Banqueting/conferences for 20/30. No dogs. No private parking though there's a car park and plenty of meters nearby. Forte. *Rooms 86. Coffee shop (7am-11pm). Access, Amex, Diners, Visa.*

The Heights   NEW   £70

New room, new chef, new experience! The roof-top setting is a bonus, and though the split-level restaurant's design seems to have been effected by committee – painted grand piano, light woods, quite bold fabrics on banquette seating, pristine white tablecloths, and waiting staff in beige smocks – the overall ambience is one of relaxation. Roux-trained chef Adam Newell proposes an eclectic menu of colourfully and artistically-presented dishes: a thin tart of rouget and tapénade with rouille sauce and roast cod with fennel

See over

tarte tatin, an exemplary terrine of pressed duck and winter vegetables, a perfect daube of beef, served with braised pig's trotters which was superfluous to the dish, a tangy iced orange and Pernod parfait and an exquisite caramel tart with hazelnut ice cream. Fine cheeses come from Neal's Yard. Early days yet, but the making of a fine restaurant – just a little more consistency is needed. Incidentally, the bread rolls are great and so is the coffee. Half a dozen house wines under £15 on the shortish list of mostly young wines. *Seats 85. Parties 8. Private Room 25. L 12-2.30 D 7-10. Closed L Sat, all Sun & Bank Holidays. Set L £14/£18.*

SW1	St James Court	73%	£180

Tel 0171-834 6655   Fax 0171-630 7587   Map 19 D4   **HR**
41 Buckingham Gate Victoria SW1E 6AF

Within walking distance of the magnificent Queen Elizabeth II conference centre opposite Westminster Abbey, and also very close to Buckingham Palace. A grand-scale Edwardian redbrick building has been converted into an almost palatial hotel, at the heart of which is a self-contained business centre offering an extensive range of rooms and services for up to 250 delegates. In the middle of the hotel is a fine open-air courtyard with ornamental trees and a period fountain – an ideal setting for alfresco receptions. Bedrooms are furnished and equipped to a high standard, with smart reproduction furniture and luxurious bathrooms. 72 apartments, 10 studios and 19 suites are also available. Children under 12 may share their parents' room (extra bed £25). The Olympian health club includes a health bar and an aerobic dance studio. The choice of restaurants includes the French (see below), Szechuan-orientated Chinese and the all-day Café Mediterranée serving brasserie-style meals. NCP a minute away (£20 per day). No dogs. European flagship of Taj International Hotels. *Rooms 471. Gym, sauna, steam room, spa bath, solarium, squash, beauty therapist, business centre, brasserie (7am-11pm). Access, Amex, Diners, Visa.*

Auberge de Provence   £90
Tel 0171 821 1899

The restaurant is closely linked to L'Oustau de Baumanière, in the beautiful village of Les Beaux de Provence. Chef Bernard Briqué is in charge of the kitchen over here, offering interesting menus of classic French dishes. One of the evening options is le menu provençal, whose typical choices include salad of artichoke hearts, green beans and pine nuts, terrine of red mullet with a coriander and tomato coulis, sole in a saffron-scented bouillon, chicken breast stuffed with foie gras and pan-fried noisettes of lamb with tapénade. French cheeses from the trolley. The well-designed wine list includes a selection from Baumanière. Excellent formal service. Reservations on 0171-821 1899. *Seats 65. L 12.30-2.30 D 7.30-11. Set L £24.50 Set D £32. Closed L Sat, all Sun, 2 weeks Aug, 26-30 Dec, 1-7 Jan.*

> Set menu prices may not always include service or wine.

EC1	St John	NEW	£60St

Tel 0171-251 0848   Fax 0171-251 4090   Map 16 D3   **R**
26 St John Street EC1

St John Street, once a dull street of small offices in converted Victorian buildings, now has yet another new-wave restaurant attracting the youngish and modish crowd that now frequents the area. Decor couldn't be simpler, the only contrast to the starkness of the bare white walls being the rows of black utility lamps suspended from the ceiling. Additionally there are plain wooden chairs, paper napkins and cheerful staff in crumpled white jackets and long aprons. The menu begins with whelks and pickled onions and continues through wild garlic and bean soup, jellied ham and parsley and lamb's brain terrine – all quite gutsy stuff – to grilled quail, leeks and olives, skate and sea kale, grilled lamb's tongues with parsnip and green sauce and mince and tatties. Quite simple but enjoyable food. To finish, if not a Welsh rarebit or cheese, then crème caramel, plum and almond tart or steamed pudding – though this comes with cold custard. Rae (hard to believe she's a grandmother), provides the smiles and chat of anyone there – apart from the rather boisterous clientele – those in the bar a particularly lively set. *Seats 120. Parties 8. Private Room 20. L 12-3 D 6-11.30. Closed D Sun, all Bank Holidays, 2 weeks Christmas. Access, Amex, Diners, Visa.*

W1   St Moritz   £55

Tel 0171-734 3324   Fax 0171-734 8995   Map 18 D2   **R**
161 Wardour Street Soho W1V 3TA

A small, charming Swiss establishment on two floors whose extensive menu offers meat and cheese fondues for two or more as well as other Swiss specialities including air-cured beef, rösti potatoes, spatzle noodles and veal zurichoise (cream and mushroom sauce). Venison appears in season, notably in the classic Grand Veneur – saddle with wild mushrooms, spatzle, brussels sprouts, red cabbage, cherries, chestnuts, pears and apples. *Seats 50. Parties 12. L 12-3 D 6-11.30. Closed L Sat, all Sun, Bank Holidays. Access, Amex, Diners, Visa.*

SW1   Sale e Pepe   £70

Tel 0171-235 0098   Map 19 C4   **R**
9-15 Pavilion Road Knightsbridge SW1X 0HB

The complete Italian job, with singing waiters, a permanent party atmosphere and a menu of well-prepared dishes from the standard repertoire. Long list of Italian wines. *Seats 75. Parties 10. L 12-2.30 D 7-11.30. Closed Sun, Bank Holidays. Access, Amex, Diners, Visa.*

SW1   Salloos   £70

Tel 0171-235 4444   Map 19 C4   **R**
62-64 Kinnerton Street Knightsbridge SW1X 8ER

Established in Lahore in 1966, Salloos has been in London since 1977. Tandoori grills – fat-free, long marinated and with no added colour – have a great reputation here, especially the lamb chops, and other special dishes which include haleem akbari (shredded lamb cooked in whole wheat germ, lentils and spices), chicken karahi (diced boneless chicken with tomato, ginger and green chili). Halwa gajar is a hot sweet prepared from shredded carrots, milk, almonds and pistachios, topped with real silver leaf. *Seats 65. L 12-2.30 D 7-11.15. Closed Sun. Set L from £16 Set D from £25. Access, Amex, Diners, Visa.*

SW3   Sambuca   £70

Tel 0171-730 6571   Map 19 C5   **R**
6 Symons Street Chelsea SW3

Straightforward Italian cooking in a popular, bustling restaurant by Sloane Square (opposite the rear door of Peter Jones). The menu sticks mainly to established favourites, with pasta for starters or mains and oven-braised lamb a speciality for two. Long list of Italian wines. *Seats 75. Parties 12. L 12.30-2.30 D 7-11.30. Closed Sun, Bank Holidays. Access, Amex, Diners, Visa.*

SW3   San Frediano   £55

Tel 0171-584 8375   Fax 0171-589 8860   Map 19 B5   **R**
62 Fulham Road SW3 6HH

Buzzing with atmosphere and old-fashioned Italian charm, San Fred is one of the real survivors among London's trattorias. Honest cooking, decent wine, ungreedy prices and slick service have provided nearly 30 years of customer satisfaction and a long list of daily dishes adds interest to a menu whose specialities include veal, pasta and seafood. *Seats 120. Parties 20. L 12.15-3 D 7-11.45. Closed Sun, Bank Holidays. Access, Amex, Diners, Visa.*

We welcome bona fide complaints and recommendations on the tear-out pages at the back of the book for readers' comments. They are followed up by our professional team.

SW3   San Lorenzo   £100

Tel 0171-584 1074   Fax 0171-584 1142   Map 19 C4   **R**
22 Beauchamp Place Knightsbridge SW3 1NL

High prices are no deterrent to the smart set who keep this Beauchamp Place hot spot permanently in the gossip columns. Favourite dishes are the spaghetti with clams or langoustines, bollito misto and tagliata with rugola. Almost a club, not always easy to get a booking, and a huge success down the years due to the effervescent owners Mara and Lorenzo Berni. *Seats 150. Parties 10. L 12.30-3 D 7.30-11.30. Closed Sun, Bank Holidays, 4 days Easter, 1 week Christmas. No credit cards.*

SW3   San Martino   £60

Tel 0171-589 3833   Fax 0171-584 8418   Map 19 B5   **R**
103 Walton Street SW3 2HP

One of London's busiest and friendliest Italian restaurants, where Costanzo Martinucci and his family are completely involved. The owner himself grows herbs, beans and ingredients for the splendid made-to-order salads and in the summer their land produces courgette flowers by the thousand for the kitchen. These may be fried or stuffed or put into risotto or tagliatelle. The ever-changing menu provides great variety and three of the most renowned dishes are fish soup, tagliatelle with hazelnuts, tarragon and wild mushroom sauce, and spaghetti cooked with seafood in a paper bag. Seasonal game plus chef's recommendations such as wild boar sausages or carpaccio of swordfish add to the choice. *Seats 130. Private Room 42. L 12-3 D 6.30-11.30 (Sat meals 12-11.30). Closed L Sun, all 25 & 26 Dec, Easter Monday. Access, Amex, Diners, Visa.*

SW3   Sandrini   £70

Tel 0171-584 1724   Map 19 B5   **R**
260 Brompton Road SW3 2AS

High marks for comfort and smart modern decor. Above-average marks for Italian cooking throughout a menu which mixes the traditional (penne arrabbiata, trout with almonds, liver and onions Venetian style) with the occasional out-of-the-ordinary (wind-dried venison with ricotta cheese). Tables outside in appropriate weather. *Seats 75. L 12-3 D 7-11.30. Access, Amex, Diners, Visa.*

SW1   Santini   £100

Tel 0171-730 4094   Fax 0171-730 0544   Map 19 C4   **R**
29 Ebury Street Victoria SW1W 0NZ

Venetian cuisine – top-quality produce cooked in a simple, honest way – is the main offering here. House specialities include ribbon pasta with artichoke sauce, poached sea bass in a sauce of herbs and balsamic vinegar, and fillet of beef in a cream, brandy and Dijon mustard sauce. To finish, try torta di pinoli, a traditional Italian flan with pine nuts and lemon filling. A 'Venetian specialities' menu changes monthly. Major expansion plans were afoot as we went to press. L'Incontro in Pimlico Road is a sister restaurant. *Seats 55. Parties 25. L 12.30-2.30 D 7-11.30 (Sun to 10.30). Closed L Sat & Sun, 25 & 26 Dec. Set L £15/£18.30. Access, Amex, Diners, Visa.*

N1   Satay Hut   £30

Tel 0171-359 4090   Fax 0171-482 4513   Map 16 D3
287 Upper Street Islington N1 2TZ

Larger and more comfortable than the name would suggest, Satay Hut has a menu that runs through Singapore, Malaysia and Thailand. Satay is the unsurprising speciality (lamb, beef, chicken, prawns or vegetarian). *Seats 95. D only 6-12. Closed 25 & 26 Dec. Access, Amex, Diners, Visa.*

W1   Les Saveurs   ★★★   £120

Tel 0171-491 8919   Fax 0171-491 3658   Map 18 C3   **R**
37a Curzon Street Mayfair W1V 8EY

A change of personnel at front-of-house, where the service under new restaurant manager Frederic Serol continues to be correct and proper, while in the kitchen, chef Joël Antunès and his team continue to perform at the height of their powers, producing dishes of stunning complexity and visual appeal. The basement restaurant itself provides all the trappings of sophisticated luxury from the exquisite place settings and artistic floral arrangements to tasteful decor and comfortable seating. Further proof, if proof were needed, that you're dining at one of the country's top restaurants, comes with those special extras that define real excellence – savoury nibbles, quality bread rolls, an amuse-bouche, say, a tiny tart of salmon rillettes with cucumber sauce, a magnificent (French) cheese trolley with every offering in tip-top condition, and a tray of petits fours, almost a dessert in itself with a choice of four treats per person. The differing menus are all fixed-price, though too many dishes attract supplements, with the daily-changing table d'hote a steal at both lunch and dinner (£38 for four courses), particularly the former when you are offered a choice of four dishes in each section. A typical example is a delicate courgette flower filled with crab, roast lamb served with zucchini, and a gratin of red fruits (mostly strawberry and raspberry at the time of our visit) in orange sauce, a perfect interpretation of a hot and cold dessert. Turning to the major menu, you'll encounter perhaps a chilled crab fondant with almond and herb mousse or terrine of duck foie gras and smoked pigeon with truffle oil, to be followed by roast sea bass on a bed of red sweet peppers and apricots or pan-fried sweetbreads in beetroot sauce. For dessert you could try the rather bizarre, but nevertheless delicious, fennel ice cream served with biscuit and red fruits, or peach and champagne soup with verbena ice cream (sometimes strawberry soup with tea sorbet), though the word soup is something of a misnomer. A very grand wine list for a grand restaurant, though most wines are on the expensive side. Best value obviously in lesser-known wines and sommelier Claude Douard's daily recommendations, and a surprisingly good New World selection for an oh! so French restaurant. Plenty of half bottles. **Seats** 50. *Parties 16. Private Room 10. L 12-2.30 D 7-11. Closed Sat & Sun, Bank Holiday Mons, 2 weeks Aug, 2 weeks Christmas/New Year. Set L £17/£22.50 D £36/£42 & £38.*

WC2   The Savoy   91%   £303

Tel 0171-836 4343   Fax 0171-240 6040   Map 20 A2   **HR**
The Strand WC2R 0EU

A household name for over one hundred years, The Savoy continues its fine traditions under new General Manager Duncan Palmer, as well as Group Managing Director Ramón Pajares, one of London's leading hoteliers for more than twenty years. Innovative when built, the hotel always seems to move with the times, introducing the latest technology without compromising its trademark standards of typically British sang-froid, efficiency and splendour. It is above all a hotel of grandeur, of contrasting styles, the marble-pillared Thames Foyer with a gazebo where a pianist or harpist plays during teatime and the cocktail hour, the imposing entrance hall, always a hive of activity with both guests and staff going about their business, the quiet drawing room, and the famous American Bar, one of London's favourite meeting places. Bedrooms, in styles ranging from traditionally English to art deco, benefit from having beds and mattresses made by the Savoy's own manufacturer, and boast such luxuries as real linen bedding, huge cosseting bath sheets, a nightly turn-down of beds and personal maid, valet and

See over

waiter bell service. River view rooms attract a supplement, and the much sought-after river suites are arguably the capital's finest. Even when originally built, bathrooms were huge and luxurious, and today, through constant renovation and refurbishment, they remain so. Another of the hotel's attractions is the Fitness Gallery, created when the adjoining Savoy Theatre was rebuilt. Favoured by natural daylight and fresh air, it is centred around the roof-top swimming pool, and includes his and hers saunas, steam rooms, warm-up and work-out rooms, and a massage room. Guests also have temporary membership of the renowned Wentworth golf and country club, a short drive from London, which has tennis courts and an outdoor pool in addition to several golf courses (proof of handicap required). Banqueting, without equal, is available for up to 500 in the Lancaster Ballroom, and theatre-style conferences can accommodate up to 600; smaller parties can take advantage of a number of elegant private rooms named after Gilbert and Sullivan operas. Own garage (£23 overnight charge). No dogs. **Rooms** 202. *Indoor swimming pool, gym, sauna, steam room, beauty & hair salon, gift and flower shops, valeting. Access, Amex, Diners, Visa.*

River Restaurant   ★   £130

This is a restaurant of two moods – at lunchtime busy and buzzy, at dinner, a more sedate affair with dancing to a live band (not Sunday) an additional attraction – in which to enjoy the grand setting (and the view if you're lucky enough to bag a window table overlooking the Thames). The chief protagonists, namely *maitre chef des cuisines* Anton Edelmann and restaurant manager Luigi Zambon, arrived here at the same time in the early 80s. Both are consummate professionals, orchestrating large brigades to provide admirable cooking and smooth service, no small feat given the number of guests fed each day. Long established as perennial favourites are the trolleys, whether accommodating oak-smoked Scotch salmon, 'roast of the day' under a silver dome, or desserts and puddings. Alternatively, choose à la carte (dishes, incidentally, are written in French with English translations), perhaps paupiettes of salmon filled with crab meat and topped with caviar; noisettes of lamb with truffle sauce, and peach Melba in an open sugar cage. A typical fixed-price menu, with several choices at each course, might offer home-made tagliatelle with foie gras, mignons of venison with wild mushrooms and juniper berry sauce, and chocolate terrine. In addition, there's a five-course dinner menu (£55) which includes a glass of wine, chosen by sommelier Werner Wissmann, to complement each dish, as well as a two-course (£27) theatre menu served from 6 to 7 pm with first and main courses before the show, returning for coffee and pastries (add another £5) in the Thames Foyer afterwards. The health-conscious and vegetarians are not neglected – note the Régime Naturel options (artichoke and wild mushroom salad in pumpkin seed oil, or ratatouille wrapped in courgettes on a potato purée with garlic, leek and extra virgin oil, vegetable cannelloni and vegetable cage). An impressive wine list, clarets especially, with wines from around the world, though unpatriotically none from this country! *Seats 160. Parties 50. Private Rooms 8/80. L 12.30-2.30 D 6-11.15 (Sun 7-10.30). Set L £27.50 (Sun £24.50) Set D £32.90 (Fri/Sat £39.50) and £55.*

Grill Room   ★   £120

Regular diners consider this yew-panelled dining-room to be almost their own club, some expecting to be seated at their favourite table whenever they book (essential by the way), occasionally testing the diplomatic skills of *maitre d'hotel* Angelo Maresca. Maitre *chef de cuisine* David Sharland's menus rarely change, though he does add the odd modern nod to classic dishes: sweet pepper salsa with smoked eel and quail's eggs, wilted greens and carrot butter sauce with fish cakes, an onion marmalade with a herb butter sauce with pan-fried calf's liver. Otherwise, the day of the week dictates les plats du jour, which differ at lunch and dinner; for instance, on a Tuesday lunch either hocks of ham with lentils or steak and kidney pie with sweetbreads are served, while the evening sees fillet of beef Wellington. Sausage and mash-lovers pinpoint Monday lunch, while those who prefer roast chicken with calvados and apple black pudding choose Wednesday evening. If your choice is roast saddle of lamb, it's served every day. For dessert, the trolley carries the usual selection, but if you're feeling daring, try the banana mousse with a ginger snap and a light custard, or iced lemon parfait with a warm blueberry compote topped with praline. There's a theatre menu here too (see River Restaurant above, similarly the wine list). Service is polished, professional, and skilful with much emphasis on carving and flambéeing. *Seats 100. Parties 8. L 12.30-2.30 D 6-11.15. Closed Sun, Aug. Set D £29.75 (pre/post-theatre only).*

Upstairs at the Savoy   £60

You can sit either at the long marble bar counter or at small tables overlooking the courtyard for an informal meal, and enjoy seafood specials and fine wines by the glass from Le Grand Cruvinet. Each month there's a different champagne (by the glass or pint silver tankard) to wash down some oysters, dressed crab, fish cakes or cod and salmon kedgeree. If you're really hungry, 'Jaks Plate' consists of smoked salmon, crab meat, avocado, prawns, bacon, scrambled eggs and sweet pepper salsa. Finish with sherry trifle or crème brulée. *Seats 38. Parties 6. 12-midnight (Sat 3-midnight). Closed Sun & Bank Holidays.*

SW3   Scalini   £70

Tel 0171-225 2301   Map 19 C5   **R**
1 Walton Street SW3 2JD

Traditional Italian cooking in smart surroundings. Freshly made risotti (with seafood, vegetables or chicken) are a speciality, and the pasta is all home-made: try penne with sausage and pesto, or spaghettini with crab, olive oil and garlic. Veal chop with truffles is a tempting main-course choice, as is foil-baked sea bass. *Seats 100. Parties 18. L 12-3 D 7-12 (Sun till 11.30). Closed Bank Holidays. Access, Amex, Diners, Visa.*

SE16   Scandic Crown Nelson Dock   69%   £129

Tel 0171-231 1001   Fax 0171-231 0599   Map 17 D4   **H**
265 Rotherhithe Street SE16 1EJ

Impressive modern hotel in the revitalised Nelson Docks. The stylish building offers two restaurants, a bar, a pub, a small leisure centre and comprehensive function/conference facilities (the two major rooms each have a capacity of 350). Efficiency is the keynote here as in all Scandic Crown hotels. Rooms are spacious and well equipped, with desk, seating area, mini-bar, trouser press, tea and coffee facilities, satellite TV and in-house movies. Children up to 16 stay free in parents' room. Club bedrooms are larger, with a view of the Thames. No dogs. *Rooms 390. River terrace, indoor swimming pool, gym, sauna, spa bath, solarium, tennis, games room, snooker, hotel river bus. Closed 4 days Christmas. Access, Amex, Diners, Visa.*

SW1   Scandic Crown Victoria   67%   £177

Tel 0171-834 8123   Fax 0171-828 1099   Map 19 D5   **H**
2 Bridge Place Victoria SW1V 1QA

A centrally located hotel which combines Scandinavian practicality and efficiency with agreeably appointed surroundings. Air-conditioned bedrooms are comfortable, with sturdy Scandinavian furniture, duvets and even Scandinavian beers in the mini-bar. Children free up to the age of 13 in parents' room. 24hr room service. Buffet breakfast served 7-10. Extensive conference and function facilities. No dogs. *Rooms 210. Indoor swimming pool, mini-gym, sauna, spa bath, solarium, beauty & hair salons. Access, Amex, Diners, Visa.*

W1   The Selfridge   75%   £181

Tel 0171-408 2080   Fax 0171-409 2295   Map 18 C2   **HR**
Orchard Street Marble Arch W1H 0JS

A porte-cochère with brass lanterns and greenery makes a good first impression at this modern hotel to the rear of the famous department store. Warm cedar panelling lends a traditional English feel to the foyer and a smart first-floor lounge with leather wing armchairs. In complete contrast, Stoves Bar is rustic, with wheelback chairs and genuine old beams and timbers recovered from a medieval barn. Bedrooms of various sizes are very comfortable, with darkwood units and TV remote controls wired to the bedside; all have air-conditioning and telephones by the bed, at the desk and in the modestly-sized bathrooms that also offer good towelling and marble vanitory units. Children up to 14 stay free in parents' room. Valet parking. Conferences and banqueting for up to 300. Thistle & Mount Charlotte. *Rooms 295. News kiosk, coffee shop (7am-11pm). Access, Amex, Diners, Visa.*

See over

Fletchers   £65

The restaurant is named after the architectural artist whose drawings adorn the walls. Mark Page's modern British menu offers well-thought-out and carefully prepared dishes. Starters might include a salad of langoustines with spiced white cabbage, warm home-smoked duck with a chilled basil pear or chargrilled seafood with crispy thyme polenta. Main courses are equally tempting – roast lamb with thyme and tongue hot pot, sirloin steak with an oxtail timbale or beautifully cooked partridge with a baby cabbage and bacon pie. A short list of good wines is preceded by guidance notes. Mostly France, some from Italy and the New World; fair prices. Cosy little perimeter booths offer intimate dining. Discreet, but enthusiastic service is under the direction of Michael D'Atria. *Seats 65. Private Room 14. L 12.30-2.30 D 6.30-10.30. Closed L Sat, all Sun. Set L £16.50 Set D £ 19.75.*

SE22   Sema   £50

Tel 0181-693 3213   Map 17 D6   **R**
57 Lordship Lane SE22 8EP

Small, friendly Thai restaurant, offering helpful service, and careful cooking. Flavours are often enhanced by the use of the charcoal grill. Particularly recommended are "golden sema" (a selection of deep-fried starters), khao pad (egg-fried rice with ham and prawns) and pad thai noodles used to good effect as the stuffing for a wafer thin omelette, something of a house speciality. The strength of the curries can be obligingly adjusted to suit the individual. Weekend buffet lunch £4.95, child £2.95. *Seats 70. Parties 18. Private Room 15. L (Sat, Sun only) 12-3 D 6-11.30. Closed L Mon-Fri, 2 days Christmas. Set meals £17/£19. Access, Amex, Diners, Visa.*

EC3   Seoul   £30

Tel 0171-480 5770   Map 20 D2   **R**
89a Aldgate High Street EC3

A tiny, one-room café/restaurant with the plainest of decor and offering an enjoyable selection of traditional, simple Korean dishes. Starters include spring onion pancakes with seafood or dumpling soup, followed, perhaps, by marinated sirloin steak, Korean pickled cabbage (kimchi) fried with pork fillet, fish and vegetables in hot spicy soup or fried thick noodles with vegetables and beef. Spicing can be quite strong. *Seats 28. L 12-3 D 6-10. Closed Sat, Sun & Bank Holidays. Access, Visa.*

E1   Shampan   ↑   £40

Tel 0171-375 0475   Map 16 D3   **R**
79 Brick Lane E1 6QL

One of the smarter restaurants on Brick Lane, with plush seating, attractive pink napery and helpful staff. The extensive menu covers a range of tandoori, biryani, dhansak and balti dishes. Fish (rarely found in most Indian restaurants) is well represented here. Dishes are carefully spiced, with the use of fresh herbs another notable feature. *Seats 62. Parties 25. L 12-3 D 6-12. Closed 26 Dec. Access, Amex, Diners, Visa.*

W1   Shampers   £50

Tel 0171-437 1692 Fax 0171-437 1217   Map 18 D3   **R**
4 Kingly Street W1R 5LF

Between Regent Street and Carnaby Street, this is one of the West End's favourite drinking spots and has a thriving food side, too. The menu runs from oysters, mussels, gravad lax and salads to grilled noisettes of lamb, chargrilled squid, bangers and mash and a fresh fish of the day. Ham and cheese pie, the day's casserole and steak sandwich are other popular choices. Silly prices on a far from silly wine list! Bargains galore, super wines, fantastic choice – sensational! *Seats 50. Private Room 45. Restaurant Mon-Fri 12-3, Wine bar 11-11 (Sat 11-3). Closed D Sat, all Sun, Bank Holidays. Access, Amex, Diners, Visa.*

W8   Shanghai   £60

Tel 0171-938 2501   Map 19 A4   **R**
38c Kensington Church Street W8 4BX

Stylish Chinese restaurant on two floors, ground and basement, offering well-cooked food in relaxing surroundings. As well as hot and sour soup, lemon chicken, crispy

Szechuan duck and other standard dishes, the menu is strong on seafood: crab with black beans and ginger, braised lobster, 'sea-spiced' scallops and sumptuous eel with a salt and pepper crust. Peking dumplings are a house speciality (griddled, boiled or steamed). Friendly service from smart and efficient staff. A pianist plays every night in the comfortable, but window-less basement. On the bend of Kensington Church Street, at the Kensington High Street end. *Seats 65. L 12-2.15 D 6.30-11.30. Closed Sun, 4 days Christmas. Set D from £17.50. Access, Amex, Diners, Visa.*

SW7   Shaw's   £70

Tel 0171-373 7774   Fax 0171-370 5102   Map 19 B5   **R**
119 Old Brompton Road South Kensington SW7 3RN

In a converted coach house, Shaw's offers serious cooking and friendly service in civilised, quietly formal surroundings. Decor is elegantly modern, with large feature mirrors (the work of one of the owners), and tables are correctly and prettily laid. Gerald (Bill) Atkins conducts front-of-house operations and his wife Frances is in charge of the kitchen. Her dishes strike a happy balance between safe and fashionable, with some very nice ideas but nothing to startle the worthy clientele which is the restaurant's target. Menus are basically modern British style, as shown by terrine of quail with a game stuffing; charlotte of asparagus, leeks and artichokes; roast duck with mangetout and a port and dark cherry sauce; and peppered noisettes of venison with a purée of celeriac and a sauté of mushrooms, pine nuts and crisp potatoes. Desserts keep up the good work with temptations like tiramisu terrine, a plate of sorbets and berries or hot vanilla soufflé with chocolate sauce. Excellent petits fours served with coffee. Tasting notes alongside each wine on a pleasing list; fair prices, but more half bottles needed. *Seats 44. Parties 10. L 12-2 (Sun to 3.30) D 7-10. Closed L Sat, D Sun, Easter, last 2 weeks Aug, Christmas-New Year. Set L £14/£17.50 (Sun £16/£19.50) Set D £26.75/£29.75. Access, Amex, Diners, Visa.*

WC2   Sheekey's   £65

Tel 0171-240 2565   Fax 0171-379 1417   Map 21 B2   **R**
28-32 St Martins Court Leicester Square WC2N 4AL

A famous fish restaurant long favoured by theatre folk and theatre-goers – its walls are lined with images of stars of stage and screen. Chef Jonathan Twinam prepares a menu which will appeal to both traditionalists and modernists: for the former, native or rock oysters, potted shrimps, poached salmon, sole meunière, stewed eels and lobster thermidor; for the latter halibut fillet in a split pea sauce flavoured with prawns and vermouth, brill steaks glazed with crab and coconut or grilled sea bass stuffed with endives. Fish pie and fishcakes are popular items on the set menu. The restaurant, Josef's Brasserie (sharing the same kitchen and entrance) and a cocktail/wine bar are now open throughout the day – the brasserie with a slightly restricted menu. 1996 sees Sheekey's centenary, and there will no doubt be some celebrations. *Seats 90. Parties 12. Private Room 50. Meals 12-11.15 (Sat 6-11.15). Closed Sun (exc May-Aug), 25 & 26 Dec, Easter & some Bank Holidays. Set L & pre-theatre D £15.95/£18.75. Access, Amex, Visa.*

SW1   Shepherd's   £60

Tel 0171-834 9552   Fax 0171-233 6047   Map 19 D5   **R**
Marsham Court Marsham Street Westminster SW1P 4LA

The portraits of Richard Shepherd, Michael Caine and their inspirer, Peter Langan, loom large from the menu, which remains a bastion of British cooking. Fixed-price menus offer a pleasing mix of traditional and modern, from hot salmon and potato salad with dill dressing, asparagus vinaigrette and black pudding with bubble and squeak among the starters, to kipper and haddock fishcakes, mackerel with mustard sauce, shepherd's pie and – from the trolley – roast beef and Yorkshire pudding. Burnt Cambridge cream, cherry crumble and home-made raspberry jelly and ice cream feature among the desserts. A good percentage of wines on the shortish list come from the New World. Very little over £20. Even an '85 Dom Perignon champagne is not unreasonably priced at £76. *Seats 70. Private Room 32. L 12.30-2.45 D 6.30-11.30. Set L & D £18.95/£20.95. Closed Sat, Sun, Bank Holidays, Easter weekend, Christmas. Access, Amex, Diners, Visa.*

SW1   Sheraton Belgravia   75%   £259

Tel 0171-235 6040   Fax 0171-259 6243   Map 19 C4   **HR**
20 Chesham Place Belgravia SW1X 8HQ

Personal service is high on the list of priorities at this luxurious modern hotel and its relatively small size allows it to be achieved. That service starts with valet parking in the NCP (at discounted rates) and a glass of champagne or orange juice at the reception desk in the panelled lobby. Day rooms, including a split-level lounge and library bar, offer abundant comfort, and bedrooms sport freestanding yew furniture; two floors are designated non-smoking. Guests have free use of two nearby health clubs, where facilities include a gym, sauna, solarium and swimming pool. Children stay free in parents' room. Unmanned business centre. No dogs. *Rooms 89. Access, Amex, Diners, Visa.*

Chesham's   £70

Modern international is the style of cooking in an attractive restaurant designed in sections – one of them with a palm tree, glass-domed roof and wall mirrors. The back section is designated non-smoking. Typical dishes include seafood chowder with garlic croutons, marinated Thai beef salad, sautéed lamb sweetbreads with roasted shallots and glazed vegetables, breast of chicken with a spinach mousse, wild mushrooms and pesto jus, and pan-fried salmon with a brioche crust, garlic potatoes and a lobster jus. Set meal prices (except Sunday lunch) include wine. Pianist Monday to Thursday evenings. *Seats 45. Parties 16. Private Room 22. L 12.30-3 D 6.30-11. Closed L Sat. Set L £21.95/£24.95 (Sun £15.95) Set D £19.95.*

SW1   Sheraton Park Tower   79%   £308

Tel 0171-235 8050   Fax 0171-235 8231   Map 19 C4   **HR**
101 Knightsbridge SW1X 7RN

One of the most distinctive of London's hotels, a circular high-rise tower within a stone's throw of Harrods and Hyde Park. Bedrooms, apart from the 31 luxury suites, are identical in size and feature rather pleasing burr walnut-veneered furniture. Thick quilted bedcovers, turned down at night, match the curtains; TVs and mini-bars are discreetly hidden away. There are telephones by the bed, on the desk and in the bathrooms, which have marble-tiled walls, good shelf space, towels and toiletries. 24hr room service is available. Children up to 14 stay free in parents' room. Extra services on Executive floors include valet unpacking, two-hour laundering, a special check-out service and fax machines. Meeting facilities can handle up to 70 theatre-style. Secure parking for 100 cars – £9 for 24 hours. *Rooms 295. Beauty & hair salon, coffee shop (7am-7pm). Access, Amex, Diners, Visa.*

Restaurant 101   £70

Ceiling-high trees and large skylights give the busy dining room a smart conservatory feel. Chef Gerd Jacobmeyer's secret of success is his flexible menu, designed to please both the shopper and the business person. Thus, a single-course option is available between noon and 7pm, which includes a selection varying from a focaccia club sandwich to steak and oyster pie. For the more ambitious, scallops with black linguini and warm coriander oil, wild mushroom soup and lightly fried calf's sweetbreads with a confit of shallots are tempting starters, followed by perhaps a lobster soufflé, venison with salsify and blackcurrants, or perfectly roasted partidge with honey-glazed parsnips. A two-course lunch menu is available at £12.50 (plus service), and features a wide choice from the carte. The cooking is precise, but standards can slip when kitchen shifts change mid-afternoon – lemon tart arriving fridge-cold rather than warm as advertised. *Seats 80. Open 12-11. Set L £12.50 (Sun £25).*

W1   Sherlock Holmes Hotel   66%   £121

Tel 0171-486 6161   Fax 0171-486 0884   Map 18 C2   **H**
108 Baker Street W1M 1LB

Tastefully decorated in the Victorian style, the walls of the large public rooms are covered with pictures of Holmes and Dr. Watson in scenes from their adventures. The bedrooms are comfortable, en suite bathrooms have tubs with overhead showers, other amenities include TVs with in-house movie channel and direct-dial phones. From some rooms of

modest size, the range extends through Plaza rooms – with sitting areas, upgraded
furnishings and spa baths, to two suites, one of which – The Reichenbach – sports
a splendid free-standing Victorian bath. Children up to ten stay free in parents' room. Air-
conditioned banquet/conference facilities for 50/80. No dogs. Useful price concessions
make the nearby NCP in Chiltern Street an attractive prospect. *Rooms 125. Access, Amex,
Diners, Visa.*

Set menu prices may not always include service or wine.

SW7   Shezan   £70

Tel 0171-584 9316   Map 19 B4   **R**
16-22 Cheval Place Knightsbridge SW7 1ES

A stairway runs down from street level to a bar area and a room of quiet elegance, which
together comprise one of London's most elegant and civilised Indian restaurants. The
menu is fairly standard, with tandoori barbecues and grills and a variety of speciality
curries. Friendly, attentive staff. Cover charge £1.75. 15% service charge. *Seats 100.
L 12-2.30 D 7-11.30. Closed 25 Dec. Set L £12.95. Access, Amex, Diners, Visa.*

W1   Shogun   £90

Tel 0171-493 1877   Map 18 C3   **R**
Britannia Inter-Continental Hotel Adams Row W1A 3AN

A basement restaurant at the rear of a modern hotel. The vaulted room is transformed by
samurai weapons, pictures of ancient warriors and traditionally clad staff into a passable
replica of a medieval Japanese dungeon. In keeping with Japanese custom, the menu is
fish based with a few nods in favour of the carnivorous. Japanese standards, various
teriyakis and sushis are supplemented by six set dinners – tempura, sashimi, salmon,
chicken, duck or beef – and provide an excellent initiation, all taking dishes from the
carte. The beautifully presented sashimi includes five types of the freshest fish. There is
a sushi/sashimi bar which provides a fascinating insight into the preparation of these
intricate dishes as the chefs work 'on view'. *Seats 60. Parties 20. D only 6-11. Closed Mon,
1 week Christmas. Set D £30 & £32. Access, Amex, Diners, Visa.*

W13   Sigiri   £30

Tel 0181-579 8000   Map 17 A4   **R**
161 Northfield Avenue West Ealing W13 9QT

Sri Lankan restaurant decorated with drawings inspired by those found on the rocks around
the ancient island fortress from which Sigiri takes its name. Among the Sinhalese offerings
are unusual rice-flour hoppers, deep-fried green banana slices, coconut-based curries and
sizzling dishes (yoghurt-marinated chicken with cashew nuts). Help-yourself buffet Sundays.
*Seats 65. Parties 24. L Sun 12.30-3 (Tue-Sat by arrangement for parties of 12 or more only)
D 6.30-11 (Sun till 9.30). Closed Mon, 25 & 26 Dec, Bank Holidays. Access, Visa.*

SW1   Signor Sassi   £60

Tel 0171-584 2277   Fax 0171-225 3953   Map 19 C4   **R**
14 Knightsbridge Green SW1X 7LG

Italian restaurant close to Harrods, with a straightforward menu of classic dishes – bresaola
with mango and rucola salad, chicken broth with tortellini, calf's liver with butter and
sage. Specialities include sea bass, lamb with mint, and veal cooked in brandy and cream.
Seats 80. Parties 15. L 12-2.30 D 7-11.30. Closed Sun. Access, Amex, Diners, Visa.

SE5   Silver Lake   £40

Tel 0171-701 9961   Fax 0171-708 5718   Map 17 D5   **R**
59 Camberwell Church Street SE5 8TR

A busy and homely Chinese restaurant offering a mix of Peking, Cantonese and Szechuan
cooking. Seafood is favoured – try mussels in black bean sauce, crispy fried oysters, stewed
garlic eels, steamed whole fish with exotic Chinese vegetables – but there's plenty of other
choice among the 130+ dishes on the menu. *Seats 40. L 12-1.45 (parties of 10 or more
only) D 5.30-11 (Fri & Sat to 12.30, Sun & Bank Holidays from 6). Closed Mon, 10 days Aug,
1 week after Christmas. Set D from £12. Access, Amex, Visa.*

SW1   Simply Nico   ★   £65

Tel 0171-630 8061   Fax 0171-355 4877   Map 19 D4   **R**
48a Rochester Row Westminster SW1P 1JU

Nico and Dinah-Jane Ladenis's smallest restaurant lives up to its name, offering delightful, straightforward menus and wine lists (all include service) without compromising quality in any way. Tim Johnson is now the chef, cooking according to Nico's priciples and creating such splendid starter dishes as a gratin of crab with fresh pasta and lobster sauce, fillets of Dover sole with sweet garlic purée and seared escalope of foie gras with brioche and chopped oranges (a simplified version of a Nico classic). Main courses range from a superb charcoal-grilled rib of Scotch beef with red wine sauce and best end of lamb with a herb crust and couscous to breast of duck with honey, peppercorns and a maize pancake and seared salmon fillet with lettuce and an Oriental sauce. Dishes are accompanied by excellent chips or pommes purée. Wonderful desserts such as double chocolate tart with orange crème anglaise and caramelised apple tart round off a genuinely enjoyable meal: the only extra is £2 for coffee. *Seats 45. L 12-2 D 7-11. Closed L Sat, all Sun & Bank Holidays, 11 days Christmas, 4 days Easter. Set L £19/£23.50 Set D £26. Access, Amex, Diners, Visa.*

WC2   Simpson's-in-the-Strand   £75

Tel 0171-836 9112   Fax 0171-836 1381   Map 20 A2   **R**
100 The Strand WC2R 0EW

The quintessential English restaurant opened its doors in 1848 and has become a veritable institution. Today it continues to offer a whole range of true British classics. Since 1994 it now starts business at 7am (Mon-Fri) to serve a splendid selection of breakfast dishes. One of its traditions is the silver carving wagons which daily include roast Scotch beef with Yorkshire pudding, roast saddle of lamb with redcurrant jelly and roast Aylesbury duck with apple sauce and stuffing. Each day of the week also brings its own warming favourite: on Sunday there's Lancashire hot pot, Tuesday sees steak, kidney and mushroom pudding and on Thursday boiled silverside with pease pudding, carrots and dumplings is offered. Puddings will also delight Anglophiles with apple pie and cream, Spotted Dick and rhubarb crumble among the many offerings. *Seats 240. Parties 12. Private Room 145. L 12-2.30 D 6-11 (Sun till 9). Closed 25 & 26 Dec, 1 Jan, Good Friday. Set L & D £10 (Sun L £17.50). Access, Amex, Diners, Visa.*

NW6   Singapore Garden   £45

Tel 0171-328 5314   Fax 0171-624 0656   Map 16 B3   **R**
83 Fairfax Road Swiss Cottage NW6 4DY

Extensive menu of far Eastern dishes served in pleasant Swiss Cottage surroundings. There are daily specials as well as Malaysian specialities – try squid blachan, fried hokkien mee (egg noodles with prawns, eggs, pork and fish cake), rogak (fresh fruit and vegetables tossed in a shrimp paste) or oyster omelette, Singapore-style. Good range of sweet and fruity desserts. *Seats 100. Private Room 60. L 12-2.45 D 6-10.45 (Fri & Sat to 11.15). Closed 5 days Christmas. Set L & D from £16. Access, Amex, Diners, Visa.*
Also at:
NW1 154 Gloucester Place NW1 6DT Tel 0171-723 8233   Map 18 C2

W6   Snows on the Green   £70

Tel 0171-603 2142   Map 17 B4   **R**
166 Shepherds Bush Road Brook Green W6 7PB

Huge pictures of lavender and sunflower fields and bunches of lavender on the half-tiled tables combine to provide an almost Provençal feel to this corner of Hammersmith whose Mediterranean menu includes some intriguing combinations. A gratinated cheese, onion and red wine soup, confit of lamb's tongues with lentils and marrow or perhaps chicken liver parfait with toasted brioche to begin, followed by beef pot-au-feu with pickled vegetables, rack of lamb with aubergine, anchovy and tomato gratin or steamed John Dory with mussels and chives. Simple desserts include some fine home-made ices. *Seats 70. Private Room 24. L 12-3 D 7-11. Closed L Sat, D Sun, Bank Holiday Mondays, 1 week Christmas. Set L £11.50/£13.50 (Sun £13.50/£16.50).*

W1   Soho Soho   ↑   £70

Tel 0171-494 3491   Fax 0171-437 3091   Map 21 A2   **R**
11-13 Frith Street Soho W1

♟ 🍓

The Rotisserie and all-day Wine Bar on the ground floor provide a raucously noisy, lively and crowded environment that continues to draw in the young and the fashionable. Upstairs, the Restaurant is equally popular but more select, with bookings and punctuality essential. Decor is Provençal – furniture and floors are in scrubbed, sky-blue-washed blue, yellow ochre, terracotta and deep azure, while walls in both have gigantic Picasso-esque drawings. Cooking is also of classic Provençal inspiration with an informal menu of omelettes, pasta and grills in the Rotisserie and more complex dishes upstairs. Soupe de poisson à la marseillaise, gateau de risotto forestière and magret of duck with a wild mushroom mousse are typical starters, while main courses might include grilled mullet with a fennel purée and anchovy and orange sauce and roasted calf's liver with a turnip gratin. Desserts such as tarte au citron or chocolate marquise are a fitting finale to a meal of exemplary standards and quality. Classy service. Ask about the free local NCP parking offer for restaurant diners (only) after 6.30pm. Part of the upstairs rooms is non-smoking. *Seats 60 (Ground-floor Rotisserie 80). Parties 8. Private Room 55. L 12-2.45 D 6-11.45 (Rotisserie Mon-Sat Meals Noon-12.45am). Closed L Sat, all Sun, 25 & 26 Dec. Set D £12.95/£15.95. Access, Amex, Diners, Visa.*

N16   Le Soir   £35

Tel 0171-275 8781   Map 16 D2   **R**
226 Stoke Newington High Street N16 7HU

Popular neighbourhood restaurant run by a husband-and-wife team. A varied menu could include filo parcels of smoked chicken and mushroom, fried Camembert with apple and calvados jelly, poussin dijonnaise, lamb steak in mint sauce and pork escalope with mashed potato and tarragon sauce. Also fish of the day, salads, a vegetarian dish and simple desserts like chocolate mousse. *Seats 46. Parties 10. D only 6-midnight. Closed Mon, 25-30 Dec. Access, Visa.*

N1   Sonargaon   £50

Tel 0171-226 6499   Map 16 C3   **R**
46 Upper Street Islington N1 OPN

A discreetly-lit intimate setting for some carefully spiced classic Indian dishes. The not overlong menu includes a few non-standard items such as ginger chicken, where fresh ginger is used to excellent effect with tender cubes of chicken. Saucing is subtle with the judicious use of spices. Butter chicken or lamb pasanda cooked with fresh cream, nuts and sultanas is as tempting as king prawns cooked with a delicious sweet and sour masala sauce. *Seats 60. Parties 30. L 12-3 D 6-12. Closed 25 Dec. Access, Amex, Diners, Visa.*

SW13   Sonny's   £65

Tel 0181-748 0393   Map 17 A5   **R**
94 Church Road Barnes SW13 0DQ

♟ 🥐

A café at the front and a split-level restaurant at the rear with a few tables overlooking what must be one of the tiniest patio gardens anywhere. The menu is modern British-based, with influences from the Med and the States: Caesar salad, roast lobster risotto with basil and rare beef with aubergines and truffle oil are typical starters, preceding baked cod with leeks, fennel and squid ink sauce, roast wild rabbit with cannellini beans or daube of beef with parsnip purée. Try prune and armangac ice cream or chocolate mousse with pistachio tuile for a delicious ending. *Seats 100. Parties 10. Private Room 20. L 12.30-2.30 D 7.30-11. Closed D Sun, all 25 & 26 Dec. Set L £13.50 (2-course), Sun L £16.50 (3-course). Access, Amex, Visa.*

We welcome bona fide complaints and recommendations on the tear-out pages at the back of the book for readers' comments. They are followed up by our professional team.

SW1   The Square   ★ ↑   £80

Tel 0171-839 8787
32 King Street St James's SW1 6RJ

Map 18 D3   **R**

Just off St James's Square, the restaurant has a smartly contemporary decor of brightly coloured upholstery and cream-coloured walls which complements Philip Howard's menus. The daily-changing choice includes modern interpretations of Mediterranean as well as a smattering of British classics. Combinations of ingredients are excitingly original, producing food that truly excites the senses. Begin with a warm salad of game with port and raisins, oxtail soup with baked roseval potatoes and bone marrow, seared scallops with squid ink risotto and gremolata and parfait of foie gras and chicken livers with toasted granary bread. Main dishes include a sauté of John Dory with pesto noodles and sauce vierge, thinly sliced veal with a Jerusalem artichoke purée and fondant potatoes, roast Tuscan squab with a sauté of trompettes and balsamic jus and rump of lamb with tomato confit and rosemary. Desserts are no less innovative: witness a superb baked chocolate sponge with a chocolate and orange sauce, a soup of fruits served with an apple sorbet or tarte bourdalou with a pear sabayon. Improved lay-out of the wine list makes selection much easier, but choose carefully to avoid too deep a hole in your pocket. *Seats 65. Parties 8. Private Room 20. L 12-3 D 6-11.45. Closed L Sat & Sun, most Bank Holidays. Set D £32/£38. Access, Visa.*

SW17   Sree Krishna   £25

Tel 0181-672 4250
192-194 Tooting High Street SW17

Map 17C6   **R**

Sound South Indian cooking making good use of freshly ground spices and herbs and sparing use of oil and fat. Vegetarian dishes are the real speciality but there are also plenty of meat, chicken and prawn preparations. *Seats 120. Parties 50. Private Room 60. L 12-3 D 6-11 (Fri/Sat to midnight). Closed 25 & 26 Dec. Access, Amex, Diners, Visa.*

W1   Sri Siam   £55

Tel 0171-434 3544
16 Old Compton Street Soho W1V 5PE

Map 21 A2   **R**

Traditional Thai food cooked to order in a lively Soho atmosphere. Good range of dishes on à la carte and set menus, and a separate vegetarian list. Among the specialities are *tom yum* soups, *homok kai* (chicken cooked in spicy coconut gravy flavoured with lemon grass and presented in banana baskets), *sia rong hai* (sliced grilled sirloin of beef with mint, coriander and green salad) and *kaeng kurry koong* (a yellow curry of king prawns). *Seats 80. Parties 40. Private Rooms 20/25. L 12-3 D 6-11.15 (Sun to 10.30). Closed L Sun, 24-26 Dec, 1 Jan. Set L £10.50 Set D from £15.50. Access, Amex, Diners, Visa.*

EC2   Sri Siam City   £55

Tel 0171-628 5772
85 London Wall EC2M 7AD

Map 20 C1   **R**

Stylish Thai basement restaurant and bar that's a good alternative to City wine bars. The main menu, supplemented by various set meals, includes classics like tom yum soup, stuffed chicken wings and curries of various hues. Specialities include neua phad prig (sliced beef pan-fried with fresh herbs and chili) and koong kratiem prig thai (stir-fried king prawns with garlic and pepper). Separate vegetarian menu. *Seats 150. Meals 11.30am-8pm. Closed Sat, Sun & Bank Holidays. Set meals £14.90/£24.90. Access, Amex, Diners, Visa.*

SW1   The Stafford   74%   £223

Tel 0171-493 0111   Fax 0171-493 7121
16 St James's Place SW1A 1NJ

Map 18 D3   **H**

In keeping with its clubland address the Stafford puts the emphasis on discreet, personal service. Paintings line the foyer walls and leather chesterfields create a scene of cultured calm. Deeper in, the drawing room, made elegant with antiques and fresh with cut

flowers, offers refreshments throughout the day, and the American Bar features
a collection of American club and university ties, caps and badges. Outside the bar is
a terrace in a cobbled mews. Accommodation ranges from singles with queen-size beds
through doubles and junior suites in the Carriage House to the Terrace Garden suite
complete with terrace and fountain. Decor is individual, with fabrics and furniture of
a high standard. The 1996 improvement programme planned by the new owners includes
air-conditioning in all bedrooms. No dogs. *Rooms 74. Access, Amex, Diners, Visa.*

W2	Stakis London Coburg	60%	£102

Tel 0171-221 2217   Fax 0171-229 0557   Map 18 A3   **H**
129 Bayswater Road W2 4RJ

Overlooking Hyde Park, and close to Queensway underground station, this hotel has
been revitalised since being acquired by the Stakis Group in 1994. Refurbishment
continues in the public rooms, but all bedrooms now have TVs, direct-dial telephones,
tea/coffee-making facilities, good desk space and en-suite bathrooms (most with tubs and
showers). Some have irons and fold-out boards, trouser presses and mini-safes. Bedrooms
on the fourth floor are reserved for non-smokers. Cots provided free. *Rooms 132.
Access, Amex, Diners, Visa.*

SW1	Stakis St Ermin's	71%	£159

Tel 0171-222 7888   Fax 0171-222 6914   Map 19 D4   **H**
Caxton Street Victoria SW1H 0QW

The Stakis St Ermin's is a peaceful haven in an area highly populated by tourists, giving it
the double appeal of plenty of activity and the perfect retreat from it all. Extensive
conference facilities (for up to 200 delegates theatre-style) also make it a primary choice
for functions and banquets. Behind an opulent Edwardian facade day rooms are equally
sumptuous: luxurious furnishings follow a green theme and the elegant furniture, much
of it antique, finds an ideal setting among marble and ornate plasterwork. A splendid
Baroque staircase leads to the five floors of bedrooms, which offer every modern comfort
and are well appointed and furnished with taste. 54 rooms are designated non-smoking.
Children stay free in parents' room. 24hr room service. 22 parking spaces (£8 for 24
hours). *Rooms 290. Coffee shop (24hrs). Access, Amex, Diners, Visa.*

W2	Standard		£40

Tel 0171-727 4818   Map 18 A3   **R**
23 Westbourne Grove W2 4UA

One of the best-known establishments (Indian) on a street of predominantly ethnic
restaurants. Consistently enjoyable food has been produced here since 1970, the menu
featuring such classic standards as rogan josh (their most popular lamb dish), chicken
biryani and kulfi (Indian ice cream). *Seats 130. Parties 12. Private Room 25. L 12-3
D 6-11.45. Closed 25 Dec. Access, Amex, Visa.*

W1	Stephen Bull		£80

Tel 0171-486 9696   Map 18 C2   **R**
5-7 Blandford Street W1H 3AA

♟ ❦

Of the three restaurants associated with Stephen Bull's name this is the original (the other
two being *Stephen Bull's Bar & Bistro* and *Fulham Road* – see entries). Its starkly
minimalist monochromatic decor remains as appealing and up to date as the menus.
These continue to offer ingredients of a quality that rivals its younger siblings in that
imaginative and well-prepared foods, largely a modish mix of influences taken from the
Orient, Mediterranean region and our own islands, are combined to create a pastiche that
delights the senses. Begin with Scotch broth, a selection of Spanish delicacies including
Serrano ham, Mahen cheese and chorizo with quince paste, prawn wun tuns with soy,
ginger and lime sauce or a warm tart of spinach and roasted peppers. Main dishes could
be a tartlet of hare, foie gras, Swiss chard, blood oranges and peppercorns, roast middle
neck fillet of lamb with a Roquefort and herb crust and John Dory and scallops with
a saffron cream and shallots. Delectable sweets to finish include a baked lemon and ginger
pudding, pistachio bavarois with panettone and an apricot tarte tatin or there are
farmhouse cheeses with home-made oatcakes. Fair prices on an enterprising wine list.
*Seats 55. L 12.15-2.15 D 6.30-10.45. Closed L Sat, all Sun, Bank Holidays, 10 days
Christmas/New Year. Access, Amex, Visa.*

EC1   Stephen Bull's Bistro & Bar   £60

Tel 0171-490 1750   Map 16 D3   **R**
71 St John Street EC1 4AN

Newly expanded into an adjoining property with the creation of a stylish seafood bar, used mainly for the preparation of a range of cold dishes and starters, the bistro offers a selection of very fashionable dishes prepared by the deft hands of Steven Carter, who has returned here after a year at the Blandford Street restaurant (qv). The daily-changing menu offers a short but varied choice including smoked haddock and bacon chowder, courgette and pesto risotto and grilled vegetables with focaccia and herb dressing among the starters. From the seafood bar come crab and cucumber salad, ceviche of queen scallops served in the half shell and topped with a salsa cruda of finely diced mixed peppers, juniper-cured salmon with horseradish cream and a selection of sushi. For a main course you could choose between braised lamb shank with kidneys, peas and mint, duck breast or a confit of spring greens, bacon and star anise, grilled plaice with artichokes, mushrooms and crab juices or roast monkfish with ratatouille, basil and garlic cream. To finish there are delicious desserts like the ubiquitous but nevertheless highly enjoyable sticky toffee pudding with hot toffee sauce and cinnamon crème caramel with strawberries or dark chocolate torte with a chocolate and rum sauce. Little over £20 on a sensible wine list, some good beers too! Delightful place and equally charming staff. *Seats 120. Parties 25. L 12-2.30 D 6-10.30 (Sat from 7). Closed L Sat, all Sun, Bank Holidays, 1 week Christmas. Access, Amex, Visa.*

SW8   The Stepping Stone   NEW   £55

Tel 0171-622 0555   Map 17 C5   **R**
123 Queenstown Road SW8 3RH

This ultra-modern dining room avoids the tedious minimalist bleakness of the 90s restaurant designers, with clever use of splashes of colour, pictures and a profusion of flowers. Intelligent buying ensures high-quality produce: starters might include grilled goat's cheese with first-class leaves from Appledore, griddled scallops (perfectly cooked) with soy, ginger, spring onion and coriander or cheese beignets, bravely served with tomato ketchup. To follow – maybe roast Barbary duck with red cabbage and chestnuts, a moist rabbit and prune casserole (the prunes remained elusive) or perhaps baked black bream with braised chard. Desserts include some excellent home-made ice creams. Interesting selection of Belgian beers. Service, under the enthusiastic direction of Gary Levy, is friendly and clued-up. *Seats 54. L 12-2.30 D 7-11. Set L £10. Closed L Sat, D Sun, all Bank Holidays. Access, Amex, Diners, Visa.*

W8   Stratfords   NEW   £70

Tel 0171-937 6388   Fax 0171-938 3435   Map 19 A4   **R**
7 Stratford Road W8 3JS

Mrs Martin takes over the helm at this re-named restaurant (formerly Le Quai St Pierre), though the piscine emphasis remains unchanged. The dining rooms, on two floors, have a cool feel with white paintwork, high-quality framed prints and crisp blue linen napery. Oysters, both French and Irish, grilled baby squid and an excellent fish soup accompanied by correct rouille as starters are followed by the day's fish (monkfish, sea bass, turbot, mullet or sole) and a tempting choice of ways to eat them; roast with garlic (with a delicious hint of fennel), plain grilled, or with either tomato and basil or beurre blanc sauce. Carnivores are not neglected with roast poussin, rib-eye steak or lamb brochettes on offer. Short list of classic dishes, but disappointingly the only cheese offered is warm goat's cheese on toast. Friendly French service. £1.50 cover charge, 15% 'optional' gets you very good bread and olives. *Seats 50. Parties 10. Private Room 30. L 12-3 D 7-11. Closed Sun. Set L £12. Access, Amex, Diners, Visa.*

We welcome bona fide complaints and recommendations on the tear-out pages at the back of the book for reader's comments. They are followed up by our professional team.

SW7   Stuart Hotel   £70

Tel 0171-373 1004   Fax 0171-370 2548   Map 19 B5   **B**
110 Cromwell Road SW7 4ES

Bed and breakfast hotel conveniently situated for all points west including Heathrow. Modestly furnished bedrooms have satellite TV, direct-dial phones and tea- and coffee-making facilities. Most have en-suite bathrooms with showers. One child under 12 can stay free in parents' room. A comfortable lounge is ideal for meeting friends. Unlicensed. No dogs. *Rooms 50. Access, Amex, Visa.*

W6   Sumos   £35

Tel 0181-741 7916   Map 17 A4   **R**
169 King Street Hammersmith W6 9JT

An unassuming Japanese snack restaurant on Hammersmith's main shopping street. Besides sushi and sashimi there's tempura, miso soup, griddle-fried dumplings, beef with ginger and chicken yakitori and sushi. *Seats 40. Parties 10. L 12-2.30 D 6.30-11.30. Closed L Sat, all Sun, Bank Holidays, 10 days Christmas-New Year. Set L from £7 Set D from £12. No credit cards.*

SW1   Suntory   £120

Tel 0171-409 0201   Fax 0171-499 0208   Map 18 D3   **R**
72 St James's Street SW1A 1PH

One of London's longest-established Japanese restaurants, with more of a Western style than Oriental; the cooking is of a high standard and staff have an exemplary attitude towards politeness, patience and understanding. The main dining area is on the ground floor, but there are several teppanyaki tables on the lower ground. The complete teppanyaki experience (£68 per head) includes appetisers, dobin-mushi soup, sashimi, foie gras, mixed seafood, fillet steak, mixed salad, rice, miso soup, pickled vegetables, dessert and coffee or green tea. Alternatives include turbot, lobster, salmon and -wait for it!- chateaubriand with prawns. 'Lamb Chops Monkey's Favourite' is teppanyaki chops with sautéed bananas. The traditional side of the menu is also long in choice and ranges from sushi and tempura to one-pot dishes such as shabu-shabu and yosenabe cooked at your table. Prices at lunchtime are considerably lower than in the evening. Suitably stylish for expense-account dining. *Seats 101. Parties 15. Private Room 7. L 12-2 D 7-10. Closed Sun, Bank Holidays (Easter & Christmas only). Set L from £15 Set D from £49.80. Access, Amex, Diners, Visa.*

W9   Supan   £35

Tel 0181-969 9387   Map 18 A2   **R**
4 Fernhead Road W9 3ET

Just round the corner from Harrow Road, this comfortable Thai restaurant has recently expanded into the next-door premises and proudly displays a modern new look. The menu offers carefully prepared Thai standards. Begin with chicken satay, one of the delicious tom yum soups or chicken wings stuffed with crabmeat. Choosing a main course is made easy, as most dishes are listed by sauce type – eg "green curry", where one simply chooses beef, chicken or prawn and then decides how hot to have it. Stir-fried rice noodle dishes, such as paht Thai (with prawns, ground peanuts, egg and salted turnip) are delicious and almost make a meal on their own. Vegetarians have their own menu. Prices are reasonable, so much so that the thriving take-away trade can cause delays from the kitchen. Friendly and helpful service. *Seats 60. Parties 8. L 12.30-2.30 D 6.30-10.45. Closed 2 days August, 25 & 26 Dec, 1 Jan. Access, Visa.*

SW3   Le Suquet   ★   £70

Tel 0171-581 1785   Fax 0171-225 0838   Map 19 B5   **R**
104 Draycott Avenue SW3 3AE

In surroundings inspired by the seafront at Cannes, fresh fish and shellfish get traditional treatment on a menu whose only changing element is the plats du jour. These often include sea bass (sold by weight), sole grilled or meunière and seafood pot-au-feu. Otherwise it's shellfish almost all the way, and the langoustines, coquilles St Jacques, mussels and clams may be ordered in either full or half-portions. For a major treat the

See over

mighty plateau de fruits de mer (£16) is a must. Steaks are always available for meat-eaters. Good salads and feuilletés. Note that Le Suquet is now open all day at weekends. *Seats 70. Private Room 18. L 12.30-2.30 D 7-11.30, Sat & Sun Meals 12.30-11.30. Set L £12. Access, Amex, Diners, Visa.*

N1   Suruchi   £30

Tel 0171-241 5213   Map 16 D2   **R**
82 Mildmay Park Newington Green N1 4TR

Classical music and pastel prints provide the background to Indian cooking notable for judicious use of fresh herbs and spices. Tandoori lobster is a major treat. Nearly half the menu is vegetarian. Thalis (set meals) provide particularly good value for money. Additional seating in the garden in summer. *Seats 34. L 12-2.30 D 6-11.30. Closed 25 Dec. Access, Diners, Visa.*

SW6   Sushi Gen   £50

Tel 0171-610 2120   Fax 0171-386 9846   Map 19 A6   **R**
585 Fulham Road SW6 5UA

A split-level restaurant right on the bend of Fulham Broadway. Walls are of old stock bricks and you walk and eat on blond wood. The menu comprises a wide selection of various sushi and makizushi (seaweed rolls) – all meticulously prepared and simply presented. Additionally, there are a few grilled and deep-fried dishes such as beef with miso sauce and the familiar tempura. *Seats 50. Parties 15. L 12-2.30 D 6-11. Closed 1 week Christmas. Access, Amex, Diners, Visa.*
Also at:
NW6 243 West End Lane Tel 0171-431 4031   Map 16 B2

SW5   Swallow International Hotel   68%   £142

Tel 0171-973 1000   Fax 0171-244 8194   Map 19 A5   **H**
Cromwell Road SW5 0TH

Comfortable modern hotel close to Gloucester Road tube station and on the main route to Heathrow and all points west. Public areas include the Fountain Brasserie (open 7am-midnight), the smart Blayneys cocktail bar and a comprehensive modern leisure club. Double-glazed bedrooms are modestly furnished and range from good-sized singles to spacious triples, all having satellite TV (with extra "pay as you view" channels) and all modern amenities. Luxurious suites have king-size beds and marble-clad bathrooms with spa baths. 24hr room service. Limited on-site parking (£17 for 24 hours). Children up to 12 stay free in parents' room. *Rooms 416. Indoor swimming pool, gym, sauna, spa bath, steam room, solarium, hair salon, news kiosk, coffee shop (7am-midnight). Access, Amex, Diners, Visa.*

EC4   Sweetings   £60

Tel 0171-248 3062   Map 20 C2   **R**
39 Queen Victoria Street EC4N 4SA

Arrive early for lunch at this busy and very traditional fish restaurant, as no reservations are taken. Most customers sit on stools at the various bars, each supervised by its own waiter, although a few long tables are available at the rear of the dining room. Prawn and crab cocktail (both very generous), or perhaps smoked eel or native oysters (in winter months) could launch your lunch, followed perhaps by fish pie, grilled herrings with mustard sauce, skate with black butter or Dover sole. It's worth noting that 'fried' here always means in breadcrumbs. Fresh fish is the strength of this establishment, not their accompanying vegetables. School desserts, including excellent steamed syrup pudding, or savouries (Welsh rarebit, roes on toast). Very short, but high quality, wine list; Black Velvet and Pimms are also popular with city 'suits'. Delicious sandwiches, and a take-away service available. *Seats 70. L only 11.30-3. Closed Sat, Sun, Bank Holidays, 1 week Christmas. No credit cards.*

NW3   Swiss Cottage Hotel   62%   £85

Tel 0171-722 2281   Fax 0171-483 4588   Map 16 B3   **H**
4 Adamson Road Swiss Cottage NW3 3HP

An unusually individual hotel converted from terraced houses in a quiet residential street a few minutes from Swiss Cottage underground station. The bedrooms have plenty of character, with some Victorian/Edwardian pieces of furniture, plush settees and nice old pictures. Some rooms are not all that large, and they're linked by warrens of corridors and stairs. The price quoted is for a standard double/twin. Superior and Executive rooms are priced considerably higher. Children up to 8 stay free in their parents' room. 24hr room service. The lounge is very appealing: ornate gold wallpaper under a moulded ceiling, sofas and button-back chairs on bright Oriental rugs, carved antique furniture and oil paintings. The hotel also has self-catered studio, one- and two-bedroom serviced apartments nearby, let by the week. No dogs. *Rooms 81. Garden. Access, Amex, Diners, Visa.*

> Set menu prices may not always include service or wine.

SW3	**Sydney House**	**£197**

Tel 0171-376 7711   Fax 0171-376 4233   Map 19 B5   **PH**
9-11 Sydney Street SW3 6PU

Jean-Luc Aeby's background as an interior designer is displayed to marvellous effect at his luxurious Chelsea hotel, converted from two elegant town houses with almost no expense spared. Each bedroom is individually decorated, from the Paris room with its heavy red fabrics and tented bed, to the penthouse, wallpapered with original ancient manuscripts and including a terrace overlooking the roofs of London. Some of the rear bedrooms are more modest in size but no less opulent. En-suite marble bathrooms, some with tubs, others with walk-in showers, offer bathrobes, enormous bath sheets and an enviable display of fine toiletries. Standards of housekeeping are high. Public rooms are few, but include an elegant lobby with comfortable sofas – ideal for a meeting point. There is a cosy residents' bar. 24hr room service. *Rooms 21. Access, Amex, Diners, Visa.*

W10	**Tabac**	**NEW**	**£65**

Tel & Fax 0181-960 2433   Map 16 B3   **R**
46 Golborne Road Notting Hill W10

Despite the very French Tabac logo, this minimalist dining room evokes nothing of the cluttered charm of those Gallic tobacconists. Pip Wylie and Bennie Neville's menu is influenced by that of the River Café (qv), where both have worked. Breakfast offerings include eggs benedict and a pancetta, mushroom and tomato hash with egg or buckwheat pancakes with maple syrup and fresh fruit. Lunch is a less expensive and shorter version of the dinner menu and might feature mixed Tabac antipasti, Jerusalem artichoke and chestnut soup with truffle oil or oysters with shallots and balsamic vinegar as starters, followed by good baked John Dory fillets with peperonata, chargrilled chicken breast with braised fennel (rather dry chicken and stringy fennel when we tried the dish) and an excellent sweet potato and chili gratin – the chili perked up a sometimes pedestrian vegetable! This is a no-frills restaurant, prices are reasonable and the design presents the food as the shining star – let's hope the kitchen can keep it polished. *Seats 85. Private Room 45. Meals 11am-11pm. Closed L Mon, all 24-26 Dec. Set L £7.50. Access, Diners, Visa.*

W1	**Tamarind**	**NEW**	**£60**

Tel 0171-629 3561   Map 18 C3   **R**
20 Queen Street Mayfair W1

With a few brush strokes from the talented interior designer Emily Todhunter, this smart basement dining room now sets the scene for some serious cooking. Atul Kochhar and his team have recently arrived from New Delhi and, with their tandoors blazing (visible too – behind a glass fronted kitchen), have devised a menu to make the jaded British "two pints of lager and a vindaloo" mentality sit up and take notice. A short list of starters includes jalpari chaat (prawns and fish marinated in mint and coriander); spiced chicken livers or light soups such as shorba badam pasanda (lamb with almonds and coriander). Main courses from the tandoor might include marinated chicken with mustard or a mildly spiced pomfret, or even a whole cauliflower! The curry aficionado is not forgotten, with karahi chicken or hari machli – fried fish with crisp spinach leaves – or a perfectly spiced rogan josh. Accompaniments are equally impressive: bindi masala (spiced okra), which managed to avoid its customary stickiness; delicious dal bukhari (lentils in a mild dark sauce), or nan bread straight from the tandoor. A sampler menu is available at lunchtime, offering an ideal introduction to the delights of this kitchen. Same ownership as *The Halcyon* (see entry), also under the direction of Robin Wauters. *Seats 80. L 12-3 D 6-11.30. Closed Sun. Access, Amex, Diners, Visa.*

SW6   Tandoori Lane   £35

Tel 0171-371 0440   Map 17 B5   **R**
131a Munster Road Fulham SW6 6DD

East Indian and Bangladeshi cooking in a congenial local restaurant. House specialities include chicken tikka roshoni and king prawn delight. Balti dishes are also available. Book for dinner. *Seats 58. Parties 18. L 12-1.30 D 6-11.15. Closed 25 & 26 Dec. Access, Visa.*

SW3   La Tante Claire   ★★★   £140

Tel 0171-352 6045   Fax 0171-352 3257   Map 19 C5   **R**
68 Royal Hospital Road SW3 4HP

One of the marks of a great restaurant is consistency, and there is no more consistent performer than the chef here, Pierre Koffmann. Since he opened his restaurant almost twenty years ago, he has been one of this country's leading chefs, if not the leader. And yet he is the quiet man of the kitchen, rarely venturing out, hardly a TV appearance, little publicity or controversy, in short, a chef at his stoves. His dishes are much copied, but seldom, if ever, improved upon, and just about the only change this year is the very smart, bolder and brighter name above the restaurant's entrance. Inside, the elegant dining room is relatively small, but not uncomfortably so, as it's airy and tables are reasonably well spaced. There's a crisp look to the decor – some modern paintings, immaculate table settings, but certainly no clutter. Staff, under the guidance of restaurant manager Bruno Bellemère, are supremely professional and very, very French, and if sometimes they appear aloof, do not confuse this trait with unfriendliness. The atmosphere at lunchtime is usually more animated, while at dinner a hushed tone prevails, but then at lunch you can eat three courses for an almost giveaway £25. In fact, there are two table d'hote menus side by side, offering the likes of *mousseline de St Jacques au beurre d'herbes; tarte aux poireaux, moules et safran; filet de barbue aux graines de moutarde; magret de canard au poivre vert;* and *savarin au rhum* or French cheeses. Coffee and petits fours are included, as is service. Divert to à la carte, and seek out Pierre's specialities, such as *galette de foie gras au Sauternes et échalotes roties, pied de cochon aux morilles* and *croustade de pommes à l'armagnac.* Whatever you choose, this is cooking in the premier league, based on classical foundations and executed in exemplary fashion. Flavours, aromas, combinations of tip-top ingredients, precise timing – they all contribute to mouthwatering perfection, enhanced by presentation that positively invites you to enjoy. Perhaps surprisingly, but very commendably for a restaurant of this class, the wines (excusably French-only) are not priced beyond the reach of mere mortals. *Seats 43. Parties 10. L 12.30-2 D 7-11. Closed Sat & Sun, Bank Holidays, 1 week Christmas, 3 weeks August. Set L £25. Access, Amex, Diners, Visa.*

SW1   Tate Gallery Restaurant   £55

Tel 0171-887 8877   Fax 0171-887 8902   Map 19 D5   **R**
Millbank SW1P 4RG

A basement, lunchtime-only setting useful for more than Gallery visitors: it is a destination restaurant rather than a Gallery snack stop (the separate self-service Gallery coffee shop is open daily 10.30-5.30). The restaurant menus are straightforward, mostly English and change monthly (some stalwarts are available year-round). Buttered crab, scallop mousse with pink grapefruit and watercress soup are typical starters. Main courses could be corn-fed chicken with ratatouille, roast leg of English lamb with garlic and rosemary, or cold poached Wiltshire pink trout with salad and new potatoes. Puddings come with a complimentary glass of champagne. There's a good selection of British farmhouse cheeses. There are usually one or two imaginative choices for vegetarians. Those in the know come here to drink some very fine wines at ridiculously low prices (eg Ch Mouton-Rothschild 1981 at £60, Ch Ducru-Beaucaillou 1979 at £37). Some bin ends too, but not many bottles left! *Seats 100. Parties 16. L only 12-3. Closed Sun, most Bank Holidays. Access, Visa.*

Consult the blue pages for summary tables and lists of
recommended establishments.

EC2   Tatsuso   ★   £85

Tel 0171-638 5863   Fax 0171-638 5864   Map 20 D1   **R**
32 Broadgate Circle EC2M 2QS

A split-level restaurant on one of the lower levels at Broadgate Circle. Immediately next to the entrance lobby is a smart, spacious teppanyaki bar. A wide staircase leads down to an elegant, formal Japanese restaurant and there's also a sushi counter and two private rooms. Ash is used to create the tables and chairs as well as the low screens that divide them, the blond wood strikingly modern, contrasting with the traditional look of kimono-clad waitresses. An extensive à la carte offers exquisitely prepared sushi and sashimi with authentic garnishes such as imported Japanese oba leaves – these leaves also turn up deep-fried in batter in some tempura dishes adding a refreshing and delicate taste. This is a serious restaurant with no compromise made on quality and the finest raw materials are assembled with infinite precision. Appetisers on the à la carte menu include salmon roe with grated Japanese radish, stewed taro potatoes topped with sweetened miso, and deep-fried turbot fins. Among the main courses are one-pot dishes (dinner only, minimum two), some of which are prepared at your table. All the dishes that comprise each of the many set dinners are balanced in perfect harmony, the small portions carefully worked out to allow the diner maximum enjoyment and nutritional benefit from the chefs' labours. *Seats 120. Private Room 20. L 11.30-2.30 D 6.30-9.30. Closed Sat, Sun & Bank Holidays. Set L from £23 Set D from £32. Access, Amex, Diners, Visa.*

W2   Tawana Thai   £40

Tel 0171-229 3785   Map 18 A3   **R**
3 Westbourne Grove W2 4UA

On the corner of Westbourne Grove and the bottom of Queensway, a pleasant little Thai restaurant offering the likes of spicy prawn and mushroom soup with lemon grass and lime, mousseline-style fish curry with basil steamed in a banana leaf, green vegetable curry, fried rice with taro root, and fresh Thai mango. *Seats 50. Parties 15. L 12-3 D 6-11. Closed 4 days New Year. Access, Amex, Diners, Visa.*

SW5   Terstan Hotel   £52

Tel 0171-835 1900   Fax 0171-373 9268   Map 19 A5   **B**
29 Nevern Square Earls Court SW5 9PE

Run by Stanley and Teresa Tabaka for over thirty years, this bed and breakfast hotel stands in a quiet garden square a couple of minutes from Earls Court Underground station. Bedrooms are modestly furnished but well maintained, with all except a few budget singles having en-suite bathrooms. All have telephone, remote TVs and tea/coffee-making facilities. Licensed bar and games room with a pool table. No dogs. *Rooms 50. Closed 24-26 Dec. Access, Amex, Visa.*

W2   Thai Kitchen   £50

Tel 0171-221 9984   Map 18 A2   **R**
108 Chepstow Road W2 5QS

The decor, kept simple, is full of refined touches like carved wood artwork set off by simply painted walls, an orchid on each table and interesting crafted crockery. The cooking, prepared with authentic Thai ingredients, emphasises freshness and true flavours. Original dishes include fried marinated chicken in pandanus leaves, spare ribs in red wine and fried shrimps with young coconut leaves. Vegetarians are well catered for. Light desserts like pumpkin or coconut custard are freshly made daily. *Seats 40. D only 6.30-11. Closed Sun, 25 Dec. Access, Amex, Diners, Visa.*

SE14   Thailand Restaurant   £35

Tel 0181-691 4040   Map 17 D6   **R**
15 Lewisham Way SE14 6PP

North-East Thailand pinpoints the MSG-free cooking in this unpretentious little place. Lao dishes are a speciality, among them hot and sour bamboo shoots, steak cooked over charcoal with lime juice, pounded toasted rice, chilis, herbs and spices, and a complete meal comprising hot and sour minced chicken with beef or pork and spiced rice balls, to be eaten wrapped in lettuce. *Seats 25. D only 6-10.30. Closed Sun & Mon, 2 weeks April. Access, Amex, Visa.*

SW3   Thierry's   £60

Tel 0171-352 3365   Map 19 B6   **R**
342 Kings Road Chelsea SW3 5UR

Cosy and romantic French bistro with window booths and red check tablecloths. Coq au vin, cassoulet and boeuf bourguignon are main-course specialities, which could follow soup, roasted vegetables on couscous or garlic snails and be followed by ices, Paris–Brest or a plate of French cheeses. Besides the carte there's a menu bistro at lunchtime, an evening menu and party menu. *Seats 70. Private Room 40. L 12.30-4.30 (Mon till 2.30) D 7-11 (Fri & Sat till 11.30, Sun till 10.30). Closed 4 days Christmas. Set D from £13.50. Access, Amex, Diners, Visa.*

SW6   Tien Phat   £30

Tel 0171-385 7147   Map 19 A6   **R**
1 The Arcade Fulham Broadway Station SW6 1DG

Vietnamese and Chinese food in café surroundings. Choose from the 133-item à la carte or house special set dinners (minimum two people). *Seats 40. L 12-3 D 5.30-11.30. Set L £5.50 Set D £11.90/£13.90. Closed 24-26 Dec. Access, Amex, Visa.*

SW1   Tophams Ebury Court   55%   £115

Tel 0171-730 8147   Fax 0171-823 5966   Map 19 C4   **HR**
28 Ebury Street Victoria SW1W 0LU

Old-fashioned courtesy and charm in five adjoining houses a few minutes walk from Victoria railway and coach stations, go some way to make up for declining standards of accommodation. Some bedrooms have simply not kept pace with the modern world in terms of maintenance and amenity; many are not en-suite. *Rooms 42. Access, Amex, Diners, Visa.*

Tophams   £50

👑 Ⅴ

Three elegantly appointed rooms, their walls adorned with paintings by the owners' ancestors, are the setting for meals that combine traditional and modern elements. Fillets of lamb with marinated mushrooms and olives, smoked salmon on ginger vinaigrette or 'an assortment of livers' in a Madeira and tarragon sauce are typical à la carte starters, with seafood patties, grilled Dover sole or roast duckling with black cherries in a pineapple sauce among the main courses, which also include a choice for vegetarians.
Simpler set menu of two or three courses. *Seats 30. Parties 12. Private Room 24. L 12-2.30 D 6-10. Closed L Sat, all Sun. Set L & D £10.50/£14.50.*

W1   Topkapi   £35

Tel 0171-486 1872   Fax 0171-486 2063   Map 18 C2   **R**
25 Marylebone High Street W1M 3PE

Turkish cuisine in an all-day restaurant named after the ancient Ottoman palace in Istanbul. Hot and cold hors d'oeuvre (stuffed vine leaves, meat balls, aubergines, yoghurt, peppers); main-course kebab grills. Quick lunches, relaxed dinners. *Seats 50. Meals 12-11.30. Closed 25 & 26 Dec. Set meals from £12.50. Access, Amex, Diners, Visa.*

E1   Tower Thistle   66%   £166

Tel 0171-481 2575   Fax 0171-488 4106   Map 20 D3   **H**
St Katharine's Way Tower Bridge E1 9LD

Positioned between the river and St Katharine's Dock, this hotel enjoys both escape from the noise of the city and some of the best views in London. Public rooms include the Which-Way-West Café (open 7am-10pm), the comfortable Gallery Lounge and the nautically themed Thames Bar, with its south-facing balcony (used for barbecues in summer). A recently refurbished carvery has its best tables overlooking the marina of St Katharine's Dock. Air-conditioned bedrooms range from modestly furnished doubles to rooms with elegant bathrooms, modem lines and a priority check-in system. The best of the luxury suites offer impressive views. 24hr room service. Secure parking (mainly covered) for 116 cars. Children up to 14 stay free in parents' room. No dogs. *Rooms 765. News kiosk, coffee shop (7.30am-10pm), covered garage. Access, Amex, Diners, Visa.*

NW1   Trattoria Lucca   £45

Tel 0171-485 6864   Map 16 C3   **R**
63 Parkway Camden Town NW1 7PP

Popular Italian restaurant whose standard trattoria menu is supplemented by daily specials
which usually include some very good stuffed vegetables. Pasta, fish and chicken each have
their own menu section, and grills are a speciality, as are some of the steak dishes and fegato
alla veneziana. Sweets from the trolley. *Seats 60. Parties 24. L 12-3 D 6-10.45 (till 11.30 Fri &
Sat). Closed Sun, Bank Holidays. Set L & D £8.50/£10.75. Access, Amex, Diners, Visa.*

We publish annually, so make sure you use the current edition
— it's well worth it!

SW7   Tui   £45

Tel 0171-584 8359   Fax 0171-352 8343   Map 19 B5   **R**
19 Exhibition Road South Kensington SW7 2HE

Tom yum, a traditional clear spicy soup scented with lemon grass, lime leaves and fresh
chilis and served in a fire pot, is a national dish and an almost essential element in a meal
at this civilised Thai restaurant, which recently celebrated its tenth birthday. It comes in
three versions – with chicken, prawns or mixed seafood. Stir-fries are other specialities,
along with mee grorb (crisp-fried rice noodles tossed in a tamarind-based sauce of pork
and shrimps), an excellent green curry and spicy cod rissoles. *Seats 56. Parties 12. L 12-
2.15 (Sun 12.30 to 2.45) D 6.30-10.45. Closed Bank Holidays. Access, Amex, Diners, Visa.*

N1   Tuk Tuk   £30

Tel 0171-226 0837   Map 16 D3   **R**
330 Upper Street Islington N1 2XQ

Named after the rickshaw-style taxis that ply the streets of Bangkok, this small, stylish and
informal Thai restaurant offers satay, chicken wings, fish patties, hot and sour soup with
prawns and rice, a mild or chili-hot curry, garlicky fried beef and noodles with mixed
seafood. *Seats 40. L 12-3.30 D 6-11. Closed L Sat, all Sun, Bank Holidays. Access, Amex, Visa.*

We welcome bona fide complaints and recommendations on the
tear-out pages at the back of the book for readers' comments.
They are followed up by our professional team.

SW3   Turner's   ↑   £100

Tel 0171 -584 6711   Fax 0171-584 4441   Map 19 B5   **R**
87/89 Walton Street SW3 2HP

In his smart dining room, restfully decorated in blue, cream and gold, Brian Turner
continues to exercise his apparently effortless charm despite dodging between kitchen,
front of house and TV studios. The kitchen, now in the capable hands of Jonathon
Bibbings, mostly refuses to be influenced by modern fashion. Lunch remains a bargain at
under a tenner for two courses (£13.50 for three) from a small menu du jour: perhaps
salad of smoked salmon and prawns or pan-fried lamb's kidneys in a sherry vinegar sauce
to start, followed by grilled pork loin with wild mushrooms and celeriac or a panaché of
fish with sun-dried tomato sauce. The salad bar menu at £8.50 offers a light alternative
and is popular with the "ladies who lunch". Dinner is a more expensive affair. Menus are
in French with English translations and might include salade niçoise, chicken liver paté
with foie gras or a salad of chargrilled tuna with sun-dried tomatoes and an excellent basil
dressing; followed by a ragout of monkfish, mussels and salmon in a saffron sauce; breast
of duck in a port and green peppercorn sauce or rack of lamb in a herb crust. Desserts are
equally good though perhaps not for the calorie-conscious! Note the William Fèvre
Chablis and Italian Sassicaia collections on the mostly French wine list, which includes an
inexpensive house selection. Prices are inclusive of service. *Seats 50. L 12.30-2.30 D 7.30-
11.15 (Sun till 10). Closed L Sat, Bank Holidays, 1 week Christmas. Set L £9.95/£13.50 Set
Sun L £19.50. Access, Amex, Diners, Visa.*

SW9   Twenty Trinity Gardens   £45

Tel 0171-733 8838   Map 17 C5   **R**
20 Trinity Gardens Brixton SW9 8DP

A popular neighbourhood restaurant that's a stone's throw away from Acre Lane – by car, approach from Brighton Terrace. The walls are crammed with a mixture of original artistic photographs (some erotic) and woven tapestries. A plant-filled conservatory makes an ideal setting for Sunday lunch, as well as for a romantic dinner. Chef Paul Churchill offers a modern French menu with lobster ravioli in a tomato and vodka sauce, wild mushroom tartlets or pigeon and duck liver terrine with onion confit to begin. Main dishes might typically include duck confit with five spice lamb steak marinated in red wine and garlic served with a haricot bean casserole. Monday and Tuesday are bargain nights, with a 2-course table d'hote menu for £10, including a 25cl carafe of wine. Vegetarians are well catered for. Charming, informal service. *Seats 54. Parties 20. Private Room 20. L (Sun only) 12-4 D 7-10.30. Closed Bank Holidays & 4 days Christmas. Set Sun L £9.95/£13.50 Set D from £14.25. Access, Visa.*

SW1   22 Jermyn Street   £230

Tel 0171-734 2353   Fax 0171-734 0750   Map 18 D3   **PH**
22 Jermyn Street SW1Y 6HL

The discreet entrance to this chic private hotel is tucked between a bespoke hatter and a shirtmaker typical of this stylish street. 1995 saw its 80th anniversary and Henry Togna continues into the third generation of family owners with as much devotion as his predecessors. Five spacious studios and 13 suites are tastefully decorated with deep carpets, period furniture, a profusion of fresh flowers and interesting objets d'art. TVs with satellite, fax points and computer modems keep the businessman in touch. 24hr room service, from enthusiastic staff, provides everything from breakfast and dinner (there is no restaurant) to personal shopping. Laundry/dry cleaning service. Business and secretarial service. Car parking can be arranged nearby. *Rooms 18. Access, Amex, Diners, Visa.*

W2   Veronica's   £65

Tel 0171-229 5079   Map 18 A3   **R**
3 Hereford Road Bayswater W2 4AB

For a taste of history, there's no better place to go than Veronica and Philip Shaw's amazing restaurant facing Leinster Square (there's been a restaurant on this site since the turn of the century). Food through the ages is an endless fascination to Veronica, and any celebration day is cause for a special menu – Burns Night, St David's Day, St George's Day, St Andrew's Day, Halloween, Guy Fawkes. New in 1995 was Georgian food, influenced by Jane Austen's novels. Dishes are well described, not just with their ingredients and history but also showing if they're low in fat, or suitable for vegetarians or vegans. The restaurant prides itself on its selection of British cheese. Outdoor tables in good weather. British wines come first on a somewhat eccentric list. *Seats 60. Parties 30. Private Room 30. L 12-3 D 7-12. Closed L Sat, all Sun, Bank Holidays. Set L & D £11.50/£15. Access, Amex, Diners, Visa.*

> **Consult the blue pages for summary tables and lists of recommended establishments.**

NW6   Vijay   £25

Tel 0171-328 1087   Map 16 B3   **R**
49 Willesden Lane NW6 7RF

Popular preparations of lamb, chicken and prawns supplement vegetarian specialities at this unpretentious establishment, opened more than 30 years ago and among the oldest South Indian restaurants in England. Adai is a pancake made from rice and three varieties of lentils; iddly (a speciality) is a steamed cake made of rice and garam flour; avial mixes several vegetables cooked with ground coconut, yoghurt, butter and curry leaves. *Seats 78. Parties 25. L 12-2.45 D 6-10.45 (Fri & Sat till 11.45). Closed 25 & 26 Dec. Access, Amex, Diners, Visa.*

W1   Villandry Dining Room   £45

Tel 0171-224 3799   Map 18 C2   **R**
89 Marylebone High Street W1M 3DE

A tiny, often crowded restaurant at the rear of a well-stocked, up-market delicatessen. The small, bare wood tables are quite tightly packed, thereby creating a rather cramped environment. The daily-changing lunchtime menu includes starter dishes like leek and parmesan soup, new potato and French sausage salad, mains such as smoked haddock brandade, Irish stew, courgette and fresh thyme risotto with salad and to finish moist chocolate cake, lemon and orange tart, or pear bread-and-butter pudding. Notwithstanding the lack of space the food and friendly attitude of the staff make it a very worthwhile experience. Once a month, usually the first Thursday of each month, they open the whole place for dinner. The menu is longer and the event is a relaxed, informal affair. The only drawback is that dinner bookings must be made very well in advance – like several weeks. No smoking. *Seats 50. Parties 30. L 12.30-3 D once a month. Closed Sun, Bank Holidays, 10 days Christmas-New Year. Access, Amex, Visa*

WC1   Wagamama   £25

Tel 0171-323 9223   Fax 0171-323 9224   Map 21 B1   **R**
4 Streatham Street off Bloomsbury Street WC1 1JB

No reservations are taken at this ever-busy, trend-setting Japanese noodle restaurant, set in a basement just off New Oxford Street and Bloomsbury Street. 'Positive eating, positive living' is the message, noodles (ramen) the medium. Expect to queue at peak times, but not for long as customers are happy with the fast serve, fast out concept. Parties should expect food to arrive as and when it is ready. A successful, self-styled 'non-destination food station' catering for upwards of 1200 customers a day. Raw energy juices and salads, gyoza dumplings, rice dishes and sake complete the picture. *Seats 104. Meals 12-11 (Sat from 12.30 Sun 12.30-10). Closed 1 week Christmas, Easter Sunday. No credit cards.*

NW3   Wakaba   £70

Tel 0171-586 7960   Map 16 B2   **R**
122a Finchley Road NW3 5HT

Behind curved glass frosted from busy Finchley Road the decor is designer-zero, canteen-style, basically plain white. The menu provides an interesting span of Japanese dishes with a particularly extensive choice from the sushi bar. Sushi is priced either à la carte (more than 30 choices) or by 5, 7 or 9 pieces. Some dishes, including sukiyaki, shabushabu and yosenabe (Japanese-style bouillabaisse), are prepared at the table. *Seats 55. D only 6.30-11. Closed Sun, 4 days Easter, 4 days Christmas. Set D from £23.60. Access, Amex, Diners, Visa.*

WC2   The Waldorf   83%   £212

Tel 0171-836 2400   Fax 0171-836 7244   Map 20 A2   **HR**
Aldwych WC2B 4DD

Opened in 1908, the Waldorf was, in 1958, the first hotel to be acquired by Charles Forte. Public areas remain unchanged in style, including the Club Bar with its polished wood panelling, leather chesterfields and marble fireplaces, the pubby Footlights Bar and traditional Aldwych Brasserie. At the heart of the hotel the truly grand Palm Court Lounge is where Saturday and Sunday tea dances (£20.50) are a veritable institution, with their origins in the Waldorf's famous Tango Teas of the 1920s and 30s. Bedrooms all have air-conditioning, secondary sockets for fax or modems and even 110-volt outlets for the convenience of transatlantic guests. Every bedroom has its own entrance lobby, new traditionally-styled polished darkwood furniture and one of nine bold decorative schemes. Elaborately draped curtains and chandeliers hark back to the opulence of the hotel's Edwardian origins, as do the period-style washstands in marble-trimmed bathrooms that all have both fixed and hand-held showers over the tubs; bathrobes, speaker extensions and good toiletries also provided. Well-turned-out staff provide a proper turn-down service in the evenings and valet parking, but overnight room service is limited to sandwiches and snacks. Banqueting/conference facilities for up to 420. *Rooms 292. Beauty & hair salon, gift shop. Access, Amex, Diners, Visa.*

See over

Restaurant   £90

A grand, high-ceilinged room with Corinthian columns and French doors opening on to the Palm Court. The menu mixes traditional and modern: Bresse pigeon with cabbage, Southdown lamb à la niçoise, John Dory with braised fennel, olives and artichokes, yellow fin tuna tataki with wasabi and pickled vegetables. The wine list is very modest for a hotel of this class. *Seats 60. Parties 10. L 12.30-2.30 D 6-11 (Sun 7-10). Set L & D £21/£25. Closed L Sat & Sun.*

SW3 Waltons of Walton Street	£100

Tel 0171-584 0204   Fax 0171-581 2848   Map 19 B5   **R**
121 Walton Street South Kensington SW3 2PH

Polished service matches the luxuriously comfortable surroundings and the à la carte menu offers well thought-out modern dishes such as hot mussel chowder, pigeon and grilled pepper terrine with baby spinach and a tomato and coriander chutney and sauté of scallops with endive salad and French dressing as starters. Main courses are equally imaginative, including rack of lamb with a herb crust, served with a leek purée and rosemary gravy, baked Scottish salmon with tagliatelle and a tomato and saffron sauce or breast of Norfolk duck served pink with sea haricots and lingonberries. Well-priced 'Simply Waltons' lunch menu, traditional three-course Sunday lunch, two-course after-theatre supper menu. Some good names on the mostly French wine list, with a fair sprinkling under £20. *Seats 65. Parties 20. L 12.30-2.30 (Sun & Bank Holidays till 2) D 7.30-11.30 (Sun & Bank Holidays 7-10). Closed D 25 & all 26 Dec. Set L £14.75 (Sun £16.50) Set D £21. Access, Amex, Diners, Visa.*

W1 Washington Hotel	73%	£200

Tel 0171-499 7000   Fax 0171-495 6172   Map 18 C3   **H**
5 Curzon Street Mayfair W1Y 8DT

As befitting a hotel, at this, one of London's smartest addresses, the public rooms are comfortable and stylish: from the marble-floored reception to Madison's lounge/bar with its handsome Indian carpets, pine panelling and elaborately draped curtains. Air-conditioned bedrooms are designed on an art-deco theme, with splendid bird's-eye maple fitted furniture. They range from good-sized singles, with all the usual modern comforts, to lavish suites with marble bathrooms and spa baths; the best have conservatories and one – the Garfield – a rooftop patio. Two floors are reserved for non-smokers. Children up to 16 stay free in parents' room. Buffet-style breakfast only, in the restaurant, but the "designer" room service Continental breakfast offers a huge choice. Conference rooms, for up to 100, are light and airy. No dogs. Sarova Hotels. *Rooms 173. Access, Amex, Diners, Visa.*

W1 The Westbury	77%	£191

Tel 0171-629 7755   Fax 0171-495 1163   Map 18 D3   **H**
Conduit Street W1A 4UH

Named after the famous polo ground on Long Island, the sister hotel to New York's Westbury is situated suitably smartly on the corner of New Bond Street. The Polo bar and the comfortable Polo lounge are decorated with the trappings of the game – the former offers a live pianist in the evenings (Tue-Sat) the latter light meals all day and decent afternoon tea. Air-conditioned bedrooms range from generously sized suites the best with roof-top patios. Full valet service. Banqueting/conference facilities for 80/120. Use of the nearby Metropolitan Club with its excellent leisure facilities. Small private car park. Forte. *Rooms 244. Access, Amex, Diners, Visa.*

Consult the blue pages for summary tables and lists of recommended establishments.

WC2   Westzenders   £60

Tel 0171-497 0376   Fax 0171-497 0378   Map 21 B2   **R**
Orion House 4a Upper St Martin's Lane WC2H 9EA

Formerly Now & Zen and still owned by the Zen group, the restaurant retains its innovative decor though some of the sparkle has faded. The food is imaginative, featuring regional specialities from Northern China. A noodle bar is a new addition. Cooking is enjoyable but sadly service isn't always on the ball. *Seats 180. Parties 30. L 12-3 D 6-11.30 (Sun to 11). Closed 25 & 26 Dec. Access, Amex, Diners, Visa.*

NW1   White House   71%   £132

Tel 0171-387 1200   Fax 0171-388 0091   Map 18 D1   **H**
Albany Street NW1 3UP

Set well back from the Euston Road traffic, but handy for Regent's Park and Great Portland Street tube, this listed building was once an exclusive block of flats, before its 60s conversion into a hotel. An elegant marble-floored foyer leads to extensive public rooms including a basement wine bar – The Winery – and a comfortable cocktail bar with an accompanying evening pianist. Double-glazed bedrooms vary from modestly sized singles with satellite TV and direct-dial phones with additional American voltage sockets, to comfortable rooms where the new owners have completed a costly programme of refurbishment. The air-conditioned "Reserve" floor, with its exclusive check-in, has plush studios, luxury suites, queen-sized beds and marble bathrooms with spa baths and luxury toiletries. 24hr room service. Conference and banqueting facilities for 120/100. Staffed business centre (Mon-Fri 9-5). No dogs. *Rooms 584. Gym, sauna, coffee shop (7am-11.30pm), news kiosk & gift shop. Access, Amex, Diners, Visa.*

W1   White Tower   £90

Tel 0171-636 8141   Map 18 D2   **R**
1 Percy Street off Tottenham Court Road W1P 0ET

A durable and civilised restaurant, endearingly old-fashioned – some of the staff have seen more than 40 years service, with George Metaxas and Mary Dunne in charge of the dining-room – so much so that you still pay a cover charge. Competent cooking, mainly Greek-based with a hint of French, sees such famous dishes, described in chatty style on the menu, as a rich, satisfying beef-based moussaka or Aylesbury duckling *farci à la cypriote* – weighty chaps stuffed with bourgourie, chopped almonds and livers, and roasted to a crisp dark brown. Each provides a festal dish for two (though a single helping may be ordered). Start with mixed patés, mezedes or fish salad; finish with fresh salad. The menu states "desserts are not our strong point"! Several wines on a humdrum list are overpriced *Seats 75. Parties 8. Private Room 16. L 12.30-2.30 D 6.30-10.30. Closed L Sat, all Sun, Bank Holidays, 1 week Christmas, 3 weeks Aug. Access, Amex, Diners, Visa.*

W2   Whites Hotel   77%   £201

Tel 0171-262 2711   Fax 0171-262 2147   Map 18 B3   **H**
90 Lancaster Gate Bayswater W2 3NR

Separated from the road by its own narrow car park and a cobbled forecourt, this comfortable hotel, in an elegant Victorian terrace, overlooks Kensington Gardens. The public rooms exude an atmosphere of peaceful relaxation, with oil paintings and quiet corners in which to relax in front of open fires. Air-conditioned bedrooms range from comfortable singles with deep carpet, swagged silk drapes and marble bathrooms, to two suites, one in Louis XV style, the other with an Oriental inspiration. Valet service. No dogs. *Rooms 54. Access, Amex, Diners, Visa.*

EC4   Whittington's   £70

Tel 0171-248 5855   Map 20 C2   **R**
21 College Hill EC4 2RP

🍷

Off Upper Thames Street, just north of Southwark Bridge, these 14th-century wine cellars were once owned by Dick Whittington. These days, it's a restaurant/wine bar whose short menu changes every three weeks or so and is supplemented by a daily specials board. Typically, the choice runs from warm timbale of chicken mousse dressed on a chive sauce or pan-fried scallops with lentils and chili dressing to grilled fillet of Seychelles parrot fish,

See over

brill with pepper, calf's liver with a basil-flavoured mash and red wine sauce, and medallions of venison with celeriac purée and a honey-scented jus. *Seats 52. Parties 18. L only 11.45-2.15. Closed Sat & Sun, Bank Holidays. Access, Amex, Diners, Visa.*

SW1   Wilbraham Hotel   55%   £94

Tel 0171-730 8296   Fax 0171-730 6815   Map 19 C5   **H**
Wilbraham Place Sloane Street SW1X 9AE

Modest hotel, with an old-fashioned charm, in a quiet location off Sloane Square. Most of the simply furnished bedrooms have TVs and en-suite bathrooms. Children up to 10 stay free in parents' room. Limited 24hr room service. No dogs. *Rooms 52. No credit cards.*

SW1   Willett Hotel   £92

Tel 0171-824 8415   Fax 0171-730 4830   Map 19 C5   **B**
32 Sloane Gardens SW1W 8DJ

Close to Sloane Square, the Willett offers bed and breakfast accommodation. Modestly furnished bedrooms all have TVs with satellite, direct-dial phones, hairdryers and trouser presses. All except those on the top floor have recently been refurbished and have en-suite bathrooms with showers above the tubs. *Rooms 19. Access, Amex, Diners, Visa.*

SW1   Wilton's   £110

Tel 0171-629 9955   Fax 0171-495 6233   Map 18 D3   **R**
55 Jermyn Street SW1Y 6LX

Oysters, fish and game are the specialities in one of London's best-known restaurants – and one of its oldest, having opened its doors in 1742. The classic à la carte menu offers a mainstream choice that includes potted shrimps, crab cocktail, poached or filled halibut and turbot, roast partridge and woodcock, and lemon sole stuffed with pike and spinach mousse served with a champagne sauce. Savouries, British cheeses and traditional puds complete the picture. Service is of the old school, in keeping with and enhancing the club-like atmosphere. *Seats 100. Parties 16. Private Room 18. L 12.30-2.30 D 6.30-10.30. Closed Sat, 1 week Christmas. Access, Amex, Diners, Visa.*

W5   Wine & Mousaka   £40

Tel 0181-998 4373   Map 17 A4   **R**
30 & 33 Haven Green Ealing W5 2NX

Two separate Greek restaurants; no 30, the smaller of the two, is lighter at lunchtime but both are candle-lit by night. Traditional Greek favourites are the mainstay of the menu with kebabs and spit-roast meats cooked at open-to-view charcoal grills. Set menus, including grand meze, offer the best value. Sister restaurant in Kew (see entry). *Seats 92 (34 at no 30). L 12-2.30 D 6-11.30. Closed Sun, Bank Holidays. Set L & D £7.95 (not Sat eve) & £11.95. Access, Amex, Diners, Visa.*

W8   Wodka   £45

Tel 0171-937 6513   Fax 0171-937 8621   Map 19 A4   **R**
12 St Albans Grove Kensington W8 5PN

A popular drinking and eating spot away from the general Kensington bustle, south of Kensington Square. The menu is Polish and Eastern European, with favourite dishes including veal and wild mushroom or spinach and curd cheese pierogi, blinis with toppings of herring, smoked salmon, aubergine mousse or caviar, excellent chunky fish cakes with dill sauce, veal or venison goulash, and pork shank roasted in beer. Upwards of a dozen vodkas are available by glass or carafe and also form the basis of some excellent sorbets. *Seats 60. Private Room 30. L 12.30-2.30 D 7-11. Closed L Sat & Sun, all Bank Holidays. Set L £10 Access, Amex, Diners, Visa.*

We welcome bona fide complaints and recommendations on the tear-out pages at the back of the book for readers' comments. They are followed up by our professional team.

SE9   Yardley Court   £46

Tel 0181-850 1850   Fax 0181 850 8319   Map 17 D5   **B**
18 Court Yard Eltham SE9 5PZ

Converted Victorian house, set back from the road. Simply furnished bedrooms all have TVs and tea/coffee-making facilities. All but one single have en-suite facilities, with walk-in showers. Breakfast is served in a pleasant conservatory overlooking the garden. Cots are added free, extra beds for just £5. Free car park. *Rooms 9. Access, Visa.*

W5   Young's Rendezvous   £40

Tel 0181-840 3060   Map 17 A4   **R**
13 Bond Street Ealing W5

Small, smart, air-conditioned Chinese restaurant one street down from the Broadway Centre, with smooth service from waiters and waitresses in tunics. Good sizzling dishes, seafood and Szechuan dishes; particularly fine lobster feast set menu. Try the chef's specials, which now feature up-to-date Hong Kong dishes. *Seats 150. Private Room 30. L 12-2.30 D 6-11.30. Closed 25 & 26 Dec. Set D from £12.50. Access, Amex, Diners, Visa.*

N16   Yum Yum   £45

Tel 0171-254 6751   Fax 0171-241 3857   Map 16 D2   **R**
26 Stoke Newington Church Street N16 0LU

Ⅴ

Now much enlarged and moved into the restaurant next door, Yum Yum is something of a hit in a popular North London street. Booking is advisable, particularly at weekends. Decor is colourful and very Thai with lots of ornate carving, mirrored wall hangings and other authentic artefacts. The food is a careful blend of spicing – some dishes hot and fiery, others milder and gentler. There's a good choice of vegetarian options – a possible throwback to the days of Spices, the Indian vegetarian restaurant which was under the same ownership as the present set-up. *Seats 100. Parties 40. L 12-2.30 D 6-11. Closed 1 week Christmas. Set L £6.50 Set D £13.50. Access, Amex, Diners, Visa.*

W1   Yumi   £80

Tel 0171-935 8320   Fax 0171 224 0917   Map 18 C2   **R**
110 George Street W1H 6DJ

Simplicity is the key at this traditional Japanese restaurant, so much so that upstairs in the private rooms diners sit cross-legged at low tables (more conventionally Western seating is to be found downstairs and at the bar). Set meals offer better value for money and à la carte choices run the gamut of familiar Japanese dishes. Some of the appetisers are more unusual and worth trying, such as *chawan mushi* (egg custard gently steamed with morsels of seafood and vegetables), *hotate isobe-yaki* (grilled scallops sandwiched with nori seaweed), or *kani shumai* (home-made crab dumplings). Owner Yumi Fujii is always on hand with a smile, a bow and advice. The private room is only for a set meal of 8 dishes at £55, £65 or £75 per head. *Seats 76. Parties 30. Private Room 14. L 12.30-2.30 D 5.30-10.30. Closed Sat & Sun, 2 weeks Christmas. Set L from £15 Set D from £26. Access, Amex, Diners, Visa.*

SW1   Zafferano   NEW   £65

Tel 0171-235 5800   Map 19 C4   **R**
16 Lowndes Street SW1X 9EY

Chef-proprietor Giorgio Locatelli's new restaurant is very rustic-chic and the burghers of Knightsbridge have taken to it readily as prices are surprisingly kind considering the location. The menu of modern Italian creations features dishes such as a salad of wind-dried tuna with French beans and tomato, marinated grilled vegetables or minestrone with pesto. Pasta dishes include potato and mint parcels with a red pepper sauce and pappardelle with broad beans and rocket in a creamy cheese sauce while for a main course the choice could be roast rabbit with Parma ham and polenta, chargrilled chicken breast with spinach or cod with lentils. Cooking is enjoyably uncomplicated, with well-defined flavours. Service is cheerfully efficient. Italian wine only, except for a couple of champagnes, one served at a very reasonable £5 per glass. *Seats 52. Parties 8. L 12-2.30 D 7-11. Closed L Mon, all Sun, 2 weeks Aug, 1 week Christmas, Bank Holidays. Access, Amex, Visa.*

W1   Zen Central   £95

Tel 0171-629 8089   Fax 0171-493 6181   Map 18 C3   **R**
20 Queen Street Mayfair W1X 7PJ

Up-market Chinese restaurant with eye-catching modern design by Rick Mather. The 'culinary art form' encompasses popular specialities like crispy duck, baked lobster and steamed sea bass as well as more unusual dishes such as beef fillet rolls with petite mushrooms, or sautéed breast of pigeon in oyster sauce. At £70 for 2 people, double-boiled supreme shark's fin will cut a swathe through the average budget – but this is well-heeled Mayfair. *Seats 70. Parties 12. L 12.15-2.30 D 6.30-11.15. Set L £20/£28 Set D £20-£50. Closed 4 days Christmas. Amex, Diners, Access, Visa.*

SW3   Zen Chelsea   £80

Tel 0171-589 1781   Fax 0171-584 0596   Map 19 B5   **R**
Chelsea Cloisters 86 Sloane Avenue SW3

The first of the Zen chain (opened in 1983) has a restrained decor with a pink hue, low ceilings, Chinese zodiac on the windows and a small waterfall near the entrance. The extensive menus span the regions of Chinese cuisine including dim sum, lettuce-wrapped chicken with green herbs, smoked fish and specials such as braised abalone, double-boiled shark's fin, Peking duck, lobster with soft noodles and a choice of four sauces, and crispy aromatic duck. *Seats 85. Parties 14. Private Room 22. L 12-2.45 D 6-11.15 Closed 3/4 days Christmas. Access, Amex, Diners, Visa.*

W1   Zen Garden   NEW   £90

Tel 0171-493 1381   Map 18 D3   **R**
16 Berkeley Street W1X 5AE

Deep carpet, polished brass pillars and well-spaced tables at this opulent Chinese restaurant, which is tastefully decorated with framed antique Chinese costumes and screen prints. The whole takes more in menu style and feel from Hong Kong, unlike its peers in the neighbourhood. For the adventurous, braised eel with glutin, crispy ox tongue and sea-spiced aubergine are all excellent. There are some regular favourites too, like sesame prawn fingers, spare ribs, lemon chicken, Singapore noodles and Peking duck (available here without the need to pre-order). Desserts are more comprehensive than normally found, with red bean paste pancake and delicate, delicious, and expensive, supreme double-boiled swallow nest. Good range of dim sum at lunchtime, particularly popular on Sundays, when booking is essential. Helpful service under the direction of Joe Sham, who gives good advice to the uninitiated. Helpings are generous, which to some degree negates the high prices. *Seats 120. Private Room 30. L 12-2.30 D 6-11.15 (Sun till 10.30). Closed 3 days Christmas. Access, Amex, Diners, Visa.*

Set menu prices may not always include service or wine.

NW3   ZeNW3   £45

Tel 0171-794 7863   Fax 0171-794 6956   Map 16 B2   **R**
83 Hampstead High Street NW3 1RE

A health-conscious MSG-free zone. The menu is shorter than the usual Chinese, with the emphasis on steaming and quick-frying. Among the more esoteric dishes are cuttlefish cakes wrapped in lettuce with herbs, giant prawns steamed with fennel seeds, and chicken fillet with spring onions cooked in a paper bag. *Seats 140. Parties 15. Private Room 24. L 12-5 D 6-11.30. Set L from £9.50 Set D from £23.50. Closed 4 days Christmas. Access, Amex, Diners, Visa.*

SW3   Ziani   £65

Tel 0171-351 5297   Fax 0171-244 8387   Map 19 C5   **R**
45/47 Radnor Walk SW3 4BP

A small, brightly decorated Italian restaurant named after an ancient Venetian family and specialising in Venetian cooking. Among the specialities are pasta with mushrooms, courgettes and truffle, warm salad of scallops, mushrooms and rucola, charcoal-grilled fish, mixed offal and wild boar sausage with polenta. Daily specials are always worth a try. Decent Italian wine list. Be sure to book in the evenings – this is a very popular place, with above-average cooking and unfailingly friendly staff. *Seats 50. L 12-2.45 (Sun to 3.15) D 7-11.30 (Sun to 10.30). Closed 25 & 26 Dec, 1 Jan. Set Sun L £12.50. Access, Amex, Diners, Visa.*

W1	**Zoe**	**£65**

Tel 0171-224 1122   Fax 0171-935 5444   Map 18 C2   **R**
St Christopher's Place W1M 5HH

Ⅴ

Beneath the all-day café the restaurant, decorated in a multitude of earthy, sunbaked colours, offers cooking with a Mediterranean slant. Order country breads, roasted chili and garlic oil, fava bean purée and sweet aubergine with poppy seed paste to nibble while pondering the list: asparagus and blue cheese tart with spinach salad; baked globe artichoke with polenta and roast chestnuts; oxtail and sweetbread terrine; penne with confit of salmon, gremolata and lemon butter; fish stew with shrimps and mussels; oven-roasted quail wrapped in Serrano ham with turnip and sage gratin. Apricot flummery and chocolate rice krispie layered torte show equal imagination when it comes to desserts. Good food, good fun, pleasant staff. *Seats 150. Parties 25. L 11.30-2.30 D 6.30-11.30. Closed L Sat (but the café is open), all Sun, Bank Holidays. Access, Amex, Diners, Visa.*

We welcome bona fide complaints and recommendations on the tear-out pages at the back of the book for readers' comments. They are followed up by our professional team.

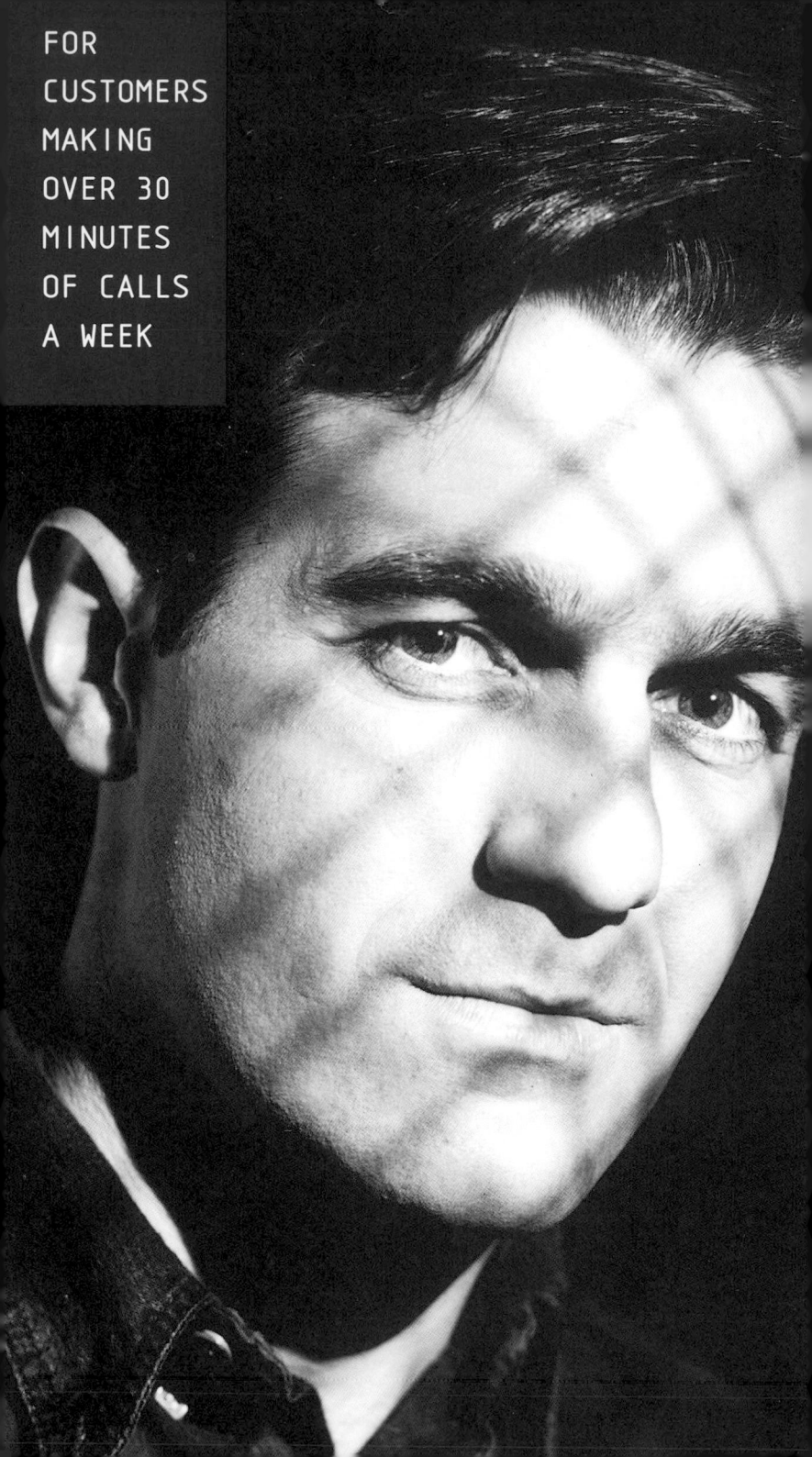

FOR
CUSTOMERS
MAKING
OVER 30
MINUTES
OF CALLS
A WEEK

FREQUENT
CALLER PLUS

FOR BUSINESS USERS WHO TRAVEL EXTENSIVELY IN THE UK AND ABROAD

If you're likely to make over 30 minutes of calls per week, and must be contactable at all times – in the UK and overseas – you need Cellnet Frequent Caller Plus.

Connected to Cellnet's digital service, you'll enjoy clearer calls and optimum call security. And you'll be able to keep in touch around the world.

What's more with 2-way data flow – including FAX – Cellnet sets the pace for mobile data communications.

For users who need a mobile phone for use in the UK only, and wish to benefit from a wide choice of low cost handsets, Frequent Caller offers connection to Cellnet's analogue service.

KEY BENEFITS

- Digital call quality*
- Optimum security*
- International roaming* – the ability to make and receive calls abroad.
- 2-way data communications*
- National UK coverage

NETWORK FEATURES

- Call Divert
- Call Waiting
- Operator enquiries

OPTIONAL SERVICES

- Callback¹ intelligent messaging
- Short Message Service*

Features and services asterisked above cannot be accessed from an analogue phone.*

THE NET THAT SETS YOU FREE

for further information call
0800 214000

FOR
CUSTOMERS
MAKING
8 - 30
MINUTES
OF CALLS
A WEEK

REGULAR
CALLER PLUS

LOCAL CALLS ANYTIME ANYPLACE

Regular Caller Plus is Cellnet's digital tariff for personal and business customers who make between 8 and 30 minutes of calls a week.

While Regular Caller Plus enables you to keep in touch – in the UK and overseas – we recognise that many mobile calls are local calls.

That's why on Regular Caller Plus, you can take advantage of Call Saver, an exclusive Cellnet service offering low cost flat rate local calls, 24 hours a day.

Only on Cellnet, does local stretch this far.

KEY BENEFITS
- Digital call quality
- Optimum call security
- International roaming
- National UK coverage
- Call Saver, offering low cost local calls, 24 hours a day.

NETWORK FEATURES
- Call Divert
- Call Waiting
- Operator enquiries

OPTIONAL SERVICES
- Callback intelligent messaging*
- Short Message Service – enabling up to 160 characters to be displayed on your handset

THE NET THAT SETS YOU FREE

for further information call
0800 214000

*Callback is a value added service provided by Cellnet Solutions Ltd, a company in the Cellnet Group. Other messaging services may be available that use the Cellnet Callback advanced network feature. Using these services will incur extra charges.

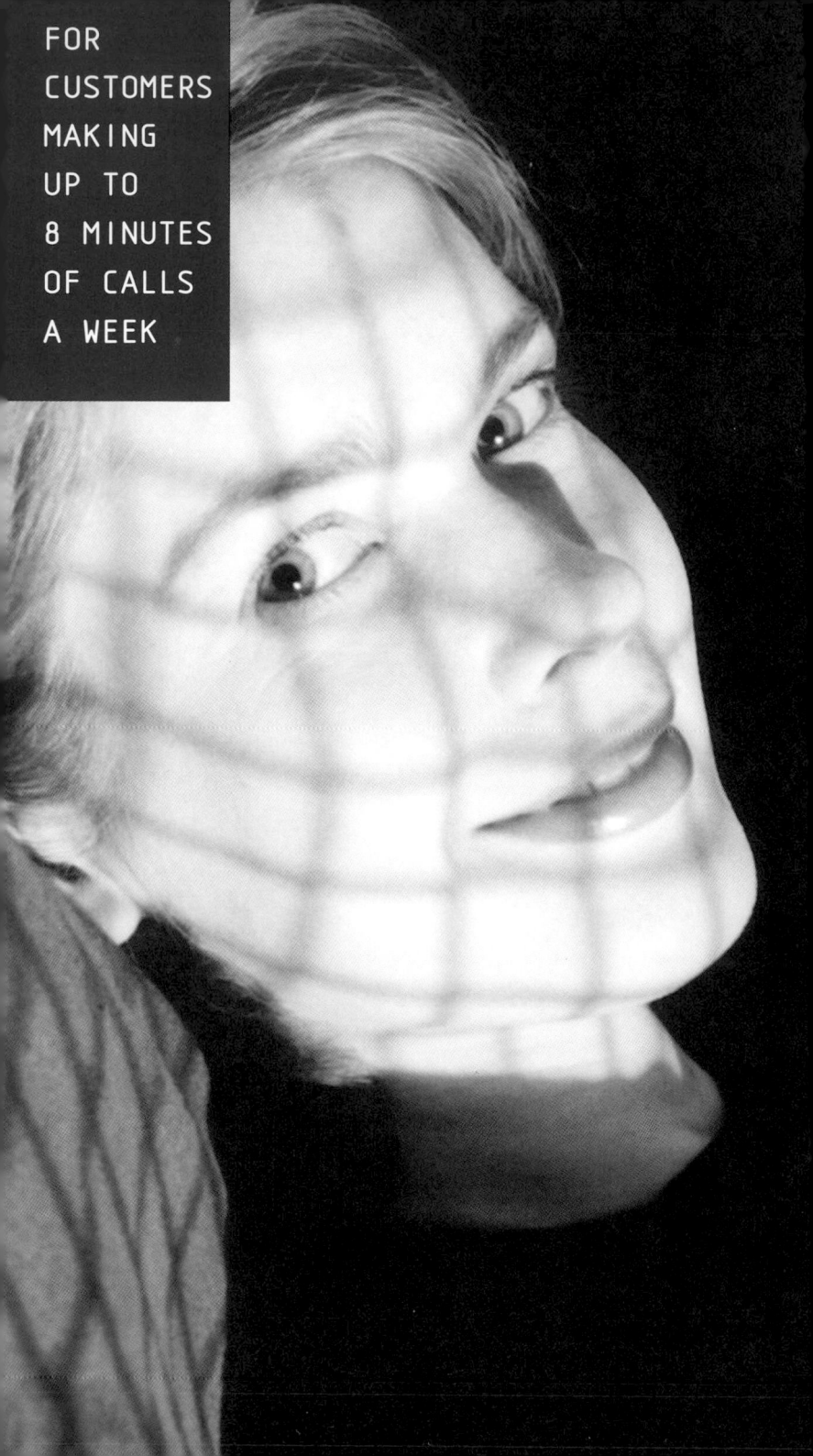

FOR
CUSTOMERS
MAKING
UP TO
8 MINUTES
OF CALLS
A WEEK

OCCASIONAL
CALLER

THE EASILY AFFORDABLE TARIFF FOR LESS FREQUENT USERS TO KEEP IN TOUCH

Occasional Caller is ideal if you're only likely to make up to 8 minutes of calls a week – mainly during off-peak hours.

It's ideal, too, if you simply need to be contactable when you're out and about.

And if you really want a mobile phone just to help you cope with the unexpected – Occasional Caller, giving you access to Cellnet's national UK network, is the perfect tariff.

No matter where you are – if you break down, miss the train, the plane, or a bus – on Cellnet you'll be covered.

KEY BENEFITS
- National UK coverage
- Low cost off-peak calls
- A wide choice of low cost analogue handsets

NETWORK FEATURES
- Call Divert
- Call Waiting
- Operator enquiries

OPTIONAL SERVICES
- Callback intelligent messaging*
- AA and RAC breakdown lines

THE NET THAT SETS YOU FREE

for further information call
0800 214000

CALL SAVER

LOCAL CALLS. ANYTIME. ANYPLACE.

Most mobile phone calls are local calls.

Most networks, however, only offer cheaper local calls, if they're made in your home area. At Cellnet, we've taken a much wider view.

We've introduced Call Saver – an exclusive Cellnet service offering low cost flat rate local calls, 24 hours a day. No matter how far you are from home.

If you live in Nottingham, but happen to be in Newcastle, and wish to phone a friend or customer in the Newcastle area – you'll be charged the Call Saver rate.

And while you'll be able to enjoy low cost local calls wherever you go in the UK – connected to Cellnet's digital service, you'll be able to keep in touch even when you're travelling abroad.

THE NET THAT SETS YOU FREE

for further information call

0800 214000

*Call Saver is only available in the UK, subject to Cellnet coverage.

England

ABBERLEY   Elms Hotel   70%   £120

Tel 01299 896666   Fax 01299 896804   Map 14 B1   **H**
Stockton Road Abberley Hereford & Worcester WR6 6AT

The sweet, welcoming aroma of a year-round log fire greets guests in the entrance hall of this substantial Queen Anne mansion just off the A443 surrounded by gardens that enjoy fine views of the countryside. Dotted with antiques, the day rooms have a gracious, country-house feel enhanced by board games and magazines. There's a mixture of antiques and reproduction pieces in bedrooms that are in good order and well appointed, with extras like fresh fruit, sherry and books. Nine Coach House rooms are in similar style but without mini-bar or remote-control for the TV. Bathrooms vary in size but all have telephone, loudspeaker extension and generously-sized towels. Beds are turned down in the evenings and room service is 24hr. The price quoted is for coach house rooms, a standard room in the main house is £159. Queens Moat Houses. **Rooms 25.** *Garden, croquet, tennis, putting. Access, Amex, Diners, Visa.*

ABBOT'S SALFORD   Salford Hall   66%   £105

Tel 01386 871300   Fax 01386 871301   Map 14 C1   **H**
Abbot's Salford Evesham Hereford & Worcester WR11 5UT

A fascinating Tudor building beside the A439 about eight miles west of Stratford-upon-Avon. Once a guest residence for the monks of nearby Evesham Abbey, it retains considerable historical and architectural interest. Stained-glass windows depict coats of arms, and there's a half-timbered, whitewashed wing and a fine walled garden. The central courtyard has been glassed in to form a pleasant conservatory, giving striking views of its gabled roofs. The lounge, once the Abbot's kitchen, displays original meat hooks suspended from oak beams. Bedrooms, named after historical characters connected with the hall and split between the main house and the gate house, are furnished mainly with reproduction pieces; many have exposed timberwork and mullioned windows. Conferences for up to 50. No dogs. **Rooms 33.** *Garden, croquet, tennis, sauna, sun beds, snooker. Closed 1 week Christmas. Access, Amex, Diners, Visa.*

ABINGDON   Abingdon Lodge   61%   £94

Tel 01235 553456   Fax 01235 554117   Map 15 D2   **H**
Marcham Road Abingdon Oxfordshire OX14 1TZ

Clean-lined, modern low-rise hotel at the junction of the A34 and A415. Day rooms include a distinctive octagonal bar. Several conference rooms cater for up to 150 delegates. Twenty-six bedrooms reserved for non-smokers. Children up to 16 stay free in parents' room. Ample car parking. **Rooms 63.** *Patio. Access, Amex, Diners, Visa.*

ABINGDON   Upper Reaches   62%   £112

Tel 01235 522311   Fax 01235 555182   Map 15 D2   **H**
Thames Street Abingdon Oxfordshire OX14 3TA

Six miles from Oxford, a former corn mill once operated by Benedictine monks, standing on a virtual island between the Thames and the Abbey Stream. Some bedrooms enjoy river views. The restaurant features a working water wheel and mill race. River moorings for those guests who wish to arrive by boat. Children up to age 16 free in parents' room. Free parking for 70 cars. Forte. **Rooms 25.** *Garden, fishing. Access, Amex, Diners, Visa.*

ALCESTER   Arrow Mill   £72

Tel 01789 762419   Fax 01789 765170   Map 14 C1   **I**
Arrow Alcester Warwickshire B49 5NL

The Arrow Mill was listed in the Domesday Book, when it was a working flour mill valued at three shillings and sixpence (17½p)! The stream-driven mill wheel still turns in the restaurant, and day rooms feature heavy beams and flagstones. Bedrooms of individual character use light, attractive fabrics and pine furniture. There's parking space for 200 cars. Banqueting/conferences for up to 120/100. Dogs in kennels only. **Rooms 18.** *Garden, fishing. Closed 2 weeks Christmas. Access, Amex, Diners, Visa.*

Consult the blue pages for summary tables and lists of recommended establishments.

| ALDEBURGH | **Brudenell Hotel** | 60% | £82 |

Tel 01728 452071   Fax 01728 454082
Map 10 D3   **H**
The Parade Aldeburgh Suffolk IP15 5BU

A traditional seaside esplanade hotel, where public rooms and many of the bedrooms look
out to sea. 10 bedrooms are designated non-smoking. Under-16s can share their parents'
room free. The elegant Music Room can accommodate up to 50 people for meetings
and conferences. The price for a sea-view room is £97. Forte. *Rooms 47.*
Access, Amex, Diners, Visa.

| ALDEBURGH | **Uplands** | 60% | £60 |

Tel 01728 452420   Fax 01728 454872
Map 10 D3   **H**
Victoria Road Aldeburgh Suffolk IP15 5DX

A Regency house, just opposite the parish church and a stone's throw from the seafront,
which maintains the best aspects of a snug guest house. Public areas include a rear
conservatory which opens on to the landscaped gardens where there's a wing of chalets.
Remaining bedrooms in the house retain some period features and have character and
charm; all but three are en suite. No dogs. *Rooms 20. Garden. Access, Amex, Diners, Visa.*

| ALDEBURGH | **Wentworth Hotel** | 68% | £86 |

Tel 01728 452312   Fax 01728 454343
Map 10 D3   **H**
Wentworth Road Aldeburgh Suffolk IP15 5BD

Just back from the beach opposite the fishermen's huts and boats, the Wentworth has
been in the same family ownership since 1920. This continuity has built up a reputation
for service and civilised comfort which brings many repeat visits. Many of the bedrooms
look out to sea, and almost all have bathrooms en suite. There are two tastefully
appointed lounges and a cosy bar. *Rooms 38. Garden. Closed 2 weeks from 27 Dec.*
Access, Amex, Diners, Visa.

| ALDERLEY EDGE | **Alderley Edge Hotel** | 72% | £117 |

Tel 01625 583033   Fax 01625 586343
Map 6 B2   **HR**
Macclesfield Road Alderley Edge Cheshire SK9 7BJ

It's always been a foodie place, and the public areas at this red-sandstone Victorian hotel
have been rearranged to the advantage of the restaurant, which now occupies the split-
level conservatory. The bar and lounge are formed out of the opened-up ground floor
rooms of the original house and still have a period feel with dado pine panelling and
plenty of comfortable armchairs and magazine-spread coffee tables. About half the
bedrooms, designated Executive, are rather small but have pleasant orangey floral fabrics
and wall coverings; best are the spacious deluxe rooms with pine furniture, spa baths and
extras like fresh fruit and decanters of sherry. Four of these rooms are cottagey in style
with wooden beams and some exposed stone walls. Bathrobes are standard throughout.
Rooms 32. Garden. Access, Amex, Diners, Visa.

Restaurant   £90

The eleven strong team of chefs is now led by Steve Kitchen, who is admirably
maintaining standards here as is immediately evident when the large basket of home-
baked breads – at least five including perhaps caraway seed, sun-dried tomato and olive
– arrives at the table. A light lunch menu is served in the lounge and there are no-
choice Market and Vegetarian menus and the à la carte. Dishes like scallops with a salad
of spring lettuce, rocket and oregano; skate wing under a gratin of parmesan and pickled
peppers; roulade of chicken breast with wild mushrooms and spinach, and a grill of
mixed meat and livers on a fondue of tomatoes and garden herbs demonstrate the
modern style. With a specialist pastry chef the desserts are also notable and varied: sugar-
glazed lemon tart, rhubarb jelly with scrumpy parfait, swede and apple 'streusel' pie with
vanilla cream. Equal thought goes into the selection of hand-made cheeses that always
includes three or four local varieties that are sometimes imaginatively used, as in a parfait
of Cropwell Bishop Stilton and Munster with Cheshire ham and walnuts. The wine list
is extraordinary – is there really a market for 100 champagnes? The rest is pretty
spectacular too, with a fair choice under £20. Plenty of magnums and half bottles.
Seats 80. Parties 22. Private Rooms 15/20. L (by arrangement only) 12-2 D 7-10.
Set L £9.50/£11.50 Set D £15.

ALDRIDGE Fairlawns 64% £80

Tel 01922 55122   Fax 01922 743210   Map 6 C4   **H**
Little Aston Road Aldridge Walsall West Midlands WS9

A Victorian house with modern redbrick extensions, set in farmland near the junction of the A452 and A454. A comfortable dado-panelled bar with leather armchairs and a rattan-furnished conservatory extension is the main day room and there are several attractively decorated conference/function rooms. Solid oak fitted units provide good, well-lit work space in neat bedrooms which include six split-level suites with sofa beds in the lounge area (good for families) and mezzanine bedrooms. Room service can provide hot food 24hrs a day. *Rooms 35. Garden. Access, Amex, Diners, Visa.*

ALL STRETTON Stretton Hall Hotel 59% £79

Tel 01694 723224   Fax 01694 724365   Map 6 A4   **H**
All Stretton nr Church Stretton Shropshire SY6 6HG

A Victorian hotel on the A49 between Ludlow and Shrewsbury. Most recent improvements concern the bedrooms – all redecorated and refurbished, a new bar, revamped lounge and an expansion of the function facilities – a new room with a capacity of 120 is added to the original 60-seat room. Some rooms are suitable for family use. *Rooms 14. Garden. Access, Amex, Diners, Visa.*

ALNWICK Blackmore's Restaurant £60

Tel 01665 604465   Map 5 D1   **R**
1 Dorothy Foster Court Narrowgate Alnwick Northumberland NE66 1NL

John Blackmore's restaurant occupies the second oldest building in town. Built in 1632, it is Grade II listed and the interior retains many attractive features including an old range which stands in an alcove in the cottagey ground-floor dining room. Upstairs there's a cosy lounge for pre- and after-dinner drinks. The menu changes seasonally and uses local produce to good effect. Typical of the starters are baked mussels with a mushroom and onion stuffing, glazed with a mornay sauce, a tartlet filled with creamed leek purée with goat's cheese, sunflower seeds and a chive sauce or a hot carrot mousse surrounded by lightly sautéed scallops in a creamy coriander sauce. Main dishes too are varied, the selection including tender breast of mallard with red cabbage and a rosemary-scented sauce, pork fillet with a creamed grapefruit and chervil sauce, beef fillet with a whisky and mushroom sauce or baked salmon with a basil and mustard crust and watercress sauce. Lovely puddings are typified by a giant profiterole with ice cream and hot fudge sauce, lemon and lime cheesecake and a rich hot chocolate sponge with hazelnut ice cream. Very charming service completes a delightful experience. No smoking. *Seats 28. Parties 8. D only 7-9. Closed Sun, Mon, Bank Holidays (except Good Friday) & all Jan. Set D £37 (Tue & Wed only, includes bottle of house wine). Access, Amex, Diners, Visa.*

ALNWICK White Swan 58% £74

Tel 01665 602109   Fax 01665 510400   Map 5 D1   **H**
Bondgate Within, Alnwick Northumberland NE66 1TD

A 300-year-old former coaching inn with a traditional ambience. The most characterful public room is the function suite with its carved panelling taken from the *Titanic's* sister ship, the *Olympic*. The bar too has charm with its memorabilia associated with the town's House of Hardy museum. 23 of the comfortable bedrooms are in the original building with 20 in a modern rear wing and the rest in a recently completed side conversion. *Rooms 55. Access, Amex, Visa.*

ALSAGER Manor House 65% £74

Tel 01270 884000   Fax 01270 882483   Map 6 B3   **H**
Audley Road Alsager Cheshire ST7 2QQ

Just three miles from Junction 16 of the M6, the Manor House is a modern hotel set in its own grounds but, since the site dates back in parts to the 17th century, old beams preserve a traditional feel in the restaurant, bars and several meeting rooms. Bedrooms are divided between the original part and a new wing; in the latter are two rooms adapted for disabled guests and two Executive rooms with jacuzzis. Children up to 14 stay free in parents' room. Conference facilities for 200. *Rooms 57. Garden, indoor swimming pool. Access, Amex, Diners, Visa.*

ALSTON   Lovelady Shield   68%   £98

Tel 01434 381203   Fax 01434 381515   Map 5 D3   **HR**
Nenthead Road Alston Cumbria CA9 3LF

A long tree-lined drive leads to this secluded 1830s house set among the wild Pennine fells east of Alston on the A689. Bordered on one side by the River Nent, the hotel bottles its own mineral water (though this is from a source higher up in the hills). Public rooms include a delightful and peaceful lounge decorated in pale cream and a convivial bar. Bedrooms are of good size and are attractively homely in character with some fine old pieces of furniture and carefully co-ordinated colour schemes. Bathrooms, though compact, are neat and have decent shower risers. Sustaining breakfasts, for which last orders are at 9am. **Rooms** 12. *Garden, croquet, tennis. Closed Jan.* *Access, Amex, Diners, Visa.*

Restaurant   £60

A charming, informal, candle-lit setting for a short, four-course fixed-price dinner which is simple in both style and presentation. A fruit cocktail or baked avocado could start the meal; then comes a soup; a choice of three main courses (fish, poultry, meat); a couple of desserts and coffee in the lounge. The wine list is pretty standard, but includes a good and inexpensive house selection. No smoking. **Seats** 30. *D only 7.30-8.30. Closed Jan (except by arrangement). Set D £24.50.*

ALTON   Grange Hotel   61%   £65

Tel 01420 86565   Fax 01420 541346   Map 15 D3   **H**
London Road Alton Hampshire GU34 4EG

The two-acre garden, overlooked by the lounge and sun terrace, is quite a feature at the Levenes' friendly hotel, where new function rooms catering for over 100 have recently been built. Individually appointed bedrooms include two honeymoon suites and the penthouse suite with a sunken bath. **Rooms** 29. *Garden, croquet, putting, coffee shop (9.30am-10pm). Access, Amex, Diners, Visa.*

ALTON   The Swan   58%   £77

Tel 01420 83777   Fax 01420 87975   Map 15 D3   **H**
High Street Alton Hampshire GU34 1AT

White-painted former coaching inn offering neat, practical accommodation alongside comfortable, unfussy public areas. Banqueting and conference facilities for 100. Forte. **Rooms** 36. *Access, Amex, Diners, Visa.*

Many hotels offer reduced rates for weekend or out-of-season bookings. Always ask about special deals.

ALTRINCHAM   Bowdon Hotel   65%   £79

Tel 0161-928 7121   Fax 0161-927 7560   Map 6 B2   **H**
Langham Road Bowdon Altrincham Cheshire WA14 2HT

Victorian hotel with sympathetic extensions, on the B5161 and convenient for the motorway network (M56 exit 7 two miles). Neat, practical accommodation, several conference rooms and banqueting suites and a bar called Silks and an ample car park. Ramps have been added for visitors in wheelchairs. Children up to 12 stay free in parents' room. New owners from March 1995. **Rooms** 82. *Access, Amex, Diners, Visa.*

ALTRINCHAM   Cresta Court   61%   £70

Tel 0161-927 7272   Fax 0161-926 9194   Map 6 B2   **H**
Church Street Altrincham Cheshire WA14 4DP

Handy for the motorway network and Manchester Airport, the privately owned Cresta Court offers well-kept, up-to-date accommodation and a variety of air-conditioned conference and function rooms (max 300). Children up to 12 stay free in parents' room. **Rooms** 138. *Mini-gym, solarium, coffee shop (9.30am-6pm). Access, Amex, Diners, Visa.*

ALTRINCHAM — Francs — £45

Tel 0161-941 3954 Fax 0161 929 0658   Map 6 B2   **R**
2 Goose Green Altrincham Cheshire WA14 1DW

First-floor French bistro with wide à la carte choice – moules marinière, chèvre niçoise en croute, mushroom omelette, confit of duck, liver lyonnaise, grilled salmon – plus various prix-fixe of which Le Braziard is of particular interest. With this menu starters and puds are chosen from the main menu but the main dish of fillet steak, chicken and pork you cook yourself on a hot stone brought from the kitchen; served with dauphinoise potatoes. Sunday lunches, when the à la carte is much shorter, are very popular, with children under ten eating free. *Seats 90. Parties 25. Private Room 12. L 12-3 D 6-10.30 (Fri & Sat till 11). Closed D Sun & 27 Dec. Set L (Sun) £8.75 Set L & D (Mon-Fri) £9.95. Set D (6-7.30pm) £6.95 & (Mon-Wed, Le Braziard) £12.95. Amex, Diners, Access, Visa.*

ALTRINCHAM — George & Dragon — 60% — £46

Tel 0161-928 9933 Fax 0161-929 8060   Map 6 B2   **H**
Manchester Road Altrincham Cheshire WA14 4PH

Smartly kept accommodation, Victorian-inspired bar-lounge. Children up to 16 stay free in parents' room. No room service. No dogs. Part of the Premier Lodge group. *Rooms 46. Garden. Access, Amex, Diners, Visa.*

ALVELEY — Mill Hotel — 72% — £120

Tel 01746 780437 Fax 01746 780850   Map 6 B4   **H**
Birdsgreen Alveley nr Bridgnorth Shropshire WV15 6HL

The D'Aniello family has created, from a 16th-century mill, a fine hotel with unusually spacious public areas that include a comfortably furnished lounge and cocktail bar. The mill workings can still be seen in the public bar. Beautifully landscaped grounds provide plenty of photo opportunities – lake, rustic bridge, gazebo – making this a popular venue for weddings; there are also several well-planned function rooms. Upstairs, dado-panelled corridors are broad, and well-appointed bedrooms generally large, with phones at both desk and bedside. Superior rooms are particularly large and have either four-posters or elaborate bedhead drapes plus sofa and armchairs. Good bathrooms, with either corner or alcoved tubs, boast large bath sheets, and often have twin basins; five have separate shower cubicles. A well-run hotel with notably friendly staff, 24hr room service and turn-down service in the evenings. Conference/banqueting facilities for up to 200; ample parking. No dogs. *Rooms 21. Garden, games room. Access, Amex, Diners, Visa.*

ALVESTON — Alveston House — 65% — £80

Tel 01454 415050 Fax 01454 415425   Map 13 F1   **H**
Alveston nr Bristol Avon BS12 2LJ

Popular commercial hotel on the A38 close to Bristol and the M4 and M5. The majority of bedrooms are singles, and the hotel is geared up to the business trade with conference suites catering for up to 85 delegates. Ample free parking. *Rooms 30. Garden. Access, Amex, Diners, Visa.*

ALVESTON — Forte Posthouse — 62% — £72

Tel 01454 412521 Fax 01454 413920   Map 13 F1   **H**
Thornbury Road Alveston nr Bristol Avon BS12 2LL

11 miles north of Bristol, close to the M4/M5 intersection, an extended Tudor inn with a good conference trade (facilities for up to 100). *Rooms 74. Outdoor swimming pool, pitch & putt. Access, Amex, Diners, Visa.*

AMBERLEY — Amberley Castle — 81% — £130

Tel 01798 831992 Fax 01798 831998   Map 11 A6   **HR**
Amberley nr Arundel West Sussex BN18 9ND

A real castle this, dating back to the 11th century, with its remarkably complete curtain walls concealing the prettiest of gardens – very much the creation of owner Martin Cummings, who is often mistaken for the gardener. Just oozing history and with all sorts

of fascinating details to discover, Amberley nevertheless manages to defy the draughty castle image with day rooms (dotted with antiques, the odd suit of armour and rack of pikes) that are positively cosy. While husband Martin is out in the garden it is Joy Cummings who has the flair for interior design, best seen in individually decorated bedrooms that come with every comfort from video players (the hotel has a library of films) and books to fruit and iced water. Bathrooms all have spa baths and come with good toiletries, bathrobes and generous towelling. High-quality staff provide a level of service to match the surroundings. No children under seven. No dogs. *Rooms 15. Garden, croquet. Access, Amex, Diners, Visa.*

Queens Room Restaurant £110

The 13th-century dining room is suitably baronial with ribbed, barrel-vaulted ceiling, lancet windows and a mural at one end commemorating the visit here in 1685 of Catherine of Braganza. A little crystal animal on each table adds charm to very proper place settings. As we went to press a change of chef was imminent. No smoking. *Seats 40. Parties 8. Private Room 12. L 12-2 D 7-9.30. Set L £13.50/£16.50 (Sun £21.50) Set D £25.50.*

AMBERLEY	Amberley Inn	57%	£70

Tel 01453 872565 Fax 01453 872738
Amberley nr Stroud Gloucestershire GL5 5AF

Map 14 B2 **H**

High on Minchinhampton Common, this sturdy, stone-built inn enjoys spectacular views of Woodchester Valley, particularly from the residents' lounge. There are two bars, the oak-panelled Lounge and the locally popular Country. Bedrooms share the views or overlook the garden. Four especially pleasant rooms are in the Garden House. Children up to 16 stay free in parents' room. *Rooms 14. Garden. Access, Amex, Diners, Visa.*

AMBLESIDE	Kirkstone Foot Hotel	65%	£108*

Tel & Fax 015394 32232
Kirkstone Pass Road Ambleside Cumbria LA22 9EH

Map 4 C3 **H**

The original 17th-century manor house and its extensions and outbuildings offer hotel accommodation plus self-catering cottages and apartments (dogs welcome in the latter only). Many guests return year after year and the place has a homely feel, especially in the lounge and bar areas, which look out on fine gardens and over Ambleside's rooftops. Bedrooms mainly have floral fabrics, colour co-ordinated schemes and smart modern furniture. They come in various sizes, among which front-facing rooms are decidedly superior. The three master bedrooms have king-size beds, and two rooms are particularly suitable for families. Currently undergoing a major refurbishment programme. *★Half-board terms only. Rooms 15. Garden. Closed Jan. Access, Amex, Diners, Visa.*

AMBLESIDE	Nanny Brow	62%	£90

Tel 015394 32036 Fax 015394 32450
Clappersgate Ambleside Cumbria LA22 9NF

Map 4 C3 **H**

An interesting Edwardian building, built in 1908 in Tudor style a mile and a half from Ambleside on the A593 Coniston/Langdale road. Nanny Brow has fine, stepped gardens and views over the Brathay Valley. Lounge and bar retain a cosy feel with open log fires. Chintz decor predominates in the main-house bedrooms; those in the Garden Wing are generally larger, with good views. The ground floor has access to a garden terrace, the first-floor suite to a private balcony. Fishing is available on a private stretch of the River Brathay and guests have free use of a local private leisure club. *Rooms 18. Garden, croquet, spa bath, sauna, solarium, tennis, fishing. Access, Amex, Diners, Visa.*

We welcome bona fide complaints and recommendations on the tear-out pages at the back of the book for readers' comments. They are followed up by our professional team.

AMBLESIDE — Rothay Manor — 71% — £113

Tel 015394 33605 Fax 015394 33607   Map 4 C3   **HR**
Rothay Bridge Ambleside Cumbria LA22 0EH

A balconied Regency frontage is echoed by an elegant, restful interior of cool decor, deep-cushioned seating and garden views which are shared by the best, front-facing bedrooms. A convenient location on the Coniston road is handy for Ambleside yet well protected from its bustle in secluded grounds. The Nixons have been here since it opened in 1967 and personal touches are evident throughout; service is very friendly and attentive. Guests have free use of a nearby leisure club (swimming pool, sauna, steam room, spa bath) and permits may be obtained for trout fishing. Traditional afternoon tea is served every day between 3.30 and 5.30. Phone about the special themed holidays and weekends. Two rooms are equipped for the use of disabled guests. No dogs. *Rooms 18. Garden, croquet. Closed 3 Jan-9 Feb. Access, Amex, Diners, Visa.*

Restaurant   £70

The setting of polished mahogany tables and soft candle-light is thoroughly traditional, and both cooking and service are in keeping. Lunchtime sees a cold buffet Monday to Saturday, roasts on Sunday (book), while dinner is a fixed-price meal. Typical dishes on the evening list include potted char, creamy curried parsnip soup, lemon sole stuffed with a purée of spinach and prawns, chicken à la crème and beef stroganoff. Very fair prices on an excellent wine list that is extremely well balanced between Europe and the New World. Note the hotel's policy when half bottles are unavailable in your choice: pay 60% of the full bottle price, or pay the lot and take home what you don't drink – admirable! No smoking. *Seats 70. Parties 20. Private Room 36. L 12.30-2 (buffet only Mon-Sat) (Sun 12.30-1.30) D 8-9. Set L £14.50 (Sun) Set D £21/£24.*

AMBLESIDE — Wateredge Hotel — 63% — £98

Tel 015394 32332 Fax 015394 31878   Map 4 C3   **HR**
Waterhead Bay Ambleside Cumbria LA22 0EP

On the outskirts of Ambleside, the Wateredge is set right at the tip of Lake Windermere and takes full advantage of its location with gardens stretching down to the shore, a jetty and rowing boat – hence no children under seven. It was originally a pair of fishermans' cottages but modern extensions have added garden rooms with private balcony or patio and two spacious ground-floor suites. A cosy bar, bright airy lounge and lake views provide the unifying theme; the Cowap family and cheerful staff provide the welcome. Guests have free membership of a nearby leisure club. *Rooms 23. Garden, boating, coarse fishing. Closed mid Dec-early Feb. Access, Amex, Visa.*

Restaurant   £80

Chefs Michael Cosgrove, Mark Cowap and Kathryn Cosgrove offer what they describe as traditional farmhouse cuisine, making all their own breads, pastries, ice creams, preserves and after-dinner truffles. Six courses include some choice on a well-balanced menu which could result in seafood crepes with scallops, mussels, prawns and cockles in a creamy mushroom and shallot sauce, celery and apple soup served with wholemeal bread, a sorbet, roast leg of English lamb with spiced poached pears and caper gravy, chocolate and orange soufflé or lemon tart and British cheeses to finish. Friendly service is again a plus, as is a non-smoking policy. Lighter lunches (12.15-2pm) and afternoon teas (3-5pm) are served out on the patio in warm weather, otherwise in the lounges – but in either case there's a good view of the lake. *Seats 50. Parties 12. D only 7-8.30. Set D £25.90.*

AMPFIELD — Potters Heron Hotel — 60% — £80

Tel 01703 266611 Fax 01703 251359   Map 15 D3   **H**
Ampfield nr Romsey Hampshire SO51 9ZF

White-painted thatched building on the A31 with ample free parking, conference facilities for up to 140 and all-day informal eating in Potters Pub. The majority of the bedrooms are designated non-smoking. Children up to 16 stay free in parents' room. Country Club Hotels. *Rooms 54. Garden, sauna, children's playroom. Access, Amex, Diners, Visa.*

Set menu prices may not always include service or wine.

| AMPNEY CRUCIS | The Crown of Crucis | £64 |

Tel 01285 851806   Fax 01285 851735   Map 14 C2   **I**
Ampney Crucis Cirencester Gloucestershire GL7 5RS

A conservatory extension is the latest addition to this 400-year-old Cotswold village inn alongside the A417. The refurbished oak-beamed bar and two-tier restaurant are housed in the old hostelry, while bedrooms are in a purpose-built extension around a garden courtyard. Most rooms enjoy a view over Ampney Brook to the village cricket ground. 14 ground-floor rooms for the less active; one is equipped for disabled guests. *Rooms 25. Garden. Closed 24-30 Dec. Access, Amex, Diners, Visa.*

| ANDOVER | White Hart Hotel | £65 |

Tel 01264 352266   Fax 01264 323767   Map 14 C3   **I**
Bridge Street Andover Hampshire SP10 1BH

Former coaching inn with a history going back 300 years. Period character (c. 1900) is created by pictures, posters and bric-a-brac in the day rooms. The Oak Room can host functions of up to 70 delegates. *Rooms 20. Access, Amex, Diners, Visa.*

| ANSTY | Ansty Hall | 70% | £100 |

Tel 01203 612222   Fax 01203 602155   Map 7 D4   **H**
Ansty nr Coventry Warwickshire CV7 9HZ

Just two minutes from Junction 2 of the M6, yet this mellow Caroline house dating from 1678 enjoys a peaceful rural setting. The entrance hall, with real log fire in winter, features wood panelling that is old rather than fine and the period day rooms tend to be multi-purpose – meeting room one day, lounge the next. Bedrooms are spacious with those in the original building sporting reproduction antique furniture, but perhaps the best are the 12 in a new wing which come with comfortable wing armchairs and stylish individual decor. Almost all rooms have bedhead drapes or canopies. Dogs are only allowed in the six characterful stable-block bedrooms. 24hr room service. *Rooms 30. Garden. Access, Amex, Diners, Visa.*

| APPLEBY-IN-WESTMORLAND | Tufton Arms | 66% | £80 |

Tel 01768 351593   Fax 01768 352761   Map 5 D3   **H**
Market Square Appleby-in-Westmorland Cumbria CA16 6XA

An unusual and rather evocative conversion of a 16th-century building which became a Victorian pub, restored by the Milsom family with authentic pieces, period prints and atmospheric appeal. Clubby bar, restful drawing room, conservatory restaurant. More Victorian features and carefully updated bathrooms in the original bedrooms; a more modest modern wing is fitted out with the businessman in mind. In the centre of Appleby, by the A66. Residents can fish free on a stretch of the Eden. Shooting parties welcome. *Rooms 21. Fishing. Access, Amex, Diners, Visa.*

| APPLEBY-IN-WESTMORLAND | Appleby Manor | 66% | £98 |

Tel 01768 351571   Fax 01768 352888   Map 5 D3   **HR**
Roman Road Appleby-in-Westmorland Cumbria CA16 6JB

A relaxing and friendly, family-owned hotel overlooking Appleby Castle and the Eden valley. Most of the original (1870s) architectural features remain, including the main fireplace and old hooks that used to carry rods to hang tapestries and pictures. Bright and cheerful bedrooms, whether those in the main house and modern wing or the seven in the coach house annexe that have just been refurbished, provide everything you need, from powerful hairdryers to in-house video films; four-poster beds attract a small supplement. Sink into one of the comfortable armchairs in the three lounges, warm yourself in front of a real log fire and sample one of the 71 single-malt whiskies on offer. Pool, snooker and table tennis in the games room. Dogs in annexe rooms only. *Rooms 30. Garden, croquet, indoor swimming pool, spa bath, sauna, steam room, sun bed, keep-fit equipment, snooker. Closed 3 days Christmas. Access, Amex, Diners, Visa.*

Oak Room Restaurant   £55

A panelled room (with a hand-painted tiled fireplace) where interesting British food is served in decent portions on four fixed-price menus, all available both lunch and dinner. Beefsteak and oyster pudding, Gypsy Hill chicken (pastry-wrapped chicken breast stuffed

See over

with pigeon breast topped with leek butter) and cinnamon-roast Gressingham duck might feature on the 'speciality' menus, with the likes of paupiette of young halibut on a bed of creamed spinach, chargrilled guinea fowl marinated in Alpine herbs, and a hot carrot and almond tart as the vegetarian option appearing on the table d'hote. Sweets from the trolley or a choice of six local Cumbrian cheeses that come with a selection of home-baked breads. There's a fixed mark-up on wines (excluding champagnes and three French classics), so nothing exceeds £15 on the list. Youngsters' menu served in the restaurant from 5pm. *Seats* 70. *Parties* 30. *L* 12-1.45 *D* 7-9. *Set L & D* £17.95, £19.95, £22.95 & £25.95.

APPLETHWAITE   Underscar Manor   74%   £150*

Tel 01768 775000   Fax 01768 774904   Map 4 C3   **HR**
Applethwaite Keswick Cumbria CA12 4PH

Overlooking Derwentwater and set in 40 acres of peaceful and tranquil grounds, the hotel is under the same direction (Pauline and Derek Harrison) as *Moss Nook (qv)*, near Manchester airport. Just one mile from the Keswick roundabout on the A66, the hotel, an Italianate house built in Victorian times, retains many original architectural features – fireplaces, mouldings, plasterwork ceilings – with period furniture to match. Opulent fabrics, deep carpets and exquisite flower arrangements all add to this splendour, carried through to the luxurious and spacious bedrooms which command breathtaking views. Bathrooms are equally well appointed with smart fittings, decent toiletries and good towels. No children under 12. No dogs. *Half-board terms only. Prices vary according to room size and outlook: that quoted above is for the four least expensive rooms. *Rooms* 11. *Garden. Access, Amex, Visa.*

Restaurant   £65

The twin dining-rooms, one with a conservatory extending into the garden, are quite sumptuous with rich drapes, chandeliers, lacy cloths and French-style armed dining chairs. In the kitchen nothing is too much trouble for head chef Robert Thornton, who smokes his own salmon (served hot as a starter with a green bean and pickled cucumber salad and a yoghurt, honey and herb dressing), makes his own pasta, bottles his own jams and preserves and even bakes his own bread. Other dishes from the à la carte might include fresh asparagus grilled with parmesan cheese and served with scallops and bacon, local Hardwick lamb cutlets with a lamb and herb cake on a chive and tarragon sauce and, among the desserts, a hot banana and frangipane tart with pistachio cream sauce. At night, for the whole table only, his six-course surprise menu is the adventurous option although the menu states that it does not include "controversial" ingredients. Few half bottles and no non-champagne sparklers on the wine list. Pleasant service, alfresco eating in fine weather. No smoking. *Seats* 55. *Parties* 10. *Private Room* 20. *L* 12-1 *D* 7-8.30. *Set L* £18.50 *Set D* £25.

ARUNDEL   Norfolk Arms   60%   £80

Tel 01903 882101   Fax 01903 884275   Map 11 A6   **H**
22 High Street Arundel West Sussex BN18 9AD

Arundel Castle is the seat of the Duke of Norfolk so it's natural to find the Norfolk Arms occupying a prime site in the town's high street – it was actually built by the 10th Duke some years ago. Bedrooms are bright, with pale floral patterns and modern bathrooms. Newer rooms are in a detached wing to the rear. Children up to 14 stay free in parents' room. Arundel Castle is an easy walk away. *Rooms* 34. *Access, Amex, Diners, Visa.*

ASCOT   Berystede Hotel   67%   £136

Tel 01344 23311   Fax 01344 872301   Map 15 E2   **H**
Bagshot Road Sunninghill Ascot Berkshire SL5 9JH

Just south of Ascot, this hotel is based on a large Victorian house standing in its own 6 acres of wooded grounds. As popular with racegoers as business people, the public rooms and the best of the bedrooms are in the original house and share its period feel. The majority of the bedrooms, however, are in a modern extension. The hotel has its own conference centre, including a business centre and can cater for up to 120 delegates. Forte. *Rooms* 91. *Garden, croquet, outdoor swimming pool, putting, games room. Access, Amex, Diners, Visa.*

ASCOT — Hyn's — £50

Tel 01344 872583   Map 15 E2   **R**
4 Brockenhurst Road Ascot Berkshire SL5 9DL

Peking, Szechuan and Cantonese all have their place on the menu (neatly and clearly printed, and no numbers!). Most of the dishes will be familiar to habitués of this most varied of cuisines, but a few are a little out of the ordinary. There's also a small choice of Thai dishes. *Seats 90. Parties 12. L 12-2.30 D 6-11. Closed 25 & 26 Dec. Set L & D from £16. Access, Amex, Diners, Visa.*

ASCOT — Royal Berkshire — 74% — £217

Tel 01344 23322   Fax 01344 874240   Map 15 E2   **H**
London Road Sunninghill Ascot Berkshire SL5 0PP

Superb setting for this Queen Anne mansion (located between Ascot racecourse and the Polo Club) whose previous occupants have included the Churchill family and a certain Colonel Horlicks (of malted drink fame) who developed the 15 acres of superb gardens and woodlands. Elegant public areas. Bedrooms in the original house are spacious and stylish with freestanding furniture and plenty of extras; those in the extensions are a little simpler. The largest of the nine conference rooms can accommodate up to 70 delegates theatre-style. *Rooms 63. Garden, croquet, indoor swimming pool, gym, sauna, spa bath, tennis, squash, putting. Access, Amex, Diners, Visa.*

ASHBOURNE — Ashbourne Lodge Hotel — 66% — £78

Tel 01335 346666   Fax 01335 346549   Map 6 C3   **H**
Derby Road Ashbourne Derbyshire DE6 1XH

On the A52 from Derby to Leek, this modern redbrick hotel is lent some old-world style by rustic-designed public areas. Bedrooms are neat and light but not over-large, although family rooms for two adults and two children are available. Banqueting/conference facilities for 200/220. Children up to 14 stay free in parents' room. No dogs. *Rooms 50. Garden, indoor swimming pool, gym, sauna, steam room, spa bath. Access, Amex, Diners, Visa.*

ASHBOURNE — Callow Hall — 69% — £105

Tel 01335 343403   Fax 01335 343624   Map 6 C3   **H**
Mappleton Road Ashbourne Derbyshire DE6 2AA

Five minutes' drive from the centre of Ashbourne, the Spencer family's Victorian mansion is an ideal retreat. Approached by a tree-lined drive through 44 acres of woodland, it enjoys a mile of private fishing on the nearby Bentley Brook. Besides fishing, it attracts shooting parties and is also popular for small conferences. Quality antiques and family memorabilia are the main features of the drawing room and homely little bar. Bedrooms with tasteful design and elegant furnishings of the highest standard provide plenty of extras – from books and magazines to fresh fruit and mineral water; one spacious ground-floor room faces the house and is equipped for disabled guests. Sumptuous tiled bathrooms boast bathrobes and locally made toiletries. Children up to 10 stay free in their parents' room. No dogs. *Rooms 16. Garden, fishing. Closed 1 week Feb. Access, Amex, Diners, Visa.*

ASHFORD — Ashford International — 71% — £102

Tel 01233 611444   Fax 01233 627708   Map 11 C5   **H**
Simone Weil Avenue Ashford Kent TN24 8UX

A smart hotel by Junction 9 of the M20. The lobby is part of a long, glass-roofed boulevard which also houses an art gallery, a lively bar and a brasserie with tables spilling out on to the tiled concourse. A fountain and a large, four-face hanging clock complete the rather pleasing Continental air. Spacious bedrooms are well maintained and equipped. Staffed business centre. Queens Moat Houses. *Rooms 200. Indoor swimming pool, gym, sauna, whirlpool bath, solarium, beautician, hair salon, brasserie (7am-11pm). Access, Amex, Diners, Visa.*

Consult the blue pages for summary tables and lists of recommended establishments.

ASHFORD   Eastwell Manor   81%   £142

Tel 01233 635751   Fax 01233 635530   Map 11 C5   **HR**
Eastwell Park Boughton Aluph Ashford Kent TN25 4HR

There's an air of faded gentility at this Jacobean-style mansion set in 62 acres of grounds and built in the 1920s. The scale of the rooms is as grand as the approach, with real log fires, flagstoned floors, oak panelling and moulded plasterwork ceilings setting the tone. Bedrooms are comfortable and well appointed, as are the bathrooms. *Rooms 23. Garden, croquet, tennis, pitch & putt, snooker. Access, Amex, Diners, Visa.*

Restaurant   £95

Patterned carpets and wallpaper in the Elizabethan-style dining room make an unexpected backdrop for the accomplished cooking of chef Ian Mansfield, who provides several set lunch and dinner menus. Current specialities include air-dried 'Eldon wild blue' ham with warm goat's cheese and aubergine, roast turbot with savoy cabbage and a sauce of foie gras and lemon grass, shin of veal braised with spices, fennel and carrots, and game from the Eastwell Estate. The confident cooking is also on display in puds such as a warm hazelnut tart with orange sauce and honey ice cream, cinnamon and poppy seed parfait with caramelised pears and a plate of rhubarb desserts. There's also a good, well-annotated menu of mostly French cheeses. Courteous and friendly service. No smoking. *Seats 65. Parties 12. Private Room 65. L 12.30-2 D 7.30-9.30 (Fri/Sat to 10). Set L £19.50 & £36.50 Set D £28.50, £36.50 & £42.*

ASHFORD   Forte Posthouse   66%   £75

Tel 01233 625790   Fax 01233 643176   Map 11 C5   **H**
Canterbury Road Ashford Kent TN24 8QQ

Half a mile out of Ashford on the A28 to Canterbury and one mile from junction 9 of the M20. A modern hotel based around a 17th-century barn, now the restaurant. Conferences for up to 120 delegates. *Rooms 60. Garden. Access, Amex, Diners, Visa.*

ASHFORD   Holiday Inn Garden Court   65%   £72

Tel 01233 713333   Fax 01233 712082   Map 11 C5   **H**
Maidstone Road Hothfield Ashford Kent TN26 1AR

A no-frills Holiday Inn offering only limited services and public areas, but spacious bedrooms with comfortable beds. Good value, with free accommodation for children in parents' room and greatly reduced rates at weekends. Conferences for up to 30. *Rooms 104. Keep-fit equipment. Access, Amex, Diners, Visa.*

ASHFORD-IN-THE-WATER   Riverside Hotel   66%   £95

Tel 01629 814275   Fax 01629 812873   Map 6 C2   **HR**
Fennel Street Ashford-in-the-Water Derbyshire DE45 1QF

Sue and Roger Taylor's ivy-clad Georgian house is set in mature, secluded gardens on the banks of the River Wye, near the centre of the village. Two comfortable sitting rooms, one with an inglenook fireplace, are complemented by an airy conservatory. Individually decorated bedrooms have four-posters or half-tester drapes. Luxury rooms, in a new wing, carry a small supplement. All are non-smoking. A cottage on the river is let on a self-catering basis. *Rooms 15. Garden, croquet. Access, Amex, Diners, Visa*

Restaurant   £75

Modern English cuisine makes fine use of fresh and seasonal produce, including daily market seafood and game from the Chatsworth Estate. Salad of roast red peppers on anchovy toast with pesto, grilled fillet of smoked haddock with spicy lentils or cream of Jerusalem artichoke soup could precede pan-fried fillet of salmon with roast fennel and a tomato and ginger sauce, or roast pork with an apricot and apple chutney and a port sauce. For dessert, perhaps chocolate and orange terrine served with jasmine tea sauce, or date and toffee crumble tartlet with banana ice cream. Interesting wine list, with plenty of half bottles. No smoking. 'Lite Bite' meals are served all day in the Terrace Room. *Seats 50. Parties 18. Private Room 30. L 12-2 D 7-9.30. Set L (Sun) £16.95 Set D £19.50 & £31.*

ASHINGTON   Mill House Hotel   £77

Tel 01903 892426   Fax 01903 892855   Map 11 A6   **I**
Mill Lane Ashington West Sussex RH20 3BZ

Comfortable, friendly and homely, this 300-year-old cottagey hotel is clearly signposted on the northbound carriage of the A24 (it's less easy to find from the London side). Both the public areas and the bedrooms are characterised by low ceilings and uneven floors. Rooms are quite well equipped but simply decorated and generally on the small side; the cottage next door contains two extra rooms. There are two four-poster rooms. *Rooms 12. Garden. Closed 24 Dec-30 Jan. Access, Amex, Diners, Visa.*

ASHINGTON   The Willows   £55

Tel 01903 892575   Map 11 A6   **R**
London Road Ashington West Sussex RH20 3JR

Look for signs on the A24 to Ashington, where you will find this 15th-century farmhouse with inglenook fireplace and old black beams. Chef-patron Carl Illes offers fixed-price lunch and dinner menus which include a selection for vegetarians. Dishes range from the simple and familiar (smoked salmon and prawns in a 'Maryrose' sauce, grilled Dover sole, chicken stuffed with herbs and breadcrumbs, fillet steak with creamy pepper sauce) to the slightly more elaborate and less usual (home-made cheese and spinach gnocchi, pan-fried scallops with savoy cabbage, bacon and cream, venison with spiced orange cranberries in a port sauce). Satisfying desserts, particularly for chocoholics; ice-cream lovers should seek out the Willows' home-made delights. There are some excellent wines (several top burgundy growers) on a good list with all four *marque* champagnes under £30 – commendable. *Seats 30. Parties 15. L (Sun only) 12-2 D 7-10. Closed D Sun, all Mon. Set L £16.50 Set D £18.95. Access, Amex, Visa.*

ASKRIGG   King's Arms Hotel   £85

Tel 01969 650258   Fax 01969 650635   Map 5 D4   **I**
Market Place Askrigg Wensleydale North Yorkshire DL8 3HQ

Liz and Ray Hopwood's characterful, friendly inn has an unbroken history dating back to 1760 when outbuildings, where now the Back Parlour is, housed John Pratt's racing stables. Turner is known to have stayed here while recording on canvas the tranquil Dales scenery of the early 1800s; while today the main bar is universally recognised as 'The Drovers Arms' as depicted on TV in *All Creatures Great and Small*. Each and every bedroom retains original features in keeping with the inn's manor house style, the many oak beams and uneven floors complemented by antique furniture, four-poster, half-tester and canopied brass beds, and colour co-ordinated fabrics of commensurate quality. Good bar snacks. *Rooms 10. Access, Amex, Visa.*

ASPLEY GUISE   Moore Place   70%   £90

Tel 01908 282000   Fax 01908 281888   Map 15 E1   **H**
The Square Aspley Guise nr Woburn Bedfordshire MK17 8DW

Built by Francis Moore, the elegant mansion set in neat lawns dominates the village centre. The frontage is restored Georgian, but beyond the original entrance the overall atmosphere is of a much more recent period. Reception is actually at the rear, housed in a smartly decorated, lofty conservatory/lounge. The majority of the bedrooms are in a modern, purpose-built block with a further 15 in a separate block. All are smartly decorated and have neat bathrooms. Thoughtful touches, apart from satellite TV, include bathrobes, fresh fruit, a measure of whisky and of sherry and a cafetière with fresh ground coffee. There's more complimentary drinking upon checking in too. Friendly, helpful staff. Children up to 12 stay free in parents' room. *Rooms 54. Garden. Access, Amex, Diners, Visa.*

Lodges are now listed by county in the reference section

Aston Clinton   Bell Inn   78%   £64

Tel 01296 630252   Fax 01296 631250   Map 15 E2   **HR**
London Road Aston Clinton Buckinghamshire HP22 5HP

In the 17th century the Bell was a coaching inn and these origins are immediately
apparent from its location (set back on the A41 London-Buckingham Road) and
configuration – the former stables across the now flower-filled courtyard have discreetly
become an integral block of bedrooms and suites. Now in its 50th year under the Harris
family's ownership, it has a unique blend of homely charm and serious professionalism,
while an appealing mix of log-burning fire, fresh flowers and pine panelling sets the scene
in the public rooms, where the mark of time and history is firmly stamped. The
flagstoned smoking room, with its brass ornaments and sporting pictures, is particularly
notable. Enjoyable breakfasts. Conference (up to 250) and banqueting (up to 220)
facilities in a purpose-built suite across the road.. *Rooms 21. Garden, croquet. Access,
Amex, Visa.*

Restaurant   £100

Giles Stonehouse has worked in some prestigious kitchens, including the *Moulin de
Mougins* under Roger Vergé, and the Bell is now reaping the benefits. The menu retains
many of the inn's old favourites such as the Bell Inn smokies and, of course, roast
Aylesbury duck. Otherwise begin with duck rillettes with warm brioche, or pan-seared
scallops with a lemon butter sauce. To follow, perhaps roast best end of lamb with an
olive and herb crust and *sauce niçoise*, baby sea bass cooked *en papillote* or rosette of
beef with *pommes Maxime* and a truffle sauce. For dessert there's a splendid choice
including a duo of vanilla and coffee soufflés, hot sticky toffee pudding with butterscotch
sauce or iced kumquat and banana parfait with a fruit coulis. Good choice of both British
and European cheeses. A short 'bistro' menu is proving popular as a lighter option.
Excellent service from an enthusiastic team under the direction of George Bottley.
A quite marvellous and comprehensive wine list, from the house recomendations with
tasting notes to the red Bordeaux vintage chart. In addition, there's a wine menu for
those who wish to accompany the three courses of their meal with a different wine (by
the glass: choice of two). *Seats 150. Private Room 24. L 12.30-1.45 D 7.30-9.45 (Sun
& Mon till 9). Set L £13.50/£17 (Sun £25) Set D £22.50.*

Axbridge   Almshouse Bistro   £35

Tel 01934 732493   Map 13 F1   **R**
The Square Axbridge Somerset BS26 2AR

A charmingly appointed bistro in a converted 15th-century almshouse overlooking the
village square. Owner-Chef Tim Collins operates an eat-as-you-please policy, so you're
welcome to order a bowl of soup or a three-course meal. The blackboard lists at least 20
dishes a day, from smoked haddock with Welsh rarebit to pasta, lamb with couscous and
fillet of beef with foie gras and truffles. Children's portions. No smoking. *Seats 32.
Private Room 6. L 12-2 D 6.45-9.45. Closed winter L except by arrangement, D Sun,
all Mon. Set L & D £9.95. Access, Visa.*

Axbridge   Oak House   £51

Tel 01934 732444   Fax 01934 733112   Map 13 F1   **I**
The Square Axbridge Somerset BS26 2AP

More ancient than it looks (it dates from the 13th century), the inn overlooks the town
square. The residents' lounge has a couple of inglenooks providing cosy comfort in
winter. Inexpensively furnished bedrooms are well kept and offer the usual amenities.
Three of the sparsely appointed bathrooms have shower/WC only. *Rooms 9.
Access, Amex, Visa.*

Aylesbury   Forte Posthouse   69%   £72

Tel 01296 393388   Fax 01296 392211   Map 15 D2   **H**
Aston Clinton Road Aylesbury Buckinghamshire HP22 5AA

A purpose-built modern hotel constructed around a central courtyard, alongside the A41
three miles east of the town centre. Public areas are open-plan and very smart. The tile-
floored foyer leads to spacious lounges, furnished in contemporary fashion and making

good use of attractive, colourful fabrics. Bedrooms are of a fair size and decorated in restful shades, with solid furniture and fully tiled bathrooms. 22 rooms are designated non-smoking. Banqueting facilitites for 100, conferences up to 120. *Rooms 94.* *Indoor swimming pool, gym, sauna, sun beds. Access, Amex, Diners, Visa.*

AYLESBURY	Hartwell House	86%	£176

Tel 01296 747444   Fax 01296 747450   Map 15 D2   **HR**
Oxford Road Aylesbury Buckinghamshire HP17 8NL

Dating back to the 16th century, Hartwell House is the epitome of luxury, a magnificent country house set in 80 acres of parkland. Day rooms have many notable features like rococo ceilings, choice antiques, oil paintings and chandeliers. Wonderful plump-cushioned seating spreads through the grandly proportioned reception rooms. Bedrooms show high standards of luxury and comfort; sumptuously appointed in impressive fashion, they employ antiques, rich fabrics and a host of pampering extras, plus huge beds. Bright, neatly fitted bathrooms. Motivated staff provide high levels of service. 100 yards from the main house is the Hartwell Spa, modelled on an orangery inspired by Sir John Soane and incorporating fine leisure facilities – the grand 50-foot swimming pool is surrounded by an arched arcade and overlooked by a gallery where you will find the Spa Bar and Buttery. The function rooms are situated in a restored 18th-century coach house and can accommodate up to 80 delegates; the rooms are named after distinguished architects who have contributed to the evolution of Hartwell House – James Gibbs, James Wyatt, Henry Keene and Eric Throssell. There are also interesting rooms in the main house for private dining. In addition to the leisure and meeting facilities Hartwell Court houses the 16 most recent bedrooms and suites. No children under 8. Dogs are not allowed in the grounds, but good kennels are nearby. *Rooms 45. Garden, croquet, indoor swimming pool, spa bath, steam room, sauna, gym, beauty & hair salon, solarium, fishing. Access, Amex, Diners, Visa.*

Restaurant   £100

The surroundings are most impressive – the elegantly vaulted, pale yellow Soane Room overlooking the croquet lawn and obelisk in parkland beyond, tail-coated waiters and fine table settings including Royal Doulton bone china. Fixed-price menus offer plenty of choice – about a dozen main dishes at night – with the likes of chicken consommé with tortellini and terrine of goose liver with apples and cinnamon among the starters and main dishes such as carpaccio of monkfish and tuna, sautéed sea bass with a sage butter sauce, fillet of beef with horseradish cream and red wine sauce and roast mallard on creamed savoy cabbage with truffle and port sauce. Several interesting wines on a splendid and very comprehensive list that would benefit greatly if presented in a more orderly and user-friendly manner. Excellent half bottle choice. No smoking. Jacket and tie for gentlemen. *Seats 70. Parties 8. Private Room 60. L 12.30-2 D 7.30-9.45.* *Set L £18.70/£24.50 Set D £39.50.*

AYLESBURY	Holiday Inn Garden Court	58%	£49

Tel 01296 398839   Fax 01296 394108   Map 15 D2   **H**
Buckingham Road Watermead Aylesbury Buckinghamsire HP19 3FY

Follow the A413 Buckingham Road out of the town centre to find this smart, cream-painted neo-colonial-style hotel. Spacious bedrooms each with a sofa bed make up for the lack of public areas. Continental breakfasts only at weekends. *Rooms 40. Garden. Access, Amex, Diners, Visa.*

Many hotels offer reduced rates for weekend or out-of-season bookings. Always ask about special deals.

BAGSHOT   Pennyhill Park   75%   £166

Tel 01276 471774   Fax 01276 473217   Map 15 E3   **H**
London Road Bagshot Surrey GU19 5ET

Just off the A30, this well-equipped hotel and country club retains some notable architectural features of its 19th-century origins, including the baronial-style foyer-lounge with stained-glass windows, exposed stone walls and slate floor, and the lounge, on two levels, with a beamed gallery upstairs and panelling downstairs. Bedrooms in the main building are spacious and charming, and those around the redeveloped courtyard vary from cosy and intimate to elegant mini-suites; all are named after flowers or shrubs, except for the luxurious Hayward suite. Children up to 14 stay free in parents' room. Parking for 120 cars, banqueting/conferences for 80/60, on-the-spot tuition in a number of sporting activities. No dogs (they can stay in the stables). *Rooms 76. Garden, croquet, outdoor swimming pool, sauna, solarium, tennis, 9-hole golf course, clay-pigeon shooting, riding, stabling, fishing. Access, Amex, Diners, Visa.*

BAKEWELL   Hassop Hall   74%   £93

Tel 01629 640488   Fax 01629 640577   Map 6 C2   **H**
Hassop nr Bakewell Derbyshire DE45 1NS

From Bakewell take the Sheffield road, then turn left on to the B6001 to Hassop and the Hall. Owned and run by Thomas Chapman since 1975, the Hall, originally the ancient seat of the Eyre family, stands among trees and parkland at the heart of the Peak District National Park. From the impressive approach you enter the marbled hallway with antiques and oil paintings. There is a chandeliered lounge in Regency style, a drawing room, a room for non-smokers and a relaxing oak-panelled bar. The large, luxurious bedrooms are individually decorated and furnished, with embroidered bed linen and splendid bathrooms. *Rooms 13. Garden, croquet, tennis. Closed 3 days Christmas. Access, Amex, Diners, Visa.*

BAMBURGH   Lord Crewe Arms   £68

Tel 01668 214243   Fax 01668 214273   Map 5 D1   **I**
Front Street Bamburgh Northumberland NE69 7BL

Friendly old inn in the middle of Bamburgh, a town dominated by its massive castle. Public areas include two rustic-style bars and two unpretentious lounges. Upstairs, bedrooms offer modest comforts with TVs and beverage trays but no telephones; all but a couple have en-suite bathrooms. No children under 5. Bar open lunchtime only in winter. *Rooms 25. Accommodation closed Nov-Mar (or Easter if earlier). Access, Visa.*

BANBURY   Banbury House Hotel   62%   £97

Tel 01295 259361   Fax 01295 270954   Map 15 D1   **H**
27-29 Oxford Road Banbury Oxfordshire OX16 9AH

A handsome Georgian house offering all the modern comforts. Star of the accommodation is the Blenheim Suite with a four-poster bed and whirlpool bath. Functions (up to 120) and conferences (to 70) are a speciality. Access to the car park (free parking for 50 cars) is from Lucky Lane. Formerly a Moat House. *Rooms 48. Access, Amex, Diners, Visa.*

BANBURY   Whately Hall   65%   £99

Tel 01295 263451   Fax 01295 271736   Map 15 D1   **H**
Banbury Cross Banbury Oxfordshire OX16 0AN

Dating from 1632, Whately Hall stands in gardens opposite Banbury Cross. The Cross is remembered in a nursery rhyme, and Jonathan Swift stayed here while writing Gulliver's Travels. Fine panelling, mullion windows and antiques give character to the day rooms. Bedrooms, some in a modern wing, all have well-lit, tiled bathrooms. Children up to 16 stay free in parents' room. Forte Heritage. *Rooms 74. Garden, croquet. Access, Amex, Diners, Visa.*

BARFORD   Glebe Hotel   68%   £110

Tel 01926 624218   Fax 01926 624625   Map 14 C1   **H**
Church Street Barford Warwickshire CV35 8BS

Originally an 1820s rectory, the hotel now has a splendid leisure club and conference facilities for up to 150. Chintzy bedrooms include those with tented ceilings or four-poster beds. All are well equipped, having satellite TVs and the usual modern amenities including up-to-date marble-floored bathrooms. Children up to 14 stay free in parents' room. Good service throughout. *Rooms 41. Garden, croquet, indoor swimming pool, keep-fit equipment, spa bath, sauna, steam room. Access, Amex, Diners, Visa.*

BARNARD CASTLE   Jersey Farm Hotel   59%   £60

Tel 01833 638223   Fax 01833 631988   Map 5 D3   **H**
Darlington Road Barnard Castle Co Durham DL12 8TA

This informal and friendly little hotel stands a mile east of town on the A67 (turn off the A1(M) on to the B6275 for Piercebridge), surrounded by a working farm. John, Jean and Mark Watson offer a warm welcome in unpretentious surroundings – public areas are homely and unfussy and the bedrooms, in the old farmhouse and in extensions, are modest but comfortable. Superior rooms are larger, with more extras, and there are six suites. The conference centre can cater for banquets up to 150 and conferences up to 200. A new leisure complex is planned. *Rooms 20. Garden. Access, Visa.*

BARNBY MOOR   Ye Olde Bell   60%   £68

Tel 01777 705121   Fax 01777 860424   Map 7 D2   **H**
Barnby Moor nr Retford Nottinghamshire DN22 8QS

On the edge of Sherwood Forest, just a mile from the A1, Ye Olde Bell has been offering hospitality to travellers for hundreds of years. Old oak panelling, open fireplaces and diamond-pane leaded lights retain the character of the public rooms while bedrooms offer modern conveniences. Conferences for up to 250 delegates. Under-12s stay free in parents' room. Principal Hotels. *Rooms 55. Garden. Access, Amex, Diners, Visa.*

BARNHAM BROOM   Barnham Broom Hotel   62%   £82

Tel 01603 759393   Fax 01603 758224   Map 10 C1   **H**
Honingham Road Barnham Broom nr Norwich Norfolk NR9 4DD

A large modern complex comprising hotel, golf and country club and conference centre (up to 150 delegates). The club bar and lounge overlook the grounds. All the bedrooms have writing desks and other extras include radios in the bathrooms. *Rooms 52. Indoor swimming pool, children's splash pool, gym, squash, sauna, steam room, solarium, beauty salon, hairdressing, tennis, two championship golf courses, snooker. Access, Amex, Diners, Visa.*

BARNSLEY   Ardsley Moat House   59%   £88

Tel 01226 289401   Fax 01226 205374   Map 6 C2   **H**
Doncaster Road Ardsley Barnsley South Yorkshire S71 5EH

Extended 18th-century mansion (only the cocktail bar still shows period features) on the A635 to the east of town. Biggest bedrooms are Executives; half the rooms are designated non-smoking. Extensive conference/function families for up to 400. Friendly staff. *Rooms 73. Garden. Access, Amex, Diners, Visa.*

Many hotels offer reduced rates for weekend or out-of-season bookings. Always ask about special deals.

BARNSLEY   Armstrongs   £55

Tel 01226 240113   Map 6 C2   **R**
6 Shambles Street Barnsley South Yorkshire S70 2SQ

Chef-patron Nicholas Pound's cooking is inventive without being gimmicky, and thoroughly enjoyable. Dinner might include chicken breasts with tarragon, fillet of beef with a garlic sauce, roast duck with orange and onion confit and seared salmon fillet with soy. Leave room for desserts such as iced butterscotch meringue cake, chocolate millefeuille or plum and cinnamon tart with Amaretto ice cream. A similar lunch menu includes a selection of lighter dishes for those wishing to eat less substantially (and more economically). A short fixed-price (£12.95) menu is available between 7 and 8pm. Modest wine list, albeit at fair prices. *Seats 60. Parties 16. L 12-2 D 7-10. Closed L Sat, all Sun & Mon, Bank Holidays. Access, Amex, Visa.*

BARNSTAPLE | Imperial Hotel | 60% | £112

Tel 01271 45861   Fax 01271 24448   Map 13 D2   **H**
Taw Vale Parade Barnstaple Devon EX32 8NB

A solid Edwardian building overlooking the river Taw. Front-facing rooms catch the afternoon sun. Meeting rooms for up to 60 people. Forte Hotels. *Rooms 56. Access, Amex, Diners, Visa.*

BARNSTAPLE | Lynwood House | | £70

Tel 01271 43695   Fax 01271 79340   Map 13 D2   **RR**
Bishop's Tawton Road Barnstaple Devon EX32 9DZ

On the edge of Barnstaple, the restaurant has been owned and run by the Roberts family for the past 26 years. Meals are taken in the quiet elegance of a Victorian dining room and comprise a choice of mostly classic dishes including duck liver paté with Cumberland sauce, cheese fondue pancakes or warm prawn salad followed perhaps by pot-roasted partridge with a pear and white wine sauce, local scallops sautéed with fresh ginger soy sauce and bean sprouts or local Dover sole grilled with butter and parsley. There are sweets such as home-made meringue with praline ice cream and hot butterscotch sauce, bread-and-butter pudding and chocolate truffle mousse to finish. A 'lighter meal' menu is also available. No smoking. *Seats 60. Private Room 20. L 12-2 D 7-9.30. Closed Sun except to residents. Set L £11.95/£13.95. Access, Amex, Visa.*

Rooms   £61
Overnight guests are accommodated in five Executive bedrooms, all with armchairs and plenty of creature comforts. Separate breakfast room; fresh Scottish kippers.

BASILDON | Forte Posthouse | 59% | £72

Tel 01268 533955   Fax 01268 530119   Map 11 B4   **H**
Cranes Farm Road Basildon Essex SS14 3DG

Modern exterior, bright and pleasant accommodation, plus lake views from the conservatory-style bar. Banqueting facilities for up to 250, conferences to 300. Guests have free use of the nearby Pipps Hill Leisure Centre. *Rooms 110. Access, Amex, Diners, Visa.*

BASINGSTOKE | Audleys Wood | 75% | £128

Tel 01256 817555   Fax 01256 817500   Map 15 D3   **HR**
Alton Road Basingstoke Hampshire RG25 2JT

Alongside the A339 Alton road, close to Junction 6 of the M3. Built in the late 1880s for Sir George Bradshaw (whose railway timetables made his fortune) and set in seven wooded acres, the overtly Victorian house had a varied history before being transformed into a hotel of some luxury (it opened in 1989). A splendid carved oak fireplace graces the panelled lounge, which also features a minstrel's gallery. Similar darkwood panelling and a handsome fireplace are to be found in the bar. The majority of the bedrooms are in sympathetically-designed extensions: roomy and tastefully appointed, with marble-tiled bathrooms; main-house bedrooms are even larger and more luxurious; 26 rooms are reserved for non-smokers. Several rooms are suitable for disabled guests. Children up to 16 can share their parents' room at no charge; interconnecting rooms available. Friendly staff. Thistle & Mount Charlotte. *Rooms 71. Garden, croquet, pétanque, putting, archery, golf practice net. Access, Amex, Diners, Visa.*

Conservatory Restaurant   £80

The glass in the pitched roof of this former conservatory and palm house was replaced with wood to create a striking and unusual restaurant that comes complete with minstrel's gallery where a player-piano tirelessly entertains diners. New chef Christopher Cleveland has stuck to the fixed-priced plus à la carte format at both lunch and dinner but with less flowery dish descriptions than his predecessor. Terrine of sole and lobster with lobster and herb dressing; medallion of veal with pan-fried scampi and Pernod sauce; saddle of venison with mushroom ravioli, beetroot, woodland mushrooms and a port and raspberry vinegar sauce and grilled lamb cutlets with chasseur sauce typify the soundly cooked dishes coming from the kitchen. *Seats 70. Parties 12. Private Room 14. L 12-1.45 (Sun until 2) D 7-9.45 (Fri & Sat to 10.15, Sun to 9.15). Closed L Bank Holidays, all 27-30 Dec. Set L £14.95/£17.95 (Sun £17.50) Set D from £19.35.*

BASINGSTOKE	Forte Posthouse	64%	£72

Tel 01256 468181   Fax 01256 840081   Map 15 D3   **H**
Grove Road Basingstoke Hampshire RG21 3EE

Leave the M3 at Junction 6 and follow signs for Alton on the A339. Accommodation includes 12 Executive rooms. Conference and banqueting facilities for up to 180 delegates. *Rooms 84. Access, Amex, Diners, Visa.*

BASINGSTOKE	Hee's		£40

Tel 01256 464410   Fax 01256 59470   Map 15 D3   **R**
23 Westminster House Basingstoke Hampshire RG21 1CS

Decent MSG-free Szechuan and Peking cooking on the edge of Basingstoke's huge central shopping centre. Special cocktails liven things up, and cheerful staff provide attentive service. *Seats 80. L 12-2 D 6-11. Closed L Sun, 2 days Christmas. Set meals from £14.50. Access, Amex, Diners, Visa.*

BASINGSTOKE	Hilton National	66%	£94

Tel 01256 460460   Fax 01256 840441   Map 15 D3   **H**
Old Common Road Black Dam Basingstoke Hampshire RG21 3PR

Bright, open-plan public areas, neat accommodation and numerous meeting rooms at a modern hotel a mile from Junction 6 of the M3 (follow signs for Eastrop). Children up to 14 stay free in parents' room. Family rooms, indoor playroom. *Rooms 141. Indoor swimming pool, keep-fit equipment, sauna, assault course. Access, Amex, Diners, Visa.*

BASINGSTOKE	The Ringway Hotel	65%	£75

Tel 01256 20212   Fax 01256 842835   Map 15 D3   **H**
Aldermaston Roundabout Ringway North Basingstoke Hampshire RG24 9NU

Bedrooms here range from small singles to roomy, well-appointed suites. 34 rooms are designated non-smoking. Banquets and conferences for 100/150. Ample parking. Leave the M3 at J6, follow signs for Newbury (A339). At the third roundabout take the Popley turn. *Rooms 135. Indoor swimming pool, keep-fit equipment. Closed 1 week Christmas. Access, Amex, Diners, Visa.*

BASLOW	Cavendish Hotel	71%	£118

Tel 01246 582311   Fax 01246 582312   Map 6 C2   **HR**
Baslow Derbyshire DE45 1SP

A solid, local stone-built former inn backing on to the A619. The front, in contrast, commands superb views over acres of green pasture that form part of the Chatsworth Estate. Eric Marsh took over the leasehold in 1975 and has created a splendid hotel radiating comfort and hospitality. Public rooms include a bright, sunny conservatory, flower-filled chintzy lounge and dark, intimate bar where log fires burn in the winter. Bedrooms are very attractive, each with a full complement of homely comforts including good beds, armchairs and writing desks. Two have four-posters. *Rooms 23. Garden, putting, fishing, gift shop (11-11). Access, Amex, Diners, Visa.*

Restaurant   £75

During the day, a bright, sunny dining-room with super views over part of the Chatsworth estate. At night, the soft pastel colours of the decor come into their own with subtle light creating an elegant setting for imaginative and carefully constructed dishes. The choice is varied with a menu of supplementary dishes additional to the fixed-price options. Chef Nick Buckingham has also been here since 1975 and has developed his own imaginative style creating renditions of classics such as double-baked cheese

See over

soufflé and smoked haddock rarebit followed by an intermediate course of warm fish salad, or rose petal sorbet with pink grapefruit and maraschino with, for main course, supreme of pheasant roasted with almonds and wild mushrooms, fillet of salmon wrapped in filo pastry on a bed of black noodles with a tomato and basil sauce or medallions of beef with a burgundy sauce. Desserts are equally imaginative and enjoyable: chocolate tart with coconut sorbet; choux pastry filled with two sauces or the hot dessert of the day. A superb selection of British cheeses can be taken instead. A good, though not the clearest, list has European and New World wines lumped together under red or white. However, plenty of good drinking under £20 in both the house and everyday selections. You can even buy fancy clarets and ports by the case – Ch Petrus 1990 a snip at £3,250 plus VAT & delivery! No smoking. *Seats 50. Parties 20. Private Room 18. L 12.30-2 D 7-10. Set L & D £23.75/£27.75.*

BASLOW   Fischer's Baslow Hall ★★   £95

Tel 01246 583259   Fax 01246 583818   Map 6 C2   **RR**
Calver Road Baslow Derbyshire DE4 1RR

From humbler beginnings in Bakewell, and in the face of considerable adversity (including a major fire six years ago), Max and Susan Fischer have fought their way to the top and were worthy winners of our Restaurant of the Year award last year. Built in 1907 of local stone, their attractive hilltop property stands on the village outskirts and is approached up a steep, snaking, tree-lined drive. Drinks and delicious canapés are taken in a lounge created from the former entrance hall. The room is dominated by a carved stone open fireplace and is furnished in a genteel country-house style. The pretty dining-room, with candlelit tables and fine plaster ceiling is an apt setting for Max's superb culinary talents. His cooking (for fixed-price-only menus) demonstrates flair and endeavour. Flavours are deliberately distinct, ensuring stunning levels of complexity that enthral the palate. Visiting Sheffield market at 5am, he selects the cream of the crop to create his regularly changing menus. The style is modern European as exemplified by starters of buckwheat blinis layered with tuna and smoked salmon topped with caviar and a parcel of duck and its foie gras wrapped in savoy cabbage on Madeira sauce. Fish is a speciality, a fine example being tian of sea bass on a beurre blanc sauce or steamed turbot on risotto nero. Meat dishes too are brilliantly executed, as in Derbyshire lamb wrapped in garden herbs on a tomato-flavoured jus. The selection of cheeses (all in good condition) is from both home and abroad and precedes outstanding desserts such as a gratin of spring rhubarb served with stuffed prunes and crème anglaise. Superb value lunch menus might offer pan-fried lamb's sweetbreads and kidneys on an onion soubise followed by beef medallions with shallots in red wine and marrowbone, with a trio of chocolate mousses to finish. Sunday lunch usually includes a traditional roast. No smoking. Quite fair prices on a mainly French wine list, that includes a few bottles from the New World (Australia and New Zealand only). Simpler, but equally well-executed meals – including breakfast and afternoon tea – are served from 10am to 10pm (not Sun) in the 30-seater Café Max, a former living room off the entrance hall, and at tables on the terrace in summer. *Seats 40. Parties 17. Private Rooms 12/30/40. L 12-2.30 D 7-9.30. Closed L Sat, D Sun (except residents), 25 & 26 Dec. Set L £16.50/£19.50 Set D £36. Access, Amex, Diners, Visa.*

Rooms   £120

There are six bedrooms, all upstairs in the main house. Of these, three are on the small side but all are very tastefully decorated, with clever use of bold, striking colour schemes to complement the mostly antique pine furniture. Bathrooms have a plentiful supply of towels and toiletries though only one has a shower. The latter forms part of a huge enamel bath that stands in the centre of the room. Excellent breakfasts commence with a refreshing exotic fruit salad and continue on to freshly baked warm brioches and croissants. Banqueting rooms for 12, 30 and 40; conference room for 40. No dogs.

Set menu prices may not always include service or wine.

BASSENTHWAITE   Armathwaite Hall   65%   £100

Tel 01768 776551   Fax 01768 776220   Map 4 C3   **H**
Bassenthwaite Lake nr Keswick Cumbria CA12 4RE

The Graves family has been in residence at Armathwaite since 1977, and their commitment to making a welcoming haven means an ongoing programme of refurbishment, ensuring that the building lives up to its splendid setting. Lawns and parkland bordered by woodlands lead down to the foreshore. Best bedrooms in the historic stately house have fine views and plenty of space, while rooms in the coach house/stable block are also spacious. There are extensive leisure facilities, and the equestrian centre offers hacking and lessons. Families are well catered for, with accommodation free for under-12s when sharing parents' room; cots and high-chairs provided; junior gourmet menu; children's club and activities such as a nature trail. An animal park with a variety of farm animals and rare breeds is open between April and October. Two self-catering units are within the grounds. A choice of conference rooms caters for up to 100. *Rooms 43. Garden, croquet, tennis, riding, 9-hole pitch and putt, coarse and game fishing, indoor swimming pool, gym, sauna, steam room, solarium, spa bath, beauty and hair salons, snooker, mountain bikes. Access, Amex, Diners, Visa.*

BASSENTHWAITE LAKE   Pheasant Inn   65%   £68

Tel 01768 776234   Fax 01768 776002   Map 4 C3   **H**
Bassenthwaite Lake nr Cockermouth Cumbria CA13 9YE

Originally a farm, the long and low Pheasant Inn, just off the A66 seven miles west of Keswick, nevertheless looks like an archetypal Victorian roadside inn. It displays abundant period appeal: open fires, beams hung with brasses, old prints and antique firearms. There are three lounges (one non-smoking) and an atmospheric bar with tobacco-brown walls. Well-kept gardens (where afternoon tea and bar snacks can be taken) are an added summer attraction and are overlooked by tastefully furnished bedrooms in varying styles. Adequate, simply fitted bathrooms are the only obvious nod to modernity. One twin is in a bungalow adjacent to the inn. No phones, TVs or dogs in bedrooms; no piped music or fruit machines in the public rooms – just the pervading Lakeland peace and quiet. *Rooms 20. Closed 25 Dec. Access, Visa.*

BATH   Apsley House   67%   £55

Tel 01225 336966   Fax 01225 425462   Map 13 F1   **H**
141 Newbridge Hill Bath Avon BA1 3PT

On the A431 a mile from the city centre on the road to Bristol, the house, built in 1830 reputedly for the Duke of Wellington, is now in the hands of Anne and Christopher Baker. Together they have restored some of the period elegance, creating a hotel of charm and warmth. Fine paintings, antiques and gilt-framed mirrors adorn the public rooms, hallways and splendid staircase. Bedrooms are pretty and homely, furnished with attractive floral fabrics and ornaments. Most bathrooms have separate shower installations with huge shower roses. *Rooms 7. Garden. Access, Visa.*

BATH   Bath Spa Hotel   87%   £176

Tel 01225 444424   Fax 01225 444006   Map 13 F1   **HR**
Sydney Road Bath Avon BA2 6JF

Opened in 1990, the hotel seems to go from strength to strength, under the superb direction of General Manager Robin Sheppard and a more than capable team of dedicated staff. There's a relaxed and friendly atmosphere in elegant country house surroundings in a building of handsome proportions. The original house dates back to the 1830s with a Grecian facade, a Georgian portico, and a classical entrance hall, resplendent with oriental carpets, flower displays, antiques, a fine plasterwork ceiling and mice....! The mice, it must be said, are of the pastry and chocolate variety and something of a hotel trademark. The gracious drawing room affords panoramic views of the landscaped grounds and gardens – seven acres in all – while past

See over

the distinctive murals and greenery of the Colonnade, you'll find the clubby bar. Walk a little further and chance upon the water collection, a display of mineral and spring waters from around the world, including the hotel's own brands of Bath Spa and canned Alfresco. Individually decorated bedrooms, including nine suites, are models of good taste, providing a host of extras, with particularly luxurious bathrooms in mahogany and marble, boasting large tubs, powerful showers, bathrobes that are all-enveloping and exquisite toiletries – the place to wallow in. In addition, there's a splendid health and leisure spa, a purpose-built staffed nursery for children between the ages of 2 and 9 (ask for rates), several functions rooms (max banqueting 150/conferences 140), even well-behaved dogs are welcome, with some bedrooms on the garden level facilitating 'walkies'. 24hr room service,. *Rooms 98. Garden, croquet, indoor swimming pool, gym, sauna, spa bath, solarium, beauty & hair salons, tennis, playroom, outdoor playground, car valeting service. Access, Amex, Diners, Visa.*

Vellore Restaurant  £90

The formal, non-smoking restaurant of the hotel, with a pianist playing at weekends, often with accompaniment. With a varying clientele, it's always difficult to design and balance menus to suit everyone, though chef Jonathan Fraser succeeds by not only changing them monthly, but also by combining traditional British dishes, albeit sometimes spiced up, with those from other parts of the world. Thus, you are likely to find tempura-fried monkfish, served with Asian stir-fry vegetables, mirin and rice wine sauce, alongside blackened Gressingham duckling with cloves, Thai spices and pea and onion confit; or celery soup with glazed Stilton sippets (olde English for croutons), and salmon supreme poached in a fennel and tarragon nage with caviar cream. There are daily-changing fixed-price menus, a separate vegetarian menu and themed menus for two persons (a tasting of different parts of duck perhaps). End with choice British farmhouse cheeses, an *amuse bouche* of puddings (patisserie) or a plate of chocolate desserts. Restaurant manager Simon Roberts orchestrates his team perfectly, while sommelier David Greenhouse will advise, if necessary, on wines from a good list which balances France and Europe with the New World, though prices are on the high side. Gentlemen are respectfully requested (though it's not insisted upon) to wear a jacket and tie. *Seats 120. Parties 12. L (Sun only) 12.30-2 D 7-10. Set Sun L £16.50 Set D £35.*

Alfresco Restaurant £65

In the Colonnade, overlooking the patio rose garden (outdoor seating 30), eating is more informal with seasonal and eclectic dishes, such as an Oriental crab salad with mung bean noodles, coriander and ginger-fried spinach; crispy duck leg, pancakes and dip dip sauce, or rich man's cod and chips. For a dessert try the sticky toffee pudding and vanilla ice cream or tiramisu with mascarpone and Jamaica rum. Splendid home-made bread, good coffees, and easy-to-use wine list with most available by the glass. *Seats 80. Meals 12-9.30. Closed Sun.*

BATH	Clos du Roy	£65

Tel 01225 444450   Fax 01225 460218   Map 13 F1   **R**
1 Seven Dials Sawclose Bath Avon BA1 1EN

Sited on the first floor under the prominent wrought-iron dome of the recent Seven Dials development near the Theatre Royal, Philippe Roy's smart restaurant is a fine setting for his culinary flair. Having originally opened the first Clos du Roy in Bath in 1984, he moved out to nearby Box before returning here in 1992. The interior plays around a musical theme – the white grand piano in the centre of the room is put to good use several nights a week. A picture window to the kitchen allows one to view chefs preparing the two-or three-course menu du jour (lunch, 6-7pm and post-theatre, in addition to a lower-priced carte at these times), which offers particularly good value and a choice of four dishes at each stage. At night, there's also a pair of fixed-price, three-course menus. Typical starters could be lemon-thyme-flavoured cream of chicken soup, mousseline of goose liver paté with Sauternes served with toast or timbale of Cornish white crab meat served with an orange and tomato dressing. Follow with Provence-style rack of lamb with a thyme sauce, supreme of guinea fowl with a honey and peppercorn sauce or steamed fillet of salmon with a tarragon butter sauce. To finish there are farmhouse cheeses or desserts such as profiteroles with butterscotch ice cream with warm chocolate sauce, milk chocolate and cinnamon mousse with a vanilla and apple sauce and a Grand Marnier crepe soufflé with an orange butter sauce. *Seats 85. L 12-2.30 D 6-10.30. Closed 25 Dec. Set L £8.95/£11.95 (Sun £9.50) Set D £18.50. Access, Amex, Diners, Visa.*

BATH	Fountain House	£120

Tel 01225 338622   Fax 01225 445855   Map 13 F1   **PH**
9/11 Fountain Buildings Lansdown Road Bath Avon BA1 5DV

An 'all-suite hotel', Fountain House comprises one-, two- and three-bedroom suites with sitting room and smart, fully-equipped kitchen, within a Palladian mansion on the northern edge of the city centre. The idea is that one gets privacy and space with the level of service (except room service) one would expect of a conventional hotel – full maid service with fresh linen and kitchen servicing daily. Unfussy decor and good-quality furnishings are immaculately maintained. Continental breakfast only is provided in the form of a basket of fresh bread, milk, yoghurt etc and a daily newspaper which are left outside the door at 7am. Reception staff can organise most things from car hire and theatre tickets to a personal in-room fax or shooting on the owners' own 750-acre estate. Unlike in a serviced apartment there is no minimum stay and indeed many guests stay for just one night. There are no public rooms. Lock-up garages, laundry and drying room, iron and ironing board, cots and valet service all provided. *Suites 14. Access, Amex, Diners, Visa.*

BATH	Francis Hotel	67%	£112

Tel 01225 424257   Fax 01225 319715   Map 13 F1   **H**
Queen Square Bath Avon BA1 2HH

Forte hotel set in what were Georgian town houses overlooking the gardens of Queen Square in the centre of the city. Public areas have a traditional feel – sofas and chesterfields in the clubby bar, old oil portraits and lacy cloths on the coffee tables in the residents' lounge. Bedrooms in the original building generally have freestanding furniture and an attractive colour scheme of red and green. Rooms in a newer wing are more functional (but spacious) with older-style, shelf-type furniture and somewhat dated bathrooms. Parking for 55 cars. *Rooms 93. Access, Amex, Diners, Visa.*

BATH	Garlands	£60

Tel 01225 442283   Map 13 F1   **R**
7 Edgar Buildings George Street Bath Avon BA1 2EE

Friendly, relaxed little restaurant that appeals to both locals and visitors to Bath. Tom Bridgeman's careful cooking tales its inspiration from all over with dishes like a Cornish crab pancake with a lime, coriander and garlic relish; grilled goat's cheese with roast Mediterranean vegetables and couscous; supreme of chicken with tarragon and sliced mushrooms; cutlet of salmon with Thai-style crust, and pheasant with lightly-curried parsnip purée and a shallot sauce. Lunchtimes there are two short, two-course set menus – both excellent value; in summer there is also an individually priced list of lighter dishes served in the bar area or outside in a small garden. *Seats 28. Parties 12. L 12-2.15 D 7-10.30. Closed Mon, 25-28 Dec. Set L £7.50 & £10.50 (£13.95) Set D £17/£20. Access, Amex, Diners, Visa.*

BATH	Hilton National	67%	£126

Tel 01225 463411   Fax 01225 464393   Map 13 F1   **H**
Walcot Street Bath Avon BA1 5BJ

Spacious and smart public rooms are a feature of this centrally located hotel which also benefits from a business centre and leisure club. Of the bedrooms, the Plaza rooms are the best and 50% of the rooms are reserved for non-smokers. Banqueting/conference facilities for 200/250. There's free parking for 20 cars on the forecourt. *Rooms 150. Indoor swimming pool, keep-fit facilities, sauna, steam room, sun beds, coffee shop (9am-11pm). Access, Amex, Diners, Visa.*

Lodges are now listed by county in the reference section

BATH   The Hole in the Wall   † £70

Tel & Fax 01225 425242   Map 13 F1   **R**
16 George Street Bath Avon BA1 2EH

Chris and Gunna Chown are bringing back the good times to the Hole in the Wall, which saw its greatest glory under George Perry-Smith in the 50s and 60s. Much of the scene is as then, including bits of original pottery. The main room features white walls, banquettes, rush floor covering and polished unclad tables, all combining to create a feel that is at once cheerful and fairly sober. A second room in contemporary style was created by moving back the kitchen. The entrance to the restaurant is from the level of the upper pavement, and not from the original 'hole in the wall' at roadside. The chef is Adrian Walton, whose main menu (one price for everything in each course – the printed prices include service) is an amalgam of his ideas, Chris Chown's and George Perry-Smith's. The menu incorporates ingredients from far and wide: grilled brochette of turbot with lemon grass and tomato salad, salmon and mushroom cutlets with tartare sauce and warm spiced pork rillettes with apple and sage chutney among the starters; roasted red bream with fennel purée, pan-fried calf's kidneys with Madeira and bubble'n'squeak, and rack of lamb with butter bean purée and rosemary sauce among the mains. Mulled figs and kumquats with white chocolate ice cream is just one of many hard-to-resist puddings. At lunchtime there's also a fixed-price lunch of one, two or three courses. There are plenty of wines by the glass on an excellent and sensible list that features most wine-growing regions, though neither New Zealand nor South Africa gets a look-in. Good choice under £20. *Seats 75. Parties 18. L 12-2 D 6-11. Closed Sun, Christmas, 2 weeks Jan. Set L £7/£9.50/£11.50. Set D £19.50. Access, Amex, Visa.*

BATH   Lansdown Grove   65%   £85

Tel 01225 315891   Fax 01225 448092   Map 13 F1   **H**
Lansdown Grove Bath Avon BA1 5EH

Set in delightful gardens high up above the city, the privately owned Lansdown Grove has benefited from continuity of care and attention. Individually decorated bedrooms reflect the good taste of the proprietor's wife with fresh, bright colour schemes and a variety of well-chosen fabrics. Furniture varies from limed oak to more traditional freestanding pieces. Public areas are equally well kept and include a comfortable residents' lounge of grand proportions. Children up to 14 can stay free in parents' room, charged for meals as taken. Ample parking, plus a lock-up garage for 6 cars. *Rooms 44. Garden. Access, Amex, Diners, Visa.*

BATH   The New Moon   £50

Tel 01225 444407   Fax 01225 318613   Map 13 F1   **R**
Seven Dials Sawclose Bath Avon BA1 1ES

Bright premises in a Georgian-style development next to the Theatre Royal. The simple brasserie menu (available until 7) spans a good range of dishes in the modern mode, from mixed leaf salad and goat's cheese beignets and salmon and chive fishcakes with ginger and lime butter to burgers, omelettes and wild boar, mustard and chili sausages with creamed potatoes and apple compote. Chilled bitter chocolate pavé with lime glaze could be one of half a dozen or so desserts. Similar evening choice. Note that the New Moon is no longer open for breakfast, and the bring-your-own-wine facility has been discontinued. *Seats 70. Meals noon-11pm. Closed 25 & 26 Dec, 1 Jan. Set D £10/£12.50. Set L £6.25 Set D £10/£12.50/£18.50. Access, Amex, Visa.*

BATH   Priory Hotel   £155

Tel 01225 331922   Fax 01225 448276   Map 13 F1   **HR**
Weston Road Bath Avon BA1 2XT

Just a mile from the city centre, yet this Gothic-style house, built of honey-coloured Bath stone in 1835, feels more like a country mansion, especially when viewed from the large, beautifully kept garden to the rear. In the early summer of 1995 new owners had just begun work on bedroom refurbishment, there having been a lack of such attention in recent years, and what we saw bodes well for the future. Good antique furniture will

remain, to be complemented by stylish fabrics and new bathrooms with marble very much in evidence. Some of the smaller rooms will disappear completely. Things like fresh flowers, magazines and mineral water provide the homely touches and the servicing of rooms in the evening – drawing curtains, turning-down beds, putting on bedside lights, placing fresh towels in the bathroom – add the cosseting element. After the bedrooms, attention will turn to the day rooms. In the circumstances we leave the hotel ungraded this year. Children are welcome with under-10s staying free in parents' room and some interconnecting rooms that can become family suites. *Rooms 21. Garden, croquet, outdoor swimming pool. Access, Amex, Diners, Visa.*

Restaurant   £85

Dinner is a fixed-price affair (priced for three or four courses) that is fully inclusive of coffee, petits fours, and service. Fairly short, just seven main dish choices, chef Michael Collom's carefully thought-out menu nevertheless manages to offer plenty of variety with dishes such as chargrilled chicken breast served with a grapefruit and orange salad, oven-baked John Dory with a wholegrain mustard and tarragon sauce, roast best end of Welsh lamb, entrecote Café de Paris, braised quail with wild mushrooms and foie gras, and home-made egg pasta with sun-dried tomatoes, shiitake mushrooms and parmesan all appearing recently. Lunch brings an à la carte menu of similar dishes. The wine list, with few bargains, is pretty standard. No smoking. *Seats 60. Parties 12. Private Room 35. L 12.15-1.45 D 7.15-9.15. Set Sun L £20.50. Set D £32/£38.*

BATH	**Queensberry Hotel**	**75%**	**£133**

Tel 01225 447928   Fax 01225 446065   Map 13 F1   **HR**
Russel Street Bath Avon BA1 2QF

In a quiet street just to the north of the town centre, this small hotel is part of an attractive terrace built by John Wood in 1772. Individually decorated rooms boast antique furniture, deep comfortable seating and homely touches like books, magazines, fruit and, in the spacious carpeted bathrooms, large towelling robes and quality toiletries. Day rooms include an elegant, intimate period drawing room and cosy bar overlooking secluded courtyard gardens. Full of charm and immaculately kept throughout. No dogs. *Rooms 22. Garden. Closed 1 week Christmas. Access, Amex, Visa.*

Olive Tree Restaurant   £55

Oriental rugs over white ceramic tiles, rag-rolled walls, modernistic (though comfortable) chairs and the crispest of white linen all add up to a cool sophistication which finds its match in Stephen Ross's contemporary and always exciting menu. Griddled scallops with an avocado, tomato and tarragon sauce, spiced couscous broth of chicken breast with red onions and peppers, beef rump braised with prunes and armagnac, and Gressingham duck breast with Oriental spices and plums poached in ginger show his style. There's always a vegetarian main course. Fish dishes depend on market availability but Tuesday is an extra-special day in that there's a delivery of fish from the West Country. The choice then could include double-baked crab soufflé, sauté of squid with chili, lime and coriander and grilled John Dory with sweet peppers and black olives. Desserts are as tempting as the rest: rich rice pudding with black cherry purée, pink grapefruit and mint sorbet, hot apple feuilleté with cinnamon ice cream. Of some four dozen well-chosen wines about half are priced under £15. No smoking. *Seats 50. Private Room 16. L 12-2 D 7-10.30 (Sun till 9). Closed L Sun. Set L £12 Set D £18.*

BATH   Royal Crescent Hotel   84%   £188

Tel 01225 319090   Fax 01225 339401   Map 13 F1   **HR**
16 Royal Crescent Bath Avon BA1 2LS

John Wood's magnificent crescent comprises a row of houses in a sweeping 500ft curve, and the two central houses form this fine hotel. Day rooms, both here and in the Dower House to the rear of the enclosed garden, retain their 18th-century elegance along with some fine original oil paintings and a scattering of antiques. The best suites are very grand, with some fine architectural features, but even standard rooms have elaborate bedhead drapes or a half-tester along with antique furniture and extras like mineral water, fruit and a flowery plant. Bathrooms are suitably luxurious with towelling robes and quality toiletries. The Beau Nash suite has its own spa pool room. Standards of service match the surroundings, albeit a little faded around the edges, with full evening maid service and valet parking (space for 30 cars). Other exclusive offerings include hot air ballooning and the four of the best front row circle seats for Saturday night at the Theatre Royal. Queens Moat Houses is the operating group. *Rooms 46. Garden, croquet, outdoor plunge pool. Access, Amex, Diners, Visa.*

Dower House Restaurant   £95

Steven Blake is an accomplished chef and the elegant surroundings complement perfectly his cooking, as does the very polished service by knowledgeable staff. The menu offers starters such as lightly browned scallops with crisp ratatouille, terrine of duck confit, foie gras and shallots, or fine slices of marinated salmon with beetroot and eau de vie cream. Main courses follow in the similar well-thought out, imaginative style with a tranche of salmon, creamed potato, mussels and parsley vinaigrette; lamb cutlets with tarragon mousse and paillasson potatoes; beef fillet with parsley purée, girolle mushrooms and French quail with braised red cabbage, lardons, wild mushrooms and baby onions. Wonderful desserts such as iced orange and cinnamon parfait, dark chocolate mousse with raspberry coulis and sorbet or warm chocolate tart with white chocolate mousse are a suitable climax to an immensely enjoyable experience. Somewhat confusingly the wine list is presented by style (New World grapey white for instance), therefore wines from countries of origin are listed in several sections. A lot under £20, though some of the better wines are quite steeply marked up. Valet parking even for non-residents. *Seats 60. Parties 8. Private Room 45. L 12.30-2 D 7-9.30 (Sat till 10). Set L £14.50/£18.50 Set D £25.*

BATTLE   Netherfield Place   78%   £105

Tel 01424 774455   Fax 01424 774024   Map 11 C6   **HR**
Battle East Sussex TN33 9PP

Surrounded by 30 acres of gardens and parkland, this neo-Georgian, 1920s-built mansion offers peace and comfort in a relaxing atmosphere. Day rooms include an elegant lounge with antique walnut coffee tables and attractive soft furnishings in shades of pink and green, a cosy bar and small sun lounge giving on to a wisteria-draped patio. Bedrooms have considerable charm with reproduction antique furniture, well-chosen (often floral) fabrics and all sorts of extras from fresh fruit and flowers to mineral water, books and a jar of sweets. Good bathrooms, many with marble tiling, come with bathrobes, generous towelling and quality toiletries. The Pomeroy Room has a four-poster bed and, along with the Mandeville Suite, attracts a supplement. Beds are turned down in the evening and room service is available throughout the day and evening. Banqueting/conference facilities for 75/40. *Rooms 14. Garden, croquet, putting, tennis. Closed 2 weeks Christmas/New Year. Access, Amex, Diners, Visa.*

Restaurant   £70

👑 🦢 🍓 V

Well stocked with soft fruits, vegetables and herbs, a one-acre walled kitchen garden makes a considerable contribution to the kitchens here. Spinach and goat's cheese ravioli on fennel butter sauce, scallop and mussel tartlet, breast of mallard duck with braised lentils and bacon and pithiviers of chicken liver on a sage and shallot sauce, Sussex lamb cutlets with Stilton mousse and a fricassee of flageolet beans demonstrate the style of well-balanced, fixed-price (lunch includes a half bottle of house wine) and evening à la carte menus. There's also a notably good vegetarian menu. Good finales might include plum tart with mascarpone cheese, rhubarb compote in a tulip basket with ginger ice cream, and crusty brie parcels with a walnut dressing. Sunday lunch begins with hors d'oeuvre from the buffet table before traditional roasts and perhaps a steak and kidney pudding. Lots of space between tables in this redwood-panelled dining-room. *Seats 80. Parties 14. Private Room 16/40. L 12.30-2 D 7-9.30 (Sun to 9). Set L £15.95 (inc. wine, Sun £15.50) Set D £23.95.*

BAWTRY	The Crown	64%	£67

Tel 01302 710341   Fax 01302 711798   Map 7 D2   **H**
High Street Bawtry South Yorkshire DN10 6JW

A sturdy old coaching inn, over 300 years old, encompassing conference/function rooms for up to 150. Most bedrooms are in a modern wing: 17 non-smoking, two four-poster rooms, another equipped for disabled guests and three sets interconnecting. Forte. *Rooms 57. Garden. Access, Amex, Diners, Visa.*

BEACONSFIELD	Bellhouse Hotel	67%	£120

Tel 01753 887211   Fax 01753 888231   Map 15 E2   **H**
Oxford Road Beaconsfield Buckinghamshire HP9 2XE

De Vere hotel on the A40, close to junction 2 of the M40, with an impressive Spanish-style frontage. Half the bedrooms are reserved for non-smokers. Six separate conference suites accommodate up to 450 delegates. Popular leisure club includes beauty therapy. Children up to 14 stay free in parents' room. *Rooms 136. Terrace, indoor swimming pool, children's splash pool, gym, squash, sauna, steam room, spa bath, sun beds, beauty salon, snooker. Access, Amex, Diners, Visa.*

BEANACRE	Beechfield House	70%	£80

Tel 01225 703700   Fax 01225 790118   Map 14 B2   **H**
Beanacre nr Melksham Wiltshire SN12 7PU

Built in 1878 of Bath stone, the ornate house is reached by a driveway off the A350 between Melksham and the National Trust village of Lacock. It is surrounded by eight acres of gardens containing many specimen trees, after which individual bedrooms are named. A white marble fireplace in the reception area houses a real log fire to welcome guests in winter. The two main day rooms are appropriately furnished with reproduction period-style easy chairs plus an incongruously modern, low-backed settee. Bedrooms vary in size but all have pretty, matching fabrics and most an antique or two plus fruit, flowers and mineral water. Good carpeted bathrooms. *Rooms 24. Garden, tennis, outdoor swimming pool. Access, Amex, Diners, Visa.*

BEARSTED	Tudor Park	67%	£94

Tel 01622 734334   Fax 01622 735360   Map 11 C5   **H**
Ashford Road Bearsted nr Maidstone Kent ME14 4NQ

The 18-hole golf course with its covered practice ground, shop and tuition is a major attraction at this modern hotel near Junction 8 of the M20 and just two miles from Leeds Castle. There are many other leisure facilities, plus conference facilities for up to 275 delegates. The public rooms are interestingly laid out and include an intimate piano bar, a garden restaurant overlooking the golf course and a plum-coloured cocktail bar. Bedrooms are of a good size and feature large, comfortable beds. Country Club Hotels. *Rooms 117. Indoor swimming pool, spa bath, sauna, steam room, solarium, gym, aerobics studio, snooker, tennis, car hire, coffee shop (10am-10pm), beautician, children's playroom, golf (18). Access, Amex, Diners, Visa.*

BEAULIEU   Montagu Arms   67%   £99

Tel 01590 612324   Fax 01590 612188   Map 14 C4   **H**
Beaulieu New Forest Hampshire SO42 7ZL

At the head of the Beaulieu river, in the heart of the famous village, this is a fine base for touring the New Forest, visiting the National Motor Museum or viewing Lord Montagu's Beaulieu Palace. It's a welcoming, old creeper-clad inn, cosy in winter with real fires and cool in good weather with a small conservatory overlooking a paved terraced area; the latter is a fine spot for afternoon tea in summer, overlooking a circular lawn and immaculately kept, compact terraced gardens. Public rooms include an intimate, bookcase-lined bar, comfortable sitting room and a rather dark dining-room, only the front part of which benefits from the lovely garden views at breakfast. Bedrooms range from a single overlooking the gardens to three antique-furnished suites, one with two bathrooms, another with a corner aspect and a four-poster bed heavily draped with floral fabric. Guests have the use of the health and beauty centre and indoor swimming pool at sister hotel Careys Manor, 6 miles away in Brockenhurst. Bucklers Hard and Exbury Gardens (with 200 acres and a fine display of azaleas and rhododendrons) are also nearby. *Rooms 24. Garden. Access, Amex, Diners, Visa.*

BECCLES   Waveney House   59%   £58

Tel 01502 712270   Fax 01502 712660   Map 10 D2   **H**
Puddingmoor Beccles Suffolk NR34 9PL

Situated in the heart of the Norfolk Broads, Waveney was built as a private house around 1592, extended from 1750 onwards, and is now a Grade I listed building. It's right on the River Waveney and there's a certain amount of nautical chat in the bar and residents' lounge. Even bedrooms have a shipboard feel with creaking floorboards, uneven walls and beams beneath which to duck. One room has a four-poster bed. *Rooms 13. Garden, fishing, mooring. Access, Amex, Diners, Visa.*

BECKINGHAM   Black Swan   £55

Tel 01636 626474   Map 7 E3   **R**
Hillside Beckingham Lincolnshire LN5 0RF

A converted village pub with a country atmosphere and a charming riverside garden where light summer lunches are served. The à la carte menu provides an interesting selection of dishes, classically based but often with original touches: twice-baked cheese soufflé with mushroom sauce, garlic sautéed Black Tiger prawns with mixed leaf and omelette salad and chili and red pepper dressing, wild duck breast topped with herb mousse and served with apple chutney and parsnips on a caraway seed sauce, roast pheasant pie in a brown beer sauce served with sage and onion stuffing and bread sauce. Good puds, with soufflés like almond with amaretto sauce, and honey and date, something of a speciality. Children under 11 eat Sunday lunch free (one child per adult). Parking for 10 cars. No smoking. *Seats 35. Private Room 28. L 12-2 (bookings only) D 7-10. Closed D Sun, all Mon, 1 week Jan & 2 weeks Aug. Set L (Sun only) £12.50. Access, Visa.*

BECKINGTON   Woolpack Inn   £65

Tel 01373 831244   Fax 01373 831223   Map 14 B3   **IR**
Beckington nr Bath Somerset BA3 6SP

A splendidly restored former coaching inn dating back to the 16th century with an easy-going atmosphere and an interestingly versatile attitude towards dining. Bedrooms are individually designed and incorporate many original features that are supplemented by custom-built freestanding furniture. The bathrooms are particularly well appointed, with plenty of bright light, generous supplies of towels and toiletries and very powerful over-bath showers. In addition to an 'Executive' room with a four-poster there are two larger, new rooms with direct access to the residents' garden; these three rooms attract a higher tariff of £84.50. New first-floor residents' lounge and a boardroom conference facility seating up to 20. *Rooms 12. Garden. Access, Visa.*

Restaurant   £65

Diners are encouraged to consume simply what they'd like just how and where they'd like, and there is plenty of choice wherever one chooses to eat, be it in the bar, in the recently-extended Garden Room (where smoking is not encouraged) that leads on to a split-level, walled terrace, or in the smaller no-smoking Oak Room dining-room;

booking is advised throughout. Chef David Woolfall offers one menu, with a dozen dishes such as warm salad of king prawns and mushrooms with a lemon dressing or ceviche of scallops with avocado dual-priced as starters or more substantial dishes; main courses that include honey-glazed Wiltshire gammon with fried egg and chips, Bath sausages with onion gravy and coriander mash, and Oriental duck breast with stir-fried vegetables show that both quality bar food and restaurant-style dishes are cleverly integrated. Round off with hot apple, sultana and calvados pancakes with orange sauce or a plate of interesting cheeses. Informal service. *Seats 40 (Garden Room) & 20 (Oak Room). Private Room 20. L 12-2 D 7-10 (Sun to 9).*

BEDFORD	The County Hotel	65%	£77

Tel 01234 799955   Fax 01234 340447   Map 15 E1   **H**
2 St Mary's Street Bedford Bedfordshire MK42 0AR

Modern tower block (formerly the Moat House and still owned by Queens Moat Houses) in a prime position in the town centre, overlooking the river Great Ouse and town bridge. Banqueting and conference facilities for 400/450. Weekend tariff reductions. *Rooms 100. Keep-fit equipment, sauna, snooker. Access, Amex, Visa.*

BEDFORD	Woodlands Manor	72%	£85

Tel 01234 363281   Fax 01234 272390   Map 15 E1   **H**
Green Lane Clapham Bedford Bedfordshire MK41 6EP

Two miles north of Bedford and set in its own grounds off the A6, Woodlands Manor is a large Victorian manor house. The porticoed entrance leads into a spacious and elegant hall with a carved stone fireplace, a wide, polished-oak staircase and groups of settees and armchairs which create the feel of a lounge. A further lounge, with a small bar in one corner, offers additional comfortable seating. Bedrooms include eight Executive rooms in a sympathetically added wing. These are larger than the remainder but all rooms are decorated and furnished to a good standard. Some bathrooms have white marble tiling, others are carpeted. Extras include satellite TV, hairdryers and trouser presses, with mini-bars in the better rooms. Three bedrooms are in a separate cottage in the grounds. *Rooms 25. Closed 3 days Christmas. Access, Amex, Diners, Visa.*

BELFORD	Blue Bell Hotel	63%	£88

Tel 01668 213543   Fax 01668 213787   Map 5 D1   **H**
Market Square Belford Northumberland NE70 7NE

Creeper-clad, the Bell stands at the head of the village on a cobbled forecourt. In front are the old Market Place and stone cross, recently restored by English Heritage; the Norman parish church stands on a hill behind. The hotel's stone-flagged foyer leads to a stylish cocktail bar boasting a collection of miniature hand bells, and a restful residents' lounge. Bedrooms are classified by type and tariff from those in the annexe (with shower/WC only) to superior and deluxe rooms with full bathrooms and lovely views of the Blue Bell's 2-acre "garden of 10,000 blooms". Children are made truly welcome as two of the hotel's "Australian Directors" are, in fact, Mrs Shirley's own grandchildren. *Rooms 17. Garden. Access, Amex, Visa.*

BELTON	Belton Woods Hotel	72%	£115

Tel 01476 593200   Fax 01476 74547   Map 7 E3   **H**
Belton nr Grantham Lincolnshire NG32 2LN

Just off the A607, north of Grantham, a modern complex standing in 475 acres of grounds, with outstanding sports facilities that are matched by equally impressive accommodation. Ambassador rooms (£140) are particularly spacious, and some of them, like the suites, have patios or balconies affording views over the golf course. A spacious, high-ceilinged lounge leading off the main foyer is filled with parlour plants and hanging baskets, and also overlooks one of three golf courses (two 18-hole and one 9-hole). The cocktail bar on the first floor is more club-like, with easy chairs and rich decor; there's a conservatory and a 'spike bar' for golfers; and the Plus Fours restaurant. Excellent facilities for children. 24hr room service. No dogs. De Vere. *Rooms 136. Garden, croquet, tennis, golf (2 18-hole, 1 9-hole), golf driving range, putting green, indoor swimming pool, children's splash pool, gym, squash, sauna, steam room, spa bath, solarium, beauty & hair salon, young children's playroom, children's playground, snooker, coffee shop (7am-10pm). Access, Amex, Diners, Visa.*

BERKSWELL   Nailcote Hall   67%   £115

Tel 01203 466174   Fax 01203 470720   Map 6 C4   **H**
Nailcote Lane Berkswell Warwickshire CV7 7DE

A black and white timbered Jacobean building is at the heart of a hotel that enjoys a rural location (on the B4101) yet is just a few minutes from the Midlands motorway network and the NEC. Beyond a rug-strewn, oak-floored lobby the main day room in the original building is a small flagstone-floored cocktail bar; a further bar is attached to an informal atrium restaurant in a stylish barn conversion that also houses the leisure centre and half the bedrooms. Of good size and comfortably appointed, bedrooms in the main building have reproduction furniture. Four period rooms have real antiques. Well-appointed bathrooms come with generously sized bath robes. *Rooms 38. Garden, croquet, golf (9), tennis, indoor swimming pool, children's splash pool, gym, solarium, spa bath, steam room, snooker.*

BERWICK-UPON-TWEED   Funnywayt'mekalivin   £50

Tel 01289 308827   Map 3 D6   **RR**
41 Bridge Street Berwick-upon-Tweed Northumberland TD15 1ES

Elizabeth Middlemiss's unusually named restaurant has built up a loyal following with menus continuing to offer honest, robust, freshly made dishes in well-thought-out combinations. Lunch offers a short carte of similarly attractive cooking. Interesting, concise wine list. *Seats 32. Private Room 8. L 11.30-2.30 D at 7.30. Closed D Sun & Tue, all Mon, 25 & 26 Dec, 1 Jan. Set D £22.50. Access, Visa.*

Rooms   £40

There are now 3 bedrooms available for cosy, overnight accommodation.

BERWICK-UPON-TWEED   Kings Arms   59%   £70

Tel 01289 307454   Fax 01289 308867   Map 3 D6   **H**
Hide Hill Berwick-upon-Tweed Northumberland TD15 1EJ

Dating from the 18th century, this town-centre hotel offers agreeable overnight accommodation that includes three rooms with four-posters. Solid oakwood furnishings give a reassuringly traditional feel, and there's plenty of room to relax in the chandelier-hung lounge and the cocktail bar. The Royal Suite is a popular venue for banquets and conferences (max. 200). *Rooms 36. Garden, coffee shop (9-5.30). Access, Amex, Diners, Visa.*

BEVERLEY   Beverley Arms   62%   £88

Tel 01482 869241   Fax 01482 870907   Map 7 E1   **H**
North Bar Within Beverley Humberside HU17 8DD

300-year-old coaching inn that retains a certain period interest. Bedrooms are mostly in a modern block. 20 are designated non-smoking. Children up to 14 stay free in parents' room. Ample free parking. Forte. *Rooms 57. Access, Amex, Diners, Visa.*

BEXLEY   Forte Posthouse   56%   £75

Tel 01322 526900   Fax 01322 526113   Map 11 B5   **H**
Black Prince Interchange Southwould Road Bexley Kent DA5 1ND

Beside the A2 this much extended former public house provides simple, no-frills accommodation in a purpose-built bedroom block. Self-contained business centre with support services. *Rooms 102. Garden, children's play room. Access, Amex, Diners, Visa.*

BEXLEYHEATH   Swallow Hotel   71%   £98

Tel 0181-298 1000   Fax 0181-298 1234   Map 11 B5   **H**
1 Broadway Bexleyheath Kent DA6 7JZ

This comparatively recent addition to the Swallow chain, purpose-built and conveniently situated just off the A2, sports up-to-the-minute decor and state-of-the-art technology, providing all possible comforts and facilities. 52 of the well-proportioned bedrooms are reserved for non-smokers, two are especially adapted for disabled guests. Conferences and banquets for up to 250. Parking for 80 cars. Children up to 15 stay free in parents' room. *Rooms 142. Indoor swimming pool, gym, spa bath, steam room, sun beds. Access, Amex, Diners, Visa.*

BIBURY The Swan 78% £128

Tel 01285 740695   Fax 01285 740473   Map 14 C2   **HR**
Bibury Gloucestershire GL7 5NW

Elizabeth and Alex Furtek run a really splendid hotel on the banks of the River Coln. The setting, in neatly kept gardens, is a real delight, and the first impressions continue throughout, from the foyer, where a grand piano plays in the evenings, through to the comfortably furnished parlour (for non-smokers) and the charming writing room, which was once the village post office. Explore further through and one finds a splendid long bar with pale oak panelling, leather tub chairs on flagstone floor, log fire and one wall covered with a mural depicting various folk involved in the hotel's transformation. Press on and the mood changes yet again in a stylish all-day brasserie (an unexpected find in a sleepy Cotswold village) complete with Italian wrought-iron furniture: a useful alternative to the hotel's rather grand dining-room and the place where late-risers will find breakfast. There are all sorts of fine decorative fabrics throughout the hotel including a collection of Charles Rennie Mackintosh chairs. Upstairs even the standard bedrooms have great appeal with antique furniture and individual decor; the best might have a four-poster bed, crystal chandelier, spa bath or luxuriously large, old-fashioned freestanding tub. Fine toiletries and bathrobes are standard. Quality of service from friendly, well-motivated staff is high, with nice touches like the linen mat placed by the bed when rooms are serviced in the evenings. No dogs. *Rooms 18. Garden, croquet, fishing, brasserie (10am-10pm). Closed 5 days Christmas. Access, Amex, Visa.*

Restaurant £100

Guy Bossom's menus are enticing and, alongside the à la carte, the set-price dinner offers four courses after a Bibury trout appetiser: perhaps a salad of duck leg confit with white grapes, fricassee of fish and shellfish with saffron cream as a starter. For the main course there's a choice which could include fillet of sea bass with thyme, potato purée and courgette ribbons with a red pepper oil, wood pigeon on a potato galette with celeriac and parsley or Barbary duck with oyster mushrooms and cep cream. A classical French créme brulée, warm apple tart with vanilla ice cream and caramel sauce are examples of the excellent desserts – or there's a good cheese selection. A constantly evolving wine list has a huge array of sweet whites, plenty of half bottles with the best value to be found in the New World section. No smoking. *Seats 65. Parties 10. Private Room 12. L 12.30-2.30 D 7.30-9.30 Set Sun L £15.95 Set D £35.*

BIGBURY-ON-SEA Burgh Island Hotel 66% £208*

Tel 01548 810514   Fax 01548 810243   Map 13 D3   **H**
Burgh Island Bigbury-on-Sea Devon TQ7 4AU

Unique is an overworked word, but it certainly applies to Beatrice and Tony Porter's 22-acre island and art deco hotel. They acquired the hotel in 1985 and set about restoring it to its 1929 glory. That glory includes the Palm Court with its Peacock Dome and cocktail bar, a glass sun lounge, jet-black glass and pink mirrors on the staircase, and a magnificent ballroom. Original art deco furniture graces day rooms and the bedrooms, all of which are suites. The island boasts its own pub – the 14th-century Pilchard Inn – and in the summer boat trips can be arranged. There are also banqueting and conference facilities (100/150). Guests park their cars in a lock-up garage on the mainland and are transported to the island either by Land Rover or on a giant sea tractor. *Half-board only. No dogs. *Rooms 14. Garden, croquet, tennis, sauna, solarium, mini-gym, games room, snooker, sea fishing. Closed mid-week during Jan & Feb. Access, Amex, Diners, Visa.*

Set menu prices may not always include service or wine.

BILBROUGH | Bilbrough Manor | 75% | £105

Tel 01937 834002   Fax 01937 834724   Map 7 D1   **H**
Bilbrough nr York North Yorkshire YO2 3PH

An attractive manor house among fine Georgian gardens in a quiet village off the A64,
six miles from York. Though the present house 'only' dates from 1901, there's been
an abode here for some 700 years, and it's probably best known as the family home of
Thomas Fairfax, Cromwell's right-hand man. The Manor was restored by Colin and Sue
Bell and opened as a country house hotel in 1987. Day rooms include a foyer-bar and
a splendid lounge with lightwood panelling and comfortable sofas. Prettily decorated
bedrooms are light and airy with carefully matched colour schemes and soft furnishings,
but rather plain modern furniture. Compact, carpeted bathrooms. No children under 10
(or dogs). *Rooms 15. Garden, keep-fit equipment, sauna. Closed 24-30 Dec. Access, Amex,
Diners, Visa.*

BILLESLEY | Billesley Manor | 75% | £168

Tel 01789 400888   Fax 01789 764145   Map 14 C1   **HR**
Billesley Alcester nr Stratford-upon-Avon Warwickshire B49 6NF

Signposted from the A46 about halfway
between Stratford and Alcester, this
Queens Moat Houses-owned, 16th-
century manor sits in 11 acres of
grounds that include a splendid topiary
garden. Oak panelling is the unifying
theme of public areas that include
a lounge and galleried cocktail bar plus
a good indoor swimming pool that in
summer opens on to a sheltered patio.
Bedrooms in the original building are
the more characterful but most are in
two newer wings of which the Topiary

Wing is marginally to be preferred as having fresher, more stylish decor. Rooms are
properly serviced in the evenings. Conference and banqueting facilities for up to 100.
No dogs. *Rooms 41. Garden, croquet, tennis, pitch & putt, indoor swimming pool.
Access, Amex, Diners, Visa.*

Stuart Restaurant   £85

Lots more oak here in the panelling and square, unclothed tables that are surrounded by
comfortable armed, button-back leather chairs – encouraging one to linger over chef
Mark Naylor's reliably good cooking. Dishes reflect modern trends and come in generous
portions. Splendid desserts. A good all-round wine list offers some familiar names, with
sensible tasting notes. Outdoor eating for 16 on a terrace. *Seats 80. Parties 8.
Private Room 16. L 12.30-2 D 7.30-9.30. Set L £18 Set D £27.50.*

BILLINGSHURST | The Gables | £55

Tel 01403 782571   Map 11 A6   **R**
Pulborough Road Parbrook Billingshurst West Sussex RH14 9EU

Chef-patron Nicholas Illes is very much following the family tradition at this black and
white timbered 15th-century restaurant just south of town on the A29; Dad runs
Cisswood House at Lower Beeding (qv) and brother Carl the *Willows Restaurant* at
Ashington (qv). They take it in turns to make early morning trips to the London markets
to pick the best of ingredients for their respective kitchens. The same, seasonally-
changing menu is served at both lunch and dinner (though differently priced) with
a good choice of dishes both simple – pan-fried squid in garlic butter, fillet steak with
tomatoes and mushrooms, grilled Dover sole – and more adventurous – chicken breast
stuffed with fresh mango and glazed with a tarragon cream sauce, fillet of sea bass with
a herb and brioche crust on a julienne of vegetables with a lime sauce. Partner Rebecca
Gilroy runs front of house with charm and efficiency. Terrific prices (including vintage
clarets) on the wine list here: six *marque* champagnes under £30, including Pommery at
£22.50. No children on Friday or Saturday nights. *Seats 50. L 12.15-1.45 D 7.15-9 (Fri
& Sat to 10). Closed L Sat, D Sun, all Mon, 1 week Jan/Feb. Set L £13.50/£15.95 Set D
£18.95. Access, Amex, Visa.*

| BINGLEY | **Bankfield Hotel** | 61% | £96 |

Tel 01274 567123   Fax 01274 551331   Map 6 C1   **H**
Bradford Road Bingley West Yorkshire BD16 1TU

On the A650 Bradford/Skipton road, a castellated Gothic frontage that "wouldn't look out of place on a Hollywood film set". Inside, handsome Victorian day rooms and mainly modern, decent-sized bedrooms. Conference facilities for up to 300 and winter dinner dances. Jarvis Hotels. **Rooms** 103. Garden, croquet. Access, Amex, Diners, Visa.

| BIRDLIP | **Kingshead House** | | £55 |

Tel 01452 862299   Map 14 B2   **RR**
Birdlip nr Cheltenham Gloucestershire GL4 8JH

Judy and Warren Knock run a relaxed, informal and welcoming country restaurant which began life in the 17th century as a coaching inn. Judy offers fixed-price-only dinner menus that vary weekly plus lighter, value-conscious lunch options available in the bar as well as the restaurant. On the dinner menu you might find swede and ginger soup and terrine of smoked haddock among the starters, then perhaps a scallop and prawn brioche and a choice of about five main courses that includes one fish and one vegetarian (salmon with lime butter sauce, rack of lamb with garlic crust and courgette and tomato sauce, risotto of field and button mushrooms). Desserts are just as appealing, and the meal price includes coffee or tea and petits fours. Traditional (and other) dishes on the Sunday lunch menu. Popular culinary evenings have recently covered Austria-Hungary and 'back to the twenties'. Diners taking a taxi home are entitled to taxi vouchers (£2.50 per person up to 4 per party). Prices are fair on a short but enterprising hand-written wine list. Sensible tasting notes, plenty of halves. Smoking is discouraged by table cards. **Seats** 32. L 12.30-1.45 D 7.30-9.45. Closed L Sat, D Sun, all Mon. Set Sun L £16 Set D £22.50/£24.50. Access, Amex, Diners, Visa.

Room   £54

The one and only en-suite double bedroom is a delightful place to stop over for a night. Birdlip lies on the lovely Cotswold Way and is equidistant (8 miles) from Gloucester and Cheltenham. Accommodation closed at Christmas.

| BIRKENHEAD | **Bowler Hat Hotel** | 65% | £85 |

Tel 0151-652 4931   Fax 0151-653 8127   Map 6 A2   **H**
2 Talbot Road Oxton Birkenhead Merseyside L43 2HH

One mile off the M53, Junction 3, a large Victorian house with the majority of rooms (all recently refurbished) in a redbrick extension to the rear. Function facilities for up to 250. Free parking for 100 cars. 24hr room service. **Rooms** 32. Garden. Access, Amex, Diners, Visa.

| BIRMINGHAM | **Adil Tandoori** | | £30 |

Tel 0121-449 0335   Map 6 C4   **R**
148-150 Stoney Lane Sparkbrook Birmingham West Midlands B11 8AJ

Basic balti house with a spreading reputation. Unlicensed, and the splendid nan bread does the work of knives and forks. **Seats** 80. Parties 40. Private Room 25. Meals 12-12.45. Closed 25 Dec. Access, Amex, Diners, Visa.

| BIRMINGHAM | **Birmingham Metropole** | 72% | £195 |

Tel 0121-780 4242   Fax 0121-780 3923   Map 6 C4   **H**
National Exhibition Centre Birmingham West Midlands B40 1PP

Room prices here depend upon what's on at the National Exhibition Centre and are often considerably less than the 'rack rate' we quote above. The only hotel within the complex, and with its own conference facilities for up to 2000 delegates, the Metropole has 800 rooms in three wings – Standard (all singles), Executive (the majority) and Crown (with extras like bathrobes, sofa, air-conditioning and separate walk-in shower in the bathroom). All have lightwood furniture, good desk space, restful colour schemes and poly-cotton bedding. Best of the Crown rooms overlook an ornamental lake. The main bar/lounge off the multi-floored lobby provides plenty of comfortable easy chairs and a singer/pianist most evenings. Other watering holes include a lakeside cocktail bar and

See over

the red-plush Cotswold Arms pub. Comprehensive 24hr room and lounge service. Breakfast, in the least formal of the hotel's three restaurants, is an extensive and well-tended buffet affair. *Rooms 802. Access, Amex, Diners, Visa.*

BIRMINGHAM   Chamberlain Hotel   £35

Tel 0121-627 0627 Fax 0121-606 9001   Map 6 C4   **B**
Alcester Street Birmingham West Midlands B12 0PJ

Originally one of the Rowton Houses built in 1903 to provide decent, affordable accommodation for working men, the Chamberlain today still offers budget prices for bed and breakfast. The rooms are small and fairly basic, with TVs, phones and beverage kit (no room service), plus en-suite shower/WC. Eight rooms are larger, with bathtubs. The main public room is a large Victorian-themed bar – also with keen prices. Breakfast is a buffet affair where eggs only come scrambled and beverages from a self-service machine. Conference/banqueting for 400/350. Secure, covered parking at £2 per day is a big plus. *Rooms 250. News kiosk. Closed 5 days Christmas. Access, Amex, Diners, Visa.*

BIRMINGHAM   Chung Ying   £40

Tel 0121-622 5669 Fax 0121-622 5860   Map 6 C4   **R**
16 Wrottesley Street Birmingham West Midlands B5 4RT

The Chinese flock to this well-established, traditionally appointed restaurant for its long Cantonese menu. The choice extends to well over 300 dishes, including more than 40 dim sum items and a 'special dishes' section with stuffed peppers, crabmeat on straw mushrooms, frog's legs and venison among the choice. Also of note are the casseroles and the Sunday lunchtime hot pots from which you help yourself. *Seats 220. Meals 12-11.30 (Sun to 11). Closed 25 Dec. Access, Amex, Diners, Visa.*

BIRMINGHAM   Chung Ying Garden   £40

Tel 0121-666 6622   Map 6 C4   **R**
17 Thorp Street Birmingham West Midlands B5 6RT

Sister and neat neighbour of the original *Chung Ying*, this has more modern decor, with pillars, plants, and murals, and a similar Cantonese menu. *Seats 350. Parties 18. Private Room 100. Access, Amex, Diners, Visa.*

BIRMINGHAM   Copthorne Hotel   70%   £136

Tel 0121-200 2727 Fax 0121-200 1197   Map 6 C4   **H**
Paradise Circus Birmingham West Midlands B3 3HJ

Occupying part of the central island of Paradise Circus close to the International Convention Centre, and overlooking Centenary Square, the hotel has a striking black glass exterior to complement the sleek and contemporary public areas which include a marble-floored foyer and raised bar-lounge. Connoisseur bedrooms offer guests extras to the standard rooms, though all enjoy excellent bathrooms with large mirrors and plenty of shelf space. Children up to 16 stay free in parents' room. Comprehensive conference (200), banqueting (150) and fitness facilities. Own limited free parking, and nearby multi-storey car park. *Rooms 212. Indoor swimming pool, gym, sauna, spa bath, steam room, solarium, news kiosk. Access, Amex, Diners, Visa.*

BIRMINGHAM   Forte Crest   66%   £111

Tel 0121-643 8171 Fax 0121-631 2528   Map 6 C4   **H**
Smallbrook Queensway Birmingham West Midlands B5 4EW

A high-rise hotel by the inner ring road geared primarily to business people (facilities include 'in-house' pagers and a Business Support Centre) and conferences (up to 630 theatre-style in the largest of 11 meeting rooms). Bedroom decor tends to be rather masculine although Lady Crest rooms have softer schemes. Some two-thirds of the rooms are singles. Bathrooms are compact but well thought-out with corner vanity units in marble and angled mirrors above – good for 'making up'. Comprehensive 24hr room service. Children up to 16 stay free in parents' room. Park in the adjacent NCP multi-storey (overnight included in room rate). *Rooms 251. Indoor swimming pool, gym, squash, sauna, solarium, table tennis. Access, Amex, Diners, Visa.*

Set menu prices may not always include service or wine.

| BIRMINGHAM | Forte Posthouse | 60% | £72 |

Tel 0121-357 7444 Fax 0121-357 7503   Map 6 C4   **H**
Chapel Lane Great Barr Birmingham West Midlands B43 7BG

Practical, modern hotel on the A34, near Junction 7 of the M6. Conference and
banqueting facilities for 150. Half the bedrooms are designated non-smoking. Plenty of
parking, front and rear. *Rooms 192. Garden, indoor swimming pool, gym, sauna, solarium,
spa bath, children's playroom and playground. Access, Amex, Diners, Visa.*

| BIRMINGHAM | Henry Wong | £45 |

Tel 0121-427 9799   Map 6 C4   **R**
283 High Street Harborne Birmingham West Midlands B17 9QH

Sister restaurant to *Henry's*, this is a bright and airy restaurant at the top end of
Harborne, some four miles from the city centre with similar Cantonese menu. Sound
cooking, good staff. *Seats 140. Parties 60. Private Room 40. L 12-1.45 D 6-11 (Fri & Sat to
11.30). Closed Sun, Bank Holidays. Set meals from £13. Access, Amex, Diners, Visa.*

| BIRMINGHAM | Henry's | £45 |

Tel 0121-200 1136   Map 6 C4   **R**
27 St Paul's Square Birmingham West Midlands B3 1RB

A short drive from the city centre is this purpose-built restaurant on split levels, serviced
by friendly staff. As at its sister restaurant in Harborne the Cantonese menu is extensive
and dishes are competently cooked, covering a range from crispy aromatic duck and
soups to scallops, sizzling dishes, roast pork with ginger and spring onions and sweet and
sour vegetarian wun tun. Set vegetarian menu (£12.50). *Seats 140. Private Room 40.
L 12-2 D 6-11. Closed Sun, Bank Holiday Mons. Access, Amex, Diners, Visa.*

| BIRMINGHAM | Holiday Inn Crowne Plaza | 72% | £128 |

Tel 0121-631 2000 Fax 0121-643 9018   Map 6 C4   **H**
Central Square Holliday Street Birmingham West Midlands B1 1HH

The hotel's promotion to Holiday Inn's 'Crowne Plaza' brand has been supported by some
£3 million of expenditure that has involved complete refurbishment of 188 Executive
bedrooms, a smart new entrance and triple glazing to all rooms ensuring a peaceful night's
sleep despite the city-centre location. All rooms are air-conditioned. The International
Convention Centre is just a step away. There's an NCP car park beneath the hotel with
free parking for residents between 5pm and 10am. *Rooms 284. Indoor swimming pool, gym,
sauna, steam room, spa bath, solarium, kiosk. Access, Amex, Diners, Visa.*

| BIRMINGHAM | Hyatt Regency | 75% | £144 |

Tel 0121-643 1234 Fax 0121-616 2323   Map 6 C4   **HR**
2 Bridge Street Birmingham West Midlands B1 2JZ

A canalside setting in the heart of Birmingham for the
impressive, mirrored 25-storey Hyatt Regency, which has
a direct link to the International Convention Centre next
door. Inside, the huge glazed atrium is the epitome of
style and elegance, bedecked with plants, and awash with
marble. The luxuriously appointed bedrooms include 12
suites; all have quality modern furniture and fashionably
uncluttered decor, plus equally splendid, marble-floored
bathrooms. Three rooms are adapted for the disabled, one
floor of 17 rooms is reserved for non-smokers and three
floors make up the Regency Club of superior rooms; the
latter has its own Club Lounge on the 22nd floor. Floor-
to-ceiling windows afford fine views over the Second
City. Excellent leisure facilities. Conference and
banqueting facilities for up to 240. Children up to 16 stay
free in parents' room. Parking £7 for 24 hours. *Rooms 319. Garden, indoor swimming
pool, gym, sauna, solarium, steam room, spa bath, business centre, café (6.30am-11.30pm).
Access, Amex, Diners, Visa.*

See over

Number 282 £80

Tagged as a Brasserie on Broad Street, though 'broadsheet' might be even more appropriate with the day's news headlines, weather, entertainment and even a personalised message on the paper place mat. The menu itself (on the same sheet) ranges from French onion soup, roasted monkfish tail wrapped in bacon and savoy cabbage with red wine sauce and a seafood medley to poached egg with bubble and squeak, and black pudding with mashed potato. Familiar puds like sherry trifle, bread-and-butter pudding and tarte tatin. Plenty of New World as well as European wines. Other eating venues include the all-day Court café and the Atrium itself. *Seats 75. Parties 16. L 12.30-2.30 D 6.30-11. Set L £12.75 Set D £15. Closed L Sat, all Sun.*

BIRMINGHAM	**Midland Hotel**	

Tel 0121-643 2601 Fax 0121-643 5075　　　　　Map 6 C4　　**H**
New Street Birmingham West Midlands B2 4JT

The hotel closed in December 1994 and is due to reopen as the Burlington in August 1996 after a major refurbishment programme.

BIRMINGHAM	**New Happy Gathering**	**£35**

Tel 0121-643 5247 Fax 0121-643 4731　　　　　Map 6 C4　　**R**
43 Station Street Birmingham West Midlands B5 4DY

The Chan family claims that theirs was the first (1970) Cantonese restaurant in Birmingham, and it can be found a short walk from Chinatown, above street level at the back of New Street Station. A tented fabric ceiling above the staircase and carved wood panels within the restaurant lend an opulent air, while traditional Chinese cuisine holds few surprises on the neatly laid-out menu. Two dozen or more dim sum and a dozen soups lead to meat, fowl and seafood sections with sizzling platters and vegetarian tofu alternatives. Set meals for two or more (set vegetarian meal for single diners); special banquets for six or more, special occasion menu for 2 or 3. *Seats 90. Private Room 100. L 12-1.45 D 5-11.15 (Fri to 11.45, Sun to 11) Sat all day 12-11.45. Set meals from £10. Access, Amex, Diners, Visa.*

BIRMINGHAM	**Novotel**	**61%**	**£94**

Tel 0121-643 2000 Fax 0121-643 9796　　　　　Map 6 C4　　**H**
70 Broad Street Birmingham West Midlands B1 2HT

Distinctive yellow- and red-brick hotel just down the street from the International Convention Centre and Birmingham Rep. Standard Novotel bedrooms, which offer practicability without frills, come with rough-textured painted walls, lightwood fitted units giving plenty of work space, open clothes hanging space, loos separate from bathrooms (all with showers over the tub) and satellite TV. A new 'canal' themed bar has a warm, cosy atmosphere in contrast to otherwise light and airy public spaces. Room service throughout the day and evening. Buffet breakfast but fried eggs cooked to order. No dogs. Underground parking for 57 cars. *Rooms 148. Gym, sauna, spa bath. Access, Amex, Diners, Visa.*

BIRMINGHAM	**Plough & Harrow**	**60%**	**£87**

Tel 0121-454 4111 Fax 0121-454 1868　　　　　Map 6 C4　　**H**
135 Hagley Road Edgbaston Birmingham West Midlands B16 8LS

A complimentary glass of mead and smiling receptionists welcome guests as they check in to this hotel based on a mellow 17th-century house at the city end of Hagley Road; a modern bedroom block was added in the 1970s. Bedrooms in the original building have recently been brightened up with new wall coverings and new matching bedcovers and curtains and it was hoped that the latter part of 1995 would see some attention to rooms in the 'new' wing which, at the time of writing, are rather masculine – darkwood fitted furniture, green button-back leather armchairs – and in need of some refurbishment. Bathrooms also have a dated feel but tubs are large and all have bidets and nice large bath sheets. The main public room is a very civilised bar/lounge with a central antique table sporting up-to-date magazines. Staff are friendly and helpful. Ample own parking. Forte. *Rooms 44. Access, Amex, Diners, Visa.*

| BIRMINGHAM | **Purple Rooms** | **£35** |

Tel 0121-702 2193   Map 6 C4

R

1076 Stratford Road Hall Green Birmingham West Midlands B28 8AD

Set at the city end of a shopping parade on a dual carriageway leading through the suburbs towards Shirley. Silver service, the usual hot plates, a floating candle atop the pink-clothed tables, plus fairly-priced Indian and Bangladeshi food. Sunday self-service buffet. No smoking in the middle dining-room. *Seats 30. Private Room 80. L 12-2.30 (Fri/Sat) D 6-12 (Sun noon-midnight). Closed L Mon-Thu. Set L & D £10.90 Set Sun L £5.95 (buffet) Set D £6.95 (Mon & Thur). Access, Amex, Diners, Visa.*

| BIRMINGHAM | **Rajdoot** | **£40** |

Tel 0121-643 8805   Map 6 C4

R

12 Albert Street Birmingham West Midlands B4 7UD

Rajdoot opened in Chelsea in 1966 and claims to be the first to use the tandoori in Europe. In the comfortable, quietly opulent Birmingham branch (as in the other outlets in Bristol, Manchester and Dublin) the clay oven turns out not only good lamb, chicken and prawn dishes but lobster, quail, venison and vegetable shashlik. *Seats 74. Parties 30. L 12-2.30 D 6.30-11.30. Closed L Sun, all 25 & 26 Dec. Set L from £6.95 Set D from £14.50. Access, Amex, Diners, Visa.*

We welcome bona fide complaints and recommendations on the tear-out pages at the back of the book for readers' comments. They are followed up by our professional team.

| BIRMINGHAM | **Royal Angus Thistle** | **65%** | **£107** |

Tel 0121-236 4211   Fax 0121-233 2195   Map 6 C4

H

St Chads Queensway Birmingham West Midlands B4 6HY

Modern city-centre hotel alongside the inner ring road, with easy parking. Summery day rooms, good-size bedrooms, up-to-date accessories. Conferences for up to 200. Free overnight parking in adjacent NCP. *Rooms 133. Access, Amex, Diners, Visa.*

| BIRMINGHAM | **Shimla Pinks** | **£50** |

Tel & Fax 0121-633 0366   Map 6 C4

R

214 Broad Street Birmingham West Midlands B15 1AY

The cooking is Indian but the decor and atmosphere anything but: one enters into a roomy lounge with widely spaced dark blue sofas, beyond which the dining space is divided between a raised section with leather armchairs around crisply-clothed tables and the main area with modernistic metal chairs and unclothed tables. Around the walls are old master paintings – but take a second look, they are not quite what they seem. The menu is more straightforward, with a good variety of well-explained dishes from throughout the sub-continent: karahi dishes from the north; kormas from Ceylon and Kashmir; achari chicken from Uttar Pradesh; chicken Jaipuri; chicken patia – originally from Persia. Dishes are well differentiated with good use of fresh herbs and spices. Special buffet nights (£10.95) Sunday and Monday in addition to the main menu. Shimla Pinks are the Indian version of Sloane Rangers. Large car park at the rear, free in the evening. Another Shimla Pinks opened mid-May at 44 Station Road, Solihull. *Seats 180. L 12.30-2.30 D 6-11.30. Closed L Sat & Sun, 25 Dec. Set L £6.95/£7.95 Set D £12.95. Access, Amex, Diners, Visa.*

| BIRMINGHAM | **Strathallan Thistle** | **63%** | **£108** |

Tel 0121-455 9777   Fax 0121-454 9432   Map 6 C4

H

225 Hagley Road Edgbaston Birmingham West Midlands B16 9RY

Circular modern building on the busy A465 just west of the city centre, very convenient for the Edgbaston cricket ground and the International Convention Centre. Flexible conference facilities (up to 170 theatre-style). Easy, mainly covered parking. 24hr room service. *Rooms 167. Access, Amex, Diners, Visa.*

BIRMINGHAM — Swallow Hotel — 77% — £145

Tel 0121-452 1144 Fax 0121-456 3442   Map 6 C4   **HR**
12 Hagley Road Five Ways Birmingham West Midlands B16 8SJ

An imposing Edwardian building, strikingly transformed into a quality luxury hotel. The foyer features sparkling Italian marble floors, rich mahogany woodwork and crystal chandeliers; there is a refined drawing room elegantly decorated with oil paintings, a quiet, dignified library and a handsome bar with colourful floral displays throughout. The air-conditioned bedrooms are stylish, well-proportioned and comfortable; one room is well equipped for disabled guests. Beautiful fabrics are complemented by fine inlaid furniture and bathrooms are impressive, with marble tiling and a host of extras. An interestingly designed leisure club is based around an Egyptian theme. Attentive, professional staff. Parking for 70 cars. *Rooms 98. Indoor swimming pool, gym, spa bath, steam room, solarium, hair & beauty salon. Access, Amex, Diners, Visa.*

Sir Edward Elgar Restaurant   £100

High-class service fits comfortably into the luxurious surroundings – murals and fine fabrics covering the walls, pianist/singer six nights a week – of this split-level, Edwardian-themed restaurant. Luxury is not hard to find on the menu, either, with the likes of caviar blinis accompanying smoked salmon, foie gras and bean casserole under roast squab, more foie gras in the apple terrine, and truffles both in the spaghetti of vegetables starter and larded into a rib of beef. From the fixed-price menus Toulouse sausage and vegetable broth, warm scallop salad with leek and balsamic dressing, casserole of veal with winter vegetables and chump of lamb on a garlic and potato purée are typical. In addition to the à la carte and table d'hote menus there is a special £25 post-theatre supper served until 10.45pm by prior arrangement only. No smoking. Perfunctory tasting notes alongside each wine on a so-so list. Langtry's list is slightly shorter. *Seats 60. Parties 10. Private Room 20. L 12.30-2.30 D 7.30-10.30 (Sun till 10). Closed L Sat. Set L £17.50 (Sun £20.50) Set D £25 (not Sat)/£30.*

Langtry's   £60

British cookery to traditional recipes produces daily lunchtime dishes from around the country: Lancashire hot pot on Wednesday, boiled ham with parsley sauce on Thursday and east-coast beer-battered cod and chips on Friday. Popular à la carte favourites include oxtail soup, English duck with cranberry and mint sauce, home-made fruit cake with Lancashire cheese and steamed treacle pudding. Outdoor seating for 16 in summer. *Seats 60. Parties 14. L 11.30-3 D 6.30-10. Closed Sun, Bank Holidays & 1 week Christmas.*

BIRMINGHAM AIRPORT — Forte Posthouse — 61% — £72

Tel 0121-782 8141 Fax 0121-782 2476   Map 6 C4   **H**
Coventry Road Birmingham Airport Birmingham West Midlands B26 3QW

30s' hotel with a modernised interior one mile from the National Exhibition Centre and seven miles from the city centre. 12 Executive rooms; half the rooms are designated non-smoking. All now have mini-bars and 'smart' TVs. Conference and banqueting facilities for up to 150. *Rooms 136. Garden. Access, Amex, Diners, Visa.*

BIRMINGHAM AIRPORT — Novotel — 65% — £84

Tel 0121-782 7000 Fax 0121-782 0445   Map 6 C4   **H**
Birmingham International Airport Birmingham West Midlands B26 3QL

Opposite the airport's main terminals and linked by monorail to the NEC, this Novotel has sound-proofed bedrooms and stylish day rooms. Children up to 16 stay free in parents' room. *Rooms 195. Restaurant (6am-midnight). Access, Amex, Diners, Visa.*

We welcome bona fide complaints and recommendations on the tear-out pages at the back of the book for readers' comments. They are followed up by our professional team.

BISHOP'S TAWTON   Halmpstone Manor   68%   £100

Tel 01271 830321   Fax 01271 830826   Map 13 D2   **HR**
Bishop's Tawton Barnstaple Devon EX32 0EA

Ask directions to find the small 16th-century manor house, which stands in gardens off a country lane and is at the heart of the Stanburys' working farm. One is quickly made to feel at home by Jane and Charles' easy friendliness while unwinding in front of a real fire in the spacious lounge dotted with family photos and ornaments. There is a homely feel to the shaggy-carpeted bedrooms too with all sorts of little comforts from fresh fruit and decanter of sherry to magazines and mineral water along with good armchairs and settees. Individually decorated in soft colours, rooms are furnished with a mixture of antique and reproduction pieces; two have four-poster beds. Bathrooms, two with shower and WC only, boast bathrobes and generously sized towels. Rooms are properly serviced in the evenings and excellent breakfasts start the day. No children under 12. *Rooms 5. Garden. Closed Nov & Jan. Access, Amex, Diners, Visa.*

Restaurant   £75

First-rate local produce – Jane can probably tell you from which of the neighbouring farms the lamb or beef on the menu originated – is the backbone of short fixed-price five-course dinners served by candle-light in the pitch-pine-panelled dining-room. Prawn-filled smoked salmon roll, artichoke soup, roast pheasant veiled in port with bread sauce, monkfish with grain mustard and steak with black peppercorns and a mushroom cream sauce show the style. No smoking. *Seats 24. Parties 16. L by arrangement D 7-9. Set D £30.*

BLACKBURN   Moat House   58%   £74

Tel 01254 264441   Fax 01254 682435   Map 6 B1   **H**
Preston New Road Blackburn Lancashire BB2 7BE

A modern Queens Moat Houses hotel with a distinctive gabled roof and extensive conference facilities (for up to 350 theatre-style). Half the bedrooms are designated non-smoking. *Rooms 98. Access, Amex, Diners, Visa.*

BLACKPOOL   Imperial Hotel   64%   £114

Tel 01253 23971   Fax 01253 751784   Map 6 A1   **H**
North Promenade Blackpool Lancashire FY1 2HB

A degree of Victorian grandeur survives at this Forte hotel overlooking the sea on the North Promenade. Generally good-sized bedrooms offer all the usual modern conveniences. Conferences/banqueting for 600/450. *Rooms 183. Indoor swimming pool, keep-fit equipment, sauna, spa bath, steam room, solarium. Access, Amex, Diners, Visa.*

BLACKPOOL   Pembroke Hotel   67%   £132

Tel 01253 23434   Fax 01253 27864   Map 6 A1   **H**
North Promenade Blackpool Lancashire FY1 2JQ

A modern conference hotel with facilities for up to 900 delegates (theatre-style) and up to 650 for banqueting. In the main holiday season families are well catered for, with a playroom, baby-sitting and a supervised creche (9am-9pm) as well as a separate children's menu. A large swimming pool and Springs night club are among the leisure amenities. Parking for 316 cars. Metropole Hotels. *Rooms 274. Indoor swimming pool. Access, Amex, Diners, Visa.*

BLACKPOOL   September Brasserie   £65

Tel 01253 23282   Map 6 A1   **R**
15-17 Queen Street Blackpool Lancashire FY1 1PU

Michael Golowicz opened the brasserie in 1989 on the first floor above his wife Pat's hairdressing salon. Monthly changing menus are short but varied. They are also very imaginative – in fact the menu terms the cooking as 'creative eclectic'. Typical choices from a well-balanced selection include starters such as Jerusalem artichoke soup with Stilton cream, smoked haddock tartare with asparagus and cuttlefish or king prawn tempura with sweet chili and *kombu* seaweed. Main course dishes range from braised oxtail in red wine, mushrooms and button onions served with olive oil mash to breast

See over

of local cock pheasant stuffed with teal and spinach and beef fillet on spiced polenta and laverbread. Good sweets too as in orange and kiwi timbale with ginger anglaise, tarte tatin with cinnamon ice cream and chocolate and pistachio sablé. The selection of British cheeses is a splendid alternative. *Seats 40. L 12-2 D 7-9.30. Closed Sun, Mon, 2 weeks summer, 2 weeks winter. Access, Amex, Diners, Visa.*

BLAKENEY   Blakeney Hotel   64%   £124

Tel 01263 740797   Fax 01263 740795   Map 10 C1   **H**
The Quay Blakeney nr Holt Norfolk NR25 7NE

Blakeney Point is part of the Heritage Coastline, in an area of outstanding natural beauty, and is owned by the National Trust, so views of it across the salt marshes from this family-owned-and-run hotel are valued by conservationists, holidaymakers and business travellers alike. Most rooms are in the main building but a few are in an annexe. All are comfortably furnished and top-of-the-range rooms usually have a feature such as four-poster bed, jacuzzi, antique furniture or a balcony. Banquets and conferences for up to 120/200. Car parking for 75. *Rooms 60. Garden, indoor swimming pool, keep-fit equipment, sauna, spa bath, hair salon, snooker. Access, Amex, Diners, Visa.*

BLAKENEY   Manor Hotel   58%   £56

Tel 01263 740376   Fax 01263 741116   Map 10 C1   **H**
Blakeney nr Holt Norfolk NR25 7ND

Privately-owned 16th-century manor house on the north coast of Norfolk, right next to salt marshes and a harbour inlet – ideal for yachtsmen and bird-watchers. A flagstoned entrance hall leads into day rooms that include a spacious lounge. Spotless, simply furnished bedrooms are arranged in converted barns and stables around neat courtyards. Charming walled garden with a seating area and a 400-year-old mulberry tree. No children under 14. *Rooms 37. Garden, bowling green. Closed 3 weeks Jan. No credit cards.*

BLANCHLAND   Lord Crewe Arms   £80

Tel 01434 675251   Fax 01434 675337   Map 5 D2   **I**
Blanchland nr Consett Co Durham DH8 9SP

Wild and remote, and some 3 miles below Derwentwater in a deep valley, Blanchland Abbey can trace its origins back to 1165; despite dissolution in 1576, the layout of its surrounding village remains unchanged to this day. At its heart is one of England's finest inns, containing remains of the abbey lodge and kitchens and set in a cloister garden which is now an ancient monument. Lord Crewe purchased the entire estate in 1704 from one Tom Forster, a Jacobite adventurer; the ghost of his sister Dorothy is claimed still to be in residence. Bedrooms, needless to say, are splendidly individual: suitably traditional in the old house with stone mullion windows and restored fireplaces and mantels, yet up-to-date accessories from colour TVs to bespoke toiletries and thoughtful extras from mending kits to complimentary sherry. More contemporary are the style and furnishings of rooms in the adjacent Angel Inn, once a Wesleyan Temperance House, a mere newcomer dating from the 1750s. In private (and caring) hands for the last few years, the Lord Crewe Arms today relives its centuries of pre-eminence. Children up to 14 stay free in parents' room. *Rooms 18. Garden. Access, Amex, Diners, Visa.*

BLEWBURY   The Blewbury Inn   £60

Tel 01235 850496   Map 15 D2   **R**
London Road Blewbury nr Didcot Oxfordshire OX11 9PD

Decorwise this is a simple pub restaurant with dado-height pine boarding, wheelback chairs and unclothed tables. The menu, however, is a bit more sophisticated with such dishes as red pepper mousse with basil sauce; baked goat's cheese with hazelnut dressing; braised lamb shank with tomato, olives and parsley sauce; chargrilled baby aubergines with pesto-flavoured ratatouille (there's always a vegetarian option) and ragout of seafood with tagliatelle on a short menu (four or five choices at each stage) that is priced à la carte to encourage snacking (the same menu is served in the bar) but with a maximum price of £21.95 if all three courses are taken. Good puds might inlcude a hot plum soufflé or freshly-baked chocolate pithiviers. No smoking. The inn is run by a keen young couple with Martine Lane providing the charming service of Paul's efforts in the kitchen. Three modest bedrooms provide overnight accommodation. *Seats 26. L 12-2 D 7-9 (weekends till 9.30). Closed D Sun, all Mon, 25 Dec. Access, Visa.*

BLOCKLEY	Crown Inn Hotel	£78

Tel 01386 700245   Map 14 C1   **I**
High Street Blockley Gloucestershire GL56 9EX

The Champion family's 16th-century coaching inn stands at the heart of a most picturesque Cotswold village. Exposed timbers and original beams, mellow stone walls and cast-iron fireplaces are appealing period features in the bedrooms, the grandest of which are suites with four-posters. *Rooms 21. Garden. Access, Amex, Diners, Visa.*

BODYMOOR HEATH	Marston Farm	65%	£95

Tel 01827 872133   Fax 01827 875043   Map 6 C4   **H**
Dog Lane Bodymoor Heath nr Sutton Coldfield Warwickshire B76 9JD

Ten minutes drive from Birmingham Airport and the NEC, Marston Farm, set in 9 acres and beside the Fazeley canal, is just off Junction 9 of the M42: follow signs to Kingsbury and Bodymoor Heath. A 17th-century farmhouse forms the main body of the hotel, deriving both character and intimacy from oak beams and inglenook fireplaces. In a converted barn are 20 uniform bedrooms and a boardroom with conference accommodation and banqueting space for 120. Satellite TV now installed in bedrooms. Children free when sharing parents' room. Greatly reduced rates at weekends. *Rooms 37. Garden, croquet, tennis, fishing, golf practice net, mountain bikes. Access, Amex, Diners, Visa.*

BOGNOR REGIS	Royal Norfolk	58%	£76

Tel 01243 826222   Fax 01243 826325   Map 11 A6   **H**
The Esplanade Bognor Regis West Sussex PO21 2LH

With sea views and its own three acres of gardens, the hotel dates from the 1830s and has played host to visiting royalty throughout the years. Bedrooms, in various styles, are generally bright and pleasant. Children up to the age of 14 stay free in parents' room. Some attention is needed to the outside of the building. Forte. *Rooms 51. Garden. Access, Amex, Diners, Visa.*

BOLLINGTON	Mauro's	£60

Tel 01625 573898   Map 6 C2   **R**
88 Palmerston Street Bollington nr Macclesfield Cheshire SK10 5PW

The Mauro family run an authentic North Italian restaurant with a feast of flavours in the *antipasti alla caprese*, served from a trolley. Home-made noodles and ravioli are served several ways and market-fresh fish heads a list of daily specials. Lighter dishes on a good-value, 3-course lunch menu; open for Sunday lunch (£14.75) only on the first Sunday of the month. Exclusively Italian wines, as one might expect. *Seats 49. Parties 12. L 12-2 D 7-10 (Sat to 10.30). Closed L Sat & all Sun (see above). Access, Amex, Visa.*

BOLTON	Beaumont Hotel	58%	£71

Tel 01204 651511   Fax 01204 61064   Map 6 B2   **H**
Beaumont Road Bolton Greater Manchester BL3 4TA

Looking very much like an older style Posthouse, which is what it actually once was, this modern hotel stands on the outskirts of Bolton near Junction 5 of the M61. There's a two-level bedroom block and conference/banqueting facilities for 120/90. Tariff reductions at weekends. Forte Hotels. *Rooms 96. Garden, children's play area. Access, Amex, Diners, Visa.*

BOLTON	Egerton House	63%	£104

Tel 01204 307171   Fax 01204 593030   Map 6 B2   **H**
off Blackburn Road Egerton Bolton Lancashire BL7 9PL

Victorian house set among trees and lawns just off the A666. Bright, comfortable lounge and bar, bedrooms graded either standard or superior. Guests have free use of the leisure facilities at the Last Drop Village Hotel, two minutes drive away. A self-contained function suite includes the Barn, catering for up to 150 delegates. Free bed and breakfast for under-10s. Owned by Macdonald Hotels. Ample parking. *Rooms 32. Garden. Access, Amex, Diners, Visa.*

BOLTON Last Drop Village Hotel 68% £105

Tel 01204 591131 Fax 01204 304122 Map 6 B2 **H**
Hospital Road Bromley Cross Lancashire BL7 9PZ

About 30 years ago, a collection of 18th-century moorland farm buildings was skilfully turned into a village with cottages, gardens, craft shops, a pub, a tea shop and, at its heart, a comfortable and well-equipped hotel. Day rooms retain some original features, while bedrooms are mainly bright and modern with all the expected amenities. Children up to 12 stay free in parents' room. There are extensive conference facilities (in a choice of rooms) for up to 200 delegates. The hotel is well signed from the A666. *Rooms 83. Indoor swimming pool, gym, sauna, steam room, spa bath, squash, beauty and hair salons, coffee shop (10am-5.30pm). Access, Amex, Diners, Visa.*

BOLTON Pack Horse Hotel 62% £55

Tel 01204 27261 Fax 01204 364352 Map 6 B2 **H**
Nelson Square Bradshawgate Bolton Greater Manchester BL1 1DP

Redbrick building in the town centre, with comfortable accommodation, cheerful bars, a thriving conference business (seven rooms handling up to 275 delegates) and free NCP parking at the rear. Children up to 14 stay free in parents' room. *Rooms 72. Access, Amex, Diners, Visa.*

BOLTON ABBEY Devonshire Arms 74% £130

Tel 01756 710441 Fax 01756 710564 Map 6 C1 **H**
Bolton Abbey nr Skipton North Yorkshire BD23 6AJ

Traditional standards of hospitality are maintained at a much-extended 18th-century coaching inn which since 1753 has been in the hands of the Dukes and Duchesses of Devonshire. Set in 12 acres of grounds in an area of outstanding natural beauty, it is furnished and appointed with much thought. Well-proportioned day rooms feature choice antiques and oil paintings from the Devonshire family home of Chatsworth in Derbyshire. The best bedrooms, in the main house, are individually themed and again show carefully chosen furnishings and fabrics. Numerous little extras like a decanter of sherry, magazines and flowers are a welcoming touch. The majority of bedrooms in more recent wings are more uniform in size and style, though they are equally inviting and comfortable. Good breakfasts in the bar. Infants in cots stay free in parents' room. Parking for 120 cars. Hotel residents have automatic membership of a luxurious health, beauty and fitness centre. *Rooms 41. Garden, croquet, indoor swimming pool, all-weather tennis, spa bath, steam room, solarium, gym, beauty therapy room, fishing. Access, Amex, Diners, Visa.*

BONCHURCH Winterbourne Hotel 64% £124*

Tel 01983 852535 Fax 01983 853056 Map 15 D4 **H**
Bonchurch Isle of Wight PO38 1RQ

Charles Dickens wrote most of *David Copperfield* here, and the bedrooms are named after characters in the novel. The setting is one of great charm, with waterfalls in the wooded, terraced garden and lovely sea views. Inside is no less appealing, and the main day room has French windows opening on to the terrace and garden. Bedrooms, most with sea views, vary considerably in size and appointments, the best perhaps being five in the converted coach house. Bonchurch is near Ventnor, on the southern tip of the island. ★ Half-board terms only. *Rooms 14. Garden, outdoor swimming pool. Closed Nov-Feb. Access, Amex, Diners, Visa.*

BOREHAM STREET White Friars Hotel 57% £75

Tel 01323 832355 Fax 01323 833882 Map 11 B6 **H**
Boreham Street nr Herstmonceux East Sussex BN27 4SE

Set in two acres of gardens on the A271 two miles from Herstmonceux, the building dates from the 1700s and has been a hotel since the 1920s. Day rooms and some bedrooms have an old-fashioned charm, complete with four-posters; nine rooms are in a separate cottage block. Characterful, beamed conference room for up to 50 delegates (banquets for 60). Children up to 16 accommodated free in parents' room, charged for meals as taken. *Rooms 20. Garden. Access, Amex, Diners, Visa.*

Set menu prices may not always include service or wine.

BOROUGHBRIDGE	The Crown	63%	£65

Tel 01423 322328   Fax 01423 324512   Map 5 E4   **H**
Horsefair Boroughbridge North Yorkshire YO5 9LB

Enjoying a prominent town-centre location this former coaching inn once boasted stabling for 100 horses. Decor throughout is smart and modern. There are conference facilities for 150 and there is ample car parking. Children up to 11 stay free in parents' room. *Rooms 42. Access, Amex, Diners, Visa.*

BORROWDALE	Borrowdale Hotel	60%	£98*

Tel 01768 777224   Fax 01768 777338   Map 4 C3   **H**
Borrowdale Keswick-on-Derwentwater Cumbria CA12 5UY

A stone's throw from Derwentwater, three miles from Keswick on the B5289, stands a solid, greystone hotel whose style of hospitality resists change. A lovely enclosed garden is overlooked by the bar and patio: two chintzy lounges have winter log fires, and the best of the comfortable, homely bedrooms have lake views. Superior rooms are spacious with four-poster beds a feature in some. For fell-walkers there's a first-floor drying room with iron and board. Free golf Mon-Fri at Keswick golf course. *Half-board terms only. *Rooms 34. Garden, playground. Closed 9 Jan to 6 Feb. Garden. Access, Visa.*

BORROWDALE	Stakis Lodore Swiss Hotel	71%	£112

Tel 01768 777285   Fax 01768 777343   Map 4 C3   **H**
Borrowdale Keswick Cumbria CA12 5UX

Overlooking Derwentwater and set in 40 acres of wooded grounds, the hotel is an ideal lakeland retreat for families. On offer is an extensive range of leisure activities. All rooms have been refurbished with best rooms taking full advantage of the splendid lake views. There are numerous price packages available from overnight bed and breakfast to stays of five nights or more (these are on half-board terms). Children are charged according to age. Conference/banqueting facilities for 80. Free golf (Mon-Fri) at Keswick golf club. *Rooms 70. Garden, indoor swimming pool, gym, squash, sauna, solarium, tennis, games room, nursery. Access, Amex, Diners, Visa.*

BOSHAM	Millstream Hotel	63%	£99

Tel 01243 573234   Fax 01243 573459   Map 15 D4   **H**
Bosham Lane Bosham West Sussex PO18 8HL

From the A27, follow signs to Bosham then Bosham Quay to reach this archetypical English village. Nestled into the curve of the stream lies the Millstream Hotel, originally a working malthouse, now a comfortable hotel furnished in country house style. The well-maintained gardens reach to the water's edge, so a duck might happily waddle across the lawn while you're taking afternoon tea under a shady tree. Indoors, the public rooms are light and airy while the bedrooms offer all modern comforts. Some have jacuzzis (in their en-suite bathrooms) and one has a charming curved wrought-iron balcony overlooking the gardens. Rooms in the newer wing tend to be slightly smaller and darker. Standards of housekeeping and service in general, are high. Children up to 16 stay free in parents' room, and there's parking for 38 cars. *Rooms 29. Garden. Access, Amex, Diners, Visa.*

BOTLEY	Cobbett's		£65

Tel 01489 782068   Fax 01489 799641   Map 15 D4   **R**
15 The Square Botley Southampton Hampshire SO30 2EA

Charming restaurant set in an old timber-framed cottage in the village of Botley, which is equally accessible from Winchester, Southampton and Portsmouth. Charles Skipwith provides the warm welcome while his wife Luce, a native of Bordeaux, is responsible for the authentic French Provincial cooking. The day's soup and fish dish depends on the market; other dishes might include a chicken mousseline with a sauce of sweet wine and wild mushrooms; grilled duck breast with an onion and beetroot marmalade; medallions of pork with apples, calvados, cream and cider; and profiteroles filled with Grand Marnier cream and coated with chocolate. The monthly-changing, fixed-price menu (priced for two or three courses) offers about half-a-dozen options at each stage. A small private dining-room can also be used for small conferences and seminars for which they have all the necessary equipment. Very short list of well-described French wines with nothing, except the fizz, breaching the £20 barrier. Ample own parking. *Seats 40.*
Private Room 14. L 12-2 D 7.30-10 (Sat from 7). Closed L Mon & Sat, all Sun, Bank Holidays, 2 weeks summer & 2 weeks winter. Set L & D £18.50/£23. Access, Visa.

BOUGHTON MONCHELSEA   Tanyard Hotel   63%   £90

Tel 01622 744705   Fax 01622 741998   Map 11 C5   **HR**
Wierton Hill Boughton Monchelsea nr Maidstone Kent ME17 4JT

From the B2163 at Boughton, turn down Park Lane opposite the Cock pub. Take the first right down Wierton Lane then fork right, and the Tanyard is on the left at the bottom of the hill. Once safely arrived you'll be subject to the caring attention of owner Jan Davies, and enjoy beautiful views over the Kenton Weald. As the name suggests, the building was once a tannery, though it now operates as a cosy, charming small hotel with a house-party atmosphere. The building itself still displays some original 14th-century beams both inside and out, as well as uneven floors and exposed brickwork. No children under six. No dogs. *Rooms 6. Garden. Closed 1 week Christmas, 2 weeks winter. Access, Amex, Diners, Visa.*

Restaurant   £60

There are plenty of genuine or imitation Tudor rooms serving as restaurants: this one is model of how it should be done. The stone walls are unencumbered by unsuitable prints or other spurious decoration between the timbers. There are no superfluous drapes ruining the windows or wall-to-wall carpets hiding the flagstones. Furniture is simple. Jan Davies is back in the kitchen after an 18-month break, producing dishes such as crab and spring onion parcels and calf's liver salad to start and main courses of pheasant casserole with shallots and chestnuts or Scottish salmon with a leek and chive sauce. For dessert you might find hot cranberry and apple soufflé or home-made brown-bread ice cream. Flavours are thought through and nicely balanced. Service is friendly. No smoking. *Seats 28. Parties 16. L 12-1.45 D 7-9. Closed L Mon, Tue & Sat. Set L £12.50/£15.50 (Sun £20) Set D £25.*

BOURNEMOUTH   Carlton Hotel   76%   £120

Tel 01202 552011   Fax 01202 299573   Map 14 C4   **H**
East Overcliff Bournemouth Dorset BH1 3DN

Large Edwardian hotel on Bournemouth's East Cliff enjoying panoramic views of the bay. Public areas were totally transformed a few years ago in opulent style with various lounges (sometimes used for private functions) including a library with some fine polished-wood panelling, a cosy room with leather upholstery, the Orangery that takes full advantage of the sea view and a bar with something of a 1920s feel all leading off a long corridor decorated in pink with mottled mirrors and marbled wallpaper. The restaurant, where good breakfasts are efficiently served, boasts no less than a dozen large chandeliers. Bedrooms, apart from a few singles, are spacious and comfortable with proper wing armchairs and attractive colour schemes. There are 12 full suites in the hotel itself and larger time-share apartments within the same building are sometimes used by the hotel. The hotel's health spa includes an outdoor pool in a sheltered position surrounded by some semi-tropical plants; a real sun-trap. Staff are friendly and key members make an effort to get to know their guests. The evening service of bedrooms extends to laying out the bathmat next to the tub in the bathroom. 24hr room service. Ample parking. *Rooms 70. Garden, outdoor swimming pool, gym, sauna, steam room, spa bath, sun beds, beauty & hair salon, games room, snooker, boutique. Access, Amex, Diners, Visa.*

BOURNEMOUTH   Chine Hotel   65%   £85

Tel 01202 396234   Fax 01202 391737   Map 14 C4   **H**
Boscombe Spa Road Bournemouth Dorset BH5 1AX

In a fine position overlooking Poole Bay to the south, the 1874-built Chine has benefited from the same conscientious family ownership since 1945. Large bedrooms, nearly half with private balcony or patio, have light-oak units and a pleasing pale-green colour scheme. Spacious public areas include a cosy residents' lounge overlooking the pine-fringed outdoor swimming pool. Business people are attracted by a number of well-equipped conference rooms (in an adjacent building) and families appreciate the

playroom, games room, coin-operated laundry room and, during school holidays,
a children's activities organiser. Children up to 12 stay free in parents' room. No dogs.
Sister hotels are the *Haven* and *Sandbanks* at nearby Poole. **Rooms** 97. *Garden, putting,
outdoor & indoor swimming pool, sauna, solarium, children's playroom and playground,
games room. Access, Amex, Diners, Visa.*

BOURNEMOUTH	Langtry Manor	62%	£99

Tel 01202 553887   Fax 01202 290115   Map 14 C4   **H**
26 Derby Road East Cliff Bournemouth Dorset BH1 3QB

Built in 1877 for Lillie Langtry by Edward VII when Prince of Wales, this romantic
manor is full of memorabilia of that heady era. Some suites in particular recall the
attachment – the Edward VII, the Jersey Lily, the Lillie Langtry – and playing fair there's
also an Alexandra suite! All suites and rooms are individually decorated and furnished
(a few are in the lodge annexe). "Not really suitable for children". **Rooms** 25. *Garden.
Access, Amex, Diners, Visa.*

BOURNEMOUTH	Norfolk Royale	70%	£138

Tel 01202 551521   Fax 01202 299729   Map 14 C4   **H**
Richmond Hill Bournemouth Dorset BH2 6EN

The Norfolk Royale's splendid two-tier cast-iron verandah looks proudly over the town,
a testament to Bournemouth's Edwardian heyday. Twin conservatories – one housing the
pool and the other part of the all-day Orangery restaurant – extend into the pretty garden
to the rear and several interconnecting rooms provide plenty of lounge/bar space. Pretty,
well-maintained bedrooms and good bathrooms. Fourteen rooms are reserved for non-
smokers, others are equipped for lady travellers, yet more are adapted for the disabled.
Disabled up to age 12 can be accommodated free in parents' room. Valet parking for 85
cars in a secure underground park is a big plus given the hotel's central location.
Well-motivated staff. No dogs. Banqueting/conferences for up to 100. **Rooms** 95.
Garden, indoor swimming pool, sauna, spa bath, steam room. Access, Amex, Diners, Visa.

BOURNEMOUTH	Ocean Palace		£45

Tel 01202 559127   Fax 01202 559130   Map 14 C4   **R**
8 Priory Road Bournemouth Dorset BH2 5DG

Behind the Bournemouth International Conference Centre and not far from the seafront,
this modern restaurant has a conservatory-style frontage, simple decor and plain walls
hung with contemporary Chinese artwork. Hing Wong's cooking skills cover Peking and
Szechuan styles, with special vegetarian and seafood sections on a long menu. **Seats** 150.
*Private Room 12. L 12-2.15 D 6-11.15. Set L from £5.95 Set D from £14. Closed 4 days
Christmas. Access, Amex, Diners, Visa.*

BOURNEMOUTH	Roundhouse Hotel	59%	£70

Tel 01202 553262   Fax 01202 557698   Map 14 C4   **H**
The Lansdowne Bournemouth Dorset BH1 2PR

This aptly named hotel is a circular building on three floors above a spiral car park. Practical
modern bedrooms and roomy open-plan public areas. Children of any age share parents'
room free. Conferences for up to 100. Forte. **Rooms** 98. *Access, Amex, Diners, Visa.*

BOURNEMOUTH	Royal Bath Hotel	73%	£115

Tel 01202 555555   Fax 01202 554158   Map 14 C4   **HR**
Bath Road Bournemouth Dorset BH1 2EW

A splendid Victorian hotel combining traditional values (courteous and helpful staff for
example) and modern amenities such as the marvellous Leisure Pavilion which features
a heated kidney-shaped swimming pool. There are also versatile conference facilities; the
largest of the seven rooms has a capacity of 350. The hotel stands in an immaculately kept
three-acre garden with clifftop views out to sea, enjoyed by many of the bedrooms (some
with terraces) which vary in style and size but are all smartly furnished with good
bathrooms. Excellent housekeeping, including a turn-down service at night, is evident
throughout. The vast public areas (bars and lounges) are comfortable and well appointed,
and breakfast in the Garden Restaurant will not disappoint. Children up to the age of 14
years free in parents' room. Supervised creche daily in high season. Covered parking for
130 cars. No dogs. De Vere Hotels. **Rooms** 131. *Garden, croquet, indoor swimming pool,
gym, sauna, steam room, spa bath, solarium, beauty & hair salon, putting, snooker, children's
playground, lounge service, garage. Access, Amex, Diners, Visa.*   *See over*

Restaurant £60

The Garden Restaurant is only open in the evenings and for Sunday lunch, offering a cuisine of English, French and International inspiration. Oscar's, a more intimate setting with Oscar Wilde memorabilia all round, offers a French-orientated carte and set menus, which at lunchtime include a roast carved from the trolley. *Seats 300. L (Sun only) 12.30-2.15 D 7-9.15. Set L £12.50 Set D £23 & £28.50. Oscar's (closed Sunday): Seats 40. L 12.30-2.15 D 7.30-10.15.*

BOURNEMOUTH   Stakis Bournemouth Hotel   71%   £118

Tel 01202 557681   Fax 01202 554918   Map 14 C4   **H**
Westover Road Bournemouth Dorset BH1 2BZ

A high-rise hotel, formerly the Palace Court, restored to its original between-the-wars splendour. Spacious public areas are in 1930s' style: the front lounge with leather armchairs in pale yellow and pale pink and the split-level lounge/bar on the first floor in darker, more sophisticated tones. Conservatory-style windows take advantage of views across the Solent to the Isle of Wight. A further café/lounge has rattan furniture and ceiling fans slowly swishing overhead. Decor in the bedrooms varies, but all have freestanding furniture, many with walnut veneer pieces, and smartly-tiled bathrooms. Eight de luxe rooms live up to their name with mirrored bedheads (containing cassette players as well as radios) and bathrooms with spa baths, private mini-saunas and exercise bicycles. Rooms at the front have balconies with outdoor seating. 24hr room service can provide hot meals even in the middle of the night. Conference/banqueting facilities for 200/250. Ample garage parking (£2 per night) and a car rental office. *Rooms 110. Indoor swimming pool, gym, spa bath, sauna, sun bed, hair salon, café-bar (10am-11pm), night club. Access, Amex, Diners, Visa.*

BOURNEMOUTH   Swallow Highcliff Hotel   70%   £120

Tel 01202 557702   Fax 01202 292734   Map 14 C4   **H**
St Michael's Road West Cliff Bournemouth Dorset BH2 5DU

An imposing Victorian hotel with a splendid clifftop location giving many of the rooms fine marine views. A funicular lift carries guests from hotel to promenade. Good-sized bedrooms in the main house have dark period-style furniture, those in the converted coastguard cottages smart lightwood pieces. Numerous public rooms include a terrace bar and a lounge for non-smokers. Magnificent conference facilities can cope with up to 350 delegates. Excellent family facilities in summer include a fenced-in outdoor play area and a creche. *Rooms 157. Garden, croquet, indoor & outdoor swimming pool, children's splash pool, spa bath, sauna, solarium, tennis, putting, games room, snooker, children's playground & playroom. Access, Amex, Diners, Visa.*

BOURTON-ON-THE-WATER   Dial House   61%   £83

Tel 01451 22244   Fax 01451 810126   Map 14 C1   **H**
The Chestnuts High Street Bourton-on-the-Water Glos GL54 2AN

This 17th-century former farmhouse, now a comfortable and gracious hotel, is located right in the centre of the popular Cotswold town of Bourton. The setting (right by the River Windrush) and the honey-coloured brick exterior make it a popular choice with tourists. Pots of flowers, glowing antiques, the inglenook fireplaces and leather sofas add to the charm, while bedrooms are individually decorated (three have four-poster beds and one a half-tester) and are not lacking in modern comforts. No children under 10. Parking for 18 cars. *Rooms 10. Garden, croquet. Access, Amex, Visa.*

BOWNESS-ON-WINDERMERE   Belsfield Hotel   62%   £113

Tel 015394 42448   Fax 015394 46397   Map 4 C3   **H**
Kendal Road Bowness-on-Windermere Cumbria LA23 3EL

From its elevated position amid 6 acres of neat gardens the hotel enjoys superb views overlooking Lake Windermere, public rooms and front-facing bedrooms affording the best vantage points. The latter command a higher price though they are also lighter and brighter. Family rooms have either bunk beds or an adjoining child's room. Leisure facilities, with smartened-up changing rooms include a heated indoor swimming pool with sliding roof. Forte Hotels. *Rooms 64. Garden, indoor swimming pool, sauna, solarium, tennis, putting, snooker. Access, Amex, Diners, Visa.*

BOWNESS-ON-WINDERMERE   Gilpin Lodge   71%   £110

Tel 015394 88818   Fax 015394 88058   Map 4 C3   **HR**
Crook Road Bowness-on-Windermere Cumbria LA23 3NE

It was the happiest of coincidences that when John and Christine Cunliffe were looking for a hotel of their own, after careers in commercial catering, the Lakeland house where John spent his childhood should have come on to the market. Now, a few years on, the love and care they have lavished on Gilpin Lodge is evident throughout. The 20 acres of grounds are well tended (despite the deer digging up the tulip bulbs as fast as they're planted), the day rooms comfortable and civilised and the generally spacious bedrooms (all but one have sitting areas) notably well appointed with a variety of antique and traditional-style furniture, books, magazines, information and maps to the area, well-stocked mini-bars and all the usual modern amenities. Excellent bathrooms, several with separate shower cubicles, the others with power showers over the tubs. There is comprehensive room service throughout the day and evening and while you dine beds are turned down, curtains drawn and bedside lights lit. First-rate breakfasts come with freshly squeezed orange juice and croissants straight from the oven. Not suitable for under-7s. Guests have free use of a nearby leisure centre. The hotel is located on the B5284 towards Kendal from Bowness. No dogs. *Rooms 9. Garden, croquet. Access, Amex, Diners, Visa.*

Restaurant £60

Not just one but three dining-rooms, each equally charming and boasting the same high-quality table settings, emphasising the importance given to the cuisine here. The fixed-price, four-course dinner menu offers a wide choice of tempting and sophisticated dishes. Originally the province of Christopher Cunliffe, the kitchen is now largely in the safe hands of Christopher Davies who very much puts his own stamp on dishes such as feuilleté of duck's liver with artichoke hearts, wild mushrooms and a *fines herbes* sauce; warm cep mousse with pesto, bacon and a plum tomato salad; chargrilled fillet of Dover sole on a purée of parsnip and celeriac with a dill and parsley butter sauce; rack of lamb with braised lentils on a roast garlic and black olive sauce; roast Goosnargh duckling with a lime, ginger and passion fruit sauce and desserts like a hot ginger and date pudding with two toffee sauces, and banana and lemon crème brulée under a nougatine crust. As an alternative to dessert there is always a well-balanced cheese plate (Long Clawson Stilton, Dewlay Lancashire and a Somerset Brie) and that almost forgotten delight – a savoury such as devils on horseback. No detail is overlooked, from nice nibbles with the menu to good home-made petits fours with the coffee or tea. The lunchtime à la carte copes equally well with a snack in the lounge or more formal meal in the restaurant. A really informative and pleasing wine list offers well-chosen wines in every section. Prices are fair, and wines by the glass are served in measures that accord with the revised legislation. No smoking. *Seats 45. Parties 24. Private Room 14. L 12-2 D 7-8.45. Set L (Sun) £14 Set D £26.*

BOWNESS-ON-WINDERMERE   Linthwaite House   72%   £115

Tel 015394 88600   Fax 015394 88601   Map 4 C3   **HR**
Bowness-on-Windermere Cumbria LA23 3JA

High standards of service combine with an amenable, unstuffy attitude in a hotel that enjoys an unsurpassed location on the B5284. With views of Lake Windermere and beyond to the Old Man of Coniston, Linthwaite's environment is conducive to relaxation with a unique, lived-in interior design which sees, for instance, old brass-cornered chests converted into practical coffee tables. Some smaller bedrooms' dimensions are similarly redeemed by stylish interiors, with hand-made pine dressers and vanity units providing the unifying theme; some rooms have lake views (room rates vary according to size and position). The best bathrooms, fully carpeted and brightly lit, feature mahogany panels and strong pulse showers. Free use of nearby leisure spa with pool, spa bath, sauna, steam room, squash and gym. No dogs. *Rooms 18. Garden, croquet, putting, practice golf hole, fly fishing. Access, Amex, Diners, Visa.*

Restaurant £68

Warming candle-light and polished mahogany tables create an intimate and cosy atmosphere for enjoying some very capable cooking in the modern British style. To supplement the à la carte there are three-course table d'hote and five-course Gourmet menus. There are four choices per course on a Sunday lunch, which could include starters such as sauté of lamb's kidneys and wild mushrooms or cream of broccoli soup

See over

with toasted almonds. To follow there's a traditional roast as well as breast of chicken with green pasta and a garlic and lemon sauce or steamed fillet of salmon topped with trout mousse and served with a pink leek sauce. Desserts like warm Spotted Dick with a fresh vanilla custard or quenelles of white and dark chocolate mousse with milk chocolate sauce or a selection of superb British cheeses (regional winner of British Cheeseboard of the Year) round off a splendid repast. There are plenty of half bottles on an enterprising wine list with pertinent tasting notes. The list is presented by style, thus a spicy, perfumed and aromatic Gewurztraminer appears in the medium dry section! No smoking. No children under 7 in the evening. *Seats 48. Parties 8. Private Room 22. L 12-1.45 D 7.15-8.45. Set L £10 (Sun £11.95) Set D from £22.*

BOWNESS-ON-WINDERMERE   Old England Hotel   65%   £127

Tel 015394 42444   Fax 015394 43432   Map 4 C3   **H**
Church Street Bowness-on-Windermere Cumbria LA23 3DF

A comfortable Georgian mansion with gardens rolling down to Lake Windermere, next to the Royal Windermere Yacht Club. The best rooms (with a small supplement) have lake views. Popular for conferences and banquets (up to 150) as well as holidaymakers. Forte. **Rooms 78.** *Garden, outdoor swimming pool, sauna, solarium, hairdressing, snooker, jetty. Access, Amex, Diners, Visa.*

BRACKNELL   Coppid Beech Hotel   72%   £125

Tel 01344 303333   Fax 01344 301200   Map 15 E2   **HR**
John Nike Way Bracknell Berkshire RG12 8TF

The privately-owned Coppid Beech is designed in striking Swiss-chalet style. A unique feature of the interior is a triangular shaft extending to the full height of the building, lined with aquaria (the largest in Europe apparently) and mirrors creating a mesmerising, watery kaleidoscope. Extensive facilities include a Bierkeller with live entertainment several nights a week, plush state-of-the-art disco night club and Waves health and fitness centre. Well-thought-out bedrooms (a significant number are full or junior suites) are well equipped – there's even an account review and check-out facility available via the advanced TV system – and the beds are large and comfortable. 24hr room service is extensive and beds are turned down at night. Children up to 12 share parents' room free; youngsters are made to feel at home with the Bobby Beech Nut club. Conference and banqueting facilities for 200/375. **Rooms 205.** *Indoor swimming pool, gym, spa bath, sauna, solarium, steam room, dry ski slope, ice rink. Access, Amex, Diners, Visa.*

Rowans Restaurant   £75

🍷 🍲 🍳 🍶 🍓

Large and comfortable with well-spaced tables, this is the hotel's main dining-room. Friendly, efficient service from smartly uniformed and numerous staff complements a kitchen that produces well-judged dishes that are as good to look at as they are to eat: a feuilleté for example in the form of a freshly-baked 'horn of plenty' from which perfectly cooked asparagus spills out on to a pool of good beurre blanc, or a coriander-flavoured shellfish consommé liberally garnished with langoustines, pieces of mullet and smoked salmon with some caviar as a finishing touch. Main dishes might include roasted salmon with tomatoes, haricot beans, herb gnocchi and a red wine sauce; loin of lamb niçoise with Mediterranean vegetables and garlic-roasted potatoes; and an aubergine gateau as the vegetarian option. Good desserts. New to the menu options is the 'Menu Specialities of the House' at £39.50 (glass of kir, four courses, coffee). Tasting notes accompany each wine on a list of a hundred or so. Fair prices, good balance, but saying "as vintage wines are produced in limited quantities, a suitable alternative will be offered when vintages become unavailable" should be avoided. You either have enough bottles in the cellar for a wine to be listed, or you don't – it's not the limited quantity of wine produced, but the limited quantity purchased by the hotel! **Seats 125. Parties 8.** *Private Room 30. L 12-2.30 (Sun to 3) D 6-10.30 (Sun 7-10). Set L £17.50 (Sun Buffet £15.95) Set D £25 & £39.50.*

BRACKNELL   Hilton National   69%   £116

Tel 01344 424801   Fax 01344 487454   Map 15 E2   **H**
Bagshot Road Bracknell Berkshire RG12 3QJ

In the heart of busy Bracknell, a modern hotel handy for the M3 (Junction 3) and M4 (Junction 10). Two floors of bedrooms are reserved for non-smokers. Large conference and banqueting facilities for up to 400. Children up to 14 free in parents' room. **Rooms 167.** *Plunge pool, keep-fit equipment, sauna, spa bath, coffee shop (10am-11pm). Access, Amex, Diners, Visa.*

BRADFORD	Nawaab	£30

Tel 01274 720371   Map 6 C1   **R**
32 Manor Row Bradford West Yorkshire BD1 4QE

Set in a former banking house, atop Manor Row, with mushroom-coloured walls and
an ornamental elephant. The extensive Pakistani menu covers tandoori specialities, more
than 40 balti dishes and around eight basic varieties of curry. Chef's specialities includes
haddock masala, lamb *dan gali* (spicy sultanas, pistachios and a garnish of sliced banana),
and a composite dish of lamb, chicken, prawns, king prawns, mushrooms and chick peas
with yoghurt. *Seats 120. L 12-2 D 6-12 (Fri & Sat to 1.30am). Closed L Sun. Access, Visa.*

BRADFORD	Novotel	60%	£55

Tel 01274 683683   Fax 01274 651342   Map 6 C1   **H**
Merrydale Road Bradford West Yorkshire BD4 6SA

Three miles south of the city centre just off the M606 on the Euroway Trading Estate,
the hotel offers smart, up-to-date and comfortable accommodation. Restaurant open
from 6am to midnight. Conference/banqueting facilities for 300/160. Free parking for
200 cars. Children up to 16 stay free in parents' room. *Rooms 127. Garden, outdoor
swimming pool. Access, Amex, Diners, Visa.*

BRADFORD	Restaurant 19	★	£70

Tel 01274 492559   Fax 01274 483827   Map 6 C1   **RR**
19 North Park Road Heaton Bradford West Yorkshire BD9 4NT

👑 🍓 🗍

Chef Stephen Smith and partner Robert Barbour, who looks after the front of house,
operate a splendid restaurant with rooms in a quiet residential suburb north-west of the
city centre. From the outside it's a substantial Victorian town house standing on a corner
overlooking Lister Park, while inside the bar and two candle-lit dining-rooms are
beautifully decorated and have a fine collection of Russell Flint prints. The fixed-price
four-course menus consist of modern, well-balanced dishes with the emphasis very much
on flavours and lightness. Fashionable ingredients are skilfully combined, as in starters
of sausage of red mullet with pesto noodles and ratatouille and roast quail with prawn
fritters and plum sauce. The soup course is served from a tureen brought to the table,
creamy fennel and courgette being a typical example. Main dishes are wonderfully
satisfying as in roast breast of corn-fed chicken, with goat's cheese, plum tomato and
tapénade; and rack of spring lamb with pistachio and mint crust and ragout of spring
vegetables. These precede deliciously simple desserts such as an orange tart with lemon
sorbet and mascarpone cheese cake with strawberry and mint. *Seats 36. Parties 12.
L by arrangement D 7-9.30 (Sat to 10.30). Closed Sun & Mon, 2 wks Sept, 2 wks Dec/Jan.
Set D £25. Access, Amex, Visa.*

Rooms   £75
The four bedrooms, furnished with cheerful, colourful chintzes and antiques, are
supremely comfortable and well equipped. Bathrooms, with top-of-the-range fittings, are
bright and spacious. Service has that welcoming, homely touch that makes a stay here so
much preferable to larger establishments. Breakfasts are superb with requirements
perfectly met.

BRADFORD	Stakis Bradford	61%	£97

Tel 01274 734734   Fax 01274 306146   Map 6 C1   **H**
Hall Ings Bradford West Yorkshire BD1 5SH

A city-centre hotel (previously the Stakis Norfolk Gardens) with an adjacent car park
(but no discounts) and facilities for up to 700 banqueting or conference delegates.
There are five bedroom floors, the lower three being smarter and more up-to-date.
Rooms 120. Access, Amex, Diners, Visa.

We welcome bona fide complaints and recommendations on the
tear-out pages at the back of the book for readers' comments.
They are followed up by our professional team.

| BRADFORD | The Victoria | 67% | £99 |

Tel 01274 728706   Fax 01274 736358   Map 6 C1   **HR**
Bridge Street Bradford West Yorkshire BD1 1JX

With the rail/bus interchange on one side, the Law Courts opposite, and St George's Hall next door, the newly renovated and refurbished hotel is in a prime position, with the added benefit of its own parking (60 cars). Taken over by Jonathan Wix (see *42 The Calls*, Leeds) the hotel once again offers style, elegance and comfort; bedrooms (20 non-smoking) – with smart granite-tiled bathrooms, good towels and quality toiletries – are in three colour schemes and have hand-made beds and, unusually, a music centre with both CD and video players (select from the library) alongside regulation TV, hairdryer, trouser press and tea- and coffee-making facilities. The grand entrance hall/lounge retains many original features, and the combination of contemporary and period furniture really pleases the eye. There's no bar as such, but its own pub the Pie Eyed Parrot (at the Old Vic), retains the hotel's theatrical connections. Conference and banqueting rooms (200/120) are in the basement together with the gym and sauna. Children free in parents' room up to 12. *Rooms 60. Gym, sauna. Access, Amex, Diners, Visa.*

Vic and Bert's   £50
Tel 01274 390321

This fin-de-siècle brasserie, specialising in grills cooked over wood, has its own entrance on Drake Street, as well as access from the hotel. The room itself is grand, yet informal, with a wood floor, oak panelling, banquettes, and chrome hat and coat rails.
An innovative touch sees daily specials print-stamped on the paper tablecloths. The cooking is overseen by Stephen Smith (see *Restaurant 19*, Bradford): typical starters (available as a main course by doubling the portion and price!) include ricotta and spinach spring roll and savoury summer pudding with tiger prawns, while for a main course you could choose a fillet of salmon marinated in olive oil, lemon grass and basil, or rack of English lamb, both from the wood-burning grill. End with a classic French lemon tart or chocolate trifle. Table d'hote dinner is served in the hotel's breakfast room on Sunday evening. Clever and fairly-priced wine list with selections under £10 or under £15 a bottle, as well as several 'fine' wines. *Seats 80. Parties 10. L 12-2.30 D 6.30-10 (10.30 Fri/Sat). Closed L Sat, all Sun, Bank Holidays. Set L & D till 7.30 £7.95/£9.95 Set D £12.95/£14.95.*

| BRADFORD-ON-AVON | Woolley Grange | 75% | £140 |

Tel 01225 864705   Fax 01225 864059   Map 14 B3   **HR**
Woolley Green Bradford-on-Avon Wiltshire BA15 1TX

The Grange is a handsome 17th-century country mansion whose comfortably lived-in day rooms are full of character, with antiques, paintings and real fires. There's a Victorian Gothic conservatory, an oak-panelled drawing room and various other rooms for whiling away a few quiet moments, and friendly young staff imbue the whole place with a friendly, relaxing feel that's a major part of the attraction. Bedrooms vary considerably in size but all have great character with a beamed bathroom here (mostly with Victorian-style fittings), a rugged stone fire breast there (about half have working gas coal fires), brass bedsteads, patchwork bedcovers, antiques and fresh flowers all helping to create an appealing 'country' feel. Don't miss the collection of interesting bicycles, which include a pre-war tandem, a modern penny farthing and a couple of Moultons. And be sure to say hello to Susie and Rosie, the Vietnamese pot-bellied pigs. The smallest doubles are priced considerably below the rate quoted above. Children stay free in parents' room, indeed this is one of the foremost family hotels in Britain, albeit at a price! There's lots for them to do – they have designated 'fun' rooms and their own garden patch.. *Rooms 20. Garden, croquet, tennis, badminton, bicycles, outdoor swimming pool, games room. Access, Amex, Diners, Visa.*

Restaurant   £75

Formerly the sous-chef here, Peter Stott took over the head chef's toque in the summer of 1995 and is admirably maintaining standards with no change of style. The fixed-price dinner menu (five choices at each stage) still offers an appealing selection of dishes with a modish slant. A typical list of mains might be roast shoulder of lamb with garlic mash and rosemary sauce; sauté of guinea fowl with fennel, olives and basil; medallions of venison with mushroom relish and port sauce; seared salmon with orange and green peppercorn sauce, and baked black bream stuffed with ginger, spring onions and coriander with a coriander salsa. Good puds like chocolate tart with espresso sauce and hot praline soufflé with apricot sauce; British cheeses are well represented on the daily selection. Lunch brings a less formal menu (also served in the conservatory or out on the terrace in summer) that might include an excellent bourride of fishes with aïoli and rouille, tagliatelle with pesto and shaved parmesan, club sandwich, hamburger with barbecue relish and a Thai-style chicken and vegetable stir-fry. A similar but slightly shorter version of this menu is also served in the conservatory in the evening as an informal alternative to the dinner served in the main dining-room with its elegant table-settings, antique balloon-back chairs and yellow walls sporting colourful paintings. No smoking in main restaurant. **Seats** 54. *Parties 40. Private Room 22. L 12-2 D 7-10. Set L (Sun) £17 Set D £28.*

We welcome bona fide complaints and recommendations on the tear-out pages at the back of the book for readers' comments. They are followed up by our professional team.

| **BRAITHWAITE** | **Ivy House** | **66%** | **£60** |

Tel 01768 778338   Fax 01768 778113   Map 4 C3   **H**
Braithwaite nr Keswick Cumbria CA12 5SY

Nick and Wendy Shill run a hotel of warmth and character in a small 17th-century house at the foot of the Lakeland fells. Walking is a favourite pastime with guests, made more appealing by ample drying facilities and log fires in the lounge. Fine old furniture and objets d'art are found in the neat bedrooms, which include a honeymoon suite with four-poster. The hotel is in the middle of the village just behind the Royal Oak pub. *Rooms 12. Closed Jan. Access, Amex, Diners, Visa.*

| **BRAMHALL** | **Moat House** | **63%** | **£106** |

Tel 0161-439 8116 Fax 0161-440 8071   Map 6 B2   **H**
Bramhall Lane South Bramhall Cheshire SK7 2EB

Built in 1972 and since expanded, this well-kept hotel appeals to both leisure and business visitors. Conference and banqueting facilities for 110/90. Ample free parking. *Rooms 65. Keep-fit equipment, sauna, sun bed. Access, Amex, Diners, Visa.*

| **BRAMHOPE** | **Forte Posthouse** | **66%** | **£86** |

Tel 0113 284 2911 Fax 0113 284 3451   Map 6 C1   **H**
Bramhope nr Leeds West Yorkshire LS16 9JJ

16 acres of grounds, swimming pool, keep-fit amenities and conference facilities for up to 160 in a hotel two miles from Leeds/Bradford Airport. Children up to 16 free in parents' room. 74 rooms reserved for non-smokers. Previously the Forte Crest. *Rooms 124. Garden, indoor swimming pool, gym, sauna, solarium, coffee shop (noon-10pm). Access, Amex, Diners, Visa.*

| **BRAMHOPE** | **Jarvis Parkway Hotel** | **62%** | **£112** |

Tel 0113 267 2551 Fax 0113 267 4410   Map 6 C1   **H**
Otley Road Bramhope nr Leeds West Yorkshire LS16 8AG

Built in 1939, the original building has a smart new colourful decor and well-equipped leisure centre. As well as a few older rooms there is an extension of attractive balconied bedrooms to the rear overlooking wooded parkland. *Rooms 105. Garden, tennis, indoor swimming pool, gym, sauna, spa bath, steam room, solarium, beauty salon. Access, Amex, Diners, Visa.*

BRAMLEY   Bramley Grange   64%   £108   H

Tel 01483 893434   Fax 01483 893835   Map 15 E3
281 Horsham Road Bramley nr Guildford Surrey GU5 0BL

Based on a mock–Tudor Victorian house, Bramley Grange now extends around three sides of a large well laid-out lawned garden (making it a popular venue for weddings) with a wooded hillside completing the square. Half the bedrooms are in the newest wing and feature limed oak furniture, plain walls and co-ordinating fabrics. Other rooms are individually decorated, from large rooms with antique furniture to a few small singles with shower and WC only. 'Standard' rooms attract a reduced weekday tariff; reductions also at weekends. All but 10 of the bedrooms are designated non-smoking. Banqueting/conference facilities for 120 in the Garden Suite. *Rooms 45. Garden, croquet, tennis. Access, Amex, Visa.*

BRAMPTON   Farlam Hall   75%   £184*   HR

Tel 01697 746234   Fax 01697 746683   Map 4 C2
Hallbankgate Brampton Cumbria CA8 2NG

The hotel stands on the A689 two miles from Brampton – not in Farlam village. Set in lovely grounds complete with stream and ornamental lake, the original 17th-century farmhouse was enlarged to form a manor house in Victorian times. The Quinion and Stevenson families' charming country house hotel features Victorian-design wallpapers and authentically re-upholstered original pieces. Plants and fresh flowers, books and board games enhance the lived-in feel. Individually decorated bedrooms are a model of taste; most have space for a sitting area, and bathrooms are modern and well equipped; the finest is a Victorian recreation in dark mahogany. Splendid breakfasts and the charm and courtesy of the resident hosts contribute greatly to a memorable stay. No children under five in the hotel. Function facilities for 45 (banqueting) and 20 (conference). *Half-board terms only. *Rooms 12. Garden, croquet. Closed 25-30 Dec. Access, Amex, Visa.*

Restaurant   £60

Guests are requested to arrive in the bar or front lounge in time to dine between 8 and 8.30. This air of formality extends to dinner. Barry Quinion's nightly fixed-price-only, 4-course menu changes daily and offers self-styled "English Country House" cooking. A small choice of three dishes at each course is typified by chicken liver parfait with home-made plum chutney, confit of Gressingham duck leg with salad or a comforting cream soup to start, followed by filo pastry basket filled with seafood in a Noilly Prat and parsley sauce, beef medallions with a brandy and pink peppercorn sauce or roast guinea fowl on a blackcurrant and cassis sauce with a blackcurrant tartlet garnish. A selection of ten excellent British cheeses precedes the dessert course which could include Austrian coffee cake, rum pie or grape and brandy trifle. Short, diverse, sensibly-priced wine list. Lunch (around £22.50) is served four times a year (Mothering Sunday, Easter Day, Christmas Day and New Year's Day). Snack lunches are available daily in the lounge to residents. *Seats 40. Parties 20. D only 8-8.30. Set D £28.50.*

BRANDON   Brandon Hall   £92   H

Tel 01203 542571   Fax 01203 544909   Map 7 D4
Brandon nr Coventry Warwickshire CV8 3FW

The hotel is situated in seventeen acres of grounds, and was undergoing a much-needed refurbishment programme at the time of our visit in summer '95. Graded at 65% in last year's guide. Most of the standard (more modern) rooms are in an extension, while the suites are in the main house. Forte Heritage. *Rooms 60. Garden, squash, pitch & putt, clay-pigeon shooting, archery. Access, Amex, Diners, Visa.*

Consult the blue pages for summary tables and lists of recommended establishments.

BRANDS HATCH Brands Hatch Thistle 70% £98

Tel 01474 854900 Fax 01474 853220 Map 11 B5 **H**
Brands Hatch nr Dartford Kent DA3 8PE

This purpose-built modern hotel definitely exploits the transport theme: situated right by the main entrance to the racing circuit on the A20, it's just 3 miles from the M25 which gives fast access also from the M20 and M26. One of the conference suites is the de Havilland, the coffee shop is the Brasserie Concorde, while the place for a quiet drink (if you're not driving!) is the Bugatti Bar. All the public areas are elegant and spacious, while the bedrooms (a quarter of which are reserved for non-smokers) offer plenty of modern amenities, especially the higher-priced Executive range. Three are also especially adapted for the disabled, There's parking for 180 cars (some spaces again reserved for the disabled). Conference/banqueting facilities for 300/250, and a hospitality suite at the track. Families are well catered for, and children up to 15 stay free in parents' room. *Rooms* 137. *Coffee shop (9.30am-10.30pm). Access, Amex, Diners, Visa.*

BRANSCOMBE Masons Arms 64% £54

Tel 01297 680300 Fax 01297 680500 Map 13 E2 **H**
Branscombe nr Seaton Devon EX12 3DJ

Surrounded by acres of unspoilt National Trust land and within a hop of the Devon Coastal Path, the Masons Arms is, unsurprisingly, popular with walkers. The 14th-century inn has slate floors, open fires and oak beams that were once the timbers of smugglers' boats. Guests may stay in the hotel itself, whose seven rooms are compact and quaint (two are without private bathrooms) or in the adjacent residential cottages, which have been sympathetically converted over the years. The proprietor of over 20 years standing, Murray Inglis, has recently taken personal charge of the day-to-day running of the Arms. *Rooms* 21. *Garden. Access, Visa.*

BRAUNTON Otter's Restaurant £50

Tel 01271 813633 Map 12 C2 **R**
30 Caen Street Braunton Barnstaple Devon EX33 1AA

Carol Cowie's realistically-priced set menu offers a choice of six or more dishes per course. She describes her cooking as 'English with French flair' and among her specialities are mushroom and bacon gratin and guinea fowl normande with gooseberries, ginger and cider. Other typical dishes include Yorkshire popover with a Stilton sauce, leek and potato soup with saffron and mussels, chicken with a bacon, chicken liver and spinach stuffing, paupiettes of lemon sole with fennel in a creamy Pernod sauce, and fillet steak au poivre. There's always a good choice of desserts, from cranachan with raspberry sauce, and roasted bananas with passion fruit and honey to a rich chocolate marquise with a Drambuie sauce. No smoking before 9.30 (but the bar is available). The restaurant stands in a little row of shops in the centre of the village, two miles from Saunton Sands. A riverside terrace is available for pre-dinner drinks or dining in the summer months. There's a large free car park opposite the restaurant. A sensible wine list offers the usual plus some lesser-known wines, particularly from the New World. *Seats* 40. *Parties* 14. *D only 7-9.30. Open L Mothers Day. Closed Sun, Mon, 2 weeks Jan, 2 weeks Nov. Set D £15.70/£17.95. Access, Amex, Visa.*

BRAY-ON-THAMES The Waterside Inn ★★★ £170

Tel 01628 20691 Fax 01628 784710 Map 15 E2 **RR**
Ferry Road Bray-on-Thames Berkshire SL6 2AT

Michel Roux's delightful and celebrated restaurant lies right on the river bank; indeed you can sit outside on the terrace for a pre/post-prandial drink or coffee and almost touch the water. Since it opened in 1972, there have been many changes here, not least the addition of bedrooms (see below), so this is *un vrai restaurant avec chambres.* Michel has surrounded himself with an enviable team of dedicated professionals, none more so than head chef Mark Dodson and restaurant manager Diego Masciaga, recently joined by Louis Abdilla. The setting is spectacular, the dining-room elegant and bright, with, naturally, the tables alongside the picture windows enjoying the best views. Cooking is, of course, very, very French, based on classic principles, but with an added

See over

lightness of touch and a nod to modern practices. You really are spoilt for choice, since there are a number of menus and the carte to choose from: a £29.50 *menu gastronomique* at lunchtime during the week, £37 on Sunday; an evening *menu du printemps* at £49.50 between October and April; *menu exceptionnel*, five courses, including a sorbet, at £66, taken from à la carte, served in smaller portions for a minimum of two persons. A typical example from the latter might include *terrine de foie gras, vinaigrette de truffes; paillard de saumon fumé sur douillet d'aubergines; aiguillettes de caneton Challandais à la vie de vin, dés d'olives au parfum d'anchois; soufflé chaud aux framboises* (note the timing for last orders of hot desserts). The other fixed-price menus are simpler (don't stray or each course will be charged separately), typified by *gourmandise de lapereau aux noisettes caramélisées; supreme de turbot poelé, timbale de crustacés, au parfum de pesto; dome aux deux chocolats et framboises*. English translations probably do not do the dishes justice, so don't be afraid to ask! Add to these delights the dainty *canapés* and *amuse-bouche*, excellent rolls, fine French cheeses, exquisite petits fours and courteous service, and you have the complete package. Yes, for the most part the wine list is pricy, but remember prices are inclusive of service. France only, the best growers, the classic names, with some less expensive bottles. No children under 12. Electric launch *The Waterside Inn II* available for hire, and the restaurant for private functions when closed. *Seats 75. Parties 10. Private Room 8. L 12-2 (Sun 2.30) D 7-10. Closed all Mon, L Tue, D Sun end Oct-mid April, Bank Holidays (open L 25 Dec), 26 Dec-end Jan. Set L £29.50 (Sun £37) Set D Oct-April £49.50, also Set L & D £66. Access, Diners, Visa.*

Rooms   £130
A new suite (bedroom, drawing room and breakfast room) situated on the river a minute's walk from the restaurant has been added to the six existing bedrooms, two of which share a large terrace. Each, with a neat bathroom, is individually and stylishly decorated, and the obvious benefit of staying here, apart from not having to drive home, is the continental breakfast with the morning's baking.

BRENTWOOD	Forte Posthouse	61%	£75

Tel 01277 260260 , **Fax 01277 264264**   Map 11 B4   **H**
Brook Street Brentwood Essex CM14 5NF

Comfortable modern redbrick hotel half a mile from the M25 (J28). Conference and banqueting facilities for 120. Children up to 18 free in parents' room. Half the rooms are designated non-smoking. *Rooms 115. Garden, indoor swimming pool, gym, sauna, solarium, beauty salon. Access, Amex, Diners, Visa.*

BRENTWOOD	Marygreen Manor	65%	£118

Tel 01277 225252   Fax 01277 262809   Map 11 B4   **H**
London Road Brentwood Essex CM14 4NR

An attractive half-timbered building dating back to the 15th century houses the public rooms and the three most characterful bedrooms, each of which has an ancient bed and antique furniture. The remainder of the bedrooms are in a cloister-like quadrangle overlooking a neat garden. 18 of them now have sparkling new black and white tiled bathrooms, with the rest to follow. All the rooms are comfortable and well equipped. Staff are obliging and cheerful. Children free in parents' room up to 14. Formerly the *Moat House. Rooms 33. Garden. Access, Amex, Diners, Visa.*

BRIDLINGTON	Expanse Hotel	60%	£65

Tel 01262 675347   Fax 01262 604928   Map 7 E1   **H**
North Marine Drive Bridlington Humberside YO15 2LS

Purpose-built in 1937, the Expanse is a traditional seaside hotel that has been owned by the Seymour family since 1948. Many of its guests are regulars, while others come for business meetings and conferences (banqueting for 120, three conference rooms for 80 in total). Public and lounge bars are agreeable places to relax, and quite a few of the bedrooms enjoy sea views; some have balconies. Children up to 15 stay free in parents' room. No dogs. *Rooms 48. Access, Amex, Diners, Visa.*

| BRIDPORT | Riverside Restaurant | £40 |

Tel 01308 422011 Map 13 F2 **R**
West Bay Bridport Dorset DT6 4EZ

The menu at this friendly, relaxed restaurant concentrates on locally caught fish and shellfish prepared plainly or with sauces. Red mullet, John Dory, Dover sole, lemon sole, plaice and sardines are grilled to order, and other choices could be skate with black butter and capers, deep-fried squid or baked brill Greek-style. Lobster is priced according to season and weight. There are a few meat dishes, too, such as Dorset air-dried ham, roast chicken and chili con carne. Breakfast, light snacks and Dorset cream teas are also served. In good weather tables are set outside on a patio overlooking the river. Opening times can vary with the seasons, so check when booking. *Seats 70. Parties 12. L 11.30-2.30 (Sun to 3.30) D 6.30-9. Closed D Sun, all Mon (except Bank Holidays), late Nov-early Mar. Access, Visa.*

| BRIERLEY HILL | Copthorne Merry Hill | 71% | £115 |

Tel 01384 482882 Fax 01384 482773 Map 6 B4 **H**
The Waterfront Level Street Brierley Hill West Midlands DY5 1UR

The renamed *Copthorne Hotel*, a fairly recent addition (1993) to the group, is a modern, stylish pupose-built hotel overlooking the marina and adjoining the shopping mall. Smart public rooms and well-appointed bedrooms (36 for non-smokers) cater largely to a business clientele. Conference/banqueting facilities cater for up to 190/250; parking for 170 cars; children up to 16 stay free in parents' room. *Rooms 138. Patio, indoor swimming pool, gym, sauna, steam room, spa bath, solarium. Access, Amex, Diners, Visa.*

| BRIGHOUSE | Forte Crest | 68% | £116 |

Tel 01484 400400 Fax 01484 400068 Map 6 C1 **H**
Coalpit Lane Clifton Village Brighouse West Yorkshire HD6 4HW

A low-rise hotel set in landscaped gardens close to J25 of the M62. Two-thirds of the bedrooms are designated non-smoking. Children up to 16 stay free in parents' room. Good leisure facilities; seven meeting/banqueting rooms accommodating 20-200. *Rooms 94. Croquet, indoor swimming pool, gym, sauna, steam room, spa bath, solarium. Access, Amex, Diners, Visa.*

| BRIGHTLING | Jack Fuller's | £35 |

Tel 01424 838 212 Map 11 B6 **R**
Brightling nr Robertsbridge East Sussex TN32 5HD

From Robertsbridge, take the Brightling road and drive about 3½ miles to the crossroads to find Jack Fuller's – if you reach Brightling church you've gone a mile too far. It's about five miles north-east of Battle. John Fuller, also known as Mad Jack of Brightling, was a Georgian builder of follies, and these are scattered around the local area, drawing visitors and locals alike to Roger and Shirl Berman's former pub. The fun atmosphere of follies extends to the interior (or the terrace for fair-weather eating) and is enhanced by generous portions of traditional English food – gammon and onion pudding, steak and mushroom pie, prawn pancakes, smoked seafood chowder. There's a good and unusual range of side dishes (cheesy spinach and brown rice, bubble and squelch, poached mushrooms, honeyed carrots) and a good choice for vegetarians. Hot puddings come with cream or proper custard and are of the crumble, pie and pudding variety; cold puds are served with unsweetened cream and range from home-made meringues to chocolate whisky charlotte. Finish with coffee, tea or hot chocolate. Excellent choice of wines by the glass. *Seats 70. Parties 30. Private Room 20. L 12-2 D 7-11. Closed D Sun, all Mon (except L Bank Holidays), Tue, 2 weeks Jan. Set L £6.95/£10.50/£12.50 (Sun £7.95) D £11/£15.50. Access, Amex, Diners, Visa.*

We welcome bona fide complaints and recommendations on the tear-out pages at the back of the book for readers' comments. They are followed up by our professional team.

BRIGHTON   Bedford Hotel   66%   £137

Tel 01273 329744   Fax 01273 775877   Map 11 B6   **H**
King's Road Brighton East Sussex BN1 2JF

The hotel comprises the lower floors of a tall seafront block. The facade has been refurbished, creating a terrace seating area with sea views. Double-glazed bedrooms are large, with quality modern furniture and compact bathrooms, all with showers. Children up to 16 stay free in parents' room. Guests may use the leisure facilities of the Metropole Hotel, just 100 yards away. Banqueting/conference facilities for 350/450. Park for 70 cars. *Rooms 129. Access, Amex, Diners, Visa.*

BRIGHTON   Black Chapati   £45

Tel 01273 699011   Map 11 B6   **R**
12 Circus Parade New England Road Brighton East Sussex BN1 4GW

The decor is plain and minimalist, the only colour other than black being provided by a few abstract prints. Stephen Funnell's Indian and Orient-derived food is equally free of clichés, and Brighton is certainly the richer for it. The frequently-changing menu (about half-a-dozen choices at each stage) might begin with dishes like crab soup with coriander and pork won tons, vegetable samosas with fresh chutney and marinated salmon with buckwheat noodles before mains such as roast haddock with wilted coriander and cauliflower pulao, Vietnamese braised beef with *kim chi* salad, and a vegetarian thali. With desserts one's on more familiar territory with the likes of crème brulée, apple caramel tart and home-made lemon and blood orange sorbets. The chef's favourite drink, Breton cider, is an excellent accompaniment. Sunday lunch is a buffet. *Seats 30. Parties 10. L Sun 1-2.30 D 7-10.30. Closed D Sun, all Mon, 1 week June & 1 week Christmas. Set Sun L £8.95. Access, Amex, Visa.*

BRIGHTON   Brighton Metropole   70%   £174

Tel 01273 775432   Fax 01273 207764   Map 11 B6   **H**
King's Road Brighton East Sussex BN1 2FU

The Metropole is one of the leading conference hotels, with a capacity of up to 1800 delegates, vast exhibition space and full secretarial services. But it's also well geared up to the needs of private guests. The broad, deep foyer leads to an elegant drawing-room with crystal chandeliers, finely detailed plasterwork and settees and armchairs round marble-topped tables. There is a second peaceful lounge and a dark, atmospheric cocktail bar. Good-size bedrooms, furnished in smart lightwood, include 16 suites with sea-facing balconies. Some rooms are large enough for settees as well as the standard two chairs and table. Good-value leisure breaks for families complete the appeal, with early suppers and a separate children's menu. Children up to 16 stay free in parents' room, their meals also free. *Rooms 328. Indoor swimming pool, sauna, steam room, solarium, spa bath, gym, sunbed, beauty salon, hairdressing, night club, coffee shop (24hr). Access, Amex, Diners, Visa.*

BRIGHTON   China Garden   £55

Tel 01273 325124   Map 11 B6   **R**
88 Preston Street Brighton East Sussex BN1 2HG

The 100-item menu at this smart roomy restaurant near the West Pier includes many Peking and Cantonese favourites: roast duck Cantonese style, 'Kung Po' prawns (in batter and braised in chili sauce), crab, lobster, Ying Yang Dover sole (one half stir-fried with vegetables, the other deep-fried with spices), iron-griddle sizzlers, bean curd with minced beef and chili. *Seats 130. Private Room 40. Meals noon-11. Closed 25 & 26 Dec. Set meals from £15.50. Access, Amex, Diners, Visa.*

BRIGHTON   Grand Hotel   74%   £165

Tel 01273 321188   Fax 01273 202694   Map 11 B6   **H**
King's Road Brighton East Sussex BN1 2FW

De Vere's Brighton flagship sits squarely on the seafront and attracts business and leisure visitors in equal measure. The atmosphere is set by the ornate entrance hall and public areas, while bedrooms continue in grand style and range from standard, seaview or de luxe seaview on to three levels of suite. Four are especially adapted for the disabled; children up to 14 stay free in parents' room. Covered valet parking is charged at £10 per day. *Rooms 200. Indoor swimming pool, keep-fit equipment, sauna, steam room, spa bath, solarium, beauty & hair salon. Access, Amex, Diners, Visa.*

| BRIGHTON | La Marinade | £60 |

Tel 01273 600992   Map 11 B6   **R**
77 St George's Road Kemp Town Brighton East Sussex BN2 1EF

Popular, unpretentious little restaurant serving straightforward bistro food. Guinea fowl in a cream, calvados and mushroom sauce; pan-fried entrecote with Dijon mustard sauce and rack of lamb with garlic are typical main dishes and there's always a fish dish of the day. Good-value three-course lunches, including Sunday. No smoking in the upstairs dining-room. *Seats 34. L 12-2 D 7-10. Closed L Sat, D Sun, all Mon & Bank Holidays. Set L £12.75 Set D £15.50/£17.50. Access, Amex, Diners, Visa.*

| BRIGHTON | Langan's Bistro | £70 |

Tel 01273 606933   Fax 01273 675686   Map 11 B6   **R**
1 Paston Place Brighton East Sussex BN2 1HA

The seaside branch of that small family of restaurants of which *Langan's Brasserie* in London is the most famous. Modern art-crammed walls follow the house style but this outpost is otherwise very much the domain of Mark (in the kitchen) and Nicole (front of house) Emmerson, who have been running things here from the beginning. The likes of scallop and monkfish salad, chicken and leek terrine, fish soup, partridge with savoy cabbage and morels, fillet of sea bass with a warm tomato vinaigrette, and rump of lamb with roasted garlic feature on the short, constantly-changing carte; at lunchtimes this is supplemented by an even shorter prix-fixe. Sunday lunch is a fixed-price menu only – about four choices of main dishes, always including a roast. Very short wine list, modest prices. *Seats 45. Parties 10. L 12.30-2.15 D 7.30-10.15. Closed L Sat, D Sun, all Mon, first 2 weeks Jan & last 2 weeks Aug. Set L £12.50/£14.50 (Sun £14.50). Access, Amex, Diners, Visa.*

| BRIGHTON | Old Ship Hotel | 65% | £80 |

Tel 01273 329001   Fax 01273 820718   Map 11 B6   **H**
King's Road Brighton East Sussex BN1 1NR

A hotel of considerable charm and with a history dating back in part to the 15th century. A central location on the seafront is a big plus as is secure parking for 70 cars. Public areas include a surprisingly spacious oak-panelled lobby dotted with antiques, a pair of quiet lounges with Adam-style ceilings and the panelled Tettersell's Bar. The Paganini Ballroom is the largest of several rooms available for conferences or banquets (max 300/200). About two-thirds of the bedrooms (mostly those in the east wing) are smartly furnished and have up-to-date bathrooms. The remainder vary somewhat in age and style but all are at least acceptable. Friendly staff. 24hr room service. Children under 12 stay free in parents' room. A children's playroom operates at weekends. *Rooms 152. Access, Amex, Diners, Visa.*

| BRIGHTON | The Brighton Thistle | 77% | £160 |

Tel 01273 206700   Fax 01273 820692   Map 11 B6   **HR**
Kings Road Brighton East Sussex BN1 2GS

This eye-catching hotel was built in 1987 and enjoys a fine seafront location just minutes from the Royal Pavilion. Light, airy and plant-filled public areas set the scene for well-equipped air-conditioned bedrooms. Three rooms were specifically designed for the disabled. Notably smart staff are both friendly and helpful. Banqueting/conferences for 250/300. Extensive 24hr room service. Free parking (for diners as well as residents) by voucher valid for the Town Hall car park under the hotel. Children up to 16 can stay free in their parents' room. *Rooms 204. Indoor swimming pool, gym, sauna, solarium, hairdressing. Access, Amex, Diners, Visa.*

See over

La Noblesse Restaurant   £85

Andrew Furrer has now settled into his kitchen and turns out modern European dishes with a light touch. Try warm scallop gateau with a light herb and tomato fondue, pan-fried calf's liver with glazed shallots and julienne of smoked bacon, and iced white and dark chocolate terrine with a duo of sauces. Predominantly French wine list with a good range of halves. *Seats 45 Parties 12. L 12.30-2 D 7-10. Closed L Sat, all Sun. Set L £16.50 D £23.*

BRIGHTON   Topps Hotel   69%   £79

Tel 01273 729334   Fax 01273 203679   Map 11 B6   **HR**
17 Regency Square Brighton East Sussex BN1 2FG

Topps Hotel looks towards the seafront, set back from the promenade in the quiet Regency Square. Owned and run by Paul and Pauline Collins it offers a friendly and comfortable base in Brighton. Bedrooms are individually decorated and well maintained offering every modern amenity backed up by homely touches like fresh flowers and a drinks tray. No dogs. *Rooms 15. Closed 25 & 26 Dec. Access, Amex, Diners, Visa.*

Restaurant   £50

The cosy basement restaurant boasts Pauline's cooking fronted by Paul, and the fixed-price menu includes the first two courses plus coffee and service with sweets available for an extra £3. Regular favourites like rough paté or prawn tart are followed by the ever-popular steak and kidney pie or saddle of venison with port and cranberry. Careful cooking ensures consistently enjoyable results with everything home-made, including the excellent bread. *Seats 20. Parties 6. Private Room 10. D only 7-9.30. Closed Sun & Wed, Jan & Christmas. Set D £18.95.*

BRIGHTON (HOVE)   QUENTIN'S   £50

Tel 01273 822734   Map 11 B6   **H**
42 Western Road Hove East Sussex BN3 1JD

Cosy pine-decorated restaurant on the borders of Brighton and Hove. A monthly-changing carte is presented by chef Quentin Fitch, whose culinary influences take in England, France, Thailand and the Middle East. Thai fishcakes or celery and walnut pie to start; lamb kebabs with mint and cucumber chutney, rib-eye steak with chips or home-smoked salmon with fresh tagliatelle, cream and chives to follow. Delicious, simple desserts such as apple pie with home-made lavender ice cream. Bargain *plats du jour* for £4.95, including bread, mineral water and coffee. *Seats 46. Parties 20. Private Room 20. L 12-2.30 D 6.30-10.30. Closed L Sat, all Sun, Mon & Bank Holidays. Set L £4.95 Set D £12.95/£14.95. Access, Amex, Diners, Visa.*

BRIGHTON (HOVE)   Sackville Hotel   61%   £70

Tel 01273 736292   Fax 01273 205759   Map 11 B6   **H**
189 Kingsway Hove Brighton East Sussex BN3 4GU

Built as four private houses in 1904, but not opened as a hotel until 1930, this seafront hotel still retains many original decorative features. The panelled bar-lounge has leather chesterfields and there is a small, rattan-furnished sun lounge. Well-kept bedrooms mostly feature darkwood furniture and soft colour schemes. Two rooms have antiques and eight have sea-facing balconies. Swimming at the King Arthur Sports Centre is free to residents. Ample parking. *Rooms 45. Access, Amex, Diners, Visa.*

BRIGHTON (HOVE)   Whitehaven Hotel   56%   £70

Tel 01273 778355   Fax 01273 731177   Map 11 B6   **H**
Wilbury Road Hove East Sussex BN3 3JP

Situated just off the seafront, the Whitehaven offers good standards of cleanliness and repair at a small, modestly comfortable hotel. Unrestricted street parking is another plus. No children under 12. One room suitable for family use. *Rooms 17. Garden. Access, Amex, Diners, Visa.*

Consult the blue pages for summary tables and lists of recommended establishments.

BRIMFIELD   Poppies Restaurant ↑   £75

Tel 01584 711230   Fax 01584 711654   Map 14 A1   **RR**
The Roebuck Brimfield nr Ludlow Hereford & Worcester SY8 4NE

Set in a former coach house attached to the village pub, this is a restaurant with a touch
of style, not just in the decor – parquet floor, comfortably upholstered rattan and wicker
chairs and crisply white-clothed tables accented by some striking dark blue glass water
jugs and glasses – but also in the cooking. Carole Evans, here since 1983, believes that
food should be fun but it takes some serious effort and talent in the kitchen to produce
dishes that are unfussy yet refined and thoroughly enjoyable. Her menus are in the
modern British mode, spanning crab ravioli, oxtail en gelée, pan-fried sea bass
on a tomato and saffron sauce garnished with crispy fried vegetables, roast saddle of rabbit
with a light grain mustard sauce and herb-crusted rack of lamb on a spinach roundel
served with a redcurrant and mint sauce. Some of the desserts sound almost too good
to eat – how about iced lime soufflé captured in a chocolate tear drop! British farmhouse
cheeses rate their own special menu with names like Pencarreg, Hereford Hop and
Longridge Fell. There's a separate menu served in the bar where, as in the restaurant,
children are made most welcome. Half bottles come first on a list with well-chosen
wines; helpful tasting notes, but only two champagne houses represented. Polished
service. *Seats 36. Private Room 18. L 12-2 D 7-10. Closed Sun & Mon, 25 & 26 Dec.
Set L £20. Access, Amex, Visa.*

Rooms   £60

Three charming, immaculate bedrooms (all en-suite, two with showers and one with
a tub) furnished in limed oak offer everything from telephones and remote-control TV
to home-made fruit cake and beverage kit with cafetière jug and real coffee. Wake
up to breakfasts in which the local cow's or ewe's milk yoghurt, bread, sausages,
marmalade and honey are all home-made (the latter from their own hives) and the
eggs free-range.

Many hotels offer reduced rates for weekend or out-of-season
bookings. Always ask about special deals.

BRISTOL   Aztec Hotel   74%   £116

Tel 01454 201090   Fax 01454 201593   Map 13 F1   **H**
Aztec West Business Park Almondsbury Bristol Avon BS12 4TS

A smart, professionally run, purpose-built, modern hotel in the Shire Inns group. It offers
a good balance of facilities between mid-week conferences – a business centre provides
secretarial services – and weekend family breaks. All bedrooms are of Executive standard
with a sitting area, writing desk and fax point; a good proportion are reserved for non-
smokers. Syndicate rooms convert to family use at weekends with wall-mounted let-
down beds; children under 16 are accommodated free in their parents' room. Day rooms
are spacious with lounges on two levels in the central 'lodge' and a smart snooker room.
The hotel also has a fine leisure club and its own Black Sheep pub. Regional specialities
at breakfast include Somerset venison sausages and Alderley trout served with scrambled
eggs. In a modern business park near Junction 16 of the M5 (south of the M4/M5
interchange). *Rooms 109. Garden, indoor swimming pool, gym, squash, sauna, solarium,
steam room, spa bath, snooker. Access, Amex, Diners, Visa.*

BRISTOL   Berkeley Square Hotel   69%   £106

Tel 0117 925 4000   Fax 0117 925 2970   Map 13 F1   **H**
15 Berkeley Square Bristol Avon BS8 1HB

Flagship of the Bristol-based Clifton Hotels, the Berkeley Square Hotel is situated
in a tranquil Georgian square. Well-equipped bedrooms vary from practical singles
to spacious suites, their names drawn from eminent Bristolians. Thirteen rooms are
designated non-smoking. Small lounge and restaurant at street level, with a state-of-the-
art basement bar and café (7.30am-10pm). Small banquets and conferences (up to 50) are
accommodated. Covered parking for 20 cars. If you have to use a meter, the hotel's staff
will 'keep an eye on it' until your departure. *Rooms 43. Access, Amex, Diners, Visa.*

BRISTOL	Blue Goose	£45

Tel 0117 942 0940 Fax 0117 944 4033   Map 13 F1   **R**
344 Gloucester Road Bristol Avon BS7 8TP

A large blue goose adorns the entrance to a roomy bistro where the shortish, fixed-price menu might include ravioli of chicken livers, mussel and saffron broth, braised rabbit and fillet of salmon with mushroom risotto; finish with the likes of upside-down pear and ginger cake and tiramisu. Inexpensive wines; there's even a champagne under £20. **Seats** 70. D only 6.30-10.30. Closed Sun. Set D £13.50. Access, Amex, Visa.

BRISTOL	Bristol Marriott	73%	£106

Tel 0117 929 4281 Fax 0117 922 5838   Map 13 F1   **H**
2 Lower Castle Street Bristol Avon BS1 3AD

Overlooking the castle ruins, the hotel stands in the city centre and although a tall and distinctive building it is best to ask for directions when booking. The lobby, with polished stone floors and exotic plant-filled Ali Baba jars, is spacious and welcoming. The remainder of the public rooms are smartly furnished and inviting too. Bedrooms are up to date and comfortable; all have double beds, even in twin rooms. They are equipped with satellite TV, full air-conditioning and a host of useful extras including 24hr room service. The majority are designated as non-smoking rooms and top of the range Executive rooms have their own dedicated lounge. Three bedrooms are suitable for disabled guests. The hotel offers an excellent range of leisure facilities and it's definitely child-friendly. The Conference venue caters for up to 600 theatre-style. Free parking in an adjacent multi-storey car park. Half-price weekend tariff. **Rooms** 289. Indoor swimming pool, gym, sauna, spa bath, steam room, solarium, beauty salon, children's playroom, games room, news kiosk, coffee shop 7am-11pm. Access, Amex, Diners, Visa.

BRISTOL	Forte Crest	67%	£112

Tel 0117 956 4242 Fax 0117 956 9735   Map 13 F1   **H**
Filton Road Hambrook Bristol Avon BS16 1QX

City-fringe hotel in 16 acres with its own lake. Health and fitness club; large conference trade, with facilities for up to 500 delegates. Close to the M32 (J1, take A4174) and M4 (from J19). Parking for 300 cars. **Rooms** 194. Indoor swimming pool, children's splash pool, gym, sauna, spa bath, solarium, snooker, children's playground & playroom. Access, Amex, Diners, Visa.

BRISTOL	The Grand	62%	£113

Tel 0117 929 1645 Fax 0117 922 7619   Map 13 F1   **H**
Broad Street Bristol Avon BS1 2EL

The central location, friendly staff and good porterage are plus points at the Grand. Bedroom refurbishment is ongoing – rooms offer a good standard of comfort and pleasing colour schemes. Conferences (600) and banquets (530) make up a lot of the Grand's business. A new 190 space security-monitored car park is a much needed and welcome addition to the hotel's amenities. 23 rooms are reserved for non-smokers. Good breakfasts. Thistle Hotels. **Rooms** 182. Access, Amex, Diners, Visa.

BRISTOL	Harveys Restaurant	£80

Tel 0117 927 5034 Fax 0117 927 5003   Map 13 F1   **R**
12 Denmark Street Bristol Avon BS1 5DQ

The ancient cellars of Harveys Wine Merchants are home to a comfortable, air-conditioned restaurant featuring the accomplished cooking of chef-manager Ramon Farthing, who brings a contemporary touch to classic skills. Specialities include chicken and black olive sausage; sauté of fresh langoustines with sugar snap peas, truffle and radishes finished with a light hazelnut cream; breast of wood pigeon on a potato and bacon rösti with foie gras, sweet shallots and a game sauce finished with grenadine. Among the sweets look out for their special apple dessert and the hot soufflé, but also cast an eye on the magnificent British cheeseboard, this year adjudged the best in the land – see awards pages. The name Harveys is of course synonymous with sherry and port, but the rest of the wine list here ain't half bad! In fact, it's exceptional and fairly priced, bearing in mind that prices include service. Clarets really excel, but the entire list is thoroughly comprehensive with many wines from the New World too. Adjoining the restaurant is a fascinating wine museum. *Seats 120. Parties 14. Private Room 50. L 12-1.45 D 7-10.30. Closed L Sat, all Sun, Bank Holidays, 4 days Christmas & 2 days New Year. Set L £16 Set D £29 & £38. Access, Amex, Diners, Visa.*

BRISTOL	Hilton National	69%	£100

Tel 0117 926 0041   Fax 0117 923 0089   Map 13 F1   **H**
Redcliffe Way Bristol Avon BS1 6NJ

Easy to find on the city's inner ring road near Temple Meads railway station. The first-floor, open-plan reception area incorporates the bar and lounge and there is a good business centre and small, unmanned leisure centre on the same level. Bedrooms are either Executive (the price quoted), Plaza rooms (£121) or Plaza suites (£151). Two floors of rooms are designated non-smoking. A buffet breakfast is served in a historic room built originally as a kiln for the Phoenix glassworks in 1785 and is and one of the last traces of Bristol's once-thriving glass industry. Free parking (some covered) for 150 cars. **Rooms** *201. Indoor swimming pool, keep-fit equipment, sauna, steam room, solarium, coffee shop (9am-2am). Access, Amex, Diners, Visa.*

BRISTOL	Holiday Inn Crowne Plaza	72%	£130

Tel 0117 925 5010   Fax 0117 925 5040   Map 13 F1   **H**
Victoria Street Bristol Avon BS1 6HY

A strikingly modern, redbrick building standing on the site of the Old City Wall, on the corner of Victoria Street and Temple Way, in the milieu of Bristol's rapidly expanding, high-tech business quarter. Catering mainly for the executive and conference market (for up to 200 delegates), the modern bedrooms mix well-lit desk space, multipoint telephone and fax line with contemporary decor and marble-effect units in the bathrooms. 58 bedrooms are designated non-smoking and two on the first floor are specially fitted for the disabled (there are also adapted toilets on the ground floor); four air-conditioned, spacious suites have spa baths and bathrobes. An open-plan foyer/lounge is noisy but reception and porterage are effectively run. Children stay free in parents' room; seven family rooms. Free underground parking (for 150) with direct lift access to reception. 24hr room service. Conference/banqueting facilities for 200/180. Queens Moat Houses. **Rooms** *128. Keep-fit equipment, solarium. Access, Amex, Diners, Visa.*

BRISTOL	Howard's		£50

Tel 0117 926 2921   Map 13 F1   **R**
1a Avon Crescent Bristol Avon BS1 6XQ

Just five minutes from the city centre in a Georgian listed building (cross the old Hotwells swing bridge and follow signs to the *SS Great Britain*), Gill and Chris Howard's restaurant continues to please. Almost everything is made on the premises, from bread to petits fours, the à la carte menu offering such dishes as wild duck terrine with pistachios, medallions of Scotch beef fillet with port sauce, Stilton mousse and spinach and cherries in kirsch or crème brulée to finish. Lots of local game and fish with extra dishes on the blackboard – try the Cornish scallops or escalope of venison. Vegetarians well catered for; small selection of British cheeses, excellent coffee. Several wines on the concise list are under £15. **Seats** *65. Parties 18. Private Room 40. L 12-2.30 D 7-11 Closed L Sat, all Sun, 25 & 26 Dec, Bank Holiday Mons. Set L £13 Set D £15 (not Sat). Access, Amex, Diners, Visa.*

BRISTOL	Hunt's		£65

Tel & Fax 0117 926 5580   Map 13 F1   **R**
26 Broad Street Bristol Avon BS1 2HG

Andy and Anne Hunt run their restaurant in small, intimate surroundings a stone's throw from St John's Gate. Daily menus (table d'hote at lunch, à la carte at both lunch and dinner) feature such main dishes as baked sea bass with roasted peppers, pesto and beurre blanc, monkfish with pink peppercorns, squid ink noodles and ginger (seafood is something of a speciality), maize-fed guinea fowl with apples, calvados and sweet marjoram, liver and bacon with parsnip purée and venison and steak suet pudding. Provençal fish soup is a good bet amongst the starters and afters include Normandy apple and almond tart with butterscotch sauce and a hot blackcurrant and cassis soufflé. Vegetarians need to advise in advance. **Seats** *40. Parties 10. Private Room 24. L 12-2 D 7-10. Closed L Sat, all Sun & Mon, 1 week Easter, 1 week Aug, 10 days Christmas. Set L £10.95/£12.95. Access, Amex, Visa.*

BRISTOL   Jameson's Restaurant   £50

Tel 0117 927 6565   Map 13 F1   **R**
30 Upper Maudlin Street Bristol Avon BS2 8DJ

Carole Jameson's popular bistro has a new 30-seat conservatory in addition to the original two-level set-up and is adorned with plenty of greenery throughout. Fresh fish is the main feature in summer and cooking is of a good standard, with some imaginative combinations such as warm smoked eel salad with chive caper sauce, and scallops with leek and white wine sauce with laverbread pancake. There are usually a couple of vegetarian alternatives. Puddings are along the lines of chocolate rum mousse with coffee sauce, lemon soufflé and gratin of soft fruits. Concise wine list and friendly service. Sunday night cabaret. *Seats 70. Private Room 40. L 12-4 (Sun to 4) D 6.30-10.30. Closed L Sat, all Bank Holidays. Set D £13.95. Access, Amex, Diners, Visa.*

BRISTOL   Jurys Bristol Hotel   66%   £92

Tel 0117 923 0333 Fax 0117 923 0300   Map 13 F1   **H**
Prince Street Bristol Avon BS1 4QF

New owners have brought not only a new name (it was formerly the *Unicorn*) but also a complete refurbishment of the bedrooms. Their number has been reduced as pairs of what were small singles have been knocked into one to create spacious rooms with fitted oak furniture, good sofas (in the doubles) or proper armchairs (in the twins), all in the same positive, pleasing colour scheme. All have spotless new bathrooms. A galleried conservatory makes the most of the hotel's waterside location with a colonial-style bar on the gallery above and a café below where tables spill out on to the cobbled quayside. Extensive conference facilities are well separated from the rest of the hotel and have their own entrance and bar. The hotel has no parking of its own but is right next to a multi-storey where guests have free parking overnight (5.30pm-9am). Check in before parking as room keys give direct access to bedroom floors at each level of the car park. 24hr room service. *Rooms 187. Access, Amex, Diners, Visa.*

BRISTOL   Restaurant Lettonie   ★   £80

Tel 0117 968 6456 Fax 0117 968 6943   Map 13 F1   **R**
9 Druid Hill Stoke Bishop Bristol Avon BS9 1EW

Martin Blunos combines natural talent with true dedication to produce the kind of dishes that makes the effort of finding this small restaurant (just seven tables) in suburban Bristol well worthwhile. The house is in a shopping arcade, and the surroundings do not immediately give a hint of the thought, skill and enterprise that go in to the cooking. Everything on the menus bears the Blunos stamp of individuality, like his starters of pan-fried scallops on parsnip purée, finished with chicken juices, duck and calvados terrine with toasted brioche or glazed pheasant with foie gras and sauerkraut. Main dishes show the same confidence with flavour combinations as in baked brill fillet with a caviar butter sauce, roast calf's sweetbreads with smoked bacon and a Noilly Prat cream sauce, rump of lamb with garlic fritters and a thyme leaf sauce or pig's trotter with a port sauce. As well as the cheeseboard there's goat's cheese tortellini with a lemon butter sauce and desserts such as chocolate marquise with a bitter orange sorbet and orange cream sauce or a vanilla and poppyseed parfait with macerated blueberries. The set menus offer two or three choices per course. Most wines on the modest list are French; practically all the classic clarets can only be found among the bin ends. *Seats 24. L 12.30-2 D 7-9. Closed Sun & Mon, 2 weeks Aug, 2 weeks Christmas. Set L £17.95 Set D £23.50 (Tue-Thurs) & £39.50. Access, Amex, Visa.*

BRISTOL   Markwicks   £65

Tel & Fax 0117 9262658   Map 13 F1   **R**
43 Corn Street Bristol Avon BS1 1HT

Right in the heart of the old merchant quarter of the city, in some converted vaults, you'll find Stephen and Judy Markwick's elegant little restaurant. The slightly unusual decor – elegance combined with fun touches – is typical also of Stephen's cooking, which he performs with an assured hand and an element of panache. There are set menus as well as a carte, from which you might be offered pan-fried scallops with sun-dried tomato risotto, crispy duck salad with a walnut and ginger dressing, breast of duck with

Puy lentils, shallots and Sauternes sauces, fillet steak with wild mushroom sauce or guinea fowl with apples and calvados. Delicious desserts such as old English rice pudding with spiced plums or hot chocolate soufflé pancakes (cooked to order, so be prepared for a 20 or so minute wait). A pleasing wine list features inexpensive, well-chosen house wines accompanied by tasting notes, and a good selection from around the world including some choice bin ends. *Seats 28. Parties 8. Private Room 16. L 12-2 D 7-10.30. Closed L Sat, all Sun, Bank Holiday Mon, 1 week Easter, 2 weeks Aug, 1 week Christmas. Set L £13.50/£16 Set D £21.50. Access, Amex, Visa.*

BRISTOL	Michael's Restaurant	£60

Tel 0117 927 6190   Map 13 F1   **R**
129 Hotwell Road Bristol Avon BS8 4RU

Long-established and popular Clifton venue where notable Victorian decor, including antiques, contributes to the sense of occasion. Typifying the menu are broccoli and almond soup, salad of chicken livers with toasted pine nuts, salmon on a saffron sauce, pigeon breasts on a Madeira jus with redcurrants and roast rack of lamb on a bed of roasted peppers with olives, tomato and basil. For dessert, try chocolate terrine with a crème de menthe sauce, crème brulée, or a trio of ice creams. Good selection of British farmhouse cheeses. Shortish wine list not lacking in quality, with brief tasting notes. No smoking in main dining-room. *Seats 50. Private Room 40. L (Sun only) 12-2.30 D 7-11. Closed D Sun, 26 Dec, 1 Jan, 4 days end Aug. Set L £9.95 Set D (2 course) £12.95 & £17.95. Access, Amex, Visa.*

BRISTOL	Rajdoot	£40

Tel 0117 926 8033   Map 13 F1   **R**
83 Park Street Bristol Avon BS1 5RJ

Part of a small group of Indian restaurants (other outlets in Birmingham, Manchester and Dublin) offering comfort, good service and decent cooking. All the familiar dishes, plus duck, venison and crab claws. *Seats 60. Parties 30. L 12-2.15 D 6.30-11.15. Closed L Sun & Bank Holidays, all 25 & 26 Dec. Set L from £6.95 Set D from £9.50. Access, Amex, Diners, Visa.*

BRISTOL	Redwood Lodge	64%	£94

Tel 01275 393901   Fax 01275 392104   Map 13 F1   **H**
Beggar Bush Lane Failand Bristol Avon BS8 3TG

Approximately ten minutes from the city centre (via Clifton Bridge) and quite close to exit 19 of the M5, Redwood Lodge offers conference facilities (for up to 250 delegates) and an impressive choice of leisure activities, notably five floodlit tennis courts and a dozen squash courts. Bedrooms, most of which are designated non-smoking, include 28 Executive rooms. Children up to 12 stay free in parents' room. Whitbread Country Club Resorts. *Rooms 108. Garden, croquet, indoor, outdoor & children's swimming pools, keep-fit equipment, sauna, steam room, solarium, beauty & hair salon, tennis, squash, badminton, snooker, children's playroom & playground, sports shop, 175-seat cinema, coffee shop (10.30am-10.30pm). Access, Amex, Diners, Visa.*

BRISTOL	Rodney Hotel	59%	£74

Tel 0117 973 5422   Fax 0117 946 7092   Map 13 F1   **H**
4 Rodney Place Clifton Down Road Bristol Avon BS8 4HY

Friendly little hotel set in a Georgian terrace in the heart of Clifton Village not far from Brunel's famed suspension bridge. There is no lounge, just a single reproduction sofa and chair in the reception hall, but a cosy cocktail bar overlooks a garden to the rear. Bedrooms are generally not large and some of the singles (about half the rooms) are very compact. All are well kept though, with simple shelf-type units, pale blue and peach colour schemes and all the usual amenities from hairdryer and trouser press to satellite TV. Half the neat bathrooms have shower and WC only. Bedrooms are all named after ships in the fleet of Admiral Rodney, who once lived here. There is no lift but two rooms are on the ground floor. Room service of snacks is available 24 hours a day. *Rooms 31. Garden. Access, Amex, Diners, Visa.*

Lodges are now listed by county in the reference section

BRISTOL	**Stakis Bristol Hotel**	61%	£117

Tel 01454 201144   Fax 01454 612022   Map 13 F1   **H**
Woodlands Lane Bradley Stoke Bristol Avon BS12 4JF

Modern low-rise hotel near junction 16 of the M5. Good-sized bedrooms have all the usual amenities. Club rooms are standard rooms with a few added extras: miniature of whisky, mineral water, fruit, chocolate. Open-plan public areas offer plenty of comfortable seating for meeting and greeting. 24hr room service. *Rooms 111. Garden, indoor swimming pool, spa bath, solarium. Access, Amex, Diners, Visa.*

BRISTOL	**Swallow Royal Hotel**	76%	£120

Tel 0117 925 5100   Fax 0117 925 1515   Map 13 F1   **HR**
College Green Bristol Avon BS1 5TA

A Victorian hotel in one of the most favourable locations in Bristol next to the cathedral and overlooking the neat lawns of College Green. The original Victorian grandeur has been enhanced by a decor with firmly traditional leanings but which also has an elegantly fashionable touch. The polished red marble-floored foyer has beautiful lounges on each side furnished in a comfortable country house style with deep-cushioned settees arranged in well-spaced groups. Light refreshments and afternoon teas are served here. The cocktail bar features huge Oriental murals at either end and a bar with gleaming glass and silverware. All the bedrooms, apart from a few smaller, inward-facing rooms, are spacious, with two armchairs and a writing desk. Every room has a whole host of extras from mini-bars with complimentary mineral water and fresh milk to irons and ironing boards for those who must press to impress. Coloured marble bathrooms have super-strong showers and most have bidets though a few, where space is more limited, have large corner baths instead. There are ten small suites with cosy sitting rooms and spa baths in their bathrooms. *Rooms 242. Indoor swimming pool, sauna, sun bed, spa bath, beauty & hair salons, keep-fit equipment, news kiosk. Access, Amex, Diners, Visa.*

Palm Court Restaurant   £70

The grand Palm Court extends up through three floors lined in Bath stone with curved balustrades and topped by stained-glass skylights. The à la carte is modern in style, taking inspiration from numerous sources: seared langoustines and scallops on a carrot and soy dressing with sesame mangetout, osso buco of monkfish(!) with squid noodles and orange oil, and loin of venison with chive creamed potatoes and baby leeks. The day's 'concept' menu (priced for two, three or four courses) offers a choice only at the main dish stage and is designed to be a balanced meal showing off the creativity of the kitchen. Service is formal yet unfussy. *Seats 60. Parties 8. D only 7.30-10.30. Closed Sun & Bank Holidays. Set D £21/£24/£27.*

BRIXHAM	**Quayside Hotel**	59%	£78

Tel 01803 855751   Fax 01803 882733   Map 13 D3   **H**
King Street Brixham Devon TQ5 9TJ

This appropriately-named hotel was originally six fisherman's cottages and the natural theme persists in the little downstairs bar. Bedrooms are all different in shape and size but all are well equipped, though bathrooms tend to be on the small side. The hotel's car park (30 spaces) is 350 yards away in Ranscombe Road. *Rooms 30. Closed Christmas & New Year. Access, Amex, Diners, Visa.*

BROADHEMBURY	**Drewe Arms**		£50

Tel 01404 841267   Map 13 E2   **R**
Broadhembury Devon EX14 0NF

Cooking with a Swedish accent in a small 15th-century thatched pub. Seafood features prominently on the blackboard menu in simple preparations like langoustines with garlic mayonnaise, marinated herrings with a glass of aquavit, Dover sole with chive butter and sea bass with ginger and lemon grass. Also gravad lax, crab and lobster. Bar menu as an alternative. *Seats 40. Parties 14. L 12-2 D 6-10. Set L & D £17.95. Closed D Sun. No credit cards.*

Set menu prices may not always include service or wine.

BROADWAY	Broadway Hotel	60%	£70

Tel 01386 852401   Fax 01386 853879   Map 14 C1   **H**
The Green Broadway Hereford & Worcester WR12 7AA

The Broadway began life as a monastic guest house, though most of the current building dates from around 1575, when it was a coaching inn. The interior courtyard now houses a pond, paved patio and white garden furniture rather than ostlers and horse troughs. Inside, the galleried lounge with its timbered gallery is an attractive feature. The bedrooms, decorated in pastel shades, are cosy, welcoming and immaculately maintained. *Rooms* 20. *Garden. Access, Amex, Diners, Visa.*

BROADWAY	Collin House	65%	£87

Tel 01386 858354   Map 14 C1   **HR**
Collin Lane Broadway Hereford & Worcester WR12 7PB

A Cotswold-stone house about a mile north-west of Broadway signposted off the A44 Evesham road (turn right at Collin Lane). John Mills and his friendly staff offer a warm welcome and plenty of advice on what to see and do in the neighbourhood (a book of handwritten notes is placed in each bedroom). Rooms are spacious and have a cottagey feel with country furnishings and pretty floral fabrics. Two rooms have four-poster beds. In the winter months blazing log fires bring cheer to the lounge and bar. 'No children under 7 except by prior discussion with parents.' *Rooms* 7. *Garden, croquet, outdoor swimming pool. Closed 24-28 Dec. Access, Visa.*

Restaurant   £60

In the oak-beamed restaurant great store is set by fresh local ingredients. 'Cotswold suppers' (minimum charge £11) are offered every evening except Saturdays, with the likes of macaroni cheese, steak and kidney pie, ham and vegetable bake and bread-and-butter pudding with brandy and cream. For the more gastronomically minded, the main menu (three-course meal priced according to main dish choice) is served in the candle-lit dining-room. Start, perhaps, with a crab and ginger soufflé with lemon grass sauce or home-cured gravlax, followed by a mixed fish grill with red pepper marmalade or noisettes of lamb with shallots, gherkins, chestnuts and a devilled sauce. Homely puds like treacle tart and Bramley apple and clove pie to finish. Tip-top bar and garden lunches (12-1.45) are also available and there's a traditional Sunday lunch (children welcome). Short wine list with all areas represented at fair prices. 'Fine wine' dinners are held every couple of months. Outdoor eating for 12 in the garden in good weather. *Seats* 24. *L* 12-1.45 *D* 7-9. *Set L* £15 *Set D from* £16.

BROADWAY	Dormy House	69%	£120

Tel 01386 852711   Fax 01386 858636   Map 14 C1   **HR**
Willersey Hill Broadway Hereford & Worcester WR12 7LF

Privately owned converted 17th-century farmhouse just off the A214, with views over the Vale of Evesham. Beams, exposed stonework and tiled floors set the tone in the main house, whose two homely lounges have fine bay windows. Converted outbuildings house cottagey, comfortable bedrooms, many also with timbered ceilings; two rooms have four-posters. Delegates at the purpose-built conference centre seem to appreciate the rustic, Cotswold-stone Barn Owl bar where less formal lunch and dinner menus are available (as well as afternoon tea). *Rooms* 49. *Garden, croquet, putting, sauna, steam room, gym, games room. Closed 25 & 26 Dec. Access, Amex, Diners, Visa.*

Restaurant   £90

A conservatory overlooks the garden and surrounding countryside, giving a brighter alternative to the more formal, dimly-lit dining-room. Alan Cutler is in charge of the kitchens, producing a wide range of English/French-inspired dishes on à la carte, table d'hote, gourmet and vegetarian menus. The table d'hote offers simple dishes such as grilled sirloin steak or Lincolnshire sausage, both with the traditional accompaniments, while the à la carte offers slightly more elaborate fare – terrine of monkfish with a mild curry mousse, fillet of beef with deep-fried beetroot and seared escalopes of tuna with grilled scallops and smoked gazpacho sauce. Fine cheeses are served with pecan rolls; sweets include a hot soufflé (notice required) and crepes flambés for two people. Ten house wines under £10, plenty of champagnes, but rather light in top-notch burgundies.

See over

However, there's a good selection of half-bottles and helpful tasting notes. *Seats 85. Parties 18. L 12.30-2 D 7.30-9.30. Closed L Sat, all 25 & 26 Dec. Set L £15/£17 Set D £26.50/£34.*

BROADWAY	Hunters Lodge	£65

Tel 01386 853247   Map 14 C1   **R**
High Street Broadway Hereford & Worcester WR12 7DT

A mellow, creeper-clad, Cotswold-stone building where cats sleep by a log fire in the bar, candles are the only illumination in the beamed restaurant and good, straightforward cooking is the order of the day. Typical dishes from the à la carte include crepe filled with prawns and stir-fried vegetables, confit of guinea fowl served warm with salad, grilled sole with lemon butter and devilled best end of lamb with a herb crust. Homely puds – crème caramel, trifle, cheesecake – are displayed on a side table. No children under 8 in the evening, but they're welcome for the weekend lunches (always a roast on Sunday). "Half portions for anyone – young or old!" *Seats 40. L (Sat & Sun only) 12.30-1.45 D (Thu-Sat only) 7.30-9.45. Closed L Thu & Fri, D Sun, all Mon-Wed, 3 weeks Feb, 3 weeks Aug, 3 days Christmas. Set L Sat £14 Sun £15. Access, Amex, Diners, Visa.*

BROADWAY	Lygon Arms	80%	£195

Tel 01386 852255   Fax 01386 858611   Map 14 C1   **HR**
High Street Broadway Hereford & Worcester WR12 7DU

Part of the Savoy Group, the hotel is quintessentially English in all the best possible ways. Enjoying a prominent position in the town since the 16th century, the front is in fact deceptive as thoughtful extensions at the rear go back some way. This is to accommodate the magnificent Country Club leisure complex, its centrepiece being the swimming pool and circular spa bath, overlooked by a gallery with comfortable seating that opens on to an outdoor terrace. For the most part, the hotel's interior enjoys real old-world charm with polished stone floors, low-beamed ceilings, wood panelling and imposing open fireplaces (even lit in summer) while the splendidly maintained bedrooms are furnished with antiques and country-style fabrics, yet provide modern amenities such as state-of-the-art satellite TV and wall safe. The bathrooms are modern too, with good toiletries, bathrobes (mini-robes for children and their own toilet bag) and vases of flowers. In fact, there are flowers everywhere – wonderful arrangements made up daily in the flower room. This a good place to bring children, who are warmly welcomed on arrival with their own play kits; there's a decent children's room service menu (or they can eat informally in the cosy and atmospheric hotel-owned Goblets wine bar next door), table tennis in the leisure complex, baby-sitting is available, and the family suites sharing a bathroom are ideal. Staff, under the dedicated and watchful eye of Managing Director Kirk Ritchie, succeed in being helpful and caring, and discreet and courteous, exemplified by the nightly-turn down service, the offer of a glass of sherry on arrival, and cleaning of car windscreens. Standards of housekeeping are superb throughout, and breakfast in the restaurant is a cut above the usual. Elegant conference facilities for up to 80. Ample parking. ***Rooms** 65. Garden, roof terrace, indoor swimming pool, spa bath, sauna, solarium, steam room, fitness studio, beauty salon, tennis, snooker, table tennis, lock-up garage, wine bar, valeting. Access, Amex, Diners, Visa.*

The Great Hall Restaurant   £85

A grand room with barrel-vaulted ceiling and heraldic frieze punctuated with stag's heads above oak wainscotting, a minstrel's gallery and no stinting on gas for the 'log' fire in its massive old stone fireplace. Tartan features in the uniform of attentive staff, who go about their work with just the right degree of friendliness but also the occasional lapse of concentration. In the kitchen first-rate ingredients are used to good effect in dishes that are full of interest without resort to gimmickry. Smoked game consommé (clear and bright) with herb dumplings, hot-pot of Cornish seafood with spicy loaf and a tartlet of caramelised red onion and curd cheese with a roasted tomato salad typify the à la carte starters, with main dishes like grilled halibut with baby leeks, apple marmalade and cider sauce; grilled fillets of thyme-marinated rabbit on fondant potato with chestnut and brandy sauce and pot-roasted Lunesdale duckling with cabbage cake and black peppercorn sauce supplemented by some straightforward char-grills. There's also a set (£25) three-course vegetarian menu. Desserts always include a Traditional Pudding of the Day like vanilla rice pudding with a compote of apricots. Good range of coffees and teas offered. Surprisingly for a hotel of this class we found no choice of bottled water, just Highland Spring. A well-balanced wine list with many fine names though you'll have to look carefully for value under £20, perhaps best found outside France. No children under 3 at night. No smoking. *Seats 120. Parties 20. Private Room 20. L 12.30-2 D 7.30-9.15. Set L £20.50 Set D £32.*

BROCKENHURST   **Balmer Lawn Hotel**   **65%**   **£90**

Tel 01590 623116   Fax 01590 623864   Map 14 C4   **H**
Lyndhurst Road Brockenhurst Hampshire SO42 72B

Lovely New Forest setting for a former hunting lodge, now a comfortable and friendly hotel which accommodates both leisure and business visitors (banqueting/conferences for up to 100). Rooms with a forest view and superior rooms attract a supplement. Children up to 16 stay free in parents' bedrooms; three family rooms. Plenty of leisure facilities both inside and out. Ladbroke Hotels, Hilton associate. **Rooms** 55. *Garden, croquet, indoor & outdoor swimming pools, gym, squash, sauna, spa bath, tennis, table tennis. Access, Amex, Diners, Visa.*

BROCKENHURST   **Careys Manor**   **65%**   **£109**

Tel 01590 623551   Fax 01590 622799   Map 14 C4   **H**
Brockenhurst Hampshire SO42 7QH

A much-extended manor house eight miles from Junction 1 of the M27 (follow signs on the A337 for Lyndhurst and Lymington). In the high-ceilinged, airy modern lounge deep-cushioned seating offers relaxation, while more active moments can be passed in the Carat Club's leisure facilities. Most of the accommodation is in the garden wing (reached via rather characterless corridors) and includes more spacious Knightwood rooms with balconies or patios overlooking the walled garden; necessary bedroom refurbishment was planned for 1995. Six rooms have four-posters. **Rooms** 79. *Garden, croquet, putting, mountain bikes, children's playground, indoor swimming pool, gym, sauna, spa bath, steam room, solarium, beauty treatment. Access, Amex, Diners, Visa.*

BROCKENHURST   **Le Poussin**   ★   **£75**

Tel 01590 623063   Map 14 C4   **R**
The Courtyard 49-55 Brookley Road Brockenhurst Hampshire SO42 7RB

A charmingly intimate restaurant off a flowery courtyard (there are four tables for alfresco dining) reached via a passageway from the main street of the village. It's very much a family affair kept deliberately small, with Alex Aitken working in the kitchen while his wife Caroline and son Justin (who is also responsible for the well-selected wine list) run front of house in correct but friendly fashion. There are chicken prints on the walls, and the theme even extends to silver cruets on the elegantly set tables. The owners seek out the best of local produce, notably game, seafood and wild mushrooms. Nage of seafoods, loin fillet of pork with prunes and hot soufflé of passion fruit are typical of dishes which are always interesting but never too elaborate. Terrines appear as both starters and desserts (white chocolate and strawberries); there are some fine British cheeses, and coffee comes with irresistible petits fours. There are some good wines on a list that could be more informative: for instance, the most expensive Alsace is listed as "Gewurztraminer Vindage" (sic) 1983 £45. No young red burgundies – two from 1989, the rest older. No smoking. *Seats 24. Parties 10. L 12-1.30 D 7-9. Closed D Sun, all Mon & Tue. Set L £10/£15 (Sun £17.50) Set D £20/£25. Access, Visa.*

Consult the blue pages for summary tables and lists of
recommended establishments.

BROCKENHURST   Rhinefield House Hotel   68%   £110

Tel 01590 622922   Fax 01590 622800   Map 14 C4   **H**
Rhinefield Road Brockenhurst Hampshire SO42 7QB

A splendid neo-Elizabethan house built in the 1890s set in 40 acres of ornamental gardens
in the heart of the New Forest, reached via a long drive signposted Rhinefield from the
A35 west of Lyndhurst. The original building houses time-share apartments and some
impressive public rooms used for meetings during the week and weddings at weekends.
All but two of the hotel bedrooms – large, and comfortable rather than luxurious – are
in a low-rise extension. Some rooms look out over the fine formal gardens, which feature
'canals' and a maze in the style of Hampton Court Palace. The main bar/lounge
is spacious and an attractive rattan-furnished Orangery offers additional lounge seating.
24hr room service; beds turned down in the evening. The leisure club has striking decor
based on the lost city of Atlantis. Good breakfasts. Friendly staff. *Rooms 34. Garden,
outdoor swimming pool, plunge pool, gym, sauna, spa bath, steam room, solarium, tennis,
games room. Access, Amex, Diners, Visa.*

BROME   The Oaksmere   67%   £75

Tel 01379 870326   Fax 01379 870051   Map 10 C2   **H**
Brome Eye Suffolk IP23 8AJ

The Oaksmere is just off the A140 Norwich to Ipswich road, two miles from Diss, and is
set in its own 20 acres of grounds which even include a cricket pitch. Ancient box and
yew topiary surrounds the part-Tudor, part-Victorian building. Stately oaks stand
proudly, and the driveway is lined with lime trees. On rough-hewn beams, time-worn
tiled floor and rustic furniture feature in the atmospheric bar and the rebuilt Victorian
conservatory makes a most appealing lounge and morning coffee room. Bedrooms in
the Tudor part have exposed timbers and oak furniture while those in the Victorian half
are furnished with antiques. *Rooms 11. Garden. Access, Amex, Diners, Visa.*

BROMLEY   Bromley Court   66%   £89

Tel 0181-464 5011 Fax 0181-460 0899   Map 11 B5   **H**
Bromley Hill Bromley Kent BR1 4JD

A large modern accommodation and conference block adjoins the original 1820s'
building at a popular hotel alongside the A21. The foyer serves as an airy lounge, and
there's a choice of attractive bars (one opens on to a patio overlooking the well-tended
gardens), plus a conservatory and coffee shop. Bedrooms of varying sizes are smartly
furnished in light wood or rattan, and bathrooms with tubs also have shower risers.
Families are well catered for with cots, extra beds and high-chairs available, and
a magician at the family Sunday lunch; children up to the age of 8 free in parents' room;
family rooms available. Saturday night dinner dances. Free membership of a local health
club, snooker club and night club. Some of the public areas have recently been
refurbished. *Rooms 118. Garden, croquet, putting, driving net. Access, Amex, Diners, Visa.*

BROMSGROVE   Bromsgrove Stakis   69%   £120

Tel 0121-447 7888 Fax 0121-447 7273   Map 14 B1   **H**
Birmingham Road Bromsgrove Hereford & Worcester B61 0JB

Modern hotel built around a charming garden courtyard, complete with fountains and
ponds, and offering large, well-designed bedrooms which include (with the businessman
in mind) a spacious, well-lit work desk with second telephone, a comfortable sofa and
mini-bar. Four rooms are adapted for the disabled; eight others are classified as Lady
Executive rooms, and there are ten King Suites. Banqueting for 60, conferences for 80.
Good bathrooms have marble vanity units and generous towelling. *Rooms 140. Garden,
indoor pool, sauna, steam room, solarium, whirlpool bath. Access, Amex, Diners, Visa.*

BROMSGROVE   Grafton Manor   70%   £125

Tel 01527 579007   Fax 01527 575221   Map 14 B1   **HR**
Grafton Lane Bromsgrove Hereford & Worcester B61 7HA

The Morris family have lived here since 1947 but it was only in the early 80s that they
opened this mellow, redbrick Elizabethan manor house, first as a restaurant and later
as a fully-fledged hotel which soon became known for its warm welcome and easy-going
atmosphere. The first-floor Great Parlour with its ribbed ceiling, red velvet walls,
splendid old fireplace and brown draylon sofas and armchairs is the sole day room

– there's a bar in one corner. All but one of the spacious bedrooms, which include two full suites, feature welcoming gas-log fires and offer extras like fresh fruit, mineral water and sherry. Furniture is antique – some pieces finer than others – and decor mostly William Morris. Six acres of grounds include a lake and water gardens. No dogs. *Rooms 9. Garden, croquet. Access, Amex, Diners, Visa.*

Restaurant £75

The same rich, gold, velvet fabric of the curtains also covers the walls of the 18th-century dining-room here but the big attraction is Simon Morris's enthusiastic cooking that makes good use of both the hotel's extensive herb garden and local produce – Simon is a keen shot and provides many of the wild duck that feature on the menu in season. His other great interest is Indian cuisine, so the fixed-price menus might include the likes of potato bondas filled with brinjal pickle served with chana dal and Mogul beef cooked with dried figs with a cardamom sauce alongside goat's cheese on a crouton with black olives and thyme, lamb's liver with bacon and green peppercorns and chicken casserole with bacon, mushrooms and sun-dried tomatoes on a bed of pasta. A separate vegetarian menu includes interesting choices at each stage. Excellent home-baked bread. No smoking. *Seats 40. Parties 14. Private Room 22. L 12.30-1.30 D 7.30-9. Closed Sat. Set L £20.50 (Sun £18.50). Set D £24.95 & £31.50.*

BROMSGROVE	Jarvis Perry Hall	56%	£102

Tel 01527 579976   Fax 01527 575998   Map 14 B1   **H**
Kidderminster Road Bromsgrove Hereford & Worcester B61 7JN

In the centre of Bromsgrove, ivy-clad Perry Hall was once the home of the poet AE Housman (who wrote *A Shropshire Lad*). Bedrooms provide all the usual modern amenities. Children up to 12 can stay free in their parents' room. Free membership of local health and leisure club. Banqueting/conference facilities. *Rooms 58. Garden. Access, Amex, Diners, Visa.*

BROMSGROVE	Pine Lodge Hotel	64%	£97

Tel 01527 576600   Fax 01527 878981   Map 14 B1   **H**
Kidderminster Road Bromsgrove Hereford & Worcester B61 9AB

Large hotel with Spanish hacienda looks and a courtyard garden just out of town on the A448 towards Kidderminster. The Iberian theme continues in the stylish foyer with its terracotta-tiled floor and timbered ceiling but the Terrace lounge (snacks served throughout the day) is furnished with Lloyd Loom chairs. Bedrooms (of which the majority are very spacious Club rooms) feature darkwood furniture and boldly patterned fabrics. 24hr room service. Children up to 16 stay free in parents' room. Conference facilities for up to 200. *Rooms 114. Patio, children's playground, indoor swimming pool, gym, sauna, steam room, spa bath, sun bed, snooker, children's indoor play room (weekends), coffee shop (9am-10pm). Access, Amex, Diners, Visa.*

BROUGHTON	Broughton Park	65%	£96

Tel 01772 864087   Fax 01772 861728   Map 6 B1   **HR**
418 Garstang Road Broughton nr Preston Lancashire PR3 5JB

Half a mile from Junction 1 of the M55, Broughton Park is based on a handsome, redbrick Victorian manor house. An open-plan bar/lounge on three different levels serves equally well for the informal business meeting or a convivial drink before dinner. Bedrooms in the newer south wing are slightly to be preferred to those in the somewhat more dated east wing, though all are equally well equipped. Nine Executive rooms, three with four-poster beds, are the most spacious. Children up to 16 share parents' room free. Conference/banqueting facilities for 200/220. Whitbread Country Club Hotels. *Rooms 98. Garden, indoor swimming pool, gym, squash, sauna, spa bath, steam room, solarium, sun beds, beauty & hair salon, snooker. Access, Amex, Diners, Visa.*

Courtyard Restaurant £65

Within the original building, with a fine white marble fireplace, this pretty restaurant offers attentive service and competent cooking. The evening à la carte might encompass creamed smoked haddock with poached quail's eggs and fondant potatoes, salad of duck confit with warm brie, sautéed monkfish with spring onions and wholegrain mustard,

See over

baked fillet of beef with a brioche crust and roasted peppers, and interesting desserts. Short daily table d'hote with four main dishes including a fish dish and a roast. No smoking. Informal eating in the poolside restaurant. *Seats 110. Parties 8. Private Room 16. L 12-2 D 7-9.45. Closed L Sat, some Bank Holiday Mons. Set L £13.95 (Sun £11.50) Set D £19.*

BROXBOURNE   Cheshunt Marriott Hotel   66%   £85

Tel 01992 451245   Fax 01992 440120   Map 15 F2   **H**
Halfhide Lane Turnford Broxbourne Hertfordshire EN10 6NG

Three miles north of the M25 alongside the A10 and approached via the Broxbourne exit, this very modern hotel offers smart open-plan public areas and bedrooms with either a king-size or two queen-size beds. Half overlook a pretty and peaceful inner courtyard with ground-floor rooms having patios. Power showers are a plus in the compact bathrooms. Three rooms are specially adapted for disabled guests. Ample parking. 24hr room service and 24hr reception. Room rates are flat rates with a maximum of 2 adults and 2 children. £20 for additional roll-away beds. *Rooms 150. Garden, indoor swimming pool, gym, spa bath, news kiosk. Access, Amex, Diners, Visa.*

BROXTED   Whitehall   69%   £105

Tel 01279 850603   Fax 01279 850385   Map 10 B3   **HR**
Church End Broxted Essex CM6 2BZ

Getting to Junction 8 of the M11 is easy enough but the ensuing journey to the hotel becomes progressively more difficult (ask for directions when booking). The hotel stands on the outskirts of a village overlooking rolling Essex countryside. The original Elizabethan manor house has been much extended, in keeping with the original style, and creates a comfortable country hotel. The interior is characterised by ancient oak beams and rough plaster walls which have been skilfully combined with modern amenities. There's a quite simply appointed bar which leads into a small sitting room dominated by the lounge behind it. Bedrooms are of good size and are furnished in a uniform scheme of cream fabrics and blond woods each possessing thoughtful extras like bathrobes and quality toiletries in the spacious bathrooms, some of which have separate shower cubicles. Free parking for 60 cars. No dogs. *Rooms 25. Garden, outdoor swimming pool, tennis. Access, Amex, Diners, Visa.*

Restaurant   £80

♔ 🍶 ❦ 🍇 🍓 🍺

The ancient timbered dining-room features a huge redbrick inglenook fireplace and a pretty, summery decor with just a few tables having views over a neat walled garden. The ambitious modern menu, abbreviated at lunchtime, is priced according to the number of courses taken. Starters include a warm game sausage with onions, chives and a hot beetroot sauce, pan-fried langoustines with a lobster sauce or smoked haddock cream soup. Main dishes could be casseroled lamb noisettes with pearl barley, sea bream with stir-fried vegetables, calf's liver with bacon and cabbage or loin of hare with apple and celeriac rösti. An extensive selection of vegetables accompanies. To finish there's a gratin of red fruits, meringue swans with fruit, coffee and cinnamon cheesecake or a reasonable hot mango soufflé. Champagne or nothing here – unusually, not one sparkling wine on the list. Cheerful staff. *Seats 40. Private Room 18. L 12.30-2 D 7.30-9.30 (Sun to 8.30). Set L £19.50 Set D from £27.50.*

BROXTON   Carden Park Hotel   71%   £125

Tel 01829 731000   Fax 01829 250539   Map 6 A3   **H**
Carden Park Broxton nr Chester Cheshire CH3 9DQ

Formerly called *The Birches*, this now more helpfully named hotel is at the heart of Carden Park (main entrance on the A534 to the west of its junction with the A41) with its golf course and wealth of other sporting and leisure facilities. The hotel looks a little like an executive housing estate with the high-quality bedroom accommodation (about 30% are full suites) located within a number of detached, redbrick, two-storey buildings set around brick-paved courtyards. All have the same stylish furniture and fabrics plus facilities that include two telephone lines, high-tech TV with numerous satellite channels, interactive CDI player for which games can be hired (the golf game is particularly addictive), a mini 'butler's pantry' with fridge and sink (room service offers Continental breakfast and sandwiches throughout the day and evening), a small 'dressing room' area and most have a fireplace – offering the possibility of a real fire – and balcony.

Bathrooms are appointed to the same high standard as the bedrooms. Public areas are dispersed between the reception building, which has a limited amount of lounge seating, an unusual 'bandstand' bar at the centre of the restaurant and, about 50 yards from the main complex, the Par 3 Brasserie which incorporates bar, brasserie and golf shop arranged open-plan style under a pitched timber roof. *Rooms 83. Garden, croquet, golf (18), driving range, golf shop, plunge pool, keep-fit equipment, spa bath, steam room, bowls, boules, mountain bikes, 4-wheel drive vehicles & course. Amex Access, Diners, Visa.*

BUCKLAND	Buckland Manor	80%	£178

Tel 01386 852626 Fax 01386 853557   Map 14 C1
Buckland nr Broadway Gloucestershire WR12 7LY

Oriental rugs strewn over parquet floors, fine paintings, an abundance of fresh flowers (even in the depths of winter when several log fires warm the day rooms), antiques and objets d'art all add up to a true country-house atmosphere at this tranquil Cotswold-stone manor, which dates back to the 13th century. Largely antique-furnished bedrooms live up to the promise of the public areas with sofas, porcelain ornaments, fresh fruit, mineral water and flowering plants all contributing to the 'house-guest' feel. Bathrooms are equally well appointed, some with twin wash basins, many with walk-in showers in addition to the tub and all with generously sized bathrobes and quality toiletries. The setting is both beautiful, in ten acres of grounds that include rose and water gardens. No children under 12. No dogs. *Rooms 14. Garden, croquet, tennis, putting, outdoor swimming pool.Access, Amex, Visa*

Restaurant   **£95**

Cream-painted panelling and stone-mullioned windows on three sides create a light airy room which, with tapestry upholstered chairs around widely spaced tables, combines elegance with comfort. In the kitchen, chef Martyn Pearn applies sound traditional skills to a well-judged à la carte that might include a pressed terrine of Dover sole, langoustines and shredded root vegetables or pithiviers of goat's cheese with a light walnut cream among the starters and main courses such as sautéed Cornish scallops with a sauce of orange juice, cream and green peppercorns, or fillet of Angus beef served in an artichoke heart, topped with fresh duck foie gras and truffle sauce. Interesting desserts (corn tart with poached pears and butterscotch sauce, Bramley apple and sultana pie with crème anglaise); farmhouse cheeses. A very grandly presented list annotates each wine. Some wines are reasonably priced (note the house selection), whereas the classic clarets seem erratically marked up. No smoking. *Seats 40. Parties 10. L 12.30-1.45 D 7.30-9. Set L £22.70 (Sun £22.50).*

BUCKLER'S HARD	Master Builder's House		£85

Tel 01590 616253 Fax 01590 616297   Map 15 D4   **I**
Buckler's Hard nr Beaulieu Hampshire SO42 7XB

Master Builder Henry Adams should still recognise the house, as the 18th-century building has been converted and extended sympathetically in meeting 20th-century requirements. Maritime memorabilia are never far away; heavy beams and rustic furnishings make the welcoming bars popular with yachtsmen and tourists alike, while residents have their own homely lounge with easy chairs, period furniture and a large inglenook fireplace. Creaky floorboards and old-world charm make the six bedrooms in the main house appealing; rooms in a purpose-built block are plainer but well equipped. The hotel's grounds run down to the Beaulieu River. *Rooms 23. Garden. Access, Amex, Visa.*

BUNBURY	Wild Boar	67%	£75

Tel 01829 260309 Fax 01829 261081   Map 6 B3   **H**
Whitchurch Road Bunbury nr Beeston Cheshire CW6 9NW

On the A49 Whitchurch to Warrington road, in the shadow of Beeston Castle, the Wild Boar is a handsome 17th-century hunting lodge with impressive, black and white timbered exterior. A lofty foyer-lounge and decent-sized bedrooms are in a modern, sympathetically designed building that adjoins the original. *Rooms 37. Garden. Access, Amex, Diners, Visa.*

BURFORD	Bay Tree	67%	£110

Tel 01993 822791   Fax 01993 823008   Map 14 C2   **H**
Sheep Street Burford Oxfordshire OX8 4LW

Situated just off the main street, the charming Bay Tree was built in 1584 for Sir Lawrence Tanfield, Chief Baron of the Exchequer in the reign of Elizabeth I. Much later it was a training school before becoming a hotel in 1938. Oak beams, flagstones and good solid furnishings give the day rooms a homely, traditional feel and bedrooms are in keeping (some have four-posters that are said never to have left the building). Ten rooms are in a cottage, while others overlook an attractive terraced garden; there are also two suites and three junior suites. *Rooms 23. Garden, croquet. Access, Amex, Diners, Visa.*

BURFORD	Lamb Inn		£86

Tel 01993 823155   Fax 01993 822228   Map 14 C2   **IR**
Sheep Street Burford Oxfordshire OX18 4LR

The mellow charm of the 14th-century Lamb Inn, tucked down a quiet side street in one of the Cotswolds' most attractive towns, is most appealing. Public rooms range from a rustic bar at one end of the building to a chintzy lounge at the other with in between a combination of the two featuring rugs on flagstone floor, a collection of brass ornaments over the fireplace, a display of china figurines on a window shelf and antique furniture – all polished and buffed to please the most exacting housekeeper. Real log fires burn for most of the year and there is a very pretty walled garden to take advantage of the English summer. Cottagey, antique-furnished bedrooms are equally appealing with old beams or pretty floral wall coverings and matching curtains at the generally small windows. Bathrooms vary from spacious to miracles of compactness, mostly with Victorian-style brass fittings and wood-panelled tubs. Bedrooms now all have telephones. Dogs (£5 per night) by arrangement only. *Rooms 16. Garden. Closed 25 & 26 Dec. Access, Visa.*

Restaurant £70

Chef Pascal Clavand's à la carte is sensibly short (about six main dishes) but with the daily changing table d'hote you won't feel pushed for choice. Rack of lamb on a blackcurrant and pepper sauce, red mullet baked in ginger and sherry on a stir-fry of winter vegetables with hollandaise sauce and medallions of pork with a peanut and chili cream show the style. Lunchtime snacks served 12-2 in the bar and lounge (except where Sunday lunch which commences with Bucks Fizz and offers a choice of roasts and 'the sweet table'). Modest and inexpensive wine list. No smoking. *Seats 50. Parties 12. L (Sun only) 12-1.45 D 7.30-9 (Sun 7.30-8.30 buffet only). Set Sun L £17 Set D £23.*

BURLEY	Burley Manor	61%	£80

Tel 01425 403522   Fax 01425 403227   Map 14 C4   **H**
Burley nr Ringwood Hampshire BH24 4BS

A Victorian manor house surrounded by 54 acres of parkland in the heart of the New Forest. Families and dogs are encouraged. Period decor includes stone fireplaces, a creaky staircase with carved balustrade and unusual commode side-tables. Bedrooms are simply decorated and have smart bathrooms; converted stable-block rooms are the largest and have the best views over open fields, plus a couple of steps leading directly down to the lawns. Riding stables in the grounds offer rides in the New Forest for both novices and experts. Banquets for up to 60, conferences to 90. *Rooms 30. Garden, croquet, riding stables, outdoor swimming pool, hairdressing, putting, coarse fishing. Access, Amex, Diners, Visa.*

BURNHAM	Burnham Beeches Moat House	68%	£122

Tel 01628 603333   Fax 01628 603994   Map 15 E2   **H**
Burnham Buckinghamshire SL1 8DP

A lovely setting for an elegant Georgian building in ten acres of lawns, with period public areas and smart modern bedrooms (children up to 5 stay free in parents' room). There are two four-poster rooms in the Georgian part. 24hr room service. Banqueting/conferences for 150/180. *Rooms 73. Garden, croquet, tennis, indoor swimming pool, keep-fit equipment, sauna, steam room, spa bath, sun beds, games room. Access, Amex, Diners, Visa.*

BURNHAM   Jarvis Grovefield Hotel   63%   £85

Tel 01628 603131   Fax 01628 668078   Map 15 E2   **H**
Taplow Common Road Burnham Buckinghamshire SL1 8LP

Usefully located about 15 minutes from Heathrow and close to Junction 7 of the M4, in the heart of the Thames Valley, the Grovefield is surrounded by seven acres of its own grounds. Main business is probably banqueting and conferences – maximum capacity 170. Children under 12 share parents' room free. *Rooms 40. Garden, croquet, putting, bowling. Access, Amex, Diners, Visa.*

BURNHAM MARKET   Fishes   £40

Tel 01328 738588   Map 10 C1   **R**
Market Place Burnham Market Norfolk PE31 8HE

Gillian Cape's simple, homely, two-roomed restaurant enjoys a very visible and central location. Pine furniture and walls crammed with local artists' work create an attractive setting for a healthy selection of well-prepared fish and seafood dishes. The starter selection includes a thick, hearty and tomatoey crab soup, oysters – plain or baked with Stilton and garlic – and dressed Cromer crab with mayonnaise. Main courses range from local sea trout with cucumber sauce, and salmon fishcakes with crab sauce to turbot fillet with hollandaise, Dover sole on the bone and lobster served either cold with mayonnaise or boiled and accompanied by melted butter and, unusually, dry Martini. To finish there's a good choice of desserts such as meringue cake, sticky toffee pudding and lemon, orange and raisin cheesecake. *Seats 42. L 12-2 D 6.45-9.30. Closed D Sun, all Mon, 25 Dec, 3 weeks end Jan. Set £8.95/£11.25. Access, Amex, Diners, Visa.*

BURNHAM MARKET   Hoste Arms   £92

Tel 01328 738257   Map 10 C1   **I**
The Green Burnham Market nr King's Lynn Norfolk PE31 8HD

A handsome 17th-century inn occupying a prime position overlooking the green and parish church of a most picturesque village. It is one of the most popular inns along the Norfolk coast thanks partly to above-average pub food based on fresh local and seasonal produce. Accommodation is also a strong point, and upstairs beyond the small gallery/lounge are fifteen charming bedrooms, two boasting four-posters. Six more bedrooms, on the ground and first floors of a barn conversion, have recently come on stream. Spotless en-suite facilities and TVs, radios, tea-makers, telephones and hairdryers. First-rate breakfasts are served in the conservatory, which is also the venue for afternoon teas (free to residents). Ideally located for exploring the Norfolk coast and its many renowned bird reserves. *Rooms 21. Garden. Access, Visa.*

BURNLEY   Oaks Hotel   63%   £89

Tel 01282 414141   Fax 01282 33401   Map 6 B1   **H**
Colne Road Reedley Burnley Lancashire BB10 2LF

A grand Victorian town house standing back from the A56 between Brierfield and Burnley, a short distance from Junction 12 of the M65 and surrounded by four acres of gardens. The house was originally built for a tea and coffee merchant, and the impressive staircase hall, one of the principal public rooms, features a magnificent stained-glass window depicting the coffee and tea trades. Other rooms, many still with original decorative features, including fine panelling, are very traditional, with red leather chesterfields. Executive bedrooms are the best appointed and a few rooms are designated for family use. All rooms have queen-size beds and satellite TVs. *Rooms 54. Garden, indoor pool, keep-fit equipment, squash, sauna, spa bath, solarium, beauty salon. Access, Amex, Diners, Visa.*

BURTON-ON-TRENT   Riverside Inn   £67

Tel 01283 511234   Fax 01283 511441   Map 6 C3   **I**
Riverside Drive Branston Burton-on-Trent Staffordshire DE14 3EP

A privately-owned hotel on the banks of the River Trent, where it has fishing rights. Staff are friendly and helpful, and can direct visitors to local places of interest. Day rooms make good use of beams, linenfold panelling, copperware and greenery, and the bar has a little thatched roof. Bedrooms, which comprise 6 doubles and 16 singles, are not large but are very well kept, with remote-control TVs with satellite channels, tea/coffee-makers, irons and boards. Immaculate bathrooms (all with showers over tubs) boast quality toiletries. Conference/banqueting facilities for up to 150 delegates. Ample free parking. *Rooms 22. Garden, golf, fishing. Access, Amex, Visa.*

BURY   Normandie Hotel   64%   £83

Tel 0161-764 3869 Fax 0161-764 4866   Map 6 B1   **HR**
Elbut Lane Birtle nr Bury Greater Manchester BL9 6UT

To find the Normandie, a corner of France within a quintessentially English part of the
country, leave the M66 at Junction 2. Approach Willow Street from Wash Lane, then
turn right on the B6222, towards Rochdale, away from Bury. Look out for signs to Old
Birtle; the hotel is one mile up the narrow Elbut Lane. It makes an ideal base from which
to explore the countryside and at the same time is well situated for the business
communities of the North West. Furnishings in the individually decorated bedrooms
range from pastel-pale to dramatic-dark, but all rooms are comfortable and welcoming.
Luxury rooms are obviously larger and even more fully equipped. Standards of
housekeeping are high; staff are genuine, helpful and friendly. *Rooms 23. Garden.*
Closed 1 week Easter, 2 weeks from 26 Dec. Access, Amex, Diners, Visa.

Restaurant   ★   £80

The restaurant is much more than just an adjunct to the hotel, and the team of Gillian
and Max Moussa proudly and personally lead a front-of-house team that provides very
'correct' service. The cooking is still in the safe hands of Pascal Pommier, who has been
in charge of the kitchen here since 1988. The French menu is reassuringly mainstream in
inspiration whilst acknowledging modern trends: salmon fillet with a red wine sauce and
fennel, pressed terrine of maize-fed chicken with a walnut oil dressing, grilled tuna
(served rare) with a tomato vinaigrette, roast duck breast, ditto, with a blackcurrant sauce,
fillet of beef with port sauce and wild mushrooms. A very moreish hot toffee pudding
(from a list that could include warm rice pudding with exotic fruits, caramel mousse and
a dark chocolate marquise) makes a splendid finale. Copious tasting notes (some helpful,
some not) on an excellent and quite individual wine list that includes a good showing
from Australia and New Zealand alongside France making up the bulk of the list.
Seats 50. Parties 18. L 12-2 D 7-9.30 (Sat to 10). Closed L Sat & Mon, all Sun,
Bank Holidays (except 25 Dec). Set L £12.50/£15 Set D £18.95.

Lodges are now listed by county in the reference section

BURY ST EDMUNDS   Angel Hotel   66%   £85

Tel 01284 753926 Fax 01284 750092   Map 10 C2   **H**
Angel Hill Bury St Edmunds Suffolk IP33 1LT

Which came first, the hill or the hotel? Either way, the Angel is an integral part of the
town, and has been in continuous use as a hotel since 1452. It comprises several adjacent
buildings (the oldest part dating back to the 12th century) that gained a unifying façade in
Georgian times, and is now completely covered in Virginia creeper. Bedrooms come in
all shapes and sizes from large rooms with four-poster beds and antique furniture to small
singles with simple white-painted fitted units; all are in good order and individually
decorated – often quite stylishly. Bathrooms are decorated to match each room.
24hr room service. Ample parking. *Rooms 42. Access, Amex, Diners, Visa.*

BURY ST EDMUNDS   Butterfly Hotel   62%   £66

Tel 01284 760884 Fax 01284 755476   Map 10 C2   **H**
Symonds Road Bury St Edmunds Suffolk IP32 7BW

Take the Bury East exit from the A14 to the Butterfly, a modern low-riser with modest
accommodation. Delegate and private dining-rooms for up to 50/22. Under-8s free
in parents' room. *Rooms 66. Access, Amex, Diners, Visa.*

BURY ST EDMUNDS   Mortimer's   £45

Tel 01284 760623 Fax 01284 752561   Map 10 C2   **R**
31 Churchgate Street Bury St Edmunds Suffolk IP33 1RG

A well-established restaurant named after the artist Thomas Mortimer, whose seascapes
adorn the light and airy interior. The menu is totally fish-oriented (apart from a couple
of vegetarian options) and changes with the Grimsby catch. Regular supplies of salmon
and oysters come from Loch Fyne. Grilled sardines, Cromer crab, smoked cod's roe

or tiger prawns with a spicy peanut sauce could launch your meal, followed perhaps by pan-fried hake, skate with black butter, chargrilled salmon or halibut baked with mushrooms in a white wine and cheese sauce. Main courses are served with new potatoes. The luncheon special – maybe fish pie or smoked haddock kedgeree – is a popular order. Wines come from their shop next door. *Seats 72. Parties 12. Private Room 12. L 12-2 D 6.30-9 (Mon to 8.15). Closed L Sat, all Sun, Bank Holidays and day after, 2 weeks Aug Bank Holiday, 23 Dec-5 Jan. Access, Amex, Diners, Visa.*

BURY ST EDMUNDS	Suffolk Hotel	59%	£82

Tel 01284 753995   Fax 01284 750973   Map 10 C2   **H**
38 Buttermarket Bury St Edmunds Suffolk IP33 1DL

Handsome town-centre inn with all-day Suffolk pantry and Viking bar. Half the rooms are designated non-smoking. Under-16s free in parents' room. Forte Heritage. *Rooms 33. Access, Amex, Diners, Visa.*

CALBOURNE	Swainston Manor	66%	£83

Tel 01983 521121   Fax 01983 521406   Map 15 D4   **H**
Calbourne Isle of Wight PO30 4HX

Set in 32 acres of parkland, the manor is Georgian in appearance although much older in parts. Classical columns grace the spacious entrance hall and there is an elegantly proportioned drawing room. Bedrooms are of a good size and feature mahogany furniture and plenty of little extras – some have a jacuzzi. Receptions are held in a 12th-century chapel adjoining the main building. Children up to 11 stay free in parents' room. Freephone 0500 131257. *Rooms 14. Garden, indoor swimming pool, fishing. Access, Amex, Diners, Visa.*

CALSTOCK	Danescombe Valley Hotel	72%	£120

Tel & Fax 01822 832414   Map 12 C3   **HR**
Lower Kelly Calstock Cornwall PL18 9RY

In a magical, hidden valley where the Danescombe meets the Tamar on a wooded bend facing south, half a mile west of the village of Calstock is where you'll find the Danescombe Valley Hotel. Originally Lord Ashburton's private residence, the beautiful Georgian balconied house is the domain of Martin Smith and his Italian wife Anna. Together they have, over the last 10 years, created a most tranquil and comfortable hotel. In addition to the five bright and spotless, well-equipped bedrooms, there's also a separate cottage, just along the lane by the river, which is let on a self-catering basis, with special provision for dinner in the hotel. Breakfasts are "long, light and lazy affairs to provide a gentle start to the day". Note unusual closing times. No children under 12. No dogs. Commission added if you pay by credit card. *Rooms 5. Garden, mooring. Closed Wed & Thu, also Nov-end Mar (but open 4 days Christmas) Access, Amex, Diners, Visa.*

Restaurant   £70

Full bedrooms mean no non-resident dinner bookings can be taken, as the dining-room (non-smoking) is not huge, so the lucky few can enjoy Anna's delightful cooking, arranged as a well-balanced, 4-course daily-changing set menu (though she is happy to discuss special needs). Local produce is used whenever possible, and there's a subtle, modern Italian influence to the superb cooking. A typical carefully composed meal might begin with asparagus baked with Parma ham, chicken breast baked with peppers, served with a sun-dried tomato sauce. West Country unpasteurised farmhouse cheeses; mascarpone and chocolate tart; and tea or coffee to finish. A marvellously opinionated wine list is presented partly by grape variety, partly by style and partly by region. Super Italian section, super prices throughout. No smoking. *Seats 12. Parties 8. D only at 8. Set D £27.50.*

We publish annually, so make sure you use the current edition. It's well worth it!

CAMBERLEY — Frimley Hall — 68% — £115

Tel 01276 28321   Fax 01276 691253   Map 15 E3   **H**
Portsmouth Road Camberley Surrey GU15 2BG

A short distance from Junction 3 of the M3, a turn-of-the-century Victorian manor house surrounded by splendid grounds that are floodlit at night. Magnificent stained-glass windows overlook an impressive carved wooden staircase – Victorian style that is carried through to the traditionally furnished main-house bedrooms, a few of which have four-poster beds. However, most of the bedrooms are located in a modern extension and are smaller, but equally appealing; several are designated non-smoking. Families are well catered for and children up to 16 stay free in parents' room. Conference and meeting rooms have Victorian character as well and cater for up to 70 delegates. Forte. *Rooms 66. Garden. Access, Amex, Diners, Visa.*

CAMBERLEY — Tithas — £30

Tel 01276 65803   Map 15 E3   **R**
31 High Street Camberley Surrey GU15 3RE

Mildly spicy, north Indian/Bengali cooking in modest surroundings. Meat and vegetarian set meals (thali) offer particularly good value. Specials include garlic chicken and lamb or chicken tikka masala. *Seats 65. Private Room 16. L 12-2.30 D 6-12. Closed 25 & 26 Dec. Access, Amex, Diners, Visa.*

CAMBRIDGE — Arundel House — 60% — £73

Tel 01223 367701   Fax 01223 367721   Map 15 F1   **H**
53 Chesterton Road Cambridge Cambridgeshire CB4 3AN

Overlooking the River Cam and open parkland beyond, Arundel House is popular with business people as well as tourists. Privately owned, the hotel is well maintained throughout with pleasing traditional standards of accommodation. There is however no provision of room service and no lifts, though the top floors enjoy splendid views. New this year is a large Victorian style extension to the rear of the hotel housing an all-day bistro. Conference facilities for 50; own parking for 70. No dogs. *Rooms 105. Garden, laundrette and ironing room. Closed 25 & 26 Dec. Access, Amex, Diners, Visa.*

CAMBRIDGE — Cambridge Lodge Hotel — 58% — £70

Tel 01223 352833   Fax 01223 355166   Map 15 F1   **H**
Huntingdon Road Cambridge Cambridgeshire CB3 0DQ

A mock-Tudor building standing in a secluded garden on the outskirts of the city. Three of the bedrooms have shower/washbasin only; top of the range is the bridal suite. The Garden Room is used for small meetings or conferences. *Rooms 11. Garden. Closed 27-30 Dec. Access, Amex, Diners, Visa.*

CAMBRIDGE — Cambridgeshire Moat House — 63% — £97

Tel 01954 249988   Fax 01954 780010   Map 15 F1   **H**
Bar Hill Cambridge Cambridgeshire CB3 8EU

Well-designed modern hotel on the A604 with extensive leisure facilities, function suites and a variety of bars and restaurants. Bedrooms are well equipped, with all the usual gadgets. Children up to 15 stay free in parents' room. Recent improvements include bedroom refurbishment and computerised reception. *Rooms 99. Garden, croquet, tennis, golf (18), putting, indoor swimming pool, children's splash pool, gym, squash, sauna, spa bath, steam room, solarium, pool table. Access, Amex, Diners, Visa.*

CAMBRIDGE — Charlie Chan — £45

Tel 01223 359336   Map 15 F1   **R**
14 Regent Street Cambridge Cambridgeshire CB1 2DB

The simply appointed ground-floor dining-room and the much plusher, air-conditioned Blue Lagoon upstairs offer the same selection of Chinese dishes. There are set meals for two or more, and the lengthy à la carte runs from a hot platter of prawns, wun tun, seaweed, squid, spring roll and spare ribs through soups, seafood (a speciality), beef, pork and poultry (book the Peking roast duck in advance) to bean curd, vegetables and crushed red bean pancake. Reliable cooking, good serving staff. The Blue Lagoon provides a night-club ambience, with musical entertainment at weekends. *Seats 160. Parties 100. L 12-2.15 D 6-11.15. Closed 25 & 26 Dec. Set meals from £13.20 per person (minimum 2 persons). Access, Amex, Visa.*

| CAMBRIDGE | Forte Posthouse | 67% | £75 |

Tel 01223 237000   Fax 01223 233426   Map 15 F1   **H**
Lakeview Bridge Road Cambridge Cambridgeshire CB4 4PH

Well geared to the needs of private guests, families and business people, this smart modern hotel stands at the junction of the A45 and B1049. Half the bedrooms are designated non-smoking. *Rooms 118. Garden, indoor swimming pool, keep-fit equipment, sauna, spa bath, solarium, children's playground & playroom. Access, Amex, Diners, Visa.*

| CAMBRIDGE | Garden House Moat House | 69% | £153 |

Tel 01223 259988   Fax 01223 316605   Map 15 F1   **H**
Granta Place Mill Lane Cambridge Cambridgeshire CB2 1RT

A modern hotel in the city centre, yet enjoying ample parking and riverside frontage; the hotel also owns the adjacent boatyard which hires out most of the punts to be seen on the Cam. The smart cocktail bar and lounge take full advantage of the setting, with the conservatory extensions and patio beyond. Standardised bedrooms offer good levels of comfort and most (attracting a supplement) overlook the river and meadows. Meeting rooms for up to 250 – the River Suite has its own entrance from the car park; Peterhouse, Cambridge's oldest college, offers additional facilities. Children up to 16 free in their parents' room. No dogs. Queens Moat Houses. *Rooms 118. Garden, fishing, punting, gift shop, coffee shop (10.30am-10pm). Access, Amex, Diners, Visa.*

| CAMBRIDGE | Gonville Hotel | 62% | £87 |

Tel 01223 66611   Fax 01223 315470   Map 15 F1   **H**
Gonville Place Cambridge Cambridgeshire CB1 1LY

An extended Victorian house overlooking the 25 acres of Parker's Piece. The ground floor is smartly attired in emerald green, brick red and cherry with an open-plan reception leading to a spacious and attractively bright and airy, Lloyd Loom-furnished bar/lounge at the rear. Smart, colourful bedrooms, where a refurbishment programme continues, are up-to-date, with chintzy fabrics and well-co-ordinated decorative schemes. The hotel has its own free parking for 80 cars. Children up to 12 free in parents' room. Banqueting and conference facilities for up to 200. *Rooms 65. Access, Amex, Diners, Visa.*

| CAMBRIDGE | Holiday Inn | 68% | £124 |

Tel 01223 464466   Fax 01223 464440   Map 15 F1   **H**
Downing Street Cambridge Cambridgeshire CB2 3DT

Modern behind its neo-classical facade, the Holiday Inn stands right in the heart of the city (follow signs towards Lion Yard). An escalator leads up from the marble-floored lobby to the first-floor reception desk and atrium-style, open-plan public areas. Air-conditioned bedrooms are the standard Holiday Inn product, combining comfort with practicality. Executive rooms get various extras plus the beds turned down in the evening. Half the accommodation is designated non-smoking. Children up to 19 stay free in parents' room. Free parking for 70 cars. Several meeting rooms can cater for up to 150 delegates. *Rooms 199. Courtyard garden, indoor swimming pool, children's play room. Access, Amex, Diners, Visa.*

| CAMBRIDGE | Regent Hotel | 57% | £74 |

Tel 01223 351470   Fax 01223 566562   Map 15 F1   **HR**
41 Regent Street Cambridge Cambridgeshire CB2 1AB

Run by the Paschalis family since 1960, and substantially modernised in recent years, the Regent offers good practical accommodation and a friendly atmosphere close to the city centre. Bedrooms are not large but come with all the usual amenities from trouser press and hairdryer to multi-channel TV. The 12 non-smoking rooms have recently been refurbished with matching bedcovers and curtains and good-quality lightwood furniture; others, though still acceptable, were due to get the same treatment during 1995. Practical bathrooms all have showers over bathtubs. A comfortable residents' lounge looks out, as do half the bedrooms, on to the green expanse of Parker's Piece. There is also a small cocktail bar. No room service is advertised but sandwiches and drinks will be served throughout the day and evening; there is no night porter. Free parking for 6 cars. No dogs. *Rooms 25. Closed 1 week Christmas. Access, Amex, Diners, Visa.*

See over

Verdi's £35

Although connected to the hotel, this bright and cheerful Italian restaurant has a separate main entrance on Regent Street. The shortish menu offers good value with a hearty minestrone soup (made to an old family recipe) and half a dozen or so antipasti to start plus pasta dishes (priced as either starters or mains) where one can mix and match various pasta shapes with a range of sauces like pesto, tomato and bolognese; and a handful of meat dishes. Good home-made bread rolls but ask which of the desserts, written up on a blackboard, are made in-house as most are bought in. *Seats 55. L 12-2 D 6-10.*

CAMBRIDGE	22 Chesterton Road	£55

Tel 01223 351880 Map 15 F1 **R**
22 Chesterton Road Cambridge Cambridgeshire CB4 3AX

By day David Carter and Louise Crompton both lecture at the local Hotel School, at night they practise what they teach at their charming, candle-lit restaurant set in a period town house to the north of the city centre on the inner ring road. The monthly-changing, fixed-price menu offers four choices at each stage with supplements for an optional fish course and the cheese (a plated selection of four British) if the latter is taken in addition to the pud. Head chef Chris Gorham is a former pupil who copes with dishes that acknowledge modern trends, such as watercress soup with spinach gnocchi, chicken liver terrine in filo pastry with red onion marmalade, ragout of fish in a saffron and herb stock, casserole of wild boar with haricot beans, grilled red mullet with ratatouille and tapénade and, for vegetarians, a ravioli of mushrooms and sun-dried tomatoes. Desserts might encompass both poached pear in tuile basket with chocolate sauce, and a traditional Spotted Dick with sauce anglaise. Four dessert wines to accompany are offered by the glass. Smokers must hang on until everyone has completed their main courses. *Seats 30. Private Room 12. L by arrangement D 7-10. Closed Sun, Mon & 1 week Christmas. Access, Amex, Visa.*

CAMBRIDGE	University Arms	65%	£115

Tel 01223 351241 Fax 01223 315256   Map 15 F1 **H**
Regent Street Cambridge Cambridgeshire CB2 1AD

19th-century hotel, with later additions, on one corner of Parker's Piece (a historic green space near the city centre). Focus of the public rooms is the central Octagon Lounge with nice plasterwork ceiling, impressive Venetian glass chandelier, attentive and friendly lounge service and a real log fire in winter. Although details of repair are not perfect the generally good-sized bedrooms are comfortable and attractively decorated with matching floral bedcovers and curtains, those in the newer section with white-painted fitted furniture and those in the original part of the building with good-quality lightwood, freestanding pieces. Bathrooms have showers over tubs (just three have shower only), generous towelling and vanity units that provide plenty of shelf space. Breakfast, served in an oak-panelled dining-room overlooking the green, includes a particularly good cold buffet. Room service can provide hot food 24hrs a day. Conference facilities include a ballroom accommodating 300 theatre-style. Children under 14 free if sharing parents' room. Parking for 100 cars. De Vere Hotels. *Rooms 115. Access, Amex, Diners, Visa.*

CAMPSEA ASHE	Old Rectory	£55

Tel 01728 746524   Map 10 D3 **RR**
Campsea Ashe nr Woodbridge Suffolk IP13 0PU

Stewart Bassett's comfortable Georgian house stands in its own grounds in a quiet village on the B1078 (from the A12). The welcome is genuinely warm and guests are shown into a drawing room where drinks are ordered and the meal announced. The meal (no choice) is served by affable young girls; Stewart cooks in splendid style and does the rounds towards the end of the evening. Starting with lemon sole with crab mousse and white wine sauce or spinach and smoked salmon tart you could proceed to breast of guinea fowl with wild mushrooms, fillet of lamb with a chestnut purée, or salmon in puff pastry. Dessert could be hot ginger and pear upside-down pudding or lemon cream cheese roulade. No smoking until after the meal. *Seats 36. Parties 18. Private Room 36. L by arrangement D 7.30-8.45. Set D £18/£21. Closed Sun, few days Christmas, 2 weeks Feb. Access, Amex, Diners, Visa.*

Rooms £52

The nine bright, comfortable bedrooms include a Victorian room and two four-posters.
Fine antiques, drawings and prints are featured. Children are "most welcome", but there
are no special facilities. No smoking. No dogs. *Garden, croquet.*

CANTERBURY	Canterbury Hotel	58%	£55

Tel 01227 450551   Fax 01227 780145   Map 11 C5   **H**
71 New Dover Road Canterbury Kent CT1 3DZ

Privately owned city-centre hotel featuring a friendly pine-clad reception area and
comfortably furnished bedrooms, with all the useful gadgets. Parking for 50 cars,
banquets and small conferences accommodated. *Rooms 27. Access, Amex, Diners, Visa.*

CANTERBURY	Chaucer Hotel	61%	£103

Tel 01227 464427   Fax 01227 450397   Map 11 C5   **H**
63 Ivy Lane Canterbury Kent CT1 1TT

A large, traditional bar also serves as the lounge in a comfortable hotel created from
an extended Georgian house opposite the cinema just off the Ring Road, very close
to the city centre. Conference/banqueting facilities for up to 100. Children up to 14
stay free in parents' room. Forte Hotels. *Rooms 42. Access, Amex, Diners, Visa.*

CANTERBURY	County Hotel	69%	£100

Tel 01227 766266   Fax 01227 451512   Map 11 C5   **HR**
High Street Canterbury Kent CT1 2RX

In the now pedestrianised High Street, the County started life as the house of a banker
way back in 1235. This heritage is best seen in the first floor residents' lounge which also
features some heavily carved antique furniture; there are lots of old timbers in evidence
in the reception area and a small bar boasts some linenfold panelling. Under manager
of nearly 20 years John Penturo, a policy of continuous refurbishment means that all
the traditionally furnished bedrooms are in excellent order and all come with immaculate,
fully-tiled bathrooms. For a small supplement there are 15 'speciality' rooms that are
more spacious and come in three styles, Georgian with half-tester beds, Tudor with four-
posters and wrought-iron light fittings and Colonial with canopyless four-posters. There
is also a splendid new suite. Standards of service are high with 24hr room service, bed
turn-down in the evening and a shoe-cleaning service. Motorists should approach the
hotel via Stour Street and ring the brass bell, just inside the side entrance, to summon
a porter, who will give access to the hotel car park (60 spaces, £2.50 per night).
Rooms 73. Coffee shop (10.30am-11pm). Access, Amex, Diners, Visa.

Sully's Restaurant £70

A windowless, 60s-style room with plush cocktail bar on a split level at the entrance,
mottled mirrors down one side, moulded ceiling, pink napery and a long-standing
reputation for sound cooking that is being upheld by new chef François Garcin. The
menu format has changed somewhat with a carte of seasonal specialities plus table d'hote
menus both priced for either two or three courses and between them offering plenty
of choice. Feuilleté of asparagus with chervil butter sauce, grilled sea bass with a coulis
of sweet peppers, veal chartreuse with a cider sauce, venison casserole with a rich
peppered sauce and chocolate-flavoured pasta, and whisky bavarois with a raspberry and
chocolate sauce demonstrate the classically-based style. There is always a generously
carved roast at lunchtime. The cheese trolley (regional winner of British Cheeseboard of
the year) majors on English cheeses at lunch with a more Continental selection at night.
A perfunctory list of mostly French wines only; a very few Australian bottles representing
the New World, a section exceeded by Italy. *Seats 50. Parties 8. L 12.30-2.30 D 7-10.
Set L from £13 (Sun £16) Set D £17.*

We welcome bona fide complaints and recommendations on the
tear-out pages at the back of the book for readers' comments.
They are followed up by our professional team.

the New World, a section exceeded by Italy. *Seats 50. Parties 8. L 12.30-2.30 D 7-10. Set L from £13 (Sun £16) Set D £17.*

CANTERBURY   Ebury Hotel   59%   £60

Tel 01227 768433   Fax 01227 459187   Map 11 C5   **H**
65 New Dover Road Canterbury Kent CT1 3DX

One mile south-east of the city centre just back from the A2, the hotel comprises two adjoining Victorian houses. There are two acres of garden, an antique-furnished lounge and a small, indoor swimming pool. Light, airy bedrooms are simply, but neatly appointed. Four self-catering flats and bungalows also available within the grounds. Family-owned and run. *Rooms 15. Garden, indoor swimming pool, spa bath, keep-fit equipment. Closed 14 Dec-14 Jan. Access, Amex, Visa.*

CANTERBURY   Falstaff Hotel   £80

Tel 01227 462138   Fax 01227 463525   Map 11 C5   **I**
8 St Dunstan's Street Canterbury Kent CT2 8AF

A centuries-old coaching inn whose well-kept day rooms get character from original beams, leaded windows and polished oak tables. Bedrooms (many of them designated non-smoking) are neat and pretty and the majority use solid modern furniture that suits the feel of the place perfectly. Children under 16 are accommodated free in their parents' room, with meals charged as taken. Within easy walking distance of the city centre, next to the Westgate Towers. No dogs. Whitbread Lansbury. *Rooms 24. Access, Amex, Diners, Visa.*

CANTERBURY   Howfield Manor   68%   £85

Tel 01227 738294   Fax 01227 731535   Map 11 C5   **H**
Chartham Hatch Canterbury Kent CT4 7HQ

An attractive old manor house on the A28 to the west of Canterbury, once part of the estate of the Priory of St Gregory and still retaining interesting architectural features. Evidence of its long history can be seen in the huge inglenook fireplace in the lounge and priesthole in the bar, which also contains some striking trompe l'oeil murals. New-wing bedrooms are spacious and have good solid oak furniture, but those in the original house are more characterful with some exposed beams; all offer numerous little comforts and have well-kept bathrooms. Conference/banqueting for 100/90. No children under 10. No dogs. *Rooms 13. Garden. Access, Amex, Visa.*

CANTERBURY   River Kwai   £40

Tel 01227 462090   Map 11 C5   **R**
49 Castle Street Canterbury Kent CT1 2PY

Thai restaurant in the city centre offering the usual range of spicy salads, fiery curries and a number of one-dish rice or noodle dishes. Pud Thai – fried rice noodles with shrimps, crab meat, bean sprouts, ground peanuts, egg and chopped salted turnips – is a speciality. Good-value fixed-price menu at lunchtime. *Seats 70. L 12-2 D 6-10.30. Closed L Mon, all Sun, 25 & 26 Dec, 1-3 Jan. Set L £7 Set D from £15. Access, Amex, Diners, Visa.*

CARLISLE   Swallow Hilltop   59%   £90

Tel 01228 29255   Fax 01228 25238   Map 4 C2   **H**
London Road Carlisle Cumbria CA1 2PQ

Leave the M6 at Junction 42 and take the A6 to find this modern hotel with conference rooms for up to 550. *Rooms 92. Garden, indoor swimming pool, gym, sauna, spa bath. Access, Amex, Diners, Visa.*

CARLYON BAY   Carlyon Bay Hotel   68%   £132

Tel 01726 812304   Fax 01726 814938   Map 12 B3   **H**
Sea Road Carlyon nr St Austell Cornwall PL25 3RD

Set in 250 acres of sub-tropical gardens and grounds, including its own championship golf course, the handsome creeper-clad hotel enjoys superb views over the bay. It was built in 1930, and, while still first and foremost a family holiday hotel, it also offers extensive conference/function facilities (for up to 250/220). Large-windowed lounges, furnished in traditional style, make the most of the splendid setting, as do most of the light, attractive bedrooms (a supplement is charged for sea-facing rooms). Families are particularly well catered for, with good outdoor facilities and an indoor pool for youngsters. **Rooms** *73. Garden, croquet, 18-hole golf course, 9-hole approach golf course, tennis, indoor & outdoor swimming pools, spa bath, sauna, solarium, snooker, playground. Access, Amex, Diners, Visa.*

CARLYON BAY	Porth Avallen Hotel	60%	£83

Tel 01726 812802   Fax 01726 817097   Map 12 B3   **H**
Sea Road Carlyon nr St Austell Cornwall PL25 3SG

About 2½ miles east of St Austell town centre and set high above Carlyon Bay, the Porth Avallen (built as a private house in the 1930s and now extended) enjoys some splendid views from its vantage point. The aim of the Perrett and Sim families is to offer peace and tranquillity in a well-ordered and modestly comfortable hotel. A small sun lounge and terrace beyond the oak-panelled lounge takes full advantage of the setting. Bedroom decor and furnishing varies in style considerably from one room to another, though all have private bathrooms and the usual gadgets. Best and largest are the five de luxe rooms. **Rooms** *24. Garden. Closed 1 week Christmas. Amex, Diners, Visa.*

CARTMEL	Aynsome Manor	60%	£87*

Tel 01539 536653   Fax 01539 536016   Map 4 C4   **H**
Cartmel nr Grange-over-Sands Cumbria LA11 6HH

Half a mile north of the village in the Vale of Cartmel is a welcoming house of 16th-century origins, run by the Varley family since 1981. Open fires, magazines and a porcelain doll collection create a homely atmosphere. Accommodation, divided between main house and converted stables across a cobbled courtyard, has an equally traditional feel. *★Half-board terms only.* **Rooms** *12. Garden. Closed 2-26 Jan. Access, Amex, Visa.*

CARTMEL	Uplands		£65

Tel & Fax 01539 536248   Map 4 C4   **RR**
Haggs Lane Cartmel Cumbria LA11 6HD

A charming country house, some two miles northwest of Grange-over-Sands, set in two acres of gardens with distant views over to Morecambe Bay. The spacious and comfortable lounge and the dining-room next door are decorated in shades of pale pink, grey and blue. Walls are hung with large, mainly impressionist prints from the New York Metropolitan Museum of Art. Pine tables and attractive pickled pine chairs create an informal backdrop to Tom Peter's delicious, well-cooked three-course luncheons or four-course dinners. Meals commence with a freshly baked, warm malty-sweet brown loaf brought to the table with a board and bread-knife. The style is simple but flavours are carefully thought-out, complementing one another successfully. A typical dinner menu in modern British style could start with hot salmon soufflé wrapped in smoked salmon and served with an asparagus sauce followed by a tureen of tomato and basil soup. The central dish could be poached fillet of fresh halibut with a chive sauce, honey-roast duckling with a calvados apple purée and green peppercorn sauce accompanied by plentiful vegetables. Finally a choice of five sweets or a cheese platter. No smoking. Coffee is served in the lounge. **Seats** *28. Parties 12. L 12.30 for 1 D 7.30 for 8. Closed Mon, Jan & Feb. Set L £14.50 Set D £25. Access, Amex, Visa.*

Rooms   £136*

Upstairs are five bedrooms all brightly decorated having white-painted furniture and light colour schemes. They are well equipped – remote TVs, hairdryers, games and books. All are en suite, three having showers only. No children under 8. *★Half-board terms only. Garden.*

CASTLE ASHBY	Falcon Hotel		£75

Tel 01604 696200   Fax 01604 696673   Map 15 E1   **I**
Castle Ashby Northamptonshire NN7 1LF

Jo and Neville Watson's charming roadside inn dates from 1594. The architecture is very characteristic of a style found throughout this region. Inside there are comfortable, homely public rooms handsomely decorated in a mix of traditional styles. Bedrooms, all

CASTLE CARY — Bond's — 63% — £64

Tel & Fax 01963 350464   Map 13 F2   **HR**
Ansford Hill Castle Cary Somerset BA7 7JP

Kevin and Yvonne Bond's listed Georgian house is just off the A371, 400yds from the station. Creeper-clad without and cosily cosseting within, it puts the emphasis on informal good living, as shown by glowing log fires in bar and lounge, and period bedrooms, each with its own personal appeal, which lack nothing in comfort. True personal service sets the seal on guests' well-being. Good breakfasts. No children under '8, but babes in arms welcome. No dogs. Private secure car park. *Rooms 7. Garden. Closed 1 week Christmas. Access, Visa.*

Restaurant   £55

Yvonne's weekly-changing menu and nightly table d'hote contain a few surprises and a good choice (spread across the menu options); her modern English cooking is substantial and nourishing, the dishes attractive. Start, perhaps, with duck and pork layered terrine served on vanilla dressing or wild mushroom and quail's egg tart, and continue with seafood in a rich white wine sauce, pot-roasted rabbit or rack of lamb served pink with redcurrant purée. Seven or so puddings, from brandy snap basket with caramel ice cream to icky sticky toffee pudding with butterscotch sauce. Lunch is a light set meal only. No smoking. *Seats 20. Parties 12. D 7-9.30. Set D £12.50 (no choice) & £19.75.*

CASTLE COMBE — Castle Inn — £55

Tel 01249 783030   Fax 01249 782315   Map 14 B2   **I**
Castle Combe nr Chippenham Wiltshire SN14 7HN

At the centre of one of England's prettiest villages, right by the ancient monument stone cross, this famous hostelry can trace its own origins back to the 12th century. Following a period of closure, it has reopened under the Hatton Hotels' banner as a smart inn. Attention to detail in exposing and retaining the intricate old stonework and centuries-old beams has been commendable, and nowhere is this better evidenced than in the new conservatory, a lovely breakfast room; it opens on to a private enclosed patio. Bedrooms are individually modelled to a very high standard; two 'superior' rooms have en-suite whirlpool baths and a third a Victorian-style slipper bath. Remote-control TVs, radio-alarms with phones, trouser presses and hairdryers are standard accessories; cosseting extras include complimentary fruit and mineral waters, boiled sweets, towelling robes, rubber ducks and resident teddy bears. No dogs. *Rooms 7. Access, Amex, Diners, Visa.*

CASTLE COMBE — Manor House — 80% — £140

Tel 01249 782206   Fax 01249 782159   Map 14 B2   **HR**
Castle Combe nr Chippenham Wiltshire SN14 7HR

Adjacent to the postcard-pretty village, the hotel is set in its own 26 acres of grounds that include gardens, a river and woodland walks. A manor house stood here in Norman times, and the current building dates back in part to the 14th century. Day rooms include an appropriately manorial front hall with some particularly fine carved-wood panelling (the reception 'desk' is an antique refectory-style table), a clubby bar with green leather upholstery and a sunny yellow drawing-room furnished in English country house style. In winter several real fires add to the cosy atmosphere. The real stars here though are the bedrooms in the main house (a little less than half the total): spacious, characterful (old timbers, some exposed stone features and various four-posters and half-testers), and stylishly decorated with rugs over oak floors and quality soft furnishings. Comforts include wing armchairs, books magazines, welcoming decanter of sherry and a teddy-bear to keep the bed warm.

Furniture is antique and always includes a piece that provides good work space because practicalities have not been overlooked; there are three telephones in each room. Bathrooms are no less luxurious, all having large walk-in showers (with huge 'deluge' shower heads and 'rain bars' in rooms in the new extension) in addition to the tub, twin washbasins and even televisions allowing one to view while having a soak. The remaining 'Mews' bedrooms are in cottages on either side of what was once part of the village street. Rooms here vary somewhat but are generally less luxurious (reproduction furniture and no sherry for example), suffer by comparison with those in the Manor and hold back our overall grading for the hotel. Things like the proper servicing of rooms at night and 24hr room service extend to all rooms. The price quoted above is for the lowest priced Main House rooms. Guests have free membership of the hotel's championship golf course: handicap certificates are required. *Rooms 36. Garden, croquet, golf (18-hole), tennis, fishing, outdoor swimming pool. Access, Amex, Diners, Visa.*

Restaurant £95

Chef Mark Taylor's high-quality food is superbly complemented by the professional service of restaurant manager Franco Campioni. Ravioli of mussels with garlic and tomato; Cornish red mullet and saffron soup; bacon, shallot and morel soufflé; smoked fillet of beef with garlic hash and wild mushroom duxelles, and confit of turbot with boulangère potatoes are typical menu dishes. A 'Classical Section' on the menu also offers roast free-range duck lyonnaise, Dover sole, chargrilled chateaubriand and locally smoked salmon served with lime. Gourmet vegetarians can work their way through a five-course dinner menu or order individual dishes as they take their fancy. Steamed chocolate sponge with Devonshire clotted cream and warm pear tart among the desserts. Good British cheeses. Choices for Sunday lunch include traditional Scottish roast beef. A grand wine list has some quite grand prices, though to be fair there are some value-for-money wines if you look carefully. Particularly fine Italian section; helpful tasting notes. No smoking. *Seats 75. Parties 8. Private Room 12. L 12.30-2 D 7.30-10. Set L £16.95 (Sun £19.50) Set D £32.*

| **CASTLE DONINGTON** | **Donington Thistle** | **70%** | **£118** |

Tel 01332 850700   Fax 01332 850823   Map 7 D3   **H**
East Midlands Airport Castle Donington Derbyshire DE74 2SH

Located within the perimeter of the East Midlands Airport, this modern two-storey redbrick hotel is also close to Donington Park motor racing circuit and the M1 (J23A, 24). The modern bedrooms are all double glazed and have individually controlled heating. Executive bedrooms, and the four suites, have mini-bars and various extras in the bathrooms like towelling robes and more luxurious toiletries. 24hr room service can rustle up a hot meal in the middle of the night. Children up to 15 stay free in parents' room. Conference/banqueting facilities for 220/200. Ample free parking. *Rooms 110. Garden, indoor swimming pool, keep-fit equipment, sauna, spa bath, solarium, airport courtesy bus. Access, Amex, Diners, Visa.*

| **CAVENDISH** | **Alfonso's** | **£60** |

Tel 01787 280372   Map 10 C3   **R**
Cavendish nr Sudbury Suffolk CO10 8BB

Alfonso and Veronica Barricella have been providing authentic Italian food in their restaurant opposite the village green for more than 20 years. Among the favourites in their repertoire are minestrone, ravioli, *scaloppine al limone, scampi rondinella* (cooked in Cointreau with onion, mushrooms, peppers wine and herbs, flamed in brandy and served on rice), and *rotondo Alfonso* – fillet steak served on a crouton with paté, artichoke, olive and brandy sauce. For dessert they whisk up an excellent zabaglione.

We welcome bona fide complaints and recommendations on the tear-out pages at the back of the book for readers' comments. They are followed up by our professional team.

CAWSTON   Grey Gables   £50

Tel 01603 871259   Map 10 C1   **RR**
Norwich Road Cawston Norwich Norfolk NR10 4EY

A small Georgian house with a Victorian façade, about a mile south of Cawston and a mile west of the B1149, provides a homely setting for Rosalind Snaith's wholesome cooking. The short, fixed-price-only menu of three, four or five courses makes good use of seasonal produce in dishes such as Norfolk ham and pease pudding (as a starter), pumpkin soup, plum sorbet or smoked salmon, trout with almonds, Stilton puff pastry parcel with peppers, celery and onions (a speciality) and roast lamb with mint and redcurrant jelly. A super wine list has wines from around the world, but no Italian whites! An obvious labour of love; some of the prices are in the 'give-away' bracket. Concise tasting notes. You can bring your own bottle(s) – why would you want to given the choice here? – for a modest corkage. No children under 5. No smoking. *Seats 30. Private Room 24. L by arrangement D 7-8.30. Closed 24-26 Dec. Set D £17/£19/£21. Access, Visa.*

Rooms   £56

Eight peaceful bedrooms (six en suite) offer traditional furnishings together with hotel comforts like direct-dial telephone, TV, radio, and en-suite, carpeted bathrooms. Children up to 10 stay free in parents' room. Bedroom number 1 is the best and carries a small supplement. *Garden, lawn tennis.*

Consult the blue pages for summary tables and lists of recommended establishments.

CHADDESLEY CORBETT   Brockencote Hall   75%   £110

Tel 01562 777876   Fax 01562 777872   Map 6 B4   **HR**
Chaddesley Corbett nr Kidderminster Hereford & Worcester DY10 4PY

Surrounded by 70 acres of pastureland, the Georgian-looking original (it actually started life as a rather ugly early Victorian building, happily re-modelled after a fire some years ago) has spawned an almost identical building next door where most of the spacious bedrooms are now to be found. Stylish individual decor, fine cherrywood furniture and extras like sherry, fruit and mineral water make for very comfortable accommodation; one room has been specially adapted for disabled guests.

Large bathrooms with alcoved tubs (three with spa baths and six with separate walk-in showers) are equally luxurious. A conservatory lounge links the two buildings. Children under 12 stay free sharing their parents' bedroom. No dogs. *Rooms 17. Garden, croquet. Access, Amex, Diners, Visa.*

Restaurant   £80

The park and the lake provide classic English views from the elegant chandeliered restaurant, but the kitchen is in French hands. Sound skills are applied to local and regional produce to create interesting, well-crafted dishes such as a ragout of snails with a salad of new potatoes and a Camembert cream sauce, salmon fillet with spinach sauce, or roast loin of lamb topped with a herb crust and served with sweet garlic-infused gravy. A separate menu of lighter, simpler dishes includes the likes of prawn salad with a dill dressing, oysters, grilled Dover sole and beef fillet béarnaise. No smoking. *Seats 50. Parties 12. Private Room 28. L 12.30-1.30 D 7-9.30. Closed L Sat. Set L from £16.50 Set D from £21.50.*

Lodges are now listed by county in the reference section

CHADLINGTON   The Manor   76%   £105

Tel 01608 676711
Chadlington Oxfordshire OX7 3LX

Map 14 C1   **HR**

David and Chris Grant's mellow stone house, set in extensive grounds in a pretty Cotswold village, has a wonderfully relaxing atmosphere and the owners and staff couldn't be more helpful and attentive. Beyond the panelled entrance lounge is a second lounge with an open fire where drinks are served in the absence of any bar. Splendid bedrooms are the high point: individually designed and tastefully furnished with antiques and period pieces, they're full of little indulgences like fresh fruit and mineral water, plus plentiful bath foam in the gold-tapped bathrooms. No dogs. *Rooms 7. Garden. Access, Visa.*

Restaurant   £60

Chris Grant's five-course dinner menu changes daily, reflecting what's best in the market, although favourite dishes often recur; space is limited and non-residents should book ahead. Soup, perhaps chicken and almond, is followed by an intermediate course such as warm goat's cheese salad or trout with ground hazelnuts; duck breast with orange, honey and ginger, pork fillet with prune sauce and grilled lemon sole with herb butter may be the main-course options; finally, home-made sweets such as hazelnut meringue with raspberry coulis or baked bananas with rum and raisins, and cheese and biscuits to top it all off. Last year's winner of our Cellar of the Year, the list here has improved yet further, expanding beyond France and Germany (note the extensive selection of sweet wines) to include England, Italy and Spain, as well as a decent New World showing. Prices, especially if you drink the best, are still ridiculously low; half bottles and vintage ports plentiful. No smoking. *Seats 20. Parties 6. Private Room 8. D only 7-8.30. Set D £25.50.*

CHAGFORD   Gidleigh Park   82%   £290*

Tel 01647 432367   Fax 01647 432574
Chagford Devon TQ13 8HH

Map 13 D2   **HR**

Forty acres of magnificent grounds are the setting for this supreme country house hotel, which lies in the shelter of the Teign Valley with splendid views of Nattadon and Meldon Hills. The grounds themselves are a source of great pride (in particular the water garden), and Paul and Kay Henderson ensure that, inside or out, guests will enjoy the highest standards. Most of the bedrooms, including two exquisite suites, are in the mock-Tudor main house, and there is a separate three-room cottage just across the river. Fine antiques, enormous sofas, top-quality English fabrics and pleasing floral arrangements are features of the panelled lounge and luxurious bar (where fine wines are served by the glass from the Cruvinet machine): discreet good taste is evident at every turn and service from the delightful staff is exceptional. The tiny hamlet of Gidleigh, settled by King Harold's mother, Gydda, dates from the eleventh century, but to find the hotel don't go there. Take Mill Street out of Chagford Square. 150 yards past Lloyds Bank, fork right. Straight on for two miles to the end of the lane. *Half-board terms only. *Rooms 15. Garden, croquet, tennis. Access, Visa.*

Restaurant   £120

Everything here combines to create a memorable dining experience: the refinement of the oak-panelled dining-room, its walls decorated with foody watercolours,

See over

immaculate table settings, correct, attentive but never overbearing service, a stunning wine list and the highly accomplished cooking of young Devonian Michael Caines, whose pedigree includes a period in Raymond Blanc's kitchen at *Le Manoir* and a stint with Joël Robuchon in Paris. Attention to detail is his hallmark, from the diverse canapés that arouse the appetite while perusing the menu to the selection of home-made breads (a different selection arrives wtih the first-rate and knowledgeably served cheese trolley) and nicely varied petits fours. Dinner begins with a complimentary starter such as the demi-tasse of langoustine bisque at a recent meal – one could have wished for a breakfast cupful – before starters like tomato tart with olives and basil, crab ravioli with ginger and lemon grass, and a ballotine of foie gras with green bean salad and mains including sea bream with an onion compote and olives served with saffron sauce and anchovy oil, roast guinea fowl with rosemary sauce and salad with truffle vinaigrette, and saddle of venison with braised chestnuts and ravioli of venison and figs. The main fixed-price menu (choice of about five main dishes) is supplemented by a five-course, no-choice speciality menu at night and a light à la carte-priced menu (soup, omelettes, sandwiches) at lunchtime. There are also two-course lunches priced at £15 (Mon-Thur), £20 (Fri & Sat) & £25 (Sun & Holiday weekends). The wine list here is a model for others to follow, though one must accept that not everyone is able to invest (passion, knowledge, time, cash etc) on such a large scale. The list has been Paul Henderson's pride and joy for many years, as well as receiving all our awards. Remarkably, for a hotel of this class, the wines are most fairly priced, in fact the better the quality (a relative term here since every wine is top-notch), the less the mark-up. Italy and America excel – there are not that many places in the UK where you can drink the quality on offer here, though the reality is that every bottle oozes class. No smoking. *Seats 40. Parties 8. L 12.30-2 D 7-9. Set L £15/£20/£25/£40/£50 Set D £50/£55.*

CHAGFORD	Great Tree Hotel	61%	£79

Tel 01647 432491   Fax 01647 432562   Map 13 D2   **H**
Sandy Park Chagford Devon TQ13 8JS

A driveway leads off the A382 two miles north of Chagford to the Eaton-Grays' relaxed hotel, a former hunting lodge in 18 acres of gardens and woodland, commanding splendid views of Dartmoor and the surrounding countryside. There's an old, rather Colonial character to the entrance hall with its ornate fireplace and a carved wooden staircase leading down to a raftered bar and lounge. Most of the bedrooms are at ground level with south-facing French windows. The Great Tree ambience is epitomised by complimentary sherry on arrival. Dogs welcome (£2.50 a day) but must be accompanied by valid vaccination certificates. The hotel has leased a 2½-mile stretch of the River Teign, and various other outdoor activities can be arranged. *Rooms 12. Garden, fishing, sun beds. Access, Amex, Diners, Visa.*

CHAGFORD	Mill End	63%	£85

Tel 01647 432282   Fax 01647 433106   Map 13 D2   **H**
Sandy Park Chagford Devon TQ13 8JN

In a setting alongside the A382 there has been a hotel since 1929. Originally it was a flour mill, whose wheel still turns in the courtyard. Located on the edge of Dartmoor in the beautiful valley of the River Teign, the hotel has 600 yards of private fishing. Bedrooms are furnished with a mixture of traditional, antique and modern pieces. Children up to 16 sharing their parents' room are accommodated free; good facilities for young families including a long children's supper menu. *Rooms 16. Garden, game fishing. Closed 10 days mid-Dec, 10 days mid-Jan. Access, Amex, Diners, Visa.*

CHAPELTOWN	Greenhead House	£75

Tel 0114 246 9004   Map 6 C2   **R**
84 Burncross Road Chapeltown nr Sheffield South Yorkshire S30 4SF

A pretty little restaurant north of Sheffield run by Neil and Anne Allen. Neil offers an absorbing monthly-changing menu written in a distinctive hand. Meals are priced according to the choice of main course – perhaps fillet steak with shallots and tarragon, scallops thermidor, roast guinea fowl with mixed mushrooms and Madeira, or Mediterranean lamb casserole. A typical selection of starters might include chicken quenelles with smoked bacon and mushroom sauce, mussels with cider and saffron, duck rillettes with a chicory and walnut salad; parsnip and coriander soup or melon may follow as an inter-course offering. Leave room for French cheeses served with grapes, apple and celery, rich chocolate cake served with fresh figs and raspberries, strawberry shortcakes or pear strudel tarts. Prices are very reasonable (including bin ends) on the short wine list. No smoking. **Seats** *32. Parties 14. L by arrangement D 7-9. Closed Sun, Mon, Tue, 2 weeks Easter, 2 weeks mid Aug & Christmas-New Year. Set D £27.50/£30. Access, Visa.*

CHARINGWORTH	Charingworth Manor	79%	£110

Tel 01386 593555   Fax 01386 593353   Map 14 C1   **HR**
Charingworth nr Chipping Campden Gloucestershire GL55 6NS

The setting (54 acres of grounds) is glorious, and the view from the well-kept garden down across the valley is, quite simply, breathtaking. The main house, which dates back to the early 14th century, retains beams showing the original medieval decoration; the spacious sitting-room has mullion windows, a patterned and painted oak beam ceiling, hand-stencilled walls, rugs on the polished wood floor and an imposing stone fireplace. Drinks are served here, straight from the cellar. The individually decorated bedrooms and suites feature antique furniture, and the Courtyard and Cottage rooms, created from the original stables and farm buildings, though more uniform and smaller, benefit from super bathrooms with separate walk-in shower as well as bathtub. Thoughtful touches abound, such as fresh fruit, home-made biscuits and welcoming decanter of sherry. Don't forget to check out the Leisure Spa, and the impressive Long Room is an ideal venue for private functions (up to 36 for a sit-down meal). **Rooms** *24. Garden, croquet, tennis, indoor swimming pool, sauna, steam room, sun bed, snooker. Access, Amex, Diners, Visa.*

John Greville Restaurant   £80

A romantic dining-room (in fact a series of interconnecting rooms) where the fixed-price dinner offers about seven choices for each course. Wild mushroom gnocchi with tomato dressing and pine kernels, salmon with a herb crust on a saffron and vegetable butter and wild venison casserole show the style. There's also a separate vegetarian menu. Lunch is a more snacky, but no less interesting, à la carte. Pleasing all-round wine list with several bottles below the £20 mark, though some of the better-known names are pricier. Introductory notes to regions only. **Seats** *48. Parties 12. Private Room 36. L 12.30-2 D 7-10. Set Sun L £17.50 Set D £29.50.*

CHARLBURY	Bell Hotel	£75

Tel 01608 810278   Fax 01608 811447   Map 14 C1   **I**
Church Street Charlbury Oxfordshire OX7 3PP

Historic Charlbury with its 7th-century St Mary's Church was royally chartered to hold cattle markets in 1256; the last one was held behind the Bell some 700 years later. With its own datestone of 1700, the mellow stone inn is full of character; the small flagstoned bar and attendant sun-lounge readily make guests at home and in fair weather the patio looking down a long, sloping garden is a picturesque one. Access to bedrooms is by steep staircases and narrow passageways, yet the rooms themselves are spacious and neatly appointed, with matching fabrics and up-to-date accessories which include hairdryers, trouser presses and welcome clock radios. The three smaller doubles have en-suite WC/showers only and one single is not en suite, though its adjacent bathroom is private. Conference facilities in the converted stable block accommodate up to 55. Children up to 16 say free in parents' room. **Rooms** *14. Garden. Access, Amex, Diners, Visa.*

We welcome bona fide complaints and recommendations on the tear-out pages at the back of the book for readers' comments. They are followed up by our professional team.

CHARLECOTE   Charlecote Pheasant   62%   £105

Tel 01789 470333   Fax 01789 470222   Map 14 C1   **H**
Charlecote nr Warwick Warwickshire CV35 9EW

Five miles from junction 15 of the M40, opposite the deer park of Charlecote Manor, this hotel combines public rooms in old beamed farmhouse buildings and bedrooms (including seven Executive rooms) in a modern block. Conference and banqueting facilities up to 120. Children up to 16 stay free in parents' room. Popular for family weekends. *Rooms 67. Garden, croquet, tennis, outdoor swimming pool, keep-fit equipment, steam room, solarium. Access, Amex, Diners, Visa.*

CHARTHAM   Thruxted Oast   £75

Tel 01227 730080   Map 11 C5   **PH**
Mystole Chartham nr Canterbury Kent CT4 7BX

In peaceful countryside four miles from Canterbury, Tim and Hilary Derouet's characterful little hotel started life in 1792 as a cluster of oast houses. There are just three bedrooms (non-smoking) with beams, pine roofs, pine furniture, patchwork quilts and many thoughtful little extras. There's a very comfortable lounge, and breakfasts are served in the farmhouse kitchen. The Oast is also home to the owners' picture-framing business. No children under 8. No dogs. Check directions, as it's slightly off the beaten track. *Rooms 3. Garden, croquet. Access, Amex, Diners, Visa.*

CHEDINGTON   Chedington Court   71%   £115

Tel 01935 891265   Fax 01935 891442   Map 13 F2   **HR**
Chedington nr Beaminster Dorset DT8 3HY

The gracious Jacobean manor, with its backdrop of beech trees and very English setting in the valley of the River Parrett, has a history documented back to at least 1316. The current facade owes much to William Trevelyan Cox, who virtually rebuilt the house in 1840. Since 1981 it has been in the loving and capable hands of Hilary and Philip Chapman. Ten acres of grounds include sweeping lawns, ponds, a grotto and a water garden, as well as a 1000-year-old yew tree. The interior lives up to the expectations promised by the approach, with stone fireplaces (open log fires), deep, comfortable upholstery, chandeliers, polished tables, and a piano in the corner. Individually named bedrooms have a variety of bathroom options (bath, shower, jacuzzi), and are furnished to a similarly high level of comfort. The hotel is situated just off the A356, 4½ miles SE of Crewkerne at Winyard's Gap. *Rooms 10. Garden, croquet, golf (9), pitch & putt, putting, sun beds, snooker. Closed Jan. Access, Amex, Visa.*

Restaurant   £65

The light, airy dining-room is fragrant with jasmine from the adjacent conservatory at the appropriate time of year, but always provides a perfect setting for Hilary Chapman's English (but French-inspired) four-course, nightly changing, menus. There are four choices each for starter and main course, typified by Brixham crab cakes with a shellfish sauce, wild mushrooms with sherry and cream, baked fillet of sea bass with garlic, fennel and bacon, and pan-fried sirloin of beef with a béarnaise sauce. One of the main courses is vegetarian – perhaps linguini with a sweet pepper and tomato sauce or blue cheese and vegetable strudel. Desserts from the trolley, splendid British cheeses. Contrasting fortunes on the excellent wine list here – take the extensive German section for instance, which has an auslese eiswein at £90 and half a bottle of Liebfraumilch at £3! For the most part, the list is inexpensive, with several gems. There's plenty of choice between Europe and the New World. *Seats 26. Parties 8. Private Room 22. D only 7-9. Set D £27.50.*

CHEDINGTON   Hazel Barton   £95

Tel 01935 891613   Fax 01935 891370   Map 13 F2   **PH**
Chedington nr Beaminster Dorset DT8 3HY

As we went to press we learnt that this idyllic house, built in the mid-19th century, was likely to become a restaurant with rooms – its present status being a de luxe 'bed and breakfast' hotel (with other meals by arrangement). Set in beautifully-maintained gardens with sweeping views, the house has two elegant lounges, both with open log fires, furnished with genuine antiques, fine paintings, luxurious fabrics and lovely flower arrangements. The four individually decorated bedrooms are models of good taste and comfort, providing all needs, and the bathrooms (some with separate walk-in shower) offer bathrobes, large towels and quality toiletries. At present the wood-panelled boardroom can accommodate 12, while 20 can be seated in the dining-room for a private party. No children under 7. *Rooms 4. Garden, croquet, snooker. Access, Amex, Visa.*

CHELTENHAM	Hotel de la Bere	64%	£82

Tel 01242 237771   Fax 01242 236016   Map 14 B1   **H**
Southam Cheltenham Gloucestershire GL52 3NH

Three miles out of town on the Winchcombe road, convenient for the racecourse. Lots of historic interest in a much-extended Tudor mansion, including a cellar bar. Conference and leisure facilities show the modern side. 20 rooms have been redecorated. *Rooms 57. Garden, outdoor swimming pool, squash, sauna, sun beds, tennis, badminton. Access, Amex, Diners, Visa.*

CHELTENHAM	Cheltenham Park	68%	£114

Tel 01242 222021   Fax 01242 226935   Map 14 B1   **H**
Cirencester Rd Charlton Kings Cheltenham Gloucestershire GL53 8EA

South of town on the A435, a predominantly conference hotel (max. 350 delegates) based on a Georgian house which gives considerable style to smart public areas, particularly the foyer/reception and bar/lounge, both of which feature marbled columns. Good, well-equipped bedrooms featuring solid lightwood furniture are mostly in a new wing. The main meeting rooms have glass doors opening on to a patio enjoying fine views (shared by some bedrooms) across the adjacent Lilleybrook golf course to hills beyond – an ideal 'break-out' area for conferences in the summer months. 24hr room service. Children up to 12 stay free in parents' room. A leisure club with swimming pool, sauna and gym was due to open at the end of 1995. *Rooms 154. Garden. Access, Amex, Diners, Visa.*

CHELTENHAM	Epicurean		£100

Tel 01242 222466   Fax 01242 222474   Map 14 B1   **R**
81 The Promenade Cheltenham Gloucestershire GL51 1PJ

Less than a year after they opened here, Patrick and Claire McDonald (coming to London as we went to press?) are no longer involved in this enterprise which encompasses a top-floor restaurant, a ground-floor bistro and a basement café. In a Grade-II listed Regency terrace building, overlooking the fashionable inner promenade, cooking is now in the hands of a very small kitchen brigade, and on the evidence of a recent lunch in the bistro, it is perhaps too early to make judgements. A salmon fishcake arrived with indecent haste, tepid on the outside, cold inside on a barely lukewarm sauce that was not the advertised hollandaise, but tarragon. On the other hand, a summer berry pudding was perfectly executed. Service from two charming waitresses was hesitant, while the restaurant manager seemed disinterested. The restaurant upstairs offers serious food at prices to match. *Seats 30. Parties 8. Private Room 16. L 12.30-2.30 D 7.30-10. Closed L Sat, all Sun, 2 weeks Jan, 2 weeks Aug. Set L £15/£20/£37 Set D £37/£55.*

CHELTENHAM	Golden Valley Thistle	69%	£112

Tel 01242 232691   Fax 01242 221846   Map 14 B1   **H**
Gloucester Road Cheltenham Gloucestershire GL51 0TS

A 70s' hotel on the outskirts of Cheltenham, one mile from Junction 11 of the M5 (next to GCHQ) and two miles from the town centre. The bright, modern Garden Lounge has wicker furniture and its own patio. Many bedrooms have recently been refurbished, and a few now have fax/modem points. Extensive conference and banqueting facilities (up to 220 delegates accommodated theatre-style). On-site parking for 250 cars. *Rooms 124. Garden, croquet, tennis, indoor swimming pool, gym, sauna, steam room, spa bath, solarium, beauty salon. Access, Amex, Diners, Visa.*

Consult the blue pages for summary tables and lists of recommended establishments.

CHELTENHAM   Le Champignon Sauvage   ★   £75

Tel 01242 573449   Map 14 B1   **R**
24-26 Suffolk Road Cheltenham Gloucestershire GL50 2AQ

Nestling among the antique shops, this cottagey restaurant offers a cosy bar for pre-dinner drinks and an elegant dining-room with well-spaced tables and some serious linen napery. David Everitt-Matthias' table d'hote menus follow a classic French theme with a few modern touches. Lunch brings three choices at each stage, dinner five. Each begins with a complimentary amuse-gueule (a delicious brie beignet with onion marmalade on one visit). Start with maybe a light black bean soup, roasted pigeon breast and boned chicken wings with Alsace potato dumplings or a perfectly fried skate wing on a concentrated parsley sauce, the whole drizzled with capers and black butter – a fine combination. To follow perhaps stuffed leg of wild rabbit on turnip sauerkraut with black pudding; fillet of cod with buttered leeks and a red wine butter sauce or roasted rump of Cinderford lamb with ratatouille – served with a wonderfully sticky sauce flavoured with fresh basil and black olives. If you can resist the splendid cheeseboard, with over 20 offerings in peak condition, the desserts are there to tempt – maybe warm chocolate tart, lemon mousse with honey jelly and a compote of berries or an apricot and walnut tart. Desserts such as these end a meal in an exciting crescendo, and thoroughly deserve our award for the best we've encountered this year – see Desserts of the Year award page. These are accompanied by home-made ice cream or sorbet. Dishes are simply described with a refreshing absence of flowery language, and invariably deliver more than promised. Helen Everitt-Matthias provides charming service. A newly introduced, no choice, *Menu Rapide* offers two courses for £12.50, including a glass of wine and mineral water. A carefully composed wine list features some lesser known but good growers/names. Excellent tasting notes, good balance, fair prices. *Seats 28. L 12.30-1.30 D 7.30-9.30. Closed L Sat, all Sun, Bank Holidays, 1 week Christmas. Set L £12.50/£14.50/£17.50. Set D £14.95, £29 & £35. Access, Amex, Diners, Visa.*

CHELTENHAM   The Greenway   80%   £110

Tel 01242 862352   Fax 01242 862780   Map 14 B1   **HR**
Shurdington Cheltenham Gloucestershire GL51 5UG

On the A46 at Shurdington, a couple of miles south west of Cheltenham town centre, this peaceful hotel, once an Elizabethan manor house, is approached via a long driveway. Named after an adjacent neolithic pathway and surrounded by parkland, it largely protects guests from the sounds of the modern world. New owner David White has maintained the high standards which have made this hotel famous over the years. The large drawing room, with its deep armchairs and sofas, polished antiques and fine paintings, has a blazing log fire in winter. Spacious bedrooms, some in the main house, others a short walk away in restored stables, all have splendid views of the surrounding countryside and are individually decorated to a very high standard. Excellent en-suite bathrooms have tubs and showers, full-length mirrors, bathrobes and decent toiletries. Housekeeping is immaculate and includes a turndown service at night. An otherwise excellent breakfast, with home-made jams and freshly squeezed juices, was spoilt on one visit by over-zealous use of the peppermill. Two meeting rooms (up to 35 theatre style). No children under seven. No dogs. Only very limited room service at night. *Rooms 19. Garden, croquet. Closed 2-7 Jan. Access, Amex, Diners, Visa.*

Restaurant   £85

Although the hotel is now under new management, chef Christopher Colmer remains and has ensured continuity of style in the restaurant. The conservatory dining-room has delightful views of the garden, with its floodlit pond and fountain, and the surrounding countryside. Table d'hote menus are offered, with cooking in the modern British style. Starters might offer a warm salad of skate wing with a confit of smoked Wiltshire ham and a split-pea dressing, a terrine of seafood with a miniature Caesar salad or half a Bresse pigeon with an excellent beetroot and pearl barley risotto – a marriage made in heaven. Follow with roasted Severn salmon with a Provence vegetable galette and a red pepper and tomato fondue; breast of guinea fowl with braised butter beans, rösti potato and a turnip-flavoured bouillon or saddle of venison with swede and carrot dauphinoise and a blackberry-scented sauce. Desserts, like all the food, are artistically arranged, but can remain curiously lacking in flavour. There are some very fine wines on the list, some quite fairly priced, others rather expensive. *Seats 50. Private Room 24. L 12.30-2.30 D 7.30-9.30. Set L £12.50/£16 Set D £27.50.*

CHELTENHAM	On The Park	76%	£101

Tel 01242 518898   Fax 01242 2511526   Map 14 B1   **HR**
Evesham Road Cheltenham Gloucestershire GL52 2AH

Darryl and Lesley-Anne Gregory's charming town house opposite Pittville Park on the northern outskirts of town (A435 Evesham Road) boasts many attractions. Not least are the luxurious and generous-sized bathrooms, some almost rooms in themselves, with a wicker chair, marble-topped vanity unit, bidet, old-fashioned tub and the usual pampering extras. Individually designed bedrooms, each named after someone with Pittville connections, are equally tasteful with fine bed linen, smart fabrics, genuine antiques, collections of porcelain and decent paintings. The suites and four-poster rooms are particularly well appointed. Special cabinets house the tea/coffee-making equipment. The civilised public areas certainly do not suffer by comparison, notably a restful drawing room/bar and cosy library/boardroom (seating up to 18), with French doors opening on to a delightful enclosed and secluded garden, both elegantly furnished and decorated. High levels of service and exemplary housekeeping include the turn-down of beds and replacement of towels at night, a welcoming decanter of mulled wine, mineral water and chocolates on arrival. Super breakfasts are served with mini-boards of assorted breads and toasts, pots of home-made jam and marmalade, good cafetière coffee and large glasses of freshly squeezed orange juice. *Rooms 12. Garden. Closed 1 week Jan. Access, Amex, Diners, Visa.*

Restaurant   £70
Tel 01242 227713

The dining-room, with its high ceiling and intricate cornices, is classically and strikingly Regency in style, with each table graced by a tall, wrought-iron, candelabra/floral display. There are both set and à la carte menus featuring well-conceived dishes that owe much to classical training but are presented in a more modern European fashion. Start with some spiced lamb's sweetbreads in a pastry case with a sweet and sour sauce; salmon marinated in coriander, mint and basil or game terrine with home-made chutney before a main dish such as grilled brill with a veal sauce, saffron potatoes and deep-fried seaweed, duck breast with creamy morel sauce and caramelised red cabbage or Cajun spiced chicken breast layered with tagliatelle, leek and courgette with a Tio Pepe sauce. Chocolate mousse, summer pudding and a crunchy praline parfait might all appear amongst the desserts. Excellent value (an '85 Léoville-Barton, 2nd growth St Julien is under £30) on a concise wine list. Service is both thoroughly pleasant and professional. Light lunches can be taken in the garden. Traditional Sunday lunch. *Seats 32. Parties 12. Private Room 18. L 12-1.45 (Sun to 2.15) D 7.30-9.30 (Sat to 10). Set L £14.50 Set D £21.50 & £45.*

CHELTENHAM	The Queen's	69%	£120

Tel 01242 514724   Fax 01242 224145   Map 14 B1   **H**
The Promenade Cheltenham Gloucestershire GL50 1NN

In the heart of the elegant spa town is the equally elegant Queen's, built early (1838) in Queen Victoria's reign, and named in her honour. The imposing white colonnaded hotel overlooks the Imperial Gardens and the lofty foyer/lounge creates an air of Regency elegance echoed in the magnificent stairwell and Napier Bar. Bedrooms (the best of which are on the first floor) include six suites and several Executive rooms; two rooms

See over

feature four-posters. All are well maintained and have desk space, armchairs and the usual extras. Children up to 16 stay free in parents' room. Conference and banquet facilities, catering for up to 350/220. 24hr room service. Free parking. Forte Heritage. *Rooms 74. Access, Amex, Diners, Visa.*

CHELTENHAM	Staithes Restaurant	£50

Tel 01242 260666   Map 14 B1   **R**
12 Suffolk Road Cheltenham Gloucestershire GL50 2AQ

Paul and Heather Lucas have dropped the "Bonnets Bistro", reverting simply to Staithes Restaurant. Paul takes care of the cooking while Heather looks after front of house. Paul's menu typically offers a mix of traditional and modern dishes: caramelised bacon salad dressed in a sherry vinegar; parsnip and apple soup; salmon en croute; puff pastry case filled with chicken livers, mushrooms, spinach and pine kernels; medallions of pork topped with a tarragon and armagnac mousseline, wrapped in crépinette. Individual baked Alaska is a favourite dessert. No smoking. *Seats 30. Private Room 10. L 12-1.30 D 7-9.45. Closed Sun, Bank Holidays, 2 weeks summer, 1 week Christmas. Access, Amex, Diners, Visa.*

CHELWOOD	Chelwood House	63%	£75

Tel 01761 490730   Map 13 F1   **HR**
Chelwood Bristol Avon BS18 4NH

A former dower house, dating from the reign of Charles II, with lovely, unspoilt views across rolling countryside towards Bath, some 10 miles away. Owners Jill and Rudi Birk, who clearly love the place, have created a warm and welcoming atmosphere. The lounge, boasting fine listed panelling, opens to an attractive staircase leading to individually styled bedrooms which some may find over-fussy. The French, Chinese and Victorian themed rooms all have four-posters, and humour is shown in naming the smallest one Lilliput. Home-made fruit compote is a feature of good, traditional breakfasts served in the sunny dining-room. No children under 8. No dogs. 200 yards south of the junction of A37 and A368. *Rooms 10. Garden, croquet. Closed 2 weeks after Christmas Day lunch. Access, Amex, Diners, Visa.*

Garden Restaurant   £50

The conservatory-style 'restaurant in a garden', with plants and fountain, is decorated with murals. Typical offerings might include celeriac and leek soup or chicken liver mousse with pumpkin preserve to start, followed by poached salmon on a bed of stir-fried vegetables with balsamic vinegar and truffle oil dressing, pan-fried supreme of Barbary duck with lemon and lime sauce, and herrentopf (a bit like beef stroganoff with spätzle) from Rudi's native Bavaria. Finish with crème brulée, meringue chantilly with peach compote, poached pear in puff pastry with hot butterscotch sauce or a selection of British cheeses. No smoking. *Seats 30. Parties 14. Private Room 12. L 12.30-1.30 (Sun only otherwise by arrangement) D 7.30-9. Closed D Sun (except residents). Set Sun L £10.50/£13.50 Set D £18.50.*

CHENIES	Bedford Arms	67%	£123

Tel 01923 283301   Fax 01923 284825   Map 15 E2   **H**
Chenies nr Rickmansworth Buckinghamshire WD3 6EQ

An attractive redbrick hotel just off the A404 on the edge of the village, two miles from junction 18 of the M25. There are two bars – a convivial public bar at the front and relaxing lounge bar to the rear. Upstairs the bedrooms are attractively decorated with good use of well co-ordinated chintzy floral fabrics and range of useful modern amenities. Banqueting facilities for 65, conferences up to 25. 24hr room service. *Rooms 10. Garden. Access, Amex, Diners, Visa.*

CHESTER	Jarvis Abbots Well	62%	£89

Tel 01244 332121   Fax 01244 335287   Map 6 A2   **H**
Whitchurch Road Christleton Chester Cheshire CH3 5QL

One mile from the M53, an angular, low-rise modern hotel standing in spacious grounds on the A41 east of Chester. Conference/banqueting facilities for 230/200, health club. Children up to 12 stay free in parents' room. *Rooms 129. Garden, indoor swimming pool, gym, sauna, spa bath, sun beds. Access, Amex, Diners, Visa.*

CHESTER	Blossoms Hotel	63%	£97

Tel 01244 323186   Fax 01244 346433   Map 6 A2   **H**
St John Street Chester Cheshire CH1 1HL

Just off one of Chester's main shopping streets, Blossoms is a characterful mix of 18th-century charm and modern amenities. Half the rooms are designated non-smoking. Forte. *Rooms 64. Access, Amex, Diners, Visa.*

CHESTER	Chester Grosvenor	84%	£220

Tel 01244 324024   Fax 01244 313246   Map 6 A2   **HR**
Eastgate Street Chester Cheshire CH1 1LT

The jewel in the crown of the Grosvenor family, acquired by them in 1800 and gracing the city's main street in its present form since 1866. The interior decor is as graceful and elegant as you could wish, with sweeping staircases, the magnificent Grosvenor chandelier, panelled library and draped drawing room all providing an air of timelessness. Suites and bedrooms are equally luxurious, with attention to every possible detail. Hand-made furniture from Italy and silks and other fabrics from France and the USA combine with quality British craftsmanship to create a reassuring feeling of solidity. Children up to 14 share their parents' room free; stylish banqueting and conference facilities cater for up to 250 delegates; and there is direct access to the hotel from Newgate Street car park. 24hr room service; no dogs. *Rooms 86.*

Closed 25 & 26 Dec. Sauna, solarium, gym, valeting. Access, Amex, Diners, Visa.

Arkle Restaurant   ★   £110

Named in honour of the triple Gold Cup-winning steeplechaser, this elegant, thoroughbred restaurant is deep in the heart of the hotel beyond the library lounge, where pre-prandial drinks are served, but with a skylight providing natural illumination. Lunchtime brings a fixed-price *menu du marché* (which always includes a roast carved at the table from a silver trolley) supplemented by a couple of fish dishes of the day, while dinner is à la carte plus a six-course *menu gourmand* temptingly described by the restaurant manager (or not, if you prefer to eat *en surprise*). High-class cooking, under executive chef Paul Reed, produces such dishes as roasted sea scallops and tomato brandade with sweet garlic and cherry tomatoes; cannelloni of wild rabbit with juniper-scented cabbage and chestnuts, and lamb fillet with boulangère potatoes and lamb's kidneys. Tempting desserts like a delicious hot passion fruit soufflé or hazelnut and banana crème brulée vie for attention with a good cheese trolley featuring a wide selection of British farmhouse cheeses along with a few of the better-known French offerings. Perhaps the best bread trolley in the country generally carries about 14 different breads – all from the hotel's own bakery. A very grand and extensive wine list at mostly grand prices – a NV Krug Rosé champagne bin end at £175 no less! Regional French, Italian and some New World wines offer best value. Many half bottles. Polished, assured service. *Seats 45. Parties 16. L 12-2.30 D 7-9.30. Closed D Sun, L Mon, Bank Holidays, 2 weeks from 25 Dec (except 31 Dec). Set L £18/£22.50 Set D £37.*

La Brasserie   £50

French-styled with a polished wood floor, painted glass dome ceiling, leather banquette seating and black bentwood chairs, this is the informal arm of the hotel open every day from early until late. Using direct access from the street, some customers come in just for croissant and coffee, or a salad and glass of wine, though a complete meal can also be enjoyed. Starters could include crostini of wild mushrooms and parmesan, fresh seared tuna fillet with Oriental vegetables, or potted rabbit with mustard and pickles. For a main course choose from Grosvenor sausages with crushed garlic potatoes and onion gravy, braised oxtail with root vegetables, grills, or charred sea bream with polenta and rouille. Decent dessert trolley and good farmhouse cheeses. Interesting choice of wines around £15; pity the price of champagne has crept up! *Seats 100. Meals 7am-10.30pm (Sun till 10). Closed 25 & 26 Dec.*

CHESTER — Crabwall Manor — 76% — £125

Tel 01244 851666   Fax 01244 851400   Map 6 A2   **H**
Parkgate Road Mollington Chester Cheshire CH1 6NE

An imposing crenellated house set in 11 acres of beautifully laid-out gardens and parkland, just north of the city on the A540. The site can be traced back to the Domesday Book, and a sense of history certainly pervades the place, combined with an awareness of the needs of the '90s. Service is professional and unobtrusive, with an attention to detail and homely touches that set it apart. A splendid stone staircase leads up to the individually decorated bedrooms, which are unusually spacious and comfortable, all with sofa or pair of substantial armchairs plus proper breakfast table and good work space. Equally impressive are the bathrooms, most with separate shower cubicle in addition to extra large bath tub and twin washbasins. All have bidets and good towels including bathrobes. There is evening turn-down service and 24hr room service. Decent breakfasts. Banqueting/conferences for up to 100. No dogs. *Rooms 48. Garden, croquet, snooker. Access, Amex, Diners, Visa.*

CHESTER — Forte Posthouse — 62% — £72

Tel 01244 680111   Fax 01244 674100   Map 6 A2   **H**
Wrexham Road Chester Cheshire CH4 9DL

Modern redbrick hotel on the A483, two miles south of the city centre. Amenities include a health and fitness club, ample car parking and five conference rooms (theatre-style capacity up to 100). Executive rooms offer a few extras and attract a small supplement. Half the rooms are reserved for non-smokers. *Rooms 105. Indoor swimming pool, gym, sauna, spa bath, sun beds, children's playroom (weekends). Access, Amex, Diners, Visa.*

CHESTER — Moat House International — 69% — £143

Tel 01244 322330   Fax 01244 316118   Map 6 A2   **H**
Trinity Street Chester Cheshire CH1 2BD

Centrally located, large modern hotel with good leisure facilities and room for up to 500 conference delegates. Accommodation includes six penthouse suites. 80 open car parking spaces (free) and 10 covered (£7.50 per night). *Rooms 152. Mini-gym, sauna, steam room, solarium. Access, Amex, Diners, Visa.*

CHESTER — Mollington Banastre — 67% — £90

Tel 01244 851471   Fax 01244 851165   Map 6 A2   **H**
Parkgate Road Chester Cheshire CH1 6NN

Comfortable accommodation (children up to 16 free in parents' room), plus good leisure and conference facilities (for up to 300 delegates) in an extended Victorian mansion surrounded by gardens. It stands a mile and a half from junction 16 of the M56. Ample free car parking. Children up to 16 share parents' room free. *Rooms 64. Garden, croquet, indoor swimming pool, gym, squash, sauna, solarium, whirlpool bath, beauty salon, hairdressing, coffee shop (11am-11pm). Access, Amex, Diners, Visa.*

CHESTER — Rowton Hall — 64% — £88

Tel 01244 335262   Fax 01244 335464   Map 6 A2   **H**
Whitchurch Road Chester Cheshire CH3 6AD

Built as a private residence in 1779, the hall stands three miles out of Chester on the A41, on the site of a Civil War battle. There's a spacious reception area and a lounge bar looking out on to the smart indoor pool. Rooms in the old house are stylish and individual, those in the adjoining wing more functional. Good amenities (Hamiltons Leisure Club) and conference facilities for up to 200 – also parking for 200 cars, with garaging available on request. *Rooms 42. Garden, croquet, tennis, indoor swimming pool, mini-gym, sauna, spa bath, sun beds, squash, coffee shop (10am-10pm). Closed 25-27 Dec. Access, Amex, Diners, Visa.*

CHESTER-LE-STREET — Lumley Castle — 69% — £110

Tel 0191-389 1111   Fax 0191-389 1881   Map 5 E2   **H**
Chester-le-Street Co Durham DH3 4NX

Set in spacious grounds, high above nearby Chester-le-Street (take the A167 towards Durham off the A1M North), parts of the castle date back to the 9th century. Authenticity abounds (have a look at the dungeons and the medieval banquet hall which is dominated by a giant stone fireplace and minstrel's gallery) and the interior oozes character, with furnishings that have been carefully chosen to harmonise. The lounge has period furniture, oil paintings and ornaments, and there are some 3000 books in the elegant library. Illuminated statues line the passage that leads to the function rooms (catering for banquets/conferences of up to 250/120), and the pillared and multi-domed Black Knight restaurant, which serves a good breakfast. Main bedrooms are spacious and appealing, with heavy drapes and beautiful decor combined with good antique furniture; feature Castle rooms have some added attractions like a raised sleeping area or a Queen Anne four-poster. A night in the King James suite (£180) includes a 20ft-high four-poster, a whirlpool bath, champagne and flowers. Most rooms, however, are in the courtyard and are smaller, but equally stylish, with decent bathrooms. Helpful and pleasant staff wear period costume. Children up to 14 stay free in parents' room. *Rooms 60. Garden. Closed 25 & 26 Dec, 1 Jan. Access, Amex, Diners, Visa.*

CHESTERFIELD	Chesterfield Hotel	59%	£75

Tel 01246 271141   Fax 01246 220719   Map 6 C2   **H**
Malkin Street Chesterfield Derbyshire S41 7UA

A one-time railway hotel, just off the bypass. Purpose-built Peak Leisure Centre (with a large swimming pool) and conference suite for up to 120 delegates. Children under 16 stay free in parents' room. Accommodation includes 12 Executive rooms. No dogs. *Rooms 73. Indoor swimming pool, gym, sauna, spa bath, steam room, solarium, beauty salon, snooker. Access, Amex, Diners, Visa.*

CHICHESTER	Comme Ca	£55

Tel 01243 788724   Map 11 A6   **R**
67 Broyle Road Chichester West Sussex PO19 4BD

North of town on the A286, and close to the Festival Theatre (3 minutes walk), this French restaurant with a bar is in a converted pub. Chef-patron Michel Navet cooks in a sound, classically-based style, offering a good choice of dishes, from the day's soup and vegetable pancake to fillets of Dover sole sautéed with cream, mushrooms and prawns (a house speciality), fish in brioche with a crab bisque, calf's liver with a sage butter sauce and bacon, and grilled fillet of beef topped with Dijon mustard, caramelised and flambé (another speciality). Popular family Sunday lunches (special children's menu) and bar lunches. Six tables in the garden in good weather. Large car park. *Seats 80. Parties 28. Private Room 35. L 12-2 D 5.30-10.30. Closed D Sun, all Mon, Bank Holidays. Set L £13.75/£16.75 (Sun £15.50) Set D (after-theatre) £14.50/£16.50. Access, Amex, Visa.*

CHICHESTER	Dolphin & Anchor	63%	£102

Tel 01243 785121   Fax 01243 533408   Map 11 A6   **H**
West Street Chichester West Sussex PO19 1QE

Built in the 17th century, the Dolphin and the Anchor were rivals until united in 1910. Best bedrooms (which attract a supplementary charge) are at the front, with views of the cathedral opposite. Children up to 16 stay free in parents' room. The conference and banqueting ballroom (once the Liberal Assembly Rooms) caters for up to 180. Forte. *Rooms 49. Access, Amex, Diners, Visa.*

CHICHESTER	The Droveway	£80

Tel 01243 528832   Map 11 A6   **R**
30a Southgate Chichester West Sussex PO19 1DR

Bookshelves, Old Master sketches and a comfortable bar/lounge area at one end of this large upstairs room create a cosy, traditional ambience. A short fixed-price dinner menu (changing every few days) supplements an appealing à la carte – roast wood pigeon and walnut salad, oyster and champagne charlotte, roast monkfish Wellington, Sussex jugged hare, tapénade of lamb, tournedos Roquefort. Imaginative list of puds or excellent, mostly English, cheese selection. Notably good coffees with names like Yemen Ismaili or Sumatra Mandeling plus a choice of quality loose-leaf teas. Wine list concentrates on value for money. After-theatre (Chichester Festival) suppers by prior booking only. *Seats 38. Private Room 10. L 12.30-2 D 7-10. Closed Sun, Mon, 1st 2 weeks Jan. Set L £12/£15 Set D £19.50. Access, Amex, Visa.*

CHIDDINGFOLD   Crown Inn   £57

Tel 01428 682255   Fax 01428 685736   Map 11 A5   **I**
The Green Chiddingfold Surrey GU8 4TX

Established as a hostelry in 1285, the mellow half-timbered Crown is one of the oldest recorded inns in England. Linenfold panelling, stained glass in mullioned windows, creaking stairs and passages leading to atmospheric bedrooms with sloping floors, bowed walls, beams and solid furniture show its age. Annexe rooms are contrastingly light and modern. *Rooms 8. Access, Amex, Diners, Visa.*

CHILGROVE   White Horse Inn   £60

Tel 01243 535219   Fax 01243 535301   Map 15 E3   **R**
High Street Chilgrove nr Chichester West Sussex PO18 9HX

Instead of a nice picture of a white horse, the pub sign here is a wine glass – which is entirely appropriate as this wisteria-clad, 18th-century hostelry boasts one of the finest wine lists in the country. But good wine deserves good food and chef-partner Neil Rusbridger's cooking fits the bill admirably. There's plenty of interest on his menus, from ravioli of crab and ginger served on a watercress sauce to lamb *en croute* with Madeira sauce, Barbary duck on a galette of bubble and squeak and, for vegetarians, creamed artichoke and spring onion vol-au-vent. The list of desserts is recited at the table and can include home-made ice cream as well as such adventurous ideas as chocolate ravioli with orange sauce. After-theatre suppers by arrangement. If there's a finer wine list anywhere in the world, please let us know! The German section alone runs to over two hundred wines, and there are well over fifty double magnums of classic clarets, not to mention dozens and dozens of vintage Lafite, Latour, Margaux etc. Vintage port is available by the bucketful, half bottles plentiful; to do the list justice, allow lots of time to peruse – think of the effort that Barry Philips has put into its compilation. Twice winner of our Cellar of the Year award. *Seats 70. Parties 24. Private Room 12. L 12-2 D 7-9.30. Closed D Sun, all Mon, 3 weeks Feb, last week Oct. Set L £17.50 Set D £23 (4-course). Access, Diners, Visa.*

CHIPPING   Gibbon Bridge Hotel   65%   £70

Tel 01995 61456   Fax 01995 61277   Map 6 B1   **H**
The Forest of Bowland Chipping Lancashire PR3 2TQ

Owned by Janet and Margaret Simpson, the hotel, in the remote Lancashire fells, was once a farmhouse, converted by local craftsmen using local materials whenever possible. It stands on the banks of the River Loud and is surrounded by 20 acres of lovingly tended gardens, floodlit at night. Attention to detail shows here – note the graceful 19th-century statue, gazebo, bridges and gas lamps. However, considerably less attention was encountered at a much below par breakfast – pity, because the conservatory restaurant is an attractive room. And, at the time of our latest visit, the bedroom information folder, still indicating old telephone numbers, was two years out of date. 22 of the bedrooms are magnificent indeed, covering two floors with a large ground-floor lounge and a separate upstairs bedroom, furnished with king-size beds with brass bedsteads (half-testers and four-posters being almost standard), and excellent and thoughtfully equipped bathrooms. However, the other bedrooms, despite pleasant views, have small windows allowing little fresh air, and are poorly soundproofed. Conferences up to 70. *Rooms 30. Garden, croquet, fishing, tennis, gym, steam room, sauna, spa bath, solarium, beauty salon, bakery. Access, Amex, Diners, Visa.*

CHIPPING CAMPDEN   Cotswold House   70%   £95

Tel 01386 840330   Fax 01386 840310   Map 14 C1   **HR**
The Square Chipping Campden Gloucestershire GL55 6AN

A late 17th-century town house right on the High Street (with a fine garden to the rear) run with great charm and easy-going hospitality by the Greenstocks. There's a 'country house' feel to civilised day rooms, which boast antiques, fresh flowers and nice architectural features like the fine cantilevered spiral staircase that sweeps up to the bedroom floors. For a change, beyond there's a courtyard garden, also run by the hotel, in a Georgian building next door. Each bedroom is tastefully themed as reflected in their names, Indian, Ribbons and Bows, Gothic, Honeysuckle – some, like Paradise and Aunt Lizzie's room, are less obvious than others. Antiques often feature in the decor and beds are turned down at night. Just one small single has shower and

WC only. Room service operates throughout the day and evening. No children under 8. No dogs. *Rooms 15. Garden, croquet, café/bar (9.30am-11pm). Closed 24 – 28 Dec. Access, Amex, Visa.*

The Garden Room   £70

Its name inspired by the charming walled garden over which it looks, the dining-room here has some fine period features – Corinthian columns, moulded ceiling, comfortable chairs around widely spaced tables and a grand piano (sporting a fine flower display) that accompanies dinner a couple of times a week. The main, fixed-price menu (there's also a short 'House Dinner') offers about seven choices at each stage including a trio of ravioli with a chive and lemon grass sauce, warm salad of lamb and veal sweetbreads with mangetout and a herb dressing, roast fillet of turbot with sweet potato, olive oil and coriander, noisettes of Cotswold lamb on a bed of Chinese spiced leeks with foie gras butter and the day's fish dish followed by desserts like warm prune and armagnac tart or chocolate and coffee millefeuille with Kahlua sauce. Careful cooking produces pleasing results and service is both attentive and friendly. An authoritative wine list, very decently priced, presented by grape style. Plenty of quality names, growers and vintages; sensible tasting notes. No smoking. *Seats 40. Private Room 20. L (Sun only) 12-2. D 7.15-9.30. Set Sun L £15.75 Set D £18.50.*

CHIPPING CAMPDEN	Noel Arms	61%	£80

Tel 01386 840317   Fax 01386 841136   Map 14 C1   **H**
High Street Chipping Campden Gloucestershire GL55 6AT

When Charles II rested here in 1651 after defeat at the Battle of Worcester this renowned hostelry was already 300 years old. Many reminders of the past remain, including swords, shields and muskets in the foyer. There's a cosy beamed bar, a bright conservatory and an oak-panelled restaurant. Bedrooms are divided more or less evenly between those in a rustic style with antique furniture in the main part to a modern look in the wing. Some rooms have four-poster beds. *Rooms 26. Access, Amex, Diners, Visa.*

CHIPPING CAMPDEN	Seymour House	64%	£90

Tel 01386 840429   Fax 01386 840369   Map 14 C1   **H**
High Street Chipping Campden Gloucestershire GL55 6AH

In the main street of town, a mellow Cotswold-stone hotel with a pretty garden to the rear. Bedrooms are the main strength here, varying in size and shape; some have characterful old beams and all but three (of which one has shower and WC only) boast reproduction antiques in a number of different styles. There are three full suites. Public rooms comprise a single lounge with firm easy chairs and settees, the restaurant where breakfast is taken and which features an ancient vine and a new bar that was due to open during 1995. Limited room service throughout the day and evening but a flask of fresh milk is provided for the beverage tray. *Rooms 16. Garden. Access, Amex, Visa.*

CHIPPING NORTON	Crown & Cushion		£69

Tel 01608 642533   Fax 01608 642926   Map 14 C1   **I**
High Street Chipping Norton Oxfordshire OX7 5AD

Accommodation at this privately-owned former coaching inn (dating in parts from 1497) ranges from 11 'standard' rooms in the coach house annexe (one minute's walk away) up to suites with separate lounge, writing bureau, sofa and traditional cast-iron bath – prices vary considerably according to size of room. Top of the range are rooms with four-poster or half-tester beds; one room is on two levels with an old four-poster up a few steps from a separate lounge area. Public areas include a cosy lounge, beamed bar, numerous conference rooms (for up to 200) and a leisure club. *Rooms 40. Indoor swimming pool, gym, squash, solarium, snooker. Access, Amex, Diners, Visa.*

CHISELDON	Chiseldon House	66%	£90

Tel 01793 741010   Fax 01793 741059   Map 14 C2   **HR**
New Road Chiseldon nr Swindon Wiltshire SN4 0NE

A charming Regency house forms the backbone of this comfortable hotel, now much enlarged with a modern extension. Brightly decorated bedrooms are modestly furnished, but all mod cons, including satellite TV, direct-dial phones, mini-bars and en-suite bathrooms. Executive rooms have four-poster beds and upgraded bathrooms with

See over

separate tubs and showers. Two stylish conference rooms provide private facilities for up to 65. *Rooms 21. Garden, outdoor swimming pool. Access, Amex, Diners, Visa.*

Orangery Restaurant   £65

The restaurant overlooks the garden and is colourfully decorated, like much of the hotel. John Farrow offers short table d'hote menus with dishes to please both the traditionalist and the more adventurous. Perhaps sautéed mushrooms with shallots and bacon or warm salad of pigeon to begin; roast sirloin of beef with rösti potatoes, chargrilled pheasant with an apple and cider sauce to follow. Generally an interesting vegetarian option – mushroom and pepper stroganoff on one visit – but prior notice is appreciated. *Seats 48. Private Room 20. L 12-2 D 7-9. Closed L Sat. Set L £11.95/£14.95 (Sun £14.95) Set D £22.95.*

CHITTLEHAMHOLT	Highbullen	60%	£105

Tel 01769 540561   Fax 01769 540492   Map 13 D2   **H**
Chittlehamholt nr South Molton Devon EX37 9HD

A splendid Victorian mansion standing in parkland which includes an 80 acre wood on high ground between Exmoor and Dartmoor (M5 Junction 27, A361 to South Molton, B3226 5 miles, turn right to Chittlehamholt, through village, half a mile to hotel). Bedrooms are in a comfortably traditional style whether in the main house, an adjoining property in a country-style garden or in a group of nearby cottages. Sports and leisure facilities are excellent (unlimited free golf, and a resident professional). There's always plenty to do, but there are also restrictions – no children under eight, no dogs, no smoking in the restaurant or breakfast room. A four-bedroomed house in the grounds is suitable for a family group. *Rooms 39. Garden, indoor & outdoor swimming pools, squash, sauna, spa bath, steam room, massage, solarium, hair & beauty salon, indoor & outdoor tennis, 9-hole golf course with resident professional, coarse fishing, indoor putting, table tennis, snooker, sports shop. No credit cards.*

CHOBHAM	Quails Restaurant	£55

Tel 01276 858491   Map 15 E3   **R**
1 Bagshot Road Chobham Surrey GU24 8BP

The interior is light and airy (and air-conditioned) with sturdy country chairs around crisply-clothed tables, each sporting a mini-parlour plant. The regularly-changing à la carte menu is of French inspiration with some more exotic touches shown by such dishes as pigeon terrine with red onion marmalade, salmon salad niçoise and bang bang chicken among the starters with such main dishes as marinated lamb fillet with a bell pepper and couscous timbale and oregano jus, entrecote of wild boar with orange and Thai ginger, and a mélange of seafood in filo with lime and coriander on a crab sabayon. Desserts include fruit sorbets, pecan and date bread-and-butter pudding and blackcurrant flummery in a dark chocolate ramekin. A limited-choice set dinner menu includes a half bottle of wine. Good Sunday lunches. There are many good wines at reasonable prices on the list. *Seats 40. Parties 12 (8 at weekend). L 12.30-2 D 7-10. Closed L Sat, D Sun & all Mon. Set L £11/£14.50 (£12.95 Sun) Set D (not Sat) £13.95 (inc wine).* *Access, Amex, Diners, Visa.*

CHOLLERFORD	George Hotel	59%	£110

Tel 01434 681611   Fax 01434 681727   Map 5 D2   **H**
Chollerford nr Hexham Northumberland NE46 4EW

A riverside setting with delightful gardens and good leisure facilities. Most bedrooms have garden or river views and are furnished in up-to-date style. Children up to 14 free in parents' room, two family rooms, four Executive rooms. Banqueting/conferences for 40/70. Swallow Hotels. *Rooms 48. Garden, indoor swimming pool, spa bath, sauna, steam room, solarium, fishing, putting. Access, Amex, Diners, Visa.*

Consult the blue pages for summary tables and lists of recommended establishments.

| CHRISTCHURCH | **Splinters** | ↑ | **£55** |

Tel 01202 483454   Fax 01202 483454   Map 14 C4   **R**
11 Church Street Christchurch Dorset BH23 1BW

Timothy Lloyd's and Robert Wilson's restaurant near the Priory in the centre of town also houses Number 11 Brasserie (10.30-2.30), a raised bar area with wicker chairs, serving light lunches and snacks. The cosy restaurant itself, with polished wooden floors and tables, combines three ground-floor rooms, one surrounded by wine racks, the other two with alcove-style seating and old church pews. Upstairs there's a first-floor lounge with open fire and comfortable sofas for the after-dinner coffee, a small terrace and a private dining-room overlooking the Priory. Chef Eamonn Redden's prix-fixe menus (a shorter version at lunch) has half-a-dozen or so choices at each stage along the lines of cod and potato rösti with split peas or ravioli of crab with a butter sauce or tomatoes and dill to start, followed by half a roast Gressingham duckling with a pear and cinnamon sauce or roasted sea bass with caramelised broad beans and parsley. End with a good selection of British and Irish cheeses, a delectable dessert such as crème caramel with fresh raspberries and a coulis, or hot rhubarb crumble tart with ginger clotted cream. Olives to start, good fresh baguette bread and coffee served with hand-made petits fours. *Seats 40. Parties 10. Private Room 22. L 12-2.30 D 7-10.30. Set L £11.50/£14.50. Set D £19.75/£24 Closed 2 weeks Jan. Access, Amex, Diners, Visa.*

| CHURT | **Frensham Pond Hotel 62%** | **£88** |

Tel 01252 795161   Fax 01252 792631   Map 11 A5   **H**
Churt nr Farnham Surrey GU10 2QB

Frensham Great Pond is a large lake with a busy weekend dinghy sailing club and the hotel overlooking it was originally built as a private residence in the 15th century. Features include four conference suites (up to 150 delegates) and a leisure club with its own bar and restaurant. Most of the bedrooms are in an extension in the gardens to the rear. 24hr room service. *Rooms 51. Garden, indoor swimming pool, sauna, solarium, squash, spa bath, keep-fit equipment, beauty salon, squash, games room, coffee shop (8am-10pm). Access, Amex, Diners, Visa.*

| CIRENCESTER | **Fleece Hotel** | **64%** | **£94** |

Tel 01285 658507   Fax 01285 651017   Map 14 C2   **H**
Market Place Cirencester Gloucestershire GL7 2LE

Timber-fronted Tudor inn in the centre of a town that once supported a thriving wool trade. Accommodation includes a couple of four-posters and a room with spa bath. Children under 16 stay free in their parents' room. The coffee shop closes between 3pm and 6pm in winter. Resort Hotels. *Rooms 30. Coffee shop (10am-11pm). Access, Amex, Diners, Visa.*

| CIRENCESTER | **Stratton House** | **64%** | **£80** |

Tel 01285 651761   Fax 01285 640024   Map 14 C2   **H**
Gloucester Road Cirencester Gloucestershire GL7 2LE

On the A417 to the north of town this former wool merchant's house dates back to the 17th century. The period feel has been retained in public areas like the flagstoned entrance hall, the beamed bar with real log fire and leather chairs and the comfortable lounge overlooking a walled garden. Pretty bedrooms are individually decorated, those in the original building often retaining original fireplaces. Good bathrooms offer large bottles of shampoo and bath essence. Limited room service. *Rooms 41. Garden, croquet. Access, Amex, Diners, Visa.*

| CIRENCESTER | **Tatyan's** | **£45** |

Tel 01285 653529   Fax 01285 641126   Map 14 C2   **R**
27 Castle Street Cirencester Gloucestershire GL7 1QD

Szechuan, Hunan and Peking regional cooking provide the specialities on a wide-ranging evening menu. Order Peking duck a day in advance. Good set lunch. Friendly and helpful service. Unusually for a Chinese restaurant, the wine list here is an excellent one and good value too. *Seats 50. Parties 20. L 12-2 D 6-10.30. Closed Sun, 25 & 26 Dec. Set L £8.50 Set D from £11.50. Access, Amex, Diners, Visa.*

CLANFIELD   Plough at Clanfield   £85

Tel 01367 810222   Fax 01367 810596   Map 14 C2   **IR**
Bourton Road Clanfield Oxfordshire OX18 2RB

Roses and wisteria clinging to the Cotswold stone walls of this small 16th-century manor house make a pretty picture in early summer and the atmosphere within is very much that of a superior inn; a single bar/lounge has a few old beams and posts and smart velour upholstered wing chairs and settees in pink and blue. Cosy bedrooms come with baby teddy bears to keep you company and bathrooms – four with whirlpool tubs, two with shower and WC only – are shared with families of plastic ducks along with towelling robes and good toiletries. No dogs. *Rooms 6. Garden. Access, Amex, Diners, Visa.*

Tapestry Room Restaurant   £70

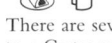

There are several choices of menu in the Tapestry Room, from a 3-course house menu to a Gastronome menu which features an optional middle course. Typical dishes include fillets of red snapper with tapénade croutons and spicy tomato compote, broccoli and cheddar tartlet with apple and hazelnuts and rack of lamb with kidneys turbigo and roast potatoes. Snacks are served in the lounge (and in the Rose Garden weather permitting). *Seats 30. Private Room 12. L 12-2 D 7-10 (Sun to 9.30). Set L £10.95/£14.50 Set D from £19.50.*

CLAWTON   Court Barn   61%   £69

Tel 01409 271219   Fax 01409 271309   Map 12 C2   **H**
Clawton Holsworthy Devon EX22 6PS

Robert and Susan Wood have been running their charming little manor house (set in five acres of well-tended gardens) since 1986, and a steady stream of returnees fills the relaxing day rooms and comfortable bedrooms, all of which are non-smoking. 1995 saw the installation of new bathrooms in most rooms and some new carpets and furnishings as well – improvements are continuing this year. Two rooms are suitable for family use, and children up to 14 stay free in parents' room; cots and high-chairs are available. Small receptions (40) and conferences (25) can be accommodated, as can 16 cars. *Rooms 8. Garden, croquet, badminton, tennis, pitch & putt, putting. Closed 2-10 Jan. Access, Amex, Diners, Visa.*

CLAYGATE   Les Alouettes   £70

Tel 01372 464882   Map 15 E2   **R**
7 High Street Claygate Surrey KT10 0JW

The restaurant's pretty decor features a rose-entwined trellis painted on the walls and the tableware is Royal Doulton bone china. A good mix of dishes features on the quite lengthy à la carte – hot duck croustade with orange sauce, warm terrine of sole and langoustines with a langoustine cream, Dover sole (grilled or meuniére) and grills. There are also more adventurous creations such as roast boned quails with a traditional French grape sauce, 'tournedos' of salmon with mushroom and dill duxelles on a smoked salmon and mushroom sauce with crispy leeks, maize-fed chicken fillet with an orange butter sauce garnished with a courgette ratatouille and crispy roast duck with caramelised pear and a cassis sauce. All dishes are based on good-quality ingredients, carefully handled. Only French wines on the Connoisseur list, but several classic names are keenly priced. *Seats 60. Parties 65. L 12-2.15 D 7-9.30 (Sat till 10). Set L £15.50 (Sun £12.95/£14.95) Set D £19.50 (Sat £22.50). Closed L Sat, D Sun, Bank Holidays, 2 weeks summer & 1 week Christmas. Access, Amex, Visa.*

CLAYTON-LE-WOODS   Pines Hotel   65%   £55

Tel 01772 38551   Fax 01772 629002   Map 6 B1   **H**
Preston Road Clayton-le-Woods nr Chorley Lancashire PR6 7ED

A much-extended Victorian house on the A6, just off the M6 (Junction 28/29), with spacious bedrooms offering good modern facilities. Four acres of wooded grounds, ideal for business meetings and conferences (up to 200 delegates), live cabaret at weekends in the Dixon suite. "Music installed with speakers all round the hotel". No dogs. Free parking for more than 100 cars. Current projects include redesigning the public areas. *Rooms 39. Garden, 24hr shop. Closed 25 & 26 Dec. Access, Amex, Diners, Visa.*

| CLEARWELL | **Clearwell Castle** | 69% | £90 |

Tel 01594 832320   Fax 01594 835523   Map 14 B2   **H**
Clearwell nr Coleford Gloucestershire GL16 8LG

Located in the Royal Forest of Dean, the site dates back to Roman times, but the current castle is of 18th-century origins, in Gothic Revival style, with a castellated exterior and stately halls. The bar is less stately, having instead a clubby appeal. Bedrooms combine four-posters and half-testers with up-to-date amenities. **Rooms** 14. Garden. Closed Jan & early Feb. Ring to confirm other winter closures. Access, Amex, Diners, Visa.

Set menu prices may not always include service or wine.

| CLEARWELL | **The Wyndham Arms** | £61 |

Tel 01594 833666   Fax 01594 836450   Map 14 B2   **I**
Clearwell nr Coleford Gloucestershire GL16 8JT

John and Rosemary Stanford have completed over 20 years as imperturbable hosts at the tranquil Wyndham, where accommodation is divided between original bedrooms in the evocative 600-year-old main building and a recent stone extension. Good bar snacks. **Rooms** 17. Garden. Access, Amex, Diners, Visa.

| CLEETHORPES | **Kingsway Hotel** | 62% | £75 |

Tel 01472 601122   Fax 01472 601381   Map 7 F2   **H**
Cleethorpes Humberside DN35 0AE

A traditional seafront hotel, run by the Harris family for four generations. Regular refurbishment keeps things smart in the day rooms and in the bedrooms, most of which have solid reproduction furniture. One of the lounges is non-smoking. No children under five (5-14s free in parents' room). No dogs. Leisure centre 300yds from hotel. **Rooms** 50. Roof garden, garage. Closed 25 & 26 Dec. Access, Amex, Diners, Visa.

| CLIMPING | **Bailiffscourt** | 74% | £125 |

Tel 01903 723511   Fax 01903 723107   Map 11 A6   **HR**
Climping nr Littlehampton West Sussex BN17 5RW

England's greatest folly? This 'medieval manor' with its associated buildings was actually constructed in the 1930s by Lord Moyen (of the Guinness family) but entirely of recycled 13th-century building materials and architectural 'antiques'. Its old timbers, heavy iron-studded doors, ancient stonework and mullioned windows imbue it with a genuinely mellow atmosphere. Since taking over in 1993 the owners have done a fine job in refurbishing both public rooms and bedrooms with solid oak furniture, including many antique pieces, and appropriate fabrics plus Oriental rugs, numerous fires and fresh flowers adding warmth and comfort to the former and splendid new bathrooms enhancing the modern amenities in the latter. Eleven of the bedrooms – some of which are in adjacent, equally 'old' buildings – boast four-posters and several can have real fires. **Rooms** 27. Garden, croquet, outdoor swimming pool, tennis. Access, Amex, Diners, Visa.

Restaurant   £80

Chef Simon Rogan produces an interesting, eclectic menu, based on the finest quality raw materials, which includes sabayon of oysters with truffled scrambled eggs, boulangère of scallops smoked à la minute with lemon and thyme and a salad of duck confit à la niçoise as starters with fillet of bass with a pistou of clams and a jus of oysters, cutlets of venison St Hubert with sauce poivrade or pot-au-feu of English lamb with a ravioli of sweetbreads to follow. Delicious desserts: a pyramid of pineapple or a soup of chocolate with ravioli of bananas. Many dishes carry a supplement in the evening, boosting prices considerably. A well-rounded list has tasting notes alongside each wine; several good names under £20. Light lunches are available in the bar (except Sun). No smoking. **Seats** 50. Parties 15. Private Room 30. L 12.30-2 D 7-9.30. Set L £17.50 Set D £29.50.

Lodges are now listed by county in the reference section

CLITHEROE — Browns Bistro — £55

Tel 01200 26928   Map 6 B1   **R**
10 York Street Clitheroe Lancashire BB7 2DL

🍷 🍾

Bare boards and check cloths lend Browns a French café atmosphere, while daily-changed blackboards emphasise the freshness of supplies. Fish and shellfish from Manchester markets, Angus beef, complimentary *petits pains* and salad bowl, generous portions – all enlivened by a general sense of fun. Ignore the spelling mistakes and the lay-out of the wine list – it offers fantastic value for money, eg house champagne at £16.50 and Louis Roederer Cristal at £75. Extensive Italian section and vintage ports by the glass. *Seats 66. Parties 12. L 12-1.45 D 7-10. Closed L Sat, all Sun, 3 days Christmas, 3 days New Year. Access, Visa.*

COATHAM MUNDEVILLE — Hall Garth — 66% — £81

Tel 01325 300400   Fax 01325 310083   Map 5 E3   **HR**
Coatham Mundeville nr Darlington Co Durham DL1 3LU

Situated just off the A167 within two minutes of the A1(M). Day rooms include three most civilised country house-style lounges warmed by real fires in winter and with drinks service from a dispenser bar, while for a change of mood there's the separate Stables Bar with a more lively, pubby atmosphere. Best of the bedrooms are perhaps those furnished with antiques in the original building (£90); the majority, in a new wing, have darkwood freestanding pieces and co-ordinating fabrics while those in the annexe above the bar feature solid lightwood furniture. Three of these have shower and WC only. Bedroom seating is generally limited to low, armless easy chairs and a stool at the desk. Ongoing refurbishments during 1995 should see bedrooms improved and the 9-hole golf course launched. 24hr room service. *Rooms 41. Garden, tennis, golf (9), putting green, indoor swimming pool, sauna, steam room, spa bath, solarium, children's outdoor playground. Closed 24-26 Dec. Access, Amex, Diners, Visa.*

Hugo's — £60

🍷 🍮 🍶

Choose between the dark red dining-room or conservatory extension to enjoy generally soundly cooked dishes from a fixed-price menu that offers a good choice. Terrine of aubergine wrapped in smoked salmon, panaché of seafood with saffron noodles in a cream and wine sauce, and supreme of chicken on a lemon and pistachio risotto show the style. Shorter lunch menu. A champagne under £20, even the '83/'85 Dom Perignons are under £60, setting the tone for all-round fair prices. Bravo! *Seats 80. Parties 12. Private Room 20. L 12-2 D 7-9.30. Closed L Sat, D Sun & D 25 Dec. Set L £10.95 (Sun £11.95) Set D £15.95/£19.95.*

COBHAM — Hilton National — 65% — £142

Tel 01932 864471   Fax 01932 868017   Map 15 E3   **H**
Seven Hills Road South Cobham Surrey KT11 1EW

Near Junction 10 of the M25, the hotel is based around Neville Chamberlain's former home, now surrounded by various modern extensions. Both public areas and bedrooms are well-kept, with good desk space (to which the telephone can be moved) and Plaza rooms come with extras like mineral water, chocolates and miniatures of whisky. The pool is small but with a 'jet stream' for more serious swimmers; the fitness room is in a separate part of the building. Conferences are an important part of the business during the week. *Rooms 152. Garden, tennis, indoor swimming pool, keep-fit equipment, squash, sauna, steam room, spa bath, solarium. Access, Amex, Diners, Visa.*

COBHAM — Woodlands Park — 68% — £154

Tel 01372 843933   Fax 01372 842704   Map 15 E3   **H**
Woodlands Lane Stoke D'Abernon Cobham Surrey KT11 3QB

A fine late-Victorian mansion, formerly home to the match-making Bryant family, set in ten acres of landscaped grounds. Very much a conference hotel during the week, at weekends it's a popular venue for weddings; most of the period meeting rooms lead off the splendid, galleried Grand Hall that serves as both lounge and 'break-out' area for delegates. There's table service of drinks here but the main bar is now incorporated into the fairly new Langtry Brasserie (Lillie Langtry and the Prince of Wales were frequent visitors to the house). Good-sized bedrooms vary in shape and decor but all are comfortably furnished with reproduction antiques. Bathrooms all have showers over tubs and guests are provided with nice large towels. Beds are turned down in the evening and room service operates day and night. Children under 12 stay free in parents' room. No dogs. **Rooms** 58. *Garden, tennis, croquet. Closed 1 week Christmas. Access, Amex, Diners, Visa.*

COCKERMOUTH	Quince & Medlar	£30

Tel 01900 823579   Map 4 C3   **R**
13 Castlegate Cockermouth Cumbria CA13 9EU

Next to Cockermouth Castle, a wood-panelled, candle-lit vegetarian restaurant in a Georgian building, run on informal lines by Colin and Louisa Le Voi. Colin's menu is short but full of interest, with starters like warm forest mushroom salad with quail's eggs and main courses which should arouse even carnivorous taste buds: spinach and tomato layered blinis topped with cheese sauce and pine kernels and served with a mixed side salad. Desserts lack nothing in appeal with the likes of rhubarb and cinnamon crunch or lime and pineapple icebox pudding. No smoking. **Seats** 26. *Parties 14. D only 7-9.30. Closed Mon, also Sun between New Year and Easter, 1 week mid-Nov & 2 weeks Jan. Access, Visa.*

COGGESHALL	White Hart	69%	£82

Tel 01376 561654   Fax 01376 561789   Map 10 C3   **HR**
Market End Coggeshall Essex CO6 1NH

A centuries-old inn that still retains all its character with flagstone floors, low beams, inglenook fireplace and not one but two resident ghosts. One bay of the original (1420) Guildhall is now the residents' lounge, whose decor adds style and comfort to the atmospheric surroundings. Individually decorated bedrooms, 12 in an extension, offer little extras like fresh fruit and mineral water. **Rooms** 18. *Garden. Access, Amex, Diners, Visa.*

Restaurant   £60

A long, low and narrow dining-room with sturdy beams and cheerful staff. An Italian menu ranges from a variety of pasta dishes (a speciality) to *fritto misto di mare,* scampi Newburg, guinea fowl flamed in Marsala wine and blackcurrant sauce and charcoal-grilled T-bone steak. Traditional Sunday lunch and a good selection of desserts. **Seats** 70. *L 12-2 (Sun 12.30-2.30) D 7-10. Closed D Sun & 25 Dec, all 26 Dec. Set Sun L £14.95.*

COLCHESTER	Butterfly Hotel	61%	£62

Tel 01206 230900   Fax 01206 231095   Map 10 C3   **H**
Old Ipswich Road Ardleigh Colchester Essex CO7 7QY

Part of a small chain offering practical accommodation (there is separate work space in all the bedrooms) that includes four rooms specially equipped for ladies (door-chains, spy-holes) and 14 reserved for non-smokers. Located on the A12/A120 near the Business Parks. **Rooms** 50. *Access, Amex, Diners, Visa.*

COLCHESTER	Forte Posthouse	61%	£72

Tel 01206 767740   Fax 01206 766577   Map 10 C3   **H**
Abbotts Lane Eight Ash Green Colchester Essex CO6 3QL

Off the A604 to the north-west of the A12. There's a Canadian log cabin-themed informal restaurant and good leisure centre. More than half the bedrooms are designated non-smoking. Children free when sharing parents' room. **Rooms** 110. *Terrace, indoor swimming pool, gym, spa bath, sauna, steam room, sun bed, beauty salon. Access, Amex, Diners, Visa.*

Lodges are now listed by county in the reference section

COLCHESTER — Red Lion Hotel — £60

Tel 01206 577986 Fax 01206 578207   Map 10 C3   **I**
High Street Colchester Essex CO1 1DH

Almost directly opposite the Hippodrome (now a nightclub) in the town centre, the Inn was built in 1465. Now restricted to the upper floors, only the wrought-iron signage at the front indicates what lies within. The main public room is the spacious and very characterful beamed bar/lounge. There are seven bedrooms in the original building, and front rooms are double-glazed. The rooms are comfortable and cosy, with a good range of modern amenities including mineral water. *Rooms 24. Access, Amex, Diners, Visa.*

COLCHESTER — Rose & Crown — £55

Tel 01206 866677 Fax 01206 866616   Map 10 C3   **I**
East Street Colchester Essex CO1 2T2

A lovely old beamed inn in the heart of the historic town. There are rough white-painted plaster walls and gnarled, blackened beams and timbers a-plenty creating a cosy and characterful setting. Bedrooms include three with four-posters. All have satellite TV and other up-to-date amenities. *Rooms 30. Closed 27-29 Dec. Amex, Access. Diners, Visa.*

Set menu prices may not always include service or wine.

COLCHESTER — Warehouse Brasserie — £50

Tel & Fax 01206 765656   Map 10 C3   **R**
Chapel Street North Colchester Essex CO2 7AL

A converted chapel down a small lane in the town centre (a few hundred yards up from Osborne Street car park). Inside, the split-level restaurant has a very relaxed, informal atmosphere. There's a long bar-counter down one side and facing it rows of plain wooden tables and chairs. The menu fits the bistroish setting with starters such as grilled tuna niçoise and home-made duck confit. Excellent garlic bread could accompany. Main dishes range from beef in Adnams ale to monkfish and salmon brochette, roast Suffolk duckling breast with spiced pear tartlet and twice-baked tomato and basil soufflé. All main dishes are accompanied by delicious vegetables. There are excellent desserts to finish such as pear crumble tartlet, pecan and praline parfait or chocolate and pear brownie with hot chocolate sauce and vanilla ice cream. Very friendly staff. *Seats 90. Parties 30. L 12-2 D 7-9.30. Closed D Sun, most Bank Holidays. Set L £7.95/£9.95. Access, Amex, Visa.*

COLERNE — Lucknam Park — 83% — £171

Tel 01225 742777 Fax 01225 743536   Map 14 B2   **HR**
Colerne Wiltshire SN14 8AZ

Approached by a straight mile of beech-lined drive, a gracious Georgian house in a tranquil setting, six miles from Bath on the southern edge of the Cotswolds. The house has a particularly English feel and is luxuriously fitted with sound taste. Day rooms are spacious and extremely elegant with soft colours, choice antiques and oil paintings plus deep-cushioned sofas. Sumptuously comfortable bedrooms are appointed to the highest standards with handsome furnishings and fittings which a house of this stature merits. Each is individually decorated in quintessential English style, and most of the marble-tiled bathrooms boast double basins. Housekeeping is immaculate. The leisure spa is contained in an eighteenth-century Roman villa and set in the old walled garden. There are two floodlit tennis courts and four individually decorated health and beauty rooms (for men and women). Impeccably dressed young staff. 24hr room service. Banqueting and conference facilities for up to 80/100. No dogs, but kennelling can be arranged. *Rooms 42. Garden, croquet, tennis, indoor pool, spa bath, sauna, solarium, steam room, gym, beauty & hair salon, snooker. Access, Amex, Diners, Visa.*

Restaurant   £100

👑 🍾 🍇 🍷 🍮 🍺

Menus are fixed-price, offering an interesting selection of dishes that might include cannelloni of crab with mango and tarragon, braised and chargrilled calamares with rocket salad and Provençal dressing, and salad of wild duck and smoked bacon with truffle vinaigrette amongst the starters and mains like a supreme of Trelough duck with foie gras and Sauternes sauce, sea bass scented with rosemary and thyme, and roast loin of venison rolled in cracked pepper and coriander with gnocchi and tomato confit. Desserts such as lasagne of seasonal fruits with Grand Marnier sauce and hot chocolate pudding simply served with Devonshire clotted cream are equally tempting. A frustrating though comprehensive wine list offers the oldest vintages first; comparisons are difficult as each wine comes from a different grower eg five vintages of Vosné Romanée, five different growers. Quite greedy mark-ups – French country wines offer best value. Water is bottled from their own spring. No children under 8 for dinner (families can eat informally in the leisure centre's Pavilion). No smoking. Gentlemen are required to wear a jacket and tie in the evenings. Sous-chef Alex Venables has recently taken over from Michael Womersley, now at the *Three Lions*, Stuckton. **Seats** 80. *Parties 8. Private Room 30. L 12.30-2 D 7.30-9.30. Set L £20.50/£24.50 (Sun £19/£22) Set D £42.50.*

CONISTON	Sun Hotel	63%	£66

Tel 01539 441248   Map 4 C3   **H**
Coniston Cumbria LA21 8HQ

The Old Man of Coniston creates a spectacular backdrop to this handsome Victorian house in a hillside setting overlooking the village. Views from a stylish, book-filled lounge are conducive to relaxation, while the adjacent 16th-century inn will appeal to the more convivial. Generally spacious bedrooms incorporate seating areas and are carpeted through to bright, airy bathrooms. Two rooms have four-posters. **Rooms** *11. Garden. Closed 24-27 Dec. Access, Diners, Visa.*

CONSTANTINE BAY	Treglos Hotel	65%	£102

Tel 01841 520727   Fax 01841 521163   Map 12 B3   **H**
Constantine Bay St Merryn Padstow Cornwall PL28 8JH

In the same ownership since 1965, this is a friendly, well-run hotel just five minutes from the sea, overlooking Constantine Bay and Trevose Golf Course. It's a popular place with many regular guests, so balcony rooms are booked well in advance. All the public rooms except the bar have sea views; the three comfortable and traditional lounges are bright and airy. Bedrooms have simple white laminate units, large windows and compact bathrooms. In the hotel jackets and ties are requested after 7pm. Special arrangements for families at the end of July and end of August. **Rooms** *44. Garden, croquet, indoor swimming pool, spa bath, games room, children's playroom, snooker, lock-up garages. Closed 5 Nov-10 Mar. Access, Visa.*

COODEN	Jarvis Cooden Beach Hotel	60%	£80

Tel 01424 842281   Fax 01424 846142   Map 11 B6   **H**
Cooden Beach Bexhill-on-Sea East Sussex TN39 4TT

Right on the beach, with views across Pevensey Bay, this white-painted half-timbered-style 30s' hotel caters well for both leisure and business guests. There are facilities for up to 160 conference delegates, a health and leisure club, a modern lounge, a cocktail bar and a tavern serving real ale. One of the bedrooms has been adapted for disabled guests; 12 are suitable for family use. Under-16s share parents' room free. **Rooms** *41. Garden, croquet, indoor & outdoor swimming pools, gym, sauna, steam room, sun beds, beauty & hair salon. Access, Amex, Diners, Visa.*

COPDOCK	Ipswich Moat House	64%	£79

Tel 01473 209988   Fax 01473 730801   Map 10 C3   **H**
London Road Copdock Ipswich Suffolk IP8 3JD

Modern hotel set in four acres of grounds just off the A12, three miles south of Ipswich. Besides practical, up-to-date accommodation the hotel offers extensive conference facilities (up to 500 delegates) and a well-equipped health and fitness club. Popular for weddings at weekends. **Rooms** *74. Children's splash pool, keep-fit equipment, sauna, spa bath, solarium. Access, Amex, Diners, Visa.*

CORBRIDGE　　　Angel Inn　　　£54

Tel 01434 632119　　　Map 5 D2　　**I**
Main Street Corbridge-on-Tyne Northumberland NE45 5LA

The oldest inn in a Saxon village, standing above the 17th-century stone bridge across the Tyne. Run in friendly fashion by Mandy McIntosh-Reid, it's a good place to pause for a drink, a snack or an overnight stay in one of the boldly decorated, pine-furnished bedrooms. Satellite TVs in all rooms. *Rooms 5. Access, Amex, Diners, Visa.*

CORBY　　　Rockingham Forest　　60%　　£65

Tel 01536 401348　　Fax 01536 266383　　　Map 7 E4　　**H**
Rockingham Road Corby Northamptonshire NN17 2NL

Off the A6116 to the north of town, this modern low-rise hotel was originally privately built, which explains the more spacious public areas and somewhat larger bedrooms than those found in most Posthouses – its most recent incarnation. Two very large mini-suites offer particularly good value for a small supplement. Meeting rooms for up to 250 theatre-style. Half the bedrooms are designated non-smoking. Children free up to 16 when sharing parents' room. Forte. *Rooms 69. Garden, games room, snooker. Access, Amex, Diners, Visa.*

CORBY　　　Stakis Corby　　67%　　£89

Tel 01536 401020　　Fax 01536 400767　　　Map 7 E4　　**H**
Geddington Road Corby Northamptonshire NN18 8ET

Situated on the A43 south-east of the town, this modern hotel was until recently the Carlton Manor. Public rooms include two bars (The Heritage decorated with a motoring theme), an all-day coffee shop, a lounge with comfortable chesterfields and a smart leisure centre with helpful and friendly staff. Large bedrooms (some brand new in 1995) have good solid wood furniture and all the usual amenities including satellite TV. En-suite bathrooms have tubs with showers over, ample shelf space and huge bathsheets. Standards of repair and housekeeping are high throughout the hotel. Ask for a rear-facing bedroom to avoid traffic noise. Banqueting/conference facilities for 180/200. Mediocre buffet-style breakfasts. 24hr room service including hot food overnight. *Rooms 68. Indoor swimming pool, gym, sauna, steam room, spa bath, solarium, beauty salon, hair salon, snooker. Access, Amex, Diners, Visa.*

CORFE CASTLE　　　Mortons House Hotel　　62%　　£80

Tel 01929 480988　　Fax 01929 480820　　　Map 14 B4　　**H**
45 East Street Corfe Castle Dorset BH20 5EE

An Elizabethan manor house, almost in the shadow of the castle, and linked to it by tunnels. The entrance hall with its original minster stone fireplace leads to a handsome oak-panelled drawing room with friezes carved by Indonesian sailors. Bedrooms are in a sympathetic 1966 extension. *Rooms 17. Garden, croquet. Access, Amex, Diners, Visa.*

CORNHILL-ON-TWEED　　Tillmouth Park　　68%　　£95

Tel 01890 882255　　Fax 01890 882540　　　Map 5 D1　　**H**
Cornhill-on-Tweed Northumberland TD12 4UU

Built in 1882, the hotel lies in lovely grounds high above the River Till where it joins the River Tweed, famous for its fishing (the hotel has its own rod and drying room). The public rooms reflect the atmosphere of the Victorian era – a galleried lounge, stained glass windows, fine pictures and artefacts, while the individually decorated antique-furnished bedrooms provide modern comforts. Two garden rooms are situated some yards from the main house. Well-kept bathrooms have wood-panelled tubs, and, like the rest of the hotel, benefit from good maintenance and housekeeping. *Rooms 14. Garden, croquet, snooker. Access, Amex, Diners, Visa.*

CORSE LAWN　　　Corse Lawn House　　71%　　£90

Tel 01452 780771　　Fax 01452 780840　　　Map 14 B1　　**HR**
Corse Lawn nr Gloucester Gloucestershire GL19 4LZ

Baba and Denis Hine continue in fine form at their handsome Queen Anne house where they and their family run this most hospitable of establishments. Day rooms are designed in a country house style and spacious bedrooms (just two are rather smaller) are individually decorated, with plain walls and attractive matching bedcovers, curtains and bedhead drapes and furnished with antiques which include marble-topped washstands to house beverage equipment (cafetière, ground coffee, loose tea, vacuum flask of fresh milk and home-made biscuits). Full room service is also available all day. The rooms are practical as well as pretty: there's a proper leather-topped desk near a light fitting and extras like fruit, mineral water and satellite TV. Good bathrooms, with ruffled blinds to match the room, offer generous towelling and bathrobes. Breakfasts include home-made marmalade and sausages plus home-cured bacon – the sort of attention to detail one might expect from a place with such an emphasis on good food. *Rooms 19.* *Garden, croquet, tennis, outdoor swimming pool. Access, Amex, Diners, Visa.*

Restaurant   £75

Everything from the bread to delicious chocolates served with coffee is home-made by Baba Hine and her team here, using only the best of fresh ingredients to produce some thoroughly satisfying dishes. Menus in the elegant L-shaped dining-room are always full of interest. Feuilleté of wild mushrooms, avocado guacamole or hot crab sausage with tomato sauce and chick peas could precede pigeon breasts in red wine, chargrilled salmon with caper sauce or fillet of pork with mustard sauce; in addition, there's always a separate, interesting vegetarian menu. Desserts might include chocolate indulgence (gateau, mousse, ice cream) and a super light and fruity hot passion fruit soufflé. Less formal but equally good eating is to be had in the bar/bistro. Denis Hine's pertinent comments enhance a marvellous wine list that includes many half bottles. Well-chosen wines and fine growers throughout. *Seats 50. Private Room 30. L 12-2 D 7-10.* *Set L £12.95/£15.95 (Sun £17.95) Set D £23.50.*

CORSHAM	Methuen Arms	£50

Tel 01249 714867   Fax 01249 712004   Map 14 B2   **I**
2 High Street Corsham Wiltshire SN13 0HB

Housed around the remains of a 14th-century nunnery, and converted into a brewery and coaching inn around 1608, the place abounds in history. Among notable features in public areas are the 100-foot Long Bar containing its own skittle alley, and outstanding examples of stonemasonry through the ages to be found in the Winter's Court restaurant. Bedrooms are in the main, Georgian, house to the rear, or set around a courtyard facing the serene garden. Newer bedrooms include some four-poster and half-tester beds. Banqueting/conferences for 120. New owners, who took over in February 1995, are refurbishing all parts of the hotel. *Rooms 25. Garden, skittle alley. Access, Visa.*

CORSHAM	Rudloe Hall	64%	£80

Tel 01225 810555   Fax 01225 811412   Map 14 B2   **H**
Leafy Lane Corsham Wiltshire SN13 0PA

The Park's wooded drive leads off the A4 between Chippenham and Bath, at the top of Box Hill. It's a distinctive Bath-stone manor house standing in ten acres of award-winning gardens. Decor within is fittingly traditional, both in the day rooms and throughout the bedrooms, which have four-posters, half-testers or crown canopies. New owners, who arrived in February 1995, plan a conservatory leisure area with heated pool, sauna and solarium, and a pitch-and-putt course. *Rooms 11. Garden, croquet. Access, Amex, Diners, Visa.*

COVENTRY	Chace Hotel	61%	£89

Tel 01203 303398   Fax 01203 301816   Map 6 C4   **H**
London Road Toll Bar End Coventry West Midlands CV3 4EQ

On the B4110, a Victorian main building with modern extensions. Children up to 14 stay free in parents' room. Banqueting/conference for 80/100. Ample parking. Forte. *Rooms 67. Garden, children's playground. Access, Amex, Diners, Visa.*

COVENTRY	Coventry Hill Hotel	60%	£81

Tel 01203 402151   Fax 01203 402235   Map 6 C4   **H**
Rye Hill Allesley Coventry West Midlands CV5 9PH

High-riser just outside the city on the A45. Two new meeting rooms among the facilities – conferences maximum 120. Ample parking. *Rooms 184. Access, Amex, Diners, Visa.*

COVENTRY	De Vere Hotel	69%	£95

Tel 01203 633733   Fax 01203 225299   Map 6 C4   **H**
Cathedral Square Coventry West Midlands CV1 5RP

A large modern hotel which overlooks the magnificent cathedral and which enjoys direct access to the square through a conservatory. Attractive public areas include a spacious foyer and the Daimler bar-lounge decorated with pictures of one of Coventry's most famous cars. Generously-sized bedrooms are smart and well equipped, with plenty of working space and colourfully tiled bathrooms. Conference and banqueting facilities for up to 450. Children up to 14 stay free in parents' room. *Rooms 190. Access, Amex, Diners, Visa.*

COVENTRY	Forte Posthouse	66%	£72

Tel 01203 613261   Fax 01203 621736   Map 6 C4   **H**
Hinckley Road Coventry West Midlands CV2 2HP

A purpose-built hotel with a fully equipped leisure club. Banqueting/conferences for up to 450. All-day snacking in the lounge. Parking for 200 cars. *Rooms 147. Gym, spa bath, sauna, steam room, solarium, beauty salon, putting, games room. Access, Amex, Diners, Visa.*

COVENTRY	Hilton National	72%	£111

Tel 01203 603000   Fax 01203 603011   Map 6 C4   **H**
Paradise Way Walsgrave Triangle Coventry Warwickshire CV2 2ST

Bedrooms at this large modern hotel by Junction 2 of the M6 come with air-conditioning, phones at the well-lit work/breakfast table as well as the bedside, special 'make up' desk with angled mirrors, iron and ironing board, glass-doored mini-bar and satellite TV; plus roomy bathrooms boasting marble floors and vanity units. One room is equipped for the disabled. The spacious lobby with central flower display and three curved, free-standing reception counters, sets the tone for semi-open-plan public areas that combine comfort with a sense of style. 24hr room service. Under-12s share parents' room free. Conference/banqueting facilities for 600/500; staffed business centre. *Rooms 172. Indoor swimming pool, gym, sauna, steam room, spa bath, sun beds, beauty salon. Access, Amex, Diners, Visa.*

COVENTRY	Novotel	62%	£58

Tel 01203 365000   Fax 01203 362422   Map 6 C4   **H**
Wilsons Lane Longford Coventry West Midlands CV6 6HL

Practical, modern accommodation close to Junction 3 of the M6. 1995 saw bedroom decoration, two new conference rooms and the 're-landscaping' of the front of the hotel. Children up to 16 stay free (B&B) in parents' room. *Rooms 100. Outdoor swimming pool, children's playground. Access, Amex, Diners, Visa.*

COWAN BRIDGE	Cobwebs		£60

Tel & Fax 01524 272141   Map 4 C4   **RR**
Leck Cowan Bridge nr Kirkby Lonsdale Lancashire LA6 2HZ

♛   🍴   🍇   🍷   🗋

At junction 36 of the M6 take the A65 towards Kirkby Lonsdale. Then at Cowan Bridge, follow signs for Leck, go under a railway bridge and on the left you'll come upon a charming Victorian house in a picturesque rural setting. Yvonne Thompson single-handedly cooks a balanced fixed-price, five-course dinner that might offer chilled Stilton and hot tomato and thyme soup (served in the same bowl), smoked chicken and avocado strudel, sorbet, whole fillet of beef rolled in crushed peppercorns with port and mushrooms (served with a selection of lightly cooked vegetables); choux pastry filled with lemon mousse; and coffee and petits fours. There's a stunning New World choice on an outstanding wine list with an excellent and inexpensive house selection but with rather too many POAs in evidence. Booking essential. No smoking in the dining-room. *Seats 25. D only 7.30 for 8. Closed Sun & Jan-mid Mar. Set D £28. Access, Visa.*

Rooms   £60

Five bedrooms in individual, charming style, with good creature comforts and excellent breakfasts.

COWAN BRIDGE　　　Hipping Hall Hotel　　64%　　£78

Tel 01524 271187　Fax 01524 272452　　　Map 4 C4　　**H**
Cowan Bridge nr Kirkby Lonsdale Lancashire LA6 2JJ

Ian Bryant and Jocelyn Ruffle, here since 1988, pride themselves on creating a relaxed country-house atmosphere; guests meet for drinks round the fire and dine together at one table in the characterful, beamed Great Hall, complete with minstrel's gallery. There is also a help-yourself bar in the old stone-flagged conservatory. Bedrooms are bright, pretty and comfortable, with gleaming bathrooms. The hall is the sole survivor of a 15th-century hamlet and stands on the A65 three miles east of Kirkby Lonsdale. No children under 12. *Rooms 7. Garden, croquet. Closed Jan & Feb. Access, Amex, Visa.*

CRANBROOK　　　Hartley Mount　　62%　　£70

Tel 01580 712230　Fax 01580 715733　　　Map 11 C5　　**H**
Hartley Road Cranbrook Kent TN17 3QX

A handsome Edwardian manor house set in spacious gardens off the A229. There are views over farmland and the Weald of Kent from the hotel and a non-smoking policy in all rooms but the conservatory (where breakfast is served). The informal atmosphere is exemplified by a lack of formal reception facilities, as the owners Lionel and Lee Skilton prefer to greet guests personally. Bedrooms include a four-poster room with period bathroom and a very large family room. No dogs. *Rooms 6. Garden, croquet, tennis, pitch & putt. Access, Amex, Visa.*

CRANBROOK　　　Kennel Holt Hotel　　66%　　£118

Tel 01580 712032　Fax 01580 715495　　　Map 11 C5　　**H**
Goudhurst Road Cranbrook Kent TN17 2PT

Family-run by Sally and Neil Chalmers, this little Elizabethan manor house with distinctive brick chimneys, just off the A262, three miles from Goudhurst, is a most welcoming home from home. There are two beamed lounges, one with floral sofas and brick inglenook fireplace, the other, with oak panelling, acting as the bar. Popular for weddings, with a marquee in the garden for larger affairs, and also well set up for small business meetings (up to 20). Parking for 25 cars. No dogs. *Rooms 9. Garden, croquet, putting green. Access, Amex, Diners, Visa.*

CRANLEIGH　　　La Barbe Encore　　　£65

Tel 01483 273889　　　　　　　　Map 15 E3　　**R**
High Street Cranleigh Surrey GU6 8AE

Jean-Pierre Bonnet can be seen in the kitchen of his cheerful, friendly bistro producing generally mainstream French dishes. A winter menu offers a deliciously warming cream of chestnut soup, coarse game terrine with an onion compote or a puff pastry case filled with prawns, scallops, mussels, squid and salmon. For a main course choose perhaps from breast of pheasant with a chartreuse sauce, roast fillet of pork with Vallée d'Auge sauce or entrecote chasseur. Simple but good desserts complete a very satisfying experience. *Seats 55. Parties 30. L 12-2 D 7-10. Closed D Sun, all Mon, Bank Holidays. Set L £14.95 Set D £17.95. Access, Amex, Visa.*

CRATHORNE　　　Crathorne Hall　　72%　　£125

Tel 01642 700398　Fax 01642 700814　　　Map 5 E3　　**H**
Crathorne nr Yarm Cleveland TS15 0AR

Set in 15 acres of grounds not far from the village centre and a short distance from the A19, Crathorne Hall was the last of the great stately homes built in the Edwardian era. Public rooms and the best of the bedrooms enjoy an elevated view over parkland with not a human habitation in sight. The drawing room is of classical proportions with a fine carved overmantel, large portraits in oil and brass chandeliers. Knoll sofas and buttoned leather Queen Anne style armchairs form part of a comfortable and very traditional decor. The cocktail bar has the air of a gentleman's club with its bottle-green walls, mahogany panelling and pillars and plush red velour chairs. Bedrooms are splendid though top floor and back rooms are smaller. Furniture is period style in keeping with the character of the building and all rooms are well equipped, superior rooms in particular. Bathrooms, some with bidets, have quality toiletries and bathrobes. Children under 12 share parents' room free. Conference/banqueting facilities for 140/120. *Rooms 37. Garden, croquet, riding, fishing, clay-pigeon shooting. Access, Amex, Diners, Visa.*

CRAWLEY   George Hotel   64%   £80

Tel 01293 524215   Fax 01293 548565   Map 11 B5   **H**
High Street Crawley West Sussex RH10 1BS

An old gallows sign announces this town-centre former coaching inn. Some parts are beamed and atmospheric, others modern. All bedrooms and public areas have recently been refurbished. Forte. *Rooms 81. Access, Amex, Diners, Visa.*

CRICK   Forte Posthouse   64%   £72

Tel 01788 822101   Fax 01788 823955   Map 7 D4   **H**
Crick Northamptonshire NN6 7XR

Low-rise modern hotel near Junction 18 on the M1, 7 miles from Rugby. 15 meeting rooms, conference facilities for 150. Forte. *Rooms 88. Garden, indoor swimming pool, gym, sauna, steam room, solarium, children's outdoor playground. Access, Amex, Diners, Visa.*

CROOK   Wild Boar Hotel   60%   £90

Tel 01539 445225   Fax 01539 442498   Map 4 C3   **H**
Crook nr Windermere Cumbria LA23 3NF

Abundant character still pervades this old coaching inn, whose name commemorates the spot where Westmorland's last wild boar was killed (in King John's time). Public rooms are a mass of blackened beams, log fires and ancient oak furniture, the oldest dating from 1635. Much of this character is reflected in the main-house bedrooms with four-posters and two suites, one with a spa bath. Children up to 15 stay free in parents' room. Free leisure facilities at a sister hotel a few miles away, discounted green fees at Windermere golf club (1 mile away). *Rooms 36. Garden. Access, Amex, Diners, Visa.*
4

CROOKLANDS   Crooklands Hotel   60%   £75

Tel 01539 567432   Fax 01539 567525   Map 4 C4   **H**
Crooklands nr Kendal Cumbria LA7 7NW

Just over a mile from the M6 (Junction 36) on the A65 in a peaceful rural location, the Crooklands is housed in a collection of farm buildings adjoining an original ale house. Superior rooms are in the more modern extension. *Rooms 30. Garden, snooker. Access, Amex, Diners, Visa.*

CROSBY-ON-EDEN   Crosby Lodge   66%   £90

Tel 01228 573618   Fax 01228 573428   Map 4 C2   **HR**
High Crosby Crosby-on-Eden nr Carlisle Cumbria CA6 4QZ

Leave the M6 at Junction 44 and follow signs for Brampton. Approximately 3 miles on, just off the A689, you should find this delightful crenellated Georgian country house, overlooking parkland and the river. The walled garden is ideal for a relaxing stroll. Indoors there's an elegant and professional air to the day rooms and bedrooms – those in the converted stable block are slightly less grand. Smoking is discouraged. Banqueting for 50, conferences 20. *Rooms 11. Garden. Closed 1st week Jan. Access, Amex, Visa.*

Restaurant   £65

Plenty of choice on daily-changing fixed-price menus that are supplemented by an à la carte of straightforward dishes like grilled Dover sole and steaks. Cooking is by Michael Sedgwick and service by Patricia. He describes the style as 'traditional with a Continental influence' and this seems an apt turn of phrase, perhaps slightly underplaying the reality of such dishes as parcels of prosciutto ham filled with asparagus mousse and garnished with spiced pears, fresh salmon marinated in red wine with herbs and walnut oil, escalope of venison with Madeira sauce and chestnuts and slivers of Solway salmon filled with scampi in a cream and grape sauce. Everything is home made, from amuse-gueule to petits fours. Helpful notes against each wine on the diverse list. No children under 5 after 7.30pm. Jacket and tie required for gentlemen. No smoking. *Seats 50. Private Room 14. L 12.15-1.30 D 7.15-9. Set L £15 Set D £25. Closed D Sun (except for residents).*

Lodges are now listed by county in the reference section

| CROYDON | **Croydon Park Hotel** | 68% | £102 |

Tel 0181-680 9200 Fax 0181-760 0426   Map 11 B5   **H**
7 Altyre Road Croydon Surrey CR9 5AA

Modern, redbrick medium-rise hotel near the law courts. The large lobby has some comfortable beige leather sofas and armchairs while the gas-lit Whistlers Bar offers more characterful and intimate surroundings. Standardised bedrooms are more practical than luxurious but provide plenty of work space, good-sized beds (with poly-cotton bedding) and air-conditioning. Compact bathrooms boast marble vanity units and all have good showers over tubs. The leisure centre has just been refurbished. Free covered parking. Children up to 14 years stay free in parents' room and there is a separate children's section on the 24hr room service menu. Conference/banqueting facilities for 300/200. *Rooms 212. Indoor swimming pool, children's splash pool, keep-fit equipment. Access, Amex, Diners, Visa.*

| CROYDON | **Forte Posthouse** | 61% | £75 |

Tel 0181-688 5185 Fax 0181-681 6438   Map 11 B5   **H**
Purley Way Croydon Surrey CR9 4LT

Convenient location, aside the A23, with flexible meeting conference facilities for up to 170 delegates. Half the bedrooms are designated non-smoking. *Rooms 83. Access, Amex, Diners, Visa.*

| CROYDON | **Hilton National** | 69% | £109 |

Tel 0181-680 3000 Fax 0181-681 6171   Map 11 B5   **H**
Waddon Way Purley Way Croydon Surrey CR9 4HH

Polished granite hotel with plenty of parking at the Croydon end of Purley Way. Quality public areas combine comfort and space with a considerable sense of style. Good bedrooms offer large beds and ample work space plus wing armchairs and proper breakfast table. White marble features in equally good bathrooms. Suites (actually just large rooms) have sophisticated wide-screen TVs that incorporate CD players and a video games feature, spa baths and separate shower cubicles in addition to the tub. Children up to 12 can stay free in parents' room. One floor out of three is designated non-smoking. 24hr room service. Conferences for up to 400. *Rooms 168. Indoor swimming pool, gym, sauna, spa bath, steam room, solarium, beauty salon, coffee shop (10.30am-10.30pm). Access, Amex, Diners, Visa.*

| CROYDON | **Selsdon Park** | 68% | £109 |

Tel 0181-657 8811 Fax 0181-651 6171   Map 11 B5   **H**
Addington Road Sanderstead Croydon Surrey CR2 8YA

200 acres of parkland are the setting for ivy-clad Selsdon Park, whose amenities combine those of hotel, golf course, leisure club, conference venue and business centre. It's also a good place for weekending families, who enjoy special rates. The baronial-style entrance hall has stone walls, an elaborate plaster ceiling and leather armchairs that are also to be found in the oak-panelled bar-lounge with its heavily carved antique furniture and brass ornaments. Bedrooms come in a variety of sizes and appointments from freestanding lightwood furniture to fitted units, and soft floral to bright fabrics. All have mini-bars and room safes in addition to the usual extras. The very best rooms enjoy views across the Surrey Hills. Regular dinner dances, and children's activity club on weekends and holidays; golf-and tennis-mad parents will be in seventh heaven (coaches on site). Unusual 40m circuit indoor swimming pool. Reservable lock-up garages and courtesy car service to East Croydon station. *Rooms 170. Garden, croquet, golf (18-hole), putting green, driving range, tennis (grass and all-weather), indoor & outdoor swimming pools, gym, spa bath, sauna, solarium, beauty salon, boules, squash, snooker, children's playground, news kiosk. Access, Amex, Diners, Visa.*

| CUCKFIELD | **Murray's** | | £66 |

Tel 01444 455826   Map 11 B6   **R**
Broad Street Cuckfield West Sussex RH17 5LJ

Several cottagey rooms, one reserved for non-smokers, provide a cosy setting in which to enjoy Sue Murray's skilled and imaginative cooking. Start, perhaps, with onion tart, or aubergine quenelles followed by chicken breast with a cherry brandy sauce, walnut-crusted lamb or salmon in pastry. Relaxed and informal – "where children can

See over

be introduced to good food". Parking in the village car park opposite. Short wine list with almost all bottles under £20. *Seats 32. L 12-1.30 D 7.15-9.30. Closed L Sat, all Sun, Bank Holidays. Access, Amex, Visa.*

CUCKFIELD	Ockenden Manor	71%	£105

Tel 01444 416111   Fax 01444 415549   Map 11 B6   **HR**
Ockenden Lane Cuckfield West Sussex RH17 5LD

Fresh flowers and a real log fire feature in the beamed entrance hall of an original Tudor building that has been sympathetically extended in the 19th and 20th centuries. There are attractive views of the South Downs from the rear of the hotel, which overlooks a grand garden. Day rooms include a pub-like, oak-panelled bar, a sunny sitting-room and a non-smoking dining-room. Bedrooms, five of which have four-poster beds, come in a variety of styles and include both reproduction and original antiques and many extras. A room by the kitchen could be subject to noise from the extractor. Banqueting (70) and conference (50) facilities available. No dogs. *Rooms 22. Garden. Access, Amex, Diners, Visa.*

Restaurant   £80

Seafood is chef Scott Welch's favourite ingredient – bisque of Chichester crab and Cornish mussels with saffron and cognac; salmon cured with sea salt, juniper, lemon and dill and served with Whitstable rock oysters; brill braised in white wine with roasted shallots and chervil butter sauce, and, a permanent feature of the menu this, a comprehensive seafood platter – but it is not allowed to dominate a carte which might also include haunch of venison with walnuts and port wine, Southdown lamb with onion confit, broad beans and mint sauce, and a vegetarian option such as wild mushroom pithiviers. The kitchen's attention to detail is exemplified by the neatly tied bundles of French beans and sticks of carrot that come as part of the vegetable side dish. Among the puds a clootie dumpling is served with custard sauce and a glazed pear and almond tartlet with clove-scented ice cream. A plated selection of about eight British farmhouse cheeses with walnut bread and oatcakes is on offer for those lacking a sweet tooth. The setting is a splendid Tudor dining-room with mellow oak panelling and a fine plaster ceiling. No smoking. *Seats 45. Parties 8. Private Room 14. L 12.30-2 D 7.30-9.30. Set L £13.50/£16.50 (Sun £18.50) Set D £26.50.*

DANE END	Green End Park	62%	£95

Tel 01920 438344   Fax 01920 438523   Map 15 F1   **H**
Dane End nr Ware Hertfordshire SG12 0NY

Off the A602 between Ware and Stevenage, this 18th-century manor house stands in eight acres of gardens. There's an elegant air to the day rooms, which include an impressive bar with a patio. Banqueting/conference facilities for up to 120/100. No dogs. *Rooms 9. Garden, croquet, tennis, putting. Access, Amex, Diners, Visa.*

DARLINGTON	Blackwell Grange	62%	£103

Tel 01325 380888   Fax 01325 380899   Map 5 E3   **H**
Blackwell Grange Darlington Co Durham DL3 8QH

Formerly the Moat House, Blackwell Grange is based around a Georgian mansion set in 15 acres of parkland. The 11 rooms in the original house have a period feel but most are in a more modern extension. Children under 14 share parents' room free and get half-price meals. 24hr room service. Dinner dances on Saturdays. *Rooms 99. Garden, indoor swimming pool, spa bath, sauna, sun bed, gym, putting, pétanque. Access, Amex, Diners, Visa.*

DARLINGTON	St George Thistle	56%	£80

Tel 01325 332631   Fax 01325 333851   Map 5 E3   **H**
Teesside Airport nr Darlington Co Durham DL2 1RH

Redbrick, two-storey hotel serving the airport rather than the town. Smart, modern bedrooms. Conferencing for up to 160. Guests have free membership of nearby Top Spin Leisure Centre. Children up to 12 stay free in parents' room. *Rooms 57. Sauna, sun bed. Access, Amex, Diners, Visa.*

Lodges are now listed by county in the reference section

DARLINGTON   Sardis   £50

Tel 01325 461222   Map 5 E3   **R**
196 Northgate Darlington Co Durham DL1 1QU

On Northgate, smart and fashionable Sardis is a five-minute walk from the pedestrian
town centre. It's bright inside with a high-windowed frontage and tables set on three
tiers in an open-plan layout – crisp white table linen, good bread, Italian-inspired menu
(baked aubergines with tomato and cheese, pasta carbonara, beef involtini, escalopes of
pork siciliana, saltimbocca), Italianate wine list, smooth, friendly service. *Seats 60.
Parties 18. L 12-2.30 D 7-9.45. Closed Sun, Mon, 1 week Jan, 1 week Apr, 2 weeks Aug.
Set L £9 Set D £16. Access, Visa.*

DARLINGTON   Swallow King's Head   57%   £95

Tel 01325 380222   Fax 01325 382006   Map 5 E3   **H**
Priestgate Darlington Co Durham DL1 1NW

Victorian hotel located above shops in the town centre. Conference and banquets are big
business (up to 200 theatre-style in the Wellington Suite) and guests have free use of the
Dolphin Leisure Centre 200 yards away. Valet parking. *Rooms 85. Coffee shop (10am-
5pm). Access, Amex, Diners, Visa.*

DARLINGTON   Victor's   £55

Tel 01325 480818   Map 5 E3   **H**
84 Victoria Road Darlington Co Durham DL1 5JW

To the west and north of the station just off one of the inner ring road roundabouts,
Victor's is a friendly, informal and totally unpretentious restaurant decorated in palest grey
with simple lighting. Jayne Robinson, here since 1984, gets all her supplies locally, and
everything possible is made on the premises. Her cooking is honest and quite
straightforward, with the emphasis on freshness and flavour. Lunch offers particularly
good value for money with appealing dishes such as tomato and fresh herb gratin, fish
strudel or grilled lamb's liver with onions and smoked bacon. On the evening menu
could be a warm salad of pigeon breast with pine kernels, Dover sole with fennel butter
and lamb kebab with raisin sauce and couscous. *Seats 30. L 12-2 D 7.30-10.30.
Closed Sun & Mon, 1 week Christmas. Set L £6.50/£8.50 Set D £20. Access, Amex,
Diners, Visa.*

DARTMOUTH   Carved Angel   ★★   £110

Tel 01803 832465   Fax 01803 835141   Map 13 D3   **R**
2 South Embankment Dartmouth Devon TQ6 9BH

The restaurant is an absolute must on any grand gastronomic itinerary of these islands.
Established in 1975, it is the domain of the doyenne of British chefs, Joyce Molyneux,
who is assisted by fellow head chef Nick Coiley. Together they continue to offer menus
that are always innovative and exciting. The style of cooking is an exhilarating blend
of modern British with strong Italian and Provençal influences. In recent years subtle
Oriental flavourings have been introduced, keeping the food very much at the forefront
of culinary creativity. Dinner could begin with pan-fried scallops with a spiced lentil
sauce, pheasant and wild duck terrine with an apricot and red onion relish, or a pimento
soufflé suissesse with aubergine and tomato. Follow with best end of lamb with spinach
and fried garlic, braised ox tongue with beetroot, celeriac and a piquant cream sauce or
venison brochette with leek, juniper and potato cake. Very delectable desserts include
chocolate pithviers and hot raspberry soufflé. The selection of Ticklemore cheeses is
another notable feature. While no-one can quibble with the quality on the outstanding
wine list, a glass of house champagne at £7.50 is a bit steep. That said, it's a terrific list
with not only wines of the month at well under £20. Check out the bin ends. The
dinner price includes 2 or 3 courses, mineral water, sorbet or cheese, coffee, petits fours
and service charge. *Seats 45. Private Room 16. L 12.30-1.45 D 7.30-9.30. Closed D Sun,
all Mon, Bank Holidays except Good Friday, 6 weeks Jan/Feb. Set L £24/£29 Set D £40/£45.
No credit cards.*

Lodges are now listed by county in the reference section

DARTMOUTH — Royal Castle Hotel — £80

Tel 01803 833033   Fax 01803 835445   Map 13 D3   **I**
11 The Quay Dartmouth Devon TQ6 9PS

Right on the quay, in the centre of town, two Tudor merchants' houses became
a hostelry in the early 1700s and the castellated facade (a Regency addition) explains the
name. Antique furniture, Tudor fireplaces, oak beams fashioned from ships' timbers and
a 300-year-old cooking range are among many reminders of the past, and in some of the
bedrooms four-poster and brass beds are in use. River-view rooms are the most sought
after (and attract a supplement); six have jacuzzis. Children under 16 sharing their parents'
room can stay free. The owners are committed to "going green": all purchasing is as
'green' as possible and they recycle as much as they can. Mountain bikes are available for
hire and guests are encouraged to use public transport. *Rooms 25. Limited covered
parking. Access, Visa.*

DARTMOUTH — Stoke Lodge — 60% — £74

Tel 01803 770523   Fax 01803 770851   Map 13 D3   **H**
Stoke Fleming Dartmouth Devon TQ6 0RA

In an area where tourism is one main industry and all things maritime another, Stoke
Lodge offers the best of both worlds, catering primarily for family holidays, and is well
situated at the top of the village to observe marine activity. Leisure facilities are good
(a mixture of indoor and outdoor, in keeping with the climate), while public areas and
bedrooms continue to be comfortable and well maintained. Parking for 50 cars.
*Rooms 24. Garden, indoor & outdoor swimming pools, putting, keep-fit equipment, sauna,
spa bath, solarium, outdoor play area, snooker, giant chess. Access, Visa.*

DAVENTRY — Daventry Resort Hotel — 69% — £107

Tel 01327 301777   Fax 01327 706313   Map 15 D1   **H**
Ashby Road Daventry Northamptonshire NN11 5SG

Located due north of Daventry town centre off a roundabout on the A361 and some
8 miles south of junction 18 of the M1. This is a large, sprawling, low-rise modern
building geared almost exclusively to a business clientele – a business centre is located in
one corner of the reception area. Automatic doors lead into a vast and elegant American-
style lobby with highly-polished coloured marble floors, Chinese-style rosewood
furniture and dark, flame-patterned long settees. Numerous Chinese table lamps provide
low-key lighting, recessed lights and spots adding soft background illumination. The Cat's
Whiskers Bar, although spacious, has a warm, clubby atmosphere created by effective soft
lighting and attractive rosewood panelling. The night club area (Friday evenings)
is at other times a conference room – one of many catering for 10-600 people. Bedrooms
range from good-sized standard to Executive and suites. All have up-to-date quality
fittings and are provided with useful extras. Four rooms have been specially designed for
disabled guests. Children up to 16 can stay free in their parents' room. Bright, modern
leisure facilities. *Rooms 138. Garden, indoor swimming pool, children's swimming pool,
gym, sauna, steam room, spa bath, solarium, beauty salon. Access, Amex, Diners, Visa.*

DEDHAM — Fountain House & Dedham Hall — £50

Tel 01206 323027   Map 10 C3   **RR**
Brook Street Dedham nr Colchester Essex CO7 6AD

Just outside the village, Dedham Hall stands in 5 acres of grounds. A loud clanging bell
announces your arrival and drinks are taken in a tiny, cosy front lounge. The dining-
room has a charming, country cottage air of informality with its wheelback chairs and
pretty pink decor. The fixed-price menu changes weekly offering a choice of simple but
carefully prepared dishes; prawn cheesecake, fresh dressed crab or Stilton soup could start
the meal, followed by beef fillet with mushrooms and Madeira, goujons of chicken breast
with fresh tomato sauce, or fillet of pork provençale. Chocolate fondue (for 2) is
a speciality dessert. The informative and educational wine list is very comprehensive
(note the lengthy Alsace, Italian and German sections) and contains a splendid half bottle
selection. *Seats 32. Parties 14. Private Room 16. L Sun only 12.30-2 D 7.30-9.30.
Closed D Sun, all Mon, Bank Holidays. Set L £16.50 Set D £18.50. Access, Visa.*

Rooms   £57

There are six neat, homely bedrooms with residents having their own lounge and
a convivial breakfast room. Further accommodation is used for the residential painting
courses.

DEDHAM	Maison Talbooth	78%	£120

Tel 01206 322367   Fax 01206 322752   Map 10 C3   **H**
Stratford Road Dedham nr Colchester Essex CO7 6HN

This peaceful Victorian country house
stands in an area of great beauty
immortalised in the paintings of George
Constable's better-known brother John.
When Gerald Milsom came here in
1952 it was a simple tea room, which
has grown down the years into
a hotel and restaurant (see entry below)
of considerable renown. *The Pier*
at Harwich is in the same ownership.
All is calm and restful in the sunny
lounge with its deep-cushioned
armchairs, profusion of fresh flowers
and views down Dedham Vale. The bedrooms, suites almost, strike a happy balance
between the shameless luxury of fine co-ordinated fabrics and crown canopied beds and
the quiet homeliness of abundant magazines, fresh fruit and a drinks tray. Bathrooms are
superb, some with jacuzzis or vast sunken tubs, all containing quality bath sheets and
bespoke toiletries. The hotel lies just moments from the A12. No dogs. *Rooms 10.
Garden, croquet. Access, Amex, Visa.*

DEDHAM	Le Talbooth	£100

Tel 01206 323150   Fax 01206 322309   Map 10 C3   **R**
Gunhill Dedham nr Colchester Essex CO7 6HP

Alfresco dining under large canvas parasols is a fine summertime option at this beautifully
located restaurant housed in a splendidly preserved half-timbered Tudor building right on
the banks of the River Stour. The bar and lounges are very traditional, comfortable and
welcoming and the dining-room overlooks the terrace and river. Fixed-price menus of
two or three courses are available lunchtime and evening and the à la carte offers a good
choice of starters, mains and desserts. Lunchtime brings an hors d'oeuvre table, a daily
roast and old favourites such as trout *en colère* or escalope of pork Holstein, and the
evening fixed-price menu is similar. A la carte, the choice is either 'traditional' or
'creative', the latter typified by deep-fried ravioli of goat's cheese, poached loin of lamb
wrapped in Swiss chard, and zarzuela, 'a musical comedy of fish'. Chateaubriand is a
fixture on the traditional side. Hot bitter chocolate soufflé is a speciality dessert. Pianist
Sunday lunchtime. Note the exceptionally keen prices on the personal selection of the
wine list, a good blend between France and The New World. Overall, the list offers value
for money at every glance, with several *marque* champagnes under £30. *Seats 85.
Parties 16. Private Room 24. L 12-2 (Sun till 5.30) D 7-9. Set L £12.50/£15 (Sun £19.95)
Set D £16.95/£19.95. Access, Amex, Visa.*

DENMEAD	Barnard's	£45

Tel 01705 257788   Map 15 D4   **R**
Hambledon Road Denmead Hampshire PO7 6NU

David Barnard's French-inspired cooking may be enjoyed in either à la carte or fixed-
price menus, as well as occasional wine tasting and gourmet evenings. Swiss cheese
soufflé garnished with ham and celery, chicken with a creamy calvados sauce, lamb cutlets
with mint hollandaise and strips of steak served in a seed mustard sauce show the style.
There are always some fish specials, perhaps diced monkfish in a creamy red wine sauce
with mushrooms and bacon. *Seats 30. L (Wed-Fri with prior booking) 12-1.45 D 7-9.45.
Closed L Tue & Sat, all Sun & Mon, 2 weeks Aug, 1 week Christmas. Set L & D £14.50.
Access, Amex, Visa.*

Set menu prices may not always include service or wine.

DERBY   European Inn   £48

Tel 01332 292000   Fax 01332 293940   Map 6 C3   **B**
Midland Road Derby Derbyshire DE1 2SL

Modern and attractive budget hotel with bright bedrooms and bathrooms. Two rooms
are equipped for disabled guests. Half the rooms are for non-smokers. Breakfast is from
a buffet selection and there are vending machines for alcohol, snacks and sundries;
no restaurant. Two meeting rooms cater for up to 120. Reduced tariff at weekends.
Rooms 88. Access, Amex, Diners, Visa.

DERBY   Forte Posthouse   61%   £72

Tel 01332 514933   Fax 01332 518668   Map 6 C3   **H**
Pastures Hill Littleover Derby Derbyshire DE23 7BA

Neat, unfussy businessman's accommodation three miles west of the city centre on the
A5250. Extensive grounds include a children's play area. Conference and banqueting
for up to 60. *Rooms 62. Access, Amex, Diners, Visa.*

DERBY   International Hotel   62%   £60

Tel 01332 369321   Fax 01332 294430   Map 6 C3   **H**
Burton Road Derby Derbyshire DE3 6AD

On the A5250 south-west of the city centre, the privately owned International, once
a Victorian school, concentrates very much on conference and exhibition business.
Bedrooms offer many extras and the suites boast spa baths. 24hr room service.
Children up to 12 stay free in parents' room. *Rooms 62. Access, Amex, Diners, Visa.*

DERBY   Midland Hotel   65%   £92

Tel 01332 345894   Fax 01332 293522   Map 6 C3   **H**
Midland Road Derby Derbyshire DE1 2SQ

Adjacent to Derby railway station and built in 1841, the Midland is now a smart modern
hotel which caters admirably for the business traveller. It currently offers 50 stylishly
decorated Executive rooms in a rebuilt section which feature multiple phone points, fax
and PC points, as well as splendid bathrooms with both steel baths and separate shower
cubicles. There is ample seating and writing space too. All the hotel's bedrooms have
attractive darkwood furniture. The 50 standard rooms aren't as well equipped and their
bathrooms are smaller and more functional. One room is equipped for disabled guests.
Conference facilities for 120. Children up to 11 stay free in parents' room. *Rooms 100.
Garden. Access, Amex, Diners, Visa.*

DISS   Weavers   £45

Tel 01379 642411   Map 10 C2   **R**
Market Hill Diss Norfolk IP22 3JZ

William and Wilma Bavin describe Weavers as a wine bar and eating house – versatility
therefore seems to be the order of the day at what was originally a chapel for the
Weaver's Guild, then a butcher's shop, and a wig maker's en route to becoming a
restaurant. Try perhaps sautéed chicken livers in a Madeira and cream sauce, then saddle
of hare in red wine and juniper with diced bacon and game faggots, with cranberry and
orange upside-down sponge served with custard. Interesting vegetarian dishes. No
smoking before 2pm at lunchtime or 9.30pm in the evening. Practically nothing over
£20 on the enterprising wine list, half of which is devoted to the New World. *Seats 80.
Parties 22. Private Room 50. L 12-1.30 D 7-9. Closed L Sat, all Sun, 2 weeks end Aug, 2
weeks Christmas. Set L £7.95/£9.95 Set D £10 (not Sat). Access, Diners, Visa.*

DONCASTER   Danum Swallow Hotel   64%   £90

Tel 01302 342261   Fax 01302 329034   Map 7 D2   **H**
High Street Doncaster South Yorkshire DN1 1DN

An Edwardian building in the centre of town; inside it's been thoroughly modernised
(except for the Crystal Suite, which can accommodate up to 350 delegates in period
style) with comfortable, spacious public areas and bedrooms which boast irons and
ironing boards in addition to the usual amenities. *Rooms 66. Coffee shop (9am-4pm).
Access, Amex, Diners, Visa.*

DONCASTER   Grand St Leger   64%   £80

Tel 01302 364111   Fax 01302 329865   Map 7 D2   **H**
Racecourse Roundabout Bennetthorpe Doncaster South Yorkshire DN2 6AX

Just a five minute walk from the Doncaster Dome Leisure Park and with the racecourse opposite and bloodstock sales yard behind, this 19th-century building was once used as a hostelry for stable lads, but today, it provides comfortable, unassuming accommodation. Pretty floral fabrics and freestanding furniture feature in the cosy bedrooms. Day rooms include a bar-lounge with a host of racing prints and photos. Banqueting up to 65, conferences 80. Children under 12 free in parents' room. No dogs. *Rooms 20. Access, Amex, Diners, Visa.*

DONCASTER   Moat House   64%   £106

Tel 01302 310331   Fax 01302 310197   Map 7 D2   **H**
Warmsworth Doncaster South Yorkshire DN4 9UX

Next to the junction of the A630 with the A1(M), this modern hotel is stone-clad to fit in with surrounding buildings, most notably the 17th-century Warmsworth Hall, which is now part of the hotel's extensive conference/function facilities (up to 400 theatre-style). A spacious marble-floored reception/lounge creates a good first impression for decent bedrooms. *Rooms 100. Garden, croquet, indoor swimming pool, gym, sauna, spa bath, solarium, children's outdoor playground. Access, Amex, Diners, Visa.*

DORCHESTER   The Mock Turtle   £55

Tel 01305 264011   Map 13 F2   **R**
34 High West Street Dorchester Dorset DT1 1UP

A charming restaurant formed from a number of interconnecting rooms in a town house dating back to the late 17th century. Decor is predominantly green with exposed stonework here and there, old photographs, crisp white napery and a welcoming fire in the comfortable lounge area. It's been run for six years by the Hodder family; Raymond's menus are fixed-price only, but offer a good choice at both lunch and dinner that is likely to please all tastes. Fish is a feature and there's usually a long list of daily specials, perhaps including fillet of cod garnished with mussels and prawns on a herb sauce or délice of halibut with fresh lemon and lime. Sound cooking is complemented by friendly service. *Seats 55. Parties 16. L 12-2 D 7-9.30. Closed L Mon & Sat, D Sun. Set L £10/£12.50 Set D £16.50/£19.50. Access, Visa.*

DORCHESTER-ON-THAMES   George Hotel   £70

Tel 01865 340404   Fax 01865 341620   Map 15 D2   **I**
High Street Dorchester-on-Thames Oxfordshire OX10 7HH

With a history spanning more than 500 years, the George is one of the oldest inns in the land. Focal point of the public area is a fine beamed bar. Bedrooms in the main building have a solid, old-fashioned feel, some cosy and snug under oak beams, two with four-posters. Other rooms have less character but are still very adequate. Small meetings and seminars (for up to 40) are held in the two rooms of a self-contained annexe; the beamed Stable room is particularly characterful. No children under 10. *Rooms 18. Garden. Access, Amex, Diners, Visa.*

DORKING   Partners West Street   £70

Tel 01306 882826   Map 15 E3   **R**
2 West Street Dorking Surrey RH4 1BL

Civilised, intimate restaurant of considerable charm in a 16th-century building just off the main street. Partners Andrew Thomason and Tim McEntire continue to maintain high standards here, now with talented young chef Anthony Robinson in the kitchen. The menu has a distinctly modern slant and is always full of interest. Recent offerings included a tartlet of roasted John Dory with caramelised endive and orange, millefeuille of veal kidneys on brussels sprout mash with bay leaf sauce and an intriguing wild mushroom cappuccino (it comes in a cup looking just like the coffee complete with froth on top but has a lovely, complex, wild mushroom flavour) among the starters and

See over

Provençal braised shoulder of lamb with olive oil mash and grilled vegetables, ragout of monkfish in red wine sauce with artichokes, mushrooms and pancetta for mains. Nicely varied afters range from plum pudding with cinnamon ice cream and brandy sauce to lemon tart with crème Chantilly and an exotic fruit fool with shortbread biscuits or a selection of four British cheeses. The wine list includes half a dozen dessert and three port wines by the glass. No smoking in the dining areas. *Seats 45. L 12-2 D 7-9.30. Set L £8.95/£11.95 (Sun £14.95) Set D (Mon-Fri) £15. Closed L Sat, D Sun. Access, Amex, Diners, Visa.*

DORKING   White Horse   62%   £92

Tel 01306 881138   Fax 01306 887241   Map 15 E3   **H**
High Street Dorking Surrey RH4 1BE

A former coaching inn with parts dating back to the 15th century. Oak beams and log fires give a cosy, traditional feel to the day rooms, while in summer the patio comes into its own. Good modern bedrooms, one with a four-poster, two with half-testers. Families are well catered for. There's a choice of meeting and syndicate rooms, the largest with a capacity of 60 (banqueting for up to 100). Leave the M25 at Junction 9 on to the A24. Forte. *Rooms 68. Garden. Access, Amex, Diners, Visa.*

DORRINGTON   Country Friends   £65

Tel 01743 718707   Map 6 A4   **RR**
Dorrington nr Shrewsbury Shropshire SY5 7JD

A half-timbered house turned into a comfortable restaurant with rooms. Chef-patron Charles Whittaker offers two-or three-course fixed-price menus lunchtime and evening. Duck is a speciality, appearing perhaps as confit with butter beans or breast presented on a bed of cabbage and bacon with mustard sauce. Venison is a seasonal favourite, served typically with an elderberry sauce and caramelised shallots. Other choices might be pickled vegetables with garlic mayonnaise, rabbit paté with pear and cranberry jelly and slices of fillet steak with home-made pasta and a dill sauce. To finish, perhaps apple and walnut crumble with cinnamon ice cream and toffee sauce, Welsh rarebit, or British cheeses. Light lunches are served Mon-Sat in the bar. No smoking. *Seats 40. L 12-2 D 7-9 (Sat to 9.30). Closed Sun (except last Sun of the month), Mon, Bank Holidays, last 2 weeks Jul, last week Oct. Set L & D £21.50/£24.85/£28.65 Set Sun L £15.50. Access, Amex, Visa.*

Rooms   £98*
Three good-quality coach-house bedrooms are attractive with antiques, if sparing with extras. Two are not en suite. None has phone or TV. *Room price includes dinner and a breakfast of Bucks Fizz and scrambled eggs with smoked salmon. No dogs.

DOVEDALE   Izaak Walton Hotel   59%   £95

Tel 01335 350555   Fax 01335 350539   Map 6 C3   **H**
Dovedale nr Ashbourne Derbyshire DE6 2AY

Owned by the Duke of Rutland, the 17th-century farmhouse building, where Izaak Walton once stayed, affords rolling views of Thorpe Cloud and Dovedale in the Peak District Park. Fly fishing is available on a 4-mile stretch of the River Dove, which flows through the estate. Leather chesterfield sofas and open fires add comfort and warmth to the public rooms; bedrooms are more noteworthy for the vistas without than the space within. Conference facilities for up to 60. Under-16s stay free in parents' room. *Rooms 33. Garden, fishing. Access, Amex, Diners, Visa.*

DOVEDALE   Peveril of the Peak   60%   £102

Tel 01335 350333   Fax 01335 350507   Map 6 C3   **H**
Thorpe Dovedale nr Ashbourne Derbyshire DE6 2AW

Easily reached from the M1 and the M6, at the foot of the 900ft Thorpe Cloud mountain in the heart of the Peak District, Peveril of the Peak has been attracting ramblers and country lovers for over 100 years. It features much local Derbyshire stone in the public rooms. Bedrooms are traditional. Banqueting/conferences for 70/60. Forte. *Rooms 47. Garden, tennis. Access, Amex, Diners, Visa.*

DOVER — County Hotel — 66% — £87

Tel 01304 509955   Fax 01304 213230   Map 11 D5   **H**
Townwall Street Dover Kent CT16 1SZ

The former Moat House, still owned by Queens Moat Houses, stands near the sea and caters well for both business and leisure visitors. Large beds in spacious bedrooms. Children under 15 stay free in parents' room. Banqueting/conference facilities for 120/80. *Rooms 79. Indoor swimming pool. Access, Amex, Diners, Visa.*

DOVER — Forte Posthouse — 63% — £72

Tel 01304 821222   Fax 01304 825576   Map 11 D5   **H**
Singledge Lane Whitfield Dover Kent CT16 3LF

Modern low-riser on the Whitfield roundabout alongside the A2, 3 miles from the ferry terminal. Children up to 13 stay free in parents' room. Banqueting/conference facilities for up to 50/65. 24hr lounge menu. *Rooms 67. Garden, outdoor playground, children's playroom (weekends). Access, Amex, Diners, Visa.*

DRIFFIELD — Bell Hotel — £75

Tel 01377 256661   Fax 01377 253228   Map 7 E1   **I**
Market Place Driffield Humberside YO25 7AP

Period charm and modern amenities (business and leisure) combine in a coaching inn that's more than 250 years old. The restored Old Town Hall has function facilities for up to 250. Day rooms include the 18th-century wood-panelled Oak Room and the flagstoned Old Corn Exchange buffet/bar. Bedrooms boast antique furniture and contemporary comforts. No children under 12. No dogs. *Rooms 14. Garden, indoor swimming pool, spa bath, steam room, massage, aromatherapy, sauna, solarium, keep-fit equipment, squash. Closed 24-30 Dec. Access, Amex, Diners, Visa.*

DROITWICH SPA — Chateau Impney — 70% — £140

Tel 01905 774411   Fax 01905 772371   Map 14 B1   **H**
Droitwich Spa Hereford & Worcester WR9 0BN

Chateau Impney is a perfect example of classical French architecture in the chateau style and makes an unexpected and delightful sight in the heart of England. The grand stone staircase and fountains surrounded by gilded cherubs enhance the first impression. However, the principal business here is as a residential conference centre and banqueting suite and the capacity is now 1250 delegates. Main-house bedrooms are spacious (but with surprisingly small bathrooms) while the separate Impney Court building offers newer but smaller accommodation. Nine apartments are also in a separate block. Children are only welcome by prior arrangement. No dogs. *Rooms 120. Garden, tennis, sauna, solarium, gym, games room. Closed Christmas. Access, Amex, Diners, Visa.*

DROITWICH SPA — Raven Hotel — 66% — £140

Tel 01905 772224   Fax 01905 797100   Map 14 B1   **H**
Victoria Square Droitwich Spa Hereford & Worcester WR9 8DU

Specialising in conferences and banqueting (for up to 150/250), the Raven also takes very good care of private guests, putting a premium on courtesy and professionalism. It's a handsome timber-framed building, parts of it going back to the 16th century. Overnight accommodation is more up-to-date than the exterior might suggest. *Rooms 72. Garden. Closed August, 24-31 Dec. Access, Amex, Diners, Visa.*

DULVERTON — Ashwick House — 68% — £95

Tel & Fax 01398 323868   Map 13 D2   **HR**
Dulverton Somerset TA22 9QD

Turn left at the post office in Dulverton, drive up to the moor, turn left after the second cattle grid and follow the hotel sign. Richard Sherwood's Ashwick House, dating from the turn of the century, stands in isolation 1000 feet above the valley of the Barle, providing all the peace and fresh air anyone could want. The William Morris interior still boasts original wallpapers; although the present reconstruction dates only from 1980, an evocative Edwardian atmosphere has carefully been retained. Thus, beside your turned-down bed you'll find a goodnight sweet and an Edward Bear hot-water bottle. Bedrooms are spacious, with lovely parkland views and rather dated, chintzy decor.

See over

Fine days start with breakfast on the terrace. Sweeping lawns lead down to water gardens, thus no children under 8. No dogs. *Rooms 6. Garden, solarium. No credit cards.*

Restaurant £60

Richard's capable one-man show extends to the kitchen and dinner, when a named, hand-written scroll menu is presented to each diner. Cooking is house-party British, exemplified by mushroom and coriander soup, baked spinach crepes, roast poussin served with sherry sauce, chocolate hazelnut truffle slice and bread-and-butter pudding. No smoking. *Seats 35. Parties 18. L (Sun only) 12.30-1.45 D 7.15-8.30. Set Sun L £14.75 Set D £22.50.*

DULVERTON	Carnarvon Arms	60%	£80

Tel 01398 23302   Fax 01398 24022   Map 13 D2   **H**
Dulverton Somerset TA22 9AE

Purpose-built by the 4th Earl of Carnarvon in 1874 to accommodate railway passengers arriving at Dulverton station, the Carnarvon Arms is now very much geared to walkers, horse-riders (the hotel will put you in touch with nearby stables) and particularly fishermen, with just over five miles of trout and salmon fishing on the rivers Exe and Barle. The spacious lounges are large, old-fashioned and relaxing, with open fires, splendid views and flower displays. Bedrooms are modest but comfortable enough. Children up to 7 stay free in their parents' room in low season (high season from £12). Owner Mrs Toni Jones has run the hotel for over 35 years. *Rooms 24. Garden, croquet, outdoor swimming pool, children's splash pool, tennis, fishing, snooker, hair salon. Access, Amex, Visa.*

DUNBRIDGE	Mill Arms Inn	£50

Tel 01794 340401   Map 14 C3   **R**
Dunbridge nr Romsey Hampshire SO51 0LF

Owner Niall Morrow continues improvements at the Mill Arms, but the fresh local produce is still cooked in a traditional style as in deep-fried tiger prawns with garlic mayonnaise, sea bass with lemon and chive butter and 10oz pork chop with either apple sauce or rich onion gravy. The wine list includes a connoisseurs' selection. Sunday lunch is popular and booking is recommended. *Seats 60. Private Room 40. L 11-3 D 6-11. Set Sun L £7.95/£9.95. Access, Amex, Diners, Visa.*

DUNKIRK	Petty France Hotel	65%	£90

Tel 01454 238361   Fax 01454 238768   Map 13 F1   **H**
Dunkirk Badminton Avon GL9 1AF

This well-proportioned Georgian house set in eye-catching gardens alongside the A46 (five miles north of M4 junction 18) stands between Bristol, Bath, Gloucester and Cheltenham. It thus satisfies tourists as well as users of the banqueting and conference facilities. Day rooms are spacious and tranquil, and bedrooms are divided between the main house and a converted stable block; a traditional feel with period furniture and floral fabrics in the former gives way to cottagey curtains and lightwood fittings in the latter. *Rooms 20. Garden, croquet. Access, Amex, Diners, Visa.*

DUNSTABLE	Old Palace Lodge	66%	£101

Tel 01582 662201   Fax 01582 696422   Map 15 E1   **H**
Church Street Dunstable Bedfordshire LU5 4RT

A usefully situated hotel, on the A505 on the Luton side of the town centre, quite near junction 11 of the M1. Creeper-clad and welcoming, it offers a good choice of accommodation, all spacious and well appointed. Executive wing rooms have extra amenities. *Rooms 50. Access, Amex, Diners, Visa.*

Consult the blue pages for summary tables and lists of

DUNSTER   Luttrell Arms   64%   £112   H

Tel 01643 821555   Fax 01643 821567   Map 13 E1
High Street Dunster nr Minehead Somerset TA24 6SG

A creeper-clad hotel of great historical interest, built in the 15th century as a guest house for the monks of Cleeve Abbey. Impressive architectural features include a superb Gothic hall (now the lounge) with a twelve-light window, hammer-beam roof and huge fireplace, and a timbered Tudor bar in the former kitchen. Bedrooms offer solid 20th-century comforts and functional modern bathrooms. Garage parking £3 per night. Forte Heritage. *Rooms 27. Garden, garage. Access, Amex, Diners, Visa.*

DURHAM   Royal County Hotel   67%   £124   H

Tel 0191-386 6821   Fax 0191-386 0704   Map 5 E3
Old Elvet Durham Co Durham DH1 3JN

A large business-orientated hotel created from a series of Jacobean town houses, close to the cathedral and castle and overlooking the River Wear. Attractively decorated bedrooms all have a mini-bar and a trouser press among the usual amenities. One large room is adapted for disabled guests. 24hr room service. Fine leisure facilities (with views over the river) attract weekend guests. Children under 14 free in parents' room. Own free parking. Swallow Hotels. *Rooms 150. Indoor swimming pool, spa bath, sauna, sun bed, gym, beauty & hair salons, coffee shop (7am-9.30pm). Access, Amex, Diners, Visa.*

> Set menu prices may not always include service or wine.

DUXFORD   Duxford Lodge   65%   £88   HR

Tel 01223 836444   Fax 01223 832271   Map 10 B3
Ickleton Road Duxford nr Cambridge Cambridgeshire CB2 4RU

The hotel enjoys a peaceful setting in its own well-tended grounds in the sleepy village of Duxford, a short distance south of Cambridge and one mile from Junction 10 of the M11. The exterior is as inviting as the interior is comfortable and homely. The spacious bar contrasts with the small residents' lounge, both of which are furnished in attractive soft autumnal colour schemes. Walls are decorated with an extensive collection of fighter aircraft pictures – both prints and paintings, appropriate as the Imperial War Museum's Duxford Airfield is only a short distance away; the lodge itself was the wartime headquarters of Douglas Bader. Bedrooms, of which four are in an attractive garden wing, are all of a good size and neatly furnished. Colour schemes are restful and decor well maintained. Top-floor bedrooms have characterful sloping ceilings. There are four bridal suites, two of them with four-posters. *Rooms 15. Garden. Closed 27-30 Dec. Access, Amex, Diners, Visa.*

Restaurant   £50

Chef-patron Ron Craddock has stepped into the background, having appointed a head chef to take over the main duties in the kitchen. Cooking continues in the modern style with a strong classical foundation resulting in a varied choice of dishes that are visually appealing and a real joy to eat. The dining-room is light and airy. *Seats 46. Parties 22. Private Room 10. L 12-2 D 7-9.30. Closed L Sat. Set L & D £15 (Sun L £9/£11.95).*

EASINGTON   Grinkle Park   70%   £80   H

Tel 01287 640515   Fax 01287 641278   Map 5 E3
Easington Loftus nr Saltburn-by-Sea Cleveland TS13 4UB

Sweeping lawns and mature pines and rhododendrons surround a formidable mansion set in parkland just off the A174. The atmosphere inside is refined and quietly elegant, much as when it was a private house from the 1880s to 1947. The delightful Camellia Room, with picture windows, festoon blinds and wicker seating, has camellias actually growing up through the floor, and in the foyer-bar the roaring winter fire is reflected in the darkwood panelling. Bedrooms are named after local flora, birds and places; they're stylishly decorated, with light, restful colour schemes. *Rooms 20. Garden, croquet, tennis, snooker. Access, Amex, Diners, Visa.*

EAST BOLDON   Forsters   £65

Tel 0191-519 0929   Map 5 E2   **R**
2 St Bedes Station Road East Boldon Tyne & Wear NE36 0LE

In the centre of Boldon, close to the A814 Sunderland to Gateshead road, Barry Forster's restaurant has a distinctive bottle-green exterior and stands in a small row of shops with limited parking at the front. Comprising a single room with a bar occupying the corner, it has pretty, peachy pastel decor. The few tables are quite closely spaced but this does not detract from the place's comfort and appeal. An eclectic menu of imaginative and enjoyable food is offered. Starters might range from green pea soup with mint and croutons, or salmon and smoked salmon paté with herb mayonnaise to toasted muffin with creamy smoked haddock, poached egg and béarnaise sauce. Main dishes include grilled fillet steak with roasted shallots and red wine sauce, roast loin of venison with red cabbage and chestnuts or breast of Lunesdale duck with an orange and Grand Marnier sauce and buttered mashed potato. Sweets are typified by sticky toffee pudding, chocolate and honey slice with coffee bean sauce and vanilla crème brulée. Friendly service is provided by Sue Forster. No children under 8. Simple, jumbled wine list, sensibly priced. *Seats 28. D only 7-10. Set £15 (Tue-Fri). Closed Sun, Mon & Bank Holidays, 1 week Jun, 1 week Aug, 1 week Christmas. Access, Amex, Diners, Visa.*

EAST BUCKLAND   Lower Pitt   £50

Tel & Fax 01598 760243   Map 13 D2   **RR**
East Buckland Barnstaple Devon EX32 0TD

Just on the western edge of Exmoor National Park (two miles off the A361), an old stone farmhouse has been converted into a charming restaurant with rooms, owned and run since 1978 by the immensely capable and welcoming Jerome and Suzanne Lyons. Suzanne is in charge in the kitchens, and uses good local produce to great effect. Typical starters might be a brandade of salmon, twice-baked cheese soufflé with Double Gloucester and chives and Cornish 'hot-smoked' salmon with grain mustard mayonnaise with dishes such as Thai prawn stir-fry, lamb Kashmir-style, game 'bourguignonne' and organically reared duckling with apple sauce. Delicious puds like sticky toffee banana split, tiramisu and *gateau lyonnais*. Good English cheeses. Over twenty half bottles on the wine list. Three tables outside on a terrace in good weather. No smoking in restaurant. No children under 8 after 8.30pm. *Seats 32. Private Room 16. D only 7-9. Closed Sun, Mon (except for residents), 2 days Christmas. Access, Amex, Visa.*

Rooms   £60

Three double rooms, all en-suite and all non-smoking, are comfortably furnished and equipped. No children under 8. Excellent breakfasts.

EAST DEREHAM   King's Head   £55

Tel 01362 693842   Fax 01362 693776   Map 10 C1   **I**
Norwich Street East Dereham Norfolk NR19 1AD

A modest but immaculately kept 17th-century coaching inn near the town centre. A cosy red-carpeted bar, busy with locals, looks out past the patio to an attractive lawn (once the bowling green) with tables and chairs. Five bedrooms are located in the light and airy converted stable block. The remainder lie beyond gloomily-lit corridors in the main building. Families are made welcome. 15 miles from Norwich. *Rooms 17. Garden, tennis, games room. Access, Amex, Diners, Visa.*

EAST GRINSTEAD   Gravetye Manor   84%   £200

Tel 01342 810567   Fax 01342 810080   Map 11 B5   **HR**
Vowels Lane East Grinstead West Sussex RH19 4LJ

Peter Herbert and his staff continue to provide an object lesson in how a country house hotel should be run. The care and attention to every last detail shows everywhere, both within the splendidly transformed Elizabethan stone mansion (built in 1598) and in the 1000 acres of grounds that incorporate the William Robinson English garden recently restored to its former glory. Flower displays fill the gracious day rooms, which include a really delightful sitting room with oak panelling and an ornate moulded ceiling, and the entrance hall with its carefully selected chair patterns. Bedrooms, with their comfortable beds, antique furniture and sumptuous fabrics, are models of good taste; books,

magazines, post cards, bedside radios and TVs concealed behind tapestry screens are among a long list of thoughtful extras. The bathrooms, too, with his and her washbasins, bidet and power shower over the bath, provide for every conceivable need, and are havens of comfort. No children under 7, but babes in arms welcome – cots provided. Fly fishing on the lake between May and September. No dogs in the hotel; kennels at the head of the drive. This most civilised of hotels stands 5 miles south-west of East Grinstead off the B2110 at the West Hoathly sign. ***Rooms 18. Garden, croquet, fishing. Access, Visa.***

Restaurant   £105

A comfortable restaurant whose enviable reputation for consistently high standards is certain to be maintained by Mark Raffan, who was returning to Gravetye's kitchen (he was head chef from 1989-91) in the summer of 1995 after spending, among other posts, three years as personal chef to King Hussain of Jordan. Mark earned a star for his cooking last time around but his return was just too late for a proper assessment so we are unable to give him a star rating this year or to quote specific dishes. One can be sure that ingredients will be of the best, with a walled kitchen garden providing much of the produce in summer, their own smokehouse the smoked salmon, duck breast and the like and the spring which has served the Manor from the start still providing water for the tables. The dining-room, with mellow oak panelling beneath a Tudor ceiling, is a lovely setting and service is silky smooth and attentive without being overbearing. Menu prices include service but not VAT. Sommelier Thierry Morigeon presides over a quite magnificent wine list that seems to get better and better each year. All the top names and growers are present, from classic clarets and burgundies to vintage champagnes and the very best the New World has to offer. Both Germany and Italy feature prominently too. No smoking. ***Seats 42. Parties 8. Private Room 18. L 12.30-2 D 7.30-9.30 (Sun to 9). Closed D 25 Dec to non-residents. Set L £22 (+VAT) (Sun £28 +VAT) Set D £28 (+VAT).***

| EAST GRINSTEAD | Woodbury House | 61% | £85 |

Tel 01342 313657   Fax 01342 314801   Map 11 B5   **H**
Lewes Road East Grinstead West Sussex RH19 3UD

Small hotel set in a Victorian house on the A22 just south of town and popular with business people. After the second change of ownership in recent years all bedrooms have now been upgraded to include fresh fruit, satellite TV, trouser press, tea- and coffee-making facilities and hairdryers. All have attractive matching fabrics, reproduction antique furniture, and good-sized, well-lit desks with sensible upright chairs. Public areas include a spacious lounge and a combined bar/bistro with conservatory extension overlooking the road. ***Rooms 14. Garden, bistro (11.30am-11pm). Access, Amex, Diners, Visa.***

| EAST HORSLEY | Jarvis Thatchers Hotel | 62% | £108 |

Tel 01483 284291   Fax 01483 284222   Map 15 E3   **H**
Epsom Road East Horsley Surrey KT24 6TB

Formerly Thatchers Resort Hotel, this is an attractive mock-Tudor building set back from the road behind a lovely garden. The main public area is a comfortable open-plan bar-lounge beyond a spacious parquet-floored reception area. Choose from prettily decorated accommodation in the main house, smaller motel-style rooms around the open-air pool and a few more cottagey bedrooms in an adjacent building. ***Rooms 59. Garden, outdoor swimming pool (May-Sep). Access, Amex, Diners, Visa.***

Consult the blue pages for summary tables and lists of recommended establishments.

EAST STOKE   Kemps Country House   56%   £80

Tel 01929 462563   Fax 01929 405287   Map 14 B4   **H**
East Stoke nr Wareham Dorset BH20 6AL

A quiet and welcoming country hotel converted from a Victorian rectory, situated on the A352 between Wareham and Wool. Five bedrooms are in the main building, four in a converted coach house; the best six pine-furnished rooms are in a recent addition, facing the Purbeck Hills. Two ground-floor rooms are suitable for disabled guests. Some rooms have whirlpool baths, and one boasts a modern four-poster. Children under 7 stay free in parents' room, meals charged as taken. Banqueting/conference facilities for 120/70. *Rooms 15. Garden. Access, Amex, Diners, Visa.*

EASTBOURNE   De Vere Cavendish Hotel   68%   £85

Tel 01323 410222   Fax 01323 410941   Map 11 B6   **H**
Grand Parade Eastbourne East Sussex BN21 4DH

Well-maintained and imposing seafront hotel with a modern corner extension. Banqueting facilities for up to 350 and conferences for up to 220. Families are made welcome with helpful amenities provided and early suppers served at flexible times. Children up to the age of 7 are accommodated free in parents' room. 24hr room service. *Rooms 112. Games room. Access, Amex, Diners, Visa.*

EASTBOURNE   De Vere Grand Hotel   75%   £140

Tel 01323 412345   Fax 01323 412233   Map 11 B6   **HR**
King Edward's Parade Eastbourne East Sussex BN21 4EQ

At the west end of the seafront, the hotel maintains much of the style and grace of its Victorian origins with marble pillars, crystal chandeliers, vast corridors and high-domed day rooms evoking a more leisurely, bygone age, with everything kept in good order by means of an ongoing refurbishment programme (this year the main hallway, lounges and leisure club). Some of the more expensive sea-facing bedrooms have balconies and are huge, with bright furniture and up-to-date fabrics, though other rooms are smaller, so it's best to check when booking. 24hr room service, comprehensive leisure and exercise facilities, themed weekend breaks and children's hostesses keep the Grand apace with its more modern competitors. Families are well catered for with children under 14 free in parents' room. Function facilities for up to 400. *Rooms 164. Garden, putting green, indoor & outdoor swimming pools, spa bath, sauna, steam room, solarium, beauty & hairdressing salons, keep-fit equipment, snooker. Access, Amex, Diners, Visa.*

Mirabelle Restaurant   £70

Long-serving executive head chef Keith Mitchell and head chef Mark Jones produce some classic dishes, albeit with a modern approach. Fixed-price lunch (2-or 3-course) and dinner (4-course, priced by choice of main course) menus offer a small but varied choice, and in addition there's an à la carte showing an eclectic style with the likes of fresh pasta ravioli of shellfish with lobster gravy and crisp-fried leek; lightly roasted veal sweetbreads wrapped in Parma ham, served with a watercress butter sauce; loin of lamb wrapped in aubergine on a bed of ratatouille with a red pepper jus; and lightly roasted turbot with braised fennel, grilled scallops and red wine fish jus. At lunchtime there's always a traditional roast, served from a silver trolley. British and French cheeses served with home-made walnut and raisin bread, and desserts such as hot apple and pear tatin with brown bread ice cream or a classic French lemon tart end the meal in fine style. Reasonable prices on the run-of-the-mill wine list. *Seats 50. Parties 12. Private Room 40. L 12.30-2.30 D 7-10. Closed Sun & Mon, Bank Holidays, 2 weeks Aug, 1st 2 weeks Jan. Set L £15.50/£18.50 Set D from £22.50.*

EASTBOURNE   Wish Tower Hotel   66%   £96

Tel 01323 722676   Fax 01323 721474   Map 11 B6   **H**
King Edward's Parade Eastbourne East Sussex BN21 4EB

The hotel stands on the seafront opposite the Wish Tower, a martello tower that is now a Napoleonic and World War II museum. Bedrooms are in attractively up-to-date style, with modern comforts like double-glazing, and many enjoy sea views. A range of function facilities can cater for up to 120 banqueting, 100 conference delegates. Children up to 14 stay free in parents' room. Residents have free membership of the David Lloyd Tennis and Sports Leisure Centre (10 minutes drive). Park on the street or int the NCP, or book one of the hotel's three lock-up garages (£3 per day). Principal Hotels.
Rooms 65. Access, Amex, Diners, Visa.

We welcome bona fide complaints and recommendations on the tear-out pages at the back of the book for readers' comments. They are followed up by our professional team.

EASTLEIGH   Forte Posthouse   66%   £72

Tel 01703 619700   Fax 01703 643945   Map 15 D3   **H**
Leigh Road Eastleigh Hampshire SO50 9PG

Modern low-rise hotel just off junction 13 of the M3 or junction 5 of the M27. Features include a leisure centre and children's playground. Conference facilities for up to 250.
Rooms 120. Indoor swimming pool, keep-fit equipment, spa bath, steam room, solarium, beauty salon, pool table. Access, Amex, Diners, Visa.

ECCLESHALL   St George Hotel   £70

Tel 01785 850300   Fax 01785 851452   Map 6 B3   **I**
Castle Street Eccleshall Staffordshire ST21 6DF

Behind the white-painted frontage of this 17th-century coaching inn is a mixture of modern and old that includes an inglenook fireplace in the bar – the focal point of the inn, with old beams and copper-topped tables. Bedrooms are kept in immaculate order and have plenty of character, some with fireplaces and exposed timbers. The Old Library is no more, so there's no longer a conference facility. What they have instead is a brewery producing and selling Slaters Ales – the brew is named after the owners.
Rooms 10. Access, Amex, Diners, Visa.

EDENBRIDGE   Honours Mill Restaurant   £60

Tel 01732 866757   Map 11 B5   **R**
87 High Street Edenbridge Kent TN8 5AU

A converted mill is the charming setting for some careful French cooking from the kitchen of Martin Radmall. Well-balanced fixed-price menus (Tues-Fri) are inclusive of coffee, petits fours and service; from three choices at each stage you might choose clam chowder followed by entrecote of beef and cheese or dessert at both lunch and dinner, the latter including a half bottle of house wine per person. Also offered is an à la carte with sausage of lamb sweetbreads with a sorrel sauce, fish soup with rouille, fricassee of chicken with sherry and wild mushrooms, and a rich stew of salt pork, oxtail, lamb tongue and confit of duck typifying the style. Among the desserts you might find Sussex Pond pudding (a traditional steamed lemon suet pudding), bananas *en papillote* and crème brulée au cassis. Since last year prices have crept up on the decent wine list, though to be fair the more expensive wines have not. Children welcome for Sunday lunch. *Seats 38. L 12.15-2 D 7.15-10. Closed L Sat, D Sun, all Mon, 2 weeks Christmas. Set L £15.50 (Sun £23.50) & £32.75 Set D £26 & £32.75. Access, Amex, Visa.*

Consult the blue pages for summary tables and lists of recommended establishments.

EGHAM   Great Fosters   67%   £99

Tel 01784 433822   Fax 01784 472455   Map 15 E2   **H**
Stroude Road Egham Surrey TW20 9UR

The imposing facade of this stately Elizabethan house sets the tone for the quintessentially English public rooms with their ornate plaster ceilings, oak panelling and carved antique furniture. The best are on the first floor and feature richly embroidered fabrics and tapestry wall hangings; there are some period suites and four-poster rooms. Other rooms are plainer – some in the house, others in the conference centre. Get to Egham then follow the brown Historical Interest signs marked Great Fosters. No dogs. *Rooms 44. Garden, tennis, outdoor swimming pool, sauna, steam room, snooker. Access, Amex, Diners, Visa.*

EGHAM   Runnymede Hotel   74%   £162

Tel 01784 436171   Fax 01784 436340   Map 15 E2   **H**
Windsor Road Egham Surrey TW20 0AG

Leave the M25 at J13 and take the A308 Egham/Windsor road to find this riverside building whose rather unpromising redbrick exterior conceals a smart hotel with light, airy public areas and high levels of service: room service runs to cooked meals 24hrs a day and beds are turned down in the evening. Latest improvements include the refurbishment of over 80 rooms. The stylish Runnymede Spa leisure centre is particularly luxurious. The best (Executive) bedrooms are most appealing with yellow and blue colour scheme, good armchairs and fine marble bathrooms. Standard rooms are more variable in size (a few are on the small side) and decor, but all have the same amenities – air-conditioning, mini-bars, bathrobes – and benefit from the same high standards of housekeeping. Numerous, well-equipped conference rooms can cope with up to 400 delegates theatre-style. Children (up to the age of 12 £10 when sharing parents' room) are made welcome with their own menu in the hotel's informal restaurant, Charlie Bells, and a large children's pool in the Spa. Thorpe Park is only just down the road. *Rooms 171. Garden, croquet, indoor swimming pool, children's pool, gym, dance studio, sauna, steam room, spa bath, solarium, beauty salon, hair salon, snooker, dinner-dance (Sat). Access, Amex, Diners, Visa.*

ELCOT   Jarvis Elcot Park   67%   £112

Tel 01488 658100   Fax 01488 658288   Map 15 D2   **H**
Elcot nr Newbury Berkshire RG16 8NJ

Set back from the A4 almost exactly halfway between Newbury and Hungerford and surrounded by 16 acres of its own grounds this hotel, based around an original 1786 family hosue, majors on conferences during the week (nine meeting rooms vary from elegant period rooms to a modern air-conditioned venue with every modern aid) and weddings at the weekends. Day rooms are in the original building, with some nice architectural features, along with a few antique-furnished bedrooms. Most rooms are in a fairly new extension but varying decor and layout give them an individual feel. Lastly there are 17 individually furnished rooms in a 'mews' a short distance from the house. Wherever they are rooms are spacious, well equipped and appealing. Go for the Executive option and you will get one of the largest rooms kitted out with various extras from bathrobe and complimentary wine to fruit and a little basket of goodies. 24hr room service extends to at least one hot item being available overnight. Children up to 16 stay free in parents' room. In addition to the leisure facilities listed below hot air ballooning, something of a speciality here, can also be arranged. *Rooms 75. Garden, croquet, tennis, indoor swimming pool, keep-fit equipment, weekly aerobics class, softball, sauna, spa bath, solarium, beauty salon, shop. Access, Amex, Diners, Visa.*

ELTON   Loch Fyne Oyster Bar   £40

Tel 01832 280298   Fax 01832 280170   Map 7 E4   **R**
The Old Dairy Elton nr Peterborough Cambridgeshire PE8 5SH

100 yards from the A605 bypass to Oundle and eight miles from Peterborough, this is an informal seafood restaurant and retail outlet located in a converted dairy building which dates back to 1901. The decor is simple with much Scots pine, while the food consists of the freshest of seafood brought down from Scotland overnight. Rock oysters come from their own oysterage and smoked fish from their own smokehouse. See also entry under Cairndow (Scotland). *Seats 80. Meals 9am-9pm (Fri & Sat to 10, Sun to 5). Closed 25 & 26 Dec. Access, Visa.*

| ELY | **Lamb Hotel** | 57% | £70 |

Tel 01353 663574   Fax 01353 662023   Map 10 B2   **H**
2 Lynn Road Ely Cambridgeshire CB7 4EJ

New owners have smartened up the bar at this former coaching inn right in the town centre. The lounge is to follow. Bedrooms offer clean, comfortable accommodation, each room possessing a hairdryer, trouser press and remote-control TV. No dogs. *Rooms 32. Access, Amex, Diners, Visa.*

| ELY | **Old Fire Engine House** | | £50 |

Tel 01353 662582   Map 10 B2   **R**
25 St Mary's Street Ely Cambridgeshire CB7 4ER

An 18th-century town house, near the cathedral, that gained its present name at the turn of the century when Ely's horse-drawn fire engine was kept here. It's a place of enormous charm and friendliness; you pass through the kitchen to reach the main eating room with its uneven tiled floor, kitchen tables and pew seating. When busy, other more elegant rooms are used, one is a comfortable lounge, and there is also a cosy bar. All rooms boast a changing collection of pictures by various artists, many local, as the whole house is as much an art gallery as restaurant. Cooking, by a team of local ladies, tends towards the homely rather than the sophisticated but does not lack interest with dishes, often from local recipes, such as herrings pickled in dill with yoghurt and cucumber, game terrine, beef in Guinness and port, fresh plaice stuffed with smoked salmon and watercress, and jugged hare plus a vegetarian dish like lasagne with a spiced bean pot. Good fresh ingredients are drawn as much as possible from the surrounding Fens and the bread is home-made. Tempting puds might include meringues with cream, sherry trifle, apple pie (made with delicious, sugary, melt-in-the-mouth short pastry), and home-made chocolate and Grand Marnier ice cream. Very long notes accompany each wine on a fairish list. In summer some tables are set out in a pretty walled garden. *Seats 36. Parties 22. Private Rooms 22. L 12.30-2 D 7.30-9. Closed D Sun, Bank Holidays, 2 weeks Christmas. Access, Visa.*

| EPPING | **Forte Posthouse** | 63% | £75 |

Tel 01992 573137   Fax 01992 560402   Map 11 B4   **H**
High Road Bell Common Epping Essex CM16 4DG

Public rooms here show their 16th-century origins while bedrooms are in a modern wing. Banqueting for 85, conferences facilities for 100. *Rooms 79. Access, Amex, Diners, Visa.*

| ERPINGHAM | **The Ark** | | £55 |

Tel 01263 761535   Map 10 C1   **RR**
The Street Erpingham Norfolk NR11 7QB

An old flint cottage set deep in rural Norfolk four miles north of Aylesham off the A140. Sheila and Becky Kidd's very individual cooking style shows many influences on fixed-price, handwritten menus that change daily and derive from local suppliers and their own garden. Typical dishes run from ricotta and spinach terrine with fresh pear dressing and Cantonese-style braised shin of beef (as a starter) to roast goose with potato and leek stuffing, lamb tagine with apricots and grilled monkfish with a pepper ragout. Farmhouse cheese and a choice of four sweets. Vegetarian dishes are always available – discuss when booking. With house wines priced at only £7.50/£8, the wine list offers terrific value, especially with its increased New World selection. Sound tasting notes. No children under 7 in the evenings. Outside eating in fine weather. *Seats 36. Parties 12. Private Rooms 16. L (Sun only) 12.30-2 D 7-9.30. Closed D Sun, all Mon & 25-30 Dec. Set L £12.50 Set D £16.75/£19.50/£21.50. No credit cards.*

Rooms   £95*

Three non-smoking bedrooms, the downstairs room allows dogs. * Half-board terms only. *Garden, croquet.*

ESHER — Good Earth — £55

Tel 01372 462489   Map 15 E2   **R**
14-18 High Street Esher Surrey KT10 9RT

A long-time fixture in Esher's main street, the Good Earth continues to provide reliably good cooking from a menu that, although not as long as in some Chinese restaurants, runs to nearly 160 items. High-quality ingredients like lovely plump scallops and the rump steak used for all the beef dishes are key to dishes that represent all the main styles from Cantonese and Peking to spicy Szechuan, plus a few from further afield like Malaysian satay. Decor is smart as are the staff, with uniforms featuring striped shirts, bow ties and braces, who are notably attentive and pleasant. For two sister restaurants with the same menu see the London section. There is also a Wimbledon take-away outlet, with home delivery service, called Good Earth Express. *Seats 85. L 12-2.30 D 6-11.*
Set L £12/£17.50/£24.50 Set D £17.50/£24.50. Closed 24-27 Dec. Access, Amex, Diners, Visa.

ETON — The Eton Wine Bar — £55

Tel 01753 854921   Fax 01753 868384   Map 15 E2   **R**
82-83 High Street Eton Berkshire SL4 6AF

Behind its smart dark green frontage this would appear at first sight to be a rather small wine bar/restaurant – stools at a wooden bar counter, pew seating, colourful pictures around the walls – but a long passageway at the back leads to a much larger conservatory dining-room. Here for 20 years, the Gilbeys know just what their customers want and offer it from a menu from which you can have just a single dish (before and after a visit to the Windsor Theatre perhaps, just a short walk away across the footbridge over the Thames). Typical dishes from the evening menu include a spiced mussel soup and smoked haddock fishcake amongst the starters and mains like plainly grilled salmon with lemon and parsley butter, chicken tandoori and stir-fried vegetarian risotto. Lunchtime, prices are a little lower and a number of dishes are priced as either starters or light main dishes, butterfly pasta in wild mushroom sauce, smoked salmon and scrambled eggs, and grilled goat's cheese sandwiched between slices of aubergine on a bed of leaves with black olive and anchovy dressing being examples. Sound cooking throughout the carte, and leave room for some good puds like amaretto and praline pot or Eton lemon tart – the latter made with a tangy lemon curd and served with vanilla ice cream. Few half bottles on the all-French wine list, but it's inexpensive enough not to matter. *Seats 100.*
Private Room 40. L 12-2.30 D 6-10.30 (till 11 Fri & Sat). Closed 2-3 days Christmas. Access, Amex, Diners, Visa.

EVERSHOT — Summer Lodge — 78% — £125

Tel 01935 83424   Fax 01935 83005   Map 13 F2   **HR**
Evershot Dorchester Dorset DT2 0JR

A former Georgian dower house, sympathetically enlarged in keeping with the original building, and fully justifying its name. Set in extensive, well-maintained, mature gardens, it feels like a country house set in a rural landscape, yet it more or less abuts the village's main street. From a few windows there are views over the picturesque village, while others look out over the gardens to the surrounding rolling hills. A wealth of beautiful flower arrangements adorns both public areas and bedrooms, adding more colour to the already fresh and summery decor. The main drawing-room is spacious with ample, deep-cushioned sofas. There is a further smaller, quieter lounge referred to as the reading room. Both rooms have the welcoming touch of open fires. Bedrooms are furnished with attractive light rattan furniture which complements the pastel tones of the quality upholstery and drapes. Home-made biscuits and tea/coffee facilities (among a host of extras) are provided for out-of-hours service but the afternoon teas are unmissable, including such delights as moist lemon sponge cake and banana bread. Breakfasts, too, are exceptionally good, with all requirements well catered for. All is maintained in the highest order and bathrooms are pristine with thick towels and quality bathtime products. Standards of service and hospitality continue second to none. **Rooms** 17. *Garden, outdoor swimming pool, tennis. Access, Amex, Diners, Visa.*

Restaurant   £100

👑 🍾 🍇 🦆 🗍

Once again there's been a change in the kitchen, with Donna Horlock now in charge, though the style of cooking and presentation of menus remain the same. The quite grand dining-room has French windows on to the garden, so there are fine views in daylight hours, always enhanced by splendid floral arrangements. Alongside the à la carte menu, there are daily-changing lunch and dinner 'country cooking' menus offering such dishes as potted brown shrimps, braised oxtail, and dark treacle tart or local farmhouse cheeses, the last treated very seriously – note the collection of cheese dishes around the hotel – with around a dozen to choose from. Should you decide to select from the à la carte, expect to encounter the likes of marinated scallops and potatoes with a lemon oil dressing; fillet of beef on a bed of wild mushrooms with a confit of shallot, concluding with a prune and armagnac soufflé served with a hot ginger sauce. At dinner there's a choice of soup, sorbet or fish (the last attracting a supplement) as an intermediate course, while Sunday lunch is a four-course affair, always with a roast available. Few '82 clarets, but this is a very fine, serious and comprehensive wine list with the best producers represented. Plenty of half bottles, good drinking under £20, and some local English wines. Terrace seating for 10. No children under 8 after 7.30pm. No smoking. *Seats 50. Parties 20. Private Room 20. L 12.30-1.45 D 7.30-9. Set L £12.50 (Sun £18.50) Set D £32.50.*

EVERSLEY	New Mill Restaurant	£80

Tel 01734 732277   Fax 01734 328780   Map 15 D3   **R**
New Mill Road Eversley Hampshire RG27 0RA

👑 🍾 🍷 🍇 🦆 🗍 �V

It's the idyllic setting that is the big attraction here; a 16th-century watermill (the wheel still working) alongside the slow-moving, green-fringed Blackwater River. The main restaurant has an open fireplace, player-piano, quality table settings and, at one end, picture windows overlooking the river. Typical starters from the à la carte menu might include a twice-baked cheese soufflé, melon with Parma ham and a puff pastry nest filled with sautéed snails, garlic, hazelnuts and green Chartreuse, and main dishes like salmon with lime hollandaise, game suet pudding with red cabbage and blackcurrants, beef Wellington and a selection of chargrills. Prices reflect the surroundings (although service is included) but there are also table d'hote menus at lunchtime representing particularly good value. The low-beamed Grill Room offers a simpler, less expensive menu with less formal service (you can have just a single dish) and one can eat from this menu in the garden where ducks wander around between the tables. There is also a characterful bar with flagstoned floor. On Sundays and Mondays the Grill Room menu only is available. Half bottles perhaps in short supply, but with ten good wines available by the glass it doesn't matter so much. There's quality in the New World and France on the list, but the rest of Europe doesn't get a look in. The New Mill is signposted from the A327. *Seats 80. Private Room 40. L 12-2 D 7-10 (Sun 12.30-9). Closed L Sat (Sun & Mon Grill Room Menu only), 26 Dec & 1 Jan. Set L £12.50 Set D £19.50. Access, Amex, Diners, Visa.*

EVESHAM	Evesham Hotel	65%	£84

Tel 01386 765566   Fax 01386 765443   Map 14 C1   **HR**
Cooper's Lane off Waterside Evesham Hereford & Worcester WR11 6DA

A largely Georgian hotel, with Tudor origins, set in several acres of secluded grounds on the edge of town and run in their own jolly style by the Jenkinson family for almost 20 years. The 'Jenkinson' humour breaks out all over the place from the 'seaside postcard' mural by the pool (Evesham-by-the-Sea) to the padlocked perfume in the (award-winning) public loos that also come with magazines and a portable radio in each cubicle. Bedrooms (keys are attached to a teddy bear) have a traditional feel with candlewick bedspreads and all sorts of extras from playing cards to rubber ducks and clothes-washing liquid in the bathroom. Some rooms have characterful beams and others a period feel with painted Georgian panelling. Public rooms centre around a comfortable, chintzy bar. "Well-behaved youngsters are as welcome as well-behaved grown-ups" according to the 'Junior à la carte', which also requests no pipes, cigars or bubble-gum in the restaurant, and there are all sorts of board games and other amusements about the place to keep younger guests happy plus an outdoor play area with swings, trampoline and slide.

See over

Freephone reservation number: 0800 716969. *Rooms 40. Garden, croquet, indoor swimming pool, table tennis, indoor play area & outdoor playground. Closed 25 & 26 Dec. Access, Amex, Diners, Visa.*

Cedar Restaurant £60

A jokey menu (changing weekly), but the setting is elegant (Regency style) and the results on the plate quite satisfactory with well-judged dishes like smoked bacon-wrapped breast of chicken filled with mozzarella on a red wine sauce; lemon sole shallow-fried with grapes, prawns and walnuts; and noisettes of lamb grilled on a bed of onion chutney with a redcurrant and mint sauce. Separate menus provide for vegetarians, children and those looking for simpler dishes – smoked salmon, grills, cold meats and salads. Good puds include white chocolate cheesecake, Cointreau chocolate mousse and raspberry yoghurt ice cream. Good selection of British cheeses. At lunchtime there is a buffet option (£6.65) in addition to the regular menu. The outstanding wine symbol here equals over the top! Seriously, the eccentric list is fantastic, having specialised in not having either French or German wines for almost twenty years. The actual list is housed in five photo albums; it's most generously priced, thoroughly and unusually comprehensive from, say, Argentina to Uruguay via Kenya! Superb section of New World wines. *Seats 55. Parties 8. Private Room 15. L 12.30-2 D 7-9.30.*

EVESHAM	Riverside Hotel	68%	£80

Tel 01386 446200   Fax 01386 40021   Map 14 C1   **HR**
The Parks Offenham Road Evesham Hereford & Worcester WR11 5JP

Vincent and Rosemary Willmott's white pebbledash house stands in three acres by the River Avon. It's a touch tricky to find, up a private road off Offenham Road (which is not accessible from the bypass). A colourful fresco of river life greets guests on entering, while downstairs an attractive lounge is decorated in corals and greens with plenty of comfortable seating. Bedrooms, with river views, are pretty and appealing, soft colours and co-ordinated fabrics being well employed. Staff are smartly attired, keen and obviously enjoy their jobs. The hotel is closed Sunday night and all Monday. No dogs. *Rooms 7. Garden, fishing. Access, Visa.*

Restaurant £55

Fine views over the River Avon from the dining-room, where Rosemary Willmott offers fixed-price, hand-written, daily-changing menus with a good choice of dishes. English and French are the basis of her methods, but there are also some influences from further afield: spicy vegetable samosas with yoghurt and chutney, steamed fillet of sea bass with ginger and soy, breast of local pheasant with Madeira and thyme jus. Other dishes are more traditional: roast duckling with sage and onion stuffing and rack of lamb with a mustard and herb crust. British cheeses. Light, tangy passion fruit cream with shortbread, hot apple pancake with ice cream and chocolate and brandy mousse – three tempting desserts. No smoking. *Seats 45. Parties 8. L 12-2 D 7.30-9. Closed D Sun, all Mon. Set L £15.95 (£17.95 Sun) Set D £21.95.*

EXETER	Buckerell Lodge	64%	£93

Tel 01392 52451   Fax 01392 412114   Map 13 D2   **HR**
157 Topsham Road Exeter Devon EX2 4SQ

Based around a Regency house, the privately owned Lodge is a business hotel set in several acres of grounds about one mile south-west of the city centre on the B3128. Most bedrooms are in a modern extension and feature an exposed brick wall behind the bedhead, lightwood, shelf-type fitted units and open hanging space; more luxurious are the Executive rooms (mostly in the original house) with colourful decor of soft yellows, blues and pinks and such extras as fresh flowers, mineral water and towelling robe. Bathrooms come with wall-mounted dispensers for liquid soap and shampoo. Some oak panelling and chandeliers help to give the open-plan public areas something of a period feel. The whole place is very well kept and staff notably smart, friendly and attentive. *Rooms 52. Garden. Access, Amex, Diners, Visa.*

Raffles Restaurant £65

There's a sense of adventure to the cooking here – leek soup with mussels; stir-fried vegetables and a lavender jus with a honey-roasted rack of lamb; grilled wild rabbit with apple, pistachio nuts and lemon and wild thyme jus – which relies on good-quality ingredients. The à la carte is fairly short, about half a dozen main dishes, with three more on the set menus, but one does not feel short of choice. No smoking. The spacious dining-room is three steps down from a comfortable cocktail bar. *Seats 45. L 12-2 D 7-9.30. Set L £14.50 Set Sun L £12.50 Set D £19.95.*

EXETER	Forte Crest	69%	£112

Tel 01392 412812   Fax 01392 413549   Map 13 D2   **H**
Southernhay East Exeter Devon EX1 1QF

A recently-built hotel with cathedral views from some of the bedrooms. Conference facilities in seven rooms for up to 160 delegates. 40 of the bedrooms, where children up to 16 stay free with parents, are reserved for non-smokers. Three rooms for disabled guests. *Rooms 110. Indoor swimming pool, gym, sauna, spa bath, solarium. Access, Amex, Diners, Visa.*

EXETER	Rougemont Thistle	63%	£83

Tel 01392 54982   Fax 01392 420928   Map 13 D2   **H**
Queen Street Exeter Devon EX4 3SP

"Rougement" is a reference to the red clay soil of the area and is an apt name for the redbrick building, which is in good order outside and in. It's handily located in the city centre, close to the station and not very far from the oldest parts, around the cathedral. Conferences for up to 300; 24hr room service. *Rooms 90. Access, Amex, Diners, Visa.*

EXETER	Royal Clarence	71%	£117

Tel 01392 58464   Fax 01392 439423   Map 13 D2   **H**
Cathedral Yard Exeter Devon EX1 1HD

On the green facing the 14th-century cathedral, the Royal Clarence claims to be the first inn in Britain to receive the title 'hotel'. Behind its white, Georgian facade the building contains several architectural styles and retains an atmosphere steeped in the past. Every one of the bedrooms is in Tudor, Georgian or Victorian style. A wealth of oak panelling, moulded friezes and covings, gilt-framed mirrors and period furniture contrive to unify the theme. By comparison, bathrooms are thoroughly modern, though smallish. The stately Georgian-style Clarence Room accommodates conferences/banquets for up to 120/90. No dogs. Parking is limited, but special overnight rates have been arranged with local car parks. Queens Moat Houses. *Rooms 56. Access, Amex, Diners, Visa.*

EXETER	St Olaves Court	63%	£90

Tel 01392 217736   Fax 01392 413054   Map 13 D2   **HR**
Mary Arches Street Exeter Devon EX4 3AZ

Built in 1827 by a wealthy merchant, St Olaves Court is now a comfortable and secluded private hotel, situated close to the cathedral. The front of the building overlooks a pretty walled garden and circular pond with fountain, and parking space for a few cars. Well-equipped bedrooms and bathrooms – jacuzzis in the executive range – are also Georgian in style. *Rooms 17. Garden. Access, Amex, Diners, Visa.*

Restaurant   £60

Chef Jason Horn's menus aim to use good British produce, prepared with a touch of French influence, strong on local and seasonal specialities. You might try terrine of pheasant with mixed salad leaves and cranberry vinaigrette, roast rack of Devon lamb with ratatouille and roasted garlic served with a rich rosemary jus, and finish with glazed blackcurrant mousse with shortbread biscuits and a vanilla sauce. *Seats 45. Parties 24. Private Room 14. L 12-2 D 6.30-9.30. Closed L Sat & Sun. Set L £12/£20.50 Set D £12/£23/£27. Closed 1 week Christmas.*

EXMOUTH	Imperial Hotel	60%	£102

Tel 01395 274761   Fax 01395 265161   Map 13 E3   **H**
The Esplanade Exmouth Devon EX8 2SW

Popular whitewashed Forte holiday hotel set in its own grounds on the esplanade with many bedrooms overlooking the gardens and sea. Children up to the age of 16 free in parents' room. *Rooms 57. Garden, outdoor swimming pool, tennis. Access, Amex, Diners, Visa.*

EYTON   Marsh Country Hotel   65%   £110

Tel 01568 613952   Map 14 A1   **HR**
Eyton Leominster Hereford & Worcester HR6 0AG

Personally run by the owners, with some part-time help, the Gillelands' lovingly restored, 14th-century, black and white timbered home makes a charming rural hideaway. Surrounded by 1½ acres of splendid gardens – one of their passions – the hotel is a couple of miles north of Leominster. The main day room is a fine medieval hall with rug-strewn, flagstoned floor and plenty of deep sofas and armchairs. The bar, with coal-burning stove, is in the adjacent Solar Wing which also houses a small, characterful meeting room on the first floor. Pretty bedrooms, mostly pine-furnished, come with comforts like fresh fruit, mineral water and a bowl of sweets in addition to TVs and direct-dial phones. No smoking in bedrooms. No children under 12. No dogs. *Rooms 4. Garden, croquet. Closed 3 weeks Jan. Access, Amex, Diners, Visa.*

Restaurant   £60

Sunny yellow walls, a few old beams and comfortably upholstered, high-backed chairs set around crisply clothed tables all combine to create an elegant dining-room with a cottagey feel. The fixed-price menu (with four choices at each stage) might include creamed leeks in puff pastry and warm pigeon breast salad with pine nuts among the starters and mains such as salmon filled with haddock mousse in a fennel and thyme cream sauce with rösti potato and calabrese, and beef fillet with a Stilton sauce, parsnip timbale and broccoli. Herefordshire duck is a regular feature and there is always a vegetarian option. A well-stocked herb garden is put to good use and they now grow much of the fruit and vegetables used in the kitchen. Booking essential as restaurant may not open in the absence of residents. No smoking. *Seats 24. L Sun only 12.30-2 D 7.30-9. Set Sun L & Set D £21.*

FAIRFORD   Bull Hotel   60%   £44

Tel 01285 712535   Fax 01285 713782   Map 14 C2   **H**
Market Place Fairford Gloucestershire GL7 4AA

Visitors to the Bull have been many and varied since its first recorded appearance as a hotel in 1745. It's right on the Market Square, and as such would have provided refreshment to merchant men and travellers alike. Perhaps, then, little has changed in some respects! Less obvious are signs of its even earlier incarnation, as a monks' chanting house – though neither did monks turn away a tired or hungry visitor. Inside, it's atmospheric and attractive, and each room has its own feature, be it beams and sloping ceilings, four-poster bed or a sunken bath. Conference facilities for up to 80 delegates. *Rooms 20. Terrace, fishing. Access, Amex, Diners, Visa.*

FALMOUTH   Falmouth Hotel   63%   £68

Tel 01326 312671   Fax 01326 319533   Map 12 B4   **H**
Castle Beach Falmouth Cornwall TR11 4NZ

The advantages of the natural harbour that is Falmouth really blossomed in Victorian times, which is when this hotel – the town's first purpose-built – came into being. It's quite surprising to find an example of the French Chateau style in the depths of Cornwall but the rest of the setting – neat gardens, light and airy day rooms (especially the conservatory) are typically English. Half the bedrooms have a view of the sea (other rooms overlook the river), and three Executive bedrooms have balconies and whirlpool baths. There are also self-catering cottages (5) and apartments (24) within the grounds, and facilities for conferences and banquets for up to 300, plus a leisure centre. Families with young children are admirably catered for. *Rooms 73. Garden, pitch & putt, indoor swimming pool, sauna, spa bath, solarium, keep-fit equipment, beauty & hair salon, snooker. Access, Amex, Diners, Visa.*

FALMOUTH   Greenbank Hotel   69%   £116

Tel 01326 312440   Fax 01326 211362   Map 12 B4   **H**
Harbourside Falmouth Cornwall TR11 2SR

The call of the sea is strong at the Greenbank, which looks across the vast natural harbour to Flushing on the far bank. The picture-windowed bar and the traditionally appointed lounges make the most of the marvellous setting, as do the majority of the bedrooms, many of them named after former resident captains and their vessels. Some rooms have balconies, including the honeymoon suites, which also have jacuzzis. The hotel is on the edge of the town centre: keep to the harbourside when approaching from Truro and follow the signs from the roundabout after Penryn. Covered parking for 30 cars. *Rooms 61. Gym, sauna, solarium, beauty & hair salon, snooker. Closed 24 Dec-17 Jan. Access, Amex, Diners, Visa.*

FALMOUTH	The Pipe Restaurant	£50

Tel 01326 315273   Map 12 B4   **R**
46 Arwenack Street Falmouth Cornwall TR11 3JH

On the main 'through' street', just opposite the turn down to Custom House Quay, a low-ceilinged, nautically-decorated, atmospheric restaurant with a proper bar just inside the door, a kitchen in view of diners down at the back and plenty of partitions to allow privacy for groups. Tables are laid in pleasing bistro style and local seafood is the main attraction, with daily blackboard specials augmenting the carte. Typical starters might include deep-fried squid with a dipping sauce or Helford mussels marinière, followed perhaps by monkfish cooked with bacon pieces and thermidor sauce, or a splendid, plainly-grilled sole served on the bone. There are a few concessions to non-fish eaters (mainly Cornish lamb) and a vegetarian menu is available on request when booking. *Seats 45. Parties 8. D only 7-10.30. Closed Sun in winter, 25 & 26 Dec. Access, Amex, Diners, Visa.*

FALMOUTH	Royal Duchy Hotel	66%	£119

Tel 01326 313042   Fax 01326 319420   Map 12 B4   **H**
Cliff Road Falmouth Cornwall TR11 4NX

Originally built in 1893, the hotel sits atop the cliffs between the town and Gyllyngvase beach commanding fine sea views. It's a good place for both exercise and relaxation; public rooms range from sun lounge to spacious dining-room with live entertainment during the summer season. A small leisure area has plenty of facilities, and bedrooms have Regency-style freestanding furniture and modern accessories. Bathrooms are clean and functional. Friendly staff, typical of the Brend Hotel group. Creche facilities. *Rooms 47. Garden, indoor swimming pool, children's pool, sauna, spa bath, sun beds, indoor & outdoor children's play areas, games room. Access, Amex, Diners, Visa.*

FALMOUTH	St Michael's Hotel	63%	£96

Tel 01326 312707   Fax 01326 211772   Map 12 B4   **H**
Stracey Road Falmouth Cornwall TR11 4NB

Located directly opposite Gyllyngvase beach, this hotel provides basic yet comfortable accommodation for the tourist or business visitor. Banquets/conferences for 200/250. There's a spacious bar/lounge with a sun terrace which overlooks award-winning gardens. Children's entertainment in high season. No dogs. *Rooms 66. Garden, indoor swimming pool, keep-fit equipment, sauna, sun beds, outdoor play area. Access, Amex, Visa.*

FALMOUTH	Seafood Bar	£45

Tel 01326 315129   Map 12 B4   **R**
Quay Street Falmouth Cornwall TR11 3HH

Down a few steps in a steep passageway near the Custom House Quay, this lively bar serves the very freshest of seafood, from scallops sautéed with lemon in garlic butter, salt cod crostini, crab claws 'Chinese' style and Helford oysters to lobster, John Dory, red mullet, monkfish hollandaise and chunky squares of cod fillet in an 'apple' batter with a tart apple sauce. Also steaks (sirloin or oyster-stuffed carpetbagger fillet). *Seats 26. Parties 14. D only 7-10.30. Closed Sun in winter, 2 weeks end Nov-early Dec. Access, Visa.*

FAREHAM	Forte Posthouse	61%	£72

Tel 01329 844644   Fax 01329 844666   Map 15 D4   **H**
Cartwright Drive Titchfield Fareham Hampshire PO15 5RS

One of the newest (and largest) Posthouses, with a leisure centre and a range of meeting rooms (up to 140 people theatre-style, ample parking). Half the bedrooms are non-smoking and four are adapted for disabled guests. From M27 Junction 9 take the A27 south towards Fareham. *Rooms 126. Garden, indoor swimming pool, gym, sauna, solarium, snooker, children's playground. Access, Amex, Diners, Visa.*

| FAREHAM | Red Lion Hotel | 57% | £65 |

Tel 01329 822640   Fax 01329 823579   Map 15 D4   **H**
East Street Fareham Hampshire PO16 0BP

A former coaching inn equidistant from Portsmouth and Southampton. Some period character remains. Function facilities for up to 100. Family-friendly, with cots and extra beds free of charge. *Rooms 43. Garden, sauna. Access, Amex, Diners, Visa.*

| FAREHAM | Solent Hotel | 75% | £108 |

Tel 01489 880000   Fax 01489 880007   Map 15 D4   **HR**
Solent Business Park Whiteley Fareham Hampshire PO15 7AJ

In a most unexpected location – adjacent to Junction 9 of the M27 (10 miles from both Portsmouth and Southampton) – this gabled hotel dating from 1990 almost has the feel of a New England inn, successfully balancing wood and brick in its design and happily satisfying the contrasting needs of business and leisure guests. All the bedrooms are of Executive standard, in traditional style, with both working and relaxing space plus comprehensive comforts – from bathrobes to mini-bars. Suites accommodate syndicate, business and interview requirements in the week and have ample space for families at weekends; children up to 16 are accommodated free in their parents' room. Committed young staff and expert management show good direction throughout. A stylish leisure club has a private membership and access from within the hotel; a floodlit tennis court is the latest feature. Plenty of easy parking. Conference facilities for 250. Shire Inns. *Rooms 88. Garden, tennis, indoor swimming pool, children's splash pool, gym, squash, sauna, spa bath, steam room, solarium, snooker. Access, Amex, Diners, Visa.*

Woodlands Restaurant   £55
♈ ♗ ✑

One room in the stone-floored dining area overlooks grass and woodlands beyond, carefully segregating conference diners when required, leaving other guests to enjoy the open fire in the main, split-level room. An enterprising carte and table d'hote offer familiar favourites with an interesting twist – 'market specials' include brioche of chicken livers, pork escalope and roast monkfish. No smoking. *Seats 80. Parties 10. L 12.30-2 D 7.15-9.45 (Sun to 8.45). Closed L Sat. Set L £13.95 (Sun £11.95) Set D £20.*

| FARNBOROUGH | Forte Crest | 66% | £130 |

Tel 01252 545051   Fax 01252 377210   Map 15 E3   **H**
Lynchford Road Farnborough Hampshire GU14 6AZ

Handsome Edwardian building alongside the A325. Day rooms have period appeal, bedrooms are mainly modern. Banqueting and conference facilities for 150/100. Children up to 16 free in parents' room. *Rooms 110. Garden, indoor swimming pool, keep-fit equipment, spa bath, sauna, solarium, beauty salon, coffee shop (12-10). Access, Amex, Diners, Visa.*

| FARNHAM | Bishop's Table Hotel | 62% | £85 |

Tel 01252 710222   Fax 01252 733494   Map 15 E3   **H**
27 West Street Farnham Surrey GU9 7DR

A small, Georgian town-centre hotel (next to the public library) with individually decorated bedrooms, most now including some antique furniture and French pine beds. The bridal suite features a Victorian half-tester bed. Kass and Mariam Verjee, a brother and sister team, run the place in friendly style. Peaceful, secluded garden with a magnificent cedar tree to the rear. Children up to 10 free in parents' room. Guests may park in the library car park next door during the evening and overnight. *Rooms 18. Garden. Closed 24 Dec-3 Jan. Access, Amex, Diners, Visa.*

| FARNHAM | Bush Hotel | 62% | £87 |

Tel 01252 715237   Fax 01252 733530   Map 15 E3   **H**
The Borough Farnham Surrey GU9 7NN

17th-century buildings cluster around a cobbled courtyard at a well-kept Forte hotel in the town centre. Most bedrooms are in a newer wing that overlooks the garden. Children can stay free in parents' room. Plenty of free parking. *Rooms 66. Garden, coffee shop (10am-6pm). Access, Amex, Diners, Visa.*

FARNHAM — Krug's Austrian Restaurant — £50

Tel 01252 723277
84 West Street Farnham Surrey GU9 7EN

Map 15 E3   **R**

Behind its pretty 16th-century, bow-windowed frontage, Karin and Gerhard Krug's restaurant mixes old English beams with Alpine-style chairs and tables, the latter sporting colourful folksy cloths. The menu is full of hearty Austrian specialities like smoked pork with home-made bratwurst and dumplings on sauerkraut; veal schnitzel with a fresh herb sauce and fillet steak with dill sauce. They're all served in generous portions, as are the various fondues. Soups – spicy ones with paprika, smoked bacon and cabbage, clear with dumplings or sliced pancake – make good starters and to finish there is a classic apple strudel plus various pancake and ice cream dishes. Drink Austrian beer or choose something from the short list of Austrian and French wines. *Seats 80. Private Room 40. D only 7-11. Set D £10. Closed Sun. Access, Amex, Visa.*

FAUGH — String of Horses Inn — £68

Tel 01228 70297   Fax 01228 70675
Heads Hook Faugh nr Carlisle Cumbria CA4 9EG

Map 4 C2   **I**

Built as a packhorse inn late in the 17th century, the String of Horses stands in a tiny village (pronounced Faff locally) off the A69. The rustic bar and lounges sport a plethora of panelling, oak beams, polished brass and similar trappings. Those in the bedrooms are rather more surprising: Hollywood-style brass fittings, large corner baths (some jacuzzis) and proprietor Eric Tasker's complimentary hangover kit; several rooms have four-poster beds. Family and leisure facilities. *Rooms 14. Terrace, outdoor swimming pool (heated all year), spa bath, sauna, solarium, games room. Access, Amex, Diners, Visa.*

FAVERSHAM — Read's — £75

Tel 01795 535344   Fax 01795 591200
Painter's Forstal Faversham Kent ME13 0EE

Map 11 C5   **R**

David and Rona Pitchford are well established in their smart little restaurant just outside Faversham, David leading the way from the kitchen and Rona charming the guests at front of house. There's a precise touch to the cooking, a sureness of flavouring and saucing, a deftness to the presentation on the plate. Set meals are well balanced, and Read's Traditional Menu, for example (available at lunch and dinner from Tuesday to Friday) might offer savoury nibbles, then a surprise appetiser at the table, next sautéed soft herring roes on a croute with parsley butter, a main course of roast duck breast with caramelised oranges and a Grand Marnier sauce, a choice of sweet or cheese then finally coffee and sweet nibbles. Desserts are as delicious as the preceding courses with iced pistachio parfait served with caramelised bananas and a hot Drambuie soufflé being typical offerings. The wine list is superb, very informatively presented, with great depth and prices to suit every pocket. For those not prepared to peruse the whole list, the condensed list of 40 wines around the £15 mark is a terrific idea. There's a nice note on the lunch menu to the effect that if you're short of time, just say, and Rona will pace your meal accordingly. *Seats 40. Private Room 20. L 12-2 D 7-10. Closed Sun & Mon. Set L £15.50 Set D £25/£32. Access, Amex, Diners, Visa.*

FAWKHAM — Brandshatch Place — 64% — £95

Tel 01474 872239   Fax 01474 879652
Fawkham Valley Road Fawkham Kent DA3 8NQ

Map 11 B5   **H**

Not far from the entrance to Brands Hatch racing circuit (look out for small signs to "hotel and leisure club"), this redbrick Georgian house built for the Duke of Norfolk is now a hotel specialising in conferences during the week and weddings (it's set in 12 acres of garden and parkland for the photos) at weekends. The two lounge rooms, one houses the bar counter, have just been redecorated although the armchairs and sofas are looking a little tired. There are further public areas – bar, roof terrace and informal restaurant – in the adjacent Fredericks Health and Leisure club. Bedrooms are generally of good size with armchairs and all the usual amenities although not all the TVs are remote control. Eleven new bedrooms, making 40 in all, are due to come on stream in September 1995. Room service is available but not advertised. No dogs. *Rooms 40. Garden, indoor swimming pool, gym, squash, sauna, steam room, spa bath, solarium, snooker. Closed 25 Dec. Access, Amex, Diners, Visa.*

| FELIXSTOWE | Orwell Hotel | 69% | £90 |

Tel 01394 309955   Fax 01394 670687   Map 10 D3   **H**
Hamilton Road Felixstowe Suffolk IP11 7DX

Renamed Moat House but run by the same team, usefully located in the centre of town opposite the railway station. Bedrooms offer all the usual modern comforts, there are conference facilities for up to 200 and comfortable public rooms offer 24hr lounge service. Ample free parking. *Rooms 58. Garden. Access, Amex, Diners, Visa.*

| FELSTED | Rumbles Cottage | £55 |

Tel 01371 820996   Map 11 B4   **R**
Braintree Road Felsted Essex CM6 3DJ

In the centre of Felsted, a whitewashed, 16th-century cottage with low, beamed ceilings and four dining-rooms. It's run in a friendly and relaxed style by enthusiastic chef-proprietress Joy Hadley, whose eclectic, monthly-changing English menu offers a choice of five dishes per course. Her enduring specialities include Stilton, cauliflower and onion soup; salmon, cucumber and lemon bavarois; chicken and asparagus Wellington; twice-baked soufflés; Arabian lamb casserole; lavender ice cream, and Stilton, pear and sultana crumble – but don't expect to find them all on the same menu! Turkish delight ice cream has reappeared by popular demand. Many of the vegetables, including white aubergines, salsify, curly kale, dwarf sugar peas and a variety of lettuces, come from Joy's own garden. There is always an unusual vegetarian dish. The three-course 'guinea pig menu' is used to try out new dishes on regular customers. All-British cheeses. (Regional winner of our British Cheeseboard of the Year award). *Seats 50. Parties 16. Private Room 22. L Sun only 12-2 D 7-9. Closed D Sun, all Mon, 2 weeks Feb. Set Sun L £12.50 Access, Visa.*
Also at:
Rumbles Castle Restaurant, 4 St James Street, Castle Hedingham, Essex
(Tel 01787 461490)
Open L Sun only & D Wed-Sat.

| FERNDOWN | Dormy Hotel | 71% | £110 |

Tel 01202 872121   Fax 01202 895388   Map 14 C4   **H**
New Road Ferndown nr Bournemouth Dorset BH22 8ES

Manager Derek Silk has kept standards high here since 1977. Guests will find plenty to please them: public rooms include an all-day bar and brasserie with well-upholstered rattan furniture, and a further bar with oak-panelled walls, red plush chesterfields and a real log fire. The leisure club's facilities are extensive: there's a club room with snooker, pool, darts and table tennis, and a children's games room with supervised activities during holiday periods; both the gym and pool are wonderfully light and airy. Bedrooms offer good standards of modern comfort; 40 rooms for non-smokers; children under 14 share parents' room free. Well geared-up for conferences with some 10 meeting rooms, the largest of which can accommodate up to 250 delegates in theatre style. De Vere.
Rooms 130. Garden, tennis, putting green, driving net, indoor swimming pool, gym, squash, sauna, steam room, spa bath, solarium, beauty salon, snooker, brasserie (10am-10pm), indoor & outdoor children's play areas. Access, Amex, Diners, Visa.

| FINDON | Findon Manor | 58% | £70 |

Tel 01903 872733   Fax 01903 877473   Map 11 A6   **H**
High Street Findon West Sussex BN14 OTA

The front door of this flint-faced former rectory, dating in part back to the 16th century, opens direct into a beamed lounge that also serves as reception area. The other main public room is the bar, made more comfortable in recent years and still attracting much local village trade. Bedrooms vary considerably in shape and size. There's a planned gradual and necessary refurbishment programme. *Rooms 11. Garden, croquet. Access, Amex, Visa.*

| FLITWICK | Flitwick Manor | 73% | £125 |

Tel 01525 712242   Fax 01525 718753   Map 15 E1   **HR**
Church Road Flitwick Bedfordshire MK45 1AE

A late 17th-century Georgian manor house set in rolling parkland just a couple of minutes from the M1 (Junction 12). Approached down a long, tree-lined drive with guests arriving into a welcoming flagstoned entrance hall with a warming open cosy fire.

The high-ceilinged music room (the main day room) features homely touches like magazines and chessboard set up ready for play. Bedrooms come in all shapes and sizes, from small singles to one with a large four-poster and original panelling; all rooms get the same extras including ice and slices of lemon with the well-stocked drinks tray, mineral water, fresh fruit, home-made biscuits, books, magazines and fresh flowers. Bathrooms are equally variable – two have shower and WC only, one with his 'n' hers 'kissing' bath tubs. Banqueting/conference facilities for 60. No children under 8. *Rooms 15. Garden, croquet, tennis. Amex, Diners, Access, Visa.*

Restaurant   £100

Between the good canapés that arrive with the menu and nicely varied petits fours with the coffee Duncan Poyser's fixed-price menu offers a selection of thoroughly modern dishes: purée of broad beans, fricassée of lamb's kidneys with wild thyme; gateau of home-cured salmon, smoked oyster beignets with lemon beurre blanc; pot-roast pork with honey and clove crust; grilled Aylesbury duck with a compote of onions and peppered cider sauce are examples of his style. Unusual menu reading, surprises on the plate too, with vegetables forming an integral part of the garnish of each main dish. Plenty of interest for afters: caramelised hazelnut soufflé with a rum sauce, a study in plum, a partition of chocolate or tarte tatin of apples and cinnamon with a calvados sauce. The lunchtime selection (including Sunday lunch) is more limited, but always interesting. No smoking. Over £7 for a glass of non-marque champagne is a bit steep; in fact the list has rather too many pricey wines. *Seats 40. Parties 8. Private Room 60. L 12.30-2 D 7-9.30 Set L £16.95/£19.50 (Sun £24.50) Set D £37.50.*

FOLKESTONE	Paul's	£45

Tel 01303 259697   Fax 01303 226647   Map 11 C5   **R**
2a Bouverie Road West Folkestone Kent CT20 2RX

Paul and Penny Hagger continue to flourish at their popular, colourful restaurant where recent developments include additional seating, a new bar and an instantly-successful Sunday carvery menu. Fish and shellfish are particularly good, some of the dishes being just that little bit different: dressed crab baked in cream and topped with brie, halibut poached in a light burgundy fish stock. Equally interesting meat options, vegetarian dishes, sweets from the trolley. Fair prices on a decent wine list – note the handwritten section, which has some real gems (Ch. Giscours '71 at £29.95). *Seats 120. L 12-2.30 D 7-9.30. Closed 4 days Chriatmas. Set Sun L £9.95. Access, Visa.*

FOLKESTONE	La Tavernetta	£45

Tel 01303 254955   Map 11 C5   **R**
Leaside Court Clifton Gardens Folkestone Kent CT20 2ED

Chef-partner Felice Puricelli has been providing sound Italian cuisine since 1965 in his friendly basement restaurant. The menu offers reliable favourites such as eggs florentine, lasagne verdi, scampi with cream and mushrooms, summer seafood and winter warmers like pheasant with cognac, venison and wild boar. *Seats 65. Parties 25. L 12-2.30 D 6-10.30. Closed Sun, Bank Holidays. Set L from £9.50. Access, Amex, Diners, Visa.*

FRAMLINGHAM	The Crown	62%	£97

Tel 01728 723521   Fax 01728 724274   Map 10 D2   **H**
Market Hill Framlingham Suffolk IP13 9AN

A Forte hotel with much 16th-century charm. A flagstoned foyer/lounge and public bar have beamed ceilings and open fires, with a creaking staircase leading up to simple bedrooms furnished with freestanding oak units. The best bedroom has a panelled oak four-poster and floral print settee. Children free in parents' room up to 14. *Rooms 14. Access, Amex, Diners, Visa.*

Consult the blue pages for summary tables and lists of
recommended establishments.

| FRESHFORD | **Homewood Park** | **78%** | **£135** |

Tel 01225 723731   Fax 01225 723820   Map 13 F1   **HR**
Hinton Charterhouse Freshford Avon BA3 6BB

Don't turn off into Freshford itself but look out for the hotel's sign alongside the A36 about 5 miles south of Bath. The drive to the largely Georgian house (the cellars date back to the 13th century) leads through gardens that are well tended except where they seem to be trying to engulf the house as various plants climb its walls, creating a very pretty picture. A splendid red Afghan rug floors the entrance hall where a warm welcome awaits from staff who combine professionalism with just the right degree of friendliness. Other day rooms include a sitting-room furnished in traditional country-house style and a bright, comfortable bar that features framed Hermès scarves. There are plans to create a second sitting-room. A sunny breakfast room looks out over the garden and when the weather allows French windows are opened on to a small terrace with tables allowing for an alfresco start to the day. Rooms vary in size (and price, that quoted above is for a larger, garden-facing room) but all have equally appealing individual decor with an antique or two and often with bedhead drapes. Little comforts include a decanter of sherry, books and, in the pretty bathrooms, towelling robes and good toiletries. In the evening beds are turned down, curtains drawn and bedside lights lit. No dogs.
Rooms 15. Garden, tennis, croquet. Access, Amex, Diners, Visa.

Restaurant   £90

The summer of '95 saw Steve Morey take over the reins in the kitchen here and an early test meal from his first menu bodes well for the future. A classic dish of pan-fried foie gras with caramelised apple and cider jus was given an individual touch by the addition of a little herby spätzle (the herbs all come from their own kitchen garden, which is currently being expanded to increase the production of home-grown vegetables) and a main dish of lobster mousse-filled ravioli with roasted Cornish scallops and *fonds d'artichaut* in a marjoram flavoured shellfish stock was equally successful. From the list of desserts a prune and mascarpone tartlet with armagnac caramel was a little less exciting; hot chocolate and hazelnut soufflé with butterscotch sauce and vanilla-flavoured rice pudding with cherry compote were among the other options. A good, if unspectacular wine list with lesser-known producers from France. The dining-room has a simple elegance with comfortable chairs, views of the garden and staff who are smart, attentive and friendly. *Seats 60. Parties 20. Private Room 90. L 12.30-2 D 7.15-9.45. Set L from £16.50 (Set Sun L £20) Set D £28.50.*

| FRESHWATER | **Farringford Hotel** | **57%** | **£90** |

Tel 01983 752500   Fax 01983 756515   Map 14 C4   **H**
Bedbury Lane Freshwater Isle of Wight PO40 9PE

Owners Mr and Mrs Cerise have been running the Farringford since 1980, and have created a peaceful retreat with gardens bordering National Trust downland. Day rooms at this 18th-century Gothic-style house include a French-windowed drawing room, a small bar and a library with Tennyson memorabilia (the poet once lived here). Bedrooms (15 in the main house, 4 accessed outside) are modest and neat, and there are also 24 bungalows and 4 flats in the grounds let on a self-catering basis. *Rooms 19. Garden, croquet, outdoor swimming pool, golf (9), putting, bowling green, tennis, children's play area, games room, snooker. Access, Amex, Diners, Visa.*

| FRESSINGFIELD | **The Fox & Goose Inn** | | **£65** |

Tel 01379 586247   Fax 01379 588107   Map 10 C2   **R**
Fressingfield nr Diss Suffolk IP21 5PB

Next to the churchyard and the village pond, the Fox & Goose was built around 1500 as a Guildhall and later became a pub. These days it's more restaurant than pub with the single bar quickly filling up with diners looking at the menu when they are busy, but there is also a bar menu or you can just have a drink. The word eclectic might have been invented to describe a menu which ranges from Peking duck with pancakes and hoisin sauce, Japanese fish and vegetable tempura, and potted Morecambe Bay brown shrimps to roasted red pepper, sweet garlic and saffron risotto with parmesan; smoked fish, potato and spring onion chowder; grilled Greek halloumi with gremolata and pitta bread and much else besides. Many dishes are available as either starter or main course. Steak and kidney pudding remains a great favourite – order in advance for Friday dinner and the weekend. Round things off with British, Irish and French cheeses and/or a dessert such as Sussex Pond pudding or prune and armagnac ice cream with prune compote. The decor is very 'country' with old black beams and red-tiled floor in the main dining-room (which was the kitchen in olden days) and a further room with sea-grass matting and 'stable' booths, used when busy. The atmosphere is informal and obliging, children are made welcome with their own menu plus a 'toy box', crayons for drawing on the paper tablecloths and, out in the garden, where one can also eat and drink, a see-saw and sandpit. All Ruth and David Watson's expertise has gone into the marvellous wine list here; in fact there are two lists – the short and inexpensive list perhaps for the less knowledgeable "where any bottle that does not please will be replaced regardless of whether it is faulty, or you just don't like it". Vintage notes for clarets and burgundies, prefaces elsewhere. Serious stuff, even suppliers get a mention. No smoking in the dining-room. **Seats** *50. Parties 20. Private Room 24. L 12-2.15 D 7-9.30. Set L £9.95/£13.50 (except Sun). Closed Mon & Tue, 10 days Christmas/New Year (but open New Year's Eve), 2 weeks Jan. No credit cards.*

FRILFORD HEATH	Dog House Hotel	£69

Tel 01865 390830 Fax 01865 390860   Map 15 D2   **I**
Frilford Heath nr Abingdon Oxfordshire OX13 6QJ

The 17th-century Dog House (a ten-minute drive from Oxford) has rooms in contemporary cottage style. Furniture is good-quality pine (one room has a pine four-poster), and accessories include remote-control TVs with satellite channels. Bathrooms have smart modern tiling, large mirrors and good lighting. Plenty of free parking. *Rooms 19. Garden, children's play area. Access, Amex, Diners, Visa.*

GARFORTH	Hilton National	61%	£90

Tel 0113 286 6556 Fax 0113 286 8326   Map 7 D1   **H**
Wakefield Road Garforth nr Leeds West Yorkshire LS25 1LH

Stylish public areas raise expectations for the bedrooms, which, although well kept, are small and fairly ordinary. Staffed leisure centre, recently enlarged. Meeting 2000 is a conference package which includes a manager/supervisor to look after the event – capacity is for up to 350 delegates theatre-style. Children free in parents' room. *Rooms 144. Garden, indoor swimming pool, keep-fit equipment, steam room, sauna, solarium, beautician, children's outdoor playground. Access, Amex, Diners, Visa.*

GATESHEAD	Jarvis Springfield Hotel	63%	£95

Tel 0191-477 4121 Fax 0191-477 7213   Map 5 E2   **H**
Durham Road Low Fell Gateshead Tyne & Wear NE9 5BT

Business hotel by the A167, 4 miles from A1(M) junction. Conference/banqueting facilities for 120/100. Children up to 10 stay free in parents' room. A 50-space secure car park is now available to guests. *Rooms 60. Access, Amex, Diners, Visa.*

GATESHEAD	Newcastle Marriott	70%	£129

Tel 0191-493 2233 Fax 0191-493 2030   Map 5 E2   **H**
MetroCentre Gateshead Newcastle Tyne & Wear NE11 9XF

Just off the A1 (Newcastle Western bypass) and opposite the MetroCentre (Europe's largest indoor shopping and leisure complex), the Marriott is tall and faced entirely in darkened glass. The spacious and modern white marble-floored foyer is stylishly appointed with wide brown leather settees and armchairs. Bedrooms have smart lightwood furniture and soft pastel colour schemes; all are well equipped – even to the extent of having video recorders with a selection of video cassettes for hire. Bathrooms have power showers and good towels. Ten highly distinctive, themed rooms are very original, well thought out and popular. Children up to 18 free in parents' room. Conference facilities for up to 450. *Rooms 150. Indoor swimming pool, spa bath, gym, sun beds, sauna, steam room, beauty salon. Access, Amex, Diners, Visa.*

GATESHEAD   Swallow Hotel   60%   £95

Tel 0191-477 1105 Fax 0191-478 7214   Map 5 E2   **H**
High West Street Gateshead Tyne & Wear NE8 1PE

A leisure club, ample secure car parking and conference facilities for up to 350 are among the amenities at this modern hotel three miles from the A1(M) and one mile from the city centre – check directions. Children up to 14 can stay free in their parents' room. *Rooms 103. Indoor swimming pool, keep-fit equipment, sauna, spa bath, steam room, solarium. Access, Amex, Diners, Visa.*

GATWICK AIRPORT   Chequers Thistle   63%   £107

Tel 01293 786992   Fax 01293 820625   Map 15 E3   **H**
Brighton Road Horley Surrey RH6 8PH

At a roundabout on the A23 to the north of the airport, this white-painted building with beamed gables was indeed once a Tudor coaching inn, though inside only the beamed bar hints at its past. Standardised bedrooms, all in a two-storey 'system built' extension to the rear, are in good order with all the usual creature comforts and practical bathrooms. 24hr room service. There's free parking if you stay at the hotel prior to flying from Gatwick. *Rooms 78. Outdoor swimming pool, coffee shop (10.30am-10.15pm). Access, Amex, Diners, Visa.*

Lodges are now listed by county in the reference section

GATWICK AIRPORT   Copthorne Effingham Park   72%   £128

Tel 01342 714994 Fax 01342 716039   Map 15 E3   **H**
West Park Road Copthorne West Sussex RH10 3EU

Follow signs to East Grinstead, off Junction 10 of the M23. Six sequoia trees, originally imported from Oregon to commemorate Wellington's victory at Waterloo, line the driveway. There's lots more of interest in the modernised stately home, including a large rotunda conference centre (catering for up to 600 delegates). Decent-sized bedrooms have reproduction furniture including a breakfast table. Best rooms have private balconies. 34 rooms reserved for non-smokers. Under-16s share parents' room free. *Rooms 122. Garden, croquet, golf (9), indoor swimming pool, children's splash pool, gym, steam room, sauna, spa bath, solarium, beauty & hair salon. Access, Amex, Diners, Visa.*

GATWICK AIRPORT   Copthorne London Gatwick   69%   £118

Tel 01342 714971 Fax 01342 717375   Map 15 E3   **H**
Copthorne nr Crawley West Sussex RH10 3PG

Set in 100 acres of gardens and woodland, the Copthorne is centred round a 16th-century farmhouse. Oak beams and log fires keep the period feel in the White Swan pub, and many of the bedrooms are also in traditional style. Connoisseur rooms feature king-size beds and spa baths; rooms are available for non-smokers (100) and disabled guests. There are several places to eat, and a variety of conference and function rooms. Families are well catered for, and under-16s can stay free in their parents' room. The hotel is just six minutes from the airport, and two from the M23 (Junction 10, then A264 towards East Grinstead). *Rooms 227. Garden, croquet, tennis, pitch & putt, jogging track, children's playground, gym, sauna, solarium, squash. Access, Amex, Diners, Visa.*

GATWICK AIRPORT   Europa Gatwick   68%   £97

Tel 01293 886666 Fax 01293 886680   Map 15 E3   **H**
Balcombe Road Maidenbower nr Crawley West Sussex RH10 7ZR

On the B2036 about 15 minutes from the airport this modern low-rise hotel is built in an unusual hacienda style with whitewashed walls and terracotta roofs. Inside, it's just as distinctive, and reception impresses first with its tall rafters, terrazzo marble floor and dark mahogany furniture. There is one restaurant (the Méditerranée), a lounge bar for lighter meals, a cocktail bar, numerous syndicate rooms and Studio 4 – a well-equipped health and leisure centre with a dance studio. Smart bedrooms with polished wood and autumnal colour schemes range up to suites with whirlpool baths. Parking for 250 cars. Britannia Hotels. *Rooms 211. Garden, indoor swimming pool, gym, steam room, spa bath, sauna, solarium, dance studio, beautician, hairdressing. Access, Amex, Diners, Visa.*

GATWICK AIRPORT   Forte Crest Gatwick   74%   £125

Tel 01293 567070   Fax 01293 567739   Map 15 E3   **H**
North Terminal Gatwick Airport West Sussex RH6 0PH

Gatwick's most distinctive hotel is 100 yards from the north terminal and has a covered walkway, leading directly into the unusual, eight-storey-high atrium, under which a bright cocktail bar and café take on an open-air feel. Public areas are modernistic, even a bit austere, and the uniformly furnished bedrooms are stark, though well lit and comfortable, with chrome fittings and black and white decor; striped bedcovers provide a dash of colour; glazing is thoroughly efficient with little or no air traffic noise. Children up to 14 stay free in parents' room. A surprisingly easy-to-use, high-tech TV system displays messages, flight information, a running total of the bill and even a check-out facility in addition to regular viewing. Service throughout is helpful, knowledgeable, friendly and efficient. 24hr room service. Guests booking in for even one night can park their cars for 15 days in the long-term car park (NCP). Banqueting/conference facilities for up to 280. Staffed business centre. *Rooms 468. Indoor swimming pool, sauna, solarium, gym, news kiosk, hair & beauty salon, coffee shop (5am – 1am). Access, Amex, Diners, Visa.*

GATWICK AIRPORT   Forte Posthouse   63%   £72

Tel 01293 771621   Fax 01293 771054   Map 15 E3   **H**
Povey Cross Road Horley Surrey RH6 0BA

On the A23 a mile north of the airport. Good modern bedrooms, choice of conference and meeting rooms (up to 150 delegates), large long-term car park. Courtesy airport coach every 30 minutes (6.15am-11.45pm). Extensive refurbishment to the bedrooms was planned during 1995. *Rooms 210. Outdoor swimming pool in summer, coffee shop (7am-10.30pm), airport courtesy coach (from 6.15am). Access, Amex, Diners, Visa.*

GATWICK AIRPORT   Hilton International   72%   £164

Tel 01293 518080   Fax 01293 28980   Map 15 E3   **H**
Gatwick West Sussex RH6 0LL

A pedestrian walkway directly connects Gatwick's south terminal with this large hotel's four-storey central atrium; a full-size replica of Jason, Amy Johnson's biplane, hangs from the ceiling. Good-sized bedrooms have easy chairs, breakfast tables, large beds and all the extras one would expect from an international hotel; TVs even display flight information, very useful if your plane is delayed. Over half the rooms are now set aside for non-smokers. The Jockey Bar's horse-racing theme harks back to the days when Gatwick racecourse was on this site. Banquets for up to 360. Lloyds Bank cashpoint machine. 24hr room service. *Rooms 550. Terrace, indoor swimming pool, sauna, solarium, spa bath, steam room, gym, beauty salon, hairdressing, kiosk, car rental desk, business centre. Access, Amex, Diners, Visa.*

GATWICK AIRPORT   Gatwick Moat House   62%   £93

Tel 01293 785599   Fax 01293 785991   Map 15 E3   **H**
Longbridge Roundabout Horley Surrey RH6 0AB

Purpose-built, five-storey hotel by a roundabout on the A23, half a mile north of the airport. Bedrooms have individual heat and air controls. Business centre, conferences up to 180. Airport courtesy coach; long-term car parking. Children up to 16 free in parents' room. *Rooms 124. Access, Amex, Diners, Visa.*

GATWICK AIRPORT   Holiday Inn Gatwick   68%   £102

Tel 01293 529991   Fax 01293 515913   Map 15 E3   **H**
Langley Drive Crawley West Sussex RH11 7SX

Modern hotel on the A23 four miles south of the airport. Good leisure and conference facilities (for up to 250) and a business centre. *Rooms 217. Gym, indoor swimming pool, children's splash pool, spa bath, sauna, solarium, snooker. Access, Amex, Diners, Visa.*

We welcome bona fide complaints and recommendations on the tear-out pages at the back of the book for readers' comments. They are followed up by our professional team.

GATWICK AIRPORT   Ramada Hotel Gatwick   70%   £114

Tel 01293 820169   Fax 01293 820259   Map 15 E3   **H**
Povey Cross Road Horley Surrey RH6 0BE

Well-signposted, large, modern, efficient and friendly hotel just off the A23. Spacious public areas include the Brighton Belle bar (based on an old Pullman carriage). Over half the bedrooms are reserved for non-smokers. The best bedrooms are spacious and well equipped, with efficient sound-proofing, good air-conditioning and neutral decor. Children up to 18 stay free in parents' room. The extensive leisure centre includes two squash courts. The self-contained conference facilities (for up to 180 delegates) and business centre were refurbished in 1995. Courtesy coaches to the airport. Ample parking. *Rooms 255. Coffee shop (10am-10.30pm), beauty salon, indoor swimming pool, sauna, solarium, spa bath, gym, squash. Access, Amex, Diners, Visa.*

GATWICK AIRPORT   Scandic Crown   64%   £109

Tel 01293 561186   Fax 01293 561169   Map 15 E3   **H**
Tinsley Lane Three Bridges Crawley West Sussex RH11 1NP

At the first roundabout towards Crawley from junction 10 of the M23, this modern, glass and brick hotel offers good-sized, air-conditioned bedrooms appointed in uncluttered Scandinavian style. Bright, cheerful public areas include a bar hung with very professional-looking abstract paintings created by sixth-formers from a local school. 24hr room service Courtesy coach to airport terminals. Ample parking. *Rooms 151. Indoor swimming pool, sauna, steam room, sun bed, gym, beauty salon. Access, Amex, Diners, Visa.*

GERRARDS CROSS   Bull Hotel   63%   £125

Tel 01753 885995   Fax 01753 885504   Map 15 E2   **H**
Gerrards Cross Buckinghamshire SL9 7PA

Some glimpses still of coaching days; mostly modern bedrooms which children up to 14 share free with parents. 20 rooms are designated non-smoking. Conferences for up to 200. De Vere. *Rooms 95. Garden. Access, Amex, Diners, Visa.*

GILLINGHAM   Stock Hill House   76%   £180*

Tel 01747 823626   Fax 01747 825628   Map 14 B3   **HR**
Stock Hill Gillingham Dorset SP8 5NR

A few miles south of the A303 on the A3081 on the village outskirts a long, winding, tree-lined drive leads to Peter and Nita Hauser's splendid Victorian country mansion. Set in 10 acres of well-tended wooded grounds, the house has, over the years, been lovingly decorated to create an almost home-from-home ambience, made even more welcoming by the Hausers' warmth and hospitality. The entrance hall features a pair of virtually life-size Indian mules carved in 1840. They stand before a huge ornate gilt mirror. Other interesting pieces, though on a lesser scale, are scattered throughout the hotel. Occupying a corner of the entrance hall is an intimate lounge area with an open fire. The drawing room offers an equal level of cosy homeliness. Bedrooms, all recently refurbished, are finished to a high standard with colourful designer chintzes and a smattering of antiques and unusual objets d'art. Creature comforts abound including fresh fruit, books and magazines. The carpeted bathrooms are spotless, a few have bidets. As Peter and Nita say, they aim to create something very special. They succeed. *Half-board terms only. No children under 5. No dogs. Smoking is discouraged in the bedrooms. *Rooms 9. Garden, croquet, tennis, sauna, putting. Access, Visa.*

Restaurant   ★ ↑   £80

The restaurant has relocated, but there's no change in Austrian-born Peter's cooking style, chich is based on that country's traditions, albeit with modern interpretations. Starters could include lamb sweetbreads and asparagus in velout, or grilled Somerset goat's cheese on cabbage vinaigrette; a middle course consists of a choice of two soups, for instance a very fine cream of lovage soup with sweet water crayfish. Main dishes can include escalope of Cornish venison with wild mushrooms; grilled noisettes of lamb with foie gras on a Madeira sauce; or red sea bream topped with a sesame and soya crust. Vegetables and herbs come more often than not from the kitchen gardens. Sweets can be elaborate as in a meringue Suchard, simple, like home-made sorbets with seasonal fruits, or classically Austrian as in *gebackene apfelspalten mit zimtzucker* – thinly sliced Bramley apples cooked in Austrian rum butter dusted with cinnamon icing sugar. A good selection of British cheeses. The wine list is rather incomplete (no vintage champagnes for example) for a hotel and restaurant with obvious pretensions. Helpful tasting notes. No smoking. *Seats 30. Parties 12. Private Rooms 12. L Sun 12.30-1.45, otherwise by arrangement D 7.30-8.45. Set L £19 Set D £28.*

GITTISHAM	Combe House	73%	£97

Tel 01404 42756   Fax 01404 46004   Map 13 E2   **H**
Gittisham nr Honiton Devon EX14 0AD

Owners Thérèse and John Boswell, here since 1970, are both very much involved in the day-to-day running of their stately Elizabethan mansion, which enjoys a peaceful, attractive setting on a 3000-acre estate. Peaceful it certainly is, but not remote, being less than two miles from the A30. Public rooms have carved panelling in the entrance hall, ancestral portraits in the panelled drawing room, a charming pink sitting room, a cosy bar with pictures of John's horse-racing activities and everywhere architectural features, antiques and personal touches by painter and sculptress Thérèse (and her mother). Bedrooms vary in size and price, larger rooms tending to have better views and more interesting furniture and pictures. One suite and two rooms have four-poster beds. The hotel owns fishing rights on the River Otter, with a season running from April to the end of September. *Rooms 15. Garden, croquet, fishing. Closed last week Jan & 1st week Feb. Access, Amex, Diners, Visa.*

GLOUCESTER	Forte Posthouse	66%	£72

Tel 01452 613311   Fax 01452 371036   Map 14 B1   **H**
Crest Way Barnwood Gloucester Gloucestershire GL4 7RX

Modern hotel on the A417, strong on conference (up to 110) and leisure facilities. Children up to 16 stay free when sharing adult rooms. *Rooms 123. Garden, indoor swimming pool, gym, beauty salon, sauna, spa bath. Access, Amex, Diners, Visa.*

GLOUCESTER	Hatherley Manor	65%	£78

Tel 01452 730217   Fax 01452 731032   Map 14 B1   **H**
Down Hatherley Lane Gloucester Gloucestershire GL2 9QA

The origins of Hatherley date back to the days of Edward the Confessor, and a sense of history pervades the elegant 17th-century building, set in its own 40 acres of parkland. Usefully located 3 miles from the M5, 2 miles from Gloucester and 6 from Cheltenham, the Manor serves business and leisure customers with equal flair. A few standard bedrooms are in the old part, but the majority are in the 'de luxe' category in the Jacobean wing. A few are suitable for family use (baby-listening and baby-sitting by arrangement; children up to 12 stay free in parents' room) and there's a four-poster honeymoon suite. Plenty of free parking. *Rooms 56. Garden, croquet. Access, Amex, Diners, Visa.*

GLOUCESTER	Hatton Court	72%	£95

Tel 01452 617412   Fax 01452 612945   Map 14 B1   **H**
Upton Hill Upton St Leonards Gloucester Gloucestershire GL4 8DE

On the B4073 Gloucester-Painswick road on the edge of Upton St Leonards, Hatton Court enjoys panoramic views over the Severn Valley. Day rooms, and 18 of the bedrooms, are in the original, creeper-clad 17th-century building and comprise a lounge (which incorporates the reception desk) and bar, both with dado oak panelling and French-style reproduction easy chairs, the bar featuring a pair of bow-windowed 'shop front' cabinets displaying porcelain and craft goods. Bedrooms, the rest of which are in an adjacent building, come with teddy bears on the pillow to keep you company and lots of extras like fruit, mineral water, sweets and home-made biscuits. Almost all the bathrooms have large corner tubs (two have regular baths and two shower and WC only) with those in the 'superior' and 'executive' rooms having a spa feature and each gets its family of plastic ducks along with bathrobes and good toiletries. Staff are notably friendly and beds are turned down at night. No dogs. *Rooms 45. Garden, croquet, outdoor swimming pool, sauna, spa bath, solarium. Access, Amex, Diners, Visa.*

Set menu prices may not always include service or wine.

GOATHLAND   Mallyan Spout   61%   £65

Tel 01947 896486   Fax 01947 896327   Map 5 F3   **H**
Goathland Whitby North Yorkshire YO22 5AN

Peter and Judith Heslop have owned and run the Mallyan Spout for over 20 years, and
have built a reputation for hospitality. Set on the village green and prettily covered in ivy,
the hotel's unusual name comes from a waterfall which cascades into a nearby wooded
valley. The three lounges and two bars provide ample space for relaxation and have views
of the garden. Cottage-style bedrooms include six rooms in a converted coach house.
The two best rooms have balconies and views of the valley and moors beyond. Two studio
flats are also available for self-catering. *Rooms 24. Garden. Access, Amex, Diners, Visa.*

GODALMING   Inn on the Lake   £75

Tel 01483 415575   Fax 01483 860445   Map 15 E3   **I**
Ockford Road Godalming Surrey GU7 1RH

On the A3100 just south of Godalming, this charming country house inn is set in 2 acres
of lovely gardens with lawns leading down to the lake. Guests will find stylish
accommodation with thoughtful extras such as magazines, sewing kits, trouser presses and
hairdryers in the best bedrooms; six rooms have spa baths and balconies. One room is
suitable for family use. There's a convivial pubby bar with a welcoming log fire in winter.
Guests have temporary membership of the Willows Club (squash, sun beds, sauna) about
one mile from the hotel. Function facilities for up to 120. *Rooms 19. Garden. Access,
Amex, Diners, Visa.*

GOLANT   Cormorant Hotel   63%   £84

Tel & Fax 01726 833426   Map 12 C3   **H**
Golant nr Fowey Cornwall PL23 1LL

The riverside setting in a small fishing village just north of Fowey is a great attraction,
and the bedrooms, day rooms and swimming pool all enjoy the views. Boats may be
hired for sea or river fishing, and the area is also a centre for sailing and water-skiing.
Bedrooms are airy, warm and comfortable, and there's a honeymoon room. The
swimming pool, set higher than the hotel, has a sliding roof for summer days. New
owners George and Estelle Elworthy took over this summer. No children under 12.
Rooms 11. Garden, indoor swimming pool. Access, Amex, Visa.

GOODWOOD   Goodwood Park   67%   £90

Tel 01243 775537   Fax 01243 533802   Map 11 A6   **H**
Goodwood nr Chichester West Sussex PO18 0QB

Within the 12,000-acre grounds of Goodwood estate, a much modernised and extended
old house plays host to hotel, golf and country club rolled into one. Residential
conferences and banqueting are the mainstay of mid-week business (there's a dedicated
conference centre catering for up to 120), while weekends are busy with guests who
make full use of the extensive leisure facilities. Theatre breaks include tickets to the
nearby Chichester Festival Theatre and racing breaks at Glorious Goodwood are also
popular. Under-16s stay free in parents' room. Free parking for 300 cars. 24hr room
service. Country Club Hotels. *Rooms 88. Garden, tennis, indoor swimming pool, sauna,
solarium, spa bath, snooker, squash, gym, beauty salon, golf course (18), driving range,
golf shop, coffee shop (9.30am-10pm). Access, Amex, Diners, Visa.*

GORING-ON-THAMES   The Leatherne Bottel ↑   £70

Tel 01491 872667   Map 15 D2   **R**
Goring-on-Thames Berkshire RG8 0HS

It would be hard to find a more idyllic setting for a restaurant than here, and equally
difficult to find a more engaging couple than owners Keith Read and Annie Bonnet. The
building, in fact a little row of white-painted cottages, stands right on the edge of the
river, with a large terrace that really comes into its own in summer. Annie's spectacular
and colourful hanging baskets, flower beds and herb garden are a real feature here, with
everything possible going into the preparation of dishes, whether it's nasturtiums into pasta
and jelly, chive and clover flowers into butter, or home-made rolls made with sweet
ginger and coriander. These flavours play an important role in the cooking, shared by

Keith and Clive O'Connor, yet it is the simplicity and freshness of dishes that appeals, albeit with quite unusual accompaniments: smoked salmon and spring nettle ice cream with smoked halibut, crispy spring roll and salmon caviar oil; sea bass roasted whole with lemon leaves and lemon grass, with chickweed and herb vinaigrette, or rack of spring lamb, roasted with mint and clover, served with minted mushy peas and baby pea asparagus shoots (sic!). Desserts are a little more traditional, as in a steamed marmalade and ginger pudding with custard; rice pudding ice cream with caramel and raspberry jam, or brandy snap basket with summer berries. Alternatively, sample some fine British farmhouse cheeses, served with walnuts, home-made green tomato or pumpkin chutney, celery, radishes and home-made biscuits. During the week (Mon-Fri) lunch can be a very casual affair – pop in for just a salad, a bowl of mussels, mushrooms on olive toast, perhaps with a glass of champagne even! The wine list is fairly short, fairly priced and any bottle up to the value of £20 will be opened and charged on how much is drunk. *Natasha*, an Edwardian saloon launch, is available for hire. **Seats 50. Parties 6. Private Room 12.** *L 12.15-2 (Sat & Sun to 2.30) D 7.15-9 (Sat to 9.30, Sun to 8.30). Closed 25 Dec. Access, Amex, Visa.*

GOUDHURST	Star & Eagle Inn	£45

Tel 01580 211512   Fax 01580 211416   Map 11 B5   **I**
High Street Goudhurst Kent TN17 1AL

The bedrooms at this gabled 14th-century inn come in all shapes and sizes, and one sports a restored four-poster bed. In the public areas period appeal survives in exposed beams, open brick fireplaces and old settles. No dogs. This Whitbread hotel stands less than two miles from the A21. **Rooms 11.** *Garden, children's indoor playroom. Closed 25 Dec. Access, Amex, Visa.*

GRANTHAM	Swallow Hotel	67%	£98

Tel 01476 593000   Fax 01476 592592   Map 7 E3   **H**
Swingbridge Road Grantham Lincolnshire NG31 7XT

A modern low-rise hotel on the Grantham side of the junction of the A1 with the A607 to Melton Mowbray; it features good-sized, smart bedrooms and a comprehensively-equipped leisure centre. **Rooms 90.** *Indoor swimming pool, children's splash pool, keep-fit equipment, sauna, steam room, spa bath, solarium. Access, Amex, Diners, Visa.*

GRASMERE	Michael's Nook	79%	£210*

Tel 015394 35496   Fax 015394 35765   Map 4 C3   **HR**
Grasmere nr Ambleside Cumbria LA22 9RP

Originally built as a summer home and named in remembrance of the humble home of the shepherd in Wordsworth's poem, this grand Victorian house stands a short distance back off the A591 surrounded by three acres of landscaped gardens and ten acres of woodland. Reg Gifford, the owner, opened it as a hotel in 1969 and since then it has firmly established itself as one of the premier country house hotels in the Lake District. The doorbell is rung to gain admittance into a beautiful entrance hall which is typical of the gracious and supremely comfortable day rooms. An Oriental carpet on the polished parquet floor, antiques, a ticking grandfather clock, potted plants and fresh flowers create an immediate sense of well-being. The drawing room, approached through double doors, is also immensely impressive, the flower arrangements arrestingly beautiful. Decor is classically elegant, with deep-cushioned settees and armchairs in which to relax. The bar has a delightful farmhouse ambience with its china-filled antique Welsh dresser and polished oak tables and chairs. Log fires warm the bar and drawing room in inclement weather. A fine balustrade staircase leads up to the bedrooms which, again, are very traditional in character and decor. Exquisite satinwood suites grace some rooms and the original furniture has been restored in one room with mahogany, oak and even Chinese lacquer in others, together with a whole host of extras making for very comfortable rooms. Three de luxe and superior rooms on the second floor are approached by steps from the garden behind the house. Beautiful bathrooms have thick towels, flannels, bathrobes and a range of Floris toiletries. Guests can use the keep-fit facilities, sauna and solarium at the sister hotel, the

See over

Wordsworth. There's also free golf Mon–Fri at Keswick. No dogs. ★Half-board terms only. *Rooms 14. Garden, croquet. Access, Amex, Diners, Visa.*

Restaurant   ★🏔   £100

Orders and pre-dinner drinks are dealt with in the charming, cosy bar with dinner taken in one of the two splendid dining-rooms. The first room has a striking decor of red gloss walls, gilt-framed mirrors and a crystal chandelier. The oak room is grander with fine oak-panelled walls. Highly polished antique mahogany tables, crystal glassware and gleaming silver create an ambience of relaxed but traditional formality. Kevin Mangeolles' cooking reflects the high quality and painstaking attention to detail exhibited in the decor and upkeep of the hotel as a whole. The five-course (four at lunchtime), fixed-price menu offers a number of alternatives at each stage plus a daily-changing recommended dish for each course. In high season there is also a six-course, no-choice gourmet menu. Kevin's base is traditional English, his influences modern, his inspiration international, the results of which are dishes of great appeal and finely judged combinations of texture and flavour: millefeuille of red mullet served with a mushroom and tomato dressing; chick pea soup garnished with foie gras; poached oysters in a pastry case with wild mushrooms and a Gewurztraminer sauce; roast mallard duck with red cabbage and a parcel of lentils on a cardamom sauce. Desserts are no less alluring and no less accomplished, as shown by a roulade of white chocolate parfait and griottine cherries wrapped in chocolate sponge on a vanilla sauce. Good British cheeses too with wonderful names like Celtic Promise and Mr Appleby's Cheshire. Look carefully for bargains (eg Chateau Musar from Lebanon) on an excellent wine list that includes two *marque* champagnes under £30 – though a glass of the same will set you back £7. Copious choice of half bottles. No smoking. *Seats 32. Parties 10. Private Room 40. L 12.30-1 D 7-8.30. Set L £28.50 Set D £39.50 & £47.50.*

GRASMERE	The Swan	65%	£108

Tel 015394 35551   Fax 015394 35741   Map 4 C3   **H**
Grasmere nr Ambleside Cumbria LA22 9RF

Public areas have a mellow country inn-like atmosphere with their carved furniture, horse brasses, copper jugs and pewter, and are little changed since Wordsworth mentioned The Swan in his poem *The Waggoner.* By contrast, the bedrooms, many with views of the surrounding fells, offer more up-to-date comfort; the five Feature rooms are the most characterful, one with a four-poster, one half-tester and one a canopied bed. After wet days walkers will appreciate the Drying Room – the Swan attracts more tourist than business trade. Forte. *Rooms 36. Garden. Access, Amex, Diners, Visa.*

GRASMERE	White Moss House	69%	£120*

Tel 015394 35295   Fax 015394 35516   Map 4 C3   **HR**
Rydal Water Grasmere Cumbria LA22 9SE

Sue and Peter Dixon are always cooking, serving or greeting guests at their tiny Lakeland hotel, built in 1730 and once owned by William Wordsworth. It's a very quiet, intimate place, very popular with walkers, and the views over Rydal Water from its wooded hillside location are another bonus. Bedrooms in the main house are full of antique pieces, and Sue's homely touches abound. Above the hotel, the hideaway Brockstone Cottage has two bedrooms (one a four-poster) and a kitchen. Good breakfasts extend to kippers, Cumberland sausage and black pudding. Guests have free use of a nearby leisure club (gym, squash, swimming pool). ★Half-board terms only. Children are welcome (under-10s stay free in parents' room) but this is not really suitable for toddlers. No dogs. *Rooms 6. Garden, game fishing. Closed mid Dec-mid Mar. Access, Visa.*

Restaurant   £60

The availability of seats for non-residents is very limited, so booking is essential for Peter Dixon's splendid five-course dinners served at 8 in a little cottage-style room. His meal is always well planned and executed, with no choice except at the dessert stage. Soup – maybe spiced celeriac, cauliflower and chive – gets dinner under way, followed by a terrine, a fish dish, or perhaps a soufflé. The centrepiece could be crispy roast Lakeland mallard with sage and onion stuffing and a damson, port and pinot noir sauce, or roast beef marinated with real ale and served with a tarragon and Pomerol sauce. This main dish is always accompanied by particularly interesting vegetables. Next comes a choice of three sweets (cabinet pudding, coconut ice cream and chocolate and amaretto slice with cherry sauce are typical) and British traditional cheeses. A very fine wine list tempts with

some unbelievably low prices (Charles Heidsieck Champagne £22). Informative
introductory notes, many old vintages, comprehensive choice from both Europe and the
New World. No smoking. *Seats 18. Parties 8. D at 8. Closed Sun.
Set D £27.50.*

GRASMERE   Wordsworth Hotel   72%   £105

Tel 015394 35592   Fax 015394 35765   Map 4 C3   **HR**
Grasmere nr Ambleside Cumbria LA22 9SW

The hotel stands in two peaceful acres located in Grasmere village, next to the
churchyard where Wordsworth is buried. The conservatory bar and adjacent lounge have
bold floral fabrics, some cane seating and the best of the views. There's also a pub – the
Dove and Olive Branch – and a leisure centre whose swimming pool opens on to a sun-
trap terrace. Individually decorated bedrooms vary widely in size and aspect; the best are
two suites with whirlpool baths and an antique-furnished four-poster room. Many rooms
are suitable for family use and there's a children's menu plus high tea served between 5.30
and 6.30 either in bedrooms or the Garden Room. Free golf at Keswick mid-week.
*Rooms 37. Garden, indoor swimming pool, keep-fit equipment, spa bath, solarium,
games room. Access, Amex, Diners, Visa.*

Prelude Restaurant   £75

Bernard Warne's menu, priced for three or four courses at night with a slightly shorter
version at lunchtime, makes good use of local produce in dishes like galantine of pheasant
with pistachios and Cumberland ham, Lakeland lamb casseroled with rosemary and
orange and a sautéed breast of Lunesdale duck with a parcel of duck confit. One might
also find things like cream of rabbit soup with basil, roast turbot with crushed sweet
potatoes on a red wine sauce finished with a parsley fondue and, with vegetarians in
mind, a lightly curried lentil and sesame ravioli on a tomato coulis with vegetables and
fruit fritters. The Sunday lunch menu always includes rib of beef with Yorkshire
pudding. Desserts like spiced bread-and-butter pudding with Drambuie cream, toffee apple mousse
and chocolate trifle are alternatives to the fine British cheeses. Size apart, the wine list is
manageable, with something for everyone, whether the choice is by price or region.
The New World is represented; the wine recommendations are carefully chosen and
offer excellent value for money. *Seats 65. Parties 12. L 12.30-2 D 7-9 (Fri & Sat to 9.30).
Set L £17.50 (Sun £12.95) Set D £28/£29.50.*

GRAYSHOTT   Woods Place   £58

Tel & Fax 01428 605555   Map 11 A6   **R**
Headley Road Grayshott nr Hindhead Surrey GU26 6LB

Continental cuisine with Swedish specialities is the attraction at Dana and Eric Norrgren's
former butcher's shop in a village just off the A3 south of Hindhead. The à la carte menu
features hearty, fairly straightforward dishes like French onion soup, medallions of lamb
with garlic and cream sauce, venison steak with wild mushroom sauce, Cajun salmon
with white wine sauce and supreme of chicken stuffed with crabmeat mousse, along with
Swedish hash and Jansson's Temptation, the latter consisting of sliced potatoes baked with
fish and cream. Leave room for upside-down apple tart or pancakes with blueberry ice
cream. Short list (about 2 dozen) of fairly priced wines. *Seats 36. Parties 16. L 12-2.30
D 7-12. Closed Sun & Mon. Access, Amex, Diners, Visa.*

GREAT AYTON   Ayton Hall   70%   £105

Tel 01642 723595   Fax 01642 722149   Map 5 E3   **H**
Low Green Great Ayton nr Middlesbrough North Yorkshire TS9 6PS

Approached down a narrow tree-lined avenue, the Hall, a Grade II listed building, stands
in six acres of mature grounds. The entrance hall is also the bar. It is dark and intimate,
with red velour upholstered Gothic-style high-back chairs around the curved walls. The
drawing room is charming with its very traditional furnishings and a baby grand in one
corner. In the dining-room there's a steadily growing collection of some 500
commemorative plates adorning the walls. Bedrooms on the first floor are named after
James Cook's ships, following his association with the place, while on the next floor
bedrooms have Maori names. All are of good size and are well equipped. Sherry, fresh
fruit and mineral water are among the pampering extras. The second-floor rooms also
have a cosy atmosphere created by the sloping ceilings, pickled pine furniture and brass
bedsteads. Neat, carpeted bathrooms. No dogs. *Rooms 9. Garden, croquet, tennis,
shooting. Access, Amex, Diners, Visa.*

GREAT BADDOW   Pontlands Park   70%   £130

Tel 01245 476444   Fax 01245 478393   Map 11 B4   **H**
West Hanningfield Road Great Baddow nr Chelmsford Essex CM2 8HR

An extended mid-Victorian hotel with an attractive health and leisure centre. Bedrooms in the wing are huge, with high ceilings, separate sitting areas, large beds, quality reproduction furniture and bright, stylish fabrics. Rooms in the main house are similar but smaller; all bathrooms boast bidets, high-class toiletries and good carpeting and decor. Public areas include a marble-effect entrance hall, a comfortable bar, an elegant lounge and a bright little garden coffee shop with lots of plants and Lloyd Loom chairs. Dogs in kennels only. Children not allowed in health centre during members' hours. *Rooms 17. Garden, indoor & outdoor swimming pools, sauna, spa bath, sun bed, keep-fit equipment, beauty & hair salons, dance studio. Closed 24-30 Dec. Access, Amex, Diners, Visa.*

GREAT DUNMOW   Saracen's Head   58%   £97

Tel 01371 873901   Fax 01371 875743   Map 10 B3   **H**
High Street Great Dunmow Essex CM6 1AG

Forte hotel blending Tudor and Georgian architectural features with a modern wing of bedrooms. Banqueting and conference facilities for around 40. Families with children well catered for, with baby-sitting and listening available. Ten minutes drive from Junction 8 of the M11. *Rooms 24. Access, Amex, Diners, Visa.*

GREAT DUNMOW   The Starr   £80

Tel 01371 874321   Fax 01371 876337   Map 10 B3   **R**
Market Place Great Dunmow Essex CM6 1AX

The Starr is a small restaurant housed in a 400-year-old timber-framed hostelry overlooking Great Dunmow's market place and has been run by Brian and Vanessa Jones along with Terry and Louise George since 1980. London markets and local sources supply the raw materials for chef Mark Fisher's careful hand: tomato, basil and mozzarella tart with yoghurt dressing and toasted pine nuts; broccoli soufflé with almonds and goat's cheese sauce; roast sea bream with a shellfish and rice pancake and a saffron butter sauce; rosette of English lamb roasted with gratin potatoes and Mediterranean vegetables with a thyme sauce are all typical dishes. The same menu is priced à la carte at lunchtime and as a prix-fixe at night. A different Sunday lunch menu is more traditional in style. A superb wine list great depth and excellent choice throughout. Sensible prices include a *marque* champagne under £30. No smoking. *Seats 50. Parties 12. Private Rooms 36. L 12-1.30 D 7-9.30 (Sat till 10). Closed L Sat, D Sun & 1st week Jan. Set Sun L £16.50/£21.50 Set D £24.50/£32.50 (Sat £35). Access, Amex, Visa.*

Rooms   £85

Eight en-suite bedrooms, with names like the Oak Room, the Brass Room and the Poppy Room, are in the old stable block and individually furnished, mainly with antiques. The Oak Room and Pine Room are superior; all rooms are non-smoking. Chidren up to six stay free in parents' room. Special weekend rates. Only "good" dogs are welcome. Parking in the rear courtyard. 15 minutes from Stanstead Airport. *Rooms closed 1st week Jan.*

GREAT GONERBY   Harry's Place   ★   £95

Tel 01476 61780   Map 7 E3   **R**
17 High Street Great Gonerby nr Grantham Lincolnshire NG31 8JS

An elegant, double-fronted village-centre Georgian house is both home and workplace to Harry and Caroline Hallam. With only three tables the restaurant has all the charm and intimacy of a gracious, yet relaxed and informal, country dining-room. Deep salmon-pink walls, varnished stripped-pine doors and tables, fresh flowers and innumerable pretty ornaments and wall hangings create a beautiful and comfortable setting enhanced by candle-light and the soft illuminations of four table lamps, the latter arranged on side furniture. The menu changes according to supplies and is short, only two choices per course, but is prepared with an eye for detail resulting in food that is both visually delightful and sensational on the palate. Raw materials, from herbs to meat, fish, poultry and even the cheeses, are purchased from top suppliers to ensure the best flavours and textures. Both of these are combined with immense skill as in Scottish mussels poached in white wine with saffron, leeks, parsley and a little cream. Main courses could be a fillet of baby halibut sautéed in olive oil with white wine, Pernod, basil and fennel or breast of French guinea fowl roasted with bacon, shallots, red wine and tarragon. Lovely desserts, such as *tarte au citron* served with vanilla ice cream or caramel *mousse brulée* with raspberries round off a memorable meal. "Usually no children under 5" to spoil the unique atmosphere. No smoking. *Seats 10. L 12.30-2 D 7-9.30. Closed Sun & Mon (except by prior arrangement), 25 & 26 Dec, Bank Holidays. Access, Visa.*

GREAT MILTON	Le Manoir aux Quat'Saisons	86%	£204

Tel 01844 278881 Fax 01844 278847 Map 15 D2 **HR**
Church Road Great Milton Oxfordshire OX44 7PD

Raymond Blanc's renowned and very special country house hotel is only a short drive from the M40. From London leave the motorway at Junction 7, approaching from the north at Junction 8. Imposing wide gates in the high surrounding stone walls lead up to a graceful 15th-century manor house built of mellow Cotswold stone. The 27 acres of carefully tended gardens include a three-acre kitchen garden and a newly created authentic Japanese tea garden. The flagstoned entrance hall leads into luxurious and comfortable lounges that are immaculately furnished with antiques, fine paintings and splendid flower arrangements and warmed in winter by open fires. The theme continues in the individually decorated bedrooms, which provide every conceivable luxury, from a decanter of Madeira to a bowl of fresh fruit. Several garden-wing rooms have their own private terrace with wrought-iron patio furniture, while the medieval dovecote has been converted into a romantic honeymoon suite. There are jacuzzi and whirlpool baths in the magnificent bathrooms, not to mention huge towels, generous bathrobes and exquisite toiletries. Of course, all this would be wasted without service and excellent housekeeping to match, and this, under the direction of General Manager Simon Rhatigan, proceeds smoothly and efficiently. Breakfasts, naturally, are quite delicious. Small conferences (40). Dogs in kennels. *Rooms 19. Garden, croquet, tennis, outdoor swimming pool, limousine. Access, Amex, Diners, Visa.*

Restaurant

 ★ ★ ★ £195

One of the country's premier country houses also has one of its leading restaurants – a true haven of comfort and gastronomy. Dining is in one of three stylish rooms which include the spacious conservatory, filled with greenery but also with splendid garden views, and the more intimate Loxton room decorated in summery yellows and blues. Chef-patron Raymond Blanc, who began in humbler surroundings in Oxford, is assisted by Clive Fretwell, who together with a strong kitchen brigade produces dishes that are both highly creative and technically superb. The grounds and kitchen gardens provide most of the quality produce used – whether it's organic herbs, vegetables or fruit – and head gardener Anne-Marie Owens gets a well-deserved mention on the menu. The style has changed little down the years – it has evolved, but still displays the lightest of touches, with influences from the Far East adding intriguing and exotic flavours to captivate the palate. A three-course *menu du jour* offers two choices in each section following an appetiser. The eight-course *menu gourmand* offers the opportunity of sampling a well-balanced selection of specialities while the carte offers a further exercise in studied perfection. Typical starters include ravioli of quail's eggs, spinach, parmesan and black truffles in a delicate chicken jus with meunière butter and Swiss chard or a trio of scallop tartare with shiso leaves, poached oyster in a cucumber butter and crab croustillant in seaweed. Main dishes range from a pan-fried fillet of gilt-head sea bream in a bouillabaisse jus with a fricassée of squid and herbs from the garden to a breast of *Landes* chicken in a white port wine sauce with leeks and truffles and pan-fried venison fillet with a bitter chocolate sauce, braised chestnuts and winter vegetables. Desserts (try Le Café Crème) and farmhouse cheeses, from both France and Great Britain, are a delight, petits fours and chocolates, mini-masterpieces. A fantastic wine list, yes, value for money, no!! Just over

See over

half a dozen wines are priced under £20, otherwise the list is hugely expensive. However, there's no doubting the quality – great names from France and Italy, fine wines from the New World. If you want to learn how to emulate the dishes here, ask for details of their cookery school. *Seats 110. Parties 10. Private Room 24/46. L 12.15-2.15 (Sun to 2.30) D 7.15-10.15. Set L £29.50 (not Sun) D £65.* 🐷

GREAT SNORING	Old Rectory	61%	£87

Tel 01328 820597 Fax 01328 820048   Map 10 C1   **H**
Barsham Road Great Snoring nr Fakenham Norfolk NR21 0HP

Behind the church on the Barsham road, the Old Rectory retains some pleasing architectural features, including stone-mullioned windows bordered by frieze tiles. Day rooms are peaceful and old-fashioned and there are some fine period furnishings in the handsomely proportioned bedrooms. The Shelton Suites, brick-and-flint self-catering cottages in the grounds, offer a greater degree of privacy and seclusion, each having its own living room and kitchen; servicing and breakfast provisions are provided daily. No children under 8 in the main house, although families with babes in arms may find the cottages a wonderfully relaxing country retreat. Six miles from the Norfolk coast. No dogs. *Rooms 6. Garden. Closed 24-27 Dec. Amex, Diners.*

GREAT YARMOUTH	Carlton Hotel	67%	£79

Tel 01493 855234 Fax 01493 852220   Map 10 D1   **H**
Marine Parade Great Yarmouth Norfolk NR30 3JE

The Carlton has a fine seafront location directly opposite Wellington Pier. The hotel's impressive interior houses conference facilities for up to 180. Bedrooms (refurbished during 1995) have bright colour schemes and smart tiled bathrooms. Children up to 12 free in parents' room. Covered parking for 22 cars. Free admission to a nearby leisure centre. *Rooms 95. Games room, hair salon. Access, Amex, Diners, Visa.*

GREAT YARMOUTH	Seafood Restaurant	£55

Tel 01493 856009   Map 10 D1   **R**
85 North Quay Great Yarmouth Norfolk NR30 1JF
🍇

Chris and Miriam Kikis have been running this friendly little restaurant since 1979 and have built up a loyal following. It's actually housed in a converted railway station and can be a little difficult for first-timers to find, so ask for directions when booking (which is advised). Fresh fish and seafood are the order of the day here: the mixed platters – fresh or smoked – are always popular, and other specialities include oysters from the tank, lobster thermidor, turbot with herb butter and monkfish with a curry or creamy black pepper sauce. Steaks also available, or a bit of both (surf & turf). Summer pudding is a seasonal favourite. Several champagnes under £30 on a good wine list. *Seats 40. L 12-1.45 D 7-10.45. Closed L Sat, all Sun, Bank Holidays (except Good Friday), 3 weeks Christmas. Access, Amex, Diners, Visa.*

GRETA BRIDGE	Morritt Arms Hotel	£70

Tel 01833 627232 Fax 01833 627392   Map 5 D3   **I**
Greta Bridge Rokeby nr Barnard Castle Co Durham DL12 9SE

New owners are in the process of restoring the charm to this 17th-century former coaching inn approached over a narrow bridge off the A66. Sue Atkinson and Barbara-Anne Johnson intend re-creating the warmth and style of days gone by. The traditional atmosphere of the public rooms is characterised by polished block floors laid with Chinese carpets and deeply comfortable loose-covered armchairs arranged in small groups in the cosy lounge, which features an open log fire. The main bar has a mural painted in 1946 by John Gilroy who took well-known local figures and created a Dickensian theme around them. Bedrooms are simple and homely each with a trouser press, hairdryer and mineral water, as well as remote-control TV. Currently the majority of the very neat carpeted bathrooms are without shower facilities. *Rooms 17. Garden, croquet, bowls, pool table, children's playground. Access, Amex, Diners, Visa.*

Set menu prices may not always include service or wine.

GRIMSBY	Forte Posthouse	64%	£72

Tel 01472 350295   Fax 01472 241354   Map 7 F1   **H**
Littlecoates Road Grimsby Humberside DN34 4LX

Friendly and peaceful late-60s' hotel on the outskirts of town, overlooking a golf course. Business-oriented in the week (conferences for up to 250), popular with families at weekends. Half the bedrooms are non-smoking. *Rooms 52. Access, Amex, Diners, Visa.*

Lodges are now listed by county in the reference section

GRIMSTON	Congham Hall	75%	£99

Tel 01485 600250   Fax 01485 601191   Map 10 B1   **HR**
Lynn Road Grimston King's Lynn Norfolk PE32 1AH

A short drive out from King's Lynn, the Hall is a beautifully proportioned, elegant Georgian manor house set in 40 acres of grounds which include a very noteworthy herb garden and the village cricket pitch. It is run by Christine and Trevor Forecast who converted it into a hotel in 1982. Original features have been retained as has a traditional style of decor which is very much in keeping with the property's original character. Public rooms lead off the long, wide entrance hall, the bar on one side and a spacious, well-appointed drawing-room on the other. At the rear of the building a new patio has been created which in fine weather makes full use of the available afternoon sun. Bedrooms are large and comfortable (there's a small single and a couple of top-floor rooms have restricted views). They are all well equipped. Books, magazines, fresh fruit as well as iced water (placed in rooms each evening) complement the colourful chintzes and furniture (rattan in some, antique in others). Excellent bathrooms are spotless and have good-quality toiletries. A feature of the house is the wealth of both fresh and dried flowers that adorn public areas and bedrooms alike. The heady perfume from myriad bowls of pot-pourri from flowers grown mostly on the premises further enhances the enjoyment of one's stay. Very friendly, efficient and helpful service. No children under 12. Dogs in kennels only (£1 per night). *Rooms 14. Garden, croquet, tennis, outdoor pool, spa bath, stabling. Access, Amex, Diners, Visa.*

Orangery Restaurant   ★   £70

An elegant and summery room with French windows looking out over lawns to ancient trees. A patio, newly created, offers the prospect of alfresco dining, weather permitting, while in the kitchen, head chef Jonathan Nicholson, having worked in a number of restaurants around the country, has returned to his roots, bringing with him a wealth of experience and expertise. Not only is there prime local produce at his disposal but there is also the multitude of flavours from the hotel's wonderful herb garden, which features some 550 different varieties. Menus have been slightly simplified with the availability now of a light lunch option as well as the full carte. Dinner is a formal affair with gentlemen requested to wear jackets. On offer is a varied choice of intricate and imaginative dishes beginning with pan-fried prawns in a Thai cream sauce with a spaghetti of vegetables and apple, marinated scallops on a saffron risotto with spinach, or roulade of duck confit and foie gras with brioche and warm wild mushroom vinaigrette. Intermediate dishes include a chicken consommé with tomato and chives and grilled fresh sardines with pesto and potato salad. For a main course there's steamed brill with a langoustine mousseline, pan-fried rib of beef served with polenta and grilled Mediterranean vegetables. The pot-roast honey-glazed shank of lamb with parmentier potatoes and rosemary jus is absolutely delicious. One of the most popular items, it is only for those with the heartiest appetites. Desserts are an eyecatching and fitting finale to a superb meal served with style. No children under 12. No smoking. Accompanying notes on some wines on a decent enough list that includes half a dozen from South Africa. Lots of half bottles. *Seats 50. Parties 8. Private Room 18. L 12.30-2 D 7.30-9.30. Closed L Sat. Set L £13.50/£15 (Sun £15) Set D £24.*

GRINDLEFORD — Maynard Arms — £65

Tel 01433 630321   Fax 01433 630445   Map 6 C2   **I**
Main Road Grindleford Derbyshire S30 1HP

A solid-stone roadside inn located in the Peak National Park on a hillside outside the village. Public rooms include a spacious and attractive public bar, The Longshaw, and smart cocktail bar with deep-green velour upholstery. Bedrooms, some with secondary glazing to help with heat retention in winter, are cottagey in style with pretty fabrics and old-fashioned furniture. Two have four-posters and all have a good selection of extras including remote TV, trouser press, hairdryer and radio-alarm. Bathrooms have gleaming dark-blue wall tiling; three sport corner baths. *Rooms 11. Access, Amex, Visa.*

GRIZEDALE — Grizedale Lodge — 61% — £65

Tel 015394 36532   Fax 015394 36572   Map 4 C4   **H**
Grizedale nr Hawkshead Cumbria LA22 0QL

A small, homely, hidden hotel whose new owners Pat and Vincent Dawson intend to 'maintain and enhance' the reputation established by Jack and Margaret Lamb, who have retired. Comfortable rewards are found in the roomy lounge, cheery bar and spick-and-span cottage-style bedrooms; two rooms are in an extension; one is a family room with a double and two single beds; two have four-posters. No smoking. No dogs. Follow the signs for the Theatre in the Forest on the road between Hawkshead and Newby Bridge. *Rooms 9. Garden. Closed 2 Jan-10 Feb. Access, Visa.*

GUILDFORD — The Angel — 73% — £122

Tel 01483 64555   Fax 01483 33770   Map 15 E3   **H**
91 High Street Guildford Surrey GU1 3DP

A feature of Guildford's cobbled High Street since the Middle Ages, the Angel's stucco facade, incorporating the signs 'posting house' and 'livery stables', was added to the original timber-framed building in the 1800s during the height of the coaching era. Under new and caring ownership since 1990, it is today an intimate and luxurious hotel. The central galleried lounge with its ancient red-brick inglenook fireplace, old black timbers and 17th-century parliament clock has, in the last year, been extended into the oak-panelled former restaurant (the restaurant itself has moved to an air-conditioned 13th-century stone-vaulted crypt) and a stylish new cocktail bar (also air-conditioned) with tartan upholstery has been created overcoming the former lack of public space. Spacious bedrooms, of which more than half are full suites, are individually decorated in some style with canopied bedheads, proper sofas and armchairs, traditional polished-wood freestanding furniture and extras like a welcoming decanter of sherry and home-made biscuits. There's a second telephone line to accommodate fax machines and three telephones in each room, including in the good bathrooms many of which have twin washbasins and separate walk-in showers in addition to the tub; all have bathrobes and quality toiletries. In the summer of 1995 ten new rooms and suites were nearing completion. Room service is particularly extensive for such a small hotel with a selection of hot meals available throughout the night. Arrive before 11am or after 4pm (between these hours the High Street is traffic free) and valet parking is offered. *Rooms 21. Terrace. Access, Amex, Diners, Visa.*

GUILDFORD — Forte Crest — 68% — £130

Tel 01483 574444   Fax 01483 302960   Map 15 E3   **H**
Egerton Road Guildford Surrey GU2 5XZ

Darkwood panelling and a white marble fireplace lend a very civilised air to the public areas at this smart modern hotel on the outskirts of town (follow signs for the Cathedral orUniversity then the Surrey Research Park). It's very much geared-up to the requirements of business travellers and there are conference facilities for up to 120 delegates. Comprehensive 24hr room service. Children up to 14 stay free in parents' room. One room is equipped for disabled guests. Considerable tariff reductions Fri & Sat. Hard by the A3 northbound. *Rooms 111. Patio, indoor swimming pool, gym, sauna, solarium. Access, Amex, Diners, Visa.*

Set menu prices may not always include service or wine.

| GUILDFORD | **Mandarin** | **£45** |

Tel 01483 572293   Map 15 E3   **R**
13 Epsom Road Guildford Surrey GU1 3JT

Modern, cool decor with black lacquered chairs and spotlit tables add up to a quietly chic ambience in a friendly restaurant at the top of the town (opposite the Odeon cinema). Cooking covers Szechuan and Peking styles with both outstanding crispy aromatic duck and scallops, squid and prawns served sizzling with ginger and spring onions showing flair in the kitchen. Mongolian lamb and beef are filling hot pot dishes. No children under 5. *Seats 50. L 12.30-1.30 D 6-10.30. Closed L Sun. Set D from £17.50. Access, Amex, Diners, Visa.*

| GUISELEY | **Prachee** | **£45** |

Tel 01943 872531   Map 6 C1   **R**
6 Bradford Road Whitecross Guiseley West Yorkshire LS20 8NH

At a major intersection just to the north of the town centre this Indian restaurant has smart decor and an extensive menu featuring a good number of set meals as well as à la carte dishes. All is very carefully prepared and highly enjoyable with clear spicing and particularly good bread. *Seats 56. Parties 25. L 12-2 D 6-12. Closed 25 Dec. Access, Visa.*

| GULWORTHY | **The Horn of Plenty** ★ | **£100** |

Tel & Fax 01822 832528   Map 12 C3   **RR**
Gulworthy nr Tavistock Devon PL19 8JD

Signposted off the A390 to the west of Tavistock, the 200-year-old house stands in four acres of gardens and orchards. The welcome from Elaine and Ian Gatehouse is warm and friendly and the views across the Tamar valley from the restaurant are glorious. The well-balanced fixed-price menus are the responsibility of Peter Gorton, (finalist in our Chef of the Year competition – see award pages), whose modern international cooking ranges from salt cod with lentils and shallot cream to charred breast of pigeon with truffle sauce for starters, and, at main course, from roast duckling with red wine and orange sauce to fillet of lemon sole coated with chopped prawns, scallops and coriander and cooked in tempura batter. Some interesting combinations appear at dessert as well – warm pear charlotte with a liquorice sauce is typical – plus a selection of English and Continental cheeses. There are tasting notes (not always very helpful) on an easy-to-use wine list with house wines under £12. No children under 12. No smoking. *Seats 50. Parties 20. Private Room 12. L 12-2 D 7-9. Closed L Mon, 24-26 Dec. Set L from £10.50 Set D £27.50. Access, Amex, Visa.*

Rooms   £108

Six of the seven pine-furnished bedrooms, each with its own balcony overlooking the valley, are in the converted coach house. Direct-dial phones, remote-control TVs and well-stocked mini-bars provide the modern comforts. No children under 12. Garden.

| HACKNESS | **Hackness Grange** 61% | **£126** |

Tel 01723 882345   Fax 01723 882391   Map 5 F3   **H**
Hackness nr Scarborough North Yorkshire YO13 0JW

An attractive 19th-century house standing in its own grounds by the River Derwent in the North York Moors National Park. Bedrooms are divided between the main house and the courtyard. Free parking for 50 cars. No dogs. *Rooms 28. Garden, croquet, tennis, pitch and putt, fishing, indoor swimming pool. Access, Amex, Diners, Visa.*

| HADLEY WOOD | **West Lodge Park Hotel** 66% | **£117** |

Tel 0181-440 8311   Fax 0181-449 3698   Map 15 E2   **HR**
Cockfosters Road Hadley Wood nr Barnet Hertfordshire EN4 0PY

An extended 19th-century country house set in parkland that includes an arboretum and a lake. Inside there's an orderly, civilised feel in the lounge, plentifully supplied with armchairs, in the brick-walled bar and in the four conference rooms (catering for up to 80 delegates). Bedrooms are individually decorated and furnished all now with cosseting little extras, and the majority have small entrance lobbies. The hotel is on the A111 halfway between the M25 (exit 24) and Cockfosters Underground station. Free membership of, and taxi to, local leisure club. 24hr room service. Ample free parking. No dogs. *Rooms 45. Garden, croquet, golf practice net, putting, bar billiards. Access, Amex, Visa.* *See over*

Cedar Restaurant   £65

A split-level dining-room furnished in a homely country style with pine furniture and pretty pink napery. Peter Leggat produces daily-changing menus with a choice of one, two or three courses from a well-thought-out, varied selection of between 8 and 10 dishes for each course. There is a modern inflection to his style though it has to be said that conservative and traditional elements are also very apparent, dictated by the tastes of the largely business and suburban clientele. The food is none the worse for this with noteworthy careful cooking. Cream of broccoli and almond soup; sea trout and prawn mousseline wrapped in lemon sole with a watercress mayonnaise; roast breast of Barbary duck on a bed of creamed celeriac with roasted shallots and garlic; braised lamb shank and pan-fried fillet of beef with cocotte potatoes and bubble and squeak on a Madeira and truffle jus. Excellent British cheeses are available as well as delicious sweets such as a confit of strawberries in a rich suet crust with custard or steamed walnut pudding with a chestnut and butterscotch sauce and Bailey's ice cream. There are also superb Bowmans Farm ices. Friendly, old-fashioned service. No smoking. *Seats 85. Parties 10. L 12.30-2 D 7.15-9.45. Set L £15.50/£17.50 (Sun £17.50) Set D £16.50/£19.50.*

HAILEY   The Bird in Hand   £50

Tel 01993 868321   Fax 01993 868702   Map 14 C2   **I**
Hailey nr Witney Oxfordshire OX8 5XP

A delightful "residential country inn" and popular eating pub in a rural setting surrounded by open fields, one mile north of Hailey on the B4022 between Witney and Charlbury. Sixteen spacious, cottage-style bedrooms (non-smoking) are in keeping with the original Cotswold-stone former coaching inn, in a U-shaped building on two storeys with wooden balconies, all overlooking an attractive grassed courtyard. Two twin-bedded, ground-floor rooms have facilities for disabled guests and a couple of large family rooms sleep up to five; pine furnishings, thoughtful touches like full-length mirrors and cotton wool plus good housekeeping bring all rooms up to a good hotel standard. Light meals and a good pint can be enjoyed in the cosy stone-walled bar rooms (one of which features a fine inglenook) and on picnic tables outside on the patio and in the walled front garden. *Rooms 16. Garden. Closed 3 days Christmas. Access, Visa.*

HALIFAX   Design House Restaurant   NEW   £55

Tel 01422 383242   Fax 01422 322732   Map 6 C1   **R**
Dean Clough Halifax West Yorkshire HX3 5AX

Follow the signs to Dean Clough (formerly Europe's largest carpet mill, now largely offices plus some workshops, an art gallery and, soon, a theatre space) and then Gate 5 to find this smart, modern restaurant where low, black leather and chrome sofas by the entrance set the contemporary tone for the decor and furnishings within. Created by David Watson, formerly of *Pool Court,* the menu is no less aggressively modern with such starters as seared venison with roquette, paremsan and truffle oil; a salad of warm French beans with spinach, walnuts and Cashel Blue cheese, and a cold seafood risotto before mains like duck breast with olive mash, mixed beans and red wine; scallops and king prawns with lobster, ginger and spring onion, and aubergine tart with spicy tomato risotto. Afters always include a savoury – perhaps potato and Munster cakes with herb salad – and cheese, along with the likes of Charentais melon soup and warm cherries with kirsch sabayon. Lunchtime brings a shorter version of the à la carte plus a set menu (priced for two or three courses). There is also a café menu served during the day. Italian wines receive their own heading, while others are listed by grape style. Fair prices, sensible tasting notes – a well-compiled list with interesting and well-chosen wines. Pleasant, unpretentious service. *Seats 70. L 12-2 D 6-10.30. Closed L Sat, all Sun (except café), 25 & 26 Dec. Set L £9.50/£12.75. Access, Amex, Visa.*

HALIFAX   Holdsworth House   69%   £103

Tel 01422 240024   Fax 01422 245174   Map 6 C1   **H**
Holdsworth nr Halifax West Yorkshire HX2 9TG

Three miles north of Halifax stands a 17th-century manor house which the Pearson family have turned into a really charming hotel. Period appeal remains in the day rooms, notably the three handsome oak-panelled rooms that make up the restaurant. The entrance hall also features polished panelling, and the lounge opens on to an attractive courtyard. The best bedrooms are four split-level suites and the rest are both neat and comfortable, with colourful fabrics and mainly period furniture. Two rooms are specially adapted for disabled guests. Good facilities for children (under-10s free in parents' room). Characterful meeting rooms (recently expanded) hold up to 150. *Rooms 40. Garden. Closed 1 week Christmas. Access, Amex, Diners, Visa.*

HAMBLETON	Hambleton Hall	84%	£152

Tel 01572 756991   Fax 01572 724721   Map 7 E3
Hambleton nr Oakham Leicestershire LE15 8TH

In the small village of Hambleton, which is on a peninsula jutting out into Rutland Water, the Victorian hall is well placed to enjoy some fine views of the surrounding countryside. Very much a country house in style, it is professionally run by general manager Jeffrey Crocket and his charming staff, who provide a high standard of friendly, personal service. Day rooms like the refined drawing room with its happy blend of elegance and homely comfort, and the warm red bar with inglenook fireplace, receive the finishing touch with Anne Taylor's artistic floral displays – something of an institution here. Fresh flowers also add to the appeal of bedrooms, where fine fabrics, antiques, armchairs and sofas combine in stylish individual schemes. Extras range from home-made biscuits, mineral water and portable radio to extra-large towelling robes and bathsheets. Rooms are properly serviced in the evening with curtains drawn, beds turned down and fresh towels for the bathroom. *Rooms 15. Garden, tennis, outdoor pool. Access, Amex, Visa.*

Restaurant    ★★   £110

Aaron Patterson and his team are not only seriously ambitious but have the talents to match. First-rate ingredients, the *sine qua non* of good cooking, include a plentiful supply of game from the surrounding countryside and produce from the hotel's own walled kitchen garden (they even grow their own peaches along with blackcurrants for the breakfast jam). A dainty complimentary taster sets up the taste buds for dishes such as a salad of roast scallops with a light lemon and candied onion vinaigrette, terrine of foie gras with a salad of artichokes, green beans and hazelnuts bound in a truffle jelly, wild salmon with a sorrel sauce, fillet of veal with a feuilleté of asparagus and a truffle and Madeira sauce and lemon tart with sliced of figs, honey ice cream and red wine sauce. The full à la carte is served both at lunch and dinner as is the no-choice set menu of the day with dishes like *quenelles de brochet* with a capuccino of freshwater crayfish, locally farmed chicken with a morel sauce and baby vegetables and hot passion fruit soufflé with its own ice. A hugely impressive wine list suits all tastes and pockets. Of particular interest are the 'wines of the moment', some thirty wines drinking especially well, categorised by price from as little as £14.50. *Seats 60. Parties 10. Private Room 20. L 12-2 D 7-9.30. Set L & D £29.50.*

HAMPTON WICK	Le Petit Max	£65

Tel 0181-977 0236   Map 15 E2
97a High Street Corner Vicarage Road Hampton Wick Surrey KT1 4DG

From Kingston, cross the bridge over the Thames and turn right following the main road until turning left immediately before the first railway bridge and you've found Bonzo's! Well that's the big name over the shop front that refers to the workman's 'caff' which occupies these modest premises during the day. A smaller sign over the door heralds *Le Petit Max* which takes over in the evenings and on Sunday. Red-check cloths and paper squares are thrown over the closely packed tables and the rough brick walls sport framed menus from famous French restaurants: this is a very francophile establishment. The twice-weekly-changing prix-fixe is written half in French and half in English. The French staff will probably greet you with a cheery "bon soir" and chef-manager Simon Gale, who has been given a largely free hand since owners Max and Marc Renzland

See over

opened *Chez Max* in Ifield Road (see London section), has just returned from four years working in France. The formula remains much the same with only the freshest of raw materials used in essentially simple dishes that are strong on flavour and low on unnecessary frills. A recent meal included a *terrine de lapin aux herbes* loosely held together with a rich jelly (and clearly made that day) and served with a celeriac rémoulade, and a large piece of turbot with crispy skin sitting on a bed of fresh leaf-spinach surrounded by a flavoursome beurre blanc along with some carrots and new potatoes. On the same menu were grilled merguez sausages with red peppers, smoked salmon and eel with pickled cucumber and mustard sauce, guinea fowl – the breast chargrilled, a confit of the leg – with a cream sauce and large, flat noodles, a rich *pot au chocolat, tarte tatin aux poires* and a *crème brulée à la cassonade*. Unlicensed (corkage £2) but there's an off-licence right next door. *Seats 35. L Sun only at 3.30. D 7-10.30 (Sun from 8). Set L & D £23.50. Closed Mon, Bank Holidays. No credit cards.*

HANCHURCH   Hanchurch Manor   £75

Tel 01782 643030   Fax 01782 643035   Map 6 B3   **PH**
Hanchurch nr Stoke-on-Trent Staffordshire ST4 8SD

Within earshot of the M6, close to Junction 15 (but ask for exact directions when booking), this Tudor-style mansion stands in nine acres of its own gardens that include a fishing lake. Just five bedrooms are now being let, on a bed-and-breakfast basis, so there's lots of space in the civilised public rooms. Comfortable, individually-decorated bedrooms are furnished with good darkwood, freestanding pieces and come with all the usual amenities and good bathrooms. Although not currently being run as a fully-fledged hotel the whole place is kept in apple-pie order, and guests are well looked after by resident manager-caretaker Patricia Farr and her husband. No dogs. *Rooms 5. Garden, fishing. Closed 25 & 26 Dec, 1 Jan. Access, Amex, Visa.*

HANDFORTH   Belfry Hotel   69%   £88

Tel 0161-437 0511   Fax 0161-499 0597   Map 6 B2   **HR**
Stanley Road Handforth nr Wilmslow Cheshire SK9 3LD

Professionalism and service – luggage porterage is the norm, beds are turned down at night, room service is 24hrs – are the great strengths of a hotel run by the Beech family since 1962. Behind a rather utilitarian exterior public rooms include a very pink reception; spacious lounge with button-back leather chairs, reproduction antique table and glass chandeliers (that look a little incongruous given the rather functional architecture of the room). Bedrooms are not large (though a number have been converted into good-sized singles as this is predominantly a business hotel) but have good freestanding furniture and pleasant, mostly Sanderson, fabrics. Bathrooms are practical rather than luxurious. Five full and four junior suites are more spacious and come with larger bathrooms. Banqueting/conferences for up to 180. Courtesy coach to Manchester Airport. No dogs. *Rooms 80. Garden. Access, Amex, Diners, Visa.*

Restaurant   £80

Excellent service under the watchful eye of long-serving restaurant manager James Moore accompanies equally reliable and satisfying cooking by Mark Fletcher and his brigade who cope with table d'hote, gourmet and extensive à la carte menus with confidence and without short cuts. The range includes something for everyone with simple dishes like cream of asparagus soup, liver and bacon (from a section of the menu called 'Return to the Traditional English Table') and grilled Dover sole; classics such as fried whitebait, poached Scotch salmon with hollandaise, and chateaubriand; and more exotic offerings like pan-fried scallops tossed in five spices with a warm mango dressing and seared wafers of foie gras on a potato galette with calvados butter. A nice old-fashioned touch is the well-stocked hors d'oeuvre trolley – a rarity these days. The wine list is a cross-section of the great – for instance, many vintage clarets at very fair prices – and the mundane, though the former easily outweigh the latter. The room is comfortable rather than elegant, with a sunken area in the centre that comes into its own for the regular Friday night dinner dances. *Seats 120. Private Room 20. L 12.30-2 D 7-10. Set L £14 (Sun £14.75) Set D £16 & £21.50.*

Set menu prices may not always include service or wine.

HANDFORTH   Handforth Chinese Restaurant.   £45

Tel 01625 531670   Map 6 B2   **R**
8a The Paddock Handforth Cheshire SK9 3NE

A straightforward restaurant in a parade of shops in suburban Manchester serving good, honest Chinese food. Sound cooking and professional service. A special vegetarian menu offers a choice of some ten dishes, mostly based on bean curd. *Seats 80. Parties 18. L 12-1.45 D 5.30-11.30. Closed L Sat & Sun, 3 days Christmas. Set L from £5.50 Set D from £23.80. Access, Amex, Visa.*

HARLOW   Green Man   60%   £97

Tel 01279 442521   Fax 01279 626113   Map 15 F2   **H**
Mulberry Green Old Town Harlow Essex CM17 0ET

Forte hotel with the heart of a 14th-century coaching inn (the building is listed) and modern bedroom blocks. Two bars, but no lounge. Conference and banqueting facilities for 60. *Rooms 55. Garden. Access, Amex, Diners, Visa.*

HARLOW   Moat House   68%   £84

Tel 01279 829988   Fax 01279 635094   Map 15 F2   **H**
Southern Way Harlow Essex CM18 7BA

Modern hotel with a squat, faceless exterior on the A414 close to Junction 7 of M11 (one mile). Stylish, spacious public rooms and bedrooms. Conference facilities for 160; ample parking. *Rooms 118. Access, Amex, Diners, Visa.*

HAROME   Pheasant Hotel   68%   £117*

Tel 01439 771241   Map 5 E4   **H**
Harome nr Helmsley North Yorkshire YO6 5JG

The pretty and unspoiled village of Harome is about three miles from Helmsley (take the Scarborough road), in the North York Moors National Park; and the Pheasant (converted from the former smithy and shop, as well as a couple of cottages) is peacefully set alongside the pond and millstream. Day rooms comprise a little oak-beamed bar, a restaurant and a lounge that opens on to a flagstoned terrace. Bedrooms include three suites in buildings around a courtyard and one with facilities for the disabled. No children under 6. *Half-board terms. *Rooms 14. Garden, indoor swimming pool. Closed Christmas Eve-end Feb. No credit cards.*

HARPENDEN   Glen Eagle Hotel   63%   £91

Tel 01582 760271   Fax 01582 460819   Map 15 E2   **H**
1 Luton Road Harpenden Hertfordshire AL5 2PX

A functional-looking redbrick hotel with ample free parking. Decent-sized bedrooms, 24hr room service, and several function rooms. The Glen Eagle stands on the A1081, near the railway station. Children up to 14 stay free in parents' room. *Rooms 50. Garden. Access, Amex, Diners, Visa.*

HARPENDEN   Harpenden House Hotel   68%   £110

Tel 01582 764111   Fax 01582 769858   Map 15 E2   **H**
18 Southdown Road Harpenden Hertfordshire AL5 1PE

Elegant redbrick Georgian house, just off A1081. Tastefully decorated day rooms and well-equipped bedrooms (20 of which are reserved for non-smokers). Family facilities. Banqueting conferences for 120/150. Formerly the Moat House. *Rooms 53. Garden, croquet. Access, Amex, Diners, Visa.*

We welcome bona fide complaints and recommendations on the tear-out pages at the back of the book for readers' comments. They are followed up by our professional team.

HARROGATE — Café Fleur — £45

Tel 01423 503034   Map 6 C1   **R**
3 Royal Parade Harrogate North Yorkshire HG1 2SZ

Behind a red and gold frontage opposite the Crown Hotel, this is a friendly French brasserie-style restaurant with a wooden floor, cane-backed chairs and neatly set mahogany tables. A straightforward selection on the various menus runs from grilled sardines and sautéed mushrooms to pasta, omelette, roast chicken in garlic, poached salmon with mustard and dill, and spinach and wild mushroom fricassee. Steak sandwich is a popular quick-snack speciality. Set menus include *Petite Fleur*, which is very cheap (and even cheaper before 7.30 Sun-Thurs). No smoking. *Seats 56. Parties 14. D only 6-9.30. Closed 25 & 26 Dec, 1 Jan. Set D from £4.95. Access, Visa.*

HARROGATE — The Crown — 67% £100

Tel 01423 567755   Fax 01423 502284   Map 6 C1   **H**
Crown Place Harrogate North Yorkshire HG1 2RZ

Forte hotel originally built in 1740 as a coaching inn, but of the grander variety. Guests have free use of the Majestic's(qv) leisure facilities. Conferences/banquets for up to 450/300. Parking for 60 cars. *Rooms 121. Young children's playroom. Access, Amex, Diners, Visa.*

HARROGATE — Drum & Monkey — £45

Tel 01423 502650   Map 6 C1   **R**
5 Montpellier Gardens Harrogate North Yorkshire HG1 2TF

Bustling fish restaurant on two floors with cramped tables. Simple dishes fare best on a menu that ranges from oysters, mussels and scallops to lobster (bisque, cocktail, cold with a salad, steamed with garlic butter, Thermidor and Drouant – cream and mustard sauce), sole, monkfish and the popular seafood pie. Lunch prices lower than dinner. *Seats 50. Parties 8. L 12-2.30 D 6.45-10.15. Closed Sun & 1 week Christmas. Access, Visa.*

HARROGATE — Hospitality Inn — 61% £96

Tel 01423 564601   Fax 01423 507508   Map 6 C1   **H**
West Park Prospect Place Harrogate North Yorkshire HG1 1LB

On the A61, a row of town-centre converted Georgian town houses, close to the parkland of The Stray. Children up to 14 free in parents' room. Busy conference and banqueting facilities for 150/100 and free parking for 40 cars. No dogs. Thistle & Mount Charlotte. *Rooms 71. Access, Amex, Diners, Visa.*

HARROGATE — Imperial Hotel — 65% £95

Tel 01423 565071   Fax 01423 500082   Map 6 C1   **H**
Prospect Place Harrogate North Yorkshire HG1 1LA

Overlooking the Stray in the centre of town the hotel looks out over flower-filled borders with balconied first-floor bedrooms at the front making the most of the view. Public areas are smart with white marble-tiled floors, the bar and lounge having buttoned, dark red-upholstered settees and armchairs. Bedrooms with traditional style darkwood furniture are neat and come with a range of useful amenities. Bathrooms are simple, with vinyl floors. *Rooms 85. Access, Amex, Diners, Visa.*

HARROGATE — The Majestic — 64% £122

Tel 01423 568972   Fax 01423 502283   Map 6 C1   **H**
Ripon Road Harrogate North Yorkshire HG1 2HU

Completed in 1900, the hotel stands in 12 acres on a hillside directly above the town's major conference venue. Public rooms are impressively spacious with much marble in evidence. Bedrooms are all recently refurbished. Good family facilities include holiday entertainment and bedrooms which can accommodate up to six people. *Rooms 156. Garden, indoor swimming pool, gym, squash, sauna, spa bath, solarium, tennis, golf driving net, beauty & hair salons, pool table, snooker. Access, Amex, Diners, Visa.*

Lodges are now listed by county in the reference section

| **HARROGATE** | **Miller's, The Bistro** | **£60** |

Tel 01423 530708 Map 6 C1 **R**
1 Montpelier Mews Harrogate North Yorkshire HG1 2TG

Simon Gueller (finalist in out Chef of the Year competition – see award pages) may have moved to Leeds (see Rascasse entry), but he still remains in control of this attractive little courtyard restaurant in the town centre. The menu remains largely unchanged with such dishes as risotto of peas and saffron, lobster and ginger spring rolls, Mediterranean fish soup and a parfait of chicken livers and foie gras with toasted brioche as starters. Main courses follow in the same innovative style with baked cod with a parsley crust and herb salad, fresh tuna salade niçoise, fillet of beef Bercy with fondant potato and caramelised shallots and chicken breast wrapped in Bayonne ham with peas and thyme being typical of an early summer menu. *Seats 40. Parties 14. L 12-2 D 7-10. Closed Sun, Mon, Bank Holidays. 10 days Christmas, 2 weeks August. Amex. Access, Diners, Visa.*

| **HARROGATE** | **Moat House** | **64%** | **£143** |

Tel 01423 500000 Fax 01423 524435 Map 6 C1 **H**
King's Road Harrogate North Yorkshire HG1 1XX

Large hotel conveniently sited right next door to the Exhibition and Conference centre and linked directly to it. Modern, redbrick building with lots of mirrored glass. Conference/banqueting facilities for 400/250. 24hr room service. Six rooms adapted for disabled guests. *Rooms 214. Access, Amex, Diners, Visa.*

Set menu prices may not always include service or wine.

| **HARROGATE** | **Old Swan Hotel** | **69%** | **£132** |

Tel 01423 500055 Fax 01423 501154 Map 6 C1 **HR**
Swan Road Harrogate North Yorkshire HG1 2SR

The present building dates back to 1840, and additional character to its exterior is provided by a luxuriant growth of Virginia creeper. The interior maintains much of its original Victorian ambience, though the lounge bar has a somewhat more modern appearance with its pastel pink walls, contrasting upholstery and mirror-fronted bar counter. Breakfasts are served in the splendid Wedgwood room with its skylight supported by pillars and elaborate plasterwork on the walls. Bedrooms overlooking the lawns and flower beds at the front are sunny and spacious – not that any rooms are small. This is the hotel where Agatha Christie stayed in 1926 when she disappeared from the public eye and aspiring private eyes return now for the Super Sleuth weekends held every few months. Children under 12 stay free in parents' room. *Rooms 136. Garden, croquet, tennis. Access, Amex, Diners, Visa.*

Library Restaurant £70

An elegant and delightfully traditional room offering standards a cut above many provincial hotels of this size. Appealing modern dishes are offered, such as confit of duck with spring onions and herbed pancakes, fillet of Cornish turbot with a vegetable casserole, and pork tenderloin with peperoni and black pudding served with cinnamon-glazed apples and a pool of mild chilis, basil and red peppers. For dessert you could choose an individual steamed toffee sponge with an orange sabayon or Grand Marnier crème brulée. Decent cheeses, and there's a modest and well-priced wine list – in fact two vintage champagnes really are good value. No smoking. *Seats 40. Parties 8. Private Room 20. L 12.30-2 D 7-10 (Sun to 9.30). Set L from £9.95 (Sun £11.95) Set D £18.*

| **HARROGATE** | **St George Swallow** | **63%** | **£105** |

Tel 01423 561431 Fax 01423 530037 Map 6 C1 **H**
1 Ripon Road Harrogate North Yorkshire HG1 2SY

Edwardian-styled interiors and good-sized bedrooms behind an ivy-clad facade. Extensive conference facilities (for up to 150 delegates) and a modern leisure club. Accommodation with breakfast is free for children under 16. *Rooms 93. Garden, indoor swimming pool, keep-fit equipment, sauna, spa bath, steam room, solarium, beauty therapy. Access, Amex, Diners, Visa.*

HARROGATE — Studley Hotel — 64% — £98

Tel 01423 560425   Fax 01423 530967   Map 6 C1   **H**
28 Swan Road Harrogate North Yorkshire HG1 2SE

A large, well-tended rockery at the front and just about sufficient car-parking at the rear
are two differing but good features of this homely town-centre hotel not far from the
main conference venues. There's a lively public bar on the ground floor and reception
and the residents' bar are on the first floor. Natural, polished lightwood is used to good
effect throughout. Bedrooms are cosy and attractively decorated. They have a lot of the
usual extras, from biscuits to satellite TV channels. Bathrooms are carpeted. Friendly,
helpful staff. Near the entrance to Valley Gardens. No children under 7. *Rooms 36.
Garden. Closed 2 days Christmas. Access, Amex, Diners, Visa.*

HARROGATE — Tannin Level — £35

Tel 01423 560595   Fax 01423 563077   Map 6 C1   **R**
5 Raglan Street Harrogate North Yorkshire HG1 1LE

Basement wine bar on the corner of Raglan Street and Princes Street with brick walls,
slate floors, old pews and assorted kitchen-style chairs, and green boards on which are
written the daily menu. This usually includes an interesting, well-balanced mix of dishes
of international provenance: rillettes of goose, fresh parmesan and Bayonne ham,
cassoulet, Cajun-style minute steak, warm salad of peppered chicken and cashew nuts,
sea bass with caper butter. The motto here is that "life's too short to drink poor wine",
confirmed by a marvellous and inexpensive world-wide list that offers terrific value,
especially the 'short' selection of some twenty wines from less than a tenner to £15. Not
much further up the scale are outstanding wines, ie an '89 Chablis Grand Cru, Vaudésir
at just over £25. One room is non-smoking. *Seats 75. Parties 12. Private Rooms 12/36.
L 12-2 D 6.30-10 (Sat to 10.30). Closed L Bank Holidays, all Sun, 25 & 26 Dec,
1 Jan. Access, Visa.*

HARTLEPOOL — Grand Hotel — 59% — £55

Tel 01429 266345   Fax 01429 265217   Map 5 E3   **H**
Swainson Street Hartlepool Cleveland TS24 8AA

A balconied Victorian ballroom tops the function/conference facilities at this handsome
redbrick hotel opposite the main shopping centre. There's an evening disco/jazz bar.
Rooms 47. Sun beds, young children's playroom, games room. Access, Amex, Diners, Visa.

HARVINGTON — The Mill — 65% — £85

Tel & Fax 01386 870688   Map 14 C1   **HR**
Anchor Lane Harvington nr Evesham Hereford & Worcester WR11 5NR

A Georgian mill, with lawns running down to a peaceful stretch of the River Avon,
converted into a hotel run in friendly, informal fashion by partners Simon and Jane
Greenhalgh and Richard and Susan Yeomans. Small, button-back armchairs in red or
green furnish the low-ceilinged lounge (where drinks are also served – there's no separate
bar) given character by a few old beams and some old bakery oven doors above the gas
coal fire. Artificial plants and pictures for sale complete the decor. Pleasant, well-kept
bedrooms all face the morning sun and overlook the river. Decent cooked breakfasts. Not
suitable for children under 8 except for infants in arms. No dogs. Signposted off the B439
opposite Harvington village. *Rooms 15. Garden, croquet, tennis, fishing, outdoor swimming
pool. Closed 1 week Christmas. Access, Amex, Diners, Visa.*

Restaurant — £60

The choice of main dishes dictates the price of a three-course dinner (the fixed-price
lunch is a limited selection of the evening dishes) in the pretty, pale-peach and grey
restaurant. Tuna with mustard sauce, guinea fowl with calvados and apple, and spicy
medallions of beef with port sauce typify the main-course choices. There is also a separate
vegetarian menu. Wines are listed twice – once by style (from dry to sweet for whites
and light to rich for reds) and again in ascending order of price, although over three-
quarters are under £20 so there is no need to take out a second mortgage and there's
a useful list of halves. A less formal lounge/terrace menu is served weekdays and most
Saturday lunchtimes. *Seats 35. Private Room 14. L 11.45-1.45 D 7-9. Set L £12.25/£13.95.
(Sun £11.75/£13.45) Set D from £20.*

HARWICH	**Pier at Harwich**	£70

Tel 01255 241212   Fax 01255 551922   Map 10 C3   **RR**
The Quay Harwich Essex CO12 3HH

Overlooking the harbour (and within a mile of the ferry port), the first-floor restaurant is just the place to enjoy good, fresh seafood which comes both plain (dressed crab, oysters, sole meunière, fish and chips, grilled sea bass) and sauced (monkfish with a herb butter sauce, poached salmon with hollandaise, and plaice fillets with a salmon mousseline on a dill and vermouth sauce). Steaks and a chicken dish also on the menu. Even allowing for the 10% service charge added to the prices on the wine list, it offers remarkable value (half a dozen champagnes under £30) and demonstrates that quality can be achieved without necessarily resorting to quantity. Merchants Lay & Wheeler also deserve a pat on the back! The Ha'penny Pier on the ground floor is a second, family-orientated restaurant also with a mainly fish menu. *Seats 70. Parties 30. Private Room 50. L 12-2 D 6-9.30. Set L £9.50/£12.50 (Sun £14.50) Set D £13.25/£16.50. Closed D 25 & 26 Dec. Access, Amex, Diners, Visa.*

Rooms   £63

The third-floor accommodation comprises six bedrooms of varying standards, all with a nautical theme, some with views down the estuary. All have en-suite bathrooms and televisions.

HASLEMERE	**Fleur de Sel** ★ NEW	£70

Tel 01428 651462   Fax 01428 661568   Map 11 A6   **R**
23-27 Lower Street Haslemere Surrey GU27 2NY

To take over a restaurant with the reputation of *Morel's* (the restaurant's former name) is no easy task, but Michel and Bernadette Perraud are just the couple to carry it off, with his expertise with Michel Roux at the *Waterside Inn* and Bernadette's front-of-house skills honed at *La Tante Claire*. The change took place just after our last edition was published so they are already well settled in, despite our 'new' tag, and attracting new customers, as well as satisfying the old, with classic French cooking that concentrates on time-tested combinations rather than gimmickry. That prices are rather kinder than formerly is a distinct bonus. Rather than being individually priced the à la carte offers 2 courses for £21 and three for £26. An additional lunch menu comes at £9.50 and £12.50 for two and three courses respectively. Fish terrine with herbs and a piquant beurre blanc, millefeuille of wild mushrooms in a port sauce, fillet of turbot filled with fish mousse and a Noilly sauce, crisply roasted Gressingham duck with honey and ginger, best end of lamb with a sauce borderlaise flavoured with juniper and noisettes of venison with chestnuts and savoy cabbage are typical of dishes that are impeccably prepared and attractively presented. For dessert try an individually cooked, flat apple tart served with ice cream flavoured with real vanilla or crème brulée with prunes and armagnac. Decor remains as before with restful pale cream and blue colour scheme, a few exposed beams lending a cottagey feel and lots of fresh flowers adding the finishing touch. Situated on a raised pavement between the High Street and the station it's not an easy restaurant to find but if you park in the main town car park (entrance off the High Street) you'll be quite close. Best to ask for directions. Shortish French-only wine list with reasonable half bottle selection. *Seats 50. Parties 10. L 12-2 D 7-10. Set L £9.50/£12.50 Set D £21/£26. Closed L Sat, D Sun, all Mon, 2 weeks Summer.*

HASLEMERE	**Lythe Hill Hotel** 71%	£111

Tel 01428 651251   Fax 01428 644131   Map 11 A6   **H**
Petworth Road Haslemere Surrey GU27 3BQ

A beautiful listed building with parts dating back to 1475. The location is an attractive one too – east of the town on the B2131 in 20 acres of grounds which include lakes, well-tended lawns and woods which in spring are awash with bluebells. Elegant, relaxing lounges and a convivial cocktail bar are complemented by characterful, well-equipped bedrooms. Decor throughout is chintzy with quality furnishings and a mix of antiques and good-quality reproduction furniture. Three bedrooms are the splendid original Tudor house, one having a 1614 four-poster bed. Bathrooms are excellent, all with good toiletries. To accompany there is 24hr room service and beds are turned down at night. Conference/banqueting facilities for 60/130. *Rooms 40. Garden, croquet, tennis, fishing, games room. Access, Amex, Visa.*

HASTINGS   Cinque Ports Hotel Periquito   66%   £59

Tel 01424 439222   Fax 01424 437277   Map 11 C6   **H**
Summerfields Bohemia Road Hastings East Sussex TN34 1ET

Modern low-rise American-style hotel standing on the A21 leading into town. Bright, spacious public areas are furnished with good-quality period-style settees and armchairs. There are seven purpose-built conference rooms for up to 300 delegates. Guests may swim free of charge at nearby Hastings Leisure Centre. Children up to 14 stay free in parents' room. *Rooms 40. Access, Amex, Diners, Visa.*

HASTINGS   Röser's   ★   £65

Tel 01424 712218   Map 11 C6   **R**
64 Eversfield Place St Leonards-on-Sea nr Hastings East Sussex TN37 6DB

A pretty bow-windowed restaurant with ruffled Dutch blinds has a welcoming, cosy decor more in keeping with that of a Bavarian country inn than that of a place on Hasting's seafront. Opened in 1984 the restaurant is the best in East Sussex and Gerald Röser maintains his premier position by adhering to very high standards in the kitchen. The menu, always very varied, begins with dishes such as wild boar sausages with wild marjoram and port sauce, a ragout of shellfish with a chive sauce and truffle or cream of Jerusalem artichoke soup with a crisp julienne of vegetables. Main courses could include roast scallops with a saffron sauce, fillet of Scottish beef with a red wine sauce and parsnip crisps, grilled sea bass with coriander seeds, basil and tomato or chargrilled venison saddle fillets with a bean and savoury purée and juniper butter. A proper veal stock forms the base of many of the sauces and everything from the choice of breads to the selection of sorbets is home-made. Among the puds, Röser's chocolate mousse, made with the finest Belgian chocolate, and an apple millefeuille have become fixtures by popular demand and there are cheeses (mostly local) served with fresh fruit and nuts. Note that the prices on the wine list are inclusive so a *marque* champagne under £30 really is good value. The list is terrific, almost catholic, with the best on offer – top menus, top growers, top of the tree! *Seats 30. Parties 8. Private Room 30. L 12-2 D 7-10. Closed L Sat, all Sun & Mon, Bank Holidays, 2 weeks Jan, 2 weeks end Aug. Set L £14.95/£16.95 Set D £17.95/£19.95. Access, Amex, Diners, Visa.*

HASTINGS   Royal Victoria Hotel   70%   £75

Tel 01424 445544   Fax 01424 721995   Map 11 C6   **H**
The Marina St Leonards-on-Sea nr Hastings East Sussex TN38 0BD

The seafront Royal Victoria retains the grand style of architecture that graced the Victorian age. An elegant marble staircase sweeps up from the foyer and in the first-floor piano lounge-cum-bar there are pillars, arches and ornate plaster mouldings, plus sea views. All the bedrooms are designated as suites, with either a separate sitting room or a large sitting area. Children up to 16 free in parents' room. Conferences/banquets for up to 150/120. *Rooms 50. Access, Amex, Diners, Visa.*

HATCH BEAUCHAMP   Farthings Hotel   70%   £65

Tel 01823 480664   Map 13 E2   **H**
Hatch Beauchamp nr Taunton Somerset TA3 6SG

On the edge of the rolling Blackdown Hills just south of Taunton, and a few minutes from Junction 25 of the M5, lies the pretty village of Hatch Beauchamp and the equally pretty Farthings Hotel. Bedrooms with a well co-ordinated, traditional decor are spacious and well-equipped. There are neat bathrooms too. Public rooms are smart and quietly inviting. The attractive, well-laid lawns are the perfect setting for a leisurely afternoon tea when the weather is favourable. Banqueting and conference facilities for 40/25. *Rooms 8. Garden, croquet. Closed 2 weeks Jan. Access, Diners, Visa.*

Consult the blue pages for summary tables and lists of recommended establishments.

HATFIELD HEATH   Down Hall   71%   £134

Tel 01279 731441   Fax 01279 730416   Map 11 B4   **H**
Hatfield Heath nr Bishops Stortford Hertfordshire CM22 7AS

Down Hall is a large Italianate mansion set in 100 acres of parkland with landscaped gardens. The handsome exterior is matched in the day rooms; the focal point is the main lounge with its Italian stone fireplace, huge crystal chandeliers and furniture ornate with ormolu. Bedrooms are divided between the main house and the sympathetically designed west wing, the latter with larger and more luxurious bathrooms. Well geared up for conferences of up to 290. *Rooms 103. Garden, croquet, putting, indoor swimming pool, sauna, spa bath, tennis, snooker, gift shop. Access, Amex, Diners, Visa.*

HATHERLEIGH   George Hotel   £70

Tel 01837 810454   Fax 01837 810901   Map 13 D2   **I**
Market Street Hatherleigh nr Okehampton Devon EX20 3JN

When a building is nearly 600 years old it's bound to have a bit of history and the George Hotel has been by turns a sanctuary for monks, brew-house, coaching inn and law court. Today, under its thatched roof, it offers a mellow old bar (reached via a cobbled courtyard) with ancient settles and a convivial atmosphere and clean, simple bedrooms featuring old timbers and antiqueish furniture. Just two are not en suite. All have direct-dial phones and TVs. *Rooms 11. Garden, outdoor swimming pool, snooker. Access, Amex, Visa.*

HATHERSAGE   Hathersage Inn   £62

Tel 01433 650259   Fax 01433 651199   Map 6 C2   **I**
Hathersage Derbyshire S30 1BB

From the family who have presided here for over 20 years, David Bowie is the current host at this ivy-clad, stone-built inn standing by Hathersage's steep main street. At the front, the Cricketers Bar is full of local memorabilia while the neatly kept bedrooms are at the back of the building. Creature comforts include a drinks tray and fresh fruit. There are two four-poster honeymoon suites. Children are not encouraged. Many special occasion breaks – it's a good base for exploring the Peak District. *Rooms 15. Access, Amex, Diners, Visa.*

HAVANT   Bear Hotel   59%   £60

Tel 01705 486501   Fax 01705 470551   Map 15 D4   **H**
East Street Havant Hampshire PO9 1AA

Historic town-centre coaching inn with modest accommodation and good parking. Conference facilities for up to 120, banqueting up to 100. Children up to 12 free in parents' room. No dogs. Owned by Countryside Inns & Hotels. *Rooms 42. Access, Amex, Diners, Visa.*

HAVANT   Forte Posthouse   62%   £72

Tel 01705 465011   Fax 01705 466468   Map 15 D4   **H**
Northney Road Hayling Island Havant Hampshire PO11 0NQ

Practical modern hotel on the north shore of Hayling Island. Two bars, health and fitness club, free car park, conferences for up to 140. *Rooms 92. Indoor swimming pool, gym, sauna, spa bath, solarium. Access, Amex, Diners, Visa.*

HAWKCHURCH   Fairwater Head Hotel   65%   £104

Tel 01297 678349   Map 13 E2   **H**
Hawkchurch nr Axminster Devon EX13 5TX

The garden and the views over the Axe valley are major attractions at the Austin and Lowe families' peaceful Edwardian hotel, which numbers many loyal returnees among its guests. Housekeeping is diligent in both the main-house bedrooms and those in the wing; attention to detail includes fresh Devon milk for the tea and coffee-making facilities. The garden wing is not connected to the house but offers the most up-to-date rooms, with compact bathrooms and views over the gardens. *Rooms 21. Garden, croquet, keep-fit equipment, children's playground, snooker. Closed Jan & Feb. Access, Amex, Diners, Visa.*

Set menu prices may not always include service or wine.

HAWKHURST   Tudor Court   61%   £78

Tel 01580 752312   Fax 01580 753966   Map 11 C6   **H**
Rye Road Hawkhurst Cranbrook Kent TN18 5DA

On the Rye road (A268) about a mile from Hawkhurst half way between Tunbridge
Wells and the coast, this well-kept redbrick hotel has equally spruce gardens. Comfortably
appointed bedrooms include some with four-posters. Children up to 16 free in parents'
room. There's a conference suite and two syndicate rooms, catering for up to 70 delegates.
Rooms 18. Garden, croquet, tennis, children's play area. Access, Amex, Diners, Visa.

HAWORTH   Weavers   £50

Tel 01535 643822   Map 6 C1   **RR**
15 West Lane Haworth nr Bradford West Yorkshire BD22 8DU

Follow signs for the Bronte Parsonage Museum (and use its car park – free after 6pm) to
find a characterful restaurant in a row of old weaver's cottages. There's a light touch in
the kitchen from chef-proprietors Colin and Jane Rushworth and mainly local produce is
used. Comforting soups usually feature among starters like steamed mussels with garlic
butter and gruyére cheese and smoked Ribblesdale cheese wrapped in air-dried ham
served with a warm potato salad; roast salmon with shredded vegetables and a butter
sauce; traditional wild rabbit pie and pan-fried calf's liver with bubble and squeak and
a gin and lime sauce are among the main courses. Crispy roast breast of Gressingham
duck served on a rhubarb sauce is considered a speciality, along with roast fillet of pork
with sage stuffing, 'cracklin', and cider apple gravy. Afters include homely favourites.
'Sampler' menu served 6.45-7.15 Tue-Fri and Sunday lunch. Cheerful service completes
the satisfying picture. *Seats 60. Parties 16. L (Sun Oct-Easter only) 12-2 D 7-9.*
Closed Sun (except L in winter, Mon, last 2 weeks July, 2 weeks after Boxing Day.
Set meals £9.95/£11.95. Access, Amex, Diners, Visa.

Rooms   £70
Four bedrooms, each with en-suite bathroom, combine antique pieces with modern
touches like satellite TV, direct-dial phone and trouser press. All have views over the
Parsonage and village to the moors beyond. No dogs. Closed after Sunday lunch to
Tuesday afternoon.

HAYDOCK   Haydock Forte Posthouse   65%   £64

Tel 01942 717878   Fax 01942 718419   Map 6 B2   **H**
Lodge Lane Newton-le-Willows Haydock Merseyside WA12 0JG

Smart, modern and well-organised hotel, by Junction 23 of the M6, next to Haydock
racecourse. 24 of the bedrooms are of the better Executive standard. All rooms have
mini-bars and new TVs with in-house movies. Health club; conference/banqueting
facilities for up to 200. Children up to 18 stay free in parents' room. *Rooms 136.*
Garden, indoor swimming pool, gym, sauna, spa bath, solarium. Access, Amex, Diners, Visa.

HAYDOCK   Haydock Thistle   67%   £107

Tel 01942 272000   Fax 01942 711092   Map 6 B2   **H**
Penny Lane Haydock St Helens Merseyside WA11 9SG

Neo-Georgian, low-rise lodge by Junction 23 of the M6 with spacious lounge and
bedrooms – half the rooms are designated non-smoking. Leisure spa and conference
facilities for up to 300. Children up to 16 stay free in parents' room.
Rooms 139. Garden, indoor swimming pool, gym, sauna, steam room, spa bath, solarium,
beauty salon, games room, snooker. Access, Amex, Diners, Visa.

We welcome bona fide complaints and recommendations on the
tear-out pages at the back of the book for readers' comments.
They are followed up by our professional team.

HAYFIELD   Bridge End Restaurant   £65

Tel 01663 747321   Fax 01663 742121   Map 6 C2   **RR**
7 Church Street Hayfield Derbyshire SK12 5JE

Bridge End is in the middle of Hayfield, opposite the church, with the River Sett running through the village. The attractive 19th-century stone building is a very English canvas on which chef Jonathan Holmes paints an international picture. Menus change regularly and you might be offered skate wings sautéed with nut oil, new potatoes and celeriac, confit of chicken, cassoulet of wild rabbit, or Jerusalem artichoke mousse. Desserts are equally intense: sweetened mascarpone with raspberries, strawberries, passion fruit and kirsch or a Grand Marnier and orange soufflé. The 'unabridged' is a selection of all the desserts in miniature, and there's a separate cheese menu with several unusual farmhouse varieties, our regional winner of British Cheeseboard of the Year. There's a good-value wine list with many wines under and around £15. House policy of reduced mark-ups on fine wines – other restaurants note! *Seats 50. Parties 12. Private Room 20. L Sun only 12-2.30 D 7-10. Closed D Sun, all Mon, 1st week Jan. Set Sun L £13. Access, Amex, Diners, Visa.*

Rooms   £45

Four en-suite bedrooms in attractive cottage style with pine furnishings and bedsteads have a secure separate entrance. 5% dinner discount for residents. Children up to 5 stay free in parents' room. *Closed 1st week Jan.*

HAYTOR   Bel Alp House   72%   £138

Tel 01364 661217   Fax 01364 661292   Map 13 D3   **H**
Haytor nr Bovey Tracey Devon TQ13 9XX

In a hillside location commanding splendid views over the rolling Devonshire countryside, this fine Edwardian house and its gardens have been much improved by Roger and Sarah Curnock since they arrived in 1983. Peace and quiet reign in the antique-furnished day rooms, amply supplied with armchairs, sofas and a host of pot plants. The atmosphere is more that of being a house guest in a large family home than of staying in a hotel. Light, airy bedrooms have plain walls, matching floral fabrics, more armchairs and pot plants, and carpeted bathrooms (two with the original Edwardian tubs on marble plinths) with quality toiletries. Housekeeping and repair are immaculate throughout. Smoking discouraged. The hotel lies two and a half miles west of Bovey Tracey off the B3387 before Haytor. *Rooms 9. Garden, croquet, games room, snooker. Closed Dec-Feb. Access, Visa.*

Consult the blue pages for summary tables and lists of recommended establishments.

HEATHROW AIRPORT   Excelsior Hotel   71%   £117

Tel 0181-759 6611   Fax 0181-759 3421   Map 15 E2   **H**
Bath Road West Drayton Middlesex UB7 0DU

A huge, modern hotel near the airport terminals with 248 Executive rooms, 16 suites, 100 non-smoking rooms and two equipped for wheelchair-bound guests. A spacious, marble-floored foyer sets the tone for the day rooms, which include two bars, one in plush and mahogany, and two restaurants. Children up to 14 free in parents' room. Conference/banqueting facilities for 750. Forte. *Rooms 827. Indoor swimming pool, sauna, spa bath, solarium, beauty & hair salons, flower shop, coffee shop (6.15am-midnight). Access, Amex, Diners, Visa.*

HEATHROW AIRPORT   Forte Crest   68%   £117

Tel 0181-759 2323   Fax 0181-897 8659   Map 15 E2   **H**
Sipson Road West Drayton Middlesex UB7 0JU

Familiar landmark by the M4 turn-off to Heathrow, ten storeys high and dating from the mid-70s. Public areas include an informal American-style bar with juke box and pool table, and a traditional cocktail bar. Conference facilities for up to 200. *Rooms 572. Garden. Access, Amex, Diners, Visa.*

HEATHROW AIRPORT   Forte Posthouse (Ariel)   65%   £75

Tel 0181-759 2552 Fax 0181-564 9265   Map 15 E2   **H**
Bath Road Hayes Middlesex UB3 5AJ

Bedrooms at this long-established airport hotel have recently been equipped with mini-bars and 'smart' TVs. Secure parking £5 per day. **Rooms 180.** *Access, Amex, Diners, Visa.*

HEATHROW AIRPORT   Heathrow Hilton   74%   £179

Tel 0181-759 7755 Fax 0181-759 7579   Map 15 E2   **HR**
Terminal 4 Heathrow Airport Hounslow Middlesex TW6 3AF

An ultra-modern hotel with many striking features, notably the massive atrium covering the foyer and the major public areas. Central lifts split the ground floor – the entrance, foyer-lounge and reception area, to one side; the brasserie, Oscar's (the American-style restaurant), and an open-plan bar and lounge to the other. Adequately sized bedrooms have effective double-glazing, and provide a tranquil escape from the hustle of an international airport. They also all have multi-channel TV which, thanks to the miracles of modern technology, keeps one informed of airport activities and the state of one's bill at the touch of a button. Three rooms are specially designed for disabled guests. A well-equipped gym provides excellent facilities for the excesses suffered by the modern traveller. A covered walkway gives direct access to Terminal 4. There are banqueting/conference facilities for 240/300. Valet parking. **Rooms 400.**
Indoor swimming pool, gym, sauna, steam room, solarium, beauty & hair salon, news kiosk, coffee shop (24hrs). Access, Amex, Diners, Visa.

Zen Oriental   £60

This modern dining-room avoids the hubbub generated by airport life. Far Eastern, rather than strictly Chinese, most of the dishes will be recognisable to those familiar with the Zen concept. The table d'hote menu may not be automatically produced, but can be a worthwhile alternative, as à la carte prices can be steep if you're not prudent. Three hours' free parking is available, for customers, in the main car park at the front of the hotel. **Seats** 70. L 12-3 D 6-10.30. Closed L Sat, 26 Dec, 1 Jan. Set L £12.50 Set D £23.50 & £28.

HEATHROW AIRPORT   Holiday Inn Crowne Plaza   74%   £148

Tel 01895 445555 Fax 01895 445122   Map 15 E2   **H**
Stockley Road West Drayton Middlesex UB7 9NA

Holiday Inns' top-of-the-range Crowne Plaza brand offering higher levels of service – 24hr table service in the lounge/bar, extensive room service with a good range of hot meals available throughout the night, a turn-down service in the evenings, valet parking – and generally more comfort than one might expect in a more standard Holiday Inn. Spacious bedrooms, with a pleasing maroon and dark blue colour scheme, have proper armchairs and breakfast table plus plenty of work space – even more in the Business Study rooms that have a more masculine black and grey decor; half the rooms are non-smoking. Two rooms are specially designed for disabled guests. Poly-cotton bedding and shortish baths (but with good showers above them) in otherwise well-appointed bathrooms which include face cloths and towelling robes. Most luxurious of the bedrooms are the Directors and Presidential suites. Under-19s are accommodated free in their parents' room. There's a large swimming pool in the leisure centre, where there are also facilities for disabled guests and mothers with babies. Conference/banqueting facilities for up to 200/150; staffed business centre. Just north of the M4. **Rooms 374.** *Golf (9), indoor swimming pool, spa bath, gym, sauna, solarium, steam room, beauty salon, coffee shop (24hrs), news kiosk. Access, Amex, Diners, Visa.*

HEATHROW AIRPORT   Jarvis International   67%   £85

Tel 0181-897 2121 Fax 0181-897 7014   Map 15 E2   **H**
Bath Road Cranford Middlesex TW5 9QE

On the A4 two miles from Heathrow, a hotel that offers practical accommodation and state-of-the-art conference facilities for up to 120. Plenty of free parking. **Rooms 56.** *Access, Amex, Diners, Visa.*

Set menu prices may not always include service or wine.

HEATHROW AIRPORT   Novotel   62%   £88

Tel 01895 431431   Fax 01895 431221   Map 15 E2   **H**
Cherry Lane West Drayton Heathrow Airport Middlesex UB7 9HB

With Novotel's familiar red-and-yellow-brick construction and blue paintwork the hotel is easy to spot just to the north of junction 4 of the M4. Attractive atrium public areas and practical if rather plain bedrooms. Courtesy bus to airport (terminals 1-3 only). *Rooms 178. Patio, indoor swimming pool, keep-fit equipment, coffee shop (6am-midnight). Access, Amex, Diners, Visa.*

HEATHROW AIRPORT   Park Hotel   61%   £113

Tel 0181-759 2400   Fax 0181-759 5278   Map 15 E2   **H**
Bath Road Longford West Drayton Middlesex UB7 0EQ

Triple-glazing and air-conditioning in all the bedrooms are big pluses at a low-rise hotel located between the A4 and the airport's runways. Banqueting for up to 1000. Free use of Morley's Health Club across the road. *Rooms 306. Kiosk, coffee shop (10.30am-11.30pm). Access, Amex, Diners, Visa.*

HEATHROW AIRPORT   Radisson Edwardian   76%   £210

Tel 0181-759 6311   Fax 0181-759 4559   Map 15 E2   **H**
Bath Road Hayes Middlesex UB3 5AW

Behind its glass and marble facade the Edwardian International offers abundant style, comfort, service and modern amenities five minutes from the airport. Public areas include a vast foyer with carpet-strewn pink marble floor, cocktail bar-cum-lounge with deep sofas in a variety of rich fabrics and polo-themed bar sporting real saddles in place of bar stools. Bedrooms, though not large, are visually appealing with decoratively painted satinwood furniture and stylishly colourful matching bedcovers and curtains. There are 17 luxurious suites with marble-lined bathrooms, spa baths, separate impulse showers and twin washbasins with gold fittings; some rooms have four-posters. 150 rooms are reserved for non-smokers. An extensive room service menu is available 24hrs a day. Conferences are an important part of the business – 550 delegates in the largest suite – and there's a fully equipped business centre. Ample parking £5 per day. *Rooms 459. Indoor swimming pool, gym, sauna, spa bath, solarium, beauty & hair salon, news kiosk, brasserie (6am-11pm). Access, Amex, Diners, Visa.*

HEATHROW AIRPORT   Ramada Hotel Heathrow   66%   £135

Tel 0181-897 6363   Fax 0181-897 1113   Map 15 E2   **H**
Bath Road Hounslow Middlesex TW6 2AQ

The £3 million refurbishment during 1994 concentrated on public areas, bar and restaurant, while the programme during 1995 emphasised the bedrooms and leisure facilities, all due for completion by the end of 1995. Bedrooms are well equipped with every modern amenity (including adjustable air-conditioning); likewise bathrooms have a condensation-free mirror and TV loudspeaker. Extensive 24hr room service and high-tech conference facilities for up to 500 theatre-style. There's a courtesy coach to the terminals. *Rooms 638. Indoor swimming pool, gym, sauna, solarium, beauty & hair salons, kiosk, coffee shop (8am-1am). Access, Amex, Visa.*

HEATHROW AIRPORT   Sheraton Heathrow   72%   £195

Tel 0181-759 2424   Fax 0181-759 2091   Map 15 E2   **H**
Colnbrook bypass West Drayton Middlesex UB7 0HJ

Formerly one of the uglier airport hotels with its brutalist concrete exterior, this modern, low-rise hotel on the A4 to the west of the airport tunnel entrance has been totally transformed with a brand new rendered facade in almost classical style, complete with an imposing porte-cochère, making it now one of the most attractive. Public areas have also undergone a transformation with new marble-floored lobby and imaginatively lit ceiling to the lounge area (where the comfortable red leather sofas remain) separated from the all-day restaurant by a stone balustrade. Three nights a week there is live entertainment in this area. Practical, good-quality bedrooms remain as before except for the addition of three full suites, of which the Presidential suite is the most impressive. All rooms have multi-channel TVs with flight information and quick check-out facility. Pristine bathrooms all have marble vanity units and good thermostatically controlled showers over the tub. 24hr room service with a couple of hot items available overnight. Children up to 17 stay free in parents' room. *Rooms 431. Garden, courtesy bus to airport. Access, Amex, Diners, Visa.*

HEATHROW AIRPORT   Sheraton Skyline   73%   £204

Tel 0181-759 2535 Fax 0181-750 9150   Map 15 E2   **H**
Bath Road Hayes Middlesex UB3 5BP

The focal point of this hotel on the A4 is the most unusual Patio Caribe, a large indoor tropical garden complete with palm trees, swimming pool, bar and music. Rooms range from standard to Executive categories, but all are right up-to-the-minute, with air-conditioning, computer links, sprinklers and smoke detector system (20% of the rooms are designated no-smoking). Conference and banqueting facilities for up to 500. Children stay free in family room. Parking £3 per day. *Rooms 353. Indoor swimming pool, gym, florist, gift shop, coffee shop (6am-1am). Access, Amex, Diners, Visa.*

HELFORD   Riverside   £80

Tel 01326 231443 Fax 01326 231103   Map 12 B4   **R**
Helford nr Helston Cornwall TR12 6JU

In an idyllic setting by a wooded tidal creek, the Riverside is a pretty, cottagey restaurant with rooms run in welcoming style by Edward and Susie Darrell. The kitchen is at the heart of the enterprise, and Susie makes fine use of local produce, particularly seafood, for her four-course dinner menus. Scallop, lobster and clam pancake with a lobster sauce or layered mozzarella and plum tomatoes with a balsamic vinegar dressing might feature among the starters, followed by a choice of about three fish main courses (monkfish wrapped in Parma ham on a bed of creamed leeks) and two meat. Next come English and French cheeses, then perhaps bread-and-butter pudding or an iced mango parfait with a passion fruit syrup. A spectacularly good wine list, fully deserving of the South-West regional award, offers a huge array of half bottles and a comprehensive selection from the New World, including well over a dozen from South Africa. Very knowledgeable tasting notes, keen prices. *Seats 32. Parties 6. D only 7.30-9. Closed end Oct-end Mar. Set D £30. No credit cards.*

HELLAND BRIDGE   Tredethy Country Hotel   56%   £60

Tel 01208 841262 Fax 01208 841707   Map 12 B3   **H**
Helland Bridge Bodmin Cornwall PL30 4QS

Take the A389 from Bodmin, then the B3266 to Camelford to find this grey-stone country house, standing in a tranquil setting of nine wooded acres. Best bedrooms are in the light and sunny front half. No dogs. *Rooms 11. Garden, outdoor swimming pool, solarium. Access, Amex, Diners, Visa.*

HELMSLEY   Black Swan   69%   £120

Tel 01439 770466 Fax 01439 770174   Map 5 E4   **H**
Market Place Helmsley North Yorkshire YO6 5BJ

Plenty of history at the Black Swan – it has been an Elizabethan coaching inn, a Tudor rectory, a Georgian private residence; if anything it has come full circle, offering hospitality to travellers in the second Elizabethan era. Day rooms, including several lounges, have heavy timbers, low beamed ceilings and cottagey decor. Residents have their own bar as well as the public bar, both being small, cosy and welcoming. Bedrooms are individually decorated and 12 are designated non-smoking; the restaurant is another smokeless zone. Children under 16 stay free in parents' room (5-16s meals charged as taken). Forte. *Rooms 44. Garden. Access, Amex, Diners, Visa.*

HELMSLEY   Feversham Arms   66%   £70

Tel 01439 770766 Fax 01439 770346   Map 5 E4   **H**
1 High Street Helmsley North Yorkshire YO6 5AG

Rebuilt in 1855 by the Earl of Feversham, the hotel combines modern comforts with traditional charm, and is a good base for touring the Yorkshire Moors and Dales. Bedrooms, all centrally heated, include some with four-posters, and a couple of rooms on the ground floor are suitable for less mobile guests. Day rooms offer a choice of lounge and bars. All children are now accepted, and up to 15 stay free in parents' room. *Rooms 18. Garden, tennis, outdoor swimming pool. Access, Amex, Diners, Visa.*

HEMEL HEMPSTEAD   Boxmoor Lodge Hotel   57%   £65

Tel 01442 230770   Fax 01442 252230   Map 15 E2   **H**
London Road Hemel Hempstead Hertfordshire HP1 2RA

The Lodge was originally the Gatehouse of Boxmoor House, which dates back to the early 17th century. It opened as a hotel in 1989, and accommodation largely comprises chalet-style bedrooms and suites. Bedrooms are smart, spacious and well maintained, and offer the usual extras like remote TV, trouser press, hairdryer and mineral water. Tariff reductions at weekends when there's a good-value family room. 10 are reserved for non-smokers, one for the disabled. The main house has a tiny bar-cum-reception area with a cosy beamed lounge down two steps. *Rooms 18. Garden. Access, Amex, Diners, Visa.*

Set menu prices may not always include service or wine.

HEMEL HEMPSTEAD   Forte Posthouse   62%   £75

Tel 01442 251122   Fax 01442 211812   Map 15 E2   **H**
Breakspear Way Hemel Hempstead Hertfordshire HP2 4UA

On the A414 near the M1 (J8), one of the newer Posthouses has Canadian log cabin-themed public areas and a good leisure centre. Children up to 16 free when sharing parents' room. *Rooms 146. Terrace, indoor swimming pool, gym, spa bath, sauna, steam room, solarium, beauty salon, hair salon. Access, Amex, Diners, Visa.*

HENLEY-ON-THAMES   Red Lion   62%   £112

Tel 01491 572161   Fax 01491 410039   Map 15 D2   **H**
Hart Street Henley-on-Thames Oxfordshire RG9 2AR

A classic redbrick wisteria-clad hotel by the finishing post of the Henley Royal Regatta rowing course, right by the bridge. Antique pine panelling is a feature in some of the day rooms, and in the bar flagstones and a log fire produce a rustic air. Two small banqueting/conference suites cater for up to 70. Bedrooms combine period appeal with modern comfort. Families welcome. *Rooms 26. Access, Amex, Visa.*

HEREFORD   County Hotel   63%   £84

Tel 01432 354301   Fax 01432 275114   Map 14 A1   **H**
Belmont Road Hereford Hereford & Worcester HR2 7BP

Formerly a Moat House, the hotel is a mile and a half from the city centre on the Abergavenny road. Accommodation is divided between discreet motel-style units and a spacious new extension. Two family rooms, conference facilities for up to 300. *Rooms 60. Garden. Access, Amex, Diners, Visa.*

HERNE BAY   L'Escargot   £55

Tel 01227 372876   Map 11 C5   **R**
22 High Street Herne Bay Kent CT6 5LH

Here since 1984, Alain and Joyce Bessemoulin are charming hosts and their friendly, informal restaurant has an uncomplicated appeal. Alain cooks in a competent and unfussy fashion using good fresh ingredients in largely classic French dishes on a menu supplemented by daily blackboard specials. Deep-fried camembert with gooseberry sauce, country-style paté or lobster bisque could be your starter, followed by fish of the day (perhaps salmon with hollandaise), breast of chicken in a light cream sauce of shallots and asparagus, carré d'agneau with rosemary or pork normande. *Seats 40. Parties 24. L 12.30-2 D 7-9.30. Closed L Sat & Mon, all Thur in winter, 1 week Jan, 1 week Jun, 1 week Sep. Set L £7.80 Set D £13.95. Access, Visa.*

We publish annually, so make sure you use the current edition
— it's well worth it!

HERSHAM   The Dining Room   £55

Tel 01932 231686   Map 15 E2   **R**
10 Queens Road The Village Green Hersham Surrey KT12 5LS

Scrubbed pine tables, pews and Laura Ashley wallpaper give a country feel to the five small dining-rooms (one for non-smokers) of this informal restaurant created from two old cottages. The English menu ranges from traditional – steak and kidney pudding, duck liver paté with Cumberland sauce, toad-in-the-hole and beef and ale pie – to more unusual offerings like grilled Scottish salmon steak with lime and saffron butter and chicken breast with an orange sauce. Good selection of classic English puddings include steamed Spotted Dick with custard, Dorset apple cake with rum butter and sticky toffee pudding with hot caramel sauce. Cooking is uncomplicated and portions are generous. *Seats 90. Parties 12. Private Room 30. L 12-2 (Sun to 2.30) D 7-10.30 (Sat from 6.30). Set L £12.75 (Sun £11/£12.75) Set D £12.75. Closed L Sat, D Sun, Bank Holidays & 1 week Christmas. Access, Amex, Visa.*

HERSTMONCEUX   Sundial Restaurant   £90

Tel 01323 832217   Map 11 B6   **R**
Gardner Street Herstmonceux East Sussex BN27 4LA

The Bertolis describe the Sundial as a 17th-century cottage restaurant offering Continental cuisine – mostly French but, not surprisingly, with plenty of Italian overtones. Imaginative food is served in an informal atmosphere – the terrace is particularly popular in summer. From a classic menu choose quenelles de brochet or moules marinière, roast crispy duckling with strawberry sauce or breast of pheasant in a calvados sauce, and finish with desserts or cheese from the central display. Comprehensive French selection including many classics on the wine list with a token offering from Italy – nothing else! Parking for about 20 cars. *Seats 55. Parties 20. Private Room 60. L 12-2 (Sun to 2.30) D 7-9.30 (Sat to 10). Closed D Sun, all Mon, 2/3 weeks Aug/Sep, Xmas-mid Jan. Set L £15.50 (Sun £17.50/£22.50) Set D £24.50/£35. Access, Amex, Diners, Visa.*

HERTINGFORDBURY   White Horse Hotel   63%   £107

Tel 01992 586791   Fax 01992 550809   Map 15 F2   **H**
Hertingfordbury Road Hertingfordbury Hertfordshire SG14 2LB

Once a coaching inn on the Cambridge-Reading run, now a mix of Georgian facade, earlier interiors and modern bedroom blocks. Children up to 16 stay free in parents' room. Small banquets/conferences (25/40) only. Forte. *Rooms 42. Garden. Access, Amex, Diners, Visa.*

HETHERSETT   Park Farm Hotel   64%   £70

Tel 01603 810264   Fax 01603 812104   Map 10 C2   **H**
Hethersett nr Norwich Norfolk NR9 3DL

Five miles south of Norwich, the Gowing family's hotel has expanded considerably over the years from the original Georgian farmhouse. Bedrooms in various styles (Executives have four-posters and whirlpool baths) are arranged around the landscaped gardens, some in the old buildings, others in a renovated Norfolk barn. 22 of the rooms are designated non-smoking. Also in outbuildings are a well-equipped leisure complex and the six conference rooms, the largest with a capacity of 120. There's a helipad and light aircraft landing strip in the grounds. *Rooms 38. Garden, croquet, tennis, putting, indoor swimming pool, gym, sauna, spa bath, steam room, solarium, beauty & hair salon, games room, snooker. Access, Amex, Diners, Visa.*

HETTON   Angel Inn   £70

Tel 01756 730263   Fax 01756 730363   Map 6 C1   **R**
Hetton nr Skipton North Yorkshire BD23 6LT

To find the Angel, take the B6265 from Skipton to Grassington, and turn left at Rylestone for Hetton. Menus are fixed price but offer plenty of choice from an eclectic mix of cooking backgrounds. Starters might be queen scallops grilled with gruyère and garlic, a pressing of ham shank and foie gras, or a terrine of Tuscan vegetables; main courses range from calf's liver pan-fried with sweet-cured bacon, set on grilled polenta and served with Marsala sauce to salmon en croute wrapped in filo and served with a lobster sauce; while puddings might include rozanne of two chocolates or a warm pear tarte tatin. Many fine wines – well over half the list in fact – are priced considerably under £20. The excellent South African Pinot Noir Hamilton Russell is a steal at just over £15. *Seats 50. L (Sun only) 12-1.30 D 7-9.30. Closed D Sun (except by arrangment). Set D £21.95. Access, Visa.*

HEXHAM	Beaumont Hotel	62%	£80

Tel 01434 602331   Map 5 D2   **H**
Beaumont Street Hexham Northumberland NE46 3LT

The family-owned and run Beaumont at Hexham is about 20 miles west of Newcastle, on the A69. It's ideally situated in the centre of town, overlooking the Abbey. The glass-fronted foyer/lounge and a convivial bar are the extent of day rooms at street level, with a cocktail bar and boardroom on the first floor overlooking the abbey gardens. Pastel papers and bright bedspreads enliven well-equipped bedrooms (15 of them are non-smoking), the best of which sport large Georgian-style windows. There are six rather smaller single rooms. Children under 5 stay free in parents' room). One family room. No dogs. Conference/banqueting for up to 100. *Rooms 23. Keep-fit equipment, sun beds. Closed 25 & 26 Dec. Access, Amex, Diners, Visa.*

HIGH ONGAR	Shoes Restaurant		£60

Tel 01277 363350   Fax 01277 723849   Map 11 B4   **R**
The Street High Ongar Essex CM5 9ND

A characterful restaurant with lots of china shoe ornaments, a galleried upper floor and a wealth of old oak timbers in a village setting in what was once the Horseshoes pub. Sue Kesseck's menus are innovative and very well put together, with well-balanced, clear flavours. The menu offers starters such as ravioli filled with smoked salmon and fresh crab meat on a crisp bean sprout salad, whole boned quail filled with game mousse and glazed with a tarragon hollandaise, seafood risotto with chargrilled squid or terrine of duck confit, pork fillet, truffle and leek served with balsamic vinaigrette. Main courses include pan-fried sesame-coated collops of monkfish with a tomato sauce, roast rack of lamb with roasted red peppers and mozzarella and pan-fried breast of duck with a fricassée of wild mushrooms and baby roast potatoes with a port sauce. Excellent desserts such as a hot Spotted Dick soufflé with a vanilla custard, Sue's own version of tiramisu served with plums poached in red wine or an iced pistachio nut parfait topped with sliced Bramley apples and caramelised bananas. *Seats 60. Parties 12. Private Room 25. L 12-2.30 D 7-9.30. Closed D Sun, all Mon, Tue & 1 week Christmas. Access, Diners, Visa.*

HIGH WYCOMBE	Forte Posthouse	65%	£75

Tel 01494 442100   Fax 01494 439071   Map 15 E2   **H**
Crest Road High Wycombe Buckinghamshire HP11 1TL

Low-riser by Junction 4 of the M40, with conference and banqueting facilities for around 100. *Rooms 106. Garden, children's playground, pool table. Access, Amex, Diners, Visa.*

HIGHAM	The Knowle		£68

Tel 01474 822262   Map 11 B5   **R**
School Lane Higham nr Rochester Kent ME3 7HP

Set in three acres of secluded gardens, making it a popular wedding venue on Saturdays, Lyn and Michael Baragwanath's large Victorian rectory is both an easygoing restaurant and a family home. Sit in the eclectically furnished bar to choose from an equally varied menu of dishes more notable for fresh ingredients and generous portions than modern fads. Cheese soufflé royale; salmon and cucumber mousse; chicken Portuguese; steak, mushroom and ale vol-au-vent, spicy fried chicken and various sauced steaks show the range. Lunchtimes (except Sunday) and Tuesday to Thursday evenings there is an additional 'Bistro' menu that is considerably less expensive than the standard carte. *Seats 70. Private Room 40. L 12-1.30 D 6.30-10. Closed D Sun, all Mon. Set L £14.95. Access, Visa.*

HIGHCLERE   The Yew Tree   £50

Tel 01635 253360   Map 15 D3   **R**

Hollington Cross Andover Road Highclere nr Newbury Berkshire RG15 9SE

A delightful 15th-century inn just south of the village on the A343. Several cottagey interconnecting rooms form the restaurant where owner Jenny Wratten is sticking to the established Yew Tree menu. The emphasis is firmly English, with many traditional and old-fashioned items: South Coast plaice on or off the bone, tweed kettle tart (salmon in a pastry case with a leek, chive and parsley sauce), hot crab ramekins, breast of duck with a honey and orange sauce. Finish with a savoury (perhaps herring roes on a toasted muffin), chocolate and brandy mousse or rhubarb and champagne jellies. There's a pretty patio for summer eating. Six cottagey rooms offer comfortable overnight accommodation.
Seats 60. Parties 24. Private Room 24. L 12-2.30 (Sun to 3) D 6.30-9.30 (Fri & Sat to 10, Sun to 9). Access, Amex, Visa.

HINCKLEY   Hinckley Island Hotel   64%   £91

Tel 01455 631122   Fax 01455 634536   Map 7 D4   **H**

The A5 Hinckley Leicestershire LE10 3JA

Adjacent to exit 1 of the M69, at the junction of the A5, this conference-oriented hotel covers some 15 acres. A huge statue of Neptune greets arrivals in the marble-floored, mirror-ceilinged foyer. Accommodation is all comfortable but the stylish de luxe rooms are more spacious. Standard rooms have been refurbished in the last year. Children up to 16 stay free in parents' room. No dogs. The conference facilities can handle up to 400 delegates. *Rooms 270. Terrace, fishing, indoor swimming pool, gym, sauna, spa bath, steam room, solarium, beauty & hair salon, snooker, news kiosk, coffee shop (8am-4.30pm). Access, Amex, Diners, Visa.*

HINSTOCK   Goldstone Hall   59%   £80

Tel 01630 661202   Fax 01630 661585   Map 6 B3   **HR**

Goldstone Market Drayton Shropshire TF9 2NA

From Hinstock (halfway between Newport and Market Drayton) follow the signs to Goldstone Hall Gardens to find this plant-covered, mellow, redbrick house that in summer sprouts a marquee extension for the weddings and other functions that are an important part of its trade. The oldest part of the building dates back to the 16th century as evidenced by the old timbers on show in the bar/reception area. There are several other public rooms, including a lounge with lovely old oak panelling but inappropriate shaggy carpet and rather lived-in furniture and another sitting-room with reproduction French-style furnishings that are in a better state. Antique-furnished bedrooms are individually decorated in a variety of styles but all have small remote-control TVs, portable radios and bathrooms well supplied with generously-sized towels. Run in friendly informal style by mother and son team Helen Ward and John Cushing. Room service throughout the day and evening. *Rooms 8. Garden, croquet, snooker. Closed 25 Dec & 1 Jan. Access, Amex, Diners, Visa.*

Restaurant   £60

Exposed brickwork at the fire-place end of the room and a few lightwood beams and timbers give something of an Edwardian feel to the dining-room. The menu is rather more up-to-date and takes its inspiration from chef Simon Smith's time in Australia and "surfing the hotels and brasseries of the Pacific Rim" for some dishes like New Zealand green lip mussels with a champagne and garlic cream sauce and sautéed prawns in Thai spices; the latter much enjoyed on a recent visit as was a perfectly cooked loin of lamb with whole roast garlic and an intense red wine glaze; dessert of banoffi pie was rather less successful. Strong clear flavours are to the fore. Other dishes from a sensible-length à la carte included local asparagus baked with mayonnaise and flakes of ewe's milk cheese and a vegetarian option of roast vegetables with sun-dried tomatoes, olives and cheese croquettes. Lobsters come from their own sea-water tank. *Seats 45. L 12-2.30 (Sat by arrangement only) D 7.30-10.30. Set Sun L £15.45.*

Set menu prices may not always include service or wine.

| HINTLESHAM | Hintlesham Hall | 82% | £153 |

Tel 01473 652268   Fax 01473 652463   Map 10 C3   **HR**
Hintlesham nr Ipswich Suffolk IP8 3NS

Originally built in the 1570s by Thomas Timperley, grandson of the 3rd Duke of Norfolk, Hintlesham's Tudor origins (more recognisable from the rear gardens) are more familiarly clad in a Georgian facade and entrance. The Hall is about four miles west of Ipswich, on the A1071. The elegance of the setting is matched by the style of the interior, from the cosy book-lined library to the calm and airy Garden Room. The bedrooms and bathrooms are equally well equipped, and maintained to a luxurious standard. Notably friendly staff offer a high standard of care, from automatic luggage porterage to 24hr room service. **Rooms 33.** Garden, croquet, tennis, golf (18), outdoor swimming pool, game fishing, gym, sauna, steam room, spa bath, solarium, beauty salon, snooker. Access, Amex, Diners, Visa.

Restaurant   £95

The same menus (set and à la carte) are available, in both the smaller, more intimate parlour and the grander salon. Alan Ford's menus are a joy to read and pose some pretty difficult choices. Crab risotto with a ragout of scallops, chicken and pistachio terrine with a walnut dressing, carpaccio of grilled vegetables with a warm tomato and brioche gateau are just a few of the starters. Main courses could include baked fillet of red snapper with leaf spinach, poppyseed noodles and aubergine fritters, breast of Hintlesham pheasant with a chestnut and sage farce and a dark watercress sauce, or sliced chump of lamb with caramelised button onions. Delicious desserts such as smooth chocolate tart with a clear orange sauce or warm pear jalousie with crème anglaise to finish or excellent British and French cheeses. A lot of though and work has gone into the compilation of the wine list here. It's a marvellous tome with quality everywhere you look. Introductory notes to each section are both knowledgeable and helpful; even some of the prices are not unreasonable! Excellent house recommendations, plenty of half bottles. **Seats 120.** Parties 10. Private Room 40. L 12-2 D 7-10. Set L £18.50/£19.50 Set D £24.

| HINTON | Hinton Grange | 62% | £105 |

Tel 0117 937 2916   Fax 0117 937 3285   Map 13 F1   **HR**
Hinton nr Dyrham Wiltshire SN14 8HG

The Lindsay-Walkers' conversion of a stone farmhouse and outbuildings in six acres of grounds has brought a touch of country living only minutes from Bath and the M4 (from Junction 18). The main building comprises a 15th-century stone-flagged bar and a lounge in simple Chinese style. Bedrooms in the surrounding buildings are Victorian-style recreations, with period washstands and bathing alcoves. There are antique four-posters and open fires (£7.95 charge for the thrill of being greeted by it lit, 2 hours' notice required). The Palm Court conservatory pool-side bar area is kept at tropical heat all year round, nurturing palm trees and orchids, and even providing bananas for the restaurant. Banqueting/conference facilities for 55/25. No children under 14. Separate high-season tariff. **Rooms 18.** Garden, 9-hole pitch & putt, indoor swimming pool, sauna, solarium, tennis, fishing. Access, Amex, Diners, Visa.

Inglenook Restaurant   £50

Informal surroundings for sound cooking by chef Neil Cooper, whose short à la carte is typified by a choice of home-made soups, roulade of chicken with mushroom mousse on a bed of lettuce with beetroot and a garlic dressing, pan-fried best end of lamb coated in honey, pink peppercrons and coriander seeds on a red wine and rosemary sauce and rosette of lemon sole and salmon with a watercress sauce. Vegetarians are well catered for. Seating for 15 on a terrace in summer. No children under 16. **Seats 60.** Parties 12. Private Room 15. L 12.30-2 D 7-9.30. Set L £14 Set D £17.95.

HOCKLEY HEATH   Nuthurst Grange   74%   £125

Tel 01564 783972   Fax 01564 783919   Map 6 C4   **HR**
Nuthurst Grange Lane Hockley Heath Warwickshire B94 5NL

The original redbrick house has been added to a number of times over the last 100 years, but the overall result is a surprisingly handsome building, helped by its setting in extensive landscaped grounds. The restaurant takes pride of place on the ground floor along with a pair of plush chesterfield-furnished lounges (one for non-smokers) where drinks are served; there is no bar. Pretty, individually-decorated bedrooms are spacious and comfortable with sofas and armchairs alongside the freestanding, darkwood furniture and extras ranging from books, chocolates and fruit to more mundane fly-spray and shoe-cleaning kit. Bathrooms all have 'air spa' baths, telephone extensions, bathrobes and personal room safes. "Suitable for children who are well behaved." Conference and banqueting for 90/100. No dogs. M40 J16 is northbound only, so, from the south, take M42 northbound and then exit at J4, proceeding via A3400 to Hockley Heath. *Rooms* 15. *Garden, croquet. Access, Amex, Diners, Visa.*

Restaurant   £60

The restaurant is very much the centrepiece of the hotel. Chef-proprietor David Randolph sources and handles fine, fresh produce with great care, creating dishes on the variety of fixed-price-only menus that are notable for honest, distinctive flavours and attractive presentation. A simpler, short choice table d'hote might offer fennel and cashew nut soup, sliced bacon joint with oranges and garlic, finishing with steamed banana pudding; the à la carte extends to cover terrine of foie gras and leek, confit of game with peppercorns, salmon marinated in limes, whole roasted, boneless quails with grapes and Madeira, Dover sole and mushroom stroganoff. Desserts might include warm marinated fruits, dark chocolate terrine with coffee bean sauce and bitter lemon tart. Fresh herbs come from their own Victorian walled garden. No smoking (smokers can use the lounge if desperate). The easy-to-use wine list shows that there is plenty available under £20, indeed the entire New World section does not breach this threshold. Toilets equipped for disabled guests. *Seats* 50. *Parties* 12. *Private Room* 90. *L* 12-2 *D* 7-9.30. *Closed L Sat. Set L £16.50 & £18.90/£23.90 Set D £23.90 & £29.90/£39.90/£45.*

HOLBETON   Alston Hall   64%   £100

Tel 01752 830555   Fax 01752 830494   Map 13 D3   **H**
Alston Cross Holbeton nr Plymouth Devon PL8 1HN

A couple of miles from the village but easy to find if you follow the signs to Alston, without going into Holbeton itself, this creeper-clad Edwardian mansion stands in four acres of parkland with views across rolling countryside to the sea. Public areas centre on the galleried Great Hall with its oak panelling and stained-glass windows. Bedrooms are attractively decorated in a variety of styles, those on the top floor a little smaller than those on the first. Room service is available throughout the day and evening. Popular for conferences (for up to 100) during the week and weddings at weekends. *Rooms* 20. *Garden, croquet, indoor swimming pool, keep-fit equipment, sauna, solarium, tennis. Access, Amex, Diners, Visa.*

HOLLINGBOURNE   Jarvis Great Danes   64%   £106

Tel 01622 631163   Fax 01622 735290   Map 11 C5   **H**
Ashford Road Hollingbourne Kent ME17 1RE

Great Danes stands in 22 acres of grounds next door to Leeds Castle off Junction 8 of the M20. It has very extensive, up-to-the-minute conference facilities and also on site is the Sebastian Coe Health Park whose attractions include a running track and floodlit tennis courts. Some rooms suitable for family use; conferences for up to 600, theatre-style. *Rooms* 126. *Garden, indoor swimming pool, gym, aerobics studio, beauty salon, sauna, solarium, tennis, 9-hole pitch & putt, children's playground, clay-pigeon shooting, rifle range. Access, Amex, Diners, Visa.*

Consult the blue pages for summary tables and lists of
recommended establishments.

HOPE COVE	Cottage Hotel	56%	£94*

Tel 01548 561555   Map 13 D3   **H**
Hope Cove nr Kingsbridge Devon TQ7 3HJ

The village of Hope Cove rests in the curve of Bigbury Bay and this popular family hotel makes the most of the views. The sun terrace is the place to be in summer, while inside there are three lounges and a cocktail bar which was built from timbers salvaged from a wrecked windjammer, the *Herzogin Cecilie*. 25 bedrooms now have en-suite facilities and some have balconies. A few singles at the back miss out on the sea views and are priced lower. Much reduced rates for children. ★Half-board terms only. *Rooms 35. Garden, games room, tots' outdoor play area. Closed Jan. No credit cards.*

HOPE COVE	Lantern Lodge	59%	£74

Tel 01548 561280   Map 13 D3   **H**
Grand View Road Hope Cove nr Kingsbridge Devon TQ7 3HE

Well located in a pretty corner of Devon, Lantern Lodge has the best of sea views and rolling countryside, making it a popular holiday destination. The ivy-clad exterior and well-tended gardens set the scene, enhanced indoors by comfortable lounges and smart bedrooms, some with four-posters. There's parking for 18 cars. No children under ten. No dogs. *Rooms 14. Garden, putting, indoor swimming pool, sauna, sun beds. Closed Dec-Feb. Access, Visa.*

HORLEY	Langshott Manor	73%	£106

Tel 01293 786680   Fax 01293 783905   Map 11 B5   **HR**
Langshott Horley Surrey RH6 9LN

Personally run by the Noble family, this small Elizabethan manor house has enormous charm. Domestic-scale day rooms with mellow panelling, old timbers and rug-strewn floors gain a real homely atmosphere from family photos, fresh flowers (from the delightful gardens), objets d'art and the house labrador dozing in front of the open-hearth fire with its smouldering logs. Bedrooms are no less characterful or appealing with antique furniture, stylish fabrics and all sorts of personal touches plus high-quality beds with the finest Egyptian cotton bedding. Smoking is allowed downstairs but not in the bedrooms. Three acres of "peaceful, English gardens". An added attraction is a one-way courtesy car on departure to nearby Gatwick airport and free parking for up to two weeks. No dogs. *Rooms 7. Garden, croquet. Closed 24-30 Dec. Access, Amex, Diners, Visa.*

Restaurant   £65

A tiny dining-room with just a few lace-clothed tables, so for non-residents it is strictly by prior reservation only. Christopher, the son of the house, cooks and the food is unpretentiously good and satisfying. The fixed-price-only menus generally offer a choice of three or four dishes at each stage beginning perhaps with sorrel soup, whisky-cured smoked salmon and sweet mustard sauce or moules marinière. Main courses could be salmon florentine, duck à l'orange, lamb noisettes with a rosemary and perry sauce or Herefordshire beef olives with a cider sauce. Vegetables are simply cooked and desserts might include crème brulée or country apple pie. The well-chosen wine list is more than adequate, the Nobles' native New Zealand being well represented. No smoking. *Seats 14. Parties 6. Private Room 8. L by arrangement D 7-9.30. Set L £22.50 Set D £25.*

HORNDON-ON-THE-HILL	The Bell Inn & Hill House	£50

Tel 01375 642463   Fax 01375 361611   Map 11 B4   **IR**
High Road Horndon-on-the-Hill Essex SS17 8LD

Two adjacent and quite separate buildings, the Bell dating from the 15th century and Hill House, which was built in the latter part of the 17th century. Bedrooms are in two parts too. There are ten to the rear of Hill House and a further four upstairs in the Bell. The latter are larger, each with a sitting area. They are a little more expensive as a result. All the rooms are comfortable and well maintained, with neat bathrooms. Breakfasts are served in the dining-room at Hill House. *Rooms 14. Access, Amex, Visa.*

Hill House Restaurant   £65

A prettily decorated dining-room with a formal air, though staff are friendly and relaxed.

See over

Sean Kelly's fixed-price menu offers seven choices per course commencing with dishes such as baked chicken and chive sausage, game and bacon terrine with home-made piccalilli and steamed mussels with garlic and coriander. Main dishes could include breast of duck with apricots and thyme, fillet of lamb in filo with a tarragon mousse, grilled skate with noodles and a lemon and chive sauce or saddle of venison with stewed onions and a red wine sauce. Desserts range from a dark chocolate marquise with roast plum coulis, bread-and-butter pudding with vanilla anglaise or, as a good alternative, a weekly-changing choice of unusual British cheeses. *Seats 30. Parties 12. L 12.15-2 D 7.15-10. Closed Sun & Mon, 25-31 Dec. Set L £14.95 Set D £17.95. Access, Amex, Visa.*

The Bell Restaurant   £60

A dining section created to the rear of the bar offers a relaxed, informal setting with oak beams galore as well as wooden tables and a flagstone floor. The menu is chalked up on a large blackboard and consists of a choice of seven individually priced dishes per course. In the same modern style as at Hill House but fractionally simpler, the dishes are well put together. Begin with chicken liver paté with spiced pepper chutney, plum tomato and pesto tart, or smoked salmon and vegetable strudel. Follow perhaps with fillet of cod wrapped in Parma ham with mushrooms, roast duck breast with honey and soy or braised shoulder of lamb with lentils and bacon. Finish with toasted sesame seed parfait with a plum sauce or sticky toffee pudding with butterscotch sauce. Good selection of British cheeses too. *Seats 40. Parties 12. Private Room 30. L 12-2 D 6.30-10 (Sun from 7). Closed 25 & 26 Dec. Set Sun L £11.50.*

HORTON	French Partridge	£70

Tel 01604 870033   Fax 01604 870032   Map 15 D1   **R**
Horton nr Northampton Northamptonshire NN7 2AP

A charming country restaurant run with care and dedication by Mary and David Partridge for the past 32 years. The decor is solidly traditional with oil paintings on the bottle green walls, comfortable, well-worn black leather banquettes and large polished mahogany tables. Thankfully, this is one restaurant which, although keeping abreast of developments, doesn't fall into the tedious trap of adopting every passing fad. Innovation is kept within the constraints of classic cooking and good taste. Dinners comprise four well-balanced courses with a short choice at each stage. A typical menu (they change on a monthly basis) could include a Normandy onion soup with cider and cream, skate with brown butter sauce and pan-fried pheasant breast with stuffed cabbage. There's a greater choice for dessert, ranging from pear and almond tart to profiteroles with chocolate sauce and rum baba with oranges in a butter sauce. Smoking is discouraged. The restaurant is on the B526 Northampton-Newport Pagnell road. Very fair prices on a sensible wine list with interesting choices from the New World. *Seats 40. Parties 10. D only 7.30-9. Closed Sun & Mon, 2 weeks Christmas, 2 weeks Easter, first 3 weeks Aug. Set D £22 (Sat £23). No credit card.*

HORTON-CUM-STUDLEY	Studley Priory	64%	£98

Tel 01865 351203   Fax 01865 351613   Map 15 D2   **H**
Horton-cum-Studley nr Oxford Oxfordshire OX33 1AZ

Set in 13 acres of wooded grounds seven miles from Oxford, this Elizabethan manor house has impressive day rooms that include a splendid hall panelled in pitch pine, a lofty drawing room and a Victorian bar with oak panelling. Six bedrooms are in the main house (one with a half-tester bed dating from about 1700), while the majority are in the Jacobean wing reached through a labyrinth of corridors. These rooms are smaller and more modern. Children up to 16 share parents' room free of charge. Small conferences (for up to 45, theatre-style) are big business here, so you'll sometimes be sharing the drawing room with the delegates. *Rooms 19. Garden, croquet, tennis. Access, Amex, Diners, Visa.*

We welcome bona fide complaints and recommendations on the tear-out pages at the back of the book for readers' comments. They are followed up by our professional team.

HOUNSLOW   Hee's   £50

Tel 0181-577 3817   Map 15 E2   **R**
476 Great Western Road Hounslow Middlesex TW5 0TA

Smart Chinese restaurant hidden behind a smoked-glass frontage in a parade of shops just back from the A4, one mile west of Brentford. Set 'feasts' are offered in both Peking and mildly-spiced Szechuan styles, covering dishes that range from bang bang chicken and crispy lamb with lettuce to sizzling dishes, crispy aromatic (or roast Peking) duck and tip-top toffee apple. Sliced sole with red pepper and vinegar soup, cold smoked fish, mandarin fillet steak, pancake with mashed red beans and almond bean curd with mixed fruit are among the less ubiquitous dishes. *Seats 80. L 12-2.30 D 6-11.15. Set meals from £13.50. Closed 4 days Christmas. Access, Amex, Diners, Visa.*

HOVE

See under Brighton (Hove)

HOVINGHAM   Worsley Arms   £105

Tel 01653 628234   Fax 01653 628130   Map 5 E4   **I**
Hovingham North Yorkshire YO6 4LA

A lovely setting with easy access to the Moors and the Dales, and its own wooded parkland, provide a backdrop for the late-Georgian Worsley Arms, owned and run from its creation in 1841 by the Worsley family (owners of nearby Hovingham Hall). Elegant and spacious sitting rooms and bedrooms lend an air of gracious living, while the homely quality of the Cricketers Bar, HQ of the local team, reminds the visitor that the inn is still also the centre of village life. *Rooms 22. Garden, tennis, squash, mountain bikes. Access, Amex, Visa.*

Set menu prices may not always include service or wine.

HUDDERSFIELD   George Hotel   62%   £89

Tel 01484 515444   Fax 01484 435056   Map 6 C1   **H**
St George's Square Huddersfield West Yorkshire HD1 1JA

In the main square opposite the railway station, a large Victorian building with sizeable conference and banqueting rooms (up to 200 delegates) plus stylish, well-equipped bedrooms. Guests enjoy free admission to Huddersfield Sports Centre, whose facilities include an Olympic-size swimming pool. Children under 14 stay free in parents' room. The hotel's bar contains a plaque commemorating the inaugural meeting of the Rugby League in 1895. *Rooms 60. Access, Amex, Diners, Visa.*

HUDDERSFIELD   Hilton National   66%   £98

Tel 01422 375431   Fax 01422 310067   Map 6 C1   **H**
Ainley Top Huddersfield West Yorkshire HD3 3RH

Above the town centre, conveniently located by junction 24 of the M62, a modern, low-rise hotel with attractive, contemporary-style bedrooms with small, but bright, bathrooms. Children up to 12 stay free in parents' room. Leisure Centre and conference facilities for up to 400. Ample free car parking. *Rooms 118. Indoor swimming pool, sauna, steam room, gym. Access, Amex, Diners, Visa.*

HULL   Ceruttis   £60

Tel 01482 328501   Fax 01482 587597   Map 7 E1   **R**
10 Nelson Street Hull Humberside HU1 1XE

The Cerutti family arrived in 1974 at their friendly harbourside restaurant, where seafood is naturally the speciality. Dover sole remains a favourite (grilled, meunière or six other ways) and several dishes, including fishcakes, scallops, moules marinière, scampi and goujons of plaice, are available as either starter or main course. King prawns – cold, or hot in garlic butter – are sold by the unit, and Ceruttis' fish grill is an appetising platter of lightly grilled mixed fish. A few meat and vegetarian dishes, but this really is a classic restaurant for seafoodies. *Seats 40. Parties 12. Private Room 24. L 12-2 D 7-9.30. Set D from £11.50. Closed L Sat, all Sun, 1 week Xmas. Access, Visa.*

HULL   Forte Crest   69%   £115

Tel 01482 225221   Fax 01482 213299   Map 7 E1   **H**
Castle Street Hull Humberside HU1 2BX

Alongside the impressive dock development, the best rooms in this purpose-built hotel have balconies and fine views over the marina. Conferences and banqueting for 120. Children up to 16 free in parents' room. *Rooms 99. Patio, indoor swimming pool, gym, sauna, solarium, beauty salon. Access, Amex, Diners, Visa.*

HULL   Forte Posthouse   62%   £70

Tel 01482 645212   Fax 01482 643332   Map 7 E1   **H**
Ferriby High Road North Ferriby Hull Humberside HU14 3LG

Purpose-built comfortable hotel outside Hull, overlooking the remarkable suspension bridge. About half the bedrooms are reserved for non-smokers. Banqueting/conferences for up to 100. *Rooms 95. Access, Amex, Diners, Visa.*

HUNGERFORD   The Bear at Hungerford   60%   £96

Tel 01488 682512   Fax 01488 684357   Map 14 C2   **H**
Charnham Street Hungerford Berkshire RG17 0EL

Located on the A4 as it brushes past the northern edge of town, this ancient inn has its origins in the 14th century and was reputedly once owned by Henry VIII. In winter a real fire warms and welcomes guests in the beamed reception/lounge area and another brings cheer to the pubby bar, where a stuffed bear presides from its glass-fronted niche. Modern bedrooms are in good order and are divided between those in the main building, the majority with pine furniture in an attached courtyard block (former stables) and nine in a separate building across the car park, called Bear Island. No room service is advertised but sandwiches and bar snacks are available at some times. Children up to 16 stay free in parents' room. Listed as **Jarvis Bear Hotel** last year; the ownership remains the same but they have now reverted to using the hotel's former name. *Rooms 41. Garden. Access, Amex, Diners, Visa.*

HUNSTRETE   HUNSTRETE HOUSE   79%   £145

Tel 01761 490490   Fax 01761 490732   Map 13 F1   **HR**
Hunstrete Chelwood nr Bath Avon BS18 4NS

Archetypal Georgian mansion a few miles south of Bath/Bristol and set in nearly 100 acres of its own grounds which include woodland and a deer park in addition to immaculately kept gardens by the house. Reception is a leather-topped desk in an inner hall that is warmed by a real fire in winter. Other day rooms include a sitting room, library and small bar where drinks are set out on a sideboard. The atmosphere throughout is very much that of a classic English country house. Bedrooms are particularly fine being individually decorated in great style with quality fabrics, good antiques, pictures, framed samplers and all sorts of extras like books, magazines and a decanter of sherry. All have sitting areas with proper armchairs and sofas. Excellent bathrooms are equally luxurious. Beds are turned down at night and room service is available throughout the day and evening. *Rooms 23. Garden, croquet, outdoor swimming pool, tennis. Access, Amex, Diners, Visa.*

Restaurant   £100

Antique crystal chandeliers with matching wall lights, heavy drapes at windows which open out on to a delightful stone-flagged courtyard, crisp white napery and high-quality table settings all help to create a suitably opulent setting for chef Robert Clayton's refined and careful cooking. Well-judged saucing with clear, strong flavours and thoughtful presentation enhance the enjoyment of dishes like spinach, smoked ham and truffle soup served under a pastry lid; sautéed wood pigeon with lentils, caramelised carrots and an 'old oak' Madeira sauce; mushroom boudin with creamed leeks, glazed apples and cep sauce; grilled sea bass stuffed with trompette mushrooms and herbs with a vanilla sauce, and honey-baked Deben duck with Sarladais potatoes and calvados sauce. On the dessert front items such as a warm chocolate tart with praline custard and vanilla ice cream, and passion fruit soufflé with hot raspberry sauce will tempt the sweet-toothed while those with more savoury tastes go for the trolley of English cheeses that comes with grapes, home-made breads, chutney and biscuits. A lovingly cared for walled kitchen garden provides much of the produce used and is a very pleasant place to stroll before dinner on a summer evening. A few inexpensive wines can be spotted on a very good list that includes the rare Le Pin from Pomerol, not a snip at £575! *Seats 50. Parties 10. Private Room 35. L 12.30-2.30 D 7.30-9.30. Set L £15 (Set Sun L £19.50) Set D £29.50.*

HUNTINGDON	Old Bridge Hotel	68%	£95

Tel 01480 452681   Fax 01480 411017   Map 7 E4   **HR**
1 High Street Huntingdon Cambridgeshire PE18 6TQ

A town-centre hotel overlooking the River Ouse, the creeper-clad Old Bridge Hotel caters to business and leisure customers equally well – the Cromwell Room and business centre showing the versatility (Cromwell was born in Huntingdon). The lounges and public rooms have an air of comfort and elegance – a highlight is the continuous mural in the Terrace, a single work of art (extending over all walls) which took Julia Rushbury over four months to complete. Bedrooms are furnished with regard to the overall atmosphere of the place, but are also well equipped with modern amenities. Free parking for about 100 cars. *Rooms 26. Garden. Access, Amex, Diners, Visa.*

Restaurant   £80

Chef-Patron Nick Steiger recruited Philip Guest as head chef in late 1994, thereby bolstering the reputation for good food enjoyed by the Old Bridge. Sensibly, one menu is available throughout the hotel, either in the more relaxed setting of the Terrace or the more formal, bookable, half non-smoking restaurant. However you can eat as much or as little as you wish from the menu, regardless of location. The cooking is mainly British, so the likes of olive mash, vegetable spaghetti, confit and goat's cheese rub shoulders with seized chicken teriyaki or forest mushroom soup. Try perhaps chargrilled scallops with pappardelle and pesto, cassoulet of rabbit and duck with garlic sausage, white beans, onions and a purée of root vegetables, and finish with chocolate and pear brulée or plum pudding soufflé with orange, clove and brandy butter – well worth the 20-minute ordering time. Accompany or follow with a choice from an extensive range of sweet wines, port, cognac, armagnac, marc, grappa, calvados, malts or liqueurs. There's always a roast on Sundays, and from Monday to Friday a lunchtime buffet of cold roast meats, poached salmon and fresh salads. A *marque* champagne at just over £20 (a merc £3.95 by the glass), friendly prices everywhere you look, several quality wines by the glass, lots of half bottles, magnums, bin ends and helpful notes – get the picture! This is a model list for others to follow, which is why it's a dual winner of Cellar of the Year – see award pages. *Seats 44. Parties 14. Private Room 28. L 12-2.30 D 6.30-10.30. Closed D 25 Dec.*

HUNTSHAM	Huntsham Court	68%	£115

Tel 01398 361365   Fax 01398 361456   Map 13 D2   **HR**
Huntsham nr Bampton Tiverton Devon EX16 7NA

A rather gaunt Victorian Gothic pile run in friendly, very casual style by owners Mogens and Andrea Bolwig. Eating is communal, there's an honour system in the bar, and you just wander into the kitchen if you need anything. There's great atmosphere in the day rooms (log fires, a panelled great hall, splendid pieces of furniture) and in the roomy bedrooms, named after composers, there are Victorian beds and baths and pre-war radios with an authentic crackle – not a teasmaid in sight! The hotel is dedicated to music, with the classical variety played forte in the evening. The day starts with an excellent buffet breakfast. No dogs, however "good" or "small". Private house parties and group functions are a speciality and their mood is likely to determine the atmosphere. It's about as far away from the world of chain hotels as you could imagine. *Rooms 14. Garden, croquet, tennis, sauna, snooker. Closed 2 weeks winter. Access, Diners, Visa.*

See over

Restaurant   £75
🍷 🌸

Five-course dinners (no choice, but variations possible in advance) are served by candle-light in leisurely fashion at an often convivial, communal table. Non-residents must book in advance as if the house is full there are no spare seats around the table. There's no wine list as such – guests choose from the cellar before dinner. Particularly well represented are the New World (Australia especially) and Spain. *Seats 30. D only 8-10. Set D £25 (Fri & Sat £30).*

HURLEY	Ye Olde Bell	65%	£114

Tel 01628 825881   Fax 01628 825939   Map 15 D2   **H**
High Street Hurley nr Maidenhead Berkshire SL6 5LX

Built in 1135 as a guest house for a Benedictine monastery, this black-and-white inn has claims to be England's oldest. You enter through a Norman arch to find a heavily beamed bar with comfortable armchairs, old brass and lots of character, while adjacent to it is the tiny Hogarth Bar. The comfortable bedrooms vary from handsome, traditionally furnished rooms in the inn and neighbouring Malt House to more modern ones in an annexe. There are some four-poster rooms. Children up to 14 stay free in parents' room. Function facilities include a tithe barn with medieval beams and rafters. Resort Hotels. *Rooms 36. Garden, croquet. Access, Amex, Diners, Visa.*

HURSTBOURNE TARRANT	Esseborne Manor	72%	£120

Tel 01264 736444   Fax 01264 736473   Map 14 C3   **HR**
Hurstbourne Tarrant nr Andover Hampshire SP11 0ER

A stylish, civilised country house hotel set back off the A343 about a mile to the north of Hurstbourne Tarrant. The building dates from the end of the last century and benefits from obvious attention to detail both in the public rooms and in the overnight accommodation, with fresh flowers, carved ducks, glossy magazines, family ornaments and some antiques. Bedrooms are decorated and furnished to a very high standard in both fabrics and materials, enjoying views of the well-kept gardens or rich farmland beyond. The six most spacious rooms are housed in a converted stable block. Extras provided include thick bath robes, books and fresh fruit. Bathrooms boast full-length mirrors, spacious surfaces and vividly coloured bath toys. No children under 12. No dogs. *Rooms 12. Garden, croquet, tennis. Access, Amex, Diners, Visa.*

Restaurant   £80
🌸 🍴 ☕

Friendly, cheerful service and a cosy atmosphere make it a pleasurable environment in which to enjoy capable cooking which shows a mix of traditional and contemporary influences. Seafood and game dishes are both specialities, the former typified by trout cooked in a paper bag or baked cod on a bed of spinach noodles with a spicy tomato fondue; the latter by pan-fried breast of pheasant with a salmis of leg meat with a swede and parsnip purée and a claret gravy. A favourite on the luncheon menu is "Esseborne's very own mixed grill" – beef fillet, liver, bacon, sausage, mushrooms and tomato with French toast. *Seats 40. Parties 22. L 12-2 D 7-9.30. Set L £14/£17.50/£22.50 (Sun £17.50).*

HYTHE	Hythe Imperial	71%	£108

Tel 01303 267441   Fax 01303 264610   Map 11 C5   **H**
Princes Parade Hythe Kent CT21 6AE

Right on the seafront at Hythe, the Imperial still manages to be set in 50 acres of grounds, and its wide frontage means that all bedrooms face the gardens and sea. Bedrooms range from singles to doubles to suites, some with jacuzzis, some with four-posters or half-testers. The polished mahogany reception area is adorned with brown leather chesterfields and leads through to comfortable bars and lounges. Pleasant staff and excellent leisure facilities that include go-karting and a children's play area with Scalextric. Families are particularly well catered for with baby-sitting, baby-listening and creche facilities available on Saturday mornings; they can eat informally in the leisure centre bistro. Banqueting/conferences for 160/200. Sunday Plus is an interesting idea – extend a weekend stay (keeping the use of your room) until 5pm on Sunday for a nominal charge that includes Sunday lunch. No dogs. *Rooms 100. Garden, croquet, indoor swimming pool, gym, spa bath, sauna, solarium, steam room, beauty & hair salons, squash, tennis, games room, snooker, 9-hole golf course, putting, young children's playroom, children's outdoor playroom, coffee shop (7.30am-10.30pm). Access, Amex, Diners, Visa.*

HYTHE   Stade Court   62%   £83   H

Tel 01303 268263   Fax 01303 261803   Map 11 C5
West Parade Hythe Kent CT21 6DT

There are Channel views from many of the traditionally-styled bedrooms, the majority of which have little sun lounges; there's also an upstairs lounge looking out to sea. Children up to 16 can stay free in their parents' room. Free use of the extensive leisure facilities at sister hotel the Hythe Imperial 600 metres away, excluding golf (for which a green fee is charged). *Rooms 42. Garden, coffee shop (7.30am-10.30pm). Access, Amex, Diners, Visa.*

IDE   Old Mill   £55   R

Tel 01392 59480   Map 13 D2
20 High Street Ide nr Exeter Devon EX2 9RN

Set menus and à la carte are available both lunchtime and evening in the tranquil surroundings of a converted 16th-century mill, just off the A30 Okehampton road roundabout, 2 miles west of Exeter. Fish dishes feature prominently on chef-proprietor Jon Cruwys's menus and wild duck, pheasant and seafood are considered house specialities. *Seats 40. Parties 22. Private Room 8. L 12-1.30 D 7-9.30. Closed Sun, 26-30 Dec. Set L £8.95/£9.95 Set D £14. Access, Amex, Visa.*

ILKLEY   Box Tree   ★   £85   R

Tel 01943 608484   Fax 01943 607186   Map 6 C1
37 Church Street Ilkley West Yorkshire LS29 9DR

Decor-wise, little has changed here over the years save a picture or two; the cottagey restaurant (very pretty outside) is in fact a series of small, intimate rooms with gilt-framed oils, wall cabinets of fine china, the odd cherub, and a Baccarat glass tree on each table. Both cooking and service are exemplary, the former under Thierry Le Pretre-Granet, whose cuisine is a mixture of classical French and modern British, with the emphasis on the finest and freshest ingredients. Presentation is impressive, flavours equally so, and with saucing spot-on, the dishes emanating from the kitchen are models of correctness. Both lunch (3 courses) and dinner (four) offer fixed-price menus with several choices in each section, typical examples being a sausage of chicken mousseline with a sherry vinegar sauce; charlotte of young vegetables, haricot beans and fresh herbs; medallions of monkfish with fresh pasta and lobster sauce, and loin of venison with roast pear and a game sauce flavoured with chocolate. Good desserts might include roasted apple with a blackcurrant and red wine coulis and cinnamon ice cream, and a gratin of pink grapefruit flavoured with acacia honey. After-meal coffees and teas, accompanied by excellent petits fours, are treated very seriously with a huge range available. Well-chosen wines on a fine list that includes many champagne and claret vinatges. Quite extensive house selection at keen prices. No smoking. *Seats 50. Parties 35. Private Room 15. L 12-2.30 D 7-10. Closed D Sun, all Mon, 1 week Christmas and last 2 wks Jan. Set L £22.50 Set D £29.50. Access, Amex, Visa.*

ILKLEY   Rombalds Hotel   61%   £84   HR

Tel 01943 603201   Fax 01943 816586   Map 6 C1
West View Wells Road Ilkley West Yorkshire LS29 9JG

Part of a period sandstone terrace just yards from the edge of Ilkley Moor. The main day room is a comfortable, traditionally furnished bar/lounge busy with diners having pre- and post-prandial drinks. Bedrooms, which include four suites, are modestly comfortable, mostly with inexpensive white melamine furniture and functional bathrooms – about half with shower and WC only. The coach-house meeting room combines character with high-tech facilities. Friendly staff. 24hr room service. Children up to 12 stay free in parents' room. *Rooms 15. Garden. Closed 27-30 Dec. Access, Amex, Diners, Visa.*

Restaurant   £65

Food is a very important part of life here, and perhaps the best-known offering is the "Edwardian Breakfast" served every Sunday (and Boxing Day) from 9am till 1. There's a buffet and a short set menu each lunchtime, and an additional more extensive evening carte. The dinner menu on Sunday features the speciality of roast beef with a separate

See over

course of Yorkshire pudding and onion gravy. Vegetarian main courses. No smoking. *Seats 36. Parties 10. Private Room 50. L 12-2 (Sun 9am-1) D 7.30-9.30 (Sun till 9). Set L & D £10.*

INGATESTONE   Heybridge Hotel   68%   £103

Tel 01277 355355   Fax 01277 353288   Map 11 B4   **H**
Roman Road Ingatestone Essex CM4 9AB

Smart motel-style rooms each with satellite TV, hairdryer and trouser press stand round a central courtyard, and there are purpose-built conference facilities for up to 600 delegates. Just off the A12. *Rooms 22. Garden. Access, Amex, Diners, Visa.*

IPSWICH   Belstead Brook Hotel   68%   £79

Tel 01473 684241   Fax 01473 681249   Map 10 C3   **H**
Belstead Road Ipswich Suffolk IP2 9HB

On the southern outskirts of Ipswich (ask for directions when booking), the 16th-century Belstead Brook is set in eight acres of gardens and woodland. Public rooms and the four-poster honeymoon suite are in the original house with most of the other well-appointed bedrooms in a modern extension. Accommodation ranges from studio singles via standard and Executive to presidential suites. Some of the suites have whirlpool baths. Children up to 12 stay free in parents' room. Purpose-built syndicate rooms cater for functions of up to 65. *Rooms 76. Garden, croquet. Access, Amex, Diners, Visa.*

IPSWICH   Constable Country Hotel   63%   £69

Tel 01473 690313   Fax 01473 680412   Map 10 C3   **H**
London Road Ipswich Suffolk IP2 0UA

On the A1214, about two miles from Ipswich on the London side, this Forte hotel offers stylish public areas and decent-sized bedrooms. Conferences for up to 140. *Rooms 112. Outdoor swimming pool (May-Sep), play area. Amex Access, Diners, Visa.*

IPSWICH   Marlborough Hotel   65%   £69

Tel 01473 257677   Fax 01473 226927   Map 10 C3   **H**
Henley Road Ipswich Suffolk IP1 3SP

Peacefully located north of the town centre, the Marlborough is in the same ownership as the *Angel*, Bury St Edmunds. The tasteful public areas and the comfortable bedrooms (the best have antique furniture) are both well kept. 24hr room service. Ample own parking. *Rooms 22. Garden. Access, Amex, Diners, Visa.*

IPSWICH   Novotel   61%   £67

Tel 01473 232400   Fax 01473 232414   Map 10 C3   **H**
Greyfriars Road Ipswich Suffolk IP1 1UP

Five minutes' walk from the pedestrianised town centre and only a brisk ten from the station; purpose-built facilities include all-day brasserie, conferences for up to 200 (banquets 150) and 3 bedrooms suitable for disabled guests. Under-16s stay free in parents' room, with breakfast also free. *Rooms 100. Access, Amex, Diners, Visa.*

IXWORTH   Theobald's   £72

Tel 01359 231707   Map 10 C2   **R**
68 High Street Ixworth nr Bury St Edmunds Suffolk IP31 2HJ

Simon and Geraldine Theobald set up their restaurant in a village seven miles north of Bury St Edmunds in 1981; consistency has been the name of their game ever since. Oak beams and log fires make a traditional English setting for enjoying Simon's capable and confident cooking. The price of a three-course meal is dictated by the price of the main dish (an allowance is made for any course not required); at lunchtime there is also a good-value table d'hote with three or so choices (more on Sundays) at each stage. The cheapest main-course option is vegetarian (perhaps basil-flavoured noodles baked with broccoli, herbs and tomatoes with a cheese sauce), continuing with main dishes like breast of corn-fed chicken wrapped in smoked bacon with a thyme-flavoured sauce, fillet of monkfish braised on a bed of leeks with a white port sauce or best end of lamb roasted with artichokes, served with a Madeira sauce. An additional 'fish supper' (4 set courses

£29.50 including half a bottle of Chablis per person) is also offered on Friday evenings; game features in season and good saucing is a notable highlight. Super prices (well over half under £20) on a carefully chosen wine list that has many bottles. The list demonstrates that quality does not suffer through lack of quantity. No smoking during service – puffers can repair to the lounge. No children under 7 at dinner. *Seats 36. L 12.15-1.30 D 7-9.30. Closed L Sat, D Sun, all Mon, Bank Holidays, 1 week Aug. Set L £12.50 (Sun £16.95) Set D £27.50. Access, Visa.*

Set menu prices may not always include service or wine.

JERVAULX   Jervaulx Hall   70%   £125*

Tel 01677 460235   Fax 01677 460263   Map 5 D4   **H**
Jervaulx Masham nr Ripon North Yorkshire HG4 4PH

On the A6108 between Masham and Middleham, the hall stands in attractive grounds next to the ruins of the 12th-century abbey. A dignified yet homely atmosphere prevails with watercolours, period furnishings, ornaments and family photos in the quiet and appealing day rooms. Peace is the main objective in the bedrooms and there's an abundance of quality toiletries in the carpeted bathrooms. John and Margaret Sharp are the resident hosts. *Half-board terms. **Rooms** 10. Garden, croquet. Closed Nov-Mar. No credit cards.*

JEVINGTON   Hungry Monk   £60

Tel 01323 482178   Fax 01323 483989   Map 11 B6   **R**
The Street Jevington nr Polegate East Sussex BN26 5QF

Nigel and Sue Mackenzie's delightful little restaurant has a quaint exterior and charmingly rustic interior. The fixed-price menu offers plenty of choice and might include fresh haddock with fresh salmon and foie gras purée, roast guinea fowl with apple and calvados sauce; daube of venison, pigeon and pheasant with horseradish dumplings; roast rack of lamb with tapénade crust and fennel and cream sauce or a vegetarian option such as aubergine and goat's cheese croustade. Delicious puddings like steamed pear and ginger pudding with lavender ice cream or chocolate marquise with coffee cream. They claim that banoffi pie was invented here. Serious farmhouse cheeses, deserving of regional award for British Cheeseboard of the Year. A very fine wine list, eccentrically but not greedily priced, with the odd tasting note ("extraordinarily delicious") adding to the fun! Plenty of half bottles. Smoking is only allowed in the lounge. No children under 3. *Seats 44. Parties 7. Private Room 16. L (Sun only) 12-2.30 D 7-10.30. Closed Bank Holiday Mons, 3 days Christmas. Set Sun L £21.90 Set D £21.90. Amex.*

KENDAL   The Moon   £35

Tel 01539 729254   Map 4 C3   **R**
129 Highgate Kendal Cumbria LA9 4EN

Eye-catching bistro opposite the Brewery Arts Centre (park here) where attention to quality and loyalty to local produce are paramount. The monthly-changing blackboard menu is about 40% vegetarian with main dishes like mushroom, fennel and spinach brioche or raisin, feta cheese and aubergine timbale alongside monkfish, cod and prawn gratin with a dill sauce, and wild mushroom and tarragon-stuffed chicken with watercress sauce. To the monthly 'pudding club' (one starter followed by five puds, mostly traditional like their richly spiced suet pudding with brandy butter) has been added, also monthly, a 'starters club' when the menu is composed of five starters with a single pud to finish. Children's portions. Around a dozen wines on the list, with nothing over £10. No smoking. *Seats 64. Parties 22. Private Room 40. D only 6.30-10 (Sat from 6). Closed 24, 25 & 31 Dec, 1 Jan & 2 weeks late Jan/early Feb. Access, Visa.*

We welcome bona fide complaints and recommendations on the tear-out pages at the back of the book for readers' comments. They are followed up by our professional team.

KENDAL   **Woolpack Hotel**   59%   £80

Tel 01539 723852   Fax 01539 728608   Map 4 C3   **H**
Stricklandgate Kendal Cumbria LA9 4ND

17th-century former coaching inn (its ground floor was once Kendal's wool auction room) with old-fashioned original bedrooms, a modern annexe and a private car park at the rear. Banqueting/conferences for up to 120/150. Children up to 12 stay free in parents' room. No dogs. *Rooms 54. Access, Amex, Visa.*

KENILWORTH   **Restaurant Bosquet**   £75

Tel 01926 852463   Map 6 C4   **R**
97a Warwick Road Kenilworth Warwickshire CV8 1HP

Bernard and Jane Lignier have been here since 1981, and their cosy little restaurant has a strong local following. French in concept and execution, the menus nevertheless draw on good British produce, with an English translation below each French dish. Accurate saucing and good flavour/texture combinations are one of Bernard's strengths, as in partridge and foie gras en croute with game sauce; fillet of local beef on wild mushrooms with a mushroom and Madeira sauce. The day's fish dish is dependent on the market. Dishes sometimes appear on both the carte and the fixed-price menu – the latter offers choices at each stage and is not available on Saturdays. *Seats 26. L by arrangement D 7-9.15. Closed Sun, Mon, 1 week Christmas & 3 weeks Aug. Set D £21 (exc Sat). Access, Amex, Visa.*

KENILWORTH   **De Montfort Hotel**   63%   £85

Tel 01926 55944   Fax 01926 57830   Map 6 C4   **H**
Kenilworth Warwickshire CV8 1ED

Modern hotel with spacious day rooms and a good standard of accommodation including some larger family rooms. Conference facilities up to 300. Residents have free use of the Abbeyfields Leisure Centre. *Rooms 96. Snooker. Access, Amex, Diners, Visa.*

KENILWORTH   **Simpson's**   £50

Tel 01926 864567   Map 6 C4   **R**
101 Warwick Road Kenilworth Warwickshire CV8 1HL

French café chairs surround crisply clothed tables behind the twin 'shop' windows of this friendly main-street restaurant, while the walls sport menus from some of the famous restaurants where chef-patron Andreas Antona and head chef Andy Waters have worked. The fixed-price menu offers a fair choice of dishes of mainly British or Mediterranean provenance, typified by confit of duck leg with colcannon, crostini of glazed goat's cheese with pesto, ballotine of chicken bourguignonne, sea bream with fennel and green sauce, and roast belly of pork with braised cabbage. One of the two rooms is designated non-smoking. Own parking to the rear. *Seats 75. Private Room 85. L 12.30-2 D 7-10. Closed L Sat, all Sun & Bank Holidays. Set L from £13.95 Set D £16.95/£19.95. Access, Diners, Visa.*

KESWICK   **Keswick Country House Hotel**   60%   £80

Tel 01768 772020   Fax 01768 771300   Map 4 C3   **H**
Station Road Keswick Cumbria CA12 4NQ

Solid Victorian hotel set in four acres of gardens, an easy walk from the town centre. Lovely lakeland views attract families and walkers as well as business trade. A fine Victorian conservatory has a grapevine and is an ideal place for afternoon tea. Guests can play golf free (Mon to Fri) at Keswick Club. Children free in parents' room up to 14. Conferences/banqueting facilities for up to 80/150. Principal Hotels. *Rooms 66. Garden, putting. Access, Amex, Diners, Visa.*

KETTERING   **Kettering Park Hotel**   71%   £105

Tel 01536 416666   Fax 01536 416171   Map 7 E4   **H**
Kettering Parkway Kettering Northamptonshire NN15 6XT

Looking like a large Jacobean manor house though actually built only recently, Kettering Park stands above a roundabout south of Kettering next to the A1/M1 link road. Stone floors laid with Oriental carpets, oak panelling, deep-coloured, richly patterned upholstery, dark polished wood tables and furniture, tapestry wall hangings – all create an ambience that feels traditional and long-established. Public areas, structured on differing levels, flow into one another culminating in a spacious, well-laid-out bar/lounge. Bedrooms are well designed and up to date offering a good range of amenities. Executive rooms have a sitting area and all rooms have a writing desk. Decor features polished wood and well-matched, colourful fabrics. Bathrooms have excellent showers with a selection of quality toiletries. Fine leisure facilities, plenty of parking, families well catered for, conferences up to 250 delegates. Shire Inns. *Rooms 88. Garden, indoor swimming pool, children's swimming pool, gym, squash, sauna, spa bath, steam room, solarium, snooker. Access, Amex, Diners, Visa.*

KEW	Wine & Mousaka	£35

Tel 0181-940 5696　　　　　　Map 15 E2　　**R**
12 Kew Green nr Richmond Surrey TW9 3BH

Friendly Greek restaurant opposite Kew Green and next to the Coach & Horses pub. The menu covers the usual favourites including both meat and vegetarian moussaka; other specialities include souvla (lamb cooked on the bone on a charcoal spit), *kleftiko* and *kalamarakia yemista* – small squid with a filling of rice, spinach and dill, oven-baked on a bed of tomatoes. *Triada* comprises stuffed courgette, pepper and vine leaves with pork mince, rice and herbs. Seats in the garden in summer. See also entry under London W5 (Ealing). *Seats 50. Parties 20. L 12-2.30 D 6-11. Closed Sun, Bank Holidays, 4 days Christmas. Access, Amex, Diners, Visa.*

KEYSTON	The Pheasant ↑	£50

Tel 01832 710241　Fax 01832 710340　　　Map 7 E4　　**R**
Village Loop Road Keyston nr Bythorn Cambridgeshire PE18 0RE

A mile and a half off the A14 between Kettering and Huntingdon the peaceful village of Keyston has, as its claim to fame, one of the most delightful inns in the country. Standing at its heart, the Pheasant, a long, low white-washed building with a thatched roof, looks much older than its 150 or so years. Inside there are heavy dark oak beams and thick walls hung with old hunting prints. The interior is divided into a number of inter-connecting rooms, of which the bar with its open log fireplace is the focal point. That's the 'friendly village local' side of things, but the Pheasant has a growing reputation for great food and superb wines. All the food is home-made, from bread, biscuits and pasta to ice creams, and a young, enthusiastic brigade changes the modern Mediterranean-influenced menu twice weekly. Haricot bean and truffle soup, ricotta cheese and farmhouse terrine with apricot chutney and Melba toast are typical starters, while main courses run from tagliatelle with sun-dried tomatoes, rosemary and parmesan to wild boar sausages, baked salmon in puff pastry with pesto sauce and pan-fried tenderloin of pork with sage noodles, spinach and a calvados sauce. More exotic elements appear in curried lamb's kidneys with a timbale of rice and pickled chilis, or hot Thai chicken curry with a vegetable stir-fry. Cheeses are all unpasteurised and British, from Neal's Yard Dairy. Sweets could include baked rum and raisin cheesecake, Spotted Dick and custard, and passion fruit sorbet. Roast sirloin of beef with Yorkshire pudding, roast potatoes and onion gravy is the star turn Sunday lunchtimes. John Hoskins MW is indeed a master when it comes to compiling a wine list. This one is no different, both enterprising and keenly priced, spanning the globe. Authoritative tasting notes too. (See Cellar(s) of the Year awards page). One part of the dining area – the Red Room – is a no-smoking area. Tables there are larger, and the napkins are linen; the menu is the same throughout. *Seats 100. Parties 18. Private Room 24. L 12-2 D 6.30-10 (Sun 7.30-9.30). Closed D 25 & 26 Dec. Access, Amex, Diners, Visa.*

KIDDERMINSTER	Stone Manor	65%	£73

Tel 01562 777555　Fax 01562 777834　　　Map 6 B4　　**H**
Stone nr Kidderminster Hereford & Worcester DY10 4PJ

Set in 25 acres of gardens, the mock-Tudor manor was built in 1926. Many of the bedrooms overlook the rose gardens and swimming pool; some rooms have four-posters. A choice of four suites can cater for up to 150 conference delegates. 24hr room service. *Rooms 52. Garden, croquet, outdoor swimming pool, tennis, pitch & putt, children's outdoor playground. Access, Amex, Diners, Visa.*

Set menu prices may not always include service or wine.

KILVE   Meadow House   70%   £75

Tel 01278 741546   Fax 01278 741663   Map 13 E1   **H**
Sea Lane Kilve nr Bridgwater Somerset TA5 1EG

Howard and Judith Wyer-Roberts operate a civilised home-from-home at their former rectory in the foothills of the Quantocks, five minutes from a quiet, fossil-strewn beach (the inspiration for Wordsworth's *On Kilve's Beach*). Among the eight acres of hotel grounds there are immaculate landscaped gardens with a stream feeding a duck pond. It's a peaceful setting and the main-house bedrooms are spacious, attractive and well appointed. Stable rooms across the car park have sitting rooms and a pleasant, cottagey look. Antiques, original paintings and log fires are features in the drawing room, lounge and study. Children under 4 share parents' room free; sensible considerations are made for children. Banqueting/conference facilities for 24/20. Turn right off the A39 at the Hood Arms when coming from Bridgwater. *Rooms 10. Garden, croquet. Access, Amex, Visa.*

KING'S LYNN   Butterfly Hotel   62%   £65

Tel 01553 771707   Fax 01553 768027   Map 10 B1   **H**
Beveridge Way Hardwick Narrows King's Lynn Norfolk PE30 4NB

A modern, town-fringe hotel at the A10/A47 roundabout; part of a small East Anglian group aiming at the middle market. Conferences up to 40; banqueting up to 30. *Rooms 50. Garden. Access, Amex, Diners, Visa.*

KING'S LYNN   Duke's Head   60%   £87

Tel 01553 774996   Fax 01553 763556   Map 10 B1   **H**
Tuesday Market Place King's Lynn Norfolk PE30 1JS

Forte Heritage hotel with an imposing 17th-century frontage. Rooms are in a more modern extension to the rear. Children up to 16 stay free in parents' room. Conference facilities for up to 250. *Rooms 71. Access, Amex, Diners, Visa.*

KING'S LYNN   Knights Hill Hotel   62%   £89

Tel 01553 675566   Fax 01553 675568   Map 10 B1   **H**
Knights Hill Village South Wootton King's Lynn Norfolk PE30 3HQ

Located north-east of King's Lynn at the intersection of the A148 and A149 this once working farm now occupying 11 acres of grounds and its numerous buildings readily give the impression of being in a small village. Bedrooms are arranged in the original buildings as well as in a chalet-like courtyard complex. All are neat and well-equipped with satellite TV, trouser press and hair dryer among the extras. Excellent leisure and conference facilities are also provided including a beauty salon and two tennis courts. No dogs in the main hotel. *Rooms 52. Garden, tennis, croquet, indoor swimming pool, gym, sauna, spa bath, steam room, solarium, beauty salon, snooker. Access, Amex, Diners, Visa.*

KINGHAM   Mill House   66%   £100

Tel 01608 658188   Fax 01608 658492   Map 14 C1   **H**
Kingham nr Chipping Norton Oxfordshire OX7 6UH

Privately-owned Cotswold hotel in a quiet pastoral setting complete with trout stream. Local stone and exposed beams give character to the day rooms, and features from earlier days include two fine old bread ovens. Most of the prettily decorated bedrooms enjoy pleasant views. The hotel is situated halfway between Stow-on-the-Wold and Chipping Norton. No children under five. No dogs. *Rooms 23. Garden, croquet, fishing. Access, Amex, Diners, Visa.*

KINGSBRIDGE   Buckland-Tout-Saints Hotel   73%   £150*

Tel 01548 853055   Fax 01548 856261   Map 13 D3   **H**
Kingsbridge South Devon TQ7 2DS

Signposted off the A381 to the north of Kingsbridge, this classic Queen Anne house overlooks the Buckland-Tout-Saints valley just outside the small hamlet of Goveton. It is personally run by the hospitable Taylors – John, Tove and son George. Day rooms like the oak-panelled Grand Hall with log fire smouldering in marble fireplace and the convivial leather chesterfield-furnished bar, are given a homely feel by family photos and the Taylors' own collection of antiques, pictures and objets d'art. Grandest bedrooms are the seven on the first floor furnished with antiques and boasting 'deluge' showers over the bathtubs. Remaining rooms on the second floor are a little smaller, with hand-held showers at the tub, but they are equally attractively decorated and all are provided with plenty of magazines and a flask of iced water. Room service is limited to Continental breakfast plus light snacks and drinks throughout the day and evening. Excellent cooked breakfasts start the day in fine style. Children are now welcome, with under-eights staying free in parents' room. ★Half-board terms only. *Rooms 13. Garden, croquet, putting green. Access, Amex, Diners, Visa.*

KINGSTON	**Restaurant Gravier**	£70

Tel 0181-549 5557   Map 15 E2   **R**
9 Station Road Norbiton Kingston Surrey KT2 7AA

French cooking, with seafood a speciality, is the attraction at this well-liked suburban restaurant, whose decor features exposed-brick walls and hop swags. The short printed menu is more or less doubled by dishes of the day, recited at the table, the result of Jean-Philippe Gravier's early morning trips to Billingsgate. Joanne Gravier (the only English member of an otherwise exclusively French team) rules in the kitchen with a sure touch, producing excellent, generally quite straightforward dishes like, clams provençale, sea bass *au beurre nantais* (a particularly good choice), sole normande and lobster (Thermidor, l'armoricaine, flambé with calvados). A couple of meat dishes. Good desserts. Outside eating in fine weather. *Seats 40. L 12.15-2 D 7-10. Closed L Sat, all Sun, Bank Holidays, 1 week Aug, 1 week Christmas. Set L £16.50. Access, Amex, Visa.*

KINGTON	**Penrhos Court**	£75

Tel 01544 230720   Fax 01544 230754   Map 9 D4   **RR**
Penrhos Kington Hereford & Worcester HR5 3LH

Set back from the A44, an ancient farm with parts dating back to 1280 is the setting for a marvellous restaurant with rooms. Owners Martin Griffiths and Daphne Lambert have spent many years rebuilding and refurbishing the site. The dining-room is the restored 13th-century Cruck Hall, complete with heavy beams and flagstone floors. Menus change daily and consist of a short selection of well-prepared dishes using locally produced ingredients, organic where possible. There's an excellent vegetarian choice. Typical dishes include vegetable kebabs with brown rice, supreme of guinea fowl with oyster mushrooms and leeks and king prawns in a tarragon cream sauce. Good desserts to finish such as vanilla cheesecake and white chocolate mousse. No smoking. *Seats 70. Private Room 20. D only 7.30-10. Closed last 2 weeks Jan. Set L Sun £15 Set D £23.50/£30. Access, Amex, Diners, Visa.*

Rooms   £70

Nineteen individually-styled bedrooms, named after birds, show some fine taste. Eight rooms are in skilfully converted Elizabethan barns; of a fair size, they use lightwood and mahogany furniture, and co-ordinated contemporary fabrics contribute to a bright, clean decor. Bathrooms (some with shower/WC only) have attractive fittings and quality toiletries. Limited hotel-style public areas, but high bedroom standards. The Swallow Room features a four-poster bed and private balcony. Children up to 9 free in parents' room. No dogs. Garden, tennis.

KINTBURY	**Dundas Arms**	£65

Tel 01488 658263   Fax 01488 658568   Map 14 C2   **IR**
53 Station Road Kintbury nr Newbury Berkshire RG15 0UT

The Kennet and Avon canal runs by this 18th-century inn with roomy, traditionally-styled accommodation in a converted livery and stable block. Sliding picture windows offer access to a terrace with garden furniture; all rooms enjoy views over the water. *Rooms 5. Access, Amex, Visa.*

Restaurant   £65

Views over the canal from this comfortable dining-room where chef-proprieter David Dalzell-Piper offers fresh local ingredients cooked with skill and confidence. These talents show up well on the understated, hand-written menu with dishes like warm ratatouille

See over

with grilled Italian bread, home-cured gravlax with mustard and dill sauce, duck breast with lemon sauce, baked cod with a herb crust and aïoli, and casseroled beef with kumquats. Luscious puddings and fine British cheeses. Really silly prices on an outstanding wine list, silly in the sense that the classy wines are genuinely cheap and offer terrific value for money. Go on, push the boat out! *Seats 36. Parties 20. L 12-2 D 7-9.15. Closed D Mon, all Sun & Christmas-New Year. Set L £17.50.*

KINVER   Berkleys   £55

Tel 01384 873679   Map 6 B4   **R**
5 High Street Kinver West Midlands DY7 2HG

In the Piano Room (a pianist plays Fri & Sat eves) Andrew Mortimer's short menu is cautiously contemporary: hot salmon and asparagus mousseline, wild boar terrine with kumquat and redcurrant jelly, steamed sea bass with lemon and seaweed, baked loin of lamb in coriander puff pastry. Desserts from a trolley. The bistro, with a different selection of dishes, is open lunchtime and evening. *Seats 35. D 7-10 (Bistro also 12-2). Closed L Sat, all Sun, Christmas-New Year, first 2 weeks Feb. Access, Amex, Diners, Visa.*

KNARESBOROUGH   Dower House   63%   £82

Tel 01423 863302   Fax 01423 867665   Map 6 C1   **H**
Bond End Knaresborough nr Harrogate North Yorkshire HG5 9AL

A town-centre ivy-clad red-brick former dower house – the main building dates from Tudor times – that retains considerable appeal in period furnishings and features. Some of the bedrooms have an old-fashioned feel, while others, along with the conference (for up to 70) and leisure facilities, are modern. Children up to 15 stay free in parents' room. Four standard rooms are priced at £75. *Rooms 32. Garden, indoor swimming pool, gym, sauna, steam room, spa bath, solarium. Access, Amex, Diners, Visa.*

KNUTSFORD   Brasserie Belle Epoque   £60

Tel 01565 633060   Fax 01565 634150   Map 6 B2   **R**
60 King Street Knutsford Cheshire WA16 2DT

An eccentric and fascinating building constructed in 1906 right in the centre of town. The interior is an evocation of Parisian Belle Epoque with many original fittings. On offer in the recently created brasserie is a light menu of modern, imaginative dishes. Starters include Cheshire cheese sausages, Worcestershire snails with garlic, braised endive with bacon and cheese and home-smoked haddock fillet with Welsh rarebit. Main dishes could be Cheshire pork fillet in a spiced Marsala and apricot sauce, braised Gressingham duck breast with a plum and sage sauce, traditional hot pot and chargrilled fresh tuna with new potatoes with onions and balsamic vinegar. Excellent desserts range from sweet pancakes filled with caramelised strawberries to chocolate fondant with a redcurrant sauce. In good weather a few tables are put out on the roof garden. Not many wines over £20, and with champagne at £4 a glass (another dozen or so wines available by the glass), this is a user-friendly and enterprising list that offers terrific value for money. *Seats 110. Parties 15. Private Room 80. L 12-2 D 7-10.30. Closed L Sat, all Sun, Bank Holidays, 1 week Jan. Set L £10.95 Set D from £15. Access, Amex, Diners, Visa.*

Rooms   £60

Seven mostly antique-furnished bedrooms, with generally rather masculine decor, come with remote-control TVs and good bathrooms – all with tubs and generous towelling. Most rooms overlook an Italianate terrace and the herb garden. Room rates include a good and substantial Continental breakfast complete with boiled eggs and home-baked croissants.

KNUTSFORD   Cottons Hotel   65%   £114

Tel 01565 650333   Fax 01565 755351   Map 6 B2   **H**
Manchester Road Knutsford Cheshire WA16 0SU

Five minutes from the M6 (junction 19) and just 15 from Manchester Airport, Cottons was designed with a New Orleans theme. There's plenty of free parking and versatile facilities for conferences (up to 200 delegates theatre-style). Two bars – the Bourbon Street and the Rose Revived – provide a choice for the thirsty. Considerable reductions

for children, whether or not in parents' room. A new leisure complex and 17 additional bedrooms were due to open in the summer of '95. Shire Inns. *Rooms 82.*
Indoor swimming pool, gym, squash, sauna, spa bath, sun beds. Access, Amex, Diners, Visa.

LACOCK	At The Sign of The Angel	£75

Tel 01249 730230   Fax 01249 730527   Map 14 B2   **IR**
6 Church Street Lacock nr Chippenham Wiltshire SN15 2LB

A 15th-century wool-merchant's house situated in a National Trust village and run by the Levis family since 1953. Beams, creaking floors, huge fireplaces and heavy oak furniture offer plenty of character in the bedrooms. The lounge is shared by residents and diners. Rooms in the cottage annexe are no longer part of the inn. *Rooms 6. Garden. Closed 1 week Christmas. Access, Amex, Visa.*

Restaurant   £70

Polished antique tables, candlelight and log fires all help to create a suitably olde-worlde atmosphere for some sound English cooking: Stilton and walnut paté, wild boar sausages with Cumberland sauce, pan-fried lamb's kidneys in Madeira, salmon with lemon hollandaise, lamb cutlets with mint sauce and onion gravy and for dinner, and Sunday lunch, there is always a traditional roast. The day's hot pudding shares the dessert list with things like treacle and walnut pudding with clotted cream and almond crème brulée – or try the English cheeseboard. *Seats 45. Parties 20. Private Room 20. L 12.30-2 D 7.30-9. Closed L Mon (except Bank Holidays).*

LAMORNA COVE	Lamorna Cove Hotel	65%	£49

Tel 01736 731411   Map 12 A4   **H**
Lamorna Cove nr Penzance Cornwall TR19 6XH

Lamorna Cove is on the southern edge of the Penwith Peninsula about 15 minutes drive from Penzance (first take the Newlyn road, then the B3315 towards Porthcurno and Treen, from which the cove and hotel are signposted). Set into the steeply sloping wooded hillside, it enjoys splendid views. Malcolm and Lisa Gray have created a home from home full of style and comfort. Rooms and suites are priced according to their view – cove, valley, or both. Well-equipped and maintained day rooms and sun terraces make ideal spots in which to relax. *Rooms 12. Garden, outdoor swimming pool. Closed Nov-mid Feb. Access, Amex, Visa.*

LANCASTER	Forte Posthouse	69%	£72

Tel 01524 65999   Fax 01524 841265   Map 6 A1   **H**
Waterside Park Caton Road Lancaster Lancashire LA1 3RA

Well-designed, practical accommodation and smart public rooms in a low-rise hotel overlooking the River Lune. Banqueting and conference facilities for 100. *Rooms 115. Indoor swimming pool, gym, sauna, spa bath, solarium. Access, Amex, Diners, Visa.*

LAND'S END	Land's End Hotel	64%	£75

Tel 01736 871844   Fax 01736 871599   Map 12 A4   **H**
Land's End Sennen Cornwall TR19 7AA

Part of the Land's End complex that includes a museum, 'Man and the Sea' exhibition, farm animal and craft area and a multi-sensory presentation of Cornish history (well worth seeing) amongst other things, all of which are free to hotel guests. Conversely, visitors to the centre have access to the hotel's public rooms which consist of a smart reception/lounge with rugs over woodblock floor, and a rattan-furnished Observatory Bar with a breathtaking view of the Atlantic from its clifftop position. Bedrooms have light, soft colour schemes with original pictures on the walls, limed lightwood furniture and Lloyd Loom easy chairs and glass-topped tables. Many have sea views. Good bathrooms except for the lack of shelf space. Conference facilities can cope with up to 200 delegates theatre-style. Children up to 14 stay free in parents' room. *Rooms 34. Terrace, children's playground, gift shops, coffee shop (10am-6pm). Access, Amex, Visa.*

Consult the blue pages for summary tables and lists of recommended establishments.

LANGAR   Langar Hall   70%   £80

Tel 01949 860559   Fax 01949 861045   Map 7 D3   **HR**
Langar Nottinghamshire NG13 9HG

The village of Langar (signposted via Bingham on the A52 or Cropwell Bishop on the
A46) is tucked away in the lush Vale of Belvoir, and the Hall itself is virtually hidden
behind the church. Built in 1830 of local sandstone, it is now the family home of Imogen
Skirving and as such is crammed full of antiques and homely artefacts. Large oil paintings
of past family members line the wide stone staircase in the entrance hall, which has an
informality continued throughout the hotel. There's very much an air of loving care,
which applies to furnishings and guests equally. Public rooms comprise a dark, intimate
library and bright, sunny drawing room both furnished in a comfortable, lived-in style.
Bedrooms upstairs in the main house vary in size and character; the courtyard rooms are
more up-to-date but all the rooms have oodles of appeal including a wide selection of
books and fine views over the extensive grounds. No smoking in bedrooms. *Rooms 12.
Garden, croquet, coarse fishing. Access, Amex, Visa.*

Restaurant   £70

With pillars and a huge fireplace, the restaurant occupies what was an inner hall. Silver
candelabra and fresh flowers decorate tables which are large and well spaced. The
cooking is basically English but with Continental influences: black pudding ravioli with
mushy peas, watercress and potato soup, venison bresaola with rocket and a mango and
sesame seed relish, salmon with sorrel sauce, pot-roast chicken with morels, rabbit
casserole with pearl barley, mascarpone cheesecake with poached fruit, treacle tart and
custard. There are some good wines on the list, though there's a huge difference in price
between the least expensive claret and the next one up! About once a month there is
some opera or theatre to accompany dinner. On such evenings the Indian dining-room
is available to diners who prefer to eat without the entertainment. *Seats 30. Parties 12.
Private Room 20. L 12-2 D 7-9.30 (Fri & Sat till 10). Closed Sun (D for residents only).*

LANGDALE   Langdale Hotel   71%   £134

Tel 01539 437302   Fax 01539 437694   Map 4 C3   **H**
Great Langdale nr Ambleside Cumbria LA22 9JD

Thirty-five acres of woodland make a secluded setting for a well-run hotel and country
club. Bedrooms, all doubles or twins, are in several satellite blocks built of Lakeland
stone, and there are some family rooms with bunk beds. Decor is either modern or
Edwardian with four-posters or canopied beds, and there are some self-catering lodges
for weekly rental. There's an open-plan bar-lounge, and a nearby slate-walled pub bar.
Rooms overlooking Great Langdale Beck have private balconies. Guests have full use of the
hotel's considerable leisure facilities. *Seats 65. Garden, croquet, tennis, fishing, indoor
swimming pool, children's splash pool, gym, children's playground, games room, snooker,
shop, coffee shop (9am-11.30pm), riding. Access, Amex, Diners, Visa.*

LANGHO   Northcote Manor   67%   £85

Tel 01254 240555   Fax 01254 246568   Map 6 B1   **HR**
Northcote Road Langho nr Blackburn Lancashire BB6 8BE

About ten miles from the M6 (Junction 31), the extended Victorian redbrick house looks
down over the Ribble Valley, though not all the hotel's rooms enjoy this view. Inside,
the atmosphere is almost 'olde worlde' with beams, oak panelling and roaring log fires
(even in summer if the night is chilly). The entrance hall-cum-bar has two lounges
leading off it and a fine staircase that ascends to the bedrooms. These are spacious and
attractively decorated and furnished, retaining much of their original character, with good
antiques, bric-à-brac, bold and colourful fabrics, and nice touches such as board games,
magazines, music alarm and remote-control satellite TV. Bathrooms vary from modern to
old-fashioned (with Victorian tiles and cast-iron tubs), all splendidly equipped, even
boasting Nina Ricci toiletries. Under the direction of joint owners Craig Bancroft and
Nigel Haworth (see below), service is of a high standard (for example afternoon tea and
warm shortbread on arrival) with excellent housekeeping and maintenance.
Improvements to the grounds continue with a new herb garden the latest project along
with the planting of yet more trees. Breakfasts are sensational, with freshly squeezed
juices, seasonal fruits, local yoghurt, home-made jams and marmalade, as well as farm
eggs, local sausages and black pudding. Banqueting for 100, conferences for 40, with the
boardroom ideal for small numbers up to 26. No dogs. *Rooms 14. Garden. Access, Amex,
Diners, Visa.*

Restaurant £90

The main dining-room has an attractive bay window and a pair of gilt and crystal chandeliers with matching wall lights creating a suitably civilised setting for some quite splendid cooking. Nigel Haworth leads a gifted team (William Reid is credited on the menu as head chef) producing such carefully composed dishes as crisp duck confit with warm tarragon potato salad and a mustard dressing, and a risotto of forest mushrooms with Italian parsley and shavings of *tete de Moine* cheese among the starters and main dishes like a rack of Pendle lamb with coriander, chargrilled Mediterranean vegetables and olive'd potatoes; breast of Goosnargh duckling with chicken liver samosas on glazed winter vegetables, fondant potatoes and a mild pepper sauce, and steamed Scottish salmon with hollandaise. There are also a couple of regional dishes such as Bury black pudding and buttered pink trout served together with a mustard and watercress sauce. Desserts are equally delicious: banana custard with a caramel crust, sticky toffee pudding with butterscotch sauce, iced bread-and-butter pudding with apricots and raspberries. Good selection of British and Irish farmhouse cheeses too plus a special plate of Lancashire cheeses. Lunchtimes there's a limited choice table d'hote in addition to a shortened version of the evening à la carte and at night there is also a no-choice, six-course gourmet menu. Sunday lunch brings a short à la carte that always includes a traditional roast. A good all-round wine list notable for the number of half bottles available. *Seats* 80. *Parties* 12. *Private Room* 40. *L* 12-1.30 (Sun till 2) *D* 7-9.30 (Sat till 10). *Set L £18.95 Set D £35.*

LANGLEY-ON-TYNE	**Langley Castle**	**63%**	**£85**

Tel 01434 688888   Fax 01434 684019   Map 5 D2   **H**
Langley-on-Tyne nr Haydon Bridge Northumberland NE49 0LY

A tall square structure originally built in 1365 but gutted by fire in 1405. The castle remained a shell for 500 years until, at the turn of this century, it was rebuilt. It became a hotel 10 years ago but there still remains plenty to remind one of the castle's origins – from the four foot thick walls to the garde-robes, thankfully no longer in use, and the spiral staircases which lead to some of the bedrooms. The lounge occupies a large portion of the first floor. It has a tiny, cosy bar through a door in one corner. Five 'feature' bedrooms each has either a 4-poster or half-tester bed. Additionally one has a spa bath and another a circular bath and private sauna. 8 new bedrooms are planned in a conversion of separate outhouses. The hotel is on the A686, a mile or two south of Haydon Bridge. *Rooms 10. Garden. Access, Amex, Diners, Visa.*

LAVENHAM	**Great House**	**£45**

Tel 01787 247431   Fax 01787 248007   Map 10 C3   **RR**
Market Place Lavenham Suffolk CO10 9QZ

The Great House is 15th-century with a Georgian facade, and stands just opposite the historic Guildhall in this well-preserved medieval town. Frenchman Régis Crépy provides excellent food, served in cosy surroundings. *Moules au curry, terrine de canard forestière, turbot braisé au champagne, noisettes d'agneau au basilic* and *tournedos Rossini au Madére* indicate the style; parcels of cheese fondue, confit of duck with beans, tarte tatin and crème brulée are considered specialities. Wide selection of French cheeses. Long, brasserie-style lunch menu (not Sun) and both fixed-price (not D Sat) and à la carte in the evening. French-style Sunday lunch, when there's a choice of around six or dishes at each stage, is always popular. Every wine is accompanied by tasting notes; plenty under £20. Seating for 25 on a patio. Smoking is not encouraged. *Seats 40. Private Room 50. L 12-2.30 D 7-9.30 (Sat to 10.30). Closed D Sun, all Mon, 5-25 Jan. Set Sun L £16.95, children £9 Set D £16.95 (not Sat). Access, Amex, Visa.*

Rooms   £68

There are four charming, traditionally furnished bedrooms all with either a separate lounge or a sitting area; one room has two double beds. Thick beams, antique furniture and floral fabrics create the look of village England. Walled garden with swings. The tariff increases to £78 on Saturday nights and £88 on Bank Holidays; children under 4 share free (cot supplied), 4- to 12-year-olds are charged £10.

LAVENHAM   The Swan   71%   £128

Tel 01787 247477   Fax 01787 248286   Map 10 C3   **HR**
High Street Lavenham nr Sudbury Suffolk CO10 9QA

A splendid example of Elizabethan architecture in an attractive and much visited village. Bristling with timbers, the cosy alcoves meander one into another, creating charming public areas. The lounge has long been the setting for relaxing afternoon tea, while the earthy real-ale bar has the warm feel of a much-loved local. Walkways overlooking pretty little gardens lead to the variously sized bedrooms, designed to retain the period feel; stylish furniture and extras like fruit and chocolates set the the tone for the attention to detail in evidence throughout the hotel; half the rooms are reserved for non-smokers. If you want to get the real feel of the place, ask for a room with a four-poster bed and private sitting-room. Three function suites, the largest holding 130. Forte. *Rooms 47. Garden. Access, Amex, Diners, Visa.*

Restaurant   £75

The restaurant, though but thirty years old, is in keeping with the hotel's origins and has a lofty, open-raftered ceiling and a minstrel's gallery. Chef Andrew Barrass has a sure touch and his menus offer a good choice of carefully cooked dishes, based on traditional British methods: chicken and leek broth, fillet of salmon and herbs, breast of pheasant with wild mushrooms, peppered sirloin steak. Modest wine list, fair prices. Informal snacks served 9.30-5.30 in the lounge areas. No smoking. *Seats 70. Parties 20. Private Room 40. L 12.30-2 D 7-9.30. Set L £12.95/£14.95 (Sun £16.95) Set D £21.95.*

LEAMINGTON SPA   Courtyard by Marriott   65%   £82

Tel 01926 425522   Fax 01926 881322   Map 14 C1   **H**
Olympus Avenue Europa Way Leamington Spa Warwickshire CV34 6RJ

Roomy and practical accommodation next to an industrial park, aimed mainly at the business traveller. Conference and banqueting facilities for up to 50. Half the bedrooms are designated non-smoking. Free car parking. *Rooms 94. Keep-fit equipment. Access, Amex, Diners, Visa.*

LEAMINGTON SPA   Inchfield Hotel   63%   £78

Tel 01926 883777   Fax 01926 330467   Map 14 C1   **H**
64 Upper Holly Walk Leamington Spa Warwickshire CV32 4JL

A large, double-fronted, Victorian house with a more modern bedroom extension to the side, just five minutes from the town centre. Bedrooms are of a good standard, quietly stylish and equipped with the usual modern comforts. No dogs. *Rooms 22. Garden. Access, Amex, Visa.*

LEAMINGTON SPA   Mallory Court   80%   £173

Tel 01926 330214   Fax 01926 451714   Map 14 C1   **HR**
Harbury Lane Bishop's Tachbrook Leamington Spa Warwickshire CV33 9QB

Two miles south of Leamington Spa, off the B4087 towards Harbury, and standing in 10 acres of beautifully landscaped gardens, Mallory Court has an air of luxury and refinement. It's one of the original country house hotels and still one of the very best, built in 1910 in the Elizabethan style of tall chimneys and stone-mullioned windows with leaded lights. A small entrance hall leads directly into the main lounge, complete with deep-cushioned couches and armchairs, quality drapes, deep carpets and fine period furniture; the drawing room boasts green leather chesterfields and there's a delightful conservatory sun-trap. Bedrooms are generally of a good size and impeccably designed, with stylish fabrics, light, fresh colours and quality freestanding furniture; some have four-posters. Extras in the rooms include bath robes, mineral water, flowers and magazines. The Blenheim suite is nothing short of luxurious with its own balcony, two tubs in the bathroom and a painted ceiling. Attentive staff and highly efficient housekeeping. Unsuitable for children under the age of 9. Parking includes six garage spaces. No dogs – kennels nearby. **Rooms 10**. *Garden, croquet, outdoor swimming pool, squash, all-weather tennis. Access, Amex, Visa.*

Restaurant   ★   £120

Oak panelling, yellow table cloths, chintzy curtains and comfortable leather dining chairs set the scene for new chef Stephen Shore's modern French cuisine. Lunch is a 2- or 3-course, fixed-price affair with four choices at each stage: spinach and coconut soup or quenelle of game mousseline with beetroot purée may be followed by pink roasted duck with glazed orange or fillet of red mullet with roulade of Dover sole and crab. In the evening there is a set dinner and a wider choice available on the à la carte menu, or diners can opt for the five-course, no-choice gourmet menu from which pink roasted squab pigeon with cannelloni of wild mushrooms and glazed shallots and lightly poached oysters with an avocado mousse and salad of baby broad beans dressed in saffron are considered specialities. Desserts include Grand Marnier soufflé with orange sorbet and strawberry bavarois and there are eleven good British cheeses on the board. Only the excellently-chosen recommended house wines, all available by the glass, attract tasting notes, but this does not detract from a fine list that includes some first-rate clarets and burgundies. Excellent service for which "no charge is made or expected". No children under 9. **Seats 50. Parties 22.** *L 12.30-2 D 7.30-9.45. Set L £19.50/£23.50 (Sun £25). Set D £30.*

Many hotels offer reduced rates for weekend or out-of-season bookings. Always ask about special deals.

| **LEAMINGTON SPA** | **Regent Hotel** | 68% | £89 |

Tel 01926 427231   Fax 01926 450728   Map 14 C1   **HR**
77 The Parade Leamington Spa Warwickshire CV32 4AX

The Regent was the largest hotel in the world when built in 1819, and George IV, when still Prince Regent, graciously allowed it to be named after him. In the same family ownership since 1904, the hotel has benefited from a consistent policy of refurbishment and modernisation over the years. Charmingly 'old-fashioned' touches include eiderdowns on the beds, the overnight cleaning of shoes left outside bedroom doors at night and genuinely friendly, helpful service from often long-serving staff. Free parking. 24hr room service. **Rooms 80**. *Games room. Access, Amex, Diners, Visa.*

Vaults Restaurant   £65

Head chef of 25 years standing Roland Clark is happily still at the helm, presiding over à la carte and fixed-price menus which offer fairly traditional dishes. You might find home-cured smoked salmon trout with supreme of chicken princess, medallions of veal à la crème, lamb and duck casserole and sirloin steak garni along with a reassuringly British cabinet pudding with apricot sauce. The setting, as the name suggests, is the barrel-vaulted cellars of the hotel, most of it reserved for non-smokers. On the wine list there's a mixture of real quality with the banal. The New World selection is disappointing. **Seats 50. Parties 14.** *L 12.30-2. D 7-10.45. Closed Sun & Bank Holidays. Set L £9.75/£11.75 Set D £12.50/£16.50.*

| **LEDBURY** | **The Feathers** | £85 |

Tel 01531 635266   Fax 01531 632001   Map 14 B1   **❙**
High Street Ledbury Hereford & Worcester HR8 1DS

Right in the town centre, a distinctive timber-framed coaching inn dating from 1564 with characterful, en-suite, double-glazed bedrooms (including one with a four-poster), original Elizabethan wall paintings, uneven, creaky floors and drunken staircases. Good snacks in the hop-bedecked Fuggles Bar and small rear patio in good weather. Conferences for up to 100. **Rooms 11**. *Squash. Access, Amex, Diners, Visa.*

Lodges are now listed by county in the reference section

LEDBURY   Hope End   70%   £120

Tel 01531 633613   Fax 01531 636366   Map 14 B1   **HR**
Hope End Ledbury Hereford & Worcester HR8 1SQ

Elizabeth Barrett-Browning's former home, largely of 18th-century origin, is at the centre of a triangle formed by the three cathedral cities of Hereford, Gloucester and Worcester. It nestles in 40 acres of wooded parkland and a beautiful Georgian landscaped garden which includes a temple, grotto and island ruin. Today's incumbents John and Patricia Hegarty run this haven of tranquillity in suitably informal fashion, setting piles of books by the deep sofas in front of the log-burning stoves. Simply decorated bedrooms, one in a little rustic cottage, have exposed beams along with country oak and antique stripped-pine furniture, fresh flowers and yet more books; no TV unless requested. Cork and tile bathrooms come with a selection of bath oils. The rate quoted is for a standard room. Two small rooms are priced at £97, the three best rooms £140. No children under 12. No dogs. **Rooms** 9. Garden. Closed mid Dec-1st weekend Feb. Access, Visa.

Restaurant   £70

Patricia Hegarty is the definitive home cook, her chutneys, breads and jellies as integral a part of production as her nightly fixed-price dinner. The kitchen garden provides vegetables, herbs and fruit for many dishes; a typical meal might start with carrot and coriander seed soup or rabbit hot-pot with bacon and mushroom sauce; continue with Herefordshire beef olives with cider sauce and end with cheese or a dessert such as bitter chocolate rum tart or raspberry and yoghurt ribbon pudding. There are many half bottles on mostly classic French wine list. The Australian section is very keenly priced. No smoking. **Seats** 24. Parties 6. D only at 7.30. Set D £30.

LEEDS   Adriano Flying Pizza   £30

Tel 0113 266 6501   Fax 0113 266 5470   Map 6 C1   **R**
60 Street Lane Roundhay Leeds West Yorkshire LS8 2DQ

A success story that started more than 20 years, Adriano offers much more than just pizzas. Apart from the extensive carte of standard Italian main courses (plenty of veal, chicken and steak dishes), the daily (except Monday) list of fresh fish dishes is particularly worthy of note. In good weather eat outside on the cobbled pavement under a colourful awning. **Seats** 140. Parties 20. L 12-2.30 D 6-11.30. Closed Easter Sun, 25 & 26 Dec, 1 Jan. Access, Amex, Visa.

LEEDS   Bibis   £50

Tel 0113 243 0905   Fax 0113 234 0844   Map 6 C1   **R**
Minerva House 16 Greek Street Leeds West Yorkshire LS1 5RU

Smart yet informal restaurant in Roman forum style squeezed in between city-centre office blocks. An extensive menu – everything from lobster ravioli with shrimp sauce and osso buco alla milanese to pizzas – is supplemented by daily specials: smoked pigeon and quail's egg salad, charred tuna steak with salsa verde. Cooking is distinctly above average, as is the service, which is particularly swift at lunchtime to meet the needs of the local business community. Children under 12 have their own "Sunday Funday" menu. **Seats** 160. Parties 40. L 12-2.15 (Sun to 2.30) D 6-11.15 (Sun to 10.30). Closed 25 Dec. Access, Amex, Visa.

LEEDS   Brasserie Forty Four †   £70

Tel 0113 234 3232   Fax 0113 234 3332   Map 6 C1   **R**
44 The Calls Leeds West Yorkshire LS2 7EW

The restaurant enjoys an enviable riverside location with a balcony for alfresco dining. Originally a grain-mill, it is located adjacent to and under 42 The Calls, the hotel, with which it shares a similar modern design concept. Huge colourful artwork hangs on the white-painted brick walls and tables and chairs are of simple contemporary design. The menu reflects this simplicity of decor and is a lengthy selection of modern Mediterranean dishes augmented by a few of Oriental and American origin. Roast peppers with tomato, basil and garlic, scrambled eggs basquaise and deep-fried duck pancakes with plum sauce are typical starters, while favourites among the main courses are chargrilled vegetables with olive tapénade, cod with mash, sirloin of beef with mushrooms and a rich red wine sauce (with Yorkshire pud if you want) and the B44's Grill comprising Toulouse sausage, black pudding and pancetta. Desserts include agreeably citrous crepes Suzette, classic lemon tart and an indulgent (for 2) chocolate fondue with Cointreau-laced chocolate, marshmallows and fresh fruit pieces. An inexpensive wine list has New World wines outweighing their European counterparts, and South Africa with a section all to itself. Splendid service. Booking essential. *Seats 112. Private Room 60. L 12-2 D 6.30-10.30 (Fri & Sat 6-11). Closed Sun, Bank Holiday Mons, 1 week Christmas. Set L £8.75/£11.95 (also D before 7.15). Access, Amex, Diners, Visa.*

LEEDS	Dawat	£30

Tel 0113 287 2279   Map 6 C1   **R**
4-6 Leeds Road Kippax nr Leeds West Yorkshire LS25 7LT

Indian home cooking Delhi-style – from lamb pasanda and king prawn pepper masala to makhani and tandoori specialities – from owner Mrs Arora in two 19th-century cottages. *Seats 26. Parties 12. D only 6.30-11. Closed Sun, 25 & 26 Dec. Access, Diners, Visa.*

LEEDS	42 The Calls	£140

Tel 0113 244 0099 Fax 0113 234 4100   Map 6 C1   **PH**
42 The Calls Leeds West Yorkshire LS2 7EW

A once unsalubrious riverside a stone's throw from the city centre has, in the last few years, undergone a major transformation, and here, derelict and neglected grain mills have been completely refurbished to create very distinctive, high-calibre accommodation (see also separate entries for *Brasserie 44* and *Pool Court at 42*, which are under the same ownership). While the public rooms may not amount to much in terms of size they are nevertheless quite adequate for the needs of this establishment. Revolving doors lead into a light reception area with a small bar and mezzanine lounge leading from it. The bedrooms are, quite simply, stunning. Virtually every conceivable extra has been included to create the nearest to a home-from-home in the spacious, well-designed rooms, including CD stereo system, fully stocked mini-bar and filter coffee machine. There's ample seating, too, as well as large writing desks, while from the windows there are views over the attractive new developments that border the river. Beds are wide and comfortable ensuring a good night's sleep and bathrooms are very thoughtfully equipped. Excellent standards of discreet service. *Rooms 41. Closed Christmas week. Access, Amex, Diners, Visa.*

LEEDS	Haley's Hotel	72%	£112

Tel 0113 278 4446 Fax 0113 275 3342   Map 6 C1   **HR**
Shire Oak Road Headingley Leeds West Yorkshire LS6 2DE

An elegant Victorian town house down a quiet leafy lane off Headingley's main thoroughfare. Transformed four years ago into a charming small hotel it possesses a homely lounge-cum-bar which is furnished in an elegant country house style. Bedrooms are the best feature. Each is decorated differently, all in good taste with fine fabrics that include colourful quilted chintzes. Furniture is of good quality with lots of polished natural wood. All expected amenities from tea/coffee-makers to satellite TVs are provided. Each room also has its own 'Haley the Cat', a delightful life-size kitty which guests leave outside the door when they do not wish to be disturbed. Bathrooms are neat and thoughtfully equipped. Large shower roses over the baths provide a reviving deluge in the morning. *Rooms 22. Garden. Closed 25-30 Dec. Access, Amex, Diners, Visa.*

Restaurant   £60

The price for the main course denotes the cost of a three-course dinner at this dining-room with a restful colour scheme of browns and creams. A menu of modern dishes offers starters such as a terrine of mixed seafood in a saffron jelly, sautéed lamb's kidneys with noodles and a Madeira sauce and marinated salmon with a lemon vinaigrette and a hazelnut salad. Main dishes could be pan-fried sea bass with fennel and tarragon, baked guinea fowl breast in a pastry trellis, saddle of lamb with polenta, tomatoes and basil and roast venison with figs, chestnuts and a port sauce. Desserts are equally imaginative: tangy

See over

lemon tart; iced gingerbread parfait with a prune and armagnac syrup and hot apple and cinnamon crepe. Less than fifty wines on a somewhat modest list here. Restaurant open to residents only on Sundays evening. *Seats 45. Parties 12. Private Room 25. L (Sun Sep-May only) 12.30-2 D 7.15-9.45. Set Sun L £12.95.*

LEEDS	Hilton National	69%	£114

Tel 0113 244 2000 Fax 0113 243 3577   Map 6 C1   **H**
Neville Street Leeds West Yorkshire LS1 4BX

Escalators in glass 'antechambers' lead to the cool marble reception/lounge in this modern, well-kept, well-run hotel which has a brand new leisure centre this year. One bedroom is equipped for disabled guests. Conference/banqueting facilities for 400/350. *Rooms 206. Indoor swimming pool & children's splash pool, gym, sauna, spa bath, sun beds, garage, coffee shop (10am-11pm). Access, Amex, Diners, Visa.*

LEEDS	Holiday Inn Crowne Plaza	69%	£142

Tel 0113 244 2200   Fax 0113 244 0460   Map 6 C1   **H**
Wellington Street Leeds West Yorkshire LS1 4DL

Ten minutes walk westwards from the city centre, this tall modern hotel stands en route to the airport. It offers all the expected modern comforts. The leisure facilities include a splendid blue-mosaic-tiled swimming pool. Well equipped for families. Children can stay free in parents' room. Full porterage. No dogs. The addition of 'Crowne Plaza' to the name has also involved a second restaurant and a major, ongoing, refurbishment programme. *Rooms 125. Indoor swimming pool, children's pool, keep-fit equipment, sauna, spa bath, solarium, beauty salon, beauty salon, snooker. Access, Amex, Diners, Visa.*

LEEDS	Leeds Marriott	74%	£100

Tel 0113 236 6366   Fax 0113 236 6367   Map 6 C1   **H**
4 Trevelyan Square Boar Lane Leeds West Yorkshire LS1 6ET

Part of an attractive new office development overlooking a pretty, part-lawned quadrangle with fountain due east of the station at the junction of Boar Lane and Briggate. Boasting impressive public rooms, the Marriott, opened in October '93, features a spacious foyer with large, square stone pillars and rich mahogany panelling. John T's Bar has a clubby, almost traditional ambience which is created in part by more mahogany panelling, etched frosted glass windows and leather-upholstered seating. Bedrooms are comfortable and up-to-date, each with at least a double (queen-size) bed, some with two. Executive rooms have king-size beds mini-bars and bathrobes. Each has all the expected amenities, including fax points, remote satellite TVs. 24hr room service. Park in the next-door NCP (free to residents from 5pm-10am): for an additional £5 the hall porters will valet park your car. *Rooms 244. Indoor swimming pool, children's splash pool, gym, sauna, sunbeds, spa bath, news kiosk. Access, Amex, Diners, Visa.*

LEEDS	Leodis Brasserie		£80

Tel 0113 242 1010 Fax 0113 243 0432   Map 6 C1   **R**
Victoria Mill Sovereign Street Leeds West Yorkshire LS1 4BJ

The ground floor of a former Victorian mill, just south of the city centre in a fast-developing area now firmly on the circuit of the Leeds smart set. Curved plate-glass screens, halogen spots and stylish modern furniture contrast with the old timbers and exposed redbrick of the walls and arched ceilings. The menu affords a lengthy, varied choice of starters, mains and sweets, and the speciality of the house is traditional ribs of beef carved from the trolley (lunchtime only). The rest of the dishes mainly strike a more contemporary note with the likes of red lentil soup with coriander and crème fraiche, wild mushroom and garlic tart, deep-fried pancake of smoked haddock, confit of duck with braised butter beans, loin of lamb in puff pastry with spinach pancake and chicken mousse and roast fillet steak with Madeira sauce on chargrilled polenta. An easy-to-use and varied wine list with helpful notes offers very fair prices (several *marque* champagnes under £30 and many good wines under £20, even £15). It's good to see a list that complements the style and price of the food. *Seats 169. Parties 20. L 12-2 D 6-10 (Fri & Sat to 11). Closed L Sat, all Sun. Set L & D £11.95. Access, Amex, Visa.*

LEEDS	Maxi's Chinese Restaurant	£40

Tel 0113 244 0552 Fax 0113 234 3902 Map 6 C1 **R**
Bingley Street Leeds West Yorkshire LS3 1LX

The largest purpose-built Chinese restaurant in the North, serving Cantonese and Peking cuisine to 300 diners. Hardly worthy of a foodie pilgrimage, but worth knowing about; plenty of room for families and a couple of private suites for functions. *Seats 300. Meals 12-12. Closed 25 & 26 Dec. Set meals from £16. Access, Amex, Diners, Visa.*

LEEDS	Merrion Thistle Hotel	65%	£107

Tel 0113 243 9191 Fax 0113 242 3527 Map 6 C1 **H**
Merrion Centre Wade Lane Leeds West Yorkshire LS2 8NH

A smartly decorated business oriented hotel (the majority of the rooms are singles) forming part of a shopping precinct. Public rooms are located on the first floor. Bedrooms on the third floor have longer beds but all rooms are well-equipped including some with trouser press, others with an iron and ironing board. There is complimentary overnight parking at the adjacent NCP. *Rooms 109. Access, Amex, Diners, Visa.*

LEEDS	New Asia	£35

Tel 0113 234 3612 Map 6 C1 **R**
128 Vicar Lane Leeds West Yorkshire LS2 7NL

Mr Xuan Truong Hoang produces inexpensive Vietnamese specialities in slightly old-fashioned surroundings. Fine spring rolls made to order, mung bean flour *(luk dao fan)* noodles and char siu. There's a long list of seafood and over a dozen soups. *Seats 60. L 12-2 D 5-12. Set L from £4.20 Set D from £9.50. Access, Visa.*

LEEDS	The Olive Tree	£55

Tel 0113 256 9283 Map 6 C1 **R**
Oaklands Rodley Lane Leeds West Yorkshire LS13 1NG

Above-average Greek cooking in a lively atmosphere. Meze are the most popular order, available in meat, seafood or vegetarian versions. Greek coffee comes with some excellent Turkish delight. Every Tuesday and Friday there is a 'bouzouki' evening with live music and dancing at no extra charge. *Seats 150. Private Room 60. L 12-2 D 6-11. Closed L Sat, 25 Dec, 1 Jan. Set L & D £13.50. Access, Amex, Visa.*

LEEDS	Oulton Hall Hotel	75%	£115

Tel 0113 282 1000 Fax 0113 282 8066 Map 6 C1 **H**
Rothwell Lane Oulton Leeds West Yorkshire LS26 8HN

Opened in 1993, the hotel recreates a semblance of the original Grade II classical Italianate mid-19th century mansion. Surrounded by Leeds City Council golf courses (reception is able to book guests on to these), the hotel also has its own extensive leisure complex. A fine black-and-white tile-floored entrance hall leads to a series of very impressive public rooms. The beautifully proportioned and furnished library and drawing room open one to another and share the services of a tail-coated butler. Here walls are covered in fine damask and, as elsewhere in the public areas, huge glittering crystal chandeliers hang from the ornate ceilings. The galleried Great Hall offers additional very comfortable seating and leads to the Calverley Bar with its elegant red leather-upholstered seating. Doors open on to the south terrace, which in turn overlooks a formal garden. The majority of the bedrooms have very much an 'international air' being uniform in size and equipped with a host of modern amenities including mini-bars and remote satellite TVs. The majority of the rooms are non-smoking. Bathrooms feature good showers. Friendly staff. De Vere Hotels. *Rooms 152. Garden, indoor swimming pool, gym, sauna, solarium, spa bath, beauty salon, snooker. Access, Amex, Diners, Visa.*

LEEDS   Pool Court at 42   ★   NEW   £80

Tel 0113 244 4242 Fax 0113 234 3332   Map 6 C1   **R**
42-44 The Calls Leeds West Yorkshire LS2 8AQ

Michael Gill has created this star-worthy reincarnation of the original Pool Court (in Pool-in-Wharfedale: the restaurant had an enviable reputation for its very elegant setting as well as the quality of its food). Eating is either in the brasserie (see entry for *Brasserie Forty Four*) or via its own private side entrance from the street. The decor is now very much more modern but retains the essentials of style and refinement. The cooking, too, while preserving its previously high standards, is now lighter and less complex. There are 2- and 3- course menus as well as a splendidly well-balanced menu gourmand. The latter could offer an amuse-bouche of a sun-dried tomato muffin with tapénade followed by chargrilled asparagus with morels and shaved parmesan on a bed of baby spinach, rocket and glass lettuce. Next, rolls of lightly smoked salmon with potato blinis and horseradish cream. For main course could come marinated loin of venison on a bed of red cabbage and a red wine sauce enriched with a hint of chocolate. A single cheese -Richard III Wensleydale accompanied by a slice of rich fruit and nut cake precedes the dessert – perhaps an aniseed parfait served with a compote of cherries in a butter chocolate cup. The cooking, by Jeff Baker, is accomplished and the restaurant is managed by Steve Ridealgh, who was the maitre d' at the original location. In fine weather the terrace overlooking the river is a very desirable spot. A cleverly compiled list of well-chosen wines with tasting notes alongside Michael's selection and 1985 clarets. Fair prices, quality throughout. *Seats 38. Parties 8. L 12-2 D 6-10.30 (Sat to 11). Set L £17.50/£22 Set D £22.50/£26.50/£37. Closed Sun & Bank Holidays. Access, Amex, Diners, Visa.*

LEEDS   Queen's Hotel   68%   £106

Tel 0113 243 1323   Fax 0113 242 5154   Map 6 C1   **H**
City Square Leeds West Yorkshire LS1 1PL

Right in the city centre and just opposite the station, the Queen's was built in the 1930s and many original features have been retained. Particularly impressive are the Palm Court lounge, the large oval lobby with domed ceiling and the clubby, mahogany-panelled bar. Authentic 30s furniture and light fittings distinguish bedrooms, which also offer all the modern comforts including up-to-date bathrooms. Five rooms are adapted for use by the disabled. 62 are designated non-smoking and children up to 16 are free in their parents' room. 24hr room service and free valet parking. Conference facilities for 600. Forte. *Rooms 190. Shop, Palm Court (7.30am-11pm). Access, Amex, Diners, Visa.*

LEEDS   Rascasse

Tel 0113 266 4411   Map 6 C1   **R**
Canal Wharf off Water Lane Leeds West Yorkshire LS11 5BB

A major move for a bright young chef who, when at Miller's Bistro at Harrogate (see entry), was awarded a star by us. Due to open in September just before our publication. We hope the restaurant will continue to offer food of the calibre found at his previous establishment.

LEEDS   Sang Sang   £50

Tel 0113 246 8664   Map 6 C1   **R**
7 The Headrow Leeds West Yorkshire LS1 6PU

Over 200 dishes are listed on the long menu at this popular Chinese restaurant. All the favourites are represented including sizzling dishes, noodles with mixed meat and Peking duck. *Seats 90. Parties 80. Private Room 16. L 12-1.45 D 5.30-11. Closed Sun & Bank Holidays. Set L from £4.95 Set D from £9.50. Access, Amex, Diners, Visa.*

LEEDS   Sous le Nez en Ville   £55

Tel 0113 244 0108 Fax 0113 245 0240   Map 6 C1   **R**
Basement Quebec House Quebec Street Leeds West Yorkshire LS1 2HA

A deservedly popular, intimate and informal cellar-like basement restaurant with polished pine furniture and quarry-tiled floors. The menu is imaginative and very enjoyable, comprising well-prepared dishes such as tagliatelle with Thai-spiced spinach, terrine of pork and duck livers with prunes wrapped in smoked bacon to begin and some mostly modern mains such as grilled fillet of pork with baby black pudding in a filo basket with Dijon mustard and chargrilled venison with brioche, plum and coriander, chutney and lime jus. Sweets are a mixture of old favourites and the new. Baked rice pudding with fruit marmalade and steamed jam and coconut sponge with custard feature alongside a thin apple tart with cardamom ice cream and individual iced white chocolate paté with a lime syrup. Very cordial service even at peak times. Terrific and expertly compiled wine list – comprehensive, knowledgeable tasting notes, and fair prices. Several come from the best growers. Regional award for Cellar of the Year. Booking very advisable. *Seats 86. Parties 16. Private Room 20. L 12-2.30 D 6-10.30 (Fri & Sat to 11). Closed L Sat, all Sun, Bank Holidays. Set D (6-7.30) £12.95 incl ½ bottle of wine. Access, Visa.*

| **LEEDS** | **Thai Siam** | **£40** |

Tel 0113 245 1608   Map 6 C1   **R**
68-72 New Briggate Leeds West Yorkshire LS1 6NU

Friendly service from traditionally clad staff in simple, uncluttered first-floor surroundings. The menu offers 60+ dishes, with a further 30 in the vegetarian part. MSG-free. *Seats 60. L 12-2.30 D 6-11. Closed L Sun & Mon. Set L from £5.50 Set D from £11. Access, Visa.*

| **LEICESTER** | **Belmont Hotel** | **65%** | **£90** |

Tel 0116 254 4773 Fax 0116 247 0804   Map 7 D4   **H**
De Montfort Street Leicester Leicestershire LE1 7GR

In the ownership of the Bowie family since 1934, the Belmont stands in a quiet street just off the A6. Good-quality darkwood furniture is used in the bedrooms, the larger of which are designated Executives. Among the day rooms are two bars and a brasserie. Children up to 16 stay free in parents' room. Free parking for 70 cars. *Rooms 65. Closed 5 days Christmas. Access, Amex, Diners, Visa.*

| **LEICESTER** | **Curry Pot** | **£45** |

Tel 0116 253 8256   Map 7 D4   **R**
78 Belgrave Road Leicester Leicestershire LE4 5AS

Tandoori restaurant offering a short menu of Indian favourites that are a cut above the average. Particularly good samosas, chicken tikka and masala, plus lamb shahi korma. *Seats 55. Parties 30. L 12-2 D 6-11. Closed Sun, 25 & 26 Dec. Set meals from £16.25. Access, Amex, Diners, Visa.*

| **LEICESTER** | **Forte Posthouse** | **64%** | **£72** |

Tel 0116 263 0500 Fax 0116 282 3623   Map 7 D4   **H**
Braunstone Lane East Leicester Leicestershire LE3 2FW

Modern low-riser equidistant from Junction 21 of the M1 and the city centre. Conference/banqueting facilities for 85. Children free up to 16 in parents' room. *Rooms 172. Garden. Access, Amex, Diners, Visa.*

| **LEICESTER** | **Holiday Inn** | **72%** | **£119** |

Tel 0116 253 1161 Fax 0116 251 3169   Map 7 D4   **H**
129 St Nicholas Circle Leicester Leicestershire LE1 5LX

At the hub of a major road interchange, near Junction 21 of the M1, Leicester's Holiday Inn is a tall building reaching high over the city. The marbled reception area makes a splendid first impression, and the lounge area that adjoins it is no less appealing. Bedrooms provide plenty of space, large beds, fitted units and good tiled bathrooms. Two floors (76 rooms) are designated non-smoking. The well-equipped health and leisure club is a great family attraction at weekends. Free covered parking in adjacent NCP. Conference facilities for 300. *Rooms 188. Indoor swimming pool, children's splash pool, sauna, solarium, spa bath, steam room, news kiosk, coffee shop (7am-10.15pm). Access, Amex, Diners, Visa.*

Consult the blue pages for summary tables and lists of
recommended establishments.

LEICESTER   Jarvis Grand Hotel   66%   £106

Tel 0116 255 5599 Fax 0116 254 4736   Map 7 D4   **H**
Granby Street Leicester Leicestershire LE1 6ES

A city-centre Victorian building with ample parking, close to the railway station. Public rooms live up to the name and bedrooms (half designated non-smoking) are stylish and of a good size. 24hr room service; children up to 14 can stay free in parents' room. Two themed bars; carvery restaurant; vast banqueting and conference facilities for up to 450. *Rooms 92. Coffee shop (7-7). Access, Amex, Diners, Visa.*

LEICESTER   Leicester Stakis   69%   £118

Tel 0116 263 0066 Fax 0116 263 0627   Map 7 D4   **H**
Braunstone Leicester Leicestershire LE3 2WQ

Ten minutes from the city centre, just off Junction 21 of the M1, at the end of the M69, this modern, business-oriented hotel offers good-sized bedrooms (four adapted for wheelchair users), an extensive range of conference facilities (up to 180 delegates), a new business centre, a well-equipped leisure club and 250 free parking spaces. Children under 16 stay free in parents' room. *Rooms 141. Garden, indoor swimming pool, gym, sauna, spa bath, steam room, solarium, beauty salon. Access, Amex, Diners, Visa.*

LEICESTER   Man Ho   £40

Tel 0116 255 7700 Fax 0116 254 5629   Map 7 D4   **R**
16 King Street Leicester Leicestershire LE1 6RJ

Comprising two houses in a low Georgian terrace behind New Walk Centre, Man Ho probably offers the best Chinese cooking in Leicester. Space, comfort and tasteful modern decor make a fine setting in which smartly-suited waitresses serve a mix of Peking, Cantonese and Szechuan cooking. Good choice à la carte or on various set menus. Sunday lunch (12-4) sees a dim sum buffet (£9 adult, £6 child). *Seats 130. Private Room 60. L 12-2.30 D 6-11.30 (Sat & Sun 12-11.30). Closed 25 & 26 Dec. Set L from £6.50 Set D from £12.50. Access, Amex, Visa.*

LEICESTER   Rise of the Raj   £35

Tel 0116 255 3885   Map 7 D4   **R**
6 Evington Road Leicester Leicestershire LE2 1HF

Indian cooking in a homely restaurant on two floors. The menu is fairly standard, with many variations on lamb, chicken and prawns providing the bulk of the dishes. Specialities include chicken or king prawn masala, lamb pasanda and tandoori rainbow trout. Good-value thali (set meals), both meat and vegetarian. Popular Sunday buffet (£5.95, children half price). *Seats 40. Parties 20. Private Room 70. L 12-2 D 6-11.30. Access, Amex, Diners, Visa.*

LEICESTER   Welford Place   £55

Tel 0116 247 0758 0116 247 1843   Map 7 D4   **R**
9 Welford Place Leicester Leicestershire LE1 6ZH

Follow signs for the Phoenix Arts Centre, whose car park is almost directly opposite this former Victorian gentlemen's club, restored in 1991, retaining an aura of grandeur. Michael and Valerie Hope have created a spacious bar and restaurant. In the latter, a quietly civilised room, two great chandeliers are suspended from the lofty ceiling. The menus operate throughout the day all year and any item is available at any time, but the restaurant is reserved for full meals. There are two set menus as well as the carte. The style of cooking is modern while retaining traditional elements. Typical starters include Stilton soup with blue cheese sablé, galantine of free-range chicken with apple and ginger chutney or a warm salad of prawns and butter beans. Main dishes could be fillet of sea bass with salmon mousseline, spinach and hollandaise sauce, roast quail with lemon and coriander stuffing on couscous, roast rack of lamb with minted pea purée and pan-fried breast of Gressingham duck with pears. Enjoyable cooking with friendly service. *Seats 60 (plus 50 in the bar). Parties 14. Private Room 60. Meals 8am-11pm (Sun till 10.30). Access, Amex, Diners, Visa.*

Set menu prices may not always include service or wine.

LENHAM   Chilston Park   71%   £95

Tel 01622 859803   Fax 01622 858588   Map 11 C5   **H**
Sandway Lenham nr Maidstone Kent ME17 2BE

Four miles from Junction 8 of M20, between Ashford and Maidstone, this is a remarkable hotel set in 250 acres complete with a lake: 17th-century diarist John Evelyn called it "a sweetly watered place", and the atmosphere thus evoked is reverently maintained. The Grade I listed house contains a treasure trove of antique furniture, oil paintings, water colours, rugs and objets d'art. Over 200 candles are lit by tail-coated staff throughout the public areas at dusk, evoking a sense of the past. The Marble Hall and Drawing Room are fine examples of elegant comfort and each bedroom in the house has its own very individual style and character; some have open fires. The Hogarth Room has an 18th-century four-poster and a splendid view of the lake. Bedrooms in the stable block are simpler but not without charm. Characterful conference and meeting rooms (for up to 100). On balmy summer days, you can take a punt across the lake. *Rooms 38. Garden, croquet, tennis, putting green, coarse fishing, games room, snooker. Closed 26-30 Dec. Access, Amex, Diners, Visa.*

LETCHWORTH   Broadway Toby Hotel   59%   £62

Tel 01462 480111   Fax 01462 481563   Map 15 E1   **H**
The Broadway Letchworth Hertfordshire SG6 3NZ

A smartly-kept hotel with a friendly, non-chain feel (even though it is in the Toby Restaurant Group, a division of Bass Taverns Ltd.). Well-furnished bedrooms and a calm cocktail bar-cum-lounge. Conference and banqueting facilities for up to 180. No dogs. *Rooms 35. Access, Amex, Diners, Visa.*

LEWDOWN   Lewtrenchard Manor   73%   £98

Tel 01566 783256   Fax 01566 783332   Map 12 C2   **HR**
Lewdown nr Okehampton Devon EX20 4PN

James and Sue Murray create the atmosphere of a large and happy family home at their handsome 17th-century mansion, where hymn-writer and novelist the Rev. Sabine Baring Gould once lived. The setting is particularly peaceful and delightfully rural, and the bedrooms all enjoy fine views through leaded windows. The rooms vary in size, the larger with antique furniture including a couple with four-posters, but all benefit from well-chosen fabrics, fresh flowers, mineral water and, in the carpeted bathrooms, towelling robes, good toiletries and huge soft bath sheets. Room service offers drinks and light snacks throughout the day and evening and beds are turned down at night. No children under eight. *Rooms 8. Garden, croquet, fishing. Access, Amex, Diners, Visa.*

Restaurant   £75

A grand room with oil portraits of some of the former occupants of the house gazing down at the crisply clothed tables where today's guests tuck in to chef Patrick Salvadori's sound cooking. The fixed-price dinner menu offers half-a-dozen choices of main dish that largely stick to tried and tested combinations: pork tenderloin with apple and calvados sauce, fillet of sea bream on a bed of basil with a tomato compote, roast boneless quail with a grape sauce, beef fillet en croute with foie gras and Madeira sauce. Puds range from a hot banana and ginger soufflé with a chocolate sauce to a selection of sorbets in a crisp nougatine basket with fresh fruit. Decent and fairly-priced wine list, remarkable for its thirty South African listings. Service is a happy combination of friendliness and formality. No smoking. *Seats 35. Parties 8. Private Room 26. L Sun 12.15-1.45 otherwise by arrangement D 7.15-9.30. Set L £16 Set D £26.*

LEWES   Shelleys Hotel   60%   £110

Tel 01273 472361   Fax 01273 483152   Map 11 B6   **H**
High Street Lewes East Sussex BN7 1XS

One of the original Mount Charlotte hotels (acquired in 1977), Shelleys is located on the main road through Lewes. Built originally (16th century) as an inn, it was later a manor house, military hospital and a number of flats and has recently undergone a complete refurbishment. Children up to 16 stay free in parents' room. *Rooms 19. Garden. Access, Amex, Diners, Visa.*

LICHFIELD   Jarvis George Hotel   59%   £92

Tel 01543 414822   Fax 01543 415817   Map 6 C3   **H**
Bird Street Lichfield Staffordshire WS13 6PR

Regency style survives in the spacious, peaceful day rooms and the pastel-decorated bedrooms of this hotel. The ballroom can accommodate up to 100 guests for a banquet or conference. Children up to 12 stay free in parents' room. *Rooms 38. Access, Amex, Diners, Visa.*

LIFTON   Arundell Arms   65%   £93

Tel 01566 784666   Fax 01566 784494   Map 12 C2   **HR**
Lifton Devon PL16 0AA

With 20 miles of its own water on the Tamar and a three-acre lake, the 16th-century Arundell Arms is a haunt for serious fisherfolk, although come the autumn it's shooting parties who take over the country-furnished bar and rug-strewn, slate-floored sitting room. In the garden, a 250-year-old circular stone cockpit – one of the few remaining in England – is now a tackle shop and rod room. Anne Voss-Bark, owner here for more than 30 years, is herself a keen fisherwoman and co-author of the *Beginner's Guide to Fly Fishing*. Well-kept bedrooms, a few in an annexe across the street, have pleasant pastel colour schemes and all the usual modern amenities; some have period furnishings, others freestanding pine pieces, while the singles feature built-in furniture. Neat bathrooms, just a couple with shower and WC only. Children up to 16 stay free in parents' room. Banqueting for 80, conference facilities for 100. *Rooms 29. Garden, fishing, skittle alley. Closed 2 days Christmas (but restaurant open for lunch). Access, Amex, Diners, Visa.*

Restaurant   £75

🍸 🍷 🍶

An elegantly proportioned room with a central glass chandlier. Chef Philip Burgess has been running the kitchen here for 15 years cooking in modern British style with classical French influences and using the pick of seasonal local produce including sea bass, scallops from Looe, Tamar salmon and South Devon beef. Lamb is another speciality and might be found as a fillet, marinated with honey, thyme and rosemary, pan-fried and served with a warm salad and a sauce from its own cooking juices, or roasted rack with a celeriac dauphinoise and a mint and saffron sauce. Daily-changing selection of desserts, home-made chocolate truffles. Shortish wine list with several inexpensive bottles. Alternative menu available in the bar (12-2.30 & 6-10). No smoking. *Seats 70. Private Room 30. L 12.30-2 D 7.30-9.30. Set L £13/£16 & £23/£27 (Sun £13/£16) Set D £23/£29.25.*

LINCOLN   Courtyard by Marriott   65%   £78

Tel 01522 544244   Fax 01522 560805   Map 7 E2   **H**
Brayford Wharf North Lincoln Lincolnshire LN1 1YW

Principally aimed at the business traveller – but also good value for the family at special weekend rates – this link in Marriott Hotels' 'junior' chain overlooks the River Witham where it broadens out into Brayford Pool in the centre of the city. Air-conditioned bedrooms offer good work space, underfloor heating in bathrooms and double beds throughout. In the absence of room service there are 24hr vending machines for soft drinks and snacks and a 'carry away' service from the galleried all-day bar-brasserie. Children up to 16 stay free in parents' room. Ample free parking. *Rooms 95. Keep-fit equipment. Access, Amex, Diners, Visa.*

LINCOLN   D'Isney Place   £64

Tel 01522 538881   Fax 01522 511321   Map 7 E2   **PH**
Eastgate Lincoln Lincolnshire LN2 4AA

D'Isney Place, an 18th-century building a short distance from the Cathedral, offers a warm and comfortable atmosphere. David and Judy Payne run it as an up-market bed and breakfast hotel. Well-loved antique furniture abounds and there's a homely feel throughout. The rooms vary from large, with four-posters and spa baths or steam showers, to compact and charming singles, one with shower/WC only. Also available is a cottage with two double en-suite bedrooms, living room, dining-room and kitchen. All bedrooms have tables and breakfast is served to order in the rooms. Limited parking within the grounds. *Rooms 17. Garden. Access, Amex, Diners, Visa.*

| LINCOLN | Lincoln Forte Posthouse | 63% | £72 |

Tel 01522 520341   Fax 01522 510780   Map 7 E2   **H**
Eastgate Lincoln Lincolnshire LN2 1PN

A modern hotel right beside the Cathedral and handy for visiting old Lincoln. Well-equipped bedrooms. Children stay free in parents' room. Conference facilities for up to 90. *Rooms 70. Garden. Access, Amex, Diners, Visa.*

| LINCOLN | The Jew's House | | £60 |

Tel 01522 524851   Map 7 E2   **R**
15 The Strait Lincoln Lincolnshire LN2 1JD

🍷 🍓

At the bottom of a steep hill leading up to the cathedral, the Jew's House dates back to 1180 (its fascinating history is related on the back of the menu) although Richard Gibbs' largely French-inspired menu is rather more up-to-date with the likes of grilled goat's cheese with bacon and croutons, oyster mushrooms in puff pastry with thyme, supreme of chicken with cucumber and ginger, fillet steak with pink peppercorns, tomato and pesto tartlette with herb vinaigrette (there are always a couple of vegetarian options) and desserts such as lemon tart with crème fraiche and crème brulée. An à la carte, which has some dishes in common with the prix-fixe, extends the savoury choices a little and the range of puds considerably: the latter generally includes an excellent hot Grand Marnier soufflé. The £10.50, three-course lunch (three choices at each stage) is particularly good value. There are just six tables in the rough stone-walled dining-room plus a little lounge on the first floor for pre- or post-prandial drinks. Plenty of wines under £20 worth trying; brief tasting notes, good variety. Certainly the best restaurant in Lincoln, and indeed for miles around. No smoking. *Seats 28. L 12-1.30 D 6.45-9.15. Closed L Mon, all Sun, Bank Holidays (except Good Fri). Set L £10.50 Set L & D £19.95. Access, Amex, Diners, Visa.*

| LINCOLN | White Hart | 69% | £117 |

Tel 01522 526222   Fax 01522 531798   Map 7 E2   **H**
Bailgate Lincoln Lincolnshire LN1 3AR

There has been an inn on this city-centre site (close to the cathedral) for over 600 years, and the place is redolent with history: Richard II stayed here in 1387, but today's visitors tend to be taking advantage of the tourist attractions of Lincoln and the surrounding countryside. There's a roof-top patio where you can take cocktails on balmy summer evenings. Bedrooms are fitted out in traditional English style (some are walnut-panelled) and public rooms display fine antiques. Some bedrooms, and the exterior of the hotel, are due for refurbishment during autumn 1995. Secure parking opposite (beneath the ancient city walls). Forte. *Rooms 48. Access, Amex, Diners, Visa.*

Set menu prices may not always include service or wine.

| LINCOLN | Wig & Mitre | | £60 |

Tel 01522 535190   Fax 01522 532402   Map 7 E2   **R**
29 Steep Hill Lincoln Lincolnshire LN2 1LU

🍷 🍮 🍴

An ancient ale house halfway down the appropriately named Steep Hill from the western end of the cathedral close, the Wig & Mitre won awards for its restoration in the late 70s. Downstairs it's a pub where you can get sandwiches (and dishes from the restaurant menu) along with the beer and where a substantial breakfast menu is served from 8am to noon and again from 3 to 6 in the afternoon. Upstairs under the steeply pitched roof with its wealth of old beams is a fully-fledged restaurant whose varied and interesting offerings are available from 8am right through until 11pm. The Daily Menu (it actually changes twice a day) might include a creamy chicken, sweetcorn and potato soup; sauté of chicken livers with orange salad; pan-fried skate wings with scallops and tomatoes in a nut brown butter; a succulent chicken supreme stuffed with a root vegetable and chicken mousse on a tarragon mustard sauce; and medallions of pork loin in a spicy lentil cream sauce, while the more permanent à la carte ranges from a marinated potato and spiced sausage salad and excellent baked cheese soufflé to duck confit with yellow split

See over

peas and balsamic vinegar, fillet steak with mushrooms and onions and rack of lamb with herb and garlic crumbs on a bed of leek and potato mash. The selection of English farmhouse cheeses might include such recherché items as Jersey Blue and Davidstone vintage Cheddar and there are puds like tiramisu, lemon cream tart and apple crumble with crème anglaise. Deservedly popular, so it's necessary to book for peak mealtimes. *Seats 80. Meals 8am-11pm. Closed 25 Dec. Access, Amex, Diners, Visa.*

LINTON	Wood Hall	76%	£98

Tel 01937 587271   Fax 01937 584353   Map 6 C1   **HR**
Tripp Lane Linton nr Wetherby West Yorkshire LS22 4JA

Almost at the top of a hill, surrounded by 100 acres of wooded parkland and with a Carmelite monastery at the rear, the hotel is approached from the centre of Linton along a winding single-track road. Its high hillside position gives front bedrooms commanding views over the valley below. Dating from 1750, the house is fronted by an elegant semi-circular portico and the intimate entrance hall has polished flagstone floors and beautiful floral arrangements creating a welcoming feeling. Public rooms are invitingly relaxing, particularly a classically proportioned drawing-room with deep-cushioned settees, antiques and a few ornaments. The bar next door is more sombre, with dark oak-panelled walls. It features a baby grand as a dispensing counter. Bedrooms above a newish leisure complex are all uniformly spacious and attractively decorated. Front-facing bedrooms have the lightest and best aspects. Bedrooms in the original house vary in size though they tend to be larger and have more character. Bathrooms, however, are a little simpler. The new-wing bathrooms have excellent showers. All rooms are well equipped. *Rooms 43. Garden, coarse fishing, indoor swimming pool, spa bath, sun bed, beauty salon, steam room, gym, snooker. Access, Amex, Diners, Visa.*

Restaurant   £85

Stephanie Moon has been promoted from sous chef to head the kitchen team serving the elegantly appointed restaurant. Her modern menu takes its inspiration from around the world, as demonstrated by tomato consommé with brie-filled wun tuns under a choux pastry cage, steamed salmon parcel with shiitake mushrooms and yellow pea sprouts on Thai green curry and coconut sauce, and roast leg of lamb with an olive and sun-dried tomato stuffing on a rosemary couscous with a Merlot sauce. Vegetarian main courses always available. The wine list is serious indeed, with a comprehensive selection from around the world. Introductory and tasting notes are helpful, though prices for known wines are on the high side. Best value is in the New World, with some rarely seen wines from New York State. No smoking. *Seats 70. Parties 12. Private Room 40. L 12.30-2.30 D 7-10. Set L £15.95 (Sun £13.95) Set D £26.95. Closed L Sat.*

LISKEARD	Well House	74%	£105

Tel & Fax 01579 342001   Map 12 C3   **HR**
St Keyne Liskeard Cornwall PL14 4RN

From the church in St Keyne take the left fork to St Keyne Well to find this tranquil spot set in small landscaped gardens that include an enchanting duck pond. Built at the turn of the century by a tea-planter, it is the most charming retreat, and owner Nick Wainford and his staff are never anything but friendly, helpful and discreet. Off the tiled hall are a relaxing drawing room and an inviting little bar; across the hall, the dining-room has magnificent bay windows overlooking the sun terrace and lawns. Individually designed bedrooms and well-equipped bathrooms are immaculately kept. First-rate breakfasts. *Rooms 7. Garden, croquet, outdoor swimming pool, tennis. Access, Amex, Visa.*

Restaurant   £65

Lunch and dinner menus of 2, 3 or 4 courses plus canapés, coffee and petits fours feature what's best and freshest from the local markets. Dishes run from terrine of Provençal vegetables with olive and basil vinaigrette, goat's cheese soufflé with apple and walnut salad and smoked haddock topped with Welsh rarebit to steamed sea bass on a herb salad and lime and grapefruit sauce, roast loin of lamb with braised red cabbage and redcurrant sauce, and breast of corn-fed chicken with wild mushroom compote and port sauce. Finish with tangy lemon tart with cassis sorbet, chocolate marquise and/or some West Country cheeses. *Seats 32. L 12.30-2 D 7.30-10. Set L & D £19.95/£24.95/£29.70.*

LIVERPOOL	Atlantic Tower	65%	£106

Tel 0151-227 4444 Fax 0151-236 3973   Map 6 A2   **H**
Chapel Street Liverpool Merseyside L3 9RE

A city-centre hotel, rising like a great liner on the Liverpool skyline, with a refurbished exterior and public areas that include a bar inspired by Nelson's *Victory*. Well-equipped bedrooms make good-sized singles but rather compact doubles and twins. Corner rooms are larger and there are ten suites. Children up to 15 can stay free in parents' room. Conference/banqueting facilities for 120/100. *Rooms 226. Access, Amex, Diners, Visa.*

LIVERPOOL	Britannia Adelphi Hotel	68%	£105

Tel 0151-709 7200 Fax 0151-708 0743   Map 6 A2   **H**
Ranelagh Place Liverpool Merseyside L3 5UL

Leisure facilities and Spindles health club, conferences for up to 800 delegates, six bars and a night club are among the amenities of a large hotel with many grand original Edwardian features. Bedrooms range from singles to suites and jacuzzi rooms. Children up to 12 stay free in parents' room. 200-space garage – £4 overnight. The hotel is next door to Lime Street station. *Rooms 391. Indoor swimming pool, sauna, spa bath, squash, hairdressing & beauty salon, snooker, coffee shop (11am-2am Mon-Sat). Access, Amex, Diners, Visa.*

LIVERPOOL	Gladstone Hotel	60%	£90

Tel 0151-709 7050 Fax 0151-709 2193   Map 6 A2   **H**
Lord Nelson Street Liverpool Merseyside L3 5QB

Modern Forte hotel (formerly the *Crest*) to the rear of Lime Street Station. 24hr room service menu. Extensive conference facilities can cope with up to 600 delegates theatre-style. Ample free parking. *Rooms 154. Snooker. Access, Amex, Diners, Visa.*

LIVERPOOL	La Grande Bouffe		£50

Tel 0151-236 3375   Map 6 A2   **R**
48a Castle Street Liverpool Merseyside L2 7LQ

Informal basement restaurant, mainly self-service at lunchtime. The evening à la carte offers a tureen of fresh mussels steamed in a pesto broth, fresh salmon and dill mousse and deep-fried avocado with a spicy tomato salsa among the starters. Main courses could be braised venison sausage with celeriac and Stilton mash, escalope of salmon with chargrilled red peppers and fresh basil velouté or lamb cutlets flavoured with mint and baked in filo pastry. *Seats 60. Parties 16. Private Room 16. L 12-3, D 6-10.30. Closed L Sat, D Mon, all Sun & Bank Holidays. Access, Amex, Visa.*

LIVERPOOL	Moat House	67%	£114

Tel 0151-709 0181 Fax 0151-709 2706   Map 6 A2   **H**
Paradise Street Liverpool Merseyside L1 8JD

Spacious bedrooms, large beds, smart public areas and a leisure centre with swimming pool. Conference/banqueting for 450/300. Children stay free in parents' room. Three floors of bedrooms are designated non-smoking. Guests can use neighbouring NCP free. *Rooms 251. Indoor swimming pool, gym, sauna, spa bath, solarium, news kiosk, coffee shop (10.30am-midnight). Access, Amex, Diners, Visa.*

LIVERPOOL	St George's Hotel	58%	£81

Tel 0151-709 7090 Fax 0151-709 0137   Map 6 A2   **H**
Lime Street Liverpool Merseyside L1 1NQ

Early 70s' Forte hotel in the centre of town. Guests can use the leisure facilities of the Britannia Adelphi for a fee of £5. Children up to 16 stay free in parents' room. 30 car parking spaces, plus free use of Euro car park 4pm-10am. *Rooms 155. Closed 24-28 Dec. Access, Amex, Diners, Visa.*

LOCKINGTON   Hilton National East Mids Airport   69%   £133

Tel 01509 674000   Fax 01509 672412   Map 7 D3   **H**
Derby Road Lockington Leicestershire DE4 2YW

Near Junction 24 of the M1 and just 1½ miles from the airport; Donington Park race track is also nearby. A modern low-rise hotel with conference facilities for up to 300. Children up to 14 stay free in parents' room. *Rooms 152. Indoor swimming pool, sauna, spa bath, solarium, gym, beauty salon, coffee shop (7am-11pm). Access, Amex, Diners, Visa.*

LONG CRENDON   The Angel Inn   £50

Tel 01844 208268   Fax 01844 208652   Map 15 D2   **R**
Bicester Road Long Crendon Buckinghamshire HP18 9EE

♟ ⚘ ⬠

A charming pub-restaurant dating back to the early 1500s. In one of the eating rooms, which include a Lloyd Loom-furnished conservatory, one can see part of the original wattle and daub construction. Chef-patron Mark Jones's cooking has a strong Mediterranean slant although the likes of Lancashire black pudding with noodles and mustard sauce, bangers 'n' mash and rack of lamb are also to be found. A variety of fresh seafood dishes written on the specials board depends upon twice-weekly deliveries direct from Billingsgate: the choice might include roast cod with scallops and spinach, chargrilled squid with chili and tapénade and baked hake with mussel risotto. A short wine list puts the emphasis on New World wines, with about eight available by the glass. Open for Sunday lunch, but not always – phone to find out. *Seats 70. Private Room 40. L 12-2.30 D 6.30-10. Closed D Sun (all Sun in summer). Access, Visa.*

Set menu prices may not always include service or wine.

LONG EATON   Sleep Inn   £50

Tel 0115 946 0000   Fax 0115 946 0726   Map 7 D3   **B**
Bostock Lane Long Eaton Nottingham Nottinghamshire NG10 5NL

Comprising spacious, brightly decorated double and family rooms this American-inspired overnighter stands adjacent to the M1 at Junction 25. Triple-glazed on the motorway side, the bedrooms have modern open-plan design, all with good-sized shower rooms; four rooms equipped for disabled guests. Amenities include video recorders with a supply of rental tapes; alcohol, soft drinks, snacks and toiletry items are available from vending machines on the ground floor. Meeting rooms for up to 75. *Rooms 101. Closed Christmas-New Year. Access, Amex, Diners, Visa.*

LONG MELFORD   Black Lion   65%   £70

Tel 01787 312356   Fax 01787 374557   Map 10 C3   **H**
The Green Long Melford Sudbury Suffolk CO10 9DN

Count the Toby jugs and admire the maps and copper collection or relax in deep sofas in the charming lounge. There's also a library, and games for both adults and children. Bedrooms are bright and comfortable, attractive fabrics complementing neutral walls and carpets. Each room has antique pine furniture and an easy chair or sofa. The top-of-the-range Green Room boasts an antique mahogany half-tester. *Rooms 9. Garden. Closed 23 Dec-2 Jan. Access, Amex, Visa.*

LONG MELFORD   Bull Hotel   65%   £102

Tel 01787 378494   Fax 01787 880307   Map 10 C3   **H**
Hall Street Long Melford Suffolk CO10 9JG

Built by a wealthy wool merchant in the 15th century, becoming a posting house with the arrival of the coaching era, the real-Tudor Bull is now a Forte Hotel combining character with comfort. 10 bedrooms are designated non-smoking. 60-seat conference room, banquets for 60. Parking for 30 cars. Children up to 16 stay free in parents' room. *Rooms 25. Access, Amex, Diners, Visa.*

Lodges are now listed by county in the reference section

LONG MELFORD   Chimneys   £80

Tel 01787 379806   Fax 01787 312294   Map 10 C3   **R**
Hall Street Long Melford Sudbury Suffolk CO10 9JR

A black and white timbered building in the centre of the village as charming inside – a wealth of ancient timbers and mellow brickwork setting off crisp white napery and bone china tableware – as out. Owner Sam Chalmers is a consummate professional who, although no longer cooking himself, ensures that the kitchen maintains a consistently high standard. Warm mousseline of chicken and Stilton, duck liver parfait, casserole of rabbit with thyme and pot-roast guinea fowl with lime demonstrate the style of the à la carte menu. Dinner or Luncheon Club membership offers significant price advantages among other things like wine tastings. The wine list includes an excellent selection of over a dozen recommended and keenly priced wines, all available by the glass as well. Tasting notes where considered necessary. *Seats 50. Parties 16. L 12-2 D 7-9.30. Closed D Sun. Set L £15.50 (Sun £16.50) Set D £17.50. Access, Amex, Diners, Visa.*

LONGHAM   Bridge House   61%   £60

Tel 01202 578828   Fax 01202 572620   Map 14 C4   **H**
2 Ringwood Road Ferndown Longham Dorset BH22 9AN

Anna Joannides' hotel on the Stour has a distinctly Mediterranean air; the sunny reception and lounge have white walls with tiles depicting Greek goddesses and the large bar opens on to a terrace overlooking the water. Bedrooms have plain white walls and pink draylon headboards; some large rooms have canopied or four-poster beds and many rooms enjoy river views. Children free in parents' room up to 10. Several conference suites are available, for up to 120 delegates. No dogs. *Rooms 37. Garden, coarse fishing, children's play area. Access, Amex, Diners, Visa.*

LONGHORSLEY   Linden Hall   75%   £125

Tel 01670 516611   Fax 01670 788544   Map 5 D2   **H**
Longhorsley nr Morpeth Northumberland NE65 8XF

An imposing, listed Georgian house stands at the centre of a much-extended hotel surrounded by 450 acres of mature park and woodland. For the individual guest there are choices of the imposing Inner Hall, drawing room (where afternoon tea is taken) and two bars (one of them the Linden Pub in the grounds) in which to relax, generally uninterrupted by users of the Health Spa and Conference Centre (capacity 300). Sporting facilities are first-class, for both individuals and business groups. The latest Garden Rooms (opened in 1993) are set in enclosed courtyards closest to the indoor pool and afford a high degree of seclusion. State-of-the-art satellite TVs, complimentary fruit, decanted sherry and all-enveloping bathrobes are all the high-quality trappings of gracious living. Children up to 14 share parents' room free. *Rooms 50. Garden, tennis, croquet, pitch & putt, indoor swimming pool, gym, sauna, solarium, beauty & hair salon, snooker, mountain bikes, coarse fishing, clay-pigeon shooting, all-weather cricket pitch. Access, Amex, Diners, Visa.*

LONGRIDGE   Paul Heathcote's Restaurant   ★★   £90

Tel 01772 784969   Fax 01772 785713   Map 6 B1   **R**
104-106 Higher Road Longridge nr Preston Lancashire PR3 3SY

On the edge of the village, and dating back to the early 1800s, this row of three cottages had a chequered history (quarryman's pub, café, Indian restaurant) before the arrival of Paul Heathcote in 1990 and its transformation into one of the very best restaurants in Britain. The interior retains something of a cottagey feel but with the elegance and style of a sophisticated restaurant. With impeccable culinary credentials gained in such eminent kitchens as those of *The Connaught, Sharrow Bay* and *Le Manoir Aux Quat' Saisons*, Paul has gone on to develop his own exciting brand of modern British cooking. Only one menu is available at lunchtime (Fri & Sun only except in December) but at the fixed price of only £22.50 for four courses plus coffee it's a real bargain. At night there are three menus to choose from, an à la carte, a six-course, no-choice Gourmet Menu, both of which are amended daily to take account of the market and seasonal produce, and Paul's ten-course Signature (tasting) Menu which rarely changes and includes such wonderful dishes as black pudding with crushed potatoes, lobster roasted with dried citrus

See over

fruit and herbs, wing of skate with a tartare of mussels and parsley, Goosnargh duckling with buttered potatoes, prunes and jasmine-scented juices, and a down-to-earth bread-and-butter pudding with apricot coulis and clotted cream. From the other menus dishes such as pig's trotters filled with ham hock and sage and served with a tartlet of pea purée and onion sauce; lightly poached oysters served with herb purée, braised leeks, ginger and a champagne sauce (both starters), roast sea bass with thyme potatoes, pan-fried scallops, a pistou of vegetables and red wine sauce, and fillet of beef garnished with braised oxtail and preserved and roasted winter vegetables, mashed potato, glazed button onions and ale sauce demonstrate Paul's sophisticated but robust style. Desserts receive as much thought as everything else here and if you go for Heathcote's Assiette you get a selection of seven, in suitably small-sized portions, all on one plate. Just as well that you'll receive sensible advice from sommelier Paul Wiltshire, since there are no tasting notes (apart from his own recommendations) on the youngish wine list on which the New World is prominently featured. A further opportunity to sample Paul's cuisine has just opened-up in the centre of Preston in the guise of *Heathcote's Brasserie* (see entry). *Seats 55. Private Room 18. L 12-2 (Sun to 2.30) D 7-9.30. Closed L Tues, Wed, Thurs, Sat (but open those L in Dec), all Mon. Set L £22.50 Set D £35 & £50 (dégustation) Access, Amex, Visa.*

| LOOE | Talland Bay Hotel | 67% | £100 |

Tel 01503 72667   Fax 01503 72940   Map 12 C3   **H**
Talland Bay nr Looe Cornwall PL13 2JB

Ten bedrooms have been refurbished at this white-painted hotel set high above Talland Bay, but the general style and tune of the hotel are unchanged and Maureen Le Page (manageress for 15 years) remains a familiar face to greet returning guests. The main lounge boasts a real log fire whenever there is the slightest chill in the air and a smaller non-smoking lounge also houses a small library. Fresh flowers abound even in the bedrooms, which vary considerably in size and furnishings with everything from inexpensive melamine units to antiques. Many of the practical bathrooms come with bidets and all have hot water bottles hanging up behind the door. Beds are turned down at night. The hotel is surrounded by 2½ acres of terraced gardens, and the area around the heated outdoor pool is particularly delightful. *Rooms 21. Garden, croquet, putting green, outdoor swimming pool, sauna. Closed Jan. Access, Amex, Diners, Visa.*

| LOUGHBOROUGH | King's Head | 58% | £99 |

Tel 01509 233222   Fax 01509 262911   Map 7 D3   **H**
High Street Loughborough Leicestershire LE11 2QL

Neat and comfortable hotel in the Jarvis group. Banqueting/conferences for 120. Children up to 12 stay free in parents' room. Guests enjoy membership of a gym across the road. *Rooms 78. Pool table. Access, Amex, Diners, Visa.*

| LOUGHBOROUGH | Quality Friendly Hotel | 63% | £96 |

Tel 01509 211800   Fax 01509 211868   Map 7 D3   **H**
New Ashby Road Loughborough Leicestershire LE11 0EX

Very modern low-rise redbrick hotel on the A512 near Junction 23 of the M1. Bedrooms are generally well equipped, with accessories such as trouser press, mini-bar and teletext TV. 12 suites have small sitting-rooms. Half the rooms are designated non-smoking. Public areas are open-plan in style and there is a small leisure centre. Banqueting/conferences for up to 180/225. *Rooms 94. Indoor swimming pool, gym, spa bath, sauna, solarium. Access, Amex, Diners, Visa.*

We welcome bona fide complaints and recommendations on the tear-out pages at the back of the book for readers' comments. They are followed up by our professional team.

LOW LAITHE   Carters Knox Manor   £35

Tel 01423 780607   Map 6 C1   **R**
Low Laithe Summerbridge nr Harrogate North Yorkshire HG3 4DQ

An old flax mill on the B6165 three miles South of Pateley Bridge is the unlikely setting for a characterful bar and restaurant. In the former, inventive light meals are the order of the day, while upstairs in the galleried restaurant the choice is a little more formal, English/French in style and featuring seasonal fish, shellfish and game. *Seats 80. Parties 12. L 12-2.30 D 6.30-10. Closed D 25 & 26 Dec. Set L & D from £8.*

Set menu prices may not always include service or wine.

LOWER BEEDING   Cisswood House Hotel   66%   £100

Tel 01403 891216   Fax 01403 891621   Map 11 A6   **HR**
Sandygate Lane Lower Beeding nr Horsham West Sussex RH13 6NF

Built in the late 1920s by the then chairman of Harrods, using many of that store's craftsmen, the mock-Tudor house has since been twice sympathetically extended to create this hotel, owned and run by Othmar and Elizabeth Illes since 1979. Oak timbers and panelling feature in public rooms that include a comfortable bar and separate residents' lounge that sometimes becomes part of an adaptable function suite. Traditionally furnished bedrooms have plain walls with a variety of different fabrics and all have a breakfast table and good desk space. Rooms are generally of a good size but the nine in the most recent extension are particularly spacious and have separate walk-in showers in their bathrooms. Room service throughout the day and evening. Conference and banqueting rooms cater for up to 200/150. No dogs. Eight miles from Gatwick Airport, on the A279 where it meets the A281. No children under 12. *Rooms 34. Garden, croquet, indoor swimming pool. Closed Easter, August Bank Holiday, 10 days Christmas/New Year. Access, Amex, Visa.*

Restaurant   £55

Othmar Illes makes regular trips to the London markets, ensuring that only the best quality ingredients arrive at the kitchen, where they are sympathetically handled in fairly straightforward dishes that are served in generous portions. Smoked meat platter, moules marinière, crab cakes with orange butter sauce, half a roast duck with sage and onion stuffing, Dover sole Colbert, king scallops meunière, and grilled liver and bacon show the style from a fixed-price menu (the same, though differently priced at lunch and dinner) that offers a good choice. Puds range from floating island and pecan pie to a refined apple and almond crumble served with a very alcoholic kirsch cream sauce. The dining-room looks out through leaded light windows on to a peaceful, mature garden. Fantastic prices (half a dozen *marque* champagnes under £30) on a splendid wine list, so it's well worth drinking a classic (or two!) here. *Seats 72. Parties 25. Private Rooms 12/25. L 12-2.15 D 7-9.15. Closed Sun. Set L £16.50/£18.50 Set D £18.25/£20.50.*

LOWER BEEDING   South Lodge   76%   £154

Tel 01403 891711   Fax 01403 891766   Map 11 A6   **H**
Brighton Road Lower Beeding West Sussex RH13 6PS

A fine house built by a noted Victorian explorer and botanist, Frederick Duncan Godman, with 90 acres of grounds full of rare trees and shrubs, including the largest rhododendron in England. The nearby Mannings Heath Golf Club is in the same ownership and the hotel's guests have members' rights there. Day rooms still have a strong Victorian feel with lots of carved oak panelling and some nice ribbed ceilings. Good-sized bedrooms, which include four full suites, are appealing and comfortable with individual decor and proper armchairs and/or sofas; one room is equipped with extra handrails for disabled guests. Italian marble bathrooms are particularly luxurious, most with separate showers and twin wash basins and all with bidets and bathrobes. Bedrooms are properly serviced in the evening, room service is round the clock and staff are notably friendly and helpful. Conference/banqueting rooms for up to 85/80. No dogs. *Rooms 39. Garden, croquet, tennis, golf (18), coarse fishing, snooker. Access, Amex, Diners, Visa.*

LOWER BOCKHAMPTON   Yalbury Cottage Hotel   £58

Tel 01305 262382   Fax 01305 266412   Map 13 F2   **IR**
Lower Bockhampton nr Dorchester Dorset DT2 8PZ

Follow the sign to Bockhampton from the A35 on the Dorchester by-pass to find the
Furmingers' cosy little hotel. Many of the comfortable cottage style bedrooms have
country views; all have colour TVs, modern bathrooms and a home-from-home
atmosphere. Popular with literary buffs, as the village was Thomas Hardy's Mellstock and
is within easy reach of his birthplace (now a National Trust property). Peaceful river
walks. A good place to unwind away from the pressures of modern life. *Rooms 8.*
Garden. Closed 2 weeks January. Access, Visa.

Restaurant   £50

Unpretentious home-style cooking, using local ingredients whenever possible, in this
cottage-style dining-room. Perhaps home-made soup, red mullet with a tapénade and
mustard crust or baby black pudding and mushroom parcels to begin; then maybe rack
of lamb with redcurrant and thyme sauce, vegetable Wellington with pesto or carefully
cooked calf's liver with a lime sauce. They are particularly proud of their desserts and
quite justly so; one visit included an excellent chocolate mousse with a fresh rhubarb
compote. *Seats 26. Private Room 8. L Sun only 12-1.30 (bookings preferred) D 7-9.*

Set menu prices may not always include service or wine.

LOWER SLAUGHTER   Lower Slaughter Manor   80%   £190*

Tel 01451 820456   Fax 01451 822150   Map 14 C1   **HR**
Lower Slaughter nr Bourton-on-the-Water Gloucestershire GL54 2HP

A peaceful Georgian manor surrounded
by its own grounds which include the
finest 15th-century dovecote in the
country, on the edge of one of the
prettiest villages in the Cotswolds. It is
the home of experienced hoteliers Peter
and Audrey Marks, who personally
welcome guests and whose family
photos add to the country house feel of
antique-furnished public areas that boast
some fine plasterwork ceilings,
particularly in the panelled drawing
room, and impressive chimney pieces.
Bedrooms are well appointed, with
chintzy floral fabrics favoured for the drapes, matching padded headboards and fabric-
draped kidney-shaped dressing tables. Numerous extras include fruit, magazines, toffees,
home-made biscuits, sherry and mineral water. Roomy bathrooms, many with bidets and
twin washbasins and some with separate walk-in showers (others have splendid 'deluge'
shower heads over the tub in addition to a hand-held attachment for hair washing), are
well supplied with towelling and toiletries and decorated to match their bedrooms.
Bedrooms in the coach house are of the same high standard as those in the main house.
No children under 10. No dogs. *Half-board terms only. *Rooms 14. Garden, croquet,
tennis, putting, indoor swimming pool, sauna. Access, Amex, Visa.*

Restaurant   £80

Stone-mullioned windows, rich drapes, comfortably upholstered chairs and immaculately
laid tables set the scene for some very civilised dining. The four-course dinner menu
offers a well-balanced selection of some seven dishes at each stage (except the cheese
course when some fine British examples are accompanied by oatcakes and home-baked
breads). Terrine of duck foie gras with Provençal vegetables and toasted honey-bread;
poached morel mushrooms filled with chicken and served with green asparagus and
a tarragon-flavoured jus; braised brill served with crab ravioli, deep-fried ginger and
lemon grass-flavoured sauce; and a ragout of rabbit cooked in truffle fumet with tarragon,
Dijon mustard and braised celery give a flavour of chef Michael Benjamin's cooking. To
avoid difficult decisions, go for the seven-course tasting menu. The lunch menu is a little

shorter and is now supplemented by a three-course 'Light Lunch'. On a very fine and ever-expanding wine list New World wines on the whole offer better value than France. Note that Italy is not represented at all, and the dessert wines are not listed separately, except Californian. No children under 10. No smoking. *Seats 26. Private Room 16. L 12-2 (Sun till 2.30) D 7-9.30 (Fri & Sat till 10). Set L £12.95 & £17.95 (Sun £17.95 only) Set D £32.50 & £55 (dégustation).*

LOWER SWELL   Old Farmhouse   £66

Tel 01451 830232   Fax 01451 870962   Map 14 C1   **I**
Lower Swell Stow-on-the-Wold Gloucestershire GL54 1LF

A very relaxed and unpretentious place with everything under the personal supervision of Dutch owner Erik Burger. The premises were a working farm until the 1960s, and the original 16th-century farmhouse contains the bar-lounge and restaurant. Above are neat country-style bedrooms, two of which share a bathroom. Further bedrooms are in former stables opening on to the car park; best rooms are in the old coach house, where there's also a quiet residents' lounge with TV, magazines and board games. Pictures and prints for sale are displayed throughout the public rooms. Mountain bikes are available for hire and air-pistol target shooting can be arranged in a corner of the garden. Lower Swell is a little village one mile west of Stow on the B4068. *Rooms 14. Garden. Closed 2 weeks Jan. Access, Visa.*

LOWICK BRIDGE   Bridgefield House   60%   £70

Tel 01229 885239   Fax 01229 885379   Map 4 C4   **HR**
Lowick Bridge Ulverston Cumbria LA12 8DA

A late 19th-century house built of local stone, overlooking the Crake Valley on the back road from Lowick Bridge to Spark Bridge. Bedrooms, though spacious, are modestly appointed with mostly freestanding furniture, telephones and clock radios but no TVs. Families are made very welcome. *Rooms 5. Garden. Closed 25 Dec eve. Access, Visa.*

Restaurant   £60
🍇

Dinner at candle-lit dark mahogany tables is courteously overseen by David Glister. His wife Rosemary's daily-changing six-course, fixed-price-only menus show all that's best in traditional British cooking. Starting with potted smoked sea trout or lamb sweetbreads in a grainy mustard and cream sauce, you'll then be served a soup, then the centrepiece dish, perhaps salmon poached in white wine served on a bed of braised leeks, or Herdwick lamb with sweet cinnamon spiced apricot sauce. Next comes a water ice, then something delicious in the dessert line like individual date and butterscotch pudding with almonds and pouring cream. The feast concludes with blue Stilton or sautéed kidneys in Madeira on toast, and coffee or tea with brandy colettes. Concise wine list, plenty of half bottles and decent prices, with Australia the pick of the bunch. No smoking. Booking essential. *Seats 24. Parties 6. D only 7.30 for 8. Set D £20.*

LUDLOW   Dinham Hall   64%   £93

Tel 01584 876464   Fax 01584 876019   Map 6 B4   **H**
By the Castle Ludlow Shropshire SY8 1EJ

Georgian town house in a quiet street opposite Ludlow Castle. The lounge features an intriguing oversized fireplace (with real log-fire in winter) that incorporates medieval carvings, Georgian panels and even a bit of art deco. The bar is part of an informal brasserie. Pleasant bedrooms, which vary in size, are mostly furnished with solid darkwood 'hotel' furniture and all have fridges and tea and coffee-making kit. Bathrooms nearly all have shower and WC only. *Rooms 12. Garden, sauna, keep-fit equipment. Access, Amex, Diners, Visa.*

We welcome bona fide complaints and recommendations on the tear-out pages at the back of the book for readers' comments. They are followed up by our professional team.

LUDLOW   Feathers Hotel   70%   £98

Tel 01584 875261   Fax 01584 876030   Map 6 B4   **H**
Bull Ring Ludlow Shropshire SY8 1AA

The stunning timber-framed facade dates from 1620 and inside there are other fine
architectural features, most notably perhaps the panelled first-floor lounge with carved
overmantel and remarkable Tudor ceiling. The real appeal of this historic town-centre
hotel though is the loving care lavished on it since the 1940s by the Edwards family
– adding an antique here, a pair of gilt-framed mirrors on a landing there, some new oak
panelling somewhere else – and numerous long-serving staff who ensure that everything
runs smoothly. It's difficult to generalise about bedrooms that range from fairly plain
standard rooms (but with all the usual amenities) with fitted units to luxurious Comus
rooms with air-conditioning and locally-made oak furniture. Bathrooms are equally
varied, some having older-style tiling, others colourful Spanish tiles, separate shower
cubicles and twin wash basins. All come with towelling robes and hot water bottles and
most have bidets. Children up to 8 stay free in parents' room. *Rooms 39. Patio, snooker.*
Access, Amex, Diners, Visa.

Set menu prices may not always include service or wine.

LUDLOW   The Merchant House   ★ ↑   NEW   £70

Tel 01584 875438   Map 6 B4   **R**
Lower Corve Street Ludlow Shropshire SY8 1DU

Since Shaun Hill's arrival here to set up his own business after nine years at the stoves of
Gidleigh Park, this medieval half-timbered building has become a gastronomic magnet.
The dining-room seats 20 and operates on a strict one-sitting-only basis. Shaun displays
all the enthusiasm of a chef reborn. A short market-driven table d'hote, with three
choices at each course, is offered, and a deceptively simple style resurrects old favourites
such as artichoke *nissarda*. A spring dinner started with moist wholemeal raisin and
excellent white breads, and amuse-gueule included scrumptious sesame goat's cheese tarts.
Starters offered steamed John Dory with sauerkraut and juniper sabayon; spring leaves
with roast quail and walnut dressing or calf's sweetbreads and kidney with a potato cake
studded with black olives – the sweetbreads beautifully crisp on the outside, perfectly
moist in the centre, the whole served with a caper sauce with just enough cutting edge
to avoid any over-richness. Main courses included roast corn-fed pigeon with spring
vegetables and a morel sauce, roast rack of lamb with North African spices and sautéed
monkfish with a mustard and cucumber sauce. A perfectly cooked saddle of venison was
accompanied by a marvellous fried goat's cheese and potato cake and a spinach-stuffed
globe artichoke base, along with a simple jus. Desserts continue the direct flavour school
of cookery – a brandy snap basket filled with rhubarb and strawberry fool, the textures
just right and the quality of the ingredients shining alone without the need for irrelevant
fripperies (feathered coulis, compulsory icing sugar and redundant mint leaves) so beloved
of the modern pastry kitchen. There's a no-nonsense approach to the wines, with
ridiculously low prices for some excellent bottles. House champagne, for instance, is only
£20, a 1985 Lanson under £30. Not many halves perhaps, but at these prices it hardly
matters. Booking essential. No smoking. *Seats 20. L 12.30-2 D 7-10. Closed L Tue, Wed,*
Thu, all Sun & Mon & 3 days Christmas. Access, Amex, Visa.

LUTON   Chiltern Hotel   60%   £88

Tel 01582 575911   Fax 01582 581859   Map 15 E1   **H**
Waller Avenue Luton Bedfordshire LU4 9RU

Forte-owned hotel halfway between the M1 (junction 11) and Luton town centre. Caters
well for families; also popular for functions and conferences (up to 350). 24hr room
service. Parking for 120 cars. *Rooms 91. Access, Amex, Diners, Visa.*

LUTON   Hotel Ibis   60%   £54

Tel 01582 424488   Fax 01582 455511   Map 15 E1   **H**
Spittlesea Road Luton Bedfordshire LU2 9NZ

Usefully located by Luton Airport, this reasonably priced hotel offers efficient, well-
equipped bedrooms, public rooms and conference facilities for up to 100. There's free
parking for 60 cars, and about a third of the bedrooms are reserved for non-smokers.
Children up to 12 stay free in parents' room. *Rooms 98. Coffee shop (6.30am-10.30pm).*
Access, Amex, Diners, Visa.

| LUTON | **Leaside Hotel** | 55% | £55 |

Tel 01582 417643   Fax 01582 34961
72 New Bedford Road Luton Bedfordshire LU3 1BT

Map 15 E1

H

Near the town centre but a touch tricky to find (ask for a map showing directions), Leaside is a modest but very agreeable little hotel run since 1980 by Carole and Martin Gillies. The building is Victorian, and a certain period charm survives in the panelled bar. Many bedrooms are smallish singles, but the basic needs are supplied and housekeeping is good. Lounge with open fire and snooker; the lounge bar opens on to a terrace surrounded by trees. Access to the car park at the back is via Old Bedford Road and Villa Road. *Rooms 12. Terrace, snooker. Closed 24, 25 & 26 Dec. Access, Amex, Diners, Visa.*

| LUTON | **Luton Gateway Hotel** | 57% | £76 |

Tel 01582 575955   Fax 01582 490065
641 Dunstable Road Luton Bedfordshire LU4 8RQ

Map 15 E1

H

Practical accommodation suitable for overnight stop-over. Popular with business folk , hence the high proportion of single rooms (70) in a modern building right next to Junction 11 of the M1. This was formerly a Forte Posthouse and is still owned by Forte. *Rooms 111. Access, Amex, Diners, Visa.*

| LUTON | **Strathmore Thistle** | 63% | £110 |

Tel 01582 34199   Fax 01582 402528
Arndale Centre Luton Bedfordshire LU1 2TR

Map 15 E1

H

High-rise hotel next to town-centre shopping and railway station. Banqueting facilities for up to 250, conferences to 300. Video-monitored car park. *Rooms 150. Coffee shop (11am-11pm). Access, Amex, Diners, Visa.*

| LUTTERWORTH | **Denbigh Arms** | 66% | £65 |

Tel 01455 553537   Fax 01455 556627
High Street Lutterworth Leicestershire LE17 4AD

Map 7 D4

H

An extended Georgian coaching inn right on the high street just over a mile from Junction 20 and the M1. The Fielding Room, largest of three function rooms, can accommodate 50 for a meeting or banquet. Good housekeeping and pleasant, friendly staff. *Rooms 32. Access, Amex, Diners, Visa.*

| LYME REGIS | **Alexandra Hotel** | 58% | £95 |

Tel 01297 442010   Fax 01297 443229
Pound Street Lyme Regis Dorset DT7 3HZ

Map 13 E2

H

Built in 1735 as a dower house and converted to a hotel at the beginning of this century, the Alexandra occupies a fine hillside position in its own grounds with a pathway to the beach. Most of the individually-decorated bedrooms overlook Lyme Bay and Cobb Harbour. *Rooms 27. Garden, croquet. Access, Amex, Diners, Visa.*

| LYMINGTON | **Gordleton Mill** | 67% | £103 |

Tel 01590 682219   Fax 01590 683073
Silver Street Hordle nr Lymington Hampshire S041 6DJ

Map 14 C4

HR

Given its wonderful location, in France this would be classified as a *restaurant avec chambres*, since the hub of the operation is the restaurant. However, with skilful building, refurbishment and landscaping, the creeper-clad 17th-century mill is more than just a restaurant. Some two miles west of town, and set in over five acres of grounds that include a stream, mill pond, sluice gates, weir and painted bridges, the hotel with its own terrace overlooks delightful gardens, a magnet for wildlife. The bedrooms (four non-smoking) have polished pine furniture, smart decor and a host of extras, such as a bottle of champagne on arrival, fresh flowers, fruit bowl, mineral water and magazines, while the bathrooms (all but one with spa tubs) offer superb toiletries, bathrobes and cosseting towels. Service, including free tea and coffee throughout your stay, housekeeping and maintenance are top-notch, with beds turned down at night, and a porter at the ready to carry suitcases. There are two beamed lounges (one designated non-smoking), and from one you can see the original mill workings, which are also accessible from the outside. Meeting/conference room for up to 30. Ample car parking from where you cross a bridge on foot to reach the hotel. No children under 7. *Rooms 7. Garden. Closed 1st 2 weeks Jan. Access, Amex, Diners, Visa.*

See over

Provence Restaurant ★ £105

🍸 🍷 🍇 🍷 🥂 🍓

Put to one side the very French and occasionally over-attentive service and the seemingly annual change of chef, and instead dwell on the exceptional quality of the cooking and surroundings. New chef Toby Hill has come up through the brigade's ranks and cooks with a sure touch and flair – dishes are artistically presented, but not to the detriment of taste and flavour. The cornerstone of the various menus is the à la carte, with several choices in each section at a set price, though there is a supplement for dishes that include foie gras. In addition, there's a *menu surprise* on Saturday night, weekday menus with matching wines, and a £20 luncheon *menu du jour* that includes three courses and coffee. There's also a set Sunday lunch, though courses from this can be taken individually. As the name of the restaurant implies, the style of food is French, with dishes written in that language and English. After an amuse-gueule of, say, marinated salmon, starters include a layered terrine of local wood pigeon and beetroot served with its own vinaigrette, colourful yes, though somewhat light on the pigeon content, steamed langoustines served with shredded courgettes and crab ravioli, or a *brandade de poisson*, a puff pastry case of fish cooked in cream and garlic with a mussel sauce. For a main course, perhaps steamed fillet of sea bass filled with a scallop and oyster mousse, served with a lightly poached oyster and noodles, a daube of beef, or a classic tournedos Rossini. Wonderful desserts might include an orange tart served with a raspberry coulis and sorbet encased in a tuile, a hot soufflé (Grand Marnier, black cherry), or a tarte tatin served with caramel ice cream. Good-looking cheese trolley with mostly French cheeses, splendid coffee and petits fours, and decent bread. The wine list is certainly exceptional, if somewhat pretentiously presented, with a good choice of house wines, backed up by tasting notes. Super selection of half bottles, quite fair prices; push the boat out and check out the *Hospices de Beaune* section. Patio dining in good weather. No smoking.
Seats 45. Parties 10. Private Room 16. L 12-2.30 D 7-9.30. Closed Mon (except D residents). Set L £20 Set D £35/£43.

LYMINGTON	Passford House	70%	£110

Tel 01590 682398   Fax 01590 683494   Map 14 C4   **H**
Mount Pleasant Lane Lymington Hampshire SO41 8LS

Just off the A337, on the edge of the New Forest between Lymington (2 miles) and Sway, this elegant white house was originally the home of Lord Arthur Cecil. Two bedroom wings and the Dolphin leisure complex have since been added, but the traditional look survives in the four lounges – one oak-panelled with an open fire, another with French windows opening on to a patio and ornamental pool. Upstairs there are bright and airy bedrooms (15 designated De Luxe and attracting a small supplement) with mostly white furniture; carpeted bathrooms have showers and useful toiletries. Children are catered for admirably, with cots, high-chairs, a separate play area and separate meal times; first child under 12 sharing parents' room is accommodated free. *Rooms 55. Garden, croquet, tennis, putting, indoor & outdoor swimming pools, sauna, solarium, spa bath, keep-fit equipment, children's outdoor playground. Access, Amex, Visa.*

LYMINGTON	Stanwell House	65%	£85

Tel 01590 677123   Fax 01590 677756   Map 14 C4   **H**
High Street Lymington Hampshire SO41 9AA

The hotel dates from the 18th century, but careful modernisation has extended its scope. Attractive day rooms include a smart cocktail bar and a chintzy lounge. Well-equipped bedrooms (including one with a four-poster) are named after Bordeaux wine chateaux. Children up to 10 stay free in parents' room. Guests have free use of leisure facilities – pool, tennis, squash, sauna – at the Elmers Court Country Club about ½ mile from the hotel. No dogs. *Rooms 35. Garden. Access, Amex, Visa.*

We welcome bona fide complaints and recommendations on the tear-out pages at the back of the book for readers' comments. They are followed up by our professional team.

LYMPSHAM · Batch Farm Country Hotel · 56% · £54

Tel 01934 750371   Fax 01934 750501   Map 13 E1   **H**
Lympsham nr Weston-super-Mare Somerset BS24 0EX

The setting is 50 acres of open farmland through which flows the River Axe. Origins of the former farmhouse are evident in the beams which adorn the bar and residents' lounges. The neat, practical bedrooms enjoy views of either the Mendip or Quantock hills. The adjoining Somerset Suite is a popular venue for functions up to 70. Lympsham is about 3 miles from Junction 22 of M5. Personally run by owners Mr and Mrs Brown. Family friendly. No dogs. *Rooms 8. Garden, croquet, fishing. Closed 1 week Christmas. Access, Amex, Diners, Visa.*

LYMPSTONE · River House · £80

Tel 01395 265147   Map 13 E3   **RR**
The Strand Lympstone Devon EX8 5EY

There are lovely views over the River Exe to Powderham Castle from Michael and Shirley Wilkes' restaurant with rooms, and when the tide is in the water laps against the walls. The menu is priced for either two, three or four courses with an alternative, individually priced menu of lighter dishes available at lunchtimes. The latter might include a lovage, cheese and onion tart with salad or large spinach and local crab-filled ravioli baked in a light parmesan sauce. Fish is always a winner here and main menu offerings are typified by grilled red mullet with an orange, tomato and fresh herb sauce, and River Exe salmon served with fresh sorrel from their garden along with the likes of braised oxtail, tagine of lamb and chicken tandoori. Vegetarians are well catered for, there's a good choice of puddings, and home-made fudge, praline and chocolates are a treat with coffee. *Seats 34. Parties 18. Private Room 14. L 12-1.30 D 7-9.30 (Sat to 10.30). Closed Sun & Mon (except for residents), Bank Holidays, 27 Dec & 2 Jan. Set L & D £25.95/£29.50/£34.50. Access, Amex, Visa.*

Rooms   £87

The four pretty bedrooms, two reserved for non-smokers, have en-suite bathrooms and many thoughtful extras. No children under six. No dogs.

LYNDHURST · Lyndhurst Park · 63% · £66

Tel 01703 283923   Fax 01703 283019   Map 14 C4   **H**
High Street Lyndhurst Hampshire SO43 7NL

On the edge of town – where it meets the New Forest – the Georgian origins of this now much-extended hotel (it boasts the largest conference/function facilities in the area – up to 500 theatre-style) are largely lost except in the cocktail bar and chandeliered reception hall, both decorated in warm red tones. Apart from a small lounge the main public room is a characterfully rustic bar. Bedrooms are notably well kept and appealing, often with brass bedheads and always with well-lit dressing/work table. Good, fully tiled and carpeted bathrooms each come with a huge bottle of shampoo and a family of plastic ducks. 24hr room service can provide a cooked meal throughout the day and evening with sandwiches and drinks overnight. Children free in parents' room to age 14. *Rooms 59. Garden, tennis, outdoor swimming pool, sauna. Access, Amex, Diners, Visa.*

LYNDHURST · Parkhill Hotel · 69% · £106

Tel 01703 282944   Fax 01703 283268   Map 14 C4   **HR**
Beaulieu Road Lyndhurst Hampshire SO43 7FZ

Parkhill enjoys a glorious New Forest setting, just off the B3056 Lyndhurst to Beaulieu road. A constant programme of upgrading is typical of the attention to detail lavished on the place, from the 12 acres of private grounds and lake to the immaculate public rooms and bedrooms. *Rooms 20. Garden, croquet, putting, coarse fishing, outdoor swimming pool. Access, Amex, Diners, Visa.*

Cedars Restaurant   £70

Modern British cooking predominates on a menu which nevertheless has international influences. Try marinated cajun spiced duck, grilled fillets of cod with an Emmental and

See over

potato gratin on a herb cream sauce and iced orange and rosemary parfait with baked kumquats to finish. No smoking. Friendly prices on a diverse list – many bottles under £20. Credit cards not accepted for less than £25. *Seats 80. Parties 36. Private Room 48. L 12-2 D 7-9. Set L £12.75/£15 (Sun £15) Set D £25.50/£28.90/£38.*

LYNDHURST   The Crown   65%   £93

Tel 01703 282922   Fax 01703 282751   Map 14 C4   **H**
High Street Lyndhurst New Forest Hampshire SO43 7NF

A solid gabled building in the high street opposite the church (follow the one-way traffic signs). Ample lounge areas provide space to relax with pleasant views of the gardens; the bar is a fine period piece with library-style wood panelling. Decent-sized bedrooms have stylish repro and antique furniture and good bathrooms. Children under 16 are accommodated free when they share a room with a parent. The New Forest surrounds the village, and walking and cycling are popular pastimes. *Rooms 40. Garden. Access, Amex, Diners, Visa.*

LYNMOUTH   Rising Sun Hotel   £89

Tel 01598 753223   Fax 01598 753480   Map 13 D1   **I**
Harbourside Lynmouth Devon EX35 6EQ

Medieval character in the form of oak panelling, uneven floors and crooked ceilings survives in a 14th-century thatched inn overlooking the picturesque harbour (leave the M5 at Junction 23 signposted to Minehead and follow the A39 to Lynmouth). Bedrooms are in keeping, being snug and cottagey. Shelley's Cottage, where the poet spent his honeymoon with his 16-year-old bride, consists of a double bedroom with four-poster bed, a sitting room and a private garden. The inn owns a stretch of river for salmon fishing. No children under five. *Rooms 16. Garden, fishing. Access, Amex, Diners, Visa.*

LYNTON   Lynton Cottage   65%   £78

Tel 01598 752342   Fax 01598 752597   Map 13 D1   **H**
North Walk Lynton Devon EX35 6ED

The Joneses' family-run hotel high above Lynmouth Bay offers spectacular sea views from the day rooms (and all but three bedrooms). Well modernised and smartly kept, it's a warm, friendly place, particularly the bar, with comfortable, old-fashioned seats and Victorian pine panelling. Bedrooms, many with corner baths in the smart bathrooms, are individually decorated with character and style. No children under ten, except babes in arms. *Rooms 16. Garden. Closed Jan. Access, Amex, Diners, Visa.*

LYTHAM   Clifton Arms   63%   £91

Tel 01253 739898   Fax 01253 730657   Map 6 A1   **H**
West Beach Lytham Lancashire FY8 5QJ

Best bedrooms at this redbrick Victorian building on the seafront (A584) are the 'Executives' at the front, overlooking the Ribble Estuary; standard rooms are smaller. Winged armchairs and settees fill the lounge. Conference/banqueting facilities for 200. *Rooms 44. Access, Amex, Diners, Visa.*

LYTHAM ST ANNES   Dalmeny Hotel   60%   £81

Tel 01253 712236   Fax 01253 724447   Map 6 A1   **HR**
19 South Promenade St Annes Lytham St Annes Lancashire FY8 1LX

A seaside hotel of wide appeal, in the ownership of the Webb family since 1945. There are several restaurants, ample roomy lounges and bars, leisure facilities, family recreational activities and accommodation that runs from singles to apartments with kitchens. Parking for 120. Friendly, helpful staff add to the pleasure. *Rooms 109. Garden, indoor swimming pool, gym, squash, sauna, solarium, beauty salon, children's playroom, games room, coffee shop (8am-10.30pm). Closed 24-26 Dec. Access, Amex, Visa.*

C'est La Vie   £60

The main restaurant serves an à la carte selection that ranges from fresh oysters, leek and bacon tartlet and goujons of Dover sole poached in white wine with grapes to fillet of beef with roast garlic and a red wine sauce and roast breast of guinea fowl with a cream and wild mushroom sauce. *C'est La Vie* is in a vaulted basement. There's also a popular carvery and a patio restaurant. **Seats** *40.* **Parties** *10.* **D** *only 6.30-10.* *Closed Sun, Mon, 3 days Christmas.*

MACCLESFIELD	Sutton Hall	£85

Tel 01260 253211   Fax 01260 252538   Map 6 B2   **I**
Bullocks Lane Sutton Macclesfield Cheshire SK11 0HE

Run by Robert Bradshaw for the last 14 years, Sutton Hall began life as an endowment to a monastery in the 11th century before becoming a baronial residence in the 16th century and then a nunnery. Now describing itself as a public house, restaurant and hotel, it's full of old-world atmosphere: black oak beams, flagstones and open log fires characterise the day rooms, and all the bedrooms feature lace-draped four-posters, Gothic windows and sturdy English furniture. Banqueting/conference facilities for 60/30. **Rooms** *10.* *Garden.* *Access, Visa.*

MADINGLEY	Three Horseshoes	£65

Tel 01954 210221   Fax 01954 212043   Map 15 F1   **R**
High Street Madingley nr Cambridge Cambridgeshire CB3 8AB

Richard Stokes has an all-round winner on his hands in that here is a picturesque, very well maintained thatched inn in the centre of a pretty village, together with an imaginative, fashionable menu of delicious, carefully prepared, mostly Mediterranean dishes and very kind prices to boot. Begin with buffalo mozzarella and tomato crostini with chopped black olives and herb salad, chargrilled scallops with chili, mint, sherry and wilted greens or duck confit with red and yellow peppers, black olives and fried basil. Main dishes range from grilled fillet of salmon with parsley salad, daube of beef with celeriac and potato purée, roast wild duck breast and leg with caramelised red cabbage to roast loin of lamb with rosemary, garlic, chargrilled Italian vegetables and spiced couscous. Delectable desserts such as caramelised lemon tart with lime and vanilla marmalade, prune and armagnac ice cream or the ever-popular sticky toffee pudding to finish. Very good cheeses are all from Neal's Yard Dairy. Attentive service. John Hoskins MW is indeed a master when it comes to compiling a wine list. This one is no different, both enterprising and keenly priced, spanning the globe. Authoritative tasting notes too. (See Cellar(s) of the Year awards pages). **Seats** *94.* **L** *12-2* **D** *6.30-10.* *Access, Amex, Diners, Visa.*

MAIDEN NEWTON	Le Petit Canard	£55

Tel 01300 320536   Map 13 F2   **R**
Dorchester Road Maiden Newton Dorset DT2 0BE

Geoff and Lin Chapman describe their cooking as "pretty much global" but will narrow it down to "Pacific Rim" if you insist! Whatever, it translates as a light modern touch to ingredients drawn from far and near – chargrilled kangaroo fillet with mustard and shallot sauce, slow-roasted Chinese-glazed duck on sautéed Chinese leaf, fish from Brixham, local vegetables, West Country artisan cheese. Bourbon-Pecan crème brulée could complete a 3-course set meal. The menu changes monthly and the wine list is updated weekly by computer, ensuring a well-priced selection of bin ends and half bottles. **Seats** *28.* **Parties** *16.* **D** *only 7-9.* *Closed Sun & Mon.* *Set D £21.50/£24.50.* *Access, Visa.*

MAIDENHEAD	Fredrick's	75%	£168

Tel 01628 35934   Fax 01628 771054   Map 15 E2   **HR**
Shoppenhangers Road Maidenhead Berkshire SL6 2PZ

In a quiet residential road, yet only minutes from Junction 8/9 of the M4, Fredrick Losel's attractive redbrick hotel offers luxury and high-quality service to a predominantly senior executive clientele. The reception area, with strikingly modern chandeliers, marble waterfall and complimentary glass of champagne on check-in, sets the tone of public rooms that include a verdant

See over

winter garden looking out over a patio, and a sumptuous cocktail bar. A novel feature of the decoratively more restrained bedrooms is that beds are set upon solid plinths. Standard rooms have a pair of easy chairs around a breakfast table while the five larger rooms have settees in separate sitting areas. All have mini-bars, satellite TV and well-appointed bathrooms – most with bidets. Three single rooms have shower and WC only. Rooms are properly serviced in the evenings and staff are notably smart. 24hr room service. Free parking for 90 cars. The conference/banqueting facilities are currently being refurbished. No dogs. *Rooms 37. Garden, croquet. Closed 24-30 Dec. Access, Amex, Diners, Visa.*

Restaurant   £100

An overtly luxurious room – gilt and crystal chandeliers, painted wall panels, monogrammed china and glassware – is matched by formal service under the eye of maitre d' Tony Guttilla and Brian Cutler's highly professional cooking based on classic French and English methods. Top-quality produce is the starting point for stylishly presented dishes like grilled wild salmon with potato and celeriac rösti, winter vegetable broth with ravioli, grenadin of English veal with fresh chanterelles and linguini, and steamed monkfish with mussels and scallops in saffron. Sunday lunch includes roast rib of beef served from the trolley. Home-made ices and sorbets among the desserts. *Seats 60. Parties 15. L 12-2 D 7-9.45. Closed L Sat. Set L £19.50 (Sun £23.50) Set D £28.50.*

Set menu prices may not always include service or wine.

MAIDENHEAD   Holiday Inn   66%   £136

Tel 01628 23444   Fax 01628 770035   Map 15 E2   **H**
Manor Lane Maidenhead Berkshire SL6 2RA

Set in 18 acres of grounds close to junction 8/9 of the M4 and junction 4 of the M40, this hotel is usefully situated for visitors to the Thames Valley area. Top-notch, large conference and banqueting facilities (for up to 400) include the characterful, reconstructed Elizabethan Shoppenhangers Manor house in the grounds. Straightforward accommodation, but good leisure facilities, including a children's pool. Playroom provided for children at weekends. *Rooms 189. Garden, indoor swimming pool, children's splash pool, spa bath, sauna, sun beds, squash, gym, snooker, coffee shop (7am-11pm). Access, Amex, Diners, Visa.*

MAIDSTONE   Larkfield Priory   62%   £77

Tel 01732 846858   Fax 01732 846786   Map 11 B5   **H**
812 London Road Maidstone Kent ME20 6HJ

Leave the M20 at Junction 4 taking the A228 Tonbridge road, then the Maidstone road from the first roundabout, to find a Forte hotel centred around a Victorian priory. A popular conference venue with facilities for up to 70 delegates. Discounts are offered at the well-equipped Larkfield Leisure Centre half a mile away. All the usual amenities in the bedrooms, which include, at a premium, a four-poster room. *Rooms 52. Garden. Access, Amex, Diners, Visa.*

MAIDSTONE   Mandarin Chef   £35

Tel 01622 755917   Map 11 B5   **R**
35 Lower Stone Street Maidstone Kent

Friendly service and sound Chinese cooking by chef Ken Lai make this a popular town-centre restaurant with a regular clientele. Peking and Cantonese regions are well represented with dishes such as braised beef fillet, sweet and sour pork, hot and sour soup, pickled cabbage, diced chicken with cashew nuts in yellow bean sauce and baked crab in ginger and spring onion sauce. Ring ahead for an off-the-menu feast of specials. The well-priced special lunch is available Mon-Fri. *Seats 70. Parties 25. L 12-2.15 D 5-11.30. Set L from £7 Set D from £14. Access, Amex, Diners, Visa.*

Consult the blue pages for summary tables and lists of recommended establishments.

| MAIDSTONE | Stakis Maidstone Hotel | 67% | £113 |

Tel 01622 734322   Fax 01622 734600   Map 11 B5   **H**
Bearsted Weavering Maidstone Kent ME14 5AA

Next to the M20 at Junction 7, the hotel, formerly the Stakis Country Court, is set around a landscaped courtyard. Spacious bedrooms have double beds, modern furnishings, speed-dial phones, smart tiled bathrooms and good showers. Ladies rooms and rooms adapted for disabled guests are available. Leisure club and extensive high-tech meeting and conference facilities. Ample car parking. *Rooms 139. Garden, indoor swimming pool, gym, sauna, spa bath, solarium, beauty salon. Access, Amex, Diners, Visa.*

| MALDON | Blue Boar | 59% | £92 |

Tel 01621 852681   Fax 01621 856202   Map 11 C4   **H**
3 Silver Street Maldon Essex CM9 7QE

An ancient inn (parts go back to the 14th century) located just off the High Street, notable for its elegant Georgian facade, heavy oak beams, open fires and timbered wings overlooking a stable yard. The majority of bedrooms (17) are designated non-smoking. Forte. *Rooms 29. Garden. Access, Amex, Diners, Visa.*

| MALDON | Francine's | | £50 |

Tel 01621 856605   Map 11 C4   **R**
1a High Street Maldon Essex CM9 7PB

An unpretentious restaurant, sited in one of Maldon's oldest buildings. The minuteness of John Brotherton's kitchen is not something he lets constrain him. Care is taken over the preparation of French-inspired dishes using the freshest of produce. The menu, now fixed-price 2 or 3 courses with coffee, changes on the first Tuesday of each month and offers the likes of mushroom feuilletés, smoked salmon bavarois, chicken breasts stuffed with crabmeat, halibut cooked in whisky and orange juice and fillet steak with Madeira and caper sauce. To finish perhaps walnut pie with calvados cream or hot winter fruit salad. John's wife Sara produces meals from her native Thailand on the third and fourth Wednesdays of each month. *Seats 24. L by arrangement D 7.30-9.30. Closed Sun & Mon. Set D £16/£18.75. Access, Visa.*

We welcome bona fide complaints and recommendations on the tear-out pages at the back of the book for readers' comments. They are followed up by our professional team.

| MALMESBURY | Old Bell Hotel | 65% | £70 |

Tel 01666 822344   Fax 01666 825145   Map 14 B2   **H**
Abbey Row Malmesbury Wiltshire SN16 OAG

The Old Bell lays claim to being England's oldest hotel. Founded by the Abbot of Malmesbury in the reign of King John, it was originally a guest house for visitors to the Abbey library. Little of the original core remains, but Edwardian and more recent additions have largely kept the atmosphere intact. Bedrooms in the main house are graded as standard, de-luxe or superior; but all have en-suite bathrooms (some with splendid freestanding tubs) and are modestly comfortable – the labelling really denotes size. Since its takeover by Luxury Family Hotels a supervised children's playroom has opened and is proving popular. By the summer of '96 an outdoor equivalent should be available in fine weather. Car park. *Rooms 31. Garden. Access, Amex, Visa.*

| MALVERN | Abbey Hotel | 62% | £80 |

Tel 01684 892332   Fax 01684 892662   Map 14 B1   **H**
Abbey Road Malvern Hereford & Worcester WR14 3ET

A mix of impressive, ivy-clad exterior and modern bedrooms (including 10 Executives) in an extension block. Conference/banqueting facilities for up to 350/300 but the hotel is also much used by tourists to the area. Children under 14 accommodated free in parents' room. De Vere Hotels. *Rooms 107. Access, Amex, Diners, Visa.*

MALVERN   Anupam   £40

Tel 01684 573814   Fax 01684 893945   Map 14 B1   **R**
85 Church Street Malvern Hereford & Worcester WR14 2AE

Indian cooking of a dependable quality, plus efficient service and a list of complementary wines compiled by the nearby *Croque-en-Bouche*. The standard menu is supplemented by interesting new arrivals such as chicken *dilkush* (with split green chilis and prunes), lamb *maharajah* flavoured with fenugreek and coriander leaves, and *achanka* vegetables in a spiced yoghurt sauce enriched with cream and almonds. *Seats 54. L 12.30-2 D 6-12. Closed 25 & 26 Dec. Set meals from £11.95. Access, Amex, Diners, Visa.*

MALVERN   Colwall Park Hotel   62%   £86

Tel 01684 540206   Fax 01684 540847   Map 14 B1   **H**
Walwyn Road Colwall Malvern Hereford & Worcester WR13 6QG

At the foot of the Malvern Hills, in the centre of Colwall village on the B4218 between Malvern and Ledbury, this mock-Tudor hotel offers simple, well-kept accommodation. The large panelled lounge bar has a roaring log fire, and an elegant staircase leads to bedrooms which are light and spacious, with quality furniture. Conference/banqueting for 120/100. *Rooms 20. Garden, croquet. Access, Amex, Visa.*

MALVERN   The Cottage in the Wood 65%   £89

Tel 01684 575859   Fax 01684 560662   Map 14 B1   **HR**
Holywell Road Malvern Wells Hereford & Worcester WR14 4LG

A particularly relaxing, family-run hotel with a glorious setting looking out over the Severn Plain from high on the steep wooded slopes of the Malvern Hills. It comprises three distinct buildings; the public rooms and eight cottagey bedrooms are in a fine Georgian dower house, with further accommodation in the nearby Beech Cottage and Coach House (with access to balconies or patios). Children under 12 are charged £1.50 for each year of life to include slip bed and full English breakfast. Private conference room for up to 14. *Rooms 20. Garden. Access, Amex, Visa.*

Restaurant   £65

Kathryn Young's Options lunch menu offers "light bites" with a roll and butter or "mega bites". In the first category come mushroom kiev, crispy prawn balls and kangaroo burger; in the latter rabbit and mushroom pie, kidneys epicure and smoked salmon. This is available (along with a set menu) every day except Sunday, when a traditional four-course menu is served (£12.95, half price for children). The evening à la carte selection is typified by fried chicken livers with apple, smoked haddock croquettes, leek and lamb pudding and guinea fowl with pineapple. Desserts could include Black Forest crepes, apple and orange pie and white chocolate and hazelnut ice cream. Good English cheeses. No smoking until coffee in the bar or lounge. The wine list is extensive and most fairly priced, with England very seriously represented. Great burgundies apart, it lacks nothing, with background notes where necessary. Smashing New World section – in fact it's a terrific list all round. *Seats 50. Parties 14. Private Room 12. L 12.30-2 D 7-9. Set L £9.95 (Sun £12.95).*

MALVERN   Croque-en-Bouche   ★   £90

Tel 01684 565612   Map 14 B1   **R**
221 Wells Road Malvern Wells Hereford & Worcester WR14 4HF

The imposing Victorian house built on a steep hillside stands directly on the A499 some two miles south of Malvern. There have been changes here of late including, midweek, both a reduction in prices as well as the option of just four or three courses. There has been absolutely no dropping of standards however with Marion Jones continuing to excite and enthral using herbs and salads, even vegetables and fruits, from her own garden to create dishes with delicious flavours. Dinner always commences with a soup such as a vegetable broth flavoured with salt cod and pesto. A choice of three second courses could include a tiger prawn, crab and skate terrine with a globe artichoke and tomato relish while for a main course there's parsleyed roast leg of Welsh lamb stuffed with aubergine, braised garlic and spinach and accompanied by a shallot, thyme and Provençal red wine sauce, French free-range corn-fed chicken roasted with a spicy orange glaze and haunch of venison escalopes with a port, redcurrant jelly and cinnamon mousse. A gratin of potato accompanies. Next come salad leaves, which precede a superb selection of British cheeses. Finally there are desserts such as lemon tart with lemon geranium leaf ice cream and the grand dessert – six tastes from the menu served with a glass of sweet Muscat wine. Superlatives do not do justice to the wine list(s) here. Past winner of all our awards it offers prices throughout which are, frankly, ridiculously cheap (e.g. over half a dozen champagnes under £30, that of the house under £20) and inclusive of VAT and service, even cheaper if you purchase them retail to take home! Observe not only the extraordinary 'world-wide' coverage of all wine-growing regions, but also the witty and knowledgeable tasting notes. Robin Jones is more than happy to offer advice on the list at any time, but be warned, his passion is intense and you don't want Marion's cooking to spoil or get cold. *Seats 22. Parties 6. Private Room 6. D only 7.30-9 (Sat to 9.30). Closed Sun-Tue, Wed Oct-May, Christmas/New Year, 2 weeks Sep. Set D £33.50 (£21/£22/£25 Weds & Thu). Access, Visa.*

MALVERN	Foley Arms	61%	£92

Tel 01684 573397 Fax 01684 569665   Map 14 B1   **H**
14 Worcester Road Great Malvern Hereford & Worcester WR14 4QS

Said to be the town's oldest hotel (built as a coaching inn in 1810), the Foley Arms stands at the top of the town, commanding magnificent views over the Severn valley. Public areas include two homely lounges (one non-smoking), a pubby bar and a summer dining terrace. Good-sized bedrooms, the best with fine views, are comfortable and unfussy, with duvets and freestanding units. Under-16s stay free in parents' room. Own parking. Free use of leisure club. *Rooms 28. Garden, giant chess. Access, Amex, Diners, Visa.*

MANCHESTER	Britannia Hotel	66%	£123

Tel 0161-228 2288 Fax 0161-236 9154   Map 6 B2   **H**
Portland Street Manchester Greater Manchester M1 3LA

Converted from a cotton warehouse in the early 80s and resplendent with its over-the-top furnishings, the Britannia is a peculiar mix of showy public rooms (note the fine cantilever staircase and chandelier) and simply decorated bedrooms. 50 fancier suites are split-level and bedecked in floral prints. Two discos, together with numerous bars and restaurants, keep up the lively pace. 24hr room service, NCP parking adjacent to the hotel, banqueting (220) and conferences up to 250. *Rooms 362. Indoor swimming pool, keep-fit equipment, sauna, steam room, spa, solarium, beauty & hair salons, pizzeria (11am-2am). Access, Amex, Diners, Visa.*

MANCHESTER	Copthorne Hotel	70%	£134

Tel 0161-873 7321 Fax 0161-873 7318   Map 6 B2   **H**
Clippers Quay Salford Quays Manchester Greater Manchester M5 2XP

Standing next to the quays in the Salford Docks redevelopment area (just a mile from the city centre) is a modern redbrick hotel. A high ceiling, exposed brickwork and polished tile floor combine to give an up-to-date feel to the foyer, with other day rooms continuing the contemporary theme. The Clippers Bar has tinted mirror walls and is a genuinely comfortable place to relax. The most popular bedrooms overlook the quay and have large bay windows, allowing in plenty of natural light; coloured-wood furniture and bathrooms tiled in two colours continue the bright theme. Superior 'Connoisseur' rooms occupy the top floor along with two suites. Two bedrooms are specifically adapted for use by wheelchair-bound guests and sixty are non-smoking. 24hr room service. Conference and function facilities for 150. No dogs. *Rooms 166. Indoor swimming pool, sauna, solarium, spa bath, steambath, gym. Access, Amex, Diners, Visa.*

MANCHESTER	Forte Posthouse	60%	£72

Tel 0161-998 7090 Fax 0161-946 0139   Map 6 B2   **H**
Palatine Road Northenden Manchester Greater Manchester M22 4FH

Mid-70s high-rise hotel, 3 miles from the airport, 7 miles from the city centre, close to junction 9 of M63. Cosy day rooms and comfortable bedrooms, where children up to 16 can stay free with parents. Interactive TVs recently installed. Banqueting/conference facilities for 100/150. *Rooms 190. Garden. Access, Amex, Diners, Visa.*

| MANCHESTER | Gaylord | £50 |

Tel 0161-832 4866 Fax 0161-832 6037   Map 6 B2   **R**
Amethyst House Spring Gardens Manchester Greater Manchester M2 1EA

In a city-centre location this is one of Manchester's best Indian restaurants, offering tandoori, Mughlai and Kashmiri cuisine. Outstanding dishes include home-made cottage cheese (in kebabs, in *pakoras,* with spinach, with peas or in *kulcha* (leavened bread)), lamb korma *badami,* and a splendidly rich chicken tikka masala. Lotus roots are an unusual item in the vegetable section. By the main post office, but not too easy to find (approach via King Street if coming by car, as it's half a block from the Market Street precinct). Excellent value lunches. *Seats 92. L 12-2.30 D 6-11.30. Set L £5.95 Set D from £11.95. Closed 25 Dec & 1 Jan. Access, Amex, Diners, Visa.*

| MANCHESTER | Holiday Inn Crowne Plaza | 73% | £158 |

Tel 0161-236 3333 Fax 0161-228 2241   Map 6 B2   **H**
Peter Street Manchester Greater Manchester M60 2DS

A grand city-centre hotel (adjacent to the G-Mex centre) restored at great expense to its past glory with ornate ceilings, arches and pillars. The foyer area is vast, with a glass roof and hanging plants crowning white columns. Cane chairs and comfortable couches adorn the adjoining terrace lounge. The high-ceilinged Octagon, one of three bars, is decorated in similar style; there are also three restaurants. Corridors that lead to the bedrooms are wide and reminiscent of a former age of spacious and luxurious hotels. Bedrooms, all recently refurbished, are generously sized and have a high standard of decor, with tiled bathrooms throughout. Extensive conference and banqueting (including kosher) facilities for up to 700. Under-19s stay free in parents' room. No dogs. *Rooms 303. Indoor swimming pool, sauna, spa bath, gym, squash, beauty & hair salon, osteopath, coffee shop (midday-10.30pm). Access, Amex, Diners, Visa.*

Consult the blue pages for summary tables and lists of recommended establishments.

| MANCHESTER | Jarvis Piccadilly | 73% | £144 |

Tel 0161-236 8414 Fax 0161-228 1568   Map 6 B2   **H**
Piccadilly Plaza Manchester Greater Manchester M60 1QR

In the heart of the city opposite Piccadilly Gardens, a high-rise hotel that is considerably smarter inside than the surroundings would suggest. Fast lifts lead up to an elegant reception area on the second floor, with an expanse of sparkling, coloured-marble flooring, and the Club Bar, both of which set the standard for decor throughout. On the lower ground floor there's a well-equipped leisure club centred around a good-sized pool. Bedrooms – 175 singles, 34 twins, 57 double and 9 suites – are also generously sized with darkwood furniture contrasting against lighter, contemporary colour schemes and well-lit bathrooms. Very extensive conference and banqueting facilities. *Rooms 275. Indoor swimming pool, gym, spa bath, sauna, solarium, steam room, beauty & hair salon, coffee shop (10am-9pm, Sun till 6). Access, Amex, Diners, Visa.*

| MANCHESTER | Market Restaurant | £55 |

Tel 0161-834 3743   Map 6 B2   **R**
Edge Street/104 High Street Manchester Greater Manchester M4 1HQ

Close to the city centre, in what is now the garment district, Peter and Anne O'Grady's friendly, homely restaurant has enormous appeal. Decorwise it's like stepping back in time with everything from the crockery and green wicker chairs to the light fittings and background music dating back to the 1940s – even the wine carafes are old-fashioned milk bottles. The monthly-changing menu takes its inspiration from all over the place. Starters might include turnip and dill soup, Thai pork sausage with sweet chili and cucumber relish and Westphalian ham with celeriac rémoulade, while main courses span wild mushroom pancakes, salmon with a mousseline of hake baked in filo, breast of tuna with a redcurrant and port sauce and top rib of beef in a green peppercorn sauce. There are always a couple of interesting vegetarian choices. Puds are important here too, as is fitting for the home of the famous Pudding Club, whose members meet six times a year to indulge in a feast of desserts like steamed puddings, fruit pies, chocolate confection, syllabubs and the like all helped down with lashings of real custard and extra thick cream. For those with more savoury tastes there is also a Starters Society. Beers, even ciders, receive equal billing with wine on an inexpensive drinks list. *Seats 42. Private Room 24. D only 6-9.30 (Sat from 7). Closed Sun, Mon, Tue, 1 week Easter, most of Aug, 1 week Christmas. Access, Amex, Visa.*

MANCHESTER	Novotel	62%	£67

Tel 0161-799 3535 Fax 0161-703 8207   Map 6 B2   **H**
Worsley Brow Worsley Manchester Greater Manchester M28 2YA

Modern hotel in its own grounds by Junction 13 of the M62. Ample free parking. Banqueting/conferences for up to 200/220. Up to two children under 16 are accommodated free, with breakfast included, when sharing their parents' room. Ample free parking. *Rooms 119. Garden, outdoor swimming pool. Access, Amex, Diners, Visa.*

MANCHESTER	Penang Village		£45

Tel 0161-236 2650   Map 6 B2   **R**
56 Faulkner Street Manchester Greater Manchester

A first-floor Malaysian restaurant on the south corner of Chinatown, near the Chinese Arch. Chicken satay or one of the range of soups is a popular prelude to a wide range of main courses including grilled king prawns or sizzling chili beef or a squid curry. Hot, 4-course buffet lunch Tue-Thur (£6). Plenty of vegetarian options. Charming service from sarong-clad waitresses. *Seats 70. Parties 80. L 12-2 D 5.30-11.30. Set L £5/£6.50 Mon & Fri, £6.50 Tue-Thur Set D from £15. Access, Amex, Diners, Visa.*

MANCHESTER	Portland Thistle	69%	£132

Tel 0161-228 3400 Fax 0161-228 6347   Map 6 B2   **H**
3/5 Portland Street Manchester Greater Manchester M1 6DP

A rather grand period facade, overlooking Piccadilly Square, belies the Portland's warehouse origins and there's no clue inside either with the newly refurbished foyer/lounge sporting a large chandelier, yellow-drag painted walls above mahogany dado panelling and plenty of comfortable seating. Other public areas include an equally comfortable bar with gilt wall-lights and mirrored ceiling, an informal bar/bistro where guests can feel at home in casual dress, and be-cushioned wicker armchairs set around a pool in the basement spa where there is a further bar. An ongoing refurbishment programme is giving the air-conditioned bedrooms a face-lift and new light grey-stained units. New TVs with satellite channels were due to be installed before we published. The main drawback here is that rooms tend to be on the small side although 'Executives' have a bit more room and 12 Junior suites are large enough to have a separate sitting area. Staff are smart and friendly. 24hr room service. Valet parking. *Rooms 205. Indoor swimming pool, keep-fit equipment, sauna, solarium. Access, Amex, Diners, Visa.*

MANCHESTER	Rajdoot		£40

Tel 0161-834 2176   Map 6 B2   **R**
Carlton House 18 Albert Square Manchester Greater Manchester M2 5PR

Rajdoot is a small chain of restaurants (established in 1966) serving well-prepared Indian food in comfortable surroundings. Tandoori dishes are a speciality, with mackerel, crab claws, lamb kidneys and venison joining more familiar variations on lamb, chicken and prawns. Other branches are in Birmingham and Bristol (also Dublin and Fuengirola on the Costa del Sol). *Seats 67. L 12-2.30 D 6.30-11.30. Closed L Sun, 25 & 26 Dec. Set L £6.95 Set D from £14.50 (£13.50 vegetarian). Access, Amex, Diners, Visa.*

MANCHESTER	Ramada Hotel	73%	£129

Tel 0161-835 2555 Fax 0161-833 0731   Map 6 B2   **H**
Blackfriars Street Manchester Greater Manchester M3 2EQ

A tall modern hotel with extensive conference and banqueting facilities (up to 450 guests). Day rooms include a large, luxurious lounge off the marble-clad lobby. The muted, pastel-shaded bedrooms are all spacious (mini-suite size), with seating areas, desk space, all the expected modern accessories and bright, well-equipped bathrooms. *Rooms 200. Hairdressing. Access, Amex, Diners, Visa.*

MANCHESTER   Sachas Hotel   64%   £83

Tel 0161-228 1234 Fax 0161-236 9202   Map 6 B2   **H**
Tib Street Piccadilly Manchester Greater Manchester M4 1SH

Formerly a C&A store, now a bright hotel with major conference facilities (up to 650 delegates) and a health club. Bedrooms vary from inner ones with neither windows nor natural light to superior versions with whirlpool baths and four-poster beds. There are lively eating and drinking spots in the basement (the pizzeria is open 6pm–2am). Sister hotel to the *Britannia*. *Rooms 223. Indoor swimming pool, keep-fit equipment, sauna, sun bed, beauty & hair salons, night club. Access, Amex, Diners, Visa.*

MANCHESTER   Siam Orchid   £60

Tel 0161-236 1388 Fax 0161-236 8830   Map 6 B2   **R**
54 Portland Street Greater Manchester M1 4QU

A friendly Thai restaurant on the edge of Manchester's Chinatown, a few steps from both the Britannia and Piccadilly hotels. A long menu covers the whole Thai range from soups and satay to fish cakes, spicy salads, curries from bright red to dull green, noodle platters, rice platters and many variations on pork, chicken, beef, crab, fish, prawns, lobster, squid and eggs. There's plenty of choice, too, for vegetarians, plus business lunch menus (£5, £7) and other set menus for four or more. Thai New Year celebrations take place on 13th April. Sister to Royal Orchid (see entry). *Seats 50. Parties 20. L 11.30-2.30 D 6.30-11.30. (meals Sat 12-11.30 Sun 12-11). Closed 25 Dec, 1 Jan. Set L from £5 Set D from £16. Access, Amex, Visa.*

Set menu prices may not always include service or wine.

MANCHESTER   Sonarga   £45

Tel 0161-861 0334   Map 6 B2   **R**
269 Barlow Moor Road Chorlton-cum-Hardy Greater Manchester M21 2GJ

On the edge of south Manchester's residential fringe at Chorlton-cum-Hardy. A well-judged modern style of Bangladeshi cooking and service is offered and the kitchen appears eager to offer new ideas without forsaking traditional values. The menu is overhauled thoroughly at least once a year. 'Sonarga supreme' dishes, such as *koowazi* lamb – a whole leg, marinated then roasted and served for four or more – need to be ordered a day in advance. Other unusual dishes include salmon *kaljeera* and chicken *jaratree*. Undoubtedly one of the best Indian restaurants in the area. *Seats 150. D 5.30-12 (Fri to 12.30, Sat 3.30-12.30, Sun 3.30-11.30). Closed L Mon-Fri & 25 Dec. Set D £15.95. Access, Visa.*

MANCHESTER   That Café   £45

Tel 0161-432 4672   Map 6 B2   **R**
1031 Stockport Road Levenshulme Greater Manchester M19 2TB

A friendly, unpretentious restaurant by the A6, south of the city. An à la carte menu operates six evenings a week, with a short set menu as an additional offering Tuesday to Thursday. Dishes on both are straightforward, from the day's soup, pork with orange, fillet of beef with onions and polenta, broccoli and Stilton parcel (there are always a couple of vegetarian options) to the fish of the day (consult the mirrors in the dining-room). *Seats 80. Private Room 35. L (Sun only) 12.30-4 D 7-11. Closed D Mon & 25-28 Dec. Set D £14.50 (exc Sat & Sun). Access, Amex, Visa.*

MANCHESTER   Victoria & Albert Hotel   73%   £148

Tel 0161-832 1188 Fax 0161-834 2484   Map 6 B2   **HR**
Water Street Manchester Greater Manchester M3 4JQ

Between their TV studios and the River Irwell, Granada's flagship hotel is a cleverly converted mid-19th-century warehouse. Original oak-timbered ceilings and cast-iron pillars feature in the smart galleried reception area, Watsons bar/lounge with its comfortable Victorian drawing room atmosphere and conservatory overlooking the river, and in the all-day French-style café/bistro. Bedrooms, which vary in size and shape, also boast timbered ceilings and some exposed brickwork; each is named after, and subtly themed with stills from, a different Granada TV drama or series. King- or queen-sized beds and a high level of equipment – the TV offers account review, quick check-out and breakfast ordering facilities – make for a comfortable stay aided by keen staff offering an above average level of service. Children under 12 years free in parents' room. Free Granada Studios tour. 24hr room service. No dogs. Conference facilities for up to 350. *Rooms 132. Garden, keep-fit equipment, sauna, solarium, café (8am-midnight), news kiosk. Access, Amex, Diners, Visa.*

Sherlock Holmes Restaurant £75

Cooking alongside executive chef John Benson-Smith, Steve Chesnutt and his team cook with confidence and style. The menu might be a bit gimmicky, but the dishes, essentially British with Oriental influences, are always enterprising, starting perhaps with potted lobster and leeks with chicken livers or hot Thai-style pork with red onions, followed by a pot roast English duck with honey and bottled cherries or roast halibut set on a vegetable Italian stew. Plain and simple dishes (chicken liver paté, best end of English lamb) are also available. To end, try the toasted rice pudding or baked filo parcel of caramelised bananas with sticky toffee sauce. Fabulous British farmhouse cheeses from around the country, good selection of breads, and a variety of teas. Simple and balanced wine list. *Seats 70. Parties 8. Private Room 60. L 12-2 D 7-10. Closed L Sat & all Sun. Set D £28.50.*

MANCHESTER	Woodlands		£70

Tel 0161-336 4241   Map 6 B2   **RR**
33 Shepley Road Audenshaw Manchester Greater Manchester M34 5DJ

A restaurant with rooms in a solid Victorian house alongside B6169. Chef William Mark Jackson's menus are based on sound, classical French traditions and offer a good choice – five or six on the table d'hote (not available Saturday), eight or so on the carte at each stage. The style is straightforward – seafood salad with Marie Rose sauce, Lancashire black and white pudding with mustard sauce, grilled plaice with parsley butter, steak with onions and peppers in a red wine sauce, and, from the carte, mussel and scallop soup flavoured with saffron, turbot baked with a herb topping and lemon butter sauce, and duck breast with a tangy mango and spring onion sauce. Lesley Ann Jackson runs front of house with friendliness and efficiency. Descriptive, mainly French wine list. Smoking is discouraged (as are credit cards). *Seats 40. Parties 24. L 12-1.45 D 7-9. Closed L Sat, all Sun (except L on last Sun of month) & Mon, 1 week after Christmas, 1 week Easter & 2 weeks mid-Aug. Set L & D £15.95. Access, Visa.*

Rooms £60

Three rooms with en-suite shower and WC. All have beverage trays, teletext TVs and direct-dial phones.

MANCHESTER	Yang Sing	★	£50

Tel 0161-236 2200 Fax 0161-236 5934   Map 6 B2   **R**
34 Princes Street Manchester Greater Manchester M1 4JY

The class of cooking and the length of the menus make this the most appealing Chinese restaurant in town, and its popularity remains undiminished. Tanks of live carp, eels and lobsters testify to the importance chef-proprietor Harry Yeung places on freshness and quality of ingredients. Some 40 different dim sum (even more on Sundays) can be chosen from trolleys parked in the middle of the restaurant or ordered from the waiting staff. A selection of pastries (all from their own kitchen) or fresh fruit for afters. Banquets for up to 200 guests can be held in the largest of several private rooms. Booking advisable except for Sunday lunch when you just have to join the queue. *Seats 140. Parties 40. Private Room 220. Meals noon-11pm. Closed 25 Dec. Set meals from £28 for two. Access, Amex, Visa.*

Consult the blue pages for summary tables and lists of recommended establishments.

MANCHESTER AIRPORT   Etrop Grange   66%   £116

Tel 0161-499 0500 Fax 0161-499 0790   Map 6 B2   **H**
Outwood Lane Manchester Airport Greater Manchester M22 5NR

The hotel is based on a small Georgian house, whose ground floor has been opened up to create public spaces that though not extensive are stylishly furnished with ribbon-hung pictures and rather low-hanging crystal chandeliers (six-footers need to duck). The bar is essentially the corridor leading to the dining-room and there is a small conservatory. Bedrooms are generally a bit on the small side but are well equipped (mini-bar, room safe etc) and all have armchairs and/or sofas. They are stronger on decor – fine fabrics, mostly antique beds – than practicality in that where there is a desk it is often rather small and sometimes there is no upright chair; similarly, bathrooms come with wood-panelled tubs and lacy shower curtains but minimal shelf space. Helpful staff. Good choice of cooked breakfasts including Manx kippers with herb butter and fresh limes, and kedgeree as well as the fry-up that comes with a brace of free-range eggs. Juices are freshly squeezed. Room service 24hrs. *Rooms 41. Courtesy car to airport. Access, Amex, Diners, Visa.*

MANCHESTER AIRPORT   Forte Crest   65%   £120

Tel 0161-437 5811 Fax 0161-436 2340   Map 6 B2   **H**
Ringway Road Wythenshawe Greater Manchester M90 3NS

Between terminals A & B, 8 miles from the city centre. Banqueting and conference facilities for 120/200, plus a leisure centre. Plenty of free parking. 24hr room service. Children up to 16 stay free in parents' room. Changes afoot as we went to press include an Oriental restaurant and a grill/bar/espresso bar. *Rooms 290. Garden, indoor swimming pool, gym, sauna. Access, Amex, Diners, Visa.*

MANCHESTER AIRPORT   Four Seasons Hotel   68%   £121

Tel 0161-904 0301 Fax 0161-980 1787   Map 6 B2   **H**
Hale Road Hale Barns nr Altrincham Greater Manchester WA15 8XW

A privately owned hotel two miles from the airport (at junction 6 of the M56). Smart modern bedrooms overlook central courtyard gardens. The top-of-the-range suites have lounges and jacuzzis. Well geared-up for business people, with up-to-date conference facilities (maximum 120) and secretarial support services available. There's a good choice of spots in which to relax, including the Lobby Bar, Vivaldi's cocktail bar, Mulligans snug and Mollenski's conservatory. Children up to 12 stay free in parents' room. *Rooms 94. Access, Amex, Diners, Visa.*

MANCHESTER AIRPORT   Hilton International   71%   £159

Tel 0161-436 4404 Fax 0161-436 1521   Map 6 B2   **H**
Outwood Lane Manchester Airport Greater Manchester M90 4WP

Convenient for both the airport and the motorway network (junction 5 off M56), this modern hotel caters admirably for travellers and general businessmen alike with its good business and meeting facilities (for up to 300), which have recently been expanded and refurbished, as have the restaurants and bars. Plaza bedrooms are larger and more impressive than the standard rooms, but all are smartly furnished with contemporary fabrics and surprisingly spacious bathrooms. Double-glazing features throughout, so noise is not a problem, despite the location. Children under 18 years free in parents' room. 24hr room service. Business centre. *Rooms 222. Garden, indoor swimming pool, children's pool, gym, solarium, spa bath, sauna, steam room, coffee shop (6am-10pm). Access, Amex, Diners, Visa.*

Set menu prices may not always include service or wine.

MANCHESTER AIRPORT   Moss Nook   £80

Tel 0161-437 4778 Fax 0161-498 8089   Map 6 B2   **RR**
Ringway Road Moss Nook Manchester Greater Manchester M22 5WD

♔

Well signed from the airport (one mile away). Red suede walls, heavy drapes, stained glass, silver plate, heavy crystal glassware, and lace slips over the tablecloths lend an air of opulence. The French-style à la carte menu is supplemented by a *menu surprise* (five small courses at lunchtime, seven in the evening). Luxury ingredients and an outsize menu typify the style. Everyone should leave room for the grand selection of desserts, while chocoholics should head straight for the chocolate medley. Outdoor terrace seating for 16 in good weather. Including a fine wine section on the list suggests perhaps that others are not! Not so here, there are many good wines throughout. No children under 8. No smoking. *Seats 65. Parties 10. L 12-1.30 D 7-9.30. Closed L Sat, all Sun & Mon, Bank Holidays & 2 weeks from 26 Dec. Set L £16.50 Set D £29. Access, Amex, Diners, Visa.*

Room   £140*

An adjacent, self-contained cottage has one double bedroom with two en-suite bathrooms, a lounge, TV and telephone. The makings of a Continental breakfast are provided. No children under 12. Accommodation closed for 2 weeks from Christmas Eve. *Price for two including dinner.

| MARKET HARBOROUGH | Three Swans Hotel | 65% | £77 |

Tel 01858 466644   Fax 01858 433101   Map 7 D4   **H**
21 High Street Market Harborough Leicestershire LE16 7NJ

Charles I slaked his thirst here in 1645, by when this friendly coaching inn was already more than 200 years old. Several bars ensure that today's visitors don't go thirsty, and there's an attractive conservatory/lounge and a patio. Bedrooms are in the main building or a block across the courtyard. All are of a good size, decorated in restful pastels and furnished with smart modern units; all have private bathrooms with tubs, shower and toiletries. The Old School House self-contained conference centre caters for up to 100 delegates, with further rooms in the main building. No dogs. *Rooms 36. Terrace. Access, Amex, Diners, Visa.*

We welcome bona fide complaints and recommendations on the tear-out pages at the back of the book for readers' comments. They are followed up by our professional team.

| MARKINGTON | Hob Green | 70% | £90 |

Tel 01423 770031   Fax 01423 771589   Map 6 C1   **H**
Markington nr Harrogate North Yorkshire HG3 3PJ

870 acres of farm and woodland make a fine setting for a mellow stone hotel, and the gardens have won many prizes as well as providing pleasant views of the rolling Yorkshire countryside. The garden room is bright and summery, while the hall and drawing room have a traditional appeal that's helped along by antiques and log fires. Books, magazines and games are available for relaxation. Bedrooms are individually appointed in homely style and furniture is a mix of period and modern. Most have a little sitting area. *Rooms 12. Garden, croquet. Access, Amex, Diners, Visa.*

| MARKYATE | Hertfordshire Moat House | 57% | £84 |

Tel 01582 840840   Fax 01582 842282   Map 15 E1   **H**
London Road Markyate Hertfordshire AL3 8HH

Only one mile from the M1 (Junction 9) alongside the A5, a modern hotel with adequate bedrooms and bathrooms, a good gym and a thriving conference trade (for up to 300). Tariff reductions at weekends. Children up to 16 stay free in parents' room. *Rooms 89. Gym, solarium. Access, Amex, Diners, Visa.*

| MARLBOROUGH | Ivy House | 61% | £68 |

Tel 01672 515333   Fax 01672 515338   Map 14 C2   **H**
High Street Marlborough Wiltshire SN8 1HJ

Resident owners David Ball and Josephine Scott offer purpose-built conference facilities (up to 80 delegates) as well as hotel amenities at their Grade II listed Georgian house, which was once a school for boys known as Marlborough Academy. Bedrooms, some with separate sitting areas, are spread between the main house, the conference block and an annexe across the High Street. Children up to 10 stay free in parents' room. *Rooms 30. Coffee shop. Access, Amex, Visa.*

MARLOW   Compleat Angler Hotel   73%   £169

Tel 01628 484444   Fax 01628 486388   Map 15 E2   **HR**
Marlow Bridge Marlow Buckinghamshire SL7 1RG

Much extended over the years from an original 16th-century inn, the Compleat Angler enjoys a splendid riverside position between bridge and weir and just a short walk over the bridge from the main shopping street. Finding that reception is an antique desk in the entrance hall sets the civilised tone of the whole hotel. There is a smallish lounge but the heart of the public areas is the bar with its twin rooms, one panelled in pine, the other in oak, offering plenty of comfortable seating. Bedrooms are a particular strength, being individually decorated in English house style and boasting traditional polished wood furniture. Modern comforts are not forgotten, with things like a phone at the desk as well as bedside (just one if it's convenient to both) and smart bathrooms with marble trimmings. 18 de luxe rooms in a new wing in the same style are particularly spacious, have balconies and get mini-bars and, in their bathrooms, separate showers, phones and bathrobes. All rooms are properly serviced in the evening and about half have river views. The hotel is named after Izaak Walton's seminal book on fishing (bedrooms are all named after fishing flies) although his connection with the hotel was actually the invention of a 19th-century owner. 24hr room service. Children up to 15 stay free in parents' room. Forte. *Rooms 62. Garden, croquet, tennis, fishing, hotel boats, conservatory (10am-11pm). Access, Amex, Diners, Visa.*

Valaisan Restaurant   £130

An oak-beamed restaurant where quality table settings, splendid views of the river and weir, and exemplary service go some way towards justifying the high prices. The cooking itself is workmanlike rather than memorable with the fixed-price lunch and dinner menus offering the best value. Typical main-dish choice from the latter might be between salmon with glazed cucumber and crayfish sauce, rack of lamb with Niçoise vegetables and red wine jus, and a breast of chicken with forest mushrooms and basil cream sauce. Just why wines by the glass are assigned to the last page is a mystery, but consistent with a somewhat confusing, otherwise excellent, list. For instance, to seek out an exceptional Bordeaux you must look through the connoisseur's selection, bin ends and the clarets. No smoking. *Seats 96. Parties 20. L 12.30-2.30 (Sun to 3) D 7-10. Set L £17.95/£22.95 (Sun £28.50) Set D £29.50.*

MATLOCK   Riber Hall   71%   £98

Tel 01629 582795   Fax 01629 580475   Map 6 C2   **HR**
Matlock Derbyshire DE4 5JU

Approached via the A615 at Tansley some twenty minutes from Junction 28 of the M1, the atmospheric Elizabethan manor house stands in the hills high above Matlock. It is graced throughout with antiques, beams and fresh flowers. There's a lovely conservatory and walled garden, making it a wonderfully peaceful location. Bedrooms are located in converted stables across a courtyard where the original beams and rough stone walls remain; all are filled with thoughtful extras, centrally heated and have period four-poster or half-tester beds. Best rooms face south and east and overlook the large garden. Five of the neat bathrooms sport whirlpool baths. A tennis trainer ball machine is available on the all-weather tennis court. No children under 10. No dogs. *Rooms 11. Garden, croquet, tennis. Access, Amex, Diners, Visa.*

Restaurant   £70

Two elegantly appointed, very traditional dining-rooms, which are very much in keeping with the character of the house, are the setting for sound cooking by Jeremy Brazelle. Luncheon is fixed-price, with dishes running from chicken liver terrine on a bed of lettuce and Cumberland sauce to toasted brioche filled with mushrooms and bacon lardons in a Madeira cream via a selection of sorbets to breast of chicken with tarragon and lime in a cream sauce, grilled Scottish salmon with fresh herbs in a white port and grape sauce and beef medallions on a bed of onion purée and port wine jus. Desserts might include iced chocolate terrine or hot coffee and amaretto soufflé. Similar style in the evening. Vegetarian dishes available on a separate menu (£18.50). Some good names (notably burgundies) on a wine list with tasting notes for everything except champagnes. *Seats 60. Private Room 40. L 12-1.30 D 7-9.30. Set L £11.50/£14.50.*

MATLOCK BATH — New Bath Hotel — 63% — £97

Tel 01629 583275   Fax 01629 580268   Map 6 C3   **H**
New Bath Road Matlock Bath Derbyshire DE4 3PX

Standing on the A6 in five acres of landscaped gardens overlooking the river Derwent the hotel has good leisure facilities including an outdoor swimming pool fed by a thermal spring. Conference/banqueting for up to 200 and family facilities reflect the midweek/weekend balance of business. Forte Hotels. *Rooms 55. Garden, indoor & outdoor swimming pools, sauna, solarium, tennis, putting. Access, Amex, Diners, Visa.*

MAWGAN PORTH — Bedruthan Steps Hotel — 65% — £97

Tel 01637 860555   Fax 01637 860714   Map 12 B3   **H**
Mawgan Porth Cornwall TR8 4BU

Sister hotel to the *Trevelgue Hotel* (see entry under Porth), another family hotel par excellence. Superb, carefully-conceived family facilities offer separate activities for babes in arms, toddlers and active teenagers: from organised sporting activities to a wind-down 'wee willie winkie club' (7.30-10pm) for under-5s. Parents are a serious part of the equation, with nightly entertainment, a health and beauty hydro with the latest high-tech gym equipment, and, perhaps most importantly, "a chance to relax and enjoy your holiday". Some facilities are charged for, others provided at no charge: the beach and its rock pools, of course, are free! A variety of comfortable accommodation is offered, from family rooms sleeping four to apartment suites; the off-season tariff is extremely reasonable and those rooms with sea views attract a small supplement (single-parent family and grandparent offers for week-long stays in April, early May and October). The majority of their business is week-long holiday bookings, so book well in advance for shorter stays. Children's activities and services vary during the season according to the numbers and the ages of the children staying, so confirm exact availability when booking; it is refreshing to see so much effort made to accommodate children's needs. Above all, the caring staff understand the requirements of hassled parents who need a holiday as much as their children. No dogs. *Rooms 100. Garden, croquet, miniature golf, tennis, squash, gym, outdoor, indoor, plunge & children's splash pools, spa baths, sun beds, children's playrooms & outdoor play areas. Closed early Nov to end Mar (office open all year). Access, Diners, Visa.*

MAWNAN SMITH — Budock Vean Hotel — 65% — £128

Tel 01326 250288   Fax 01326 250892   Map 12 B4   **H**
Mawnan Smith nr Falmouth Cornwall TR11 5LG

There's a resident golf professional at Budock Vean, but there are plenty of other activities also on offer at this elegant sporting hotel set in 25 acres of sub-tropical gardens, which include a private foreshore to the Helford river. Spacious bedrooms include some with sitting rooms. There are also three self-catering cottages in the grounds, two adjoining with a private garden, and a larger separate one. 2% surcharge when paying by Diners Card. *Rooms 54. Garden, croquet, indoor swimming pool, tennis, golf (18), putting, young children's playroom, coarse fishing, snooker, golf-shop. Closed 2 Jan-13 Feb. Access, Diners, Visa.*

MAWNAN SMITH — Meudon Hotel — 69% — £170*

Tel 01326 250541   Fax 01326 250543   Map 12 B4   **H**
Mawnan Smith nr Falmouth Cornwall TR11 5HT

The Pilgrim family, here since 1964, put the accent on peace, quiet and personal service, with no conferences or even large parties to intrude. Sub-tropical gardens, laid out by 'Capability' Brown, are a major attraction of staying here and lead down to a private beach. The house itself was built at the turn of the century, and the new wing, connected at first-floor level, is in matching stone. The main lounge is very comfortable and appealing, with paintings, photographs, fresh flowers and antiques. Bedrooms are individually appointed in elegant style, with furnishings and fittings of a uniformly high standard; all overlook the gardens. Two balcony suites have their own sitting rooms. Residents can enjoy free golf at the Falmouth Golf Club (two miles away) and both sea and river fishing are available. A really charming and friendly place where most of the guests are regulars. Take the A39 from Truro towards Falmouth. Turn right at Hillhead roundabout; the hotel is 3½ miles along on the left. *Half-board terms. *Rooms 32. Garden, hair salon, snooker. Access, Diners, Visa.*

458   England

MAWNAN SMITH · Nansidwell · 70% · £123

Tel 01326 250340   Fax 01326 250440 · Map 12 B4 · **HR**
Mawnan Smith nr Falmouth Cornwall TR11 5HU

A traditional country hotel with ample supplies of friendliness, peace and beautiful scenery. Built at the turn of the century, although the wisteria clad exterior looks older, it enjoys an idyllic location in five acres of gardens surrounded by National Trust land between Helford River and the sea. Day rooms have a comfortably lived-in feel, with family photos creating a genuinely homely atmosphere. Individually decorated bedrooms with 'country' and near-antique furniture vary considerably in size but all boast fresh flowers and generous quantities of books and magazines. No room service.
Rooms 12. Garden, tennis. Closed Jan. Access, Visa.

Restaurant   £66

An appealing dining-room with decorative plates adorning yellow rag-painted walls and views over the terraced gardens. Equally appealing are Anthony Alcott's well-executed dishes from a fairly sophisticated menu that includes speciality fish dishes such as steamed fillet of turbot with a lime and chervil hollandaise, Dover sole with almond and basil butter and red mullet with local shellfish on a tomato and tarragon sauce. Meaty options might include duck in a red wine and honey sauce, roast partridge with sweet chestnuts and glazed apples and tenderloin of pork with apricot and sage stuffing. Finish with good puds like baked pistachio and orange pudding on a caramel and Drambuie sauce and hot pear and ginger meringue cake on a lemon and apricot purée. *Seats 45. Parties 18. L 12.30-1.30 D 7-9. Set L £14.75 (Sun £15.75) Set D £25.*

MEDMENHAM · Danesfield House · 77% · £145

Tel 01628 891010   Fax 01628 890408 · Map 15 D2 · **HR**
Medmenham Marlow Buckinghamshire SL7 3ES

Danesfield is the third house since 1964 to occupy this splendid site overlooking the River Thames between Marlow and Henley. This latest incarnation was completed around 1900 in a rather grand neo-Tudor style of stone-mullioned windows, crenellations and twisted redbrick chimney stacks that acknowledges its forebears. A large stone terrace, beyond which are formal parterre gardens as the land drops away to the river below, is a grand spot in summer. The main day room is the tapestry-hung Grand Hall with its high windows, hammerbeam roof and minstrel's gallery (now home to the snooker table); impressive rather than cosy and sometimes used for conferences – a significant part of the business here. The bar has an Italian feel and extends into a glassed-in loggia. Bedrooms are quite ornate, often with plaster or painted-wood panelled walls, marble fireplace complete with gas log fire and always with a glass chandelier whose coloured drops match one of three colour schemes – apricot, blue or pink – that extends to the tiling in gold-tapped bathrooms. Bathrobes, face cloths and the turning down of beds at night are among the pampering features and all rooms come with two separate telephone lines (but at 50p per unit it might be best to take your 'mobile' along). *Rooms 89. Garden, croquet, outdoor swimming pool, squash, tennis, snooker. Access, Amex, Diners, Visa.*

Oak Room   £100

Oak panelling and a fine 'ribbon' plaster ceiling maintain the period style while the loggia extension is the most popular choice at breakfast time. Chef Colin Flood's fixed-price menu (about eight main-course choices plus another four on the additional lunch menu) offers competently cooked and accurately described dishes that are in the mainstream of current trends. Baked haddock on a tomato and courgette stew; roasted scallops on grilled Provençal vegetables with pepper oil dressing; and roast loin of venison with fresh figs, braised red cabbage and gratin potatoes in a fruity pepper sauce show the style. Several dishes attract a supplement to the menu price but coffee (or the good choice of well-served teas) and petits fours are included. Few surprises on an easy-to-use wine list arranged by price. *Seats 50. Parties 10. L 12-1.45 D 7-9.45. Set L £17.50/£22.50 (Sun £22.50) Set D £32.50.*

| **MELBOURN** | **Pink Geranium** | ↑ | **£105** |

Tel 01763 260215   Fax 01763 262110   Map 15 F1   **R**
Station Road Melbourn nr Royston Hertfordshire SG8 6DX

In one of the prettiest and most romantic cottage restaurants in the country Steven Saunders remains firmly at the helm. This ensures a consistency of standards from a dedicated and highly professional team. Approached through a well-tended garden, the restaurant is pink outside and pink within. Rose-pink geraniums feature in the curtains and upholstery as well as in the wide borders around the walls. The effort is to create a cosy, traditional ambience. The menu keeps firmly abreast of the times while retaining a strong element of classicism. For example, game consommé with ravioli of soft quail egg and coriander; Provence gateau of crab with Thai ginger beurre blanc; breast of Barbary duck with its own confit, caramelised figs and armagnac jus, navarin of fish and shellfish with 'spaghetti' of lemon linguine and shellfish cream; and saddle of wild venison with *saladaise* potatoes, star anise and thyme scented juices. Sweets range from hot banana soufflé with butterscotch sauce to rich chocolate tart with cassis ice cream. Some good British cheeses come with celery, grapes and warm walnut bread. An excellent wine list (our Home Counties regional winner of Cellar of the Year) is clearly laid out with helpful tasting notes; a good mix between classic France, the rest of Europe and the New World. House champagne at £25, plenty of half bottles. No children in the dining-room after 8pm, however a creche facility is offered (or a private room for families with children). Limousine service offered at taxi prices – distance no object. *Seats 65. Parties 18. Private Rooms 55/18. L 12.30-2.30 D 7-10.30. Closed D Sun, all Mon, 26 Dec. Set L £15.95/£18.95 (Sun £18.95) Set D £29.95 & £50. Access, Amex, Visa.*

| **MELKSHAM** | **Toxique** | **£75** |

Tel 01225 702129   Map 14 B3   **RR**
187 Woodrow Road Melksham Wiltshire SN12 7AY

Take the Calne road from the town-centre mini roundabout, turn left after half a mile into Forest Road and continue for nearly a mile – eventually you'll find Toxique. However, you must book in advance as it's 'famine or feast round these parts', meaning it's closed when not busy and very busy when booked up. Nevertheless, Peter Jewkes and chef-partner Helen Bartlett's slightly eccentric restaurant with its farmhouse look and out-of-the-ordinary colourful modern decor is worth a visit. A fixed-price-only menu offers six dishes at each stage (four at lunchtime): perhaps a warm salad of pan-fried scallops with chicory and orange to start, followed by monkfish and langoustine cassoulet; loin of venison, Puy lentils, aubergine and celeriac tian with a port sauce and breast of duck with sliced red cabbage, onion tart and potato rösti. Two diners can order a plate of sampling desserts (for a small supplement). No smoking at the table (but it's allowed in the bar area). Some tasting and introductory notes on a decent wine list that, surprisingly, includes but one, hardly-known champagne. Outside tables for drinks in good weather. *Seats 30. Parties 20. Private Room 20. L 12.30-2 D 7-10. Closed 2 weeks Jan, 2 weeks late Aug-early Sep. Set L £16.50 Set D £24.50. Access, Amex, Visa.*

Rooms   £84
The old stone farmhouse offers very distinctive, individually decorated and stylish modern bedroom suites. They are bright, spacious and well equipped. No dogs. Garden.

| **MELLOR** | **Millstone Hotel** | **£88** |

Tel 01254 813333   Fax 01254 812628   Map 6 B1   **I**
Church Lane Mellor nr Blackburn Lancashire BB2 7JR

Ten minutes from Junction 31 of the M6, next to St Mary's church in a quiet village off the A59, this small, friendly hotel effectively mixes modern conveniences with the charm of a traditional roadside inn. One of the two bars also acts as the village local. Bedrooms are neat and well maintained. Children up to the age of 14 are free in parents' room. Shire Inns. *Rooms 19. Access, Amex, Diners, Visa.*

MELMERBY — Village Bakery — £30

Tel 01768 881515   Fax 01768 881848   Map 4 C3   **R**
Melmerby Penrith Cumbria CA10 1HE

A converted barn built of local stone with a bright, airy conservatory and pine furniture overlooks the green of a beautiful fellside village, ten miles east of Penrith on the A686 Alston road. One of the pioneers of true wholefood and organic cuisine, the bakery continues to produce superb breads and pastries which are baked on the premises in a wood-fired brick oven. Any fruit and vegetables not coming from the five-acre organic smallholding to the rear are obtained, together with the few meats on offer, from local organic and wholefood suppliers. Breakfast is served until 11am (raspberry porridge, oak-smoked Scottish kippers, free-range boiled eggs, croissants, spicy buns, full fried breakfast and a vegetarian version). Lunch starts at noon, with last orders at 2: soup comes first, then perhaps pork chop with apples and maple syrup, grilled Cumberland sausage or nutty mushroom and Stilton pie or the Baker's lunch with bread and North Country cheeses; for dessert, fruit pie, sherry trifle or perhaps Christmas pudding. Also savoury snacks, sandwiches and a super cream tea. Children's portions are reduced by a third. No smoking. *Seats 45. Meals 8.30-5 (Sun from 9.30). Closed 25-27 Dec, 1 Jan. Access, Diners, Visa.*

MELTON MOWBRAY — George Hotel — 57% — £45

Tel 01664 62112   Fax 01664 410457   Map 7 D3   **H**
High Street Melton Mowbray Leicestershire LE13 0TR

The entrance hall at this very old former coaching inn was once the archway through which the stage coaches drove. The arrival and departure clock still stands on display, and another traditional touch is provided by four-posters in some of the bedrooms. Special rates for families in adjoining rooms. There are three bars, one with beams and hunting prints, and a patio. *Rooms 14. Access, Amex, Diners, Visa.*

MERIDEN — De Vere Manor Hotel — 64% — £95

Tel 01676 522735   Fax 01676 522186   Map 6 C4   **H**
Main Road Meriden West Midlands CV7 7NH

Impressive, extended Georgian-style building with comfortable bedrooms in a smart modern wing. Popular for conferences and banquets (275/250) but no leisure facilities. Children up to 14 free in parents' room. Two rooms are specially equipped for disabled guests. *Rooms 74. Access, Amex, Diners, Visa.*

MERIDEN — Forest of Arden Hotel — 70% — £127

Tel 01676 522335   Fax 01676 523711   Map 6 C4   **H**
Maxstoke Lane Meriden West Midlands CV7 7HR

Just over a mile off the A45 (west of Coventry), near the M6/M42 intersection, this purpose-built hotel, golf and country club stands at the end of a country lane in 400 acres of rolling countryside. The Mediterranean-style interior is welcoming. Bedrooms are comfortable and furnished in contemporary fashion; bathrooms are carpeted and have good-quality showers. Extensive leisure facilities are housed in the impressive Country Club and include a large pool. A supervised creche can be provided by arrangement (as can baby-sitting). Country Club Hotels. *Rooms 154. 2 golf courses, fishing, indoor swimming pool, sauna, steam room, spa bath, solarium, squash, tennis, snooker, fitness studio, beauty salon, dance studio. Access, Amex, Diners, Visa.*

MICKLETON — Three Ways House — 59% — £76

Tel 01386 438429   Fax 01386 438118   Map 14 C1   **H**
Mickleton nr Chipping Campden Gloucestershire GL55 6SB

Standing at the heart of a Cotswold village between Broadway and Stratford, this is a privately-run hotel built from mellow, local stone. Bedrooms are practical rather than luxurious, with modest en-suite facilities. Friendly and relaxing atmosphere; family facilities (children up to 16 stay free in parents' room). Three conference/function suites, one opening onto a patio. New owners took over as we went to press, at which time the famous Pudding Club was in abeyance. *Rooms 41. Garden. Access, Amex, Diners, Visa.*

MIDDLE WALLOP	Fifehead Manor	61%	£90

Tel 01264 781565   Fax 01264 781400   Map 14 C3   **H**
Middle Wallop nr Stockbridge Hampshire SO20 8EG

Standing in well-kept gardens and grounds on the A343, the manor has a long and interesting history that includes a spell as a nunnery. Central to the house is the medieval dining hall with its mullioned windows and there is a small bar plus a lounge. Large bedrooms in the main house have good-size bathrooms; smaller singles (with showers only) are in an annexe, but attractive colour schemes are used throughout, and the furniture is mostly modern, although a few antiques help contribute to the atmosphere. Fine cooked breakfasts. *Rooms 16. Garden, croquet. Access, Amex, Diners, Visa.*

MIDDLECOMBE	Periton Park	67%	£90

Tel & Fax 01643 706885   Map 13 D1   **HR**
Periton Road Middlecombe nr Minehead Somerset TA24 8SW

Occupying a wonderful location at the northern edge of Exmoor National Park, Richard and Angela Hunt's Periton Park (built in 1875) is set in its own splendidly maintained gardens against a backdrop of rolling woodlands and streams. Walking is a favourite guest pastime, along with riding (stables next door), shooting and fishing. Off the entrance hall, a comfortable and pleasingly furnished lounge provides log fires in winter, and there's also a boardroom-style meeting room for 14. Each bedroom (three non-smoking), all with fine views, has its own character with freestanding furniture, good fabrics and neat bathroms with notably hot water; one ground-floor room, with French windows opening on to the garden, allows dogs. No children under 12. *Rooms 8. Garden, croquet, riding. Closed Jan. Access, Amex, Visa.*

Restaurant   **£55**
Angela is in the kitchen and the ubiquitous Richard looks after the sunny restaurant, where you'll encounter sound cooking based on local ingredients and leaning towards an English style. The fixed-price three-course dinner menu allows several choices in each section, say, seafood gratin or goat's cheese salad to start with, followed by pan-fried halibut steak served with a warm lime and coriander vinaigrette or medallions of Exmoor venison in a classic black cherry sauce. Traditional desserts include trifle, lemon tart and a Portuguese version of cream caramel made with added orange. Afterwards, relax in the drawing room with good cafetière coffee and mints. No smoking. *Seats 24. Parties 18. Private Room 14. L by arrangement only D 7-9. Set D £20.*

MIDDLESBROUGH	Hotel Baltimore	62%	£85

Tel 01642 224111   Fax 01642 226156   Map 5 E3   **H**
250 Marton Road Middlesbrough Cleveland TS4 2EZ

Popular executive hotel south of the town centre on the A172, handy for Teesside airport (9 miles). Bedrooms are double-glazed and have colour TV and radio, direct-dial telephones and tea/coffee-making facilities. Children up to 14 free in parents' room. Free secure parking. *Rooms 31. Access, Amex, Visa.*

MIDDLESBROUGH	Hospitality Inn	59%	£98

Tel 01642 232000   Fax 01642 232655   Map 5 E3   **H**
Fry Street Middlesbrough Cleveland TS1 1JH

High-rise hotel in the town centre. Five banqueting and conference suites have a maximum capacity of 400. Thistle & Mount Charlotte. *Rooms 180. Access, Amex, Diners, Visa.*

MIDDLETON STONEY	Jersey Arms		£80

Tel 01869 343234   Fax 01869 343565   Map 15 D1   **I**
Middleton Stoney nr Bicester Oxfordshire OX6 8SE

A 17th-century Cotswold-stone inn alongside the B430 (between Junctions 9 & 10 of the M40) offering comfortable accommodation in cottagey style. Bedrooms are divided between the main house (where wooden beams and creaking floors abound) and the courtyard, where they are a little more up-to-date; the Langtry Suite has a four-poster bed and sitting room. Day rooms include a low-ceilinged bar warmed by an open fire and a lounge with half panelling and comfortable seating. Children free in parents' room up to age 11. No dogs. *Rooms 16. Garden. Access, Amex, Diners, Visa.*

MIDDLETON-IN-TEESDALE   Teesdale Hotel   £61

Tel 01833 640264   Fax 01833 640651   Map 5 D3   **I**
Market Place Middleton-in-Teesdale nr Barnard Castle Co Durham DL12 0QG

At the centre of a rather austere stone-built village deep in the High Pennines, the Streit family have been practising their own brand of hospitality for nearly 20 years. Over those years the day rooms have been carefully modernised throughout, tastefully furnished and immaculately kept. Individually decorated bedrooms are for the most part full of colour and natural light, with those on the first floor being the best, with neatly-kept (if rather basic) en-suite bathrooms; one large family room, where children under 4 share with parents free. *Rooms 10. Terrace. Access, Visa.*

MIDHURST   Angel Hotel   £80

Tel 01730 812421   Fax 01730 815928   Map 11 A6   **IR**
North Street Midhurst West Sussex GU29 9DN

Behind a non-committal white-painted Georgian facade the Angel is a warm and welcoming place. Public rooms are largely centred around the two bars and restaurants with a relatively quiet residents' lounge at the front. Furnishings throughout are a mix of well-maintained polished antiques, deep relaxing armchairs and settees, with paintings and prints on the walls – the usual traditional trappings that befit a well-cared-for establishment such as this. Bedrooms, all on upper floors and all of a good size, are in either the original building or a purpose-built modern block to the rear. No dogs. *Rooms 21. Garden. Access, Amex, Diners, Visa.*

The Cowdray Room and Brasserie   £60

The brasserie, adjacent to the bar, is rustic in style and hence informal in character while the Cowdray Room, in contrast, is spacious and classically elegant with large, well-spaced tables. The scope of the two menus is similar, but prices are lower in the brasserie. Seafood (often from Brixham) is a particular strength, as evidenced in deep-fried squid with chili, salmon en croute with sorrel and saffron sauce or grilled brill with olive oil mash and sauce vierge. Many dishes are a little out of the ordinary: warm asparagus salad with smoked eel and a truffle dressing, cannon of roe deer with a chestnut crépinette and lentils, millefeuille of Cornish scallops and monkfish with an aniseed cream. Pianist in Cowdray Room. *Seats 45. Private Room 80. L 12-2.30 D 6.30-10. Set L from £12.50 Set D £17.50.*

MIDHURST   Spread Eagle   69%   £92

Tel 01730 816911   Fax 01730 815668   Map 11 A6   **H**
South Street Midhurst West Sussex GU29 9NH

The characterful 15th- and 17th-century buildings combine here with friendly staff and pleasing decor to form a most appealing hotel. The lounge bar – recently refurbished – with log fire, polished ship's timbers and fresh flowers, has great charm, as do the other public areas, including the residents' lounge with its high, beamed ceiling. Bedrooms are individually decorated with quiet good taste and are furnished with a mixture of reproduction and antique pieces. Many, including the five four-poster rooms, have old exposed timbers or mellow wood panelling. Smart bathrooms offer huge towels and good toiletries. The 17th-century Jacobean Hall is a splendid setting for banquets and meetings (for around 110/60). *Rooms 41. Garden. Access, Amex, Diners, Visa.*

MILBORNE PORT   The Old Vicarage   65%   NEW   £64

Tel 01963 251117   Fax 01963 251515   Map 13 F2   **H**
Sherborne Road Milborne Port Dorset DT9 5AT

Unique is an understatement for the Gnoykes' new venture – a Victorian vicarage in its own spacious grounds. Plans are under way to develop the coach house and to add a veranda to the conservatory sitting room. Nothing is too much trouble, and willingness to provide breakfast whenever a guest might want it, is a measure of their dedication. Bedrooms in the main house are individually decorated, some in period style and some more idiosyncratic. Those in the coach house are more uniformly modern and all offer mineral water, fruit and fresh flowers. Ample parking. *Rooms 8. Garden. Closed Jan. No credit cards.*

MILFORD-ON-SEA — Rocher's — £65

Tel 01590 642340   Map 14 C4   **R**
69-71 High Street Milford-on-Sea Hampshire SO41 0QG

Behind the pink-washed exterior of this high-street restaurant the atmosphere is friendly and inviting, with Rebecca providing charming service while French husband Alain Rocher works single-handedly in the kitchen. Dishes on the fixed-price menu (there's also a shorter, less expensive menu available during the week) are listed in French but come with clear English descriptions. Poached egg florentine, quail with a sherry-dressed seasonal salad, halibut with a basil sauce, tenderloin of pork with grain mustard and entrecote bordelaise show the style. Reliably good cooking has attracted a strong local following and with just seven tables booking is advisable. The wine list has been expanded from France to the New World. Helpful tasting notes. No children. *Seats 30. L (Sun only) 12.30-1.45 D 7.15-9.45. Closed D Sun (except Sun before Bank Holidays), all Mon & Tue, 2 wks Jun. Set Sun L £13.50 Set D £15.95 (Wed, Thur, Fri) & £18.40/£21.90 (except Sat & Bank Holiday Sundays) & £19.40/£22.90. Access, Amex, Diners, Visa.*

MILFORD-ON-SEA — South Lawn — 66% — £84

Tel 01590 643911   Fax 01590 644820   Map 14 C4   **H**
Lymington Road Milford-on-Sea nr Lymington Hampshire SO41 0RF

The high proportion of repeat business here says much for the standards of hospitality, service and maintenance, provided by Ernst and Jennifer Barten, owners since 1971 of this rambling black-and-white former dower house. Fresh flowers make a colourful show both outside and in the roomy lounge, and the bedrooms have views over paddocks and garden. Three rooms are on the ground floor, the rest on the first. Golf, sailing, windsurfing and riding are all available nearby. No children under seven. No dogs. *Rooms 24. Garden. Closed 20 Dec-20 Jan. Access, Visa.*

MILTON COMMON — Belfry Hotel — 60% — £93

Tel 01844 279381   Fax 01844 279624   Map 15 D2   **H**
Brimpton Grange Milton Common nr Thame Oxfordshire OX9 2JW

Driving from London on the M40, the hotel is next to Junction 7 but from the Birmingham approach take Junction 8. The original building has been much extended over the years and as a result offers bedrooms that differ in style and character. There are small, old-fashioned rooms and larger, brighter, more modern ones. They share a spacious dark oak-panelled bar and an attractive small leisure centre. *Rooms 77. Garden, indoor swimming pool, mini-gym, sauna, solarium. Closed 24-31 Dec. Access, Amex, Diners, Visa.*

MILTON KEYNES — Forte Crest — 68% — £117

Tel 01908 667722   Fax 01908 674714   Map 15 E1   **H**
500 Saxon Gate West Central Milton Keynes Buckinghamshire MK9 2HQ

Modern atrium hotel in the centre of town, next to the huge covered shopping centre. 24hr room service. Free car park. Banqueting facilities for up to 120, conferences to 150. *Rooms 150. Indoor swimming pool, gym, sauna, sun beds, beauty treatment. Access, Amex, Diners, Visa.*

MILTON KEYNES — Hilton National — 64% — £111

Tel 01908 694433   Fax 01908 695533   Map 15 E1   **H**
Timbold Drive Kents Hill Park Milton Keynes Buckinghamshire MK7 6HL

Follow the signs for the University to find this smartly decorated modern hotel located off H9 Groveway. Club rooms feature additional extras like mineral water, bathrobes and magazines. *Rooms 138. Garden, indoor swimming pool, gym, sauna, steam room, spa bath. Closed 27-30 Dec. Access, Amex, Diners, Visa.*

Many hotels offer reduced rates for weekend or out-of-season bookings. Always ask about special deals.

MILTON KEYNES   Quality Friendly Hotel   £87

Tel 01908 561666   Fax 01908 568303   Map 15 E1   **H**
Monksway Two Mile Ash Milton Keynes Buckinghamshire MK8 8LY

Practical, modern low-rise hotel at the junction of the A5 and A422. Twelve Premier Plus suites with small kitchenette and small lounge, come with fax machine and are favoured by both business people and families. Children stay free in parents' room. Conference facilities for up to 150. *Rooms 88. Indoor swimming pool, gym, sauna, spa bath, steam room, sun bed. Access, Amex, Diners, Visa.*

Many hotels offer reduced rates for weekend or out-of-season bookings. Always ask about special deals.

MINSTER LOVELL   Lovells at Windrush Farm   ★   £85

Tel & Fax 01993 779802   Map 14 C2   **RR**
Minster Lovell Oxfordshire OX8 5RN

From Minster Lovell head for Old Minster Lovell (going straight ahead rather than turning left over the little bridge into the old village itself) to find this 16th-century gentleman farmer's house. Very much a place for an evening out, rather than just somewhere to have dinner, they like guests to arrive by 8 o'clock in order to take a drink and peruse the wine list (the menu offers no choices) while sitting on damask sofas in the galleried inner hall before being summoned into the comfortable but rather uninteresting dining-room at 8.30. Dinner is a multi-course affair, served at a leisurely pace, and chef Marcus Ashford's talent lies not just in the excellence of his cooking but also in the overall balance and composition of his menus so that even after six or seven courses (it depends how you count, is a 'pre dessert' a course?) the feeling is one of happy well-being rather than over-indulgence. After a canapé of Welsh rarebit enlivened with a little home-made rhubarb chutney, a recent meal comprised an appetiser of slices of game sausage with a Cumberland dressing; a demi-tasse of root vegetable soup glazed with horseradish cream; brill on vegetable tagliatelle with champagne sauce; an assiette of duck consisting of the liver on a mushroom mousse, the breast on a bed of Puy lentils and leeks with a blackcurrant sauce and a confit of the leg on fondant potato (Marcus is fond of 'trio' dishes); cheese – each table getting its own straw mat of six different cheeses each in perfect condition and lovingly described with advice on the order in which they should be eaten; 'pre dessert' – a warm chocolate and raisin tartlet; dessert itself which was another trio of mini hot passion fruit soufflé, prune and armagnac brulée and honey and almond ice cream, and finally three petits fours including Turkish delight and a little lemony square served on a tuile biscuit. Lunch, by arrangement only, is a no-choice menu of three courses plus canapés and petits fours. Manageable wine list, mostly French, light in the New World; fair prices. No smoking. Booking is essential. *Seats 18. Parties 10. L by arrangement D 8 for 8.30. Closed D Sun, Mon (except by arrangement) & Jan. Set D (7-course) £29.50. Access, Amex, Diners, Visa.*

Rooms   £95
Two comfortable, traditionally furnished bedrooms provide for overnight guests. Both are en-suite, one with shower and WC only. Both TV and telephone are available on request. An added bonus is the 80 acres of grounds with fishing on the Windrush River.

MINSTER LOVELL   Old Swan   67%   £80

Tel 01993 774441   Fax 01993 702002   Map 14 C2   **H**
Minster Lovell nr Witney Oxfordshire OX8 5RN

A half-timbered Cotswold inn close to the River Windrush retaining many of its original pub features. There are three lounges with polished flagstone floors and open log fires, and a beamed restaurant opening on to a picturesque rear garden. Sixteen superior bedrooms offer a comfortable and relaxing stay, while the smaller bedrooms of the adjacent conference centre (five conference rooms and eight syndicate rooms) are offered at a lower rate when not in use by resident delegates. Children up to 14 stay free in parents' room. *Rooms 57. Garden, croquet, putting, tennis, fishing, punting. Access, Amex, Diners, Visa.*

MONK FRYSTON   Monk Fryston Hall   65%   £96

Tel 01977 682369   Fax 01977 683544   Map 7 D1   **H**
Monk Fryston nr Leeds North Yorkshire LS25 5DU

There has been a dwelling on this site since William the Conqueror's time, though the present building looks back only a couple of centuries. It remained a private residence until purchased by the Duke of Rutland, who turned it into a hotel in 1954. The grey stone walls and mullioned windows gracefully absorb the new wing added in 1986. In the grounds, formal gardens embrace an ornamental lake; indoors, open log fires and fine oak panelling set the scene. An oak staircase leads up to bright, traditionally furnished bedrooms. Rooms in the new wing have more modern furnishings, but all are well equipped and maintained. *Rooms 28. Garden. Access, Amex, Visa.*

MONKTON COMBE   Combe Grove Manor   71%   £175

Tel 01225 834644   Fax 01225 834961   Map 13 F1   **H**
Brassknocker Hill Monkton Combe Bath Avon BA2 7HS

Perched high up above the Limpley Stoke valley and set within its own 68 acres of wooded grounds, the manor has extensive leisure facilities belonging to the associated country club (which even offers 7-day morning creche facilities for parents with youngsters). Elegant day rooms and the best of the bedrooms – individually decorated in some style with reproduction furniture – are in the original Georgian house beneath which, in the old cellars reached via some external steps, is an informal bar/bistro decorated in ancient Roman style. The majority of more standardised bedrooms are some 50 yards away in the Garden Lodge, designed to take full advantage of the splendid view (just four rooms are rear-facing) with most having a private patio or balcony. Beds are turned down at night. 24hr room service. Conference/banqueting facilities for 100/80 in the Tapestry Room of the Garden Lodge and in the Roman Room in the Manor House. No dogs. 2 miles from Bath city centre and 18 miles from M4 Junction 18. *Rooms 40. Garden, indoor & outdoor swimming pools, gym, sauna, spa baths, steam room, sun beds, beauty salon, aerobics studio, indoor & outdoor tennis, golf (5-hole), putting, golf driving range, crazy golf, bowling green, creche. Access, Amex, Diners, Visa.*

MONTACUTE   King's Arms Inn   £69

Tel 01935 822513   Fax 01935 826549   Map 13 F2   **I**
Montacute Somerset TA15 6UU

A 16th-century hamstone inn, standing opposite the church in a picturesque and unspoilt village, that was once an ale-house owned by the abbey. Today's comfortable, modernised little inn offers characterful accommodation in en-suite rooms, either standard or deluxe, the best with a four-poster or half-tester bed. The Windsor room is a relaxing lounge; the Pickwick Bar remains the centre of village life, with real ales and bar snacks. Follow a relaxing night with a decent buffet-style breakfast and a walk on the National Trust's wooded St Michael's Hill behind the hotel. No dogs. *Rooms 13. Garden. Access, Amex, Visa.*

MORETON-IN-MARSH   Annie's   £60

Tel 01608 651981   Map 14 C1   **R**
3 Oxford Street Moreton-in-Marsh Gloucestershire GL56 0LA

In a romantic cottagey setting of candle-light and soft music, David Ellis is in the kitchen while Anne runs front of house in the most friendly fashion. David's is French and English country cooking, quite straightforward and without pretension: chicken liver parfait with melba toast, smoked salmon with lemon and chive mayonnaise, pan-fried pork tenderloin with mushrooms, thyme and a Madeira sauce, rack of lamb with a spiced crust and mint cream sauce. Sultana and lemon sponge with a lemon sauce or meringue with clotted cream and fresh fruit could be among the desserts. Sunday lunch always includes a traditional roast. Modest wine list, mostly French. *Seats 30. Private Room 10. L (Sun only) 12-2 D 7-10 Set Sun L £17.50 Set D (Mon-Fri) £20. Closed D Sun, 2 weeks Jan/Feb. Access, Amex, Diners, Visa.*

Set menu prices may not always include service or wine.

MORETON-IN-MARSH   Manor House   66%   £85

Tel 01608 650501   Fax 01608 651481   Map 14 C1   **H**
High Street Moreton-in-Marsh Gloucestershire GL56 0LJ

Parts of this roadside, Cotswold-stone manor house set in an attractive garden date back to 1545, but others are nearly new. The hall and lounges both have a period feel, while the bar is more modern. Among the bedrooms, too, there's a choice between traditional and modern. No dogs. *Rooms 39. Garden, putting, indoor swimming pool, sauna, spa bath. Access, Amex, Diners, Visa.*

MORETON-IN-MARSH   Marsh Goose   £65

Tel 01608 652111   Map 14 C1   **R**
High Street Moreton-in-Marsh Gloucestershire GL56 0AX

An intimate and agreeably informal restaurant where chef Sonya Kidney's menus are an excellent advertisement for her skills, and even in a part of the country densely populated by quality restaurants her cooking stands out for its reliability and individual flair. Lunchtime sees a no-choice three-course menu as well as a carte of five choices per course. Gruyère soufflé, marinated salmon with spicy avocado relish, calf's liver with smoked bacon and black pudding, deep-fried sole fillet with chips, and pan-fried saddle of rabbit with ginger, lime and sultanas typify the style. Among the desserts you might find sticky toffee pudding, apple fritters with maple syrup parfait and warm pear and frangipane tart with vanilla ice cream. Similar evening choice on the fixed-price menu (three courses and coffee). The wine list is presented by style (eg aromatic dry or unoaked whites/medium weight or classic reds). Really well-chosen wines at reasonable prices. No smoking, except in the bar area. *Seats 60. Parties 22. Private Room 15. L 12.30-2.30 D 7.30-9.45. Closed D Sun, all Mon, 26 Dec, 1 Jan. Set L £13.50 (Sun £18) Set D £23. Access, Amex, Visa.*

We welcome bona fide complaints and recommendations on the tear-out pages at the back of the book for readers' comments. They are followed up by our professional team.

MORETONHAMPSTEAD   Manor House Hotel   66%   £100

Tel 01647 440355   01647 440961   Map 13 D2   **H**
Moretonhampstead Devon TQ13 8RE

Perched above the confluence of two rivers that run through the estate, the large Jacobean-style manor (built in 1907 by the son of WH Smith) is reached via a drive through its well-established golf courses. This is predominantly a golfing hotel. Oak panelling and carved stonework feature in the public rooms and bedrooms, all refurbished in recent years, are in traditional style with freestanding darkwood furniture. Largest rooms are on the first floor and the top floor is mostly moderately-sized singles. Staff are friendly and helpful: a glass of sherry is offered on check-in, as is luggage porterage, and beds are turned down in the evening. Buffet breakfast. The entrance to the hotel lies a couple of miles to the west of Moretonhampstead on the B3212. *Rooms 70. Garden, croquet, tennis, golf (18-hole), pitch & putt, putting green, game fishing, squash, games room, snooker. Access, Amex, Diners, Visa.*

MORETONHAMPSTEAD   White Hart Hotel   £63

Tel 01647 440406   Fax 01647 440565   Map 13 D2   **I**
The Square Moretonhampstead Devon TQ13 8NF

A landmark inn in a small former woollen town, the inn was originally a Georgian posting house. Owner Peter Morgan with his managers and staff keep up high standards of hospitality for both residents (comfortable, old-fashioned bedrooms, a cosy lounge where afternoon tea is served) and locals (in the oak-beamed bar with its polished wood and gleaming copper). Though the style is mainly traditional, the bathrooms boast telephone extensions and modern power showers. Children up to 10 are accommodated free in their parents' room. *Rooms 20. Terrace. Access, Amex, Diners, Visa.*

MORLEY   **Breadsall Priory**   69%   £111

Tel 01332 832235   Fax 01332 833509   Map 6 C3   **H**
Moor Road Morley nr Derby Derbyshire DE7 6DL

Very much geared to the conference and leisure market, Breadsall Priory is usefully located off the A61 (via Breadsall Village) just north of Derby. Although its origins lie in the 13th century (evident in the gracious proportions and tiled-and-arched reception area) the design and facilities are all totally up to date, as befits its target market. Bedrooms are well equipped and comfortably furnished. No dogs. Country Club Hotels. *Rooms 91. Garden, croquet, tennis, two golf courses (18), golf driving range, indoor swimming pool, gym, squash, sauna, spa bath, steam room, solarium, beauty salon. Access, Amex, Diners, Visa.*

MORSTON   **Morston Hall**   73%   £140*

Tel 01263 741041   Fax 01263 740419   Map 10 C1   **H**
Morston Holt Norfolk NR25 7AA

Dating back to the 17th century, Morston Hall is a substantial flint house with secluded grounds to the front and side including a tranquil walled garden with ancient ice-house in one corner. It stands on the A149 coast road close to Morston's tidal quay from where boats depart for the seal sanctuary at Blakeney Point, which is due north. Galton Blackiston, his wife Tracy and partner Justin Fraser have combined their experience and talents to create a hotel offering country hospitality in good measure. The welcome is apparent as soon as you enter the rug-strewn flagstone-floored hall. Fresh flowers and smiles greet you and there is genuine warmth in the welcome. To one side of this entrance hall is a comfortable, relaxing and homely lounge with more flowers, most from the garden. The bedrooms, some with dual-aspect windows, are large, sunny, bright and traditional, overlooking the gardens and rolling farmland beyond. Each room is equipped with almost every conceivable amenity – even a back-scratcher! Good bathrooms and in the morning excellent fruit among the breakfast offerings. Two more rooms have recently come on stream. *Half-board terms only. **Rooms** 6. Garden. Closed Jan 1-late Feb. Access, Amex, Visa.*

MOTTRAM ST ANDREW   **De Vere Mottram Hall**   70%   £140

Tel 01625 828135   Fax 01625 829284   Map 6 B2   **H**
Mottram St Andrew Prestbury Cheshire SK10 4QT

De Vere Hotels' impressive Georgian mansion stands in 270 acres of mature parkland adjacent to the A538. Extensive leisure facilities include a championship golf course and clubhouse. Spacious day rooms in the original Mottram Hall feature restored Adam ceilings and fine panelling. Most of the bedrooms are in newer extensions. Banqueting/conferences for 180/275. *Rooms 133. Garden, croquet, putting green, golf (18), indoor swimming pool, gym, squash, sauna, spa bath, steam room, solarium, beauty salon, snooker, tennis, children's outdoor playground. Access, Amex, Visa.*

Lodges are now listed by county in the reference section

MOULSFORD-ON-THAMES   **Beetle & Wedge**   71%   £95

Tel 01491 651381   Fax 01491 651376   Map 15 D2   **HR**
Moulsford-on-Thames Oxfordshire OX10 9JF

An enviable Thameside location, immortalised in *The Wind in the Willows*, is approached down a narrow lane off the A329. Once the home of Jerome K Jerome of *Three Men in a Boat* fame it is now in the very capable hands of Kate and Richard Smith (our 1995 Hosts of the Year). Through the entrance lobby a pretty, cosy bar affords fine river views; the lounge continues to be decidedly homely and very comfortable, and in inclement weather a fire wards off chills. Bedrooms, most with river views, are very desirable, possessing both charm and style. Antique pine furniture and sleep-inducing bedding characterise all, while the deep-carpeted bathrooms have splendid freestanding cast-iron Victorian bathtubs as well as such modern conveniences as bidets. In the summer, a water garden with long-established water lilies comes into its own with light grills, salads and fish served alfresco. Own parking for 35 cars. *Rooms 10. Garden. Access, Amex, Diners, Visa.*

See over

The Dining Room ⭐ £100

The choice is whether to eat in the simple conviviality of the Boat House or in the formal elegance of the wall-to-wall-windowed dining-room where Richard Smith supervises a cuisine that's both sophisticated and very fashionable. There is also an inner dining-room decorated in pretty shades of pink, a room eminently suitable for dining when the weather becomes cooler. Starters, from a daily-changing menu, range from a wonderful stir-fry of spicy squid, scallops, tomato and coriander to a salad of duck livers and smoked pheasant. Main dishes are mouthwateringly good – grilled fillet of sea bass with mussels, olives, tomato and basil or roast best end of new season's English lamb with couscous and aubergine. Served alongside are delicious vegetables such as fresh asparagus with hollandaise, rösti potatoes, leeks and fennel. A range of superb desserts includes the likes of a pear and armagnac tart with vanilla ice cream or a perfectly formed hot Cointreau soufflé with a raspberry sauce. Cafetière coffee and excellent petits fours complete a superbly satisfying repast. The almost entirely French wine list has been very carefully and knowledgeably compiled by Kate, so it's worth seeking advice on what to drink, depending on your budget. Note the "dipstick" policy in lieu of half bottles. No smoking. **Seats** 30. *Parties 10. Private Room 55. L 12.30-2 D 7.30-10. Closed D Sun, all Mon & 25 Dec. Set L £17.50/£21.50 (Sun £27.50).*

The Boat House ⬛ £70

Perched on the banks of the Thames, a skilfully converted boathouse with a terrace (6 tables) overlooking the water. Decor is rustic with uneven terracotta floors, rough redbrick walls and heavy beams and struts overhead. An imaginative and varied menu can cause problems when it comes to choosing as everything sounds so good. Starters merge into main dishes with no distinct boundary between the two. Thus crispy duck and frisée salad and avocado, chicken and smoked prawn salad are available under both headings. Duck liver and cognac terrine is served with toasted brioche, while other starters could be warm goat's cheese with croutons, lardons and mixed leaves or fish soup with rouille and gruyère followed perhaps by chicken with scallops, wild mushrooms and creamy curry sauce, tagliatelle with pesto and seared scallops or monkfish tail with wild mushrooms and Dijon mustard. From the charcoal grill come fish such as whole Dover sole or escalope of salmon; and meat dishes could be calf's kidneys and black pudding with a grain mustard sauce or a simple but good fillet steak béarnaise. Excellent sweets and cafetière coffee together with highly personable staff make this an occasion to remember. **Seats** 60. *Parties 8. L 12.30-2 D 7.30-10. Closed 25 Dec.*

MOULTON	Black Bull	£55

Tel 01325 377289   Fax 01325 377422   Map 5 E3   **R**
Moulton nr Richmond North Yorkshire DL10 6QJ

The Pagendam family, here since 1963, have built a wide and still growing reputation for the food served at their splendid pub/restaurant a mile south of Scotch Corner. That reputation rests largely, but by no means exclusively, on seafood and Aberdeen Angus beef. The former ranges from oysters, and spicy skewered prawns with garlic bread to halibut and smoked salmon in filo pastry with a sorrel butter sauce and lobster thermidor. The latter includes chateaubriand b,arnaise (for two), peppered fillet with cream sauce and grilled sirloin with red wine and shallots. As well as the carte there's a lunchtime prix-fixe, Sunday lunch and a lunchtime (Mon-Sat) bar snack menu. Eight *marque* champagnes under £30 (even Dom Perignon and Louis Roederer Cristal 1985s are under £60) set the tone for wine prices, which are quite remarkable for the quality offered. **Seats** 100. *Parties 30. Private Room 36. L 12-2 (Sun to 3) D 6.45-10.15. Closed Sun, 24-27 Dec. Set L £13.75 (Sun £15). Access, Amex, Visa.*

MOUSEHOLE	Lobster Pot	57%	£70

Tel 01736 731251   Fax 01736 731140   Map 12 A4   **H**
Mousehole nr Penzance Cornwall TR19 6QX

Mousehole is the epitome of a quaint Cornish fishing village, and the Lobster Pot by natural extension an archetypal atmospheric hotel. It overlooks the harbour, whose activity can be watched from most of the public rooms and some of the well-maintained bedrooms. There's extra accommodation in four cottages across the narrow street. Very much a holiday rather than a business base, with families well catered for. **Rooms 25.** *Closed Jan-mid Mar. Access, Visa.*

MUCH BIRCH	Pilgrim Hotel	64%	£89

Tel 01981 540742   Fax 01981 540620   Map 14 A1   **H**
Much Birch nr Hereford Hereford & Worcester HR2 8HJ

Set back from the A49 between Hereford and Ross-on-Wye, this much-extended former rectory stands in four acres of grounds with views over Golden Valley and the Black Mountains. Stone walls, oak furniture and a log-burning stove give character to the bar, and the bedrooms have good-quality furnishings, armchairs and useful desk space. Children aged 12 or under are accommodated free in parents' room. Five of the bedrooms are designated non-smoking. **Rooms 20.** *Garden, croquet, 3-hole pitch & putt. Access, Amex, Diners, Visa.*

MUDEFORD	Avonmouth Hotel	59%	£107

Tel 01202 483434   Fax 01202 479004   Map 14 C4   **H**
Mudeford Christchurch Dorset BH23 3NT

A Forte hotel, clearly signposted off the A35, with a private jetty, slipway and moorings at the end of lawns leading down to Christchurch Harbour. Best bedrooms (with a small supplement) have balconies and/or sea views. Room service throughout the day until 10pm. **Rooms 41.** *Garden, croquet, putting, outdoor swimming pool, children's splash pool, games room. Access, Amex, Diners, Visa.*

MULLION	Polurrian Hotel	66%	£134

Tel 01326 240421   Fax 01326 240083   Map 12 B4   **H**
Mullion Helston Cornwall TR12 7EN

On a cliff above a secluded beach and cove, Polurrian is a family holiday hotel par excellence, with a wide range of activities on the premises and many more in the neighbourhood. Comfortable lounges take full advantage of the views and so do many of the bedrooms (rooms without the view are cheaper). Free accommodation for 6-14 year olds sharing adults' room, with breakfast and high tea charged at £10 per day. For under-5s breakfast and high tea are also free if parents have booked on dinner, bed & breakfast terms. 200 yards from the hotel are six bungalows let out on a weekly self-catering basis. **Rooms 39.** *Garden, indoor & outdoor swimming pools, children's splash pool, children's playground, tennis, keep-fit equipment, squash, badminton, sauna, spa bath, solarium, putting, snooker. Closed Jan & Feb. Access, Amex, Diners, Visa.*

MYLOR BRIDGE	Pandora Inn		£50

Tel 01326 372678   Map 12 B4   **R**
Restronguet Creek Mylor Bridge Falmouth Cornwall TR11 5ST

🍷 🍇

Parts of the building date back to the 13th century, and the flagstone floors, low beamed ceilings and nautical memorabilia all add to the sense of history. In the restaurant, there's good use of local ingredients (especially fish and shellfish) – mussels steamed in white wine flavoured with herbs and fennel seeds, monkfish in garlic butter, seafood platter, roast duck with plum sauce, supreme of chicken on a lightly curried sherry and coconut cream sauce, vegetable and nut stroganoff with wild rice. It's worth checking the board for daily specials, and there's a separate, substantial bar menu available at both lunch and dinner. Excellent range of wines by the glass on a concise, kindly priced list. Ask for directions when booking. **Seats 46.** *D only 7-10 (9.30 in winter). Closed Sun in winter, 25 Dec. Access, Amex, Visa.*

We welcome bona fide complaints and recommendations on the tear-out pages at the back of the book for readers' comments. They are followed up by our professional team.

NANTWICH   Churche's Mansion   £70

Tel 01270 625933   Fax 01270 74256   Map 6 B3   **R**
Hospital Street Nantwich Cheshire CW5 0RY

The restaurant is housed in a four-gabled 16th-century building with original oak beams,
exposed brickwork, open fireplaces and complementary furnishings. Chef Graham
Tucker's monthly-changing fixed-price menus offer plenty of choice (about a dozen main
dishes) and excellent value for money with everything from the bread to the petits fours
home-made. Full of interest, dishes range from starters such as creamed butternut squash
and Jerusalem artichoke soup flavoured with truffles, roast scallops with ventreche bacon
and rocket flavoured with carrot juice and lime, and filo parcels filled with ratatouille on
a black olive purée with gazpacho sauce to mains like chargrilled slices of calf's liver with
crisp pancetta bacon, seafood stew in a saffron liquor with rouille croutons and pot-
roasted pheasant filled with foie gras and chestnut stuffing on Jerusalem artichoke and
sweet potatoes with a lentil sauce. Desserts are a little more mainstream and might
include a hot prune and armagnac soufflé with caramel ice cream and apricot tarte tatin.
Some excellent British cheeses are well described on their own separate menu. Good
coffee. The three champagnes offered are well under £30, setting the very fair pricing
policy on the list. Wine merchant Bibendum rightly receive much credit for help in
compiling the list. No smoking in the dining-rooms. No children under 10 at dinner;
families welcome for Sunday lunch (half price, half portions offered). Parking for 40 cars.
*Seats 50. Private Room 24. L 12-2.30 D 7-9.30. Closed D Sun, all Mon & 2nd week Jan. Set
L £12.50/£15.50 Set D £24. Access, Diners, Visa.*

NANTWICH   Rookery Hall   80%   £150

Tel 01270 610016   Fax 01270 626027   Map 6 B3   **HR**
Worleston nr Nantwich Cheshire CW5 6DQ

Set in 200 acres of parkland and
originally built as a private house in
1816, the hotel has had many
additions over the years (most
recently a new wing, with extended
conference facilities), but is still
largely Regency in style. The public
rooms have splendid moulded
ceilings, deep sofas, fine antiques and
original panelling. All bedrooms are
individually decorated and
luxuriously furnished; those in the
main building are in a more
sumptuous, multi-tasselled style; the
new block is equally palatial, though
more restrained in decoration. Bathrooms are fitted to the highest standards. 24hr room
service. The hotel stands on the B5074 north of Nantwich. *Rooms 45. Garden, croquet,
tennis, putting, coarse fishing. Access, Amex, Diners, Visa.*

Restaurant   £85

Elegant oak-panelled dining-room, with views over the gardens and countryside beyond.
Chef David Alton cooks in the Modern British style with light saucing and flavours
gathered from around the world. The table d'hote menu might offer grilled bream on
a salad of smoked salmon and chives, tartare of venison and blue cheese with basil
mayonnaise or a broth of mussels, scallops and oysters finished with coconut milk to
begin; maize-fed Lancashire chicken with coriander tagliatelle and a ginger-flavoured
sauce, fillet of beef with a roasted parsnip purée, onion marmalade and celeriac or
a panaché of seafood with cucumber and pink peppercorns to follow. The beautiful
arrangement of some dishes unfortunately promises more than the flavours deliver. Lunch
offers less choice, perhaps four options at each course. A new candle-lit cellar restaurant is
available for private parties. A two-part wine list is divided between 'cellar' and 'hotel'.
It's difficult to understand the separation or need, since there are some excellent wines on
the latter list and some ordinary ones on the former. Few half bottles. *Seats 30. Parties 10.
Private Room 65. L 12-2 D 7-9.45. Closed 26-30 Dec.*

| NEEDHAM MARKET | Pipps Ford | 60% | £55 |

Tel 01449 760208   Fax 01449 760561   Map 10 C3   **H**
Needham Market nr Ipswich Suffolk IP6 8LJ

Raewyn Hackett-Jones personally welcomes guests to her 16th-century farmhouse
in a delightful garden just off the A45/A140 roundabout. Winter log fires burn in huge
inglenooks, and a fine breakfast featuring home-produced honey, eggs and bread is served
in the plant-filled conservatory. Bedrooms, all named after flowers, are split between the
house and adjacent Stables Cottage, up a steep spiral staircase. In the main house, Sweet Pea
and Forget-Me-Not share a shower room. Hollyhock has a four-poster. No phones or TV
in the bedrooms. No children under 5. No dogs. No smoking. ***Rooms*** *7. Garden, croquet,
outdoor swimming pool, tennis, coarse fishing. Closed mid Dec-mid Jan. No credit cards.*

| NETHER LANGWITH | Goff's Restaurant | £65 |

Tel 01623 744538   Map 7 D2   **RR**
Langwith Mill House Nether Langwith nr Mansfield Nottinghamshire NG20 9JF

An old, dilapidated cotton mill forms a striking landmark alongside the A632 about
a mile east of the village. Owners the Goffs converted the adjacent Mill House into
a charming, homely restaurant with rooms. The front entrance is actually at the back
(when approached from the road) and on the ground floor there's a simple, cosy lounge
and two pretty, candle-lit dining-rooms – one spacious, the other intimate. The 'bistro
menu' (all mains £9, all starters and desserts £4) might include salmon fishcakes with
basil mayonnaise, grilled pork chop with roast vegetables, coriander chicken curry and
tarte tatin. At night there is also a set-price, monthly-changing 'gourmet' menu (five
choices at each stage) where chef Darren Shears might start with town with starters such as
a chicken liver parfait with a breast of pigeon on toasted brioche with orange sauce, and
shellfish consommé with fresh herbs and a julienne of vegetables before main dishes like
salmon with a pine kernel crust and basil butter sauce, and fillet of beef with roasted
shallots, a small kidney pudding and port sauce. Desserts include sticky toffee pudding
and raspberry meringue with pistachio sauce. ***Seats*** *45. Parties 12. Private Room 28.
L 12-1.30 D 7-9.30. Set L & D £13/£17. Set D £27.50. Closed L Sat, D Sun, all Mon & Tue
after Bank Holidays & 26-31 Dec. Access, Amex, Diners, Visa.*

Rooms   **£50**
The two bedrooms are spacious and comfortable. Storage heaters provide ample heat
on chilly nights and remote-control TVs, books, magazines and fresh fruit are among the
homely extras.

| NEW ALRESFORD | Hunters | £55 |

Tel 01962 732468   Map 15 D3   **RR**
32 Broad Street New Alresford Hampshire SO24 9AQ

Wine bar/brasserie with two distinctive bow-fronted windows, awnings and candle-light
within, run by the Birmingham family. Morning coffee is served from 11, followed an
hour later by the luncheon menu of starters, light snacks and main courses. Chicken
mousseline with a tomato vinaigrette, filo parcels of Stilton cheese with honey jus, boeuf
bourguignon and wild boar and apple sausages show the style. Sunday lunch in winter is
a simpler affair. In the evenings there are table d'hote (not Sat) and à la carte menus
whose offerings include home-smoked wood pigeon salad with leek and mustard
dressing, fresh salmon terrine with fine beans and quail's eggs, grilled lamb cutlets with
a herb jus and confit of duck leg with rosemary cream sauce (the chef specialises in
sauces). Dark chocolate pavé and bread-and-butter pudding are typical desserts. The
Garden Room is a popular venue for parties, accommodating up to 75 guests. ***Seats*** *30.
Parties 12. Private Rooms 15/75. L 12-2 D 7-10. Closed Sun except lunch in winter,
1 week Christmas. Set D £13.95/£15.95. Access, Amex, Diners, Visa.*

Rooms   **£48**
The three bedrooms, all with shower and WC en suite, are in an old Georgian building.

Set menu prices may not always include service or wine.

NEW BARNET — Mims ↑ £75

Tel 0181-449 2974 Fax 0181-447 1825   Map 15 F2   **R**
63 East Barnet Road New Barnet Hertfordshire EN4 8RN

The surprises here are on the plate rather than in the unprepossessing surroundings.
In a parade of shops right next to a petrol station partners Moustafa Abouzahrah and
Ismail Al-Sersy, the chef, have created a jewel of a restaurant. Menus change daily and
dishes are not only imaginative but also very artistically presented. Initial choices could be
a cappuccino of smoked leek and cinnamon, spicy pork sausage with a lettuce, tomato
and onion salad, roast leg of lamb with a lamb's sweetbread and onion tart, sauté of baby
chicken with lemon and olive oil mash and seared salmon with spinach, tomato and herb
jus. Desserts might include a dark chocolate gateau with blueberries, cinnamon ice cream
with caramelised apples or banana crepes. Flavours are wonderfully distinct and unsullied
by over-elaboration, sauces are simple, delicate jus. Charming and attentive service.
No children under 6 after 7pm. Special parking arrangements behind the garage next
door during the evenings and all day Sunday. *Seats 45. Parties 8. L 12-2.30 D 6.30-11
Sun meals 12-10.30. Closed L Sat, all Mon, 2 weeks August, 1 week Christmas.
Set L £9.50/£14.50. Set D £15/£19. Access, Visa.*

> Set menu prices may not always include service or wine.

NEW MILTON — Chewton Glen — 89% — £214

Tel 01425 275341   Fax 01425 272310   Map 14 C4   **HR**
Christchurch Road New Milton Hampshire BH25 6QS

Half-way between Bournemouth and
Lymington, Martin and Brigitte Skan's
magnificent 'hotel, health and country
club' justly enjoys a worldwide
reputation not only for what it offers
today, but for consistently maintaining
the highest standards since 1966. Great
hotels rely on the quality of their staff
and here they are unquestionably
professional, courteous and efficient
under the direction of Peter Crome.
Set in 70 acres of grounds, including
a superlative croquet lawn, the hotel has evolved over the years into one of the country's
finest, pioneering styles and setting standards that others have followed. The stunningly-
designed leisure and health club, whose facilities guests share with non-resident club
members, epitomises the quality to be found throughout the hotel; its centrepiece is a
swimming pool of magnificent proportions. The bedrooms, some with balconies and
private terraces, are equally luxurious with high-quality fabrics, beautiful colour schemes,
period furniture and fine bathrooms, complete with fresh flowers, that positively pamper;
it goes without saying that fruit, sherry, mineral water, home-made biscuits and 24hr
room service are all provided. Such elegance is also apparent in the public areas where
the tastefully decorated rooms with their exquisite antiques, fine paintings and
memorabilia still provide the atmosphere of a large, modern private house. No children
under seven; families can eat informally in the balcony lounge of the health club or
formally in the restaurant between 6 and 7. Breakfast, as befits an establishment of this
calibre, is fit for a king, ranging from freshly-baked pastries to stewed prunes, kedgeree
and kippers. No dogs. Elegant conference/banqueting facilities for 100. Minimum two
nights' weekend stay at certain times of year. *Rooms 58. Garden, croquet,
indoor & outdoor swimming pools, sun beds, sauna, steam room, spa bath, beauty & hair
salon, gym, golf (9), indoor & outdoor tennis, putting, snooker, valeting, boutique.
Access, Amex, Diners, Visa.*

Marryat Room Restaurant — ★ — £100

There is no longer an à la carte here but the fixed-price menus (priced for two or three
courses at lunchtime) have been extended and favourite dishes from the previous carte,

like the double-baked Emmental soufflé with fondue sauce, are still to be found. Chef Pierre Chevillard handles first-rate ingredients with admirable assurance, producing sauces with subtle flavours and perfect textures. His prowess at combining complementary flavours can be seen in such dishes as a tartare of salmon seasoned with a light anchovy mayonnaise and lime, escalope of hot foie gras on a wafer-thin savoury apple tart, braised pork cheeks cooked in lemon grass and ginger with a fricassee of scallops, pan-fried skate with Cajun spices, and roast leg of Pauillac lamb on a bed of couscous with a rosemary-flavoured jus. Desserts range from a thoroughly English Bramley apple pie to caramelised lemon tart with poached cherries and an exotic fruit salad with a refreshing coconut sorbet, and there are both English and French cheeses. Lovely petits fours are served with various styles of coffee. Summer eating here is delightful, both on an outdoor terrace area where tables are laid out overlooking the gardens (and swimming pool) and in the delightful conservatory dining-room. The wine list is fantastic, and if you're not prepared to push the boat out there's a section of wines under £20. However, for the most part exceptional wines attract exceptional prices, though note that the latter are inclusive of service – it all helps! The list is hugely comprehensive with quality throughout. No smoking. No children under 7. *Seats 120. Parties 8. L 12.30-2 D 7.30-9.30. Set L £18.50/£23.50 (Sun £25.50) Set D £39.50.*

NEWARK	Gannets Bistrot '94	£50

Tel 01636 610018   Map 7 D3   **R**
35 Castlegate Newark Nottinghamshire NG24 1AZ

Experienced food-lovers Gwen and her chef-husband Colin White run the delightful little upstairs bistrot, access to which is still via the main entrance below. A seasonally changing menu is backed up by daily blackboard specials. Summer offerings could include excellent home-made paté flavoured with fresh herbs and supported by good onion marmalade, fish soup with croutons and rouille and baked goat's cheese salad with a herb and walnut dressing to begin; with perhaps omelette Arnold Bennett, guinea fowl sausage with lentils and apples or roast skate with a warm butter bean and potato salad to follow. Desserts are complimentary to diners who have had two courses. On the ground floor, the Café (Tel 01636 702066) is open from 9.30 to 4.30 seven days a week, offering a wide selection of snacks and lunchtime specials, including plenty of choice for vegetarians. No smoking. Bistrot: *Seats 40. L 12-2 D 6.30-9.30. Closed (Bistrot) Sun, Mon & Bank Holidays, (café 25 & 26 Dec, 1 Jan). Access, Visa.*

NEWARK	Grange Hotel	58%	£55

Tel 01636 703399   Fax 01636 702328   Map 7 D3   **H**
73 London Road Newark Nottinghamshire NG24 1RZ

An unassuming, family-run Victorian hotel on the edge of town. Free parking at the back of the hotel. No dogs. *Rooms 15. Garden. Closed 24 Dec-3 Jan. Access, Visa.*

NEWBURY	Chequers Hotel	66%	£102

Tel 01635 38000   Fax 01635 37170   Map 15 D2   **H**
Oxford Street Newbury Berkshire RG13 1JB

A handsome Georgian facade conceals an even older town-centre coaching inn. Bedrooms have all the usual modern comforts and about half are non-smoking. Forte. *Rooms 56. Garden. Access, Amex, Diners, Visa.*

NEWBURY	Donnington Valley Hotel	74%	£108

Tel 01635 551199   Fax 01635 551123   Map 15 D2   **H**
Old Oxford Road Donnington nr Newbury Berkshire RG16 9AG

Alongside its own golf course, this very modern, privately-owned hotel conceals a surprisingly stylish interior behind a rather less remarkable redbrick exterior. Beneath a vast, steeply-pitched timber ceiling the main, split-level public areas boast a real log fire, Oriental carpets over parquet floor and numerous comfortable sofas and armchairs with intriguing antique knick-knacks dotted about. The effect created is one of Edwardian elegance (though with modern comfort as the whole hotel is air-conditioned), a theme that extends to the bedrooms, many of which have period-style inlaid furniture and hand-painted tiles in the good bathrooms. There is a turn-down service in the evenings and extensive 24hr room service. Children up to 12 stay free in parents' room. Some rooms are equipped for disabled guests. Purpose-built conference facilities cater for up to 140 delegates. *Rooms 140. Garden, golf (18), putting, fishing, shooting. Access, Amex, Diners, Visa.*

NEWBURY   Foley Lodge   71%   £115

Tel 01635 528770   Fax 01635 528398   Map 15 D2   **H**
Stockcross Newbury Berkshire RG16 8JU

A mile and a half west of Newbury on the B4000, this former Victorian hunting lodge is approached via a winding, tree-lined drive. The entrance is through a glass conservatory with black-and-white tiled floor and wicker chairs, overlooking the landscaped gardens. A "modern Victorian" ambience is cleverly created in both the public rooms and bedrooms by using fringed floral drapes and smart reproduction antiques. There is a high standard of accommodation throughout, with rooms in a new block being equally comfortable. Top of the range is the luxurious Sycamore Suite with a four-poster bed and a large bay window. A bright and airy octagonal pagoda is an unusual setting for the bubbling, circular swimming pool. Meeting rooms for up to 200 persons. Children can stay free in parents' room. *Rooms 69. Garden, croquet, indoor swimming pool, snooker.* *Access, Amex, Diners, Visa.*

NEWBURY   Hilton National   69%   £108

Tel 01635 529000   Fax 01635 529337   Map 15 D2   **H**
Pinchington Lane Newbury Berkshire RG14 7HL

Modern low-rise hotel one mile south of Newbury with a variety of conference rooms (catering for up to 200) and a leisure complex. Best of the bedrooms are the Plaza rooms, with bigger beds and more accessories than the others. Children up to 14 stay free in parents' room. *Rooms 109. Indoor swimming pool, keep-fit facilities, sauna, steam room.* *Access, Amex, Diners, Visa.*

NEWBURY   Millwaters   67%   £78

Tel 01635 528838   Fax 01635 523406   Map 15 D2   **H**
London Road Newbury Berkshire RG13 2BY

Eight charming acres of gardens surround Millwaters, the specific waters being those of the Rivers Kennet and Lambourn which meander through the gardens. Conference and banqueting (for up to 80) are the mainstays, in addition to fishing. Bedrooms and dayrooms are all comfortably furnished. Children up to 10 stay free in parents' room. Tariff reductions at weekends (when weddings are popular). *Rooms 30. Garden, croquet, fishing. Access, Amex, Diners, Visa.*

NEWBURY   Regency Park Hotel   70%   £109

Tel 01635 871555   Fax 01635 871571   Map 15 D2   **H**
Bowling Green Road Thatcham Newbury Berkshire RG18 3RP

Five minutes from Newbury (signposted off the A4 Reading road), and standing in 5 acres of grounds, the original Edwardian house is now rather lost within more modern extensions. Spacious bedrooms offer guests comfortable, carefully planned accommodation in rooms that are light and well appointed. Picture windows in the sun lounge overlook the patio and an ornamental fountain. Keen, helpful management and a variety of special weekend themes and special rates throughout the year. Children up to 12 stay free in parents' room. *Rooms 50. Garden, all-weather tennis, news kiosk. Access, Amex, Diners, Visa.*

NEWBURY   Stakis Newbury Hotel   67%   £100

Tel 01635 247010   Fax 01635 247077   Map 15 D2   **H**
Oxford Road Newbury Berkshire RG16 8XY

Just off Junction 13 of the M4, the Stakis Newbury is well designed for business people. Bedrooms feature good desk/work space, and there are four conference/seminar rooms with up-to-date equipment catering for up to 60 attendees. Under-5s stay free in parents' room. *Rooms 112. Indoor swimming pool, gym, sauna, spa bath, steam room, sun beds.* *Access, Amex, Diners, Visa.*

Consult the blue pages for summary tables and lists of recommended establishments.

NEWBY BRIDGE   The Swan   61%   £88   H

Tel 01539 531681   Fax 01539 531917   Map 4 C4
Newby Bridge nr Ulverston Cumbria LA12 8NB

Attractively situated opposite the five-arched stone bridge over the River Leven by Windermere's southern shore, the Swan is a comfortable family hotel and fisherman's haunt, popular also for themed weekend breaks. In addition to one suite and four de luxe bedrooms with balconies and a river view, there are five spacious family rooms (children £18 per night) and bright, neatly-kept bathrooms throughout. Facilities for conferences of up to 65 delegates; ample parking. No dogs. **Rooms 36.** *Garden, croquet, coarse fishing, mooring. Access, Amex, Diners, Visa.*

NEWBY WISKE   Solberge Hall   69%   £80   H

Tel 01609 779191   Fax 01609 780472   Map 5 E4
Newby Wiske nr Northallerton North Yorkshire DL7 9ER

Leisure and business visitors are both well looked after at the Hall, a country mansion dating from 1824 and set in 16 acres of gardens and woodland. The views are impressive and inside there's a delightful wood-panelled foyer with a blue-and-white-tiled fireplace, a homely lounge and a comfortable bar. Bedrooms are good-sized, some having four-posters, with plenty of thoughtful extras. Children under 14 stay free in parents' room. Conference capacity 120. **Rooms 25.** *Garden, clay-pigeon shooting, snooker. Access, Amex, Diners, Visa.*

NEWCASTLE-UNDER-LYME   Clayton Lodge   60%   £97   H

Tel 01782 613093   Fax 01782 711896   Map 6 B3
Clayton Road Newcastle-under-Lyme Staffordshire ST5 4AF

On the A519, a mile from the M6 (J15) this Jarvis-owned conference and meeting hotel has views over the Lyme Valley. The largest of the several conference rooms can accommodate 270. Well-equipped bedrooms, where children up to 16 can stay free in parents' room. **Rooms 49.** *Access, Amex, Diners, Visa.*

NEWCASTLE-UNDER-LYME   Forte Posthouse   60%   £72   H

Tel 01782 717171   Fax 01782 717138   Map 6 B3
Clayton Road Newcastle-under-Lyme Staffordshire ST5 4DL

100 yards from Junction 15 of the M6, this Posthouse provides decent modern accommodation for the family, keep-fit amenities and conference facilities for up to 70. Children up to 16 stay free in parents' room. **Rooms 119.** *Garden, indoor swimming pool, gym, sauna, spa bath, sun beds, children's playroom, playground. Access, Amex, Diners, Visa.*

Set menu prices may not always include service or wine.

NEWCASTLE-UPON-TYNE   The Blackgate Restaurant   £70   R

Tel 0191-261 7356   Map 5 E2
Milburn House The Side Quayside Newcastle-upon-Tyne Tyne & Wear NE1 3JE

One of Newcastle's oldest restaurants, with an unbroken history since 1905, the Blackgate is housed in the bottom of Milburn House, just off Dean Street. Chef Douglas Jordan enjoys the celebration of British cooking in deceptively simple dishes with a carefully constructed range and balance of flavours. A "Menu Select" at lunch and early evening produces skilfully cooked main dishes at bargain prices: baked cod fillet with parsley sauce and cumin-flavoured carrot purée and first-class marinated rib of beef, pan-fried and served with garlic butter. A la carte are breast of chicken with buttered spring onions, king prawns and fresh ginger; salmon baked in a mustard and pistachio crust; tenderloin of Northumberland venison with caramelised sour apple and port sauce; and peppered duck breast with mandarin and garlic marmalade. Fine British puddings such as apricot and sultana Bakewell and brown bread trifle, and good local cheeses from Dunsyre Blue to Haltwhistle. Hard to push the boat out on the wine list here – short and modest in the extreme. **Seats 40. Parties 18.** *Private Room 12. L 12.30-2 D 6.30-10. Closed L Sat, D Mon, all Sun, Bank Holidays, 1 week Christmas. Set L £10.90/£17.45 D £19.10/£24.75. Access, Amex, Diners, Visa.*

NEWCASTLE-UPON-TYNE   Copthorne Hotel   73%   £138

Tel 0191-222 0333   Fax 0191-230 1111   Map 5 E2   **H**
The Close Quayside Newcastle-upon-Tyne Tyne & Wear NE1 3RT

To the west of the Tyne Bridge and built straight alongside the Tyne, the hotel makes
the most of its riverside location. All the bedrooms are at the front, some with balconies.
It's stylishly modern in design – with an impressive marble-floored five-floor atrium at its
heart. Space and high standards of comfort are its hallmarks. Here, in what is also
a lounge, there are tan leather seats and burr-walnut tables while in Claspers Bar, named
after the rower, the ambience is a little more clubby. Classic bedrooms are well equipped
but Connoisseur bedrooms have the edge on comfort with king-size beds, bathrobes,
a later check-out and various little extras. All rooms are fully air-conditioned and have
satellite TVs. Excellent power showers in the bathrooms. Free overnight parking in the
multi-storey car park which occupies the rear of the hotel. Executive conference and
banqueting facilities (150/200), a business centre and a fitness and leisure centre are
further services offered. Children up to 16 can stay free in parents' room. *Rooms 156.*
Gym, sauna, spa bath, steam room, solarium, news kiosk, shop. Access, Amex, Diners, Visa.

NEWCASTLE-UPON-TYNE   County Thistle   68%   £106

Tel 0191-232 2471   Fax 0191-232 1285   Map 5 E2   **H**
Neville Street Newcastle-upon-Tyne Tyne & Wear NE99 1AH

A handsome Victorian building opposite Central station. Popular for conferences
(up to 130). Decent bedrooms, studios being the best equipped. *Rooms 115.*
Access, Amex, Diners, Visa.

NEWCASTLE-UPON-TYNE   Courtney's   £55

Tel 0191-232 5537   Map 5 E2   **R**
5-7 The Side Quayside Newcastle-upon-Tyne Tyne & Wear NE1 3JE

Ⅴ

Michael and Kerensa Carr's small split-level restaurant in what can be described as the
city's gastronomic quarter is simple and without frills, but therein lies its success. No
surplus of staff here, just a couple of well-mannered and keen enthusiasts assisting the
owners (Michael does the cooking, which is precise and correct). A blackboard indicates
the evening specials of the day and the lunchtime fixed-price menu in addition to the
regular menu. There's a distinctive English slant to the cooking with a range of dishes
from starters such as blackened red snapper with a tomato salsa or cheese and ham soufflé
suissesse to main courses that include veal escalopes with a wild mushroom cream sauce
or Toulouse sausage with a lentil gravy and basil mash. For dessert, try the caramelised
rice pudding with a cinnamon anglaise or darjeeling blancmange with a pink grapefruit
sauce. Vegetarians are well catered for. Inexpensive wines with a good house selection.
*Seats 28. L 12-2 D 7-10.30. Closed L Sat, all Sun, Bank Hols, 2 weeks May, 1 week
Christmas. Set L £13. Access, Amex, Visa.*

NEWCASTLE-UPON-TYNE   Europa Hotel   59%   £82

Tel 0191-262 8989   Fax 0191-263 4172   Map 5 E2   **H**
Coast Road Wallsend Newcastle-upon-Tyne Tyne & Wear NE28 9HP

Modern low-riser set in its own grounds on the Silverlink Business Park, by the A19 just
north of the Tyne Tunnel. Plenty of free car parking, numerous large conference rooms
(up to 400 delegates) and a health complex. Good tariff reductions at weekends;
children under 14 stay free in parents' room. Formerly Newcastle Moat House.
*Rooms 147. Gym, indoor pool, children's splash pool, spa bath, sauna, plunge pool,
steam room, solarium, games room. Access, Amex, Diners, Visa.*

NEWCASTLE-UPON-TYNE   Fisherman's Lodge   £85

Tel 0191-281 3281   Fax 0191-281 6410   Map 5 E2   **R**
7 Jesmond Dene Jesmond Newcastle-upon-Tyne Tyne & Wear NE7 7BQ

In a deep wooded valley two miles from Newcastle city centre, Fisherman's Lodge has
been among the best known of north-eastern restaurants for many years (it opened in
1979). Variety is allied to fine cooking throughout the various menus, which include one

for vegetarians. 'Chef's classics' put the emphasis on seafood with dishes such as lobster with garlic butter, surf and turf, and grilled salmon with scallops, asparagus tips and a sorrel sauce. Daily specials increase the choice, and desserts include home-made ice creams. There are a few meat dishes including roast grouse in season, as well as braised and roasted lamb shank with leek pudding and Madeira sauce. No children under 10 after 8pm. No smoking in the dining-room (it's permitted with coffee in the lounge). Patio/garden seating for 30 in good weather. *Seats 60. Parties 14. Private Room 40. L 12-2 D 7-11. Closed L Sat, all Sun, Bank Holidays. Set L £17.80 Set D £26.50. Access, Amex, Diners, Visa.*

NEWCASTLE-UPON-TYNE	Forte Crest	61%	£101

Tel 0191-232 6191 Fax 0191-261 8529   Map 5 E2   **H**
New Bridge Street Newcastle-upon-Tyne Tyne & Wear NE1 8BS

City-centre hotel with a business centre and many meeting/conference rooms (for up to 600 delegates). Computer link-up and satellite TV in all rooms. Free overnight (only) parking in the adjacent council car park. *Rooms 166. Access, Amex, Diners, Visa.*

NEWCASTLE-UPON-TYNE	King Neptune		£45

Tel 0191-261 6657   Map 5 E2   **R**
34 Stowell Street Newcastle-upon-Tyne Tyne & Wear NE1 4XB

The Mak brothers are first-generation Geordie Chinese and take great pride in their Peking and Szechuan cooking. Seafood is a particularly strong point, with a dozen prawn dishes, scallops, oysters, squid, crab and fish fillets. Specialities include steamed sea bass in spring onion/soy sauce and sea-spiced lobster in chili sauce. Vegetarian menu. Booking is usually essential, even on Sundays. The restaurant is in the heart of Newcastle's Chinatown. *Seats 120. Parties 20. Private Room 70. L 12-1.45 D 6-10.45 (Sat 6-11.30). Closed 25 & 26 Dec, 1 Jan. Set L from £6.50 Set D from £14.80. Access, Amex, Diners, Visa.*

NEWCASTLE-UPON-TYNE	Novotel	63%	£78

Tel 0191-214 0303 Fax 0191-214 0633   Map 5 E2   **H**
Ponteland Road Kenton Newcastle-upon-Tyne Tyne & Wear NE3 3HZ

Very modern Novotel just off the A1 on the western by-pass. Spacious bedrooms (half designated non-smoking), air-conditioning, four rooms adapted for disabled guests. Conference facilities for up to 250. Children up to 15 stay free in parents' room. Ample free car parking. Special early room service breakfast available 4am-6am. *Rooms 126. Indoor swimming pool, gym, sauna, restaurant (6am-midnight). Access, Amex, Diners, Visa.*

NEWCASTLE-UPON-TYNE	Swallow Hotel	63%	£90

Tel 0191-232 5025 Fax 0191-232 8428   Map 5 E2   **H**
Newgate Arcade Newcastle-upon-Tyne Tyne & Wear NE1 5SX

A modern hotel in the city centre, with suites that include an ample free car park, conference facilities for up to 100 and a sixth-floor cocktail bar affording panoramic views. Children up to 14 stay free in parents' room. *Rooms 93. Access, Amex, Diners, Visa.*

NEWCASTLE-UPON-TYNE	Swallow Gosforth Park	73%	£100

Tel 0191-236 4111 Fax 0191-236 8192   Map 5 E2   **H**
High Gosforth Park Newcastle-upon-Tyne Tyne & Wear NE3 5HN

A splendid modern hotel in 12 acres of wooded parkland next to Newcastle racecourse and just off the A1. Neat, well-tended grounds form a good first impression. Stylish day rooms include an elegant foyer/lounge and two bars, and there are good conference (up to 500 delegates) and leisure facilities. Accommodation includes luxury suites, studios and spacious Executive rooms. The standard bedrooms are not large, but nevertheless attractive with modern lightwood furniture and an armchair, their bathrooms tidy and well equipped. Half the rooms are designated non-smoking. Free parking for 300 cars. Refurbishments were planned to be completed in all bedrooms by the end of 1995. *Rooms 178. Garden, indoor swimming pool, gym, squash, sauna, spa bath, solarium, hairdressing, beauty salon, games room, tennis, courtesy car Access, Amex, Diners, Visa.*

Set menu prices may not always include service or wine.

NEWCASTLE-UPON-TYNE   21 QUEEN STREET   ★ ↑   £95

Tel 0191-222 0755 Fax 0191-230 5875   Map 5 E2   **R**
21 Queen St Princes Wharf Quayside Newcastle-upon-Tyne Tyne & Wear NE1 3UG

The new minimalist decor of Newcastle's foremost restaurant suits Terry Laybourne's style perfectly. The plain white walls are decorated with a raised motif of 21 Queen Street with crisp white-linen-clad tables and effective spotlighting providing a suitably modish setting for ambitious and very sound cooking. Menus are composed of an extremely varied and imaginative selection of dishes including a mussel, cockle and saffron soup with dill pesto, tomato risotto with a small herb salad and brown butter vinaigrette or a fricassee of asparagus, morel mushrooms and roast chicken wings. Plump, tender griddled scallops are accompanied by a cod brandade whose delicate saltiness is a perfect counterpoint for the subtle sweetness of the molluscs. A garnish of wafer-thin crisp pancetta and a liberal dribble of saffron oil completes a wonderful taste sensation. Main courses follow in the same vein with poached Tweed salmon, lobster potatoes (potato purée with a dice of lobster, as well as tiny crispy bits of pancetta and drops of lobster oil) and veal stock reduction, griddled snapper with chorizo, fennel and olive oil, Chinese-spiced crispy roast duck and slow-cooked knuckle of veal with pasta and herbs. Finish on a high note with a warm bitter chocolate tart with coconut ice cream, strawberry 'club sandwich' with a passion fruit sauce or a hazelnut rice pudding with a honey ice cream. Good prices on a wine list that includes a separate selection of around two dozen under £20, though the whole list is most certainly worth browsing through. *Seats 50. L 12-2 D 7-10.45. Closed L Sat, all Sun, Bank Holidays, 2 weeks Aug. Set L £15/£17. Access, Amex, Diners, Visa.*

Set menu prices may not always include service or wine.

NEWCASTLE-UPON-TYNE   Vermont Hotel   72%   £80

Tel 0191-233 1010 Fax 0191-233 1234   Map 5 E2   **HR**
Castle Garth Newcastle-upon-Tyne Tyne & Wear NE1 1RQ

Plumb in the city centre next to the castle and sharing the same courtyard as the Moot Hall (Law Courts) the Vermont is Newcastle's newest luxury hotel. Built of Portland stone in 1910 on the side of a hill, it was originally the County Hall building. It comprises 12 floors and has the unusual aspect that the main entrance, leading to reception, the spacious lounge and hotel bar and brasserie, is on the 6th floor. A further entrance is down below on Dean Street, with Martha's bar and bistro. Public rooms are elegantly furnished and there are plenty of staff on hand to attend to one's needs. Bedrooms have a uniform decor of smart, contemporary mahogany furniture with ample writing space, a settee and an armchair. Of good size, they are also well equipped, featuring a mini-bar, satellite TV and fresh fruit among a range of useful amenities. There is also excellent room service. Bedrooms additionally offer very good views across the river taking in the Tyne Bridge as well as the High Level Bridge. No dogs. *Rooms 134. Gym, solarium, beauty salon, news kiosk. Access, Amex, Diners, Visa.*

Blue Room   £80

On the third floor of the hotel, with midnight blue walls, cream upholstery and soft lighting, the main hotel restaurant is an elegant and sophisticated setting for Stephen Waite's enjoyable cooking. The imaginative menu offers starters such as an individual shortcrust pie filled with scallops, truffle and a champagne sauce, parfait of chicken and goose livers or feuillantine of wild mushrooms and asparagus. Main dishes range from roast monkfish with olives and pavé of lamb with sweetbreads to breast of guinea fowl braised in red wine and port served with truffled pommes purée, braised vegetables and pulses. To finish there's a tarte tatin or nougatine parfait with caramelised honey and citrus zest speckled with almonds and pistachios and served with a raspberry sauce or poached pears in syrup with toffee ice cream. *Seats 90. L 12.30-2.30 D 7-10. Closed Sun & Mon. Set D £27.50. Access, Amex, Diners, Visa.*

Brasserie   £65

A smart, brightly-lit room with a varied choice of imaginative, mostly modern, Mediterranean-style dishes. Begin with, for example, carpaccio of beef, wild mushroom risotto with parmesan and game chips, tagliatelle carbonara or warm tomato and mozzarella tart with a hazelnut salad. Main courses include steamed salmon with shredded vegetables and a tomato and chive vinaigrette, noisettes of lamb with couscous and a Provençal sauce and, from the grill, chicken breast with a lemon and thyme broth. Among the desserts is an excellent pecan crème brulée. Other choices could be hot chocolate pudding with vanilla ice cream and hot apple pie with almond cream. *Seats 145. Open 10.30-3 & 6-midnight. Set L £13.50 Set D £15.50.*

NEWCASTLE-UPON-TYNE AIRPORT   Moat House   62%   £114

Tel 01661 824911   Fax 01661 860157   Map 5 E2   **H**
Woolsington Newcastle-upon-Tyne Tyne & Wear NE13 8DJ

Low-rise modern redbrick hotel just north of the Tyne Tunnel. Conference/banqueting facilities for 400/350. Children up to the age of 16 are accommodated free in parents' room. 22 rooms are reserved for non-smokers, all are sound-proofed. Guests have temporary membership of the Ponteland Leisure Centre about two miles away. Free parking throughout your holiday if you stay the night here before flying off from the airport – free transport to the terminal. *Rooms 100. Access, Amex, Diners, Visa.*

NEWLYN   Higher Faugan   62%   £86

Tel 01736 62076   Fax 01736 51648   Map 12 A4   **H**
Newlyn nr Penzance Cornwall TR18 5NS

Built by Stanhope Forbes at the turn of the century, this sturdy greystone house stands at the end of a winding drive in 10 acres of lawns and woodland. Day rooms are peaceful and traditional, and the best bedrooms feature Victorian or Edwardian furnishings; rooms with superior views attract a small supplement. Children under 12 sharing parents' room stay free. *Rooms 12. Garden, outdoor swimming pool, tennis, keep-fit equipment, putting, sun beds, snooker, games room. Access, Amex, Diners, Visa.*

NEWMARKET   Heath Court Hotel   62%   £70

Tel 01638 667171   Fax 01638 666533   Map 10 B3   **H**
Moulton Road Newmarket Suffolk CB8 8DY

Modern hotel behind the town clock tower, with well-appointed bedrooms, a lounge with board games and versatile function rooms (up to 70 for conferences, 120 for banquets). Children up to 6 stay free in parents' room. *Rooms 44. Access, Amex, Diners, Visa.*

NEWMARKET   White Hart   60%   £50

Tel 01638 663051   Fax 01638 667284   Map 10 B3   **H**
High Street Newmarket Suffolk CB8 8JP

A redbrick hotel in the High Street opposite the Jockey Club. Comfortable bedrooms have either an art deco or a country look. Conferences for up to 120 delegates. *Rooms 23. Access, Amex, Diners, Visa.*

NEWQUAY   Hotel Bristol   64%   £80

Tel 01637 875181   Fax 01637 879347   Map 12 B3   **H**
Narrowcliff Newquay Cornwall TR7 2PQ

The Young family, at the helm since the hotel opened in 1927, put courtesy and comfort high on their list of priorities. The redbrick Bristol enjoys a fine situation overlooking the sea and the beach (some distance below the cliff), and there are splendid views from many of the bedrooms; these come in various styles, some traditional, others more modern. There are also some self-catering holiday houses. Day rooms provide ample space to relax over a drink, a chat or one of the board games available from reception. Conferences (for up to 250 delegates) and banquets (up to 265) are catered for. Parking for 100 cars and 5 lock-up garages available behind the hotel. *Rooms 74. Indoor swimming pool, sauna, solarium, beauty & hair salon, games room, snooker. Access, Amex, Diners, Visa.*

Consult the blue pages for summary tables and lists of recommended establishments.

NEWQUAY   Hotel Riviera   63%   £83

Tel 01637 874251   Fax 01637 850823   Map 12 B3   **H**
Lusty Glaze Road Newquay Cornwall TR7 3AA

Popular for family holidays, functions and conferences (for around 120), the hotel overlooks a lovely stretch of coastline. Three bars, a lounge and a garden provide plenty of space to relax, and in summer there's evening entertainment. Most of the bedrooms enjoy sea views. Free parking for 60 cars. **Rooms 50.** *Garden, outdoor swimming pool, squash, sauna, snooker, children's playroom and play area. Access, Amex, Diners, Visa.*

Set menu prices may not always include service or wine.

NEWTON ABBOT   Passage House   65%   £75

Tel 01626 55515   Fax 01626 63336   Map 13 D3   **H**
Hackney Lane Kingsteignton Newton Abbot Devon TQ12 3QH

Follow the racecourse signs from the A380 to find this modern hotel, which enjoys fine views along the Teign estuary. Contemporary decor, spacious bedrooms, friendly staff and purpose-built spa and conference facilities. Self-catering apartments are also available. **Rooms 38.** *Garden, indoor swimming pool, keep-fit equipment, sauna, spa bath, steam room, solarium. Access, Amex, Diners, Visa.*

NEWTON SOLNEY   Jarvis Newton Park   67%   £112

Tel 01283 703568   Fax 01283 703214   Map 6 C3   **H**
Newton Solney Burton-on-Trent Derbyshire DE15 0SS

Three miles from the centre of Burton-on-Trent, the 17th-century, creeper-clad Newton Park enjoys a peaceful setting in landscaped grounds overlooking the river. Conference facilities for up to 120 delegates. **Rooms 50.** *Garden, croquet. Closed 3 days Christmas. Access, Amex, Diners, Visa.*

NIDD   Nidd Hall   76%   £120

Tel 01423 771598   Fax 01423 770931   Map 6 C1   **H**
Nidd nr Harrogate North Yorkshire HG3 3BN

Follow the signs to Nidd on the B6165 a few miles north of Harrogate off the A61. A long tree-lined drive leads up to this stately mansion set in 45 acres of parkland which includes a splendid three-acre lake used for fishing and boating. The entrance hall, surmounted by a glass cupola, is impressive with its white marble floor and very summery yellow ragged walls hung with copies of old masters. Public rooms are very spacious and comfortable with ample seating. The decor is of a reasonably high standard, the style reminiscent of a lived-in country house. Best of the bedrooms are in the main house, those at the front enjoying wonderful vistas, through the trees and over the seemingly uninhabited surrounding countryside. The quite separate courtyard rooms were converted a few years ago from stables and are pleasant enough but not quite as appealing as the 38 in the Hall. All are attractively furnished in a traditional style with a plethora of colourful fabrics and mahogany furniture, and all are well equipped. Breakfasts are from a hot and cold buffet, though special requests are eagerly complied with. Particularly well geared-up for families, the hotel has its own nursery facilities that can provide everything from baby-sitting to a private nanny and out in the grounds there's a paddock of child-friendly animals including various goats, a small pony and 'Bambi' deer. **Rooms 59.** *Garden, croquet, tennis, indoor swimming pool, children's splash pool, gym, sauna, sun beds, beauty salon, squash, snooker, table tennis, children's outdoor playground, boating. Access, Amex, Diners, Visa.*

Lodges are now listed by county in the reference section

NORTH HARROW — Percy's — £70

Tel 0181-427 2021 Fax 0181-427 8134   Map 15 E2   **R**
66 Station Road North Harrow Middlesex HA2 7SJ

Almost next to North Harrow station and originally a wine bar, Percy's is now a restaurant with a cool, summery decor. Tony Bricknell-Webb looks after the front of house while his wife Tina cooks. She is completely self-taught and uses produce originating primarily from the South-West. They even have their own 40-acre farm in North Devon and are self-sufficient in herbs and most vegetables. Game, in season, and fish are particularly strong points, the fish arriving daily to ensure as near-perfect freshness as possible. The cooking is involved, with sometimes unusual and interesting combinations, for example king prawns with bacon and papaya and pan-fried chicken with mango, pineapple, coriander and lime, in a lightly spiced coconut cream sauce. Some more straightforward main courses include breast of pheasant with cranberry and chestnut stuffing, wild venison steak cooked pink with mild peppercorn sauce and roast rack of Welsh lamb; with lemon tart, tropical fruit meringue or chocolate and rum truffle pudding for dessert. Organic coffee to finish. A non-smoking restaurant. No children under 10. **Seats** 70. *Parties 10. L 12-2.30 D 6.30-10.30. Closed Sun & Mon, 1 week Christmas. Access, Amex, Diners, Visa.*

NORTH HUISH — Brookdale House — 69% — £90

Tel 01548 821661   Fax 01548 821606   Map 13 D3   **H**
North Huish nr South Brent Devon TQ10 9NR

A Tudor-Gothic style Victorian rectory set in 2½ acres of gardens (which include a pretty waterfall), within the beautiful South Hams area. The main day room is a most civilised lounge, with real log fire when needed, where drinks are also served. Antique-furnished bedrooms vary somewhat in size; three are in an adjacent cottage, but all are equally appealing with decor featuring soft floral fabrics set off by plain walls. Fresh fruit, flowers and magazines add a homely touch and in the evening beds are turned down, curtains drawn and bedside lights turned on. Room service is offered throughout the day and evening and good cooked breakfasts make a good start to the day. **Rooms** 8. *Garden. Access, Amex, Diners, Visa.*

We welcome bona fide complaints and recommendations on the tear-out pages at the back of the book for readers' comments. They are followed up by our professional team.

NORTH PETHERTON — Walnut Tree Inn — 65% — £68

Tel 01278 662255   Fax 01278 663946   Map 13 E2   **H**
Fore Street North Petherton nr Bridgwater Somerset TA6 6QA

A carefully modernised, 18th-century coaching inn on the A38 (one mile from J25 M5), with conference and function facilities. Business people will appreciate the good work space in both standard and larger Executive bedrooms, while more romantically-inclined weekenders may plump for one of the spacious four-poster suites. Five rooms have been added since last year. Friendly service from resident proprietors. Conference/banqueting facilities for 90/80. Weekend tariff reductions. **Rooms** 33. *Garden, sun beds. Access, Amex, Diners, Visa.*

NORTH STIFFORD — Stifford Moat House — 61% — £93

Tel 01708 719988   Fax 01375 390426   Map 11 B4   **H**
High Road North Stifford nr Grays Essex RM16 1UE

Based on a Georgian mansion, the Stifford Moat House stands in 6 acres of grounds next to the A13 about one mile east of junction 30/31 of the M25. Most bedrooms are in a modern block and those in the original building are very similar. Children up to 16 stay free in parents' room. Conferencing for up to 530 delegates. **Rooms** 96. *Garden, tennis, pétanque. Closed 27-30 Dec. Access, Amex, Diners, Visa.*

NORTH STOKE   Springs Hotel   70%   £155

Tel 01491 836687   Fax 01491 836877   Map 15 D2   **H**
Wallingford Road North Stoke Oxfordshire OX9 6BE

The thirty acres of grounds which surround the mock-Tudor building include a spring-fed lake from which it gets its name. Public areas include a panelled lounge of old-world appeal and a small cosy bar. Bedrooms generally are spacious and pleasantly appointed with quality fabrics, smart furniture and subtle colours; best are those with private balconies. 24hr room service. No dogs. The hotel stands halfway between the M4 (J8/9) and the M40 (J6) between Goring and Crowmarsh on the B4009 New owners as we went to press.. *Rooms 38. Garden, putting, croquet, outdoor swimming pool, sauna, tennis. Access, Amex, Diners, Visa.*

NORTHAMPTON   Courtyard by Marriott   65%   £80

Tel 01604 22777   Fax 01604 35454   Map 15 D1   **H**
Bedford Road Northampton Northamptonshire NN4 7YF

Five minutes from Junction 15 of the M1, just off the A45 alongside the A428, one mile from the town centre. Large bedrooms, with desks plus fax and data sockets. Children up to 17 free in parents' room, and families are well catered for. Modern meeting rooms for up to 40. Plenty of free, secure parking. *Rooms 104. Garden, keep-fit equipment, coffee shop (11am-10.15pm). Access, Amex, Diners, Visa.*

NORTHAMPTON   Moat House   63%   £112

Tel 01604 739988   Fax 01604 230614   Map 15 D1   **H**
Silver Street Northampton Northamptonshire NN1 2TA

A tall and distinctive blue and white building in the town centre. Numerous function and meeting rooms (the largest, the Buckingham Suite, can accommodate 600) make it a popular conference venue. Considerable tariff reductions at weekends. All bedrooms have been refurbished this year; a gym was being planned as we went to press. *Rooms 140. Access, Amex, Diners, Visa.*

NORTHAMPTON   Stakis Country Court   68%   £124

Tel 01604 700666   Fax 01604 702850   Map 15 D1   **H**
100 Watering Lane Collingtree Northampton Northamptonshire NN4 0XW

Just a few hundred yards from Junction 15 of the M1, this very modern business-oriented hotel is built around a central courtyard with a fountain. Large bedrooms, all with king-size beds, are bright and summery with floral fabrics; each has a spacious work desk in addition to the usual unit furniture. Midweek trade tends to be business oriented while the weekends are more family-minded. *Rooms 139. Garden, indoor swimming pool, gym, sauna, steam room, spa bath, solarium, beautician. Access, Amex, Diners, Visa.*

NORTHAMPTON   Swallow Hotel   72%   £102

Tel 01604 768700   Fax 01604 769011   Map 15 D1   **H**
Eagle Drive Northampton Northamptonshire NN4 7HW

The low-rise, modern red-brick hotel is set in landscaped grounds, next to the Delapre Lake and golf course, some three miles east from Junction 15 of the M1 on the A45. Inside, the public areas are stylishly contemporary: a marble foyer with black leather seating, a sunny conservatory lounge with patio doors to the gardens, and an Oriental-themed bar. Energy-saving bedrooms (the keycard controls the electricity) are smart and practical, offering the usual amenities such as satellite TV, mini-bar, trouser press, iron and board. 40% designated no smoking, two specially designed for disabled guests, several interconnecting and therefore particularly suitable for families. Bathrooms (some with bidet) are on the small side, but kept exceptionally clean, confirming the excellent housekeeping encountered throughout the hotel. Fresh grapefruit and orange segments lift breakfast above the ordinary. Conference and banqueting facilities for up to 200. Next door to the hotel is the Cambridge Building, a purpose-built management training centre with observation studios, one-way mirrors and hi-tech sound system. *Rooms 120. Garden, indoor swimming pool, sauna, sun beds, spa bath, steam room, keep-fit equipment. Access, Amex, Diners, Visa.*

Set menu prices may not always include service or wine.

NORTHAMPTON   Westone Hotel   59%   £95

Tel 01604 739955   Fax 01604 415023   Map 15 D1   **H**
Ashley Way Weston Favell Northampton Northamptonshire NN3 3EA

Built in 1914, the Westone is a warm, honey-coloured stone mansion set in its own grounds off the A4500 to the east of town. Public rooms have some interesting architectural features and bedrooms are well equipped with modern comforts. Children up to 14 stay free in parents' room. Theatre-style conferences for up to 180. No dogs in the main house. Note that the hotel (formerly a Moat House) no longer has any leisure facilities. *Rooms 66. Garden. Access, Amex, Diners, Visa.*

NORTHLEACH   Old Woolhouse   ★   £90

Tel 01451 860366   Map 14 C2   **R**
Market Place Northleach Gloucestershire GL54 3EE

Time has definitely not marched on here, and the restaurant is all the better for it. Why change a successful formula? A husband and wife team, Jacques Astic in the kitchen, Jenny at front of house; a lovely Cotswold-stone building, intimate within with a low ceiling and old timbers, an open fireplace, antiques, and tables set with gleaming silver and household china. The kitchen is domestic in size, indeed the entire restaurant is no larger than a country house dining-room, but therein lies the charm of the place. The menu, usually read out at 8pm, changes daily depending on the freshest ingredients available; fish, for instance, relies on the catch delivered, producing, perhaps, a dish of turbot, mussels and scallops with a very spicy sauce. Jacques is not averse to cooking offal: calf's sweetbreads and kidneys in cassis are a house speciality. *Poulet au porto* is a favourite and game appears notably in *lièvre à la royale*. Desserts such as *tarte aux pruneaux* and almond meringue *daquoise* with an apricot sauce are not to be missed. First-class bread and coffee, plus super wines – ask, there are some real bargains to be had. *Seats 18. D only 8-9.30. Closed Sun, Mon & 1 week Christmas. Set D £37.50. No credit cards.*

NORTHLEACH   Wickens   £55

Tel 01451 860421   Map 14 C2   **R**
Market Place Northleach Gloucestershire GL54 3EJ

Right in middle of one side of the Market Square of this quintessentially Cotswold village is Chris and Joanna Wicken's typically English restaurant. Menus change with the seasons, at least weekly, and each month they also carry a special red and white wine selection. From the light luncheon menu you can put together as many or as few courses as you like. Typical spring dinner offerings might be a salad of mixed leaves with marinated herring, then a Cotswold cassoulet of local lamb, pork and sausages with haricot beans and vegetables in a cider gravy, with one of Joanna's luscious puddings to finish. There's usually a witty literary quote on the menu. Extensive range of English wines on the list. No smoking. *Seats 38. Parties 20. L 12-1.30 (summer only) D 7.20-8.45. Closed Sun & Mon. Set D £19.50. Access, Amex, Visa.*

> We welcome bona fide complaints and recommendations on the tear-out pages at the back of the book for readers' comments. They are followed up by our professional team.

NORTHWICH   Friendly Floatel   56%   £75

Tel 01606 44443   Fax 01606 42596   Map 6 B2   **H**
London Road Northwich Cheshire CW9 5HD

A novel hotel that floats in the basin where the Rivers Dane and Weaver meet in the centre of town. Cabins (bedrooms) are not large but are practical and ship-shape with good, well-lit workspace. All but the six Premier Plus rooms (two with four-posters) have shower and WC only; one room is equipped for disabled guests. Ask for a river view, there's no extra charge. Main day room is a pleasant panelled bar with rattan furniture. Landlubbers should note that although it's normally rock steady there can be some movement in rough weather. Although not advertised, room service is available throughout the day and evening. Children under 12 share parents' room free. Parking for 100 cars. *Rooms 60. Keep-fit equipment, sauna, sun bed. Access, Amex, Diners, Visa.*

| NORTHWICH | Hartford Hall | 63% | £75 |

Tel 01606 75711   Fax 01606 782285   Map 6 B2   **H**
School Lane Hartford Northwich Cheshire CW8 1PW

Mock-Victorian is the style of the day rooms at this 16th-century gabled house just off the A556 (M56 Junction 7, M6 Junction 19). Good desk space in the bedrooms, where children up to 7 can stay free if sharing with their parents. Parking for 60 cars. *Rooms 20. Garden. Access, Amex, Diners, Visa.*

| NORTHWICH | Nunsmere Hall | 77% | £147 |

Tel 01606 889100   Fax 01606 889055   Map 6 B2   **HR**
Tarporley Road Oakmere Northwich Cheshire CW8 2ES

Almost surrounded by a 60-acre lake, turn-of-the-century Nunsmere Hall enjoys a delightfully secluded setting off the A49 in Delamere Forest. A fine galleried entrance hall sets the tone for appealing day rooms which include a comfortable, oak-panelled bar, leather-furnished library and a lounge with a huge floral centrepiece. Notably large, antique-furnished bedrooms are individually decorated, with comfortable sitting areas. Some rooms boast four-posters. Sybaritic bathrooms, many with separate shower cubicle in addition to a large tub, all have bidets, generous towelling and attractive basins sunk into marble-topped wash stands. Rooms are properly serviced in the evenings and there is 24hr room service. No dogs. Previously listed under Sandiway. *Rooms 32. Garden, croquet. Access, Amex, Diners, Visa.*

Garden Room Restaurant   £70

The restaurant features brass chandeliers hanging from the moulded plaster ceiling and floor-length undercloths on tables which boast pretty, high-quality tableware. Chef Paul Kitching's style is modern on a classical base, producing such dishes as braised quail with Parma ham and shallots, fish terrine with asparagus, chargrilled salmon *dugléré*, and roasted fillet of beef with sun-dried tomatoes and tarragon sauce. Desserts might include orange mousse with tangerine ice cream, or a layered meringue filled with a white and dark chocolate bavarois served with sliced caramelised bananas and lime syrup. There's a separate vegetarian menu. British farmhouse cheeses are served with home-made date and walnut bread. Particularly good *amuse gueule* arrive with the menu. There are few half bottles on the decent wine list, which is notable for some good New world bottles. A light menu is served in the lounge or on the terrace throughout the day. No smoking. A harpist plays on Saturday night. *Seats 48. Parties 10. Private Room 42. L 12-2 D 7-10. Set L from £16.95 (Sun £18.50) Set D from £28.50.*

| NORTON | Hundred House Hotel | £69 |

Tel 01952 730353   Fax 01952 730355   Map 6 B4   **IR**
Norton nr Shifnal Shropshire TF11 9EE

A creeper-covered, redbrick Georgian inn standing alongside the A442. Personally run by the Phillips family, it has great charm, with mellow brick walls, stained glass, colourful patchwork, leather upholstery and (hanging from the ceiling beams) dozens of bunches of dried flowers and herbs, all from Sylvia's splendid garden, which you are encouraged to visit. Enchanting antique-furnished bedrooms have lots of nice touches like patchwork bedcovers (often on antique brass beds), fresh flowers and pot-pourri. All have good en-suite bathrooms and room service of drinks and light snacks is available throughout the day and evening. *Rooms 10. Garden. Access, Amex, Visa.*

Restaurant   £65

There's a distinctly modern touch to the dishes on Stuart Phillips' sensibly short à la carte menu. Salad of duck confit on a red cabbage salad, warm roulade of salmon and sole served with a crayfish and tarragon sauce (their own herbs are well used and appear in the little posy of flowers on each table), fillet of beef topped with marinated goat's cheese with balsamic sauce, rack of lamb braised in a mustard sauce with shallots and baby turnips served with lentils show the style. Fish dishes, fillet of cod with spinach and a parsley sauce for example, appear on the list of the day's specials. Notably good puds range from tarte tatin and crème brulée to iced prune and armangac terrine with hot chocolate sauce and tiramisu. *Seats 60. Parties 12. Private Room 30. L 12-2.30 D 6.15-10 (Sun 7-9).*

NORWICH   Adlard's   ★   £85

Tel 01603 633522   Map 10 C1   **R**
79 Upper St Giles Street Norwich Norfolk NR2 1AB

Adlard's is a classic example of a restaurant run by a thoroughly dedicated chef-patron and his wife – David and Mary Adlard. Crisp white linen tablecloths add a classic touch and a cosy and welcoming air pervades the whole restaurant. David Adlard's cooking, modern British with French undertones, makes the most of prime seasonal produce, and his passionate zeal in sourcing and synergising ingredients is apparent in every dish. Lunchtime brings a two- or three-course fixed-price menu that offers remarkable value for money with such dishes as a tart of softly boiled quail's eggs with mushroom duxelles; warm smoked salmon mousse with horseradish and crème fraiche; herb-crusted cod with celeriac and saffron purée, tapénade sauce and tagliatelle; and navarin of lamb. The evening choice is also four or five dishes per course, with either individual prices per course or a set price for three or four courses. Sauté of duck foie gras with brown lentils and duck sauce infused with sherry vinegar is well worth the small supplement as a starter, and main courses are typified by breast of pheasant on parsnip and potato purée with caramelised apple and five spice sauce, or rack of lamb with glazed winter vegetables, boulangère potatoes and thyme cream sauce. Superb cheeses or a salad, then an 'assiette' of chocolate, or savarin of Yorkshire rhubarb sorbet. Super half bottle selection on a quite marvellous wine list that features the New World and Europe equally. Very fair prices, especially among the 'bin beginnings'. East of England regional winner, Cellar of the Year. No smoking until after the main course. *Seats 40. L 12.30-1.45 D 7.30-10.30. Closed L Mon, all Sun. Set L £13.50/£16.50 Set D £27.50/£31/£34. Access, Amex, Visa.*

NORWICH   Brasted's   £60

Tel 01603 625949   Map 10 C1   **R**
8-10 St Andrew's Hill Norwich Norfolk NR2 1DS

John Brasted's cosy little restaurant has just benefited from a complete refurbishment including armchairs replacing the former pine cottage chairs. Tucked away in the old part of the city, it's only a short walk from both Cathedral and Castle. Chef Adrian Clarke's carefully-planned menus take their inspiration from all over the place with dishes like cassoulet, Thai crab cake spiced with chili, ginger and fresh coriander, vegetable korma on Basmati rice and beef stroganoff (a speciality) sharing the carte with such creations as a boned rack of lamb rolled around lemon zest, herbs and pine nuts, Loch Fyne langoustines on a bed of noodles and a haddock and leek tart with watercress sauce. England is not forgotten either with a classic steak and kidney pudding or perhaps more novel interpretations like a twice-baked Stilton soufflé or a warm salad of fish and chips, the last two found among the starters. There's always a grilled fish of the day and game is a speciality in season. Desserts might inlcude treacle tart, steamed ginger pudding and pavlova; or go for a savoury like angels on horseback or Welsh rarebit. The thoughtful and fairly-priced wine list includes a vintage chart and notes on the house selection. *Seats 22. Parties 12. L 12-2 D 7-9.30. Closed L Sat, all Sun & Bank Holidays. Set L £8.50/£12.50/£16. Access, Amex, Diners, Visa.*

NORWICH   Forte Posthouse   63%   £72

Tel 01603 56431   Fax 01603 506400   Map 10 C1   **H**
Ipswich Road Norwich Norfolk NR4 6EP

Modern building in secluded grounds just off the A140, to the south of town. Under-16s share their parents' room free; 54 rooms have an extra bed. The largest of several conference rooms can hold up to 100 delegates theatre-style. *Rooms 116. Garden, indoor swimming pool, gym, sauna, spa bath, solarium, outdoor children's play area. Access, Amex, Diners, Visa.*

NORWICH   Friendly Hotel   60%   £77

Tel 01603 741161   Fax 01603 741500   Map 10 C1   **H**
2 Barnard Road Bowthorpe Norwich Norfolk NR5 9JB

Modern, purpose-built, low-rise hotel 4 miles west of the city centre, on the A1074, offering straightforward accommodation. Fully-equipped leisure centre; conference and banqueting facilities for up to 250. Easy parking. *Rooms 80. Indoor swimming pool, gym, spa bath, sauna, steam room, sun bed. Access, Amex, Diners, Visa.*

NORWICH   Greens Seafood Restaurant   £60

Tel 01603 623733   Fax 01603 615268   Map 10 C1   **R**
82 Upper St Giles Street Norwich Norfolk NR2 1LT

Local supplies of fresh fish form the basis of the menu at Dennis Crompton's popular restaurant with appropriate nautical decor. Crab and avocado, oysters, deep-fried squid or herring fillet might get a meal under way, while main courses run from cod with a shrimp butter sauce to skate with black butter, basil-sauced salmon and fresh lobster. Simple sweets; well-chosen, fairly-priced wines. *Seats 48. L 12.15-2.15 D 7-10.45. Closed L Sat, all Sun & Mon, Bank Holidays, 1 week Christmas. Set L £12.50/£15. Access, Visa.*

NORWICH   Marco's   £80

Tel 01603 624044   Map 10 C1   **R**
17 Pottergate Norwich Norfolk NR2 1DS

Here since 1970, Marco Vessalio still greets diners from the door of his kitchen, the master of all he surveys; his is quintessential provincial Italian food, steadfastly untrendy, with wonderful ingredients unfailingly well cooked. Cannelloni filled with spinach and ricotta, served with a pistachio sauce, potato pancake with sour cream and smoked salmon or wild boar bresaola with buffalo mozzarella, olive oil and lemon juice could be your starter, followed perhaps by steamed salmon fillet with a lemon cream sauce, baked saddle of lamb with a redcurrant, mint and orange sauce or chicken breast with onion, ginger, garlic, sweet peppers, king prawns, white wine and a touch of tomato sauce. Desserts include a classic zabaglione and Italian style bread-and-butter pudding (*budino di pane*). Few half bottles on the all Italian wine list (champagnes apart). Tasting notes are a help. No smoking in the dining-room, but you may indulge in the Marco Polo bar lounge. *Seats 22. Parties 12. L 12-2 D 7-10. Closed Sun & Mon, last 2 weeks Sep & first week Oct. Set L £14. Access, Amex, Diners, Visa.*

NORWICH   Hotel Nelson   65%   £87

Tel 01603 760260   Fax 01603 620008   Map 10 C1   **H**
Prince of Wales Road Norwich Norfolk NR1 1DX

Keep one eye open for the railway station, opposite which stands this modern red-brick hotel alongside the River Wensum. Picture windows in the spacious lounge overlook the water and one of the two bars displays memorabilia of Nelson's flagship Victory. Best bedrooms include a sitting area and some have private balconies. One twin-bedded room is adapted for the use of disabled guests, with its own car-parking space and entrance from the car park. The largest of five conference rooms can accommodate up to 90 delegates. *Rooms 132. Garden, indoor swimming pool, gym, sauna, steam room, spa bath, solarium, beauty & hair salon. Access, Amex, Diners, Visa.*

NORWICH   Hotel Norwich   62%   £73

Tel 01603 787260   Fax 01603 400466   Map 10 C1   **H**
121 Boundary Road Norwich Norfolk NR3 2BA

Modern, privately-run redbrick hotel on the outer ring road (A47) north-east of the city. Roomy, well-equipped bedrooms with ample writing surfaces, some undergoing refurbishment as we went to press. Popular for functions, with facilities for around 300 in 13 different rooms. Children under 16 stay free in parents' room. 24hr room service. Sister establishment to the Hotel Nelson (see entry). No dogs. *Rooms 107. Indoor swimming pool, gym, spa bath, sauna, solarium. Access, Amex, Diners, Visa.*

Set menu prices may not always include service or wine.

NORWICH Sport Village Hotel 63% £69

Tel 01603 788898 Fax 01603 406845   Map 10 C1   **H**
Drayton High Road Hellesdon Norwich Norfolk NR6 5DU

Practical, roomy bedrooms are at the centre of a very extensive sports complex situated just off the outer Norwich ring road on the A1067 to Fakenham. All the rooms have en-suite facilities, half showers, half tubs. Children up to 16 share parents' room free. Sporting facilities are the most impressive feature, with over 60 sports and activities available. They include seven squash courts and no less than a dozen tennis courts, seven of them indoors. Hotel guests share the lively open-plan bar, bistro and restaurant with the other users of the complex. The Aquapark swimming complex includes a competition pool, a shallow, warm playpool with two slides and rapids and a paddling pool for toddlers. There's a soft play area for the very young. All the rooms are suitable for families and cots, potties, nappies, high-chairs and baby food can be provided; supervised creche for six hours a week. No dogs. Conference facilities for thousands. Dinosaur Park (open mid Apr-Nov) is 9 miles away. *Rooms 55. Garden, indoor swimming pool, gym, squash, sauna, steam room, solarium, spa bath, multi-sports hall, aerobics, beauty salon, tennis, badminton, snooker. Access, Amex, Diners, Visa.*

Lodges are now listed by county in the reference section

NORWICH Sprowston Manor 69% £102

Tel 01603 410871 Fax 01603 423911   Map 10 C1   **H**
Sprowston Park Wroxham Road Norwich Norfolk NR7 8RP

Built around a 16th-century manor house, once the home of the Gurney banking family, this extended hotel by the A1151 contains a wealth of up-to-date facilities. A leisure club is at the heart of the most recent development, resplendent with palms and stone balustrades. Meeting and conference rooms (catering for up to 120 theatre-style) are kept discreetly apart from the main hotel day rooms, with a separate entrance to the ballroom. Bedrooms benefit from views of the surrounding parkland, home to the adjacent Sprowston Golf Club; they also combine stylish fitted furniture and floral fabrics with up-to-date accessories including mini-bars and wall safes. Eight bedrooms are in the original manor house. Children under 16 stay free in parents' room. *Rooms 94. Garden, golf (18), indoor swimming pool & children's splash pool, spa bath, sauna, solarium, beauty salon, gym. Access, Amex, Diners, Visa.*

NORWICH AIRPORT Stakis Ambassador 65% £82

Tel 01603 410544 Fax 01603 789935   Map 10C1   **H**
Cromer Road Norwich Airport Norwich Norfolk NR6 6JA

Modern redbrick hotel whose aeronautical associations include the Concorde Bar and a replica Spitfire in the garden. Practical accommodation in decent-sized bedrooms; the honeymoon suites feature four-poster beds and jacuzzis. Children up to 14 stay free in parents' room; purpose-built facility for conferences and banquets (up to 500/400). *Rooms 108. Indoor swimming pool, gym, sauna, steam room, solarium, whirlpool bath. Access, Amex, Diners, Visa.*

NOTTINGHAM Forte Crest 70% £100

Tel 0115 947 0131 Fax 0115 948 4366   Map 7 D3   **H**
St James's Street Nottingham Nottinghamshire NG1 6BN

Large city-centre hotel whose higher-floor rooms have good views. Public areas include a striking black and white decorated foyer. Extensive conference and function rooms (catering for up to 600). Free NCP parking. Recent months have seen refurbishments to the bar and the opening of a new bar and restaurant. *Rooms 130. Access, Amex, Diners, Visa.*

NOTTINGHAM Forte Posthouse 61% £72

Tel 0115 939 7800 Fax 0115 949 0469   Map 7 D3   **H**
Bostocks Lane Sandiacre Nottingham Nottinghamshire NG10 5NJ

One of the original Posthouses, in a residential area close to Junction 25 of the M1. Practical accommodation plus conference/meeting rooms (maximum 60). Children's playroom at weekends. *Rooms 93. Garden. Access, Amex, Diners, Visa.*

NOTTINGHAM — Higoi — £50

Tel 0115 942 3379   Map 7 D3   **R**
57 Lenton Boulevard Nottingham Nottinghamshire NG7 2FQ

Japanese chef Mr Kato, assisted by his English wife, continues to educate customers in the delights of his native cooking. Helpful and informative staff will guide you through the complete range of specialities and menus. *Teriyaki, shogoyaki* and *tempura* dinners are preceded by selected hors d'oeuvre; choice of à la carte or set meals (book two days ahead for the multi-course Kaiseki feast). *Seats 35. L 12-2 D 6.30-10 (Sun to 9.30). Closed L Sun-Thur, all Bank Holiday Mon, 3 days Christmas. Set L £6.90/£8.90 Set D from £17.95. Access, Amex, Diners, Visa.*

Lodges are now listed by county in the reference section

NOTTINGHAM — Holiday Inn Garden Court — 65% — £80

Tel 0115 950 0600   Fax 0115 950 0433   Map 7 D3   **H**
Castle Marina Park Nottingham Nottinghamshire NG7 1GX

Spacious rooms with large beds are a big plus at this bright modern hotel off the A6005, near the marina; good value, too – particularly for families, as the room price covers up to four occupants. Significant tariff reductions at weekends. *Rooms 100. Access, Amex, Diners, Visa.*

NOTTINGHAM — Man Ho — £40

Tel 0115 947 4729   Map 7 D3   **R**
35 Pelham Street Nottingham Nottinghamshire NG1 2EA

A city-centre restaurant specialising in the cooking of Canton, Peking and Szechuan. At lunchtime, the busiest period, the emphasis is very much on the selection of some 60 dim sum dishes. *Seats 156. Meals 12-11.30. Set meals from £13.50 (min 2). Access, Amex, Diners, Visa.*

NOTTINGHAM — Moat House — 59% — £99

Tel 0115 935 9988   Fax 0115 969 1506   Map 7 D3   **H**
Mansfield Road Nottingham Nottinghamshire NG5 2BT

A modern block hotel to the north of the city centre. Conferences/banqueting for up to 200/160. Children up to 12 free in parents' room. 50% of bedrooms designated non-smoking. Not to be confused with the Royal Moat House nearer the heart of the city. *Rooms 172. Access, Amex, Diners, Visa.*

NOTTINGHAM — Novotel — 62% — £58

Tel 0115 946 5111   Fax 0115 946 5900   Map 7 D3   **H**
Bostock Lane Long Eaton Nottingham Nottinghamshire NG10 4EP

Practical, modern accommodation just off junction 25 of the M1. Up to two children under 16 stay free of charge (inc breakfast) when sharing their parents' room. 46 rooms are reserved for non-smokers. The hotel restaurant is open for à la carte service from 6am to midnight. Conference facilities for up to 200. *Rooms 105. Garden, outdoor swimming pool. Access, Amex, Diners, Visa.*

NOTTINGHAM — Ocean City — £40

Tel 0115 941 0041   Fax 0115 924 0369   Map 7 D3   **R**
100-104 Derby Road Nottingham Nottinghamshire NG1 5FB

A cavernous restaurant just out of the city centre; highly popular with the local Chinese community. The long Cantonese menu is strong on sizzling dishes and assorted seafood that includes lobster, crab and monkfish; these are well complemented by some more unusual dishes on the freshly cooked lunchtime dim sum selection. *Seats 250. Parties 12. L 12-2.30 (Mon & Tue to 4) D 6-11.30 (Fri to 12), Sat 12-12, Sun 12-10.30. Closed 25 Dec. Set L from £6.50 Set D from £13.50. Access, Amex, Visa.*

NOTTINGHAM   Royal Moat House   70%   £118

Tel 0115 941 4444 Fax 0115 947 5667   Map 7 D3   **H**
Wollaton Street Nottingham Nottinghamshire NG1 5RH

An internal atrium planted with tropical trees and plants is a major attraction at this strikingly modern city-centre hotel next to the Theatre Royal. The Penthouse Bar offers panoramic views over the city. Bedroom size varies from roomy doubles and twins to rather more compact singles. Decor is light and contemporary in style and all rooms have a mini-bar and the usual modern comforts. 24hr room service. Conference facilities for up to 600 delegates. Free multi-storey car parking. No dogs. *Rooms 201. Squash, kiosk, coffee shop (10am-6pm). Access, Amex, Diners, Visa.*

NOTTINGHAM   Rutland Square Hotel   63%   £78

Tel 0115 941 1114 Fax 0115 941 0014   Map 7 D3   **H**
St James Street Nottingham Nottinghamshire NG1 6FJ

Reached by following the signs to the castle, this city-centre hotel has been cleverly converted from a warehouse. Public rooms are smart and spacious, with a large marble-floored foyer incorporating a comfortable sitting area and a mezzanine level bar with a glass roof. Bedrooms are modestly furnished but have TVs with satellite, mini-bars and en-suite bathrooms with spa baths, while a penthouse suite has splendid views of both the castle and the city. Free parking in an adjacent car park. *Rooms 105. Access, Amex, Diners, Visa.*

NOTTINGHAM   Sonny's   ↑   £60

Tel 0115 947 3041   Map 7 D3   **R**
3 Carlton Street Hockley Nottingham Nottinghamshire NG1 1NL

A laid-back, modern setting for a short, progressive, modern menu. Graeme Watson's cuisine is nothing if not fashionable, with 90s favourites bang bang chicken, salmon carpaccio and Caesar salad among the starters and sweet potato gnocchi with roast cherry tomatoes, basil and smoked mozzarella available as either starter or main course. Other mains run from blackened salmon with coriander and spring onion butter to leek and cheese sausage with fennel dauphinoise and grilled beef fillet with wild mushrooms, smoked bacon and baby onions. Main courses come with frites or new potatoes, with other vegetables or salads charged separately. The pudding list is every bit as enticing, containing as it does the likes of hot peppered strawberries with sorbet or gooseberry crème fraiche tart with elderflower ice cream. There are some excellent wine on the list, most with knowledgeable tasting notes. Fair prices – note the 'grand' section. The café, in one corner, is open from 11 to 3 for sandwiches and snacks. *Seats 80. Parties 30. L 12-2.30 D 7-10.30 (Fri & Sat to 11, Sun to 10). Closed Bank Holidays. Set Sun L £10.95. Access, Amex, Visa.*

NOTTINGHAM   Stakis Nottingham Hotel   62%   £85

Tel 0115 9419561 Fax 0115 9484736   Map 7 D3   **H**
Milton Street Nottingham Nottinghamshire NG1 3PZ

Formerly the Stakis Victoria this 19th-century Edwardian building enjoys a good central location. Three grades of room; Standard, Executive and Club in ascending order of quality and price. The price we quote above is for a mid-range Executive room. Nine conference rooms handle from 6 to 200 delegates. *Rooms 167. Access, Amex, Diners, Visa.*

NOTTINGHAM   Strathdon Thistle   66%   £110

Tel 0115 9418501 Fax 0115 9483725   Map 7 D3   **H**
44 Derby Road Nottingham Nottinghamshire NG1 5FT

Neat, practical bedrooms and comfortable day rooms in a modern hotel in the heart of the city near the Cathedral, directly opposite the Albert Hall conference and exhibition centre and Playhouse theatre. Choice of bars and 24hr room service. Children up to 14 free in their parents' room. Guests have free use of the leisure facilities at the sister hotel the *Donington Thistle* at Castle Donington (see entry). Banqueting/conferences for 100/150. Own parking for only eight cars but some price concessions for hotel guests at a nearby NCP. *Rooms 68. Access, Amex, Diners, Visa.*

NUTFIELD   Nutfield Priory   71%   £135

Tel 01737 822066   Fax 01737 823321   Map 11 B5   **H**
Nutfield Redhill Surrey RH1 4EN

East of Redhill on the A25, Nutfield Priory is an extravagant Victorian-Gothic pile built on a ridge commanding extensive views over the Surrey and Sussex countryside. Day rooms include the galleried main hall that comes complete with stained-glass windows and pipe organ, panelled library with some fine carving on the ribbed ceiling, and the bar set within a country house-style lounge. Individually decorated bedrooms have considerable appeal with elaborate bedhead drapes or canopies and a variety of furniture from rattan to reproduction antique pieces. A number of beamed rooms are particularly characterful. All have safes and bathrooms are decorated to match individual bedrooms. It's a popular conference venue with 10 different meeting rooms and guests have free membership of the separately run Fredericks sports and leisure club situated within the hotel's grounds. No dogs. *Rooms 52. Garden, indoor swimming pool, children's splash pool, young children's playroom, sauna, solarium, spa bath, steam room, gym, beauty salon, hair salon, badminton, squash, snooker. Closed 1 week Christmas. Access, Amex, Diners, Visa.*

Many hotels offer reduced rates for weekend or out-of-season bookings. Always ask about special deals.

OAKHAM   Barnsdale Lodge Hotel 69%   £70

Tel 01572 724678   Fax 01572 724961   Map 7 E3   **H**
The Avenue Rutland Water nr Oakham Leicestershire LE15 8AH

Standing above Rutland Water alongside the A606 three miles east of Oakham, this comfortable hotel was originally a 16th-century farmhouse. Recent extensions, including a roomy conservatory and a new wing adding a further 12 bedrooms, have been harmoniously incorporated, cleverly retaining the cottagey feel. Edwardian antiques, period prints and ornaments fill the bedrooms and public rooms; indeed, an antique centre (under the same ownership) is situated next door. Cosy bedrooms, some with four-posters, have been refurbished to a high standard with comfortable armchairs and good-quality soft furnishings. All have the expected modern amenities. Two rooms for disabled guests have been incorporated into the new wing. *Rooms 29. Garden. Access, Visa.*

OAKHAM   Whipper-in Hotel   66%   £67

Tel 01572 756971   Fax 01572 757759   Map 7 E3   **HR**
Market Place Oakham Leicestershire LE15 6DT

A 17th-century town-centre hotel furnished with antiques, old prints and pictures. The traditional country ambience is further enhanced by log fires which burn in the lounges and bars. A popular meeting place for locals. Bedrooms are tastefully furnished, each with a mix of antiques and reproduction pieces as well as a range of modern amenities. *Rooms 24. Courtyard. Access, Amex, Visa.*

Restaurant   £70

Hunting prints around the walls, a couple of old beams and comfortable high-backed chairs create a cosy 'county' setting for some sound cooking. Fillet of brill topped with curry sauce with a mussel and watercress sauce on the side; supreme of chicken coated with a tarragon cream sauce; pan-fried duck breast with a compote of apricots, oranges and almonds; 8oz charcoal grilled steaks are all typical dishes. Vegetables are given as much care as the rest of the meal. Pleasant service. *Seats 50. Private Room 40. L 12.30-2.30 D 7.30-9.30 (Sun till 9). Set L £7.95 Set D £14.95.*

ODIHAM   George Hotel   £75

Tel 01256 702081   Fax 01256 704213   Map 15 D3   **I**
High Street Odiham nr Basingstoke Hampshire RG25 1LP

First granted a licence in 1540, the privately-owned George has kept a good deal of its period character. Timber framing can be seen throughout, and in the Oak Room – a popular place for afternoon tea or private parties – the wattle and daub walls are exposed. The oak-panelled, flagstone-floored restaurant was at one time an assize court.

Main-house bedrooms have creaking floors, beams and antiques, while rooms in the converted barn and coach house are modern behind original exteriors. Four-poster rooms attract a small supplement and in one of them some Elizabethan wall paintings are carefully protected. One mile from the M3 (junction 5). *Rooms 18. Garden. Access, Amex, Diners, Visa.*

OLD AMERSHAM	The Crown	64%	£90

Tel 01494 721541   Fax 01494 431283   Map 15 E2   **H**
16 High Street Amersham Old Town Buckinghamshire HP7 0DW

A picturesque former coaching inn with Georgian facade and Elizabethan interior complete with beamed ceilings and inglenook fireplaces. As is to be expected in a building of this age, rooms vary considerably in both size as well as style; unfortunately, standards of service, furnishing and maintenance are also very variable. One of the hotel's bedrooms features the now-famous four-poster bed used in the recent British film success *Four Weddings and a Funeral.* Free parking to the rear of building. Forte. *Rooms 22. Garden, patio. Access, Amex, Diners, Visa.*

OLD AMERSHAM	Gilbey's	£55

Tel 01494 727242   Fax 01494 431243   Map 15 E2   **R**
1 Market Square Amersham Old Town Buckinghamshire HP7 0DF

An early 17th-century building with low-beamed ceiling and old red brick fireplace that has been given a bright, informal feel with sunny yellow walls and a series of fine paintings of southern France (by Alexandra Haynes, a niece of the owner) in bold primary colours. There's a strong Mediterranean flavour to chef Stephen Spooner's well-judged dishes too: chilled gazpacho, roasted sweet peppers with spicy aubergine relish, roasted red mullet wrapped in radicchio leaves with oregano and lemon, calf's liver and bacon with a sage jus and creamed leek tartlet, and pan-fried entrecote with a mustard and herb butter and chips. Many of the same dishes appear at lunchtime and on Sunday night (when they are happy to serve just a single dish) along with a pasta dish of the day, mussels provençale with parmesan shavings and an open sandwich (grilled chicken and bacon with avocado and sun-dried tomato salsa on toasted tapenade bread). Desserts might include their rather good lemon tart with vanilla ice cream, passion fruit mousse with summer fruits, and poached tamarillos with cassis sorbet. Very affordable prices on the enterprising French-only (apart from two English) wine list. Authoritative tasting notes. *Seats 50. Parties 10 (Fri & Sat). Private Room 10. L 12-2.30 D 7-10. Closed 26-28 Dec & 1 Jan. Access, Amex, Diners, Visa.*

OLD AMERSHAM	Heddons	£40

Tel 01494 431491   Map 15 E2   **R**
20 Market Square Amersham Old Town Buckinghamshire HP7 0DW

This aromatic patisserie and restaurant begins the day by serving breakfasts (including home-baked croissants), progresses through light meals and then transforms itself into a distinctly chic little French restaurant by night. The short à la carte, augmented by a blackboard with the likes of fresh fish and vegetarian specials, is strong on chargrills. Delicious home-made soups and zesty starters are served with home-baked baguettes. Good, finely-cut chips and crisp, seasonal vegetables. *Seats 47. Meals 9-5 (Sat & Sun from 8) D 7.30-9.30. Closed 25 & 26 Dec. Access, Visa.*

OLD BURGHCLERE	Dew Pond	£70

Tel 01635 278408   Map 15 D3   **R**
Old Burghclere Newbury Berkshire RG20 9LH

The 16th-century house stands in Watership Down surrounded by beautiful countryside. Inside, the two dining rooms are comfortably and pleasantly furnished with good pictures, objets d'art and smartly upholstered chairs – there's even an open fire. It's very much a family affair, with Keith Marshall and his wife Julie in charge of matters culinary. Game is a speciality, shown in such dishes as pheasant sausage with a calvados sauce and caramelised apples; roast partridge garnished with confit of the leg, port sauce and glazed baby onions;

See over

or saddle of roe deer served with a tartlet of cranberries, chestnuts and a red wine sauce. Look out, too, for the day's fish dish, best end of lamb with dauphinoise potatoes and (for a small supplement) a grand selection of desserts in miniature. Good farmhouse British cheeses, Colombian coffee and a fairly-priced wine list: with a dozen or so house wines (with tasting notes) under £15 as well as several half bottles you can't go far wrong. *Seats 44. Parties 22. Private Room 32. D 7-10. Closed Sun, Mon, 2 weeks Jan, 2 weeks Aug. Access, Visa.*

OLD HARLOW	Churchgate Manor	64%	£96

Tel 01279 420246   Fax 01279 437720   Map 11 B4   **H**
Churchgate Street Village Old Harlow Essex CM17 0JT

The original white-painted chantry house, built in 1610, overlooks the winding village main street. The remainder of the hotel stretches out to the rear in a series of added-on extensions. Public rooms have smart lightwood furniture and a comfortable, relaxing air. Bedrooms are attractive and well equipped, each with its own compact, neat bathroom. 21 Executive rooms have mini-bars, spa baths and sofas. Popular with businessfolk; there are conference facilities for up to 130. *Rooms 85. Garden, indoor swimming pool, mini-gym, sauna, spa bath, sun beds. Access, Amex, Diners, Visa.*

OSWESTRY	Wynnstay Hotel	66%	£93

Tel 01691 655261   Fax 01691 670606   Map 8 D2   **H**
Church Street Oswestry Shropshire SY11 2SZ

In the town centre opposite St Oswalds church, this is a typical Georgian building with stylish day rooms. Besides the restaurant and lounge there are conference facilities for up to 190, plus a 200-year-old crown bowling green as an unusual leisure offering. Best of the bedrooms have whirlpool baths. Children up to 13 free in parents' room. June 1995 saw the opening of a leisure centre. *Rooms 27. Garden, bowling, indoor swimming pool, keep-fit equipment, sauna, spa bath, solarium, beautician, coffee shop (9.30am-10pm). Access, Amex, Diners, Visa.*

Set menu prices may not always include service or wine.

OTLEY	Chevin Lodge	64%	£92

Tel 01943 467818   Fax 01943 850335   Map 6 C1   **H**
York Gate Otley West Yorkshire LS21 3NU

Set in fifty acres of woodlands and lakes and built of Finnish pine, the Lodge is the largest log construction in the country. Bedrooms are in either the main building or smaller log lodges scattered amongst the trees. Despite the rusticity, rooms have all the usual modern conveniences. Executive lodges have separate lounges. The well-equipped Woodlands Suite has facilities for up to 130 conference delegates. Guests have free membership of a private leisure club 5 minutes drive away. *Rooms 50. Garden, jogging trail, mountain bikes, sauna, solarium, spa bath, tennis, fishing, games room. Access, Amex, Visa.*

OUNDLE	Talbot Hotel	62%	£82

Tel 01832 273621   Fax 01832 274545   Map 7 E4   **H**
New Street Oundle Northamptonshire PE8 4EA

Built as a monks' hostel, and rebuilt in the 17th century with stones from nearby Fotheringhay Castle, the Talbot is quite splendid with its transom windows and bell-capped gables. In 1638 the castle's oak staircase descended by Mary Queen of Scots on the day of her execution in 1587 was installed. Conference/banqueting facilities for up to 120/100. Forte Hotels. *Rooms 39. Garden. Access, Amex, Diners, Visa.*

OXFORD	Al-Shami		£30

Tel 01865 310066   Fax 01865 311241   Map 15 D2   **R**
25 Walton Crescent Oxford Oxfordshire OX1 2JG

Between Somerville and Worcester Colleges, this Lebanese restaurant is open long hours and serves authentic dishes including charcoal grills of lamb, chicken and minced meat and the usual wide range of hot and cold hors d'oeuvre. The wine list includes a dozen Lebanese varieties plus arak. Set menus can be arranged for parties of six or more, and there are one or two dishes for vegetarians. *Seats 48. Private Room 30. Meals 12-12. No credit cards.*

OXFORD   Bath Place   £80

Tel 01865 791812   Fax 01865 791834   Map 15 D2   **RR**
4 & 5 Bath Place Holywell Street Oxford Oxfordshire OX1 3SU

A very pleasant little family-run restaurant in a tiny cobbled lane running off Holywell Street. The lane is opposite the Holywell music rooms just a short walk from the Bodleian Library. It's a very popular place, thanks in no small measure to the talents of chef Jeremy Blake O'Connor, and that popularity has resulted in seven-day opening and an increase in the kitchen staff. Jeremy's grounding in the classic French tradition has been developed and modernised, with influences from Britain and the Mediterranean. Among his current specialities are confit of belly pork with a salad of green beans, tomatoes, chervil and shallots; raviolo of salmon and scallops set on a bed of braised endive; galette of foie gras marinated in port; lobster Café de Paris; and seasonal game. Top of the menu offerings is the 8-course *menu surprise*, which must be ordered by everyone at a table. There are brief tasting notes alongside each wine on a fairly priced, balanced list. No smoking. *Seats 32. Parties 20. L 12-2 (Sun 12.30-2.30) D 7-10 (Fri & Sat to 10.30, Sun to 9.30). Set L £14.50/17.50 (Sun £21.50) Set D £17.50 (Sun & Mon), £24.50 & £49.50 (8-course). Access, Amex, Visa.*

Rooms   £105
The ten bedrooms are set around a courtyard.

OXFORD   Cherwell Boathouse   £50

Tel & Fax 01865 52746   Map 15 D2   **R**
Bardwell Road Oxford Oxfordshire OX2 6SR

Park your car or moor your punt, and enjoy a leisurely meal in the friendly surroundings of a converted boathouse on the River Cherwell. The evening menu is three-course, fixed-price, weekly-changing. Fresh seasonal produce gets sympathetic treatment in such dishes as deep-fried celeriac with mint chutney, fillet of cod *plaki*, and (a speciality) loin of free-range pork with prune and port sauce. Sticky toffee pudding remains a favourite dessert. Some very fair prices (the house selections are downright cheap) on a splendid wine list that includes many great names. Much from France, but quality also from the New World. Tables outside in summer. *Seats 50. L 12-2 D 7-10.30. Closed L Tues, D Sun, all Mon, Dec 24-30. Set L £10.50/16.50 (Sun £16.50) Set D £17.50. Access, Amex, Visa.*

OXFORD   Eastgate Hotel   61%   £122

Tel 01865 248244   Fax 01865 791681   Map 15 D2   **H**
High Street Oxford Oxfordshire OX1 4BE

Panelled walls complement the attractive furnishings in the public rooms of this central hotel with an 18th-century facade. Although on the High Street, the reception entrance is in Merton Street. Forte Hotels. *Rooms 43. Access, Amex, Diners, Visa.*

OXFORD   Restaurant Elizabeth ↑   £75

Tel 01865 242230   Map 15 D2   **R**
82 St Aldate's Oxford Oxfordshire OX1 1RA

There's a sombre intimacy to the dark-panelled first-floor dining-rooms of this Oxford institution set in a 15th-century building opposite Christ Church College. With chef Salvador Rodriguez here since 1978, and owner Antonio Lopez even longer, the shortish menu does not change much from year to year. Perhaps the classic meal here, and one showing the kitchen at its best, would be *quenelles de saumon sauce Nantua* followed by duck *à l'orange*, with their peerless crème brulée for dessert. To finish go for the coffee which gurgles nostalgically in veteran, meths-fuelled Cona machines placed on the table. The New World is conspicuous by its absence on the otherwise classic wine list. Order perhaps a Rioja and then graduate to a Sauternes, of which there are plenty. *Seats 40. L 12.30-2.30 D 6.30-11 (Sun 7-10.30). Closed Mon, 24-30 Dec, Good Friday. Set L £15. Access, Amex, Diners, Visa.*

OXFORD — 15 North Parade — £70

Tel 01865 513773   Map 15 D2   **R**
15 North Parade Avenue Oxford Oxfordshire OX9 1JH

Sean Wood and Benedic Gorman present exciting, innovative and eclectic menus of worldwide influence in a cool, modern restaurant in a narrow lane just north of the city centre. The menu introduces refreshingly fashionable concepts, dishes being characterised by clear, well-balanced flavours. Chilled tomato soup with basil, egg and Serrano ham, wild salmon carpaccio with radishes, mouli and horseradish, and warm pancake stuffed with herb mousse on salad could be your starter, which you might follow with a tureen of seafood in a clear fish consommé with Thai aromatics, braised sweetbreads with giant shallots and anna potatoes, or chargrilled rib-eye steak with red onion relish, salad and chunky chips. To finish there are delightful sweets such as hot chocolate brownie, Moroccan rice pudding with tangerine confit and baby rum baba with toffeed fruits. Everything including the bread is prepared with great care and served by charming staff. Shortish but interesting wine list with wines presented by style and taste. The kitchen has been moved up to the level of the restaurant, and a private room is located in the basement. 20 seats out on a walled patio for summer eating. As we went to press, a new reception area and lobby plus a toilet for the use of disabled guests were nearing completion. A really charming family concern. *Seats 55. L 12-2 D 7-11. Closed D Sun, all Mon, last 2 weeks Aug. Set L £10/£12 (Sun £13.75). Set D £15. Access, Visa.*

OXFORD — Ma Cuisine — £55

Tel 01865 201316   Map 15 D2   **R**
21 Cowley Road The Plain Oxford Oxfordshire OX4 1HP

A traditional French restaurant run with verve and panache by the chef-patron André Chavagnon and his wife Susan. Regular and old favourite dishes like *moules marinière, tarte à l'oignon, salade niçoise, coq au vin* and *steak au poivre* feature on the classical menu. The restaurant is small and unprepossessing yet full of charm, providing the kind of experience that is tantamount to a trip down memory lane. In fine weather the brick-floored patio with its hanging baskets and parasols is a delight. *Seats 30. Parties 10. L 11.30-2 D 6.30-10.30. Closed Sun, some Bank Holidays. Set L £16.50 Set D £18.50 (Mon-Thurs). Access, Amex, Visa.*

OXFORD — Moat House — 62% — £135

Tel 01865 59933   Fax 01865 310259   Map 15 D2   **H**
Wolvercote Roundabout Oxford Oxfordshire OX2 8AL

Modern business hotel two miles north of the city centre at the junction of the A34 and A40. Refurbished bedrooms, leisure centre, ten conference rooms and many more syndicate rooms, the largest with a maximum capacity of 100. Ample free car parking. *Rooms 155. Indoor swimming pool, gym, squash, sauna, spa bath, solarium, putting, snooker, coffee shop (11am-11pm). Closed New Year. Access, Amex, Diners, Visa.*

OXFORD — Old Parsonage — 70% — £140

Tel 01865 310210   Fax 01865 311262   Map 15 D2   **H**
1 Banbury Road Oxford Oxfordshire OX2 6NN

On a site dating back to the 14th century, the Old Parsonage was established in 1660 and underwent a major transformation in order to open as a small hotel of quality and individuality early in 1991. Great style and taste have been employed in its refurbishment, creating an effect that's very easy on the eye. Bedrooms, though not large, are stylishly appointed with striking soft furnishings, muted colours and harmonious fittings. Accessories include mini-bars, hairdryers and remote-control radio and TVs with satellite stations. Stunning marble-fitted bathrooms have two showers, soft towels, fine toiletries and telephone extensions. A clubby bar has walls hung with hundreds of pictures and there's a small lounge. Young, efficient staff. No dining-room as such, but light meals are served in the bar. Browns restaurant (under the same ownership as the hotel) is two minutes away. No dogs. *Rooms 30. Garden. Closed 23-27 Dec. Access, Amex, Diners, Visa.*

Lodges are now listed by county in the reference section

OXFORD · Randolph Hotel   68%   £143

Tel 01865 247481   Fax 01865 791678   Map 15 D2   **H**
Beaumont Street Oxford Oxfordshire OX1 2LN

Built in 1864 in neo-Gothic style, the Randolph is named after Dr Francis Randolph, a benefactor of the Ashmolean Museum opposite. The grand, oak-panelled foyer with vaulted ceiling and sweeping staircase sets the tone for the day rooms, which include an elegant, chandeliered lounge and clubby bar. Bedrooms vary in size from small to spacious. The hotel has a number of suites catering for anything from 20 to 300 conference visitors. Free covered parking for 70 cars. Forte. *Rooms 109. kiosk, coffee shop (10-8). Access, Amex, Diners, Visa.*

Many hotels offer reduced rates for weekend or out-of-season bookings. Always ask about special deals.

PADSTOW   The Seafood Restaurant   ★ ↑   £80

Tel 01841 532485   Fax 01841 533344   Map 12 B3   **RR**
Riverside Padstow Cornwall PL28 8BY

Rick Stein has for 20 years been chef-patron at what has become one of the country's best known seafood restaurants, one totally deserving of an emphasis on *The* in its title. His understanding of his craft and raw materials helps produce food of quality to make a meal here an experience to both savour and admire, hence our supreme award of Restaurant of the Year. Drinks taken in the conservatory come served with a simple jar of Greek black and green olives, freshly baked baguettes and brown bread – all quality hallmarks showing attention to detail. Dishes are essentially straightforward, allowing the peak freshness of the produce to shine through, and many show a French influence: roast turbot with hollandaise sauce, grilled Padstow lobster (they're kept in chilled seawater tanks until ordered) with *fines herbes*, whole Dover sole with sea salt and lime (seasoned with sea salt and cooked un-skinned on the grill, the skin becomes deliciously crispy), fillets of brill with beurre blanc. Start with mussels, cockles and clams Marsala (a Goan dish), some Helford oysters or a classic *soupe de poissons* with rouille and parmesan. There's always one non-fish dish on the menu, usually steak, but why come here and eat meat? Sweets keep up the enjoyment level: warm tart of Agen prunes with armagnac, pear bavarois with orange and passion fruit coulis, bread-and-butter pudding (there's always one 'nursery pudding'). A very classy wine list shows a fine balance between old and new. Knowledgeable tasting notes add to the expected enjoyment of fairly priced, carefully chosen wines. Having eaten here look in at Stein's Delicatessen (in Middle Street) where some of the restaurant dishes are available to take away along with home-made jams, chutneys, preserves and much else. There's a coffee shop above. *Seats 70. Parties 18. L 12.30-2.15 D 7-10. Closed Sun, May Day, mid Dec-3 Feb. Set L £20.50 Set D £27.85. Access, Visa.*

Rooms   £98

Ten individually decorated bedrooms above the restaurant provide some very comfortable accommodation; light and airy colour schemes plus televisions, mini-bars and tea/coffee making facilities are standard features. Two rooms have private balconies with views of the harbour. All rooms have stylish bathrooms en suite, most with good shower baths. Breakfast taken in the restaurant includes English, kippers or Continental, the nearby delicatessen providing many of the items. The price we quote is for a mid-range room but prices start at £58 for two B&B.

St Petroc's House
Tel 01841 532700

A small, 8-bedroom hotel (from £52 per double) 150 yards up the hill from the restaurant. It has a 30-seat Bistro (closed Monday & 3-29 Dec) offering a daily-changing, 3-course menu at £14.95 (typically smoked duck breast with new potatoes, rocket and endive; garbure béarnaise; chargrilled lamb chop with tomato and coriander; baked cod with boulangère potatoes; crème caramel and bread-and-butter pudding). Courses also priced separately.

| PAIGNTON | **Palace Hotel** | 60% | **£117** |

Tel 01803 555121   Fax 01803 527974   Map 13 D3   **H**
Esplanade Road Paignton Devon TQ4 6BJ

Traditional seaside hotel overlooking the pier and Torbay beyond. Good leisure amenities and conference facilities for up to 50. Forte. *Rooms 52. Garden, outdoor swimming pool, keep-fit equipment, sauna, spa bath, sun bed, beautician, hair salon, tennis, pool table. Access, Amex, Diners, Visa.*

| PAIGNTON | **Redcliffe Hotel** | 62% | **£92** |

Tel 01803 526397   Fax 01803 528030   Map 13 D3   **H**
Marine Drive Paignton Devon TQ3 2NL

A round tower is the central feature of this distinctive turn-of-the-century hotel on Paignton seafront, dividing Paignton and Preston beaches. Day rooms enjoy the view, as do some of the bedrooms, which include seven low-ceilinged rooms of character in the tower; family suites also available. Conference/banqueting for 160/210. A private tunnel leading to the beach is of particular appeal to children; there is a nanny available between 7 and 9 on summer evenings. No dogs. 24hr room service. *Rooms 60. Garden, indoor & outdoor swimming pool, gym, sauna, steam room, spa bath, solarium, hair salon (not Mon), putting, games room, children's playground, young children's playroom. Access, Amex, Visa.*

| PAINSWICK | **Painswick Hotel** | 70% | **£98** |

Tel 01452 812160   Fax 01452 814059   Map 14 B2   **H**
Kemps Lane Painswick Gloucestershire GL6 6YB

Tucked away down the narrow streets behind the church in one of the most architecturally interesting Cotswold villages, the Painswick Hotel is a grand Palladian mansion. Numerous intriguing features include an Italianate loggia overlooking the croquet lawn in gardens that also enclose a 'grotto' built by a vicar (this was once the Rectory) to amplify his sermons and an elaborate ribbed ceiling in the former chapel, now the bar. Elegant day rooms – some occasionally used for meetings – boast some fine antiques and paintings. It's run in relaxed style by Somerset and Hélène Moore, who create a friendly atmosphere. Accommodation varies from spacious rooms with some notable antiques, objets d'art and stylish fabrics in the original building to smaller rooms with more modest pieces and some modern furniture in a newer wing but all have extras like magazines, mineral water and bathrobes. Top of the range are two rooms with four-posters, one with feminine floral canopies, the other with a more solid, masculine, oak version. Breakfasts with freshly squeezed orange juice and some lovely smoky bacon start the day. Parking for 30 cars. *Rooms 20. Garden, croquet. Access, Amex, Visa.*

| PARKGATE | **Ship Hotel** | 56% | **£58** |

Tel 0151-336 3931   Fax 0151-353 0051   Map 6 A2   **H**
The Parade Parkgate The Wirral Cheshire L64 6SA

Overlooking the salt-marshes and the Dee estuary bird sanctuary, this stone-fronted hotel is an ideal retreat for 'twitchers' and nature-lovers alike. Modestly furnished bedrooms all have TVs, tea and coffee-making facilities and en-suite bathrooms. Four overlook the sea, two of them with four-posters and more comfortable furnishings. Among renovation plans by the new owners, the seafront bar will be restored to an atmosphere more in keeping with the historic village. *Rooms 26. Access, Visa.*

| PARKHAM | **Penhaven Country House** | 64% | **£100** |

Tel 01237 451388   Fax 01237 451878   Map 12 C2   **H**
Parkham nr Bideford Devon EX39 5PL

Maxine and Alan Wade are the friendly hosts at a small 19th-century hotel whose setting in the Devon countryside includes nine acres of woodland and gardens. Inside, all is spick and span, from the bar with its log fire to the bedrooms – these range from standard to 'super-de-luxe' and six cottage suites. All rooms have both bath and shower. No children under ten. Turn left at Horns Cross on the A39; up the hill into Parkham village then turn left when the church is on the right. *Rooms 12. Garden. Access, Amex, Diners, Visa.*

PAULERSPURY   Vine House   £55

Tel 01327 811267   Fax 01327 811309   Map 15 D1   **RR**
100 High Street Paulerspury Northamptonshire NN12 7NA

A 300-year-old village-centre limestone cottage two miles south of Towcester and a mile off the A5 is now a restaurant with rooms that exudes charm and hospitality, thanks to involved owners Marcus and Julie Springett. A tiny, cosy bar serves for pre-dinner drinks, while the dining-room is spacious, bright and, though modernised, still retains much of its original charm. Marcus offers a short, daily-changing menu using the freshest seasonal produce and creating rich, satisfying flavours in robust, well-made dishes. Mackerel croquettes with a lemon butter sauce and scampi paté with a leek salad and a cherry tomato sauce are starters you probably won't find on any other menu in the land, and the main courses also show a fine, controlled imagination: fillet of halibut with a herb sauce and a carrot and saffron jus, venison rissole topped with a button mushroom mousse, wrapped in flaky pastry, baked and served with a shallot and Madeira sauce. Fruity desserts are typified by blackberry, damson and cassis sorbet with a minestrone of fresh fruit. Some excellent wines on a shortish list – all the New World wines around £15. *Seats 45. Private Room 12. L 12.30-1.45 D 7-10.30. Closed L Mon & Sat, all Sun. Set L £13.95 Set D £19.50. Access, Visa.*

Rooms   £61

There's a quiet lounge for residents, who have the pleasure of sleeping in one of the 6 prettily decorated bedrooms. Though not large they are well equipped and each has neat en-suite facilities. One boasts a four-poster. No dogs. *Closed 24-30 Dec.*

PENKRIDGE   William Harding's House   £50

Tel 01785 712955   Map 6 B3   **R**
Mill Street Penkridge Stafford Staffordshire ST19 5AY

Leave the M6 at Junction 12 or 13 and take the A449. Built as a stable in 1693 and occupied by Cromwell's men during the Civil War, this is a small, cottagey restaurant run by Fiona and Eric Bickley. Eric's frequently-changing menu is a fixed-price-only affair and offers a good choice – perhaps creamy 'ragoo' of mushrooms and chicken, savoury poached pears on fresh pineapple with a blackcurrant dressing or chicken liver parfait to start, followed by chicken breast parcel with apricots and vine fruits, noisettes of salmon wrapped in plaice with a Harlequin sauce or escalopes of pork on a blue cheese sauce with walnuts. To finish, 'British rural cheeses' and a choice of desserts displayed on the sideboard. Sunday lunch is a relaxed occasion and offers a choice of four dishes for each course, including a roast meat. Supper Club first two Thursdays of every month, with multiple returns 'for seconds' of puddings! No children under 15. *Seats 24. Parties 16. Private Room 16. L (First & last Sun in month only) 12.30-2 D 7.30-9.30. Closed D Sun & Mon, 26 Dec and 1 Jan. Set Sun L £12.50 Set D £18.95. Access, Visa.*

PENRITH   North Lakes Hotel   71%   £108

Tel 01768 868111   Fax 01768 868291   Map 4 C3   **H**
Ullswater Road Penrith Cumbria CA11 8QT

Smart, modern hotel, by Junction 40 of the M6, comfortably dividing its function between mid-week conferences and a weekend base for Lakeland visitors. Facilities for both categories are purpose-built around a central lodge of local stone with massive railway-sleeper beams, which houses bar, lounges and coffee shop. Executive-style bedrooms include a separate study and relaxation area while interconnecting syndicate rooms convert handily for family use at holiday times. Two rooms are specially adapted for disabled guests. Children up to 14 free in parents' room. 24hr room service. Conference and banqueting facilities for up to 300 and a staffed business centre. Activities for children every weekend and during school holidays. Shire Inns. *Rooms 84. Garden, indoor swimming pool & children's splash pool, sauna, spa bath, solarium, gym, squash, snooker. Access, Amex, Diners, Visa.*

Many hotels offer reduced rates for weekend or out-of-season bookings. Always ask about special deals.

PENZANCE · Abbey Hotel · 67% · £85

Tel 01736 66906   Fax 01736 51163   Map 12 A4   **HR**
Abbey Street Penzance Cornwall TR18 4AR

The truly delightful Abbey Hotel is perched above and overlooks the quay in a quiet backwater of town (on entering Penzance take the road marked Sea Front, pass a large car park on the left, turn right just before the bridge, then turn left up the slipway). Jean and Michael Cox's house is a model of good taste, replete with their collections of antiques and fine art, deep armchairs and abundant reading material. Stylish bedrooms retain the building's uniqueness and charm, using colour and light to great advantage where space is limited. "Not a family hotel." *Rooms 7. Garden, croquet. Closed 3 or 4 days at Christmas. Access, Amex, Visa.*

Restaurant · £60

Do book as, with only six tables, non-residents are only welcomed as space allows, but don't expect any great sense of occasion. A table d'hote offers three choices per course nightly. Hot avocado with spicy hot chick peas, salmon mousse with king prawns or lentil, garlic and cumin soup could precede roast pheasant with chestnuts and a red wine sauce, salmon baked with a light tarragon cream, or the vegetarian options, perhaps tagliatelle with sun-dried tomatoes. Choice of three sweets. *Seats 18. Parties 12. D only 7.30-8.30. Set D £22.50.*

Set menu prices may not always include service or wine.

PENZANCE · Harris's · £70

Tel 01736 64408   Map 12 A4   **R**
46 New Street Penzance Cornwall TR18 2LZ

👑 🍓 🗋

Local produce, especially fish and game, feature on the menu of Roger Harris's cosy little hillside restaurant down a narrow street in the centre of town. Crab florentine, grilled goat's cheese wrapped in bacon, duck paté and grilled scallops on a bed of salad with herb dressing are among the starters. Main courses include poached John Dory with a saffron sauce, jugged hare, stuffed pheasant breast in filo pastry and rack of lamb with crab apple jelly and rosemary. There's a light lunch menu also available with fresh salmon pancakes, fresh crab salad and Cumberland sausages with onions and mashed potatoes being typical offerings. Vegetarians should give prior notice. *Seats 40. Parties 12. Private Room 20. L 12-2 D 7-10. Closed L Mon also D Mon Oct-Jun, all Sun, 25 & 26 Dec, 1 Jan, 1 week Feb, 2 weeks Nov. Access, Amex, Visa.*

PETERBOROUGH · Butterfly Hotel · 63% · £70

Tel 01733 64240   Fax 01733 65538   Map 7 E4   **H**
Thorpe Meadows Longthorpe Parkway Peterborough Cambridgeshire PE3 6GA

One of a small chain of modern, low-rise brick-built East Anglian hotels. Peterborough's Butterfly sits at the water's edge, overlooking Thorpe Meadows rowing lake. Neat, practical accommodation ranges from studio singles to four suites. Conferences (80), banqueting (50). Free parking for 80 cars. *Rooms 70. Access, Amex, Diners, Visa.*

PETERBOROUGH · Forte Posthouse · 60% · £72

Tel 01733 240209   Fax 01733 244455   Map 7 E4   **H**
Great North Road Norman Cross Peterborough Cambridgeshire PE7 3TB

Popular hotel at the Norman Cross roundabout on the A1. Mini-bars and in-house movies are the latest additions to rooms, some of which are located in an unusual rotunda block. Meeting rooms for up to 50. Children up to 16 stay free in parents' room. *Rooms 90. Indoor swimming pool, gym, sauna, spa bath, sun bed. Access, Amex, Diners, Visa.*

Consult the blue pages for summary tables and lists of recommended establishments.

| PETERBOROUGH | Moat House | 64% | £88 |

Tel 01733 260000   Fax 01733 262737   Map 7 E4   **H**
Thorpe Wood Peterborough Cambridgeshire PE3 6SG

Two miles west of the city centre by the Thorpe Wood golf course and Nene Country Park, a modern redbrick hotel offering extensive leisure and air-conditioned conference facilities; the largest room can take up to 400 delegates. Children up to 15 stay free in parents' room. One double and one single are adapted for disabled guests. *Rooms 125. Indoor swimming pool, gym, sauna, spa baths, steam room, solarium, games room. Access, Amex, Diners, Visa.*

| PETERBOROUGH | Swallow Hotel | 69% | £105 |

Tel 01733 371111   Fax 01733 236725   Map 7 E4   **H**
Peterborough Business Park Lynchwood Peterborough
Cambridgeshire PE2 0GB

Modern, low-rise hotel by the A605, two minutes from the A1 (take Alwalton-Chesterton Business Park & Showground sign). Spacious public areas are bright and airy. Conference facilities for up to 300. *Rooms 163. Garden, pitch & putt, indoor swimming pool, keep-fit equipment, sauna, spa bath, steam room, sun beds, beauty & hair salon. Access, Amex, Diners, Visa.*

| PETERSFIELD | Langrish House | 63% | £55 |

Tel 01730 266941   Fax 01730 260543   Map 15 D3   **H**
Langrish Petersfield Hampshire GU32 1RN

Built around the heart of a 16th-century farmhouse and converted to a hotel in 1979, the house stands in rolling countryside three miles out of Petersfield off the A272. Bedrooms have peaceful pastoral views, traditional furnishings and a few homely extras. The large cellar (now a bar) was reputedly excavated by Royalist prisoners taken at the Civil War's Battle of Cheriton after which they ended up in their own prison! *Rooms 18. Garden. Closed 25 Dec-1 Jan. Access, Amex, Diners, Visa.*

We welcome bona fide complaints and recommendations on the tear-out pages at the back of the book for readers' comments. They are followed up by our professional team.

| PETWORTH | L'Amico | £50 |

Tel 01798 343659   Map 11 A6   **R**
Grove Lane Petworth West Sussex GU28 0HY

Follow the High Street south as it becomes Grove Road and finally Grove Lane to find this 15th-century cottage restaurant on the right just after leaving the edge of town. The interior has been opened up but still boasts a few old timbers. Most people though choose the conservatory in which to enjoy Gino Tecchia's straightforward Italian cooking. There's nothing modern about the menu, which sticks to old favourites like *pollo alla cacciatora, scaloppine alla marsala, calamari marinara* and standard pasta dishes. Although there are no special facilities, children are made welcome and are offered smaller portions of dishes from the menu. Gino's English wife Barbara is the friendly face front of house. *Seats 40. Parties 15. Private Room 16. L 12-2.30 D 7-10. Closed D Sun, all Mon. Set L £8.50 Set Sun L £10.95 Set D £12.95/£15.50. Access, Amex, Visa.*

| PICKERING | White Swan | £76 |

Tel & Fax 01751 472288   Map 5 E4   **I**
The Market Place Pickering West Yorkshire YO18 7AA

A charming town-centre inn where guests can find quiet (in the elegant lounge) or conviviality (in the oak-panelled bar and snug). Gradual, continuous improvement of bedrooms sees the addition of good-quality pine furniture and personally selected antique pieces. Deirdre Buchanan and her loyal staff provide the warmest of welcomes, and decent bar food is produced by a quietly competent kitchen. *Rooms 13. Access, Amex, Visa.*

PINGEWOOD   Kirtons Hotel   60%   £100

Tel 01734 500885   Fax 01734 391996   Map 15 D2   **H**
Pingewood Reading Berkshire RG3 3UN

Unexceptional standardised bedrooms (those in the new wing are best), except that each
has a balcony overlooking the lake where the European water-ski championships are
sometimes held. Residential conferences (facilities for up to 110) are the main business
during the week but at weekends it's the extensive leisure facilities of the adjacent
country club (also available to hotel guests) that are the big attraction. It is here that there
are creche facilities in the mornings (reservations required) with a children's club on
Saturdays. 24hr room service. Near Junction 11 of the M4 but ask for detailed directions
when booking. *Rooms 81. Indoor swimming pool, gym, squash, spa baths, sauna, steam
room, sun beds, beauty & hair salon, snooker, tennis, children's playground, water-skiing,
jet-skiing. Access, Amex, Diners, Visa.*

PLUMTREE   Perkins Bar Bistro   £50

Tel 0115 937 3695   Fax 0115 937 6405   Map 7 D3   **R**
Station Road Plumtree Nottinghamshire NG12 5NA

🍷

A converted railway station where Tony and Wendy Perkins have been keeping
customers happy for many, many years with reliable cooking in a pleasant informal
atmosphere, with further improvements in table lay-ups and seating. The monthly-
changing menu – carrot, orange and coriander soup; salmon cakes with spinach and dill
sauce; goujons of plaice with *sauce verte*; entrecote steak with duxelles, stuffed tomato
and béarnaise sauce – is supplemented by a blackboard of daily specials (eg game in
season). Very fair prices on a concise wine list that has apposite tasting notes. No smoking
area. Given fair weather, the 'platform garden' has a number of tables, enabling one to sit
outside. Staff are terrific. *Seats 73. Parties 24. Private Room 30. L 12-2 D 6.45-9.45.
Closed Sun, Mon & Bank Holidays. Access, Amex, Diners, Visa.*

PLYMOUTH   Chez Nous   £80

Tel 01752 266793   Fax 01752 660428   Map 12 C3   **R**
13 Frankfort Gate Plymouth Devon PL1 1QA

🍓

Frankfort Gate is a pedestrianised shopping square in the town centre (use either the
Octagon or Derry's Cross car parks and you're very close) one unit of which conceals
this little corner of France behind the white-painted wooden louvres that obscure the
windows. Bistro-ish in style with dark blue-painted chairs and walls decorated with classic
French posters and framed menus from famous restaurants. Jacques Marchal describes his
cooking as *cuisine spontanée* which means that almost all the dishes from the blackboard
menu are prepared *à la minute* using the best available produce – and after 20 years
Jacques has developed some excellent sources of supply. A few dishes, like the *cassolette
d'escargots aux champignons, caneton aux lentilles* and *deux filets de Meaux* are more
or less permanent fixtures while others change from day to day. An example of the latter
is splendid *langoustines provençale* – fresh from a Spanish fishing trawler stopping off en
route home from the Scottish fishing grounds. Suzanne Marchal runs front of house with
friendly informality and verbally describes the day's desserts from amongst which a light
sponge pudding with caramel sauce makes an excellent finale. Wines, unsurprisingly, are
predominantly French. *Seats 28. L 12.30-2 D 7-10.30. Closed Sun & Mon, Bank Holidays,
3 weeks Feb, 3 weeks Sep. Set meals £30. Access, Amex, Diners, Visa.*

PLYMOUTH   Copthorne Hotel   70%   £106

Tel 01752 224161   Fax 01752 670688   Map 12 C3   **H**
Armada Way Plymouth Devon PL1 1AR

The Copthorne is an attractive hotel, with the light and elegant decor in the foyer setting
the overall tone; other public areas include a restaurant, brasserie (open 10.30-10.30),
Gallery cocktail bar and lounge. Bedrooms include Classic (singles), Connoisseur and suites
all with contemporary fitted furniture and plenty of writing space; there are rooms for
non-smokers and one for disabled guests; tiled bathrooms have good counter space and
large, well-lit mirrors. Children up to 16 stay free in parents' room. 24hr room service.

Ample free parking. Greatly reduced weekend rates (Fri–Sun). Facilities for banquets and conferences (up to 80) and Plymsoles leisure club. The hotel is at North Cross roundabout, opposite the university. *Rooms 135. Indoor swimming pool, gym, sauna, solarium, pool table, shop/news kiosk (8-10.30am & 6-8.30pm). Access, Amex, Diners, Visa.*

PLYMOUTH	Forte Posthouse	65%	£68

Tel 01752 662828 Fax 01752 660974   Map 12 C3   **H**
Cliff Road The Hoe Plymouth Devon PL7 3DL

High-riser with fine views from its prime position on the Hoe overlooking Plymouth Sound. Conferences for up to 120, banqueting to 100. Children up to 16 free in parents' room. *Rooms 106. Garden, outdoor swimming pool. Access, Amex, Diners, Visa.*

PLYMOUTH	Jarvis Boringdon Hall	67%	£90

Tel 01752 344455 Fax 01752 346578   Map 12 C3   **H**
Colebrook Plympton Plymouth Devon PL7 4DP

In a rural setting to the north of Plympton, Boringdon Hall was a monastery before becoming a manor house, at the time of the dissolution of the former, that has played host to both Elizabeth I and Sir Francis Drake. The galleried Great Hall in the original building makes a most impressive bar/lounge, despite the gas log fire, and the tower above houses the six most characterful rooms, four with four-poster beds. Most rooms are in a remarkably sympathetic courtyard extension, built only a few years ago, and feature traditional-style oak furniture, including a bureau, and matching bedcovers and curtains plus all mod cons like satellite TV. Room service, although not advertised, is available all day. *Rooms 40. Garden, pitch & putt, indoor swimming pool, keep-fit equipment, sauna, tennis. Access, Amex, Diners, Visa.*

PLYMOUTH	Moat House	70%	£123

Tel 01752 662866 Fax 01752 673816   Map 12 C3   **H**
Armada Way Plymouth Devon PL1 2HJ

Day rooms at this high-rise hotel, in particular the Penthouse restaurant and bar, command spectacular views of the Hoe and Plymouth Sound. So do many of the good-sized, picture-windowed bedrooms, which have double beds (twins have two double beds), seating areas and plenty of writing space. Conference and banqueting facilities for 300/350. Children under 16 are accommodated free if sharing their parents' room. Covered free parking below the building. *Rooms 212. Indoor swimming pool, gym, sauna, steam room, solarium, games room. Access, Amex, Diners, Visa.*

PLYMOUTH	Novotel	62%	£59

Tel & Fax 01752 221422   Map 12 C3   **H**
Marsh Mills Roundabout 270 Plymouth Road Plymouth Devon PL6 8NH

Practical modern accommodation and conference/banqueting facilities (for up to 240 delegates) on the A38 two miles from the town centre. Guests have free use of the gym at the Plympton Squash Club about two miles from the hotel. *Rooms 100. Garden, outdoor swimming pool, children's playground. Access, Amex, Diners, Visa.*

POLPERRO	Kitchen at Polperro	£55

Tel 01503 272780   Map 12 C3   **R**
The Coombes Polperro Cornwall PL13 2RQ

Park in the village car park and walk down to Ian and Vanessa Bateson's lovely little restaurant. The cooking is enjoyable and unpretentious, the menus interesting and varied: starters like gravad lax muffins, cheese paté (Miller Howe's recipe), avocado with chili dressing and pistachio nuts and Cornish sausages with onion marmalade precede a couple of dozen mains ranging from chicken *dijonnaise*, Thai beef and Moroccan lamb to scampi *jalfrezi*, coconut crab and half a dozen vegetarian options. A daily-changing list of extra dishes majors on seafood. Apart from a bottle of champagne, there's nothing over £20 on the wine list – commendable! No children under ten. No smoking. *Seats 24. Parties 4. D only 7-9.30. Closed Sun, Mon (Mar-July & Sept-Oct), Tue (Mar-May & Oct) & Nov-Easter. Access, Visa.*

PONTELAND — Café 21 — ↑ NEW — £55

Tel 01661 820357   Map 5 D2   **R**
**35 The Broadway Darras Hall Ponteland Newcastle-upon-Tyne
Northumberland NE20 9PW**

The B6323 leads from Ponteland to Darras Hall estate, where the restaurant occupies a site at the end of a parade of shops. Opposite is a modern church and almost next door, a garage. Opened in October 1994, it has an interior which is rustic and simple. The menus, chalked up above and alongside the bar, are uncomplicated too, yet the cooking is remarkably accomplished – as one might well expect from Terry Leybourne who also owns *21 Queen Street* in Newcastle city centre. Starters could include a roasted tomato soup with chorizo sausage and pesto, warm rabbit salad with broad beans, black olives and thyme or pigeon ravioli with pine nuts. Main dishes are typified by a confit of duck with braised butter beans, pan-fried sea bream with braised fennel, pan-fried salmon with garlic mash and tomato butter, or chargrilled tuna with a *salade niçoise*. Excellent desserts include old favourites like sticky toffee pudding and lemon meringue pie. Extremely pleasant service accompanies highly enjoyable food. *Seats 34. Parties 12. L 11.30-3 D 6-10.30. Closed Sun, Mon & Bank Holidays. Set L £9.95. Access, Amex, Diners, Visa.*

We welcome bona fide complaints and recommendations on the tear-out pages at the back of the book for readers' comments. They are followed up by our professional team.

POOLE — Haven Hotel — 69% — £120

Tel 01202 707333   Fax 01202 708796   Map 14 C4   **HR**
Banks Road Sandbanks Poole Dorset BH13 7QL

Follow signs to the Swanage ferry to find the Haven, right by the water's edge at the entrance to the world's second largest natural harbour giving most of the bedrooms (many with balconies) fine views either of Brownsea Island and the Purbeck Hills or across the Solent to the Isle of Wight. Comfortable rather than luxurious, with lightwood furniture and matching bedcovers and curtains, the rooms are immaculately kept, as is the whole hotel. Inviting public areas include the beamed Marconi lounge (he made the first wireless telegraph broadcast from here) with leather chesterfields, and a splendid conservatory with comfortably upholstered 'garden' furniture and waterside terrace beyond. The exceptionally comprehensive leisure centre includes both indoor and outdoor pools, just a few steps beyond which is the hotel's own sandy beach. There's also a fine, purpose-built business centre adjacent to the hotel catering for up to 160. Children up to 14 years stay free in parents' room. No dogs. *Rooms 94. Terrace, tennis, indoor & outdoor swimming pools, gym, squash, sauna, steam room, spa bath, solarium, beauty salon, hairdressing. Access, Amex, Diners, Visa.*

Sea View Restaurant   £55
🍷 🎺 ✍

Large, 20s-style dining-room with short but well-balanced table d'hote dinner menu supplemented by a varied grill menu. Well-thought-out dishes are reliably cooked and swiftly served – from starters like salad of pan-fried pigeon or creamy carrot and vanilla soup to main courses that might encompass pan-fried tournedos of lamb with rosemary on an aubergine purée, galette of pan-fried angler-fish with ratatouille, a watercress sauce and red pepper coulis. To finish, perhaps a steamed chocolate and pistachio pudding or vanilla and exotic fruit torte. Lunch is a buffet/carvery affair, including Sunday when a traditional roast is always offered. The wine list is presented by style; for the most part, wines are not expensive (half a dozen champagnes at £30 or less). Note the fine wines and bin ends at the back of the list. No children after 7pm. Light lunches are also available in the informal conservatory and on the terrace, from where there are views of Poole Bay and Studland. *Seats 150. Parties 24. L 12.30-2 D 7-9.30. Set L £14.50 Set D £22.*

La Roche   £80
♕ 🍷 🎺

The more intimate à la carte restaurant is where chef Karl Heinz Nagler gives full rein to his undoubted skills. The sophisticated black-edged decor is a suitable foil to equally sophisticated dishes such as a potted oxtail galette, steamed cannelloni of salmon on a bed of spinach with crispy leeks and a basil vinaigrette, baked fillet of cod with thyme mousse and scaled with crispy potatoes, pan-fried lamb tournedos on an aubergine purée with garlic-scented tomato and lamb jus and marinaded and roasted loin of Scottish beef with herb dumplings, wild mushrooms and a rich, red wine sauce. To round off the meal there are desserts like a pyramid of honey wafers filled with lemon and lime mousse, a simple brioche pudding enriched with whisky and served with *sauce anglaise* and caramelised apples or a délice of bananas enriched with Galliano and served with a dark chocolate sauce. Same wine list as above. No children under 10 years. **Seats** *26. Parties 12. D only 7-10. Closed Sun, 25 & 26 Dec.*

POOLE	**Mansion House**	**74%**	**£110**
Tel 01202 685666 Fax 01202 665709		Map 14 C4	**HR**
11 Thames Street Poole Dorset BH15 1JN			

Facing St James Church across a tiny square, the marble-pillared portico and tall, arched windows of the Mansion House epitomise Georgian elegance. It is only a stone's throw from bustling Poole quay, yet it is an oasis of calm within. The best bedrooms are generously proportioned and airy, although some others are rather less so. Each is decorated in individual style and furnished with fine antiques, to which today's more modern necessities have been sympathetically added. More thoughtful, homely extras extend to mineral water, fresh fruit and boiled sweets in the rooms plus complimentary early morning tea tray and choice of newspaper. Children up to 12 stay free in parents' room. No dogs. **Rooms** *28. Access, Amex, Diners, Visa.*

Benjamins Restaurant   £65

A smart dining club, also open to the public, where non-residents (or non-members) pay 15% supplement for the various fixed-price menu prices quoted below. Also note that all prices (except Sunday Lunch) are for two courses with desserts an optional extra. The style is 'modern English' with fillet of halibut topped with mushroom and herbs on a whole grain mustard sauce, grilled smoked haddock and asparagus on crostini with a peppery hollandaise, pan-fried pork with Dorset air-dried ham and sage with Marsala sauce and gnocchi, and roast best end of lamb sliced on to curried aubergines with a lamb sauce typifying the main dish choices. At lunchtime there is always a roast from the trolley and an hors d'oeuvre table, the latter forming the principal course of the slimmer's choice menu. Good vegetarian options and traditional puddings complete the picture along with a two-part wine list with over half the bottles under £20, and all accompanied by tasting notes. The clubby atmosphere successfully avoids stuffiness and service is good. JJ's Bistro offers more informal fare, but is only open to members and residents. **Seats** *40. Parties 12. Private Room 40. L 12-2 D 7-9.30. Closed L Sat & Bank Holiday Mondays, D Sun. Set L £10 (Slimmer's Choice), £11.50 (£15.50 inc wine – 50 Minute Luncheon) & £14 (£18 inc wine – Benjamin's Choice) Set L Sun £12.95 (children half price). Set D £13.95.*

POOLE	**Quay Thistle Hotel**	**63%**	**£108**
Tel 01202 666800 Fax 01202 684470		Map 14 C4	**H**
The Quay Poole Dorset BH15 1HD			

Signposted from the town centre, the hotel overlooks the harbour. Neat, practical bedrooms include 22 for non-smokers. **Rooms** *68. Patio. Access, Amex, Diners, Visa.*

POOLE	**Sandbanks Hotel**	**59%**	**£110**
Tel 01202 707377 Fax 01202 708885		Map 14 C4	**H**
15 Banks Road Sandbanks Poole Dorset BH13 7PS			

Ideal for families, with an attractive patio and garden leading on to a sandy beach, and complete holiday services that include organised activities, a children's restaurant and a nursery. 17 rooms are specifically designated as family rooms. Four tiers of balconied bedrooms look either out to sea or across Poole Bay and the open-plan bar, vast sun lounge and dining-rooms also enjoy panoramic views over the sea. Adult guests may use the leisure facilities at the *Haven Hotel* (see entry). No dogs. **Rooms** *107. Terrace, putting green, indoor swimming pool, gym, sauna, steam room, spa bath, solarium, creche (daily in summer), children's outdoor play area, coffee shop (10am-11pm). Access, Amex, Diners, Visa.*

PORLOCK — Oaks Hotel   65%   £80

Tel & Fax 01643 862265   Map 13 D1   **HR**
Porlock Somerset TA24 8ES

An Edwardian country house in an elevated position among lawns and trees (oaks, of course!), with views down to Porlock Bay. Tim and Anne Riley, here since 1986, are the most welcoming of hosts, and the lounge, with its flowers, books and magazines, is an easy place for relaxing. There's also an intimate bar. Bedrooms are light and pretty with a mix of pine and some nice old-fashioned pieces. Service is a strong point and the whole place is kept crisp and fresh. *Rooms 10. Closed Jan & Feb. Garden. Access, Visa.*

Restaurant   £45

Anne's daily-changing dinner menus start with soup (perhaps cream of watercress), Caerphilly cheese and fresh herb tart or guinea fowl and chestnut terrine; follow with the fish/shellfish course; continue with local duckling with cherry, apple and cinnamon, stuffed tenderloin of pork with cider gravy or grilled Devonshire fillet of steak; and round things off with a sorbet, ice cream, treacle tart or a selection of local cheeses. More than reasonable prices (£14 for the excellent Hamilton Russell Pinot Noir from South Africa) on a well-balanced list that includes concise tasting notes. No smoking. *Seats 24. Parties 12. D only 7-8.30. Set D £22.*

PORTH — Trevelgue Hotel   62%   £100*

Tel 01637 872864   Fax 01637 876365   Map 12 B3   **H**
Porth nr Newquay Cornwall TR7 3LX

A budget family holiday hotel par excellence. With the rolling downs of north Cornwall behind, a 180° sea vista to the front and a large, sandy beach just down the hill, the Trevelgue has a head start with its position. Self-styled as a "parents' haven" and "children's paradise", its continued success (after 13 years) is achieved by providing almost everything that families need – at no extra cost – in order to have a peaceful stay away from the comforts of home. From babes in arms to the most energetic of teenagers, due consideration is given to their requirements; you name it and they've generally thought of it, and they bring it off with panache. The arrangements for children's high tea and for parents to enjoy their modest evening meal are particularly impressive (the wine list is very keenly priced). Cots, high-chairs, bunk beds, bikes, buggies, back packs, baby walkers, baby baths, sterilisers, bottle-warmers and bouncy chairs can all be provided if booked in advance. The hotel is spacious enough never to feel like a nursery and the management have cleverly made the adult attractions as inviting as those for their junior guests. Accommodation is in 42 spacious (if somewhat spartan) family suites with 28 further rooms for additional family members. Guests without children are not encouraged. *Half-board, weekly terms only in season (highest daily rate given). Previous winner of our Family Hotel of the Year award. *Rooms 70. Garden, tennis, children's sports in high season, squash, golf practice net, 2 practice holes, mini-golf, croquet & boules, skittles, air rifle range, children's adventure playground, outdoor & indoor swimming pools, health and beauty salons, pool, table tennis, BMX track. Closed Nov-end Mar (except Feb half-term) booking office remains open. Access, Visa.*

PORTLOE — Lugger Hotel   59%   £100

Tel 01872 501322   Fax 01872 501691   Map 12 B3   **H**
Portloe Truro Cornwall TR2 5RD

17th-century inn, smugglers' haunt, boat-builders' shed, and since 1950 a cosy, friendly little waterside hotel run by the hospitable Powell family. The sea and tiny beach are virtually on the doorstep, and in fine weather the cocktail bar terrace is a popular spot. Oak-beamed lounge, library, well-equipped bedrooms divided between the original building and a modern addition. No children under 12. No dogs. *Rooms 19. Closed late Nov – early Feb. Terrace, sauna, sun beds. Access, Amex, Diners, Visa.*

Consult the blue pages for summary tables and lists of recommended establishments.

PORTSMOUTH   Forte Posthouse   65%   £72

Tel 01705 827651   Fax 01705 756715   Map 15 D4   **H**
Pembroke Road Southsea Portsmouth Hampshire PO1 2TA

Near the Hovercraft terminal at Southsea, a modern hotel with leisure and business centres (conferences for up to 250, banqueting up to 220). *Rooms 163. Indoor swimming pool, gym, sauna, spa bath, steam room, solarium, beauty salon, games room, snooker, children's playroom. Access, Amex, Diners, Visa.*

PORTSMOUTH   Hilton National   66%   £90

Tel 01705 219111   Fax 01705 210762   Map 15 D4   **H**
Eastern Road Farlington Portsmouth Hampshire PO6 1UN

Modern low-rise hotel alongside M27 ten minutes from Portsmouth city centre. Well-equipped bedrooms (children up to 16 free in parents' room), free parking and conferences for up to 230. *Rooms 118. Garden, indoor swimming pool, keep-fit facilities, sauna, spa bath, floodlit tennis, snooker. Access, Amex, Diners, Visa.*

PORTSMOUTH   Hospitality Inn   61%   £79

Tel 01705 731281   Fax 01705 817572   Map 15 D4   **H**
South Parade Southsea Portsmouth Hampshire PO4 0RN

Seafront hotel with some Victorian features, but mainly modern bedrooms. 20 rooms reserved for non-smokers. Children up to 6 share parents' room free. Popular for conferences and functions for up to 250/300 people. Thistle & Mount Charlotte Hotels. *Rooms 115. Access, Amex, Diners, Visa.*

Set menu prices may not always include service or wine.

PORTSMOUTH   Pendragon Hotel   59%   £49

Tel 01705 823201   Fax 01705 750283   Map 15 D4   **H**
Clarence Parade Southsea Portsmouth Hampshire PO5 2HY

Privately-owned hotel with some bedrooms commanding sea views over the Solent. Banqueting/conferences for up to 100, family rooms and children's menu. *Rooms 49. Patio. Access, Amex, Diners, Visa.*

PORTSMOUTH   Portsmouth Marriott   73%   £105

Tel 01705 383151   Fax 01705 388701   Map 15 D4   **H**
North Harbour Cosham Portsmouth Hampshire PO6 4SH

The hotel stands alongside the junction of the A3 and M27, a short drive from the ferry terminals and the town centre. Public areas in atrium-style include swimming pool, lounge, bar and split-level restaurant. Bedrooms on seven floors (four non-smoking) are roomy, with high standards of housekeeping, stylish wooden furniture, modern fabrics and good-sized beds – all doubles and many king-size. Satellite TV in all rooms. Compact bathrooms have good showers (but smallish baths) and plenty of toiletries. Leisure facilities include a snooker room and well-kept secluded garden with barbecue. Banqueting and conference facilities up to 450 (300 in one suite). The rate quoted is for a standard room. Premier rooms are priced at £125. Rates include parking. Children free in parents' room. *Rooms 170. Garden, indoor swimming pool, keep-fit equipment, squash, volleyball, basketball, sauna, spa bath, solarium, beauty salon, snooker, children's playroom & playground. Access, Amex, Diners, Visa.*

POUNDSGATE   Leusdon Lodge Hotel   61%   £90

Tel 01364 631304   Fax 01364 631599   Map 13 D3   **HR**
Leusdon Poundsgate nr Newton Abbot Devon TQ13 7PE

Not easy to find this oasis of a hotel, perched high on the moors above Newton Abbot, so phone for directions. The views from the public rooms and many of the bedrooms will make the effort worthwhile. The home comforts and delightful welcome will make you feel like a guest in a private house. Delicious cream teas. A good centre for walking in Dartmoor National Park. Children up to 12 stay free in parents' room. *Rooms 7. Garden, croquet. Closed 22-27 Dec & 8 Jan-7 Feb. Access, Visa.*

See over

Restaurant   £55

Good simple cooking using the best ingredients: carrot and coriander soup, melon with elderflower dressing, John Dory with vanilla, roast rack of Shrewsbury lamb, medallions of pork with orange and ginger. There is always an interesting vegetarian option. For dessert the hot chocolate soufflé is a must if it's one of the offerings on the day's fixed-price menu or try pistachio and almond loaf with apricot sauce or meringues with hot fudge sauce. Beautiful views of the Dart Valley from the dining-room. No smoking. *Seats 18. Parties 12. L by arrangement D 7.30-8.45. Set D £21.50.*

POWBURN	Breamish Country House	67%	£116*

Tel 01665 578266   Fax 01665 578500   Map 5 D1   **H**
Powburn Alnwick Northumberland NE66 4LL

Resident owners Doreen and Alan Johnson offer hospitality and tranquillity in abundance at their Georgian-style building, originating in the 17th century as a farmhouse and converted in the 19th century to a hunting lodge. Five acres of gardens and woodland provide the setting, and trees from those woods furnish the names of the individually decorated bedrooms. Children under 12 and dogs strictly by arrangement only. ★Half-board rate, bed and breakfast is available. *Rooms 11. Garden. Closed Jan & 1st 2 weeks Feb. Access, Visa.*

Consult the blue pages for summary tables and lists of recommended establishments.

POWERSTOCK	Three Horseshoes Inn	£50

Tel 01308 485328   Map 13 F2   **RR**
Powerstock Bridport Dorset DT6 3TF

The Three Horseshoes is a stone and thatch country inn with simple country furnishings and open fires, reached by narrow winding lanes. Its restaurant comprises two pine-panelled rooms, one small and cosy, the other more roomy and airy. Fish is what licensee Pat Ferguson is best known for, and the blackboard menu offers several examples of freshly caught produce, simply prepared and presented. Meat-eaters are also well provided for. Cooking is generally in traditional British mode, especially the puddings. Very popular for Sunday lunches – essential to book, especially in winter. Tables in the garden for summer eating. No smoking. *Seats 60. L 12-2 D 7-10 (to 9 Sun). Set L £10.95/£12.95. Closed 25 Dec. Access, Amex, Visa.*

Rooms   £50

Four large, traditionally-styled rooms have central heating, en-suite bathrooms and lovely views. Delightful garden. Families with children are welcome; cots available.

PRESTBURY	Bridge Hotel	63%	£89

Tel 01625 829326   Fax 01625 827557   Map 6 B2   **H**
New Road Prestbury nr Macclesfield Cheshire SK10 4DQ

Old-world charm and modern convenience meet in a privately owned hotel next to the church in the centre of a pretty village. Day rooms retain some feel of the 17th-century origins, while most of the bedrooms are in a modern redbrick extension overlooking the River Bollin. Banqueting and conference facilities for up to 100. *Rooms 23. Garden. Access, Amex, Diners, Visa.*

PRESTBURY	White House Manor	£112

Tel 01625 829376   Fax 01625 828627   Map 6 B2   **HR**
The Village Prestbury Cheshire SK10 4HP

There are no public areas as such (thus no hotel grading), just a small conservatory lounge and honesty bar where you can take a leisurely breakfast, though it's just as often served in the privacy of your own room. The very individually furnished bedrooms range from the most elegant 'Crystal Room' which has a locally crafted four-poster bed, crystal chandelier and and whirlpool bath to the sporty 'Minerva' that includes a Turkish steam room and power shower, as well as antique sporting equipment. Then there's the 'Glyndebourne' with a music centre and comprehensive library of modern and classical music, and 'The Studio' featuring art. Room service is available throughout the day and evening and in addition there are extensive bar and beverage facilities in the bedrooms, as well as remote-control TV, hairdryer and decent toiletries. Small meeting rooms 5/40, conferences (50 theatre-style) and banqueting in the restaurant. *Rooms 9. Garden. Access, Amex, Diners, Visa.*

Restaurant £65

A few minutes walk from the hotel, in the centre of the village, the pretty restaurant features exquisite table settings, Macclesfield silk and lace, and lots of greenery. Owner Ryland Wakeham and chef Mark Cunniffe are at the helm in the kitchen, and wherever possible produce is local (as in roast loin of Cheshire pork with black pudding stuffing, and sage, apple and onion sauce). Other dishes might include a seafood pancake with herb sabayon, roast leg of lamb in basil pesto and iced chocolate and chestnut parfait. A fine cheese platter features several British farmhouse varieties (Dunsyre Blue, Bonchester, Pencarreg); In addition to the tasting notes, there's a glossary of tasting terms eg "full-bodied – a wine with lots of body" and "light – opposite of full-bodied"! But it is a good list, with perhaps the best value in the New World. *Seats 70. Parties 12. Private Room 40. L 12-2 D 7-10. Closed D Sun, L Mon. Set L £11.95/£12.90 Set D £13.50/£16.50/£20.75.*

PRESTON	Forte Posthouse	63%	£72

Tel 01772 259411 Fax 01772 201923   Map 6 B1   **H**
The Ringway Preston Lancashire PR1 3AU

Tall redbrick hotel with neatly designed bedrooms, and conference facilities for up to 120. Children up to 12 stay free in parents' room. Free parking for guests' cars in an adjacent multi-storey park. *Rooms 121. Access, Amex, Diners, Visa.*

PRESTON	Heathcotes Brasserie	NEW	£55

Tel 01772 252732 Fax 01772 203433   Map 6 B1   **R**
23 Winckley Square Preston Lancashire PR1 3JJ

Modern (surprisingly comfortable chairs by Philippe Starck) and stylish – note the murals by Lubaina Hind – with colour schemes of magnolia and burnt ochre. There's a downstairs seafood counter and rotisserie serving the likes of fish (lobster, salmon) platters, bowls of mussels or spit-roast chicken, though it is perhaps the upstairs area that's making most waves, and rightly so, since the cooking is of a high standard. Paul Heathcote has placed two able lieutenants from his Longridge restaurant in charge: Max Gnoyke in the kitchen and Andrew Morris as restaurant manager together orchestrate an enthusiastic team, providing good food at value-for-money prices in a lively atmosphere. Look out for dishes such as risotto of basil pesto, and chargrilled tuna with red pepper caponata and yellow pepper coulis to start, followed by a lamb hot-pot with braised red cabbage or grilled calf's liver served on sage buttered cabbage and crisp spätzle. End with what's fast becoming a signature dish: bread-and-butter pudding scented with orange; melting chocolate tart or glazed rice pudding. Live jazz Sunday lunchtime. Short list of around twenty wines, all available by the glass. *Seats 90 (brasserie). Parties 20. L 11.45-2.15 D 6-10.30 Set L £8.50/£10.50 (Sun £13.50). Seafood & Rotisserie Bar: Seats 65. Parties 20. All Day 12-9pm (Sunday L 12-3 D 7-9). Access, Amex, Diners, Visa.*

PRESTON	Novotel	62%	£55

Tel 01772 313331 Fax 01772 627868   Map 6 B1   **H**
Reedfield Place Walton Summit Preston Lancashire PR5 6AB

Practical modern accommodation and conference facilities for 180. Children up to 16 stay free in parents' room. Situated on the A6, and handy for the M6 (J29) and M61 (J9). Free parking for up to 140 cars. *Rooms 98. Outdoor swimming pool. Access, Amex, Diners, Visa.*

Set menu prices may not always include service or wine.

PUCKRUP   **Puckrup Hall Hotel**   75%   £98

Tel 01684 296200   Fax 01684 850788   Map 14 B1   **H**
Puckrup Tewkesbury Gloucestershire GL20 6EL

Formerly a small Regency hotel, the original building (which still contains 16 of the bedrooms) is now just an annexe (linked by glass walkway) to a splendid new hotel. Exceptionally well designed and built to a high standard, it boasts many nice architectural and decorative features showing great attention to detail. A marble 'compass' floor, with mural-painted dome above, is at the centre of a reception area that sports faux-marble columns and some classical statuary. Lots of other appealing public areas include an Orangery, a cocktail bar with baronial light fittings, a clubby golfer's bar with oak panelling and leather armchairs, and a modernistic coffee shop. Well-designed bedrooms come with good lightwood furniture, armchairs, phones at both desk and bedside, extras like mineral water and books, and, when the beds are turned down at night, a cuddly hedgehog left on your pillow to keep you company and to take home as a souvenir. Smart bathrooms have good showers above, large bathtubs and quality toiletries. There are two full suites and eight 'junior' suites with charming circular sitting areas opening on to furnished balconies. An extensive room service menu can provide a choice of hot dishes 24 hours a day. *Rooms 84. Garden, croquet, golf (18), putting, coarse fishing, indoor swimming pool, gym, aerobics studio, sauna, steam room, spa bath, solarium, beauty salon, children's playroom. Access, Amex, Diners, Visa.*

PUDDINGTON   **Craxton Wood**   70%   £102

Tel 0151-339 4717   Fax 0151-339 1740   Map 6 A2   **HR**
Parkgate Road Puddington South Wirral Cheshire L66 9PB

Craxton Wood is just 6 miles from Chester, 2 miles from both the M56 and M53, and easily accessible from Manchester and Liverpool airport and their business communities. That said, the hotel itself is an oasis of calm, where old-fashioned standards of service and comfort hold sway and where owner-manager Mr Petranca has been greeting guests since 1967. Extensive wooded grounds (floodlit at night), lawns and rose gardens provide a peaceful setting and the spacious bedrooms are reassuringly traditional, with reproduction furniture, conservative decor and neat, bright bathrooms. By contrast, the bar is done out in modern greys, pinks and pastel blues, though the main feature here is the splendid view of the gardens. The lounge is more traditional in style and very formal, with the highly polished furniture that characterises the bedrooms. Parking for 45 cars, banqueting/conferences for 50/40. No dogs. *Rooms 14. Garden. Closed first week Jan, last 2 weeks Aug. Access, Amex, Diners, Visa.*

Restaurant   £70

👑 🗋 V

The French menu with English translations offers a reasonable choice, including speciality dishes *supreme de volaille Louise (*breast of chicken and lobster poached in white wine, served with a sherry and lobster sauce) and *tournedos Jean-Paul*, with a truffle-flavoured wild mushroom sauce. There's a separate vegetarian menu and a good range of English and French cheeses. *Seats 85. Parties 50. L 12.30-2 D 7.30-10. Set L & D £19.85. Closed Sun, Bank Holidays.*

PULBOROUGH   **Chequers Hotel**   61%   £75

Tel 01798 872486   Fax 01798 872715   Map 11 A6   **H**
Church Place Pulborough West Sussex RH20 1AD

Just off the A29 north of the village, an intimate hotel, formed from a charming little Queen Anne house and adjacent stone building, which has been run, and lovingly cared for, by John and Ann Searancke for 30 years. Recent changes include development of a patio garden and complete refurbishment of most rooms (2 are now designated non-smoking). Children up to 12 share parents' room free. Small car park (for 16 cars); banqueting/conference facilities for 50/20. Dogs welcome. *Rooms 11. Garden, conservatory coffee shop (9.30am-5.30pm). Access, Amex, Diners, Visa.*

We welcome bona fide complaints and recommendations on the tear-out pages at the back of the book for readers' comments. They are followed up by our professional team.

| PULBOROUGH | **Stane Street Hollow** | **£60** |

Tel 01798 872819   Map 11 A6   **R**
Codmore Hill Pulborough West Sussex RH20 1BG

Converted from two 16th-century cottages, René and Ann Kaiser's long-established, charming restaurant is built of solid Sussex stone. René has been at the stoves for 20 years, and his 'peasant-style European cooking' has won many friends. Fine, fresh ingredients are always at the base of his dishes, and many of the vegetables are home-grown. They keep ducks and chickens for their eggs, and smoke their own salmon, chicken and ham. Prawn bisque, vegetable terrine with a sun-dried tomato vinaigrette and vol-au-vents filled with chicken dumplings, mushrooms and asparagus typify the à la carte starters, while main courses could span salmon dugléré, breast of duckling with a gooseberry compote, smoked ham with duxelles and Swiss cheese baked in puff pastry, and casserole of lamb's sweetbreads cooked in red wine with rosemary, garnished with pan-cooked lamb's kidneys. Desserts keep up the high level of appeal with the likes of rich, dark chocolate truffle served on a chocolate sponge moistened with rum. *Assiette René* gives small portions of four desserts. Traditional roast among the Sunday lunch offerings. Champagne-lovers should note the modest prices of Veuve Cliquot; in fact the entire wine list offers good value. No smoking. *Seats 32. Parties 10. Private Rooms 12 & 22. L 12.30-1.30 D 7.15-9.15. Closed L Sat, all Mon & Tue, 2 weeks June, 2 weeks Nov, 24-27 Dec. Set L £8.50 (Sun £12.50/£15.50). Access, Visa.*

> Lodges are now listed by county in the reference section

| PURTON | **Pear Tree** | **75%** | **£90** |

Tel 01793 772100   Fax 01793 772369   Map 14 C2   **H**
Church End Purton nr Swindon Wiltshire SN5 9ED

This former vicarage was moved, at the beginning of the century, a mile from its original site beside the church to its present position on the outskirts of the village. It is now much enlarged, with extra bedrooms and elegant conservatories. The comfortable pink-themed sitting-rooms provide a cosy welcome. Upstairs bedrooms, continuing the pink theme, are approached via a splendid atrium, complete with central tree. The attention to detail paid by the Youngs to their guests is impressive and nothing is too much trouble: fresh flowers, complimentary mineral water and a decanter of sherry in the bedrooms, good-quality his and hers toiletries and bathrobes in the bathrooms. A comfortable upstairs conference room (seating 50), overlooks the garden. Special "Let off some steam" weekends are arranged in conjunction with the Swindon and Cricklade Railway, where you can learn to drive a steam train. *Rooms 18. Garden, croquet. Closed 1 week Christmas. Access, Amex, Diners, Visa.*

| QUORN | **The Quorn** | **72%** | **£110** |

Tel 01509 415050   Fax 01509 415557   Map 7 D3   **H**
66 Leicester Road Quorn Leicestershire LE12 8BB

With gardens reaching down to the River Soar, the Quorn offers ease of access with a touch of the country thrown in. The mahogany-panelled entrance hall with its flagstones, Oriental rugs and carved stone fireplace, has a very welcoming look, and a splendid wooden staircase featuring oil paintings and a brass chandelier heightens the country house feel. Bedrooms in a modern purpose-built part are prettily decorated and tastefully furnished; appointments include air conditioning, two armchairs and remote-control TV (some with teletext). There are various attractive function rooms, from the 12-seater Snug to the mahogany-panelled Charnwood Suite which can hold 120. Staff are very jolly and friendly. The hotel is in the centre of Quorn, a village which is now by-passed by the A6. *Rooms 19. Garden, coarse fishing. Access, Amex, Diners, Visa.*

QUORN   Quorn Grange   67%   £102

Tel 01509 412167   Fax 01509 415621   Map 7 D3   **HR**
Wood Lane Quorn Leicestershire LE12 8DB

A short drive off the A6 brings you to this extended, ivy-clad Victorian house. Stylish bedrooms offer garden views and are tastefully appointed using contemporary fabrics offset against plain walls. Impressive, brightly lit bathrooms have huge mirrors, marble surrounds and powerful showers. A bar-lounge is housed in a bright, plant-filled conservatory. *Rooms 18. Garden, croquet. Access, Amex, Diners, Visa.*

Restaurant   £65

Dining-room windows are hung with Austrian blinds – a quietly elegant setting for chef Gordon Lang's serious cooking. Grilled goat's cheese with sweet grape salad and walnut pesto or a light pastry case of scrambled eggs and smoked salmon could start the meal, followed perhaps by chargrilled tuna with deep-fried noodles, ginger and coriander, medallions of pork fillet with glazed apples and Madeira sauce or roast pheasant with smoked bacon, bread sauce and cranberry gravy. *Seats 50. Parties 24.*
Private Rooms 24/36. L 11.30-2.30 D 7-9.30 (weekend to 10). Closed L Sat, all 26 Dec, 1 Jan. Set L £9.95 (Sun £7.95/£9.95 & £20.25) Set D £15.95/£20.25.

RAMSBOTTOM   Village Restaurant   £45

Tel 01706 825070   Map 6 B1   **R**
16-18 Market Place Ramsbottom nr Bury Lancashire BL0 9HT

Ros Hunter does the cooking while partner Chris Johnson looks after front of house and the superb wines. The look is informal bistro with pew seating. Ingredients are first class, lunch is à la carte from the ever-changing blackboard, while supper (not dinner in these parts!) offers four courses. Locally reared beef, lamb and venison are among the highlights; starters always include a splendid soup, and to finish there could be chocolate rum pot, bread-and-butter pudding and a rich, dark, boozy trifle. There's always an interesting vegetarian option, a marvellous selection of mature cheeses, and a short and carefully chosen wine list with a further several hundred wines available (at an additional £4.95 corkage) from their and wine shop. *Seats 40. Parties 8.*
Private Room 10. L 12-2.30 D 7.30 for 8. Closed D Sun, all Mon & Tues. Set L from £5.95 (Sun £17.50) Set D £17.50. Access, Amex, Diners, Visa.

RAVENSTONEDALE   Black Swan Inn   £66

Tel 01539 623204   Fax 01539 623604   Map 5 D3   **I**
Ravenstonedale nr Kirkby Stephen Cumbria CA17 4NG

A ten-minute drive from J38 of the M6 via the A685 brings you into a peaceful village nestling on the edge of the Howgill Fells. The Black Swan is a quiet little turn-of-the-century Lakeland stone hotel run since 1985 by Gordon and Norma Stuart. One of the stone-walled bar rooms is very much a locals' bar, while the other has a refined pub air with highly-polished, copper-topped tables; Thomas the black cat (whose portrait hangs proudly on the wall) may already have the best seat! Three spacious, ground-floor bedrooms have particularly good disabled facilities (and ramp access into the bars), while the rest – "above stairs" – are comfortably furnished in traditional style with floral decor. On the first floor is a homely sitting room. Across the road is a delightful, sheltered garden with a small footbridge across a trickling beck. *Rooms 16. Garden, lake and river fishing, tennis. Access, Amex, Diners, Visa.*

READING   Forte Posthouse   64%   £75

Tel 01734 875485   Fax 01734 311958   Map 15 D2   **H**
500 Basingstoke Road Reading Berkshire RG2 0SL

Near Junction 11 of the M4. Good leisure amenities. Banqueting and conference facilities for 110. Parking for 300. *Rooms 138. Garden, indoor swimming pool, childrens' splash pool, gym, sauna, steam room, spa bath, solarium. Access, Amex, Diners, Visa.*

Set menu prices may not always include service or wine.

READING   Holiday Inn Reading   71%   £106

Tel 01734 391818   Fax 01734 391665   Map 15 D2   **H**
Richfield Avenue Caversham Bridge Reading Berkshire RG1 8BD

Situated right on the edge of the Thames by the side of Caversham Bridge, this three-storey hotel is ultra-modern in design with a mixture of red brick and sloping roofs. Much trade comes from the business community (banquets for 180, conferences for 200) – unsurprisingly, given its location and good communication links – but it is also a useful tourist stopover. Large, open-plan public rooms include a cocktail bar in the sunken lounge, and a spotless white marble foyer. Limed lightwood furniture graces the uniformly decorated bedrooms. Eight suites have private balconies with river views, good-sized sitting rooms and better quality furnishings. Parking for 200 cars. *Rooms 111. Indoor swimming pool, sauna, sun beds, gym. Access, Amex, Diners, Visa.*

READING   Ramada Hotel   68%   £117

Tel 01734 586222   Fax 01734 597842   Map 15 D2   **H**
Oxford Road Reading Berkshire RG1 7RH

A large modern redbrick hotel in the central area of town offering well-equipped bedrooms (all have individually controllable air-conditioning), the best of which are 32 Executives (worth the small premium) with better-quality lightwood furniture giving plenty of work space and a second telephone at the desk. Seven rooms are designated as Lady Guest rooms; one room is specially adapted for disabled guests; the presidential Suite is top of the range. Public areas include a sunken lounge with central gas-log fire feature and Froggies, an informal café/bar; buffet-only breakfast. Conference/banqueting facilities for 220/180. Free valet parking is available in a supervised reserved section of a nearby multi-storey car park. Children under 18 stay free in parents' room. *Rooms 194. Indoor swimming pool, gym, sauna, spa bath, sun beds, beauty salon. Access, Amex, Diners, Visa.*

We welcome bona fide complaints and recommendations on the tear-out pages at the back of the book for readers' comments. They are followed up by our professional team.

REETH   Burgoyne Hotel   66%   £60

Tel & Fax 01748 884292   Map 5 D3   **HR**
The Green Reeth Richmond North Yorkshire DL11 6SN

An intentionally personalised and intimate small hotel has been created here by partners Derek Hickson and Peter Carwardine with echoes of, and obliquely paying homage to, an early Sharrow Bay. Once the home of the Burgoyne Johnson family, the imposing ivy-faced house stands in a prominent position overlooking the village green with commanding views of Swaledale and the surrounding hills shared by all but one of its bedrooms. The warmth of welcome, abundant comfort in elegant if slightly fussy day rooms and the personal attention which cossets each and every guest echoes the pleasure and pride which Peter and Derek take in having you stay in their house. In the tastefully modernised bedrooms plain, rich fabrics, freestanding furniture, easy chairs and magazines engender the feeling of well-being; remote-control TV and radio/alarm clocks are provided, and direct-dial phones have just been installed. Where the bathrooms of three of the rooms cannot practically be incorporated en suite, towelling robes and slippers are provided for a short step across the corridor. *Rooms 9. Garden. Closed 2 Jan – 1st weekend in Feb. Access, Visa.*

Restaurant   £55

Dinner is a nightly-changed five-course affair where guests foregather in the lounge (there is no bar) to choose their first and middle courses. Peter's menus offer four or five starters – savoury stuffed tomatoes, prawn and melon cocktail, millefeuille of creamed mushrooms and bacon – followed by a soup and then a sorbet before the main event, which might offer a choice between salmon hollandaise, duck with orange liqueur sauce and medallions of pork fillet with grain mustard cream. Finish with the likes of egg custard with fruit compote or blackberry and apple crumble. Derek provides smooth, professional service. Space is strictly limited and non-residents, though warmly welcomed, are nonetheless required to book. *Seats 30. L by arrangement D at 8. Set D £21.*

| REIGATE | La Barbe | £65 |

Tel 01737 241966   Fax 01737 226837   Map 15 E3   **R**
71 Bell Street Reigate Surrey RH2 7AN

An informal, very Gallic bistro-like setting on the edge of the town centre. Menus, which change every eight weeks or so, offer a mixture of classical and provincial cuisine, like traditional onion quiche or mussels cooked in a white wine and mushroom sauce, followed by a fish of the day or veal kidneys cooked in caramelised shallots and port sauce. Main courses are accompanied by a selection of vegetables and the speciality *gratin dauphinois*. End with fine French cheeses from Rungis market in Paris or pancakes filled with vanilla and hazelnut custard. Dishes are helpfully cross-referenced with recommended bottles on the well-described wine list, and there are always several monthly suggestions at fair prices. Friday night is accordion night! *Seats 65. Parties 20. L 12-2 D 7.15-9.45. Closed L Sat, all Sun, Bank Holidays & 3 days after Xmas. Set L £16.45/£17.95. Set D £19.95/£23.95. Access, Amex, Visa.*

| REIGATE | Bridge House | 61% | £81 |

Tel 01737 246801   Fax 01737 223756   Map 15 E3   **H**
Reigate Hill Reigate Surrey RH2 9RP

On the A217, just off Junction 8 of the M25, 15 minutes from Gatwick Airport. From its position high on Reigate Hill, this modern hotel enjoys impressive views across the valley. Bedrooms are of a good size, with smart darkwood units; the best rooms have south-facing balconies and good views, while rear rooms have poor outlooks but are very quiet. Considerably reduced stand-by room rates after 6pm and at weekends. No dogs. *Rooms 40. Access, Amex, Diners, Visa.*

| REIGATE | The Dining Room | £65 |

Tel 01737 226650   Map 15 E3   **R**
59a High Street Reigate Surrey RH2 9AE

Smart first-floor restaurant above the High Street shops. A short à la carte (supplemented by a particularly good value fixed-price option) is determinedly modern in style with the likes of seared sea scallops on a base of sweet and sour tomatoes, tian of white crab meat and avocado, roast cutlets of lamb with basil mash and shallot purée, fillet steak with cumin purée and ravioli of langoustines – all produced in workmanlike fashion by chef Anthony Tobin in the kitchen. Desserts range from roasted baby pears with a tulip biscuit filled with honey ice cream to a chilled soufflé of two chocolates with a compote of raspberries. Clean and fairly-priced short list of wines from Bibendum, an enterprising London wine merchant. Smoking allowed only in the bar area. *Seats 50. Parties 12. L 12-2 D 7-10. Closed L Sat, all Sun, Bank Holidays, 2 weeks Christmas, 1 week Easter & 1 week August. Set L & D £13.95. Access, Amex, Diners, Visa.*

| RENISHAW | Sitwell Arms | 61% | £60 |

Tel 01246 435226   Fax 01246 433915   Map 7 D2   **H**
39 Station Road Renishaw nr Eckington Derbyshire S31 9WF

A roadside inn, dating back in parts to the 18th century, featuring a purpose-built block of bedrooms, each of a good, comfortable standard. Two large bars form the greater part of the public areas. No dogs. *Rooms 30. Garden. Access, Amex, Visa.*

| RICHMOND | Burnt Chair | £55 |

Tel 0181-940 9488   Map 15 E2   **R**
5 Duke Street Richmond Surrey TW9 1HP

A small restaurant, just around the corner from Richmond Theatre, with closely-packed, crisply-clothed tables behind a gauze-draped shop front. Formerly an accountant, chef-patron Weenson Andrew Oo has an enthusiasm for food and wine that finds expression in an interesting à la carte that changes on the first Friday of each month. The style is modern, with influences from Europe and beyond: warm salad of duck with creamed lentils, black bean cakes with tomato salsa, fettuccine of salmon with Roquefort, grilled leg of lamb with oven-roasted vegetables. English farmhouse and French country cheeses, and for dessert perhaps lemon tart or basil ice cream with red plum compote. Extensive tasting notes on a list that seems longer than it really is, because every wine has been carefully chosen. Some good and interesting red burgundies; quality throughout, with very fair prices. A short fixed-price menu is available till 7.30pm (7pm Sat). *Seats 31. L by arrangement D 6-11 (Sat from 5.30). Closed Sun, 1 week Aug, 1 week Christmas. Set D £12.50 (2 courses). Access, Visa.*

RICHMOND	Petersham Hotel	65%	£130

Tel 0181-940 7471 Fax 0181-940 9998   Map 15 E2   **HR**
Nightingale Lane Richmond Surrey TW10 6UZ

Distinctive French Gothic-style building dating from 1865 with an elevated position on Richmond Hill affording fine views of a tranquil bend of the River Thames. An impressive cantilever staircase (the largest in the country) extends from the black-and-white tiled floor of the lobby/reception to a painted ceiling five floors above. Bedrooms vary considerably in size and shape with the largest having the best views and reproduction antique furniture; others incorporate more modest shelf-type fitted units. Bathrooms are often beyond an open arch, in which case there is a separate loo. Public rooms include two small lounges furnished in traditional style and a cocktail bar in pastel shades. No dogs. *Rooms 54. Access, Amex, Diners, Visa.*

Nightingales   £65

Smart, comfortable dining-room in shades of pink and blue where smooth, professional service complements reliably good cooking from head chef Tim Richardson's kitchen. The imaginatively compiled set lunch or dinner menu offers something for everyone with English dishes like Petersham fish cakes with watercress sauce and grilled calf's liver with bacon, classics such as potted shrimps, osso buco and boeuf bourguignon, and in the modern idiom home-made quail and pigeon sausage, steamed collops of monkfish with turnips and squid ink pasta. Good puds range from a daily 'hot English Pudding' via sharp lemon tart to a rich dark chocolate frangipan. Sunday lunchtimes there is a fixed-price menu only (choice of four main dishes) and only at this meal are children specifically catered for, with those under 10 paying half price with special menu alternatives offered. One no-smoking room. *Seats 70. Parties 14. Private Room 36. L 12.15-2.15 D 7-9.45. Set L £17.50 (Sun £20) Set D £23.*

RICHMOND	Richmond Gate Hotel	65%	£123

Tel 0181-940 0061 Fax 0181-332 0354   Map 15 E2   **H**
Richmond Hill Richmond Surrey TW10 6RP

High up on Richmond Hill, with a Victorian walled tarrace garden, overlooking the edge of 2500-acre Richmond Park and the Thames, the hotel was once a collection of four 18th-century buildings. The original house contains intimate public rooms and eight luxury double rooms of grand proportions, some with four-posters. In a newer extension, to the rear, bedrooms are equally attractive and comfortable, though more uniform in design. Under-5s stay free in parents' room. Functions/conferences for up to 70. No dogs. A leisure centre is due to open when this Guide is published (Oct '95). *Rooms 64. Garden, croquet. Access, Amex, Diners, Visa.*

RICHMOND	River Terrace		£65

Tel 0181-332 2524 Fax 0181-332 6136   Map 15 E2   **R**
The Tower, Bridge Street Richmond Surrey TW9 1TQ

Lovely Thames views from a redeveloped Georgian building right on Richmond Bridge. Eat inside in the conservatory or out on the expansive terrace from a short menu offering the likes of chicken liver parfait; tartlet of grilled sea scallops, tomato and basil; grilled black and white pudding on rösti; codling fillet on braised fennel and saffron; pot-roasted pigeon with wild mushroom ravioli and cinnamon jus; and best end of lamb with couscous. Concise, reasonably-priced international wine list. *Seats 60. Parties 10. L 12-3 D 7-10.30. Closed D Sun & all Mon (both winter only), 26-30 Dec. Access, Amex, Diners, Visa.*

Set menu prices may not always include service or wine.

RIDGEWAY   Old Vicarage   ★★   £90

Tel 0114 247 5814 Fax 0114 247 7079   Map 6 C2   **R**
Ridgeway Moor Ridgeway nr Sheffield Derbyshire S12 3XW

Close to the village centre and set back from the road, the Old Vicarage is a substantial Victorian house surrounded by lawns and mature trees. As there's only the most discreet of name plates by the entrance gate it is advisable to obtain precise directions when booking. The welcome is warm and the decor is pleasingly unfussy in a country-house style with a charming, homely sitting room where pre-dinner drinks and wonderful canapés are served. The dining-room, candle-lit at night, is decorated in soft pastel shades offset by beautiful oil paintings and verdant prospects of the garden, creating a romantic and elegant setting for stunning cooking from Tessa Bramley and fellow head chef Rupert Staniforth. The use of home-grown produce, particularly herbs (and even their minuscule flowers), creates a myriad of delightful taste sensations. The style is based on robust, but still remarkably delicate and refined dishes imbued with the Bramley hallmarks of subtlety and sophistication. Thai-spiced crab cake in fragrant rice with crab sauce, quail roasted over lavender with a spinach and cep stuffing or roast monkfish tail with mint pesto and deep-fried leeks with pancetta might be offered as light appetiser courses. These are followed by such superb creations as roasted spring lamb fillet with a herb crust, chervil and spring onion and pommes Anna; roast *poulet noir* with fennel and potato stuffing, a confit of the leg served on a balsamic-dressed salad; and English sea bass steamed with five spice and ginger and served with a soy butter sauce. Desserts are equally exciting, ranging from a passion fruit crepe soufflé with passion fruit coulis and candied lime, pecan and orange pudding with butterscotch sauce, caramel ice cream and tangerine compote to the most brilliant, and rich chocolate pudding ever – a small baked chocolate sponge served with a chocolate fudge sauce and English custard – totally sensational. Coffee is served with hand-made chocolates and petits fours. A cosy and – if weather permits – beautifully bright and sunny conservatory makes a charming setting for Tessa Bramley's Bistro, her second dining-room and one which has a fixed-price menu chalked up on a blackboard against the wall. Prices here may be lower and the food marginally simpler in style but the attention to detail and the quality of the cooking is just as apparent as in the main dining-room. Roast tomato and basil soup with garlic croutons followed by pot-roasted free-range chicken on saffron risotto with chicken liver salad, then poached pear in Muscat de Beaumes with chocolate ice cream could comprise a typical extremely satisfying meal. Improved New World showing on a very decent wine list that offers some value-for-money wines, though the 'known' names are quite pricy. Champagne starts at £38. No smoking. *Seats* 50 (Bistro 30). *Private Room* 30/46. L (reservations only) 12.15-2.30 D 7-10.45. Closed D Sat (Bistro only), D Sun, all Mon, 26 & 27 Dec, 10 days Jan. Set L & D £18.50/£35 (Sun L £18.50), Bistro £17.50. Access, Amex, Visa.

RIPLEY   Boar's Head Hotel   66%   £90

Tel 01423 771888   Fax 01423 771509   Map 6 C1   **HR**
Ripley nr Harrogate North Yorkshire H53 3AY

Dating back to 1830 when the Lord of the Manor rebuilt the village next to Ripley Castle (open to the public during the summer), this former coaching inn is now a fairly up-market hotel. Oil paintings and furniture from the castle help to create the country house feel in tranquil drawing and morning rooms and the individually decorated bedrooms, which favour plain walls and stylish matching fabrics. Antique furniture features in rooms in the main building and in the larger rooms in another house across the cobbled square, while rooms in the former stable block are furnished with white-painted wicker pieces. Nice touches include porcelain ornaments and wooden toy catamarans in bathrooms that boast large soft towels and quality toiletries. *Rooms* 25. *Garden, tennis, coarse fishing. Access, Amex, Visa.*

Restaurant   £70

David Box cooks in accomplished modern English style on his short, well-chosen menus
(à la carte both sessions, fixed-price also at lunchtime). Evening choices range from
terrine of game birds with plum relish and steamed fillet of cod on a tomato and thyme
compote with a parsley sabayon to guinea fowl with a creamy pepper and morel sauce,
monkfish with braised celery and sautéed beef fillet topped with a casserole of oxtail and
wild mushrooms. Interesting sweets, too, typified by a trio comprising steamed fruit
pudding, warm berry crumble and crisp deep-fried apricots. There's a splendid wine list
– well-chosen, with fair prices, lots of half bottles and helpful notes. *Seats 38. Parties 14.*
Private Room 10. L 12-2 D 7-9.30. Set L £14.50.

RIPLEY	Michels'	★	£90

Tel 01483 224777   Map 15 E3   **R**
13 High Street Ripley Surrey GU23 6AQ

Erik and Karen Michel opened their restaurant in 1986; the setting is an elegant Georgian-
fronted Clock House. The Michels use locally grown produce whenever possible, picking
wild mushrooms in season, growing their own herbs, baking the delicious range of breads
daily. Menus change with the seasons, the fixed-price surprise menu (£19 lunch, £21
dinner) changing daily. The extensive carte might include as starters ravioli of pig's trotter
with green asparagus and truffle juice, seared scallops in a hop-flavoured butter sauce and
barley or risotto of langoustines and morels with a parmesan pancake. For main course try
the baked turbot with young fennel and a parsley sauce, duck breast with Chinese cabbage
cooked with lime and served with a crisp sesame galette. The dessert menu might also
challenge you with a pastry case filled with goat's milk curd, flavoured with rose water and
served with a blueberry salad. Karen Michel guides you through these delights charmingly
at front of house. The house wine selection has tasting notes, otherwise the list is quite
matter-of-fact, but with a good sprinkling of wines under £30. 3 glasses of wine are
included with the gourmet menu. *Seats 50. Parties 12. Private Room 12. L 12.30-1.30*
D 7.30-9 (Sat 7-9.30). Closed L Sat, D Sun, all Mon, 25 & 26 Dec, 1st week Jan. Set L £19
Set D £21/£28. Access, Amex, Visa.

RIPON	Ripon Spa Hotel	62%	£97

Tel 01765 602172   Fax 01765 690770   Map 5 E4   **H**
Park Street Ripon North Yorkshire HG4 2BU

On the B6265 to Pateley Bridge, the hotel, dating from 1909, is comfortable and has
friendly staff and commendably high standards of housekeeping. The prize-winning
gardens are a major plus, and the setting is secluded considering its proximity to the
centre. Rooms are individually decorated and furnished, and two have four-posters. Two
de luxe rooms have whirlpool baths. Most of the bedrooms enjoy garden views. The hotel has
several conference/function rooms, with a capacity of up to 160. Children up to 12 stay free
in parents' room (breakfast will be charged). *Rooms 40. Garden, croquet. Access, Amex,*
Diners, Visa.

ROADE	Roadhouse Restaurant		£55

Tel 01604 863372   Map 15 D1   **R**
16 High Street Roade Northamptonshire NN7 2NW

Once the local ale house, Christopher and Susan Kewley's village restaurant with pink
rag-roll-effect walls and a couple of old beams offers a shortish menu of dishes soundly
cooked by Chris and served in a friendly, unhurried atmosphere: pastry tartlet with
smoked haddock, tomato, poached egg and cheese sauce; breast of wild duck with sage
and onion stuffing and a compote of red cabbage and apple; chump of lamb in a rich red
wine sauce; baked fillets of salmon, cod and plaice served with mussels and a warm
mustard and tomato vinaigrette; civet of venison with red wine, bacon and mushrooms
(game is a seasonal speciality). The keenly-priced lunch menu is based on less expensive
dishes from the evening à la carte. There is a small bar for pre-dinner drinks. *Seats 45.*
L 12.30-1.45 D 7-9.30. Closed D Sun, all Mon. Set L £15 (Sun £16). Access, Amex, Visa.

ROCHESTER   Bridgewood Manor Hotel   68%   £105

Tel 01634 201333   Fax 01634 201330   Map 11 B5   **H**
Bridgewood Roundabout Maidstone Road Rochester Kent ME5 9AX

Virtually beside Junction 3 of the M2, this modern brick-built hotel offers up-to-date
meeting and conference facilities as well as a good base for the local tourist attractions.
General manager Gail Callaway and her staff provide friendly and helpful service. Public
areas, including a spacious reception lounge and bar, have an ecclesiastical decorative
inspiration. Bedrooms (37 designated non-smoking) have all the expected features,
remote TV, trouser presses and compact, clean, functional bathrooms. 24hr room service.
Children up to 16 stay free in parents' room. A central courtyard area provides
a sheltered al fresco area in the summer months. There's a wide range of facilities in the
self-contained leisure club. Small dogs only. Marston Hotels. *Rooms 100. Garden, tennis,*
putting green, indoor swimming pool, gym, sauna, spa bath, solarium, hair & beauty salon,
tennis, children's playground, snooker. Access, Amex, Diners, Visa.

> Consult the blue pages for summary tables and lists of
> recommended establishments.

ROCHESTER   Forte Posthouse   62%   £72

Tel 01634 687111   Fax 01634 864768   Map 11 B5   **H**
Maidstone Road Rochester Airport Rochester Kent ME5 9SF

Up-to-date comfort near Junction 3 of the M2 and Junction 6 of the M20. Children stay
free in parents' bedrooms. Conferences for up to 110. *Rooms 105. Indoor swimming pool,*
gym, sauna, spa bath, solarium, steam room, beauty salon, coffee shop (7am-10.30pm).
Access, Amex, Diners, Visa.

ROLLESTON-ON-DOVE   Brookhouse Hotel   62%   £85

Tel 01283 814188   Fax 01283 813644   Map 6 C3   **H**
Brookside Rolleston-on-Dove nr Burton-on-Trent Staffordshire DE13 9AA

Standing by the village brook, the William and Mary Grade II listed brick building was
converted to a hotel in 1976. Bedrooms are all individually styled, featuring antique
furniture, and many have four-posters, half-testers or Victorian brass beds trimmed with
Nottingham lace; several are in an adjacent converted barn. No children under 12.
Rooms 21. Garden. Access, Amex, Diners, Visa.

ROMALDKIRK   Rose & Crown   £75

Tel 01833 650213   Fax 01833 650828   Map 5 D3   **IR**
Romaldkirk Co Durham DL12 9EB

An imposing 18th-century coaching inn in a most picturesque village setting, and a fine
base for touring, walking, fishing and shooting. The main bar has a fine stone fireplace,
wood panelling, old black and white photos of the village, a grandfather clock and some
alarming-looking traps. Wrought iron-legged tables are surrounded by roundback chairs or
bench seating, and on the dining side of the room there are exposed stone walls, beams
and old farm implements. A residents' lounge, heavily endowed with more stripped stone
and beams, features wing chairs and period furniture, books, magazines and board games.
Everywhere there are local watercolours. Creaking floorboards, beams, old stone walls,
well-chosen antique furniture and contemporary fabrics feature in the refurbished and
improved bedrooms; duvets can be swapped for sheets and blankets. Front views overlook
the village green. Five further rooms, in an annexe, are more uniform in size and design,
with modern furniture and fittings. Excellent snacks and real ales served all sessions in the
bar and Crown Room; six tables are outside in front of the hotel. Service is friendly and
smiling throughout. *Rooms 12. Closed 25 & 26 Dec. Access, Visa.*

Restaurant   £65

In the part-panelled restaurant there are elegantly clothed tables and a civilised air. Chef
Christopher Davy's fixed-price, four-course dinners make excellent use of local produce,
typified by poached breast of corn-fed chicken with a roasted ballotine of the leg meat
and hollandaise, or chargrilled entrecote with garlic butter. Flanking these main courses
could be langoustines with aïoli, hot chive and potato pancake with smoked salmon and

sour cream, hot prune and almond tart and chocolate truffle mousse. Roast ribs of
English beef with Yorkshire pudding is a favourite centrepiece of the Sunday lunch
menu. Sensible and realistic prices on the wine list, with most wines attracting
enthusiastic tasting notes. No smoking. *Seats 24. Parties 12. L (Sun only) 12-1.30 D 7.30-9
(D Sun open for residents only). Set L (Sun) £11.50 Set D £22.*

| ROMSEY | Old Manor House | ★ | £90 |

Tel 01794 517353   Map 14 C3   **R**
21 Palmerston Street Romsey Hampshire SO51 8GF

The Old Manor House is exactly that, so it's somewhat unexpected to encounter Italian
and French dishes – until you realise that Mauro Bregoli is keeping his national heritage
alive in this corner of England. That's not to say that he doesn't take full advantage of
local produce like Test Valley trout, Lymington lobster or fresh asparagus, to serve
alongside his more familiar *pasta e fagioli, gnocchi bolognese* or breast of duck with
a reduction of honey and balsamic vinegar. Additionally, he tracks down wild mushrooms
and game, hunts truffles, hangs and smokes meat in the restaurant's giant chimney breast,
and is a dab hand at making fresh pasta (perhaps tagliatelle with Parma ham and dandelion
leaves). Desserts include crème brulée with fennel and fresh herbs, warm pear and
hazelnut tart and home-made Amaretto ice cream. A very serious and well-balanced wine
list offers quality throughout; in fact, there are some real gems to be had, albeit at a price.
However, the choice of the house provides exceptional value and the Italian especially
merits scrutiny. *Seats 45. Private Room 22. L 12-2 D 7-9.30. Closed D Sun, all Mon,
1 week Christmas. Set meals £13.50/£17.50. Access, Amex, Visa.*

| ROMSEY | White Horse Hotel | 63% | £102 |

Tel 01794 512431   Fax 01794 517485   Map 14 C3   **H**
Market Place Romsey Hampshire SO51 8ZJ

Georgian facade, oak beams, bedrooms (both period and modern) in a Forte hotel right
on the market place. Courtyard seating. Banqueting facilities for 90, conferences up to
40. Free use of nearby leisure centre. *Rooms 33. Access, Amex, Diners, Visa.*

| ROSEDALE ABBEY | Milburn Arms | 60% | £74 |

Tel & Fax 01751 417312   Map 5 E3   **H**
Rosedale Abbey nr Pickering North Yorkshire YO18 8RA

Country hotel and village pub, the Milburn Arms enjoys a tranquil and beautiful setting
in the North Yorks moors. Plants, ornaments, books and games make the lounge a good
place to spend an hour or two, and in the bar an extensive range of snacks and meals is
served. Individually-decorated bedrooms have good bathrooms and some also have fine
views; dogs in ground-floor annexe rooms only. A favoured spot in summer is the
peaceful garden, opposite the village green, with tables set out under a splendid 150-year-
old cedar. *Rooms 11. Garden. Closed 23-26 Dec. Access, Diners, Visa.*

| ROSS-ON-WYE | Chase Hotel | 64% | £80 |

Tel 01989 763161   Fax 01989 768330   Map 14 B1   **H**
Gloucester Road Ross-on-Wye Hereford & Worcester HR9 5LH

Large Georgian house – although the impressive entrance hall with colour-tiled floor and
marble columns supporting stone arches looks more Victorian – set in well-kept grounds
that make it a popular wedding venue. There's no separate lounge but the bar is smart
and comfortable. Attractive bedrooms feature co-ordinating fabrics with floral curtains
and striped bedcovers in several different colours. The furniture is sturdy light oak.
Fully-tiled bathrooms have decent toiletries. Decorative order is excellent throughout.
The four Executive rooms are the most spacious – two have four-poster beds. *Rooms 39.
Garden. Access, Amex, Diners, Visa.*

We welcome bona fide complaints and recommendations on the
tear-out pages at the back of the book for readers' comments.
They are followed up by our professional team.

ROSS-ON-WYE — Pengethley Manor — 67% — £100

Tel 01989 730211   Fax 01989 730258   Map 14 B1   **H**
Pengethley Park nr Ross-on-Wye Hereford & Worcester HR9 6LL

Pengethley is to be found at the end of a long drive off the A49 Ross (10 minutes to the south) to Hereford (20 minutes north) road. Fifteen acres of estate with a par-3 golf course, trout lake, vineyard and landscaped gardens enhance the tranquil country setting. Banqueting for up to 75 and conference rooms accommodating 50 kept discreetly separate. One purpose-built bedroom for disabled guests; children up to 16 stay free in parents' room with meals charged as taken. *Rooms 25. Garden, croquet, golf (9) outdoor swimming pool, snooker. Access, Amex, Diners, Visa.*

ROSS-ON-WYE — Pheasants — £70

Tel 01989 565751   Map 14 B1   **RR**
52 Edde Cross Street Ross-on-Wye Hereford & Worcester HR9 7BZ

A change in traffic priorities means that from having been in a side street this former pub is now on one side of the main street into town. There have been changes inside too, such as new crockery and glassware and some high-backed Italian chairs, but the atmosphere remains homely with warm, red rag-rolled walls, a few old beams, some gentle jazz/swing in the background and a distinctly unhurried atmosphere. It's a two-handed affair with New Zealander Adrian Wells serving and chef-patronne Eileen Brunnarius in the kitchen. Cooking is good dinner-party style with the likes of marinated salmon with cucumber spaghetti, smokies and spinach tart with hollandaise and tomato salsa, grilled breast of Trelough duck with beetroot 'caviar' and watercress sauce, halibut in champagne with shrimp sauce and pickled samphire, bitter chocolate and Cointreau bavarois, and Eileen's ever popular bread-and-butter pudding. Good farmhouse cheeses, mostly local, come with Bath Olivers and oatcakes, and such names as Yemen 'Ismaila' and Rooibosch (caffeine-free and low in tannin) are to be found among the coffees and teas on offer. The informed wine list (presented mostly by grape variety/style characteristics) is Adrian's passion – get him started on the subject and he might not stop! An improved New World section this year, and he's always on the look-out for varietal wines; though clarets and burgundies are not listed, there are some! *Seats 22. Private Room 10. L by arrangement. D 7-10. Closed Sun, Mon & 25 Dec-2 Jan. Set D £16/£19.50. Access, Amex, Diners, Visa.*

Rooms   £45

Two modestly furnished bedrooms (no TV or phone) share a good bathroom with Eileen and her ever-growing herd of hippopotami. Hearty breakfasts make a good start to the day.

Set menu prices may not always include service or wine.

ROTHERHAM — Carlton Park Hotel — 69% — £90

Tel 01709 364902   Fax 01709 368960   Map 7 D2   **H**
Moorgate Road Rotherham South Yorkshire S60 2BG

Formerly the Moat House, this modern redbrick hotel stands on the A618 south-east of the town centre, close to Rotherham General Hospital. Leisure facilities (no pool) and conference suites (for up to 250); elegant banqueting room for up to 200. Children up to 12 share parents' room free. 23 rooms reserved for non-smokers. *Rooms 78. Gym, spa bath, sauna, steam room, solarium. Access, Amex, Diners, Visa.*

ROTHERHAM — Swallow Hotel — 65% — NEW — £96

Tel 01709 830630   Fax 01709 830459   Map 7 D2   **H**
West Bawtry Road Rotherham South Yorkshire S60 4NA

Situated just half a mile from Junction 33 of the M1, this is a modern hotel with a foyer lounge, leisure club and secure parking. Spacious bedrooms (almost half non-smoking) have satellite TV, tea and coffee-making facilities (located some distance from an accessible power point), trouser press and hairdryer, but can suffer from extraneous noises – thin walls and bathroom fan for instance. Neat bathrooms offer good toiletries, though the overhead shower has a fixed flex and cannot be used 'telephone' fashion! Room service was very swift at the time of our last visit. Conferences for up to 300. ***Rooms*** *100. Indoor swimming pool, spa bath, steam room, sauna, solarium, gym. Access, Amex, Diners, Visa.*

ROTHERWICK	**Tylney Hall**	**79%**	**£122**

Tel 01256 764881   Fax 01256 768141   Map 15 D3   **HR**
Rotherwick nr Hook Hampshire RG27 9AZ

Signposted from the B3349 west of Junction 5 of the M3, Tylney Hall is a Grade II listed mansion built about 100 years ago but incorporating some much older architectural features like the ornate Italian ceiling in one of the lounges. Indeed, fine ceilings are a feature of the extensive public rooms here and come in various styles, Tudor in the dining-room, delicate and refined in the Wedgwood room and baronial in the ballroom that also features a minstrel's gallery and massive stone fireplace. The building is set in 66 acres of grounds with fine Gertrude Jekyll gardens that include cascading waterfalls, fountains, ornamental lakes and woodland walks. There are no small bedrooms here and many are very spacious. All share the same pink and pale green colour scheme, though in various styles, with a mixture of antique and reproduction furniture, and all have good armchairs and/or settees. Levels of service are high with notably attentive, friendly staff and the moving of telephones from desk to bedside when rooms are serviced in the evenings is a nice touch. 24hr room service. Children up to 14 stay free in parents' room. For guests seeking extra privacy there are three cottage suites in the grounds overlooking a small lake. Conference/banqueting facilities in a variety of rooms, the largest holding 100. No dogs. ***Rooms*** *91. Garden, croquet, tennis, indoor & outdoor swimming pools, gym, sauna, snooker. Access, Amex, Diners, Visa.*

Oak Room   £95

Impeccable service from engaging maitre d' Ignacio Gonzalez and his team adds lustre to the cooking in the mellow oak-panelled dining-room. Stephen Hine uses the best raw materials in his cooking, which is modern English and Continental in inspiration. Wild mushroom terrine or hot game sausage with black pudding and a lentil sauce could be your starter, followed by pot-au-feu of maize-fed chicken with parsley potatoes, pan-fried saddle of venison accompanied by a chestnut mousse and parsnip purée, or braised fillet of turbot and langoustines with a light curry and coconut sauce. British farmhouse cheeses, half a dozen desserts. The New World shows well on an otherwise quite classic list, though greedily marking up prices to the nearest 5p is plain silly (eg Mouton Cadet £16.05)! The lunchtime table d'hote concentrates on English Fayre. Outdoor dining for 20 on the terrace. ***Seats*** *100. Parties 8. L 12.30-1.45 D 7.30-9.30 (Fri & Sat to 10). Set L £12/£19.50 (Sun £19.50) Set D £28.*

ROTHLEY	**Rothley Court**	**67%**	**£102**

Tel 0116 237 4141   Fax 0116 237 4483   Map 7 D3   **H**
Westfield Lane Rothley Leicestershire LE7 7LG

By the B5328 west of Rothley (six miles outside Leicester), this imposing 13th-century manor stands in six acres of grounds, surrounded by lawns and open farmland. Much historical character is retained, including an 11th-century chapel built by the Holy Order of the Knights Templar. Day rooms feature some fine oak panelling, buttoned-leather chairs, exposed floorboards and stone fireplaces, while the main staircase boasts two fine stained-glass windows. Manor bedrooms of various sizes have antique furniture and subdued colour schemes, while annexe rooms are more uniform. ***Rooms*** *36. Garden. Access, Amex, Diners, Visa.*

We welcome bona fide complaints and recommendations on the tear-out pages at the back of the book for readers' comments. They are followed up by our professional team.

ROWDE — George & Dragon — £60

Tel 01380 723053   Map 14 C3   **R**
High Street Rowde Wiltshire SN10 2PN

A village pub in the heart of Wiltshire where the blackboard lists an extensive selection of mainly fish dishes which are a far cry from traditional pub fare. Twice-weekly deliveries from Cornwall ensure a good and constantly changing variety. Additionally the preparations, sauces and accompaniments are wonderfully innovative as in crostini of fish paté with parsley, pesto and grilled peppers, followed by halibut with a scallop and lentil sauce, Thai seafood curry of sea bream, swordfish and mussels or monkfish with cucumber, mustard and crème fraiche. There are some familiar items too as in salmon fishcakes with hollandaise, dressed Cornish crab salad, whole grilled lobster with basil and garlic butter. For the non-fish fancier there's sautéed lamb's kidneys with mushrooms in sherry vinegar; pumpkin risotto with saffron, tomato, pine nuts and raisins; wild mushroom and quail's egg tart with chervil hollandaise and cheese soufflé. Lovely old-fashioned sweets – bread-and-butter pudding, hot chocolate sponge pudding with chocolate sauce and lemon tart – as well as an interesting choice of ice creams and sorbets: marmalade, champagne, clementine. There's an inexpensive wine list (lots of wines under £10, plenty available by the glass) with helpful tasting notes. *Seats 35. L 12-2 D 7-10. Closed Sun, Mon, 25,26 Dec & 1 Jan. Set L £8.50. Access, Visa.*

ROWSLEY — Jarvis Peacock Hotel — 64% — £123*

Tel 01629 733518   Fax 01629 732671   Map 6 C2   **H**
Rowsley Matlock Derbyshire DE4 2EB

A small hotel with the River Derwent running through the gardens, so its's no surprise to find plenty of anglers among the guests – there's trout and grayling fishing on the Derwent and an additional 12 rods on the Wye. Dating back to the 17th century, the hotel has an appeal that is enhanced by mellow, antique-filled public rooms including a beamed bar with rough stone walls, while individually decorated bedrooms offer all the usual modern comforts. Children up to 14 stay free in parents' room. The hotel stands on the A6 five miles north of Matlock and three miles south of Bakewell. *Half-board rate – ask about B&B tariff. **Rooms** 14. Garden, fishing. Access, Amex, Diners, Visa.*

RUCKHALL — Ancient Camp Inn — £48

Tel 01981 250449   Fax 01981 251581   Map 14 A1   **I**
Ruckhall nr Eaton Bishop Hereford & Worcester HR2 9QX

On the site of a former Iron Age camp, the inn stands atop an escarpment overlooking a wide bend in the river Wye. Ruckhall (not on many maps) is signposted on the main A465 leaving Hereford towards Abergavenny. The building retains original stonework and flagstone floors to create an intimate atmosphere, cheered in winter by huge log fires. Home-made bar meals are served lunchtime and evening (but not on Mondays). Three neat bedrooms to the rear have showers/WC only; of two at the front one has a private sitting room, the other an en-suite bath elevated to maximise its river view. All are centrally heated. No children under eight. No dogs. Now under new ownership. *Rooms 5. Garden, fishing. Access, Visa.*

RUNCORN — Forte Posthouse — 62% — £72

Tel 01928 714000   Fax 01928 714611   Map 6 A2   **H**
Wood Lane Beechwood Runcorn Cheshire WA7 3HA

A modern hotel not far from Junction 12 of the M56, overlooking the Frodsham Hills and Weaver Valley. Ample free car parking, a leisure club and very extensive conference facilities (a choice of 19 rooms holding up to 500 delegates theatre-style). 86 rooms are designated non-smoking. *Rooms 135. Garden, indoor swimming pool, gym, sauna, spa bath, steam room, solarium, beauty salon, outdoor children's play area. Access, Amex, Diners, Visa.*

We welcome bona fide complaints and recommendations on the tear-out pages at the back of the book for readers' comments. They are followed up by our professional team.

RUSPER   Ghyll Manor   65%   £101

Tel 01293 871571   Fax 01293 871419   Map 11 A5   **H**
High Street Rusper nr Horsham West Sussex RH12 4PX

Recently acquired by CSMA (Civil Service Motoring Association, whose members benefit from discounted rates) but remaining open to the general public, Ghyll Manor is a picturesque 14th-century timbered manor house in 40-odd acres of delightful grounds deep in the peaceful West Sussex countryside. The main day room is the Library Lounge, off which is a small bar with linenfold panelling and an old stone fireplace. The most characterful bedrooms are the ten in the main building, often featuring exposed beams and furnished with traditional freestanding pieces (refurbishment planned for these rooms). Remaining rooms and two cottages are in a separate Stable Mews block and tend to be more modern, with darkwood units. A popular venue for weddings and conferences (up to 150 theatre-style). Children under 16 stay free in parents' room. Sports facilities planned. *Rooms 24. Garden, croquet. Access, Amex, Diners, Visa.*

Set menu prices may not always include service or wine.

RYE   George Hotel   62%   £94

Tel 01797 222114   Fax 01797 224065   Map 11 C6   **H**
High Street Rye East Sussex TN31 7JP

Former coaching inn dating in parts back to 1575. Day rooms are comfortably traditional, and most of the bedrooms have old beams – two are suitable for family use. The Georgian ballroom is a popular choice for banqueting functions (up to 100) and conferences (up to 80). Forte. *Rooms 22. Access, Amex, Diners, Visa.*

RYE   Landgate Bistro   £60

Tel 01797 222829   Map 11 C6   **R**
5/6 Landgate Rye East Sussex TN31 7LH

♟

Skilled cooking in the simple surroundings of a popular bistro in a picturesque tourist town. Seafood is very much a speciality on chef-patron Toni Ferguson-Lees' menu – moules marinière, crab terrine, cod with ginger and spring onion, sea bass with hollandaise and the popular 'very fishy stew', a selection of local fish poached in stock and served with aïoli, garlic bread and a salad – but there's plenty for meat-eaters too, like wild rabbit with white wine and tarragon, guinea fowl with sherry and mushrooms, lamb steak with braised butter beans and fillet of beef in pastry with béarnaise sauce. Ginger or cardamom ice cream, walnut and treacle tart and lemon and sherry syllabub typify the desserts. *Seats 30. Parties 10. D only 7-9.30 (Sat till 10). Closed Sun, Mon, 1 week June, 1 week autumn, 1 week Christmas. Set D (Tue-Thur) £15.50. Access, Amex, Diners, Visa.*

RYE   Mermaid Inn   60%   £117

Tel 01797 223065   Fax 01797 225069   Map 11 C6   **H**
Mermaid Street Rye East Sussex TN31 7EU

Rebuilt in 1420 (on foundations dating back to 1156), the Mermaid stands among the cobbled streets of ancient Rye. Once famous for its smuggling associations, it remains strong on romantic, old-world appeal, with low beams, antique furnishings, Elizabethan illustrations and linenfold panelling. Five of the bedrooms have four-posters, six are suitable for family use. Free parking at the rear of the inn. No dogs. *Rooms 28. Access, Amex, Diners, Visa.*

SAFFRON WALDEN   Saffron Hotel   57%   £65

Tel 01799 522676   Fax 01799 513979   Map 10 B3   **H**
High Street Saffron Walden Essex CB10 1AY

A listed building of 16th-century origin, in the centre of a historic and charming market town. There's an old-fashioned panelled bar with exposed brickwork and timbers. Bedrooms, a few with four-posters, vary in size and style, but their decor and appointments are generally quite modest. Some rooms are reached by winding passages with head-threatening beams. Parking for 10 cars. *Rooms 17. Garden. Access, Amex, Diners, Visa.*

ST ALBANS — Noke Thistle — 65% — £111

Tel 01727 854252   Fax 01727 841906   Map 15 E2   **H**
Watford Road St Albans Hertfordshire AL2 3DS

Located on a roundabout on the A405 conveniently close to the M1, M10 and M25, the hotel has a classic early Victorian country house-like exterior. Inside there's a characterful reception with shiny blackened carved oak panelling and furniture. There's a choice of two lounges – a small, intimate chintzy one or a more spacious, but equally comfortable, lounge bar. Half the bedrooms are designated Executive. These have more writing space, a mini bar, three phones and more toiletries differentiating them from the Club rooms. All rooms sport hairdryers and satellite TV. Banqueting and conferences to 70. Residents have membership of the vast St Albans Health & Racquet Club and nearby Mentmore Golf Club. Children up to 14 stay free in parents' room. Reduced weekend tariff. *Rooms 111. Garden, gym. Access, Amex, Diners, Visa.*

ST ALBANS — St Michael's Manor — 63% — £96

Tel 01727 864444   Fax 01727 848909   Map 15 E2   **H**
Fishpool Street St Albans Hertfordshire AL3 4RY

The manor house, which dates from the 16th century, stands in five acres of attractive gardens complete with a lake. Well-proportioned day rooms have a traditional feel, particularly the Oak Lounge, part of the original Tudor structure, with fine plastered ceilings dated 1586. The restaurant has a bright conservatory (Victorian in style but dating from 1987) that's popular for private parties. The grounds contain many specimen trees, after which all the bedrooms are named. Best of the rooms are doubles with four-posters and garden views. *Rooms 22. Garden. Access, Amex, Diners, Visa.*

ST ALBANS — Sopwell House Hotel — 69% — £137

Tel 01727 864477   Fax 01727 844741   Map 15 E2   **H**
Cottonmill Lane Sopwell St Albans Hertfordshire AL1 2HQ

Two miles south-east of the city centre, Sopwell House, once the country home of Earl Mountbatten, still retains a good degree of its original Georgian elegance even though in the last few years it has undergone considerable enlargement. Eleven acres of part-wooded, part-landscaped gardens provide a peaceful rural setting. Substantial conference facilities (for up to 400), a new bedroom wing and a splendid leisure complex are all fairly recent additions. Public rooms include an elegant, quite clubby bar furnished with brown leather chesterfields, this sets the tone for the drawing room and library. 22 of the bedrooms have four-posters and these, together with a number of other rooms, have a traditional ambience. The remainder are a little more modern in style. Decor in all is well co-ordinated and tasteful. Extras include satellite TV. Marble bathrooms are excellent, each with a power shower, scales and useful toiletries. *Rooms 92. Garden, croquet, indoor swimming pool, gym, sauna, spa bath, steam room, solarium, beauty salon, hair salon, snooker, brasserie (10am-10pm). Access, Amex, Diners, Visa.*

ST AUSTELL — Boscundle Manor — 65% — £110

Tel 01726 813557   Fax 01726 814997   Map 12 B3   **H**
Tregrehan St Austell Cornwall PL25 3RL

Secluded grounds make a peaceful setting for this lovely little 18th-century manor house, whose owners Andrew and Mary Flint have been in residence since 1978, opening for the summer season only. Seven bedrooms are in the main house, one in the Garden Room above the swimming pool and two in a cottage at the top of the garden; all the doubles (8) have spa baths. Although more suited to residents wanting a quiet holiday, self-entertaining families might find this a pleasant home-from-home, run like a private house. No functions, no lunches for non-residents, just good old peace and quiet. As we went to press, a barn at the end of the golf area was being renovated as a games room. *Rooms 10. Garden, croquet, pitch & putt, outdoor swimming pool, keep-fit equipment, children's playroom. Closed end Oct-end Mar. Access, Amex, Visa.*

Consult the blue pages for summary tables and lists of recommended establishments.

| ST AUSTELL | White Hart | £64 |

Tel 01726 72100   Fax 01726 74705   Map 12 B3   **I**
Church Street St Austell Cornwall PL25 4AT

Although the centrally located White Hart is steeped in history (it dates back to 1735) it offers every modern comfort to holidaymakers and business travellers. The saloon bar is the focal point of the day rooms. Banqueting/conference facilities for up to 60.
Rooms 18. Closed 25 & 26 Dec. Access, Amex, Diners, Visa.

| ST IVES (CAMBS) | Slepe Hall | 61% | £62 |

Tel 01480 463122   Fax 01480 300706   Map 10 B2   **H**
Ramsey Road St Ives Cambridgeshire PE17 4RB

A Grade II listed building dating from 1848 and a private boarding school for girls until its conversion in 1966. Now a small, comfortable hotel, it's kept in excellent order by Jan and Colin Stapleton. Several bedrooms feature four-poster or half-tester beds, and among the public areas is the Brunel Suite, which can cater for 220 conference delegates or banqueters. *Rooms 15. Garden. Closed 25-28 Dec. Access, Amex, Diners, Visa.*

| ST IVES (CORNWALL) | Garrack Hotel | 62% | £100 |

Tel 01736 796199   Fax 01736 798955   Map 12 A3   **H**
Burthallan Lane St Ives Cornwall TR26 3AA

Run by the Kilby family since 1965, the creeper-clad Garrack stands peacefully in two acres of gardens overlooking Porthmeor beach and the distant sweep of St Ives Bay (ask for directions or a route map). The main lounge is a busy family room with games and books, and there are two other more formal lounges plus a pleasant cocktail bar. Bedrooms in the main house are traditionally furnished and vary in size; those in the extension are more modern and roomy. Some rooms have four-posters, some spa baths and there are also family rooms with bunk beds. *Rooms 18. Garden, indoor swimming pool, keep-fit equipment, sauna, solarium, spa bath, coffee shop (9.30am-10pm). Access, Amex, Diners, Visa.*

| ST IVES (CORNWALL) | Pig 'n' Fish | £45 |

Tel 01736 794204   Map 12 A3   **R**
Norway Lane St Ives Cornwall TR26 1LZ

In a simply appointed restaurant above a back-street craft market chef-patron Paul Sellars prepares fine (mainly) seafood dishes, many with a French or Italian accent and often showing more than a little invention. Lunchtime is fixed-price, dinner à la carte, and typical dishes include warm mussel salad with parsley pesto, terrine of pig's knuckle with mustard pickle, baked cod with a confit of fennel and garlic and poached skate with onions, coriander and preserved lemon. Tempting sweets such as honey and nut parfait or port and zabaglione ice cream with strawberries and balsamic vinegar end a meal in fine style. *Seats 30. Parties 12. L 12.30-1.30 D 7-9.30. Set L £17.50. Closed Sun & Mon, also Nov to mid-Feb. Access, Visa.*

| ST MARGARET'S | Wallett's Court | 60% | £60 |

Tel 01304 852424   Fax 01304 853430   Map 11 D5   **HR**
West Cliffe St Margaret's Dover Kent CT15 6EW

Wallett's Court is a lovely old country manor house just outside St Margaret's on the B2058 (off the A258 Dover/Deal road), and it has a history documented back to the Domesday Book, explained for interested visitors on a frieze in one of the dining-rooms and evident also in the atmosphere of the house. The main building is dated 1627, inscribed on either side of the porch, and feels as though it has also always been in good and caring hands, whether those belonged to Queen Eleanor of Aquitaine or Chris and Lea Oakley, who have been here since 1977 and are now ably assisted by son Craig. Three bedrooms are in the main house and carry a small supplement (one, the Seaview Room, just gives you that glimpse, as do south-east facing ground-floor day rooms) while the remainder are in two separate sympathetic conversions (the former granary) across the gravel drive and beautifully manicured lawn. All are comfortably furnished and well maintained. The lounge and bar are beamed and feature an upright Steinway whose

See over

ivories talented guests may tinkle. Excellent breakfasts, served in a new conservatory, offer locally cured bacon and sausages, free-range eggs, locally smoked fish and home-made preserves as well as healthy options like home-made muesli and herbal teas, all served with just the right balance of efficiency and relaxation. *Rooms 10. Garden, tennis, children's outdoor playground, snooker. Closed 5 days Christmas. Access, Visa.*

Restaurant   £60

Chris Oakley produces set menus of three courses during the week but five (with choices) on Saturdays, served in the candle-lit, beamed, non-smoking dining-rooms. The menu draws strongly on local produce, carefully cooked with some well-thought-out flavour and texture combinations. Thus you might start with a seasoned pumpkin soup finished with chives and an optional splash of cream or Stilton and walnut paté, moving on to wild Hebridean salmon baked with rosemary, Barbary duck with a red wine and shallot sauce or lamb stew with 'penny royal' dumplings. There's a choice of puddings displayed, such as whisky chocolate mousse topped with raspberry syllabub and fresh raspberries, summer pudding, hot bread-and-butter pudding, or a platter of about eight British and Continental cheeses. Saturdays add a fish dish and a sorbet as the second and third courses respectively. Coffee and Belgian chocolates close the proceedings. Good, well-annotated wine list. Charming service led by Craig Oakley. *Seats 60. Parties 10. Private Room 40. D only 7-9. Closed Sun (except residents). Set D £21 (Sat £26).*

St Martin's	St Martin's Hotel	69%	£130

Tel 01720 422092   Fax 01720 422298   Map 12 A2   **HR**
St Martin's Isles of Scilly TR25 0QW

Following a flight from the mainland (or a 2½ hr sea crossing from Penzance) that arrives on St Mary's Island nearby, the hotel launch transfers guests to St Martin's Island, 28 miles out in the Atlantic; the hotel will make all travel arrangements to suit guests – there are many options via Penzance, Exeter, Plymouth and Newquay. The island provides the ultimate escape for solitude-seekers and an equally novel activity centre for families (under-16s stay free in parents' room). Public rooms include the first-floor sunset lounge, which affords wonderful views westward towards Tresco. *Rooms 24. Garden, indoor swimming pool, snooker, hotel yacht. Closed 1 Nov-1 Mar. Access, Amex, Diners, Visa.*

Tean Restaurant   £60

The restaurant, whose walls are hung with paintings by local artists, makes good use of local fish which is landed right on the hotel's quay. Lobster is a speciality and game and home-grown vegetables also feature on the choice of table d'hote menus – *menu du jour* and *menu gourmet*, from which diners can easily mix and match. The former menu offers standard favourites, while the latter might extend to smoked haddock collops poached in a fumet of wild mushrooms, lemon sole and asparagus pudding with crab and truffle cream, lamb and turkey roulade or strips of Cornish beef dusted in paprika with shallots, bacon and tarragon. Daily vegetarian dish. Cornish cheeses. No smoking. Lighter bar lunches. *Seats 60. Parties 16. L in bar only 10-5 D 7-10. Set D £22.50 & £29.50.*

St Mary's	Hotel Godolphin	58%	£92*

Tel 01720 422316   Fax 01720 422252   Map 12 A2   **H**
Church Street St Mary's Isles of Scilly TR21 0JR

In the hands of the Mumford family since 1967, the hotel stands in a delightful town-house garden just a minute from the harbour beach. It has a welcoming, homely appearance that is reinforced inside, where an oak-panelled entrance hall leads to a comfortable lounge area with gold velour seating around a marble fireplace. There is also a cosy bar. Most of the simply furnished bedrooms have functional bathrooms without showers; three are not en suite and four are suitable for family use. No dogs. *Half-board rate. B&B on application. Rooms 31. Garden, sauna. Closed mid Oct-mid Mar. Access, Visa.*

We welcome bona fide complaints and recommendations on the tear-out pages at the back of the book for readers' comments. They are followed up by our professional team.

St Mary's   Tregarthen's Hotel   60%   £126*

Tel 01720 422540   Fax 01720 422089   Map 12 A2   **H**
St Mary's Isles of Scilly TR21 0PP

Arrival on the Island is by air from Lands End, Penzance, Plymouth or Bristol. Sea crossing available from Penzance. Founded in 1840 by a Captain Tregarthen, owner of the steam packet *Little Western*, this friendly hotel with a loyal following of regular guests stands in terraced gardens overlooking the harbour. Day rooms include the Little Western bar serving good snacks at lunchtime and a roast on Sunday. Bedrooms, some looking out to sea, are neat and comfortable. The Port Light – a double room with private bathroom and sitting room – lies across the garden, 30 yards from the hotel entrance. One bathroom boasts a Victorian cast-iron tub. *Half-board terms. No dogs. *Rooms 29. Garden. Closed mid Oct-mid Mar. Access, Amex, Diners, Visa.*

St Mawes   Idle Rocks Hotel   66%   £118

Tel 01326 270771   Fax 01326 270062   Map 12 B4   **HR**
Harbourside St Mawes Cornwall TR2 5AN

On the water's edge in the lovely Roseland Peninsula, the spick-and-span Idle Rocks is a popular destination for both residents and passers-by. Public rooms – including a panelled bar and armchair-filled lounge – enjoy harbour views. Pretty bedrooms in the main building – bedhead drapes, ribbon-hung pictures, antique and reproduction furniture – are not large but have good carpeted bathrooms with darkwood panelled tubs; three, including two tiny singles, have shower and WC only. More spacious bedrooms, with equally good facilities, are in a nearby annexe. Housekeeping and maintenance are in fine order. There are also some cottages and apartments nearby, let on a self-catering basis. *Rooms 24. Access, Amex, Visa.*

Waters Edge Restaurant   £65

Fish is naturally popular here, though there's also a choice for meat-eaters on Alan Vickops's à la carte and table d'hote menus. Seafish terrine with a sweet mustard sauce, melon with Cornish crab tartare and ragout of salmon and sole served with vermouth butter sauce and asparagus show the style. The hotel has a second restaurant, the 12-03 Terrace, open for lunch every day. *Seats 65. Parties 20. L Sun only Oct-Apr 12-2.30 D 7-9.15. Set D £18.95 & £23.95.*

St Mawes   Rising Sun   62%   £79

Tel 01326 270233   Map 12 B4   **H**
The Square St Mawes Truro Cornwall TR2 5DJ

A popular and lively place on the waterfront in the centre of the village. The small conservatory frontage houses a lounge bar, and there's a public bar that's a favourite with the locals. Residents can retreat to their own little lounge at the back (six seats, with TV). Bedrooms are being completely revamped (winter 1995/6). Children up to 10 stay free with parents in the family room. Small dogs only. *Rooms 11. Terrace. Access, Amex, Visa.*

St Mawes   Hotel Tresanton   67%   £70

Tel 01326 270544   Fax 01326 270002   Map 12 B4   **H**
Lower Castle Road St Mawes Cornwall TR2 5DR

Overlooking the Fal estuary, the hotel offers peace and quiet in idyllic surroundings – log fires, antiques, paintings and comfortable sofas in the lounges, or the terraced gardens in fine weather. Charming bedrooms, some with balconies, all have sea views. Housekeeping, maintenance and breakfast disappointed on a recent visit. No children under 10. *Rooms 21. Garden. Closed 1 Nov-23 Dec, 2 Jan-5 Mar. Access, Amex, Diners, Visa.*

Salcombe   Marine Hotel   66%   £152*

Tel 01548 844444   Fax 01548 843109   Map 13 D3   **H**
Cliff Road Salcombe Devon TQ8 8JH

The Marine takes full advantage of its enviable position alongside the Salcombe Ria (an 'estuary' without a river) with picture windows in the spacious, open-plan public area

see over

looking out over the water and with all but six of the bedrooms sharing the view. Most also have usable balconies and there are lounges out on the sun deck. A mini-decanter of sherry welcomes guests to rooms that, although a bit dated, are generally light and airy and of good size. All bathrooms have tubs with shower above and large towels. Some planned refurbishment will be welcome. *Half board terms only for advance reservations. Dogs in selected rooms only. Children under 7 sharing parents' room stay free. *Rooms 51. Garden, indoor swimming pool, keep-fit equipment, sauna, spa bath, solarium, beauty & hair salon, sea fishing, mooring, games room. Access, Amex, Diners, Visa.*

SALCOMBE	Soar Mill Cove	66%	£120

Tel 01548 561566   Fax 01548 561223   Map 13 D3   **HR**
Soar Mill Cove nr Salcombe Devon TQ7 3DS

A spectacular sea view is one of the rewards of following the narrow winding country lane (follow signs to Soar from Marlborough just before you get to Salcombe) that ends at the Soar Mill Cove Hotel standing alone above a sandy beach. A purpose-built single-storey building with all its immaculate bedrooms boasting their own patios, and several their own private garden. Six rooms, including the two full suites, are suitable for families (rates start at 20% for under-6s) who also appreciate the special youngsters' high tea served from 5pm. The genteel atmosphere – reproduction antiques, glass drop and gilt chandeliers and velour upholstery – also attracts older guests, many of whom return year after year to a warm welcome from Keith and Norma Makepeace. *Rooms 16. Garden, indoor & outdoor swimming pools, tennis, pitch & putt, children's playground, games room, laundry room. Closed Nov-mid Feb. Access, Visa.*

Restaurant   £78

🍶 🍓

After an energetic day, or a lazy one, the ritual of dinner is the highlight here. It begins with the tempting array of canapés offered with pre-dinner drinks and ends with an equally impressive selection of petits fours – all home-made, as is the bread. Dinner itself is a daily-changing, four-course affair (with a choice of four main dishes) that makes good use of local produce like lobsters from the bay overlooked by the hotel, Devon beef and lamb that comes from a flock kept by one of the waiters, Luis, who also provides organically grown vegetables to supplement those from the hotel's own extensive kitchen garden. Home-made game sausage served hot on a salad of mustard dressed leaves, roast Salcombe scallops with caramelised onions and citrus zest, lamb wrapped with a herb crust on minted cream sauce, corn-fed guinea fowl on a bed of braised vegetables and garlic with an orange and rosé wine sauce, and a wonderfully fresh fillet of brill with lemon butter sauce are typical of the dishes that emerge from son-of-the-house Keith Makepeace's kitchen. Vegetables are notably well handled and might include a puff pastry star stuffed with spinach for example. Gateau pithiviers, praline bavarois and lemon crème brulée were just the first three from a list of ten desserts last time we dined. The cheese trolley sticks to English and West Country examples. Lunch is an informal affair from an individually priced menu that ranges from a bowl of soup or Soar Bay chowder via sandwiches and salads to a couple of hot dishes like steak and grilled local sole. *Seats 40. L 12.30-2.30 D 7.30-9.30. Set D £32.*

SALCOMBE	South Sands	60%	£94

Tel 01548 843741   Fax 01548 842112   Map 13 D3   **H**
Salcombe Devon TQ8 8LL

Salcombe is one of the most southerly towns in England, and South Sands is well placed to get the best of the sunshine, with great views out to sea. Under the same ownership (the Edwards family, with John and Bridget in charge here) as the *Tides Reach* (see below) but even closer to the shore with the sandy beach reaching right up to the terrace walk, the South Sands caters more for younger children with ten family suites and a special high tea for youngsters served in the terrace bar/coffee shop from 5pm. Generally good-sized bedrooms, half with freestanding pine and half with white melamine fitted furniture, are uncluttered, with carpeted, fully tiled bathrooms. Friendly staff. *Rooms 30. Terrace, indoor swimming pool, spa bath, steam room, solarium, moorings, children's playroom, pool room, coffee shop (10.30-8.30). Closed Nov-Feb. Access, Visa.*

Set menu prices may not always include service or wine

SALCOMBE   Spinnakers   £50

Tel 01548 843408   Map 13 D3   **R**
Fore Street Salcombe Devon TQ8 8JG

The waterside restaurant and bar (downstairs in the Salcombe Apartment building) is a popular spot since most of the tables have views of the estuary. There's also seating outside on the terrace. Lunchtime food is ordered and paid for at the bar, with a more formal service in the evenings – but still not very formal, and you're welcome to choose just one course. Unpretentious atmosphere, plenty of daily seafood dishes (salmon with sorrel, lemon sole with grilled banana, scallops with leeks, prawns and ginger) and a few meat alternatives. *Seats 60. Parties 14. Private Room 28. L 12-2 D 7-9.30 (last order time varies with the seasons). Closed D Sun, also all Mon except in midsummer, Tue in winter, all mid Nov-mid Feb. Set D £12.95. Access, Visa.*

SALCOMBE   Tides Reach   71%   £124

Tel 01548 843466   Fax 01548 843954   Map 13 D3   **H**
South Sands Salcombe Devon TQ8 8LJ

There's a modern yet somehow timeless air at the Tides Reach, a popular holiday destination since it was built and where the Edwards family maintain consistently high standards. It nestles snugly in the valley immediately behind South Sands beach, with clear views over the estuary and the Bolt Head. All the elegant public areas – the marble-floored, plant-filled conservatory-style entrance, the restful lounge, the stylish Aquarium Bar – enjoy sea views, as do all but three bedrooms. These range from five singles with small double beds to junior and family suites, penthouse rooms (most have balconies) and extra large Premier and Honeymoon rooms. The sunbathing deck next to the pool and a grass area around an ornamental pond are both glorious suntraps. Very friendly and willing staff and excellent leisure facilities on-site or nearby, some at a small extra charge. A small public ferry chugs its way from South Sands beach into the town and there are spectacular coastal walks straight from the hotel. No children under 8. *Rooms 38. Garden, indoor swimming pool, sauna, spa bath, solarium, keep-fit equipment, beauty and hairdressing salons, snooker, squash, sailing, windsurfing (with tuition), water skiing, moorings, boat house & dinghy park. Closed Jan & Feb. Access, Amex, Diners, Visa.*

SALISBURY   Rose & Crown   56%   £113

Tel 01722 327908   Fax 01722 339816   Map 14 C3   **H**
Harnham Road Harnham Salisbury Wiltshire SP2 8QJ

A 13th-century, half-timbered inn whose gardens border the River Avon. Public areas and a few characterful bedrooms are in the original building; other rooms, including family rooms, are in a modern extension. Queens Moat Houses. *Rooms 29. Garden. A Access, Amex, Diners, Visa.*

SALISBURY   White Hart   63%   £112

Tel 01722 327476   Fax 01722 412761   Map 14 C3   **H**
1 St John Street Salisbury Wiltshire SP1 2SD

City-centre Forte hotel with an impressive pillared portico and elegant Georgian facade, but modest bedrooms. Plenty of free parking. Banquets/conferences for 96/80. Handy for the Cathedral and main shops. Children up to 16 stay free in parents' room. The hotel was completely refurbished in 1995. *Rooms 68. Access, Amex, Diners, Visa.*

SAMLESBURY   Swallow Trafalgar   60%   £95

Tel 01772 877351   Fax 01772 877424   Map 6 B1   **H**
Preston New Road Samlesbury Lancashire PR5 0UL

Heading east from Junction 31 of the M6 and alongside the A59 at its intersection with the A677 Blackburn road is a practical, business-orientated hotel with good leisure facilities and conference capacities of up to 250. Parking for 350 cars. *Rooms 78. Indoor swimming pool, spa bath, sauna, steam room, solarium, mini-gym, squash. Access, Amex, Diners, Visa.*

Lodges are now listed by county in the reference section

SAMLESBURY　　Tickled Trout　　63%　£112

Tel 01772 877671　Fax 01772 877463　　Map 6 B1　　**H**
Preston New Road Samlesbury Lancashire PR5 OUJ

A modern hotel on the banks of the Ribble, west of junction 31 of the M6. Quiet bedrooms (most overlook the river) have fitted furniture, modern fabrics and the usual accessories. Children up to 14 stay free in parents' room. Conference facilities for up to 150. *Rooms 72. Plunge pool, fishing. Access, Amex, Diners, Visa.*

We welcome bona fide complaints and recommendations on the tear-out pages at the back of the book for readers' comments. They are followed up by our professional team.

SANDBACH　　Chimney House　　62%　£80

Tel 01270 764141　Fax 01270 768916　　Map 6 B2　　**H**
Congleton Road Sandbach Cheshire CW11 0ST

Although only moments from the M6 (Junction 17), the mock-Tudor Chimney House has a remarkably peaceful rural setting within eight acres of wooded grounds. Open-plan public areas focus on a back-to-back pair of original fireplaces. Conference facilities for up to 90 theatre-style. No dogs. Country Club Hotels. *Rooms 48. Garden, sauna, sun bed. Access, Amex, Diners, Visa.*

SANDIWAY　　Nunsmere Hall

See under Northwich

SAUNTON　　Saunton Sands　　67%　£128

Tel 01271 890212　Fax 01271 890145　　Map 12 C1　　**H**
Saunton nr Braunton Devon EX33 1LQ

A family-oriented resort hotel commanding panoramic views over the North Devon coastline: five miles of golden sands beckon, and if you resist the glorious outdoors there are extensive indoor leisure facilities instead. Bedrooms are neat, light and airy. Children's facilities include a creche (10-6 daily), play areas, a full entertainment programme during high season and school holidays, plenty of cots, baby-sitting, baby-listening and high teas. Three conference suites accommodate 20-175. Parking for over 100 cars. 24hr room service. No dogs, but kennels can be arranged nearby. *Rooms 96. Garden, putting, tennis, squash, indoor & outdoor swimming pools, spa bath, sauna, solarium, snooker, hair and beauty salons, indoor and outdoor play areas. Access, Amex, Diners, Visa.*

SCALBY　　Wrea Head　　65%　£99

Tel 01723 378211　Fax 01723 371780　　Map 5 F3　　**H**
Scalby nr Scarborough North Yorkshire YO13 0PB

Built in 1881, Wrea Head stands in 14 acres of wooded and landscaped grounds that were once part of a deer park. It's signposted off the A171 and reached by a narrow driveway. A fine oak-panelled hall features a wall-long stained-glass window, there's a minstrel's gallery in the lounge, and the bar is notable for an unusual terracotta frieze. Individually appointed bedrooms are generally neat and comfortable, with delightful views. Free use of leisure facilities at *Hackness Grange* (see entry under Hackness), 3 miles away. *Rooms 21. Garden, croquet. Access, Amex, Diners, Visa.*

SCARBOROUGH　　Lanterna　　£45

Tel 01723 363616　　　　Map 5 F4　　**R**
33 Queen Street Scarborough North Yorkshire YO11 1HQ

Run for 23 years by the Arecco family, Lanterna offers a menu of straightforward Italian dishes, from tonno e fagioli and spaghetti (bolognese, carbonara, napoletana) to scampi, chicken breast in four ways, veal escalopes and steaks. *Seats 36. D only 7-10. Closed Sun & Mon, 25 & 26 Dec. Access, Visa.*

SCARBOROUGH   The Crown   63%   £82

Tel 01723 373491   Fax 01723 362271   Map 5 F4   **H**
Esplanade Scarborough North Yorkshire YO11 2AG

Crowning the cliffs overlooking South Bay, this gracious hotel caters to both tourist and business trade (conference facilities for up to 200 delegates). Forte. *Rooms 78. Garden, snooker, hair salon. Access, Amex, Diners, Visa.*

SCARISBRICK   Master McGraths   £55

Tel 01704 880050   Fax 01704 880227   Map 6 A1   **R**
535 Southport Road Scarisbrick Lancashire L40 9RF

Situated on the A570 between Ormskirk and Southport, this is an enticing pub restaurant with hanging baskets and a gypsy caravan outside, and a traditional pub feel inside. Generously proportioned lunchtime dishes are chalked up on the board, perhaps an excellent stir-fry of lamb fillets, mangetout, peppers and puff pastry, or chicken and mushroom fricassee served with wild rice and cream sauce, accompanied by perfectly cooked mixed vegetables and new potatoes. A lemon and lime cheesecake with an apricot and apple sauce ends the meal in style. Dinner (note the fixed-price menu is only available between 5.30-7pm) offers a wider choice, say, salmon fishcake with ginger hollandaise or chicken liver parfait with tomato relish to start, followed by grilled fish of the day from the morning's market or a cut of beef from the chargrill. Good puds such as rum and apple crumble with raspberry coulis, and fresh cherry torte with kiwi fruit. *Seats 120. Parties 20. L 12-2 (Sun till 2.30) D 5.30-10. Set L £6 Set D (5.30-7pm) £8.50/£10.50. Access, Amex, Diners, Visa.*

SCOLE   Scole Inn   £66

Tel 01379 740481   Fax 01379 740762   Map 10 C2   **I**
Norwich Road Scole nr Diss Norfolk IP21 4DR

Built in 1655 by a wool merchant, this grand-looking redbrick inn is Grade 1 listed for its architectural interest. Splendid brick gables front and rear show a Dutch influence. Bedrooms in the Georgian stable block are quieter and more modern than those in the main building, which face the busy A140. These rooms, though, are full of character, many having carved oak doors, old timbers and fireplaces plus four-poster or half-oak doors, old timbers and fireplaces plus four-poster or half-tester beds. The beamed, pubby bar is also full of atmosphere with a vast brick fireplace, dark oak furniture and an 'old English Inn' ambience. Children up to 12 stay free in parents' room. *Rooms 23. Access, Amex, Diners, Visa.*

SEAHOUSES   Olde Ship Hotel   £68

Tel 01665 720200   Fax 01665 721383   Map 5 D1   **I**
9 Main Street Seahouses Northumberland NE68 7RD

Alan and Jean Glen, here since 1969, have emphasised the nautical charm of their characterful old inn overlooking the picturesque harbour and Farne Islands. The tiny cabin bar and handsome saloon bar house marine antiques, while the long gallery lounge has a collection of model ships. It's very much a traditional pub, a social centre for regulars and locals, and it has a lawn and summerhouse for fair-weather use. Good bar food is served at lunchtime, and in the evening there are sandwiches and a four-course dinner menu. Homely bedrooms; two have four-poster beds, four are annexe apartments. No dogs. *Rooms 16. Garden. Closed Dec & Jan. Access, Amex, Visa.*

SEALE   Jarvis Hog's Back Hotel   64%   £112

Tel 01252 782345   Fax 01252 783113   Map 15 E3   **H**
Seale nr Farnham Surrey GU10 1EX

A tile-hung, gable-fronted hotel set high up on the Hog's Back on the A31, with day rooms smart in pastel and pale wood, a leisure centre and conference facilities for up to 140 in the Summit Conference Centre. Children up to 14 stay free in parents' room. *Rooms 89. Garden, indoor swimming pool, children's splash pool, keep-fit equipment, sauna, steam room, spa bath, solarium, beauty salon. Access, Amex, Diners, Visa.*

SEATON BURN   Holiday Inn Newcastle   70%   £128

Tel 0191-236 5432 Fax 0191-236 8091   Map 5 D2   **H**
Great North Road Seaton Burn nr Newcastle-upon-Tyne Tyne & Wear NE13 6BP

One of the earliest Holiday Inns, set in 13 acres of grounds, off a roundabout on the A1 seven miles north of the city, six miles from the Metrocentre and five from the airport. The lobby, with its polished stone floor, is imposing and other day rooms include a bar that overlooks the indoor pool. Bedrooms offer modern extras, compact bathrooms with superb showers and a good supply of thick towels. Conference facilities for up to 400; ample parking. Children up to 19 share their parents' room free of charge. *Rooms 150. Garden, pitch & putt, indoor swimming pool, sauna, solarium, spa bath, keep-fit equipment. Access, Amex, Diners, Visa.*

Set menu prices may not always include service or wine.

SEATON BURN   Horton Grange   £80

Tel 01661 860686   Fax 01661 860308   Map 5 D2   **RR**
Seaton Burn Newcastle-upon-Tyne Tyne & Wear NE13 6BU

Located on the perimeter of a large working farm complex, the Grange was once the landowner's private home. Virtually equidistant from city centre and Newcastle airport, it is best approached by following the airport signs from the A19 junction with the A1 western by-pass. The house, converted by owners Andrew and Sue Shilton, manages to combine elegance with homeliness: traditional decor and furnishings, fine handcut crystal and 18th-century English plate produce a relaxing and unstuffy atmosphere in which to enjoy chef Steve Martin's fixed-price, five-course dinner, for which the menu changes nightly. As a preliminary, there might be canapés of smoked salmon mousse, and miniature vegetable spring rolls. A typical starter, oak-smoked chicken and pigeon with salad leaves and baby corn brushed with a blue cheese dressing, is full of well-balanced flavours and comes with good home-made bread and unsalted butter. A lemon and Chablis water ice refreshes before the main course – from a choice of five – of roast rack of English lamb served with a tartlet of buttered spinach with a thyme lamb jus. Desserts might include hot vanilla soufflé with a warm butterscotch sauce and banana millefeuilles. No smoking. *Seats 30. Parties 15. Private Room 10. L residents only D 7-8.30. Closed D Sun (except residents), 24-30 Dec & 1-5 Jan. Set D £32. Access, Visa.*

Rooms   £80

Five spacious bedrooms in the main house contain a treasure trove of heirlooms and antique pieces and have spacious, well-aired bathrooms. Facing the Grange's own herb garden and just yards from the front door is the Peach House which contains a further four rooms, described as "single suites". They each have a bright private sitting room for those "with masses of paperwork to do".

Lodges are now listed by county in the reference section

SEAVIEW   Seaview Hotel   62%   £60

Tel 01983 612711 Fax 01983 613729   Map 15 D4   **HR**
High Street Seaview Isle of Wight PO34 5EX

The epitome of a small, family-run seaside hotel. Nicholas and Nicola Hayward run this charming little hotel-cum-local inn set just back from the sea front with a most appealing efficiency. A small patio with pub-style white iron tables and chairs at the front of the hotel is a delightful sun trap from which one can watch the world, his boat, spouse and children go by; it leads into a narrow hallway, either side of which are a busy bar and a restaurant. To the rear are two snug lounges (one for non-smokers), another popular nautically-themed bar with bare boards and an open-air yard. Upstairs, the bedrooms (some with views over the Solent) are all individually decorated with predominantly blue and yellow colour schemes and feature interesting pictures, objets d'art and spotless bathrooms. Plans due to be realised before the end of 1995 were an extension at the rear, a new car park and the redecoration of some existing rooms. *Rooms 16. Closed 25 Dec. Access, Amex, Visa.*

Restaurant   £50

An intimate dining-room with close-set tables, candle-lit in the evenings; unmessed-about-with local fish and shellfish are probably the best bet. Snacks are served in the adjacent bar or out on the terrace. Realistically priced wines. *Seats 30. L 12-2 D 7.30-9.30. Closed D Sun (except Bank Holiday weekends).*

SEAVINGTON ST MARY	The Pheasant	69%	£88

Tel 01460 240502   Fax 01460 242388   Map 13 F2   **H**
Water Street Seavington St Mary nr Ilminster Somerset TA19 0QH

Look first for signs for Seavington St Michael from the South Petherton end of the A303 Ilminster bypass, then signs for the pretty village of Seavington St Mary itself, to find this converted 17th-century farmhouse, surrounded by landscaped gardens. Inside, eight pretty cottage bedrooms (two reserved for non-smokers) offer character and comfort while the public rooms are also full of old-world charm – beams, inglenooks and open fires. Children up to 5 stay free in parents' room; no dogs; parking for 40 cars. *Rooms 8. Garden. Closed 26 Dec-7 Jan. Access, Amex, Diners, Visa.*

SEDLESCOMBE	Brickwall Hotel	56%	£62

Tel 01424 870253   Fax 01424 870785   Map 11 C6   **H**
Sedlescombe nr Battle East Sussex TN33 0QA

A Tudor mansion overlooking the village green originally built for the local ironmaster. Deep-red velour fireside chairs, oak panelling, exposed beams and a log fire give character to the bar, and the residents' lounge is equally friendly. Some bedrooms boast four-posters and black beams. *Rooms 23. Garden, outdoor swimming pool (indoor pool planned). Access, Amex, Diners, Visa.*

Consult the blue pages for summary tables and lists of
recommended establishments.

SEVENOAKS	Royal Oak	66%	£70

Tel 01732 451109   Fax 01732 740187   Map 11 B5   **HR**
5 Upper High Street Sevenoaks Kent TN13 1HY

A former coaching inn with a handsome flintstone Georgian facade. Rich, bold colours perfectly complement the fabric of the building. Traditional or antique furniture is used in the bedrooms, which are decorated in individual, often striking style. Neat, bright bathrooms. Among the day rooms are a cosy pub-like bar (where imaginative bar snacks are served in a candle-lit section with scrubbed pine tables and comfortable, well-upholstered seats), a beautifully furnished drawing room and a conservatory where morning coffee and afternoon tea may be taken. Under-14s stay free in parents' room. *Rooms 39. Terrace, tennis. Access, Amex, Diners, Visa.*

Restaurant   £65

A charming and comfortable restaurant comprising several rooms that are partially panelled and cleverly lit, creating a relaxing atmosphere. A la carte and fixed-price menus provide plenty of choice and straightforward descriptions: smoked chicken consommé topped with poached quail's eggs; smoked salmon, crab and prawn fishcakes; roast fillet of lamb; banana tatin with ice cream. James Butterfill's fixed-price menus offer particularly good value. Outdoor eating in good weather on a creeper-clad patio. *Seats 60. Parties 24. L 12.30-2 D 7.30-9.45. Closed L Sat. Set L £8.95/10.95 Set D £10.95/£13.95.*

SHAFTESBURY	Grosvenor Hotel	62%	£83

Tel 01747 852282   Fax 01747 854755   Map 14 B3   **H**
The Commons Shaftesbury Dorset SP7 8JA

Former coaching inn set around a cobbled courtyard in a picturesque location with a homely, traditional feel. Nearly half the rooms are reserved for non-smokers. Conference/banqueting facilities for 150/120. Children under 14 stay free when sharing a room with their parents and eat for half-price. Under-5s even eat free. Forte. *Rooms 35. Access, Amex, Diners, Visa.*

SHAFTESBURY   Royal Chase Hotel   60%   £70

Tel 01747 853355   Fax 01747 851969   Map 14 B3   **H**
Shaftesbury Dorset SP7 8DB

To the south of the town centre on a roundabout where the A30 and A350 intersect, a friendly, family-run hotel. Until 1922 the building was used as a monastery and the present bar was once the chapel. Much has changed since those days and now the hotel offers a cosy library lounge and a popular indoor leisure area. Best of the bedrooms are the Crown rooms. Bathrooms in the older parts of the building are quite compact. Staff are friendly and obliging. Conference/banqueting facilities for 100/130. Families are well catered for, particularly in holiday periods, and children up to 15 stay free in their parents' room; informal eating in the Country Kitchen. *Rooms 35. Garden, indoor swimming pool, steam room, solarium, children's playground. Access, Amex, Diners, Visa.*

SHANKLIN   Cliff Tops Hotel   64%   £66

Tel 01983 863262   Fax 01983 867139   Map 15 D4   **H**
Park Road Shanklin Isle of Wight PO37 6BB

A modern hotel, one of the Isle of Wight's largest, with fine sea views and bright, spacious day rooms. It stands high above Sandown Bay, and a public lift leads down to the seafront. There's a choice of bars, a leisure club and conference rooms for up to 240 delegates. Most of the bedrooms have balconies. *Rooms 88. Garden, indoor swimming pool, gym, sauna, spa bath, steam room, solarium, beauty & hair salon, snooker, children's play area. Access, Amex, Diners, Visa.*

SHANKLIN OLD VILLAGE   The Cottage   £60

Tel 01983 862504   Fax 01983 867512   Map 15 D4   **R**
8 Eastcliff Road Shanklin Old Village Isle of Wight PO37 6AA

Three old cottages in a cul-de-sac on the town side of Shanklin's old village, visible from the main road. Neil Graham and Alan Priddle have been in the kitchen and at front of house respectively since 1973. Neil's daily-changing table d'hote at lunchtime and evening à la carte menus are a careful mix of English and French. The carte offers a long list of starters and classic main courses, all elegantly scripted on the handwritten menu. Tiger prawns with ginger vinaigrette, mushroom and cheese pancakes, sole véronique and lamb with mint béarnaise show the style. All puddings and desserts are home-made. No smoking in the restaurant, but there are lounges for puffers, one with access to a courtyard and garden. *Seats 32. Parties 10. L 12-2 D 7.30-9.45. Closed Sun, Mon, Mar & Oct. Set L £8.85. Access, Amex, Diners, Visa.*

SHEFFIELD   Charnwood Hotel   64%   £90

Tel 0114 258 9411   Fax 0114 255 5107   Map 6 C2   **H**
10 Sharrow Lane Sheffield South Yorkshire S11 8AA

A Georgian mansion just south of the city centre – ask for directions – converted to a hotel in 1985. Bedrooms feature brass bedheads and darkwood units incorporating a mini-bar. Carpeted bathrooms offer good shelf space and generously sized towels. Day rooms include several small lounges – one in period style, another the conservatory-style Garden Room – plus an appealing fin de siècle Parisian-style brasserie. There are seven conference rooms, the largest with a capacity of 100. Good cooked breakfasts. Friendly staff. *Rooms 22. Access, Amex, Diners, Visa.*

SHEFFIELD   Forte Posthouse   65%   £72

Tel 0114 267 0067   Fax 0114 268 2620   Map 6 C2   **H**
Manchester Road Sheffield South Yorkshire S10 5DX

A modern, stilted tower-block building with good conference (maximum capacity 300 – secretarial service available) and leisure facilities. Three-quarters of the rooms are non-smoking. Children up to 16 free in parents' room; playroom available at weekends. 8 miles from M1 junction 33, on the A57. Ample free parking. *Rooms 135. Indoor swimming pool, spa bath, sauna, solarium, gym. Access, Amex, Diners, Visa.*

Consult the blue pages for summary tables and lists of recommended establishments.

| SHEFFIELD | Grosvenor House | 67% | £73 |

Tel 0114 272 0041 Fax 0114 275 7199
Map 6 C2 **H**
Charter Square Sheffield South Yorkshire S1 3EH

Prominent tower-block hotel with direct access from its own car park. Rooms on the higher floors have good views over the city. Conference/banqueting facilities for 385/270; two boardrooms seat up to 20. *Rooms 103. Access, Amex, Diners, Visa.*

| SHEFFIELD | Holiday Inn Royal Victoria | 67% | £95 |

Tel 0114 276 8822 Fax 0114 272 4519
Map 6 C2 **H**
Victoria Station Road Sheffield South Yorkshire S4 7YE

Large redbrick Victorian building with well-proportioned, high-ceilinged day rooms. 20 bedrooms are designated non-smoking. Conference and banqueting facilities for up to 450. Children up to 19 free in parents' room. Free parking for up to 200 cars. *Rooms 100. Access, Amex, Diners, Visa.*

| SHEFFIELD | Moat House | 68% | £111 |

Tel 0114 282 9988 Fax 0114 237 8140
Map 6 C2 **H**
Chesterfield Road South Sheffield South Yorkshire S8 8BW

On the outskirts of town, by the A61 towards Chesterfield, this large, modern, redbrick hotel is wearing well since being opened by the Duke of Devonshire in 1989. Large bedrooms have solid lightwood units providing good work space plus a couple of easy chairs around a coffee table and decent-sized bathrooms with ample shelf space. The leisure centre includes a well-equipped gym, aerobics studio and creche (the last available Mon, Wed & Fri mornings only). Conference facilities can accommodate up to 500 delegates theatre-style. Cooked breakfasts are collected from a buffet. As we went to press work on the public areas included the creation of a new meeting room and business centre in what was the lounge area. *Rooms 95. Garden, indoor swimming pool, gym, sauna, spa bath, steam room, sun beds, beauty salon. Access, Amex, Diners, Visa.*

| SHEFFIELD | Nirmal's | | £40 |

Tel 0114 272 4054
Map 6 C2 **R**
189-193 Glossop Road Sheffield South Yorkshire S10 2GW

Blackboard specials supplement the regular North Indian menu at this well-established restaurant on the edge of the city centre. A good plan though is to allow the friendly, chatty owner Mrs Gupta (here for 15 years) to guide you towards the more unusual and interesting dishes. Good range of vegetarian options. *Seats 80. Private Room 50. L 12-2.30 D 6-12 (Fri & Sat to 1). Closed L Sun, all 25 & 26 Dec. Set L £6.95/£12.50 Set D from £12.50. Access, Amex, Diners, Visa.*

| SHEFFIELD | Novotel | 63% | £68 |

Tel 0114 278 1781 Fax 0114 278 7744
Map 6 C2 **H**
Arundel Gate Sheffield South Yorkshire S1 2PR

Central location opposite City Hall and close to both the Crucible and Lyceum Theatres. Cheerful, open-plan public areas are matched by practical, well-planned bedrooms that all come with extra sofa-beds (ideal for families) and WCs separate from the bathroom. Children up to 16 stay free in parents' room. 24hr room service. 75% of rooms are reserved for non-smokers. Parking for 45 cars. *Rooms 144. Indoor swimming pool, keep-fit equipment. Access, Amex, Diners, Visa.*

| SHEFFIELD | Swallow Hotel | 64% | £98 |

Tel 0114 258 3811 Fax 0114 250 0138
Map 6 C2 **H**
Kenwood Road Sheffield South Yorkshire S7 1NQ

Much-extended country house set in 11 acres of landscaped gardens (including an ornamental lake), two miles from the city centre. Continual improvements keep facilities, which include conferencing for up to 200 and a smart leisure club, right up to date. 24hr room service. Formerly the St George Swallow. *Rooms 117. Garden, indoor swimming pool, gym, sauna, spa bath, steam room, solarium, beauty salon, coffee shop (7am-7pm). Access, Amex, Diners, Visa.*

SHEPPERTON — Moat House — 61% — £110

Tel 01932 241404   Fax 01932 245231   Map 15 E2   **H**
Felix Lane Shepperton Middlesex TW17 8NP

A peaceful location by the Thames is a big plus at this modern hotel set in 11 acres of grounds and with its own private mooring. Conference facilities for up to 300 delegates, and a staffed business centre. 24hr room service. *Rooms 183. Keep-fit equipment, putting, mooring, 9-hole pitch & putt. Access, Amex, Diners, Visa.*

SHEPPERTON — Warren Lodge — £85

Tel 01932 242972   Fax 01932 253883   Map 15 E2   **I**
Church Square Shepperton Middlesex TW17 9JZ

Close to the Thames, on the corner of a pretty village square in the middle of a conservation area, this 18th-century inn offers clean, basic accommodation in a picturesque setting. There are views of the river not only from the wood-beamed bar but also from 16 rooms in a newer wing which lead on to a courtyard, motel-style. Modestly decorated bedrooms are kept in good order. Banqueting/conference facilities recently expanded. No dogs. *Rooms 50. Garden. Access, Amex, Diners, Visa.*

SHEPTON MALLET — Blostin's Restaurant — £50

Tel 01749 343648   Map 13 F1   **R**
29 Waterloo Road Shepton Mallet Somerset BA4 5HH

Nick and Lynne Reed's dark, candle-lit bistro offers consistently well-cooked meals with 2- or 3-course fixed-price menus supplemented by an additional list of à la carte seasonal specialities. Fish soup, warm chicken and smoky bacon salad, lamb's sweetbreads with a creamy mushroom sauce, saffron-sauced fillets of Dover sole, pork with black pudding, apple and cider brandy, and fillet of beef baked in puff pastry served with a Madeira sauce show Nick's style. To finish, perhaps treacle and walnut tart or a home-made ice cream. Small vegetarian menu. *Seats 32. D only 7-9.30. Closed Sun & Mon, 2 weeks Jan, 2 weeks Jun. Set L £10.95/£11.95 Set D £13.95/£14.95. Access, Visa.*

SHERBORNE — Eastbury Hotel — 67% — £65

Tel 01935 813131   Fax 01935 817296   Map 13 F2   **H**
Long Street Sherborne Dorset DT9 3BY

An elegant Georgian town house which dates, in part, as far back as the 16th century; new owners John and Alison Pickford have taken care to retain as many original features as possible. The beautifully proportioned older rooms stick to period-style furnishings, with comfortable sofas and armchairs in the drawing room. A modern conservatory has been added to the building and is elegantly decorated and used as the dining-room. Bedrooms, named after flowers, have en-suite bathrooms with tubs and showers and all the usual mod cons. The well-kept walled garden is a special attraction. Ask for directions on how to negotiate the town's one-way system to find the hotel's small car park! No dogs. *Rooms 15. Garden. Access, Visa.*

SHERBORNE — Sherborne Hotel — 58% — £74

Tel 01935 813191   Fax 01935 816493   Map 13 F2   **H**
Horsecastles Lane Sherborne Dorset DT9 6BB

The Sherborne is part of Forte's renamed White Hart Hotels group but is still under the same management. On the A30 just outside Sherborne, the low-rise modern building has conference/banqueting for 100/75. *Rooms 59. Garden, croquet, playground. Access, Amex, Diners, Visa.*

SHERE — Kinghams — £60

Tel 01483 202168   Map 15 E3   **R**
Gomshall Lane Shere Surrey GU5 9HB

"One cannot work well, feel well, love well, unless one has eaten well", proclaims the menu at Jason and Paul Baker's cottage restaurant in the pretty village of Shere, so you know exactly what to expect: good food served in a friendly atmosphere. Paul's cooking shows a deft touch and an inventive mind – try a warm winter salad of black pudding, poached quail eggs, sauté potatoes and bacon, then roast loin of lamb on a crisp polenta cake topped with mint salsa, and finish with almond cream and exotic fruit terrine. A blackboard that displays a £10 two-course menu at lunchtimes and on Tuesday-Thursday evenings is used for fish dishes on Friday night and additional specialities on Saturday night. One of the separate rooms is reserved for non-smokers and in summer there is seating for 60 out in the garden. Ample parking. *Seats 44. Parties 25. Private Room 25. L 12-2.30 D 7-9.30. Closed D Sun & all Mon, Bank Holidays. Set L £10/£13.50 (Sun £10/£13) D £10/£13.50/£20. Access, Amex, Visa.*

SHIFNAL	Park House	71%	£90

Tel 01952 460128   Fax 01952 461658   Map 6 B4   **H**
Park Street Shifnal nr Telford Shropshire TF11 9BA

Originally two adjacent country houses of completely different architectural styles, Park House has nevertheless managed to retain much of the atmosphere of a private house. An elegant garden suite and individually stylish private rooms accommodate conferences of up to 200 delegates. Bedrooms use quality furniture and fabrics, and plentiful extras include decanters of sherry and baskets of fresh fruit. Children under 12 stay free in parents' room. No dogs. The hotel lies near Junction 4 of the M54. *Rooms 54. Garden, indoor swimming pool, spa bath, sauna, solarium, fishing. Access, Amex, Diners, Visa.*

SHINFIELD	L'Ortolan	★★★	£140

Tel 01734 883783   Fax 01734 885391   Map 15 D2   **R**
The Old Vicarage Church Lane Shinfield nr Reading Berkshire RG2 9BY

There are few better restaurants in the country than this one, and a more passionate and gifted chef than John Burton-Race you will not find, confirming that the British can compete on equal terms with, or even, dare we say, surpass the French. For, make no mistake, this is as near to a grand French country restaurant as you'll get, either side of the Channel! And yet it's but an hour's drive from London, and half that from Heathrow airport (five minutes from the M4, Junction 11).

After crunching up the drive, you'll be warmly welcomed; a drink first in the plant-hung lounge/conservatory while considering the French-written menus with English translations, a dining-room decorated in apricot with bird and botanical prints, and another (dining) conservatory, leading on to a patio and overlooking a delightful garden, a great place for coffee (and a snooze after your meal). The whole operation is very much Anglo-French with a formidable British kitchen brigade alongside John: second-in-command Nigel Marriage, pastry chef Michael Taylor, and chef tournant James Race (John's brother). Front-of-house on the other hand is mostly French with John's wife Christine a charming and knowledgeable hostess, backed up by head waitress Olga Pailley and sommelier Jerome Debris, a team of premier division status. The quality of cooking continues to excite, flavours are intense, and combinations of ingredients both innovative and interesting: for instance *pommes de terre nouvelles fourrées aux escargots bourguignon*, new potatoes filled with snails cooked in red wine, garlic and herbs, served with an enriched red wine sauce, or *galette de foie gras aux figues*, a pastry case lined with sliced figs, topped with pan-fried fresh foie gras and served with onion confit with sherry vinegar. Fixed-price menus are now only available at lunchtime, perhaps *salade de coquilles St Jacques grillées et son gazpacho*, sliced grilled scallops on a gazpacho sauce garnished with a seasonal salad, *pigeon sauvage, soufflé de foie gras, fumet de Medoc*, wild pigeon breast topped with foie gras soufflé, wrapped in a 'crépinette' and roasted, and served with a red wine sauce, ending with a cappuccino framboise, a pastry case of various raspberry creations. From the à la carte you might select some of the restaurant's specialities: *gourmandise de la mer*, buckwheat pancakes, caviar, an oyster topped with a sweet and sour horseradish cream and a little crown of marinated salmon, *lasagne de langoustines à l'huile de truffe*, layers of langoustines in its mousse, between leaves of fresh pasta, then steamed and sprinkled with truffle oil, and *dome de mousse, caramel*

See over

brulée, caramel mousse served in a toffee dome. Alternatively, select from the cheeseboard, where there are never less than twenty-five varieties, each described in detail (if required) before serving. The excellent wine list, very carefully compiled under the watchful eye of Christine, does present the best from France; the New World is well represented by USA, reasonably by Australia, but hardly at all by New Zealand; however, of paramount importance is the quality of choice. **Seats** 60. *Parties 10. Private Room 40. L 12.15-2.15 D 7.15-10. Closed D Sun, all Mon, last 2 weeks Feb, last 2 weeks Aug. Set L £28/£37. Access, Amex, Diners, Visa.*

SHORNE	Inn on the Lake	61%	£70

Tel 01474 823333   Fax 01474 823175   Map 11 B5   **H**
Shorne nr Gravesend Kent DA12 3HB

A modern stopover set in landscaped grounds with ornamental lakes. Two lounge bars open off the reception area, one quieter with settees, the other with conference chairs and often occupied for that purpose. Of the pleasant and practical bedrooms, a few on the first floor overlook the lakes and have balconies. Banqueting/conference facilities for 500/800. **Rooms** 78. *Garden, fishing. Access, Amex, Diners, Visa.*

SHREWSBURY	Lion Hotel	62%	£82

Tel 01743 353107   Fax 01743 352744   Map 6 A3   **H**
Wyle Cop Shrewsbury Shropshire SY1 1UY

Former coaching inn, now a town-centre Forte hotel with characterful, beamed bedrooms and other period features amid the modern day rooms and conference facilities (up to 200 delegates). Children up to 16 stay free in parents' room. 24 rooms reserved for non-smokers. Parking for 70 cars. **Rooms** 59. *Access, Amex, Diners, Visa.*

SHREWSBURY	Prince Rupert Hotel	64%	£85

Tel 01743 499955   Fax 01743 357306   Map 6 A3   **H**
Butcher Row Shrewsbury Shropshire SY1 1UQ

Queens Moat Houses hotel in the medieval city centre (ask hotel for detailed directions). Bedrooms include two four-poster suites, and four rooms are suitable for family use: children up to 12 stay free in parents' room. Banqueting and conference facilities for up to 120. **Rooms** 65. *Access, Amex, Diners, Visa.*

SIDMOUTH	Belmont Hotel	63%	£144

Tel 01395 512555   Fax 01395 579101   Map 13 E2   **H**
The Esplanade Sidmouth Devon EX10 8RX

Serving a mixture of family and business customers, standing in substantial grounds on the seafront, the Belmont was built as a private residence in 1820, becoming a hotel exactly a century later. Attention to detail lavished by the owners pays dividends, and there's an air of elegance in the public rooms. There are views over the bay from its roomy lounges and from many of its bedrooms. Some rooms have private balconies, and de luxe rooms offer numerous cosseting extras such as bathrobes. Guests have free use of the leisure facilities of the sister hotel next door, the *Victoria* (see entry). Parking for 45 cars, banqueting/conferences for 120/40. No dogs. **Rooms** 51. *Garden, putting. Access, Amex, Diners, Visa.*

SIDMOUTH	Fortfield Hotel	59%	£70

Tel & Fax 01395 512403   Map 13 E2   **H**
Sidmouth Devon EX10 8NU

Andrew and Annabel Torjussen own and run this Edwardian redbrick hotel overlooking a cricket ground and the sea beyond. A light, sunny lounge makes the most of the location, and a number of bedrooms have balconies. Smoking not encouraged. Payments by credit card are surcharged by 2½ %. **Rooms** 55. *Garden, indoor swimming pool, sauna, solarium, games room. Access, Amex, Diners, Visa.*

We welcome bona fide complaints and recommendations on the tear-out pages at the back of the book for readers' comments. They are followed up by our professional team.

SIDMOUTH	**Hotel Riviera**	66%	£112

Tel 01395 515201   Fax 01395 577775
The Esplanade Sidmouth Devon EX10 8AY

Map 13 E2   **H**

A handsome Regency façade fronts a terrace of three-storey houses in the middle of the esplanade overlooking Lyme Bay. The Regency Bar is a relaxing spot for a drink, while cream teas can be enjoyed in the lounge or out on the patio. Most of the bedrooms have bay views; two rooms are specially equipped for disabled guests. Bedrooms and day rooms have recently been refurbished. Concessionary green fees at two nearby golf courses. Banqueting/conference facilities for 90. *Rooms 27. Terrace. Access, Amex, Diners, Visa.*

SIDMOUTH	**Victoria Hotel**	67%	£146

Tel 01395 512651   Fax 01395 579154
The Esplanade Sidmouth Devon EX10 8RY

Map 13 E2   **H**

Named after Queen Victoria, a frequent visitor to her neighbouring residence, the hotel was actually opened early in the reign of Edward VII. Lounges are roomy and relaxing, and most of the well-appointed bedrooms face south and the sea (many have French windows leading to private balconies). The swimming pool complex is a great attraction, including as it does a barbecue, bar and buttery. Families are well catered for with good leisure facilities, baby-sitting, children's menu in the dining-room (a special high tea for the younger ones) and in summer there's a creche, nanny and various activities like quizzes and swimming galas organised. Room service is available at any hour. No dogs. Ample free parking. *Rooms 65. Garden, indoor & outdoor swimming pools, sauna, spa bath, sun bed, hairdressing, tennis, putting, snooker & games room, lock-up garages. Access, Amex, Diners, Visa.*

Consult the blue pages for summary tables and lists of
recommended establishments.

SILCHESTER	**Romans Hotel**	64%	£85

Tel 01734 700421   Fax 01734 700691
Little London Road Silchester nr Reading Hampshire RG7 2PN

Map 15 D3   **H**

Built in the early years of this century, this handsome Lutyens house stands amid trim lawns and mature grounds with two hard tennis courts. Inside, polished floors, oak panelling and ornate mouldings take the eye in the day rooms, while bedrooms in the main house have space, comfort and mainly period furniture. Extension rooms are smaller. Not far from the M3 (leave at Junction 6) and the M4 (Junction 11). Children up to 16 stay free in parents' room. *Rooms 25. Garden, outdoor swimming pool, tennis. Closed 25 Dec & 1 Jan. Access, Amex, Diners, Visa.*

SILLOTH-ON-SOLWAY	**Skinburness Hotel**	67%	£63

Tel 01697 332332   Fax 01697 332549
Silloth-on-Solway nr Carlisle Cumbria CA5 4QY

Map 4 C2   **H**

The isolated Skinburness Hotel is ideally placed (on the shores of the Solway Firth) for those wishing to explore the rugged beauty of this part of England. The interior recreates a Victorian atmosphere by use of brass lamps and ceiling fans, cane furniture and a picturesque conservatory. Accommodation is divided between plainly decorated Green Rooms and generally more comfortable Red Rooms. Special terms for golfers who wish to play at the local championship course. *Rooms 25. Garden, indoor swimming pool, keep-fit equipment, sauna, spa bath, sun bed, snooker. Access, Amex, Diners, Visa.*

SIMONSBATH	**Simonsbath House**	64%	£90

Tel 01643 83259
Simonsbath Somerset TA24 7SH

Map 13 D1   **H**

Located on the B3223 in the middle of Exmoor, Mike and Sue Burns' hotel dates back over 300 years. Thick stone walls, log fires and cosy, traditional decor create a warm homely and tranquil environment. Self-catering cottages. No children under 10. No dogs. *Rooms 7. Garden. Closed Dec & Jan. Access, Amex, Diners, Visa.*

SINDLESHAM   Reading Moat House   70%   £116

Tel 01734 499988   Fax 01734 666530   Map 15 D2   **H**
Mill Lane Sindlesham nr Wokingham Berkshire RG11 5DF

Standing in its own grounds near the M4 (Junction 10 is closest), a late-80s' hotel built in sympathy with the next-door 19th-century mill house that now houses the hotel's own free-house pub (The Poacher) and night club. Features include a stylish, pine-panelled, marble-floored foyer, a roomy lounge bar and smartly appointed bedrooms and bathrooms. Two bedrooms are specially equipped for disabled guests. 24hr room service. Conference/banqueting facilities for 80/200; car parking for 360. *Rooms 96. Garden, gym, sauna, steam room, spa bath, fishing. Access, Amex, Diners, Visa.*

SISSINGHURST   Rankins   £65

Tel 01580 713964   Map 11 C5   **R**
The Street Sissinghurst Kent TN17 2JH

A charming, white clapboard cottage is the setting for Hugh Rankin to produce short but invariably interesting and enjoyable fixed-price evening meals and Sunday lunches. Dishes are very much his own: puff pastry tart of bacon, onions and gruyère; cod, smoked haddock and mussel hot-pot; grilled chicken steak with rich mushroom sauce; ragout of lamb fillets with an orange and port gravy enriched with redcurrant jelly. There's always a vegetarian main course (perhaps couscous with a mixed Mediterranean bean stew with parsley and garlic purée), and to round things off there are some hard-to-resist puddings and desserts. No smoking before 10pm (2pm on Sunday). *Seats 30. L (Sun only) 12.30-2 D 7.30-9. Closed D Sun, all Mon, Tues & Bank Holidays. Set L £17.95/£19.95/£21.95 Set D £18.95/£21.95/£23.95. Access, Visa.*

SIX MILE BOTTOM   Swynford Paddocks   74%   £107

Tel 01638 570234   Fax 01638 570283   Map 10 B3   **H**
Six Mile Bottom nr Newmarket Cambridgeshire CB8 0UE

The poet Byron was a regular visitor to this elegant country mansion, which stands on the A1304 in a 60-acre stud farm (this is very much horse-racing territory, and Newmarket is only six miles away). The dado-panelled and galleried hall/reception sets the period tone and from there you can progress to a large bar/lounge with stylishly draped curtains, comfortable easy chairs and a grand piano. The bedrooms have attractive matching bedcovers and curtains and many extras, including books and mini-bars; there's a suite, and two rooms with four-posters. *Rooms 15. Garden, croquet, golf (9), all-weather tennis, giant chess. Closed 4 days between Christmas & New Year. Access, Amex, Diners, Visa.*

SKIPTON   Randell's Hotel   65%   £85

Tel 01756 700100   Fax 01756 700107   Map 6 C1   **H**
Keighley Road Snaygill Skipton North Yorkshire BD23 2TA

Purpose-built hotel just a mile outside the town centre on the A629, with the Trans-Pennine Waterway passing to the rear and the Dales close at hand. Spacious bedrooms are light and contemporary with fully-tiled private facilities; one room has facilities for the disabled. Day rooms include an open-plan lobby and a first-floor bar. There's also a well-equipped leisure centre. A new purpose-built conference centre opened in spring 1995. Splendid facilities for youngsters, including the state-registered Playzone supervised nursery (for under-7s) with outdoor play area. 24hr room service. Children up to 16 stay free in parents' room. Parking for up to 150 cars. *Rooms 76. Terrace, indoor swimming pool, gym, squash, sauna, spa bath, steam room, solarium, hair & beauty salons. Access, Amex, Diners, Visa.*

SLOUGH   Copthorne Slough/Windsor   71%   £145

Tel 01753 516222   Fax 01753 516237   Map 15 E2   **H**
Cippenham Lane Slough Berkshire SL1 2YE

Conveniently situated next to junction 6 of the M4 and a 15-minute drive from Heathrow, the Copthorne owes 80% of its trade to corporate business. All the elegant public areas – the polished granite-floored reception area, the comfortable, spacious lounge and relaxing bar – are Art Deco in style; so, too, the variously sized conference rooms, which can handle up to 250 delegates. All bedrooms, whether Classics,

Connoisseurs or suites, are decorated to the same high standard with lightwood units and co-ordinating fabrics. Tiled bathrooms offer showers and tubs, plus good soaps and toiletries. 24hr room service. First-rate leisure club. Plenty of free covered parking with night security. No dogs. *Rooms 219. Indoor swimming pool, gym, sauna, spa bath, steam bath, solarium, snooker, shop. Access, Amex, Diners, Visa.*

SLOUGH	Courtyard by Marriott	60%	£92

Tel 01753 551551   Fax 01753 553333   Map 15 E2   **H**
Church Street Chalvey Slough Berkshire SL1 2NH

At the first roundabout towards Slough from Junction 6 of the M4, this was the first of Marriott's hotels in this country aimed primarily at the weekday business traveller, although the weekend tariff (£48) is also very attractive to families on the move. Children up to 12 free in parents' room. There's no porterage or room service but food and drink may be taken to rooms from the cheerful Number One all-day bar/brasserie or 24hr vending machines. Uncluttered bedrooms are well equipped and good bathrooms have both under-floor heating and heated mirrors. *Rooms 148. Keep-fit equipment, brasserie (6.30am-11pm). Access, Amex, Diners, Visa.*

SLOUGH	Heathrow Marriott Hotel	73%	£154

Tel 01753 544244   Fax 01753 540272   Map 15 E2   **H**
Ditton Road Langley Slough Berkshire SL3 8PT

Next to Junction 5 of the M4, a purpose-built hotel with good modern leisure and conference facilities (for up to 280) plus stylish day rooms. Bedrooms have at least one double bed and are decorated in soft shades with lightwood units. All have tiled, if rather small, bathrooms. Children up to 18 can stay free in parents' room. *Rooms 349. Indoor swimming pool, gym, sauna, spa bath, steam room, sun beds, beauty salon, all-weather floodlit tennis, coffee shop (6.30am-11pm), courtesy airport coach. Access, Amex, Diners, Visa.*

SOLIHULL	Jarvis International	66%	£105

Tel 0121-711 2121   Fax 0121-711 3374   Map 6 C4   **H**
The Square Solihull West Midlands B91 3RF

The oldest part of this town-centre hotel (formerly called the Jarvis George) dates back to the 16th century and houses the beamed Club Room bar which is furnished exclusively with comfortable tub and wing armchairs. Most bedrooms are in modern wings extending around three sides of a 16th-century bowling green. Standard rooms are just that, but there are also Executive bedrooms with bird's-eye maple veneered furniture and phones at both desk and bedside plus Town House Suites with galleried rooms. These rooms boast personal fax machines, large working tables and executive stress-relieving toys along with various other extras. Children up to 12 share parents' room free. Guests have free use of the pool, weights room and running track at a leisure centre within walking distance. Conferences up to 200. Ample free parking. *Rooms 127. Access, Amex, Diners, Visa.*

SOLIHULL	Moat House	69%	£139

Tel 0121-623 9988   Fax 0121-711 2696   Map 6 C4   **H**
Homer Road Solihull West Midlands B91 3QD

Purpose-built in 1990, this large hotel stands just out of the town centre. A marble-floored entrance hall leads to the reception, main lounge and a raised bar area. Decor is light throughout, with seating comfortable and contemporary in both design and colour. Bedrooms are equally stylish, using co-ordinating fabrics and mainly darkwood freestanding furniture. Room service can provide hot food at any time. Children up to 16 stay free in parents' room. Modern health and fitness club. Conference and banqueting facilities for up to 200. A large car park (free) surrounds the hotel. *Rooms 115. Garden, indoor swimming pool, gym, aerobics studio, sauna, steam room, spa bath, solarium. Access, Amex, Diners, Visa.*

Many hotels offer reduced rates for weekend or out-of-season bookings. Always ask about special deals.

SOLIHULL   Regency Hotel   64%   £100

Tel 0121-745 6119 Fax 0121-733 3801   Map 6 C4   **H**
Stratford Road Shirley Solihull West Midlands B90 4EB

The luxurious leisure club is a major feature at this Regency-style building on the A34, half a mile from Junction 4 of the M42. Children under 14 share parents' room free. 24 hr room service. Conference/banqueting facilities for up to 150. Ample free parking.
Rooms 112. Garden, indoor swimming pool, plunge pool, gym, sauna, steam room, spa bath, solarium, coffee shop (10am-10pm). Access, Amex, Visa.

SOLIHULL   St John's Swallow Hotel   63%   £95

Tel 0121-711 3000 Fax 0121-705 6629   Map 6 C4   **H**
651 Warwick Road Solihull West Midlands B91 1AT

Five minutes drive from the M42, this comfortable, well-appointed hotel has a distinctive gabled facade, massive conference/banqueting (for up to 700) and good leisure facilities. Children up to 15 accommodated free in parents' room; six family rooms and two rooms equipped for disabled guests. A third of the rooms are reserved for non-smokers.
Rooms 177. Garden, indoor swimming pool, spa bath, sauna, solarium, steam room, keep-fit equipment. Access, Amex, Diners, Visa.

SOMERTON   Lynch Country House Hotel   69%   £55

Tel 01458 272316 Fax 01458 272590   Map 13 F2   **H**
4 Behind Berry Somerton Somerset TA11 7PD

Set in the heart of lush Somerset countryside, the Grade II listed house is surrounded by ten acres with 2800 trees, a small lake and formal gardens. Bedrooms contain books, magazines and tourist maps; appointments are individual, from Victorian bedsteads to a Georgian four-poster. A bed and breakfast hotel only, with the breakfast room overlooking the grounds and lake. Two self-catering cottages also available. *Rooms 5. Garden, croquet. Closed 25 & 26 Dec. Access, Visa.*

SOUTH MILFORD   Forte Posthouse Leeds/Selby   65%   £72

Tel 01977 682711 Fax 01977 685462   Map 7 D1   **H**
South Milford nr Leeds North Yorkshire LS25 5LF

At the junction of the A1 and A63, between York and Leeds (close to J33 of M62). Modern hotel with a variety of conference facilities for up to 120; ample parking. Children up to 16 stay free in parents' room. 43 rooms are no-smoking. All-day, informal lounge snacks. New 'smart' TVs and mini-bars in rooms. *Rooms 105. Garden, indoor swimming pool, 9-hole pitch & putt, tennis, sauna, sun beds, children's playroom (weekends), playground. Access, Amex, Diners, Visa.*

SOUTH MIMMS   Forte Posthouse   60%   £75

Tel 01707 643311 Fax 01707 646728   Map 15 E2   **H**
Bignells Corner South Mimms nr Potters Bar Hertfordshire EN6 3NH

Up-to-date accommodation just off to the left of the South Mimms service area on the M25. Mini-bars and 'intelligent' TVs in all bedrooms. *Rooms 120. Gym, sauna, spa bath, beauty therapy, solarium, pool table. Access, Amex, Diners, Visa.*

SOUTH MOLTON   Whitechapel Manor   76%   £125

Tel 01769 573377 Fax 01769 573797   Map 13 D2   **HR**
South Molton Devon EX36 3EG

Follow the Whitechapel sign from a roundabout on the A361 near South Molton to find John and Patricia Shapland's delightfully peaceful Elizabethan manor house fronted by terraced lawns and enjoying a fine view across the Yeo Valley. A fine Jacobean carved oak screen separates the entrance from the Great Hall, where comfortable chairs are set around the fireplace under a time-bowed William and Mary ceiling. The other day room is a blue leather-furnished bar. There's a scattering of antiques both downstairs and in the bedrooms, which range from small to large – some with separate sitting/dressing rooms that are also ideal for a child's bed – with soft colour schemes and extras like games compendium and jug of iced water from their own spring. Bathrooms, decorated to match the rooms, all have panelled tubs with showers above, generously sized bottles of bath oil and towelling robes. *Rooms 10. Garden, croquet. Access, Amex, Diners, Visa.*

Restaurant   £80

Patricia Shapland masterminds the kitchen, producing enjoyable dishes that are a happy compromise between simplicity and elaboration. Good local produce features in offerings like sautéed Cornish scallops with ribbons of vegetable and a balsamic vinegar dressing, best end of Devon lamb with garlic cream sauce and Exmoor venison. Other dishes might include hot duck foie gras with roasted potato and armagnac sauce, fillet of brill with mussels and saffron and beef with glazed onions and a port wine sauce. British cheeses, half a dozen desserts. Coffee is served with petits fours in the Great Hall or bar. A sensible wine list has something to suit most tastes and pockets. No smoking. *Seats 24. L 12-1.45 D 7-8.45. Set L & D from £18.*

SOUTH NORMANTON	Swallow Hotel	69%	£105

Tel 01773 812000   Fax 01773 580032   Map 7 D3   **H**
Carter Lane East South Normanton Derbyshire DE55 2EH

Modern, low-rise hotel near Junction 28 of the M1 with spacious public areas and large, conference facilities for a maximum of 200 delegates. Two of the bedrooms have been specially designed for disabled guests. Under-14s stay free in parents' room. *Rooms 161. Indoor swimming pool, keep-fit equipment, sauna, spa bath, steam room, solarium. Access, Amex, Diners, Visa.*

SOUTHALL	Asian Tandoori Centre	£15

Tel 0181-574 2597   Map 15 E2   **R**
114 The Green Southall Middlesex UB2 4BQ

Simple Indian canteen serving hearty, unsophisticated food throughout the day. Particularly good peshwari stuffed nan. Unlicensed; non-smoking area. *Seats 80. Meals 9am-10.30pm (Fri-Sun to 11pm).*
Also at:
157 The Broadway, Southall. Tel 0181-574 3476   Map 15 E2

SOUTHALL	Madhu's Brilliant	£40

Tel 0181-574 1897   Fax 0181-813 8639   Map 15 E2   **R**
39 South Road Southall Middlesex UB1 1SW

Popular restaurant specialising in authentic Punjabi food, served in comfortable surroundings. Short delays can result from the cooked-to-order policy adopted by the conscientious kitchen team – they are worth it. Some of the dishes are for two or more people, for example the butter fried chicken, where a whole chicken is produced to be picked from at the table. To start, try the delicious *alu tikkie*, which is potato with chick peas and fresh coriander – here transformed into something magical – or perhaps the fresh samosas. Follow with masala fish, excellent *karai gosht* (lamb in a dark, pungent sauce) or one of the many vegetable curries. The crisp *bhatua* bread is not to be missed. Friendly, helpful service. *Seats 104. Parties 30. Private Room 50. L 12.30-3 D 6-11.30 (Fri & Sat till 12). Closed L Sat & Sun, all Tues. Access, Amex, Diners, Visa.*

SOUTHAMPTON	De Vere Grand Harbour	72%	NEW	£110

Tel 01703 633033   Fax 01703 633066   Map 15 D4   **H**
West Quay Road Southampton Hampshire SO15 1 AG

Striking new hotel in polished granite with stepped storeys (giving balconies to some bedrooms) and pyramidical atrium on one side next to an ornamental lake. The design makes for some exciting public spaces in a range of styles from the classic use of marble and wood panelling in the reception lobby to a wicker-furnished atrium lounge (complete with scenic elevator – there are regular ones for the vertiginous), conservatory-style restaurant complex (mediocre dinner in Allertons, and, disappointingly, carton orange juice at breakfast) and, in the leisure club, a traditional leather-furnished, wood-

See over

panelled library; only the shelf of books at browsing height is real however. Bedrooms (astonishingly, only around thirty are air-conditioned, so ask for one of these) maintain the quality and style found in the public areas with traditional polished-wood, freestanding furniture, a pair of proper armchairs in every room (some Executive rooms, which are larger, also get sofas, as well as a bowl of fresh fruit, mineral water and chocolates on arrival) and every modern convenience from teletext TV and room safe to phones at both desk and bedside and mini-bar, though the latter does not provide fresh milk for the tea- and coffee-making facilities. Bathrooms all have hand-held as well as overhead showers at the tub (some have separate walk-in showers), black polished-granite vanity units (no shaving mirrors though), and face cloths plus bathrobes in the Executive rooms. A turn-down service at night and comprehensive 24hr room service are offered. Commendably, nine rooms are specially adapted for the disabled, who will also find special facilities in the leisure club. Banqueting/conference facilities for 400/500. Ample own parking. *Rooms 172. Patio, indoor swimming pool (separate children's pool), gym, sauna, steam room, spa bath, sun beds, beauty salon, snooker. Access, Amex, Diners, Visa.*

SOUTHAMPTON	Dolphin Hotel	60%	£77

Tel 01703 339955   Fax 01703 333650   Map 15 D4   **H**
High Street Southampton Hampshire SO14 7NS

This Forte hotel is a modernised 18th-century coaching inn with banqueting/conference facilities for 90/70. Free use of nearby Posthouse health and fitness club. Children up to 16 stay free in parents' room. *Rooms 73. Access, Amex, Diners, Visa.*

SOUTHAMPTON	Forte Posthouse	58%	£72

Tel 01703 330777   Fax 01703 332510   Map 15 D4   **H**
Herbert Walker Avenue Southampton Hampshire SO15 0HJ

Ten-storey tower-block hotel with views of the liners' berths from some rooms. Well-equipped bedrooms, Traders Bar, children's playroom (at weekends) and playground. Banqueting/conferences for up to 200. *Rooms 128. Indoor swimming pool, gym, sauna, spa bath, solarium. Access, Amex, Diners, Visa.*

SOUTHAMPTON	Hilton National	68%	£96

Tel 01703 702700   Fax 01703 767233   Map 15 D4   **H**
Bracken Place Chilworth Southampton Hampshire SO16 3RB 4HB

Up-to-date leisure and business facilities in a modern redbrick Hilton hotel by the A33 and M27 (approach from Junction 5). 50 Plaza bedrooms and suites feature a queen-size bed, welcome drink, chocolates, mini-bar, bathrobe and slippers and fresh fruit; these rooms attract a considerable supplement. Two rooms equipped for disabled guests; 21 reserved for non-smokers. Children under 16 share parents' room free. 24hr room service. Banqueting/conference facilities for 120/220; ample parking. *Rooms 135. Garden, indoor swimming pool, gym, sauna, steam room, solarium, beauty salon, deli coffee shop (6.30am-11pm). Access, Amex, Diners, Visa.*

SOUTHAMPTON	Kuti's		£45

Tel 01703 221585   Map 15 D4   **R**
37 Oxford Street Southampton Hampshire SO1 1DP

A fine range of Bangladeshi-style Indian cooking is on offer at this comfortable restaurant. Besides the familiar chicken, lamb and prawn variants you'll find some more unusual items including half-a-dozen ways with duck and preparations of trout, sea bass and the exotic *ayre* fish and *chitol* fish. *Seats 78. Private Room 60. L 12-2 D 6-11.30. Closed 25 & 26 Dec. Set L £8.50 (buffet Sun-Fri) Set D £10.95. Access, Amex, Diners, Visa.*

SOUTHAMPTON	Novotel	62%	£65

Tel 01703 330550   Fax 01703 222158   Map 15 D4   **H**
1 West Quay Road Southampton Hampshire SO15 1RA

Very modern hotel convenient for railway station, ferries and Ocean Village. Geared to business use in the week (with conference facilities for up to 450, banqueting up to 350), children up to 16 stay free in parents' room. All rooms have queen-size beds and single divans. *Rooms 121. Indoor swimming pool, keep-fit facilities, sauna, games room. Access, Amex, Diners, Visa.*

SOUTHAMPTON	Polygon Hotel	65%	£71

Tel 01703 330055   Fax 01703 332435   Map 15 D4   **H**
Cumberland Place Southampton Hampshire SO9 4GD

Close by the civic centre, a 30s' structure in red brick overlooking Watts Park. Banqueting/conference facilities for 450/500 (parking for 150). Free use of Forte Posthouse health and fitness club in Herbert Walker Avenue. 38 rooms reserved for non-smokers. Forte. *Rooms 93. Access, Amex, Diners, Visa.*

SOUTHAMPTON	Southampton Park Hotel	64%	£68

Tel 01703 223467   Fax 01703 332538   Map 15 D4   **H**
12 Cumberland Place Southampton Hampshire SO15 2WY

Functional modern building overlooking Watts Park. Well-equipped bedrooms (front ones have balconies), roomy lounge areas, two restaurants, a cocktail bar, conference rooms (up to 300 delegates) and a leisure club exclusively for guests. *Rooms 72. Indoor swimming pool, sauna, spa bath, steam room, solarium. Access, Amex, Diners, Visa.*

SOUTHPORT	New Bold Hotel	58%	£51

Tel 01704 532578   Fax 01704 532528   Map 6 A1   **H**
Lord Street Southport Merseyside PR9 0BE

Family-owned and family-run, the Bold stands on the town's leafy main boulevard. Modern bedrooms include two for family use and a bridal suite with sunken bath; back rooms are the quietest. A public bar serves traditional beers and Raphael's bar/café has long-hours opening and live entertainment. Reception is upstairs, and the front door leads straight into the bar. Royal Birkdale Golf Course is just along the road. *Rooms 23. Access, Visa.*

SOUTHPORT	Prince of Wales Hotel	64%	£74

Tel 01704 536688   Fax 01704 543488   Map 6 A1   **H**
Lord Street Southport Merseyside PR8 1JS

On the town's tree-lined main street, the hotel exudes elegance. A large-scale programme of refurbishment is being undertaken by new owners, restoring both the moulded plaster ceilings of the ground floor, and the enormous leaded glass roof in the ballroom to their former glories. The comfortable Clubhouse bar features mirrors displaying the signatures of some of the world's greatest golfers. Bedrooms, all recently redecorated, are modestly furnished, but basic requirements are well provided for, with hairdryers, trouser presses, satellite TVs and modern en-suite bathrooms. Conferences are the main business, with a maximum capacity of 450 theatre-style. Children up to 16 stay free in parents' room. Parking for 90 cars. *Rooms 104. Terrace. Access, Amex, Diners, Visa.*

SOUTHSEA	Bistro Montparnasse		£55

Tel 01705 816754   Map 15 D4   **R**
103 Palmerston Road Southsea Hampshire PO5 3PS

An international menu of modern inspiration brings diners to Peter and Gillian Scott's warm and welcoming French bistro, conveniently close to Southsea's main shopping area and the ferries to France and Spain. Gillian offers a well-thought-out and often inventive choice on her à la carte menu, which changes monthly. Home-made breads and focaccia with olive oil are great to nibble and dip before the meal gets under way. Some of the starters read like mains, as in smoked ham and pease pudding with parsley sauce or steamed smoked haddock with cabbage and bacon. Main courses proper always include a fresh fish of the day among about half a dozen choices – crisp breast of duck with ginger and lemon grass jus, slow-roast shoulder of lamb with parsley and garlic mash, fillet of beef with braised oxtail and a mustard dumpling. Finish in style with lemon soufflé crepes or Grand Marnier and orange trifle with orange tuiles. A special blackboard set menu at £12.50 is also offered on weekdays. *Seats 40. Parties 12. Private Room 25. D only 7 10. Closed Sun, Mon, Tue after Bank Holiday, 2 weeks Jan. Set D £12.50 (not Sat). Access, Amex, Visa.*

Lodges are now listed by county in the reference section

SOUTHWELL   Saracen's Head   62%   £75

Tel 01636 812701   Fax 01636 815408   Map 7 D3   **H**
Market Place Southwell Nottinghamshire NG25 0HE

The ancient half-timbered inn still shows many original features, including a fine 14th-century wall painting. Characterful public areas and bedrooms that offer all the usual modern comforts and conveniences. Banqueting/conferences for up to 120. Forte. *Rooms 27. Access, Amex, Diners, Visa.*

SOUTHWOLD   The Crown   £69

Tel 01502 722275   Fax 01502 724805   Map 10 D2   **IR**
90 High Street Southwold Suffolk IP18 6DP

Restored town-centre Georgian inn in the ownership of Adnams, the Southwold brewers. To the front, facing the High Street, the Parlour is half lounge, half dining area; the front bar and attendant restaurant exude refinement. Bedrooms are well equipped, with antique or decent reproduction pieces and bright fabrics and furnishings; all have private bathrooms though three are not strictly en suite (their private bathrooms are across a corridor); one family room has a double and two single beds; another pair of rooms adjoin. Function facilities for 22 (banqueting), 45 (theatre-style conference). Car parking is limited. *Rooms 12. Closed 1 week Jan. Access, Amex, Diners, Visa.*

Restaurant   £50

A charming traditional setting for some imaginative and enjoyable dishes. Starters include cold venison sausages with a baby spinach salad, and marinated scallops with stir-fried vegetables and wun tuns. Main dishes range from baked fillet of lemon sole with a chili and lemon crust and Thai-style deep-fried rainbow trout with coriander and lime to rare fillet of beef with glazed beetroot and wilted greens. As you might expect, prices are kept down on the exceptional wine merchant's list. In addition, vintages are classified and tasting notes accompany each wine. No half bottles, but plenty available by the glass. *Seats 22 + Parlour 16. Parties 6. L 12.30-1.30 D 7.30-9.30. Set L £12.95/£15.50 Set D £17.95/£19.95.*

SOUTHWOLD   The Swan   65%   £91

Tel 01502 722186   Fax 01502 724800   Map 10 D2   **HR**
Market Place Southwold Suffolk IP18 6EG

The ancient Swan, rebuilt in 1660 after a fire that destroyed most of the town, stands facing the market square and backs on to Adnams Brewery. An old long-case clock and fresh flowers grace the flagstoned foyer and an abundance of sofas the period drawing room. Main-house bedrooms are traditional in style with freestanding furniture, including the odd antique, while simpler chalet-style rooms a garden to the rear. Banquets and conferences for up to 80/50. Good bar snacks. *Rooms 45. Garden, croquet. Access, Amex, Diners, Visa.*

Restaurant   £65

An elegant, pink dining-room and a choice of fixed-price-only menus which offer a varied range of dishes that include beef tomato filled with kipper mousse, grilled salmon with lemon butter, capers, prawns and flaked almonds, pork fillet wrapped in bacon and roasted with figs. Roast turkey with a traditional garnish and chicken supreme filled with banana and served with rice and a light curry sauce are other possibilities, with poached pears in red wine among the desserts. No smoking. Many gems on the fine wine list with succinct tasting notes alongside each wine. Some prices are exceptional (eg a 1994 New Zealand Cloudy Bay Sauvignon at £15.75). *Seats 50. Private Room 40. L 12-1.45 D 7-9.30. Closed lunchtime Mon-Fri Jan-Easter. Set L £11.50/£13.95 (Sun £12.50/£16.50) Set D from £17.50.*

We welcome bona fide complaints and recommendations on the tear-out pages at the back of the book for readers' comments. They are followed up by our professional team.

STADDLEBRIDGE	McCoy's	70%	£99

Tel 01609 882671   Fax 01609 882660   Map 5 E3   **HR**
Staddlebridge North Yorkshire DL6 3JB

Staddlebridge doesn't actually exist on the map – the hotel stands at the intersection of the A19 and the A172 with entry via the southbound lane of the latter. It's an extraordinary place, not for the more conservative-minded, but then there are hotels a-plenty catering to their tastes. Here is a unique establishment run with care and dedication by three brothers, Eugene, Peter and Tom McCoy. On the ground floor there's a long, narrow lounge and in the next room a spacious bar. Both are decorated in a very laid-back and original style   settees from around the 40s, one or two virtually coming apart, are piled with huge scatter cushions covered in flamboyantly colourful fabrics. The bar with its multicoloured foil wallpaper and palms has an ambience that wouldn't be amiss in some tropical climes. Bedrooms too are striking. Wallpaper by Hubert de Givenchy and a mix of furniture create a splendid setting with comfortable seating and even more comfortable beds. Windows have secondary glazing to reduce possible noise levels. Bathrooms have huge shower roses and good soaps. In the morning superb breakfasts range from a platter of unusual fruit to eggs from their own free-range black hens. *Rooms 6. Garden. Access, Amex, Diners, Visa.*

Restaurant  £85

The restaurant on the ground floor, open for dinner only, offers a glittering candle-lit experience with maroon mirrored-lined walls and beautiful pink napery. The menu is sophisticated and cleverly innovative, Tom and Eugene McCoy's style since the very beginning. The quality of the cooking is of a very high standard in the restaurant and also in the cellar bistro, with some dishes appropriate for both. Thus curried parsnip and apple soup, fresh langoustines grilled with garlic, mushroom tart with Muscadet sauce and stunning pan-fried scallops topped with caviar and served in a red wine sauce are eminently suitable for either venue. Main dishes include roast guinea fowl with red wine, fillet of lamb with tomato and basil tart and the likes of sea bass with deep-fried vegetables and plum vinaigrette. Many desserts are perennial favourites such as crepe San Lorenzo with a filling of amaretti biscuits in Grand Marnier and vanilla cream and the outstanding choc-o-block Stanley – a chocolate fondant with sponge soaked in Tia Maria with a coffee bean sauce or "thin, thin oh so very thin" layers of puff pastry, crème patissière and strawberries. Excellent cheeses and to finish superb coffee and home-made chocolate truffles. The wine list is mostly French, with quality offerings in every section. Brief tasting notes. Fabulous service. Booking essential. *Seats 50. Parties 12. Private Room 30. D only 7-10. Closed Sun & Mon, 25 & 26 Dec, 1 Jan.*

STAFFORD	De Vere Tillington Hall	63%	£90

Tel 01785 53531   Fax 01785 59223   Map 6 B3   **H**
Eccleshall Road Stafford Staffordshire ST16 1JJ

Half a mile from the M6 (J14), this modern De Vere hotel adds good leisure and conference facilities (200 maximum) to decent refurbished bedrooms that include attractive four-poster rooms. Children up to 14 share adult accommodation free, paying for meals as taken. *Rooms 90. Garden, indoor swimming pool, gym, sauna, spa bath, solarium, beauty salon, tennis, snooker. Closed 28 & 29 Dec. Access, Amex, Diners, Visa.*

STAMFORD	The George of Stamford	72%	£105

Tel 01780 55171   Fax 01780 57070   Map 7 E3   **HR**
71 St Martins Stamford Lincolnshire PE9 2LB

The George must be one of England's most famous old coaching inns, and it declares its history from the moment you approach its prime town-centre site. You can still just visualise a coach and four going through to the cobbled courtyard, though the ostler would be surprised to see that the livery stables now house a business centre, and instead of waiting for coaches, visitors to the London Room and York Bar are enjoying a pint of Adnams. Open fires, exposed stonework walls, flagstone floors and beams all add to the atmosphere. Bedrooms are quirky and quaint (owing to the age of the building), several have four-posters and some overlook the courtyard, but all are well equipped and well maintained. Poste Hotels. *Rooms 47. Garden. Access, Amex, Diners, Visa.*

See over

Restaurant   £85

Chris Pitman aims to use the best of British raw ingredients, presented in inspired international ways to a discerning clientele. Classics on his main menu include Dover sole, roast duck with glazed peaches, rack of lamb and roast beef served from the silver carving wagon. There's a Light Quick Lunch menu available in the restaurant (not Sundays) which takes some dishes from the carte, such as marinated salmon and haddock with salade niçoise, game terrine or spaghetti with cheese or meat sauce. Desserts and cheeses live up to the standards of the rest. We have long acknowledged that the generously priced wine list here (as in other Poste Hotels where the wines have been chosen by John Hoskins MW, hence the well-informed tasting notes) as one of the best in the country. For instance, wines by the glass are served in two measures, there are as many magnums (an '81 Ducru Beaucaillou at £75 really is a steal) as half bottles, and non-French wines receive equal billing. A house *marque* champagne is under £20. Informal eating in the Garden Lounge. Tables out on the patio in summer. *Seats 80. Parties 12. Private Room 50. L 12.30-2.30 D 7.15-10.30 (Garden Lounge 12-10.30pm). Set L £16.50/£19.50 (Mon-Sat).*

| STAMFORD | Warunee's | £35 |

Tel 01780 57291   Map 7 E3   R
43 St Mary's Street Stamford Lincolnshire PE9 2DS

The interior of this period building resembles nothing so much as an English tea shop with its wheelback chairs and lacy table-cloths but a few Oriental etchings nestling between mock timbers give the clue that this is actually a Thai restaurant. The eponymous Warunee is the lady in the kitchen responsible for the authentic cooking, while English husband David runs front of house. There's a good price/quality ratio, with many main dishes on a fairly extensive menu at less than £6. Particularly succulent chicken satay with lashings of peanut sauce makes a good starter before such dishes as pork with mushrooms, bean sprouts and ginger; chicken with chili peppers, onion and garlic (one of the hotter dishes); roast duck with plum sauce; or prawns with coconut and lemon grass – all prepared in a way which strongly emphasises the main flavouring of the dish. Best to book at weekends. *Seats 45. Private Room 16. L by arrangement D 6-10.30. Closed Sun, 3 days Christmas, 3 days New Year. Set D £12.50. Access, Amex, Diners, Visa.*

| STANDISH | Kilhey Court | 65% | £95 |

Tel 01257 472100   Fax 01257 422401   Map 6 B1   H
Chorley Road Standish nr Wigan Lancashire WN1 2XN

Built by a Wigan brewer in 1884, the main building stands in ten acres of woodland alongside the A5106. Additions such as the conference and business centres (catering for up to 180, with ample parking), a leisure club with a small pool, a bedroom block and the reception area lack much of the house's original elegance. Bedrooms are provided with a work desk and mini-bar, and finished in white ash and floral fabrics – putting practicality ahead of luxury. Rural tranquillity and proximity to the M61 and M6 are major assets. 24hr room service. A recent refurbishment programme has seen the addition of some Victorian-style suites and a marquee facility (banquets for 450). *Rooms 62. Garden, golf (18), night club (Fri & Sat), indoor swimming pool, gym, sauna, solarium, spa bath, fishing, children's playground. Access, Amex, Diners, Visa.*

| STANDISH | Wigan Standish Moat House | 63% | £90 |

Tel 01257 499988   Fax 01257 427327   Map 6 B1   H
Almond Brook Road Standish nr Wigan Greater Manchester WN6 0SR

Formerly the Almond Brook Moat House, the hotel stands 200 yards from Junction 27 of the M6. Neat, well-maintained bedrooms and conference facilities for up to 270. Families are well catered for with under-14s free when sharing parents' room. *Rooms 122. Garden, indoor swimming pool, keep-fit equipment, sauna, sun bed, night club/disco. Closed 24-30 Dec. Access, Amex, Diners, Visa.*

| STANSTEAD ABBOTS | Briggens House | 70% | £115 |

Tel 01279 792416   Fax 01279 793685   Map 15 F2   H
Stanstead Road Stanstead Abbots nr Ware Hertfordshire SG12 8LD

A grand former stately home, a few miles off the M11, set in 45 acres of grounds and splendid gardens with its own 9-hole golf course. High standards of service are typified by the smart, uniformed doormen. A magnificent carved wood staircase leads up from the entrance hall with its glass chandelier to 22 bedrooms in the main house; 32 more are in the converted coach house and have lower ceilings, but all are equally tastefully decorated with a good range of extras included as standard. Swagged drapes and stylish reproduction antiques give an elegant air. In summer, tables are set on the expansive lawns outside the French windows leading off the lounge. Function facilities for 100. Children under 16 free in parents' room. Queens Moat Houses. **Rooms** 54. *Garden, croquet, outdoor swimming pool, tennis, golf (9), pitch & putt, putting, bowls, fishing. Access, Amex, Diners, Visa.*

STANSTEAD AIRPORT	Hilton National	56%	£129

Tel 01279 680800   Fax 01279 680890   Map 10 B3   **H**
Round Coppice Road Stanstead Airport Essex CM24 8SE

Just off junction 8 of the M11, this is the only hotel within the airport perimeter and it benefits from courtesy transport to and from the terminal as well as splendid leisure and fitness facilities. Bedrooms are being gradually upgraded. Popular with conferences, with 16 meeting rooms and a maximum of 300 delegates. **Rooms** 237. *Garden, indoor swimming pool, gym, sauna, steam room, spa bath, beauty & hair salon. Access, Amex, Diners, Visa.*

STANTON ST QUINTIN	Stanton Manor	64%	£82

Tel 01666 837552   Fax 01666 837022   Map 14 B2   **HR**
Stanton St Quintin nr Chippenham Wiltshire SN14 6DQ

"Your home in Wiltshire" proclaims the brochure, and indeed Elizabeth and Philip Bullock are the friendliest and most welcoming of hosts at their stone manor house. The present main house dates from the 19th century, though some buildings are much older, notably a 14th-century dovecote. Bedrooms are individually appointed in traditional style. Children up to 18 stay free in parents' room. Two minutes from the M4 (J17) just off the A429. **Rooms** 10. *Garden, croquet. Closed 26 Dec-8 Jan. Access, Amex, Diners, Visa.*

Restaurant   £50

Ⅴ

Simple dishes appeal on a short à la carte, to which the manor's own kitchen garden contributes seasonal fruit and vegetables – and much of the rest is supplied locally. Garlicky king prawns, terrine of duck and chicken, roast rack of lamb, escalope of salmon with a green peppercorn and brandy sauce, iced chocolate parfait and warm poached pear on a light praline sauce show the style. Vegetarian menu. No smoking. **Seats** 30. *Parties 12. Private Room 24. L 12-1.30 D 7-9.30. Set L & D £15/£18. Closed L Sun.*

STAPLEFORD	Stapleford Park	87%	£155

Tel 01572 787522   Fax 01572 787651   Map 7 E3   **HR**
Stapleford nr Melton Mowbray Leicestershire LE14 2EF

Set in 500 acres of parkland laid out by Capability Brown, this beautiful country house hotel is approached via the gatehouses and protected from hundreds of grazing sheep by a splendid stone ha-ha. The core of the house was built by the Sherard family in the 17th century and their family portraits dominate the public rooms; Victorian additions blend in perfectly. Drawing rooms have comfortable sofas, splendid carved and moulded ceilings and roaring winter fires. Upstairs, luxuriously appointed bedrooms have been designed by more than 25 famous names, based on their image of life in the country – not only recognised designers such as Nina Campbell and David Hicks but also more surprising names like Turnbull & Asser (a very masculine room with shirt fabric-inspired wall coverings), and Crabtree & Evelyn with a room full of over 200 floral pictures. Marble bathrooms are equally sumptuous, with heavy bathrobes, luxury toiletries and tubs practically deep enough for a swim. New for this year is a four-bedroomed self-contained cottage with bedrooms by Coca Cola, MGM, Range Rover and IBM. Children up to 10 stay free in parents' room. Many delightful private meeting rooms, the largest having banqueting/conference facilities for 170/200. **Rooms** 43. *Garden, croquet, coarse fishing, tennis, clay pigeon shooting, putting, riding, basketball. Access, Amex, Diners, Visa.*

Restaurant   £90

👑 🍇 🍃 🍶

The Grinling Gibbons dining-room lives up to the standard of the rest of the hotel, filled as it is with his splendid swags and carvings. This room is generally only used in the

See over

evenings, when chef Malcolm Jessop offers an à la carte menu rooted in the French tradition. However, he has put his own signature on familiar favourites: so tomato and mozzarella salad comes with calamata olives, ratatouille vinaigrette and toasted pitta chips; and grilled prawns come wrapped in Parma ham with three aïolis. Main courses might include seared sea bass on a bed of spinach with saffron sauce and pernod-scented scallops or herb-crusted rack of lamb with roasted garlic and rosemary jus. Desserts are equally tempting – The Stapleford Wave is a sampler plate for those not calorie-counting and the chocolate pecan pie with caramel sauce is not to be missed. Except on Sunday, when traditional lunch is served in the winter and a comprehensive barbecue in the summer, lunch is a lighter affair, served in the vaulted Old Kitchen. An early summer visit brought a delicious broccoli soup with garlic croutons and chargrilled chicken breast and asparagus with a sweet pepper and onion chutney salad. Beetroot crisps made an interesting nibble. The unconventional wine list is presented by grape style, with each wine well annotated. Prices are very fair; few half bottles. Outdoor eating for 40 on the terrace. No smoking. *Seats 70. Parties 8. Private Room 50. L 12-2.30 D 7-9.30 (Fri & Sat to 10). Set Sun L £19.95.*

STEEPLE ASTON	Hopcrofts Holt Hotel	63%	£80

Tel 01869 340259   Fax 01869 340865   Map 15 D1   **H**
Steeple Aston nr Oxford Oxfordshire OX6 3QQ

Once a coaching inn, the hotel has now expanded its role with Executive accommodation and purpose-built conference rooms which can cater for up to 200 delegates in one room. New owners have refurbished many of the bedrooms and a new leisure centre is under construction. Just off the A4260 between Banbury and Oxford. *Rooms 88. Access, Amex, Diners, Visa.*

STEVENAGE	Forte Posthouse	58%	£72

Tel 01438 365444   Fax 01438 741308   Map 15 E1   **H**
Old London Road Broadwater Stevenage Hertfordshire SG2 8DS

On the B197 to the north of town. One of the smaller Posthouses, with public rooms in a 15th-century building and bedrooms (half designated non-smoking) in more modern extensions. Children free in parents' room. *Rooms 54. Access, Amex, Diners, Visa.*

STEVENAGE	Novotel	60%	£68

Tel 01438 742299   Fax 01438 723872   Map 15 E1   **H**
Knebworth Park Stevenage Hertfordshire SG1 2AX

Modern, open-plan hotel at Junction 7 of the A1(M). Banqueting facilities for up to 120, conferences up to 150. *Rooms 100. Outdoor swimming pool. Access, Amex, Diners, Visa.*

STILTON	Bell Inn		£64

Tel 01733 241066   Fax 01733 245173   Map 7 E4   **IR**
Great North Road Stilton nr Peterborough Cambridgeshire PE7 3RA

Reputedly the oldest coaching inn on the Great North Road (and once refuge to highwayman Dick Turpin), the Bell boasts a Roman well in the courtyard and an impressive 15th-century stone frontage. Modern additions include hotel reception glassed in under the original archway and two rear wings of bedrooms with today's trappings, tokens of antiquity sadly confined to the odd four-poster bed. Separate conference and banqueting for up to 100 in the Marlborough Suite. No dogs. *Rooms 19. Garden. Closed 25 & 26 Dec. Access, Amex, Diners, Visa.*

Restaurant   £45

The delightful, galleried restaurant with vaulted ceiling and exposed rafters is more in character with the original Old Bell. Stilton cheese was first sold to travellers here in the 1720s and it still features on the menus, just as it is with plum bread or in dishes such as puff pastry parcels with a port sauce, or scallops and prawns topped with a champagne sabayon gratinated with Stilton. Other typical menu items are individual kidney pie, trout *normande* and confit of duck with herbed sauté potatoes. Sunday lunch includes a traditional roast sirloin with Yorkshire pudding and horseradish sauce. Vegetarian options. Snacks at lunchtime in the bar. *Seats 30. Parties 22. Private Room 12. L Sun 12-2, other days by arrangement D 7-9.30 (Sun to 9). Set Sun L £9.95 Set D £15.50/£22.50.*

| STOCKBRIDGE | Grosvenor Hotel | 57% | £75 |

Tel 01264 810606   Fax 01264 810747   Map 14 C3   **H**
High Street Stockbridge Hampshire SO20 6EU

On the A30 in the village centre, the Grosvenor (owned by Countryside Inns) has kept many of its original Georgian features, including a colonnaded porch. The bar is one of the focal points of Stockbridge life. Bedrooms in the original house are larger than those in the converted stables. Banqueting and conference facilities for around 70. *Rooms 25. Garden, sauna, snooker. Access, Amex, Diners, Visa.*

| STOCKPORT | Jarvis Alma Lodge | 61% | £95 |

Tel 0161-483 4431   Fax 0161-483 1983   Map 6 B2   **H**
149 Buxton Road Stockport Cheshire SK2 6EL

Two miles from the M6 (Junction 12) on the A6 to the south of Stockport, this early-Victorian house has been greatly extended to create a business-oriented hotel. Some original features of the old house – wood panelling and open fires – survive in the public rooms. All bedrooms have showers. Banqueting/conference facilities for up to 250. Children up to 16 accommodated free in parents' room. *Rooms 52. Access, Amex, Diners, Visa.*

| STOCKTON-ON-TEES | Swallow Hotel | 67% | £96 |

Tel 01642 679721   Fax 01642 601714   Map 5 E3   **H**
10 John Walker Square Stockton-on-Tees Cleveland TS18 1AQ

Practical, town-centre business hotel with an Egyptian-themed leisure centre and an all-day brasserie – Matchmakers (closed Sun) – named after John Walker, the man who invented the match and who came from Stockton. Banqueting/conference facilities for 300. Head for Stockton town centre and follow signs to the adjoining multi-storey car park, whose 6th floor is free for hotel residents. Half the bedrooms are designated non-smoking. *Rooms 125. Indoor swimming pool, keep-fit equipment, sauna, spa bath, steam room, solarium. Access, Amex, Diners, Visa.*

| STOKE-ON-TRENT | Haydon House Hotel | 65% | £62 |

Tel 01782 711311   Fax 01782 717470   Map 6 B3   **H**
Haydon Street Basford Stoke-on-Trent Staffordshire ST4 6JD

A family-owned Victorian hotel with friendly atmosphere, dependable accommodation and six de luxe suites, each with its own entrance, in adjacent Glebe Mews. Classy Victorian-style day rooms with antique clock collection. Take the A500 from the M6 (J15 or 16) to the A53 turn-off. The hotel stands on the A53 at Basford. *Rooms 31. Closed 1 week Jan. Access, Amex, Diners, Visa.*

| STOKE-ON-TRENT | North Stafford Hotel | 61% | £92 |

Tel 01782 744477   Fax 01782 744580   Map 6 B3   **H**
Station Road Stoke-on-Trent Staffordshire ST4 2AE

Redbrick Victorian hotel with cheerful, generally good-sized bedrooms and conference/seminar facilities for up to 450 in one room. Children up to 14 stay free in parents' room. Refurbishment continues. *Rooms 69. Access, Amex, Diners, Visa.*

| STOKE-ON-TRENT | Stakis Stoke-on-Trent | 68% | £106 |

Tel 01782 202361   Fax 01782 286464   Map 6 B3   **H**
Trinity Street Hanley Stoke-on-Trent Staffordshire ST1 5NB

Situated at Hanley town centre and close to Stoke Festival Park, this Stakis combines a busy conference trade (max 300) with good family facilities and a leisure club. Two ground-floor rooms are equipped for disabled guests. Children up to 15 stay free in parents' room. Bennetts pubby lounge/bar is open all day (except Sunday). Staffed business centre. *Rooms 128. Indoor swimming pool, keep-fit equipment, sauna, spa bath, steam room, solarium. Access, Amex, Diners, Visa.*

Set menu prices may not always include service or wine.

STOKE-ON-TRENT   Stoke-on-Trent Moat House   70%   £107

Tel 01782 219000 Fax 01782 284500   Map 6 B3   **H**
Etruria Hall Festival Way Etruria Stoke-on-Trent Staffordshire ST1 5BQ

Ten minutes drive from the M6, and equidistant from Junctions 15 and 16, the hotel stands by the A53 at the heart of the 1986 Garden Festival park. Day rooms, leisure club and smart up-to-date bedrooms are in a sympathetically designed stone-clad complex which reflects within it many of the original hall's features. There are 13 conference rooms, which can handle 500+ delegates. Free parking for 350 cars. Good children's facilities include a supervised sports club; under-16s stay free in parents' room. No dogs. *Rooms 143. Indoor swimming pool, gym, sauna, spa bath, solarium, beauty salon, snooker, games room, table tennis, coffee shop (9am-10pm). Access, Amex, Diners, Visa.*

STOKESLEY   Chapters   65%   £60

Tel 01642 711888 Fax 01642 713387   Map 5 E3   **HR**
27 High Street Stokesley North Yorkshire TS9 5AD

A splendid redbrick Georgian former coaching inn standing in the heart of the town. The first floor comprises the Personal Appearance suite dedicated to bath and beauty and including a reflexologist, hypnotherapist and masseur. Bedrooms, all en suite, are neat and well-equipped. Special weekend breaks available on a half-board basis. *Rooms 13. Garden, solarium, beauty salon, hairdressing. Closed 25 Dec, 1 Jan. Access, Amex, Diners, Visa.*

Bistro   £40

Assisted by his wife Catherine, Alan Thompson continues to turn out interesting menus using fresh local produce whenever possible, presented with an international twist. Thus you might try hot gruyère cheese soufflé, rack of lamb on Puy lentils with a Dijon sauce and sticky toffee pudding to finish. *Seats 36. L by arrangement D 7-9.30. Closed Sun.*

STON EASTON   Ston Easton Park   88%   £169

Tel 01761 241631 Fax 01761 241377   Map 13 F1   **HR**
Ston Easton nr Bath Avon BA3 4DF

Built in 1740, this magnificent Palladian house is distinguished by some exceptional architectural features. Its setting is also outstanding: the Humphrey Repton gardens, including wells, a ruined grotto and bridges spanning the River Norr, and an 18th-century ice house, are not to be missed. On the river bank 75 yards from the house is the Gardener's Cottage comprising two separate suites, each with a large twin/double-bedded room, living room and private bathrooms.

The magnificence of the gardens is reflected in the wonderful floral displays you'll find in the salon – note the ornate plasterwork and trompe l'oeil murals – and in the library, which contains listed mahogany bookcases. Tastefully-decorated bedrooms, some with four-posters of the Chippendale and Hepplewhite periods, have luxurious bathroom, boasting high-quality fittings and toiletries. Impeccable staff provide excellent service (beds turned down and towels changed when guests are dining), and a real English country house-style breakfast will not disappoint. Children of seven years onwards and babes in arms welcome, and kennelling is available (free of charge) as dogs are not allowed inside. The house offers perhaps a unique glimpse into the 'Upstairs, Downstairs' world of the 18th century: ask to see 'downstairs', which has a kitchen museum, linen room, servants' hall, billiard room and wine cellars, all in use today. Period meeting rooms and banqueting (the house's original dining-room, now called the Yellow Room) for 24. *Rooms 21. Garden, croquet, tennis, bicycle hire, snooker. Access, Amex, Diners, Visa.*

Restaurant   £95

The main dining-room, with fine wood panelling painted in soft colours and bamboo-style furniture, was the old parlour. Relying on the best and freshest produce, including vegetables, herbs and fruit from the walled kitchen garden, chef Mark Harrington cooks with imagination and consistency in a style that combines the best of English and French elements. First-course choice is headed by soup; other starters could include warm terrine of duck confit with a salad of lentils and a Cabernet Sauvignon vinaigrette, or king scallops roasted in lemon oil topped with crisp-fried vegetables and soya dressing. Main dishes are mostly in the classic, traditional mould, as in roast partridge with glazed button onions, wild mushrooms and lardons, or Dover sole with a lemon butter sauce. Desserts keep up the excellent work with the likes of iced mascarpone torte studded with candied strawberries or (order the hot one with the main course) baked banana and clotted cream clafoutis served with rum and raisin ice cream. Fine British cheeses and a splendidly balanced wine list, in terms of both ages of wine offered and variety of countries of origin. Many of the famous growers are available in half bottles. Introductory paragraphs to each section and tasting notes alongside a "good-value selection" around a dozen. *Seats 40. Parties 8. Private Room 24. L 12.30-2 D 7.30-9.30 (Fri & Sat to 10). Set L £26 Set D £38.50.*

STONEHOUSE	Stonehouse Court	68%	£80

Tel 01453 825155   Fax 01453 824611   Map 14 B2   **H**
Bristol Road Stonehouse Gloucestershire GL10 3RA

Conveniently situated about a mile from Junction 13 of the M5 (A419 towards Stroud), Stonehouse Court is an imposing 17th-century building (Grade II listed) set in six acres of secluded gardens. Bedrooms are split between spacious rooms with mullioned windows in the main house and more uniform ones in redbrick extensions. Children occupying parents' room are accommodated free of charge. Day rooms include a large panelled lounge with fine carved stone fireplace, abundant seating and a bar with green leather chesterfield sofas. Conference/banqueting facilities for up to 150. Friendly management. *Rooms 36. Garden, croquet, fishing. Access, Amex, Diners, Visa.*

STONHAM	Mr Underhill's	★	£75

Tel 01449 711206   Map 10 C3   **R**
Stonham nr Stowmarket Suffolk IP14 5DW

On the A140, close to its junction with the A1120, the Bradleys' typical Suffolk 'three-box' house is older than it appears from the outside with timbers much in evidence internally. The whole effect, with Bauhaus chairs around crisply clothed tables and the work of local artists supplementing their own art collection around the warm red walls, is very pleasing. Chris Bradley works single-handedly in the kitchen on his daily-changing no-choice menu (discussed when booking to sort out likes and dislikes) priced for starter and main dish with cheese, desserts (three or four choices) and coffee (which comes with good home-made petits fours) as optional extras. First-rate ingredients are sympathetically handled in dishes that are essentially uncomplicated yet thoroughly satisfying. Modern British best describes the style, typified in favourite dishes such as warm salad of asparagus with broad beans and basil, Barbary duck with Provence herbs, fillet of beef with tarragon essence and, for dessert, a hot chocolate tart "with no pastry case in an effort to keep it lighter". Judy Bradley looks after front of house (with help when they are busy) with great charm. An informative and fairly-priced wine list contains several good names, including the outstanding Italian Angelo Gaja. *Seats 24. Parties 16. L Sun 12.30-1.45 other days by arrangement D 7.30-9. Closed D Sun, all Mon, Bank Holidays (open 25 Dec). Set Sun L £21 Set D £26. Access, Diners, Visa.*

STONOR	Stonor Arms		£80

Tel 01491 638345   Fax 01491 638863   Map 15 D2   **RR**
Stonor nr Henley-on-Thames Oxfordshire RG9 6HE

A converted 18th-century village pub offering two levels of food: informal yet serious lunchtime snacking in Blades Brasserie and a more formal menu in the elegant restaurant proper and conservatory room. Aperitifs and canapés are served in a spacious drawing room graced with antiques and comfortable sofas. Stephen Frost uses fresh produce from local sources, fish from Cornwall and some meats and vegetables from their own farm or estates in Scotland. Warm scallop mousse with scallop roe sauce, terrine of chicken, leek and truffle, roast guinea fowl with black pudding and roast apples, fillet of brill with quenelles of salmon, white chocolate mousse with mint sauce, chilled lemon tart – mouthwatering stuff. The brasserie menu is similarly enticing: guinea fowl rillettes with

See over

pickled gherkins, smoked haddock fishcakes with cream and curry sauce, leg of rabbit with roast celeriac and tomato and thyme gravy, iced armagnac parfait with prunes. Outdoor eating in summer. The excellent and comprehensive wine list will satisfy the most assiduous drinker in both price and depth of choice; there are several vintages of Chateau Batailley (Pauillac) and a dozen Olivier Leflaive burgundies, as well as helpful notes alongside the 'recommended' wines. *Seats 20 (restaurant) 40 (brasserie). Parties 10. Private Rooms 12/24. Restaurant: L 12-2 D 7-9.30 Blades: L & D 12-2 & 7-9.30 7 days. Restaurant closed Bank Holidays. Set D £29.50. Access, Amex, Visa.*

Rooms   £93

A wing of bedrooms, numbering nine (including two suites – £137.50 per night), is furnished to a high standard with some antiques. Cots and Z-beds for children are additional charges. No dogs. Garden.

| STORRINGTON | Little Thakeham | 77% | £150 |

Tel 01903 744416   Fax 01903 745022   Map 11 A6   **HR**
Merrywood Lane Storrington West Sussex RH20 3HE

A Lutyens house and Gertrude Jekyll garden, the latter restored over the last few years, individually attract admirers, but it's the way the two complement each other that is the glory of Little Thakeham. Over the last 15 years the Ractliffs have filled the public rooms with period 'arts and crafts' furniture and objets d'art with a small first-floor gallery displaying a collection of turn-of-the-century porcelain, glass and silverware that is available for sale. Bedrooms are furnished with antiques from earlier periods and individually decorated with a variety of stylish fabrics. Two full suites have sofa-beds in their lounges, making them suitable for families. Bathrooms that come with robes and bathsheets mostly have only hand-held showers at the tub – just two have 'power' showers. No room service is advertised; guests are encouraged to make use of the day rooms, but drinks and sandwiches are available in rooms throughout the day and evening – meals in suites only (of which there are two). *Rooms 9. Garden, croquet, tennis. Closed 2 weeks Christmas/New Year. Access, Amex, Diners, Visa.*

Restaurant   £90

The dining-room features a huge inglenook fireplace – one of several in the house. A new chef, Gary North, is producing sensibly short (4-5 main dishes) fixed-price menus (four courses at night) that now include Mediterranean-influenced dishes – confit of duck with green beans and hazelnuts; tomato, mozzarella and tapénade salad – along with the likes of roast Southdown lamb and fillet of cod with salmon mousseline and saffron sauce. Straightforward wine list with many of the top French names present; bits and bobs from elsewhere. There's a delightful terrace for summer dining. *Seats 30. Parties 24. Private Room 30. L 12.30-2 D 7-9. Closed D Sun, L Mon. Set L £16.50/£21.50 Set D (4-course) £32.50.*

| STORRINGTON | Manleys | £85 |

Tel 01903 742331   Map 11 A6   **RR**
Manleys Hill Storrington West Sussex RH20 4BT

Well-established restaurant in a pretty Queen Anne cottage at the foot of the South Downs, on the A283, off the A24. Inside, the beamed ceiling is a foil for smart table settings and crisp napery, and there's always a posy of fresh flowers on each table. Chef-patron Karl Löderer's cooking is sophisticated and accomplished, French by inspiration, but including also some specialities from his native Austria. Local seafood and seasonal game are much favoured, exemplified respectively by pan-fried scallops with home-made pasta flavoured with roast garlic and herbs, and venison fillets with red wine sauce, pan-fried with caramelised apples and griotte cherries. Sunday lunch always includes a traditional roast and fish option. Champagne starts at £42, which is steep to say the least! However, there are quality offerings from France; Germany and Austria OK, but little else. *Seats 48. Parties 36. Private Room 22. L 12-1.45 D 7-9.15 (to 10 Sat). Closed D Sun, all Mon, 1st 10 days Jan. Set L £19.60 (Sun £23.50) Set D £28.50 (2 courses). Access, Amex, Visa.*

Room   £102

For overnight guests a luxurious suite, with every modern comfort, overlooks the garden and Downs beyond. No dogs.

| STORRINGTON | The Old Forge | £60 |

Tel 01903 743402   Fax 01903 742540   Map 11 A6   **R**
6 Church Street Storrington West Sussex RH20 4LA

Having recently expanded into the shops next door, Clive and Cathy Roberts' charming 15th-century restaurant now comprises three cottagey rooms (one including a small lounge area) featuring low beams, rough white-painted stone walls and an inglenook fireplace. Clive's monthly-changing menus are never dull, with dishes such as rillettes of rabbit and duck flavoured with dried figs and anis, medallions of monkfish pan-fried with cumin and served on a sauce of lightly curried red onion marmalade, and loin of smoked ham braised in vin santo with peas and turnips being typical examples of his distinctive style. Everything here is home-made, including the cinnamon and calvados ice cream that comes with a super twice-baked apple soufflé, and the bread, a walnut variation of which is served with the regularly changing selection of about eight British "artisan-made" cheeses. The wine list (80% New World) is as interesting as the menu and as well as the half-dozen or so house wines served by the glass (not counting some ten dessert wines), and in lieu of half bottles, they will happily open most things on a pay-for-what-you-drink basis. A nice surprise at the end of a meal here is that coffee and petits fours are served at no extra charge. *Seats 36. Parties 12. Private Room 18. L 12.15-1.30 D 7.15-9. Set L £12/£14.50 Set Sun L £13/£16 Set D £16/£20.50. Closed L Sat & Tue, D Sun, all Mon, 1 week spring, 3 weeks October. Access, Amex, Diners, Visa.*

| STOURBRIDGE | Bon Appétit | £55 |

Tel 01384 375372   Map 6 B4   **R**
38 Market Street Stourbridge West Midlands DY8 1AG

Pleasant, unpretentious yet homely restaurant on two floors of a small town house on the edge of the town centre. Careful, uncomplicated cooking is the formula that has attracted a strong local following – booking is advisable. Starters such as tuna and sweetcorn tart, 'Creole' of Norwegian prawns with fruits and sauté of French duck are followed by main dishes like grilled halibut steak florentine, breast of guinea fowl with curried peas and sirloin of Angus beef. Leave room for some good desserts: crunchy brandy crème brulée, bread-and-butter pudding, steamed sponge pudding with two sauces. Fixed-price menus (particularly good value at lunchtimes and Tuesday-Thursday evenings when prices are almost half those on Friday and Saturday nights) offer a choice of half a dozen dishes at each stage. *Seats 60. Parties 20. L 12.30-2 D 7.30-10. Closed L Sat, all Sun & Mon, first week Jan. Set L (& D Tue-Thu) £12.50/£15, Set D (Fri & Sat) £19.75 & £22.50. Access, Amex, Visa.*

| STOURBRIDGE | Talbot Hotel | 59% | £50 |

Tel 01384 394350   Fax 01384 371318   Map 6 B4   **H**
High Street Stourbridge West Midlands DY8 1DW

A charming redbrick town-centre inn with many reminders of its coaching-days origins back in the 17th century. There are heavy doors to the coach entrance and some handsome timbers and moulded ceilings in the day rooms. A marvellous old staircase winds up to bedrooms, which vary in their size and furnishings. Some look out over the interior courtyard. Children up to 12 can stay free in parents' room. *Rooms 25. Coffee shop (9am-11pm). Access, Amex, Visa.*

| STOURPORT-ON-SEVERN | County Hotel | 62% | £86 |

Tel 01299 827733   Fax 01299 878520   Map 6 B4   **H**
Hartlebury Road Stourport-on-Severn Hereford & Worcester DY13 9LT

Well set up for business or pleasure, the Moat House stands in a wooded 20-acre site. Banqueting and conference facilities for 350/300. Children up to 10 stay free in parents' room. Take the Hartlebury Road out of Stourport; the hotel is half a mile along on the left. *Rooms 68. Garden, pitch & putt, outdoor swimming pool, gym, squash, sauna, tennis, snooker. Access, Amex, Diners, Visa.*

Set menu prices may not always include service or wine.

STOW-ON-THE-WOLD   Fosse Manor   60%   £98

Tel 01451 830354   Fax 01451 832486   Map 14 C1   **H**
Fosse Way Stow-on-the-Wold Gloucestershire GL54 1JX

Resident proprietors Bob and Yvonne Johnston and their loyal staff run a family haven that attracts many repeat visitors. Built in the style of a Cotswold manor house, it stands in its ivy coat in grounds set back from the A429 (originally the Fosse Way) about a mile south of Stow-on-the-Wold. Bedrooms (including several suitable for family occupation) overlook colourful gardens and the bright look of the day rooms is enhanced throughout by potted plants, fresh flowers and spotless housekeeping. Children up to 16 stay free in their parents' room. *Rooms 20. Garden, putting, indoor swimming pool, children's playground, sauna, spa bath, solarium, beauty salon. Closed 1 week Christmas. Access, Amex, Diners, Visa.*

STOW-ON-THE-WOLD   Grapevine Hotel   68%   £108

Tel 01451 830344   Fax 01451 832278   Map 14 C1   **HR**
Sheep Street Stow-on-the-Wold Gloucestershire GL54 1AU

Improvements continue apace at this quite charming Cotswold-stone hotel, where the addition of the wood-panelled Georgian meeting room blends perfectly with the existing building, both inside and outside, and the refurbishment of the conservatory restaurant really shows off the trailing vine, already resplendent with ripe grapes (pity they're not edible!) in late June. Owner Sam (Sandra) Elliott and her neatly uniformed staff will really make you feel welcome here – it's cosy throughout, though you'll have to mind your head on the low beams, particularly in bedroom corridors and on the stairs. Lots of exposed stonework, pine and period furniture in the immaculately serviced bedrooms that provide the normal extras. No dogs. The tennis court, belonging to the owners, is situated a mile from the hotel. Own parking at rear of hotel. *Rooms 21. Patio (front & back), tennis. Closed 24 Dec-10 Jan. Access, Amex, Diners, Visa.*

Restaurant   £50

As we went to press, a new chef, Dean Collins, had just arrived. The menu is unlikely to change in style, offering mostly modern English dishes, perhaps starting with a game terrine served with red onion marmalade, followed by grilled salmon on braised spinach with a lemon and cinnamon butter sauce, and a steamed syrup sponge pudding served with a warm *sauce anglaise* (custard, surely!). Don't miss the British farmhouse cheese selection. For lunch the Gigot menu (also available in the bar) operates: mussels, fish cakes, local bangers served on bubble and squeak with onion gravy, or beef and ale casserole. End with traditional sticky toffee or bread-and-butter puddings. Inexpensive wine list with tasting notes. *Seats 60. Parties 10. Private Room 28. L 12-2.30 D 7-9.30. Set L (Sun only) £7.95/£9.95 Set D £13/£16.*

STOW-ON-THE-WOLD   Unicorn Hotel   59%   £102

Tel 01451 830257   Fax 01451 831090   Map 14 C1   **H**
Sheep Street Stow-on-the-Wold Gloucestershire GL54 1HQ

17th-century origins with some period appeal (steep tiled roof, dormer windows and original beams). Children free in parents' room up to 14. Forte. *Rooms 20. Access, Amex, Diners, Visa.*

STOW-ON-THE-WOLD   Wyck Hill House   74%   £108

Tel 01451 831936   Fax 01451 832243   Map 14 C1   **HR**
Burford Road Stow-on-the-Wold Gloucestershire GL54 1HY

Two miles south of Stow off the A424, this hilltop manor house, built early in the 18th century, stands in 100 acres of its own grounds and gardens commanding fine views across the Windrush Valley. Day rooms combine comfort with a carefully created lived-in feel: rugs over time-worn floorboards in the cedar-panelled library and inner hall with its fine galleried staircase, leather armchairs in the clubby bar and dark oil portraits and various items of porcelain that look deceptively as if they have always been part of the house. Generally spacious bedrooms are either in the main house (traditionally furnished with antique and reproduction pieces and floral fabrics), the Orangery some 100 yards away (bright summery rooms with rattan furniture and orange patterned soft furnishings, each with French windows opening on to a patio) or, at a similar distance from the main building, in the coach house where pine-furnished rooms open directly on to a central courtyard. Rooms are all of a similar standard except that de luxe rooms get the better views and little extras like sherry, sweets and shortbread. Some rooms boast king-size or four-poster beds. Attentive, friendly staff. **Rooms 31. Garden, croquet. Access, Amex, Diners, Visa.**

Restaurant £95

👑 🍇 🦐 🍓 🍺 V

A contrast in styles here between the richly opulent inner dining-room with red damask fabric-covered walls and huge central flower display and a large conservatory which takes full advantage of the panoramic views. Plenty of choice too on Ian Smith's confidently handled, modish à la carte: grilled polenta with sautéed wood pigeon, local oak-smoked salmon, herb-crusted monkfish with a warm asparagus vinaigrette, sauté of local pheasant with pickled pears, chestnuts and elderberry sauce, roast spiced loin of lamb; plain grills are also available. For lunch there's a choice of light luncheon menu (toasted club sandwiches, cold poached salmon, lamb cutlets) or a 2- or 3-course table d'hote and four courses on Sundays. Splendid desserts such as hot bramble soufflé, coffee and chestnut roulade and warm butterscotch tart. No smoking. **Seats 70. Parties 8. Private Room 40. L 12-2 D 7.30-9.30. Set L £9.50/£11.95 (Sun £17.50) .**

STRATFIELD TURGIS	Wellington Arms	£65

Tel 01256 882214 Fax 01256 882934   Map 15 D3   **I**
Stratfield Turgis Basingstoke Hampshire RG27 0AS

Hard by the A33 behind a handsome white Georgian facade, a charming old inn with a mix of the old and the new. A small and pubby L-shaped bar leads directly round into a friendly drawing room in country-house style. Fifteen bedrooms in the original building include two "luxury doubles" (one a suite with a heavily-carved four-poster and spa bath), while the other 20 are in a two-storey modern extension to the rear, uniformly decorated in Laura Ashley pastel shades plus modern light oak furniture. A couple of modern suites serve as both small meeting rooms and family rooms with pull-down additional beds. Good light meals and snacks in the public bar/lounge. Next door to the Duke of Wellington's estate (Stratfield Saye House) and close to Wellington Country Park (ideal for family outings). The Long Room caters for banquet/conferences of up to 70/50. Busy in the week with business travellers but more restful at weekends, when reduced rates apply. **Rooms 35. Garden. Access, Amex, Diners, Visa.**

STRATFORD-UPON-AVON	Alveston Manor	67%	£125

Tel 01789 204581 Fax 01789 414095   Map 14 C1   **H**
Clopton Bridge Stratford-upon-Avon Warwickshire CV37 7HP

On the A422 Banbury road, just south of the town, this imposing half-timbered hotel partly dates back to the 16th century. Indeed, it is said that *A Midsummer Night's Dream* was first performed here under a cedar tree which still dominates the garden. At least once a year a re-enactment takes place. The main house retains much of its Elizabethan charm, with leaded light windows in the public rooms, splendid original panelling and some four-poster beds. Most bedrooms are in a new wing and have recently been refurbished to a comfortable standard. Modern amenities are not forgotten, all bedrooms having TV with satellite and freshly decorated bathrooms. Ask for a rear-facing room for views of the garden and thus avoid traffic noise. Over 20 rooms are reserved for non-smokers. Banqueting/conference facilities for 140/160. Free use of a local leisure centre. **Rooms 106. Garden, croquet, pitch & putt. Access, Amex, Diners, Visa.**

STRATFORD-UPON-AVON	Dukes Hotel	65%	£70

Tel 01789 269300 Fax 01789 414700   Map 14 C1   **H**
Payton Street Stratford-upon-Avon Warwickshire CV37 6UA

Two Georgian town houses dating from 1820 make up a civilised, privately-owned hotel not far from the town centre, shops and theatres. Friendly armchairs, antique furniture and ornaments make a homely, lived-in lounge, and there's a small bar. Bedrooms are neat and comfortable, with period pieces; there are two four-poster rooms and two suites. No children under 12. No dogs. **Rooms 22. Garden, croquet. Closed Christmas and New Year. Access, Amex, Visa.**

Lodges are now listed by county in the reference section

STRATFORD-UPON-AVON   Ettington Park   76%   £145

Tel 01789 450123   Fax 01789 450472   Map 14 C1   **H**
Alderminster Stratford-upon-Avon Warwickshire CV37 8BS

An imposing neo-Gothic stately home with a Grade 1 preservation listing. It stands five miles south of Stratford on the A34 to Oxford, in mature parkland by the Stour. The interior of the house fully lives up to the promise of the setting: notable features include a lovely plant-filled conservatory entrance, a fine Victorian drawing room, a richly panelled library bar and a very elegant and relaxing lounge. Bedrooms are no less impressive, with plenty of space, well-chosen antiques, light, restful colour schemes and all sorts of little personal touches. The majority of rooms enjoy fine country views. All bedrooms were due to be refurbished by the end of 1995. The Long Gallery is one of the most characterful meeting rooms in the country, with book-lined walls and a high, wood-panelled vaulted ceiling; it holds up to 75 delegates. Similarly, there are other interesting rooms like the 14th-century chapel with stained-glass windows, suitable for private dining and board meetings. No dogs. *Rooms 48. Garden, croquet, tennis, indoor swimming pool, keep-fit equipment, sauna, solarium, steam room, spa bath, coarse fishing, riding, clay-pigeon shooting. Access, Amex, Diners, Visa.*

STRATFORD-UPON-AVON   Falcon Hotel   63%   £99

Tel 01789 279953   Fax 01789 414260   Map 14 C1   **H**
Chapel Street Stratford-upon-Avon Warwickshire CV37 6HA

Behind a classic timbered facade there's a blend of old and new. The beamed and panelled Oak Bar is as old as the building (1640), while the conference rooms (for up to 200) are thoroughly up-to-date. 20 bedrooms, including a four-poster suite, are in the original part, the rest in a modern section. Children up to the age of 14 can stay and have breakfast free of charge if sharing a room with an adult. 27 rooms are designated non-smoking. Ample car parking. Queens Moat Houses. *Rooms 73. Garden. Access, Amex, Diners, Visa.*

STRATFORD-UPON-AVON   Forte Posthouse   59%   £72

Tel 01789 266761   Fax 01789 414547   Map 14 C1   **H**
Bridgefoot Stratford-upon-Avon Warwickshire CV37 7LT

Popular tourist, family and business base overlooking the river Avon, opposite the theatre. Seven rooms are of Executive standard. Reduced rates (£5 from £12) at a leisure centre down the road. Conferences for up to 150. *Rooms 60. Children's playground. Access, Amex, Diners, Visa.*

STRATFORD-UPON-AVON   Liaison   £65

Tel 01789 293400   Fax 01789 297863   Map 14 C1   **R**
1 Shakespeare Street Stratford-upon-Avon Warwickshire CV37 6RN

Chic, modern restaurant within what was originally a Methodist chapel, and more recently a motor museum. Patricia Plunkett's cooking is modish too, in her own appealing style, with dishes such as cappuccino of crabmeat topped with a frothy paprika cream, cannelloni of home-dried duck glazed with a black bean sauce, sea bream on a bouillabaisse sauce and fillet of lamb on a red onion, tomato and rosemary tart on the à la carte, which is supplemented by equally exciting set menus for both lunch and dinner. In addition there is a separate Liaison 'Lights' menu (now available at all times) offering single-dish meals like roast tuna on a fondue of tomatoes with chargrilled vegetables and Spanish paella with chicken, spicy sausage and seafood. There's also a separate vegetarian menu. Desserts cover more familiar ground: bread-and-butter pudding, lemon tart, strawberries Romanoff. Full meals begin with freshly made canapés and end with good petits fours, both served on mini cake stands. Inexpensive wines on a sensible list, though there are rather few half bottles. *Seats 58. Parties 12. Private Room 25. L 12-2.30 D 6-10.30. Closed L Sat, all Sun & 2 weeks Jan. Set L £12.50/£14.95 D £19.50. Access, Amex, Diners, Visa.*

Consult the blue pages for summary tables and lists of
recommended establishments.

STRATFORD-UPON-AVON The Opposition   £50

Tel 01789 269980   Map 14 C1   **R**
13 Sheep Street Stratford-upon-Avon Warwickshire CV37 9EF

Nigel Lambert's busy bistro offers a winning combination of good food, fair prices and convivial atmosphere that puts it ahead of most of the opposition. Light dishes and starters head the menu, including garlic mushrooms or snails, trio of salmon, chicken liver paté, and chargrilled king prawns. Greek and Niçoise salads may be ordered as either starter or main course, and hot mains range from pasta and stir-fry rice to chargrilled burger, Cajun-style chicken and a bowl of chili. Banoffi pie is the speciality dessert. *Seats 50. Parties 10. L 12-2 (Sat to 2.30) D 5.30-11 (Sun 6-10). Closed L Sun Jan-Mar, 25 & 26 Dec. Access, Amex, Visa.*

STRATFORD-UPON-AVON   Shakespeare Hotel   69%   £136

Tel 01789 294771 Fax 01789 415111   Map 14 C1   **H**
Chapel Street Stratford-upon-Avon Warwickshire CV37 6ER

A Forte hotel with a central location (next to the town hall) and a long history. The gabled and timbered facade is typical of its 17th-century origins, and inside are beams and flagstones, open fires and period furnishings. Floral fabrics and smart darkwood furniture are used in the bedrooms, which range from single/twins for one through four-poster rooms to luxury twin suites. Children up to 16 stay free in parents' room. Bedroom refurbishment is due to be completed by the end of 1995. Function facilities for up to 90. *Rooms 63. Garden. Access, Amex, Diners, Visa.*

STRATFORD-UPON-AVON   Stratford House   62%   £85

Tel 01789 268288 Fax 01789 295580   Map 14 C1   **H**
18 Sheep Street Stratford-upon-Avon Warwickshire CV37 6EF

Approximately one hundred yards from the Royal Shakespeare Theatre and the River Avon, this quiet little hotel in a Georgian house is a comfortable, friendly home from home, its appeal enhanced by owner Sylvia Adcock's antiques, pictures and china. An open fire warms the lounge, and there's a bright conservatory restaurant and bar. In warm weather the walled garden comes into its own. Neat bedrooms use floral fabrics and darkwood units. Families are welcome, with most facilities provided. Charged parking in a nearby car park. No dogs. *Rooms 11. Garden. Closed 4 days at Christmas. Access, Amex, Diners, Visa.*

STRATFORD-UPON-AVON   Stratford Moat House   66%   £144

Tel 01789 279988 Fax 01789 298589   Map 14 C1   **H**
Bridgefoot Stratford-upon-Avon Warwickshire CV37 6YR

A purpose-built modern hotel close to the centre of town (on the A34) with a wealth of facilities to keep the conference trade happy. Spacious public rooms beyond the redesigned entrance area include a simply furnished residents' lounge and another that overlooks the River Avon. Uniform bedrooms include some with views of the Royal Shakespeare Theatre and river; 94 are reserved for non-smokers; eight are triple rooms for families (children up to 5 stay free in their parents' room). Piano Bar. Health and fitness centre. Conference and banqueting facilities for up to 470. Children's film and puppet shows. Recent visits have shown declining standards of service and housekeeping. *Rooms 247. Garden, fishing, indoor swimming pool, gym, spa bath, sauna, steam room, solarium, beautician, hairdressing, mooring, disco (Fri & Sat), shopping arcade, news kiosk. Access, Amex, Diners, Visa.*

STRATFORD-UPON-AVON   Welcombe Hotel   74%   £125

Tel 01789 295252 Fax 01789 414666   Map 14 C1   **H**
Warwick Road Stratford-upon-Avon Warwickshire CV37 0NR   3/29/99

A large and handsome Jacobean-style mansion a mile and a half from the centre of Stratford. The 157 acres of mature parkland that surround it includes two lakes and an 18-hole, par 70 golf course, whose clubhouse is a popular spot for a drink or a snack. There's an Italian garden, a rose garden, a winter garden and a water garden. In the main building is the oak-panelled bar, named after the historian Sir George Trevelyan, who once lived here. In the oak-panelled lounge, deep sofas and armchairs provide abundant

See over

comfort, and a log fire burns in the ornate black marble fireplace. Individually furnished bedrooms in the main house have antiques and period pieces, plus marble bathrooms with separate showers. Some of the suites are most impressive – the Lady Caroline (Trevelyan) comprises four-poster bedroom, drawing room, study and a luxurious bathroom where you can wallow in the bathtub and watch television at the same time. Rooms in a garden wing are smaller but equally comfortable. *Rooms 75. Garden, tennis, golf (18), games room. Closed 28 Dec-3 Jan. Access, Amex, Diners, Visa.*

STRATFORD-UPON-AVON   White Swan   62%   £85

Tel 01789 297022   Fax 01789 268773   Map 14 C1   **H**
Rother Street Stratford-upon-Avon Warwickshire CV37 6NH

The exterior of this old inn is little changed since Shakespeare's day and public rooms are full of atmosphere, with old beams, timbers and a well-preserved wall painting dating from 1550 in the bar. Bedrooms, except for two antique-furnished rooms in the original building, are in rear extensions of various ages (the newest some 60 years old) and though varying widely in size and shape share the same solid oak furniture, pleasant matching bedcovers and curtains and the usual modern amenities. Children up to 16 stay free in parents' room. Limited on-site parking, but there's a free park very near. *Rooms 37. Access, Amex, Diners, Visa.*

STRATFORD-UPON-AVON   Windmill Park   64%   £98

Tel 01789 731173   Fax 01789 731131   Map 14 C1   **H**
Warwick Road Stratford-upon-Avon Warwickshire CV37 0PY

Four linked blocks provide practical accommodation in a modern redbrick hotel on the A439 (leave the M40 at Junction 15). Fully-equipped leisure centre (the gym has recently been enlarged); conference facilities for up to 360; many large family and interconnecting bedrooms, with under-16s staying free in parents' room. *Rooms 103. Tennis, indoor swimming pool, gym, sauna, spa bath, steam room, solarium. Access, Amex, Diners, Visa.*

STREATLEY-ON-THAMES   Swan Diplomat   68%   £134

Tel 01491 873737   Fax 01491 872554   Map 15 D2   **HR**
High Street Streatley-on-Thames Berkshire RG8 9HR

This charming hotel (the welcome is friendly and professional) spreads itself along the south bank of the River Thames, enabling the public rooms, including the pine-clad bar and the comfortable lounges, to have extensive views of the river, the boats and the ducks. Likewise, over half the bedrooms overlook the water, many of these with their own balconies. Two are reserved for non-smokers. The attractively decorated bedrooms are furnished with traditional-style mahogany pieces combining comfort with all mod cons. For the energetic, the well-equipped Reflexions fitness centre, incorporated in the building, is available free for guests. Moored alongside is the Magdalen College Barge, which, as well as looking picturesque, provides an unusual setting for meetings and cocktail parties. Spacious car park. 24hr room service. *Rooms 46. Garden, croquet, indoor 'fitness' swimming pool, sauna, solarium, gym, bicycles, rowing boats, moorings. Access, Amex, Diners, Visa.*

Riverside Restaurant   £85

👑 🍇 ⏲

Attractive, summery dining-room with trelliswork ceiling, rattan-effect chairs, crisp napery and Royal Doulton china but it's the river views which steal the show. On the food front the former sous chef has stepped into the top job and, with the rest of the team more or less unchanged, the transition has been very smooth and the Riverside Restaurant continues to serve reliably good dishes made from first-rate ingredients. Smoked haddock soup garnished with lentils and fresh herbs, fricassee of woodland mushrooms with lemon thyme and blackberry vinegar, sea bass with saffron and herbs on a bed of vegetables with red pepper essence, saddle of rabbit roasted with thyme, garlic and lavender on a pink peppercorn sauce, and breast of Barbary duck with noodles and a light parsley sauce (more like a dressing in the modern style really) give an idea of the à la carte, which is supplemented by a limited choice prix-fixe at night. Sunday lunch brings a fixed-price buffet brunch. Afters include a decent selection of French and English cheeses. There are some quite hefty mark-ups on the wine list, on which the house wines come under the heading 'cuvée maison'. Not so, since none of the wines is grown or owned by the house! For less formal dining the Duck Room Brasserie (a small area between the bar and the restaurant proper) has a menu that ranges from soup of the day and dressed crab to steak, ale and mushroom pie and a mini-baguette steak sandwich. Staff are notably polite and pleasant. *Seats 75. Parties 12. D 7.30-9.30 (Sat from 7 in summer). Closed L Mon-Sat (open Sun for brunch only), D Sun & Mon. Set Sun brunch £17.50 Set D £27.50. Access, Amex, Diners, Visa.*

We welcome bona fide complaints and recommendations on the tear-out pages at the back of the book for readers' comments. They are followed up by our professional team.

| STREET | Bear Inn | 63% | £62 |

Tel 01458 42021 Fax 01458 840007   Map 13 F1   **H**
53 High Street Street Somerset BA16 0EF

On the edge of town, just off the A39, the late-Victorian stone-built Bear retains its intimate air in the small fire-lit residents' lounge and livelier bar and patio. Bedrooms have just benefited from major refurbishment. Well-equipped conference and function facilities for up to 80. No dogs. *Rooms 17. Garden. Closed 25 Dec. Access, Visa.*

| STRETTON (LEICS) | Ram Jam Inn | | £61 |

Tel 01780 410776 Fax 01780 410361   Map 7 E3   **IR**
Great North Road Stretton nr Oakham Leicestershire LE15 7QX

Hard by a service station nine miles north of Stamford on the northbound lane of the A1 (southbound drivers take the B668 exit to Oakham and follow signs), the Ram Jam Inn, named after a special brew produced in its early days, is a very pleasing alternative to the mass of commercial hotels and eating places along the A1. Public rooms are devoted completely to informal, yet smartly furnished eating areas (bar, snack, outdoor terrace and restaurant). All the bedrooms overlooking the garden and orchard are individually and tastefully decorated with limed pine furniture, and are surprisingly quiet considering the proximity to the road. *Rooms 7. Garden. Access, Amex, Diners, Visa.*

Restaurant £40

Coffee, breakfast, snacks and full meals are all available in a pleasantly light dining-room overlooking the orchard. Granary baps for quick snacks; main-course specialities include rump steak burgers, casseroled pheasant and marinated chicken breast with honey and thyme served with *pommes lyonnaise* on a bed of spinach. *Seats 30. Private Room 25. L 12-2.30 D 7-10 (light meals 7am-10pm). Closed 25 Dec.*

| STRETTON (STAFFS) | Dovecliffe Hall | 68% | £95 |

Tel 01283 531818 Fax 01283 516546   Map 6 C3   **HR**
Dovecliffe Road Stretton nr Burton-on-Trent Staffordshire DE13 0DJ

A fine Georgian house in eight acres of gardens surrounded by farmland, Dovecliffe is as much a restaurant with rooms as a hotel. The two elegant lounges may seem excessively spacious for just seven bedrooms but come into their own for perusing the dinner menu or taking post-prandial brandies. Beneath the fine central staircase the reception desk doubles as a bar counter. Bedrooms, most large but with one small single with shower and WC only, are comfortably furnished and come with various thoughtful extras such as fruit, mineral water and bathrobes. *Rooms 7. Garden, fishing, golf (18). Closed 1 week spring, 2 weeks summer, 1 week Christmas. Access, Amex, Diners, Visa.*

Restaurant £65

Uncomplicated, but not uninteresting, cooking based on good raw materials is a formula that has attracted a strong local following to this elegantly proportioned, high-ceilinged restaurant where the ebullient owner Nicholas Hine is very much in evidence greeting diners – many by name. Dinner brings a sort of à la carte (the choice of main course determines the price of a three-course meal) plus a table d'hote menu, while lunch is a more limited (but good-value) fixed-price affair. Chargrilled venison on red cabbage

See over

with port sauce, supreme of chicken on a bed of creamed leeks, pan-fried calf's liver with smoked bacon and sweet and sour onions, and grilled fillet of sea bass typify main dishes that come with simple but accurately cooked vegetables. Bread-and-butter pudding made with double cream and Cointreau-soaked raisins and served with *crème anglaise* and caramel is considered a speciality pudding. A decent wine list offers a dozen wines and no fewer than seven vintage ports by the glass. Three tables on a terrace in good weather. **Seats** *90. Parties 24. L 12-1.45 D 7-9.30. Closed D Sun, L Mon & L Sat. Set L £9.50/£11.50 (Sun £13.95) Set D £18.50.*

STUCKTON — The Three Lions — £65

Tel 01425 652489   Fax 01425 656144   Map 14 C4   **R**
Stuckton nr Fordingbridge Hampshire SP6 2HF

In a rural setting on the edge of the New Forest, here is a mecca for lovers of good food, fine wine and conviviality. Blackboard menus proclaim a daily-changing choice of dishes making good use of local ingredients: New Forest game soup; Poole Bay oysters; hock of Wiltshire ham *alsacienne;* Dorset calf's liver with bacon, braised shallots and onion marmalade; breast of local wood pigeon and wild duck with marinated winter fruits and game sauce. Many influences from further afield are also apparent, with typical examples including brochette of tiger prawns *orientale,* trilogy of herring fillets Swedish style, grilled fresh marlin steak with pink and green peppercorn sauce, French onion soup and spinach and Edam strudels. A smashing and fairly priced list with every wine carefully chosen, including an Australian showing that's one of the best in the country. No children under 14. No smoking. As we went to press, Karl and June Wadsock were on the point of retiring, the restaurant having been taken over by Michael Womersley, recently arrived from *Lucknam Park,* Colerne. **Seats** *60. Parties 12. L 12.15-1.30 D 7.15-9 (Sat to 9.30). Closed Sun, Mon, 2 weeks Feb, 2 weeks Jul-Aug & 2 weeks Oct. Access, Visa.*

STUDLAND BAY — Knoll House — 63% £146*

Tel 01929 450450   Fax 01929 450423   Map 14 C4   **H**
Studland Bay nr Swanage Dorset BH19 3AH

Given up as a lordly residence in 1932 when the ferry road was built passing by the front of the hotel and cutting through the Studland estate, the hotel has now been in the ownership of the Ferguson family since 1959. They have greatly extended the original country house, creating a popular summertime retreat for families, particularly those with younger children. There is a special children's dining-room serving 'real' food, with non-slip floor and an attendant, specially dedicated kitchen as well as a host of amenities including a splendid outdoor Swedish-designed play area complete with a large pirate ship, climbing frame, chutes and more. The beach is a few hundred yards away across the road and can be glimpsed through the trees from the front bedrooms. All rooms are comfortably homely and possess clean, simple bathrooms, though some are not en suite. The permutations for those requiring different types of rooms are almost endless, with many interconnected rooms and simple suites. For adults there's a child-free lounge as well as a spacious bar and restaurant with much-sought-after window tables. The leisure centre is compact but comprehensively equipped. No televisions are provided, though they can be hired and there is a separate television lounge. Baby listening involves housekeepers who 'patrol the corridors' from 7.30 to 11pm. ★A somewhat complicated tariff here. The price we quote is the daily rate in early July (the second highest of seven tariff periods) for two people on half-board sharing an en-suite room. In fact most people stay long enough (3+ nights, 4 if Fri or Sat included) to qualify for full board at the same rate; weekly rates (which are the only option in the highest tariff period) are at a discount to the daily rate. **Rooms** *70. Garden, tennis, golf (par three), indoor & outdoor swimming pool, children's splash pool, gym, sauna, steam room, spa bath, solarium, children's playroom, games rooms, playground, gift shop, self-service launderette, writing/bridge room. Closed Nov-Easter. No credit cards.*

STURMINSTER NEWTON — Plumber Manor — £55

Tel 01258 472507   Fax 01258 473370   Map 14 B4   **RR**
Hazelbury Bryan Road Sturminster Newton Dorset DT10 2AF

The restaurant is definitely the centre of attraction at the Prideaux-Brune family's home in the heart of Hardy country. Built in 1665 from local stone, the house is surrounded by lawns shaded by fine old trees. Brian Prideaux-Brune's cooking generally sticks to well-tried combinations – gravad lax with dill and mustard sauce, scallop mousseline with saffron sauce, fillet of veal with sage mousse and local Denhay ham, guinea fowl Grand Veneur, rack of lamb with Shrewsbury sauce and onion soubise – and is none the worse for that. Fixed-price menus generally offer an optional fish course like lemon sole with smoked haddock mousse perhaps. Choose from about a dozen desserts such as almond pavlova with grapes, hot sticky ginger pudding with butterscotch sauce and fresh strawberries and cream. Sunday lunch, for which there's a good choice, is popular. Concise wine list with many bottles under £20; the modest house wines are half that. Small conference rooms for up to 40, and popular for boardroom meetings of up to 12. *Seats 60. Private Room 40. L (Sun only) 12.30-1.30 D 7.30-9. Closed Feb. Set L (Sun only) £17.50 Set D £20/£22.50 & £25/£27.50. Access, Amex, Diners, Visa.*

Rooms   £115

The 16 rooms are spacious and well appointed, most having antique furniture. Six are in the main house, four more in the courtyard; the rooms in a converted stone barn are more modern and even larger, with window seats overlooking a stream and the garden. Full English breakfast plus fresh fish. Free stabling is provided on a do-it-yourself basis. A fine base for a weekend touring Hardy country. Garden, croquet, tennis.

SUDBURY	**Mabey's Brasserie**	**£55**

Tel & Fax 01787 374298   Map 10 C3   **R**
47 Gainsborough Street Sudbury Suffolk CO10 7SS

After opening two new restaurants, Robert Mabey is back and cooking in his eponymous flagship. The format is more bistro than brasserie (it's only open at usual meal times); the decor is pine and pews with a blue colour scheme; and the menu, written on blackboards above the open kitchen, is varied. Chargrilled chicken, pepper and mushroom kebabs, deep-fried lemon sole with light ginger sauce and skate in black bean sauce are among the specialities. Vegetables, like the bread, are extras. Desserts range from summer pudding and vanilla crème brulée to Earl Grey tea and lemon sorbet. Air-conditioned. Separate dining-room for smokers. *Seats 50. Private Room 35. L 12-2 D 7-10. Closed Sun & Mon, 5 days at Christmas. Access, Amex, Visa.*

SUDBURY	**Mill Hotel**	**58%**	**£93**

Tel 01787 375544   Fax 01787 373027   Map 10 C3   **H**
Walnut Tree Lane Sudbury Suffolk CO10 6BD

The old mill stands on the banks of the Stour by a large mill pond. Bedrooms are either old-fashioned or extension-modern. Children up to 12 may stay free in parents' room. Note the old 16ft millwheel behind glass in the bar-lounge. *Rooms 56. Terrace, fishing. Access, Amex, Diners, Visa.*

SUNDERLAND	**Swallow Hotel**	**70%**	**£105**

Tel 0191-529 2041   Fax 0191-529 4227   Map 5 E2   **H**
Queen's Parade Seaburn Sunderland Tyne & Wear SR6 8DB

A smart, modern hotel sited north of Sunderland right on the seafront overlooking a long stretch of good sand with amusement arcades a little further along. A uniformed bell boy greets you at the entrance and carries your luggage to your room. Reception is in a part of a spacious lounge area done out, as is the whole place, in a smart, colourful, contemporary style. The Mariner Bar, as its name implies, has a nautical theme. Best of the bedrooms overlook the sea. These are spacious and have sitting areas; all rooms are well equipped, with, in addition to the usual facilities, an iron and board, mini-bar and satellite TV. Reasonable breakfasts are taken in the sunny restaurant. The Castles suite can accommodate up to 300 guests for banquets. 24hr room service and guarded parking. *Rooms 65. Indoor swimming pool, gym, steam room, sauna, spa bath, plunge pool, solarium. Access, Amex, Diners, Visa.*

We welcome bona fide complaints and recommendations on the tear-out pages at the back of the book for readers' comments. They are followed up by our professional team.

SURBITON   Chez Max   £65

Tel 0181-399 2365   Map 15 E2   **R**
85 Maple Road Surbiton Surrey KT6 4AW

Chef-patron Max Markarian's conservatory-roofed suburban restaurant is a haven of enjoyable French cooking. Some of his dishes are classics, others just that little bit different: egg and cheese soufflé with spinach and cream sauce, breast of pheasant with chestnut sherry sauce, fillet of pork with apricot and coriander. There are a few inexpensive wines on the almost exclusively French list, but hardly anything between £20 and £35 – eg a claret at £16.95, the next up being £34. *Seats 40. Parties 25. L 12.30-2 D 7.30-10. Closed L Sat, all Sun & Mon, 25-30 Dec. Set L £15.95 Set D £13.95 (Sat £14.95). Access, Amex, Diners, Visa.*

SUTTON   Heen's   £50

Tel 0181-643 1221   Map 15 E3   **R**
14 Mulgrave Road Sutton Surrey SM2 6LE

Smartish Chinese restaurant opposite Sutton railway station, run by the urbane John Man and his unusually communicative and attentive team. Fresh lobster and crab (both kept live) are something of a speciality – each is served either in black bean sauce or with ginger and spring onion – on a menu that also includes the usual range from bang bang chicken and crispy duck to stir-fried king prawns with orange and various sizzling dishes. *Seats 70. L 12-2.30 D 6-11.15. Closed 1 week Christmas & 1 Jan. Set L & D from £12.50 (min 2 persons). Access, Amex, Diners, Visa.*

SUTTON   Holiday Inn Sutton   70%   £130

Tel 0181-770 1311 Fax 0181-770 1539   Map 15 E3   **H**
Gibson Road Sutton Surrey SM1 2RF

This redbrick town-centre hotel with ample free parking offers practical and convenient accommodation. Well laid-out bedrooms have the usual Holiday Inn virtues of large beds, plenty of well-lit work space and good easy chairs around a substantial breakfast table. Bathrooms are user-friendly, too, with thermostatically-controlled showers over tubs, good shelf space and large towels. Executive Club bedrooms and suites have various extras and include seven Study Rooms equipped with fax machines. There's a separate staffed business centre. Four rooms are specially designed for guests in wheelchairs. Good breakfasts; light snacks in the Balcony Lounge overlooking the leisure club where there's a separate children's splash pool. Modern conference facilities for up to 220. Children under 12 can share their parents' room at no charge; vast tariff reductions at weekends. Ask for a map showing directions from M25. *Rooms 116. Indoor swimming pool, spa bath, sauna, solarium, steam room, beautician, mini-gym, snooker, coffee shop (9am-6pm). Access, Amex, Diners, Visa.*

SUTTON   Partners Brasserie   £50

Tel 0181-644 7743   Map 15 E3   **R**
23 Stonecot Hill Sutton Surrey SM3 9HB

In a parade of shops on the A24, this sister restaurant to *Partners West Street* (see under Dorking) is more towards the budget end of the restaurant spectrum with main courses (about seven choices) on the carte in the £8-£10 range: casserole of seafood, chargrilled rump steak with fries, brochette of lamb with pasta and grilled vegetables. Start with chicken satay with peanut dip, vegetable spring roll with plum sauce or crostini of gorgonzola and olives and end with bread-and-butter pudding, Häagen-Dazs ices or a British cheese plate. The prix-fixe (two choices at each stage) is even better value. Sound cooking and friendly staff have earned a loyal local following. Just 20 wines, but selected from around the world and realistically priced. *Seats 30. Parties 12. L 12-2 D 7-9.30. Closed L Sat, all Sun, Mon & 1 week Christmas. Set L & D £8.45/£10.95. Access, Amex, Diners, Visa.*

SUTTON COLDFIELD   Jarvis Penns Hall   66%   £115

Tel 0121-351 3111 Fax 0121-313 1297   Map 6 C4   **H**
Penns Lane Walmley Sutton Coldfield West Midlands B76 1LH

Ample grounds with a splendid lake stocked with fish are the setting for Penns Hall, a 17th-century house carefully adapted and extended into a comfortable hotel and conference venue. A covered walkway across the lake leads to the Sebastian Coe Health Park, complete with running track. Special event facilities in a variety of rooms holding up to 650. Easy access from Junction 9 of the M42 (4 miles), linking to the M6 (J6) and M40 (J4). *Rooms 114. Garden, fishing, indoor swimming pool, children's splash pool, squash, gym, spa bath, sauna, solarium, beauty salon, steam room, snooker, children's playground. Access, Amex, Diners, Visa.*

SUTTON COLDFIELD	Moor Hall	62%	£95

Tel 0121-308 3571 Fax 0121-308 8974   Map 6 C4   **H**
Moor Hall Drive Four Oaks Sutton Coldfield West Midlands B75 6LN

In a rural setting, but handy for the motorway network, the extended Edwardian building is surrounded by a golf course. It has its own leisure centre, plus facilities for up to 300 conference delegates. There are two bars, and the bedrooms include suites and Executive rooms. Families welcome – under-16s stay free in parents' room. *Rooms 75. Garden, indoor swimming pool, gym, sauna, solarium. Access, Amex, Diners, Visa.*

SUTTON COLDFIELD	New Hall	80%	£134

Tel 0121-378 2442 Fax 0121-378 4637   Map 6 C4   **HR**
Walmley Road Sutton Coldfield West Midlands B76 8QX

A mile or so south of town off the B4148 and hidden away down a long drive, this converted medieval manor is reputedly the oldest moated house in England. Public rooms include an elegantly furnished drawing-room and cocktail bar overlooking the terrace and relaxing gardens. The Great Chamber (dating from the 16th century) has magnificent Elizabethan plasterwork ceiling and oak panelling. Individually furnished bedrooms and suites offer every modern comfort, including a welcoming decanter of sherry; most are in a new courtyard wing which has been tastefully added. The moat is now splendidly full of lilies – and some of the bedrooms are named after their varieties. The hotel is under the careful management of Mr and Mrs Parkes, who are proud to go to any lengths to satisfy the needs of their guests. A 9-hole (par 3) golf course has been added this year, though guests can still play at the Belfry by arrangement. No dogs; no children under eight. Enquire about the good-value weekend champagne breaks. *Rooms 60. Garden, croquet, golf (9-hole), putting, tennis. Access, Amex, Diners, Visa.*

Restaurant   £95

Mellow oak panelling, stone-mullioned windows with leaded lights featuring some heraldic stained-glass, and quality table settings all add to the appeal of the dining-room. Simon Radley presents modern British menus typified by velouté of woodland mushrooms, aromatic herb risotto with sea scallops and ginger, turbot Rossini (simply cooked with griddled foie gras), Norfolk duckling with baked apple charlotte and port juices, and 'a composition of offals' served with a candied shallot sauce. A very comprehensive wine list was perhaps rather too enthusiastically described last year as user-friendly. It is undoubtedly a very fine list, but with a 'Discovery' section at the front and a page of house wines (some dozen available by the glass) sandwiched between white Bordeaux and burgundy, it is in fact quite difficult to find your way about. Once you do, you're spoilt for choice. Separate vegetarian menu. No smoking. *Seats 60. Parties 10. Private Room 8. L 12.30-2 (Sun to 2.15) D 7-10 (Sun to 9.30). Closed L Sat. Set L £18.50 Set D £26.95.*

Lodges are now listed by county in the reference section

SWAFFHAM   Strattons   £60

Tel 01760 723845   Fax 01760 720458   Map 10 C1   **RR**
4 Ash Close Swaffham Norfolk PE37 7NH

A former residence of Lady Hamilton, Stratton's is secreted down a narrow cul-de-sac off
the Market Square. The 18th century Palladian villa has been transformed into
a restaurant with rooms of immense charm and distiction. There are two lounges in the
original part separated by stripped pine double doors. There is a further very spacious
lounge in a Victorian addition to the property. Walls are covered with all manor of
artwork and family photographs while the furniture is crammed with ornaments,
especially China cats. Huge bunches of dried flowers and grasses, innumerable books,
magazines and games create a relaxing and homely environment. The restaurant
is in a red-brick lined semi-basement with a very rustic and informal character. A well-
filled Welsh dresser occupies part of one wall, the rest being packed with pictures, flat
surfaces and shelves with yet more china cats. Here Vanessa Scott offers dinner of five
courses with a short choice at each stage. Menus change daily and are composed of prime
local ingredients wherever possible. These are skilfully combined to create well-balanced,
simple, country-style dishes. A typical menu could offer nettle and herb soup, warm
prawn and goat's cheese salad, smoked trout paté with tomato chutney or plump, lightly
sautéed oysters on garlic and herb croutons to begin. To follow there could be boned and
braised leg of lamb with a mint butter sauce, mushroom and Cashel soufflé or a generous
slice of salmon fillet grilled under a crust of thinly sliced potato and sun-dried tomato.
After the British cheese course come desserts such as baked lemon and cherry cheesecake,
chocolate and pepper tart or ice creams. Les Scott provides the service, accompanied by
Vanessa's mother. *Seats 20. Parties 8. D only 7-9.30. Set D £23. Closed 25 & 26 Dec.
Access, Amex, Visa.*

Rooms   £78

The seven bedrooms are a colourful and lovely pastiche based on a Victorian theme with
almost everything from antique bedspreads and bowls of pot-pourri to remote-control
satellite TVs. Bathrooms are equally impressive and packed with all manner of lotions and
potions for the body beautiful. There's even a plastic duck by the bath. A very charming
and friendly set up. *Rooms 7. Garden. Closed 25 & 26 Dec.*

SWINDON   Blunsdon House   69%   £93

Tel 01793 721701   Fax 01793 721056   Map 14 C2   **H**
Blunsdon Swindon Wiltshire SN2 4AD

From Junction 15 of the M4 take the A419 Cirencester road. After about 7 miles turn
right to Broad Blunsdon. The well-kept driveway and frontage make a good first
impression as you approach the hotel. It was a farm guest house in 1958, a country club
in 1960, and a fully licensed hotel since 1962 – and the Clifford family have been here
from the beginning. It's now a popular conference rendezvous (up to 300 delegates) with
extensive leisure club facilities. There are ample lounges and bars, while all the bedrooms
are reasonably roomy and many have pleasant views. Decoration and appointments are of
smart modern business standard, and bathrooms all have shower attachments; some have
spa baths. Families are well catered for; children up to 16 stay free in parents' room.
No dogs. *Rooms 88. Garden, indoor swimming pool, children's splash pool, gym, squash,
sauna, steam room, spa bath, sun beds, beauty salon, tennis, golf (9), putting, games room,
snooker, children's indoor & outdoor play areas. Access, Amex, Diners, Visa.*

SWINDON   De Vere Hotel   69%   £115

Tel 01793 878785   Fax 01793 877822   Map 14 C2   **H**
Shaw Ridge Leisure Park Whitehill Way Swindon Wiltshire SN5 7DW

Brick-built and fronted by a clock tower and futuristic leisure club, this modern hotel
boasts extensive and well-equipped conference and banqueting areas (up to 400/270).
Two floors of well-equipped bedrooms are built around a central courtyard; half the
bedrooms are reserved for non-smokers. Two rooms are specially equipped for disabled
guests. 24hr room service. *Rooms 154. Garden, indoor swimming pool, gym, sauna, steam
room, spa bath, sun beds, beauty salon, snooker, news kiosk. Access, Amex, Diners, Visa.*

Set menu prices may not always include service or wine.

| SWINDON | Forte Posthouse | 63% | £72 |

Tel 01793 524601   Fax 01793 512887   Map 14 C2   **H**
Marlborough Road Swindon Wiltshire SN3 6AQ

70s' hotel set in five acres of grounds between Junction 15 of the M4 and the town centre. Three 80-seat conference rooms plus six 8-people syndicate rooms. Ample free parking. *Rooms 100. Garden, indoor swimming pool, keep-fit equipment, sauna, spa bath, solarium. Access, Amex, Diners, Visa.*

| SWINDON | Hilton National | 64% | NEW | £106 |

Tel 01793 881777   Fax 01793 881881   Map 14 C2   **H**
Lydiard Fields Great Western Way Swindon Wiltshire SN5 8UZ

By junction 16 of the M4. Opened in August 1994. All bedrooms are air-conditioned. *Rooms 150. Indoor swimming pool, sauna, steam room, spa bath, gym, beauty treatment room, coffee shop (11am-9.45pm). Access, Amex, Diners, Visa.*

| SWINDON | Swindon Crest Hotel | 62% | £96 |

Tel 01793 831333   Fax 01793 831401   Map 14 C2   **H**
Oxford Road Stratton St Margaret Swindon Wiltshire SN3 4TL

Modern low-rise hotel on the A420, near the A419 roundabout. Very much geared-up to the need of the business traveller with secretarial services, in-house pager facilities, 24hr room service and meeting rooms for up to 75 theatre-style. Recently re-branded to White Hart, still under the Forte banner. *Rooms 91. Access, Amex, Diners, Visa.*

| SWINDON | Swindon Marriott | 71% | £115 |

Tel 01793 512121   Fax 01793 513114   Map 14 C2   **H**
Pipers Way Swindon Wiltshire SN3 1SH

A modern purpose-built hotel standing in mature woodland next to a golf course. It's easily found when approaching from junction 15 of the M4, and only half a mile from the Old Town. Scandinavian-influenced public areas overlook the leisure area and are open-plan, with central beams and pine ceilings. Contemporary-style bedrooms have plenty of natural light and individual temperature control; under-19s stay free in parents' room. There are three suites and twelve rooms with king-size beds; 24hr room service is available. Conferences and banqueting for up to 280. Ample free parking. *Rooms 153. Garden, indoor swimming pool, gym, squash, sauna, spa bath, steam bath, solarium, beauty and hair salon, tennis, shop. Access, Amex, Diners, Visa.*

> Consult the blue pages for summary tables and lists of
> recommended establishments.

| SWINDON | Wiltshire Hotel | 62% | £79 |

Tel 01793 528282   Fax 01793 541283   Map 14 C2   **H**
Fleming Way Swindon Wiltshire SN1 1TN

Swindon's only central hotel, a short walk from bus and railway stations and with ample free parking in an adjacent public car park. Meeting rooms from 22 to 230, with banqueting for 200. Thistle & Mount Charlotte. *Rooms 95. Access, Amex, Diners, Visa.*

| SWINFEN | Swinfen Hall | 70% | £85 |

Tel 01543 481494   Fax 01543 480341   Map 6 C4   **H**
Swinfen nr Lichfield Staffordshire WS14 9RS

Splendid Palladian mansion set back from the A38 about two miles south of Lichfield. The ornate entrance hall is a 'wedding cake' confection in cream, pale blue and gold with fluted columns supporting a minstrel's gallery; beyond is a more restrained lounge with French windows opening on to a fine stone terrace overlooking formal gardens. A leather chesterfield-furnished bar is more Edwardian in style. First-floor bedrooms tend to be spacious (some very) with reproduction antique furniture and stylish fabrics, while those on the second floor are smaller with standardised lightwood furniture but the same pleasing soft furnishings. Beds are not turned down at night but there is 24hr room service. No dogs. *Rooms 20. Garden, croquet, tennis. Access, Amex, Visa.*

TADWORTH | Gemini Restaurant | £55

Tel 01737 812179
28 Station Approach Tadworth Surrey KT20 5AH

Map 15 E3

R

A friendly little restaurant located in a parade of shops near the station. Debbie Foster is at front of house while Robert concentrates on the kitchen, from where he produces a selection of set-price menus, in French style but described in English. Typical dishes might include smoked crab and tarragon sausage served with Provençal vegetables, pan-fried lamb's kidneys butter-fried with chicken liver paté, fillet of turbot in a champagne sauce studded with capers and orange, guinea fowl with buttered cabbage glazed with a fresh mustard sabayon and grilled fillet steak with mushroom and tomato or a choice of sauces. For dessert try a rhubarb and vanilla crème brulée, or a citrus fruit tart garnished with its own sauce. English and French cheeses are served with walnuts and grapes. Traditional roast Sunday lunchtime. No children under 10. *Seats* 40. *L 12-2 D 7-9.30. Closed L Sat, D Sun, all Mon, 2 weeks June, 2 weeks Christmas. Set L £11.50/£13.50/£15.50 (Sun £14.50) Set D £18.50 (Tues-Thurs)/£22.50/£26.50. Access, Visa.*

TAPLOW | Cliveden | 92% | £266

Tel 01628 668561   Fax 01628 661837
Taplow nr Maidenhead Berkshire SL6 0JF

Map 15 E2

HR

Our Hotel of the Year is both a remarkable and majestic hotel with a fascinating history – a former home of a Prince of Wales, several dukes and the Astor family – Cliveden (also a Stately Home and gardens owned by The National Trust, and therefore open to visitors at certain times) has been at the centre of Britain's social and political life for over three centuries. It overlooks the Thames and is set in over 350 acres of parkland and gardens, with a series of estate walks, some winding down to the river, where the hotel's own launch and electric canoe are moored – the boats are available for hire, whether for a summer picnic, a barbecue on one of the hotel's islands or just a trip down (or up) the river. The mansion itself, built in 1666, with the terrace, the dominant feature of the south facade, looks down on the breathtaking 17th-century parterre. Inside, observe the magnificent Great Hall with its lavish carved wood interior and stone fireplace, an apt setting for the works of art, tapestries and armour; the main staircase; the panelled library; the Adam-style boudoir (once Nancy Astor's sitting room); the panelled French Rococo dining-room, where a traditional English breakfast is served and staff wear long white gloves; the redbrick and vaulted cellar dining-room; the Mountbatten boardroom; the east and west wing corridors – all featuring wonderful portraits and paintings. Even the porte cochère houses something interesting: George Bernard Shaw's silver-topped cane. Each air-conditioned bedroom and suite (four full, six 'junior') has been named after someone connected to the house and all are sumptuously and stylishly furnished and decorated, offering every conceivable need and luxury, including fresh fruit, bathrobes and guest slippers. Bathrooms (most with his and hers washbasins) are simply stunning. Honeymooners even receive monogrammed bedside mats! In the suites (where afternoon tea and pre-supper Bucks Fizz are served) you'll also find a music centre and a video recorder (the hotel provides a very comprehensive video – plenty for the children too – and compact disc collection). The recently-added Clutton wing offers additonal bedrooms, the air-conditioned Macmillan meeting room, and Cliveden Club members-only bar/restaurant, converted from the original stables, featuring an intriguing trompe l'oeil, and retaining existing stalls and feeding troughs to create an authentic atmosphere. This wing connects with the Garden wing with its state-of-the-art and fully air-conditioned Churchill boardroom that opens directly on to its own terrace and overlooks the luxurious Pavilion Leisure complex (note the new non-slip pool surround) with its own Conservatory restaurant, housed in the original walled garden. Children under 2 are barred from the facilities at all times, while those up to the age of 12 can use them until noon; however, there is a creche and organised programmes for them. Service, from impeccably dressed staff, is outstanding; housekeeping is of the highest order. Banqueting for up to 160, conferences

for 42. Children up to five stay free in parents' room. Dogs are admirably catered for.
***Rooms** 37. Garden, indoor and outdoor swimming pools, children's splash pool, hot tub, spa
pool, saunas, plunge pool, steam room, gym, treatment rooms, hairdressing, croquet, indoor
and outdoor tennis, squash, badminton, snooker, riding, coarse fishing, boating, valeting,
Daimler Sovereign limousine. Access, Amex, Diners, Visa.*

Terrace Dining Room   £140

Once the main drawing room of the house, the room is incomparably grand, with
stunning views across the parterre, down to the river and for many miles beyond. Table
settings are immaculate, and service, under the guidance of restaurant manager Stephen
Colley, is polished and professional. Cooking is a mixture of modern and traditional
British and classical French, with dishes (fixed-price or à la carte) ranging from a tomato,
fennel and ginger consommé with smoked chicken and poached quail's eggs, or a warm
salad of smoked foie gras with marinated wild mushrooms and grilled baby leeks, to roast
corn-fed chicken with crayfish, truffle tagliatelle and spring vegetables, or grilled Dover
sole with parsley butter. Desserts such as an egg custard and pear tart with prune and
armagnac ice cream or summer pudding with elderflower ice cream end a meal in fine
style. The hotel's air-conditioned and temperature-controlled van makes daily trips to the
markets, ensuring the freshest and best produce, which when added to head chef Ron
Maxfield's talents, provide first-class dishes. A manageable wine list has the odd tasting
note – ask about half bottles and what else lurks in the cellar! No smoking. "A donation
of £2.50 to The National Trust is charged to each guest. Service is neither included nor
anticipated". ***Seats** 65. Parties 12. Private room 54. L 12.30-2.30 D 7-10.30.
Set L £28 (Sun £36.50/£45) Set D £38.*

Waldo's   ★   £120

Of the hotel's two main restaurants, this is perhaps chef Ron Maxfield's showcase, with
cooking that is more modern (British for the most part) and innovative than upstairs,
relying, of course, on the finest ingredients. Access is down a flight of stairs, past a wall of
old servants' bells, and through a lobby adorned with photos of the rich and famous
(kings and queens, dukes and duchesses, Chaplin, Roosevelt, Lloyd George and Shaw)
who stayed at the house during the Astor period. History continues in the Gents
cloakroom where there are drawings of Christine Keeler and Mandy Rice-Davies by
Dr Stephen Ward – the main protagonists in the Profumo affair that led to the downfall
of the Macmillan government in 1964. A pianist plays in the pine-panelled bar, and the
small restaurant itself resembles a private club with suitably formal service. The menu is
fixed-price (choice of three, four or six courses, the latter predestined): a typical three-
course meal might consist of Cornish crab with lime and pimentos, grilled scallops and
a warm potato and chive salad; roast corn-fed free-range guinea fowl with cepes and
morels in a light truffle and tarragon cream; apricot soufflé with a wild strawberry ice
cream. Some of the dishes owe more of a nod to the Continent than to Britain, as in
fresh gnocchi with Alba truffles, gruyère cheese and wild mushrooms in a light cream
sauce or fillet of red mullet whith chorizo. Whatever you choose, you'll encounter
cooking of precision, flair and finesse, an abundance of flavours and aromas – in short,
genuine talent. Same wine list and contributions as the dining-room. No smoking.
***Seats** 26. Parties 4. D only 7-10.30. Closed Sun & Mon. Set D £45, £49 & £60.*

TAUNTON	The Castle	76%	£110

Tel 01823 272671   Fax 01823 336066   Map 13 E2   **HR**
Castle Green Taunton Somerset TA1 1NF

Twelve centuries ago there was a Saxon settlement here, then a Norman castle. The
present building is approximately 300 years old and possesses a very distinctive West
Front which in early summer is a riot of wisteria. Inside there's a careful balance of the
old and the new. Handsome stonework, tapestries, English chintz and fine art all feature
in the evocative public areas; the great oak staircase adds to the feeling of grandeur. Such
surroundings deserve the highest standards of service, and you will not be disappointed
here. The first evidence of this is when greeted on arrival by charmingly friendly and
efficient staff; they are obviously well motivated, mainly due to the fact that two
generations of the Chapman family (with Kit at the helm) have been in situ and know
how things should be done. Of necessity (it's hard to modernise and knock down 15-foot
thick walls), not all the bedrooms are as spacious and plush as the Bow or garden suites
with their deep sofas, canopied beds and heavy fabrics, indeed some of the singles are on

See over

the small side, though they are all smartly furnished and decorated in their own individual style with those extra bits and bobs to make your stay even more comfortable. Good bathrooms (with decent toiletries) invite a long soak! Cars can be pampered as well: locked in the garage for a tenner or washed for a fiver! *Rooms 35. Garden. Access, Amex, Diners, Visa.*

Restaurant   ★ ↑   £90

Phil Vickery, here since 1990, is maintaining the great Castle tradition for fine British cooking throughout a wide choice of menus written in straightforward, unpretentious English and depending on the finest produce available. From the simplest luncheon could come curried parsnip soup, grilled fillets of red mullet with leaf spinach and a saffron cream plus warm bread-and-butter pudding with cream. Move on to the higher-priced menus and you might find some more exotic influences at work: seared salmon with a spice crust, couscous and spring onion crème fraiche (and that's just a starter!); steamed sea bass with braised leeks, saffron oil and roast garlic or pan-fried tournedos with truffle butter. There's a fine British cheeseboard and some splendid desserts such as baked egg custard tart with nutmeg ice cream and warm Bramley apple crumble tart with caramelised pecan ice cream or hot chocolate pudding with chocolate sauce. Service from a young and committed team is most professional. Sunday lunch is a traditional 3-course meal with roast sirloin of beef and Yorkshire pudding as the centrepiece. More informal lunchtime eating (not Sunday) in the Minstrel's Bar. There's some terrific value on the splendid wine list, packed with information, including who supplies what. For once, Spain is well represented, with the excellent 1986 Marqués de Griñon cabernet sauvignon a snip at just over £20. No smoking. *Seats 80. Parties 8. Private Room 25. L 12.30-2 D 7.30-9. Set L £14.50/£16.50 & £28.50/£32.50 (Sun £16.50, children half price) Set D £19.90/£23.90 & £28.50/£32.50.*

TAUNTON	Forte Posthouse	66%	£72

Tel 01823 332222   Fax 01823 332266   Map 13 E2   **H**
Deane Gate Avenue Taunton Somerset TA1 2UA

Two miles from the town centre, close to Junction 25 of the M5. Modern conference facilities for up to 280. *Rooms 97. Keep-fit equipment, sauna, children's playroom. Access, Amex, Diners, Visa.*

TAUNTON	Porters Wine Bar	£40

Tel 01823 256688   Map 13 E2   **R**
49 East Reach Taunton Somerset TA1 3EX

The blackboard menu changes several times a week, offering straightforward, enjoyable dishes such as haddock, prawn and sweetcorn chowder, pork and apricot paté, breast of duck with two sauces, monkfish with orange and green peppercorn sauce on a bed of leeks and chargrilled steaks. Three vegetarian choices; sticky toffee pudding is a favourite sweet. A dozen or more wines are available by the glass. Four courtyard tables in good weather and a non-smoking area to the rear of the restaurant. *Seats 50. Parties 16. L 12.30-2 D 7.30-9.45. Closed L Sat, all Sun, Bank Holidays & 1 week Christmas. Access, Visa.*

TEFFONT EVIAS	Howard's House Hotel	68%	£111

Tel 01722 716392   Fax 01722 716820   Map 14 C3   **HR**
Teffont Evias nr Salisbury Wiltshire SP3 5RJ

In the almost idyllic setting of a sleepy hamlet of medieval origins the families Firmin and Ford have studiously converted their Tudor stone farmhouse into a very comfortable hotel. They are direct descendants of Christopher Mayne, who bought the manor in 1692 (it was built some 70 years earlier). Two acres of gardens now provide flowers for bedrooms and day rooms, as well as herbs for the kitchen. A little gem of a place. *Rooms 9. Garden, croquet. Access, Amex, Diners, Visa.*

Restaurant   £75

Paul Firmin's fixed-price dinner menus, which offer five choices per course, are well balanced and carefully executed. You might start with baked mackerel with orange, lime and lemon balm, or mousseline of rabbit with wild mushrooms and a red wine sabayon before moving on to grilled halibut with a cardamom and saffron butter sauce, or medallions of beef fillet with rösti potatoes, morels and Madeira. Finish with whisky and oatmeal parfait with blackberry sauce, or chocolate torte with chocolate and cherry ice cream. The wine list is carefully compiled, concise and very fairly priced. Five tables on a terrace for outdoor eating. **Seats** 35. L (Sun only) 12.30-2 D 7.30-10. Set L £19.50 Set D £25.50/£29.50.

TEIGNMOUTH	Thomas Luny House	£60

Tel 01626 772976   Map 13 D3   **PH**
Teign Street Teignmouth Devon TQ14 8EG

Built by the marine artist Thomas Luny in the late 18th century, this small Georgian town house has been charmingly restored by Alison and John Allan. This means that you are essentially a guest in their home, socialising with them and fellow guests in the well-appointed drawing room that displays family photos, and sharing the non-smoking evening meal around a large polished dining table. The simple, carefully prepared set dinner (£16.50 – for residents and their guests only) is a joint effort by the Allans and there is a short, modestly-priced list of wines. A recent meal comprised tomato, avocado and watercress salad wtih a crispy bacon dressing, baked fillet of lemon sole with a herb-scented sauce, and truffle torte. Four antique-furnished bedrooms have been decorated with great style and quality and have excellent co-ordinating bathrooms (one has shower and WC only). All rooms have direct-dial telephones and remote-control TV, plus homely touches like fresh flowers, books and mineral water. It all adds up to a delightful alternative to a conventional hotel. Follow signs to the quay and turn into Teign Street just before the port entrance. The room rate includes afternoon tea. No children under 12 except babes in arms. No dogs. **Rooms** 4. Garden. No credit cards.

TELFORD	Holiday Inn Telford/Ironbridge	68%	£109

Tel 01952 292500   Fax 01952 291949   Map 6 B3   **H**
St Quentin Gate Telford Shropshire TF3 4EH

With easy access to the M54 (Junction 4) and town centre, this modern low-riser is adjacent to Telford Racquet and Exhibition Centre. Business centre serves conferences (max 290) and banqueting up to 180. Children up to 12 can stay free in parents' room. Ample free parking. **Rooms** 100. Indoor swimming pool, gym, sauna, spa bath, steam room, solarium, beautician. Access, Amex, Diners, Visa.

TELFORD	Madeley Court	67%	£98

Tel 01952 680068   Fax 01952 684275   Map 6 B3   **H**
Madeley Telford Shropshire TF7 5DW

Public areas, which include a small oak-panelled lounge/bar, are in the oldest (13th-century) part of a predominantly Elizabethan hotel that, although within the Madeley area of Telford, is next to a small lake and has a rural setting. Bedrooms are divided between eight characterful, antique-furnished, historic rooms in the old building (two in a 16th-century gatehouse) and those in the new East and South wings, the former with rag-rolled fitted units, the latter with darkwood freestanding furniture. Conference facilities (capacity 200) are in a converted 16th-century mill. **Rooms** 47. Patio. Access, Amex, Diners, Visa.

TELFORD	Moat House	67%	£109

Tel 01952 291291   Fax 01952 292012   Map 6 B3   **H**
Forgegate Telford Shropshire TF3 4NA

Close to the town centre and easily accessible from the motorways, this is a modern hotel with good conference (12 rooms catering for up to 450 delegates) and leisure facilities. Comfortable atrium lounge and Forgegate Bar. Children up to 16 free in parents' room. **Rooms** 148. Indoor swimming pool, gym, sauna, solarium. Access, Amex, Diners, Visa.

Consult the blue pages for summary tables and lists of recommended establishments.

TELFORD	Telford Hotel	64%	£110

Tel 01952 429977   Fax 01952 586602   Map 6 B3   **H**
Great Hay Sutton Hill Telford Shropshire TF7 4DT

Standing south of the town centre above Ironbridge Gorge, the hotel combines comfortable, modern accommodation with golf and country club facilities and a state-of-the-art conference centre for up to 240 delegates. Under-16s stay free in parents' room; good family facilities at weekends (the hotel is convenient for the seven Ironbridge museums), plus a children's menu and play area in the Racquets coffee shop. Queens Moat Houses. *Rooms 86. Patio, golf (18), pitch & putt, golf driving range, indoor swimming pool, gym, spa bath, sauna, solarium, steam room, young children's playroom, snooker, coffee shop (9.30am-9pm). Access, Amex, Diners, Visa.*

TETBURY	Calcot Manor	77%	£115

Tel 01666 890391   Fax 01666 890394   Map 14 B2   **HR**
Tetbury Gloucestershire GL8 8YJ

This delightful manor house complex continues to develop in all the nicest ways, without spoiling the feel of its medieval origins: additions this year include a croquet lawn, tennis courts and a pub, The Gumstool, which seems to be as popular with locals as with residents. The comfortable hotel sitting rooms remain for those who prefer more tranquil surroundings. Bedrooms vary in size from very adequate to expansive, most are in the main house but recent additions are housed in attractive stable blocks. One of these is geared to family use, with a mini-library of Beatrix Potter books, sophisticated baby-listening devices and "piped" children's videos. An enclosed garden adjacent to the family block has a play train. Children's high tea is served from 5.30pm. Banqueting and conferences for up to 60. *Rooms 20. Garden, outdoor swimming pool. Access, Amex, Diners, Visa.*

Restaurant   £65

Another change of chef this year, although Eddie Portlock has been promoted from within so the style remains the same. Lighter meals are available at the Gumstool Inn and the menu in the restaurant is now table d'hote only, seasonally changing and offering six choices at each course: Oriental chicken salad, crisp lamb sweetbreads with a flat mushroom and tarragon salad or crostini of mozzarella with Mediterranean vegetables for starters; roast duck with apples, apricots and a caramel sauce, chargrilled lemon sole with herb and lemon butter or sirloin steak with creamed celeriac and roast garlic sauce are main courses which set the style. An immaculately presented wine list with the house selection matching various wines with dishes. Some regions very lightly presented, though prices are fair. The dining-room is romantically candle-lit at night. A terrace provides four tables for outdoor eating, when weather permits. No smoking in the dining-room. *Seats 50. Private Room 35. L 12.30-2 D 7.30-9.30. Set Sun L & D £23/£26 (Sun L £15).*

TETBURY	The Close	72%	£95

Tel 01666 502272   Fax 01666 504401   Map 14 B2   **H**
8 Long Street Tetbury Gloucestershire GL8 8AQ

The original house was built in the 16th century for a local wool merchant and became a hotel in 1974. It presents a relatively modest face to the main street, but the rear elevation, which forms one side of a delightful walled garden hidden away from the market-town bustle, is more impressive. Rag, drag and stipple painting take the eye in the day rooms and in the bedrooms, which vary in size and shape; some feature old beams, one is in Art Deco style, none lacks in comfort. Beds are turned down at night. 22 car parking spaces at the rear of the hotel (access via Close Gardens on New Church Street). Children up to 12 stay free in parents' room. Managed by Virgin's Voyager Hotels. No dogs. *Rooms 15. Garden, croquet. Access, Amex, Diners, Visa.*

TETBURY — Snooty Fox Hotel — 66% — £80

Tel 01666 502436   Fax 01666 503479   Map 14 B2   **H**
Market Place Tetbury Gloucestershire GL8 8DD

Standing in the centre of the town opposite the picturesque Market House (still used on Wednesday market days) this 16th-century former coaching inn exudes period charm. The bar, with its imposing copper fire hood and pub-like atmosphere, is a popular local's rendezvous. A quiet residents' lounge provides a comfortable contrast. Individually designed bedrooms (named after hunts), some with four-poster beds, are full of character and are in the process of refurbishment. All have the expected modern gadgetry, plus little extras like a basket of fruit, bottles of mineral water and decorative "snooty foxes" (these are popular soft toys and for sale from reception). En suite bathrooms have good toiletries and plush bathrobes. Hatton Hotels. *Rooms 12. Access, Amex, Diners, Visa.*

TEWKESBURY — Bell Hotel — 57% — £75

Tel 01684 293293   Fax 01684 295938   Map 14 B1   **H**
Church Street Tewkesbury Gloucestershire GL20 5SA

The hotel bears the date 1696 but the architectural style of this substantial black-and-white timbered building alongside Tewkesbury Abbey suggests an even earlier period. Since taking over some three years ago, Peter and Gillian Hands have effected considerable refurbishment, creating cosy, bright bedrooms with pretty, matching bedcovers and curtains and a co-ordinating frieze around the top of plain walls. The best have oak furniture but not all have convenient work space for the business traveller. All come with the usual amenities such as hairdryer and trouser press plus practical bathrooms of which just a couple have shower and WC only. There are three four-poster rooms. Main day room is a comfortable bar which features linenfold panelling, some old timbers and a large stone fireplace complete with real fire in winter. *Rooms 25. Access, Amex, Diners, Visa.*

TEWKESBURY — Royal Hop Pole — 66% — £92

Tel 01684 293236   Fax 01684 296680   Map 14 B1   **H**
Church Street Tewkesbury Gloucestershire GL20 5RT

One of the smaller hotels in the Forte chain, and one of the oldest in the county, the Royal Hop Pole is mentioned by Charles Dickens in *The Pickwick Papers*. Sympathetic conversion has provided an elegant drawing room and rear-facing bar. Best of the bedrooms feature a four-poster and executive extras, but many may plump for the oak-beamed character of the older rear bedrooms, where bathroom space is at a premium. A walled garden runs down to the River Avon and the hotel's private mooring. *Rooms 29. Garden, mooring. Access, Amex, Diners, Visa.*

TEWKESBURY — Tewkesbury Park — 62% — £93

Tel 01684 295405   Fax 01684 292386   Map 14 B1   **H**
Lincoln Green Lane Tewkesbury Gloucestershire GL20 7DN

Just 5 minutes from Junction 9 of the M5, Tewkesbury Park is more country club than country house, and conferences (up to 150 people) are big business. Well-appointed bedrooms afford views of the Malvern Hills. Children up to 14 free in parents' room. No dogs. Country Club Hotels. *Rooms 78. Garden, tennis, golf (18), putting, golf pro and shop, indoor swimming pool, gym, squash, sauna, steam room, spa bath, solarium, beauty salon, snooker, children's playroom & playground, coffee shop (10am-11pm). Access, Amex, Diners, Visa.*

THAME — Spread Eagle — 65% — £90

Tel 01844 213661   Fax 01844 261380   Map 15 D2   **H**
Cornmarket Thame Oxfordshire OX9 2BW

A square-fronted redbrick former coaching inn standing in the centre of town, with free parking for 80 cars at the rear. Public rooms are divided between the small lounge area in the entrance lobby and the quite separate bars across the cobbled yard in the original part of the hotel. Decor throughout is mellow and in keeping with the hotel's character. Bedrooms in the main house have period charm while those in a wing extending into the car park have the advantage of French windows which open on to a sunny, west-facing lawn and flower beds. Equipped with the usual trappings of a modern hotel, the rooms are

See over

well maintained and staff give the impression of being only too willing to please. One bedroom is equipped for disabled guests. 24hr room service. Children under 15 are accommodated free of charge in parents' room. Banqueting suites and syndicate rooms hold up to 250. No dogs. *Rooms 33. Garden. Closed 28-31 Dec. Access, Amex, Diners, Visa.*

THETFORD	The Bell	62%	£82

Tel 01842 754455   Fax 01842 755552   Map 10 C2   **H**
King Street Thetford Norfolk IP24 2AZ

An old coaching inn overlooking the Ouse with many architectural features dating back to the 15th century. Bedrooms in the old part are beamed, several boasting four-posters; wing rooms are more up-to-date. No charge for under-16s sharing parents' room. The function facility houses banqueting for 60, conferences up to 80. Forte. *Rooms 47. Terrace, coffee shop (10-5). Access, Amex, Diners, Visa.*

THETFORD	Martine's	NEW	£55

Tel 01842 762000   Map 10 C2   **R**
17 St Giles Lane Thetford Norfolk IP24 2AE

Martine Greslon runs her charming little restaurant almost singlehandedly. Having worked for a number of years in the wine trade, she embarked on the present venture in mid-1994. The setting is a homely one with a bottle-green carpeted rectangular dining-room furnished in red pine. She prepares everything, from the breads to the ice creams, and offers a monthly-changing menu of enjoyable, imaginative dishes. Begin, perhaps, with home-made tagliatelle with langoustines and a creamy tomato sauce, Thai crab cakes with a small Oriental salad or a thick pea and ham soup. Follow with roast pork fillet with hoisin sauce, a sweetcorn pancake and crispy stir-fry vegetables, chicken breast with a creamy basil sauce, new potatoes and crisp green leaves or pan-fried fillet of cod on a potato galette with a mixed vegetable garnish. Desserts could include treacle tart with real custard, rich white chocolate mousse or a hot apple tartlet with vanilla ice cream. Ask for directions when booking as although it's in the town centre the restaurant is slightly off the beaten track. *Seats 30. Parties 10. Private Room 20. L 12-2 D 7-9.30. Closed L Sat, all Sun & Mon. Access, Amex, Diners, Visa.*

THORNABY-ON-TEES	Forte Posthouse	60%	£72

Tel 01642 591213   Fax 01642 594989   Map 5 E3   **H**
Low Lane by Stainton Village nr Thornaby-on-Tees Cleveland TS17 9LW

An older-style Posthouse in the village of Stainton. Half of the bedrooms are designated non-smoking. Children up to 16 free in parents' room. Conferences/banquets for up to 100. Ample free parking. *Rooms 135. Garden, sauna, sun beds. Access, Amex, Diners, Visa.*

THORNBURY	Thornbury Castle	80%	£105

Tel 01454 281182   Fax 01454 416188   Map 13 F1   **H**
Thornbury nr Bristol Avon BS12 1HH

History abounds at Thornbury Castle, its gardens and vineyard surrounded by high walls. Henry VIII appropriated the castle as a royal demesne for many years, after which Mary Tudor spent some time here before returning it to the descendants of the original owner, the Duke of Buckingham. Bedrooms, some reached via stone and spiral staircases, are full of character with many features (Tudor fireplaces, oriel windows, shutters, intricate ceilings) retained. Several, with fine views, have four-poster beds decked out with bold country fabrics; all greet arriving guests with a bowl of fruit and decanter of sherry, and provide good bathrooms offering pampering extras. Baronial public rooms (candle-lit each evening, which adds to the atmosphere) are impressive, none more than the panelled lounge with its magnificent stone fireplace, high mullioned windows and Tudor portraits on the walls. The room rate quoted above is the minimum for a twin/double and includes Continental breakfast; de luxe rooms are priced up to £205. No children under 12 "unless known". No smoking in the dining-rooms. No dogs. Convenient motorway access from M4 (J20/21) and M5 (J14/16). *Rooms 18. Garden, croquet. Closed 2 days early Jan. Access, Amex, Diners, Visa.*

THORNTON-LE-FYLDE	River House	£85

Tel 01253 883497   Fax 01253 892083   Map 6 A1   **RR**
Skippool Creek Thornton-le-Fylde nr Blackpool Lancashire FY5 5LF

Bill and Carole Scott's inviting restaurant with rooms, built in 1830 for a gentleman farmer, enjoys a delightful location opposite Skippool Creek and offers confidently cooked food in a relaxed setting. The menu's influence is decidedly French, and though some menu favourites recur there's always plenty of choice. Try perhaps a soufflé suissesse – a featherlight cheese soufflé with cream and gruyère cheese – followed by very rare roast venison with a game sauce, chateaubriand with béarnaise sauce or bloody young grouse with a redcurrant sauce. Ticky tacky pudding, a hot date and walnut pudding with butterscotch sauce and vanilla ice cream – first served here in 1958 – makes a really delicious finale. Bill's menu comes with the proviso of availability being dependant on supply, so you can be sure that if it's on, it's good, and if possible it will be home-made. The wine list is extensive, interesting and very reasonably priced. *Seats 40. Parties 30. Private Room 14. L & D by arrangement. Set L & D £18.50. Closed Sun, some Bank Holidays. Access, Visa.*

Rooms   £80

Five individually decorated and named rooms offer traditional comfort and modern amenities. Well-behaved children are welcome. Garden, croquet.

THUNDRIDGE	Hanbury Manor	85%	£161

Tel 01920 487722   Fax 01920 487692   Map 15 F1   **HR**
Thundridge nr Ware Hertfordshire SG12 0SD

A very handsome and substantial Jacobean-style mansion surrounded by 200 acres of golf course and mature parkland. Its history includes a period as a convent during which additional wings and a cloister were added. A long, sweeping drive leads directly from the A10 to the front entrance, where a valet is on hand to park your car. A genuinely warm greeting is extended in the entrance hall, to the right of which is the magnificent galleried oak hall with its huge tapestries, open fireplace, panelled walls and lofty ceiling from whose beams are suspended immense crystal chandeliers. The library serves as a peaceful retreat during the day but in the evening it is often used as an overflow for the splendidly elegant bar with its pale cream walls and richly coloured upholstery. Bedrooms are decorated with impeccable taste and furnished with traditional polished-wood free-standing pieces. All enjoy good views over the grounds and come with every modern convenience plus extra comforts like towelling robes in the superb marble bathrooms. There are 25 full suites. The hotel's leisure complex is most luxurious and includes a palatial indoor swimming pool and a creche (10-4 Mon-Fri, 10-4 Sat & Sun) among other things. Very friendly, obliging staff. 24hr room service. Children up to 16 share parents' room free. One night's deposit is requested to guarantee accommodation. *Rooms 96. Garden, croquet, golf (18), tennis, putting, squash, indoor swimming pool, spa bath, sauna, steam room, sun beds, gymnasium, snooker, beautician, hairdressing, news kiosk. Access, Amex, Diners, Visa.*

Zodiac Restaurant and Conservatory   £130

Taking its name from the signs of the zodiac discreetly incorporated into the fine plasterwork of its barrel-vaulted ceiling, this is an extremely elegant dining-room with caryatids and atlantes supporting the mantle above a large fireplace, cream panelled walls with fluted pilasters and high-quality table settings and appointments, all illuminated by

See over

three glittering chandeliers. Service, under restaurant manager Tony Ferrario, is faultless, with waiters never having to ask "who is having what", for example. Albert Roux of *Le Gavroche* is retained as a consultant but it is executive chef Rory Kennedy who runs the show with a menu of reliably produced dishes such as a light vegetable bouillon with medallions of poached foie gras; mousseline of langoustines au jus de crustacés; fricassee of corn-fed chicken with champagne sauce; breast of duck with a purée of carrots, red wine sauce and oysters. The à la carte is pricy (the luxurious surroundings and high level of service have to be paid for) but the fixed-price dinner represents good value. Weekday lunches, served in the Conservatory (and out on the terrace in fine weather), bring a weekly-changing à la carte (main dishes £12.50-£15.50) with a choice of six dishes at each stage. No smoking in dining-rooms. No children under eight in Zodiac room. *Seats 40. Parties 8. Private Room 8. L (Mon-Fri in Conservatory, Sun in Zodiac) 12.30-2.30 D (in Zodiac plus Conservatory Fri & Sat) 7.30-10 (Fri & Sat from 7). Closed L Sat & D Sun. Set D (& L Sun) £25.*

THURLESTONE	Thurlestone Hotel	69%	£140

Tel 01548 560382   Fax 01548 561069   Map 13 D3   **H**
Thurlestone Kingsbridge Devon TQ7 3NN

The elegance of the 20s combines with the amenities of the 90s in a handsome hotel in a lovely setting with spectacular sea views. The Gorse family have been here from the start, and 1996 is their centenary year. Splendidly geared to family holidays (particularly at half-term breaks, when dancing, competitions, film shows and parties are all laid on), with an excellent leisure club, the hotel also has an off-peak trade in conferences (for up to 120). Day rooms include The Village Inn, whose timbers are said to have come from the San Pedro, part of the Spanish Armada. Accommodation is graded as 'de luxe' (sea view, video player, private bar, undercover parking, no dogs allowed, most with balconies), 'sea view' and 'country view'. Children up to 16 can stay free of charge in their parents' room, but a minimum charge of £15 is made for breakfast and children's supper. Gentlemen are requested to wear jackets and ties for dinner in the (no-smoking) restaurant. Ample parking (100 open, 20 covered spaces). *Rooms 68. Garden, tennis, golf (9), putting, indoor & outdoor swimming pools, gym, squash, sauna, solarium, beauty & hair salon, badminton, games room, snooker, children's playroom and playground. Access, Visa.*

TICKTON	Tickton Grange	62%	£75

Tel 01964 543666   Fax 01964 542556   Map 7 E1   **H**
Tickton nr Beverley Humberside HU17 9SH

A family-owned Georgian house standing just off the A1035 east of Beverley in 3½ acres of rose gardens, where afternoon teas are served in the summer. Day rooms retain a traditional appeal, and bedrooms are decorated in a fresh, light style. There are two suites, one with a Georgian four-poster bed. Tickton truffles are offered as a welcome. The Whymant family run the hotel along friendly and informal lines. *Rooms 18. Garden, croquet. Access, Amex, Diners, Visa.*

TINTAGEL	Trebrea Lodge	66%	£64

Tel 01840 770410   Map 12 B2   **HR**
Trenale Tintagel Cornwall PL34 0HR

Set in four acres of wooded hillside, this civilised country hotel dates back 600 years, although the facade is Georgian. It's furnished throughout with antiques (one of the partners owns an antique shop in London); there's an elegant and sunny first-floor drawing room and cosy 'honesty' bar (the only place in the house where smoking is allowed). Appealing bedrooms, all enjoying fine views across fields to the sea in the distance, are individually decorated, with good bathrooms; about half have shower and WC only. One room has a four-poster. No smoking. No children under 7. *Rooms 7. Garden. Closed 8-31 Jan. Access, Visa.*

Restaurant   £40

Dinner, served at 8pm in the small candle-lit oak-panelled dining-room, is a simple no-choice affair that allows the excellent, often local, ingredients to speak for themselves. A typical menu might be smoked haddock and prawns au gratin, steak and mushroom pie, chocolate and orange mousse and a couple of cheeses. Chef-proprietor Sean Devlin numbers marinated home-cured beef among his specialities. The short wine list has no half bottles but good house wine is available by the glass. No smoking. *Seats 14. Set D £14.75.*

TONBRIDGE	Goldhill Mill	£70

Tel 01732 851626   Fax 01732 851881   Map 11 B5   **PH**
Golden Green Hadlow Tonbridge Kent TN11 0BA

Check directions when booking at this superior bed-and-breakfast hotel with luxurious accommodation. Originally a watermill, it enjoys an idyllic location beside the River Bourne surrounded by twenty acres including mature gardens and ponds containing freshwater crayfish (a breakfast speciality in summer months). Amiable hosts Shirley and Vernon Cole ensure that you relax in what has been their family home since the late 1930s. The house is stylishly decorated – a beamed farmhouse kitchen (used for breakfast) resplendent with working mill wheel, a drawing room with wood-burning stove, a small TV/video lounge. Three individually decorated bedrooms (non-smoking, like the rest of the house), beautifully furnished in chintzy soft furnishings offer an abundance of extras, remote-control TV, bowl of fruit and fresh flowers. One room has a four-poster. Lavishly appointed bathrooms include jacuzzi baths in two rooms and excellent toiletries. In the grounds, the Ciderpass Cottage is open all year for self-catering accommodation. No children under 12 or dogs. *Rooms 3. Garden, floodlit tennis court. Closed 15 Jul-31 Aug, 25 & 26 Dec. Access, Visa.*

TONBRIDGE	Rose & Crown	59%	£82

Tel 01732 357966   Fax 01732 357194   Map 11 B5   **H**
125 High Street Tonbridge Kent TN9 1DD

A 16th-century coaching inn with traditionally furnished bedrooms in the old part, modern rooms in the garden wing. 20 of the rooms are designated non-smoking. Children up to 16 stay free in parents' room. Conference/banqueting facilities for 120/80. Forte. *Rooms 48. Garden. Access, Amex, Diners, Visa.*

TORQUAY	Grand Hotel	68%	£105

Tel 01803 296677   Fax 01803 213462   Map 13 D3   **H**
Sea Front Torquay Devon TQ2 6NT

Large, white-painted Edwardian hotel where Agatha Christie honeymooned, on the seafront just 100 yards from Torquay railway station. Bedrooms have a variety of pleasant colour schemes, good easy chairs and darkwood furniture. There are seaviews from about half the rooms, of which those designated 'Riviera' are the most spacious. Beds are turned down at night and room service is 24hrs. Glass-fronted display cabinets feature in the entrance/reception area, which leads into a large central lobby with lounge seating. The main day room, though, is Boaters Bar with a sun lounge beyond. The more pubby Pullman Bar is reached from outside the hotel. Children under 12 sharing parents' room stay free. Excellent facilities for families. *Rooms 111. Garden, tennis, indoor & outdoor swimming pools, mini-gym, solarium, spa bath, hair salon, games room, snooker. Access, Amex, Diners, Visa.*

TORQUAY	Homers Hotel	64%	£60

Tel 01803 213456   Fax 01803 213458   Map 13 D3   **H**
Warren Road Torquay Devon TQ2 5TN

A small Victorian hotel, perched high above Torbay. Bedrooms have extravagantly-sized padded headboards that co-ordinate with bedcovers and curtains. A tray of mineral water, biscuits and sweets is left at the bedside when rooms are serviced in the evening. The great majority of rooms share a panoramic view of the bay. Genteel day rooms have been opened up to each other but still retain a period feel with reproduction-style easy chairs and lots of parlour plants. The bar is in an alcove off this main lounge, part of which is reserved for non-smokers. A terrace looks down on to a stepped garden that affords direct access to Torquay's famous Rock Walk Gardens. New this year is a conference suite for up to 50 delegates (theatre-style). *Rooms 15. Garden. Access, Amex, Diners, Visa.*

We welcome bona fide complaints and recommendations on the tear-out pages at the back of the book for readers' comments. They are followed up by our professional team.

TORQUAY	Imperial Hotel	83%	£120

Tel 01803 294301   Fax 01803 298293   Map 13 D3   **H**
Parkhill Road Torquay Devon TQ1 2DG

The Imperial is a grand hotel dating from the mid-19th century and looking very smart after a major refurbishment programme. An imposing marble-floored lobby with fluted Corinthian pilasters and glittering chandeliers sets the tone for extensive public areas that boast many fine period features: the colonnade with painted panels, luxurious Palm Court lounge with Lloyd Loom-furnished Sun Deck beyond, bar with deeply comfortable leather armchairs and Regency Lounge with dancing to a live band every Friday and Saturday night. Outside, ranks of sunloungers surround the pool and, from the hotel's elevated position high above the bay, terraced gardens reach right down to the shore. Most of the bedrooms have their own entrance lobbies and more than half have good-sized, furnished balconies overlooking the bay. Traditionally furnished either with reproduction antique or freestanding darkwood pieces, they come in a variety of bright, tasteful colour schemes and all have good bathrooms, with generous towels and bathrobes. High levels of service include a proper concierge, evening turn-down and extensive 24hr room service. For younger guests there is the Scallywags Club – with its own suite of rooms – and all sorts of activities from painting and model-making to dressing-up and video games organised during the summer and other holiday periods. Banquets/conferences for 350/400 in the Torbay Suite. Full business support services. *Rooms 167. Garden, croquet, tennis, indoor & outdoor swimming pools, gym, squash, sauna, solarium, beauty & hair salon, snooker, children's playroom, news kiosk. Access, Amex, Diners, Visa.*

TORQUAY	Livermead Cliff Hotel	60%	£76

Tel 01803 299666   Fax 01803 294496   Map 13 D3   **H**
Sea Front Torquay Devon TQ2 6RQ

Right by the sea, with 20 steps leading to safe beaches, this is not surprisingly a popular holiday spot and a good place for families (children up to 15 stay free in parents' room). It's also geared up to the conference trade (for up to 80 delegates), so it's quite a busy place all year round. Picture windows in the lounge look out to sea. Good housekeeping (further modernisation under way in the bedrooms), friendly staff. *Rooms 64. Garden, outdoor swimming pool, mini-gym, solarium, laundry room. Access, Amex, Diners, Visa.*

TORQUAY	Livermead House	60%	£90

Tel 01803 294361   Fax 01803 200758   Map 13 D3   **H**
Sea Front Torquay Devon TQ2 6QJ

Charles Kingsley was an early guest here, and today's water babies will appreciate the swimming pools. The sea is also at hand, providing panoramic views from the hotel's picture windows. There's plenty to keep visitors occupied both inside and out, and for relaxation there's a choice of lounges and bars. The best of the well kept bedrooms face the sea. A conference and banqueting facility – the Regency Suite – can accommodate 250 for functions, 300 for meetings. Free parking for 120 cars. No dogs. *Rooms 65. Garden, adults' and children's outdoor swimming pool, mini-gym, squash, sauna, sun beds, snooker. Access, Amex, Diners, Visa.*

TORQUAY	Orestone Manor	58%	£90

Tel 01803 328098   Fax 01803 328336   Map 13 D3   **H**
Hockhouse Lane Maidencombe Torquay Devon TQ1 4SX

Take the Teignmouth road out of Torquay to find this hotel run by the Staples family. Situated high above Babbacombe Bay and once the home of artist John Calcott Horsley, it enjoys fine views of the sea. Clean and comfortable public rooms and all the bedrooms have been recently decorated, and most have sea views. No children under ten, except under-twos. *Rooms 18. Garden, outdoor swimming pool, children's splash pool. Access, Amex, Diners, Visa.*

TORQUAY	Osborne Hotel	65%	£76

Tel 01803 213311   Fax 01803 296788   Map 13 D3   **H**
Hesketh Crescent Meadfoot Beach Torquay Devon TQ1 2LL

The Osborne describes itself as a country house hotel by the sea, and its location within a well-maintained Regency crescent on the hillside ensures good views over the bay.

Bedrooms and apartments offer a high level of comfort, while there are good business facilities (conference/banqueting for 80/100) and leisure pursuits available both within the hotel and nearby. No dogs. *Rooms 23. Garden, indoor & outdoor swimming pools, tennis, putting, snooker, brasserie (11am-11pm – hours vary in winter). Access, Amex, Visa.*

TORQUAY	Palace Hotel	68%	£120

Tel 01803 200200   Fax 01803 299899   Map 13 D3   **H**
Babbacombe Road Torquay Devon TQ1 3TG

The Palace is set in 25 acres of gardens and woodland stretching to the sea. It opened in 1921 as a hotel offering some of the finest sporting facilities in the land and still admirably provides the active guest with some of the best (golf, swimming, tennis and squash professionals on hand). Music or entertainment is provided nightly, and families are very well catered for. Out of season the hotel is often busy with conferences (handling up to 2000 delegates theatre-style and offering a full range of services). Six large bedroom suites have splendid views, individual decor and good-quality furniture; other rooms are simpler but comfortable with handsome period bathrooms. Children up to three free in parents' room. Parking for 150. No dogs. *Rooms 140. Garden, croquet, indoor & outdoor swimming pools, squash, sauna, hairdressing, indoor & outdoor tennis, 9-hole golf course, snooker, nanny, children's indoor & outdoor play areas, hair salon. Access, Diners, Visa.*

TORQUAY	Table Restaurant	↑	£70

Tel 01803 324292   Map 13 D3   **R**
135 Babbacombe Road Babbacombe Torquay Devon TQ1 3SR

In the Babbacombe suburb to the east of town, this restaurant is quite charming, with sunny yellow decor and a glittering chandelier at the centre of a small room. Working single-handedly in the kitchen, Trevor Brooks produces four or five excellent and original choices at each stage of his fixed-price dinner menus. Fish soup with parmesan and garlic croutons, terrine of foie gras and trotters or goat's cheese polenta with crispy pancetta and truffles are typical first courses; next might come salmon with Cajun spices, braised oxtail with morels or honey-glazed chicken with a yellow split pea and foie gras sauce. For dessert, perhaps tiramisu terrine or spiced orange and walnut sablé with toffee ice cream, then a selection of traditional farmhouse cheeses. Shortish, though good-value wine list is presented by style (ie drier white, lighter/softer red etc). No children under 10 years. No smoking. *Seats 20. D only 7.30-9.30. Closed Sun, Mon, 1st 2 weeks Feb, 1st 2 weeks Sept. Set D £28. Access, Visa.*

TRESCO	Island Hotel	67%	£186*

Tel 01720 422883   Fax 01720 423008   Map 12 A2   **HR**
Tresco Isles of Scilly TR24 0PU

Tresco, England's "Island of Flowers", is privately owned and maintained, its lanes free of traffic. Guests arriving at the quay or heliport are transported by tractor-drawn charabanc to the island's only hotel, set in beautifully tended gardens by the shore. Picture windows make the most of the spectacular location and the panoramic sea views: should the mists close in there's a Terrace Bar (with a wide range of snacks) and a Quiet Room stacked with books, magazines and games. Some bedrooms enjoy sea views, while others overlook the gardens. Special holiday packages for gardeners, bird-watchers and others. *Half-board terms only. No dogs. *Rooms 40. Garden, croquet, bowling green, tennis, outdoor swimming pool, fishing, boat hire and tuition, games room. Closed Nov-end Feb. Access, Amex, Visa.*

Restaurant   £95

There are bar snacks from an extensive menu available lunchtime while in the evening there's an imaginative table d'hote and short carte which places strong emphasis on local seafood (local Tresco lobster, scallops and Bryher crab). There's also Devonshire beef from the grill as well as a cold buffet. Traditional farmhouse cheeses. Luxurious Sunday buffet (£27.50, includes lobster). Plenty of half bottles on a decent, fairly priced wine list, with house champagne under £20. Children under 12 can eat half-price from the carte. No smoking. *Seats 110. Private Room 10. L 12-2.15 D 6.45-9.30. Set D £15/£19.50/£28.*

TROUTBECK   Mortal Man Inn   £100*

Tel 01539 433193   Fax 01539 431261   Map 4 C3   **I**
Troutbeck nr Windermere Cumbria LA23 1PL

The name of the inn is derived from a painting by one Julius Caesar Ibbetson, who died
in 1817, which contains the inscription 'O mortal man that lives by bread...'. An
appropriate motif for this most hospitable inn surrounded by glorious lakeland scenery
and run for more than 20 years by owners Christopher and Annette Poulsom. Join the
regulars in the Village Bar or relax in the residents' bar and sunny lounge overlooking the
Troutbeck Valley. Bedrooms are smart, bathrooms compact and housekeeping
praiseworthy. No children under five. *Half-board terms only. **Rooms** 12. Garden.
Closed mid Nov-mid Feb. No credit cards._

TRURO   Alverton Manor   70%   £99

Tel 01872 76633   Fax 01872 222989   Map 12 B3   **H**
Tregolls Road Truro Cornwall TR1 1XQ

An impressive Victorian Gothic building on the A390 from St Austell. Conferences are an
important part of the hotel's business and one of the rooms was once a chapel (the building
then being a convent). Apart from the restaurant, the only day room is an elegantly
proportioned and comfortable lounge that also incorporates the bar. Excellent, individually
decorated bedrooms are the great strength here with stylish fabrics, good-quality
reproduction antique furniture and extras like sherry and mineral water. Bathrooms, three
with shower and WC only, are equally good, with robes and generous towelling. 24hr
room service. No dogs. **Rooms** 34. Garden, snooker. Access, Amex, Diners, Visa._

TUCKENHAY   Floyd's Inn (Sometimes)   £125

Tel 01803 732350   Fax 01803 732651   Map 13 D3   **IR**
Bow Creek Tuckenhay Totnes Devon TQ9 7EQ

There's an air of laid-back eccentricity about food writer and broadcaster Keith Floyd's
pub-cum-restaurant-with-rooms set alongside a small quay on the heavily wooded, and
very beautiful, Bow Creek. The rusticated bar (on the top floor, which is at road level,
of a building dating back to 1550) consists of several interconnecting rooms and offers
a menu reflecting Keith's current culinary interest. The restaurant is one floor below, and
at quay level there is a dispense bar for alfresco drinkers; there is also a lunchtime
barbecue in summer, weather permitting. The three bedrooms in an adjacent building are
tremendous fun: one room has a strong nautical theme, another, the 'Dukes Room', is
furnished with antiques and with rather masculine decor; and the third, the Khun Akorn
room, has Thai decor and satin sheets. All sorts of extras are thrown in, from
complimentary drinks and chocolate bars in the fridge, to books, fruit and toothpicks.
Bathrooms, two with separate walk-in showers in addition to the tub, have mirrored
walls, Floris toiletries, slippers and towelling robes. Choose between an extensive cooked
breakfast or a Continental version, plus boiled egg, served in your bedroom. Overnight
guests also get to choose a jar or two of home-made preserves to take away as a souvenir.
Rooms 4. Sun bed, sauna, boat, snooker. Access, Amex, Visa._

George's Restaurant   £100

A split-level room with terrace overlooking the creek for pre-dinner drinks, it has just
five tables. The menu is now all à la carte, with specialities that include a splendid lobster
soufflé. Then there is a selection of British (mostly local) cheeses and/or puds like crème
brulee, chocolate tart with cinnamon ice cream, raspberry parfait and sticky toffee
pudding. Sound cooking and unfussy presentation achieve most satisfactory results.
Seats 26. Parties 6. L 12-2 D 7-9. Closed D Sun, all Mon, 25 & 26 Dec._

TUNBRIDGE WELLS   Cheevers   £60

Tel 01892 545524   Fax 01892 535956   Map 11 B5   **R**
56 High Street Tunbridge Wells Kent TN1 1XF

Long-established high-street restaurant where Timothy Cheevers in the kitchen and
Martin Miles front of house keep the customers well fed and happy. From Tuesday
through to Thursday in the evening, and at lunchtime, all starters are £4, all main
courses £9.50 and all desserts £4. The modern British menus change weekly, though

variations from one week to another can be small. Mussel and fennel broth, fettuccine with wild mushrooms and terrine of pork and calf's liver are typical starters, while main courses could include fillet of salmon poached with saffron, confit of duck with Puy lentils and gammon, and milk-fed lamb grilled with celeriac and aubergine. The £25 dinner menu (Fri & Sat) includes crudités and coffe or tea with sweetmeats. A pleasing, diverse and manageable wine list has only a few bottles over £20. *Seats 32. Parties 16. L 12.30-2 (Sat to 1.45) D 7.30-10.30. Closed Sun & Mon, 1 week Christmas, Bank Holidays. Set D Fri & Sat £25. Access, Amex, Visa.*

TUNBRIDGE WELLS	Downstairs at Thackeray's	£45

Tel 01892 537559 Fax 01892 571921   Map 11 B5   **R**
85 London Road Tunbridge Wells Kent TN1 1EA

Downstairs from *Thackeray's House* (qv), with its own separate courtyard entrance, this delightful little place with cosy, close-set tables and fresh flowers has the friendly, relaxed feel of a bistro, still of course under the watchful eye of Bruce Wass, though with Peter Lucas in the kitchen. Dishes like preserved duck salad, creamy fish soup and haggis with neeps 'n' tatties are in a section of the menu headed 'starters or light meals'. More robust main courses include such dishes as oxtail in red wine with butter, Scottish rib steak with shallots and grilled venison sausages with onion gravy. Delicious desserts like steamed marmalade pudding, warm pear and almond tart and an orange burnt cream round off the meal, and there's a good selection of farmhouse cheeses. Best to book.
Seats 30. Parties 20. Private Room 30. L 12.30-2.30 D 7-10. Closed Sun, Mon & 5 days Christmas. Set L £7.50/£9.75 Set D £7.50/£10.50. Access, Visa.

TUNBRIDGE WELLS	Royal Wells Inn	64%	£80

Tel 01892 511188 Fax 01892 511908   Map 11 B5   **H**
Mount Ephraim Tunbridge Wells Kent TN4 8BE

The royal coat of arms atop the family-run Royal Wells is a proud memento of the days when, during her childhood, Queen Victoria used to stay here. Inside, there's a stylish reception/lounge with columns as well as a light and attractive bar area. Best bedrooms are on the top floor – these have brass beds, pine furniture, Laura Ashley fabrics and up-to-date, tiled bathrooms; two rooms have four-posters. The hotel bus is a delightful 1909 Commer, once owned by the founder of the AA, Lord Lonsdale. Conference and banquet facilities for up to 100. *Rooms 19. Closed 25 & 26 Dec. Access, Amex, Diners, Visa.*

TUNBRIDGE WELLS	Spa Hotel	72%	£101

Tel 01892 520331 Fax 01892 510575   Map 11 B5   **HR**
Mount Ephraim Tunbridge Wells Kent TN4 8XJ

The Spa was built in 1766 as a country mansion for Sir George Kelly and remained a private home for its first century. It became a hotel in 1880 and has been in the same family ever since. Sister hotel to *The Goring* in London, it stands in 15 acres of gardens and parkland that include two lakes. The foyer opens on to a spacious lounge with Corinthian columns, darkwood panelling and a gas log fire at each end; half is reserved for non-smokers. The Equestrian Bar is a favourite place for a drink or bar food. Bedrooms vary in size and decor, but all feature freestanding furniture. De luxe rooms have king-sized beds and tend to be larger, with views across the gardens. Although conferences (for up to 300) form most of the weekday business, there is an atmosphere of a moderately grand hotel run along traditional lines, with excellent leisure facilities. Children up to 14 free in parents' room. *Rooms 76. Garden, croquet, indoor swimming pool, gym, sauna, spa bath, solarium, beauty & hair salon, tennis, children's adventure playground. Access, Amex, Diners, Visa.*

Chandelier Restaurant   £60

In the large, high-ceilinged Regency dining-room, good-quality produce is best enjoyed in the simpler dishes. Lunchtime roasts are carved and served formally from a trolley. There's a weekly list of 'old traditionals' lunch menus such as Tuesday's meal of vegetable soup, roast leg of lamb with onion sauce or fish and egg pie, with steamed golden syrup pudding to finish – just the sort of food to keep the climate at bay! Separate vegetarian section and à la carte menu. The evening table d'hote is priced according to the main course. *Seats 80. L 12.30-2 D 7-9.30. Closed L Sat. Set L £10/£17.50. Set D from £14.*

TUNBRIDGE WELLS   Thackeray's House   ★   £90

Tel 01892 511921   Map 11 B5   **R**
85 London Road Tunbridge Wells Kent TN11 1EA

Chef-patron Bruce Wass presides at this pretty restaurant facing the common, in a house where William Makepeace Thackeray once lived. There's a bar upstairs and one area of the restaurant is sufficiently detached to allow for private dinner parties of up to 24 people. Cooking is in contemporary, Anglo-French rustic mode. Hot chicken liver cake with bacon and chive sauce; tagliatelle with mussels, tomato and basil, roast monkfish with saffron, tomato and tarragon; saddle of hare with apples and green peppercorns; guinea fowl with morels; hot apple tart with calvados sauce and prune and armagnac ice cream are typical. There is an à la carte in addition to the set menu. A good variety of British and Irish cheeses is served. There's a super half-bottle selection on an enterprising list which includes a couple of dozen house wines. Italy is particularly well represented. *Seats 50. Private Room 24. L 12.30-2.30 D 7-10. Closed D Sun, all Mon, 5 days Christmas. Set L £10/£14.75 (Sun £15.50/£18.50) Set D £18.50/£22.50 (Tue-Thurs) & £42. Access, Visa.*

TURNERS HILL   Alexander House   79%   £150

Tel 01342 714914   Fax 01342 717328   Map 11 B5   **HR**
East Street Turners Hill West Sussex RH10 4QD

An imposing country mansion set in 135 acres on the B2110 between Turners Hill and East Grinstead. Distinguished buildings have occupied the site since the 14th century and the oldest part of the present house dates from the early 17th century. Numerous grand day rooms feature many high-quality antiques, paintings (including *A Jamaica Bay* by Noel Coward) and other decorative features like the painted silk chinoiserie panels in the main salon and a pair of ornate French ormolu lamps in the foyer. Many bedrooms have traditional yew furniture and boast original paintings plus many little extras like fresh flowers, fruit and magazines. Smart, friendly staff. No children under 7. No dogs. Handy for Gatwick (9 miles). *Rooms 15. Garden, croquet, putting, keep-fit equipment, tennis, sun beds, beauty salon, snooker, limousine service, valeting. Access, Amex, Diners, Visa.*

Restaurant   £120

Formal service (senior waiters wear tail-coats) tends towards the deferential but does not seem inappropriate in the elegant dining-room with its striking burnt-orange walls and pine dado panelling with ornate, carved coving above. Everything is of the highest quality, from the glass and silverware to the Royal Worcester china, and first-rate raw materials used in the kitchen by chef Timothy Kelsey. Their own oxygenated fresh and sea-water tanks ensure particularly fresh seafood which is used to good effect in dishes such as lobster bisque, a classic lobster thermidor, baked fillet of brill with a crab crust, and *brochette de fruits de mer*. Other dishes from a kitchen that is equally strong in all departments might include paté of duck and quail with redcurrant and onion chutney, deep-fried egg on seasonal leaves with bacon, marinated medallions of venison with a filo parcel of caramelised shallots, fillet of beef with either béarnaise sauce or foie gras ravioli and wild mushrooms, and grilled duck breast with rösti potatoes and caramelised pears. Puds included, on our last visit, a particularly delicious spiced apple compote served in a calvados-soaked brioche with marzipan ice cream. Opting for the fixed-price menu (the only choice for Sunday lunch) helps to keep the bill down but still offers a choice of about five main dishes. Alongside the standard wine list there are limited stocks of fine wines at hefty prices. Good half-bottle selection. No smoking. *Seats 55. Parties 12. Private Room 16. L 12.30-2 D 7-9.30 (Sun to 9). Set L £16.75/£18.75 (Sun £18.95) Set D £24.95.*

TUTBURY   Ye Olde Dog & Partridge   £73

Tel 01283 813030   Fax 01283 813178   Map 6 C3   **H**
High Street Tutbury nr Burton-on-Trent Staffordshire DE13 9LS

In the middle of the main village street, the inn has kept much of its 15th-century character, and its half-timbered frontage with diamond-leaded windows is a pretty subject for a picture postcard. Its history includes a spell as an important overnight stop on the London-Liverpool coaching route. Inside, the welcome is warm: there are two traditional bars and a restaurant where a busy buffet and carvery operate and a pianist plays nightly.

The oldest accommodation, with creaking floors and oak panelling, is the three rooms in the original buildings, while the rest are in an adjacent Georgian house with a central spiral staircase. Four-poster and half-tester rooms are available. *Rooms 17. Garden. Closed 25 Dec, 1 Jan. Access, Amex, Visa.*

TWICKENHAM	Hamiltons	£50

Tel 0181-892 3949   Map 15 E2   **R**
43 Crown Road St Margarets Twickenham Middlesex TW1 3EJ

The approach to Hamiltons is heralded by its distinctive red and gold exterior and stained-glass windows, though once it has drawn you in, you are relaxed by the calmer, welcoming apricot/cream shades. David Poole, here for almost ten years, cooks an Anglo-French menu: smoked goose breast with a red onion and sage marmalade, garlicky grilled mussels, roast baby chicken with a mushroom and lemon stuffing, trout with parsley and spring onion butter and steak and mushroom pie with a puff pastry lid. Live jazz during family Sunday lunchtimes, when roasts are the centrepiece. *Seats 48. Parties 16. Private Room 8. L 12-2.30 (Sun to 3.30) D 7-10.30. Closed L Sat, D Sun, all Mon, 1-10 Jan. Set L £11.95 (Sun £15.95, children £8.95). Access, Amex, Visa.*

TWICKENHAM	McClements	£50

Tel 0181-744 9610   Fax 0181-890 1372   Map 15 E2   **R**
2 Whitton Road Twickenham Middlesex TW1 1BJ

John McClements' newly revamped restaurant is a cosy, friendly little place just down the road from his original restaurant (now sold). The menu changes daily according to the market but the emphasis is on seafood plus game in season and there is usually an offal dish or two. A typical evening's menu might comprise a croute of red mullet with aïoli, a velouté of oysters with foie gras and guinea fowl with charlotte parmentier for starters while mains might be scallops with a fennel and garlic butter sauce, lobster salad, roast fillet of turbot with lobster garnish and saddle of venison with a confit of chestnuts and onions on a bed of cabbage. To follow there's always a hot soufflé of some kind as well as a cold dessert. Whatever the choice the execution is superb with great care taken to ensure the correct balance of flavours and textures. Staff provide the kind of friendly service you'd expect from such a charming little restaurant. *Seats 45. L 12-2.30 D 7-11. Closed 1 week Easter & 10 days summer. Set L £10/£12 (not always available) Set L & D £16/£18. Access, Visa.*

UCKFIELD	Horsted Place Hotel	79%	£136

Tel 01825 750581   Fax 01825 750459   Map 11 B6   **HR**
Little Horsted Uckfield East Sussex TN22 5TS

Off the A26 to the south of Uckfield, Horsted Place is a fine example of high-Victorian architecture with its distinctive chequered brickwork, splendidly exuberant Pugin staircase and grounds laid out by Geoffrey Jellicoe. Day rooms, which are off an elegant central hall running the length of the house, include a library and large lounge, boasting two real fires in winter. Individually decorated in some style, bedrooms vary somewhat in size but all are furnished with good reproduction antiques and offer all sorts of comforts from books and magazines to fruit and mineral water. Guests have access to the adjacent East Sussex National golf course (under the same ownership as the hotel) and Glyndebourne is but a few minutes down the road. Conference/banqueting facilities in the Horsted Management Centre for 100/80. No children under 8. No dogs. *Rooms 17. Garden, croquet, tennis, golf (18), fishing, indoor swimming pool, reflexology & holistic massage. Access, Amex, Diners, Visa.*

See over

Pugin Dining Room   £95

Designed by the eponymous architect (also responsible for the Houses of Parliament) in
one of his more restrained moments, this luxuriously appointed dining-room is an
appropriate setting for Allan Garth's sensibly short menu of dishes that are a well-judged
balance between interest, lack of complication and modern trends. Home-smoked food
(salmon in particular) is a speciality, and other choices run from cauliflower and turmeric
soup and ballotine of foie gras to pan-fried scallops with artichokes and tomatoes, roasted
guinea fowl filled with halloumi cheese and tarragon on a green peppercorn sauce, and
medallions of venison with noodles and bacon. Vegetarian options, splendid desserts and
British farmhouse cheeses. A good all-round wine list, but for a hotel of this class it still
contains too many spelling mistakes! Outdoor seating for 20 on a terrace. **Seats** 40.
Parties 12. Private Rooms 6/26. L 12-2 D 7.30-9.30. Set L £10/£14.95 Set D £28.50.

ULLSWATER	Leeming House	75%	£142

Tel 01768 486622   Fax 01768 486443   Map 4 C3   **HR**
Watermillock Ullswater nr Penrith Cumbria CA11 0JJ

Surrounded by 20 acres of beautifully
landscaped gardens on the northern
shore of Ullswater, Leeming House
dates from the early 1800s and was
converted into a hotel in 1969. Public
rooms lead off a long, pillared entrance
hall and, in keeping with the character
of the building, are classically traditional
in decor and furnishings. The library,
with book-filled shelves, and the
adjoining sitting and drawing rooms
have comfortable, deep-cushioned
settees and armchairs arranged in well-
spaced groupings. The bar is dark and
clubby with wood-panelled walls. The drawing room and a wide, tiled conservatory
which connects a wing of newer bedrooms have good views over the gently sloping
grounds, with glimpses of the lake through a fine collection of trees. Feature rooms with
balcony views carry a small supplement; eleven rooms are reserved for non-smokers.
Possessing a tasteful floral decor with smart darkwood furniture they are all elegantly
furnished and comprehensively equipped (including one for disabled guests).
Bathrooms have lovely old-fashioned fittings as well as good toiletries and bathrobes.
Forte. **Rooms** 40. *Garden, croquet, fishing. Access, Amex, Diners, Visa.*

Restaurant   £80

A long, beautifully proportioned dining-room with fine south-facing views over the
grounds to the lake. Familiar classics share the menus with slightly more unusual dishes
such as sea bass with scallops, lemon and chili sauce, salmon with beetroot butter sauce
with leeks, grapes and ginger, or breast of guinea fowl with cranberry and port coulis and
chestnut and sage stuffing. The choice for dinner is three or six courses while lunchtime
is à la carte. Sunday lunch (£16.75) sees traditional roast sirloin of Angus beef served
with light Yorkshire pudding and creamed shiitake mushrooms. The wine list is rather
modest for a hotel of this class. Friendly service. No smoking. No very young children in
the evening. **Seats** 80. *Parties 10. Private Room 30. L 12.30-1.45 D 7.30-8.45.
Set Sun L £16.75 Set D £28.50/£35.50.*

ULLSWATER	Old Church Hotel	67%	£120

Tel 01768 486204   Fax 01768 486368   Map 4 C3   **HR**
Watermillock Ullswater Cumbria CA11 0JN

Kevin and Maureen Whitemore provide a warm welcome for guests at their pleasant
lakeside hotel, which was built in 1754 on the site of a 12th-century church. Both
lounges are built for relaxation and are packed with board games and periodicals.
Maureen's bold colour schemes brighten the bedrooms (priced according to the view),
with crown canopies and half-testers framing really comfortable beds. Excellent breakfasts.
No dogs. **Rooms** 10. *Garden. Closed Nov-Mar. No credit cards.*

Restaurant   £60

The smaller lounge doubles as an aperitif bar where guests gather prior to dinner (availability is limited for outside diners and booking is essential). Kevin's menu offers a short, straightforward selection, with rack of Lakeland lamb a speciality. Goat's cheese salad with a walnut dressing, duck or chicken liver paté with Cumberland sauce and home-made oatcakes, salmon with hollandaise and stir-fried chicken supreme with ginger, soy and bean sprouts are other favourites. Several good bottles under £20 on the short wine list that includes alcoholic content as part of the tasting notes. No smoking. *Seats 24. Parties 6. D only 7.30-8.30 (order by 7). Closed Sun. Set D £23.50.*

ULLSWATER	Rampsbeck Country House Hotel	65%	£80

Tel 01768 486442   Fax 01768 486688   Map 4 C3   **HR**
Watermillock Ullswater Cumbria CA11 0LP

An 18th-century country house with 18 acres of gardens and grounds and marvellous views from its setting on Ullswater. Tom and Marion Gibb generate a warm air of hospitality that resides in the lounge, with its grandfather clocks, log fire and flowers, and the bar, which gives on to the patio and garden. All the spick-and-span bedrooms enjoy lake or garden views, and there's a small supplement for rooms with a private balcony overlooking the lake. No children under 5. ***Rooms 21. Garden, croquet. Closed Jan-mid Feb. Access, Visa.***

Restaurant   £55

Andrew McGeorge puts the pick of local produce to fine use in his updated classic cooking. Warm squat lobster mousse served with tomato and basil dressing, ratatouille tart topped with pan-fried; roast loin of Cumbrian venison with a timbale of air-dried ham filled with creamed celeriac; Baileys délice served with caramelised brioche, whisky sabayon and chocolate sorbet show a style which is at once imaginative and disciplined. The main and very fairly priced wine list with tasting notes is presented by style, though helpfully there is an abbreviated country of origin list to cross reference. No smoking in the restaurant. There's also a light and interesting bar lunch menu, and cream teas are served in the lounge. *Seats 40. Parties 12. Private Room 15. L 12-1.15 D 7-8.30. Set L £22 Set D £26 & £34.*

ULLSWATER	Sharrow Bay	82%	£260*

Tel 01768 486301   Fax 01768 486349   Map 4 C3   **HR**
Howtown Ullswater Cumbria CA10 2LZ

Among the first, and still one of the best, country house hotels, Francis Coulson's and Brian Sack's Sharrow Bay enjoys an idyllic location nestling beneath Barton Fell on the very edge of Lake Ullswater. The main lounge, with picture windows to take full advantage of the stunning view, second lounge and Victorian-style conservatory all boast deep-cushioned settees and armchairs, fresh flowers, fine ornaments and paintings that all contribute to the air of gracious living. There is no bar as such but drinks are served in the lounges, which can sometimes get a little crowded in the evening when there are non-resident diners in addition to a full-house of residents. Eleven bedrooms are in the main house (a couple of these have bathrooms which, though private, are not en suite), a further seven are in two separate buildings (Lodge Gatehouse and Garden Cottage) within a few hundred yards of the main building, and seven more are in Bank House about a mile away. The last have their own characterful Refectory breakfast room but dinner is taken in the main-house restaurant so, to quote the hotel's own literature, "It is essential that clients have their own cars". Finally, about four miles away, there is Thwaite Cottage, a suite with bedroom, dressing room, lounge and sun room. There is no room service offered at the cottage but beverage-making kit is provided. Wherever they are, every bedroom is furnished to the highest standards of comfort and luxury with fine antiques, embroidered linen sheets, porcelain ornaments, rich fabrics, plants, books and every little extra comfort imaginable. Most bedrooms have

See over

sitting areas and bathrooms boast exquisite toiletries and thick, cosseting towels. Breakfasts are as much of an institution here as their famed afternoon teas: newly-baked croissants, brioches, freshly-squeezed orange juice and a cooked breakfast sans pareil. Staff, many of whom have been here for many years, are dedicated to ensuring that every guest is thoroughly cosseted and the hotel kept in absolutely gleaming, ship-shape order. Room service till 10.30pm. No children under 13. ★Half-board terms. *Rooms 28. Garden. Closed end Nov-end Feb. No credit cards.*

Restaurant   ⭐   £100

The maxim 'Cooking is Art and all Art is Patience' is printed at the top of the menu – and haste is not something that immediately springs to mind when seated in either of the two delightful dining-rooms. The lakeside dining-room has splendid views over the water, while next door in the Victorian panelled studio dining-room there is a genteel ambience and tables are spaciously arranged. Orders are taken in one of the lounges and as you go in for dinner you pass a sample tray of that mealtime's desserts (and have them described as you go). The fixed-price, six-course menus (five at lunchtime when there is no cheese) offers a wide choice of starters such as duck foie gras served with spinach on toasted brioche with citrus fruits and an orange Curaçao sauce and ravioli of lobster mousseline in lemon pasta with a julienne of fried vegetables and lobster sauce. Next comes a fish dish, perhaps halibut fillet with marinière sauce and a soufflé suissesse, then a sorbet. Lots of choice again for the main event: grilled sea bass with confit of tomato and a caper, onion and parsley sauce; local venison with noodles, chestnuts and a gravy made from the juices with juniper berries and brandy; breast of chicken cooked with white wine, wild mushrooms and cream and served with a 'solferino' of vegetables and pilaff rice. The preparation of dishes is essentially simple, but made more complex by elaborate accompanying garnishes. As if these were not enough, vegetables are plentiful, perhaps including young carrots, baby leeks, broccoli and sweetcorn plus two different potatoes. Follow that, if you can, with a choice of up to a dozen desserts before a selection of Great British Cheeses. From the wonderful range of home-baked breads to the delightful petits fours, eating here is an experience to be savoured. Super wine lists (there are two, the second devoted to 'before and after') offer you a terrific selection from around the world at quite fair prices. Many wines are available by the glass, and there are two pages of bin ends. No smoking. No children under 13. *Seats 65. Parties 10. L 1-1.45 D 8-8.45. Set L £25/£30.75 Set D £40.75.* 🐂

ULVERSTON   Bay Horse Inn   £65

Tel 01229 583972   Fax 01229 580502   Map 4 C4   **RR**
Canal Foot Ulverston Cumbria LA12 9EL

A mile and a half from Ulverston, follow the signs for Canal Foot to find this old pub with a sympathetic conversion that includes an intimate conservatory restaurant with picturesque views over the Leven estuary. Chef Robert Lyons presents a short but alluring modern English menu based wherever possible on local produce and inspired in no small measure by co-owner John Tovey. Potato, onion and parsley soup or mussels with wine and cream under a puff pastry topping could get your meal started, followed perhaps by fillets of turbot filled with mushrooms, prawns and water chestnuts served with a Noilly Prat and chive cream sauce, or pan-fried calf's liver with garlic, shallots and smoked bacon. A popular, plainer alternative main course is an Aberdeen Angus steak, hung for at least four weeks in the cold room, grilled and served with a baked potato and salad. Put the seal on your meal with a dark and white chocolate slice, or banana, apple and butterscotch farmhouse pie, then coffee with home-made truffles. It's a New World paradise here with some 60 bottles on the list, all fairly priced with most under £20, many under £15. In fact, apart from champagne, there's not a single bottle over £30, which goes to show that enterprise and imagination do not necessarily cost! There's also a bar menu. No children under 12. No smoking. *Seats 50. Private Room 30. L 12.30 D 7.30 for 8. Closed L Sun & Mon, Jan. Set L £14.50. Access, Visa.*

Rooms   £150*

Overnight accommodation is provided in seven attractive en-suite bedrooms, five of which open on to a small terrace with a view of the estuary. No children under 12. *Half-board terms – 10% added "in lieu of staff gratuities".

UPPER SLAUGHTER   Lords of the Manor   75%   £115

Tel 01451 820243   Fax 01451 820696   Map 14 C1   **HR**
Upper Slaughter nr Bourton-on-the-Water Gloucestershire GL54 2JD

The original part of the house dates from the mid-17th century, though much has been added since, mostly in Victorian times. Both the hotel and setting (eight acres of parkland and a lake) are quintessentially English, as are the furnishings both in the lounges with their open fireplaces and Oriental rugs, and in the individually decorated bedrooms: lots of chintzy fabrics, genuine antiques, and family portraits. On arrival you'll be greeted by a welcoming decanter of sherry, a bowl of fruit, and mineral water, while in the bathroom you'll find decent-sized bathrobes and quality toiletries. Room rates vary – the price quoted is for a standard room, add £75 for a four-poster; mid-week and weekend breaks are offered inclusive of dinner, though not available at peak times, which include Cheltenham Gold Cup week. No dogs. *Rooms 27. Garden, croquet, fishing. Closed 2-11 Jan. Access, Amex, Diners, Visa.*

Restaurant   £90

The dining-room looks out on to the walled garden, where the terrace is used for drinks or coffee (or even a meal) when the weather allows. Chef Robert-Clive Dixon's appealing menus surprise and delight with ideas like terrine of salmon and brill layered with herbs and shallots served with a Caesar salad or a classic fish soup with rouille to start, followed by turbot cooked on savoy cabbage, ham hock, salami, potato and garlic or Trelough duckling on a spicy pearl barley risotto with home-made chutney. There's a short set lunch menu during the week (perhaps a salade paysanne, fillet of cod Mediterranean style, glazed rice pudding with poached fruits) and more familiar dishes such as roast Aberdeenshire beef with Yorkshire pudding and warm treacle tart with vanilla ice cream appear for Sunday lunch. Decent-size portions, good breads and excellent coffee, together with polished service under the watchful eye of general manager Richard Young ensure satisfaction here. A marvellous wine list has many quality wines by the glass and excellent house recommendations, all with tasting notes. There's a comprehensive selection throughout, particularly in the New World section, which is presented by grape style. No smoking. *Seats 65. Parties 10. Private Room 60. L 12.30-2 (Sun to 2.30) D 7.30 (Fri & Sat from 7)-9.30. Set L £14.95/£17.95 (Sun £15.50/£19.50) Set D £27.50/£33.50.*

UPPINGHAM   The Lake Isle   £65

Tel 01572 822951   Fax 01572 822951   Map 7 E4   **RR**
16 High Street East Uppingham Leicestershire LE15 9PZ

Just off the town centre, David and Claire Whitfield's charming, informal restaurant is in an 18th-century property reached by way of flower-decked Reeves Yard. Chef David gathers the ingredients for his short multi-course menus from near and far with twice-weekly deliveries from the Paris Rungis market, fish from Grimsby and Cornwall, plus herbs from his own walled garden. A sure touch is evident in dishes like an individual croustade of venison and juniper, timbale of sole and spinach with a white wine and vermouth sauce, gigot of lamb with minted rosemary hollandaise and savoury carrot cakes with a sweet Martini sauce. 'Healthy food choices' asterisked on the lunchtime menu might include a bowl of seasonal home-made soup, salmon and smoked salmon fishcakes with a tomato and basil sauce and breast of chicken with a sauce of red wine and juniper. A fine choice of British cheeses is served with walnut bread and a bowl of nuts. The splendid and well-chosen wine list has fair prices and probably the best half-bottle selection in the country; the New World is treated with respect. *Seats 40. Parties 24. Private Room 10. L 12.30-1.45 (Sun 12-2) D 7.30-9.30 (Sat 7-10). Closed L Mon & D Sun except to residents. Set L £10.50/£13.50 (Sun £13.50/£15) Set D £21/£24. Access, Amex, Diners, Visa.*

Rooms   £66

The twelve bedrooms vary in size and style and are named after French wine regions (Dom Perignon is large and has a whirlpool bath). All have direct dial phones, colour TVs and thoughtful extras like fruit, mineral water and a decanter of sherry. Two double-bedded Cottage Suites are also available, one of which is self-contained and suitable for long stays. Good breakfasts in the restaurant or Continental served in the room.

VENTNOR — Royal Hotel — 60% — £66

Tel 01983 852186   Fax 01983 855395   Map 15 D4   **H**
Belgrave Road Ventnor Isle of Wight PO38 1JJ

Neat gardens front a Victorian sandstone hotel. Bedrooms are well-maintained.
Small banquets/conferences for up to 80. *Rooms 54. Garden, outdoor swimming pool,
games room. Access, Amex, Diners, Visa.*

VERYAN — Nare Hotel — 70% — £160

Tel 01872 501279   Fax 01872 501856   Map 12 B3   **HR**
Carne Beach Veryan nr Truro Cornwall TR2 5PF

Standing above the mile-long sandy Carne Beach, the Nare has been transformed from
a simple seaside hotel to a model of good taste and a haven of tranquillity. Lounges and
drawing room face extensive patios and garden and have country house appeal with
antique furniture. The very best of the bedrooms have easy chairs and sofas, with
beautiful views out to sea and over the hotel lawns from picture windows and balconies.
Expect fruit and flowers on arrival and join fellow guests for complimentary afternoon
tea. A drying/boot room is very useful for walkers. Concessionary vouchers are given to
guests who wish to play golf at Truro Golf Club 12 miles away. *Rooms 35. Garden,
indoor & outdoor swimming pool, spa bath, sauna, sun beds, tennis, gym, snooker, riding,
boating. Closed 6 weeks Jan-mid Feb. Access, Visa.*

Restaurant £70

Pleasingly located in a modern extension that allows windows on three sides to make the
most of the sea views, the hotel's comfortably furnished and well-appointed restaurant has
a somewhat sedate atmosphere; however, well-trained staff (and a high staff/diner ratio)
and careful attention to detail ensure that the generous, traditional food is clearly enjoyed
by their loyal patrons and is right in every detail. Specialities, including hors d'oeuvre,
abound on trolleys; excellent roast beef is carved to your liking from a mobile heated
carvery and served with featherlight Yorkshire pudding and roast onions. An old-
fashioned dessert trolley is laden with predictably irresistible temptations and followed by
a terrific cheese trolley (featuring a veritable sea of little flags and, of course, the port).
Flambé dishes are also popular, attracting a supplement on the table d'hote dinner menu.
It may be fashionable to call this kind of operation out-of-date, but when it's done well
– as it is here – it inspires a special kind of respect. A children's menu (£10.50) is
available in the Gwendra from 5.30 to 6.15. "Little ones are not expected in the
restaurant in the evenings." Jacket and tie preferred in the evening. Minimum à la carte
charge £29 per person. *Seats 70. Parties 12. Private Room 20. L 12.30-2 D 7.15-9.30.
Set L (Sun) £14.50 Set D (5-course) £26.*

WAKEFIELD — Cedar Court — 59% — £92

Tel 01924 276310   Fax 01924 280221   Map 6 C1   **H**
Denby Dale Road Calder Grove Wakefield West Yorkshire WF4 3QZ

Modern, purpose-built business hotel on the roundabout at Junction 39 of the M1,
12 miles south of Leeds. Open-plan day rooms, practical accommodation including
several suites and a dozen Executive rooms; satellite TVs throughout; phone extensions in
bathrooms; some whirlpool baths. Half the bedrooms are designated no-smoking.
Conference/banqueting facilities up to 400. Free parking for up to 350 cars.
Keep-fit equipment was due to be installed as we went to press. *Rooms 150. Garden.
Access, Amex, Diners, Visa.*

WAKEFIELD — Forte Posthouse — 64% — £72

Tel 01924 276388   Fax 01924 276437   Map 6 C1   **H**
Queen's Drive Ossett Wakefield West Yorkshire WF5 9BE

Easily visible from (and very close to) Junction 40 of the M1, this purpose-built modern
hotel caters for business custom – extensive lounge, conference, banqueting and parking
facilities. Some rooms are suitable for family occupation. Refurbishment of the public
areas and upgrading of TVs was ongoing during 1995. *Rooms 99. Garden. Access, Amex,
Diners, Visa.*

WAKEFIELD   Swallow Hotel   58%   £89

Tel 01924 372111   Fax 01924 383648   Map 6 C1   **H**
Queen Street Wakefield West Yorkshire WF1 1JU

A tall hotel, with splendid views from bedrooms on the upper floors, near the Cathedral in the city centre. Public rooms are on the first and second floors. The largest of several conference rooms can take up to 200 delegates. Parking for 40 cars. Guests have free membership of a local fitness centre and a snooker club. *Rooms 64. Access, Amex, Diners, Visa.*

WALBERTON   Stakis Avisford Park Hotel   66%   £111

Tel 01243 551215   Fax 01243 552485   Map 11 A6   **H**
Yapton Lane nr Arundel Walberton West Sussex BN18 0L5

At heart a Georgian house, now much extended, set in 62 acres of grounds near Arundel. The new prefix to the name indicates a change of ownership since our last edition and plans are afoot for major refurbishment of bedrooms in the main part of the building, although the mostly spacious rooms are in any event in good order, if a little dated. Bedrooms in the fairly new Garden Lodge business centre/annexe, reached by a long enclosed walkway, are already modern and comfortable, with smart bathrooms. The main public area is a large split-level bar/lounge, amply furnished with blue velour armchairs, that opens on to a terrace overlooking the golf course. Conferences (up to 350 theatre-style) are the main business during the week, with weddings and other functions at weekends. Room service can provide hot meals 24hrs a day. Children up to 16 stay free in parents' room. On the cards are a gym and golf course (due late 95 and mid-96). *Rooms 127. Garden, croquet, golf (9), tennis, indoor swimming pool, solarium, sauna, squash, snooker. Access, Amex, Diners, Visa.*

WALKINGTON   Manor House   72%   £97

Tel 01482 881645   Fax 01482 866501   Map 7 E1   **HR**
Northlands Walkington Beverley Humberside HU17 8RT

In a wonderfully peaceful location surrounded by the Yorkshire Wolds, three minutes from Beverley on the B1230, stands this late-Victorian house run by Derek and Lee Baugh along the lines of a private house with family guests. The bedrooms, all with king-size beds, offer fine country views and are decorated in soft tones. Comfortable seating, flowers, magazines and ornaments add to the homely appeal. Bathrooms squeeze with difficulty into 19th-century rooms, but are well equipped. Day rooms include an elegant drawing room with fine antiques, oil paintings and seating made for relaxation. Friendly staff and notably good housekeeping. *Rooms 7. Garden. Access, Visa.*

Restaurant   £75

An elegant blue dining-room and adjoining conservatory provide a choice of environments in which to enjoy Derek Baugh's cooking. Fixed-price-only menus are described in refreshingly straightforward English and the style gives classical dishes modern elaboration: nine Bridlington queenies in the half-shell cooked in different flavours and sauces; terrine of rabbit and hare with port jelly; supremes of poussin, pigeon and quail with apple bubble and squeak; roasted salmon with peppercorns and red wine butter; plus one vegetarian option. Coffee is served with chocolate truffles. Simpler lunches and a good-value nightly table d'hote. Limited choice of half bottles on a decent list that leans towards France. Around £20, look to the New World. *Seats 60. Parties 24. Private Room 24. D only 7.30-9.15. Closed Sun. Set D from £15/£27.50.*

WALLINGFORD   George Hotel   60%   £72

Tel 01491 836665   Fax 01491 825359   Map 15 D2   **H**
High Street Wallingford Oxfordshire OX10 0BS

Dick Turpin took rooms at this historic coaching inn and during the Civil War Royalist troops were billeted here. Now, in a less turbulent phase, the George mixes tradition with basic modern hotel amenity. Nine of the bedrooms are reserved for non-smokers. A self-contained suite can accommodate up to 120 conference delegates. Children up to 12 stay free in parents' room. Free use of the Wave leisure centre at Didcot, 6 miles away. Thistle & Mount Charlotte. *Rooms 39. Access, Amex, Diners, Visa.*

WALLINGFORD   Shillingford Bridge Hotel   61%   £95

Tel 01865 858567   Fax 01865 858636   Map 15 D2   **H**
Ferry Road Shillingford nr Wallingford Oxfordshire OX10 8LX

The Thamesside location has been well utilised, with smart public rooms overlooking
a wide, slow-flowing stretch of the river as it passes under Shillingford Bridge. Bedrooms
have a generally pretty, floral decor. Three have four-posters and virtually all have good
views over the river. Large sliding patio windows are an appealing feature of a few
spacious bedrooms in a separate house. All bathrooms have large size bottles of family
shampoo and bath foam and come ready occupied by a family of ducks – the yellow
plastic species. *Rooms 42. Garden, outdoor swimming pool, squash, coarse fishing, mooring.
Access, Amex, Diners, Visa.*

WALSALL   Boundary Hotel   61%   £74

Tel 01922 33555   Fax 01922 612034   Map 6 C4   **H**
Birmingham Road Walsall West Midlands WS5 3AB

A Forte hotel reached by taking Junction 7 of the M6, then the A34 to the ring road
intersection. It's a modern purpose-built hotel offering facilities for small banquets (25)
and conferences (45). Half the bedrooms are designated non-smoking. *Rooms 98. Access,
Amex, Diners, Visa.*

WALSALL   Friendly Hotel   60%   £85

Tel 01922 724444   Fax 01922 723148   Map 6 C4   **H**
20 Wolverhampton Rd West Bentley Walsall West Midlands WS2 0BS

By Junction 10 of the M6, this was one of Friendly Hotel's first purpose-built units: low-
rise, open-plan public areas, small leisure centre, practical standardised bedrooms and 12
suites with small lounges and personal fax machines. Children under 12 can stay free in
parents' room. One room is equipped for disabled guests. Meeting rooms for up to 180.
*Rooms 153. Garden, indoor swimming pool, gym, sauna, spa bath, sun beds. Access, Amex,
Diners, Visa.*

WALSALL WOOD   Baron's Court Hotel   62%   £74

Tel 01543 452020   Fax 01543 361276   Map 6 C4   **H**
Walsall Wood Walsall West Midlands WS9 9AH

Tudor-inspired styling and fittings feature throughout the ground-floor areas of this
unusual hotel on the A461. Bedrooms employ Queen Anne-style furniture and soft
decor. Thorough refurbishment of the hotel has included the creation of two new suites.
Executive rooms are larger, with whirlpool baths. Banquets/conferences for up to 200.
*Rooms 94. Indoor swimming pool, keep-fit equipment, sauna, spa bath, steam room,
solarium. Access, Amex, Diners, Visa.*

WALTHAM ABBEY   Swallow Hotel   66%   £115

Tel 01992 717170   Fax 01992 711841   Map 15 F2   **H**
Old Shire Lane Waltham Abbey Essex EN9 3LX

Just north of Junction 26 of the M25, this is one of Swallow's newest hotels. Public
rooms and bedrooms radiate from an impressive lobby bar and lounge area which is
dominated by a huge, glittering, funnel-shaped fountain. Neat, well-equipped bedrooms
offer 24hr room service. Children up to 14 stay free in parents' room. Free parking for
220 cars. *Rooms 163. Garden, croquet, indoor swimming pool, children's splash pool, mini-
gym, sauna, spa bath, steam room, solarium, courtesy mini-bus. Access, Amex, Diners, Visa.*

WANSFORD-IN-ENGLAND   The Haycock   70%   £98

Tel 01780 782223   Fax 01780 783031   Map 7 E4   **HR**
Wansford-in-England Peterborough Cambridgeshire PE8 6JA

Alongside the A1 at its intersection with the A47 and almost midway between
Peterborough and Stamford, the Haycock is a familiar and welcoming sight. Built in the
17th century as a coaching inn, it combines history and character, and the present owners
are dedicated to maintaining its fine traditions. Surrounded by six acres of well-kept
gardens, the hotel is set well enough back from the road for the traffic noise not to
intrude. Public rooms are cosy with a log fire in the lounge, a quiet, comfortable library
and a convivial bar. Bedrooms include four with four-posters. All are tastefully furnished

and well-equipped – still and sparkling mineral water and a fruit basket are additional to the usual amenities. Seven ground-floor rooms have direct access to the garden. Carpeted bathrooms are neat and staff do their utmost to please. The business centre has six boardrooms and a maximum capacity of 200. The hotel offers meals throughout the day – main meals are served in the restaurant while the bar and orchard room offer lighter snacks and meals. Afternoon tea is served in the lounge. In fine weather there's alfresco dining on the patio overlooking the garden and in the central courtyard. Now owned by Arcadian Hotels **Rooms** 50. *Garden, croquet, fishing, pétanque. Access, Amex, Diners, Visa.*

Restaurant   £75

A la carte meals are served in the traditional comfort of a dining-room from whose ceiling are suspended two chandeliers. Hunting prints adorn the walls and the room is furnished in solid dark oak. In this very English setting it is a pleasant surprise to find enjoyable modern cooking as well as a smattering of classic English dishes. Thus chicken liver pat, with Cumberland sauce, cream of watercress soup, grilled Dover sole, roast rack of lamb with fresh mint sauce and roast sirloin of beef carved from the silver wagon and accompanied by Yorkshire pudding and horseradish sauce sit happily alongside pithiviers of smoked sweetbreads, baked goat's cheese on toasted brioche with salad, roast monkfish with egg noodles and marinated vegetables and breast of chicken stuffed with almond mousse and served with a tarragon and white wine sauce. The wine list is inexpensive (champagne under £20), imaginative and helpful, with good tasting notes, as well as offering a good spread from around the world. Pleasant service. **Seats** 100. **Parties** 10. *Private Room 30. L 12-2.30 D 7-10.30. Set L Mon-Fri £14.95.*

WANTAGE	Bear Hotel	58%	£65

Tel 01235 766366   Fax 01235 768826   Map 14 C2   **H**
Market Square Wantage Oxfordshire OX12 8AB

Since the 16th century the Bear has been a notable feature on the market square of the town where Alfred the Great was born (his statue is another landmark). The cobbled courtyard evokes some of the atmosphere of the past, and a few of the bedrooms are furnished with some older pieces, including brass bedsteads. A few rooms are suitable for family use – children up to 13 stay free in parents' room. The Ascot Suite provides conference facilities for up to 80. **Rooms** 32. *Access, Amex, Diners, Visa.*

WAREHAM	Priory Hotel	72%	£110

Tel 01929 551666   Fax 01929 554519   Map 14 B4   **HR**
Church Green Wareham Dorset BH20 4ND

Dating from the early 16th century, the former priory of Lady St Mary stands in landscaped gardens that reach down to the River Frome. Two beautifully decorated lounges overlook the gardens, and there is a small traditional bar. Bedrooms vary in size (and price, above is for a mid-range room) but all are thoughtfully equipped: each has mineral water, fresh fruit, books and magazines, plus bathrobes, clothes brushes and hairdryers. One room has a four-poster and a whirlpool bath and all feature handsome antique furniture. The Boathouse, converted from a 16th-century clay barn, contains two bedrooms and two luxurious suites. Moorings are available for guests arriving by boat. No dogs. **Rooms** 19. *Garden, croquet, coarse & game fishing. Access, Amex, Diners, Visa.*

Restaurant   £75

Two rooms: ground-floor dining-room for breakfast and lunch; the stone-vaulted Abbots Cellar for a candle-lit dinner. Seasonal produce, local and British, is the basis of Michael Rust's appealing menus, which apply modern accents to traditional methods: terrine of duck confit and foie gras flavoured with port and truffles with sultana brioche; warm scallop and lobster salad with mild curry butter sauce; red mullet with Pommery mustard pasta; Dorset air-cured ham and anchovy butter, and noisettes of lamb with creamed leeks and sweetbread ravioli. Steak Diane and crspes Suzette are prepared at the table; roasts carved at the table; desserts from the trolley; English cheeses, a fine selection earning our British Cheeseboard of the Year regional award. There's a super wine list – shame about some of the spelling! Regions (extensive selection of clarets especially) are prefaced by very knowledgeable notes. **Seats** 66. *Private Room 24. L 12.30-2.30 D 7.30-10. Set L £12.95/£14.95 (Sun £17). Set D £24.50.*

WAREHAM   Springfield Country Hotel   60%   £96

Tel 01929 552177   Fax 01929 551862   Map 14 B4   **H**
Grange Road Stoborough nr Wareham Dorset BH20 5AL

Set in six acres of stylishly landscaped gardens off the A351, a pleasant redbrick hotel with an appealing modern exterior. The spacious foyer is dominated by a splendid stag's head and there are two cosy bars. Bedrooms are agreeable and neatly maintained, all featuring a uniform pink decor, and include doubles, twins and singles, plus a number of family rooms and suites; bidets and avocado suites in the compact bathrooms. The function suite and impressive leisure club are approached across an uncovered, grassy patch from the hotel and has bars, an informal restaurant and banqueting/conference facilities for 160/200. Good family facilities, including high teas and Saturday morning activities. Outdoor pool heated May-Oct. *Rooms 32. Garden, tennis, indoor & outdoor swimming pool, gym, squash, sauna, steam room, solarium, beauty salon, badminton, games room (snooker, pool & table tennis), children's playroom. Access, Amex, Visa.*

WARMINSTER   Bishopstrow House   79%   £125

Tel 01985 212312   Fax 01985 216769   Map 14 B3   **HR**
Boreham Road Warminster Wiltshire BA12 9HH

An elegant, ivy-clad Georgian house in a lovely garden setting alongside the River Wylye. The entrance hall, morning room and dining-rooms are very stylish and formal, with fine oil paintings, French and English antiques, Persian carpets and deep, inviting armchairs. Flower displays add splendid splashes of colour. Spacious bedrooms are in three places: main house, garden rooms and courtyard rooms reached by long corridors. Rooms are either standard or de luxe. Fruit, biscuits and magazines are provided and some of the bedrooms feature spa baths or separate showers. A stunning indoor swimming pool looks out on to the gardens. Conference facilities for up to 60. Sister hotel to *Charingworth Manor* (entry under Chipping Campden). *Rooms 30. Garden, croquet, indoor and outdoor tennis, indoor & outdoor swimming pools, game fishing, sauna. Access, Amex, Diners, Visa.*

The Temple Restaurant   £80

Garden views accompany inventive modern cooking by Chris Suter. Refreshingly straightforward menu descriptions in English belie the effort and invention that go into his dishes: grilled sea bass with lemon and virgin olive oil-flavoured coarsely mashed potato and a velouté of leeks; pan-fried saddle of local venison with wild mushrooms, Agen prunes and a vanilla bean sauce; chargrilled rib-eye steak with braised winter vegetables and bone marrow dumpling. To finish, farmhouse cheeses, a tulip of home-made ice creams and sorbets, caramelised lemon and banana tartlet with an apricot and citrus fruit jus or toffee apple crumble with butterscotch sauce and cinnamon ice cream. An interesting and well-conceived wine list has notes on regions and vintages. Some fair prices, but also some hefty mark-ups on a few classics. No smoking. *Seats 65. Parties 8. Private Room 22. L 12.30-2 D 7.30-9.30. Set L £12.50/ £19.95 Set D £33.*

WARRINGTON   De Vere Lord Daresbury   67%   £105

Tel 01925 267331   Fax 01925 601496   Map 6 B2   **H**
Chester Road Daresbury Warrington Cheshire WA4 4BB

Conveniently located by junction 11 of the M56, this modern, conference-oriented hotel (meeting rooms for up to 400 delegates) also offers extensive leisure amenities. Half the rooms are reserved for non-smokers; some are designated as Lady Executive rooms. Children aged 5 to 14 are accommodated free and charged for all meals including breakfast. 0-4s also get dinner and breakfast free. *Rooms 140. Indoor swimming pool, gym, squash, sauna, spa bath, steam bath, solarium, beauty & hair salon, snooker, children's playground. Access, Amex, Diners, Visa.*

WARRINGTON   Holiday Inn Garden Court   65%   £74

Tel 01925 838779   Fax 01925 838859   Map 6 B2   **H**
Woolston Grange Avenue Woolston Warrington Cheshire WA1 4PX

By Junction 21 of the M6, one of the 'junior' Holiday Inns offering good bedrooms (over half for non-smokers), with limited public areas and no room service. Children up to 19 stay free (those under 12 also eat free) in parents' room. Parking for 114 cars. *Rooms 99. Patio, games room. Access, Amex, Diners, Visa.*

WARWICK   Hilton National   66%   £111

Tel 01926 499555   Fax 01926 410020   Map 14 C1   **H**
Stratford Road Warwick Warwickshire CV34 6RE

Conferences for up to 400 are catered for at this low-rise modern hotel on the A429 by Junction 15 of the M40. Executive rooms and four-bedded family rooms available. Children up to 14 free in parents' room. One floor out of the three is designated non-smoking. 24hr room service includes hot food. One bedroom is equipped for disabled guests. *Rooms 181. Indoor swimming pool, keep-fit equipment, sauna, steam room, sun beds. Access, Amex, Diners, Visa.*

WASHINGTON   Forte Posthouse   59%   £72

Tel 0191-416 2264   Fax 0191-415 3371   Map 5 E2   **H**
Emerson District 5 Washington Tyne & Wear NE37 1LB

Just south of Washington Services on A1(M), a practical modern hotel that's popular with business visitors. Children under 16 free in parents' room. *Rooms 138. Garden, 18-hole pitch & putt, children's playroom & playground. Access, Amex, Diners, Visa.*

WASHINGTON   Moat House   66%   £100

Tel 0191-417 2626   Fax 0191-415 1166   Map 5 E2   **H**
Stone Cellar Road High Usworth District 12 Washington Tyne & Wear NE37 1PH

First-class leisure facilities are the main attraction at this modern Moat House by a championship golf course. Large bedrooms have all the usual modern accessories. Popular with business people during the week and sportsmen and families at weekends. Conference/banqueting suites for 200/180. Ample free parking. *Rooms 106. Garden, indoor swimming pool, 18-hole golf course, pitch & putt, golf driving range, spa bath, sauna, solarium, keep-fit equipment, squash. Access, Amex, Diners, Visa.*

WATERHOUSES   Old Beams   ★ ↑   £80

Tel 01538 308254   Fax 01538 308157   Map 6 C3   **RR**
Leek Road Waterhouses Staffordshire ST10 3HW

An 18th-century former inn on the A523 transformed by Nigel and Ann Wallis into country restaurant of enormous charm. Oak beams, open fires and Windsor chairs feature within while the sunny conservatory boasts a splendid mural. Add an abundance of fresh flowers and urbane service, and the scene is set for Nigel's well-balanced menus that manage to give ample variety at each stage. Tortellini of Dublin Bay prawns with a fino beurre blanc, glazed pig's trotter with sweetbreads and morels served on a truffle sauce, grilled breast of duck on a sweet spicy sauce and fillet of lamb on a bed of spinach garnished with roast baby onions and garlic show a very fine balance of flavours and great attention to detail. Desserts could include hot raspberry soufflé, brulée of creamed rice and roast figs filled with vanilla ice cream served on a port wine sauce. The less expensive lunch menu changes fortnightly. Consistently high standards are evident throughout, right up to the petits fours served with coffee. Many well-sourced wines on the excellent list that is not shy on half bottles. Note the very pertinent tasting comments. The restaurant's own 'favourites' are well worth a punt. No smoking at table, but puff if you must in the reception area. *Seats 40. Parties 20. Private Room 12. L 12-2 D 7-9.30. Closed L Sat, D Sun, all Mon. Set L £10.95 (except Sun) & £17.50 Set D £18.50 & £35. Access, Amex, Diners, Visa.*

Rooms   £87

Just across the road in a converted smithy are the five luxurious bedrooms (large Premier or small De Luxe), each named after one of the famous Staffordshire potteries.

See over

Individually decorated with flair and style, the rooms boast hand-made beds, beautiful hand-embroidered Egyptian cotton bedding and splendid bathrooms with towelling robes and huge monogrammed bath sheets. Continental breakfasts – with croissants hot from the oven, freshly squeezed orange juice and home-made preserves – can be served in the room, cooked breakfasts in the restaurant. No dogs.

WATERINGBURY   Wateringbury Hotel   59%   £75

Tel 01622 812632   Fax 01622 812720   Map 11 B5   **H**
Tonbridge Road Wateringbury nr Maidstone Kent ME18 5NS

Rooms at this tile-hung roadside inn range from singles to a four-poster suite. There's a cane-furnished conservatory, a cocktail bar and two function rooms (catering for up to 80 delegates). Children up to the age of 16 are free if sharing with their parents. *Rooms 40. Garden, sauna. Access, Amex, Diners, Visa.*

WATFORD   Hilton National   64%   £115

Tel 01923 235881   Fax 01923 220836   Map 15 E2   **H**
Elton Way Watford Hertfordshire WD2 8HA

Practical accommodation, a leisure centre and extensive conference facilities (for up to 500). Children under the age of 14 are accommodated free in parents' room, but their time in the leisure centre is limited. 24hr room service. Ample free parking. No dogs. *Rooms 195. Indoor swimming pool, gym, sauna, spa bath, steam room, beauty salon. Access, Amex, Diners, Visa.*

WATFORD   Jarvis International   67%   £118

Tel 0181-950 6211   Fax 0181-950 7809   Map 15 E2   **H**
A41 Watford By-pass Watford Hertfordshire WD2 8HQ

Comfortable modern hotel, 5 minutes from junction 5 of the M1. A spacious, uncluttered lobby leads to the Arts Restaurant and 24-hour Arts Gallery coffee shop. Newly refurbished bedrooms are modestly furnished, but all have en-suite bathrooms and the expected amenities. Suites have upgraded furnishings and a separate sitting area. Luxurious studio rooms have satellite TV (in 8 languages), CD-i players and ultra-modern bathrooms with Japanese showers. A Sebastian Coe leisure centre is free for guests' use. Banqueting/conference facilities for 200. Children up to 14 free in parents' room. *Rooms 217. Garden, tennis, indoor swimming pools, sauna, spa bath, solarium, gym, beauty salon. Access, Amex, Diners, Visa.*

WATH-IN-NIDDERDALE   Sportsman's Arms   £60

Tel 01423 711306   Fax 01423 712524   Map 6 C1   **RR**
Wath-in-Nidderdale Pateley Bridge North Yorkshire HG3 5PP

Making optimum use of seasonal market availability, an ever-enthusiastic Ray Carter produces nightly dinners in a classic style as he has done here for over 15 years. Pier-fresh Whitby fish, Dales lamb and free-range chickens are served with excellent vegetables both common and exotic. Summer pudding with double cream has been a favourite from the word go, and among the alternatives is a fine selection of British and French cheeses. Almost giveaway prices on a fine wine list. *Seats 50. Parties 8. Private Room 8. Sun L 12-2 D 7-9.30. Closed 25 Dec. Set Sun L £12 Set D £19.75 (inc.wine). Access, Amex, Visa.*

Rooms   £58

Stripped pine doors are the unifying theme of the single corridor of bedrooms which are of modest size and appointment; returning guests appreciate rather the total peace and quiet and the absence of room telephones. Whilst all are equipped with wash basins only two out of seven have full en-suite facilities: two WCs and two separate bathrooms are shared by the rest. A long, leisurely and very large breakfast is served at 9.

WEEDON   Crossroads Hotel   55%   £49

Tel 01327 340354   Fax 01327 340849   Map 15 D1   **H**
High Street Weedon Northamptonshire NN7 4PX

A well-run lodge located on the busy intersection of the A5 and A45, with efficient triple-glazing for the rooms where it matters. Most of the public areas are in the original building and comprise a large, characterful bar (full of pubby artefacts) with a south-facing balcony (only 3 tables). Bedrooms are all in a U-shaped motel-style block (except for 10 in the main building). Attractively furnished and neatly maintained. Two are adapted for guests in wheelchairs. Children free in parents' room. *Rooms 48. Garden, tennis, brasserie (7am-6pm). Closed 25 & 26 Dec. Access, Amex, Diners, Visa.*

WELLS	Ritcher's Restaurant	£55

Tel 01749 679085 Map 13 F1   **R**
5 Sadler Street Wells Somerset BA5 2RR

In an alley between shops in the town centre, there's a choice of casual eating in the pine-furnished downstairs bistro and more formal dining in the comfortable upstairs restaurant – both outlets making wide use of prime local produce in a cuisine that reflects both modern English and classical French influences. Typical items on the bistro menu run from warm leek and Stilton flan with béarnaise sauce to the day's fresh fish dish, guinea fowl and tarragon fricassee and braised oxtail. From the restaurant come the likes of a warm, light spinach and brie dumpling set on a saffron cream, a summer seafood platter for two, game in winter, crème brulée and crepes Suzette. Tables outside in the bistro. Partners in this splendid operation are Nick Hart and Kate Ritcher. *Restaurant: Seats 14. L 12-2 (booking only) D 7-9 (Sat to 9.30). Closed Sun, Mon, 26 Dec, 1 Jan. Set L £12.50/£14.50 Set D £15/£18. Bistro: Seats 18. L 12-2 (Sat to 2.30) D 7-9 (Sat to 9.30). Set L £4.95/£6.95 (Sun £5.95/£7.95) Set D £11.50/£13.50. Closed 26 Dec, 1 Jan. Access, Visa.*

WELWYN	Clock Hotel	54%	£73

Tel 01438 716911   Fax 01438 714065   Map 15 E1   **H**
The Link Welwyn Hertfordshire AL6 9XA

Enjoying a prominent position on a roundabout alongside the northbound carriageway of the A1(M), from which it's approached via Junction 6, a hotel that's popular with business folk. Friendly Hotels. *Rooms 95. Mini-gym. Access, Amex, Diners, Visa.*

WEMBLEY	Hilton National	64%	£146

Tel 0181-902 8839   Fax 0181-900 2201   Map 15 E2   **H**
Empire Way Wembley Middlesex HA9 8DS

Large modern hotel just a stone's throw from the Wembley Stadium complex so it gets pretty hectic when there is a big event on. Standard-sized bedrooms are not large; best are those on the two Plaza floors where for a premium you get better furniture (wardrobe rather than open hanging space for example) and evening bed turn-down service. 24-hour room service runs to a couple of hot dishes throughout the night. Children under 8 years stay free in parents' room. Extensive conference facilities. *Rooms 304. Indoor swimming pool, keep-fit equipment, sauna, steam room, spa bath, solarium, beauty salon, news kiosk. Access, Amex, Diners, Visa.*

WENTBRIDGE	Wentbridge House	64%	£75

Tel 01977 620444   Fax 01977 620148   Map 7 D1   **H**
Wentbridge nr Pontefract West Yorkshire WF8 3JJ

Only half a mile from the A1, the house, dating from 1700, possesses beautifully laid-out grounds. The bar has fine damask-covered walls, creating, with the polished bar counter and gleaming glassware, a smart and yet convivial ambience. Carpets throughout the public areas have a distinctive Fleur de Lys design. Bedrooms are cosy and homely, furnished mostly with dark Stag furniture and pretty floral fabrics. All the usual amenities are on hand, including bottles of mineral water. One bedroom has fine oak panelling as well as the only four-poster built by the Mouseman of Thirsk. Neat, carpeted bathrooms. Excellent housekeeping. *Rooms 13. Garden. Closed 25 Dec eve. Access, Amex, Diners, Visa.*

WEOBLEY	Ye Olde Salutation Inn	£55

Tel 01544 318443   Fax 01544 318216   Map 14 A1   **I**
Market Pitch Weobley Hereford & Worcester HR4 8SJ

Chris and Frances Anthony have created an attractive hostelry out of a town-centre 14th-century ale and cider house. Stylish overnight accommodation has a Victorian theme, with one splendid four-poster available. The bedrooms, restaurant and an area of the lounge/bar are no-smoking. Good breakfasts. No children under 14, except infants (by arrangement). *Rooms 3. Gym. Closed 25 Dec. Amex, Diners, Access, Visa.*

WEST BEXINGTON   Manor Hotel   59%   £78

Tel 01308 897616   Fax 01308 897035   Map 13 F2   **H**
Beach Road West Bexington nr Bridport Dorset DT2 9DF

"Where country meets coast", says their literature, and indeed Richard and Jayne Childs'
manor house stands in a garden on a gentle slope near the famous Chesil Bank shingle
beach, overlooking Lyme Bay. Stone walls and oak panelling are much in evidence. Day
rooms include lounge/reading room, cellar bar, restaurant and conservatory. Pretty,
cottagey bedrooms, most with sea views, are furnished with old pine and enhanced with
books and ornaments. Families are very well catered for. *Rooms 13. Garden,
children's playground. Closed 25 Dec. Access, Amex, Diners, Visa.*

WEST BROMWICH   Moat House   59%   £89

Tel 0121-609 9988   Fax 0121-525 7403   Map 6 C4   **H**
Birmingham Road West Bromwich West Midlands B70 6RS

A squarish modern hotel with good-sized bedrooms, half reserved for non-smokers, and
conference facilities for up to 180 theatre-style. Take Junction 1 from M5, close to the
M6 interchange. *Rooms 171. Terrace, pitch & putt, target golf, mini-gym, solarium.
Access, Amex, Diners, Visa.*

WEST CHILTINGTON   Roundabout Hotel   61%   £83

Tel 01798 813838   Fax 01798 812962   Map 11 A6   **H**
Monkmead Lane West Chiltington nr Pulborough West Sussex RH20 2PF

"Nowhere near a roundabout", a Tudor-style hotel with leaded windows, whitewashed
walls and attractive, cottagey exterior. The cartwheel chandelier in the entrance hall, fairy
lights over the bar and armchairs upholstered in tapestry style characterise the public
rooms. Attractive oak furniture and tapestries feature in the bedrooms, the roomiest of
which are classified as Executive; some have four-poster beds. *Rooms 23. Garden.
Access, Amex, Diners, Visa.*

WEST DIDSBURY   The Lime Tree   £45

Tel 0161-445 1217   Map 6 B2   **R**
8 Lapwing Lane West Didsbury Manchester, Gtr Manchester M20 8WS

Well-established, busy bistro – wood-block floor, unclothed tables, candles in bottles –
where a frequently-changing menu of robust dishes is served with cheerful informality.
Chargrilled vegetables with olive dressing and feta cheese; pressed chicken and Parma
ham terrine; fresh mussels normande; roast duck on plum and apple sauce; fillet of salmon
with chervil, white wine and tomatoes, and fillet of beef with polenta and salsa verde on
a Madeira sauce show the range. Familiar puds like chocolate marquise, praline parfait
and sticky toffee pudding. *Seats 80. L 12-2.30 D 6-10.30. Closed L Sat & Mon, all Bank
Holidays. Set L £7.95 (Sun £10.50). Access, Amex, Visa.*

WEST RUNTON   Links Country Park Hotel   62%   £120

Tel 01263 838383   Fax 01263 838264   Map 10 C1   **H**
Sandy Lane West Runton nr Cromer Norfolk NR27 9QH

Set in 35 acres of coastal parkland, midway between Sheringham and Cromer on the
A149, the privately-owned Links is a large Edwardian mock-Tudor building. Guests are
well looked after in comfortable day rooms and decently-equipped bedrooms (satellite TV,
24hr room service). The Garden Rooms are larger. Suitable for sports-orientated families
(all facilities free to residents); children under 16 free in parents' room. *Rooms 40. Garden,
indoor swimming pool, tennis, 9-hole golf course, sauna, sun beds. Access, Amex, Visa.*

WESTON-ON-THE-GREEN   Weston Manor   61%   £105

Tel 01869 350621   Fax 01869 350901   Map 15 D1   **H**
Weston-on-the-Green Oxfordshire OX6 8QL

An imposing castellated manor house standing in 13 acres of gardens and grounds on the
B430 six miles north of Oxford. Accommodation is divided between the main house and
smaller, more modern rooms in the former coach house. Most characterful of the day
rooms is the Baronial Hall dining-room complete with minstrel's gallery. No dogs.
Rooms 38. Garden, croquet, outdoor swimming pool, squash. Access, Amex, Diners, Visa.

WESTON-SUPER-MARE Grand Atlantic 64% £77

Tel 01934 626543 Fax 01934 415048 Map 13 E1 **H**
Beach Road Weston-super-Mare Avon BS23 1BA

Modernised Victorian hotel standing in pleasant gardens with views across the broad, sandy sweep of Weston Bay. Winter conference trade, summer holiday makers. Popular venue for wedding receptions. Forte. *Rooms 76. Garden, tennis, outdoor swimming pool (Jul & Aug only). Access, Amex, Diners, Visa.*

WESTON-UNDER-REDCASTLE Hawkstone Park Hotel 61% £65

Tel 01939 200611 Fax 01939 200311 Map 6 B3 **H**
Weston-under-Redcastle Shrewsbury Shropshire SY4 5UY

In the world of golf Hawkstone is known as the course where Sandy Lyle learnt his game. There are in fact two courses (one of them recently re-designed), and a historic park with splendid cliffs and grottoes, monuments and follies created in the 18th century by Sir Rowland Hill. In the handsome restored inn are a pub, cocktail bar, lounge and restaurant, plus function suites (up to 200 banqueters or conference delegates). Comfortable, well-equipped bedrooms, fully-tiled bathrooms, children up to 13 stay free in parents' room. No dogs. *Rooms 66. Garden, croquet, outdoor swimming pool, golf (2 x 18 hole), putting, tennis, sauna, solarium, games room, snooker, coffee shop (9am-11pm). Access, Amex, Diners, Visa.*

WESTONBIRT Hare & Hounds 59% £80

Tel 01666 880233 Fax 01666 880241 Map 14 B2 **H**
Westonbirt nr Tetbury Gloucestershire GL8 8QL

A former farmhouse built of Cotswold stone and standing in ten acres of gardens and woodland by the A433. Jeremy and Martin Price have run it since 1953, and its old-fashioned charm and homely atmosphere remain a great attraction. Sturdy oak and leather are used for furnishings, and some of the bedrooms have four-posters. Five rooms are in the garden cottage, with their own adjacent parking. Children up to 16 can stay free in their parents' room. *Rooms 30. Garden, croquet, tennis, squash, snooker (½ size). Access, Amex, Diners, Visa.*

WETHERAL Crown Hotel 70% £106

Tel 01228 561888 Fax 01228 561637 Map 4 C2 **H**
Wetheral nr Carlisle Cumbria CA4 8ES

Originally an 18th-century coaching inn, the Crown stands above the River Eden, tucked away from the village itself, yet only minutes from junction 42/43 of the M6 (via the A69/B6263). Behind the bright white frontage, there's a warm and welcoming hotel. Waltons, the pubby bar, exudes atmosphere and serves a good pint of Thwaites (who own the Crown's owners Shire Inns), while the garden-facing lounge is suitably relaxing. Bedrooms are attractive and well maintained, bathrooms bright and modern. Both the conference facilities (for up to 175, complete with business centre) and the smart leisure club (with children's splash pool) are purpose-built and discreetly separate. Children under 16 stay free in parents' room. Two cottages in the grounds are let on a self-catering basis. Free parking for 80 cars. *Rooms 51. Garden, indoor swimming pool, squash, sauna, solarium, spa bath, gym, beauty therapy, massage, squash, snooker. Access, Amex, Diners, Visa.*

WETHERSFIELD Dicken's £60

Tel 01371 850723 Map 10 B3 **R**
The Green Wethersfield Essex CM7 4BS

Set in the heart of the village next to the village hall, the restaurant is full of charm and character. Drinks and orders are taken in a cosy bar at the front. The dining-room at the rear is a gem – a gallery with two tables for two overlooks the main body. There are beams everywhere and rough plaster walls painted salmon pink. The food is truly eclectic, with Oriental and Mediterranean influences and clean, fresh flavours. Asparagus and turnip top risotto, Mediterranean fish soup, confit of duck on sweet and sour cabbage, sea bass with flageolet beans and chives, and rack of lamb with a rosemary and olive jus typify the sunny style. A short selection of sweets includes the likes of crème brulée on stewed plums and ginger or sticky toffee pudding. Inexpensive house selection and wines of the month on a good, fairly priced list. Friendly service. *Seats 60. Private Rooms 10/22/36. L 12.30-2 D 7.30-9.30. Closed D Sun, all Mon & Tues. Set L £13.95/£15. Access, Visa.*

WEYBRIDGE   Casa Romana   £70

Tel 01932 843470   Fax 01932 854221   Map 15 E3   **R**
2 Temple Hall Monument Hill Weybridge Surrey KT13 8RH

Comfortable, long-established Italian restaurant in a striking pale yellow building on the side of a hill as you drop down into town from the Hersham direction. The decor features etchings of old Rome around peach-coloured, rag-rolled walls and robust service comes from waiters in colourful waistcoats. There's nothing 'new-wave' about the cooking, which uses plenty of cream, brandy and wine for dishes that are largely familiar although there are some more exotic items like breast of chicken with peaches and kiwi fruit in a champagne and cream sauce. Before ordering a starter be sure to take a look at the most impressive hors d'oeuvre trolley. The sweet trolley is less interesting, with two or three home-made items, apart from various bowls of fresh fruit and compotes along with a couple of seemingly bought-in gateaux. Mainly Italian wines. Own parking. *Seats 90. Parties 25. L 12.15-2.15 D 7-10.45 (to 10 Sun). Set L £12.95, Set L & D £16.50. Closed L Sat, 25 & 26 Dec. Access, Amex, Diners, Visa.*

WEYBRIDGE   Oatlands Park   69%   £128

Tel 01932 847242   Fax 01932 842252   Map 15 E3   **H**
146 Oatlands Drive Weybridge Surrey KT13 9HB

A late 18th-century mansion, in 10 acres of parkland, whose porticoed entrance leads into a most impressive galleried lounge with trompe l'oeil marble columns and tapestry hangings under a large glass dome. Bedrooms of various sizes are furnished in mahogany. Weekly residential conferences are the main business – the newly refurbished and fully air-conditioned York Suite holds up to 300 delegates. A new basement fitness suite was opening as we went to press. Sister to the *Swiss Cottage Hotel* in London. **Rooms** *117. Garden, coffee lounge (10am-11pm), tennis, keep-fit equipment. Access, Amex, Diners, Visa.*

WEYBRIDGE   Ship Thistle Hotel   63%   £119

Tel 01932 848364   Fax 01932 857153   Map 15 E3   **H**
Monument Green Weybridge Surrey KT13 8BQ

Originally an 18th-century coaching inn, now much extended with conference and banqueting facilities for up to 150. Open-plan public rooms have a few antiques to add period character. Well-equipped bedrooms, with room service available round the clock. Free parking for 55 cars. **Rooms** *39. Terrace. Access, Amex, Diners, Visa.*

WEYMOUTH   Perry's   £60

Tel 01305 785799   Map 13 F3   **R**
The Harbourside 4 Trinity Road Weymouth Dorset DT4 8TJ

Down by the attractively busy Old Harbour, Perry's not unsurprisingly specialises in local seafood. Consult the blackboard for daily specials of lobster, crab, oysters, bass, brill, sole etc. On the printed menu you might find potted chicken liver parfait, moules marinière, ratatouille tart, fillet of beef vert pré, medallions of venison with blackcurrants and cassis sauce and duck en croute. Desserts include Sharrow Bay's sticky toffee pudding along with apple crumble tart, iced lemon parfait and crème brulée. The covered terrace at the back of the restaurant is popular in summer. *Seats 50. Parties 26. Private Room 40. L 12-2 D 7-9.30 (Sat to 10). Set L £10/£12.50. Closed L Mon & Sat; D Sun except high season. Access, Visa.*

WHIMPLE   Woodhayes Hotel   75%   £90

Tel 01404 822237   Map 13 E2   **HR**
Whimple nr Exeter Devon EX5 2TD

Katherine Rendle and her family run their delightfully situated Georgian home-from-home just off the A30 Exeter to Honiton Road with great style and panache. Surrounded by park-like gardens, an apple orchard and sheep grazing in the distance, the setting is rural and peaceful, although Exeter is only eight miles away. The guests' wishes come first, and afternoon tea with mouthwatering cakes included in the tariff is a typically

personal touch; their policy of no nasty extras on bills (teas, coffees, sandwiches and light laundry are not charged as extra) is greatly appreciated by their guests. There are two lounges, one with green, pale blue and apricot decor and soft sofas, the second with a grey scheme, a small library and even deeper sofas. For a peaceful drink, head for the flagstoned bar with its old pine furniture. Spacious bedrooms have solidly traditional furniture. Housekeeping is good and the breakfasts excellent. An adult, friendly country retreat, with no children under 12 to disturb the peace. No dogs. *Rooms 6. Garden, croquet, putting. Access, Amex, Diners, Visa.*

Restaurant   £65

Katherine discusses her menus with guests and special diets are gladly catered for (Katherine has been a vegetarian herself for many years!). Dinners are party occasions in the lovely dining-room where tables are sensibly spaced and French doors lead out on to a paved terrace. Five-course menus (plus coffee) offer a choice only at the dessert stage. A typical night's offering might be melon with ginger and lime sorbet, grilled turbot with a crab crust and lemon sauce, and medallions of venison with pears and cranberries before a choice between crème brulée, rhubarb strudel and home-made ice creams with cheese – Quicke's unpasteurised Cheddar and Blue Vinney with grapes and walnuts – to finish. Concise wine list with a dozen house selections (all available by the glass). Four tables outside for residents' afternoon tea (although Katherine will be happy to accommodate non-residents who ring ahead). Owing to the size of the operation, dinner is only open to non-residents when the accommodation is not full. *Seats 18. L by arrangement for residents only (£15) D 7.30 for 8. Set D £25.*

WHITEWELL   **Inn at Whitewell**   **£60**

Tel 01200 448222   Fax 01200 448298   Map 6 B1   I
Whitewell Forest of Bowland nr Clitheroe Lancashire BB7 3AT

Richard Bowman, lessee of the Duchy of Lancaster, and his staff imbue this ancient stone inn with warmth, personality and a pleasing quirkiness. It's set amid the wild beauty of North Lancashire, overlooking the River Hodder and standing next to the village church. A stone-floored tap room and a library with good books and pictures are both mellow and civilised. Bedrooms feature luxurious fabrics, high-tech music systems and video recorders; some have antique furniture, peat fires and Victorian baths. Telephones are available for most rooms on request. Food in both bar and restaurant; good breakfasts. "Dogs with kind natures and good manners are very welcome . . . but no Alsatians, Rottweilers or moody dogs in public rooms." *Rooms 11. Garden, coarse & game fishing. Access, Amex, Diners, Visa.*

WHITSTABLE   **Whitstable Oyster Fishery Company**   **£45**

Tel 01227 276856   Fax 01227 770666   Map 11 C5   R
The Royal Native Oyster Stores Horsebridge Beach Whitstable Kent CT5 1BU

Sole (their pun not ours!) producers of Royal Whitstable Natives, the actual Fishery Company houses the restaurant within what was originally the oyster storage area. Nowadays the bivalves are held in the original tidal tanks, along with other live shellfish. There's a succinct piscatorial menu chalked on a board, offering for example scallops in bacon or squid pan-fried with garlic as alternative starters to the delectable oysters. Seasonal lobster, local Dover sole and Cornish cock crab are also specialities. *Seats 130. Private Room 100. L 12-2 D 7-9. Closed D Sun, all Mon, 25 & 26 Dec. Access, Amex, Diners, Visa.*

Set menu prices may not always include service or wine.

WICKHAM — Old House Hotel — 66% — £87

Tel 01329 833049 Fax 01329 833672   Map 15 D4 **HR**
The Square Wickham Hampshire PO17 5JG

A Grade II listed Georgian town house built in 1715 and overlooking the village square. It is run with dedication by Richard and Annie Skipwith, who have created a civilised and unpretentious hotel. Polished wood floorboards, rugs and period furniture grace the two lounges, one of which is panelled; solid period pieces are also to be found in the warm, comfortable and prettily decorated bedrooms. Nine of the bathrooms have stand-up showers as well as baths. No dogs. *Rooms 12. Garden. Closed 1 week Easter, 2 weeks Aug, 2 weeks Christmas, Bank Holidays. Access, Amex, Diners, Visa.*

Restaurant   £75

Polished wood tables illuminated by candlelight in the evenings make a charming setting for some good regional French cooking. A short menu offers starters such as mushroom consommé with Madeira, pigeon breast on a crouton with port sauce and celeriac garnish followed perhaps by grilled English fillet steak with a spicy tomato sauce, fillets of turbot and brill with a sauce that is somewhere between a *rémoulade* and a *sauce verte*. Invention comes in the form of guinea fowl with a sauce of red wine, cherry brandy, pink grapefruit and cream. Enjoyable desserts include a rich chocolate mousse with hazelnuts, walnuts, almonds and sultanas marinated in rum or a brandy snap basket filled with a strawberry mousse on a passion fruit coulis. *Seats 40. Parties 22. Private Room 14. L 12.30-1.45 D 7.30-9.30. Closed L Sat & Mon, all Sun. Set meals £20/£25.*

WILLERBY — Grange Park — 67% — £89

Tel 01482 656488 Fax 01482 655848   Map 7 E1 **H**
Main Street Willerby nr Hull Humberside HU10 6EA

Adjacent to the A164 and Willerby Shopping Park, Grange Park is a much-extended Victorian house standing in 12 acres of grounds four miles from the centre of Hull. Besides comfortable modern accommodation it offers extensive purpose-built conference facilities (up to 550 in 4 suites and 10 syndicate rooms). Guests have free use of the Club Tamarisk, whose attractions include a gymnasium and pool. Hydrotherapy and aromatherapy treatment rooms are planned. *Rooms 104. Garden, indoor swimming pool, gym. Access, Amex, Diners, Visa.*

WILLERBY — Willerby Manor — 62% — £89

Tel 01482 652616 Fax 01482 653901   Map 7 E1 **H**
Well Lane Willerby nr Hull Humberside HU10 6ER

An extended Victorian house set in three acres of landscaped gardens, attracting mid-week business clientele and functions at weekends. Everglades Bar is conservatory in style, and overlooks the garden. A variety of rooms provide conferences and banqueting facilities for up to 500; ample parking. Most of the bedrooms are in a modern annexe, and half have king-size beds. Weekend room rates are considerably reduced. Part of a local, family-owned wine merchant business. *Rooms 38. Garden, croquet. Access, Visa.*

WILLITON — White House — £70

Tel 01984 632306   Map 13 E1 **RR**
Williton Somerset TA4 4QW

On the main road through the village, the White House has been run since 1967 by Dick and Kay Smith, who also share the cooking. British, French and American influences can all be found on the nightly-changing menu, from which guests can opt for 3, 4 or 5 courses. Top local suppliers provide the finest raw materials, and the Smiths do the rest. Dishes cover the whole range: courgette and prawn couscous, soufflé suissesse, free-range chicken breast in hazelnut and sherry sauce with stir-fried local asparagus, *boeuf braisé au fumet de vin rouge*, seared salmon on a julienne of vegetables and mushrooms with chive-flavoured crème fraiche and saffron mashed potato, lemon soufflé cheesecake with lime and lemon sorbet, *sablé aux fraises*. Local spring lamb and Exmoor venison are specialities. English cheeses (the day's selection is listed on the menu) are served with home-made oatmeal biscuits. A mostly French and fairly-priced wine list (note the good selection of half bottles) has personal and informed tasting notes. *Seats 26. Parties 8. D only 7-8.30. Set D £25/£28/£31. Closed Nov-May. No credit cards.*

Rooms £70

Residents may choose between a bedroom in the main house or those in the former stables with individual access. 12 rooms in all, 9 of them en suite.

| WILMINGTON | Home Farm | 58% | £56 |

Tel 01404 831246   Fax 01404 831411   Map 13 E2   **H**
Wilmington nr Honiton Devon EX14 9JR

A thatched former farmhouse (a working farm until 1950) with a five-acre garden, cobbled courtyard, flagstoned bar and homely lounge with piano, books and board games. Bedrooms are divided between the main house and the Garden and Courtyard wings. Guests have free use of the nearby Woodworthy Court Leisure Centre. *Rooms 13. Garden. Closed 3 days Christmas. Access, Amex, Visa.*

| WILMSLOW | Harry's | | |

Tel 01625 528799   Map 6 B2   **R**
70 Grove Street Wilmslow Cheshire

As we went to press, Harry's Chinese restaurant had not re-opened after a serious fire. Phone Harry's for information.

| WILMSLOW | Moat House | 58% | £109 |

Tel 01625 529201   Fax 01625 531876   Map 6 B2   **H**
Altrincham Road Wilmslow Cheshire SK9 4LR

A modern hotel in Swiss chalet style offering modest accommodation, with good, on-the-spot leisure club facilities, conference facilities for 300 and a nightclub. Courtesy coaches to Manchester Airport, a mile away and free long-term parking (up to two weeks) for overnight guests on production of flight tickets. Reduced rates at weekends. Children up to 14 stay free in parents' room. *Rooms 125. Indoor swimming pool, gym, squash, sauna, spa bath, sun bed, beautician, courtesy coach to airport. Access, Amex, Diners, Visa.*

| WILMSLOW | Stanneylands | 70% | £87 |

Tel 01625 525225   Fax 01625 537282   Map 6 B2   **HR**
Stanneylands Road Wilmslow Cheshire SK9 4EY

Set in mature gardens boasting some fine specimen trees and based around an original 1920s house, Stanneylands benefits from the same high standards of professionalism and service as its sister hotel *The Belfry* (qv) at nearby Handforth, both under managing director Gordon Beech, whose family have run the hotels for many years. Day rooms include a cosy oak panelled lounge with comfortable cocktail bar beyond, both warmed by real fires in winter. Bedrooms have traditional darkwood freestanding furniture and a variety of attractive colour schemes. When you check in you'll be asked what time you would like early morning tea delivered (beverage trays can be provided on request) and beds are turned down at night. Room service can provide a hot meal at any time of day or night. *Rooms 33. Garden. Access, Amex, Diners, Visa.*

Restaurant £80

Food has always been important here and the two panelled dining-rooms, one in antique oak and the other with polished walnut, have a comfortable, clubby atmosphere appreciated by the many regular customers. The kitchen copes well with both à la carte and fixed-price menus, the latter particularly good value at lunchtime when there is a short choice of three courses (at night it's a no-choice six-course affair headed "a menu of interesting tastes and textures"). Traditionally based but with modern influences, typical dishes might include lobster consommé with tiny herb ravioli, duck and rabbit terrine with a cranberry and apple chutney, pan-fried salmon on a pimento gallette with lemon thyme and orange dressing and loin of lamb with a timbale of marinated vegetables and pimento sauce. Jacques Franke is the long-serving restaurant manager who keeps things running smoothly front of house. The wine list is old-fashioned in the best possible sense, with some real classics very fairly priced, though we would like to see some of the cheaper and 'popular' wines disappearing. There's a good sprinkling of New World wines. *Seats 80. Parties 15. Private Rooms 60/100. L 12.30-2 D 7-10. Closed (cold buffet for residents only) 1 Jan, Good Friday, 26 Dec, D Sun. Set L £10.50/£13.50 Set D (6 courses) £25.*

WIMBORNE   Les Bouviers   £60

Tel 01202 889555   Map 14 C4   **R**
Oakley Hill Merley Wimborne Dorset BH21 1RJ

Owner-chef James Coward's cottagey and sunny restaurant, which celebrated its fifth birthday in 1995, has ceiling fans, floral drapes and a conservatory that really comes into its own in good weather. Local produce is used whenever possible, and everything from bread to sorbets and petits fours on his enterprising menus is made on the premises. The style is a mix of French and English, shown in favourite dishes such as hot cheese soufflé with a watercress and horseradish sauce, hazelnut-studded game terrine, Dover sole grilled or pan-fried, and crisp-cooked duck with legs *en confit* finished with celeriac strips and a star anise sauce. There's a good sprinkling of New World wines among the traditional French offerings, plus several Piemonte Bava wines. Fair prices, helpful tasting notes. No smoking. *Seats 50. L 12-2 D 7-10. Closed L Sat, 26 Dec, 1 Jan. Set L £8.95/£11.95/£18.95 (Sun £14.50) Set D from £23.95. Access, Amex, Diners, Visa.*

WINCHESTER   Forte Crest   69%   £114

Tel 01962 861611   Fax 01962 841503   Map 15 D3   **H**
Paternoster Row Winchester Hampshire SO23 9LQ

A modern hotel next to the cathedral. Among the day rooms are a coffee shop with lots of light pine and a lounge with dark leather seating. Bedrooms boast smart Italian furniture and Executive rooms overlook the cathedral. Children stay free in parents' room. Banquets and conferences for up to 100. *Rooms 94. Coffee shop (10am-10pm). Access, Amex, Diners, Visa.*

WINCHESTER   Lainston House   75%   £145

Tel 01962 863588   Fax 01962 776672   Map 15 D3   **H**
Sparsholt Winchester Hampshire SO21 2LJ

Well-signposted off the A272 Winchester-Stockbridge road, this fine William and Mary house glories in 63 acres of classic English parkland. The entrance hall/reception is particularly welcoming in winter, when a log fire smoulders in a large Delft-tiled fireplace; those in the comfortable lounge with its floral fabrics and brass chandeliers sport flowers. The remaining public room is the library lounge displaying some fine carved cedar panelling. Main-house bedrooms have high ceilings and elegant proportions, the 14 in the Chudleigh Court extension have more uniformity but perhaps the best are six newest rooms created out of the former stable block. These are very sumptuous with some fine antiques and luxurious bathrooms that even boast TVs. All rooms have quality furnishings and stylish decor. Friendly staff and good cooked breakfasts. Various conference and function rooms (catering for up to 50 theatre-style) include a restored half-timbered barn; ample parking. *Rooms 37. Garden, croquet, tennis, pitch & putt, putting, fishing, snooker, game fishing. Access, Amex, Diners, Visa.*

WINCHESTER   The Old Chesil Rectory   £50

Tel 01962 851555   Map 15 D3   **R**
Chesil Street Winchester Hampshire SO23 8HU

The building dates back to 1450 and has enormous appeal with its old timbers, mellow brickwork and open fire in winter. The restaurant is on two floors, with crisp white linen upstairs and less formal unclothed tables downstairs. Chef-patron Nicholas Ruthven-Stuart's cooking, which he rightly describes as 'modern international', has an honesty and genuineness that is most appealing, and everything on his menus reads temptingly: specialities include a symphony of seafood, Lunesdale duck (perhaps peppered breast with spinach, mushrooms and a brandy cream sauce or Oriental-style with honey and star anise), liver with bacon and shallots, and a 'trilogy of game' – pigeon breast, rabbit and haunch of venison with a juniper game sauce. Prune and armagnac parfait is considered a speciality among good desserts that may also feature glazed French apple tart with calvados sorbet, crème brulée and a chocolate 'assiette'. There's also a selection of British and Continental cheeses. A short wine list, 30% of which is represented by the New World. Good value, with only half a dozen wines over £20. *Seats 56. Parties 14. Private Rooms 10/30. L 12-2.30 D 7-9.30. Closed Sun & Mon, last week Jul, 1st week Aug, 1 week Christmas. Set L £9.95. Access, Visa.*

WINCHESTER   Royal Hotel   68%   £97

Tel 01962 840840   Fax 01962 841582   Map 15 D3   **H**
St Peter Street Winchester Hampshire SO22 8BS

Well signposted, but tucked away down a quiet street just 100 yards from the town
centre. This former Benedictine convent has been greatly extended over the years. The
modest exterior (with attractive hanging baskets in summer) hides elegant public rooms,
all recently refurbished, but still retaining their 16th-century charm. Comfortable
bedrooms have been brought into the modern world with satellite TV (including CNN),
voice mail and computer modem points. A few rooms have four-posters (for which
a £10 per night supplement is charged) and one, part of the original chapel, sports
a splendid half-tester. The secluded garden hosts summer lunchtime barbecues – very
popular with the local community. Function rooms, including one with timber beams
cater for up to 110 delegates. Under-16s stay free in parents' room. Ample parking.
Rooms 75. Garden. Access, Amex, Diners, Visa.

WINCHESTER   Hotel du Vin & Bistro   75%   NEW   £75

Tel 01962 841414   Fax 01962 842458   Map 15 D3   **HR**
14 Southgate Street Winchester Hampshire S023 9EF

The sign of things to come perhaps? A charming and thoroughly sensible central-city
town house hotel, with, as the name suggests, wine the dominant theme, though not
overpoweringly so. The original house, dating back to 1715, has the benefit of a period
walled garden and large car park, a romantic, candle-lit, brick-arched basement wine-
tasting cellar (you're welcome to browse), a comfortable drawing room, and a small
function room (note the hand-painted vine frescos on the columns). Each bedroom,
named and sponsored by a well-known wine company (Pol Roger, Veuve Clicquot,
Courvoisier, Brown Brothers, Beringer etc), is decorated with paintings, photographs and
memorabilia from that sponsor, though the obvious attraction lies in their quality – real
linen sheets on the comfortable beds, thick curtains, antiques, good furniture and splendid
bathrooms which feature powerful overhead showers, as well as deep tubs. The addition
of mini-bar and tea/coffee-making facilities with fresh milk, both cleverly hidden in
bedside tables, satellite TV, and trouser press goes almost unnoticed. The place is
excellently run in tandem by Robin Hutson and Gerard Basset (see below), backed
by a willing and enthusiastic team, with exemplary housekeeping standards to match.
Breakfast, too, is a fine affair, with real orange juice, super baking (*pain au chocolat* for
instance), excellent coffee and a variety of teas. Banqueting/conferences 40/30. Children
free in parents' room up to 16 years. No room service. No dogs. Our Newcomer of the
Year (see award pages). *Rooms 13. Garden. Access, Amex, Diners, Visa.*

Bistro   £60

The two informal dining areas have wood floors and vinous surroundings. The place
positively buzzes. Gerard Basset is one of the country's leading sommeliers, probably the
top man, so we'll get the wine comments out of the way first! To match the daily-
changing menu, he chooses a small selection to complement the dishes, some by the
glass, by the bottle – all between £10 and £20, marque champagne excepted – and even
by the half bottle. In addition, there's a cellar list of some 160 carefully chosen bins, large
for a hotel of this size, from around the world. Quality is paramount, prices are fair, but it
is worth seeking advice. Worthy regional recipient of our Cellar of the Year award. And
what of the food? Chef James Martin offers a simple modern menu of good,
unpretentious dishes, well prepared from fresh and, wherever possible, local ingredients.
Typical starters include steamed mussels with red onions and thyme, and chargrilled
asparagus; main courses, roast salmon with sauce vierge, and best end of lamb with
honey-roasted parsnips. Vegetables are extra. Finish with strawberries in balsamic vinegar,
or a pear and almond tart with sauce anglaise. Staff are terrific, the bread is good and the
coffee great. When the weather permits, dine out in the garden. *Seats 45. Parties 12.
Private Room 40. L 12-2.30 D 7-10.*

Consult the blue pages for summary tables and lists of
recommended establishments.

WINCHESTER　Wykeham Arms　£75

Tel 01962 853834　Fax 01962 854411　Map 15 D3　**IR**
75 Kingsgate Street Winchester Hampshire SO23 9PE

Sandwiched between the Cathedral and Winchester College by the 18th-century Kingsgate Arch, the Wykeham Arms has become something of an institution in its 250-year history. Local pub, comfortable accommodation, discerning restaurant, used by destination travellers, passers-through, locals and simply those-in-the-know. Not everyone knows of the special relationship the inn has with the cathedral, for which its customers helped raise £60,000 towards a music foundation. The areas that are typically "inn" are quintessentially so: open log fires, rooms decorated with tankards and artefacts from days gone by. Bedrooms are stylish and have modern comforts. No children under 14 overnight or in restaurant. No specifically non-smoking bedrooms but guests are requested to abstain. *Rooms 7. Garden, sauna. Access, Amex, Visa.*

Restaurant　£55

The kitchen is run by four lady cooks headed by Vanessa Booth. They turn out a splendid variety of dishes on menus that change twice daily, with a different emphasis at lunch and dinner. Some interesting combinations are to be found, such as plaice, crab and chive terrine, caramelised onion tart and coarse country pork paté as starters; then fillet of cod on an onion confit topped with bacon and a Dijon mustard sauce, fillet of pork stuffed with prunes and apples served with a cider and green peppercorn sauce or roast rack of lamb with Provençal vegetables and a thyme and port wine glaze. For dessert try the unusual carrot and ginger pudding with butterscotch sauce, or raspberry trifle or cappuccino mousse cake. Concise wine list with tasting notes – plenty available by glass or carafe. For summer eating and drinking there is a neat walled garden and patio. Booking is absolutely essential. No-smoking room. *Seats 90. Parties 8. L 12-2.30 D 6.30-8.45. Closed Sun, 25 Dec.*

WINDERMERE　Holbeck Ghyll　72%　£130*

Tel 015394 32375　Fax 015394 34743　Map 4 C3　**HR**
Holbeck Lane Windermere Cumbria LA23 1LU

If approaching from Windermere on the A591, take the right turn signposted Troutbeck after the Brockhole Visitor Centre. This is about half way to Ambleside, so if coming from the other direction it's the first sign to the left. Commanding a majestic view over Lake Windermere, this was once the hunting lodge of Lord Lonsdale, whose name adorns the ceremonial belt of British Boxing Championships. Today, as the home of Patricia and David Nicholson, it possesses a timeless, lived-in feel with the welcoming scents of fresh flowers in summer and pine logs glowing in the inglenook in cold weather. Patricia and her housekeepers run an immaculate house where thoughtful decor even matches tissue boxes and pin cushions to the theme of each individually decorated bedroom. All the bathrooms are stylishly tiled and come with smart mahogany fittings, bathrobes and quality toiletries. Ebullient David fronts operations with verve and good humour, taking pride in his bespoke snooker room, which converts for use as a boardroom, and in continuous improvements to both the hotel and grounds. *Half-board terms only. *Rooms 14. Garden, croquet, tennis, putting, snooker. Access, Amex, Diners, Visa.*

Restaurant　£55

In the oak-panelled restaurant the menu changes every day, offering a tempting variety of dishes based on prime local produce and with English and European influences. King scallops with prawn, basil and tomato concassé could precede soup, scrambled egg with smoked halibut or a water ice, with a main course of baked fillet of brill with a pine nut and garlic crust, country casserole of Cumbrian lamb, or a traditional pot roast of beef cooked in the Aga and served with baby Yorkshire puddings and herb dumplings. Desserts from the buffet table. Fair prices on a pleasing wine list with something for everyone from almost everywhere. No children under 9. *Seats 36. Parties 12. Private Room 16. D only 7-8.45. Set D £27.50/£30.*

Consult the blue pages for summary tables and lists of recommended establishments.

WINDERMERE	**Merewood Hotel**	66%	£90

Tel 015394 46484   Fax 015394 42128   Map 4 C3   **H**
Ecclerigg Windermere Cumbria LA23 1LH

Almost midway between Windermere and Ambleside on the A591, the hotel dates from 1812 and is approached up a long, quite steeply inclined drive that twists through part of the 25 acres of secluded grounds. From its elevated position there are good views of the lake from public rooms and from the six large front-facing bedrooms. The conservatory bar with its mosaic-tiled floor, mahogany panelling and brown leather chesterfields has a smart Edwardian ambience. Bedrooms, some with pine, others with mahogany furniture, are of a good size and have a colourful, homely decor. There are conference facilities for up to 40 delegates. *Rooms 20. Garden. Access, Amex, Diners, Visa.*

WINDERMERE	**Miller Howe**	70%	£150*

Tel 015394 42536   Fax 015394 45664   Map 4 C3   **H**
Rayrigg Road Windermere Cumbria LA23 1EY

John Tovey's Miller Howe, an impressive Edwardian country house, stands well above Lake Windermere, with probably the grandest and most stunning views of any hotel in the Lake District. Built alongside the A592, it has well-tended grounds which sweep down almost to the water's edge. The hotel's public rooms and best bedrooms all share the panoramic vista with sunsets over the distant Cumbrian mountains particularly glorious. A heavy wooden door leads from the porch into a homely entrance hall lined with numerous past awards. Unusual objets d'art, sculptures ancient and modern, oil paintings and fine antique pieces put together unfussily create a comfortable, welcoming, lived-in feel. All three lounges are in keeping with the hotel's Edwardian origins. In the conservatory the bright decor comprises cushioned white garden furniture and window sills of potted plants. Bedrooms, though not large, have a cosy, rather old-fashioned appeal that's changed little down the years. White laminate built-in units are used in even the best rooms, compensated for in the high standards of cleanliness and amenities on offer: books, games, small stereo system with classical music cassettes, trouser press, even umbrellas. The best bedrooms have balconies with seating at white wrought-iron tables. Binoculars are provided too. Compact bathrooms have lots of extras, all of good quality – thick towels, classy toiletries and bathrobes. Coming down for breakfast guests are greeted at the foot of the stairs with a complimentary Bucks Fizz which is followed by a very extensive menu that will leave you replete till lunchtime at the earliest. *Half-board only. *Rooms 12. Garden. Closed early Dec-early Mar. Access, Amex, Diners, Visa.*

WINDERMERE	**Rogers Restaurant**		£55

Tel 015394 44954   Map 4 C3   **R**
4 High Street Windermere Cumbria LA23 1AF

Roger Pergl-Wilson is the sole cook and his wife Alena the most affable of hostesses at their cosy little restaurant in the heart of the English Lakes (located opposite Windermere Information Centre). Dishes are straightforward, robust in flavour, and highly enjoyable with inspiration from both France and England. Lentil, carrot and coriander soup, scallops with celeriac mousse and cheese glaze, and croustade of wild mushrooms are typical starters on the à la carte menu, while main courses range from halibut with tomatoes, basil and shallots through game pie to roast duck with apple sauce and stuffing and grilled sirloin steak with Parma ham and gruyère. Good desserts, French and English cheeses. Mostly youngish wines on an agreeable and fairly-priced list. Limited choice of half bottles. Particularly good-value, 3-course table d'hote includes canapés and coffee with petits fours. Phone about the regular Thursday French nights and other special events. *Seats 22. Parties 12. Private Room 28. D only 7-9.30. Closed Sun (phone for details of other closures) Set D £15.75. Access, Amex, Diners, Visa.*

WINDSOR	**Castle Hotel**	67%	£156

Tel 01753 851011   Fax 01753 830244   Map 15 E2   **H**
High Street Windsor Berkshire SL4 1LJ

Period atmosphere and modern facilities in a Forte hotel behind a Georgian facade. Children up to the age of 16 free in parents' room. Banqueting and conferences for 300/190. Ample parking. *Rooms 104. Coffee shop (7am-10pm). Access, Amex, Diners, Visa.*

| WINDSOR | Oakley Court | 78% | £183 |

Tel 01628 74141   Fax 01628 37011   Map 15 E2   **HR**
Windsor Road Water Oakley nr Windsor Berkshire SL4 5UR

Set in 35 acres of landscaped grounds that slope gently down to the banks of the Thames, Oakley Court – a grand Victorian manor – is only about half an hour from central London. The spacious lounges have open log fires, chandeliers and original, ornate plasterwork ceilings. The panelled library has over 500 volumes with which to while away the hours. Bedrooms are most appealing, with almost all rooms in separate extensions (the Riverside and Garden Wings) close to the main house; many are particularly spacious and boast splendid red granite bathrooms; the six luxurious suites in the original house have a more traditional, period feel. In the 60s and 70s the Court was used as the atmospheric setting for many films, including the *St Trinians* series, the *Rocky Horror Picture Show* and several Hammer horror productions. Boats for hire from the hotel's private jetty; weekend summer steam boat service to Windsor. Queens Moat Houses. Parking for 120. No dogs. **Rooms** 92. *Garden, croquet, 9-hole golf, boating, fishing, gym, sauna, solarium, snooker. Access, Amex, Diners, Visa.*

Oak Leaf Restaurant   £100

A pianist plays nightly in the dado oak-panelled dining-room here to accompany some fine cooking from head chef Michael Croft. His à la carte menu features dishes in contemporary style such as terrine of chargrilled vegetables with a tomato and basil vinaigrette, 'minestrone' of scallops and langoustine tails in a tomato and herb stock with fresh pasta, breast of duck with creamed parsnips and a prune and armagnac chutney, and, one of his great successes when at the Mirabelle, a galette of potato and celeriac with crispy fried foie gras, wild mushrooms and shallots in a Madeira and truffle essence. Those with simpler tastes should look to the Traditional Fayre section for potted crab, poached salmon hollandaise, whole Dover sole grilled or pan-fried, calf's liver and bacon, fillet steak béarnaise and similarly straightforward dishes. There is also a short vegetarian selection. Desserts range from wine-poached pear filled with blackcurrant mousse and exotic fruit salad to a traditional bread-and-butter pudding, there is a good French and English cheese trolley that comes with home-baked bread. Wine-growing areas on the list are prefaced with an illustrative map, and some wines are recommended not just by the sommelier but by a committee! It's a good list, but after France it rather runs out of steam. Although friendly the service lacks the polish that the kitchen here deserves.
Seats 65. *Parties 12. Private Room 18. L 12.30-2 D 7.30-10. Set L £20 (Sun £23.50) Set D £30.*

Boaters Brasserie   £50

Turn left on entering the main restaurant reception to find the hotel's less formal eaterie. Red tablecloths, a few parlour plants and punkas overhead give something of the brasserie feel to an essentially Victorian gothic room. The regular menu is eclectic, with dishes ranging from vegetable tempura with black bean salsa, terrine of duck confit with chestnuts, steamed crab and coriander wun tuns and cannelloni of mushroom, spinach and ricotta to cod and chips with tartare sauce, and Cumberland sausage and black pudding with spring onion and mustard mash. From time to time there are additional themed set menus such as French or Spanish. There's a good choice of wines by the glass.
Seats 30. *Parties 12. L 12.30-2 D 7-10. Closed L Sun.*

We welcome bona fide complaints and recommendations on the tear-out pages at the back of the book for readers' comments. They are followed up by our professional team.

WINKLEIGH — Pophams — £30

Tel 01837 83767   Map 13 D2   **R**
Castle Street Winkleigh Devon EX19 8HQ

The most intimate of restaurants, squeezed into a tiny village shop which is also a morning coffee shop and deli. Melvyn Popham produces daily-changing lunch menus in his tiny kitchen. Avocado with hot smoked bacon, leek and potato soup, Parma ham and fresh figs, roast fillet of beef with oyster mushrooms and Madeira sauce, salmon with asparagus salad and duck breast with a green peppercorn and brandy sauce show the style. Leave room for tempting desserts like chocolate roulade with chocolate bourbon ice cream, Bacardi and lime jelly and a rum, date and stem ginger tart. Unlicensed, so bring your own wine – no corkage. No children under 14. No smoking. **Seats** 10. **Parties** 10. L only 12-3. Closed Sun, 25 Dec & all Feb. Access, Visa.

WINKTON — Fisherman's Haunt — £59

Tel 01202 484071   Fax 01202 478883   Map 14 C4   **I**
Salisbury Road Winkton Christchurch Dorset BH23 7AS

James Bochan has been here for 20 years, dispensing hospitality to fishermen and non-anglers alike. The hotel stands on the B3347 Christchurch-Ringwood road about 2 miles from Bournemouth (Hurn) Airport, and the River Avon is just across the road. The building's 17th-century origins are not all that evident, but the bars, one featuring an old well with spring water, have a certain personality as well as real ale. Bedrooms, furnished in various styles, are spread around the main building (largest rooms), an old coach house and a nearby cottage. **Rooms** 20. Garden. Accommodation closed 25 Dec. Access, Amex, Diners, Visa.

WINSFORD — Royal Oak Inn — £90

Tel 01643 851455   Fax 01643 851388   Map 13 D2   **I**
Winsford Somerset TA24 7JE

At the centre of a sleepy Exmoor village, Charles Steven's lovely 13th-century thatched inn doubles as village local and celebrated haunt for the hunting and fishing folk. The hotel waters run through the village and additional beats, fishing tuition and the hire or purchase of fishing tackle can be arranged. The inn was closed for major repairs after a fire. It was due to re-open by the end of September 1995, after we went to press. **Rooms** 15. Garden, fishing. Access, Amex, Diners, Visa.

WINTERBOURNE — Jarvis Grange Hotel — 68% £100

Tel 01454 777333   Fax 01454 777447   Map 13 F1   **H**
Northwoods Winterbourne Avon BS17 1RP

Seven miles from Bristol, but only a few minutes from M4 (J20) and M5 (J16); nevertheless, you should obtain directions when booking. The much-extended Victorian building stands in 18 acres of mature parkland, just outside the village. Conference facilities (up to 150 delegates) occupy much of the main house with bedrooms and leisure club in attendant modern blocks; 19 rooms for non-smokers; children up to 16 share parents' room free. Six Executive rooms have larger work space and bay windows overlooking the grounds. No dogs. **Rooms** 52. Garden, indoor swimming pool, sauna, spa bath, sun beds. Access, Amex, Diners, Visa.

WINTERINGHAM — Winteringham Fields — ★★ £115

Tel 01724 733096   Fax 01724 733898   Map 7 E1   **RR**
Winteringham South Humberside DN15 9PF

That such a wonderful restaurant exists just south of the Humber Bridge may surprise some, but not those who have followed Germain and Anne Schwab's success since their move from Beck Farm, Wilberfoss over seven years ago. At the time of our latest visit in mid-June, the builders were evident, not only re-roofing the building(s), but also completing Germain's new kitchen (now boasting the very best French ovens), enabling expansion into the restaurant. Our award of Kitchen of the Year is well deserved. The building itself is 16th-century and retains many original features, from beams and panelling to open fireplaces and the cellar, which is well worth a look around. There are

See over

a series of characterfully furnished dining areas, a conservatory and lounge for drinks/coffee before and after, and you should take advantage of the terrace and beautifully maintained gardens in fine weather. A la carte menus change seasonally, others daily, and wherever possible local suppliers are used, with most of the vegetables and herbs coming from their own organic gardens and greenhouse, including two grape vines that supply the black grapes you see on the magnificent cheese trolley. A lunch menu might feature cream of local asparagus soup, rolled rack of Lincolnshire lamb and rhubarb tartlet; a speciality dish of, say, pig's trotter stuffed with chicken and sweetbreads, served with roast garlic; and off the à la carte, perhaps simply steamed sea bass, or, unusually, chargrilled goat with rösti and juniper berries. Desserts include their own hot Winteringham corn tart with butterscotch and fresh cream or Swiss (Germain's nationality) lemon tart with orange sorbet. Whatever you choose (note also the 6-course menu surprise) you'll be assured of quite outstanding cooking with service to match, and the Schwabs' policy of relying on 'local' extends to many of the young staff on parade. The wine list is nothing short of sensational; it's thoroughly comprehensive and well annotated, with the monthly selection offering particularly good value, though we question the wisdom of having 'recommended' symbols of differing degrees alongside many wines, almost suggesting that others are not worth drinking, which is certainly not the case here! *Seats 40. Parties 8. Private Room 10. L 12-1.30 D 7.30-9.30 Closed L Mon & Sat, all Sun, Bank Holidays, 2 weeks Christmas, 1st week Aug. Set L £12.50/£17.50 Set D £28/£43. Access, Amex, Visa.*

Rooms   £94

No ordinary bedrooms these, but charmingly and thoughtfully furnished with period pieces and a host of extras ranging from flowers, pot pourri and mineral water to a portable radio, bathrobes and fine toiletries. Four (including a four-poster) are in the main house, three in the converted courtyard stables. Excellent home-baking features on the breakfast tray with dozen of teas (loose or sachet) to choose from. No children under 9 except infants in arms up to the age of 2 (free in parents' room). No dogs. No smoking.

WISHAW	The Belfry	73%	£150

Tel 01675 470301   Fax 01675 470178   Map 6 C4   **H**
Wishaw Warwickshire B76 9PR

This large, ivy-clad hotel in the De Vere group stands amid two international standard golf courses (the Derby & Championship Brabazon) set in 360 acres of grounds. Golf is big business, so too conferences, and the facilities for both are extensive. The largest of the eight bars, with a pubby feel, overlooks one of the courses and has special spike-proof flooring. Also notable among the public areas is a sunken amphitheatre-style lounge with a glass roof and abundant greenery. Smart and stylish bedrooms with solid period furnishings are in four wings and are named after famous golfers. Choice of four restaurants. Children up to 14 can stay free in parents' room. The PGA Training Academy at the Belfry development includes a new conference centre (seating 450) and 48 woodland lodges (both due to open autumn 1995) plus a third golf course (due to open in 1996). No dogs. *Rooms 219. Garden, croquet, golf (2x18), floodlit driving range, putting green, gym, indoor swimming pool, spa bath, sauna, steam room, solarium, beautician, squash, tennis, children's playground, night club, snooker. Access, Amex, Diners, Visa.*

WITHERSLACK	Old Vicarage	68%	£98

Tel 01539 52381   Fax 01539 52373   Map 4 C4   **HR**
Church Road Witherslack Cumbria LA11 6RS

The Reeve and Burrington-Brown families offer warmth and hospitality in their delightful Georgian former vicarage. Well-appointed bedrooms are either in the Old House or the aptly-named Orchard House – the orchard in question being of damsons and apples – and offer welcome relaxation from touring the Lake District. Super breakfasts. Turn off the A590 into Witherslack village. Look for the telephone box on your right, then take the next left turn. The Old Vicarage is about ¾ mile along this lane. *Rooms 15. Garden, tennis. Access, Visa.*

Restaurant   £60

Local suppliers contribute to dishes such as black pudding with caramelised apple rings, roast Derwentwater duckling and roast leg of Lakeland lamb "served with a good gravy and St Paul's Churchyard fresh mint sauce, roast potatoes, fine green beans, broccoli, roast parsnips and sautéed celeriac". For pudding, try damson ice cream in a brandy snap basket and a red berry compote, or apricot and frangipane flan. The cheeseboard is a highlight, emphasising as it does hand-made specialities from the North of England. Breads, ices and chocolates are also all home-made. There's a good mix between old and new on the wine list, with just one (Italian) bottle priced over £30. No classics, but none the worse for that. *Seats 35. Parties 18. Private Room 10. L Sun only 12.30 for 1 D at 7.30 for 8. Set L (Sun) £13.50 Set D £25.*

WITNEY	Witney Lodge	62%	£96

Tel 01993 779777   Fax 01993 703467   Map 14 C2   **H**
Ducklington Lane Witney Oxfordshire OX8 7TJ

Just outside Witney at the junction of the A40 and A415, a modern hotel with an attractive stone frontage. Bright, practical accommodation, rustic-style bar-lounge, purpose-built leisure centre with a decent-size indoor pool. Popular for conferences (up to 140) and banquets (130). Family facilities include a splash pool for toddlers alongside the bright, daylight pool; children up to 16 stay free in parents' room. 24hr room service. *Rooms 74. Gym, indoor swimming pool, spa bath, sauna, solarium, snooker. Access, Amex, Diners, Visa.*

WIVELISCOMBE	Langley House	66%	£85

Tel 01984 623318   Fax 01984 624573   Map 13 E2   **HR**
Langley Marsh Wiveliscombe nr Taunton Somerset TA4 2UF

Peter and Anne Wilson's pale-peach Georgian house (with 16th-century origins) nestles in lovely countryside at the foot of the Brendon Hills; drive half a mile north of Wiveliscombe on the road to Langley Marsh. It's a pretty place with four acres of landscaped gardens, cobbled courtyard and attractive, lived-in drawing rooms. Bedrooms are particularly stylish and appealing with well-planned colour schemes and lots of little extras. The Wilsons' personal care and attention are of a high order and breakfasts are super. *Rooms 8. Garden, croquet, children's outdoor playground. Access, Amex, Visa.*

Restaurant   £75

The beamed, candle-lit restaurant with its silver and crystal table settings enhances the air of well-being to which Peter's four-course dinner menus, changing nightly, do full justice. Produce is first-rate, a walled kitchen garden providing the freshest of ingredients. Bavarois of sweet peppers with a tomato coulis could get things under way, followed perhaps by fillet of sea bass with Provençal breadcrumbs on a bed of leeks with beurre blanc (a speciality). The main dish might be lamb fillet with ratatouille or veal with a Dijon mustard sauce with a choice of half a dozen desserts to round things off. Some of the country's best wine suppliers are credited on the list, which is a fine one albeit with no introductory or tasting notes at all. Wines are listed by price (least expensive first), which can be helpful to the pocket but does not necessarily take quality into account. No smoking. *Seats 20. Parties 8. Private Room 20. L by arrangement D 7.30-8.30 Set D from £28.50.*

WOBURN	Bedford Arms	68%	£100

Tel 01525 290441   Fax 01525 290432   Map 15 E1   **H**
George Street Woburn nr Milton Keynes Bedfordshire MK17 9PX

A former coaching inn standing at a crossroads in the heart of the village. Behind the long Georgian frontage the Tavistock Bar has a historical air with its redbrick walls, heavy oak timbers and horsebrasses, while the cocktail bar is elegantly appointed. Bedrooms in a purpose-built block at the rear have a pleasing, well co-ordinated decor, but lack the character and charm of the ten original bedrooms in the main house. Tasteful touches include fine inlaid furniture and shell hand-basins. Satellite TVs and mini-bars are included among the extras. Thistle & Mount Charlotte. *Rooms 55. Access, Amex, Diners, Visa.*

Consult the blue pages for summary tables and lists of
recommended establishments.

WOBURN   Bell Inn   57%   £72

Tel 01525 290280   Fax 01525 290017   Map 15 E1   **H**
21 Bedford Street Woburn Bedfordshire MK17 9QD

A privately-owned hotel with a mixture of Tudor, Georgian and Victorian buildings standing on either side of the street. To one side are a beamed bar and restaurant, to the other reception and a residents' lounge. The bar is a popular spot for snacks. A conference room can accommodate up to 36 theatre-style. Bedrooms retain much of the character of the original buildings and all have en-suite facilities. Children up to 16 share family rooms without charge. No dogs. *Rooms 27. Closed 25-30 Dec. Access, Amex, Diners, Visa.*

WOBURN   Paris House   £90

Tel 01525 290692   Fax 01525 290471   Map 15 E1   **R**
Woburn Park Woburn Bedfordshire MK17 9QP

Located just off the A4012, Paris House has a splendid setting in the middle of a deer park. The eye-catching half-timbered house is fronted by a well-tended garden where, in fine weather, aperitifs and coffee are served. Inside, the dining-room has bold ivy-patterned wallpaper and some large abstract paintings. Peter Chandler, chef-patron since 1983, offers a menu of modernised classical cooking, the execution of which is belied by the simple descriptions. You might be offered confit of crispy duck in orange sauce, fisherman's chowder, sweet and sour chicken with pineapple, roast rack of lamb with aubergines and tomatoes, hot bananas Foster with chocolate chip cookie ice cream or lemon mousse with macerated strawberries. Moderately priced wine list. *Seats 44. Private Room 14. L 12-2 D 7-9.30. Closed D Sun, all Mon, Bank Holidays, Feb. Set L £25 Set D £38. Access, Amex, Diners, Visa.*

WOKINGHAM   Stakis St Anne's Manor   69%   £126

Tel 01734 772550   Fax 01734 772526   Map 15 D2   **H**
London Road Wokingham Berkshire RG11 1ST

A converted and extended manor house situated in 25 acres of grounds close to the A329(M). Well-appointed bedrooms and comfortable public areas. Good leisure amenities. Banqueting/conference facilities for 300. *Rooms 130. Garden, croquet, tennis, indoor swimming pool, keep-fit equipment, sauna, spa bath, steam room, sun beds. Access, Amex, Diners, Visa.*

WOLVERHAMPTON   Goldthorn Hotel   62%   £78

Tel 01902 29216   Fax 01902 710419   Map 6 B4   **H**
Penn Road Wolverhampton West Midlands WV3 0ER

A 19th-century house with large, modern extensions in distinctly contrasting architectural style gives a mix of atmospheres, similarly mirrored in the styles of bedrooms. One mile south of the town centre on the A449, half a mile from the Wolverhampton ring road. Conference facilities for up to 150. Parking for 100. No dogs. *Rooms 92. Garden, swimming pool, mini-gym, sauna, steam room. Access, Amex, Diners, Visa.*

WOLVERHAMPTON   Jarvis Mount Hotel   60%   £112

Tel 01902 752055   Fax 01902 745263   Map 6 B4   **H**
Mount Road Tettenhall Wood Wolverhampton West Midlands WV6 8HL

Eight miles from Junction 10 of the M6 and two miles from the centre, a solid, 1870s redbrick building with modern bedroom wings, set in extensive gardens. Banqueting and conference facilities include the Grand Library complete with Italian rococo-style ceiling and minstrel's gallery. The Club Bar is a recent addition. Free parking. *Rooms 56. Garden. Access, Amex, Diners, Visa.*

Consult the blue pages for summary tables and lists of recommended establishments.

WOLVERHAMPTON Novotel 61% £65

Tel 01902 871100 Fax 01902 870054 Map 6 B4 **H**
Union Street Wolverhampton West Midlands WV1 3JN

Difficult to miss on the town centre ring road, this large modern Novotel features the usual plain but practical bedrooms and airy open-plan public areas. An outdoor swimming pool operates from May to September. Conference facilities for 120. *Rooms 132. Outdoor swimming pool. Access, Amex, Diners, Visa.*

WOODBRIDGE Seckford Hall 68% £99

Tel 01394 385678 Fax 01394 380610 Map 10 D3 **H**
Woodbridge Suffolk IP13 6NU

Family-owned and run since 1950, this imposing Elizabethan manor house is reached by following the A12 Woodbridge by-pass (don't turn off into the town) until a distinctive sign announces the hotel on the left. The house is surrounded by 34 acres of gardens and woodlands which include a willow-fringed lake. Its interior is characterised by period features such as linenfold panelling, heavily beamed ceilings, huge fireplaces and the carved wooden doors of the Great Hall (lounge). These are offset by plush velvet furnishings and richly coloured carpets. Bedrooms are comfortably furnished more in private house than hotel style, four have four-poster beds (one dates back to 1587) and some are in a courtyard complex that includes an inspired conversion of an old tithe barn into a delightful heated swimming pool. Banqueting/conference facilities for 100. Adjacent 18-hole golf course. *Rooms 32. Garden, putting, indoor swimming pool, solarium, spa bath, gym, fishing, coffee shop (10am-10pm). Closed 25 Dec. Access, Amex, Diners, Visa.*

WOODFORD BRIDGE Prince Regent Hotel 63% £96

Tel 0181-505 9966 Fax 0181-506 0807 Map 11 B4 **H**
Manor Road Woodford Bridge Essex IG8 8AE

The main house is Georgian, although now much extended to include substantial function and conference facilities for up to 400 delegates with various secretarial services available. Smart, up-to-date bedrooms are in a converted Victorian abbey joined to the original building. *Rooms 51. Garden. Access, Amex, Diners, Visa.*

WOODHALL SPA Dower House 62% £58

Tel 01526 352588 Fax 01526 354045 Map 7 E2 **H**
Manor Estate Woodhall Spa Lincolnshire LN10 6PY

In three acres of grounds on a private road, an Edwardian hotel sheltered from the nearby town centre. Comfortable armchairs around a log fire in the entrance hall give winter visitors a warm welcome, while summer guests will enjoy the garden views from the lounge and bar. Traditional bedrooms (six en suite, one with a bathroom down the corridor) are spacious and quiet. Children under 6 share parents' room free. *Rooms 7. Garden. Access, Amex, Diners, Visa.*

WOODSTOCK Bear Hotel 66% £133

Tel 01993 811511 Fax 01993 813380 Map 15 D2 **HR**
Park Street Woodstock Oxfordshire OX20 1SZ

Longstanding landmark of local catering, the origins of the creeper-clad coaching inn going back to the 12th century. It stands in a quiet side street before the gates to Blenheim Palace. Bedrooms (half newly refurbished) come in all shapes and sizes with decorations ranging from antique to modern. There is plenty of period charm, including heavy black beams and a Cotswold-stone fireplace with roaring log fire in the downstairs lounge-bar. Forte. *Rooms 44. Access, Amex, Diners, Visa.*

Restaurant £60

Darkwood reproduction furniture, white napery and original oak beams make a good contrast in the dining-room. The short, seasonal menu offers the likes of smoked haddock tartlet, Stilton and sorrel soufflé, braised oxtail with root vegetables, noisettes of lamb with aubergine mousse and tarragon sauce, and red mullet with fresh pasta. Desserts include millefeuille of red fruit, hot fudge cake and a hot soufflé of the day. Modest wine list with prices on the high side, though there are a few reasonably-priced lesser wines. *Seats 80. Parties 20. Private Rooms 6/28. L 12.30-2.30 D 7-10. Set L £14.95/£16.95 (Sun £18.50) Set D £25.95.*

WOODSTOCK — Feathers Hotel — 73% — £119

Tel 01993 812291   Fax 01993 813158   Map 15 D2   **HR**
Market Street Woodstock Oxfordshire OX7 1SX

Eight miles north of Oxford in the centre of historic Woodstock, the Feathers stands almost next to the gates of Blenheim Palace. Converted from four separate houses, it offers a range of comfortable, characterful accommodation behind its 17th-century Cotswold-stone frontage. All bedrooms have elaborately draped curtains and a useful range of extras that includes mineral water, chocolates, fresh flowers, magazines and tea on arrival. Some rooms have draped awnings over the beds, while the best have four-posters. Bathrooms are luxuriously fitted in marble throughout, with bathrobes and an abundance of toiletries provided. The upstairs drawing room with a library and open fire is the most inviting of the day rooms and a cosy bar has flagstone flooring and an open fireplace. During warm weather the courtyard garden is a delightful spot for light meals (which are also served in the Whinchat Bar). Service is courteous and efficient. Mountain bikes are available free of charge to guests. The addition of five more bedrooms was being planned as we went to press. *Rooms 17. Patio. Access, Amex, Diners, Visa.*

Restaurant   £75

A quiet, sophisticated air pervades the dining-room, where à la carte and fixed-price menus provide a choice of interesting options. David Lewis's style is modern British, typified by baked goat's cheese in oats with smoked bacon and lentils, smoked salmon three ways, chargrilled breast of chicken with wild rice and grain mustard hollandaise and fillet of halibut with Mediterranean vegetables. British cheeses are served with walnut, onion and herb bread; desserts range from lemon soufflé with strawberry compote to white chocolate and pistachio cheesecake. The wine list is rather patchy and somewhat inconsistent in its pricing policy: £7.50 for a glass of quite ordinary champagne is a bit steep! On the other hand, New World wines are fairly priced, though in the Australian section we are advised to "look out for the South Australian and New South Wales" areas, and yet most of those listed come from Victoria! Fortunately, good wines also come from there. *Seats 60. Parties 8. Private Room 22/60. L 12.30-2.15 (Sun to 2.30) D 7.30-9.30. Set L & D £19.50/£24.50.*

WOODY BAY — Woody Bay Hotel — 59% — £66

Tel & Fax 01598 763264   Map 13 D1   **H**
Woody Bay Devon EX31 4QX

Martin and Colette Petch can offer guests at their 100-year-old hotel two major attractions: spectacular views from its woody site overlooking the bay and an abundance of peace and quiet (there are no phones in the bedroom, but TVs are available on request). All but two of the rooms enjoy the views and those two are slightly discounted. There are two four-poster rooms and a family suite. Leave the A49 at Martinhoe Cross (or go via the Valley of Rocks coastal toll road). *Rooms 15. Closed Mon-Fri Dec-Feb. Access, Visa.*

WOOLACOMBE — Woolacombe Bay Hotel — 65% — £166*

Tel 01271 870388   Fax 01271 870613   Map 12 C1   **H**
South Street Woolacombe Devon EX34 7BN

Family summer holidays, winter breaks and conferences (for up to 200 delegates) are the main business at this imposing Edwardian hotel, whose lawns and gardens reach down to three miles of golden sands. The attractions extend outside the immediate vicinity, as guests enjoy preferential rates at both Saunton Sands Golf Club and Eastacott Meadows riding stables. Public rooms are fairly grand, bedrooms (including a new twin and a new family room) bright and roomy, with mostly modern furnishings. There are self-catering suites, apartments and flats. Children's club in high season. As we went to press a new gym and health suite 'The Hot House' was about to open. No dogs. *Half-board terms only. *Rooms 61. Garden, croquet, tennis, pitch & putt, indoor & outdoor swimming pools, gym, squash, sauna, spa bath, steam room, solarium, beauty salon, indoor bowls, billiards room, children's playground and organiser in high season, games room, snooker. Closed 2 Jan-10 Feb. Access, Amex, Diners, Visa.*

Set menu prices may not always include service or wine.

WOOLTON HILL   Hollington House   83%   £130

Tel 01635 255100   Fax 01635 255075   Map 15 D3   **HR**
Woolton Hill nr Newbury Berkshire RG20 9XA

Continuous improvements have taken place at John and Penny Guy's delightful Edwardian country house (follow signs to Hollington Herb Garden on the A343 Andover road south of Newbury) since it first opened three years ago. With the recent purchase of the surrounding woodland, the hotel now stands in 24 acres of very peaceful grounds, the gardens having been designed by Gertrude Jekyll. Inside, it's a marvellous place in which to relax and wind down, starting in the galleried entrance hall with wood panelling and large fireplace, carrying through to the high-ceilinged lounges with their stone mullion windows, comfortably furnished and particularly cosy in winter with roaring log fires. Throughout, you will notice John's collection of model ships in glass cases and Penny's appliqué and patchwork cushions. The individually designed bedrooms are models of good taste, providing all manner of extras from books, magazines and fresh flowers to mineral water, powerful hairdryer, portable radio and remote-control TV with teletext. 'Do not disturb' signs are replaced by fluffy toy cats! An obvious bonus is the very posh bathrooms (arguably the most spacious you'll ever see), many with spa baths, some even double spas and additional walk-in shower, with every conceivable extra provided from bathrobe to floating toy ducks. Breakfasts are great, staff absolutely terrific. Children under 7 free in parents' room. Two new conference suites and a games room have been added. Banqueting/conferences 70/80. No dogs. *Rooms 20. Garden, outdoor swimming pool, tennis, croquet, putting, snooker, mountain bikes. Access, Amex, Diners, Visa.*

The Oak Room   £90

A splendid oak-panelled room with a high latticework ceiling is the setting for David Lake's precise cooking (English with French touches). Now in situ for over a year, he has developed a pleasing, unfussy style, offering uncomplicated dishes, allowing the tastes and flavours of good-quality ingredients to come to the fore, rather than flowery menu descriptions. Start with a warming soup (cream of leek and potato perhaps) or tortellini of scallops, and follow with braised oxtail or steamed fillet of turbot. For a dessert, look no further than the classic Eve's pudding or an iced almond parfait with a coffee bean sauce. Alternatively, there's a huge array of British farmhouse cheeses, including the nearby Waterloo from Reading and Cerney from the Cotswolds. Incidentally, Sunday lunch includes a traditional roast rib of Scotch beef carved at your table. Last year's New World Cellar of the Year gets better and better with the further addition of rare Australian wines. But, it's not just Australia that makes the list here so fabulous – wines from all over the world are well represented and have been carefully chosen. Prices are very fair and encourage you to experiment and indulge! Furthermore, any bottle under £30 on the list can be served by the glass. *Seats 50. Parties 22. Private Room 14. L 12-2.30 D 7-9.30. Set L £13.75/£16.75 (Sun £18.50/£23.50) Set D £28.*

WORCESTER   Brown's   £75

Tel 01905 26263   Map 14 B1   **R**
24 Quay Street Worcester Hereford & Worcester WR1 2JJ

A spacious, high-ceilinged restaurant converted from a corn mill, with large picture windows overlooking the river and a capacious public car park next door. Dinner is a fixed-price, three-course affair of wholesome dishes: warm chicken liver salad, devilled herring roes on brioche toast, roast duck with Seville oranges, lamb's sweetbreads with tarragon and cream in a puff pastry case, charcoal-grilled fillet of beef. Also fresh fish of the day and a vegetarian special all adding up to about half a dozen main-course choices. Desserts range from savarin of fruits, ginger treacle sponge and chocolate marjolaine to home-made water ices. Lunch is a simpler meal along the same lines. No children under 8. *Seats 95. Parties 22. L 12.30-1.45 D 7.30-9.45. Closed Bank Holiday Mon, 1 week Christmas. Set L £16 (Sun £20) Set D £30. Access, Amex, Diners, Visa.*

WORCESTER   Fownes Hotel   70%   £100

Tel 01905 613151   Fax 01905 23742   Map 14 B1   **H**
City Walls Road Worcester Hereford & Worcester WR1 2AP

On the site of a famous glove factory, by an attractive canalside walk just a short distance from the cathedral and city centre. Victorian character is evident in the stylish and spacious interior; public rooms include a large foyer, a smart cocktail bar and an intimate library, where dark green walls and green leather wing chairs allow both the books and the collection of Royal Worcester china to be seen to advantage. Spacious bedrooms, all sited away from the busy main road, are well equipped, with freestanding mahogany furniture and quiet colour schemes. Good desk space and seating are provided. One bedroom is equipped for disabled guests. The John Fownes suite caters for conferences of up to 120. Children up to 16 may share parents' room free. *Rooms 61. Garden. Access, Amex, Diners, Visa.*

WORCESTER   Giffard Hotel   61%   £79

Tel 01905 726262   Fax 01905 723458   Map 14 B1   **H**
High Street Worcester Hereford & Worcester WR1 2QR

Decent accommodation in concrete 1960s' hotel opposite the cathedral. Conferences and banqueting cater for up to 150. Residents can use the adjacent NCP for only £2 a day. Forte. *Rooms 103. Pool table. Access, Amex, Diners, Visa.*

WORFIELD   Old Vicarage   67%   £90

Tel 01746 716497   Fax 01746 716552   Map 6 B4   **HR**
Worfield Bridgnorth Shropshire WV15 5JZ

Set in two acres of grounds overlooking fields and farmland, Peter and Christine Iles's redbrick Edwardian parsonage reflects the peace and quiet of its village setting. Twin conservatories jutting out into the garden house a relaxing lounge. Individually designed bedrooms, each named after a local village, sport reproduction furniture, pretty soft furnishings and copious extras. Four rooms in the Coach House have superior fittings (larger showers, jacuzzis, safes) and open on to a private garden with unspoilt views across the valley to the River Worfe; six of the bedrooms are for non-smokers and one is adapted for the use of wheelchair-bound guests. Staff are particularly friendly and families with children are welcome – no charge for extra beds or a cot in parents' room; high tea at 6pm; children up to 10 can stay free in parents' room. *Rooms 14. Garden, croquet. Access, Amex, Diners, Visa.*

Restaurant   £72

🍾 🍷 🦐 🍖 🍓🍷

Reliably good cooking from chef John Williams including starters like parsnip soup with curried coriander cream, a twice-baked wild mushroom and herb soufflé and confit of duck with honey and rosemary glaze before such main dishes as steamed Cornish turbot with chive butter sauce and basil noodles, supreme of chicken on a bed of braised cabbage and bacon with wild mushroom jus and pan-fried entrecote with roast shallots and wholegrain mustard sauce. Good artisanal British cheeses and/or desserts like lemon tart with blackcurrant sauce and iced praline parfait. The wines are good value here so you can afford to drink the very best. Wide choice from around the world, top growers, and many half bottles. The no-nonsense tasting notes are short and to the point. Cellar of the Year regional winner for Midlands/Heart of England. *Seats 50. Private Room 16. L Sun 12-2 other days by arrangement D 7-9 (Sun at 7). Set Sun L £12.95 Set D £23.50/£27.50 (Fri & Sat £28.50/£33.50).*

WORTHING   Beach Hotel   64%   £82

Tel 01903 234001   Fax 01903 234567   Map 11 A6   **H**
Marine Parade Worthing West Sussex BN11 3QJ

In a prime seafront position, the Beach offers modest comfort behind a long terraced frontage. Public rooms are on a scale large enough to handle conferences of up to 200. The majority of the double-glazed bedrooms are singles; most are generally light and spacious with a traditional look. Some rooms have their own balconies directly overlooking the sea. No dogs. *Rooms 81. Access, Amex, Diners, Visa.*

WORTHING — Chatsworth Hotel — 57% — £90

Tel 01903 236103   Fax 01903 823726   Map 11 A6   **H**
Steyne Worthing West Sussex BN11 3DU

A conference-orientated hotel in a one-way system (turn left after the pier) with fine creeper-covered Georgian facade, overlooking Steyne Gardens and the sea. Well-kept bedrooms are not luxurious, but include the extras one now expects as standard. Children under 14 sharing with two adults charged for meals only. The games room contains two full-size snooker tables. *Rooms 107. Games room. Access, Amex, Diners, Visa.*

WRIGHTINGTON — High Moor Inn — NEW — £55

Tel 01257 252364   Fax 01257 255120   Map 6 B1   **R**
High Moor Lane Wrightington nr Wigan Lancashire WN6 9QA

A change of style here with the restaurant undergoing an expensive facelift (lots of oak, stone flagging, iron fireplaces and exposed beams, the whole adding up to an appealing rustic charm). *Master McGraths* at Scarisbrick (qv) is in the same ownership. The cooking, under the direction of chef-partner Jim Sines, also appeals, leaning as it does towards modern British dishes, though occasional intruders such as Thai crab cakes, stir-fried vegetables with calamari and hoi sin, or chicken kebab with tabouleh salad make an appearance. Otherwise, choose from, say, smoked haddock cappuccino; black pudding and melted onion; roast sea bream with lemon grass, mussels and coriander; braised boneless oxtails with bubble and squeak. Desserts include sticky toffee pudding with butterscotch sauce and hot chocolate tart, while the splendid cheeseboard features several English farmhouse cheeses. Cheerful service and 'Early Doors'/Sunday fixed-price meals encourage families, with the traditional Sunday lunch served until 4pm; on Sunday evenings only the early evening menu (extended to 8.30pm) is available, not à la carte. Fairly-priced wine list with many (chalked up on the board) available by the glass. *Seats 95. Parties 14. L 12-2 D 5.30-10 (Sun 12-8.30). Set L £9/£11 Set D (5.30-7pm only) £9.50/£11.50. Access, Amex, Diners, Visa.*

WROTHAM HEATH — Forte Posthouse — 67% — £75

Tel 01732 883311   Fax 01732 885850   Map 11 B5   **H**
London Road Wrotham Heath nr Sevenoaks Kent TN15 7RS

Located on the A20 close to Junction 2A of the M26, offering spacious, well-designed public areas and good leisure facilities. The bars and lounges are in an open-plan arrangement, one section of the lounge overlooking an inner courtyard with an ornamental pool. Meeting room for 60. *Rooms 106. Garden, indoor swimming pool, sauna, solarium, whirlpool bath, gym. Access, Amex, Diners, Visa.*

WROXTON ST MARY — Wroxton House Hotel — 66% — £95

Tel 01295 730777   Fax 01295 730800   Map 14 C1   **H**
Wroxton St Mary nr Banbury Oxfordshire OX15 6QB

On the Stratford side of Banbury (A422), three village houses dating from the 17th century have been sympathetically linked to a modern clocktower wing built of local honey-coloured stone to make this genuinely friendly hotel. Reception and a sunken lounge flank the flagstoned foyer, beyond which is a period-style bar featuring open fires in winter, and masses of flowers in summer. Bedrooms are individually decorated, with original timbers preserved in some of the older rooms; the remainder have stylish darkwood furniture. Children up to 16 free in their parents' room; family facilities provided. *Rooms 32. Garden. Access, Amex, Diners, Visa.*

WYCH CROSS — Ashdown Park Hotel — 78% — £115

Tel 01342 824988   Fax 01342 826206   Map 11 B6   **HR**
Wych Cross nr East Grinstead East Sussex RH18 5JR

From the A22 at Wych Cross take the minor road signposted Hatfield to find this extensive Victorian mansion, opened as a hotel in late 1993. The setting is splendid with the hotel's own 187 acres of mature parkland, which boasts a herd of wild deer, surrounded by Ashdown Forest. From the porte-cochère you enter into a grand, galleried entrance hall/reception with the welcoming aroma of a log fire that burns all year in a large stone fireplace. Day rooms include a row of three stately lounges and a cocktail

See over

bar from which an open stairway leads down to a convivial snooker room with two full-sized tables as well as bar billiards for less serious cue men. Five grades of bedroom differ only in size and outlook as all have the same reproduction antique-style furniture, comfortable easy chairs and extras like mineral water and fresh fruit; bathrooms all come with robes, generous towelling and quality toiletries. Keen staff are aiming at high levels of service with rooms properly serviced in the evenings and 24hr room service. Along with a smart new Country Club and 9-hole golf course guests also enjoy temporary membership of not just one but two championship courses in the vicinity. A large chapel (the house was once a nunnery – it's also been an American university and a training centre for one of the big banks) has been imaginatively converted into a pair of fine conference/function rooms holding up to 180 theatre-style. Under the same ownership as *Tylney Hall*, Rotherwick (qv). *Rooms 95. Garden, croquet, tennis, golf (9-hole), indoor swimming pool, gym, squash, sauna, spa bath, sun beds, beauty salon, snooker. Access, Amex, Diners, Visa.*

Anderida Restaurant   £80

The name comes from that given by the Romans to the forest that surrounds the hotel and which can be seen in the distance from the tall, stone-mullioned windows of the large dining-room. The kitchen is in the experienced and safe hands of John McManus, who uses only the best-quality ingredients for dishes like a cream of artichoke soup finished with scallops under a puff pastry lid; duck confit with Oriental spices; whole roast turbot (for two) with herb glaze and creamed wild mushrooms; loin of pork with salsify, smoked bacon and rosemary, and warm pigeon tart with roasted root vegetables and peppercorn sauce. Good, clear-flavoured sauces and attractive, unfussy presentation are notable features. Puds might include rice pudding with glacé fruit and Cointreau, and toffee apple crumble with vanilla ice cream and there are some good British cheeses. Many big names on a big wine list that is thoroughly well presented, informative and very comprehensive. Terrific balance between Europe and the New World, old and recent vintages. Many half bottles; house recommendations apart, mark-ups are quite steep. Prices throughout the hotel are inclusive of service. *Seats 150. Parties 10. L 12.30-2 D 7.30-9.30 (Fri & Sat till 10). Set L £12.95/£17 (Sun £18.95) Set D £27.*

WYLAM	Laburnum House	£65

Tel 01661 852185   Map 5 D2   **RR**
Main Street Wylam Northumberland NE41 8AJ

A delightful little restaurant in a Tyneside village, with inviting wicker chairs set at attractively laid tables. Traditional and modern elements are both to be found on a menu that changes frequently and always offers variety and reliable standards of cooking: moules marinière, chicken and pistachio terrine, crab and prawn bisque, grilled chicken breast with lemon and walnut sauce, rack of lamb with tarragon, medallions of pork with rosemary, tomato and mozzarella and sticky toffee pudding. *Seats 47. Parties 15. D only 6.30-10. Closed Sun, 26 Dec, 1 & 2 Jan. Set D £15.50. Access, Amex, Visa.*

Rooms   £50

Four neat bedrooms, all doubles and all quite large; three have private shower rooms and one a bathroom.

WYMONDHAM	Number Twenty Four	£45

Tel 01953 607750   Map 10 C2   **R**
24 Middleton Street Wymondham Norfolk NR18 0BH

A homely town-centre restaurant where reservations need to be made well in advance for Saturday nights. Chef-proprietor Richard Hughes offers a lunchtime blackboard menu

with individually priced dishes as well as a three-course fixed-priced menu of virtually the same dishes. There are a few more choices on the evening three-course menu. Local ingredients are put to good use in dishes such as casserole of mussels with Morston samphire and vermouth cream and chicken, leek and brie sausage with an apple and walnut salad. Tournedos of local pork loin with mustard seed crust, apple and rosemary cream gravy and tarragon mash and roast rack of lamb with fresh blackberries, noodles and sherry sauce are typical of main dishes on offer. Good vegetarian options. Desserts such as caramelised apple wafers and Nico Ladenis' rich chocolate marquise or 'the grand dessert' – a little of everything – round things off nicely. Sound, reliable, cooking without pretensions in friendly, informal surroundings. No smoking before 9.30.
Seats 65. Parties 40. Private Room 50. L 11-2.30 D 7.30-9.30. Closed D Tues, all Sun & Mon, 24-31 Dec. Set L £9 Set D £16.95. Access, Visa.

YELVERTON	Moorland Links	65%	£85

Tel 01822 852245   Fax 01822 855004   Map 12 C3   **H**
Yelverton nr Plymouth Devon PL20 6DA

Set in nine acres of grounds within the Dartmoor National Park, the hotel is off the A386 between Plymouth and Tavistock. Public rooms look out on to well-kept lawns and individually decorated bedrooms are spacious and comfortable, with well-equipped, carpeted bathrooms. Conference facilities for up to 100, banqueting up to 200. Children up to 12 stay free in parents' room. Forestdale Hotels. *Rooms 45. Garden, tennis. Access, Amex, Diners, Visa.*

YEOVIL	Little Barwick House	£70

Tel 01935 23902   Fax 01935 20908   Map 13 F2   **RR**
Barwick Village nr Yeovil Somerset BA22 9TD

Ask for directions in order to find this delightful listed Georgian Dower House set in gently sloping gardens some two miles south of Yeovil. Veronica Colley's fixed-price menus may be short on choice but certainly not on imagination. Begin with confit of duck leg on a bed of pasta or pot of baked, flaked Finnan haddock topped with cheese and move on to roast rack of local lamb with mint and cucumber, Sussex pie, West Bay fillet of sole meuniére or roast wild duck with Madeira gravy. No smoking. *Seats 40. Private Room 20. D only 7-9 (Sat to 9.30). Closed Sun (except residents), 2 weeks Jan. Set D £16.90/£22.90. Access, Amex, Visa.*

Rooms   £76

Six spotlessly kept bedrooms (no smoking) with simple decor and furnishings promise peace and quiet in an abundantly calm rural setting. Exemplary breakfasts are served in the sunlit morning room.

YEOVIL	The Manor Hotel	63%	£86

Tel 01935 231161   Fax 01935 706607   Map 13 F2   **H**
Hendford Yeovil Somerset BA20 1TG

Close to the town centre, an old mansion dating from 1735 with converted stables offering modern bedroom facilities. Conferences and private dining for up to 60; attractive conservatory opening to enclosed formal garden. Forte. *Rooms 41. Garden. Access, Amex, Diners, Visa.*

YORK	Abbey Park Resort Hotel	57%	£96

Tel 01904 658301   Fax 01904 621224   Map 7 D1   **H**
77 The Mount York North Yorkshire YO2 2BN

One mile from the city centre, this hotel offers modern facilities behind a Georgian facade. Accommodation comprises singles, doubles, twins and family rooms – some rooms enjoy fine views of the city. Children up to 16 stay free in their parents' room. *Rooms 85. Access, Amex, Diners, Visa.*

Set menu prices may not always include service or wine.

YORK   Dean Court Hotel   63%   £105

Tel 01904 625082   Fax 01904 620305   Map 7 D1   **H**
Duncombe Place York North Yorkshire YO1 2EF

Originally built to provide homes for the clergy of York Minster (opposite the west front of which it stands) Dean Court is now a privately owned hotel. The public areas boast some fine yew-veneered furniture and fittings, there's a delightful tearoom-conservatory and a private dining/conference room, the McLeod Suite. Bedrooms are light and airy, and those at the front have fine views of the Minster and its close. 24hr room service. Valet parking in the hotel's own secure car park. Children up to 16 stay free in parents' room. A refurbishment programme is under way throughout the hotel. No dogs. *Rooms 42. Coffee shop (9.30am-6.30pm). Access, Amex, Diners, Visa.*

YORK   Forte Posthouse   65%   £72

Tel 01904 707921   Fax 01904 702804   Map 7 D1   **H**
Tadcaster Road York North Yorkshire YO2 2QF

Bright and airy day rooms surround a central lawn at a practical modern hotel on the A1036, south of the city. Banqueting for 65 and conferences for up to 120 theatre-style. 30 interconnecting family rooms. Small pitch and putt course. *Rooms 139. Garden. Access, Amex, Diners, Visa.*

YORK   Grange Hotel   74%   £98

Tel 01904 644744   Fax 01904 612453   Map 7 D1   **HR**
Clifton York North Yorkshire YO3 6AA

A fine Regency town house, carefully restored from a group of flats, just 400 yards north of the city walls on the A19 road to Thirsk. The relaxed, homely atmosphere is exemplified by the elegant morning room – plump cushions on the couches, a fine open fire, oil paintings hanging on the walls and fresh flowers. The bedrooms may not be large but are individually furnished with fine-quality fabrics, antique furniture and English chintz. The young management and friendly staff have high hotel-keeping standards and help make this a good alternative to uniform, commercial rivals. Baby-sitting can be arranged in advance and there are a couple of high-chairs in the Brasserie (easiest access is via the rear car park). Meeting rooms for up to 60. *Rooms 30. Access, Amex, Diners, Visa.*

Ivy Restaurant   £60

Head chef Christopher Falcus produces two fixed-price menus, offering perhaps roulade of smoked salmon with cream cheese and fresh herbs, salad of chargrilled vegtables with pesto and tomato dressing and breast of chicken cooked with honey and mustard at lunch, plus warm scallop and bacon salad with red wine vinaigrette and breast of chicken (this time filled with white pudding on braised garlic lentils) for dinner. Vegetarian options too. An à la carte is also available. Simpler fare is offered in the 45-seat, brick-vaulted Brasserie converted from the old cellars. *Seats 55. Parties 14. Private Room 50. L 12.30-2.30 D 7-10 (Brasserie 12-3, 6-11). Closed L Sat. Set L £13 (Sun £15) Set D £23.*

YORK   Judges Lodging   64%   £95

Tel 01904 638733   Fax 01904 679947   Map 7 D1   **H**
9 Lendal York North Yorkshire YO1 2AQ

Close to York Minster, within the central footstreet zone, a fine Georgian town house which was the official residence of the Assize Court judges from 1806. It remained such until 1977, when it was restored and opened as a hotel. Two curved stone stairs lead you from the courtyard to the lovely central entrance, beyond which is a beautifully proportioned hall with a small lounge area. Arched redbrick ceilings add character to the cellar bar and the bedrooms are delightful, with antiques, fine paintings, prints and lots of extras. Own parking. *Rooms 12. Garden. Access, Amex, Diners, Visa.*

Consult the blue pages for summary tables and lists of recommended establishments.

YORK — Melton's — £50

Tel 01904 634341   Fax 01904 629233   Map 7 D1   **R**
7 Scarcroft Road York North Yorkshire YO2 1ND

A warm, inviting and family-friendly restaurant where the cooking mixes the adventurous with more standard fare, making use of local suppliers when possible. Cabbage and bacon broth, smoked haddock rarebit and coconut and aubergine loaf with a hot pepper sauce were warming starters on a winter menu, while main courses included cod with parsley purée, saffron mash and a gratin of courgettes and fennel, rack of lamb with gratin dauphinois and pan-fried breast of pheasant with spring onions and ginger. Tuesday, Wednesday and Thursday evenings bring, respectively, seafood, pudding and vegetarian specialities, and there are special menus for Saturday lunch, with a specific theme for the first Saturday in each month. Super desserts might include a white chocolate parfait with lime syrup or sticky toffee pudding. Menu prices include coffee, mineral water and service. With a maximum mark-up of £10 a bottle, the more expensive the wine the better the value, though the reality is that everything on the list, which has just a sprinkling of non-French, offers good value. *Seats 40. Parties 30. Private Room 16. L 12-2 D 5.30-10. Closed D Sun, L Mon, 1 week Aug/Sep, 3 weeks Christmas. Set L & early D £13.90 Set D £19.50 (Mon-Thur) & £28.50. Access, Visa.*

YORK — Middlethorpe Hall — 79% — £141

Tel 01904 641241   Fax 01904 620176   Map 7 D1   **HR**
Bishopthorpe Road York North Yorkshire YO2 1QB

Built in 1699, Middlethorpe is a lovely example of a William and Mary house. It stands in 27 acres of well-tended grounds some 1½ miles south of the city centre on the edge of York racecourse. Its red-brick classical exterior is complemented by a very fine interior decor and furnishings which are in keeping with the building's character. The flagstoned entrance hall has a log fire, flower arrangements and paintings which create a splendid first impression. Public rooms are liberally dotted with antiques as well as oil paintings and a multitude of flowers. The chandeliered drawing-room has well-upholstered settees and armchairs and there's also the more cosy and intimate library. Bedrooms in the main house are spacious and high-ceilinged, those in the converted courtyard rooms more cottagey, though both categories are decorated and furnished to an exacting standard, all with a host of pampering extras. Edwardian-style bathrooms have quality toiletries and plentiful thick towels. Super standards of housekeeping and service. No children under 8. No dogs. *Rooms 30. Garden, croquet. Access, Amex, Diners, Visa.*

Restaurant   £100

Dinner is a formal and elegant affair taking place in the panelled Oak Rooms. At lunchtime the full-length windows take full advantage of the garden views. Dinner comprises 3 or 4 courses with an additional gourmet menu also available. The style follows current fashionable trends, offering a mix of Mediterranean and Oriental influences. Starters from a daily-changing selection could be a salad of pigeon with bean shoots and Chinese leaves with a raspberry dressing or roast fillet of baby codling with a tapénade crust and sun-dried tomatoes. Lamb cutlets with a tarragon and wild mushroom mousse and basil gravy and maize-fed chicken poached with spicy vegetables and a light Jacqueline liquor are among the main dishes. For dessert there's a praline parfait with vanilla custard or trio of chocolate mousses with a raspberry sauce. The gourmet menu offers slightly more ambitious cooking and the Grill Room offers an intimate cellar-like setting for some more traditional cooking. Easy-to-use wine list, though only house selection and sommelier's choice have tasting notes. *Seats 60. Parties 8. Private Room 50. L 12.30-1.45 D 7.30-9.45. Set L £12.50 (Sun £14.50) Set D £25.95 & £33.95.*

YORK   Mount Royale   66%   £85

Tel 01904 628856   Fax 01904 611171   Map 7 D1   **H**
119 The Mount York North Yorkshire YO2 2DA

Located just a short distance outside the city walls on one of the principal routes into the centre, the privately owned hotel offers comfortable, homely accommodation with very pleasant staff in attendance. The best and quietest rooms overlook the well-maintained gardens at the rear though front rooms are all triple glazed. Public rooms include a very snug bar with dark oak panelling originally from a church. There's also a brighter cocktail bar-cum-coffee lounge with bamboo furniture. It serves as one of two lounges; the other, more laid-back and relaxing is located in a modern extension to the side. Bedrooms vary in size and character but all are furnished to a good standard with many thoughtful extras provided. The four garden rooms are spacious and have patio doors that open on to a small verandah overlooking, and with access to, the gardens. *Rooms 23. Garden, outdoor swimming pool, sauna, steam room, solarium, snooker. Closed 24-30 Dec. Access, Amex, Diners, Visa.*

YORK   19 Grape Lane   £75

Tel 01904 636366   Map 7 D1   **R**
19 Grape Lane York North Yorkshire YO1 2HU

♀ ❦

The restaurant is housed in a characterful timbered building close to York Minster on the corner of Coffee Yard (off Stonegate) and Grape Lane. There is a simple lunchtime menu while in the evening wider choice might include breast of chicken on a bed of noodles with a Stilton sauce, poached salmon with a spinach and white wine sauce and lamb cutlets with a redcurrant sauce. *Seats 34. Parties 12. Private Room 22. L 12-1.45 D 6-9 (Sat to 10). Closed Sun & Mon, Christmas, 2 weeks Jan/Feb, 2 weeks Sep. Set L £9.95/£12.50. Access, Visa.*

YORK   Novotel   62%   £89

Tel 01904 611660   Fax 01904 610925   Map 7 D1   **H**
Fishergate York North Yorkshire YO1 4AD

Modern redbrick hotel in the city centre (A19 Selby road), by the side of the River Ouse. All rooms have a double and a single bed. Four bedrooms equipped for disabled guests. Two children under 16 may share their parents' room free of charge, breakfast included. Conference/banqueting facilities for 210/130; parking for 150 cars. Dogs £10 per night. *Rooms 124. Indoor swimming pool. Access, Amex, Diners, Visa.*

YORK   Royal York Hotel   67%   £113

Tel 01904 653681   Fax 01904 623503   Map 7 D1   **H**
Station Road York North Yorkshire YO2 2AA

Adjacent to the railway station with its own covered entrance from it, and fronted by three acres of well-tended gardens, the hotel (1878) is a fine example of solidly-built Victorian architecture. The entrance hall features a grand staircase flanked by two impressive Italian crystal chandeliers. Spacious public rooms include a basement bar, Tiles, its walls covered in original and now listed Birmantoft tiles. There's also a leisure complex. Bedrooms are very smartly decorated with front-facing rooms enjoying good views of the Cathedral. *Rooms 145. Garden, croquet, putting, pitch & putt, gym, sauna, steam room, solarium, gents hairdressing, snooker. Access, Amex, Diners, Visa.*

YORK   Stakis York   65%   £104

Tel 01904 648111   Fax 01904 610317   Map 7 D1   **H**
1 Tower Street York North Yorkshire YO1 1SB

A modern redbrick hotel standing in the shadows of Clifford's Tower in the heart of the city. Bedrooms, all doubles or twins, are comprehensively equipped with satellite TV, mini-bars and the usual modern amenities. Bathrooms are neat but compact. *Rooms 128. Access, Amex, Diners, Visa.*

Lodges are now listed by county in the reference section

YORK — Swallow Hotel — 64% — £110

Tel 01904 701000   Fax 01904 702308   Map 7 D1   **H**
Tadcaster Road York North Yorkshire YO2 2QQ

A mile from the city centre on the A1036, the Swallow stands in its own grounds overlooking the historic Knavesmire racecourse. The purpose-built Swallow Management Centre has proved a popular addition to the facilities which include a leisure club and parking for 200+ cars. Banqueting/conferences for 120/170. Children up to 15 free in parents' room. *Rooms 112. Garden, croquet, putting, indoor swimming pool, steam room, spa bath, sauna, solarium, beautician, keep-fit equipment, coffee shop (10am-10pm). Access, Amex, Diners, Visa.*

YORK — Viking Moat House — 69% — £132

Tel 01904 659822   Fax 01904 641793   Map 7 D1   **H**
North Street York North Yorkshire YO1 1JF

Tall, modern Queens Moat Houses hotel and conference centre standing in a convenient central location by the river Ouse. Style and comfort are not lacking in the brick-walled reception, the lounge and the bar, the last two with river views. A choice of conference suites can handle up to 300 delegates. Bedrooms are well lit and amply furnished. 24hr room service. No dogs. Limited underground garaging (£5 a night). Formerly called simply *The Viking. Rooms 187. Patio, gym, sauna, spa bath, solarium, golf practice net, brasserie (10am-10pm). Access, Amex, Diners, Visa.*

YOXFORD — Satis House — 63% — £78

Tel 01728 668418   Fax 01728 668640   Map 10 D2   **H**
Yoxford Saxmundham Suffolk IP16 3EX

The Grade II listed country house is set in three acres of parkland alongside the A12. Charles Dickens was a friend of the original owner and Pip Gargery mentions the house in *Great Expectations*. The entrance hall is paved with York stone and leads to public rooms furnished with antiques. Two of the bedrooms are older in style with large, solid wood half-tester double beds and Edwardian baths and fittings, while others are more modern. No children under 14 or dogs. *Rooms 7. Garden, croquet, keep-fit equipment, sauna, solarium, spa bath. Access, Amex, Diners, Visa.*

THE INDEPENDENT

INDEPENDENT
ON SUNDAY

Your truly independent guides to life

Your **Guarantee** of **Quality** and **Independence**

EGON RONAY'S GUIDES

1996

- Establishment inspections are anonymous
- Inspections are undertaken by qualified Egon Ronay's Guides inspectors
- The Guides are completely independent in their editorial selection
- The Guides do not accept advertising, hospitality or payment from listed establishments

The **Leading** Guides

Hotels & Restaurants ● Pubs & Inns ● Europe
Ireland ● Just A Bite
And Children Come Too ● Paris
Oriental Restaurants

Egon Ronay's Guides are available from all good bookshops or can be ordered from: Leading Guides, 35 Tadema Road, London SW10 0PZ
Tel 0171 352 0172

USING YOUR MOBILE PHONE OVERSEAS

In addition to superb voice quality, and enhanced call security, Cellnet's digital service enables you to keep in touch, throughout the UK – and while travelling overseas.

International Roaming – the facility to make and receive calls while travelling abroad is made available through reciprocal agreements with individual network operators in a number of countries.

At the time of publication – October '95 – mobile coverage embraces virtually all Western Europe and many major trading areas further afield, including: Australia, Hong Kong and South Africa.

During 1996 it is expected that worldwide coverage will be extended to include: Cyprus, Gibraltar, Hungary, Iceland, Morocco, Singapore, and the United Arab Emirates.

International Roaming enables you to keep in touch with contacts in the countries you visit, as well as colleagues, suppliers, and family back home.

THE NET THAT SETS YOU FREE

for further information call

0800 214000

At the time of publication, October '95, reciprocal agreements have been signed with the following countries.

AUSTRALIA

AUSTRIA

BELGIUM

DENMARK

FINLAND

FRANCE

GERMANY

GREECE

HONG KONG

IRELAND

ITALY

JERSEY

LUXEMBOURG

NETHERLANDS

NORWAY

PORTUGAL

SOUTH AFRICA

SPAIN

SWEDEN

SWITZERLAND

UNITED ARAB
EMIRATES

THE NET THAT SETS YOU FREE

for further information call
0800 214000

Scotland

ABERDEEN   Ardoe House   70%   £146

Tel 01224 867355   Fax 01224 861283   Map 3 D4   **H**
South Deeside Road Blairs Grampian AB1 5YP

A few minutes' drive from the centre of Aberdeen, Ardoe House enjoys a secluded
setting at the end of a winding drive. Its style is Scottish Baronial, and day rooms retain
all their best original features, with carved oak panelling and handsome ceiling work. The
drawing-room and cocktail bar are warm and inviting, and there's a choice of rooms
available for conferences and banquets (for up to 300/200). Bedrooms are comfortable
and well appointed, whether in the main building (some reached by a fine oak staircase
past a stained-glass window) or in the sympathetically designed modern section, where
the majority are located. Children stay free in parents' room. *Rooms 71. Garden, croquet,
putting. Access, Amex, Diners, Visa.*

ABERDEEN   Atlantis   £65

Tel 01224 591403   Fax 01224 571621   Map 3 D4   **R**
Malacca Hotel 349 Gt Western Road Aberdeen Grampian AB1 6NW

Seafood takes pride of place here with dishes like sole bonne femme, monkfish in
a rosemary and vermouth sauce, steamed scallops on a chicory and cucumber sauce, and
simply grilled lobster, making good use of the landings at Aberdeen's famous fish market
plus salmon from the River Ugie and mussels and oysters from Orkney. The cold seafood
platter (£60 for two) is a generous selection of all their seafood presented with four
different dips. The meat section of the menu majors on prime Aberdeen Angus steaks
plus old favourites such as beef stroganoff, coq au vin and chicken cordon bleu. Sunday
lunchtime brings a three-course carvery menu in addition to the regular à la carte.
Seats 40. Private Room 25. L 12-2 D 6-10. Set Sun L £7.40/£9.25 Access, Amex, Diners, Visa.

ABERDEEN   Caledonian Thistle   68%   £115

Tel 01224 640233   Fax 01224 641627   Map 3 D4   **H**
Union Terrace Aberdeen Grampian AB9 1HE

City-centre hotel with Regency-style day rooms, double-glazed bedrooms and a choice
of eating places – the café/bar is open 10am-11.45pm (10.45 Sunday). Ongoing
refurbishment. Children up to 14 share parents' room free. Conference/banqueting for
40/26. *Rooms 78. Sauna. Access, Amex, Diners, Visa.*

ABERDEEN   Copthorne Hotel   68%   £136

Tel 01224 630404   Fax 01224 640573   Map 3 D4   **H**
122 Huntly Street Aberdeen Grampian AB1 1SU

A smart, modern city-centre hotel behind the granite facade of a converted warehouse.
Good standards of accommodation in Classic and Connoisseur rooms and suites. 24hr room
service. Conference facilities for 220. No dogs. *Rooms 89. Access, Amex, Diners, Visa.*

ABERDEEN   Gerard's   £70

Tel 01224 639500   Fax 01224 571782   Map 3 D4   **R**
50 Chapel Street Aberdeen Grampian AB1 1SN

Reliable, sound cooking – French and international – is the hallmark of Gerard Flecher's
city-centre restaurant, off the west end of Union Street. Very good value business lunches
offer an unusually wide choice, from cream soup of the day with garlic bread to
vol-au-vent of venison in a rowan jelly and cream sauce. Dinner brings a *menu complet*
and a varied à la carte choice that includes classics such as garlic snails and moules
marinière along with more innovative suggestions like veal escalope in a cheese, egg and
lemon batter, roast lamb with apricot and herb stuffing on a rosemary, claret and red
onion sauce and salmon creel filled with flaked salmon and langoustine cooked in Tokay
wine and cream. Predominantly French wine list with twenty or so fine reserve wines.
Children welcome; special menu and toybox available. *Seats 70. Private Rooms 12/16/24.
L 12-2.30 D 6-10.30. Closed Sun & Bank Holiday Mondays. Set D £23.50.
Access, Amex, Diners, Visa.*

ABERDEEN — Holiday Inn Crowne Plaza 69% £127

Tel 01224 713911 Fax 01224 714020 Map 3 D4 **H**
Oldmeldrum Road Bucksburn Aberdeen Grampian AB2 9LN

There's a courtesy coach provided between Aberdeen Airport and this modern hotel on the A96 Inverness road. All the bedrooms have double beds and the usual range of electric gadgets. Well equipped for leisure and for conferences (500 theatre-style). Parking for 250 cars. *Rooms 144. Indoor swimming pool, keep-fit equipment, sauna, steam room, sun bed. Access, Amex, Diners, Visa.*

Many hotels offer reduced rates for weekend or out-of-season bookings. Always ask about special deals.

ABERDEEN — The Marcliffe at Pitfodels 78% £120

Tel 01224 861000 Fax 01224 868860 Map 3 D4 **HR**
North Deeside Road Pitfodels Aberdeen Grampian AB1 9PA

Aberdeen's latest and best hotel is set in six acres of landscaped grounds on the western outskirts of the city, newly built, but in traditional style, by experienced local hoteliers Stewart and Sheila Spence. Day rooms like the rug-strewn, flagstoned lobby and richly furnished lounge with its red walls, real fire and scattering of antiques, demonstrate Sheila's flair for interior design. Bedroom decor is particularly striking with innovative combinations of floral patterns, checks and colourful Mediterranean prints used to great effect. Well-designed and spacious, with quality furniture – antiques in the Master bedrooms that boast such extras as video machines and decanters of sherry – and comfortable armchairs, all rooms have desk as well as bedside phones, mini-bars with fresh milk for the discreetly hidden beverage kit (there's also 24hr room service) and trouser press incorporating iron and ironing board. Good bathrooms feature a third tap at the washbasin dispensing specially purified drinking water. Immaculate staff, kitted-out in the hotel's own tartan, are numerous and attentive, providing a high level of service. Good breakfasts include 'Aberdeen Rowies', a local speciality a bit like a flat croissant. Banqueting/conferences for up to 400/600. *Rooms 42. Garden, croquet, putting, fishing, games room, snooker. Access, Amex, Diners, Visa.*

Conservatory Restaurant and Invery Room £90

A choice of eating here: the smart yet informal, split-level (divided by stone balustrade) Conservatory with terrace offering a short but varied à la carte – fillet of lamb with a garden herb crust, medallions of monkfish with a wild mushroom mousse, chargrilled steaks – and the opulent, formal, dinner-only Invery Room. The latter, sporting a handsome antique sideboard, offers a fixed-price, four-course menu that shares some dishes with the Conservatory plus the likes of cream of curried parsnip soup with chicken and herb dumplings, ravioli of lamb's sweetbreads, salmon escalope on a bed of leeks with a tomato béarnaise and roast fillet of venison on a port and rowanberry sauce. Cooking generally is uncomplicated but not unsophisticated; and the raw materials are first-rate. Price quoted is for the no-smoking Invery Room. Why present a printed and bound wine list if "prices are subject to market, duty and foreign exchange rate fluctuations and may be adjusted without prior notice?" Are not the bottles listed already in the cellar? Good value house wines, imaginative New World section, France less so.
Invery Room: Seats 32. Parties 12. Private Room 24. D only 7-10. Closed Sun & Mon.
Conservatory: Seats 74. L 12-2.30 D 6.30-10.

Set menu prices may not always include service or wine.

ABERDEEN   Silver Darling   £65

Tel 01224 576229   Map 3 D4   **R**
Pocra Quay North Pier Aberdeen Grampian AB2 1DQ

A French speciality 'barbecued seafood' restaurant overlooking the city and old port from the farthest point of the North Quay. Most of the fish is prepared in full view of diners through a large kitchen window, cooked on the barbecue and served with fennel, tomatoes and a herb butter sauce. Besides this there's a wide choice, from a soup of monkfish, mussels and smoked haddock flavoured with sorrel and a warm salad of scallops and Dublin Bay prawns with blueberry vinegar to sole, halibut and prawns poached on a bed of seaweed and fish stock finished with cream and saffron. Just three half bottles on the concise French-only wine list that includes extensive tasting notes. *Seats 35. L 12-1.45 D 7-9.45. Closed L Sat, all Sun & 2 weeks Christmas. Set L £16.50. Access, Amex, Diners, Visa.*

ABERDEEN   Stakis Aberdeen   63%   £128

Tel 01224 313377   Fax 01224 312028   Map 3 D4   **H**
161 Springfield Road Aberdeen Grampian AB9 2QH

In a residential area on the western edge of the city, a hotel offering a variety of bedrooms, including Executive and family rooms, all complete with the expected up-to-date accessories. There's a well-equipped leisure club and large, comprehensive conference facilities catering for up to 1000 delegates. Children up to 15 stay free in parents' room. 30% of the rooms are non-smoking. Previously the *Stakis Tree Tops*. *Rooms 110. Indoor swimming pool, gym, spa bath, sauna, sun beds, tennis. Access, Amex, Diners, Visa.*

Set menu prices may not always include service or wine.

ABERDEEN AIRPORT   Aberdeen Marriott   70%   £132

Tel 01224 770011   Fax 01224 722347   Map 3 D4   **H**
Riverview Drive Farburn Dyce Aberdeen Grampian AB2 0AZ

Low-rise hotel two miles from the airport built around a central leisure area with kidney-shaped pool. Standardised bedrooms – half designated non-smoking – are spacious and practical rather than luxurious. Executive rooms get various extras. One room is equipped for disabled guests. Children up to 18 share parents' room free. 24hr room service. Conference and banqueting facilities for 400/350; parking for 200 cars. Courtesy coach to and from the airport. Guests may use the squash courts at the *Skean Dhu* hotel nearby. 4 miles from the city centre. *Rooms 154. Indoor swimming pool, gym, aerobics, sauna, spa bath, solarium, gift shop (7.30am-9pm), coffee shop (all day). Access, Amex, Diners, Visa.*

ABERDEEN AIRPORT   Airport Skean Dhu   65%   £114

Tel 01224 725252   Fax 01224 723745   Map 3 D4   **H**
Argyll Road Dyce Aberdeen Grampian AB2 0DU

Conveniently close to the airport terminal, this Thistle & Mount Charlotte hotel combines roomy, well-equipped bedrooms with a busy conference trade (up to 450 delegates). Two bedrooms are equipped for disabled guests. Children stay free in parents' room. *Rooms 148. Garden, outdoor swimming pool, games room. Access, Amex, Diners, Visa.*

ABERFELDY   Farleyer House   70%   £130

Tel 01887 820332   Fax 01887 829430   Map 3 C4   **HR**
Weem Aberfeldy Perthshire Tayside PH15 2JE

A 16th-century croft transformed in the 18th century to become Dower House to nearby Menzies Castle, Farleyer House enjoys a fine position overlooking the Tay valley to the west of town on the B846. The elegant drawing-room and library bar with inner sanctum are comfortably furnished in country house style with deep armchairs and a relaxed atmosphere. Bedrooms (seven up a steep staircase on the second floor) vary in size and appeal with some built-in furniture plus a good scattering of antiques and individual decor. Rooms are serviced in the evenings and breakfasts come with freshly squeezed orange juice. Four simpler rooms in the grounds offer much cheaper accommodation. Guests have use of the leisure facilities (including an indoor swimming pool) at the nearby Kenmore Club. Children up to 14 stay free in parents' room. Dogs in kennels only. *Rooms 11. Garden, croquet, golf (6-hole), putting. Access, Amex, Diners, Visa.*

Menzies Restaurant   £75

Polished tables, dark green decor and floral curtains give a traditional look to the dining-room. Local produce, notably seafood and game, features strongly on both the fixed-price dinner menu and the Scottish Bistro menu, most notably in speciality dishes such as escalope of salmon with a fresh herb sauce, roast haunch of roe deer with red wine cream sauce and grilled Highland rib-eye with (or without) garlic butter. Look out also for bresaola (air-dried beef), duck terrine with aubergine chutney and, to round things off in style, hot sticky toffee pudding with toffee ice cream. Some decent prices on a wide-ranging wine list that includes 'fine' wines at the back. Does this mean that an '82 La Tache from Romanée-Conti in the Burgundy section is not a 'fine' wine? No smoking in Menzies, but smoking is allowed in the Scottish Bistro. *Seats 24. Private Room 35. D 7.30 for 8 (Bistro 10-2 & 6-9.30). Set L (Bistro) £12 Set D £27/£32.*

ABERFOYLE	Braeval	↑	£75

Tel 01877 382711   Fax 01877 382400   Map 3 B5   **R**
Aberfoyle Central FK8 3UY

An old stone mill by the junction of the A81 and A821 just east of town. Inside, the floor is flagstoned, the walls rough stone (softened by some arty fabric wall-hangings) and the tables clothed. The overall effect is most pleasing and is enhanced by charming service. There is no choice for the first three of four courses on the fixed-price menu, thus allowing chef-patron Nick Nairn to concentrate fully on each of the well-conceived dishes on the day's menu. Typical of his modern style might be a parsnip soup with chili oil before a gateau of roasted vegetables with Parma ham and pesto followed by Barbary duck with a confit of roots, lentils and tarragon and bacon velouté. Vegetarian options are available given notice. The dessert choice might be between cherry clafoutis, chocolate soufflé pudding with chocolate sauce, Grand Marnier parfait with citrus fruits and kumquat sauce, and a selection of British cheeses. No children under ten. Quality and fair prices throughout on the wine list where New World whites easily outscore their red counterparts. Abundance of half bottles. No smoking until coffee time. *Seats 34. Parties 12. L Sun (weekdays by arrangement) 12.30-1.30 D 7.30-9.30. Closed D Sun & all Mon, Bank Holidays, 1 week Feb, 1 week May/Jun & 1 week Oct/Nov. Set L £18.50 Set D £28.50. Access, Visa.*

ACHILTIBUIE	Summer Isles	64%	£95

Tel 01854 622282   Fax 01854 622251   Map 2 B2   **HR**
Achiltibuie by Ullapool Highland IV26 2YG

A friendly family-run hotel in a particularly beautiful spot. Public areas include a sitting room with TV, honesty bar and games, plus a small study with a telephone. There are no TVs or phones in the neat, light bedrooms, three of which are in Norwegian pine-log cabins (Verandah Rooms) a few steps from the main building. The Log House Suite, also in Norwegian pine, is a self-contained house that can accommodate 5. Owners Mark and Geraldine Irvine will be happy to give advice about fishing, bird-watching and walking. *Rooms 12. Garden, coffee shop (10.30am-9pm in high season). Closed mid Oct-Apr. No credit cards.*

Restaurant   £75

There are spectacular views of the Summer Isles to be had from the dining-room, where Chris Firth-Bernard makes good use of top-quality local produce, seafood and shellfish in particular. The five-course dinner starts with an interesting soup, perhaps mushroom and mustard with Madeira or smoked haddock and potato, continues with the likes of goujons of monkfish or beef carpaccio and majors on a main course such as Summer Isles lobster and prawns hollandaise or lamb with rosemary and caramelised garlic. Choice of five puddings, British cheeses, coffee. The restaurant is now open for lunch serving primarily local shellfish in salads, also home-cooked meats, cheese and home-baked breads. Provided you know your wines, the list is easy to use, very well chosen, with lots under £20 and many half bottles. No smoking. *Seats 26. Parties 8. L 12.30-2.30 D at 8. Set D £33.*

ADVIE   Tulchan Lodge   77%   £350*

Tel 01807 510200   Fax 01807 510234   Map 2 C3   H
Advie nr Grantown-on-Spey Highland PH26 3PW

The immaculately maintained Tulchan Lodge is one of the finest Edwardian shooting
lodges in Scotland, and it continues to offer some of the best fishing on 8 miles of the
Spey – both banks (each beat has its own ghillie and luxurious fishing cabin where lunch
is served) – and shooting on the 25,000-acre estate (grouse, pheasant, duck flighting and
roe deer stalking). Guests return year after year for the sport, but non-sporting clients are
equally welcome. It was constructed, apparently, without regard to labour and cost,
designed to offer every possible amenity and comfort, and there's still a similar philosophy
holding true today, the atmosphere being much more that of a country house weekend
party than a hotel. Dinner, for residents only, is served butler-style at a single large
polished table. *Full-board terms only. Mid-April to September is the summer fishing
season, October to January it is open only for shooting parties and February to April it is
closed altogether. No children. Dogs in kennels only. *Rooms 9. Garden, game fishing,
shooting, snooker, tennis. Closed Feb-Apr. No credit cards.*

AIRTH   Airth Castle   68%   £105

Tel 01324 831411   Fax 01324 831419   Map 3 C5   H
Airth by Falkirk Central FK2 8JF

There are lovely views over the Forth Valley from this carefully restored castle, dating in
parts from the 14th century (to get there, take Junction 7 off the M9, then the A905 to
Kincardine Bridge). Some bedrooms and two of the conference rooms (up to 400
delegates) are in a recent extension. Public areas are splendid, with fine proportions, ornate
ceilings and elegant traditional furniture. Modern-day facilities are provided in bedrooms
that range from spacious Executive-style to romantic four-poster. 36 rooms are suitable for
family use. Leisure amenities are in the country club at the end of the drive. No dogs.
*Rooms 75. Garden, tennis, indoor swimming pool, sauna, solarium, spa bath, steam room,
keep-fit equipment, aerobics studio, children's play areas. Access, Amex, Diners, Visa.*

ALEXANDRIA   Cameron House   81%   £150

Tel 01389 755565   Fax 01389 759522   Map 3 B5   HR
Loch Lomond Alexandria Strathclyde G83 8QZ

Cameron House has a wonderful setting, right on the
shores of Loch Lomond in 100 acres of lawns, gardens and
woodland. The majestic Georgian building offers
a mixture of traditional elegance (in the day rooms and
bedrooms) and state-of-the-art technology (in the
splendidly equipped Leisure Club and the bar). Bedrooms
and bathrooms are generously laid out and provide all
comforts, and service throughout is exemplary. Extensive
range of outdoor sports as well as the Leisure Club.
Families are well catered for, with a daily crèche (normally
to 5pm, but extended to 9pm on Thurs & Fri), early
suppers at 6pm and baby-sitting available. No dogs.
*Rooms 68. Garden, croquet, indoor swimming pools, steam
room, sauna, solarium, spa bath, squash, badminton,
snooker, gym, hairdressing, beauty salon, crèche, kiosk,*
9-hole golf course, tennis, watersports centre, marina, fishing, mountain bikes. Access, Amex,
Diners, Visa.*

Georgian Room   £80

The main hotel dining-room (there's also a brasserie for lighter, more casual meals) is
sumptuous and graceful, an ideal backdrop for Jeff Bland's sophisticated Scottish cooking
with a modern touch. Typical of his innovative style are a gateau of artichoke and tomato
with salad leaves and coriander vinaigrette, casserole of langoustines with wild
mushrooms, accompanied by black noodles flavoured with ginger and a lobster and lentil
sauce and for dessert, chocolate millefeuille filled with coffee cream and served on
a compote of raspberries. There are fixed-price and à la carte menus. No children under
14. No smoking in the restaurant. *Seats 42. Parties 10. Private Room 42. L 12-1.45 D 7-10.
Closed L Sat. Set L £13.95/£16.50 Set D £32.50.*

ALTNAHARRA · Altnaharra Hotel · 60% · £113*

Tel & Fax 01549 411222 Map 2 B2 **H**
Altnaharra by Lairg Highland IV27 4UE

A renowned base for salmon and trout fishing, this remote 19th-century inn keeps fishing records that go back over 100 years. Ghillies can be hired, there's a tackle shop and a chalet provides rod racks, deep freeze and drying facilities. Fishing tuition may be available by advance arrangement. Healthy walks in lovely country are another popular option. There are no TVs or telephones in the airy bedrooms, among which is an annexe cottage ideal for anglers' families. *Half-board terms only. **Rooms** 17. Garden, game fishing. Closed Nov-early Mar. Access, Visa.*

ALYTH · Drumnacree House · £55

Tel & Fax 01828 632194 Map 3 C4 **RR**
St Ninians Road Alyth Perthshire Tayside PH11 8AP

Chef-patron Allan Cull is never short of enthusiasm and a good deal of skill is evident in his short, fixed-price dinner menu. This might include crispy duck leg confit with Chinese sauce, devilled lamb's kidneys on toast, Tay salmon with balsamic vinaigrette and fillet of venison on rösti potato with chanterelle mushroom sauce; there is always a grilled steak too. Cajun dishes – prawn and okra gumbo, blackened chicken and 'dirty' rice – are a speciality and get their own separate menu. Game also features in season. Leave room for some good puds. Coffee is served with home-made truffles. Eleanor Cull looks after the front of house with its pretty pink linen and candles. No smoking. **Seats** 30. *Private Room 22. D only 7-9.30. Closed Sun & Mon (to non-residents), 15 Dec-31 Mar. Set D £19.50. Access, Visa.*

Rooms · £65

Six neat, no-smoking bedrooms offer modest comfort with duvets, TVs, tea and coffee kits and en-suite shower rooms. No charge for children under 12. Good breakfasts might include kedgeree, kippers and home-made black pudding. Garden.

ANNAN · Warmanbie Hotel · 59% · £74

Tel & Fax 01461 204015 Map 4 C2 **H**
Annan Dumfries & Galloway DG12 5LL

Home of the Duncan family since 1953, this Georgian house set in 45 acres of wooded grounds by the River Annan was converted to a hotel in 1983. There's still a homely, private house feel about the day rooms, and a traditional look to the bedrooms, which offer easy chairs, books, mini-bars and tea-makers; room 1 has a mahogany four-poster with matching furniture and a Victorian bathtub. Under-16s stay in their parents' room for £7.25 including breakfast. Free fishing on a private stretch of the Annan. **Rooms** 7. *Garden, game fishing. Access, Amex, Visa.*

ANSTRUTHER · Cellar · £75

Tel 01333 310378 Fax 01333 312544 Map 3 D5 **R**
24 East Green Anstruther Fife KY10 3AA

A cosy, fisherman's-cottagey restaurant with natural stone walls, tucked away behind the harbour. Fish from nearby Pittenweem is the mainstay of chef-patron Peter Jukes's menu, handled with skill and sympathy in dishes which combine simplicity with sophistication. Starters from the fixed-price, four-course dinner menu – warm salad of Isle of Mull scallops with sesame seed oil, cold East Neuk crab salad with toast and lemon mayonnaise, hot lobster quiche with peeled langoustines and smoked sea trout – tend to become main dishes on the less formal lunchtime carte. Back at dinner a soup course comes next – crayfish and mussel bisque gratinée or spinach and nutmeg – before the main dish choice that will always include both turbot and monkfish, the first perhaps with leeks, asparagus and a Chablis sauce, the second flavoured with herb and garlic butter and served with a Mediterranean vegetable stew. The meat option might be noisettes of new-season lamb with wild mushrooms. As always, the wine list is terrific, as well as fairly priced, offering among other gems some fabulous white burgundies, several top French growers and a decent showing from the New World. Booking is essential for dinner. **Seats** 30. *L 12.30-1.30 D 7.30-9. Closed Sun, Mon & 10 days Christmas. Set D £25/£30. Access, Amex, Visa.*

APPIN   Invercreran House Hotel   67%   £126   H

Tel 01631 730414   Fax 01631 730532   Map 3 B4
Appin by Oban Highland PA38 4BJ

A long, low-level hotel built in the 70s, standing in rugged countryside off the A828
Oban-Fort William road. A semi-circular part at the centre of the building is fronted by
balconied terracing and houses a colourful lounge and the dining areas; drinks service
comes from a neat dispense bar. Downstairs are master bedrooms with spacious tiled
bathrooms, all with showers and bidets. No children under five; 5-10s stay free in
parents' room. Dogs in kennels only. *Rooms 9. Garden, sauna. Closed 1 Nov-1 Mar.
Access, Visa.*

ARDENTINNY   Ardentinny Hotel   62%   £86   H

Tel 01369 810209   Fax 01369 810345   Map 3 B5
Loch Long Ardentinny nr Dunoon Strathclyde PA23 8TR

White-painted hotel on the very edge of Loch Long, 20 minutes' drive from Dunoon
and the car ferry to Gourock. Its position within the Argyll Forest Park (where there are
50 miles of traffic-free walks), views over the loch and moody 2000ft Creachan Mor, and
an interesting, rambling garden are the main attractions. Down-to-earth, pubby bars serve
hearty bar food and are popular with Clyde yachtsmen. The best bedrooms (all up
a narrow, winding staircase) are designated 'Fyne' and attract a considerable supplement
for their fine views, larger bathroom and remote-controlled television; accommodation is
generally modest but comfortable; some rooms have showers only and others are large
enough for families (further supplements are payable). Tariff reductions mid-Mar to end
May and during October. A few steps lead directly down from the hotel to the pebbly
shoreline; ask the way to the nearby sandy beach with its lovely, rhododendron-lined
setting. *Rooms 11. Garden, jetty/mooring, fishing, hotel boat & mountain bike hire.
Closed Nov-mid Mar. Access, Amex, Diners, Visa.*

ARDUAINE   Loch Melfort Hotel   65%   £93   H

Tel 01852 200233   Fax 01852 200214   Map 3 B5
Arduaine by Oban Strathclyde PA34 4XG

Self-styled as "the finest location on the West Coast", Loch Melfort Hotel is indeed in
a glorious setting, with a vast panorama of water and mountains unfolding across the field
that sweeps down from the hotel to the water's edge. All the public rooms (including the
simply-appointed dining-room where breakfast is taken) have picture windows to make
the most of the wonderful views down the Sound of Jura; only a cosy, wood-panelled
library is tucked away from the glorious outdoors. Larger bedrooms are in the main
house but those in the comfortable motel-style, two-storey Cedar Wing extension are
surprisingly comfortable; the latter all have patios or balconies to make the most of the
scenery. The pine-furnished Chartroom (open 10am-11pm) is an informal bar room
where chef-proprietor Philip Lewis's particularly good bar meals are served; yachtsmen
can tie up at the hotel's own moorings, row in and walk up to the hotel through the
front field (there are even showers provided for non-residents). Lawned gardens lead
around the hotel and down to Arduaine Gardens, which are run by the National Trust
for Scotland and well worth a visit to see the rhododendrons, azaleas and magnolias.
Children under 5 may share parents' room; room service from 8am-11pm. No dogs in
the main house or public rooms. 19 miles south of Oban on A816. *Rooms 27. Garden,
moorings. Closed Jan 5-Feb 25. Access, Amex, Visa.*

ARISAIG   Arisaig House   75%   £160   HR

Tel 01687 450622   Fax 01687 450626   Map 3 A4
Beasdale Arisaig Highland PH39 4NR

Three miles east of the village, Arisaig House enjoys an idyllic location surrounded by
some of the most gently beautiful scenery in Scotland and with fine views across Arisaig
Sound. Originally Victorian, the house was virtually rebuilt after a fire in the 1930s, thus
the day rooms are light and airy with plain white walls that make a perfect background
for well-chosen antiques, objets d'art and an abundance of fresh flowers – the latter all
from their own 20 acres of grounds. Personally run by the unobtrusively hospitable
Smithers family, the whole place has an air of peace and tranquillity. Bedrooms vary in
size from two full suites to a single room whose bathroom is private but not en-suite.
There's a variety of furniture too, from antiques to more contemporary pieces, but all
rooms are immaculately kept with tasteful decor and humanising touches like books, fresh

flowers and fruit. Bathrooms all have tubs but only hand-held showers; generous towelling includes bath robes and toiletries are of good quality. Conserves at breakfast are all home-made with soft fruits from the kitchen garden. No children under 10 years. *Rooms 14. Garden, croquet, snooker. Closed Nov-Mar. Access, Amex, Visa.*

Restaurant   £85

Dinner is fixed-price but with an unusual format in that chef David Wilkinson (the son-in-law of the house) proposes his own five-course menu but with a list of alternatives should your tastes and his not quite coincide. Cooking is refined yet not overcomplicated, with dishes such as filo pastry cup filled with scallops and mussels; cullen skink; maize-fed guinea fowl supreme with chanterelles; roast Highland grouse with bread sauce; fillet of Shetland salmon with lemon oil and best end of spring lamb with a port and redcurrant sauce demonstrating the style. Desserts might include fudgy pecan nut flan, peach melba or rich chocolate marquise. Cheeses are first class: regional winner of Cheeseboard of the Year for Scotland. Lunch is a much less formal affair, also served in the bar or out on the terrace – the ideal spot if the weather allows. There are plenty of French 'names' on an otherwise frankly disappointing wine list. No smoking. No children under 10 years. *Seats 36. Parties 10. L 12.30-2 D 7.30-8.30. Set D £30.*

ARISAIG   Old Library Lodge   £60

Tel 01687 450651   Fax 01687 450219   Map 3 A4   **RR**
Arisaig Highland BH39 4NH

On the road to the Isles, where it borders Loch Non Seall with fine views as far as the Inner Hebrides, the Broadhursts' 200-year-old stable has been converted into a pleasing little restaurant with white-painted rough stone walls, cork floor and black-painted tables. Alan has managed to develop a network of local sources for some of the excellent produce to be found hereabouts, most notably the first-rate seafood (which usually gets exported direct to the Continent) like langoustines, sole, crab, mussels and Mallaig scallops. Venison, duck and chicken also appear on the short (about five choices at each stage), fixed-price dinner menus in dishes that are uncomplicated but not uninteresting – courgette and mint soup, goat's cheese marinated in herbs and olive oil, fillets of lamb with a port wine sauce, scallops on a bed of celeriac. Puds are homely and the bread home-baked. Lunch is a less formal affair that also includes salads and 'toasties'. *Seats 28. Parties 12. L 11.30-2.30 D 6.30-9.30. Closed end Oct-end Mar. Set D £21. Access, Amex, Visa.*

Rooms   £62

The six bedrooms, four of them chalet-style behind the main building, are spacious, clean and bright with the modern conveniences of remote-control TV, direct-dial phones and tea and coffee-making kit. All are en suite with two having shower and WC only. Good cooked breakfasts begin with freshly squeezed orange juice.

AUCHENCAIRN   Balcary Bay Hotel   64%   £88

Tel 01556 640217   Fax 01556 640272   Map 4 B3   **RR**
Auchencairn nr Castle Douglas Dumfries & Galloway DG7 1QZ

On the shore road two miles south of Auchencairn this sophisticated, white pebbledash, early 17th-century house has a glorious location on the edge of Balcary Bay. Its seclusion made it a haunt of smugglers in years gone by and today one can see the salmon nets jutting out into the bay towards Heston Isle, where the contraband was landed. It's now a comfortable hotel run in friendly fashion by the Lambs, and peace and quiet are major attractions. Day rooms include the spacious oak-timbered general lounge with chintzy cushions enlivening the brown easy chairs, a pretty non-smoking lounge and a small cocktail bar with terrace from which to enjoy the view. Floral patterns are favoured in the individually decorated bedrooms (the majority having bay views) with darkwood 'Stag' furniture and good en-suite bathrooms. A bowl of fresh fruit welcomes guests and beds are turned down at night. *Rooms 17. Garden, snooker. Closed mid Nov-Mar. Access, Amex, Visa.*

See over

Restaurant   £60

Fish dishes, fresh from Scottish rivers and seas whenever possible, feature on the menu in the pale green dining-room although there are also plenty of meat dishes – lamb en croute, duck with soy and honey sauce, chicken with blue Stilton and red wine sauce. In addition to the à la carte there's a daily changing fixed-price dinner with a couple of choices at each stage other than the sorbet. One of each of the day's half-dozen or so desserts is displayed on a sideboard. *Seats 50. Parties 18. L Sun (other days by arrangement only) 12-1.45 D 7-8.30 (till 9 high season). Set D £19.50.*

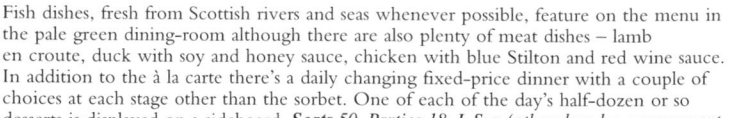

| AUCHENCAIRN | Collin House | 68% | £78 |

Tel 01556 640292   Fax 01556 640276   Map 4 B3   **HR**
Auchencairn nr Castle Douglas Dumfries & Galloway DG7 1QN

Dating from 1750, pink-painted Collin House is easily spotted in its elevated position to the east of town from which it enjoys fine views across the Solway Firth. It's the sort of place where guests soon get to know each other over pre-dinner drinks served in the civilised, homely drawing-room with its open fire, flowers, books and a nice collection of paintings. Spacious bedrooms, furnished with a variety of antiques, are light and airy with homely extras justifying the brochure promise of 'unpretentious comfort'. Good-sized bathrooms (one is huge) offer large bathsheets and good toiletries. Breakfasts, which include haggis, kippers and smoked haddock amongst the options, are worth getting up for. *Rooms 6. Garden. Closed Feb. Access, Visa.*

Restaurant   £68

Fresh flowers and bronze animals grace the polished, antique tables of the red dining-room where John Wood's short (a couple of choices at each stage plus a soup course) fixed-price menu offers sound, uncomplicated, essentially British cooking. Risotto of smoked venison with ceps (a house speciality), terrine of wild duck and mushrooms with quince jelly, rack of Scottish lamb with herb crust and port wine sauce and escalope of halibut rolled in sesame seeds with a basil sauce show the style, with the likes of hot lemon pudding, chocolate roulade and gooseberry fool for dessert. Booking is essential for non-residents. No smoking. No children under 12. *Seats 16. D only 7.30 for 8. Set D £27.*

| AUCHTERARDER | Auchterarder House | 75% | £130 |

Tel 01764 663646   Fax 01764 662939   Map 3 C5   **HR**
Auchterarder Tayside PH3 1DZ

Just a mile and a half north of Auchterarder on the B8062, this baronial-style mansion set in 17 acres of grounds was built in 1832. Nowadays it's a hotel popular with corporate clients and boasting many fine features: beautiful coloured marbles recur throughout and there's carved oak panelling in the central hall, ribbed ceilings and marble fireplaces in the day rooms, a characterful billiard room bar, and a charming conservatory. The Brown family have added the warm welcome and many homely touches like original paintings, an abundance of fresh flowers and numerous objets d'art. Bedroom decor varies, but all rooms are generously sized and have extras both luxurious (like a cut-glass decanter of good sherry) and practical (iron and ironing board). Many of the bathrooms include bidets and separate showers. *Rooms 15. Garden, croquet, pitch & putt, putting green. Access, Amex, Diners, Visa.*

Restaurant   £90

A richly, if somewhat sombrely, decorated room in Victorian baronial style with heavy woodwork, dark green flock wallpaper and elaborately moulded and ribbed ceiling, but Audrey Brown's pretty posies of fresh flowers brighten things up on tables immaculately laid with fine china and glassware and boasting silver candelabra. David Hunt's fixed-price dinner menu leans heavily on good Scottish produce in dishes like skate fishcake with a brioche crust, Arran mustard, fennel compote and nori seaweed, medallions of red deer encrusted with oatmeal and thyme and cock-a-leekie sauce and Crawfurdland Castle guinea fowl breast with a whisky and juniper essence. Interesting puds might include a hot frangipane pastry with a moneybag of amaretto sultanas and a vanilla and roast hazelnut sauce, and a spiced savarin flavoured with Earl Grey, lemon and cinnamon with a rum ice cream and figs. When he's in the mood, proprietor Ian Brown might accompany dinner at the grand piano in the main hall. The classic wine list features big names, but at sensible prices. Lots from France, but not to the exclusion of the rest of the world. Fair sprinkling of half bottles. *Seats 25. Parties 8. Private Room 40. L 12-2.30 D 6-9.30. Set L from £18.50 Set D from £27.50 Set Sun L from £15.*

AUCHTERARDER	Gleneagles Hotel	86%	£230

Tel 01764 662231   Fax 01764 662022   Map 3 C5   **H**
Auchterarder Tayside PH3 1NF

A sporting dream, but of course particularly associated with golf – Jack Nicklaus designed the new Monarch's course. In the hotel's grand arcade are illustrious names such as Harvey Nichols, Mappin & Webb, Burberry's and even a branch of the Royal Bank of Scotland. Public areas are also of a grand dimension with high-ceilinged rooms, faux-marble fluted columns, and decorative plaster ceilings. Pianists play in the bars and restaurant, and you can dance to a live band in the drawing room. Accommodation ranges from the Royal Lochnagar Suite and the Monarch's Suite, to three other grades of suite, on to four grades of bedroom – we quote a basic price, but even standard rooms are individually decorated. The Country Club encompasses Champneys Health Spa; there's also an equestrian centre (Mark Phillips) and a clay target shooting school (Jackie Stewart), even falconry. Conferences of up to 360 delegates can take equal advantage of all that's on offer. With the number of staff probably exceeding the number of guests, it's one of a kind, set in some 830 acres of beautiful scenery, yet only an hour's drive from Edinburgh and Glasgow. *Rooms 234. Garden, croquet, indoor swimming pool, sauna, steam room, solarium, whirlpool bath, gym, hairdressing, tennis, squash, golf courses, pitch & putt, indoor putting, jogging trails, bowling green, riding, clay-pigeon shooting, coarse and game fishing, falconry, mountain bikes, off-road driving, children's playground, snooker, valeting, shopping arcade, bank, post office. Access, Amex, Diners, Visa.*

AUCHTERHOUSE	Old Mansion House	68%	£120

Tel 01382 320366   Fax 01382 320466   Map 3 C5   **HR**
Auchterhouse by Dundee Tayside DD3 0QN

A 16th-century whitewashed Scottish baronial house skilfully converted by Nigel and Eva Bell to a charming and relaxed hotel. Some nice architectural features include the vaulted entrance hall, an open Jacobean fireplace and a splendidly ornate 17th-century plasterwork ceiling in the original drawing-room. Pleasantly furnished bedrooms – two are family suites with separate children's bedrooms – have good bathrooms well stocked with toiletries. The house is on the B954 seven miles from Dundee. *Rooms 6. Garden, tennis, croquet, outdoor swimming pool, squash. Closed 24 Dec-5 Jan. Access, Amex, Diners, Visa.*

Restaurant   £75

Much local produce is used for a varied carte that is supplemented by a separate vegetarian menu. Cullen skink (smoked haddock and potato soup), smoked Tay salmon, whole prawn tails with a vermouth, chutney and mushroom sauce, collops in the pan with sherry and pickled walnuts, and gingered sticky toffee pudding with a caramel sauce show the style. Also bar lunch and supper menus. No under-10s at night. No smoking. *Seats 50. Private Room 22. L 12.30-1.45 D 7-9.30 (Sun to 9). Set L £12.95/£15.95.*

AVIEMORE   Aviemore Highlands Hotel   61%   £93

Tel 01479 810771   Fax 01479 811473   Map 3 C4   **H**
Aviemore Centre Aviemore Highland PH22 1PJ

On the A9 Perth to Inverness road, a modern hotel popular for both business and pleasure, with banqueting/conference facilities for up to 120, and plenty of free parking. 24hr room service. Discounted rates at a nearby leisure centre. *Rooms 102. Garden, sun beds. Access, Amex, Diners, Visa.*

AVIEMORE   Stakis Aviemore Four Seasons   70%   £100

Tel 01479 810681   Fax 01479 810534   Map 3 C4   **H**
Aviemore Highland PH22 1PF

A seven-storey hotel at the heart of the skiing centre, a mile from the A9, with views of the Spey Valley and the Cairngorms. It was due to reopen, after a major fire, as we went to press. *Rooms 88. Garden, indoor swimming pool, gym, sauna, spa bath, steam bath, solarium, ski school. Access, Amex, Diners, Visa.*

AVIEMORE   Stakis Coylumbridge   62%   £103

Tel 01479 810661   Fax 01479 811309   Map 3 C4   **H**
Aviemore Highland PH22 1QN

Skiing is the thing at Aviemore, but this sprawling modern hotel caters admirably for all sorts of activities for both adults and children. There's a sports hall for children, a fun house and an outdoor play area. It's also geared up for large conferences (maximum 750 delegates). Most of the bedrooms are big enough for family use. A couple of rooms are suitable for disabled guests. *Rooms 175. Two indoor swimming pools, hydrotherapy pool, sauna, solarium, hair salon, tennis, archery, target shooting. Access, Amex, Diners, Visa.*

AYR   Fouters Bistro   £50

Tel 01292 261391   Fax 01292 619323   Map 4 A1   **R**
2a Academy Street Ayr Strathclyde KA7 1HS

Fran and Laurie Black's cheerful bistro is in vaulted basement premises down a cobbled lane opposite the Town Hall. Scottish produce (especially local seafood, and game in season) is cooked in French style with consistently enjoyable results which have kept the place popular for well over 20 years. Tartlet of seafood thermidor, breast of chicken with mango mousse, seared salmon with a warm hollandaise sauce, Gressingham duck with cherry apples and ginger, and chargrilled steaks show the range. The Taste of Scotland platter includes, typically, smoked chicken, salmon and trout, patés and shrimps. Tuesday to Friday dinner is à la carte with fixed-price menus taking over on Saturday and Sunday nights. Lunchtime brings a less formal menu with dishes individually priced. A short list of carefully chosen wines includes a couple from Switzerland. *Seats 38. L 12-2 D 6.30-10.30. Set Sat D £19.50 Set Sun D £14.95/£17.50. Closed L Sun, all Mon, 4 days Christmas, 4 days New Year. Access, Amex, Diners, Visa.*

AYR   Jarvis Caledonian Hotel   64%   £117

Tel 01292 269331   Fax 01292 610722   Map 4 A1   **H**
Dalblair Road Ayr Strathclyde KA7 1UG

Town-centre hotel with leisure facilities and a conference suite (for up to 175). Many bedrooms suitable for families (children up to 16 stay free in parents' room, or pay 50% in their own room). Within easy reach of eight golf courses, thus popular for sporting breaks. *Rooms 114. Indoor swimming pool, gym, sauna, spa bath, sun beds, pool table. Access, Amex, Diners, Visa.*

AYR   The Stables   £30

Tel 01292 283704   Map 4 A1   **R**
Queen's Court 41 Sandgate Ayr Strathclyde KA7 1BD

In a shopping area of restored Georgian and Victorian buildings Edward Baines and his chef William (Billy) McFadzean demonstrate the art of ethnic Scottish cooking. Anything from light snacks to full meals is available: scones, clootie dumplings, toasted sandwiches, haggis, chicken stovies (with potatoes, turnips, onions and carrots), smoked fish and meat from the family smokehouse, salad plates, ham and haddie pie. Tweed kettle is a casserole of salmon, mushrooms, celery and onions spiced with mace and cooked in white wine. The wine list includes a number of traditional country wines, one made from the sap of the silver birch, another from blackberries. No reservations. No smoking in the main dining-room. *Seats 50. Meals 10-4.45. Closed Sun out of season, 25 & 26 Dec, 1 Jan. No credit cards.*

| BALLACHULISH | Ballachulish Hotel | 60% | £82 |

Tel 01855 811606   Fax 01855 811629   Map 3 B4   **H**
Ballachulish Argyll Highland PA39 4JY

On the A828 three miles north of Glencoe and some 12 miles south of Fort William. This may be one of Scotland's oldest hotels but things are still happening here with the addition of 20 new rooms this year along with some public area refurbishment. Set above Loch Linnhe at the base of picturesque mountains, the hotel has panoramic views from all the public areas. Guests have free use of the leisure centre at the sister hotel the *Isles of Glencoe* (qv) about two miles away. Families are well catered for. *Rooms 54. Garden. Access, Visa.*

Many hotels offer reduced rates for weekend or out-of-season bookings. Always ask about special deals.

| BALLACHULISH | Isles of Glencoe Hotel | 59% | £92 |

Tel 01855 811602   Fax 01855 821463   Map 3 B4   **H**
Ballachulish nr Fort William Highland PA39 4JY

Next to the A82 Glasgow-Fort William road a mile west of Glencoe. This purpose-built modern hotel makes a useful overnight stop with comfortable uncluttered bedrooms, although their narrow sloping windows fail to make the best of the views – the loch and ancient burial island of the Clan McDonald on one side and mountains on the other. Friendly young staff. Enhanced leisure facilities. *Rooms 39. Garden, indoor pool, keep-fit equipment, spa bath, sauna, steam room, solarium, coffee shop (10am-10pm). Access, Visa.*

| BALLATER | Craigendarroch Hotel | 74% | £125 |

Tel 01339 755858   Fax 01339 755447   Map 3 C4   **H**
Braemar Road Ballater Grampian AB35 5XA

Seven miles from Balmoral on the banks of the River Dee, this fine hotel in Scottish baronial style offers comfort, peace and a wealth of sports and leisure amenities in a setting of peace and beauty. Fair-sized bedrooms are bright and modern, with plenty of toiletries in the bathrooms, and views of the Dee valley to wake up to. Thoughtful extras abound, from sewing kit to shortbread, playing cards to sherry. There are two bars (one with regular live music nights) and three restaurants. No dogs, but excellent facilities for children, including a daily creche and the Acorn Club for 5 to 15-year-olds. *Rooms 49. Garden, indoor swimming pool, children's splash pool, playroom & playground, gym, squash, sauna, steam room, spa bath, solarium, beauty & hair salon, tennis, dry ski slope, snooker. Access, Amex, Diners, Visa.*

| BALLATER | Tullich Lodge | 71% | £190* |

Tel 01339 755406   Fax 01339 755397   Map 3 C4   **HR**
Ballater Grampian AB35 5SB

An imposing but delightful pink granite mansion overlooking the Dee on the A93 Aberdeen-Braemar road. Hector Macdonald and Neil Bannister have been here since 1968, running a hotel of great atmosphere and real character which attracts a large number of regularly-returning guests. Crenellations and towers are outward distinguishing features, while inside antiques, pictures and handsome furnishings grace the drawing-room and chintzy little sitting-room (the perfect place to retire with a book); an old Broadwood piano in the drawing-room 'responds kindly to early 19th-century music'. Bedrooms are individually decorated in keeping with the rest of the place, and the Tower Room, on the third floor, provides not only exercise but a splendid Victorian bathroom; televisions are available on request only; however, a wireless is in every room. High tea is served to children at 5pm in the kitchen, and both picnic lunches and packed dinners ('for the train') can be provided. *Half-board terms only. *Rooms 10. Garden. Closed end Oct-end Mar. Access, Amex, Diners, Visa.*

See over

Dining Room £60

In the mahogany-panelled dining-room (no smoking; jacket and tie requested) Neil prepares no-choice four-course dinners based on sound classic and modern British methods. Typical offerings might include marinated Finnan haddock with lime juice, baked egg with peppers, aubergine and tomato, or cullen skink among the starters, then perhaps a soup or consommé before a main course of roast rib of Highland beef, baked whole plaice with shrimps and leek or grilled chicken with tarragon and vinegar. The fourth course is a fruit-based dessert or Scottish cheeses, and coffee is included in the meal price. *Seats 26. Parties 8. L at 1 D 7.30-9. Set L in the bar £7 Set D £25.*

BANCHORY   Raemoir House   71%   £95

Tel 01330 824884   Fax 01330 822171   Map 3 D4   **HR**
Raemoir Banchory Grampian AB31 4ED

Sixteen miles south west of Aberdeen and $2\frac{1}{2}$ miles north of Banchory on the A980 is Raemoir House, an 18th-century mansion set in a 3500-acre estate which has been in the Sabin family since 1943. Ongoing attention to refurbishment ensures that standards are maintained at the same time as the cosy ambience. Rich red brocade chairs, panelled walls and valuable antiques enhance the traditional look of the morning room, and the bar is fashioned from a Tudor four-poster. Bedrooms are all different in size and character, but most have inviting chaises longues, day beds or armchairs. Six rooms are in the historic 16th-century Ha'Hoose immediately behind the mansion. There are five self-catering apartments converted from the original coachhouse and stables. *Rooms 25. Garden, croquet, sauna, sun beds, keep-fit equipment, tennis, game fishing, pitch & putt, shooting. Closed 1st 2 weeks Jan. Access, Amex, Diners, Visa.*

The Macintyre Room £75

A lengthy international menu with a good smattering of Scottish food is on offer in this relaxed and very traditional dining-room. For a true taste of Scotland go no further than the creamed Arbroath smokies and smoked Dee salmon and Scottish langoustines cooked in herb and lemon or garlic butter available as starters. Herbs from the garden are much used and feature in pan-fried supreme of chicken stuffed with herbed garlic butter. Saddle of Highland venison comes with a rich redcurrant and wild game sauce, grilled 12oz Aberdeen Angus steak with an accompaniment of onion rings, mushrooms, tomato and French fried potatoes. In season there's pheasant from the estate. Extensive vegetarian menu. Some quite reasonable prices on a good all-round wine list. *Seats 70. Parties 16. Private Room 80. L 12.30-2 D 7.30-9. Set L £14.50 (Sun) Set D £24.50.*

BANCHORY   Tor-na-Coille Hotel   66%   £69

Tel 01330 822242   Fax 01330 824012   Map 3 D4   **H**
Inchmarlo Road Banchory Grampian AB31 4AB

Built as a private house in 1873 and run as a hotel since the turn of the century, Tor-na-Coille retains much of its Victorian character. The function room can accommodate 90 people for a banquet or conference. Bedrooms are furnished with antiques. Children under 12 stay free in parents' room. *Rooms 22. Garden, croquet, squash. Closed 25-27 Dec. Access, Amex, Diners, Visa.*

BEARSDEN   Fifty Five BC   £50

Tel 0141-942 7272   Fax 0141-942 9650   Map 3 B5   **R**
128 Drymen Road Bearsden Glasgow Strathclyde G61 3RB

Restaurant and bar with great family appeal. The style is modern Scottish/French, confident and fairly straightforward. Duck livers, steamed mussels, salmon ravioli, roast pigeon and chargrilled steaks show the style. Slightly more outré is maize-fed chicken with an onion and pearl barley compote and a chestnut-flavoured jus. On the bar menu are snackier items such as crispy potato skins, quiche and the 55BC Quarter Pounder, plus a selection of sandwiches. *Seats 24. L 12-3 (Sun 12.30-4) D 7-10. Closed 1 Jan. Access, Visa.*

BEATTOCK	Auchen Castle	64%	£76

Tel 01683 3407   Fax 01683 3667   Map 4 C2   **H**
Beattock nr Moffat Dumfries & Galloway DG10 9SH

Signposted on the A74 a mile north of Beattock, 55 miles from Glasgow and 41 miles from Carlisle, Auchen Castle offers both budget and mid-priced overnight accommodation for those wishing to break a long journey heading south or north. Panoramic views across upper Annandale to the Moffat hills from the hotel's elevated position and 50 acres of immaculately-kept grounds – complete with terraced gardens and a trout lake – are the attractions for longer stays. The grey sandstone, baronial-style Victorian mansion has a rather institutional air within, and main-house bedrooms have the best views; ten more functional, spacious rooms in the incongruous Cedar Lodge annexe have showers, attractive patchwork bedspreads and good-sized remote-controlled TVs. Bar snacks at lunchtime, but evening room service extends only to sandwiches. *Rooms 25. Garden, fishing. Closed 3 weeks Christmas/New Year. Access, Amex, Diners, Visa.*

Set menu prices may not always include service or wine.

BEAULY	Lovat Arms Hotel	59%	£74

Tel 01463 782313   Fax 01463 782862   Map 2 B3   **H**
High Street Beauly Highland IV4 7BS

Substantial red-stone hotel next to the petrol station in the centre of town. It's owned by the Fraser family, whose clan tartan is much used in the good-quality soft furnishings of the public areas, which include a banquette-seated lounge bar and an entrance hall/reception that, with its real log fire and deep armchairs, also doubles up very well as the lounge. Bespoke carpeting displays the clan crest and motto. A different tartan features in each of the bedrooms, of which the best, often with elaborate bedhead drapes or canopies, are on the first floor although rooms 10, 11 and 12 (above a noisy public bar) are best avoided if you plan an early night. Some room service is available although not advertised. *Rooms 22. Access, Visa.*

BLAIRGOWRIE	Kinloch House	70%	£152*

Tel 01250 884237   Fax 01250 884333   Map 3 C5   **HR**
Kinloch by Blairgowrie Tayside PH10 6SG

Highland cattle graze in the 25 acres of parkland and policies (Scottish for the pleasure-grounds around a mansion) that surrounds a creeper-clad 19th-century house which has been turned into a relaxing country hotel by David and Sarah Shentall. Public areas include oak-panelled hall and first-floor galleries and a period drawing-room; most guests seem to prefer the convivial atmosphere of the comfortable bar or the charm of the plant-filled conservatory with its Lloyd Loom chairs and tables. All the rooms are traditionally furnished and boast particularly luxurious bathrooms. Extras include books, magazines, ironing boards and bathrobes. Shooting parties and fishermen appreciate the Sportsman's room, which offers everything from a deep freeze to dog bowls. Room service is limited. *Half-board terms only. Three miles west of Blairgowrie, on the A923 to Dunkeld. *Rooms 21. Garden, croquet, fishing. Closed last 2 weeks Dec. Access, Amex, Diners, Visa.*

Restaurant £75

A civilised dining-room where chef Bill McNicoll's daily-changing menus bring a good choice of dishes, both simple and more elaborate – from cock-a-leekie, melon with prawns in Marie Rose sauce and pan-fried Aberdeen Angus sirloin topped with pine kernels to seafood sausage on a parsley and garlic sauce with crisply fried vegetables, breast of chicken filled with broccoli and Stilton mousse on a bed of lentils with vegetable butter sauce and vegetable coulibiac. Desserts from a trolley. Also informal lunches with interesting open sandwiches. Sunday lunch sees a small choice that usually includes good beef dishes. There's a good overall balance on the wine list with many bottles under £20 and lots of half bottles. Bordeaux are helpfully listed by vintage, cheapest first, culminating in a 1981 Pétrus at precisely £244.45, which at first glance might seem expensive but is still £100 or £150 less than on some lists! No children under 7 at night. Jackets and ties are requested in the evening. No smoking. *Seats 55. Parties 12. Private Room 30. L 12.30-2 D 7-9.15. Set Sun L £15.75 Set D £27.90.*

BONNYRIGG   Dalhousie Castle   62%   £120

Tel 01875 820153   Fax 01875 821936   Map 3 C6   **H**
Bonnyrigg nr Edinburgh Lothian EH19 3JB

Built around 1450 (though it's thought there was a dwelling on this site even earlier) from locally quarried red sandstone, Dalhousie is a real castle complete with tower and crenellations. Notable features of the public areas include Gothic-style fan vaulting in the entrance hall and a 'wedding cake' moulded ceiling in the wood-panelled library that is the main day room. Bedrooms vary considerably in furnishings and decor and are designated either Castle rooms or Historically-themed rooms; all have en-suite bathrooms. Breakfasts are served in the characterful barrel-vaulted castle dungeons thankfully cleared of any trace of what might have gone on here in the distant past. Functions and meetings are a major part of the business here – facilities for up to 120. *Rooms 25. Garden. Access, Amex, Diners, Visa.*

BRIDGE OF ALLAN   Royal Hotel   59%   £70

Tel 01786 832284   Fax 01786 834377   Map 3 C5   **H**
Henderson Street Bridge of Allan Central FK9 4HG

Built in 1842 in what was then a spa town (now most notably home to Stirling University), the Royal stands half a mile from the railway station and one mile from the M9 (Junction 11). Bedroom accessories include satellite TV, and rooms all have modern bathrooms. There's a plush bar, an oak-panelled lounge and several conference rooms (maximum capacity 150). *Rooms 32. Garden. Access, Amex, Diners, Visa.*

> Many hotels offer reduced rates for weekend or out-of-season bookings. Always ask about special deals.   ·

CAIRNDOW   Loch Fyne Oyster Bar   £50

Tel 01499 600236   Fax 01499 600234   Map 3 B5   **R**
Clachan Farm by Cairndow Strathclyde PA26 8BH

Hard by the road that sweeps round the head of expansive Loch Fyne – a fine location for the converted farm buildings that house this informal restaurant with pine and larch wood decor. Shellfish and both smoked and cured fish (much direct from the loch outside and smoked in their own smokehouse) are the main attraction and may be purchased from the shop through which you gain access to the long, L-shaped dining-room. Try bradhan rost (hot-smoked salmon with whisky sauce), oysters baked with spinach and breadcrumbs, kippers, marinated herrings, a daily fresh fish, or push the boat out with a shellfish platter (rock oysters, langoustines, queen scallops, brown crab and clams). Smoked venison and steak are the only meat options. Stick to straightforward dishes (seafood chowder and vegetables were both poor on a recent visit) and you can Rest And Be Thankful after an exhilarating drive over the pass and down through the glens. Facilities for the disabled. See also entry under Elton (near Peterborough, England). *Seats 80. Parties 50. Meals 9-9 (Nov to end Feb 9-6). Closed 10 days Christmas. Access, Amex, Visa.*

CALLANDER   Roman Camp   69%   £129

Tel 01877 330003   Fax 01877 331533   Map 3 C5   **HR**
off Main Street Callander Tayside FK17 8BG

After it started life as a modest 17th-century manor house, subsequent alterations and extensions have given the Roman Camp something of the appearance of a French chateau, complete with a pair of towers, one hiding a 'secret' chapel. The hotel's drive begins in the main street of town but the building is surrounded by fine gardens bordering the River Teith. When the house was turned into a hotel in the 1930s, much of the original furniture and objets d'art (there's even the remains of a wreath from Queen Victoria's coffin on display) remained in place both in the public rooms – which include a mellow panelled library with fine Tudor-style ceiling, and civilised drawing-room – and in the bedrooms, which feature a mixture of antique and painted pieces. There are three full suites, seven 'superior' (larger) rooms of which three are in more modern style, and four 'standard' rooms of which two have shower and WC only. Other bathrooms have suites from various periods. All rooms get extras like sherry, fresh fruit, mineral water and fresh flowers. Beds are turned down at night and room service is available throughout the day and evening. *Rooms 14. Garden, game fishing. Access, Amex, Diners, Visa.*

Restaurant   £95

The timbered ceiling of the dining-room gives it a somewhat Austrian feel, although painted with traditional Celtic patterns. Both the à la carte and no-choice, four-course tasting menu feature dishes in the modern idiom – consommé of beetroot and orange, pithiviers of crottin cheese and apple, salmon with pasta noodles and a dill butter sauce, fillet of beef with a brioche and black peppercorn crust and a carrot mousse – competently handled by the kitchen. Decent prices on a fair wine list with dogmatic tasting notes. No smoking. *Seats 45. Parties 12. Private Room 32. L 12-2 D 7-9.30. Set L £14/£18 Set D £32.*

CANONBIE   Riverside Inn   £72

Tel 01387 371512   Map 4 C2   **IR**
Canonbie Dumfries & Galloway DG14 0UX

Overlooking the River Esk in the small village of Canonbie just north of the border, Robert and Susan Phillips' Georgian inn is in immaculate order inside and out. The carpeted bar, furnished with country chairs grouped around sewing-machine tables, is happily free of piped music, fruit machines and the like. Six en-suite bedrooms (two with shower and WC only) have pretty, matching bedcovers and curtains – and even loo roll and tissue box covers – and boast extras like fresh fruit, mineral water, books and magazines plus TV but no telephone. For residents there is a domestic-scale sitting-room. *Rooms 6. Garden. Closed 2 weeks Feb, 2 weeks Nov, 25 & 26 Dec, 1 Jan. Access, Visa.*

Restaurant   £55

Concentrating on good local produce, the fixed-price dinner menu offers a choice of dishes using seasonal fresh local produce wherever possible. Grilled sardines, potted salmon, venison and pork terrine, chargrilled red snapper with coriander salsa, roast lamb with onion sauce and Angus sirloin steak show the style. Leave room for such puds as gingerbread slice with toffee sauce, rhubarb crumble ice cream and lime and grapefruit meringue pie. Small, manageable wine list; fair prices, helpful notes, good choices. At lunchtimes (except Sunday) and in the evenings there is a substantial blackboard menu in the bar. No smoking. No children under 10 years. *Seats 24. Parties 6. L 12-2 (bar – not Sun) D 7.30-8.30 (restaurant) 7-9 (bar). Closed L Sun. Set D £22.50.*

CHAPEL OF GARIOCH   Pittodrie House   65%   £115

Tel 01467 681444   Fax 01467 681648   Map 2 D3   **H**
Chapel of Garioch nr Inverurie Highland AB51 9HS

Fishing, stalking, shooting and riding are all available locally, combining with facilities on the premises to make this a fine base for sporting holidays. The house dates largely from the 17th century (rebuilt from 15th-century origins) and the reception rooms are very traditional and homely, with antiques, family portraits and log fires. The wine bar is stocked with more than ninety malt whiskies. Bedrooms are either in the main building (motley fabrics, antiques) or in a 1990-built wing, with reproduction furniture and decent modern bathrooms. There are banqueting and conference facilities for 130/150. *Rooms 27. Garden, croquet, squash, tennis, snooker, clay-pigeon shooting. Access, Amex, Diners, Visa.*

CLEISH   Nivingston House   65%   £95

Tel 01577 850216   Fax 01577 850238   Map 3 C5   **H**
Cleish Kinross Tayside KY13 7LS

Formerly a farmhouse, with parts dating back to 1725, stone-built Nivingston House enjoys a very tranquil setting in 12 acres of gardens at the foot of the Cleish Hills (yet only two miles from J5 of the M90). Public rooms include a quiet drawing-room and a cosy, plush bar whose attractions include 50 malts. Pretty bedrooms with Laura Ashley fabrics and wallpapers are well kept, like the whole hotel, and there are neat bathrooms, a few of which have shower and WC only. Children up to 12 stay free in parents' room. *Rooms 17. Garden, croquet, putting. Closed 1st 2 weeks Jan. Access, Amex, Visa.*

Consult the blue pages for summary tables and lists of
recommended establishments.

COLBOST   Three Chimneys   £60

Tel 01470 511258   Map 2 A3   **R**
Colbost by Dunvegan Isle of Skye Highland IV55 8ZT

Eddie and Shirley Spear's charming restaurant is housed in a remote former crofter's
cottage, four miles west of Dunvegan on the B884 road to Glendale. At whatever time of
day you visit, you can be assured of excellent local produce (suppliers are both cherished
and credited) prepared and cooked with care and devotion. Morning coffee and
afternoon tea frame the lunchtime session, when dishes range from potted wild duck
paté, hot kipper tart with lemon butter sauce and cream crowdie (soft cheese) with
hazelnuts to herring in oatmeal and smoked Highland venison. Among the seafood
specialities are Skye oysters, peat-smoked salmon, prawns and lobster, while sweet treats
include the renowned hot marmalade pudding served with ice cream or Drambuie
custard. Four-course dinners start with soup and freshly baked breads and end with
a selection of puddings or a Scottish cheeseboard. In between could come crab pancake
with sherry and tomato sauce, then fillet of cod grilled with anchovy butter or fillet of
Highland lamb with kidneys and mushrooms in hot mustard sauce. There's a separate
vegetarian menu, and a Grand Seafood Platter menu of 4 courses at £65 for two diners.
Pleasant wine list, fair prices, succinct tasting notes, though alongside pudding wines we
respectfully suggest 'we have a great weakness for pudding wines' rather than, as written,
'pudding wines are a great weakness of ours'! No smoking. *Seats 30. Parties 10.
Private Room 18. L 12.30-2 D 7-9. Closed Sun (except Whitsun & Easter), Nov-Mar.
Set D from £25. Access, Visa.*

CONTIN   Craigdarroch Lodge   56%   £84

Tel & Fax 01997 421265   Map 2 B3   **H**
Contin by Strathpeffer Highland IV14 9EH

Built as a shooting lodge in the early part of the 19th century, Craigdarroch stands along
a tree-lined drive off the A835 at the foot of the mountains. It's a great base for touring,
walking and all kinds of outdoor activities – much of its business now revolves around
special golfing packages. On site are a bar and lounge, plus a range of leisure pursuits.
Bedrooms are modest but provide the basic comforts. *Rooms 13. Garden, indoor
swimming pool, sauna, solarium, tennis, snooker. Closed Jan & Feb. No credit cards.*

CRAIGELLACHIE   Craigellachie Hotel   68%   £99

Tel 01340 881204   Fax 01340 881253   Map 2 C3   **H**
Craigellachie Grampian AB38 9SS

A hundred years old and still going strong, this solidly built hotel on the A95 stands in
the village where the Spey and the Fiddich rivers meet. Public areas include an airy
lounge with lace-draped grand piano, antique sideboard and plenty of armchairs and
sofas, plus a small library and snug green bar with a good choice of local malt whiskies.
Chintzy fabrics decorate the bedrooms, which have smart modern bathrooms and either
antique or contemporary traditional-style furniture. *Rooms 30. Garden, sauna, keep-fit
equipment, snooker. Access, Amex, Diners, Visa.*

CRAIGNURE   Isle of Mull Hotel   56%   £90

Tel 01680 812351   Fax 01680 812462   Map 3 A5   **H**
Craignure Isle of Mull Argyll Strathclyde PA65 6BB

A long, low modern building where all bedrooms (recently increased in a major
extension) look out across the Sound of Mull. Day rooms offer plenty of space to relax,
and one of the lounges has access to a patio. Two bars. The gardens run down to the sea.
Rooms 87. Garden. Closed Nov-Mar. Access, Visa.

CRIEFF   Crieff Hydro   64%   £103

Tel 01764 655555   Fax 01764 653087   Map 3 C5   **H**
Crieff Tayside PH7 3LQ

An enormous Victorian building, now a family hotel par excellence with an impressive
range of leisure activities to keep everyone busy and fit, from indoor cinema and table
tennis room to outdoor riding school and golf course. Most of the bedrooms are of
a decent size, furnished with either lightwood units or more traditional or antique pieces;

nine two-storey family chalets are in the woods behind. Table licence only, no bar. Banqueting for up to 200 and conference facilities for up to 350 people. A new wing incorporating 40 bedrooms and a conference suite was approaching completion as we went to press. No dogs (a few kennels are provided, but require prior booking). Good family facilities include a children's menu and programme of events. *Rooms 194. Garden, croquet, tennis, golf (9), putting, riding school, indoor swimming pool, gym, squash, whirlpool, spa bath, sauna, steam room, sun beds, boutique, hairdressing and beauty salon, badminton, putting, bowling green, snooker, football pitch, cinema, playroom, playground, coffee shop (9.30am-11pm). Access, Amex, Diners, Visa.*

CRINAN	Crinan Hotel	69%	£115

Tel 01546 830261   Fax 01546 830292   Map 3 B5   **HR**
Crinan by Lochgilphead Strathclyde PA31 8SR

At the northern end of the canal connecting Loch Fyne with the Atlantic stands a tiny fishing village and the Ryans' hotel, which has been constructed in such a way that every window has a view either westwards up the Jura sound or down over the canal's 15th, and final, lock. Major local attractions include the renowned Argyll Gardens and seal colonies (boat trips arranged). Interiors by Mrs Ryan (alias Frances MacDonald the well-known artist) add colour to Italian varnished pine bedrooms of which the pick have private balconies. 1995 saw the Ryans' 25th year here, and the transformation of the Roof Bar into the Gallery Bar – light and airy, with a 'colonial' feel and now incorporating an art gallery. *Rooms 22. Garden. Closed 1 week Christmas. Access, Amex, Visa.*

Westward Restaurant   £70

The hotel's main restaurant, decorated in soft, gentle colours, makes use of the finest seafood, prime Aberdeen Angus beef and Kintyre lamb. The four-course dinner menu starts with a choice of about five starters (three fishy), then perhaps seafood boat with a white wine sauce, before the centrepiece dish, a choice typically of River Add salmon with hollandaise or charcoal-grilled sirloin steak. Scottish cheddar or a lemon meringue pie is a favourite way to finish; Mount Kenya coffee is served in the lounge. No smoking until after main course. Light lunches are served in the public bar. Pretty fair prices on a diverse list that is, of course, personally overseen by Nick Ryan! Well-chosen wines in every section with informative and expertly written tasting notes. Seek advice if you need it – you'll have a companion for life! *Seats 45. D only 7-9. Set D £27.50.*

Lock 16 Restaurant   £95

On the hotel's top floor, this specialist seafood restaurant depends very much on the local fishing fleet which comes in (late afternoon) to unload at the quayside below. A bad catch and the restaurant might not open (it's closed on Sunday and Monday anyway), so it's always best to check. On a good day the fishermen will land jumbo prawns from Corryvreckan, lobsters from the Sound of Jura, Princess clams from Loch Fyne and mussels from Loch Craignish, so you can reasonably expect dishes such as Crinan seafood stew, moules marinière and wild salmon. How the freshest of fresh seafood is cooked is down to Nick Ryan, but it's safe to say that he's a traditionalist and doesn't muck about too much with accompaniments, allowing the fish to taste of just that. To round off the meal, perhaps French lemon tart, and either Stilton or mature Scottish farmhouse cheddar, served with oatcakes. Jacket and tie for gentlemen. *Seats 20. L by arrangment. D at 8. Closed Sun & Mon, also Oct-April. Set D £40.*

CROMARTY	Royal Hotel	£58

Tel 01381 600217   Map 2 C3   I
Marine Terrace Cromarty Highland IV11 8YN

A terrace of 18th-century coastguard's cottages on the waterfront has been converted into a hotel of considerable charm, with welcoming hosts in Stewart and Yvonne Morrison. A fire burns brightly in the homely lounge, off which runs a sun lounge overlooking the Cromarty Firth and Ross-shire mountains. There are two bars, one with pool and darts, and a function suite with a capacity of 120. Immaculate, individually decorated bedrooms in traditional style boast sea views and cotton sheets. *Rooms 10. Garden. Access, Amex, Visa.*

Set menu prices may not always include service or wine.

CUMBERNAULD   Westerwood Hotel   73%   £100

Tel 01236 457171   Fax 01236 738478   Map 3 C5   **HR**
St Andrews Drive Westerwood Cumbernauld Strathclyde G68 0EW

Set on a hill above the A80, Westerwood is a modern hotel and country club with a golf course (designed by Dave Thomas and Severiano Ballesteros) that boasts a 40ft waterfall at the 15th green and wonderful views over the Campsie Hills. For après-golf choose between the hotel's luxurious lounge and cocktail bar with fabric-covered walls and indoor garden or the less formal tartan-carpeted country club. Artificial trees are a novel form of decor in good standard bedrooms. Beds are turned down at night and staff are friendly and helpful. Families are well catered for and can eat informally by the lovely indoor pool or in the clubhouse. Children under 14 may share parents' room free. Banqueting/conference facilities for 170/220. *Rooms 49. Garden, golf (18), bowling green, pétanque, tennis, indoor swimming pool, snooker, gym, sauna, spa bath, steam room, solarium, beauty salon, hairdressing, coffee shop (7am-10pm), golf shop. Access, Amex, Diners, Visa.*

Old Masters Restaurant   £70

An unusual circular dining-room with dark-green watered-silk-effect walls and tented ceiling from which hangs a large brass chandelier. Tom Robertson's sophisticated menus typically offer River Tay salmon served from a trolley, chilled roulade of lemon sole with a fennel and sweet pepper vinaigrette, a light watercress and lime soup, Scottish salmon with scallop mousseline and cucumber and dill butter sauce, medallions of beef fillet with garlic and goose liver sausage on a burgundy truffle and pink peppercorn sauce, and tempting desserts. Reduced menu at Sunday lunchtime, when the central attraction is prime roast Scottish beef. Service is as smooth and confident as the cooking. *Seats 75. Parties 8. L Sun only 12-2.45 D 7-10. Closed D Sun, all Mon & Tue & 1-3 Jan. Set Sun L £9.50 Set D £15.50/£22.50.*

CUPAR   Ostlers Close   £60

Tel 01334 655574   Map 3 C5   **R**
25 Bonnygate Cupar Fife KY15 4BU

Wild mushrooms garnered from nearby forests, herbs and salad ingredients from his own garden, fresh local seafood, specially bred chickens and ducks and seasonal game (especially venison) all feature on Jimmy Graham's menu at an unpretentious restaurant hidden down an alleyway off Bonnygate. The choice changes constantly, typified by pan-fried mixed poultry livers with crispy Parma ham and a warm balsamic vinaigrette, seafood on a champagne sauce, roast wood pigeon and roe venison with Puy lentils, and roast saddle of lamb served with a herb-scented sauce. To finish, Scottish cheeses or some splendid sweets, often including honey, Drambuie and oatmeal ice cream. Pleasing all-round wine list with plenty of good drinking under £20. Smoking only at the end of the meal. *Seats 26. L 12.15-2 D 7-9.30. Closed Sun & Mon, 25 & 26 Dec. Access, Amex, Visa.*

DERVAIG   Druimard Country House   £55

Tel & Fax 01688 400345   Map 3 A4   **RR**
Dervaig Isle of Mull Strathclyde PA75 6QW

More comfortable family home than grand country house, Haydn and Wendy Hubbard's hillside Victorian house overlooks the wide open spaces of Glen Bellart. Within, the dining-room has pin-striped mustard and damson decor, a floral dado and unpretentious table settings. Next door to the house is the charming Mull Little Theatre (the UK's smallest professional theatre, with just 43 seats; Tel 01688 400267) and pre-theatre suppers commence between 6 and 6.45pm when the theatre is open (shows start at 8.30pm). Wendy's performance in the kitchen might open with a celeriac soup, assorted smoked fish or creamy, spiced mushrooms topped with garlic breadcrumbs and slivered almonds; the main attraction could be hand-dived local scallops (perhaps with a vivid, well-balanced saffron and Chablis sauce and matching yellow nasturtium leaf – for a small supplement to the one-price menu), wild Mull salmon with frothy lemon sabayon, year-round farmed pheasant, venison or fillet of Angus beef. Herby Mull Cheddar and other interesting Scottish cheeses or over-generous helpings of rich, home-made puddings to finish the show. Packet butter served with cheese and over-chilled wine are small disappointments; smoking is permitted in the small conservatory bar area off the no-smoking dining-room. The house's field sports theme continues in the homely drawing-room, where coffee, mints and a wee dram of Tobermory malt might amuse the culinary audience further. The 8-mile drive up and over from Tobermory is wonderfully winding, hilly and scenic. *Seats 30. Parties 12. D only 6-8.30 (from 7 non-theatre nights, 7-8 Sun residents only). Set D £14.50/£16.50. Closed Nov-end Mar. Access, Visa.*

Rooms   £85
The six bedrooms are spotlessly kept but modestly furnished. A suite under the eaves on the top floor comprises separate double and small twin bedrooms plus a sitting-room – ideal for families. Two rooms (including the suite) have en-suite bath, two have en-suite shower and two currently share a bathroom and attract a lower tariff (£56/£64). Haggis features on the breakfast menu. Packed lunches are offered. Garden.

DIRLETON	Open Arms Hotel	67%	£119

Tel 01620 850241   Fax 01620 850570   Map 3 D5   **H**
Dirleton nr North Berwick Lothian EH39 5EG

There's a cosy and friendly atmosphere at this small, family-run hotel, well situated for holidaymakers and well equipped for conferences, banquets, receptions (marquee on the lawn) and outside catering. Children up to 12 stay free in parents' room. New owners recently took over. *Rooms 7. Garden. Access, Visa.*

DRUMNADROCHIT	Polmaily House	66%	£90

Tel 01456 450343   Map 2 B3   **HR**
Drumnadrochit Highland IV3 6XT

Set back from the A831 about 1½ miles into the Glen of Urquhart from Loch Ness, Polmaily House stands in 12 acres of its own gardens and woodland. Since taking over in 1993 John and Sonia Whittington-Davis have redecorated and refurbished throughout (and in 1995 plans were afoot to cover and heat the swimming pool and add a conservatory bar extension to the lounge), creating a comfortable, relaxing hotel. Bedrooms vary in size but all are attractively decorated and include an antique or two; the largest have separate sitting areas. All are now en suite, the two small singles with shower and WC only. Families are encouraged with video players (they have a library of films for children) and toys (appropriate to age) placed in all rooms where there are to be children. One bedroom has a connecting room with bunk beds, another separate room with bunk beds is just for children and several others can be arranged to suit family needs. For breakfast try the game haggis; it goes splendidly with fried eggs, and there are freshly baked croissants too. Room service is offered throughout the day and evening. *Rooms 10. Garden, croquet, tennis, outdoor swimming pool, playground, games room. Closed mid Nov-mid Dec. Access, Visa.*

Urquhart Restaurant   £45
It's Sonia who does the cooking, using local produce as much as possible – most of the seafood comes from Mallaig for example – in straightforward, unfussy style. There's a largish à la carte ranging from whitebait and home-made patés to omelettes, Highlander's mixed grill, deep-fried fish, pasta and vegetarian dishes plus a special 'slimmers choice' in addition to the table d'hote. The day's list of homely puds is recited at the table. Smoking is allowed in the drawing-room (eating pause allowed) but not in the restaurant. *Seats 40. Parties 12. L by arrangement D 7.30-9.30. Set D £17.50.*

DRYBRIDGE	Old Monastery Restaurant	£55

Tel 01542 832660   Map 2 C3   **R**
Drybridge Buckie Grampian AB56 2JB

Up in the hills three miles inland from Buckie, the former monastery enjoys delightful views over the Moray Firth (turn off the A98 at Buckie junction on to the Drybridge road. Follow the road for 2½ miles – do not turn right into Drybridge village). Maureen Gray offers a warm welcome front of house, while Douglas in the kitchen uses the best of the local larder with fish from the Spey, seasonal game and Aberdeen Angus beef. Typical choices are: warm salad of scallops; French onion soup made using Aberdeen Angus beef stock; guinea fowl with a claret sauce; breast of duckling Seville with

See over

a bittersweet orange and Cointreau sauce and medallions of Highland venison with a redcurrant and port sauce. Desserts include a warm filo parcel of orange, banana and cinnamon with caramel and vanilla sauces and a chocolate and Tia Maria roulade. Plenty of halves on a decent wine list which includes succinct tasting notes. No smoking. *Seats 45. L 12.15-1.30 D 7-9.30 (Sat to 10). Closed Sun & Mon, 3 weeks Jan, 2 weeks Nov. Access, Amex, Visa.*

DRYBURGH	**Dryburgh Abbey**	65%	£110

Tel 01835 822261   Fax 01835 823945   Map 4 C1   **H**
St Boswells Dryburgh nr Melrose Borders TD6 0RQ

On the A68 at St Boswells take the B6404, drive through the village and follow the signs to Scott's View and Earlston (B6356). The red sandstone hotel, especially popular with the shooting and fishing fraternity, stands next to the historic ruins of Dryburgh Abbey alongside the River Tweed. Comfort and space are well supplied in the attractive public areas (two lounges − one on the first floor next to the restaurant − and a bar) and bedrooms (named after fishing flies). From the Garden View rooms to the four-poster room and suites which enjoy views across the woods to the abbey or the river, all provide hairdryer, trouser press, and remote-control teletext TV, as well as decent bathrooms. Up to 200 can be accommodated in the function suite, and there's a private dining-room/boardroom. *Rooms 26. Garden, croquet, pitch & putt, fishing, indoor swimming pool. Access, Visa.*

DRYMEN	**Buchanan Arms Hotel**	62%	£114

Tel 01360 660588   Fax 01360 660943   Map 3 B5   **H**
Main Street Drymen by Loch Lomond Central G63 0BQ

This former coaching inn now has a thoroughly modern air − as in the relaxing conservatory − whilst not forgetting its origins, as in the arched and beamed lounge bar. The bedrooms are well equipped and maintained and there's an excellent leisure centre (the Buchanan Club) as well as a versatile range of conference and banqueting suites (up to 150 delegates and 120 for a function). Children up to 12 stay free in parents' room. Six rooms are reserved for non-smokers. Baby-sitting and baby-listening are available. *Rooms 51. Garden, indoor swimming pool, gym, squash, sauna, spa bath, beauty salon, bowling green. Access, Amex, Diners, Visa.*

DULNAIN BRIDGE	**Auchendean Lodge**	62%	£69

Tel & Fax 01479 851 347   Map 2 C3   **HR**
Dulnain Bridge Grantown-on-Spey Highland PH26 3LU

Built as an Edwardian hunting and fishing lodge, this owner-run country hotel is set in spectacular scenery a mile south of Dulnain Bridge on the A95. A range of activities − golfing at six nearby courses, canoeing on the Spey, skiing in the Cairngorms, shooting, fishing and hiking − is available locally. There's period furniture in two open-fired lounges and individually-styled bedrooms (five en-suite) have electric blankets, radio/alarms and TVs, but no phones. 200 acres of woods and $1\frac{1}{2}$ acres of gardens surround the hotel. *Rooms 8. Garden, pitch & putt. Closed 4 weeks before or after Christmas. Access, Amex, Diners, Visa.*

Restaurant   £55

Dinner is a daily-changing, four-course affair making good use of local game, fish, garden vegetables and wild mushrooms − a passion of chef Eric Hart. Those mushrooms could appear on toast (wood blewits), in mushroom and sherry soup or in a yellow legs (winter chanterelles), red wine and herb beef casserole. Other choices could include baked sweet pepper or gravad lax, roast monkfish with grain mustard sauce, wild mallard with blueberry sauce or wild mountain hare fillet with juniper sauce. To finish, perhaps apple and hazelnut crumble, rum-baked banana or pears in cassis sauce. Good Scottish cheeses. The menu states that "credit card commission is charged extra". Snacks or picnics provided if prior notice given. No smoking. *Seats 18. D only 7.30-9. Set D £23.50.*

DULNAIN BRIDGE	**Muckrach Lodge**	59%	£82

Tel 01479 851257   Fax 01479 851325   Map 2 C3   **H**
Dulnain Bridge Grantown-on-Spey Highland PH26 3LY

A Victorian hunting lodge set in ten acres of grounds with fine views of the Dulnain valley all around. It's a fine base for touring the beautiful Speyside country, and a most pleasant place for just sitting back and relaxing. The feel is friendly and informal in both lounge and bar, and there are soothing views from most of the bedrooms, which include a four-poster room. Carpeted bathrooms offer good towelling and all sorts of bits and bobs from cotton wool balls to a nail brush. The former steading (stables) houses two full suites, one especially adapted for wheelchair-bound guests. Children up to 12 years stay free in parents' room. Two additional bedrooms have recently come on stream. No dogs. *Rooms 14. Garden, fishing. Access, Amex, Diners, Visa.*

DUNBLANE	Cromlix House	82%	£140

Tel 01786 822125   Fax 01786 825450   Map 3 C5   **HR**
Kinbuck by Dunblane Central FK15 9JT

A sturdy Victorian mansion set in glorious countryside on a 3000-acre estate four miles north of Dunblane. Much of the furniture, paintings and porcelain has been in the house since the last century, and the collection of fishing rods, croquet mallets and wellies in the entrance hall indicates the atmosphere as that of a treasured family home. Day rooms such as the leather-furnished library and morning room with its floral-patterned linen covers on armchairs and settees, combine elegance with comfort. Spacious, antique-furnished bedrooms (eight are full suites) often have period light fittings and other features that give something of an Edwardian feel. Bathrooms, with fittings from various periods, are all large and boast quality toiletries and towelling. *Rooms 14. Garden, croquet, tennis, clay-pigeon shooting, fishing. Closed Jan. Access, Amex, Diners, Visa.*

Restaurant   £90

Two dining-rooms, one with fluted pilasters and ornate gilt light fittings, the other in Victorian shooting lodge style. Fixed-price dinners, with just a couple of choices at each stage, make use of the best local produce, carefully prepared in modern British style and eye-catchingly presented. Baked brie wrapped in Parma ham and filo pastry set on a citrus fruit sauce with salad leaves; smooth terrine of liver paté flavoured with garlic accompanied by a port wine coulis; cream of broccoli and Dunsyre blue cheese soup; grilled Tay salmon with a green grape and basil cream; and thinly sliced fillet of Aberdeen Angus beef resting on a bed of wild mushrooms enhanced by a sherry jus show the style. Choice of hot and cold dessert; Scottish cheeses. Vegetarian menu available. Some fair prices on a decent wine list with a good New World section. No smoking. *Seats 40. Parties 8. Private Rooms 12/24/40. L 12.30-1.15 (by arrangment only Mon-Fri Oct-Apr) D 7-8.30. Set L £17/£24 Set D £35.*

DUNBLANE	Stakis Dunblane	61%	£111

Tel 01786 822551   Fax 01786 825403   Map 3 C5   **H**
Perth Road Dunblane Central FK15 0HG

Handsome Victorian building set high above the main road to Perth in 44 acres of grounds. The main attraction is the enhanced leisure facility, and bedrooms range from singles, twins and doubles to family rooms, suites and 36 non-smoking Club rooms with whirlpool baths. Four rooms are adapted for disabled guests. Children up to 4 stay free in parents' room, 5s-15s are charged £18 for high tea, bed & breakfast. Conferences are also big business, with room for up to 500 theatre-style. *Rooms 214. Garden, indoor swimming pool, keep-fit equipment, sauna, steam room, spa bath, solarium, aromatherapy, reflexology, tennis, putting, playroom. Access, Amex, Diners, Visa.*

DUNDEE   Angus Thistle   69%   £107

Tel 01382 226874   Fax 01382 322564   Map 3 C5   **H**
Marketgait Dundee Tayside DD1 1QU

A modern, six-storey city-centre hotel offering a good standard of bedroom
accommodation (including five suites) and conference facilities for up to 500 delegates;
some rooms have views across the Tay Estuary. 24hr room service; children up to 12 free
in parents' room. *Rooms 58. Access, Amex, Diners, Visa.*

DUNDEE   Invercarse Hotel   59%   £80

Tel 01382 669231   Fax 01382 644112   Map 3 C5   **H**
371 Perth Road Dundee Tayside DD2 1PG

The privately-owned Invercarse is an extended Victorian house set on a hill (some three
miles west of the city centre) affording views across the Tay to the Fife hills beyond.
Children up to 12 can share parents' room free. Conference/banqueting for 200/280.
Rooms 35. Garden. Access, Amex, Diners, Visa.

DUNFERMLINE   King Malcolm Thistle   65%   £93

Tel 01383 722611   Fax 01383 730865   Map 3 C5   **H**
Queensferry Road Dunfermline Fife KY11 5DS

Fifteen miles from the centre of Edinburgh and a short drive from Junction 2 of the
M90. Modern bedrooms have all the expected amenities plus 24hr room service. The
Malcolm Suite can accommodate up to 130 delegates theatre-style. Children up to 16
stay free in parents' room. *Rooms 48. Garden. Access, Amex, Diners, Visa.*

DUNKELD   Kinnaird   81%   £185

Tel 01796 482440   Fax 01796 482289   Map 3 C5   **HR**
Kinnaird Estate by Dunkeld Tayside PH8 0LB

With superb views, overlooking the
River Tay valley and surrounded by its
own beautifully landscaped gardens, part
of a 9,000-acre estate (making it ideal
for small sporting parties – fishing,
shooting, deer-stalking – for whom
every facility is provided, even heated
kennels for the dogs), this late 18th-
century house is a haven of relaxed and
civilised luxury. Kinnaird has all the
facilities associated with a fine country
house hotel, yet retains the atmosphere
of a private home – flower-filled day
rooms boast fine antiques, porcelain ornaments, pictures and mementoes belonging to
owner Constance Ward's family. The Cedar Room, so called for its panelling, filled with
deep sofas and with a huge fireplace where a real fire burns in winter, is the main sitting-
room and there is a superb snooker room to retire to with a wee dram after dinner.
Individually decorated bedrooms are spacious and no less comfortable with settees and easy
chairs, gas-log fires and every modern convenience. Bathrooms are particularly sybaritic.
There are now also five fully-equipped country cottages located around the estate that
enjoy all the amenities of the hotel. Turn off the A9 just north of Dunkeld on to the
B898; Kinnaird is about four miles further north. No children under 12. No dogs in the
house. *Rooms 9. Garden, croquet, tennis, game fishing, snooker. Closed Mon, Tue & Wed
from Jan-Mar. Access, Amex, Visa.*

Restaurant   🔼   £90

A fine room with glittering chandeliers and marble fireplace where 19th-century
Italianate frescoes of a sylvan landscape compete for attention with fine real-life views
from picture windows. The splendid cooking of John Webber complements the
surroundings perfectly. He uses first-rate ingredients, local whenever possible, in dishes
that are creative and interesting. This clever balance is demonstrated in such main dishes
as poached wild salmon in a light herb and vegetable liquor, braised boned oxtail cooked
with red wine and stout and Scotch fillet steak topped with parsnip and horseradish and
served with polenta and a red wine sauce. First courses might include terrine of duck

cassoulet served with warm ravioli of Toulouse sausage and a dressing of green herbs, and a shellfish minestrone and to round things off you might go for hot chocolate pithiviers or apple and cider mousse after sampling something from the mostly Scottish (the occasional English example might creep in) cheese trolley. At lunchtime cheese is an alternative to dessert on a rather shorter fixed-price menu that is priced for either two or three courses. Extensive half bottle selection on a fine list that includes some value-for-money French country wines and much from the New World. No smoking. Gentlemen should wear jackets and ties. *Seats 35. Parties 8. Private Room 20. L 12.30-1.45 D 7.15-9.30. Set L £19.50/£24 Set D £39.50.*

DUNOON	Chatters	£50

Tel 01369 706402   Map 3 B5   **R**
58 John Street Dunoon Strathclyde TA23 8BJ

With a comfortable conservatory lounge for drinks before and after eating, the style is now more that of a restaurant proper, though bar snacks are also available lunchtimes. David Craig uses local produce whenever possible including some excellent game and seafood. Menus are short and include, as starters, a warm salad of wood pigeon and bacon, garnished with quail's eggs, a trio of wild mushroom ravioli on a watercress sauce or Loch Fyne shellfish. Main courses follow in a similar modern mode: poached fillet of salmon with squid on a bed of noodles with a chervil beurre blanc; pan-fried breast of pheasant with a pistachio and lentil purée and a wild mushroom and malt whisky ragout or duet of roast pork and beef fillet with lemon glazed apricots on a Madeira reduction. *Seats 35. L 12-2.30 D 6-10. Closed Sun, January. Access, Visa.*

DUROR	Stewart Hotel	59%	£80

Tel 01631 740268   Fax 01631 740328   Map 3 B4   **H**
Glen Duror Appin Argyll Highland PA38 4BW

The hospitable Lacy family (here since 1986) and their staff offer a friendly welcome at their Victorian house, which stands in five acres of terraced gardens with beautiful views of Loch Linnhe. The oldest part was built 120 years ago in the style of a hunting lodge. Bedrooms are simple and neat, with views (most), modern furniture and tiny bathrooms. The hotel is signposted off the A828 six miles south of Ballachulish on the way to Oban. *Rooms 19. Garden. Closed mid Oct-Easter. Access, Amex, Diners, Visa.*

EAST KILBRIDE	Stakis Westpoint Hotel	74%	£115

Tel 01355 236300   Fax 01355 233552   Map 3 C6   **H**
Stewartfield Way East Kilbride Strathclyde G74 5LA

This modern hotel is unusual in both design and location. Situated on a new industrial estate, it lies close enough to Glasgow to attract the business community, though it appears the hotel's major appeal is its superb leisure facilities. There are also banqueting and conference rooms for up to 120/150. The bedrooms lack nothing in style or quality; Executive bedrooms especially are models of good taste, with spacious sitting areas and splendid bathrooms with marble-effect tiling, robes and fine Scottish toiletries. The satellite TV cabinet houses a mini-bar (with fresh milk). 24hr room service and all-day lounge menu. No dogs. *Rooms 74. Indoor swimming pool, gym, squash, sauna, steam room, spa bath, solarium, beauty salon, snooker. Access, Amex, Diners, Visa.*

EAST KILBRIDE	Stuart Hotel	62%	£80

Tel 01355 221161   Fax 01355 264410   Map 3 C6   **H**
Cornwall Way East Kilbride Strathclyde G74 1JR

A modern hotel whose day rooms include two bars and a function suite with an unusual brass ceiling. Three Executive bedrooms recently upgraded to De Luxe. Conference facilities for up to 200, banqueting for 150. 24hr room service. *Rooms 39. Access, Amex, Diners, Visa.*

We welcome bona fide complaints and recommendations on the tear-out pages at the back of the book for readers' comments. They are followed up by our professional team.

EDINBURGH	Alp-Horn	£45

Tel 0131-225 4787 Fax 0131-225 1546   Map 3 C6   **R**
167 Rose Street Edinburgh Lothian EH2 4LS

Just off Charlotte Square and two minutes from Princes Street, a Swiss restaurant with
a chalet atmosphere (Rose Street is pedestrianised – best to park in Charlotte Square or
George Street). Cheese and beef fondues (for two or more) are well-executed specialities,
and air-dried Swiss beef and ham (assiette de Grisons), veal sausage (kalbsbratwurst), plus
emincé de veau zurichoise with rösti potatoes are also faithful to their origins. Supreme
de volaille Sophia Loren is a breadcrumbed breast of chicken filled with ham and cheese,
garnished with asparagus and served with rösti. In addition a weekly-changing 'chef's
choice' menu offers the likes of avocado vinaigrette, salmon bonne femme and rump
steak with parsley butter. Apfel strudel is made on the premises. Lunchtimes see an
excellent value 'square deal lunch' of two courses and a shortened à la carte. Try the
Swiss wines, even though they may seem expensive alongside the rest of the wine list.
Separate room for non-smokers. *Seats 66. Parties 12. Private Room 25. L 12-2 D 6.30-10.
Closed Sun, 25 & 26 Dec & 2 days New Year. Set L £5.75. Access, Amex, Diners, Visa.*

EDINBURGH	Atrium	↑	£60

Tel 0131-228 8882   Map 3 C6   **R**
Cambridge Street Edinburgh Lothian EH1 2ED

Within the atrium of Saltire Court – a smart new office building next to the Usher Hall
in Edinburgh's Theatre district – the restaurant's post-modern decor is quite stunning
with railway sleeper tables, raw linen-draped chairs and glass torches based on an ancient
glass drinking horn, set in wrought-iron sconces imparting an almost medieval
atmosphere. Andrew Radford's short but truly eclectic twice-daily-changing menus utilise
the best of Scottish produce to create dishes that ably demonstrate his culinary knowledge
and skills. A typical winter's dinner could provide starters like a samosa of squat lobster
and scallops, salmon fishcake with greens or wood pigeon with champ, Parma ham and
lentils. To follow: monkfish tails with spring onion, coriander and leeks; Scottish beef,
savoy cabbage with mushrooms and bacon; wild duck with roast roots and juniper or
mackerel fillet with grilled endive, salsa and olive oil. Finish in great style with delectables
like white truffle cake with a toffee sauce and praline, strawberry tart or poached pear
with sablé and crème fraiche. There is also a short snack menu at lunchtime and for pre-
theatre diners between 6–7pm. The wine list is imaginative, fairly priced and with some
tasting notes, though seemingly there's no order to it at all! One of Andrew's brigade,
Glyn Stevens, carried off the Chef of the Year title – see the award pages at the front of
the book. *Seats 70. L 12-2.30 D 6-10.30. Closed L Sat, all Sun, 10 days Christmas. Access,
Amex, Diners, Visa.*

EDINBURGH	L'Auberge	£75

Tel 0131-556 5888 Fax 0131-556 2588   Map 3 C6   **R**
56 St Mary Street Edinburgh Lothian EH1 1SX

Owner Daniel Wencker has taken over chef's duties in the kitchen of this long-
established and comfortable French restaurant in Edinburgh's 'old town', off the Royal
Mile near John Knox House. He plans to introduce dishes from his native Alsace to
menus that include the likes of escargots sautéed with garlic, parsley and pine kernels,
a Provençal version of gravlax flavoured with fennel, medallions of venison with prunes
and chestnuts in a juniper and port sauce, and the day's fish dish. Afters might include
their speciality *tarte des demoiselles tatin* and a traditional crème brulée along with
some, mostly unpasteurised, French cheeses. There is a page of New World wines
alongside a very comprehensive French list that has many priced under £20. Several
classics and well-known names, plenty of half bottles. *Seats 65. Parties 20.
Private Room 28. L 12.15-2 D 6.15-9.30. Set L £12.50/£15.50 (Sun £16.50)
Set D £19.50/£23.50 & £31.50. Access, Amex, Diners, Visa*

**Consult the blue pages for summary tables and lists of
recommended establishments.**

EDINBURGH — The Balmoral — 83% — £167

Tel 0131-556 2414 Fax 0131-557 3747   Map 3 C6   **HR**
Princes Street Edinburgh Lothian EH2 2EQ

At the top of Forte's tree in Scotland, the Balmoral wears its total refurbishment from the early '90s very comfortably indeed. Opulence, comfort, courtesy, elegance are the watchwords here – definitely a place in which to be cosseted, and nothing is too much trouble for the very professional staff. Bedrooms (with marble bathrooms) and suites are excellently equipped and maintained, modern conveniences blending discreetly with traditional furnishings. We quote a standard price: there are superior, de luxe and suites above that. Public areas are of a similarly high standard, encompassing the Palm Court Lounge, coffee shop, bars, brasserie and the main restaurant, so that any style of refreshment can be provided. Room service is available around the clock. There are ten function suites, the largest holding 400.

Rooms *189. Gym, sauna, steam room, sunbeds, beauty & hair salon, cashmere & crystal shop. Access, Amex, Diners, Visa.*

The Grill Room, No 1 Princes Street   £110

Very much the grand hotel dining-room, where discretion and attention to detail (both in decor and in food presentation) are impeccable. On the à la carte menu the prices are written out as words not figures (slightly prolonging the shock), although the better value set lunch menus are expressed in a more straightforward manner. Many dishes are indicated with a thistle device as being a "Taste of Scotland". Try perhaps terrine of wild Crathie pigeon marbled with pistachio and oak-smoked peppers, galantine of quail served with yellow tomato chutney or grilled Oban scallops served with a broad bean salad and crispy bacon, then for main course saddle of rabbit with a farce of Scottish lamb with Lanark Blue cheese sauce and young vegetables. An extensive range of excellent quality fish and meat can be simply grilled, and with eight hours' notice two people can share pressed Rouennais duck, its preparation finished at table. The separate vegetarian menu is of similar style, and the lunch menus read more simply. Quite a comprehensive wine list, though prices are on the high side; best value is in the New World. **Seats** *45. Parties 8. L 12-2.30 D 7-10.30. Closed L Sat & Sun. Set L £17.50/£19.95 Set D £35.*

NB's Bar & Brasserie   £40

A brasserie in the Continental style, with an all-day menu of salads, snacks, appetisers (soup, fishcakes, paté) and main courses (fish and chips, pasta, charcoal grills). Also a wide selection of cakes and pastries, coffees and teas. Regular live music. The bar section is in traditional pub style. The hotel used to be called the North British, affectionately known as the NB, hence the name change from *Bridges.* **Seats** *90. Parties 16. Meals 7am-11pm. Set L £8.50 Set D £20.*

EDINBURGH — Barnton Thistle — 63% — £108

Tel 0131-339 1144 Fax 0131-339 5521   Map 3 C6   **H**
Queensferry Road Edinburgh Lothian EH4 6AS

On the A90, handy for airport and city centre, providing modern comfort for both leisure and business visitors. Conference/banqueting facilities for 150/120. Ample free parking. **Rooms** *50. Sauna. Access, Amex, Diners, Visa.*

EDINBURGH — Braid Hills Hotel — 61% — £95

Tel 0131-447 8888 Fax 0131-452 8477   Map 3 C6   **H**
134 Braid Road Edinburgh Lothian EH10 6JD

A lofty, baronial hotel whose upper-floor bedrooms afford sweeping views over Edinburgh. A strong group and function clientele enjoys neatly kept, well-equipped rooms serviced by obliging staff. A bistro has recently been added. **Rooms** *68. Garden. Access, Amex, Diners, Visa.*

EDINBURGH   **Caledonian Hotel**   79%   £280

Tel 0131-459 9988 Fax 0131-225 6632   Map 3 C6   **HR**
Princes Street Edinburgh Lothian EH1 2AB

Built at the turn of the century by the Caledonian Railway Company, the 'Caley' is
virtually a national monument. Traditional standards of hospitality and service have been
maintained while moving with the times in terms of comfort and amenities. The carpeted
foyer leads to the grand, elegantly proportioned lounge which is at the heart of the public
areas; a popular place with both locals and visitors to Edinburgh to take afternoon tea
seated on plush shot-silk sofas. For a complete change of atmosphere there's Carriages
restaurant and bar which retains the redbrick former station entrance as an inside wall.
Bedrooms, including 22 full suites, are individually styled, featuring traditional
freestanding furniture and well-chosen fabrics. 43 Superior business bedrooms have large
work stations, fax and computer points and a voicemail facility. De luxe rooms and those
with a view of the Castle attract a supplement. Towelling robes are provided in all the
bathrooms, some of which boast elegant antique-style fittings. Plus factors are the number
of telephone extensions in each room, 24hr lounge service and an evening turn-down
service. Families are particularly well catered for with children up to 16 staying free in
parents' room. No dogs. Conference facilities for up to 300. Dedicated business centre.
Free parking for 50 cars. *Rooms 236. Access, Amex, Diners, Visa.*

La Pompadour   £105

Opened in 1925 and named after Louis
XV's mistress, the Pompadour is elegant
and formal; ornate plasterwork frames
large wall-paintings of delicate flowers,
a pianist plays soothing music and
excellent staff provide impeccable
service. Executive chef Tony Binks has
been here since 1980 and, together
with his young team, he continues to
use the best of Scottish produce to
good effect. The evening à la carte (also
available on request at lunchtime) is
sensibly short with dishes like Lanark
Blue cheese mousse wrapped in cured ham and filled with creamed leeks finished with
Sauternes sauce, fillet of young turbot layered with scampi mousseline in pastry, and
medallions of wild fallow deer pan-fried and served with spiced curly kale and preserved
cherry sauce supplemented by a list of 'classics': asparagus hollandaise, cognac-flavoured
roulade of foie gras with toasted brioche, grilled Dover sole. There is also a no-choice,
four-course Signature menu. The fixed-price lunch menu claims to represent the
tradition and history of the national cuisine under the title 'Legends of the Scottish Table'
but stretches credulity somewhat with dishes such as avocado and blood orange salad with
ginger dressing, baked filo pastry of Parma ham, brie and basil with a cucumber and apple
salad, and grilled lamb's liver with red pepper sauce and a courgette and onion chutney.
A well-rounded wine list, though with no tasting notes. *Seats 60. L 12.30-2.15 D 7.30-
10.15. Closed L Sat & Sun & D Sun in winter. Set L £22.50 Set D £40.*

Carriages Restaurant   £60

The hotel's informal eaterie, open for breakfast, lunch and dinner seven days a week,
offering a range of familiar, fairly straightforward dishes on à la carte and fixed-price
menus: deep-fried mushrooms, mulligatawny soup, spaghetti bolognese, grills, mushroom
and vegetable risotto, French apple tart, cheesecake. Scottish favourites include cock-a-
leekie soup and haggis. *Seats 130. L 12-2.30 D 6.30-10. Set L £14.75/£17.75 (Sun £16.25)
Set D £24.50 & £28.*

Consult the blue pages for summary tables and lists of
recommended establishments.

| EDINBURGH | **Capital Moat House** | **66%** | **£134** |

Tel 0131-334 3391 Fax 0131-334 9712   Map 3 C6   **H**
Clermiston Road Edinburgh Lothian EH12 6UG

Located in north east Corstorphine, the hotel is quite a way from the city centre. The Terrace restaurant, an attractive conservatory-style dining-room, is the hotel's most striking feature, offering exceptional views of the surroundings. Executive bedrooms are unusually large, with discreet pink decor and well-designed bathrooms. Standard ones tend to be smaller and more ordinary. The hotel has a well-equipped leisure centre. *Rooms 111. Indoor swimming pool, gym, sauna, steam room, solarium, spa bath, beauty salon. Access, Amex, Diners, Visa.*

| EDINBURGH | **Carlton Highland** | **68%** | **£160** |

Tel 0131-556 7277 Fax 0131-556 2691   Map 3 C6   **H**
North Bridge Edinburgh Lothian EH1 1SD

Besides well-equipped bedrooms and comfortable day rooms the Carlton Highland (located between Princes Street and the Royal Mile) has a fine leisure club, conference facilities for up to 350 and a night club with dancing and live entertainment several nights a week. One room is equipped for disabled guests. Children up to 15 stay free in their parents' room. Scottish Highland Hotels. *Rooms 197. Indoor swimming pool, gym, sauna, steam room, solarium, squash, snooker, beauty & hair salon, children's playroom, coffee shop (10am-6pm). Access, Amex, Diners, Visa.*

Set menu prices may not always include service or wine.

| EDINBURGH | **Channings** | **64%** | **£135** |

Tel 0131-315 2226 Fax 0131-332 9631   Map 3 C6   **H**
South Learmonth Gardens Edinburgh Lothian EH4 1EZ

Half a mile from the west end of Princes Street is a series of fine, adjoining Edwardian town houses run as a comfortable, privately-owned hotel with a country house feel. Traditional features – oak panelling, high moulded ceilings, ornate fireplaces, antique furniture and prints – remain in the peaceful lounges, while the bedrooms (some overlooking old Edinburgh) are individually furnished in a more contemporary manner. Staff are friendly and there's a relaxed ambience throughout. No dogs. *Rooms 48. Terrace. Closed 25-27 Dec. Access, Amex, Diners, Visa.*

| EDINBURGH | **Denzlers 121** | | **£50** |

Tel 0131-554 3268   Map 3 C6   **R**
121 Constitution Street Leith Edinburgh Lothian EH6 7AE

Sister restaurant to the *Alp-Horn* and with a similarly Swiss/French menu but without the chalet-style decor. Externally forbidding former bank premises down amongst the bonded warehouses of Leith (5-minute taxi ride from the centre of Edinburgh); inside is bright and welcoming, while outside the parking is easy in the evening. Solidly traditional Swiss favourites like veal zurichoise, air-dried beef and ham (bunderplattli), cheese fondues (minimum 2 persons) and apfel strudel are favourites, along with fish soufflé in a smoked salmon 'chemise', duck with cherries and assiette Lucullus – a platter of sweets comprising profiteroles, meringue with ice cream and fruit tartlet. The set lunch offers very good value (soup, chipolatas with purée of peas, swordfish meunière, chicken pie) and includes a drink. Short, diverse wine list opens with three Swiss wines. *Seats 65. Parties 12. L 12-2 D 6.30-10. Closed L Sat, all Sun, Mon, 1st week Jan, 2 weeks end Jul, 2 days early Christmas. Set L £7.75. Access, Amex, Diners, Visa.*

| EDINBURGH | **Forte Posthouse** | **62%** | **£75** |

Tel 0131-334 0390 Fax 0131-334 9237   Map 3 C6   **H**
Corstorphine Road Edinburgh Lothian EH12 6UA

On the A8 halfway between airport and city centre, with both Murrayfield (for the rugby) and the zoo nearby. Conference facilities for up to 140 delegates. *Rooms 204. Access, Amex, Diners, Visa.*

EDINBURGH   George Inter-Continental   74%   £180

Tel 0131-225 1251 Fax 0131-226 5644   Map 3 C6   **H**
19 George Street Edinburgh Lothian EH2 2PB

Very conveniently located for the shopping on Edinburgh's Princes Street. The classical facade conceals a grand entrance lobby complete with elegant, fluted Corinthian columns, polished marble floors and a raised seating area behind a wooden balustrade from where one can observe the busy comings and goings. Other public areas include the clubby Gathering of the Clans bar sporting clan mementoes and curios from the whisky trade. Luxurious bedrooms, including ten suites, have comfortable settees or armchairs and quality freestanding furniture (mostly in yew), teletext TVs, in-house movies and beverage facilities neatly hidden away in cabinets. Conference/banqueting facilities for 200/150. Guests have free use of the nearby Flying Scots health club. No dogs. *Rooms 195. Access, Amex, Diners, Visa.*

EDINBURGH   Greenside Hotel   £80

Tel & Fax 0131-557 0022   Map 3 C6   **PH**
9 Royal Terrace Edinburgh Lothian EH7 5AB

Relatively close to the centre, the hotel benefits from a quiet location, with bedrooms overlooking the Royal Terrace gardens in front or the flowery rear gardens which the owners take great pride in keeping up themselves. Bedrooms are roomy, furnished with taste and sparkling clean. All rooms are now en suite and have telephones. A new bar doubles as a breakfast room. No dogs. *Rooms 13. Access, Amex, Diners, Visa.*

EDINBURGH   Hilton National   68%   £176

Tel 0131-332 2545 Fax 0131-332 3805   Map 3 C6   **H**
69 Belford Road Edinburgh Lothian EH4 3DG

A modern hotel just a few minutes walk from Princes Street. Public areas centre on a glitzy, split-level cocktail bar; a more pubby bar is to be found in what was an old flour mill. Business centre, several conference rooms (125 in largest room). Children up to 12 stay free in parents' room. *Rooms 144. Access, Amex, Diners, Visa.*

EDINBURGH   Holiday Inn Garden Court 65%   £95

Tel 0131-332 2442 Fax 0131-332 3408   Map 3 C6   **H**
107 Queensferry Road Edinburgh Lothian EH4 3HL

Located on the A90 a mile from the city centre. Bedrooms are somewhat smaller than the normal Holiday Inn standard, half are non-smoking rooms. Meeting rooms for up to 60. *Rooms 119. Garden, gym. Access, Amex, Diners, Visa.*

EDINBURGH   Howard Hotel   74%   £180

Tel 0131-557 3500 Fax 0131-557 6515   Map 3 C6   **H**
36 Great King Street Edinburgh Lothian EH3 6QH

Created out of three interconnected town houses in the Georgian 'New Town' area of the city, the Howard conceals behind its rather dour exterior a hotel of quiet luxury and considerable comfort. The dark greens, blues and purples of Highland heather predominate in bedrooms which boast a mixture of antiques and painted furniture. Dishes of fruit and nuts, mineral water, bowls of pot-pourri and the like are common to all rooms and all, except four rather small singles, get a second phone at the desk. Bathrooms, again except for the singles, come with separate shower cubicles, many boast twin washbasins and three or four have wonderful old-fashioned freestanding tubs – others have nice chunky reproduction-style suites with brass fittings. The main day room is the very model of a refined Edinburgh drawing-room. Staff are most helpful and friendly. Good cooked breakfasts are served in the basement restaurant. *Rooms 16. Access, Amex, Diners, Visa.*

EDINBURGH   Indian Cavalry Club   £45

Tel 0131-228 3282 Fax 0131-225 1911   Map 3 C6   **R**
3 Atholl Place Edinburgh Lothian EH3 8HP

Modern Indian cooking with an emphasis on steaming; the unusually complicated menu suggests side dishes as suitable accompaniments for main-course dishes and also suggests wines to match. The set menus are easy to follow however. Stylish setting, with enormous swagged curtains and black-and-white checked floor in the high-ceilinged ground-floor Officers' Mess and a marquee-style Club Tent downstairs; military-uniformed waiters provide attentive service. Buffet-style choice of main courses at lunchtime; interesting seafood banquet for two or more. Also at: 8-10 Eyre Place (Tel 0131-556 2404). The informal Pakora Bar, serving a mix of Western and Indian cooking in a bistro-style atmosphere, is at Glenville Place (Tel 0131-225 9199). *Seats 80. Private Room 40. L 12-2 D 5.30-11.30. Set L £6.95 Set D from £9.95 (vegetarian) & £17.95. Access, Amex, Diners, Visa.*

EDINBURGH	Kalpna	£35

Tel 0131-667 9890　　　　　　　Map 3 C6　　**R**
2 St Patrick Square Edinburgh Lothian EH8 9EZ

Gujerati and South Indian vegetarian food has few finer homes than Kalpna, a non-smoking restaurant in the student area. Their elephant logo was designed to show that you can be big, strong and intelligent without eating meat. Here you will feast on stuffed lentil pasties, vegetable cutlets, rice pancakes, mixed vegetables with nuts in a piquant sauce, roasted almonds with peas, and aubergines with spinach, tomatoes and fenugreek leaves. The lunchtime buffet costs just £4.50, and there are various price options in the evening with a choice of thali set meals. On Wednesdays there's a regional gourmet buffet (£8.50). The short wine list includes Veena, a light Riesling blended with Indian spices. *Seats 60. Parties 30. Private Room 70. L 12-2 D 5.30-11. Closed L Sat, all Sun, 25 & 26 Dec & 1 Jan. Set L from £4.50. Access, Visa.*

EDINBURGH	Kelly's	£60

Tel 0131-668 3847　Fax 0131-668 3847　　Map 3 C6　　**R**
46 West Richmond Street Edinburgh Lothian EH8 9DZ

Just off the Pleasance and particularly convenient for the new Festival Theatre, with opening times that cater for pre-theatre suppers, Jeff and Jacquie Kelly have run their restaurant in a former baker's shop in a Georgian block since 1986. The room is small and L-shaped, with wall lamps, plants, tubular chairs and pink napery. Although the short menu is essentially a fixed-price affair a footnote gives the price of each course subject to a £10 minimum charge. Cooking is modern and British with dishes such as leek and goat's cheese tartlet with a pimento coulis; monkfish tails with a lime, coriander and green peppercorn sauce, and roast loin of lamb with minted couscous and a garlic sauce showing the style. Desserts range from a lemon cream ramekin topped with hot meringue to a traditional steamed 'cloutie' dumpling. Cheeses, both British and French, like Isle of Mull truckle and Tomme de Savoie. Fair prices on the wine list, which has several house wines at £10. No smoking before 9.30 pm. *Seats 34. D only 6-10. Closed Sun, Mon, Tue, 1st week Jan & all Oct. Set D £21.50/£25.25. Access, Amex, Visa.*

EDINBURGH	King James Thistle	70%	£128

Tel 0131-556 0111　Fax 0131-557 5333　　Map 3 C6　　**H**
St James Centre 107 Leith Street Edinburgh Lothian EH1 3SW

Accommodation is first rate at this luxurious hotel in a position that's ideal for both business and tourist visitors. Double-glazing keeps traffic noise at bay, and bedrooms have good writing areas and mini-bars. En-suite bathrooms are well equipped, with powerful showers. Children up to 12 stay free in parents' room. Public areas are split between the ground and third floors. The street-level foyer-lounge is elegant, with marble-effect floor, chandelier and comfortable winged armchairs. The American-themed bar, brasserie and cocktail bar are reached by means of a swift and efficient lift. The hotel is linked to the St James shopping centre, accessible from the third floor. Conference/banqueting facilities for 250. Regular evening entertainment includes a long-popular two-hour haggis ceremony. The hotel has parking for only 20 cars, but there's a special deal with a nearby car park. *Rooms 147. Coffee shop (11am-11pm). Access, Amex, Diners, Visa.*

We publish annually, so make sure you use the current edition.
It's well worth it!

EDINBURGH   Malmaison Edinburgh   65%   NEW   £90

Tel 0131-555 6868 Fax 0131-555 6999   Map 3 C6   **HR**
1 Tower Place Leith Edinburgh Lothian EH6 7BD

With tower and turrets, this imposing Scottish Baronial-style edifice was actually built in Victorian times as a seamen's mission in what is now the up-and-coming docks area of Leith across a dock basin from the new Scottish Office building. The first of Ken McCulloch's new Malmaison hotels to open (the second is in Glasgow qv), it offers spacious, stylish bedrooms, including six full suites, that feature high-tech music centres (for which CDs can be borrowed from reception) and two telephones among their amenities. What is not offered are things like luggage porterage or room service other than Continental breakfast with either tea or coffee. On our last visit we chose tea and got a pot of hot water with tea bags on the side and no milk (there were packets of dried milk on the in-room beverage tray) so it's probably best to start the day in the café, where cooked breakfasts are also to be had. *Rooms 25. Access, Amex, Diners, Visa.*

Brasserie   £60
Tel 0131-555 6969

On one side of the hotel entrance is the bar/café serving various sandwiches and baked potatoes between noon and 2.30 pm, on the other this brasserie with an informal atmosphere and a menu of fairly standard dishes: eggs benedict, rocket and parmesan salad, seared salmon and hollandaise, steak frites, coq au vin. There are about ten main dishes in all, with puds like pot au chocolat, rice pudding with armagnac prunes and crème brulée. In summer food is served all day and tables spill out on to the cobbled quayside. Some 30 wines from around the world are on offer of which about a dozen (including two champagnes) are also available by the glass (large or small) and half-pint pot. *Seats 74. L 12-2.30 D 6-10.30 (Meals all day in summer). Set L (Sat & Sun only) £7.50.*

EDINBURGH   Le Marché Noir   £60

Tel 0131-558 1608 Fax 0131-556 0798   Map 3 C6   **R**
2 Eyre Place Edinburgh Lothian EH3 5EP

An unpretentiously comfortable restaurant whose rough plaster walls and mock ceiling beams hark back to a previous incarnation as an Italian restaurant. Since 1990, however, under proprietor and oenophile Malcolm Duck, things have taken a distinctly Gallic turn. Both lunch and dinner bring two short prix-fixe menus, written in French without translation, of essentially straightforward dishes: salmon and cod terrine, black pudding with red wine, artichoke and gruyère tart, roast tuna with garlic and red wine, hare with cassis sauce, medallions of pork with orange, pavé au chocolat, crème brulée. House champagne under £20, even a Taittinger is under £30, setting the tone for the very fair prices on the excellent list, from which several wines can be served by the glass. *Seats 35. L 12-2.30 D 7-10 (Fri, Sat till 10.30, Sun till 9.30). Closed L Sat & Sun, all 25, 26 Dec & 1 Jan. Set L £10.50/£12.50 & £17.50 Set D £19.50 & £25.50. Access, Amex, Visa.*

> Many hotels offer reduced rates for weekend or out-of-season bookings. Always ask about special deals.

EDINBURGH   Martin's   £75

Tel 0131-225 3106   Map 3 C6   **R**
70 Rose Street North Lane Edinburgh Lothian EH2 3DX

Between Frederick Street and Castle Street, in cobbled North Lane off Rose Street (vehicles must enter via Frederick Street as it's a one-way system), Martin's is run by Martin and Gay Irons, who nurture their customers in a charming atmosphere that features clever lighting and lots of fresh flowers. Chef Forbes Stott produces a short, daily-changing à la carte utilising good ingredients (most of the vegetables are organically grown and Martin's father provides the herbs from his own garden) that are simply but carefully cooked in starters like monkfish and scallops pan-fried with asparagus tips, tomatoes and chili or a salad of feta cheese, olives and salsa verde, and mains such as sea bass sautéed with sun-dried tomatoes, basil vinaigrette and leeks, and loin of lamb with shiitake and oyster mushrooms, soya and mirin. At lunch there's also a short (two choices at each stage) prix-fixe. Delicious desserts might include rhubarb compote with ginger ice cream and strawberry parfait or try the unpasteurised Scottish and Irish cheeses. No background music, no smoking and no children under 8. The main list has many good wines and growers, as well as realistic prices, carried through to the 'fine wines' which includes some splendid burgundies. *Seats 28. Parties 10. Private Room 8. L 12-2 D 7-10 (Fri & Sat to 10.30). Closed L Sat, all Sun & Mon, 4 weeks Dec/Jan, 1 week late May & 1 week late Sept. Set L £11.95/£15. Access, Amex, Diners, Visa.*

EDINBURGH	Ristorante Raffaelli	£45

Tel 0131-225 6060 Fax 0131-225 8830   Map 3 C6   **R**
10 Randolph Place Edinburgh Lothian EH3 7TA

A sophisticated setting for the all-day service of Italian cooking with the emphasis on Tuscany. Good home-made pasta features in a dish like trenette with pesto sauce and pecorino cheese; other choices might include scampi risotto, fillet of lemon sole with watercress sauce, shinbone of veal with cannellini beans or grilled T-bone of veal with garlic and rosemary. Snacks in the wine bar next door. *Seats 60. Meals 12.15-9.30 (Sat to 10.30). Closed L Sat, all Sun, Bank Holidays, 25 & 26 Dec, 1 & 2 Jan. Access, Amex, Diners, Visa.*

EDINBURGH	Ristorante Tinelli	£35

Tel 0131-652 1932   Map 3 C6   **R**
139 Easter Road Edinburgh Lothian EH7 5QA

Unassuming, modestly comfortable restaurant where chef-patron Giancarlo Tinelli's North Italian fare is offered on a short but varied menu. Bresaola, fish soup, tortelli with a trio of ricotta, chestnut and pumpkin fillings, king prawns mornay and baked rabbit with a cream and rosemary sauce sit beside more familiar dishes such as risotto alla bolognese, scampi and scaloppine alla veneziana. The three-course lunchtime menu is selected from highlighted dishes on the evening menu. *Seats 32. Parties 12. L 12-2.30 D 6.30-11. Closed Sun & Mon (except at Christmas and during Festival) and various annual closures – ring to check. Set L £8.95. Access, Amex, Visa.*

EDINBURGH	Roxburghe Hotel	64%	£110

Tel 0131-225 3921 Fax 0131-220 2518   Map 3 C6   **H**
38 Charlotte Square Edinburgh Lothian EH2 4HG

On the corner of Charlotte Square and noisy George Street; some inward-facing rooms can also suffer from extraneous noise. The smart interior manages to mix both country and town house feels. Decor in the bedrooms varies widely, but they are generally in good order. Children up to 14 stay free in parents' room. Conference/banqueting facilities for 250/275. The only parking is at meters around the square. *Rooms 75. Coffee shop (7.30am-7pm). Closed 3 days Christmas. Access, Amex, Diners, Visa.*

EDINBURGH	Royal Terrace Hotel	70%	£159

Tel 0131-557 3222 Fax 0131-557 5334   Map 3 C6   **H**
18 Royal Terrace Edinburgh Lothian EH7 5AQ

Glittering chandeliers, sumptuous carpets and elaborately draped curtains grace the elegant reception and lounge areas at a hotel consisting of six linked houses on a famous cobbled terrace built to commemorate King George IV's visit to the city in 1822. Bedrooms vary in size but all are given an appealing period feel by plaster-panelled walls and many have stylish bedhead drapes. Rooms range from singles to four-poster rooms and suites. Bathrooms mostly have spa baths and a few boast luxurious impulse showers. Children up to 14 stay free in parents' room. Paved and landscaped gardens to the rear run the length of the hotel. The hotel is ten minutes walk from Princes Street. Banqueting for 60, conferences for 80. On-street parking (free overnight and at weekends). No dogs. *Rooms 93. Garden, indoor swimming pool, gym, sauna, spa bath, solarium, beauty salon, outdoor chess. Access, Amex, Diners, Visa.*

EDINBURGH   Scandic Crown   63%   £165

Tel 0131-557 9797 Fax 0131-557 9789   Map 3 C6   **H**
80 High Street The Royal Mile Edinburgh Lothian EH1 1TH

The hotel enjoys a prime location on the historic Royal Mile, and behind its old turreted facade it's all modern and contemporary in Scandinavian style with open-plan public areas. There are different varieties of spacious bedrooms: standard, club and de luxe. Half the rooms are designated non-smoking. Adjacent car parking with direct access to the hotel is free to guests. There are several conference and syndicate rooms, catering for up to 220 delegates. *Rooms 238. Indoor swimming pool, gym, sauna, solarium. Closed 24-28 Dec. Access, Amex, Diners, Visa.*

EDINBURGH   Shamiana   £40

Tel 0131-228 2265   Map 3 C6   **R**
14 Brougham Street Edinburgh Lothian EH3 9JH

Around the corner from the King's Theatre is an Indian restaurant with decidedly untypical black, white and grey-tiled decor. North-West Indian Kashmiri cuisine is the speciality with subtle spicing ringing the changes from run-of-the-mill Indian cooking. Shahi murgh (royal chicken) and Shahi jahar kurzi (royal lamb) are festive dishes requiring 24 hours notice. *Seats 36. Parties 22. Private Room 12. L 12-2 D 6-11.30. Closed L Sat & Sun & all 25 Dec. Set L from £9 Set D £12. Access, Amex, Diners, Visa.*

EDINBURGH   Sheraton Grand Hotel   79%   £231

Tel 0131-229 9131 Fax 0131-228 4510   Map 3 C6   **H**
1 Festival Square Edinburgh Lothian EH3 9SR

A first-class modern hotel with classical elegance featuring its own tartan specially commissioned from Hunters of Brora. A grand staircase leads to the second level, housing the bar and lounge area, shopping gallery, boardroom and meeting rooms, two of which have fine views of the castle. There are three floors of superior Grand/Castle View rooms in country-house style offering bathrobes and an evening turn-down service, but all the rooms have tasteful American cherrywood furniture, tartan checks and prints of old Edinburgh, as well as the usual facilities of remote-control satellite TV, mini-bar, and hospitality tray. Bathrooms are on the small side. Two rooms are equipped for disabled guests. Excellent service from the committed and attentive staff, also attired in tartan. Children up to 17 share parents' room free. Conference and banqueting facilities for 600/485. No dogs. *Rooms 261. Indoor 'leisure' pool, gym, sauna, sun beds, 24hr lounge service, news kiosk, shop. Access, Amex, Diners, Visa.* 🐖

EDINBURGH   Stakis Grosvenor Hotel   64%   £112

Tel 0131-226 6001 Fax 0131-220 2387   Map 3 C6   **H**
Grosvenor Street Edinburgh Lothian EH12 5EF

Usefully located hotel of Victorian origin, set in a gracious street. Main business comes from conferences and banquets, for up to 500. Children up to 12 can stay free in parents' room. *Rooms 136. Access, Amex, Diners, Visa.*

EDINBURGH   Swallow Royal Scot   65%   £125

Tel 0131-334 9191 Fax 0131-316 4507   Map 3 C6   **H**
111 Glasgow Road Edinburgh Lothian EH12 8NF

Five miles west of the city centre, two miles from the airport, a large 70s' hotel with a leisure club and conference/banqueting facilities for 250. Dinner dance Saturdays October-April. Children up to 14 stay free in parents' room. Direct line for reservations is 0131-334 9292. *Rooms 259. Garden, indoor swimming pool, keep-fit equipment, sauna, steam room, spa bath, sun beds, hair salon. Access, Amex, Diners, Visa.*

EDINBURGH   Szechuan House   £30

Tel 0131-229 4655   Map 3 C6   **R**
12 Leamington Terrace Edinburgh Lothian EH10 4JN

This unpretentious little restaurant serves authentic Szechuan cooking, with spicy items underlined on the menu. These include bang bang chicken, steamed lamb and spicy beef in the starters, and various seafood, poultry and meat dishes among the mains. *Seats 150. Parties 25. Private Room 25. D only 5-12. Closed Mon & 2 days at Chinese New Year. Access, Amex, Visa.*

EDINBURGH	**Vintners Room, Vaults**	**£55**

Tel 0131-554 6767   Map 3 C6   **R**
87 Giles Street Leith Edinburgh Lothian EH6 6BZ

The old sale room of the Vintners' Guild with its 17th-century Italian plasterwork (smoke-blackened from the candles that provide the only illumination) is home to Tim Cumming's appealingly robust, well-executed cooking. Market-fresh produce gets skilful handling in dishes like terrine of duck and pork, baked turbot with crab and sherry bisque, and guinea fowl with lentils and Madeira sauce. Poached nectarine, chocolate parfait and prune and almond tart are among the desserts. Informal lunch in the wine bar offers a 2-or 3-course, fixed-price menu with a small but always interesting choice. The setting is more formal in the evening. Very fair prices (a glass of real bubbly for under a fiver) on a super wine list that includes lots of half bottles. No smoking. *Seats 60. Parties 16. L 12-2.30 D 6.30-10.30. Closed Sun, 2 weeks Christmas. Set L £8.50/£11.75. Access, Amex, Visa.*

ELGIN	**Mansion House**	**67%**	**£110**

Tel 01343 548811   Fax 01343 547916   Map 2 C3   **H**
The Haugh Elgin Moray Grampian IV30 1AW

Set in gardens next to the River Lossie, the turreted mansion built in the mid-19th century is within a stone's throw of the town centre. The chandeliered entrance hall makes a good first impression, and spruce day rooms comprise the piano lounge (a favourite pre-dinner meeting place), the Wee Bar and the Still Room with its whisky collection. Good-sized bedrooms offer a lot of extras, including a welcoming glass of sherry and a mini-bar. A staircase connects the bedrooms to the Country Club, whose facilities include an all-day snack bar. No dogs. *Rooms 23. Garden, indoor swimming pool, sauna, steam room, spa bath, sun beds, gym, snooker, beauty & hair salon, coffee shop (10am-10pm). Access, Amex, Diners, Visa.*

ERISKA	**Isle of Eriska**	**75%**	**£165**

Tel 01631 720371   Fax 01631 720531   Map 3 B5   **HR**
Eriska Ledaig by Oban Strathclyde PA37 1SD

On its own 280-acre island (reached via a private vehicle bridge) the Buchanan-Smiths' Scottish baronial-style mansion is at the heart of what is virtually a private nature reserve; it's a nightly ritual to feed the badgers that come up to the French doors of the bar each evening. After 22 years, Beppo Buchanan-Smith has largely taken over the running of Eriska from parents Robin and Sheena although the former is still often the caring, attentive host front of house and the latter retains overall control of the kitchen. Physically the hotel has a lot of appeal – chintzy drawing-room with real log fires and baby grand (well supplied with sheet music to encourage its use), panelled central hall with fine pargeted frieze, spacious, traditionally furnished bedrooms with every sort of comfort from proper sofas and armchairs to hot water bottles, real linen sheets and fresh flowers everywhere – but the real secret of Eriska is the way it combines a family-run country house atmosphere with the highest standards of professional service that extend to bedrooms being serviced three times a day and a room service menu that provides a choice of hot meals 24 hrs a day. That 60% of guests are returnees (an enviable statistic) is no surprise. A newly completed leisure centre has bought not only the usual facilities but also clay-pigeon shooting, and more unusually, an observation lounge. *Rooms 17 Garden, croquet, tennis, golf (9-hole), pitch & putt, putting, riding, fishing, indoor swimming pool, gym, sauna, steam room, spa bath, windsurfing, water-skiing, clay pigeon shooting, observation lounge. Closed Jan & Feb. Access, Amex, Visa.*

See over

Restaurant   £85

A dado-panelled dining-room with candle-lit, polished wooden tables and exemplary service delivered with an entirely appropriate degree of friendliness. Dinner is a fixed-price, multi-course affair with just a couple of choices at most stages; a typical night's offerings might be poached queen scallops in Vermouth sauce or a warm salad of wild mushrooms to start followed by a soup or fish dish (baked fillet of cod with a light ginger sauce perhaps) before the main choice of three dishes of which pan-fried guinea fowl, poached Loch Creran Salmon and best end of lamb show the style. A choice of puds and we're on the home stretch with just a savoury like Ayrshire toast to negotiate before the cheese trolley arrives and then it's off to collect coffee and petits fours from the main hall. Sheena Buchanan-Smith herself presides over the kitchen providing food designed first and last to be enjoyed. Many good names on the conventional and comprehensive wine list. Several under £15, some under £10! Tasting notes alongside house wines only. *Seats* 40. *D only 8-9. Set D £35.*

ERSKINE	Forte Posthouse	62%	£72

Tel 0141-812 0123 Fax 0141-812 7642   Map 3 B5   **H**
by Erskine Bridge Strathclyde PA8 6AN

Practical modern accommodation close to the M8 on the south side of Erskine Bridge. Half the bedrooms are designated non-smoking. Conference facilities for up to 600, banqueting to 450. *Rooms 166. Indoor swimming pool, keep-fit equipment, sauna, spa bath, solarium, beauty salon, pitch & putt, children's playground. Access, Amex, Diners, Visa.*

ETTRICKBRIDGE	Ettrickshaws	62%	£70

Tel 01750 52229   Map 4 C1   **H**
Ettrickbridge Selkirk Borders TD7 5HW

A turn-of-the-century country house set in spectacular countryside west of Selkirk on the B7009. Open fires warm the drawing-room and bar, and both they and the traditionally appointed bedrooms (no smoking) enjoy the views. *Rooms 6. Garden, game fishing. Access, Visa.*

FAIRLIE	Fins Restaurant		£60

Tel 01475 568989   Map 3 B6   **R**
Fencefoot Farm Fairlie nr Largs Strathclyde

Part of a fish farm and smokery just south of town on the A78, the restaurant is in a 350-year-old barn with whitewashed rough-stone walls, green-painted concrete floor and pine tables. Not surprisingly the menu is almost entirely seafood (just one starter and Aberdeen steaks for carnivores) with the likes of Cumbrae oysters, grilled langoustine tails with garlic or lemon butter, Atlantic salmon with red pepper sauce and Loch Etive mussels, plaice fillets stuffed with squat lobster tails in a Chardonnay sauce and a seafood platter that includes the products of their own smokehouse. Lunch is a less formal affair with such things as seafood omelette and salmon fishcakes. Homely puds. No smoking before 8.45. *Seats 30. L 12-2 D 6.30-9.30. Closed D Sun, all Mon, 25-27 Dec & 1-3 Jan. Access, Amex, Diners, Visa.*

FALKIRK	Hotel Cladhan	60%	£69

Tel 01324 27421   Fax 01324 611436   Map 3 C5   **H**
Kemper Avenue Falkirk Central FK1 1UF

Behind the somewhat unprepossessing modern exterior the Cladhan's interior is stylish and attractive. Public areas are open-plan and designed in a striking modern style with an art deco influence. The bedrooms are light and airy, with good-quality fitted furniture and thermostatically controlled heating. Most rooms overlook the Callender estate and gardens. The hotel can cater for banquets and conferences for up to 200. *Rooms 37. Garden. Access, Amex, Diners, Visa.*

Consult the blue pages for summary tables and lists of
recommended establishments.

FALKIRK	Pierre's	£50

Tel 01324 635843   Map 3 C5   **R**
140 Grahams Road Falkirk Central FK2 7BQ

A pleasant little corner of France with a largely classic menu featuring fish, shellfish and seasonal game: bourride, hare and pistachio terrine, brochette of langoustines and mussels, coq au vin, veal steak with a creamy mushroom sauce. A good-value 3-course business lunch could offer egg, bacon and cheese pancake, grilled mackerel, garlicky roast lamb and hot apple sponge. Note that Pierre's is now open on Monday. *Seats 40. Parties 14. L 12-2.15 D 6.45-9.30. Closed L Sat, all Sun, 2 weeks Jan. Set L £5.95 Set D £12.35 (£10.35 before 7.30). Access, Amex, Diners, Visa.*

FORFAR	Royal Hotel	57%	£70

Tel & Fax 01307 462691   Map 3 C4   **H**
Castle Street Forfar Tayside DD8 3AE

A modest entrance conceals a thriving, compact, well-kept hotel complete with leisure centre, ballroom and roof garden. Bedrooms, apart from one four-poster room, are small, but neat and practical. Children up to 16 share parents' room free. Conferences for up to 220. *Rooms 19. Indoor swimming pool, sauna, spa bath, solarium, hair salon. Access, Amex, Diners, Visa.*

FORT WILLIAM	Crannog Seafood Restaurant	£50

Tel 01397 705589   Map 3 B4   **R**
Town Pier Fort William Highland PH33 7NG

Converted ticket office and bait store in a quayside setting with views down Loch Linnhe. Scrubbed tables and a simple, mainly fish menu (including a vegetarian dish of the day). Langoustines (caught by their own fishing boat) and smoked salmon from their own smokehouse are specialities. Try cranachan (toasted oats with whisky, whipped cream and raspberries) or vacherin to finish. The latest outlet is at Kilninver near Oban Tel 01852 316202. Other branches are in Glasgow Tel 0141-221 1727 and Edinburgh Tel 0131-557 5589. *Seats 70. Private Room 40. L 12-2.30 D 6-9.30. Closed 25 Dec, 1 Jan. Access, Visa.*

FORT WILLIAM	The Factor's House	£70

Tel 01397 705767   Fax 01397 701421   Map 3 B4   **RR**
Torlundy Fort William Highland PH33 6SN

The former estate manager's house in the grounds of Inverlochy Castle (see below) whose head chef, Simon Haigh, now also supervises the kitchen here. The short à la carte offers just four choices at each stage although there are also some daily blackboard specials: home-smoked salmon with chive-scented crème fraiche, terrine of rabbit with home-made chutney, chicken and sweetbread pie, venison pudding, lemon tart and sticky toffee pudding show the style. Children's meal served between 6 and 7pm. *Seats 24. Parties 8. D only 7-9.30. Closed (both restaurant & rooms) Sun, Mon & 6 weeks Jan/Feb. Access, Amex, Visa.*

Rooms   £110
Bedrooms, which have views of either Ben Nevis or the surrounding hills, have just been refurbished so that all now have bathtubs as well as showers plus TV, direct-dial telephone, hairdryer, trouser press and beverage kit. Guests have the use of the facilities of Inverlochy Castle. *Rooms 5. Garden, tennis.*

FORT WILLIAM	Inverlochy Castle	90%	£276

Tel 01397 702177   Fax 01397 702953   Map 3 B4   **HR**
Torlundy Fort William Highland PH33 6SN

Staff at Inverlochy show genuine interest in the comfort and well-being of guests, and a constant programme of refurbishment means that standards throughout are always maintained. Even though it's only been a country house hotel for 27 years the castle, built in 1863 with towers and turrets, was always designed for comfort rather than defence. Perhaps the grandest of the five day rooms is the Great Hall with ornate Venetian crystal chandeliers hanging from a frescoed ceiling depicting chubby cherubs

See over

cavorting amongst the clouds. Highly polished antiques abound both in the public areas and in the luxurious bedrooms above, each individually decorated, often in summer shades, with proper sofas and armchairs, fresh flowers, books and sybaritic bathrooms (the smallest would be large by most hotel standards) many with bidets and separate showers, the others all having power showers over tubs – and finished with marble. Generous towelling, robes and quality toiletries are standard. Children under 4 stay free in parents' room. Dogs in kennels only. *Rooms 17. Garden, croquet, tennis, fishing, snooker, valeting. Closed Dec-Feb. Access, Amex, Diners, Visa.*

Restaurant ★ £100

Simon Haigh produces sophisticated dishes that are full of interest without being in any way contrived. First-rate raw materials form the basis of dishes such as ballotine of foie gras with macerated sultanas; roast turbot with baby onions; loin of venison with roasted pears, walnuts and a peppery port sauce, and caramelised rice pudding with exotic fruits. Crème brulée and orange soufflé are speciality desserts. The fixed-price dinner menu is short (five choices at each stage plus a soup course) but well balanced while the lunch menu (two or three options) is supplemented by a more snacky, individually-priced light lunch menu. There are two highly civilised dining-rooms – the larger with polished wooden tables and a couple of monumental, heavily carved sideboards, the smaller with clothed tables – both with the same fine china and silverware. Service is never less than exemplary, as one would expect from Inverlochy. Surprisingly perhaps, for such a grand castle, there are several inexpensive and quality wines on the comprehensive list. Do not overlook the house recommendations (taken from the main list) at realistic prices (eg an '89 Joseph Drouhin Pinot Noir from Oregon at £30). Huge array of half bottles. No smoking. *Seats 34. Parties 8. Private Room 14. L 12.30-1.45 D 7.15-9.15. Set L £24/£28 Set D £42.50.*

FORT WILLIAM	Mercury Hotel	58%	£93

Tel 01397 703117 Fax 01397 700550   Map 3 B4   **H**
Achintore Road Fort William Highland PH33 6RW

Modern hotel with half the bedrooms enjoying views across Loch Linnhe. 36 Executive rooms are equipped with trouser presses and irons. Very spacious and smart bar/lounge. Children up to 13 stay free in parents' room. *Rooms 86. Sauna, pool table. Access, Amex, Diners, Visa.*

GAIRLOCH	Creag Mor	66%	£80

Tel 01445 712068 Fax 01445 712044   Map 2 B3   **H**
Charleston Gairloch Highland IV21 2AH

Larry and Betty Nieto offer warm hospitality in the spectacular setting of Wester Ross, where their hotel stands in landscaped grounds overlooking Old Gairloch harbour. The two-level Gallery Lounge enjoys marvellous views and also houses an exhibition of watercolours. In the Bothan Bar and cocktail bar there's a choice of more than 100 whiskies. Bedrooms are neat, bright and well equipped for a comfortable stay. *Rooms 19. Garden, games room, coffee shop (8am-10pm). Closed Nov-Feb. Access, Visa.*

GARVE	Inchbae Lodge	57%	£60

Tel 01997 455269 Fax 01997 455207   Map 2 B3   **HR**
Inchbae by Garve Highland IV23 2PH

New owners Pat and Judy Price have brought no radical changes to this modest hotel (originally a Victorian hunting lodge) alongside the A835 a couple of miles north west of Garve and next to the Blackwater River on which the hotel has a mile of fishing rights. A motley collection of sofas and easy chairs fills the two lounges, warmed by real fires in winter and well provided with board games, and there's a small rustic bar used by the locals. Bedrooms, half in the original lodge and half in an adjacent red cedar chalet, have no TVs, radios or telephones to disturb the peace and all but three have shower and WC only. Those in the main building are prettiest, with plum and pale green colour schemes, pine and country antique furniture. Smokers should choose the chalet rooms. Children are welcome and have their own high tea served before the grown-ups' dinner. *Rooms 12. Garden, fishing. Closed 25 & 26 Dec. Visa.*

The Dining Room   £60

Pat Price does the cooking here and his fixed-price, four-course dinner might begin with
a choice between haggis with neeps, and pan-fried breast of wild duck on a bed of salad
leaves followed by a good home-made soup (cullen skink perhaps or carrot and orange)
before the main decision between steak, kidney and black olive pie, and glazed ham with
a mustard cream sauce – if neither of the night's dishes suit Pat can always rustle up
a steak or something from the bar menu. Round things off with peach upside-down
pudding or kiwi syllabub truffle before the coffee and home-made sweeties. No smoking.
Bar food only at lunchtime. **Seats** 30. *Parties 8. Private Room 30. L (bar) 12-2, Sun from
12.30 D 7.30-8.30 (dining-room) 6.30-8.30 (bar). Set D £19.50.*

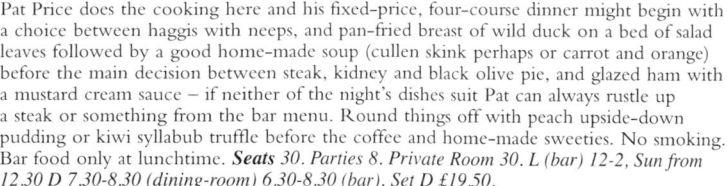

GATEHOUSE OF FLEET	Cally Palace	69%	£135*

Tel 01557 814341   Fax 01557 814522   Map 4 B2   **H**
Gatehouse of Fleet Dumfries & Galloway DG7 2DL

An 18th-century mansion with lofty public rooms decorated in Louis XIV style and
a plush cocktail bar. Bedrooms have pleasant decor, good bathrooms and thoughtful
extras; two rooms are equipped for disabled guests. Conference facilities (for up to 80) are
well patronised, and the hotel is also popular for family holidays and special occasions.
No dogs. *Half-board terms. **Rooms** 56. *Garden, croquet, golf (18), indoor swimming pool,
sauna, spa bath, solarium, tennis, children's play room & playground, fishing.
Closed 4 Jan to end Feb. Access, Visa.*

GATEHOUSE OF FLEET	Murray Arms Hotel	£79

Tel 01557 814207   Fax 01557 814370   Map 4 B2   **I**
Anne Street Gatehouse of Fleet Dumfries & Galloway DG7 2HY

A warm, friendly old posting inn (established over 300 years) whose hospitable day rooms
include the Burns Room, where the poet reputedly wrote Scots Wha Hae. There's also
a little cocktail bar. Bedrooms, all centrally heated, are by no means grand but lack
nothing to provide a good night's rest. These, and the bathrooms, are kept in very good
order. A cottage in the garden consists of a twin or double bedroom, sitting-room (with
settee bed) and bathroom, making it very suitable for families. Children up to 16 free in
parents' room. The inn stands on the A75 Dumfries to Stranraer road. **Rooms** 13.
Garden, croquet. Access, Amex, Diners, Visa.

GIFFNOCK	Macdonald Thistle	64%	£87

Tel 0141-638 2225 Fax 0141-638 6231   Map 3 B6   **H**
Eastwood Toll Giffnock nr Glasgow Strathclyde G46 6RA

Modern commercial hotel convenient for Glasgow Airport (six miles) and the city centre
(five miles). Conference facilities for up to 160, banqueting up to 130. 24hr room
service. Reduced tariff at weekends. **Rooms** 56. *Terrace, sauna, solarium. Access, Amex,
Diners, Visa.*

GLAMIS	Castleton House	71%	£90

Tel 01307 840340   Fax 01307 840506   Map 3 C4   **HR**
Glamis by Forfar Angus Tayside DD8 1SJ

On the A94 three miles from Glamis Castle, a Victorian house has been turned by
William and Maureen Little into a charming country hotel with the emphasis on
comfort, service and good food. The six bedrooms, all with en-suite facilities, are
furnished with high-quality reproduction pieces, and there are showers above the dark-
panelled tubs. The hotel can arrange fishing, shooting and pony trekking. Children up to
12 stay free in parents' room. No dogs. **Rooms** 6. *Garden, putting. Access, Amex, Visa.*

Restaurant   £55

Local produce plus fruit and vegetables from their own garden are used on a varied menu
that might include fresh chargrilled tuna on a salad niçoise, poached halibut with crispy
fried leeks and a grain mustard sauce and a loin of lamb with herb crust, confit of onion
and port wine jus among the main dishes. Good-value, five-course, no-choice 'chef
recommends' menu in addition to the carte at night. Informal eating in the Conservatory
restaurant from 12pm-10pm. **Seats** 28. *Parties 7. L 12-2.30 D 7-9.30. Set L £11.75.
Set D £19.50.*

GLASGOW · Amber £40

Tel 0141-339 6121　　Map 3 B6　　**R**
130 Byres Road Glasgow Strathclyde G12 8TD

Under colonial fans and red-tinged lights, menus, music and cutlery may appear
Westernised but the cooking is authentic at this, one of Glasgow's favourite Chinese
restaurants. Lunch choices offer remarkable value without compromising quality and the
chef's specialities include seafood and aromatic crispy duck. Peking and Cantonese dishes.
*Seats 60. L 12-2 D 5-11.30. Closed L Sun & Chinese New Year. Set L from £4.50
Set D from £15. Access, Amex, Diners, Visa.*

GLASGOW Ashoka West End £30

Tel 0141-339 0936　Fax 0141-337 3385　　Map 3 B6　　**R**
1284 Argyle Street Glasgow Strathclyde G3 8AB

Indian restaurant on the corner of Glasgow's longest and shortest streets. Dozens of
variations on lamb, chicken and prawn plus tandoori dishes and a section of specialities
from the North East Frontier. There's also a healthy option menu with dishes cooked
without excessive fats or oils. There are five other branches (three in Glasgow plus
Johnstone and Paisley) as well as three bar/diners in Glasgow. Own jokey newspaper
– The Delhi Record. *Seats 70. D only 5-12.30 (Fri & Sat till 1). Closed 25 Dec, 1 Jan.
Set meals (2 persons) from £19.95. Access, Amex, Diners, Visa.*

GLASGOW Beardmore Hotel NEW £110

Tel 0141-951 6000　Fax 0141-951 6018　　Map 3 B6　　**H**
Beardmore Street Clydebank Strathclyde G81 4SA

Opened as we went to press, this modern hotel, just fifteen minutes from the city centre
and airport, stands on the banks on the River Clyde. With a staffed business centre,
a purpose-built auditorium accommodating up to 170 and several individual meeting
rooms, the hotel will appeal as much to the business community as to the leisure traveller,
but all will enjoy the state-of-the-art fitness and leisure centre. Comfortable and spacious
air-conditioned bedrooms (half non-smoking, six specially adapted for the disabled)
provide multi-channel satellite TV, mini-bar and tea and coffee-making facilities.
Children free in parents' room up to age of 12. 24hr room service. The hotel is managed
by David Clarke, who held the same position at *The Caledonian* in Edinburgh for several
years. *Rooms 168. Garden, indoor swimming pool, gym, sauna, spa bath, news kiosk.
Access, Amex, Diners, Visa.*

GLASGOW Brasserie on West Regent Street £45

Tel 0141-248 3801　Fax 0141-248 8197　　Map 3 B6 ·　　**R**
176 West Regent Street Glasgow Strathclyde G2 4NL

Part of the Rogano stable, with the familiar tartan carpet and smart, white-aproned staff,
the Brasserie prepares fresh local and seasonal produce in both traditional and modern
styles. Wild mushrooms with garlic butter, seafood bisque, poached salmon hollandaise
and rack of lamb with shallot jus show the style. A couple of vegetarian main dishes are
always available – perhaps vegetable and nut risotto with pimento sauce and saffron pasta
with feta cheese and red chili peppers. There are also 'something lighter' and 'after-
theatre' menus. *Seats 100. Parties 22. Private Room 10. Meals 12-11. Closed Sat between
3 & 5, all Sun & Bank Holidays. After-theatre supper £9.75. Access, Amex, Diners, Visa.*

GLASGOW Buttery £75

Tel 0141-221 8188　Fax 0141-204 4639　　Map 3 B6　　**R**
652 Argyle Street Glasgow Strathclyde G3 8UF

Tastefully converted Victorian city-centre pub in the same ownership as Rogano and
Brasserie on West Regent Street. Chef Stephen Johnson prepares some unusual and
imaginative dishes, including some based on seasonal game: roast breast of pheasant on
a green leaf and pine-nut pancake with a foie gras butter sauce; sliced loin of venison on
game haggis with a game and bay leaf-flavoured jus. Other examples of his distinctive style
include curried cream of broccoli soup with a mango chutney yoghurt, brill in a stem

ginger and vegetable cream, and bee's pollen ice cream in a brandy basket with a thick
mixed berry sauce. Separate vegetarian menu. Private parking. The Belfry Bistro in the
basement is open 12-2.30 & 6-11. *Seats 50. Parties 12. Private Room 8. L 12-2.30 D 7-10.30.
Closed L Sat, all Sun, Bank and Local Holidays. Set L £14.75. Access, Amex, Diners, Visa.*

GLASGOW	Café Gandolfi	£35

Tel 0141-552 6813   Map 3 B6   **R**
64 Albion Street Glasgow Strathclyde G1 1NY

All-day à la carte eating in a bistro-style café in the old merchant district. Specialities
include stuffed peppers, salmon and sole in filo pastry and mini-boeuf en croute.
No under-14s after 8pm. *Seats 60. Parties 12. Meals 9am-11.30pm (Sun from noon).
Closed some Bank Holidays. Access, Visa.*

GLASGOW	Copthorne Hotel	64%	£125

Tel 0141-332 6711 Fax 0141-332 4264   Map 3 B6   **H**
George Square Glasgow Strathclyde G2 1DS

Overlooking busy George Square with Queen Street railway station adjacent, the
Copthorne is well situated for passers-through as well as destination visitors. Bedrooms
range from Classic or Connoisseur to suites, and all offer 24hr room service; under-12s
stay free in parents' room. Conference/banqueting for up to 100. No dogs. *Rooms 140.
Access, Amex, Diners, Visa.*

GLASGOW	D'Arcy's	£40

Tel 0141-226 4309   Map 3 B6   **R**
Basement Courtyard Princes Square Glasgow Strathclyde G1 4PR

Part café, part restaurant in the Princes Square shopping centre. Till midday it's breakfasts,
cakes and croissants, then an informal à la carte menu takes over with sections for
appetisers (chicken liver paté, stuffed mushrooms); salads such as bacon and avocado or
gingered chicken with walnut and banana; pasta; sandwiches; burgers and snacks. From
3pm there are two additional fixed-price menus, both priced for either two or three
courses, offering the likes of grilled chicken on a bed of salad, rib of beef with onion
gravy, salmon on cabbage with redcurrant coulis and vegetable millefeuille with olive and
bean sprout sauce. Until 7pm the set menus come with a free glass of wine. Between
noon and 4pm on Sundays there's a brunch breakfast in addition to the other menus.
*Seats 72. Meals 9am-10.30pm (Mon-Wed till 9.30, Sun 11-6). Closed D Sun, 25 & 26 Dec,
1 & 2 Jan. Set D & Sun L £7.95/£9.95 & £9.95/£11.95. Access, Amex, Diners, Visa.*

GLASGOW	Devonshire Hotel	£137

Tel 0141-339 7878 Fax 0141-339 3980   Map 3 B6   **PH**
5 Devonshire Gardens Glasgow Strathclyde G12 0UX

Ring the doorbell to gain admittance to this discreet, luxurious hotel at one end of an
imposing Victorian terrace set back from the main road out of the city towards the west.
The atmosphere is deliberately quiet and restful with dark, rich tones in the hallway and
mellow autumnal shades used in the lounge that also doubles up as the bar with drinks set
out on a side table. There is also a small dining-room (just four tables) that is for residents
and their guests. Spacious, antique pine-furnished bedrooms are individually decorated in
considerable style and all boast proper armchairs and/or sofas along with little extras like
magazines and mineral water. Bathrooms, decorated to match the bedrooms, are of a
good size too, with power showers over the tubs (one room has shower and WC only),
telephone extensions, bathrobes and generous towelling. Room service offers a choice of
hot meals 24 hours a day. There's no car park but easy, unrestricted street parking is
available right outside. Children up to 12 stay free in parents' room. *Rooms 14.
Access, Amex, Diners, Visa.*

Consult the blue pages for summary tables and lists of
recommended establishments.

GLASGOW | Forte Crest | 74% | £120

Tel 0141-248 2656 Fax 0141-221 8986   Map 3 B6   **H**
Bothwell Street Glasgow Strathclyde G2 7EN

Classic re-styling in marble and primary colours, customer-conscious staff and strong management all contribute to the Forte Crest's position among Glasgow's top hotels. Day rooms are stylish and relaxed while in the bedrooms touches of luxury are provided by mini-bars, remote-control TV and comprehensive grooming accessories. Bathrooms are smartly fitted and brightly lit. The hotel has no leisure amenities, but guests are offered some elite services: same-day laundry, valeting, multi-lingual reception staff and valet parking. There are excellent facilities for conferences, with room for up to 800 delegates theatre-style and first-class support services; 24hr room service. *Rooms 251.*
Access, Amex, Diners, Visa.

GLASGOW | Glasgow Hilton | 78% | £140

Tel 0141-204 5555 Fax 0141-204 5004   Map 3 B6   **HR**
1 William Street Glasgow Strathclyde G3 8HT

A modern 20-storey city-centre landmark situated close to the M8 between junctions 18 and 19. The glass and granite exterior is complemented by an eyecatching and stylish interior with public rooms arranged off a well-lit and spacious central atrium. Air-conditioned standard bedrooms (with sealed windows) are not large and have a uniform up-to-date decor and furnishings, but an extra £25 on the room-only rate brings Executive status with extras like bathrobe and slippers, and use of the top-floor Executive lounge with complimentary Continental breakfast, afternoon tea and evening drink. One floor caters specifically to Japanese guests, with green tea added to the beverage tray and a yukata (Japanese pyjamas) provided as standard. A traditional Japanese breakfast is also available. Extensive 24hr room service and conference/banqueting facilities for up to 1100. Valet parking. *Rooms 319. Indoor swimming pool, gym, sauna, steam room, spa bath, solarium, beauty & hair salons, news kiosk, coffee shop (6.30am-11pm). Access, Amex, Diners, Visa.*

Camerons Restaurant   £95

Designed to resemble several interconnecting rooms from a grand Scottish hunting lodge, the decor here is among the most appealing of any modern hotel restaurant. There's plenty to like about the menu too with dishes like a potage of Loch Fyne oysters; foie gras encased in Tay salmon on crisp artichokes; pot-au-feu of Western Isles seafood with a Keta caviar sauce; chateaubriand of Angus fillet and poached fillet of Borders lamb with couscous on a rosewater jus, combining a light, modern style with the best of Scottish produce. The grape variety sometimes appears alongside a wine on the carefully compiled and comprehensive list, which includes many half bottles and a house selection under £15. *Seats 60. Private Room 25. L 12-2.30 D 7-10.30. Closed L Sat, all Sun. Set L £16.95. Set D £29.50.*

GLASGOW | Glasgow Marriott | 73% | £100

Tel 0141-226 5577 Fax 0141-221 9202   Map 3 B6   **H**
Argyle Street Anderston Glasgow Strathclyde G3 8RR

Situated close to the city centre (by Junction 19 of the M8), the Marriott has good-sized bedrooms, all with large beds, breakfast table and ample work space plus mini-bars and individually controllable air-conditioning; one room is equipped for disabled guests. A small supplement brings Executive status with extras like bath robe and slippers, fresh fruit, complimentary wine and a turn-down service in the evening. Comprehensive 24hr room service and extensive conference/banqueting facilities for 720/650 (parking for 180+). Under-14s stay free in parents' room; children's entertainment. *Rooms 298. Indoor swimming pool, gym, squash, sauna, spa bath, solarium, hair salon, kiosk, coffee shop (8am-10.30pm). Access, Amex, Diners, Visa.*

GLASGOW   Glasgow Moat House   69%   £144

Tel 0141-204 0733 Fax 0141-221 2022   Map 3 B6   **H**
Congress Road Glasgow Strathclyde G3 8QT

Adjacent to the Scottish Exhibition Centre (follow signs from J19 of the nearby M8), with fine views across the Clyde. Historical connections with Glasgow's shipbuilding past are recalled by the vast mural which dominates one end of the spacious, glass-walled public areas. On ground and mezzanine floors conference and banqueting suites will hold up to 800, serviced by a self-contained business centre. The chief recreation area is the Waterside health and leisure club. Roomy bedrooms are identically equipped with maple-effect fitted furniture and marble-finish bathrooms; state-of-the-art TV includes a breakfast order facility, bill check and automatic payment service. Under-12s stay free in their parents' room and there are various family facilities plus a special family Sunday lunch. Two rooms are equipped for disabled guests. Ample parking space. *Rooms 283. Indoor swimming pool, gym, spa bath, sauna, solarium, coffee shop (9am-12pm). Access, Amex, Diners, Visa.*

GLASGOW   Hospitality Inn   67%   £141

Tel 0141-332 3311 Fax 0141-332 4050   Map 3 B6   **H**
36 Cambridge Street Glasgow Strathclyde G2 3HN

Situated next to the pedestrianised shopping centre this modern hotel is particularly suited to business customers, with conference suites to hold up to 1500 and a free 250-space car park for residents. Eight floors of bedrooms; especially roomy de luxe rooms and efficient 24hr room service. Sky TV in all rooms. Children up to 14 stay free in parents' room. Might change its name to the Glasgow Thistle. *Rooms 307. Access, Amex, Diners, Visa.*

GLASGOW   Jurys Glasgow   59%   £92

Tel 0141-334 8161 Fax 0141-334 3846   Map 3 B6   **H**
2 Shelly Road Great Western Road Glasgow Strathclyde G12 0XP

Overlooking the boating pond from which it takes it name, this first Scottish outlet for the Irish-based Jurys group has good leisure and conference facilities, the latter for up to 150. Well set up for families (under-14s stay free in parents' room). The hotel stands on the Great Western Road three miles west of the city centre (leave the M8 at junction 17 and follow the A82 for 2$^1/_2$ miles). No dogs. Formerly called Jurys Pond Hotel. *Rooms 133. Indoor swimming pool, children's pool, gym, sauna, spa bath, solarium. Closed 24-29 Dec. Access, Amex, Diners, Visa.*

GLASGOW   Kelvin Park Lorne   63%   £93

Tel 0141-314 9955 Fax 0141-337 1659   Map 3 B6   **H**
923 Sauchiehall Street Glasgow Strathclyde G3 7TE

Ten minutes from the city centre, a Queens Moat Houses hotel with a choice of accommodation (Standard, Executive, Superior Executive and suites) and six conference suites for up to 300 delegates. The bedrooms have recently been redecorated. *Rooms 98. Closed 25 & 26 Dec. Access, Amex, Diners, Visa.*

GLASGOW   Loon Fung   £45

Tel 0141-332 1240 Fax 0141-332 3705   Map 3 B6   **R**
417 Sauchiehall Street Glasgow Strathclyde G2 3JD

Colourful carvings of the dragon and phoenix (Loon Fung) decorate one end of this smart restaurant, which takes pride in its authentic Cantonese cooking. It's open all day, with a business lunch served from 12 to 2 Mon-Fri, and dim sum (30 varieties) available until 7. Scallops with bamboo shoots, crunchy stuffed duck, chicken with sweet ginger and pineapple, a dozen ways with prawns and sizzling lamb or steak are among the many popular choices. Vegetarian meals available. Special banquets can be ordered by prior arrangement. *Seats 190. Parties 30. Meals 12-11.30. Set L £5.70 (not Sat or Sun) Set D from £10. Access, Amex, Visa.*

We welcome bona fide complaints and recommendations on the tear-out pages at the back of the book for readers' comments. They are followed up by our professional team.

GLASGOW   Malmaison Glasgow   66%   NEW   £90

Tel 0141-221 6400 Fax 0141-221 6411   Map 3 B6   **HR**
278 West George Street Glasgow Strathclyde G2 4LL

A new hotel concept (there are two so far, the other is in Edinburgh) created by Ken McCulloch of *One Devonshire Gardens*, qv. The idea is to offer stylishly designed, quality bedrooms (complete with high-tech music centres for which CDs can be borrowed from reception) along with traditional French brasseries/cafés in architecturally interesting buildings. Costs are kept down by not providing things like room service (except for Continental breakfast – full breakfast can be had in the Brasserie), luggage porterage or turning-down of beds at night. This one has been created within an early 20th-century, former non-conformist church designed by Charles 'Greek' Thompson. Local craftsmen have been used for the conversion, the furniture specially made to complement the style of the building and with a striking wrought-iron staircase leading to the upper floor of bedrooms (there's no lift). *Rooms 21. Access, Amex, Diners, Visa.*

Brasserie   £60
Tel 0141-221 6401

Buzzy brasserie in vaulted basement where the menu (choice of about ten main dishes) covers familiar territory: eggs benedict, French onion soup, mussels with garlic and parsley, steak frites, coq au vin, salade niçoise, lamb's liver and bacon. Puds might include pot au chocolat or rice pudding with armagnac prunes. The café/bar area is open all day with coffee and croissants till midday and a bar menu of sandwiches, croque monsieur, salads and quiche between 11am and 4pm. *Seats 80. L 12-2.30 D 6-11. Set L (Sat & Sun only) £7.50.*

GLASGOW   Mata Hari   £40

Tel 0141-332 9789   Map 3 B6   **R**
17 West Princes Street Glasgow Strathclyde GB4 9BS

Malaysian cooking in a basement restaurant with a no-smoking section. Dishes to try include chicken, beef and king prawn satay (also mushroom for vegetarians), *kari daging istimewa* (rump steak slices cooked with aubergine and 'tropical spices', *rendang ayam* (chicken with 'exotic' spices and lemon grass), *ikan halia* (chunks of fish cooked with shredded ginger, chili and soya bean sauce) and *acar* (mixed vegetable pickle with sesame seeds in a spiced lemon grass sauce). Hot and sour *tom yum* soup and *char koay teow* (stir-fried noodles with chicken, shrimps, chili, egg and bean sprouts) are considered specialities. Desserts include coconut pancakes and rambutan stuffed with pineapple. Also now open for lunch with a Malaysian 'kopi shop'-style menu. *Seats 50. L 12-1.45 D 6-10.30 (Fri & Sat to 11.30). Closed Sun, 25 & 26 Dec, 1 Jan. Set L from £5 Set D £17.50. Access, Amex, Diners, Visa.*

GLASGOW   One Devonshire Gardens   82%   £145

Tel 0141-339 2001 Fax 0141-337 1663   Map 3 B6   **HR**
1 Devonshire Gardens Glasgow Strathclyde G12 0UX

One Devonshire is one of a kind. Owned by Ken McCulloch and superbly run by Beverly Payne, this is a hotel of real style and distinction. It's an unusual spot at which to find such insulated comforts, situated as it is at the junction of the Great Western and Hyndland Roads; rooms at the rear are therefore quieter. Every creature comfort imaginable (within a hotel context!) seems to be available in bedrooms, bathrooms or public rooms as appropriate, creating an air of opulence and luxury that somehow doesn't overawe. Quality is evident throughout, whether it's the level of service provided (courteous porterage, immaculate housekeeping and cheerful turning-down of beds at night), the facilities offered in the bedrooms (hi-tech TV and CD player, mini-bar, fresh flowers, books, magazines, quality toiletries, and luxurious hooded bathrobes), or the standard and degree of comfort in the lounge and bar, where you can unwind and relax in splendour, surrounded by antiques and good paintings. You really feel valued and cosseted in a manner that only a truly professional hotelier and his staff can achieve. Up to 50 can be catered for conference-style in the boardroom, study or private dining-room. Children under 16 may stay free in their parents' room. *Rooms 27. Patio garden. Access, Amex, Diners, Visa.*

Restaurant   £95

Sophisticated decor sees the crisp, spotlit whiteness of damask tablecloths set against a background of midnight blue with dense medieval-tapestry patterned drapes and wallpaper. The market-driven, fixed-price menu format offers a choice of five main dishes (four at lunchtime). Very much in the modern idiom, typical dishes might include a dodine of quail with a salad of winter endives, warm salad of globe artichoke with pleurottes on a walnut and truffle dressing, roasted king scallops with bean sprouts and crispy fried vegetables in a Thai-spiced sauce, pot-roasted poussin with braised flageolets and baby onions and mignons of pork fillet with potato and turnip gratin and glazed chestnuts; all are based on first-rate ingredients cooked with flair and skill. Puds range from lemon tart to iced aniseed parfait. Good selection of home-made breads. Sunday lunch comes with a glass of champagne and always includes prime roast joints of Scottish roast beef carved at your table. Fair section of half bottles on an enterprising, though pricey, wine list. Can an '86 Barbaresco really command a price tag of over £170? *Seats 50. Parties 8. Private Room 32. L 12.30-2 D 7-10.30. Closed L Sat. Set L £25 Set D £37.50.*

GLASGOW	**La Parmigiana**	**£50**

Tel 0141-334 0686 Fax 0141-332 3533   Map 3 B6   **R**
447 Great Western Road Glasgow Strathclyde G12 8HH

An unpretentious family-run trattoria, rather smarter than most. The menu follows a fairly familiar path, with sections for starters, pasta, main courses (including fresh fish from the market) and desserts. Popular three-course lunch offers a good choice (considering the admirably low price); booking advisable. *Seats 60. L 12-2.30 D 6-11. Closed Sun & Bank Holidays. Set L £6.80. Access, Amex, Diners, Visa.*

GLASGOW	**The Puppet Theatre** ↑	**£75**

Tel 0141-339 8444 Fax 0141-339 7666   Map 3 B6   **R**
11 Ruthven Lane Glasgow Strathclyde G12 9BQ

Venture down a narrow lane opposite Hillhead Metro station in Glasgow's West End to find one of the city's most chic restaurants. The first choice to make is whether to eat in the dark green, candle-lit, labyrinthine interior (one wall features a detail from the ceiling of the Sistine Chapel, another is mirrored, and there is an intimate padded booth) or the eccentrically-shaped conservatory to the rear of the early 19th-century building. The evening à la carte might include salad of roasted quail and pigeon; seared marinated beef fillet with radish, cucumber and roasted peanuts; baked monkfish with saffron risotto; calf's liver with lime and caramelised onions; duo of salmon with seared queenies and a creamy vermouth sauce. Puds range from the exotic – gateau of coconut ice cream, mango and banana – to a lemon tart with raspberries with cream. Just two dozen well-chosen wines on offer, almost all (except the fizz) at less than £20 a bottle. *Seats 65. Private Room 26. L 12-2.30 D 7-11. Closed L Sat, all Mon, 25 & 26 Dec, 1 & 2 Jan. Set L £13.95/£16 (Sun £21) Set D £29/£34. Access, Amex, Visa.*

GLASGOW	**Ristorante Caprese**	**£35**

Tel 0141-332 3070   Map 3 B6   **R**
217 Buchanan Street (basement) Glasgow Strathclyde G1 2JZ

Cheerful, inexpensive and atmospheric basement Italian restaurant close to the Royal Concert Hall. The menu holds few surprises but cooking is enjoyably robust and homely. House specialities include Italian sausages with spaghetti, veal cordon bleu, steak pizzaiola, chicken Kiev, lemon sole and sea bream. Also daily blackboard dishes and vegetarian choices. *Seats 60. Private Room 25. L 12-2.30 D 5.30-11. Closed L Sat, all Sun, some Bank Holidays & last 2 weeks Jul. Set L £5.50. Access, Amex, Diners, Visa.*

GLASGOW — Rogano — £75

Tel 0141-248 4055 Fax 0141-248 2608   Map 3 B6   **R**
11 Exchange Place Glasgow Strathclyde G1 3AN

♛ 𝖸 ❦ ✐

As much a part of Glasgow as Sauchiehall Street, the institution that is Rogano remains as popular as ever. The setting is ocean-liner art deco and the menu predominantly seafood: oysters, fish soup with rouille and parmesan croutons, feuilleté of mussels and scallops in a saffron cream sauce, grilled sardines with tomato and garlic concassé, grilled monkfish with red onions, crisp-fried salmon with orange and coriander. There are a couple of meat dishes such as an Angus steak with pink peppercorns and leeks, and liver and bacon with port sauce. Finish with the baked lemon tart or steamed toffee pudding with butterscotch sauce. With the cheapest bottle of champagne at £39, go for two halves at £18 each! Downstairs, the all-day Café Rogano is more informal. No smoking at lunch or dinner until 2pm and 9pm respectively. *Seats 50. Private Room 16. L 12-2.30 D 7-10.30 (Sun till 10) (Café 12-11, Fri & Sat till midnight, Sun till 10). Closed 26 Dec. Set L £16.50 (Sat & Sun £15) Access, Amex, Diners, Visa.*

GLASGOW — Stakis Grosvenor — 66% — £116

Tel 0141-339 8811 Fax 0141-334 0710   Map 3 B6   **H**
Grosvenor Terrace Glasgow Strathclyde G12 0TA

At the west end of the city, just opposite the Botanical Gardens, a Victorian frontage conceals a hotel which is kept up to date with constant refurbishment. Conference facilities for up to 450, 60% non-smoking bedrooms and 14 spacious family rooms (under-15s stay free). The West End Piano Bar is open 7am-10pm for meals and snacks. *Rooms 96. Access, Amex, Diners, Visa.*

GLASGOW — Swallow Hotel — 62% — £95

Tel 0141-427 3146 Fax 0141-427 4059   Map 3 B6   **H**
517 Paisley Road West Glasgow Strathclyde G51 1RW

A mile west of the city centre at junction 23 of the M8, near Ibrox Park, a busy modern hotel with conference facilities for 300+, a leisure club and parking for 150 cars. Almost half the bedrooms are designated non-smoking. *Rooms 117. Indoor swimming pool, gym, sauna, spa bath, steam room. Access, Amex, Diners, Visa.*

GLASGOW — Tinto Firs Hotel — 62% — £90

Tel 0141-637 2353 Fax 0141-633 1340   Map 3 B6   **H**
470 Kilmarnock Road Glasgow Strathclyde G43 2BB

A modern, if modest, hotel just off the A77 in the suburbs (three miles from the city centre) whose accommodation includes two suites. Banqueting for 130, conferences up to 200. Friendly staff create a relaxed atmosphere. Free parking for 40 cars. 24hr room service. Thistle & Mount Charlotte. *Rooms 28. Garden. Access, Amex, Diners, Visa.*

GLASGOW — Town House — 66% — £91

Tel 0141-332 3320 Fax 0141-332 9756   Map 3 B6   **H**
54 West George Street Glasgow Strathclyde G2 1NG

Created out of the turn-of-the-century former Royal Academy of Music and Drama building, the Town House enjoys a conveniently central location opposite the Stock Exchange and not far from both the Queen's Street and Central railway stations. Some nice architectural features include the vaulted lobby and bas-reliefs (honouring famous composers) adorning the staircase. There is a coffee lounge at lobby level but the main day room for residents is a cosy, armchair-furnished bar on the first floor. Bedrooms, individually decorated in some style, are generally of good size and smart bathrooms come with generous towelling and good toiletries. Beds are turned down at night and room service is offered throughout the day and evening. There are five period meeting/function rooms. Parking is difficult. *Rooms 34. Access, Amex, Diners, Visa.*

Consult the blue pages for summary tables and lists of
recommended establishments.

GLASGOW | Two Fat Ladies | £55

Tel 0141-339 1944   Map 3 B6   **R**
88 Dumbarton Road Glasgow Strathclyde G11 6NX

Chef-patron Calum Matheson specialises in seafood from Scottish waters on menus that change four times a year at his relaxed restaurant near the City Art Gallery. Starters such as cracked crab salad with basil and lemon mayonnaise, salmon spring roll with chili and soya dip or cullen skink precede main courses like whole grilled sea bass on a bed of rocket with ginger butter, sautéed king scallops with caramelised peppers and snow peas, steamed halibut fillet with a lobster and cognac sauce or spaghetti with prawns, dill and cream. There's a token meat dish, lamb being a favourite, as in roast loin with an oatmeal stuffing and a port sauce. Finish on a high note with a hot pineapple pavlova with butterscotch sauce or sachertorte with a vanilla sauce. A la carte or set menus available. *Seats 30. L 12.15-2 D 5.45-10.15. Closed Sun, 1st week Jan. Set L £7.95 Set D £9.95. Access, Visa.*

GLASGOW | Ubiquitous Chip | £75

Tel 0141-334 5007 Fax 0141-337 1302   Map 3 B6   **R**
12 Ashton Lane Glasgow Strathclyde G12 8SJ

A former Victorian coach house and stables in a cobbled lane near the university. The main restaurant is in the covered courtyard (with rampant greenery) and offers an inventive, daily-changing menu that combines a strong Scottish slant with modern touches – vegetarian haggis and neeps, shellfish bisque, stuffed Loch Fyne mussels, pan-fried scallops on a roasted potato cake with stewed garlic, and baked pear filled with mixed nuts and honey served with a rich caramel sauce. More traditional dishes include langoustines with mayonnaise, lamb's kidney pudding, Aberdeen Angus steak with onion and leek marmalade and Scots burnt cream – the long list of handwritten dishes is endlessly enticing. Cooking is more bistroish than refined, with generously-sized portions. The 'Upstairs at the Chip' bar offers a less expensive all-day menu along similar lines; several tables are set on a balcony overlooking the restaurant courtyard below. Good selection of Scottish cheeses (priced either individually or as a mixed platter). Vegetarians are unlikely to be disappointed. There's a serious wine list at sometimes giveaway prices. This is the place to come to for a comprehensive selection from around the world, from Germany to California, Italy to South Africa, and, of course, France. Single Highland malts aplenty. Friendly staff and, generally, exemplary service. *Seats 140. Parties 60. Private Room 30. L 12-2.30 D 5.30-11 (Upstairs open 12-11). Closed 25 Dec, 1 & 2 Jan. Set Sun L £10. Access, Amex, Diners, Visa.*

We welcome bona fide complaints and recommendations on the tear-out pages at the back of the book for readers' comments. They are followed up by our professional team.

GLASGOW AIRPORT | Forte Crest | 68% | £121

Tel 0141-887 1212 Fax 0141-887 3738   Map 3 B6   **H**
Abbotsinch nr Paisley Strathclyde PA3 2TR

The only hotel located directly beside Glasgow Airport. All the bedrooms are sound-proofed, double-glazed and air-conditioned. Half are reserved for non-smokers. 24hr room service. Children up to 14 share parents' room free. Banqueting/conference facilities for 450. Ask about occasional special rates to include long-stay car parking and weekend tariff reductions. Refurbishment of both day rooms and bedrooms continues. *Rooms 307. Access, Amex, Diners, Visa.*

GLASGOW AIRPORT | Stakis Glasgow Airport | 61% | £102

Tel 0141-886 4100 Fax 0141-885 2366   Map 3 B6   **H**
Inchman Road Renfrew Glasgow Airport Strathclyde PA4 5EJ

A modern hotel on the A8, some five minutes from the airport. Bedrooms offer practical comforts, and nine suites accommodate up to 1000 for conferences. *Rooms 141. Garden, golf-driving range, dinner dance every Saturday. Access, Amex, Diners, Visa.*

GLENCARSE   Newton House Hotel   58%   £90

Tel 01738 860250   Fax 01738 860717   Map 3 C5   **H**
Glencarse nr Perth Tayside PH2 7LX

Set back in gardens from the A85 four miles east of Perth, this is a substantial double-fronted dower house dating from 1840. It's well kept throughout, comfortable and genteel. There's a little lounge and a cocktail bar, and bedrooms ranging from small singles to more roomy doubles and twins. Children up to 16 stay free in parents' room. *Rooms 10. Garden, playground, news kiosk. Access, Amex, Diners, Visa.*

GLENELG   Glenelg Inn   £76

Tel & Fax 01599 522273   Map 3 B4   **IR**
Glenelg by Kyle of Lochalsh Highland IV40 8JR

It's a spectacular and somewhat precipitous drive to reach this old inn, idyllically set on the shore of Glenelg Bay, that has been sympathetically refurbished by local man Christopher Main. To a convivial, rustic bar have been added, within the original stable block, six spacious bedrooms individually decorated and furnished with antiques. Each has its own smart bathroom and a view over to Skye. The Master bedroom attracts a supplement, but is particularly well appointed with little in the way of modern paraphernalia to spoil the uncluttered homeliness. One room is above the bar and attracts a suitably lower tariff. Residents socialise after dinner in the Morning Room with its Victorian paintings and photos, green leather chesterfield, stag's head and various antiques and objets d'art – a comfortable retreat. Stay for two nights and there is a free excursion on one of the hotel's own boats – either a large motor yacht or a rigid inflatable; seven nights' stay earns a full day's Loch fishing along with other 'extras'. *Rooms 6. Garden, fishing, sun beds, boat trips. Closed Nov-Mar (bars open), except to party bookings. No credit cards.*

Restaurant   £55

The intimate dining-room has a civilised air with candles and fresh flowers on the tables and a real fire on chilly evenings. Local seafood, venison and hill-bred lamb are the mainstays of the fixed-price menu. Typical main dishes might include Loch Hourn monkfish in a lemon and lime glaze, fillet of Scotch beef and pan-fried Lochalsh scallops, sautéed in cream and sherry. Simpler starters (smoked salmon, grilled prawns in a garlic butter, venison liver paté, cream of broccoli soup) and tempting desserts such as raspberry cranachan, sticky toffee pudding and home-made lemon sorbet, along with a cheeseboard offering "three very good Scottish cheeses". Straightforward snacks at lunchtime but it's worth building up an appetite for dinner. No smoking. *Seats 20. D only 7.30-9. Set D £19.*

GLENROTHES   Balgeddie House   65%   £91

Tel 01592 742511   Fax 01592 621702   Map 3 C5   **H**
Balgeddie Way Glenrothes Fife KY6 3ET

Until recently surrounded by farmland, this 18th-century Georgian house was converted to a hotel in 1989 and is now part of a suburb of Glenrothes new town. Bedrooms on the first floor are superior and spacious, with fine modern bathrooms, those on the second floor are twins, with sloping ceilings. There's a choice of bars – cocktail for pre-dinner drinks, the Paddock serving bar lunches and suppers and the Lodge with machines and pool table – and a lounge. Outside there's a lawn the size of a football pitch and eight acres of landscaped gardens complete with palm trees. Children stay free in their parents' room. Functions/conferences for up to 70. *Rooms 18. Garden. Closed 1 Jan. Access, Amex, Diners, Visa.*

GOUROCK   Stakis Gourock Hotel   64%   £102

Tel 01475 634671   Fax 01475 632490   Map 3 B5   **H**
Cloch Road Gourock Strathclyde PA15 1AR

Friendly staff, smart day rooms and well-equipped bedrooms including Executive suites. Children up to 14 stay free in parents' room. Fine views across the Clyde. Extensive banqueting and conference facilities, including two boardrooms, plus good leisure centre. *Rooms 99. Indoor swimming pool, gym, sauna, steam room, spa bath, solarium, floodlit tennis, children's playground. Access, Amex, Diners, Visa.*

GULLANE   **Greywalls Hotel**   76%   £170

Tel 01620 842144   Fax 01620 842241   Map 3 C5   **HR**
Muirfield Gullane Lothian EH31 2EG

Built in 1901, Greywalls is one of the few examples of Lutyens' architecture north of the Border. In a lovely position next to Muirfield Golf Course, the house has a perfect unity of design. The Library is a very fine room with lightwood panelling, grand piano, 'His Master's Voice' gramophone and an open fire; to the north you glimpse the Firth of Forth, to the south Gertrude Jekyll's rose garden. There's a clubby bar and a delightful sun room. Bedrooms are generally of fine proportions and full of light; little personal touches like books and portable radios make the hotel a home from home. Enchanting cottage-style rooms in the lodge. Good breakfast, friendly service. On the A198 at the east end of Gullane village. *Rooms 22. Garden, croquet, tennis. Closed Nov-Mar. Access, Amex, Diners, Visa.*

Restaurant   £85

Paul Baron, here since 1990, is a careful chef, with neat presentation being one of his hallmarks; attention to detail (everything from bread to petits fours is home-made) is another, particularly in sourcing the good local beef and salmon that appear in dishes such as pan-fried medallions of beef with roasted baby onions and red wine sauce or simply grilled salmon served with sorrel butter. In the delightful dining-room, menus are organised daily and offer fixed-price, four-course meals with a choice of around four dishes at each stage. Terrine of leek and woodland mushrooms with a truffle vinaigrette followed by sorbet or soup and then best end of lamb with whole sweet garlic and thyme sauce before a tangy lemon tart might comprise a typical meal. Booking is essential for dinner. Lunch is from a short à la carte served in the bar or sun room if it's a light meal or in the dining-room if a more formal lunch. Traditional roast Sunday lunch. The French content on the easy-to-use wine list is excellent. *Seats 50. Parties 12. Private Room 20. L 12.30-2 D 7.30-9.30. Set L (Sun only) £20 Set D £33.*

Set menu prices may not always include service or wine.

GULLANE   **La Potinière**   ★   £75

Tel 01620 843214   Map 3 C5   **R**
Main Street Gullane Lothian EH31 2AA

An unassuming cottage in the main street is a two-hander with Hilary Brown in the kitchen and David combining the role of host and waiter. Dinner is at a fixed hour from a no-choice menu with thoughtfully composed dishes brought together in well-balanced menus mixing modern French inspiration and the finest Scottish produce. Soup – perhaps potage St Germain or cream of courgette and rosemary – comes before a fish dish like fillets of sole layered with pistou on a bed of spinach with a sweet and sour sauce. Next comes the main dish, perhaps *magret de canette* with Puy lentils and morels; after which a salad is served. Then comes the day's cheese with a pud such as a *soufflé glacé à l'orange* or *citron surprise* (a soufflé-like topping over a tangy lemon curd base) to finish. Lunch follows the same format except that you have to choose between cheese and dessert. A splendid floral display (David's department) dominates the centre of the small, pretty dining-room and bunches of dried flowers hang from rustic ceiling beams. It's essential to book well in advance, especially at weekends. The south-west of France section on the wine list continues to grow and offers real value-for-money, as does the entire list on which several fine wines do not appear. However, they are in the cellar, so it's worth discussing with David. No smoking. *Seats 30. L at 1 D at 8. Closed L Fri & Sat, D Sun-Thur, all Wed, 1 week Jun, Oct. 25 & 26 Dec, 1 & 2 Jan. Set L £18.75 (Sun £19.25) Set D £29.50. No credit cards.*

HARRAY LOCH — Merkister Hotel — 59% — £66

Tel 01856 771366   Fax 01856 771515   Map 2 C1   **H**
Harray Loch Orkney KW17 2LF

First and last a fishing hotel, with great sport on Loch Harray and three other lochs. The brown trout fishing is among the best in the world, and boats, outboards and ghillies can be arranged. Deep-freezing facilities are available, and smoking of the fish can be organised. Owner Angus MacDonald is a keen fisherman himself, and is always willing to give guidance, and his wife Elma runs the hotel with great charm. Centre of affairs is the bar or the conservatory built on to the front of the hotel. Well-kept bedrooms include two new suites and a chalet, the latter with picture windows and spectacular loch views. Birdwatchers are also attracted here, and the hotel has a bird hide in the grounds. Ask for a map showing directions from Stromness ferry terminal when booking. *Rooms 14. Garden, game fishing. Closed 25 Dec. Access, Amex, Visa.*

HELMSDALE — Navidale House — 60% — £60

Tel 01431 821258   Map 2 C2   **H**
Helmsdale Highland KW8 6JS

Built as a hunting lodge for the Dukes of Sutherland in the 1830s, and now a favourite with anglers, Navidale House is beautifully situated in woods and gardens on the A9. The views over Moray Firth and Ord of Caithness are a major asset, and inside the bar and lounge offer cosy, old-fashioned appeal. Bedrooms in the main house have period furnishings and functional tiled bathrooms. Five rooms are in a lodge in the grounds. Children up to 16 stay free in parents' room. *Rooms 15. Garden, croquet, squash, game fishing. Closed mid Nov-mid Jan. Access, Visa.*

INGLISTON — Norton House — 66% — £120

Tel 0131-333 1275   Fax 0131-333 5305   Map 3 C5   **H**
Ingliston nr Edinburgh Lothian EH28 8LX

Set on the western outskirts of Edinburgh, conveniently located for the airport, and in its own parkland with sweeping lawns and tall trees, Norton House's grand Victorian origins are instantly clear. Inside, wood panelling and marble work continue the ambience created by the approach. The Oak Room bar is in the main building while in the grounds the Norton Tavern features a walled garden, a barbecue area and a children's play area. Comfortable, well-equipped bedrooms include suites and mini-suites, superior and standard rooms. Families are well catered for, and children under 12 can stay free in their parents' room. Part of the Virgin Hotels group. *Rooms 47. Garden, croquet, outdoor play area. Access, Amex, Diners, Visa.*

INVERNESS — Bunchrew House — 67% — £124

Tel 01463 234917   Fax 01463 710620   Map 2 C3   **H**
Bunchrew Inverness Highland IV3 6TA

A couple of miles out of town on the A682, Bunchrew House is a fine-looking Scottish baronial mansion set alongside the Beauly Firth in 20 acres of woodland. The bar and appealing, restful lounge both feature dark brown painted panelling and real fires in winter. About half the comfortable bedrooms have reproduction antique furniture while more recent rooms have good-quality darkwood pieces. All have mini-bars and there is room service throughout the day and evening. The atmosphere is relaxed and friendly with obliging staff. Beds are turned down at night. *Rooms 11. Garden, fishing. Closed 2 weeks Jan. Access, Amex, Visa.*

INVERNESS — Caledonian Hotel — 69% — £117

Tel 01463 235181   Fax 01463 711206   Map 2 C3   **H**
33 Church Street Inverness Highland IV1 1DX

Alongside the River Ness, a smart city-centre hotel with modern public rooms and accommodation plus good facilities for conferences (up to 300 delegates) and leisure. Ample parking. Children free up to the age of 16 in parents' room. Now known as the Jarvis Caledonian. *Rooms 106. Indoor swimming pool, gym, sauna, spa bath, solarium, beauty salon, snooker. Access, Amex, Diners, Visa.*

INVERNESS **Culloden House** 73% £175

Tel 01463 790461 Fax 01463 792181 Map 2 C3 **HR**
Inverness Highland IV1 2NZ

An impressive mansion in Georgian style run since 1981 by resident owners Marjory and
Ian McKenzie. History abounds in the house (Bonnie Prince Charlie once seized it), the
40 acres of lawns and parkland and the surrounding countryside. The traditional feel is
preserved within the chandeliered hall, and in the grandly proportioned lounge and
dining-room with their ornate plasterwork, friezes and carved fireplace surrounds.
Accommodation ranges from single rooms via standard twins and triples to king-size
doubles, four-posters and twins with jacuzzis. Four stylish no-smoking suites are in the
imposing Garden Mansion 200 yards from the main building (don't be alarmed if you
find a little wild roe deer grazing outside your window in the morning when you wake
up). No children under ten. *Rooms 23. Garden, tennis, sauna, solarium, snooker.
Access, Amex, Diners, Visa.*

Restaurant £85

Lunch in the elegant Adam Room is à la carte and dinner an inclusive affair of five
courses. Michael Simpson's style combines Scottish country house and French, exemplified
by warm filo pastry parcel of scallops and smoked salmon, breast of guinea fowl filled with
light orange mousse and pork tenderloin with a nut, apricot and bacon stuffing. There's
always an interesting vegetarian main course (carrot and mushroom pie with tomato
coulis) and some fruity, creamy desserts. The wine list, though not particularly user-
friendly, has a good selection of half bottles and several good-value wines if you look
carefully. *Seats 50. Parties 18. Private Room 35. L 12.30-2 D 7-9. Set D £35.*

INVERNESS **Dunain Park** 69% £130

Tel 01463 230512 Fax 01463 224532 Map 2 C3 **HR**
Inverness Highland IV3 6JN

Ann and Edward Nicoll's handsome Georgian hunting lodge stands in six acres of gardens
and woodland a mile from Inverness on the A82 road to Loch Ness. Various styles of
accommodation are available, top of the range being six suites in the main building with
spacious sitting-rooms and Italian marble bathrooms. Two rooms are in cottages in the
grounds. *Rooms 14. Garden, croquet, indoor pool, sauna. Closed 3 weeks Jan/Feb.
Access, Amex, Diners, Visa.*

Restaurant £65

The walled garden provides Ann with many vegetables, fruit and herbs for use in the
kitchen. Her cooking is Scottish with French influences, based on seasonal local produce:
pastry-topped flat field mushrooms filled with wild mushrooms in a white wine and
cream sauce, game terrine on an onion confit, loin of venison stuffed with black pudding
and served with red wine sauce and apple jelly, bacon-wrapped monkfish with
a Mediterranean dressing. No smoking in the dining-room. A choice of 85 malt
whiskies should satisfy lovers of a wee dram. *Seats 45. Parties 12. L by arrangement D 7-9
Set L £16.50.*

INVERNESS **Kingsmills Hotel** 67% £130

Tel 01463 237166 Fax 01463 225208 Map 2 C3 **H**
Culcabock Road Inverness Highland IV2 3LP

One mile from the centre of town (next to Inverness golf course) and surrounded by
inspiring countryside, the 18th-century house was extensively remodelled to create
a modern hotel. Top of the range of bedrooms are seven grander 'Presidential' rooms.
One room equipped for disabled guests; thirteen reserved for non-smokers. Children up
to 16 share parents' room free; 11 family rooms available, five with bunk beds, six larger
rooms with extra beds. Six self-catering 'holiday villas' are 100yds from the hotel.
Conference facilities for up to 60, banqueting up to 80. 24hr room service. Swallow
Hotels. *Rooms 79. Garden, indoor swimming pool, mini-gym, sauna, steam room, spa bath,
solarium, beauty & hair salon, 3-hole pitch & putt, short tennis, bicycles. Access, Amex,
Diners, Visa.*

Set menu prices may not always include service or wine.

INVERNESS   Mercury Hotel   62%   £115

Tel 01463 239666   Fax 01463 711145   Map 2 C3   **H**
Millburn Road Inverness Highland IV2 3TR

Modern, purpose-built hotel at the foot of the North Kessoch Bridge, which connects Inverness with the Black Isle. The fifth floor has recently been upgraded to Executive status. Banqueting and conferences (for up to 230) are a large part of the Mercury's business. Parking for 150 cars. Thistle & Mount Charlotte. *Rooms 118. Garden. Access, Amex, Diners, Visa.*

INVERURIE   Thainstone House   76%   £126

Tel 01467 621643   Fax 01467 625084   Map 3 D4   **H**
Inverurie nr Aberdeen Grampian AB51 5NT

An extended 19th-century Palladian mansion with grand porticoed entrance from which broad stairs lead up to the main public areas. These include a galleried reception area, elegant lounge with Adam-style ceiling, and comfortable cocktail bar which in winter boasts a real fire in its black marble fireplace. There is a more pubby, informal bar on the ground floor. Bedrooms come with reproduction mahogany furniture, good armchairs and a variety of stylish, often rather masculine, decorative schemes although rather surprisingly there are no pictures on the walls. Extras include a welcoming decanter of sherry. Beds are turned down in the evening. Smart bathrooms, providing towelling robes and large bathsheets, are equipped with good showers above tubs which have a convenient thermostatically controlled filling system. Well turned-out staff offer high-quality service with friendly smiles. Extensive 24hr room service. No dogs. *Rooms 48. Garden, indoor swimming pool, gym, spa bath, steam room, snooker. Access, Amex, Diners, Visa.*

IRVINE   Hospitality Inn   68%   £118

Tel 01294 274272   Fax 01294 277287   Map 4 A1   **H**
46 Annick Road Irvine Strathclyde KA11 4LD

A Moorish theme pervades the central concourse, lounge and bar. Superior bedrooms are round the atrium and the pool. Conference facilities for up to 320, banqueting to 220. Full secretarial service available. Children up to 16 stay free in parents' room. Ample car parking. Thistle & Mount Charlotte. *Rooms 127. Indoor swimming pool, spa bath, golf (9-hole), putting. Access, Amex, Diners, Visa.*

KELSO   Ednam House   64%   £63

Tel 01573 224168   Fax 01573 226319   Map 5 D1   **H**
Bridge Street Kelso Borders TD5 7HT

A town-centre Georgian house with lawns reaching down to the River Tweed, a homely open fire, sporting paintings, cosy armchairs and waders and waterproofs in the hall. It's a popular fishing hotel, and outside high season the large majority of guests are salmon fishers (Feb/Mar & Oct/Nov). The bars (where lunches are served Monday to Saturday) are convivial and the lounges are quietly traditional. Well-kept bedrooms match modern comforts with old-fashioned courtesies. Children under 12 share parents' room free of charge. *Rooms 32. Garden, croquet, fishing. Closed Christmas & New Year. Access, Visa.*

KELSO   Sunlaws House   72%   £140

Tel 01573 450331   Fax 01573 450611   Map 5 D1   **H**
Heiton Kelso Borders TD5 8JZ

An imposing Scottish country house three miles from Kelso on the A698, at the south end of Heiton village, offering peace, quiet and plenty of sporting activities. Log fires keep things cosy in the entrance hall, the elegantly draped drawing-room, the library bar and the central hall with its ornate carved wooden fireplace. The two best bedrooms also have log fires, along with antique furnishings. Other main-house rooms use good-quality darkwood pieces, while those in the converted stable block tend to have fitted units. Bathrooms are decorated to match their individually styled bedrooms where beds are turned down at night. The hotel has its own trout loch. *Rooms 22. Garden, croquet, tennis, clay-pigeon shooting, game fishing, steam room, beauty salon. Access, Amex, Diners, Visa.* 🐂

KENMORE	Kenmore Hotel	62%	£117*

Tel 01887 830205   Fax 01887 830262   Map 3 C5   **H**
Kenmore Tayside PH15 2NU

Reputedly Scotland's oldest inn (1572), the Kenmore is a magnet for anglers (they have three miles of private beats on the Tay, which flows past the inn). The various cosy public rooms, one called the Poets Parlour to commemorate a visit by Robert Burns, are made even more inviting by real fires. Bedrooms, 14 in a Victorian gatehouse opposite, vary considerably in decor and furnishings. The hotel is situated at the east end of Loch Tay on the A827. *Half-board terms. Concessions at the nearby Kenmore Country Club and a golf club. *Rooms 39. Game fishing, tennis. Access, Amex, Visa.*

KENTALLEN OF APPIN	Ardsheal House	64%	£160*

Tel 01631 740227   Fax 01631 740342   Map 3 B4   **HR**
Kentallen By Appin Highland PA38 4BX

A long private drive that borders Ardsheal Bay and Loch Linnhe finds this beautifully located 18th-century house. A motley collection of antiques and period pieces furnishes the various small day rooms – oak-panelled entrance hall, TV lounge (there are also sets in bedrooms), library lounge, pine-boarded snooker room and tiny bar in what used to be the butler's pantry – and bedrooms that have something of an Edwardian feel. Some redecoration and refurbishment has recently taken place inside and major re-landscaping of the 16 acres of gardens is planned. Off the A828 five miles south of Ballachulish bridge between Glencoe and Appin. *Half-board terms only. Now open all year round. *Rooms 13. Garden, tennis, snooker. Access, Amex, Visa.*

Restaurant   £80

There's a garden feel in the conservatory dining-room, and good use is made of the vegetables, herbs and fruits that come from the two-acre kitchen garden. Seafood features on the daily-changing menus – there are always two choices for each course – perhaps a salad of Colonsay oysters with samphire and sauce vierge or terrine of summer vegetables to start, a soup course, then roast duck with celeriac and port wine sauce or baked monkfish with herb brioche crust and a chive and lemon butter sauce. Good desserts or cheese to finish. Although lunch is also nominally a fixed-price affair they will charge accordingly if you take less than the full three courses. In fine weather there are a couple of tables on the lawn, especially suitable for light lunches. No smoking in the dining-room. *Seats 45. L 12.30-1.45 D 8 for 8.30. Set L £18 Set D £32.50.*

KENTALLEN OF APPIN	Holly Tree	65%	£90

Tel 01631 740292   Fax 01631 740345   Map 3 B4   **H**
Kentallen of Appin Highland PA38 4BY

The Holly Tree has evolved from a former railway station, and retains some of the more interesting features of that original incarnation. However, the level of comfort and hospitality available nowadays far exceeds anything any railways board ever offered! Comfortable seats and generous fabrics and furnishings make this a delightful spot from which to enjoy the splendid views of Loch Linnhe and the hillside behind. Children under 5 stay free in parents' room; families well catered for. *Rooms 10. Access, Visa.*

KILCHRENAN	Ardanaiseig	74%	£142

Tel 01866 833333   Fax 01866 833222   Map 3 B5   **HR**
Kilchrenan by Taynuilt Strathclyde PA35 1HG

Allow plenty of time to negotiate the picturesque single-track road that leads to this baronial mansion, signposted from Kilchrenan. Its location on the shores of Loch Awe is all the more awesome for the splendid woodland gardens replete with giant azaleas and rhododendrons, as well as an equally expansive walled garden. A dour welcome from the kilted manager and resident ghillie soon thaws in front of log fires in the plump-cushioned, sofa-filled drawing-room (complete with grand piano) and small bar, both with loch views. Bedrooms, biggest and best with garden or loch views, are comfortable and well maintained, some with new four-posters, and feature mineral water, fresh fruit

See over

and plenty of reading matter, although the modern telephone system seems to be a challenge for the staff. Bathrooms fit into the constraints of a former private house, but all have robes, toiletries and unpredictable shower attachments which make it safer to run a peat coloured-bath. No children under eight. *Rooms 14. Garden, croquet, tennis, fishing, hotel boat, snooker. Closed Oct-Easter. Access, Amex, Diners, Visa.*

Restaurant   £80

A small plate of canapés appears as you peruse the five-course dinner menu, amended daily and offering alternate choices for starter, main course and dessert. Locally-sourced seafood and game are prominent, often accompanied by herbs and vegetables from the kitchen garden. Typical offerings could include home-cured gravad lax or Loch Etive prawns in a garlic and herb butter to start, then a creamy vegetable soup, before main courses ranging from roast fillet of Scottish beef with chanterelles and tarragon cream to oven-baked cod with herb crust and pimento vinaigrette. Less successful desserts but good-quality cheese to follow. Traditional Sunday lunch includes roast sirloin of Highland beef with Yorkshire pudding and a rich onion gravy. Keen prices (sometimes amazingly so) on a mainly French wine list. No smoking. *Seats 30. L 12.30-2 D 7.30-9. Set L £15 Set D £33.50.*

KILCHRENAN	Taychreggan Hotel	66%	£80

Tel 01866 833211   Fax 01866 833244   Map 3 B5   **HR**
Kilchrenan by Taynuilt Strathclyde PA35 1HQ

With a glorious location on the edge of Loch Awe, this former drovers' inn (they spent the night here before swimming their cattle across the Loch) was modestly extended in the 1970s to enclose a charming cobbled courtyard. Today Euan and Annie Paul are continuing to improve Taychreggan with five new rooms added this year plus refurbishment of other areas including the bar with its "shamefully large selection" of malt whiskies. Hill walking is a favourite pastime, and there are 13 munros (peaks over 3000ft) in the vicinity. No children under 12. *Rooms 20. Garden, coarse and game fishing, boating, snooker. Access, Amex, Visa.*

Restaurant   £70

Antique tables are set against a collection of modern paintings in the recently refurbished and extended dining-room. Dinner is a fixed-price, five-course affair with a choice only of starters – melon and grapefruit cocktail with stem ginger and Campari or chicken liver parfait with Cumberland sauce perhaps – and at the soup course, although they can generally come up with an alternative if the main dish, which might be beef fillet served with pickled walnuts and béarnaise sauce does not suit. A dessert such as crisp sablé biscuits filled with Chantilly cream, blueberries and raspberries precedes the cheese. Lunch brings an individually priced menu of dishes ranging from soup, paté with French bread and quiche to chicken pie, steak and langoustines with garlic butter. No children under 12. No smoking. *Seats 36. L 12.30-2.15 D 7.30-8.45. Set D £30.*

KILDRUMMY	Kildrummy Castle	70%	£130

Tel 019755 71288   Fax 019755 71345   Map 3 C4   **H**
Kildrummy Alford Grampian AB33 8RA

Built in 1900 as a rather grandiose castellated country house, the hotel has a lovely setting overlooking the ruins of a 13th-century castle, and gardens which feature specimen trees, alpine plants and rare shrubs. (Grampian has more than 70 castles, many just a short drive from the hotel.) The baronial entrance hall contrasts with the Adam elegance of the sunny drawing-room. Two carved lions act as sentries on a splendidly ornate staircase which leads to the bedrooms. These are less grand than the day rooms but are comfortable, spacious and warm; those in the attic with sloping ceilings are charming. Long-serving owner Thomas Hanna strongly motivates his staff, who are outgoing and friendly. Trout and salmon fishing are available on a $3^1/_2$-mile stretch of the River Don, and local centres organise shooting, stalking, riding and pony trekking. *Rooms 16. Garden, fishing, children's playground, snooker. Closed 3 Jan-10 Feb. Access, Amex, Visa.*

Many hotels offer reduced rates for weekend or out-of-season bookings. Always ask about special deals.

KILFINAN | Kilfinan Hotel | £72

Tel 01700 821201   Fax 01700 821205   Map 3 B5   **IR**
Kilfinan by Tighnabruaich Strathclyde PA21 2AP

A delightful Swiss/Scottish couple, Rolf and Lynne Mueller, run this remote white-stoned coaching inn set amid magnificent scenery on the east shore of Loch Fyne, reached down a single-track road (B8000, off the A886) between Strachur and Tighnabruaich. The Dunoon ferry is less than an exhilarating hour's drive across the moors. Purchased about ten years ago by the Laird of Kilfinan, so that it would not fall into the hands of developers, the inn has exclusive access to beautiful Kilfinan Bay (about 20 minutes walk through the garden and the estate) and is well placed for traditional outdoor pursuits. Two bars, neither of them a lounge, are both cosy and characterful with log fires, and the bedrooms – some antique-furnished – offer all the usual little luxuries, including good-quality toiletries in the carpeted en-suite bathrooms; one room overlooks St Finnan's graveyard, a surprisingly pleasant view. Good walking country begins right outside the door. No dogs in bedrooms but there are a couple of kennels available. *Rooms 11. Garden, fishing. Closed Feb. Access, Amex, Visa.*

Restaurant | £70

Inviting dining-rooms with crisp linen, gleaming glassware and candle-light. Rolf brings Swiss precision into his cooking, exemplified in the daily-changing, fixed-price dinner menu that offers a small choice for each of the four courses (except soup). Noisettes of lamb in a rosemary sauce, supreme of guinea fowl with wild mushrooms and grilled skate wing in black butter with capers typify the main dish selection. The likes of *pavé au chocolat*, strawberry sablé or a selection of local cheeses to finish, plus good coffee served with petits fours. Three-course Sunday lunch always includes a traditional roast; during the week lighter lunches are served in the bar. Concise wine list; fair prices. Outdoor eating for 20 in the garden in good weather. No smoking in restaurant. *Seats 22. Parties 10. Private Room 24. L Sun only 12-2 D 7.30-9.30. Set Sun L £12.50 Set D £25.*

KILLIECRANKIE | Killiecrankie Hotel | 64% | £145*

Tel 01796 473220   Fax 01796 472451   Map 3 C4   **H**
Killiecrankie by Pitlochry Tayside PH16 5LG

Four acres of landscaped gardens overlook the River Garry and the Pass of Killiecrankie (turn off the A9 north of Pitlochry). There's something of the feeling of an inn about the little hotel, which was built as a manse in 1840. The reception hall and small panelled bar (which has a suntrap extension) have displays of stuffed animals and an upstairs lounge offers various board games plus a variety of books as distractions. Pine-furnished bedrooms are fresh and bright. Bar menu for informal lunches and suppers. *Half-board terms (limited availability B&B at £48 per person per night). *Rooms 10. Garden, croquet. Closed 3 Jan-8 Mar. Access, Visa.*

We welcome bona fide complaints and recommendations on the
tear-out pages at the back of the book for readers' comments.
They are followed up by our professional team.

KILMORE | Glenfeochan House | 70% | £128

Tel 01631 770273   Fax 01631 770624   Map 3 B5   **HR**
Kilmore Oban Strathclyde PA34 4QR

Built in 1875 (though some parts are probably much older), the house stands in a beautiful, peaceful spot at the head of Loch Feochan, five miles south of Oban, on a 350-acre estate of hills, lochs, rivers and farmland. The eight-acre garden contains a Victorian arboretum with over 100 rhododendrons. Inside, all is spick and span, from the entrance hall and stairway featuring pitch pine to the drawing-room with a fine moulded ceiling and complementary antiques. Bedrooms have plain walls, floral curtains and more antiques. TVs and radios are provided, but no phones; no smoking. The Tulip Room has an en-suite round bathroom in the turret. Self-catering accommodation is available in the farmhouse. No children under ten. No dogs. *Rooms 3. Garden, croquet, fishing. Closed 1 Nov-1 Feb. Access, Visa.*

See over

Restaurant   £70

Guests gather for dinner at 8 and non-residents can join them by prior arrangement. Patricia Baber is an excellent cook and her short dinner menus (discussed at breakfast time) make as much use as possible of produce from the estate or local sources: salmon is served fresh or cured traditionally and smoked over oak, wild mushrooms are gathered from the estate and other favourites include Jura venison, lobster, and guinea fowl roasted and served with a raspberry and redcurrant sauce. Scottish cheeses. Concise and inexpensive wine list. No smoking. **Seats** 10. D only at 8. Set D £30.

KILWINNING	Montgreenan Mansion	70%	£92

Tel 01294 557733   Fax 01294 585397   Map 3 B6   **H**
Montgreenan Estate Torranyard by Kilwinning Strathclyde KA13 7QZ

The Mansion House was built in 1817 by one Dr Robert Glasgow, and once completed it was described as 'a very desirable residence'. Current owners the Dobson family believe this still to be true, as do their many returning regulars. It stands in 45 acres of gardens and grounds (four miles north of Irvine on the A736) and many period features, including marble and brass fireplaces and decorative plasterwork, have been retained. Day rooms are of quite grand proportions, the lounge-library being particularly appealing. There are several conference rooms (maximum capacity 100). Bedrooms, furnished with reproduction pieces or antiques, range from standard singles to suites. Children up to 10 stay free in parents' room. **Rooms** 21. Garden, croquet, tennis, 5 practice golf holes, snooker. Access, Amex, Diners, Visa.

Lodges are now listed by county in the reference section

KINCLAVEN BY STANLEY	Ballathie House	74%	£155

Tel 01250 883268   Fax 01250 883396   Map 3 C5   **HR**
Kinclaven by Stanley Tayside PH1 4QN

Built in 1850 in the baronial style, Ballathie was a private residence until 1971 when it became a hotel – it is still in the same safe hands today. The lawns slope down to the edge of the River Tay (salmon fishing a speciality) and the house is set at the heart of its own vast estate. Some fine ceilings and marble fireplaces feature in the numerous, comfortable and stylishly decorated day rooms that include an elegantly proportioned drawing-room, clubby leather-furnished bar and spacious inner hall from which a grand oak staircase leads to the bedrooms. These vary considerably in size from large master rooms to a few compact singles among the standard rooms but all are individually decorated to the same high standard and all are equally well appointed. Three rooms have been adapted for use by disabled guests. **Rooms** 37. Garden, croquet, tennis, fishing, putting, shooting. Closed 25 & 26 Dec. Access, Amex, Diners, Visa.

Restaurant   £70

Wonderful views across the River Tay from the elegant high-windowed dining-room enhance a meal that will often feature local and Scottish ingredients, though influences are drawn from further afield. After a splendid game or seafood main course finish with British cheeses or a dessert such as warm apple and sultana pie with ice cream and vanilla sauce. Lunch brings a good value à la carte during the week and a fixed-price menu on Sunday. Chef Kevin MacGillivray is happy to suggest special menus at lunch or dinner for party bookings; there's a programme of special events throughout the year. Pleasing house selection on a fairly priced wine list that includes several vintages of the excellent Chateau Musar from Lebanon. No smoking. **Seats** 80. Parties 12. Private Room 30. L 12-2 D 7-9. Set L £10/£12.95 (Sun £12.95) Set D £23.60/£26.

KINGUSSIE	The Cross		£70

Tel 01540 661166   Fax 01540 661080   Map 3 C4   **RR**
Tweed Mill Brae Ardbroilach Road Kingussie Highland PH21 1HX

From the traffic lights in Kingussie, travel uphill along Ardbroilach Road for 300 metres; then turn left at the sign down Tweed Mill Brae to find Tony and Ruth Hadley's converted old tweed mill by the River Gynack. White-painted rough stone walls and a timbered ceiling contrast with immaculately crisp white linen and luxurious table settings in the cleverly lit dining-room. Ruth's sympathetic and refined use of the best of Scottish produce is evident in limited-choice, five-course dinners that might start with a platter of salmon (gravad lax, ceviche, rillettes) or a pigeon breast salad and proceed by way of a soup to boudin of pike with leek and lemon grass sauce and a main event such as roast breast of duck with a Chinese-style sauce or fillet of beef with shallots and Madeira. Finally, choice of a couple of sweets or a splendid cheeseboard. Home hot-smoked salmon, venison 'francatelli' and chocolate whisky 'laird' are considered specialities. Vegetarians should notify in advance. So extensive is the half bottle wine list that alone it puts many full lists to shame. Overall, the choice is fantastic, the quality exceptional and the prices ridiculously low. The list is the work of a real enthusiast, so ask Tony for advice, since there are intentionally no guidance or tasting notes. There are no longer any Italian wines either: nobody bought them! Past winner of our Cellar of the Year award. Outdoor eating for 12 on a terrace overlooking the river. No children under 12. No smoking. *Seats 28. L by arrangment D 7-9 Closed D Tues, 1-26 Dec, early Jan-end Feb. Set D Sat £35. Access, Visa.*

Rooms   £170*

Upstairs, beyond a residents' lounge that successfully mixes antiques with Scandinavian-style seating, are nine individually styled bedrooms that generally combine pine and antique furniture to good effect. Good bathrooms, mostly with bidet and separate shower cubicle in additon to the tub, boast large towels and good-quality toiletries. No TVs. No smoking in the bedrooms, only in the lounge. The waterside terrace makes a good spot for Continental breakfast that comes with lovely home-made jams. No dogs. *Half-board terms only. Garden.

KINLOCHBERVIE	Kinlochbervie Hotel	64%	£84

Tel 01971 521275   Fax 01971 521438   Map 2 B2   **H**
Kinlochbervie by Lairg Highland IV27 4RP

Almost at the northernmost tip of mainland Scotland, 47 miles from Lairg, Kinlochbervie is a modern hotel high up on a hill overlooking a fishing harbour. Six bedrooms (and a first-floor residents' lounge crammed with literature for walkers and fishermen) also benefit from the setting. All rooms have showers as well as baths. A convivial bar and bistro adjacent are popular with locals. *Rooms 14. Sea and loch fishing. Closed 1 Nov-1 Mar. Access, Amex, Diners, Visa.*

KINROSS	Windlestrae Hotel	62%	£100

Tel 01577 863217   Fax 01577 864733   Map 3 C5   **H**
The Muirs Kinross Tayside KY13 7AS

Windlestrae – its name is derived from 'tall grasses swaying gently in the breeze by Loch Leven' – is a relaxing retreat set in landscaped gardens, offering a warm welcome from Terry and Jean Doyle. The lounges (one split-level) are comfortable, as are the bedrooms, while the leisure club is equipped to a high standard. Conferences/banquets for up to 250/200. Two rooms are fully equipped for disabled guests. *Rooms 46. Garden, indoor swimming pool, gym, sauna, steam room, spa bath, solarium, sun beds, beauty and hair salon, snooker. Access, Amex, Diners, Visa.*

KIRKMICHAEL	Log Cabin Hotel	59%	£66

Tel 01250 881288   Fax 01250 881402   Map 3 C4   **H**
Kirkmichael Tayside PH10 7NB

A mecca for outdoor activists (fishing, shooting, stalking and walking – bring your camera!). The hotel is built of Norwegian pine logs and stands half a mile from the A924 between Pitlochry and Blairgowrie. Quite modest accommodation (TVs on request), but in keeping with the surroundings. *Rooms 13. Garden, games room, snooker, game fishing, shooting, craft shop. Closed 25 & 26 Dec. Access, Amex, Diners, Visa.*

We welcome bona fide complaints and recommendations on the tear-out pages at the back of the book for readers' comments. They are followed up by our professional team.

KIRKNEWTON   Dalmahoy Hotel   78%   £127

Tel 0131-333 1845 Fax 0131-333 3203   Map 3 C6   **HR**
Kirknewton Lothian EH27 8EB

Situated by the Pentland Hills, seven miles west of Edinburgh just off the A71, surrounded by two mature golf courses and with a well-equipped leisure centre, Dalmahoy Hotel, Golf and Country Club is not only conveniently placed but also offers plenty of diversions. The imposing house has been carefully restored to its original Georgian splendour but the bedrooms – even the ones in period style – enjoy every modern comfort. Banqueting and conference facilities for up to 190, parking for up to 350 cars. Children up to the age of 13 accommodated free in parents' room. Informal eating in the poolside Terrace restaurant. No dogs (kennels available nearby). Country Club Hotels. *Rooms 116. Garden, 18-hole golf courses, putting, tennis, indoor swimming pool, squash, sauna, steam room, solarium, snooker, gym, spa bath, beautician, golf & leisure shop, coffee shop (9.30am-10pm). Access, Amex, Diners, Visa.*

Pentland Restaurant   £70

Chef Gary Bates offers a set menu in the stately dining-room, but there's plenty of choice at each course. Trio of West Coast seafood – terrine of red mullet, gateau of salmon rillettes, tartlet of creamed crab – could be your starter, followed perhaps by pan-fried veal kidney in a port, tarragon and Arran mustard gravy, chargrilled sirloin steak or a speciality dish of breast of Gressingham duck served with the leg braised, green lentils and roast celeriac. Good desserts, farmhouse cheese. *Seats 120. Parties 20. L 12.30-2 D 7-9.30 (Sun from 7.30). Closed L Sat. Set L £14.50 Set D £20/£23.50.*

KYLE OF LOCHALSH   Lochalsh Hotel   63%   £85

Tel 01599 534202 Fax 01599 534881   Map 2 B3   **H**
Ferry Road Kyle of Lochalsh Highland IV40 8AF

A privately owned, white-painted building opposite the ferry terminal and looking over the sea to Skye. Beauty spots abound locally, and a day's sightseeing can conclude agreeably with a dram or two from the choice of 70 whiskies in the cocktail bar. Bedrooms are fresh, bright and comfortable. *Rooms 38. Garden. Access, Amex, Diners, Visa.*

LANGBANK   Gleddoch House   68%   £140

Tel 01475 540711 Fax 01475 540201   Map 3 B5   **H**
Langbank Strathclyde PA14 6YE

The large windows of Gleddoch House look out on to a 360-acre estate and beautiful countryside over to the Clyde, and inside there's plenty to please the eye too. In the main lounge area there are leather easy chairs in which to relax, and dado panelling and more leather chairs give a period feel to the baize-lined bar, which offers a hundred different brands of whisky. The rooms are all named after Scottish birds, each engraved on the door-plate. Children under 12 stay free in parents' room. Banqueting/conference facilities for 120/100. *Rooms 39. Garden, squash, sauna, snooker, golf (18), putting, riding. Access, Amex, Diners, Visa.*

LERWICK   Shetland Hotel   62%   £82

Tel 01595 5515 Fax 01595 5828   Map 2 D2   **H**
Holmsgarth Road Lerwick Shetland ZE1 0PW

Close to the town centre and overlooking the harbour (where the ferries from Aberdeen dock), the Shetland is a skilfully designed modern hotel that caters well for both summer tourism and year-round business. Bedrooms are uniformly light and spacious, with private bathrooms throughout. There is a bright, comfortable bar and an impressive function hall. Banqueting facilities available for up to 180 and conferences for 225 delegates. *Rooms 64. Garden. Access, Amex, Diners, Visa.*

| **LETHAM** | **Fernie Castle** | **60%** | **£70** |

Tel 01337 810381   Fax 01337 810422   Map 3 D4   **H**
Letham by Cupar Fife KY7 7RU

Set in 25 acres of woodland grounds alongside the A914, the original 1300s L-shaped castle has been altered and extended in most centuries since. Public rooms include a rough-stone vaulted cocktail bar in the oldest part of the building and a small, comfortable first-floor residents' lounge in the Georgian section. Modestly comfortable bedrooms divide roughly 50:50 between 'large' and 'small' rooms, six of the latter with shower and WC only, furnished and decorated in a variety of styles. A programme of bedroom refurbishment continues. *Rooms 15. Garden. Closed 1st 2 weeks Jan. Access, Visa.*

| **LINLITHGOW** | **Champany Inn** | **★** | **£100** |

Tel 01506 834532   Fax 01506 834302   Map 3 C5   **R**
Champany Linlithgow Lothian EH49 7LU

You'll not find better Aberdeen Angus beef (hung on the bone in the restaurant's own chill rooms for at least three weeks) than here at Clive and Anne Davidson's characterful restaurant a couple of miles north-east of Linlithgow where the A904 meets the A803. The buildings at Champany Corner date from the 16th century, the time of Mary Queen of Scots, who was born two miles away at Linlithgow Palace. Steaks destined for the charcoal grill, which range from sirloin on the bone ("the nearer the bone the sweeter the meat") and wing rib to porterhouse and rib-eye, are on display; they are cut to your own specification and charged by the ounce. Some come with sauces – béarnaise, monkey gland, Bonnie Prince Charlie (honey, Drambuie and whisky) – or stuffed with smoked salmon (salmon bagger) or oysters (carpet bagger). The other speciality here is seafood such as Shetland salmon hollandaise or lobster (from the restaurant's seawater pool), and for a starter try the home-smoked salmon, local oysters, or a prawn bisque. The sweet trolley features cheesecake, crème brulée, chocolate mousse and fresh fruit tart as well as fresh fruits and a variety of home-made ice creams, or else try the superb Stilton with home-made oatcakes. The wine list is remarkable, not only for its South African section (the best in the UK), own-label wines and some 150-year-old cognacs at £90 a glass, but also for its burgundies and malt whiskies. With other areas also well represented, there's a bottle (or half) to suit every pocket – fantastic! Past winner of our Cellar of the Year award. You can eat outside in the garden in fine weather. No children under eight. *Seats 50. Parties 16. L 12.30-2 D 7-10. Closed L Sat, all Sun, 25,25 Dec, & 1, 2 Jan. Set L £13.75/£18.25 Set D £27.50/£35. Access, Amex, Diners, Visa.*

| **LINLITHGOW** | **Champany Inn Chop & Ale House** | **£50** |

Tel 01506 834532   Fax 01506 834302   Map 3 C5   **R**
Champany Linlithglow Lothian EH49 7LU

Adjacent to the main restaurant (above), this is a much less formal eaterie where the same outstanding Aberdeen Angus steaks are served – though less expensive and cut a bit smaller – together with various burgers, deep-fried Scottish prawn tails (scampi), grain-fed chicken (finished on the charcoal grill after being slowly spit-roasted) and a cold buffet with help-yourself salad bar. For afters go for the home-made, hot malted waffles or Champany's own cheesecake served with apricot purée. Ten tables are set in a courtyard for alfresco dining. *Seats 46. L 12-2 (Sun from 12.30, Sat & Sun till 2.30) D 6.30-10 (Sat from 6). Closed 25,26 Dec & 1,2 Jan. Access, Amex, Diners, Visa.*

| **LOCHINVER** | **Inver Lodge Hotel** | **70%** | **£130** |

Tel 01571 844496   Fax 01571 844395   Map 2 B2   **H**
Lochinver Highland IV27 4LU

Built at the beginning of 1988, the hotel is set high above the village in a scene of exceptional peace and beauty. It's an ideal base for fishing (10 rods on local rivers, 10 more with boats on the lochs, drying room, deep freeze), bird-watching and hill walking, and after the day's activity the lounge and cocktail bar offer comfort and conviviality. Generously sized bedrooms – each named after a nearby mountain or loch – feature bold earth tones and colourful fabrics. Two rooms, Suilven and Canisp, have dining tables and sofas. Children up to 16 are accommodated free in parents' room. *Rooms 20. Garden, sauna, solarium, fishing, snooker, shop (gifts and fishing tackle). Closed Nov-Apr. Access, Amex, Diners, Visa.*

MARKINCH   **Balbirnie House**   74%   £125

Tel 01592 610066   Fax 01592 610629   Map 3 C5   **HR**
Balbirnie Park Markinch by Glenrothes Fife KY7 6NE

A large Georgian mansion to which the Victorians added a massive classical portico, Balbirnie is surrounded by fine gardens (including some rare rhododendrons) at the centre of a 400-odd-acre country park that includes a golf course to which hotel guests have priviliged access. Backed-up by an efficient team of smartly kitted-out staff, the Russell family run the hotel (now five years old) on friendly, personal lines. Day rooms include a well-stocked (both with books and malts) library bar, peaceful drawing-room and architecturally fine Long Gallery – note the trompe l'oeil. Only a few bedrooms are less than spacious and all are individually decorated in great style and comfort with lots of extras from sherry and mineral water to towelling robes in good bathrooms that feature panelled tubs and white marble shelving; beds are turned down at night and room service is 24hrs. *Rooms 30. Garden, snooker. Access, Amex, Diners, Visa.*

Restaurant   £65

Both the four-course set dinner and less formal lunchtime à la carte (three-course set lunch on Sunday) feature chargrilled steaks along with a balanced choice of sauced dishes like fillet of salmon fried in goose fat served with crisp Bayonne ham and Provençal sauce, breast of chicken Vallée d'Auge and Perthshire venison with braised cabbage and a red wine, redcurrant and green peppercorn sauce at dinner, and beef bourguignon with parsnip purée, deep-fried sole with tartare sauce and omelettes at lunchtime. Lunch is also served in an informal bistro, The Gamekeeper's Inn. An excellent and balanced wine list is fairly priced, with the house selections well annotated. All wines are coded (dry/sweet, light/full). Plenty of half bottles. *Seats 100. Parties 10. Private Room 56. L 12-2.30 D 7-9.30. Set Sun L £13.75 Set D £25.*

MARYCULTER   **Maryculter House**   65%   £115

Tel 01224 732124   Fax 01224 733510   Map 3 D4   **H**
South Deeside Road Maryculter Grampian AB1 0BB

A fine location on the banks of the River Dee makes Maryculter a popular wedding venue, especially with its fine function suite for up to 180 people. The oldest room (now a rattan-furnished cocktail bar/lounge) has high stone walls and dates back to the 13th century. The other main public room is the Victorian-styled Poachers Bar, which opens on to a riverside patio. Bedrooms, including those in an extension, feature pine furniture and pretty fabrics with matching curtains and duvet covers. Considerable weekend tariff reductions. Children up to 12 stay free in parents' room. *Rooms 23. Garden. Access, Amex, Diners, Visa.*

Set menu prices may not always include service or wine.

MAYBOLE   **Ladyburn**   73%   £140

Tel 01655 740585   Fax 01655 740580   Map 4 A2   **HR**
by Maybole Strathclyde KA19 7SG

Set in 23 acres (4 ¹/₂ of which are well-kept gardens) near the Kilkerran estate, signposted off the B741 2 miles south of Crosshill. The family home of the Hepburns, it is run by owner/manager/chef Jane Hepburn in country-house style with family photos and pictures in the day rooms (a very pleasant drawing-room with pale pink and pale green armchairs and Chinese lacquered pieces and an equally pleasant library for smokers) along with fresh flowers, ornaments and objets d'art that are to be found throughout the hotel. Bedrooms (no smoking) feature plain cream walls setting off antique furniture, more flowers, fruit, books, ornaments and Royal Doulton bone china for tea and coffee-making facilities. Bathrooms (3 with large showers only) have generous bottles of bath oil plus huge bath sheets. Rooms are properly serviced at night. There is no bar, but drinks are served in the drawing-room or library. No children under 16 except in a flat which is sometimes available. No dogs. *Rooms 8. Garden, croquet. Closed Nov-Mar. Access, Amex, Visa.*

dining-room   £60

Dried flowers in the fireplaces, lacy cloths over yellow undercloths, bone china and fresh flowers help create a pleasant dining-room. Jane cooks in a simple, homely style making exclusive use of local supplies and preparing everything except bread on the premises. Speciality dishes include oxtail and grape casserole, fish pie, apple tart and boozy chocolate mousse. No smoking. Advance bookings only. *Seats 25. D only 7.30-8.30. Set D from £25.*

MELROSE — Burts Hotel — £74

Tel 01896 822285   Fax 01896 822870   Map 4 C1   **I**
Market Square Melrose Borders TD6 9PN

On the A6091, 3 miles from the A7 and 2 miles from the A68 in the heart of Border country and below the Eildon Hills, lies Melrose. At its heart is Burts Hotel, which has been in the Henderson family's capable hands since 1970. It's a useful centre from which to explore the area, whether you favour stately homes, salmon fishing or something in between. However you've spent your day, there's a warm welcome back at the hotel, along with impeccably maintained bedrooms. *Rooms 21. Garden, snooker. Closed 26 Dec.* *Access, Amex, Diners, Visa.*

MELROSE — George & Abbotsford Hotel — 56% — £70

Tel 01896 822308   Fax 01896 823363   Map 4 C1   **H**
High Street Melrose Borders TD6 9PD

A Victorian look has been restored to this town-centre former coaching inn, once a haunt of Sir Walter Scott. Glass-shaded brass chandeliers, red plush upholstery and dado panelling set the tone in the day rooms; separate conference rooms accommodate up to 180. Neat bedrooms range from standards with shower/WC only to four-poster rooms. Children up to 15 stay free in parents' room. *Rooms 30. Garden, children's playground.* *Access, Amex, Diners, Visa.*

MILNGAVIE — Black Bull Thistle — 59% — £93

Tel 0141-956 2291   Fax 0141-956 1896   Map 3 B5   **H**
Main Street Milngavie Strathclyde G62 6BH

A useful stopover on the A81 six miles north of the centre of Glasgow. Children up to 10 stay free in parents' room. Conferences and functions for up to 100. Ample free parking. *Rooms 27. Access, Amex, Diners, Visa.*

MUIR-OF-ORD — Dower House — £70

Tel & Fax 01463 870090   Map 2 B3   **RR**
Highfield Muir-of-Ord Highland IV6 7XN

Take the A862 Dingwall road out of Muir-of-Ord and after about a mile, by a double bend sign, turn left through green and white railing gates into the three acres of mature grounds that surround Robyn and Mena Aitchison's charming cottage orné-style Dower House. Dinner is a no-choice, four-course affair (five if you count the coffee and home-made truffles) with perhaps a chicken and apricot terrine or grilled goat's cheese salad to start before a soup and then a main dish such as breast of mallard duck with juniper berry sauce or fillet of beef with herb relish. Dessert might be a chocolate tart with caramel sauce or strawberries and white peaches steeped in Sauternes with an alternative of some fine Scottish cheeses. No children under 5 in the dining-room after 7.30pm (they can have supper from 5.30pm). Though there are no tasting notes on the wine list, there are many fine wines and good growers at quite reasonable prices. No smoking. Eight seats in the garden in fine weather. *Seats 28. L by arrangement D 7.30-9. Closed 1 week Oct, 2 weeks Mar & a few days Christmas. Set D £28. Access, Visa.*

Rooms — £100

The five bedrooms are comfortable and cottagey, and all have Victorian-style bathrooms with cast-iron baths and brass fittings, plus "colour television if required". One has its own sitting-room, three are reserved for non-smokers. No dogs. Garden, croquet, children's playground.

Lodges are now listed by county in the reference section

NAIRN   Clifton Hotel   70%   £96

Tel 01667 453119   Fax 01667 452836   Map 2 C3   **HR**
Viewfield Street Nairn Highland IV12 4HW

Turn west at the only roundabout on the A96 through Nairn to find the Clifton Hotel,
a delightful town house just minutes from the beach, next door to the Nairn Pottery
studios and run since 1952 by J. Gordon Macintyre, hotelier and patron of the arts. The
house bears witness to his individual taste, with hand-chosen antiques, fresh and dried
flowers and fragrant pot-pourri making public rooms cosy and attractive. Paintings crowd
the walls and there are antiques, too, in the bedrooms, where TVs and telephones do not
intrude. Breakfast is served right up until noon! *Rooms 12. Garden. Closed Dec-Feb.
Access, Amex, Diners, Visa.*

Restaurant   £60

On offer is a daily-changing menu, handwritten in French, with local produce used when
possible to produce a classic Auld Alliance choice. So *saumon au beurre rouge* or *sauté
de filet de porc normande* clearly display their origins and the confident touch in the
cooking pays dividends. Delicious traditional puddings could include chocolate pots,
sherry trifle and orange soufflé and Scottish cheeses. Half bottles might be in short supply
on the excellent and comprehensive wine list, but with several wines available by the
glass it's not too important. The list is extraordinary, with some New World wines
starting from as little as £6.50 ranging to a selection of over 50 champagnes. The separate
Green Room (serenely colour co-ordinated in green and white including the flowers!) is
non-smoking, and is used sometimes for lunch, and for private parties. *Seats 40.
Parties 12. Private Room 12. L 12.30-1 D 7-9.30.*

NAIRN   Golf View Hotel   67%   £112

Tel 01667 452301   Fax 01667 455267   Map 2 C3   **H**
Seabank Road Nairn Highland IV12 4HD

The most recent development at this late-Victorian hotel is a leisure centre in the garden.
The grounds extend down to a sandy beach on the Firth of Forth opposite the Black Isle,
and sunsets can be quite spectacular. Public areas all share the same decor with elaborate
floral drapes, brass chandeliers and co-ordinating soft furnishings while well-kept
bedrooms (all with proper armchairs and/or sofas) have a variety of bright fabrics for the
matching bedcovers and curtains. Greta Anderson has been running the hotel since 1980.
*Rooms 47. Garden, tennis, putting, indoor swimming pool, gym, steam room, spa bath,
solarium. Access, Amex, Diners, Visa.*

NAIRN   Newton Hotel   65%   £70

Tel 01667 453144   Fax 01667 454026   Map 2 C3   **H**
Inverness Road Nairn Highland IV12 4RX

At the bottom of a winding, tree-lined private drive, this imposing building is set
in 27 acres with sweeping views overlooking the Nairn golf course and the Moray Firth
beyond. The high-ceilinged rooms within the main house are more interesting than the
newer, more contemporary ones in the adjacent Newton Court, a converted granary and
stables. Bar meals are served in a conservatory extension to the cocktail bar. The peaceful
setting, well-chosen antiques and velvet upholstery recall the gracious Victorian era.
Families welcome: up-to-5s share parents' accommodation free, 5s-14s have a 50%
reduction. Functions for up to 100. *Rooms 44. Garden, croquet, putting, sauna, sun beds.
Access, Amex, Diners, Visa.*

NEWBURGH   Udny Arms Hotel   60%   £85

Tel 01358 789444   Fax 01358 789012   Map 2 D3   **H**
Main Street Newburgh Grampian AB41 0BL

The Victorian facade is on the main street but at the back there are pleasant views over
a golf course and the Ythan estuary. Day rooms vary: perhaps the most appealing is the
mellow cocktail bar with its pine-board banquettes, scrubbed pine tables and Windsor
chairs. Bedrooms are furnished mainly in traditional style and are all en suite; the best
rooms overlook the picturesque estuary. Children under 12 stay free in parents' room.
Theatre-style conferences for up to 130. Parking for 180 cars. *Rooms 26. Garden.
Access, Amex, Diners, Visa.*

NEWTON STEWART | Kirroughtree Hotel | 76% | £96

Tel 01671 402141   Fax 01671 402425   Map 4 A2   **HR**
Newton Stewart Dumfries & Galloway DG8 6AN

The public rooms of this 18th-century hotel are still rather obviously opulent with much flock wallpaper, ormolu-mounted furniture, onyx and gilt coffee tables and the like. Upstairs, however, the owners have been transforming the bedrooms into high-class accommodation (not all have yet been finished so ask for 'new' rooms when booking). Furniture is high-quality mahogany in traditional style with proper dining table for room service meals, stylish soft furnishings include sofas and armchairs, and extras run to mineral water, sherry, fruit and bathrobes. In the evening beds are turned down, curtains drawn and bedside lights switched on. In the same ownership as the North West Castle at Stranraer and Cally Palace at Gatehouse of Fleet. No children under 12 in hotel or restaurant. From the A75 take the A712 towards New Galloway. The hotel driveway is 300 yards on the left. *Rooms 17. Garden, croquet, tennis, badminton, putting. Closed 3 Jan-mid Feb. Access, Visa.*

Restaurant   £65

Twin dining-rooms – one in red and one in blue (both now non-smoking) – with plush banquette seating around watered-silk-effect walls, and a piano playing every night. Foodwise, Ian Bennett stays on song with his sensibly short, daily-changing menus that feature good, often local, ingredients in dishes as varied as steamed fillet of halibut in dill and mustard sauce, pot-roast partridge, roast lamb en crépinette, and guinea fowl with braised cabbage and rich port sauce. For afters go for an artistically presented pud like caramelised lemon and banana tart or some good Scottish cheeses that always include a selection of local goat's and ewe's milk cheeses along with Mull of Kintyre Cheddar matured for at least nine months. No children under 12. No smoking. *Seats 40. Parties 12. Private Room 20. D only (except Sun L 12-1.30) 7-9.30. Set D £25.*

NEWTOWN ST BOSWELLS | Le Provençale | £40

Tel 01835 823284   Map 4 C1   **R**
Monksford Road Newtown St Boswells Borders TD6 0SB

Frenchman René Duzelier in the kitchen and his Scottish wife Elizabeth front of house make a fine team in their spotless little restaurant just off the A68. The daily-changing menu is handwritten with English descriptions in a distinctive French script. Straightforward cooking covers dishes like garlic snails, cream of vegetable soup, fillet of beef au poivre, ballotine of pheasant in Madeira sauce, fillets of haddock in vermouth and, to finish, lemon pancakes or rice pudding caramel. No smoking. *Seats 40. Parties 18. L 12-2 D 7-10. Closed Sun & Mon. No credit cards.*

NORTH BERWICK | Marine Hotel | 64% | £85

Tel 01620 892406   Fax 01620 894480   Map 3 D5   **H**
Cromwell Road North Berwick Lothian EH39 4LZ

Fine coastal views of the Firth of Forth are enjoyed from this imposing Victorian hotel with a long golfing tradition (it overlooks the 16th green of the North Berwick Championship Westlinks Course and there are dozens of courses nearby). Banqueting for 300; conferences up to 350. Forte. *Rooms 83. Garden, tennis, putting, outdoor swimming pool, children's splash pool, sauna, sun bed, snooker, squash, steam room, children's playroom & playground. Access, Amex, Diners, Visa.*

Consult the blue pages for summary tables and lists of
recommended establishments.

NORTH MIDDLETON   Borthwick Castle   66%   £120

Tel 01875 820514   Fax 01875 821702   Map 3 C6   **H**
North Middleton Lothian EH23 4QY

Built in 1430 and beseiged by Cromwell in 1650, historic Borthwick Castle with its tall
twin towers once held Mary Queen of Scots as a prisoner. She escaped, dressed as a page
boy, from a window of the vast stone-vaulted main hall, which boasts a 40-foot Gothic
arch, minstrel's gallery and hooded fireplace. Spiral staircases within the massive stone
walls lead to bedrooms offering more atmosphere than luxury. Top of the range is the
Mary Queen of Scots four-poster 'double bedchamber'. Most bathrooms have shower
and WC only. Probably the most genuinely atmospheric medieval castle hotel in the
country (follow Historic Buildings sign on the A7). *Rooms 10. Garden, croquet.
Closed Jan, Feb. Access, Amex, Diners, Visa.*

NORTH QUEENSFERRY   Queensferry Lodge   63%   £75

Tel 01383 410000   Fax 01383 419708   Map 3 C5   **H**
St Margaret's Head North Queensferry nr Inverkeithing Fife KY11 1HP

A modern family-run hotel overlooking the Forth and its famous bridges. Bedrooms are
quite generous on space and accessories, and sparkling bathrooms have good showers
over the tubs and ample towelling. A tourist information office is manned from 10 to 6
throughout the year, and in a Scottish crafts shop you can find out all about the area.
Conference and banqueting facilities for 200. Plans for the next year include another 30
bedrooms and a leisure complex. *Rooms 32. Access, Amex, Visa.*

OBAN   Alexandra Hotel   59%   £90

Tel 01631 562381   Fax 01631 564497   Map 3 B5   **H**
Corran Esplanade Oban Strathclyde PA34 5AA

Built in the late 1860s, the hotel stands on the esplanade a short stroll from the town
centre. Modest accommodation, two lounges and a cocktail bar. Function facilities
for up to 120. Ample parking. *Rooms 60. Garden, indoor swimming pool, sun bed,
steam room, gym, snooker, games room. Access, Amex, Visa.*

OBAN   Columba Hotel   60%   £99

Tel 01631 562183   Fax 01631 564683   Map 3 B5   **H**
North Pier Esplanade Oban Strathclyde PA34 5QD

An Edwardian sandstone building on the North Pier, with views across the bay to the
Western Isles. Three bars offer a choice for a relaxing drink, and conference suites can
cater for up to 300 delegates. Children up to 14 stay free when sharing parents' room.
Parking for 10 cars. *Rooms 48. Access, Amex, Visa.*

OBAN   Knipoch Hotel   72%   £130

Tel 01852 316251   Fax 01852 316249   Map 3 B5   **HR**
by Oban Strathclyde PA34 4QT

The Craig family have been hands-on owners since 1981 of an elegant, well-kept
Georgian hotel standing six miles south of Oban on the A816 halfway along the shore of
Loch Feochan, an arm of the sea stretching four miles inland. Lounges and bars are filled
with family heirlooms, and there are plenty of magazines to read in the leathery comfort
of fireside armchairs. Well-proportioned bedrooms have period furniture and particularly
well-appointed bathrooms. A purpose-built bedroom extension blends well with the
original. Children under 5 half price. No dogs. *Rooms 17. Garden. Closed mid Nov-mid
Feb. Access, Amex, Diners, Visa.*

Restaurant   **£80**

Dinner is three or five courses featuring excellent produce from garden, loch and the
hotel's own smokery; their salmon is cured, marinated in juniper, rowan, Barbados sugar,
herbs and whisky then smoked over oak for three days. Smoked scallops are another
speciality and a new favourite is monkfish, Norway lobster and squid served chilled in oil
with basil and pine kernels. Centrepiece of the gourmet menu is chateaubriand with
béarnaise and a generous selection of vegetables. Next comes cheese, then dessert (orange
cake with bavarois, strawberry roulade) and coffee with petits fours. No smoking. Too
many wines are marked 'not available' on the otherwise excellent and fairly priced list,

which has some great names and outstanding growers. Helpful tasting notes, not many halves. *Seats 44. Parties 12. Private Rooms 12/24. L by arrangement D 7.30-9. Set D £29.50 & £39.50.*

OLDMELDRUM	Meldrum House	65%	£95

Tel 01651 872294   Fax 01651 872464   Map 2 D3   **H**
Meldrum House Oldmeldrum Grampian AB1 0AE

In a substantial Scottish Baronial mansion, a welcoming, year-round log fire burns in the spacious entrance hall, off which is a small, rough-stone, barrel-vaulted bar that dates back to the 13th century. The drawing-room, by contrast, is in elegant yet homely country-house style. All but one of the antique-furnished bedrooms are very large with fine views over the grounds and pretty, rather than stylish, soft furnishings. The entrance to the estate (there's an attractive drive past a lake to reach the house) is at the junction of the A947 and B9170 just out of town. *Rooms 9. Garden, fishing. Closed 3 & 4 Jan. Access, Visa.*

ONICH	Allt-nan-Ros Hotel	63%	£95

Tel 01855 821210   Fax 01855 821462   Map 3 B4   **HR**
Onich nr Fort William Highland PH33 6RY

The great glory of this white pebbledash, early Victorian shooting lodge on the A82 is its fabulous panoramic view (shared by all but one of the bedrooms) across Lochs Levin and Linnhe to the mountains beyond. On a clear day one can see as far as the Isle of Mull. Inside, all is neat and well ordered; the bar, with a real fire in its white marble fireplace in winter, opens on to a lounge with picture windows. Bedrooms all feature quality furniture and a variety of pretty, matching fabrics. Two rooms are in a converted stable annexe. Good, freshly-cooked breakfasts. The hotel's name means 'Burn of the Roses', a reference to the stream which runs through the garden. *Rooms 21. Garden, putting. Closed mid Nov-Christmas. Access, Amex, Diners, Visa.*

Restaurant   £55

♉ 🐛 🍵 🍶

While the picture windows take full advantage of the view a short, fixed-price dinner menu features a main-course selection of pan-fried sirloin steak, pork and loin of lamb with a red wine sauce, roast breast of corn-fed chicken with bacon and mangetout and baked haddock fillets coated in sesame seeds with a horseradish cream sauce. Lighter lunches. In addition to the main wine list, which includes tasting notes, there's a quite extensive house selection. Realistic prices. *Seats 50. L 12.30-2 D 7-9. Set L £7 (Sun L £8.50) Set D £19.50.*

ONICH	The Lodge On The Loch	63%	£142*

Tel 01855 821237   Fax 01855 821463   Map 3 B4   **H**
Creag Dhu Onich nr Fort William Highland PH33 6RY

A friendly little hotel set amid spectacular loch and mountain scenery just off the A82 (five miles north of Glencoe, twelve miles south of Fort William). Plump-cushioned sofas make for easy relaxation in the lounge, and there's a modern bar. Best bedrooms are the Chieftains with loch views. Guests have free membership of The Isles Club with a pool, sauna, steam room sun bed and keep-fit equipment, 3 miles away in Ballochulish at sister hotel the *Isles of Glencoe*. ★Half-board terms only (children up to 16 enjoy considerable reductions). *Rooms 18. Garden. Closed Jan. Access, Visa.*

ONICH	Onich Hotel	61%	£80

Tel 01855 821214   Fax 01855 821484   Map 3 B4   **H**
Onich nr Fort William Highland PH33 6RY

A popular family-run hotel whose location virtually at the head of Loch Linnhe makes it an ideal spot to stay and indulge in all sorts of strenuous outdoor activities of the climbing and hill-walking variety, followed by less strenuous indoor ones such as relaxing in the spa bath or the bar! There are early suppers for exhausted youngsters, substantial bar snacks for midday refuelling, and a general feeling of warmth and welcome for everyone. *Rooms 27. Closed 1 week Christmas, 1 week Jan. Garden, spa bath, solarium, pool table, children's playground. Access, Amex, Diners, Visa.*

PEAT INN | The Peat Inn ★ ↑ £85

Tel 01334 840206   Fax 01334 840530   Map 3 C5   **RR**
Peat Inn by Cupar Fife KY15 5LH

Originally a coaching inn, this renowned restaurant with rooms sits at the crossroads in the centre of a tiny village named after the inn, and its heart is chef-patron David Wilson's kitchen. With his wife Patricia (who designed the sumptuous bedrooms – see below) he has run this restaurant in true French country style for over twenty years; it's formal yet friendly, with a reception lounge with open log fire, carved sideboard, high-backed tapestry chairs, and rough white plaster walls. There are three separate dining-rooms in which to enjoy the modern cooking, which very much reflects the produce available locally. This has two beneficial effects – a guarantee of freshness and quality, and encouragement to local suppliers and growers. The menu choice lies between à la carte, the menu of the day and the tasting menu (the last may only be ordered for a complete table); there's also a vegetarian list. Some dishes have become all-time favourites, among them the wonderfully aromatic fish soup, lobster poached or in salad with a citrus vinaigrette, roast lamb in a thyme-flavoured sauce, venison in a rich red wine sauce and caramelised apple pastry with a caramel sauce. Always ask about the day's selection of fish, and consider very seriously, or an alternative to the apple pastry, a trio of nut desserts. Cheeses from the trolley. There's a quite marvellous wine list at affordable prices, with great depth and quality wherever you look, and notes where appropriate. Be bold, experiment, and if shy (David certainly isn't), seek advice. Cellar of the Year regional winner for Scotland. No smoking. *Seats 48. Parties 12. Private Room 24. L at 1 D 7-9.30. Closed Sun & Mon, 25 Dec, 1 Jan. Set L £18.50 Set D £28 & £42.*
Access, Amex, Diners, Visa.

Rooms £135

Overlooking the garden, the bedrooms are in fact suites (seven split-level and one ground-level suitable for disabled guests) with an upstairs sitting-room, where a super Continental breakfast, consisting of freshly squeezed orange juice, fruit compote, yoghurt, hot croissants etc, is served. Excellent coffee and tea (the latter comes in decent-sized cups). The rooms have been furnished by design graduate Patricia and provide the utmost comfort – smart co-ordinating fabrics, good French period furniture (a cabinet hides the remote-control teletext TV, Scottish mineral water and a variety of games), luxurious Italian marble bathrooms with Czech & Speake fittings and toiletries, bathrobes, and even slippers. There are fresh flowers, fruit, home-made biscuits, books and magazines, as well as direct-dial telephone, radio/alarm and hairdryer – these rooms are among the best you'll find anywhere. Garden.

PEEBLES | Cringletie House 65% £98

Tel 01721 730233   Fax 01721 730244   Map 4 C1   **HR**
Peebles Borders EH45 8PL

Owned and run since 1971 by the Maguire family, Cringletie is a baronial-style mansion which was built in 1861 for the Wolfe family, and it still offers a family welcome today. Set well back from the A703, three miles north of Peebles, it provides peace and quiet and enjoys views, from all rooms, of the distant Meldon and Moorfoot Hills. Marbled fireplaces, fresh flowers from the gardens and antiques enhance the traditional decor. Most impressive of the day rooms is the panelled drawing-room with fine painted ceiling. Well-maintained bedrooms offer traditional comforts. *Rooms 13. Garden, croquet, tennis, putting. Closed early Jan-early Mar. Access, Visa.*

Restaurant £65

Aileen Maguire, ably assisted since 1981 by Sheila McKellar, offers well-balanced set menus with choices at the main courses, drawing as much produce as possible from the lovely walled kitchen garden. A typical four-course dinner might start with tomato, turmeric and orange soup, and proceed via gruyère roulade filled with asparagus or king prawn bridies to the centrepiece – a choice of five could include sole with watercress hollandaise, roast duckling with brambles and gin, or Moroccan spiced lamb casserole served with couscous. To finish, perhaps tipsy sherry gateau with vanilla sauce from a choice of four. New since last year is a 35-seat conservatory. The wine list is jolly good, if somewhat higgledy-piggledy. Some top names at very reasonable prices. No smoking. *Seats 56. Parties 12. Private Room 27. L 1-1.45 D 7.30-8.30. Sun L £15.50 Set D £25.50.*

PEEBLES   Park Hotel   62%   £106

Tel 01721 720451   Fax 01721 723510   Map 4 C1   **H**
Innerleithen Road Peebles Borders EH45 8BA

A handsome, whitewashed building on the A72. Views of gardens and hills are enjoyed by many of the bedrooms, which include one with a four-poster. Guests may use the extensive leisure facilities of the *Peebles Hotel Hydro*, in the same ownership, and less than half a mile away. *Rooms 24. Garden, putting. Access, Amex, Diners, Visa.*

PEEBLES   Peebles Hotel Hydro   70%   £103

Tel 01721 720602   Fax 01721 722999   Map 4 C1   **H**
Innerleithen Road Peebles Borders EH45 8LX

In Scottish border country, Peebles Hotel Hydro is a complete resort: once installed, you are unlikely to need anything throughout your stay that is not available on-site. The list of facilities in Bubbles leisure centre is seemingly endless, and Pieter Van Dijk, in charge since 1972, keeps abreast of new trends and options, bringing them on stream as appropriate. Despite the up-to-date technology, the hotel is true to its Edwardian origins in terms of grandeur and elegance in public rooms and bedrooms, even down to weekend dances in the ballroom – and there's a disco for the younger element. Families are well catered for. Banqueting, conference and function facilities for up to 450. *Rooms 137. Garden, croquet, tennis, pitch and putt, putting, riding, indoor swimming pool, gym, squash, badminton, sauna, steam room, spa bath, solarium, beauty salon, hair salon, children's playroom and playground, games room, snooker, news kiosk, coffee shop (11am-11pm). Access, Amex, Diners, Visa.*

PEEBLES   Tontine Hotel   57%   £87

Tel 01721 720892   Fax 01721 729732   Map 4 C1   **H**
High Street Peebles Borders EH45 8AJ

Modest, practical accommodation at an agreeable hotel established in 1808. Under-14s stay free in parents' room. No dogs. No room service. A member of White Hart Hotels (Forte). *Rooms 35. Access, Amex, Diners, Visa.*

PERTH   Number Thirty Three   £55

Tel 01738 633771   Map 3 C5   **R**
33 George Street Perth Tayside PH1 5LA

Choose between the light meal menu of the oyster bar (ideal for theatre-goers) and the more substantial dishes offered in the dining area beyond at this nearly-all seafood art deco restaurant near the centre of town. The former might include seafood soup, Scottish oysters and a platter of assorted fresh, smoked and marinated fish and shellfish; the latter pan-fried lemon sole with herb butter, Loch Craignish scallops in a vermouth sauce, roast duckling and grilled fillet steak. Both menus list the same desserts, sticky toffee pudding with butterscotch sauce and elderflower ice cream with brown sugar meringue being typical. *Seats 42. Parties 10. L 12.30-2.30 D 6.30-9.30. Closed Sun, Mon & first 3 weeks Feb. Access, Amex, Visa.*

PERTH   Royal George Hotel   62%   £87

Tel 01738 624455   Fax 01738 630345   Map 3 C5   **H**
Tay Street Perth Tayside PH1 5LD

A Georgian jumble of a hotel near the city centre with some rooms facing the River Tay. Refurbished day rooms are quite extensive and offer many quiet, comfortable seating areas. Functions for up to 100 in the ballroom. A limited room service is offered. Forte. *Rooms 44. Garden. Access, Amex, Diners, Visa.*

PERTH   Stakis City Mills Hotel   60%   £94

Tel 01738 628281   Fax 01738 643423   Map 3 C5   **H**
West Mill Street Perth Tayside PH1 5QP

Right in the heart of Perth, the Stakis is based on a watermill dating back to the 15th century. Accommodation comprises singles, doubles and twins, and a suite that can be adapted for family use. Children up to 12 free in parents' room. Conferences up to 140 theatre-style. *Rooms 76. Access, Amex, Diners, Visa.*

PETERHEAD	Waterside Inn	67%	£93

Tel 01779 471121   Fax 01779 470670   Map 2 D3   **H**
Fraserburgh Road Peterhead Grampian AB42 7BN

Turn left at a grassy roundabout as you approach Peterhead from Aberdeen (A92) and follow signs to St Fergus to find this modern hotel which seems set to educate its guests in more than just the three 'Rs', including (but not restricted to) refuge, refresh, revitalise, relax, relive, reward – aiming ultimately for you to return. There's certainly plenty to do in the well-equipped leisure centre or the immediate area (the unspoilt far north-east coast of Scotland), and special breaks are offered at various times of the year. There's a series of bars to suit every taste, and several conference rooms (maximum capacity 245). 40 studio bedrooms in a separate block are compact and functional, while those in the main building are more spacious and luxurious; children under 13 stay free in parents' room. *Rooms 110. Garden, indoor swimming pool, keep-fit equipment, sauna, steam room, spa bath, sun beds, snooker, indoor and outdoor children's play areas, grill room (7am-10pm). Access, Amex, Diners, Visa.*

PITLOCHRY	Green Park Hotel	58%	£90

Tel 01796 473248   Fax 01796 473520   Map 3 C4   **H**
Cluny Bridge Road Pitlochry Tayside PH16 5JY

Graham and Anne Brown have been at the Green Park for over 25 years and their attention to detail shows throughout. Bedrooms are attractively furnished while the lounge and bar also continue to provide comfort and loch views. Neat, well-tended gardens lead right down to the shore of Loch Faskally, and when it's fine you can have light meals or snacks in the garden. Children under 5 free in parents' room. *Rooms 37. Garden, putting, game fishing. Closed Nov-Mar. Access, Visa.*

PITLOCHRY	Pitlochry Hydro Hotel	64%	£106

Tel 01796 472666   Fax 01796 472238   Map 3 C4   **H**
Knockard Road Pitlochry Tayside PH16 5JH

Set high above Pitlochry, the Hydro is a sturdily-built, well-maintained and well-run late-Victorian hotel. Its attractions are supplemented by good leisure facilities, mostly housed in the Hydro Club. Bedrooms, including a couple of suites, have modern tiled bathrooms. Children up to 14 stay free in parents' room, with breakfast also free. No dogs. *Rooms 62. Garden, croquet, putting, indoor swimming pool, gym, spa bath, sauna, solarium, snooker. Closed Jan-early Feb. Access, Amex, Diners, Visa.*

PORT APPIN	Airds Hotel	75%	£266*

Tel 01631 730236   Fax 01631 730535   Map 3 B5   **HR**
Port Appin Appin Strathclyde PA38 4DF

With glorious views across Loch Linnhe this 250-year old former ferry inn conceals a most civilised and comfortable hotel behind its modest white painted facade. Although not grand in scale the public areas lack nothing when it comes to comfort with lots of overstuffed armchairs and sofas, fresh flowers, books, magazines and real fires in the two charming lounges, an intimate bar (not much used) and a small flower-filled conservatory by the entrance. Bedrooms vary considerably in size with the smallest being rather compact but others feeling quite spacious. The best have proper armchairs, the smaller more modest seating but all get homely touches with fresh flowers and porcelain ornaments. Most feature antique furniture. Good bathrooms come with robes, generous towelling and plenty of quality toiletries and, like the bedrooms, are properly serviced in the evening. Expect a warm welcome from the Allen family, who have been here for nearly 20 years. *Half-board terms only. Rooms 12. Garden. Access, Amex, Visa.*

Restaurant   £80

A long, low-ceilinged dining-room, with elegantly laid tables – napkins neatly tied with a tartan bow – of which those in the window are the most sought after. Betty and Graeme Allen (mother and son) share the work in the kitchen producing sophisticated yet uncomplicated dishes for their daily-changing, four-course, fixed-price menu. Open ravioli of mushrooms in a Muscadet and parsley sauce, lightly cooked oysters with smoked salmon and a champagne jelly, roast saddle of roe deer on a potato cake with a thyme and juniper sauce and fillet of halibut on a bed of honeyed aubergines typify the style. Light lunches are served in the lounge. Eric Allen's constantly evolving wine list is right up there with the very best, offering a good balance of mature vintages and younger wines ready for drinking. Lots of half bottles, fair prices with house and French country wines a steal! *Seats 36. L by arrangement, D at 8. Set D £35.*

PORT APPIN — Pierhouse Hotel — £70

Tel 01631 730302   Fax 01631 730521   Map 3 B5   **IR**
Port Appin Pier nr Appin Strathclyde PA38 4DE

Turn off the A828 and head on down to the end of the road where you'll find the distinctive twin round-fronted buildings of the low, white Pierhouse; its setting is delightfully tranquil and picturesque, right on the edge of Loch Linnhe, where the little Lismore passenger ferry docks. The terrace, the picture-windowed main bar room (open all day) and small residents' sitting-room make the most of the evolving weather scene that plays out over the towering Morvern Hills beyond the Isle of Lismore. Eleven smart, pine-furnished bedrooms are in a sympathetically designed two-storey building to one side of the former ferry house; the front bedrooms have glorious loch and island views, but the bathrooms are windowless. A large family room (£80) has a double and a single bed (plus room for a cot) plus good hanging and shelf space. Owners Alan and Sheila Macleod and family are most hospitable. Advance arrangements can be made to see Castle Stalker and basking seals by boat. Generous breakfasts. No dogs. Yacht moorings available for diners and overnight guests. *Rooms 11. Terrace, bicycle and boat hire, moorings. Closed 25 Dec. Access, Visa.*

Seafood Restaurant — £55

In the four small, unpretentious dining areas (one is no-smoking) the best few tables are at the picture windows, although those by the warming fire are an attraction in winter; bright, interesting artwork – from George Devlin and Robin McGregor – adorns the whitewashed walls. Callum Macleod provides energetic, happy service with a smile and a sense of humour, taking obvious pride in his mum Sheila's particularly good cooking. 'Clam chowder', made with scallops and salmon stock, is quite superb, as are cracked clab claws with home-made mayonnaise, Lismore oysters and large langoustines from Loch Linnhe (some way from Dublin Bay!). Seafood may be served with cheese and wine, lemon and butter or garlic butter sauces, but when it's so fresh (dark blue lobsters, oysters and giant crabs are kept in submerged creels off the pier) and the quality so good it seems appropriate to let the natural ingredients' flavours speak for themselves. Half a dozen Aberdeen Angus beef, venison and chicken dishes complete the main-course picture. Those puddings that are home-made, such as bread-and-butter pudding made with French bread or a light, bitter chocolate roulade, are the ones to choose. Fine bar snacks are served at lunchtime only. If it's really quiet in winter you may need to tell them you're coming. Disabled facilities. *Seats 40. L 12-3 D 6.30-9.30. Closed D 25 Dec.*

PORT WILLIAM — Corsemalzie House — 61% — £86

Tel 01988 860254   Fax 01988 860213   Map 4 A3   **H**
Port William by Newton Stewart Dumfries & Galloway DG8 9RL

The McDougalls have been at Corsemalzie since 1981 but the stone mansion has been in its secluded forty acres of woodland for over a century. Apart from creature comforts, the main attractions are of the fishing and shooting variety (rights on the renowned Rivers Bladnoch and Tarff as well as the nearby lochs), and the comfortable lounges make an ideal place to relax after such strenuous activity. Bedrooms are generally of a decent size; all have private bath or shower. Parking for 35 cars. Banqueting/conferences for 80. *Rooms 14. Garden, croquet, putting, children's playground, game fishing, shooting. Closed 2 weeks Feb. Access, Amex, Visa.*

PORTPATRICK — Knockinaam Lodge — 73% — £104

Tel 01776 810471   Fax 01776 810435   Map 4 A2   **HR**
Portpatrick nr Stranraer Dumfries & Galloway DG9 9AD

New owners have kept out the welcome mat at this comfortable country house, which enjoys a secluded setting in a cove with a private beach (follow signs from the A77). An eclectic clock collection graces most public rooms, which include a warmly panelled bar complete with stag's head, and open-fire-warmed sitting-rooms with a wealth of plump-cushioned sofas, magazines and board games. Bedrooms, some with new decor and bathrooms, are equally gracious, pretty but not fussy, and bathrooms include a splendid

See over

tub used by Winston Churchill. Excellent breakfasts and delightful service. *Rooms 10. Garden, croquet, playground. Access, Amex, Diners, Visa.*

Restaurant   £80

☕ 🍴 ❓ 🍇 🍷 🦞

Stuart Muir's French menus make good use of home-grown and local produce: speciality dishes include fresh scallops in a potato shell with home-made courgette chutney and a balsamic vinaigrette; breast of pigeon filled with a chicken and apricot mousse; brill poached in champagne with asparagus and a purée of potatoes flavoured with olive oil, garlic and truffles; and rack of lamb topped with a honey, mustard and brioche herb crust served with a beurre noisette. To finish, a choice of dessert or Jacques Vernier farmhouse cheese. Frankly, some of the prices on the quite marvellous wine list belong in fantasy land, though there can be no doubt about the quality on show. It's an enthusiast's list, but you must look carefully for value. Do not overlook the whisky collection! Bar snacks supplement the lunchtime menu. No smoking in the dining-room. No children. *Seats 26. Parties 10. L 12-2 D 7.30-9.30. Set L £25 Set D £32.*

PORTREE	Rosedale Hotel	56%	£70

Tel 01478 613131   Fax 01478 612531   Map 2 A3   **H**
Beaumont Crescent Portree Isle of Skye Highland IV51 9DB

Situated right on the quayside of a quaint, picturesque fishing harbour, the Rosedale enjoys splendid views across the bay. The building was originally a group of fishermen's homes, and the conversion provides simple but comfortable accommodation in well-kept en-suite bedrooms reached by narrow stairs and corridors. Some of the accommodation is in Beaumont House along the waterfront. *Rooms 23. Garden. Closed Oct-April. Access, Visa.*

QUOTHQUAN	Shieldhill Hotel	73%	£104

Tel 01899 20035   Fax 01899 21092   Map 3 C6   **H**
Quothquan Biggar Strathclyde ML12 6NA

Surrounded by the rolling farmland of the Clyde Valley, this crenellated, stone-built mansion dates back to the 12th century. Inside all is relaxed and comfortable in country-house style with the main oak-panelled drawing-room boasting fresh flowers, magazines and plenty of deep armchairs. Bedrooms vary considerably in size – the largest is a huge split-level affair with a vast, sunken spa bath within the room – but all have antique furniture, good easy chairs and extras like mineral water and a decanter of sherry. Several rooms have (gas coal) fireplaces. Each has been individually decorated with pretty Laura Ashley fabrics and wall coverings that extend to the matching bathrooms (two with shower & WC only). Good breakfasts begin with freshly squeezed orange juice. No children under 11, no dogs and no smoking in the bedrooms. *Rooms 11. Garden, croquet. Access, Amex, Diners, Visa.*

ROCKCLIFFE	Baron's Craig	65%	£98

Tel 01556 630225   Fax 01556 630328   Map 4 B2   **H**
Rockcliffe by Dalbeattie Dumfries & Galloway DG5 4QF

Rockcliffe is a small village overlooking the mouth of Rough Firth, just where it joins the Solway Firth, and Baron's Craig is perfectly situated to take full advantage of the splendid views thus afforded. The house, built of local granite in the 1800s, is elegantly proportioned and public rooms are light, airy and comfortably furnished. Bedrooms are modern and well equipped. Parking for 30 cars. Small conferences (up to 20) can be accommodated. *Rooms 22. Garden, putting. Closed Nov-Easter. Access, Amex, Visa.*

ROTHES	Rothes Glen Hotel	65%	£90

Tel 01340 831 254   Fax 01340 831566   Map 2 C3   **H**
Rothes nr Elgin Grampian AB38 7AH

Forty acres of grounds at the head of the Glen of Rothes provide rural peace at a baronial house designed by the architect of Balmoral Castle. Inside, there's an elegant lounge with ribbed ceiling and white marble fireplace, plus a bar and TV room. Antique furniture graces most of the variously-sized bedrooms, which provide the normal amenities, including mini-bar. Two rooms have shower only. *Rooms 16. Garden, putting. Closed Christmas-Jan. Access, Amex, Diners, Visa.*

ST ANDREWS	The Grange Inn	£45

Tel 01334 472670   Fax 01334 478703   Map 3 D5   **R**
Grange Road St Andrews Fife KY16 8LJ

Part of a group of pretty little old cottages about a mile out of town to the south-east and with fine views over St Andrews and the Tay Estuary to the Angus Hills beyond, the Grange Inn is now almost exclusively a restaurant, although there is still a tiny, atmospheric bar with flagstone floor, ancient fireplace and beamed ceiling. Three separate dining-rooms are cottagey with bare stone walls and a charming mix of rustic and antique furniture. The menu sticks mainly to fairly straightforward grills and the excellent local seafood with details of the day's catch appearing on a blackboard menu along with seasonal items like asparagus. Sticky toffee pudding, chocolate roulade and crème brulée exhaust the pudding menu although there is also always some Stilton and a couple of Scottish cheeses to be had along with wheat wafers or oatcakes. Friendly atmosphere. *Seats 76. Private Room 36. L 12.30-2.15 D 6.30-9.15. Closed Mon & Tue Nov-Mar. Set L £9.50/£11.95 (Sun £10.50/£12.95). Access, Amex, Diners, Visa.*

ST ANDREWS	Rufflets Country House	65%	£130

Tel 01334 472594   Fax 01334 478703   Map 3 D5   **H**
Strathkinness Low Road St Andrews Fife KY16 9TX

They are justly proud of their ten acres of award-winning gardens (complete with topiary and a stream) at this 1920s-built hotel on the B939 a mile and a half west of St Andrews. Inside, the hotel is as well kept as the gardens, with pretty floral fabrics and wallpapers and mostly traditional darkwood furniture. Three particularly attractive rooms are in a rose-covered cottage in the grounds. Children up to 10 stay free in parents' room. Public areas include an appealing entrance hall, lounge, little bar and formal drawing-room. *Rooms 25. Garden, putting. Access, Amex, Diners, Visa.*

ST ANDREWS	Rusacks Hotel	74%	£138

Tel 01334 474321   Fax 01334 477896   Map 3 D5   **H**
Pilmour Links St Andrews Fife KY16 9JQ

Standing by the 18th fairway of the world-famous Old Course, this grand Victorian hotel not surprisingly attracts golf-lovers from near and far. The sun lounge provides a quiet retreat and fairway views, and the golf-themed Champion's Bar is a good place to relive the triumphs and disasters of the day's golf. Many fine features survive both in the day rooms (marble columns, crystal chandeliers) and in the bedrooms, many of which sport antiques. Smart bathrooms have generous towelling bathrobes. Well-turned-out staff provide a high level of service that includes valet parking, luggage porterage and proper bedroom service in the evenings. Children under 12 stay free in parents' room, under-5s also eat free. Forte. *Rooms 50. Golf shop, changing room, sauna, solarium. Access, Amex, Diners, Visa.*

ST ANDREWS	St Andrews Old Course Hotel	82%	£245

Tel 01334 474371   Fax 01334 477668   Map 3 D5   **H**
St Andrews Fife KY16 9SP

Arguably one of the most famous golfing hotels in the world, set beside the infamous 17th Road Hole (no problem to John Daly, 1995 winner of The Open), and by the clubhouse of the Royal and Ancient, it also has views to the bay, the city and, behind that, the Highlands: almost a microcosm of all things quintessentially Scottish. The setting is undeniably splendid, so too the hotel itself. Chandeliers and sofas to sink into typify the comfort, stencilled coving and book-lined walls the artistry that has gone into the creation of a haven of peace and luxury. Attention to detail in the bedrooms is equally meticulous, with traditional wooden furniture, TVs hidden away in cabinets and footstools with the comfortable armchairs. High-class toiletries and generously-sized bathrobes add to the exuberance in the marble bathrooms. Indoor leisure activities are centred on the Spa, the luxuriously equipped health and beauty centre, based around the stunning glass-covered, pillared and frescoed pool area. Golfing guests wishing to play the Old Course should apply to the hotel's golf steward. The hotel also provides fine facilities for banqueting and conferences (up to 300 people). Children up to 12 stay free in parents' room. Special children's menu available. *Rooms 125. Garden, indoor swimming pool, gym, steam room, solarium, golf shop, coffee shop (10am-10pm). Access, Amex, Diners, Visa.*

ST FILLANS   Four Seasons Hotel   60%   £74

Tel & Fax 01764 685333   Map 3 C5   **HR**
St Fillans nr Crieff Tayside PH6 2N6

Unremarkable at first sight, except for its stunning location at the head of Loch Earn, the Four Seasons is the sort of hotel that improves with acquaintance – a process that begins with a warm welcome from a member of the Scott family. Residents and diners share a little bar which has Oregon pine and natural stone features, and there is also a small, genteel lounge and, on the first floor, a tiny library that also offers various board games. Modestly furnished bedrooms are bright, cheerful and generally of a good size; six are in chalets above and to the rear of the hotel. Super breakfasts come with rolls hot from the oven, home-made bread and fresh orange juice. Children up to 6 stay free in parents' room. *Rooms 18. Terrace, fishing. Closed early Dec-end Feb. Access, Amex, Diners, Visa.*

Restaurant   £60

Fabulous views from the dining-room here (tables in the window are much sought after) and some pretty good cooking too from Andrew Scott (the son of the house) and his small team. Everything is home-made and generously served, from the bread and the oatcakes that accompany a board of well-kept cheeses to the fresh pasta with a scallop and West Coast lobster starter. Other dishes from the daily-changing, fixed-price dinner menu might include whole roast sea bass with garlic and olive oil, fillet of beef and wild mushrooms, supreme of chicken with tarragon and lemon, tart of rhubarb with its ice cream, double chocolate marquise and orange cheesecake. Bar lunches. *Seats 55. Private Room 16. L (Sun only) 12.15-2.15 D 7-9.30. Set Sun L £13.25 Set D 21.95/£23.95.*

SCARISTA   Scarista House   67%   £89

Tel 01859 550238   Fax 01859 550277   Map 2 A3   **HR**
Scarista Isle of Harris Highland HS3 3HX

The Callaghans' former manse on the Atlantic coast of Harris (15 miles south-west of Tarbert on the A859) must be one of the most remote hotels in Britain. Ruggedly beautiful countryside and endless deserted beaches are a magnet for walkers, bird-watchers and fishermen, who also appreciate the warm welcome and homely comforts of Scarista House. One of the two lounges is lined with books and there is a record collection available for guests' use. Bedrooms in the annexe are larger and more modern than those in the main house, which have a touch more character; all are non-smoking. No children between 2 and 8. Well-trained dogs are welcome so long as they do not disturb the hill sheep. *Rooms 8. Garden. Closed mid Sep-mid May. No credit cards.*

Restaurant   £55

Jane Callaghan's simple, hearty dinners are served in a candle-lit dining-room and are based on good local produce using only free-range eggs and meat, and avoiding farmed seafood. The choice is fixed, so advise in advance of any dislikes ("or, indeed, any likes"). Tomato and oatmeal tarts, fish stew (all locally caught) with salad and home-made hot herb rolls, and apricot whim wham. Scottish cheeses. Bread, cakes and preserves are all home-made. No smoking. *Seats 16. Parties 8. L by arrangement. D at 8.15. Set D £25.*

SCONE   Murrayshall House   72%   £125

Tel 01738 551171   Fax 01738 552595   Map 3 C5   **HR**
Scone Tayside PH2 7PH

Golf is a major attraction at this turn-of-the-century stone mansion, with its 18-hole golf course, two driving ranges, golf shop, professional on hand to give tuition, clubhouse with bar and, new this year, an indoor golf school. Fabric-covered walls feature in the stylish day rooms, dark blue damask to match the soft furnishings in the quiet lounge and a bold floral pattern in the lounge bar. Best bedrooms are those in the original part of the house, those in the newer wing being somewhat smaller, but all offer many extras like fresh flowers, fruit, magazines and mineral water. Rooms are properly serviced in the evenings as are the bathrooms, which boast robes and large bath sheets. Children up to 10 stay free in parents' room. *Rooms 19. Garden, tennis, bowling, golf (18), golf driving ranges, indoor golf school. Access, Amex, Diners, Visa.*

Old Masters Restaurant   £60

A luxuriously appointed hotel restaurant. Typical dishes from the dinner menu, priced according to the number of courses taken, are a tartlet of Arbroath smokies and gruyère cheese on a herb and cream sauce, poached salmon on a bed of fennel with a basil and tomato sauce, beef sirloin rolled in black peppercorns with a cream tarragon sauce, and date and walnut pudding with caramel sauce. There is also always a roast of the day. The well-rounded wine list has some odd mark-ups, though prices are not excessive. Apart from Sunday, lunch in the restaurant is offered only in winter but sandwiches and light meals can be found in the Clubhouse. *Seats 80. Parties 12. Private Room 40. L (Sun only in summer) 12-2.30 D 6.30-9.30. Set L (winter only) £6.95 (Sun £13.50 all year) Set D £12.95/£16.50.*

SCOURIE	Eddrachilles Hotel	60%	£72

Tel 01971 502080   Fax 01971 502477   Map 2 B2   **H**
Badcall Bay Scourie Highland IV27 4TH

This 200-year-old hotel enjoys a setting of outstanding peace and rugged beauty in a 320-acre estate at the head of Badcall Bay. Handa Island bird sanctuary is a few miles to the north, and boat trips can be made from nearby Tarbet. To the south are Britain's highest waterfalls, of Eas-coul-Aluin. It's also a great base for walking, exploring, climbing and fishing and packed lunches are available for serious outdoor types. Seven of the neatly-kept bedrooms have shower/WC only. No children under 3. No dogs. *Rooms 11. Garden, fishing, boat hire. Closed Nov-mid Mar. Access, Visa.*

SCOURIE	Scourie Hotel	60%	£72

Tel 01971 502396   Fax 01971 502423   Map 2 B2   **H**
Scourie Highland IV27 4SX

Built by the second Duke of Sutherland as a coaching inn, this is now a fishing hotel par excellence. Brown trout, sea trout and salmon are all to be found in the 50 hotel-controlled beats in the 25,000 acres of grounds, and boats can be supplied for many of the beats. Tackle and packed lunches are available. Tales swapped in the lounges and cocktail bar are naturally fairly fishy. Bedrooms, including two garden suites, are modern and well kept, with fitted furniture and good-sized bathrooms (two rooms are without en-suite facilities). There are no TVs, but the views from the windows are very watchable. Children under 16 stay free in parents' room, being charged only for meals as taken. *Rooms 20. Garden, game fishing. Closed 15 Oct-1 Apr. Access, Amex, Diners, Visa.*

SELKIRK	Philipburn House	60%	£97

Tel 01750 20747   Fax 01750 21690   Map 4 C1   **H**
Linglie Road Selkirk Borders TD7 5LS

Set back from the A707/A708 junction, a mile from the town centre on the Peebles road, this extended 18th-century house has been turned into a delightful family hotel with a Tyrolean-style interior. The Hill family, owners since 1971, cater for all kinds of visitors – business, fishing, tourist, family – and friendly hospitality is their watchword. Bedrooms – in the house, by the pool or in the 'log cabin' – feature pine, pretty fabrics and a host of extras. Parents will appreciate the privacy provided by many separate but connecting children's rooms. *Rooms 16. Garden, outdoor swimming pool, games room, children's playground. Access, Visa.*

SKEABOST BRIDGE	Skeabost House	60%	£92

Tel 01470 532202   Fax 01470 532454   Map 2 A3   **H**
Skeabost Bridge by Portree Isle of Skye Highland IV51 9NP

Twelve acres of woodland and gardens surround a former hunting lodge on Loch Snizort. It's a comfortable place, with the same family owners since 1970, and relaxation is easy in the lounges, the flagstoned sun lounge, the 60-seat conservatory, the cosy bar and the billiard room. Pretty bedrooms include one with a four-poster and a few in the nearby Garden House. One is a large family room. The hotel owns eight miles of the River Snizort, which runs through the grounds, and has a boat on a nearby loch. *Rooms 26. Garden, golf (9-hole), putting, fishing, snooker. Closed 23 Oct-27 Mar. Access, Visa.*

SKELMORLIE   Manor Park   61%   £85

Tel & Fax 01475 520832   Map 3 B6   **H**
Skelmorlie nr Largs Strathclyde PA17 5HE

A 1840s' built hotel above the A78 coast road between Skelmorlie and Largs just a quarter of an hour from Greenock and the M8 motorway. There are spectacular views from the 15 acres of immaculately kept and landscaped grounds and from the Adam-style house – note the intricate coving, oak staircase and galleried landing. Nine bedrooms are in the main building, the rest in the nearby converted stables. The largest of several conference rooms can accommodate up to 150 delegates, the smallest was used by Churchill and Eisenhower when planning the D-Day landings. *Rooms 23. Garden. Access, Amex, Diners, Visa.*

SLEAT   Kinloch Lodge   67%   £130

Tel 01471 833214   Fax 01471 833277   Map 3 A4   **HR**
Sleat Isle of Skye Highland IV43 8QY

Kinloch Lodge is a white stone building at the head of Loch Na Dal in the south of the island. Built in 1680 as a farmhouse, it is now the home of Lord and Lady Macdonald where guests are made to feel like family friends. Its isolated position makes it a haven of peace and the views are truly outstanding. Two stylish drawing-rooms enjoy the spectacular setting and are adorned with ancestral portraits, fine antiques, porcelain pieces and each with a roaring fire provides a perfect spot for afternoon tea or a pre-dinner drink. Bedrooms, mostly rather small, are comfortable and quiet, with no phones or TVs to disturb the peace; prices vary to reflect their size, outlook and the time of year – the price quoted above is for a mid-range room in high season. Furniture is a mixture of antique and modern pieces and the two rooms not en suite have bathrooms across the corridor. Children by arrangement only. *Rooms 10. Garden, fishing. Closed 1 Dec-end Feb. Access, Amex, Visa.*

Dining Room   £75

♛ ⚜

Expert home cooking by Lady Macdonald and Peter Macpherson makes good use of excellent local ingredients and comes in hearty portions. A typical five-course dinner might begin with a choice between mushroom and cheese-filled herb profiteroles and tartare of fresh salmon followed by a soup, carrot and tomato perhaps, before the main decision between saddle of venison with a port and redcurrant sauce or baked fillet of cod with a julienne of vegetables and a creamy *sauce messine*. Finally a dark chocolate roulade or lemon *suédoise* with vanilla meringues before fresh fruit and cheese to finish. No smoking in the dining-rooms. Coffee with fudge is served in the drawing-rooms. Concise, carefully selected wine list with a good choice under £20. The hotel holds regular cookery demonstrations. *Seats 28. Parties 12. D at 8. Set D £25-35 (depending on the time of year).*

SOUTH QUEENSFERRY   Forth Bridges Hotel   61%   £116

Tel 0131-469 9955   Fax 0131-319 1733   Map 3 C5   **H**
South Queensferry Lothian EH30 9SF

A former Queen's Moat House, now owned by County Hotels, about five miles from Edinburgh Airport. Built in the 60s, the hotel boasts spectacular views of both Forth Bridges. Good leisure facilities. Conference/banqueting for up to 250. Children up to 16 stay free in parents' room. *Rooms 108. Garden, indoor swimming pool, gym, squash, sauna, spa bath, hair salon, snooker, coffee shop (9-6 summer only). Access, Amex, Diners, Visa.*

SPEAN BRIDGE   Old Station Restaurant   £45

Tel 01397 712535   Map 3 B4   **R**
Station Road Spean Bridge Highland PH34 4EP

As the name implies, a railway station where the former ticket office and waiting rooms that line the platform have been turned into a most appealing restaurant by Richard (in the kitchen) and Helen (front of house) Bunney. The sensibly short à la carte (about five dishes at each stage) nevertheless offers plenty of variety with mains ranging from a simple chargrilled Aberdeen Angus steak to grilled teriyaki salmon fillet, duck breast with apricot and lemon sauce, and always a vegetarian option. Notable among the starters is the soup of the day while puds might include home-made Amaretto liqueur ice cream along with a good sticky toffee pudding. *Seats 30. Parties 10. Private Room 12. L 12-2.30 (private parties of 8 or more only) D 6.30-9. Closed D Mon-Wed in winter, 25 Dec & 1 Jan. Access, Visa.* 🐂

STEWARTON   Chapeltoun House   71%   £99

Tel 01560 482696   Fax 01560 485100   Map 3 B6   **H**
Stewarton-Irvine Road (B769) Stewarton Strathclyde KA3 3ED

Chapeltown House was built at the turn of the century for a Glasgow merchant and his English bride and still retains many original features, the pale pink-washed walls and stone balustrades of the exterior highlighting its serene position amid 20 well-kept acres of gardens. The oak-panelled entrance hall, friezes, plasterwork and teak floors all add to the sense of occasion and, to its many regulars, of homecoming. Bedrooms (several refurbished this year) range in style and character from the super-king-size four-poster room, with bay windows to catch the early morning sun, to master and superior rooms, but all have thoughtful extras. Not really suitable for children under 12. *Rooms 8. Garden. Closed 1st 2 weeks Jan. Access, Amex, Visa.*

STORNOWAY   Cabarfeidh Hotel   64%   £88

Tel 01851 702604   Fax 01851 705572   Map 2 A2   **H**
Manor Park Stornoway Isle of Lewis Highland PA87 2EU

An early-70s hotel (the name means stag's head) with a rather faceless exterior belying the inviting interior, a brisk walk from the Ullapool ferry terminal on the largest of the Outer Hebrides islands. The Viking Bar (with a longship for a counter), a cocktail bar and a restaurant divided into three differently styled areas comprise the public rooms. Cheerful bedrooms, all en suite (children up to 14 stay free in parents' room). Banquets and conferences for up to 330/400. Spectacular scenery and an abundance of peace are major assets. *Rooms 47. Garden, croquet. Access, Amex, Diners, Visa.*

STRACHUR   Creggans Inn   61%   £98

Tel 01369 860279   Fax 01369 860637   Map 3 B5   **H**
Strachur Strathclyde PA27 8BX

Sir Fitzroy and Lady Maclean's white-painted inn stands amid magnificent scenery by Loch Fyne on the Road to the Isles. It's a great part of the world for fishing, walking and touring, after which a glass of the hotel's own Old MacPhunn ten-year-old vatted malt goes down well in either bar. There's a peaceful sitting-room and a large garden lounge, both with delightful views. Decor varies in the small but charming bedrooms, almost all of which have bathrooms en suite. Special winter breaks offer good value. *Rooms 21. Garden, fishing, games room. Access, Amex, Diners, Visa.*

STRANRAER   North West Castle   68%   £70

Tel 01776 704413   Fax 01776 702646   Map 4 A2   **H**
Stranraer Dumfries & Galloway DG9 8EH

Tastefully extended since being built in 1820, the hotel stands opposite the ferry port. It was once the home of the Arctic explorer Sir John Ross, whose name is commemorated in the panelled bar, and was the first hotel in the world to have its own indoor curling rink. Bedrooms include six suites, and many rooms have enough space for an extra bed or cots. Conference and banqueting facilities for 100/180; enquire about special arrangements for residents at two local golf courses and nearby squash courts. Children up to 5 stay for £5 in parents' room, 5-15s £10; children's holiday entertainment. Sister establishment to the *Cally Palace Hotel* in Gatehouse of Fleet and *Kirroughtree Hotel*, Newton Stewart. No dogs. *Rooms 71. Garden, indoor swimming pool, curling rink (Oct-Apr), sauna, sun beds, spa bath, keep-fit equipment, snooker, children's playroom, coffee shop (10am-11pm), shop. Access, Visa.* 🐂

We welcome bona fide complaints and recommendations on the tear-out pages at the back of the book for readers' comments. They are followed up by our professional team.

STRATHBLANE   Kirkhouse Inn   £73

Tel 01360 770621   Fax 01360 770896   Map 3 B5   **I**
Glasgow Road Strathblane Central G63 9AA

Substantial inn/hotel on the A81 just south of town at the foot of the Campsie Fell
(popular with hill walkers). Bedrooms are done out in a variety of pleasant colour
schemes, those at the back have 'woodchip walls' and most have either light or darkwood
units. All the usual hotel facilities are here (remote-control TV, trouser press, beverage
tray) plus a room service menu that runs to hot meals 24 hours a day. En-suite bathrooms
all have tubs. Downstairs choose between the cocktail bar with brown plush banquette
seating and the large public bar which, with its new tartan carpet, is less basic than its
designation might suggest but does come with pool table, fruit machine and juke box.
Friendly staff. *Rooms 15. Garden, beauty treatment. Access, Amex, Diners, Visa.*

STRONTIAN   Kilcamb Lodge Hotel   68%   £135*

Tel 01967 402257   Fax 01967 402041   Map 3 B4   **HR**
Strontian Argyll Highland PH36 4HY

Fronted by natural lawns leading down to the edge of Loch Sunart and surrounded by
the most glorious scenery in Scotland, Kilcamb Lodge is ideal for both walkers and those
just looking for peace and quiet. The age of the original stone building is not known but
the Victorians added a bit and so have the hospitable Blakeway family who have
renovated and refurbished with both good taste and comfort in mind. For the less
energetic there are plenty of books about and in one of the lounges there's usually
a communal jigsaw on the go. Bedrooms – four quite spacious, four rather less so – all
have dark stained pine furniture, quality beds, TVs and loch views but no telephones to
interrupt the idyll. Good bathrooms come with bathrobes and nice soft towels. Stay for
three nights or more and the reward, weather permitting, is a cruise on the hotel yacht
– Peter Blakeway is ex-RN. Good breakfasts come with freshly squeezed orange juice
and eggs from their own hens. No smoking in bedrooms. Two traditionally built self-
catering cottages in the grounds are particularly suitable for families. No smoking.
*Half-board terms. *Rooms 8. Garden, fishing. Closed Nov-late Mar. Access, Visa.*

Restaurant   £70

The daily-changing fixed-price dinner menu always follows the same pattern with
a choice of three starters (one fishy such as salmon fishcakes with red pepper sauce, one
meaty, chicken liver terrine with home-made chutney and mint salad perhaps, and one
vegetable), before a soup and then a meat or fish main dish – saddle of venison with red
cabbage and a port and juniper sauce and baked cod with herb crust and lobster sauce for
example. To finish there is a selection of puds, fresh fruit platter or a good selection of
Scottish cheeses. The kitchen is in the hands of mother-and-son team Ann and Peter
Blakeway whose cooking is careful, with clear flavours to the fore creating most
satisfactory results. An intelligently composed wine list has something for most tastes. It's
coded for sweetness (whites) and body (reds) and very few bottles breach the £20 barrier.
No smoking. *Seats 26. D only at 7.30. Set D £25 (4 courses).*

TALLADALE   Loch Maree Hotel   £80

Tel 01445 760288   Fax 01445 760241   Map 2 B3   **I**
Talladale by Achnasheen Highland IV22 2HL

A purpose-built fishing hotel beautifully situated on the banks of the loch between
Gairloch and Kinlochewe. The glorious outdoors is certainly a major attraction, and
inside things have changed dramatically from the former time-warp Victorian cosiness.
One twin room is equipped for disabled guests. The hotel owns eight boats (complete
with mandatory ghillies) for sea trout and salmon fishing on the loch; tackle and gifts
available in the hotel shop. *Rooms 30. Garden, fishing, boating. Access, Visa.*

TARBERT   Stonefield Castle   58%   £130*

Tel 01880 820836   Fax 01880 820929   Map 3 B6   **H**
Loch Fyne Tarbert Strathclyde PA29 6YJ

Sixty acres of grounds surround this 19th-century former baronial home and many of the
rooms command spectacular views over Loch Fyne. It's great walking country, and many
outdoor sporting activities are available in the vicinity. Day rooms are in comfortable,

traditional style, so too the bedrooms in the main house. Wing rooms are more ordinary but certainly adequate. Two miles north of Tarbert – look out for hotel signs.
*Half-board terms only. **Rooms 33.** *Garden, outdoor swimming pool (summer only), fishing, sauna, sun beds, snooker. Access, Amex, Diners, Visa.*

TOBERMORY   Tobermory Hotel   57%   £66

Tel 01688 302091   Fax 01688 302254   Map 3 A4   **H**
53 Main Street Tobermory Isle of Mull Strathclyde PA75 6NT

Ring the bell to gain access to this small, carefully maintained hotel on the waterfront of Tobermory Bay. Owners Martin and Kay Sutton put hospitality top of their list, and two cosy lounges furnished with floral sofas and easy chairs, well-chosen ornaments and pictures offer welcoming touches like magazines and fresh flowers. Compact bedrooms (all non-smoking) include some king-size beds. The bathrooms are well kept; nine are currently en suite. Two ground-floor rooms have been adapted to the needs of guests in wheelchairs. **Rooms 17.** *Access, Visa.*

TROON   Marine Highland Hotel   67%   £146

Tel 01292 314444   Fax 01292 316922   Map 4 A1   **H**
Crosbie Road Troon Strathclyde KA10 6HE

This handsome Victorian sandstone structure overlooks the 18th fairway of Royal Troon championship golf course. Accommodation options are standard, de luxe or top-of-the-range Ambassador suites. Since last year there has been a complete refurbishment of the lounge and 30 bedrooms plus a gym extension. Children up to 18 share parents' room free. Good conference facilities for up to 250. Leave the A77 and follow the B789 to Troon. Scottish Highland Hotels. **Rooms 72.** *Indoor swimming pool & children's splash pool, gym, squash, sauna, steam room, solarium, beauty salon, putting, snooker, news kiosk, brasserie (10am-midnight). Access, Amex, Diners, Visa.*

TROON   Piersland House   64%   £98

Tel 01292 314747   Fax 01292 315613   Map 4 A1   **H**
15 Craigend Road Troon Strathclyde KA10 6HD

Built in the 1890s for the grandson of Johnnie Walker (of whisky fame). From the reception, stairs lead up to a galleried landing with exposed roof timbers. Further pleasing architectural features are to be found in the bar/lounge, which boasts stone-mullioned windows, an embroidered frieze and a ribbed ceiling. Bedrooms are individually and prettily appointed; four cottage suites are situated next to the hotel. Banqueting and conference facilities can cater for 100+. The hotel stands opposite Royal Troon golf club, with upwards of a dozen more courses in the neighbourhood. **Rooms 23.** *Garden, putting. Access, Amex, Diners, Visa.*

TURNBERRY   Turnberry Hotel   84%   £210

Tel 01655 331000   Fax 01655 331706   Map 4 A2   **HR**
Turnberry Strathclyde KA26 9LT

When Turnberry opened in 1906 it became the world's first hotel and golf resort, and the country club and health spa keep it today in the forefront of sporting hotels. It is also established as a top-flight conference and banqueting venue (up to 150 delegates in the self-contained Turnberry Suite). The hotel overlooks the famous links of Ailsa and Arran, to the islands of that name and towards the Mull of Kintyre beyond. Day rooms combine comfort and splendour at a high level, and bedrooms, too, are notably stylish, with luxuriously equipped bathrooms. There are ten suites, with luxury apartments including four-posters and jacuzzis. The Clubhouse offers an informal setting for simple eating, from sandwiches and salads to the daily roast. The Bay at Turnberry offers health-conscious menus (closed for dinner between October and April) and there is a Halfway House by the 10th tee on the Ailsa Course. There are several other bars, including the

See over

Deck lounge above the spa. *Rooms 132. Garden, tennis, 2 18-hole championship golf courses, 12-hole pitch & putt, putting, indoor swimming pool, children's splash pool, gym, sauna, steam room, spa bath, solarium, beauty & hair salon, health spa, tennis, squash, snooker, Clubhouse restaurant (8am-7pm). Access, Amex, Diners, Visa.*

Restaurant   £130

The à la carte menu is strong on luxury items – caviar, foie gras, oysters, lobster, champagne-poached turbot, poussin filled with lobster mousse – while the fixed-price dinner menu has a daily roast along with dishes such as bresaola with parmesan flakes and black olive, tomato and lemon vinaigrette, 'cassoulette' of halibut, scampi and scallops with a cognac and lobster sauce, and risotto of woodland mushrooms. Sunday lunch comprises a glass of champagne, three courses, coffee and petits fours. Surprisingly for a hotel that must attract many international visitors from English-speaking overseas countries, the New World section on the wine list is minimal. On the other hand, there's an abundance of French classics, and even Switzerland is better represented. *Seats 180. Parties 10. Private Room 110. L (Sun only) 1-2.30 D 7.30-10. Set Sun L £20.50 (Sun £19.50) Set D £37.50.*

TWEEDSMUIR	Crook Inn	59%	£52

Tel 01899 880272   Fax 01899 880294   Map 4 C1   **H**
Tweedsmuir nr Biggar Borders ML12 6QN

Standing on the A701 Moffat-Edinburgh road and set in the ruggedly beautiful Tweed valley, the Crook is a good base for walking, climbing and touring holidays. Guests can also enjoy free fishing on 30 miles of the River Tweed. Burns wrote Willie Wastle's Wife in what is now the bar, and locally-born John Buchan set many of his novels in the area. Neat bedrooms are simple in their appointments, with no TVs or telephones. There are a few Art Deco features in the lounge and some of the bathrooms. The success of the glass-making centre in the former stable block has led to the subsequent creation of the Upper Tweed Heritage Centre. Light meals can be enjoyed in the garden. *Rooms 8. Garden, fishing, putting, pétanque. Access, Amex, Diners, Visa.*

UIG	Uig Hotel	59%	£86

Tel 01470 542205   Fax 01470 542308   Map 2 A3   **H**
Uig Isle of Skye Highland IV51 9YE

On a hillside at the north end of the island, this white-painted former coaching inn (a hotel since 1946) is handy for the ferry to Uist and Harris. You come here to enjoy the peace and solitude, the wonderful scenery, the walks and the wildlife. Day rooms are neat and homely, and provide fine sea views. Comfortable bedrooms with smart co-ordinated colour schemes include six in Sobhraig House, a converted steading next to the hotel. Self-catering apartments are available. Children under 12 can share their parents' room free. *Rooms 17. Garden, pony trekking. Closed mid Oct-Mar. Access, Amex, Diners, Visa.*

ULLAPOOL	Altnaharrie Inn	73%	£280*

Tel 01854 633230   Map 2 B2   **HR**
Ullapool Wester Ross Highland IV26 2SS

There is a timeless, magical quality about a journey to this passionately run former drover's cottage nestling in splendid isolation by the shores of Loch Broom. Fred Brown and Gunn Eriksen have not only created a place of pilgrimage, but almost unbelievably also manage to ensure that no matter if it is your first or fifteenth visit, it is still fresh, remarkable and of unfailing quality. *Mother Goose* has been pensioned off in favour of a smart, new launch that ferries customers and their baggage across from Ullapool (phone first to ascertain the time of the next crossing and which jetty to use depending on the tide), and willing staff are on hand to assist on the narrow jetty that leads to the delightfully pretty garden and Fred Brown's warm welcome at Altnaharrie. There are two main sitting-rooms, the smaller with log and peat fire by the entrance, a larger room upstairs, both models of restrained simplicity and elegance with hints of Gunn's Norwegian background and her passion for ceramics and textiles. Bedrooms, eight in all, share the same style and influences, those in separate cottages above the main house having a particular charm and benefiting most recently from Gunn's sense of colour and design. Elegant furniture, wonderfully comfortable beds and pristine linen are typical, as are books, fruit platters and the torch by the bedside table for when the generator is switched off at night. Flora abound, from a leaf adorning the seashell soap in sparkling bathrooms to a tiny flower on the napkin at breakfast, itself a star-worthy meal with beautifully prepared fruits, porridge, jams, breads and perfect eggs. Not a cheap experience but perfection such as this rightly carries a premium. No smoking anywhere. No children under 8. Private hotel car park in Ullapool. ★Half-board terms only. *Rooms 8. Garden. Closed Nov-Easter. Access, Amex, Visa.*

Restaurant ★ ★ ★ £150

Gunn Eriksen's approach to cooking is now the stuff of legend. Her almost obsessional zeal for exploring the unusual has given way to a calm, sure hand that unerringly seems to find the quintessential marriage of flavour, texture and colour. Dinner in the elegantly informal dining-room, with its myriad artistic touches and enchanting views of Loch Broom, is the closest thing most of us will get to a state of culinary ecstasy. The first indication of this experience is at the time of booking (essential as there are only 18 seats) when any dislikes, allergies etc are discussed. Then, when one has settled down to study the wine list before leaving a note of one's selection on the sitting-room desk, the evening's five-course dinner (no choice except at dessert stage) is carefully explained by Fred. Finally, at 8pm when all sit for dinner, the anticipation is matched by a wonderful performance from both the kitchen, where Gunn, invisible for most of the day, is creating her magic almost unaided, and from a small team of charming helpers assisting Fred with service. A typical menu might start with a warm salad of scallops on a bed of spinach with green lentils, morels and a champagne vinegar sauce, followed by an ethereally fragrant clear broth of crab with a vivid dribble of virgin olive oil, then a fillet of Sika (deer) with Spanish onions and green juniper berries, a single raviolo of mushroom and grapes and, a trademark, two sauces, one a reduction of the meat juices and burgundy, the other a light juniper cream. A remarkable choice of classic French, British and Norwegian cheeses precedes dessert (often all three are served) that could include a banana baked in a thin shell of pastry with a sauce of Cointreau, orange and cream or an impossibly rich chocolate cake with a soft runny centre and chocolate ice cream. With nowhere to drive to, you can afford to push the boat out here – the half bottle list itself is as good as most main lists! One slight drawback is the price of champagne (the cheapest is £19.20 per half bottle and a glass is £9), otherwise all tastes are catered for, and most wine-growing regions represented; good house selection. *Seats 18. D only at 8pm (Light lunch available to residents only). Set D £65.*

ULLAPOOL	Ceilidh Place	£100

Tel 01854 612103   Fax 01854 612886   Map 2 B2   **IR**
14 West Argyle Street Ullapool Wester Ross Highland IV26 2TY

Although we list Ceilidh Place as an Inn, it is in truth impossible to classify, being bookshop, arts centre, picture gallery, coffee shop, bar and hotel all created out of a row of whitewashed cottages one street back from the harbour side. Upstairs are 13 spotless bedrooms (three not en suite) simply but appealingly appointed, some with dark-stained fitted units, some with the odd antique and most with beamed ceilings. Dado-boarded bathrooms all have tubs with hand-held shower attachments. Telephones are standard, with TVs and beverage trays available on request. The first-floor residents' lounge with large windows on two sides is quite delightful. Families are welcome with cots provided free; extra beds are charged for. A separate Club House offers budget accommodation with bunk beds and communal showers and it is here that live entertainment – anything from jazz, folk or classical concerts to poetry readings – is to be found several nights a week in summer. *Rooms 13. Garden, bookshop. Closed two weeks Jan. Access, Amex, Diners, Visa.*

Restaurant £40

By day the coffee shop-cum-bar offers counter service of soups, baked potatoes, haddock and chips, chicken pie, nut roast, Bakewell tart, scones and the like. From early evening there's table service and a printed menu from which you can have just a single dish in the coffee shop or create a more formal meal in the conservatory area with its white-clothed tables. Mushroom and walnut paté with oatcakes, falafel with minty yoghurt dip, bouillabaisse, wild salmon poached in white wine, lemon and dill, beef stroganoff and casserole of local venison are just a sample of the wide variety of dishes on offer. There's a good vegetarian section too. Children can have half portions of most things and there are three high-chairs available, one an antique. *Seats 30. Open 9.30-9.30.*

UPHALL   Houstoun House   69%   £133

Tel 01506 853831   Fax 01506 854220   Map 3 C5   **H**
Uphall Lothian EH52 6JS

A classic Scottish Tower House is at the heart of this hotel set in 20 acres of mature gardens adjacent to the Uphall Golf Club, of which guests enjoy temporary membership. The vaulted bar, where a real fire burns most of the year, dates back to the 1500s. A new reception/lounge was being created in the summer of 1995 linking the main part of the building with bedrooms in the Steading (former stables); a couple more rooms are in the 16th-century Woman's House across a flagstoned courtyard. Bedrooms, generally spacious and furnished in traditional style, have benefited from some refurbishment (especially the bathrooms) in the last couple of years and come with extras like fresh fruit and bathrobes. As we go to press a new bedroom wing and function room, designed to match the surrounding buildings, should be complete. *Rooms 42. Garden. Access, Amex, Diners, Visa.*

WHITEBRIDGE   Knockie Lodge   71%   £90

Tel 01456 486276   Fax 01456 486389   Map 3 B4   **HR**
Whitebridge Highland IV1 2UP

Just 20 minutes from Fort Augustus but a world away from the tourist-beaten track, Knockie Lodge enjoys a glorious setting high above Loch Nan Lann. Built as a hunting lodge in 1789, it is immensely civilised, with a timelessly tranquil atmosphere nurtured by the warm hospitality of Ian and Brenda Milward, here since 1983. Peat and log fires warm the antique-filled hall and appealing morning room (where the honesty bar is to be found) with family photos and ornaments adding to the charm. Traditionally furnished bedrooms (some with antiques) are prettily decorated and boast fresh flowers, mineral water and lots of books. All have direct-dial phones but no radio or TV. No children under ten. The rate quoted above is for a Standard room; Superior rooms are £130, Master rooms £150 and there are a couple of singles at £50; also note that "Due to the remoteness of our situation we will always assume that guests will require dinner each night of their stay for which they will be charged accordingly unless we are advised to the contrary." *Rooms 10. Garden, fishing, sailing, snooker. Closed end Oct-end Apr. Access, Amex, Diners, Visa.*

Restaurant   £70

Chris Freeman's no-choice five-course dinners, served in a delightful panelled room, make good use of local supplies. A typical starter might be game and pork terrine or hot stuffed mushrooms in crispy batter with a tangy sauce before a soup course (cullen skink, Highland lentil). The main event might be a fillet of lamb en croute with mushroom and garlic stuffing and a Madeira sauce or some Scottish beef fillet wrapped in bacon and herbs with red wine sauce. Choice of two desserts – mincemeat roulade and orange crème brulée for example – before the cheeseboard and coffee round things off. No smoking. Bar lunches for residents only. *Seats 20. D at 8. Set D £26.*

We welcome bona fide complaints and recommendations on the tear-out pages at the back of the book for readers' comments. They are followed up by our professional team.

Wales

ABERCYNON   Llechwen Hall   £70

Tel 01443 742050   Fax 01443 742189   Map 9 C6   **I**
Abercynon nr Llanfabon Mid Glamorgan CF37 4HP

About a mile and a half from Abercynon (signposted from the A4054), Llechwen Hall is a 17th-century farmhouse, converted to a gentleman's residence in 1905, and to the present hotel in 1988. The name means "a place of shelter" or "refuge", and seems very appropriate, as the atmosphere is warm and welcoming. There are period pieces in both day rooms and bedrooms, one of which has a four-poster. A lively local trade adds welcoming warmth to the bars and restaurant and there are banqueting and conference facilities (for up to 80) in the Nelson suite. *Rooms 11. Garden. Access, Amex, Diners, Visa.*

ABERDOVEY   Penhelig Arms Hotel   £68

Tel 01654 767215   Fax 01654 767690   Map 8 C3   **IR**
Aberdovey Gwynedd LL35 0LT

Built in the early 18th century, this totally delightful black-and-white inn stands right on the A193 with unrivalled views across the Dyfi estuary to Ynyslas. Robert and Sally Hughes are the most attentive of hosts, ensuring every comfort in a relaxed atmosphere that makes guests immediately feel at home. All but a couple of the bedrooms enjoy the views; three 'superior' rooms have a little more space than the rest, plus easy chairs and balconies; what the others lack in space they make up in interior design and up-to-date comforts. Days start with a comprehensive Welsh breakfast. *Rooms 10. Terrace. Closed 25 & 26 Dec. Access, Visa.*

Restaurant   £55

Fish always features strongly on the evening menu, notably in the likes of salmon with lemon hollandaise or sea bass baked with fresh herbs with a green garlic sauce. Terrine of pork with Cumberland sauce, roast beef with roast potatoes and a béarnaise sauce, and pheasant cooked in burgundy with celery and shallots are other favourites, and farmhouse cheeses are an alternative to some good puds. Less formal lunches in the bar or restaurant, with a set menu on Sunday. Good-quality wines. *Seats 34. Parties 18. L 12.15-2 D 7-9.15. Set Sun L £12 Set D £18.50.*

ABERDOVEY   Plas Penhelig   62%   £80

Tel 01654 767676   Fax 01654 767783   Map 8 C3   **H**
Aberdovey Gwynedd LL35 0NA

A steep, twisting, drive leads from the A493 up to the house, whose seven acres of award-winning grounds include a walled kitchen garden. The views are splendid, whether over the gardens or out across the Dovey estuary. Inside, the feel is Edwardian in the oak-panelled hall and in the south-facing lounge, while bedrooms are more modern in aspect. The terrace is an agreeable spot for an alfresco drink. *Rooms 11. Garden, croquet, putting. Closed 23 Dec-end Feb. Access, Amex, Visa.*

ABERDOVEY   Trefeddian Hotel   60%   £70

Tel 01654 767213   Fax 01654 767777   Map 8 C3   **H**
Aberdovey Gwynedd LL35 0SB

In the Cave-Brown-Cave family for over 70 years, Trefeddian stands back from the A493, half a mile north of Aberdovey, with fine views across Cardigan Bay. Day rooms, which include refurbished lounges and bar, offer a choice of peace and quiet or conviviality. Neat, practical bedrooms include several with balconies. Eight sea-facing rooms have recently been upgraded. Self-catering accommodation is also available in a house, flat and bungalow. Family facilities include three family rooms and children's playroom and playground. *Rooms 46. Garden, indoor swimming pool, children's splash pool, tennis, pitch & putt, solarium, games room, table tennis, pool table, snooker. Closed 3 Jan-1 Mar. Access, Visa.*

ABERGAVENNY   Llanwenarth Arms Hotel   £59

Tel 01873 810550   Fax 01873 811880   Map 9 D5   **I**
Brecon Road Abergavenny Gwent NP8 1EP

A refurbished roadside inn on the A40 standing on an escarpment above the Usk valley between Abergavenny and Crickhowell. Residents enjoy the use of their own lounge and a Victorian-style conservatory furnished with comfortable cane furniture. Bedrooms, approached by way of a sheltered courtyard, are attractively furnished and immaculately kept, each one enjoying its fair share of the view across to Sugar Loaf mountain. Good bar snacks. No dogs. *Rooms 18. Garden. Access, Amex, Diners, Visa.*

ABERGAVENNY	Walnut Tree Inn	★	£80

Tel 01873 852797   Fax 01873 859764   Map 9 D5   **R**
Llandewi Skirrid Abergavenny Gwent NP7 8AW

Three miles north-east of Abergavenny on the B4521 stands this delightful restaurant, which was once a coaching inn for scholars seeking the spires of Oxford. Ann and Franco Taruschio have been spreading their culinary gospel since 1963 and what started as an inn with three tables is now a restaurant of literally worldwide repute. Back in the 60s Franco was single-handedly responsible for introducing such previously unheard of things as bresaola to the Principality; today his market-driven menus (handwritten in unpretentious style) are still abreast of the times with dishes such as goujonettes of sole with Thai dip, roast duck with kumquats, panaché of fish with balsamic vinaigrette and escalope of salmon with rhubarb and ginger sharing the carte with crostini of peppers with home-made Italian sausage, venison pie, *vincigrassi masceratese* (an 18th-century recipe involving pasta with porcini mushrooms, truffles and parma ham), brodetta (a mixed fish casserole) and roast partridge with crostone and rocket. Side dishes might include parsnip chips, purple sprouting broccoli and rocket salad. Desserts are no less enticing with Toulouse chestnut pudding, fresh strawberry and mascarpone gratinée and home-made ices such as whinberry ice cream, cassata and elderflower sorbet among some two dozen choices. A quite marvellous wine list naturally features a fantastic Italian section, but not to the detriment of the rest of the world. The list is prepared with the assistance of Bill Baker of Reid Wines, acknowledged in the trade as one of the best and most helpful in the business. At lunchtime meals are only served in the 60-seat rustic bistro/bar. In the evening the dining-room proper is opened, with its brown linen napery. Space is at a premium, so booking is essential. *Seats 46. L 12.15-3.15 D 7.15-10.15. Closed Sun & Mon, 4 days Christmas & 2 weeks Feb (Check dates). No credit cards.*

ABERKENFIG	New Garden		£35

Tel 01656 724361   Map 9 C6   **R**
40 Pandy Road Aberkenfig nr Bridgend Mid Glamorgan CF32 9PP

Stylishly modern behind an unassuming frontage, New Garden offers a mainly Cantonese menu that keeps the crowds rolling in. Stuffed crab claws, black bean mussels or honey-roast spare ribs could precede soup, then perhaps grilled fish with crabmeat sauce, a filling hot pot dish or one of a dozen ways with duck. Various set meals for 2 or more. *Seats 160. L 12-2 D 5.30-12. Closed L Sun, 3 days Christmas. Set meals from £11.50. Access, Amex, Diners, Visa.*

ABERSOCH	Porth Tocyn Hotel	69%	£94

Tel 01758 713303   Fax 01758 713538   Map 8 B3   **HR**
Bwlchtocyn Abersoch Gwynedd LL53 7BU

Run in commendable style since 1948 by the Fletcher Brewer family, the hotel has gained a reputation for attentive hospitality. Once a row of lead-miners' cottages, it stands high above Cardigan Bay; it's about 2½ miles south of Abersoch, through the hamlets of Sarn Bach and Bwlchtocyn. The chintzy lounges contribute just the right degree of homeliness. Bedrooms, though generally small, are individually furnished in a similar style, many with restful sea views (these rooms attract a small supplement), all with private bathrooms and showers. Families with children are well catered for (children stay free in parents' room) – ask for their 'useful information for families' info sheet which sets out their aims and expectations. Flexibility is the key here. *Rooms 17. Garden, tennis, indoor playroom. Closed mid Nov-week before Easter. Access, Visa.*

Restaurant   £60

The focal point of Louise Fletcher Brewer's self-styled "dinner party cooking" is her short-choice two- or five-course dinner menu that is changed completely each day. In practice, the style is less 'cordon bleu' than one might expect, with sautéed crab cakes

See over

with chive and crab sauce, grilled fruit kebabs with ginger syrup, roast leg of Welsh lamb with mushroom strudel and red wine sauce, poached chicken supremes with apricot and lime sauce, pan-fried sea bass and trout fillets with a lobster, mussel and spinach cream all typical dishes. There's always an inter-course fresh soup (perhaps celery and sweet pea or watercress and potato) and the nursery puddings are a popular dessert, especially at the all-you-can-eat hot and cold buffet on Sundays. Welsh and other cheeses and coffee with home-made petits fours. There's a fair wine list, though only the house selections have tasting notes. £21 for a decent house champagne is excellent value. Lunch is casual, maybe alfresco by the pool. High tea for youngsters is 5-6pm. *Seats 50. Parties 20. L 12.30-2 D 7.30-9.30. Set L (Sun) £15.50 Set D £19/£25.50.*

ABERSOCH	Riverside Hotel	59%	£70

Tel 01758 712419   Fax 01758 712671   Map 8 B3   **H**
Abersoch Gwynedd LL53 7HW

John and Wendy Bakewell, here since 1967, say that like monks they took a solemn vow of hospitality when they made the move from farming all that time ago. They have remained true to their word, as the many returning visitors will attest. Family-run and family-friendly, the hotel is well situated on the Lleyn peninsula. The River Soch actually flows next to the garden. Bedrooms are neat, modern and functional. Reduced rates for children with many facilities supplied including cots, high-chairs, a laundry room and high tea served at 5.30pm. No dogs. *Rooms 12. Garden, indoor swimming pool (open Apr-end of Sept). Closed mid Nov-Apr. Access, Amex, Diners, Visa.*

ABERYSTWYTH	Conrah Country Hotel	63%	£93

Tel 01970 617941   Fax 01970 624546   Map 9 B4   **H**
Chancery Aberystwyth Dyfed SY23 4DF

Tucked away at the end of a long drive lined by rhododendrons, three miles south of Aberystwyth, set in 22 acres of grounds and woods, the Conrah puts peace, friendliness and fine views high on the agenda, and the three drawing rooms provide them in abundance. 11 of the bedrooms are in the main house, the rest around a courtyard. No children under 5 (or dogs). *Rooms 20. Garden, croquet, indoor swimming pool, sauna, table tennis. Closed 1 week Christmas. Access, Amex, Diners, Visa.*

BARRY	Bunbury's		£50

Tel 01446 732075   Map 9 C6   **R**
14 High Street Barry South Glamorgan CF6 8EA

30s' sounds and setting behind the Barry Hotel. The main menu covers a good range of dishes, in individual and often fairly adventurous style. Cheese-topped savoury stuffed tomatoes and chicken breast filled with mushrooms set on a bed of lentils are two favourites. There's also a lunchtime blackboard menu with dishes priced at around £4. *Seats 32. L 10.30-2.30 D 7.30-10 (Sat to 10.30). Closed Sun, Mon & Bank Holidays. Open Tues for bookings only. Access, Visa.*

BARRY	Mount Sorrel Hotel	59%	£90

Tel 01446 740069   Fax 01446 746600   Map 9 C6   **H**
Porthkerry Road Barry South Glamorgan CF62 7XY

Converted from two Victorian houses some 30 years ago, with more recent additions for extra accommodation, meeting rooms (conferences for up to 150) and leisure facilities. Comfortable day rooms (named after Welsh castles), very acceptable bedrooms (children up to 16 stay free when sharing with parents); two suites have interconnecting rooms and six other rooms are suitable for families. *Rooms 43. Indoor swimming pool, keep-fit equipment, sauna. Access, Amex, Diners, Visa.*

BEAUMARIS	Bulkeley Arms	59%	£67

Tel 01248 810415   Fax 01248 810146   Map 8 B1   **H**
Castle Street Beaumaris Anglesey Gwynedd LL58 8AW

A sturdy Georgian building opposite the pier with splendid views across the Menai Straits to Snowdonia. Bedrooms include some suites and several family rooms. Children up to 12 stay free in parents' room. Banquets/conferences for 130/200; plenty of parking. *Rooms 42. Garden, beauty salon, news kiosk, night club. Access, Amex, Visa.*

BEDDGELERT	Royal Goat Hotel	60%	£68

Tel 0176 686224   Fax 0176 686422   Map 8 B2   **H**
Beddgelert Gwynedd LL55 4YE

The Roberts family play host to the regulars who come for Snowdonia's fishing, walking and climbing. Beyond the white-painted facade an entrance hall/reception has heavily carved furniture and brass ornaments, more of which feature in the comfortable residents-only bar. Some of the bedrooms boast four-posters and ten are reserved for non-smokers. Children up to ten stay free in parents' room. *Rooms 34. Garden, fishing. Access, Amex, Diners, Visa.*

BETWS-Y-COED	Royal Oak	59%	£74

Tel 01690 710219   Fax 01690 710603   Map 8 C2   **H**
Holyhead Road Betws-y-Coed Gwynedd LL24 0AY

A centrally located solid stone edifice across from the River Llugwy with a traditional and welcoming air in reception and bar. Bedrooms have a restful decor and simple modern furniture; six annexe rooms with glossy laminated furniture with eye-catching bedheads. No dogs. *Rooms 27. Garden, coffee shop (7.30am-10pm). Access, Amex, Diners, Visa.*

BONTDDU	Bontddu Hall	62%	£90

Tel 01341 430661   Fax 01341 430284   Map 8 C3   **H**
Bontddu nr Dolgellau Gwynedd LL40 2SU

One of the main attractions at Michael and Margaretta Ball's unspoilt Victorian Gothic country mansion is, quite simply, peace and quiet, though its setting in Snowdonia means there's also plenty of activity in the area for those so desiring – golf, hill walking, pony trekking, sea fishing, the narrow gauge railway, gold mining. For relaxation there are splendid, elegant, period day rooms from which to enjoy the stunning views. Bedrooms, the majority also offering fine views over the Mawddach estuary, include a four-poster room and one with a spa bath. Six lodge suites are in the hotel grounds. No children under 3, but up-to-12s stay free in parents' room. *Rooms 20. Garden. Closed Nov-Mar. Access, Amex, Diners, Visa.*

BRECHFA	Ty Mawr		£60

Tel 01267 202332   Fax 01267 202437   Map 9 B5   **RR**
Brechfa nr Carmarthen Dyfed SA32 7RA

Tiny Brechfa village stands by the Marlais river bridge below the 1200-year-old forest which covers its steep valley. Once part of the managed estate with a history traceable back at least to early Elizabethan times, Ty Mawr ("The Big House") also has a big heart, personified in Dick and Beryl Tudhope's warm hospitality. Their philosophy of "simplicity with style" is evidenced both by the restaurant's gleaming and immaculately restored interior and in the style and quality of Beryl's food. At dinner the house speciality is her hat-shaped dominicans (a twice-baked cheese soufflé). Aubergine, mushroom and coriander paté and herb pancakes filled with cockles, bacon and laverbread exhibit an assured range of skills with a leaning deliberately away from undue fussiness. Noisettes of Welsh lamb with a creamy garlic and haricot bean sauce and breast of duck roasted with honey, orange and thyme show the sound classical basis of the cooking. Dark chocolate and almond slice with black cherry sauce, pear and gingerbread pudding or a plate of Welsh and English cheese for fine finishing. The 3-course dinner, including coffee and sweetmeats, is priced according to choice of main course. Booking is essential. *Seats 35. Parties 10. Private Room 24. D only 7-9.30. Closed last 2 weeks Jan, last week Dec. Access, Amex, Visa.*

Rooms   £76

The five cottagey bedrooms, all with private facilities, have varnished pine furniture and pretty, floral duvets. There are no phones or radios in the rooms nor is there a TV on the premises. Quiet children are welcome overnight. A conference room accommodates 20.

Consult the blue pages for summary tables and lists of recommended establishments.

CAPEL COCH   Tre-Ysgawen Hall   76%   £110

Tel 01248 750750   Fax 01248 750035   Map 8 B1   **HR**
Capel Coch nr Llangefni Anglesey Gwynedd LL77 7UR

A long tree-lined drive off the B5111, about five miles north of Llangefni, leads to this substantial Victorian stone mansion. Handsomely restored by Pat Craighead, it has elegantly furnished high-ceilinged public rooms, all of which lead off a spacious galleried central hall with skylight high above. Bedrooms, all individually decorated in considerable style, vary in size from ample to huge, the largest having high-quality mahogany furniture, the others a variety of antique pieces. Carpeted bathrooms, all with towelling robes and good toiletries, also vary from large with spa bath and bidet to some rather smaller with deep burgundy suites and limited shelf space. Decent breakfasts make a good start to the day. Room service is 24hrs and luggage porterage is always offered. Conference/banqueting facilities for up to 150/120. *Rooms 20. Garden, kennels. Access, Amex, Diners, Visa.*

Restaurant   £80

The main dining-room is a large conservatory-like extension jutting out into the garden; when less busy a smaller, more cosy room is used. Chicken liver parfait layered with foie gras on Cumberland sauce with brioche toast; wild mushroom mousse in puff pastry; roast boneless quail stuffed with blue cheese mousse; ravioli of lobster and sole with warm sherry vinaigrette; loin of Welsh lamb coated in mint mousse and wrapped in spinach on a potato and onion bhajee with a mild curry sauce; chocolate soufflé in a sweet pastry case with Grand Marnier ice cream typify the freshly prepared, soundly cooked dishes to be found on the à la carte (dinner only) and short table d'hote menus. Pleasant, friendly service. *Seats 64. Parties 12. Private Room 30. L 12-2.30 D 7-9. Closed Jan. Set L £14 Set D £19.95.*

CARDIFF   Angel Hotel   64%   £111

Tel 01222 232633   Fax 01222 396212   Map 9 D6   **H**
Castle Street Cardiff South Glamorgan CF1 2QZ

Between the Castle and Arms Park rugby stadium, the distinctive Angel retains some of its individual, 100-year-old character. Bedrooms are generally roomy, though both housekeeping and maintenance need attention, and there are several function rooms catering for up to 300 theatre-style in the galleried Dragon Suite (parking for 70). 24hr room service. Children under 16 share parents' room free. Now owned by Paramount Hotels, who will no doubt make improvements. *Rooms 91. Gym, sauna, solarium, beauty salon, snooker. Access, Amex, Diners, Visa.*

CARDIFF   Armless Dragon   £50

Tel 01222 382357   Map 9 D6   **R**
97 Wyeverne Road Cathays Cardiff South Glamorgan CF2 4BG

A popular bistro whose monthly à la carte is supplemented by light lunch menus of two or three courses plus tea or coffee. Vegetable soup, laverbread with mushrooms, escabeche with mango and tamarind and crab soup with lemon grass are typical starters, followed by a main course of fish (poached, grilled, fried or in a sauce) or meat – chicken with leeks and bacon, perhaps, or a winter casserole with duck, lamb, sausage, beef and beans. There's always a choice for vegetarians. *Seats 45. L 12.15-2.15 D 7-10.15. Closed L Sat, all Sun & Mon, 1 week Christmas. Set L £7.90/£9.90.*

CARDIFF   Cardiff International   67%   £103

Tel 01222 341441   Fax 01222 223742   Map 9 D6   **H**
Mary Ann Street Cardiff South Glamorgan CF1 2EQ

A striking modern hotel opposite Cardiff International Arena and next to the National ice rink. Victorian brick and cast iron are cleverly matched, and an arcade-style interior echoes the architecture of Cardiff's markets. Bedrooms, all twin or double-bedded, include two floors of Executive standard; eight rooms are equipped for the disabled and there's a ramp at the main entrance. Smart and keen staff. Children up to 12 are accommodated free in their parents' room. Banqueting/conference facilities for 40. 24hr room service. Free, covered parking for up to 55 cars; car rental outlet on site. No dogs. *Rooms 143. Access, Amex, Diners, Visa.*

| CARDIFF | **Cardiff Marriott Hotel** | 68% | £116 |

Tel 01222 399944   Fax 01222 395578   Map 9 D6   **H**
Mill Lane Cardiff South Glamorgan CF1 1EZ

A stylish city-centre hotel especially convenient for St David's Hall, the national rugby stadium and the central railway station. Modish decor of much steel and glass incorporates a view of the indoor pool and leisure areas from the spacious open-plan lounge. Large American-configuration bedrooms (with two double beds in all twin rooms) provide comfortable easy chairs and plenty of well-lit work space, and include non-smoking (half the rooms) and Executive rooms. Children up to 18 free in parents' room. Ample free parking. Conference and banqueting facilities for 300. *Rooms 182. Indoor swimming pool, gym, squash, sauna, spa bath, solarium, beauty salon. Access, Amex, Diners, Visa.*

| CARDIFF | **Copthorne Hotel** | 70% | £122 |

Tel 01222 599100   Fax 01222 599080   Map 9 D6   **H**
Culverhouse Cross Cardiff South Glamorgan CF5 6XJ

Leave the M4 at junction 33 to reach this very modern five-storey hotel near the HTV studios. Lots of wood panelling and rich autumnal colour schemes predominate in appealing public areas, some of which overlook the hotel's own small lake. All the good-sized bedrooms are well laid out, with large desks (to which the phone is easily movable) and comfortable armchairs in addition to breakfast table and proper armchair. Good bathrooms feature polished red-granite vanitory units. Rooms on the Connoisseur Floor get extras like bathrobes and slippers plus use of an Executive lounge with free soft drinks and Continental breakfast. Two rooms are equipped for disabled guests. Children up to 15 stay free in parents' room. Banqueting/conference facilities for 200/300; parking for 225 cars. *Rooms 135. Indoor swimming pool, gym, sauna, spa bath, steam room, hairdresser. Access, Amex, Diners, Visa.*

| CARDIFF | **Forte Posthouse Cardiff** | 63% | £72 |

Tel 01222 731212   Fax 01222 549147   Map 9 D6   **H**
Pentwyn Road Cardiff South Glamorgan CF2 7XA

Modern hotel near Junction 29 of the M4 (take A48M). Conference facilities (up to 140) with ample parking. *Rooms 142. Garden, indoor swimming pool, gym, sauna, steam room, spa bath, solarium. Access, Amex, Diners, Visa.*

| CARDIFF | **Forte Posthouse Cardiff City** | 69% | £86 |

Tel 01222 388681   Fax 01222 371495   Map 9 D6   **H**
Castle Street Cardiff South Glamorgan CF1 2XB

City-centre hotel (formerly the Forte Crest) located between the River Taff and Arms Park. Children up to 16 stay free in parents' room. Conferences up to 180. Parking for 150 cars. *Rooms 155. Snooker. Access, Amex, Diners, Visa.*

| CARDIFF | **Moat House** | 70% | £94 |

Tel 01222 732520   Fax 01222 549092   Map 9 D6   **H**
Circle Way East Llanederyn Cardiff South Glamorgan CF3 7XF

Travelling west on the M4, leave at Junction 29 and take the A48(M). Heading east from West Wales, take the A470 at Junction 32 to arrive at this Moat House, set in its own grounds east of Cardiff. It's smart, comfortable and practical behind its unexciting modern exterior. Day rooms are in open plan, providing plenty of space in which to unwind. The conference complex (for up to 320 delegates) is on the first floor. Good-sized bedrooms, with extra touches of luxury plus evening maid service in Executive rooms. The most recent addition is an in-house pub The Daff & Leek. *Rooms 132. Indoor swimming pool, keep-fit equipment, spa bath, sauna, solarium, children's playground. Access, Amex, Diners, Visa.*

Many hotels offer reduced rates for weekend or out-of-season bookings. Always ask about special deals.

CARDIFF   Le Monde   £40

Tel 01222 387376   Map 9 D6   R
60 St Mary Street Cardiff South Glamorgan

One of a trio of dark, intimate restaurants-cum-wine bars, this one appeals primarily to fish-eaters with a wide array of shell, sea and freshwater fish. Its siblings are *La Brasserie* (01222 372164) specialising in grilled meats and seasonal game and offering a £5 set lunch, and *Champers* (01222 373363) with a Spanish slant to both decor, menu and wine list – over 100 Riojas! *Champers* is also open Sunday evening to 12.15am and seats 150. *Seats 180. L 12-2.30 D 7-12.15. Closed Sun, 25 & 26 Dec. Access, Amex, Diners, Visa.*

CARDIFF   Park Hotel   70%   £116

Tel 01222 383471   Fax 01222 399309   Map 9 D6   H
Park Place Cardiff South Glamorgan CF1 3UD

The Park's impressive stone-clad facade is a striking landmark on Cardiff's pedestrianised Queen Street and today's lack of traffic is a bonus for those occupying the best, front-facing bedrooms. All the bedrooms – singles, twins/doubles and top-of-the-range studios – have been refurbished, and attention has now turned to the public rooms, notably the reception area, the main restaurant (to be enlarged) and a new public bar. The lounge and residents' bar keep their traditional atmosphere. There are several conference and function suites, the largest accommodating 250. As we went to press there were plans to build a 22-room 'ladies' wing'. Thistle & Mount Charlotte. *Rooms 119.* *Access, Amex, Diners, Visa.*

CARMARTHEN   Ivy Bush Royal   59%   £75

Tel 01267 235111   Fax 01267 234914   Map 9 B5   H
Spilman Street Carmarthen Dyfed SA31 1LG

Once a favoured retreat of Lord Nelson and Lady Hamilton, today a Forte hotel on the West Wales heritage trail, popular with coach tours and conferences (max 250). Note the stained glass window in the lounge commemorating the formation of the first Circle of Bards. Children up to 16 stay free in parents' room. *Rooms 75. Garden. Access, Amex, Diners, Visa.*

CHEPSTOW   Castle View Hotel   £61

Tel 01291 620349   Fax 01291 627397   Map 9 D6   I
16 Bridge Street Chepstow Gwent NP6 5EZ

This small hotel was built in the 17th century as a private residence, perhaps with stones from neighbouring Chepstow Castle. Ivy-covered, and genuinely welcoming, it's immaculately kept by Martin and Vicky Cardale. Original walls and timbers may still be seen, both in the public area and in some bedrooms. One room, with its own lounge and sleeping up to four, is in a small cottage next door and there are two spacious family rooms overlooking the garden. Good snacks in the bar. *Rooms 13. Garden.* *Closed 1st 2 weeks Jan. Access, Amex, Diners, Visa.*

CHEPSTOW   St Pierre Hotel   70%   £123

Tel 01291 625261   Fax 01291 629975   Map 9 D6   H
St Pierre Park Chepstow Gwent NP6 6YA

St Pierre enjoys an enviable reputation for its golfing (two 18-hole courses) and extensive recreational facilities set in 400 acres of mature parkland just two miles from the Severn Bridge (leave the M4 at J22 and take the A48 towards Newport). The 14th-century mansion at the hotel's heart includes a spacious and well-lit foyer and reception lounge, beyond which you can relax in a fine oak-panelled bar and lounge overlooking the final greens. Access for banqueting, conferences (for up to 220) and ever-present golf societies is kept sensibly apart, through the Trophy Bar. Poolside grill and sports bar and the self-contained leisure centre are interconnected. A varied choice of bedrooms ranges from ground-floor courtyard suites and mansion bedrooms overlooking the park to the dozen detached lodges, with from three to six bedrooms, in St Pierre's Lakeland Village, which is much favoured for golf or house parties and family get-togethers. Public areas and bedrooms have both benefited from a recent refurbishment programme. Children up to 16 years are accommodated free in parents' room. Country Club Resorts Group. *Rooms 141.* *Garden, croquet, tennis, golf (2x18), indoor swimming pool, gym, squash, sauna, steam room, spa bath, solarium, bowls, children's outdoor playground, snooker, beauty salon.* *Access, Amex, Diners, Visa.*

CHIRK	Starlings Castle	£60

Tel & Fax 01691 718464   Map 8 D2   **RR**
Bronygarth Chirk nr Oswestry Clwyd SY10 7NU

The address is of little help in finding the Pitts' 17th-century sandstone farmhouse in its isolated position high up on the Welsh side of the border not far from Offa's Dyke; best ask for directions – they will happily fax you a map. Once found, the reward is a delightfully civilised, slightly rustic, away-from-it-all hideaway with the bonus of Anthony Pitt's highly accomplished cooking. The menu, with five or so choices at each stage, changes frequently with dishes that are at the same time sophisticated and unpretentious: pork, pigeon and pistachio terrine with paw paw chutney; langoustines with a coriander and chili sauce; baked hake with an olive and caper vinaigrette; grilled maize-fed chicken with grilled Provençal vegetables and aïoli. Puds like mango and rhubarb fool, tarte au citron and hot chocolate soufflé or a selection of Welsh and Borders farmhouse cheeses. Fair prices and many misspellings on the wine list. The dining-room is in a converted barn with rough stone walls, flagstone floor and wood-burning stove; another such stove warms a homely bar/lounge. Ask about their occasional special evenings which might be anything from a Thai Feast or Goanese Night to a medieval banquet or Salsa Night with live music and dancing. *Seats 65. Private Room 50. L (Sun only) 12-2.30 D 7.30-10. Access, Amex, Diners, Visa.*

Rooms   £58
Antique-furnished bedrooms come with non-remote TVs, beverage kits and comforts like thick duvets, hot water bottles and collections of books. Eight rooms share two bathrooms (silk dressing gowns are provided for the trip) while two rooms have en-suite facilities. Families welcome; high-chairs, cots and Z-beds provided. Garden.

CLYDACH	The Drum and Monkey	£50

Tel 01873 831980   Map 9 D5   **R**
Clydach Blackrock Abergavenny Gwent NP7 0LW

Skilful conversion of a derelict pub alongside the A465 has created a refined restaurant and lounge bar whose views of Clydach Gorge are superb. Jon West's cooking skills are to the fore throughout a varied menu that might include rillettes of duck with pistachio nuts and onion marmalade, a filo basket of chicken in tikka spices with a cucumber and mint raita and Cajun seasoned pork tenderloin with creamed parsnip and wholegrain mustard sauce alongside lamb's liver with bubble and squeak, braised lamb shank with roast vegetables and steaks. Lighter bar snacks daily; early evening menu £12.45 for three courses. Check directions when booking. *Seats 50. Parties 14. L 12-2 D 6-9.30 (Sun 7-9). Set Sun L £8.95/£10.95 Set D (till 7.30) £12.45. No credit cards.*

COLWYN BAY	Café Niçoise	£45

Tel 01492 531555   Map 8 C1   **R**
124 Abergele Road Colwyn Bay Clwyd LL29 7PS

Traditional and modern French cooking in Carl and Lynne Swift's romantic setting with French background music. Carl's specialities include roast saddle of Anglesey hare with wild mushrooms and celeriac, and roast monkfish with basil and Provençal vegetables. It is not surprising to find salade niçoise among the regular items. French and Welsh cheeses. Good-value, three-course table d'hote offers a choice of around four dishes at each stage. *Seats 32. L 12-2 D 7-10. Closed L Mon-Wed, all Sun, 1 week June, 3 days Christmas. Set meals £10.75/£12.95 (not D Fri & Sat). Access, Amex, Visa.*

COLWYN BAY	Colwyn Bay Hotel	61%	£53

Tel 01492 516555   Fax 01492 515565   Map 8 C1   **H**
Penmaenhead Colwyn Bay Clwyd LL29 9LD

All the bedrooms enjoy sea views at this distinctive hotel which stands on a clifftop above Colwyn Bay. Children up to 12 stay free in parents' room. Conference facilities for up to 200 delegates. *Rooms 43. Access, Amex, Diners, Visa.*

Set menu prices may not always include service or wine.

CONWY   Sychnant Pass Hotel   60%   £60

Tel 01492 596868   Fax 01492 870009   Map 8 C1   **H**
Sychnant Pass Road Conwy Gwynedd LL32 8BJ

Self-styled as "a little bit of Switzerland in Wales", the three acres of grounds (just within
the Snowdonia National Park) around this substantial white-pebbledash house include
a stream, a pond and woods. It's lovely walking country, but when the weather's not so
kind the lounge and bar are good places to relax. Fine views can be enjoyed from the
bedrooms, the best and largest of which are those in the original part of the house, where
furnishings are traditional; other rooms have modern units. One ground-floor room is
adapted for disabled guests. The Conwy Tunnel considerably eases access to this pleasant
location. Children up to 12 stay free in parents' room. Banqueting/conferencing for 40.
Rooms 13. Garden, sauna, spa bath. Access, Amex, Diners, Visa.

COYCHURCH   Coed-y-Mwstwr Hotel   70%   £140

Tel 01656 860621   Fax 01656 863122   Map 9 C6   **H**
Coychurch nr Bridgend Mid Glamorgan CF35 6AF

High above the Vale of Glamorgan, the "whispering trees" of this Victorian hotel's name
are easily heard among the 17 acres of ancient woodland in which Coed-y-Mwstwr
stands, one of the most attractively positioned country mansions in South Wales. True to
its Victorian origins, decor and furnishings are a blend of homely charm and elegant
period style: private suites and function rooms have high ceilings, chandeliers, oak
panelling and huge fireplaces. Bedrooms throughout are spacious and comfortable with
crown-canopied beds and carpeted bathrooms containing bathrobes and a good supply of
toiletries. Conference/banqueting facilities for 185/160. Leave the M4 at Junction 35.
Virgin Hotels. *Rooms 23. Garden, outdoor swimming pool, tennis, snooker. Access, Amex,
Diners, Visa.*

CRICKHOWELL   Bear Hotel   £54

Tel 01873 810408   Fax 01873 811696   Map 9 D5   **I**
High Street Crickhowell Powys NP8 1BW

Dating back to the 15th century, the Bear bristles with personality and continues its
tradition of hospitality as the focal point of the market town. The evocative, busy bars,
with low black beams, sturdy old furniture and open fires, are good places for a drink or
a chat with locals, and upstairs there's a quiet residents' lounge. Bedrooms, some grouped
round a Tudor-style courtyard, have good-quality furniture and warm, well-chosen
fabrics. Top of the range is a four-poster room with jacuzzi. *Rooms 29. Garden. Access,
Amex, Visa.*

CRICKHOWELL   Gliffaes Country House   63%   £85

Tel 01874 730371   Fax 01874 730463   Map 9 D5   **H**
Crickhowell Powys NP8 1RH

Fishing is the favourite pastime at this distinctive late-Victorian Italianate house (spot the
campanile) that is set in 29 acres of grounds (including 7 acres of gardens) and overlooks
a mile of water on the left bank of the Usk, west of Crickhowell. Many other outdoor
activities have a following here, while the sitting room and drawing room are splendid
places for doing nothing. Bedrooms are spacious and attractively furnished with old or
antique pieces. Dogs permitted in the lodge. *Rooms 22. Garden, croquet, game fishing,
tennis, snooker. Closed 5 Jan-23 Feb. Access, Amex, Diners, Visa.*

EGLWYSFACH   Ynyshir Hall   70%   £120

Tel 01654 781209   Fax 01654 781366   Map 8 C3   **HR**
Eglwysfach Machynlleth Powys SY20 8TA

A Georgian manor house, once owned by Queen Victoria, set on the Dovey estuary by
an extensive bird reserve. Owner Rob Reen is an accomplished artist, whose work is to
be found in the bedrooms, each named after a famous painter, and throughout the
immaculate day rooms which also feature a collection of Oriental rugs. An artist's eye is
also evident in the stylish decor of the bedrooms, which are furnished with antiques and
come with magazines, books and mineral water (best rooms also get sherry) among other
comforts. Top of the range (£140) are the suites – the Degas and Renoir (both non-
smoking) and the Vermeer with an 1860 walnut bed and blue-tiled bathroom. New this
year is the Monet garden suite with conservatory sitting room. Breakfast includes freshly

squeezed orange juice and home-made conserves. No children under 9 years. *Rooms 8. Garden, pitch & putt. Access, Amex, Diners, Visa.*

Restaurant   £60

Local produce features on fixed-price menus that offer four choices at each stage, fewer at lunchtime (which is by arrangement only unless opting for a light snack in the bar). Starters like baked Welsh goat's cheese on a bed of honeyed vegetables, ravioli of potato and truffles with a Sauternes cream and a warm salad of smoked goose with hazelnut dressing precede main dishes such as Dyfi salmon with a trio of fettuccine on a shellfish sauce, fillet of black Welsh beef with mushrooms and mangetout topped with black pudding purée and, as the vegetarian option, roast pimento with wild rice, Provençal vegetables and saffron noodles. For afters choose between a good selection of Welsh cheeses – Pencarreg, Teifi, Pantygywen goat's cheese, Llanboidy, Pencarreg Blue – or the likes of hot bread and butter soufflé, and peach and plum crème brulée with Drambuie cream. Good-value, including house wines, all under £20, on a decent list that has plenty from the New World. *Seats 40. Private Room 16. L by arrangement D 7-8.30. Set L £17.50 Set D £27.50.*

EWLOE	St David's Park Hotel	69%	£107

Tel 01244 520800   Fax 01244 520930   Map 8 D2   **H**
St David's Park Ewloe Clwyd CH5 3YB

Smart, modern hotel, with some neo-Georgian features, at the junction of the A55 and A494. Inside, the several areas that make up the bar/lounge include a couple of 'rooms' with fireplaces, floral armchairs and busy wallpaper giving something of a Victorian feel, plus an airy orangery with black-and-white tiled floor. Spacious, well-planned bedrooms have good, solid oak furniture and roomy bathrooms; 30 rooms for non-smokers. The seven 'junior suites' have separate walk-in showers and extras like robes and slippers. Beds are turned down at night and room service is 24hrs. Under-16s stay free in parents' room. Banqueting/conferencing for 220/325 (ample parking). The Northop Country Park golf and country club is just 5 minutes away from the hotel – courtesy transport provided. *Rooms 121. Garden, tennis, golf (18), indoor swimming pool, gym, spa bath, steam room, sauna, solarium, beautician, games room, snooker. Access, Amex, Diners, Visa.*

FISHGUARD	Fishguard Bay Hotel	59%	£55

Tel 01348 873571   Fax 01348 873030   Map 9 A5   **H**
Quay Road Goodwick Fishguard Dyfed SA64 0BT

Ten acres of woodland stand at the back while Cardigan Bay is straight ahead as well as the ferry service to Rosslare. A popular venue for functions, with banquets for up to 300. Best and brightest bedrooms have bay-facing balconies. The lounge and bar areas have recently been refurbished. Children up to 12 stay free in their parents' room. *Rooms 62. Garden. Access, Amex, Diners, Visa.*

GOWERTON	Cefn Goleu Park	69%	£80

Tel 01792 873099   Map 9 B6   **HR**
Cefn Stylle Road Gowerton West Glamorgan SA4 3QS

Bought by Emma and Claude Rossi in 1987, the manor house, which stands in 48 acres of gardens, has been restored with love, patience and the skills of local craftsmen. A stunning vaulted central hall contains unique showcases of china dolls and is ringed by a minstrel's gallery leading to four master bedrooms where Victorian elegance has been recreated. No children under 10. No dogs. *Rooms 4. Garden. Closed 2 weeks Jan. Access, Visa.*

Restaurant   £60

From Claude and son Bernard's kitchen come hearty, full-flavoured dishes for an essentially French menu that holds few surprises: paté and melba toast, escargots bourguignon, sole véronique, chicken in mustard sauce, fillet steak forester style, escalope viennoise. Daily specials follow the seasons with saddle of roebuck deer with sauce poivrade and pheasant with a white wine, brandy and game sauce from a winter menu. The fixed-price Sunday lunch always includes a traditional roast and a fish dish amongst around four main dish choices. Vegetarian meals by prior arrangement only. Sweets from the trolley. Smoking is not encouraged. *Seats 30. Parties 14. Private Room 20. L (Sun only) 12-2 D 7-9. Closed D Sun & all Mon (except to residents). Set Sun L £12.50.*

GWBERT-ON-SEA   Cliff Hotel   60%   £59

Tel 01239 613241   Fax 01239 615391   Map 9 B4   **H**
Gwbert-on-Sea Cardigan Dyfed SA43 1PP

Thirty acres of private headland provide outstanding sea views from this privately owned hotel, whose convivial atmosphere is augmented by friendly staff and high-profile management. There's a wealth of recreational facilities, both on and off site, for all the family (under-12s free in parents' room); fishing on a private stretch of the River Teifi, conference and banqueting (max 200). Self-catering apartments offering full use of the hotel facilities are also available. The room rate quoted is for a standard room; sea view rooms are £73, Executives £94, Premiers £115. *Rooms 73. Garden, fishing, outdoor swimming pool, gym, squash, sauna, golf (9), snooker. Access, Amex, Diners, Visa.*

HOLYHEAD   Trearddur Bay Hotel   65%   £98

Tel 01407 860301   Fax 01407 861181   Map 8 B1   **H**
Holyhead Anglesey Gwynedd LL65 2UN

A family-run and family-friendly coastal hotel on the western tip of Anglesey just two miles from Holyhead and the Irish ferry terminal. Smart public areas provide a choice between the newly named and furbished Inn at the Bay and the cocktail bar and lounge overlooking the bay. A self-contained indoor swimming pool is in the garden, while for hardier types the real thing, and a safe, sandy beach, are just across the road. The majority of bedrooms, decorated in muted colours, share views of the sand dunes and rocky coastline; those facing west with new private balconies are certainly the pick. Friendly, cheerful staff; children welcome, cots and bunk beds available. *Rooms 30. Garden, indoor swimming pool, games room. Access, Amex, Diners, Visa.*

LAMPHEY   Court Hotel   68%   £85

Tel 01646 672273   Fax 01646 672480   Map 9 A5   **H**
Lamphey Pembroke Dyfed SA71 5NT

Much extended and improved since its opening as a hotel in 1978, The Court is peacefully situated in extensive grounds just a mile from the south Pembrokeshire coast (take the A48 from the M4 to Carmarthen, then A477 Pembroke Road, at Milton village turn left for Lamphey). A handsomely-proportioned staircase dominates the reception hall, from which radiate the day rooms. The pick is a cocktail bar leading to the conservatory and patio which make a fine-weather alternative for breakfast service, as well as children's high teas. Nonetheless, the Georgian elegance of the Court's origins is carefully retained and reflected also in main-house bedrooms, which are spacious, elegantly furnished and enjoy fine views. Children up to 16 stay free in parents' room, cots available. General refurbishment recently carried out and leisure centre expanded. Conference and banqueting facilities for up to 100. *Rooms 32. Garden, indoor swimming pool, gym, sauna, spa bath, solarium, floodlit tennis, beauty salon. Access, Amex, Diners, Visa.*

LLANARMON DYFFRYN CEIRIOG   Hand Hotel   £58

Tel & Fax 01691 600666   Map 8 D2   **I**
Llanarmon Dyffryn Ceiriog nr Llangollen Clwyd LL20 7LD

Originally a 16th-century farmhouse, the Hand stands in beautiful countryside in a picturesque village at the head of the Ceiriog Valley. An old black range in reception, antiques in lounge and bar plus a log fire all add up to a cosy, traditional atmosphere. Bedrooms are neat and simple, with plain walls and white fitted furniture. The hotel has its own all-weather tennis court and fishing can be arranged. *Rooms 13. Garden, tennis. Access, Amex, Diners, Visa.*

LLANARMON DYFFRYN CEIRIOG   West Arms Hotel   £100

Tel 01691 600665   Fax 01691 600622   Map 8 D2   **I**
Llanarmon Dyffryn Ceiriog nr Llangollen Clwyd LL20 7LD

Nestling in the lovely Ceiriog Valley, this 400-year-old country inn offers cosy comfort within and well-manicured gardens without. Slate-flagged floors, vast inglenooks and beams offset by period furnishings preserve the atmosphere of a bygone age. Though six of the bedrooms are fairly modern, the rest retain exposed beams, brass bedsteads and antique furniture, to which neatly added bathrooms provide the requisite modern comforts. TVs in all rooms, tea-makers in all. A private garden suite accommodates dinner parties for up to 90 guests. Families are well looked after. Take the B4500 from Chirk. *Rooms 12. Garden, croquet, fishing. Closed 2 weeks Jan/Feb. Access, Amex, Diners, Visa.*

LLANBERIS   Y Bistro   £50

Tel 01286 871278   Map 8 B2   **R**
43-45 High Street Llanberis Gwynedd LL55 4EU

The bilingual (English and Welsh) menu at Danny and Nerys Roberts' friendly restaurant makes as much use as possible of local Welsh produce in dishes like scrambled egg with locally smoked salmon on toasted brioche; Penrhyn mussels cooked with leeks, garlic and Cariad wine (from the Vale of Glamorgan), and penne baked with Llanboidy cheese and grain mustard sauce with a breadcrumb and pine kernel topping. Good puds like pineapple Romanov, chocolate and coffee mousse and fruit tart or cheese or the fresh fruit basket to follow. The menu price includes canapés, side salad, home-baked bread, coffee and florentines. *Seats 50. Private Room 20. L by arrangment D 7.30-9.45. Closed Sun (except before Bank Holidays) & Mon in Nov, Jan & Feb. Set D £19/£21/£23.50. Access, Visa.*

We publish annually, so make sure you use the current edition
— it's well worth it!

LLANDEILO   Cawdor Arms   65%   £70

Tel 01558 823500   Fax 01558 822399   Map 9 C5   **H**
Rhosmaen Street Llandeilo Dyfed SA19 6EN

Clearly signposted at the end of the M4, and attractively situated in the Vale of Towy, the hotel bears the Cawdor family coat of arms as its emblem. Of handsome proportions, the Georgian day rooms have benefited from refurbishment since the arrival of new owners; work on bedrooms was to follow. *Rooms 12. Sauna. Access, Amex, Diners, Visa.*

LLANDRILLO   Tyddyn Llan   66%   £88

Tel 01490 440264   Fax 01490 440414   Map 8 C2   **HR**
Llandrillo nr Corwen Clwyd LL21 0ST

This lovely Georgian house on the B4401 between Corwen and Bala is where the Kindreds live. Once a shooting lodge for the Dukes of Westminster, it stands amid beautifully tended gardens in the Vale of Edeyrnion above the Dee (on which it has four miles of fishing rights) and below the Berwyn mountains in some of the finest countryside in Wales. It is also a special place developed and extended over the years to his own design by Peter Kindred and replete with antiques, period furniture and unusual art, some of it his own. No more house-proud proprietor could be found either than Bridget and it shows in the immaculate condition of everything within from fresh flowers and pot pourri to bathroom towels and bed linen. Residents are made instantly welcome and at home: each individually furnished bedroom reflects the calm of Tyddyn Llan's idyllic setting and nothing appears too much trouble for hosts whose hospitality transcends mere hotelkeeping. *Rooms 10. Garden, croquet, fishing. Closed last 3 weeks Jan. Access, Amex, Diners, Visa.*

Restaurant   £60

Dinner begins, as it were, in the bar and lounge with an informal introduction to the highlights of a nightly-changed fixed-price menu which places high emphasis on original and forceful flavours. Balsamic dressing and sautéed peppers enliven the delicate hot fish terrine; orange, thyme and red wine sauce richly augment a navarin of local Welsh lamb; and a brandy snap basket of fresh fruit is refreshingly enhanced by rose-water ice cream. However, it is perhaps the attention paid to Welsh cheeses, fully deserving of our Regional Cheesboard of the Year award, that sets the restaurant apart. Of course, the informal and warm hospitality, aligned with friendly service, also helps hugely. No smoking. *Seats 60. Parties 20. Private Room 44. L 12.30-2 D 7-9.30. Set L £10.75/£12.75 (Sun £14.50) Set D £21.50/£23.50.*

We welcome bona fide complaints and recommendations on the
tear-out pages at the back of the book for readers' comments.
They are followed up by our professional team.

| LLANDUDNO | **Bodysgallen Hall** | 77% | **£140** |

Tel 01492 584466   Fax 01492 582519   Map 8 C1   **HR**
Llandudno Gwynedd LL30 1RS

Splendid pink sandstone manor house, mainly Jacobean (a 13th-century tower is the oldest part), set in the most glorious gardens: a formal parterre, winding paths descending through rock gardens, decorative lily-strewn ponds, a walled-rose garden where all the blooms are either white or yellow – most impressive at the right time of year, through an arch to the kitchen garden with its vast fruit cages, cordon fruit trees and ranks of blooms waiting to be cut for the house, extensive woodland walks. More than enough to keep the four full-time gardeners employed. Historic House Hotels have expended just as much care on the inside of the building with careful restoration creating a real 'country house' atmosphere. Antiques, Oriental rugs and oil paintings complement the mellow wood panelling and pargeted friezes of the various lounges where the plumping of feather-filled cushions keeps the indoor staff almost as busy as the gardeners. Bedrooms, which include nine one- or two-bedroom cottage suites (with kitchenettes) set around a charming courtyard garden, vary considerably in size and shape but all boast the odd antique along with fabric-draped pieces and nice touches like porcelain ornaments, magazines, books, mineral water, flowering plants and home-made biscuits. All have two phones but the easy chairs tend to be on the small side. Cork-floored bathrooms come with towelling robes, Crabtree & Evelyn toiletries and brass fittings but no shaving-mirrors. First-rate breakfasts include home-baked croissants, freshly-squeezed orange juice and de-crusted toast. Staff are friendly (sometimes almost motherly) and attentive. The leisure centre, which was originally due for completion by early in the year, should now be ready by the end of 1995. No children under eight; dogs in the Cottage Suites only. The hotel is signposted off the A470 just out of town.
Rooms 29. Garden, croquet, tennis. Access, Amex, Diners, Visa.

Restaurant   £75

Twin dining-rooms have fine views over the estate from their stone-mullioned windows and provide a most civilised setting for a meal. The main fixed-price dinner menu offers just four choices for each of three courses (slightly more choice at lunch which is priced for either two or three courses), although a vegetarian dish or grilled steak is available on request. A typical selection of main dishes might be breast of duck on a tea-infused sauce, beef sirloin with a thyme potato purée, cold poached salmon with minted potatoes and salad leaves, and roast local sea bass on a compote of smoked bacon, broad beans and garlic. The five-course Gourmet menu (dinner only) offers a further three, rather more elaborate, main dishes like a trio of Welsh spring lamb with thyme rösti and champagne vinegar sauce, Dublin Bay prawn risotto with scallop tortellini and chive sauce, and roast milk-fed squab with baby vegetables and Gewürztraminer sauce. Good-value house selection and cellarman's choice on an altogether pleasing wine list that has many half bottles. New World wines listed by style. No smoking. No children under nine.
Seats 60. Private Room 40. L 12.30-2 D 7.30-9.45. Set L £11.50/£13.50 Set D £27.50 & £36.

| LLANDUDNO | **Empire Hotel** | 70% | **£70** |

Tel 01492 860555   Fax 01492 860791   Map 8 C1   **H**
Church Walks Llandudno Gwynedd LL30 2HE

The Maddocks family have been here for 50 years and their dedication is obvious throughout from the exterior, which has recently undergone major renovation, to the extremely well-equipped bedrooms. There's a wide choice from budget singles to de luxe rooms in the Victorian house next to the main building but antiques, cast-iron beds, silk drapes and marble-floored bathrooms with whirlpool baths feature throughout. Satellite TV and video recorders (large library of films available) and personal safes are also standard. *Rooms 58. Indoor & outdoor swimming pools, spa bath, sauna, steam room, roof garden and sun terrace, beauty salon, dinner dance (Sat). Closed 10 days Christmas. Access, Amex, Diners, Visa.*

LLANDUDNO	St George's Hotel	61%	£78

Tel 01492 877544   Fax 01492 877788   Map 8 C1   **H**
St George's Place Llandudno Gwynedd LL30 2LG

Situated right on the promenade, Llandudno's oldest hotel offers up-to-date conference and banqueting facilities for up to 290/260 and the Shape Club offers top-to-toe health, hair and cosmetic care. Many bedrooms afford views of the sea and Great Orme, and the best have balconies. Under-14s stay free in their parents' room. No dogs. *Rooms 87. Keep-fit equipment, sauna, spa bath, steam room, solarium, beauty & hair salon. Closed 1st week Jan. Access, Amex, Diners, Visa.*

Set menu prices may not always include service or wine.

LLANDUDNO	St Tudno Hotel	69%	£110

Tel 01492 874411   Fax 01492 860407   Map 8 C1   **HR**
The Promenade Llandudno Gwynedd LL30 2LP

Martin and Janette Bland came here in 1972, since when their charming seafront hotel has been known for its friendliness and good service. Either side of the entrance hall the bar/lounge and sitting-room (reserved for non-smokers) are Victorian in style – parlour plants, original fire places – in contrast to a bright coffee lounge to be found beyond the reception desk where fresh flowers compete with the receptionists' smiles. A small bottle of sparkling wine greets guests in bedrooms that, though generally not large, are individually decorated in pretty co-ordinating fabrics and wall coverings with a good eye for detail. Rooms are properly serviced in the evenings as are the bathrooms with their generous towelling and good toiletries. In 1861 Alice Liddell, later to be immortalised in Lewis Carroll's Alice's Adventures in Wonderland, spent a holiday here. Very much family-friendly. High tea is served from 5 to 6 in the coffee lounge. Parking for six cars. *Rooms 21. Patio, indoor swimming pool. Access, Amex, Diners, Visa.*

Garden Room Restaurant   £70

Although it is windowless, walls painted with greenery and trellis-work, potted plants, conservatory-style furniture and air-conditioning all help to provide the garden feel promised in the restaurant's name. Dinner runs to five courses with soup, sorbet or a salad after starters such as melon with mango and Grand Marnier; hot-pot of Conway mussels with laverbread and saffron sauce, or poached eggs with asparagus and a butter sauce. Main dishes, of which there are usually eight including two vegetarian options, range from rack of Welsh lamb with Anna potatoes and grilled local sea bass with Llanboidy cheese sauce and fried leeks, to pan-fried calf's sweetbreads with a Pernod sauce. Organically produced Welsh cheeses and Stilton come after, or before, some nicely varied desserts including roast nut savarin filled with an amaretto cream, a platter of seasonal fruits with a claret granita and elderflower sorbet, and a hot soufflé. There are, unusually, a couple of savouries like Welsh rarebit or smoked haddock glazed with a cayenne and shrimp sauce offered as an alternative for those lacking a sweet tooth. Lunch is a shorter three-course affair and a good range of lighter dishes is served in the coffee lounge and bar. Ian Watson represented Wales in our Chef of the Year competition (see awards pages). Under £20 for a bottle of house champagne is a bargain, over £3 for the same amount of Welsh water is excessive! Pleasant wine list with cellarman's choice offering best value. No smoking. *Seats 66. L 12.30-1.45 D 7-9.30 (Sun till 8.30). Set L £15.50 Set D £27.50.*

LLANGAMMARCH WELLS	Lake Country House	69%	£115

Tel 01591 620202   Fax 01591 620457   Map 9 C4   **HR**
Llangammarch Wells Powys LD4 4BS

Standing in 50 acres of parkland, this mainly Edwardian hotel has grandly proportioned day rooms including a drawing room where traditional Welsh teas are served. In the summer, teas are also served under the chestnut tree in the garden overlooking the River Irfon. Bedrooms have fine views and are individually styled with a combination of antiques and restful colour schemes. All bathrooms have recently been refurbished. Smart, efficient staff mirror the owners' enthusiasm. Fishing is available on three rivers and the hotel's lake and riding can be arranged locally. The calm of the hotel is occasionally disrupted by seminars.. *Rooms 19. Garden, pitch & putt, tennis, fishing, games room. Access, Amex, Diners, Visa.*

See over

Restaurant   £65

Richard Arnold's fixed-price dinners always start with a soup, perhaps courgette and rosemary or lightly spiced parsnip. The next courses are invariably imaginative and sometimes quite intricate, typified by twice-baked Teifi cheese soufflé with leeks and hazelnuts, or escalope of salmon topped with a couscous crust set on a crayfish sauce. Home-made ice cream among the desserts and both Welsh and English cheeses. In general, quite favourable prices on the comprehensive wine list – a good balance between France and the rest of the world – that also has sensible tasting notes. *Seats 50. L 12.15-2 D 7-8.45. Set L £15.50 Set D £24.50.*

LLANGOLLEN	Hand Hotel	55%	£68

Tel 01978 860303   Fax 01978 861277   Map 8 D2   **H**
Bridge Street Llangollen Clwyd LL20 8PL

Country hotel (once a posting house for the Irish Mail coaches) with gardens reaching down to the River Dee. Simple, attractive rooms include some suitable for family use. Banqueting and conference facilities for 100/90. *Rooms 57. Garden, fishing. Access, Amex, Diners, Visa.*

LLANGOLLEN	Royal Hotel	59%	£82

Tel 01978 860202   Fax 01978 861824   Map 8 D2   **H**
Bridge Street Llangollen Clwyd LL20 8PG

Looking just a little like a fairy-tale castle, the Royal overlooks a 14th-century stone bridge on the banks of the Dee. Simple bedrooms, two bars and a comfortable lounge. Children under 16 stay free in parents' room. Banqueting/conferences for up to 80. Forte. *Rooms 33. Access, Amex, Diners, Visa.*

LLANGYBI	Cwrt Bleddyn Hotel	71%	£102

Tel 01633 450521   Fax 01633 450220   Map 9 D6   **H**
Tredunnock nr Usk Gwent NP5 1PG

A large house standing in 17 acres of countryside three miles from Caerleon, between Llangybi and Tredunnock, Cwrt Bleddyn can trace its heritage back to the 14th century. Some original features date back just to the 17th century but the interior is modernised to a great extent, including 25 spacious bedrooms and 11 suites. Children up to 16 can stay free in parents' room. The lounge and private meeting rooms feature carved panelling and fireplaces and the sun lounge/cocktail bar has a spectacular high-domed glass ceiling. Good family facilities; coffee shop in leisure club 11am-11pm. Conference facilities for up to 200. Ample parking. Ask about the wine appreciation and murder weekends. *Rooms 36. Garden, croquet, tennis, indoor swimming pool, gym, sauna, squash, steam room, solarium, spa bath, beauty salon, hair salon, snooker, children's playground. Access, Amex, Diners, Visa.*

LLANRUG	Seiont Manor	71%	£100

Tel 01286 673366   Fax 01286 672840   Map 8 B2   **H**
Llanrug Caernarfon Gwynedd LL55 2AQ

Developed from the farmstead of a Georgian manor house, the hotel stands on the A4086. 150 acres of parkland provide pleasant walks, and Snowdonia National Park and the Isle of Anglesey are both a short drive away. Fishing is available on the River Seiont, and guests have complimentary access to a nearby golf course. Public rooms, including a traditional oak-panelled bar, a lounge and a very comfortable library (the last two serving morning coffee, lunch and afternoon tea), are also furnished in a manner that befits the ancient character of the building. Bedrooms are in two purpose-built blocks which extend from the original stone building and are in a style sympathetic to it. Rooms have either little balconies or patio doors, are of a good size and all boast antique or good-quality period furniture. Conference facilities for up to 100 delegates. Virgin Hotels. *Rooms 28. Garden, indoor swimming pool, keep-fit equipment, sauna, solarium, fishing. Access, Amex, Diners, Visa.*

Set menu prices may not always include service or wine.

LLANSANFFRAID GLAN CONWY	Old Rectory	73%	£84

Tel 01492 580611   Fax 01492 584555   Map 8 C1   **HR**
Llanrwst Road Llansanffraid Glan Conwy Gwynedd LL28 5LF

Standing above the A470, the Old Rectory (dating from 1740) enjoys splendid views across the Conwy estuary from Conwy Castle to Snowdonia. It's personally run by the Vaughans, with Michael presiding over front of house in chatty, friendly style. The main day room is a comfortable, pine-panelled lounge where drinks are also served – there is no separate bar. Antique-furnished bedrooms come with all sorts of homely comforts from fresh flowers and fruit to piles of books and magazines. Each room also has an iron and ironing board plus tea- and coffee-making kit, although room service of beverages and sandwiches is available throughout the day and evening. Dogs, children (not under 5) and smokers are all restricted to two rooms in an adjacent converted stable block. *Rooms 6. Garden. Closed 20 Dec-1 Feb. Access, Amex, Diners, Visa.*

Restaurant £70

A most civilised dining-room, originally two rooms but now joined by twin arches, with collections of silverware and decanters on antique side tables, fine china in glass-fronted cabinets, chandeliers and some fine paintings on the walls – an ideal setting in which to enjoy Wendy Vaughan's excellent four-course set dinners unhurriedly served by Michael. The menu announces, in Welsh as well as English, that only Welsh black beef and Welsh mountain lamb are served. Conwy fish is another speciality, and to end the meal there's a choice of splendid desserts followed by Welsh farmhouse cheeses. Everything from the bread rolls to the nibbles served with pre-dinner drinks is freshly prepared and cooked with a sure touch. There are tasting notes for each wine on a very reasonably priced, list with plenty of half bottles. No smoking. *Seats 16. D only 7.30 for 8. Set D £27.50.*

LLANVIHANGEL GOBION	Llansantffraed Court	66%	£75

Tel 01873 840678   Fax 01873 840674   Map 9 D5   **H**
Llanvihangel Gobion nr Abergavenny Gwent NP7 9BA

A neo-classical Lutyens house with strong Georgian influences standing on the B4598 Abergavenny road on the fringe of the Usk valley. Set against a backdrop of the Black Mountains, the house is surrounded by 19 acres of parkland including a lake and woods. Most characterful of the bedrooms are on the top floor, with oak beams and dormer windows. Children up to 14 stay free in parents' room. The lounge and bar provide ample space for a relaxing chat or drink. Conference/banqueting for 50/120. Privately owned but managed by Thistle and Mount Charlotte group. *Rooms 21. Garden. Access, Amex, Diners, Visa.*

LLANWDDYN	Lake Vyrnwy Hotel	67%	£77

Tel 01691 870692   Fax 01691 870259   Map 8 C3   **HR**
Lake Vyrnwy Llanwddyn Montgomery Powys SY10 0LY

The magnificent, if austere, stone mansion high on a wooded hillside looks across 1,100 acres of man-made lake set amid the vast the Vyrnwy Estate. Built at the same time as the dam in 1890 (drinking water from here is still supplied to Liverpool 68 miles away) this is indeed a magical spot and, now as then, "a retreat for all country lovers". True to their Victorian origins, the generously proportioned public rooms, have an ageless feel, with chintz sofas, Bechstein piano, tapestries and oil paintings gracing the lounge, while a clubby atmosphere in the bar is enhanced by pitch pine, leather armchairs and sporting prints. For an informal drink, the spectacular views can be enjoyed from the balcony of the adjacent Tavern. The majority of bedrooms share this aspect; each is individually designed with much antique and period furniture in evidence and many special features of unique appeal, from private sitting areas and balconies to four-poster beds and jacuzzi baths. Conference and banqueting facilities accommodate up to 120. Children welcome overnight; cots provided. *Rooms 35. Garden, tennis, shooting, fishing, boat hire, sailing, bicycles. Access, Amex, Diners, Visa.*

Restaurant £65

The kitchen's home production runs from breakfast marmalade to petits fours at dinner, with the estate and gardens providing their fair share of seasonal produce. A light soufflé of Cornish crab with lemon grass and mussels, roast Welsh black beef with Yorkshire

See over

pudding, and whisky and orange sponge pudding typify nightly choices from a fixed-price varied-choice menu. One or two good names on the wine list, which includes three bottles of traditional Welsh mead. No smoking. *Seats 120. Private Room 70. L 12.30-1.45 D 7.30-9.15. Set L £13.75 (Sun £14.75) Set D £22.50.*

LLANWNDA	Stables Hotel	57%	£49

Tel 01286 830711   Fax 01286 830413   Map 8 B2   **H**
Llanwnda nr Caernarfon Gwynedd LL54 5SD

Three miles south-west of Caernarfon on the A499, this is a modest single-storey hotel set around original Victorian stables which now house a small bar and restaurant. Children up to 12 stay free in parents' room. Four-room suite also available. *Rooms 14. Garden, outdoor swimming pool. Access, Amex, Visa.*

LLYSWEN	Llangoed Hall	81%	£155

Tel 01874 754525   Fax 01874 754545   Map 9 D5   **HR**
Llyswen Brecon Powys LD3 0YP

This site has played host to a number of distinguished buildings over the centuries, including, it is thought, the home of the first Welsh Parliament. The house as it stands now dates from the 1600s, but was completely restored and largely redesigned earlier this century by Sir Clough Williams-Ellis, who later went on to build Portmeirion, the renowned Italianate village in North Wales. Sir Bernard Ashley bought the hotel in 1987, and masterminded its restoration returning it to its Edwardian splendour. The Great Hall and other public rooms boast open fires, original paintings, large sofas and some fine antiques. Unsurprisingly, the whole hotel is decorated with Laura Ashley fabrics and wall coverings and, apart from the antiques, utilises their own range of furniture. A sweeping staircase leads up to the bedrooms, each individually decorated and all having thoughtful touches such as decanters of sherry, Welsh spring water and bowls of fruit. Luxurious bathrooms with hand-held showers and huge towels retain something of the old-fashioned quality – even the tubs fill at a leisurely pace, and Floris toiletries add to the classy feel. Delicious breakfasts offer a wide choice from salmon kedgeree, grilled kippers and vegetarian Glamorgan sausages to English muffins with smoked salmon, poached egg and hollandaise sauce as well as a traditional full Welsh breakfast. *Rooms 23. Garden with maze, tennis, croquet, fishing, snooker. Access, Amex, Diners, Visa.*

Restaurant   £90

An elegant room with fluted pilasters and some fine pictures from Sir Bernard's personal collection around pale yellow walls. Posies of fresh flowers adorn immaculately set tables. Whether choosing from the à la carte or opting for the evening's no-choice, four-course dinner menu, the offerings will have a distinctly modish slant with such dishes as red pepper soup with aubergine croutons, steamed turbot with cucumber 'spaghetti' and carrot sauce, saddle of rabbit wrapped in croustillant pastry with tarragon sauce, and Welsh lamb with a lemon grass sauce. Desserts are full of interest too with the likes of apple and ginger sweet lasagne with blackcurrant dressing and a mango tarte tatin with butterscotch sauce to tempt the sweet-toothed. Lunch offers a limited-choice, set-price menu. There's a very fine wine list indeed with a good-value cellarman's choice and an interesting 'recommended' section with tasting notes. Lots of half bottles. No smoking. *Seats 40. Private Room 16. L 12.30-2.15 D 7.15-9.30. Set L £13/£16 (Sun £16.50) Set D £29.50.*

Consult the blue pages for summary tables and lists of
recommended establishments.

| MACHYNLLETH | **Wynnstay Arms** | 60% | £53 |

Tel 01654 702941   Fax 01654 703884   Map 8 C3   **H**
Maengwyn Street Machynlleth Powys SY20 8AE

The day rooms have recently been smartened up (albeit in a rather corporate manner) at this townhouse hotel. Bedrooms are functional and half are designated non-smoking. The hotel is well placed in the valley of the River Dovey as a base from which to visit Snowdonia. Children up to 16 stay free in parents' room. *Rooms 20. Access, Amex, Diners, Visa.*

We welcome bona fide complaints and recommendations on the tear-out pages at the back of the book for readers' comments. They are followed up by our professional team.

| MERTHYR TYDFIL | **Baverstock Hotel** | 57% | £55 |

Tel 01685 386221   Fax 01685 723670   Map 9 C5   **H**
Heads of the Valley Road Merthyr Tydfil Mid Glamorgan CF44 0LX

Modern hotel in an elevated position on the A465. A good deal of business comes from conferences and meetings in a variety of rooms for up to 300 delegates. Children up to 12 stay free in parents' room. Ample parking. *Rooms 53. Garden, snooker. Access, Amex, Diners, Visa.*

| MISKIN | **Miskin Manor** | 70% | £95 |

Tel 01443 224204   Fax 01443 237606   Map 9 C6   **H**
Penddylan Road Miskin Pontyclun Mid Glamorgan CF7 8ND

Built of mellow grey Welsh stone, the present manor dates from the 1850s. Overlooking both the M4 (1 mile from Junction 34) and the River Ely, the hotel stands in 20 acres of garden and woodland. Oak linenfold panelling is a predominant feature of the elegantly proportioned day rooms, which are brightly decorated to reflect their pastoral aspect. Individually furnished bedrooms, notable for their size and luxurious appointments, have their share each of the view. Crown-canopied beds, two four-posters and a suite occupied in the 1920s by the future Edward VIII imbue this fine house with a tangible legacy of its own history. A short walk from the hotel, the self-contained Health and Leisure club with playroom and creche is shared, at no charge for residents, with local members. *Rooms 32. Garden, croquet, indoor swimming pool, gym, squash, spa bath, steam room, sauna, solarium, beauty salon, badminton, coffee shop (11am-9.30pm), creche (9am-3pm Mon-Fri), outdoor children's playground. Access, Amex, Diners, Visa.*

| MUMBLES | **Norton House** | 65% | £65 |

Tel 01792 404891   Fax 01792 403210   Map 9 C6   **HR**
17 Norton Road Mumbles Swansea West Glamorgan SA3 5TQ

The Power family's elegant Georgian home overlooking the seashore was once a master mariner's house. Focal point of the day rooms is the mirror-lined bar with its unusual umbrella-vaulted ceiling, though residents seeking peace and quiet have use of a first-floor lounge over the old coach house. Bedrooms are practical and neatly appointed with those on the ground floor having access to their own patios. Four main-house rooms have four-poster beds, generous seating areas, smart bathrooms and welcoming extras. *Rooms 15. Garden. Closed 25 & 26 Dec. Access, Amex, Diners, Visa.*

Restaurant   **£65**

The influence and enthusiasm of first son Mark Power brings touches of originality to dinner menus which, though written in Welsh, have a broad, traditional English and French base. Fillet of trout stuffed with laverbread, cockles and bacon appears alongside warmed smoked salmon on creamed spinach with a chive sauce; breast of Aylesbury duck with sage and onion stuffing and apple sauce; baked Alaska and banana cheesecake with toffee sauce follow for dessert. Equally traditional restaurant furnishings, flambé and liqueur trolleys and the proprietors' personally-selected wine list are all reminiscent of the private entertaining which Norton House's style still echoes. *Seats 30. Parties 12. Private Room 22. L (Sun only) 12.30-2.30 D 7-9.30 (Sun 7-9). Set D £19.50/£23.50.*

NEWPORT   Celtic Manor   75%   £120

Tel 01633 413000   Fax 01633 412910   Map 9 D6   **H**
The Coldra Newport Gwent NP6 2YA

Just one minute from Junction 24 of the M4, this 19th-century manor house is set in a 300-acre estate. Well set up for both business and pleasure, the hotel maintains high standards of decor, maintenance and service. Six conference suites cater for up to 350 delegates, and the leisure facilities are impressive. There is an elegant drawing room and a large patio conservatory which is used for breakfast. Bedrooms are of a good size and feature triple glazing, freestanding darkwood furniture with ample writing space, attractive window seating and smartly tiled, well-lit bathrooms. By the time this guide goes to press the Ian Woosnam Golfing Academy (including an 18- and a 9-hole course) should have opened as part of the hotel. The remaining nine holes and a tennis club are planned for 1996. *Rooms 73. Garden, indoor swimming pool, gym, sauna, solarium. Access, Amex, Diners, Visa.*

NEWPORT   Hilton National   61%   £84

Tel 01633 412777   Fax 01633 413087   Map 9 D6   **H**
The Coldra Newport Gwent NP6 2YG

In an attractive woodland setting, the hotel entrance is just 100 yards from Junction 24 of the M4. Facilities, much geared to business conferences (up to 500), exhibitions, seasonal coach parties and banqueting (300), swing over to more general family use at weekends with swimming, games room and evening entertainment. Children up to 12 can stay free in parents' 3-bedded rooms. Cots available free of charge. *Rooms 119. Indoor swimming pool, keep-fit equipment, sauna, steam room, solarium, games room. Access, Amex, Diners, Visa.*

NEWPORT   Stakis Cardiff-Newport   69%   £113

Tel 01633 413737   Fax 01633 413713   Map 9 D6   **H**
Chepstow Road Langstone Newport Gwent NP6 2LX

Stakis hotel built round a courtyard garden. Roomy overnight accommodation, leisure centre, self-contained facilities for business meetings. Children up to 16 free in parents' room. 50 non-smoking rooms. Ample free parking. *Rooms 141. Indoor pool, gym, sauna, steam room, spa bath, solarium, lounge service 10.30am-10pm. Access, Amex, Diners, Visa.*

NORTHOP   Soughton Hall   79%   £99

Tel 01352 840811   Fax 01352 840382   Map 8 D2   **H**
Northop nr Mold Clwyd CH7 6AB

Watch out for the sheep as you drive down a long avenue of lime trees to approach this creeper-clad, former Bishop's Palace dating from 1714. The grandeur of some of the public rooms, like the high-ceilinged first-floor sitting room with its decorated beams and tapestry wall hangings, is moderated by personal touches like family photos and objets d'art at what is the Rodenhursts' family home as well as a hotel. A real log fire warms the entrance hall and there is a tiny bar hidden behind a 'secret' door in the small library. Antiques abound, particularly in the bedrooms, which come with all sorts of extras such as fresh fruit, mineral water and comfortable armchairs plus various ornaments helping to create a 'house guest' ambience. Antiques also feature in some of the good bathrooms, all of which have views of the surrounding countryside. Breakfast is taken in the original servants' hall which still features an old black range. Golf can be arranged at a course adjacent to the hotel. *Rooms 14. Garden, croquet, snooker, tennis, archery. Closed first 2 weeks Jan. Access, Amex, Visa.*

PANT MAWR   Glansevern Arms   £55

Tel 01686 440240   Map 9 C4   **I**
Pant Mawr nr Llangurig Powys SY18 6SY

On the A44, four miles west of Llangurig, personally owned and managed for 30 years by
Mr Edwards and family, the Glansevern Arms commands a magnificent position
overlooking the upper reaches of the Wye. An intimate bar and lounge soak in the glorious
hill scenery by day and glow with warmth from log fires at night. Residents equally enjoy
the peace and quiet afforded by bedrooms with private sitting areas, uninterrupted by any
phones, where the views should provide a greater attraction than television. Under-12s free
in parents' room. *Rooms 7. Closed 1 week Christmas. No credit cards.*

PENALLY   Penally Abbey   65%   £90

Tel 01834 843033   Fax 01834 844714   Map 9 B6   **HR**
Penally nr Tenby Dyfed SA70 7PY

Set in five acres of gardens and woodland overlooking sand dunes and Carmarthen Bay,
Penally Abbey is a Gothic-style stone-built mansion with an adjoining coach house.
There's a tiny bar, a vine-shaded conservatory and a homely lounge where guests can
play various musical instruments. Four bedrooms have four-posters (two are in the Coach
House), others pine wardrobes and period wash-stands. Cheerful staff and welcoming
hosts. Good breakfasts. Children up to 14 share parents' room free. No dogs. *Rooms 12.
Garden, croquet, small indoor swimming pool, children's pool, snooker. Access, Amex, Visa.*

Restaurant   £50

Elleen Warren makes excellent use of prime local ingredients on her fixed-price dinner
menus. Smoked salmon terrine with salmon mousse, spinach soufflé and cream cheese
roulade, grilled lemon sole with garlic butter, fillet of lamb with cranberries and a port
and orange sauce, and vegetable creole show the style. No children under seven (resident
children have their own high tea at 5). No smoking. *Seats 46. Parties 6. Private Room 12.
L by arrangement D 7.30-9.30. Set D £23.*

PENMAENPOOL   George III Hotel   £88

Tel 01341 422525   Fax 01341 423565   Map 8 C3   **I**
Penmaenpool nr Dolgellau Gwynedd LL40 1YD

Magnificent views are shared by all but two of the bedrooms at the Cartwright family's
17th-century inn at the head of the Mawddach estuary. Focal point of the day rooms is
the Dresser Bar (the bar counter is made from part of an old Welsh dresser). There's also
a cellar bar (actually at ground level) and a cosy residents' lounge. Bedrooms, half of them
in the adjacent Victorian former railway station, are pretty and traditional, bathrooms
smart and modern. *Rooms 12. Garden, fishing. Access, Visa.*

PORTHKERRY   Egerton Grey   68%   £85

Tel 01446 711666   Fax 01446 711690   Map 9 C6   **H**
Porthkerry nr Cardiff South Glamorgan CF6 9BZ

This handsome former rectory, standing in seven acres of woodland at the fringe of the
Vale of Glamorgan, is hidden in a lush valley at the foot of a single-track road; rather
surprisingly, it is just two minutes' drive from Cardiff Wales Airport. Follow the signs to
Rhoose from the M4 at Junction 33, and the hotel is indicated off the airport perimeter
road. A parquet-floored foyer leads to elegantly-proportioned day rooms: the lounge with
deep-cushioned sofas, family portraits and grand piano; a restful library replete with
magazines and board games; and a mahogany-furnished breakfast room that doubles (as
required) for conferences or private dining. Bedrooms abound with antique furniture,
including a vast four-poster in the honeymoon suite. The decor of each is a striking mix
of bold colour schemes and plush fabrics with thick carpeting running through to
spacious, well-lit bathrooms, the pick of which feature Edwardian baths, with exposed
brasswork and huge deluge shower heads. *Rooms 10. Garden, tennis, croquet.
Access, Amex, Diners, Visa.*

Consult the blue pages for summary tables and lists of
recommended establishments.

PORTMEIRION   Hotel Portmeirion   74%   £132

Tel 01766 770228 Fax 01766 771331   Map 8 B2   **HR**
Portmeirion Gwynedd LL48 6ER

Portmeirion was created (and opened in 1926) by Sir Clough Williams-Ellis on the
secluded, Aber Iâ peninsula on the Traeth Bach estuary, though it was 1973 before the
whole fairy-tale village, comprising 50 buildings arranged round a central piazza, was
completed. The hotel is based on an early-Victorian villa near the shore and contains
some stunning public rooms: among others the black and white marble-floored hall and
the Indian-themed Jaipur Bar particularly take the eye. Guests stay either in the main
hotel building with the pick of the sea views or in the surrounding suites and cottages
that make up the village, all within very comfortable walking distance of the hotel. Five
de luxe suites in the Anchor and Fountain building overlook the swimming pool and
estuary. Conference/banqueting facilities for up to 100. Guests have free use of
Porthmaddog golf course two miles away. No dogs. *Rooms 34. Garden, outdoor swimming
pool, tennis, coffee shop (10am-5pm), village shops (closed Jan-Mar). Closed early Jan-early
Feb. Access, Amex, Diners, Visa.*

Restaurant   £65

The stunning, light, spacious, curvilinear dining-room (added to the hotel during the
1930s) with fine vistas across the estuary is a fitting backdrop for Craig Hindley's light
touch in the kitchen, utilising first-rate local raw materials in modern style. Paté of North
Wales fish with a sweet pepper dressing and a terrine of venison and chicken livers with
ginger are typical starters; fillet of beef with beetroot and a red wine sauce and baked
salmon with a truffle butter sauce typical main course dishes, with chocolate terrine with
caramel sauce or a warm kiwi flan with vanilla sauce for dessert. The fixed-price dinner
menus offer about six choices at each stage, the good-value lunch menu about half that
number. Even some of the tasting notes on the fine and very enterprising wine list are in
Welsh! Prices are on the generous side of fair with house champagne under £25 (£4.50
a glass) and a house selection offering around 40 wines at under £13.50. No smoking.
*Seats 100. Parties 16. Private Room 30. L 12.30-2 D 7-9.30. Set L £10.50/£13.50 (Sun £16)
Set D £20/£25. Closed L Mon.*

PRESTEIGNE   Radnorshire Arms   £92

Tel 01544 267406 Fax 01544 260418   Map 9 D4   **I**
High Street Presteigne Powys LD8 2BE

Built in 1616 by Sir Christopher Hatton, a favourite of Queen Elizabeth I, the main
house on Presteigne's historic High Street is a magnificent example of 17th-century
magpie architecture. It opened as a coaching inn in 1792, and the town's stocks in front
of it remained in use until 1851. Fine Jacobean panelling in the lounge, and black oak
beams, high-backed settles and log fires in the hotel bar are splendidly evocative of
a bygone era, to which the main-house bedrooms (despite up-to-date additions of
telephones, TVs and en-suite bathrooms) add their own sense of history. Conference
facility for 30. *Rooms 16. Garden. Access, Amex, Diners, Visa.*

PWLLHELI   Plas Bodegroes   £75

Tel 01758 612363 Fax 01758 701247   Map 8 B2   **RR**
Nefyn Road Pwllheli Gwynedd LL53 5TH

A small Georgian house, hidden away in woodland two miles out of town on the Nefyn
road, is the idyllic setting for Chris and Gunna Chown's stylish restaurant with rooms.
Duck-green walls crammed with contemporary Welsh art and lit by mini-spotlights
suspended from wires strung across the ceiling create a modern setting for some modish
cooking. Galantine of quail with red pepper chutney, mushroom tart with rocket and
salami salad, baked fillet of brill with a herb crust and a smoked prawn sauce, Hereford
duck with apple and calvados and mulled figs with white chocolate ice cream are typical
of the appealing dishes Chris creates out of largely local ingredients for his fixed-price,
five-course menu that offers three or four choices at each stage. Prominent Alsace section
within the manageable and well-presented wine list, which is both comprehensive and
fairly priced. Helpful notes. No smoking. *Seats 35. Private Room 16. D only 7-9.30
(Sun to 9). Closed Mon & Nov-Feb. Set D £30. Access, Amex, Visa.*

Rooms   £140 *

Gunna's Scandinavian flair for interior design is evident in the eight immaculate, individually styled bedrooms that combine charm and style. Rooms at the top of the house are given added character by some exposed beams and all have smart modern bathrooms. Enjoy the garden from the wisteria-draped veranda or there's croquet for the more energetic. No smoking in bedrooms. *Half-board terms only. Accommodation closed Monday nights (for other seasonal closure see above). Garden, croquet.

| REYNOLDSTON | **Fairyhill** | 65% | £85 |

Tel 01792 390139   Fax 01792 391358   Map 9 B6   **HR**
Reynoldston Gower Swansea West Glamorgan SA3 1BS

The hotel is set in beautiful countryside at the heart of the peninsula (best located by following signs to Gower from J47 of the M4); its own 24 acres include a meandering trout stream and lake, and abundant wild life. Within, Fairyhill's quiet intimacy is perhaps its greatest asset, to which proprietors, brother and sister Andrew Hetherington and Jane Camm, contribute a homely style of personal service. The drawing room and leafy patio are an idyllic setting for afternoon tea or pre-dinner drinks, and there's a more modest, convivial, bar. Bedroom accoutrements include remote-control TVs and CD players (reception has a CD library); fresh fruit on arrival and beds turned down during dinner. Splendid country breakfasts. No children under 8. *Rooms 9. Garden, fishing. Access, Amex, Visa.*

Restaurant   £70

Partner Paul Davies runs the kitchen with Kate Cole, offering lunch daily and a fixed-price dinner, with a balanced range of choices which changes every night. Champions of local produce, they might offer cockles, bacon and laverbread tartlets as an appetiser, along with game terrine with apple and prune chutney, warm salad of skate and bacon, and poached sewin in season (with cucumber sauce, perhaps) to follow. Prime fillet of beef with rösti potatoes and sun-dried tomato butter and supreme of Pembrokeshire duckling with white onion sauce and sherried jus are typical alternatives. Certain desserts such as tarte tatin need ordering at the beginning of the meal, otherwise the selection includes chocolate marquise and sticky toffee pudding with toffee sauce. Much work has gone into the compilation of the exceptional wine list, regional winner of our Cellar of the Year award, which offers many wines below £15 and very keen prices everywhere you look, for instance half a dozen *marque* champagnes including Pommery under £30. *Seats 68. Parties 24. Private Room 44. L 12.30-2.15 D 7.30-9. Set L from £6.95 Set D from £19.50.*

| ROSSETT | **Llyndir Hall** | 71% | £110 |

Tel 01244 571648   Fax 01244 571258   Map 8 D2   **H**
Llyndir Lane Rossett nr Wrexham Clwyd LL12 0AY

Ten minutes drive from the centre of Chester, this 'Strawberry Gothic' hall is surrounded by beautiful parkland. Bedrooms are well sized and furnished with antique pieces, the effect being both tasteful and elegant without being ostentatious. Most of the rooms are in a sympathetic new building. Some rooms are suitable for family use and children up to 16 stay free in parents' room. A gracious and sunny drawing room looks out over the lush lawns and diners have the benefit of a newly-added conservatory. Banquet and conference facilities for up to 90/130. *Rooms 38. Garden, indoor swimming pool, spa bath, steam room, solarium, coffee shop (7am-10pm, till 11 weekends). Access, Amex, Diners, Visa.*

| RUTHIN | **Ruthin Castle** | 62% | £85 |

Tel 01824 702664   Fax 01824 705978   Map 8 C2   **H**
Corwen Road Ruthin Clwyd LL15 2NU

Extensive gardens and parkland surround ancient Ruthin Castle, where relics of the past include a drowning pool, whipping pit and dungeons. The castle has known attack, siege and virtual destruction, but more peaceful diversions today centre around the cocktail bar, splendid lounge, or comfortable bedrooms appointed in traditional style. The Great Hall is the scene of regular medieval banquets, which hotel guests may attend. Conference/banqueting facilities for up to 150, free ample parking. No dogs. *Rooms 60. Garden, snooker, fishing. Access, Amex, Diners, Visa.*

St David's · St Non's Hotel · 56% · £64 · H

Tel 01437 720239   Fax 01437 721839   Map 9 A5
St David's Dyfed SA62 6RJ

Named appropriately after the mother of St David, this friendly family hotel half a mile
from the town centre offers some of the best children's terms around: under-5s stay free
in parents' room and enjoy free breakfast and high tea. Other bonuses include five
ground-floor bedrooms for the less mobile, and free golf at the picturesque St David's
9-hole course. *Rooms 24. Garden. Access, Amex, Diners, Visa.*

St David's · Warpool Court · 64% · £104 · H

Tel 01437 720300   Fax 01437 720676   Map 9 A5
St David's Dyfed SA62 6BN

Bordering National Trust parkland, Warpool Court enjoys spectacular scenery and
panoramic views over St Brides Bay to the offshore islands beyond. Equally eye-catching
within is the Ada Williams collection of unique armorial and ornamental hand-painted
tiles which bedeck the public areas and a number of the bedrooms. Private rooms for
conferences accommodate up to 40 people. Children under 14 stay free in parents' room;
outdoor playground for children. Free golf at the St David's course. The hotel was built
in the 1860s as St David's Cathedral School. *Rooms 25. Garden, croquet, tennis, covered
outdoor swimming pool (Easter-Oct), keep-fit equipment, sauna, games room, children's play
area. Closed Jan. Access, Amex, Diners, Visa.*

Swansea · Forte Posthouse · 69% · £86 · H

Tel 01792 651074   Fax 01792 456044   Map 9 C6
39 The Kingsway Swansea West Glamorgan SA1 5LS

High-riser in the city centre, updated from its 60s' look. Leisure and business centres
(conference facilities for 230). Two-thirds of the bedrooms are designated non-smoking.
Children up to 16 stay free in parents' room. Free overnight parking in NCP opposite.
Formerly the Forte Crest. *Rooms 99. Indoor swimming pool, gym, sauna, solarium.
Access, Amex, Diners, Visa.*

Swansea · Hilton National · 65% · £68 · H

Tel 01792 310330   Fax 01792 797535   Map 9 C6
Phoenix Way Enterprise Park Llansamlet Swansea
West Glamorgan SA7 9EG

Two-storey, purpose-built redbrick hotel three miles from the city centre and two from
the M4 (Junctions 44 or 45). Conference facilities for up to 180. 24hr room service.
Undergoing refurbishment to public areas as we went to press. *Rooms 118. Indoor
swimming pool, solarium. Access, Amex, Diners, Visa.*

Swansea · Langland Court Hotel · £76 · I

Tel 01792 361545   Fax 01792 362302   Map 9 C6
31 Langland Court Road Langland Swansea West Glamorgan SA3 4TD

Take the A4067 coastal road from Swansea to Mumbles (five miles) and follow signs to
Langland Bay (turn left at Newton Church) to find this comfortable clifftop inn. Public
areas take the form of a Tudor-style residence, to which Polly's, the Dylan Thomas-
themed wine bar, adds much character. Period-style main-house bedrooms mostly have
fine views of the Bristol Channel, while further rooms occupy the former coach house
(dogs allowed here only). Children up to 16 stay free in parents' room. Popular for
conferences and functions (for up to 150). *Rooms 21. Garden. Access, Amex, Diners, Visa.*

Swansea · Number One · £55 · R

Tel 01792 456996   Map 9 C6
1 Wind Street Swansea West Glamorgan SA1 1DE

The atmosphere at Kate Taylor's bistro is convivial and it's immensely popular, so
booking is advised. There's nothing pretentious about either the surroundings or her
no-nonsense cooking. Seafood is a popular choice on a daily-changing menu: sweet-
cured herring with potato and mustard salad, warm terrine of fresh lobster and hake,
coquilles St Jacques, poached salmon with sorrel sauce, fillets of monkfish with Ricard

sauce. Meaty options, too, and separate vegetarian, dessert and cheese menus. Good-value 2- and 3-course lunches with a small choice. Short wine list with the New World represented only among dessert wines. *Seats 40. L 12-2.30 D 7-9.30. Closed D Mon & Tue, all Sun. Set L £9.95/£11.95. Access, Amex, Visa.*

SWANSEA	Swansea Marriott	67%	£126

Tel 01792 642020   Fax 01792 650345   Map 9 C6   **H**
Maritime Quarter Swansea West Glamorgan SA1 3SS

Modern, four-storey redbrick hotel in the Maritime Quarter. Good-size bedrooms (50% non-smoking) look out over either the bay or the marina. Children up to 18 stay free in parents' room. Ample free parking. Banquets/conferences for up to 180/250. *Rooms 117. Indoor swimming pool, keep-fit equipment, spa bath, sauna. Access, Amex, Diners, Visa.*

TALSARNAU	Maes-y-Neuadd	72%	£107

Tel 01766 780200   Fax 01766 780211   Map 8 C2   **HR**
Talsarnau nr Harlech Gwynedd LL47 6YA

Signposted off the B4573 between Talsarnau and Harlech, Maes-y-Neuadd enjoys a tranquil setting on one side of an almost secret valley with fine views across the Snowdonia National Park. The oldest part of the building, now the bar with stone inglenook and leather upholstery, dates from the 15th century with later additions from the 16th and 19th. Other day rooms include a central lobby/lounge with large skylight and bedrooms vary considerably in style from a small single with shower and WC only, a few with pine furniture, others with antique pieces and a four-poster with oak furniture to a splendidly large room (one of four in the adjacent stable block) with black beams, high pitched ceiling and log-burning stove. All have armchairs and/or sofas and bathrooms (three with spa baths) offer good towelling and robes. Meeting rooms for up to 40, banqueting for up to 50 (which can also be arranged on the nearby Ffestiniog Railway). Personally run in friendly fashion by Malcolm and Olive Horsfall and Mike and June Slatter. *Rooms 16. Garden, croquet. Access, Amex, Diners, Visa.*

Restaurant   £70

Peter Jackson's longest dinner menu option is officially a five-course affair but add the complimentary starter and the fact that one is encouraged to sample the outstanding Welsh cheeses plus both puds before rounding off with one of their unusual ice creams and it can be more like eight or nine. The well-balanced, daily-changing menu offers a small choice at some stages; terrine of crab and salmon or salad of locally smoked meats with crispy bacon and a carrot dressing to start, strips of chicken with coarse mustard and mushrooms or fillet of beef with saffron potatoes and a rich Madeira sauce for the main course. In between come a soup and a light fish dish. The Grand Finale – Diweddglo Mawreddog in Welsh – comprises Welsh cheese, two desserts (strawberry delice, gratin of fruits) and ice creams, then coffee and sweetmeats. Read the introductory notes for an insight into how a wine list is compiled. We are pleased to say that last year's positive comment was ours! It is indeed, an excellent list, comprehensive too, with a good balance between Europe and the New World. Fair prices, helpful tasting notes, and some good bin ends. A variety of home-baked breads testifies to the care taken in the kitchen, where good use is also made of the extensive herb garden. Three-course Sunday lunch includes a traditional roast and a fish dish among the choices. No smoking. No children under 7 at dinner. *Seats 50. Parties 12. Private Room 12. L 12.15-1.45 D 7-9. Set L £11.75 (Sun £14.25) Set D £28.*

TALYLLYN	Tynycornel Hotel	59%	£90

Tel 01654 782282   Fax 01654 782679   Map 8 C3   **H**
Talyllyn Tywyn Gwynedd LL36 9AJ

Fishing is the main attraction here, but the marvellous setting on Talyllyn Lake in Snowdonia National Park makes it a popular base for hikers and lovers of all aspects of the great outdoors, particularly birdwatching. The hotel has its own fleet of small boats for hire and there's also an angler's tackle shop, a drying room and a rod room. The atmosphere is cosy and relaxed in the lounge and bar. Accommodation is comfortable and functional. Children up to the age of 12 stay free in parents' room. Banqueting and conference facilities for up to 60. *Rooms 16. Garden, outdoor swimming pool, sauna, solarium, fishing. Access, Amex, Diners, Visa.*

| TINTERN ABBEY | **Beaufort Hotel** | 60% | £92 |

Tel 01291 689777   Fax 01291 689727   Map 9 D5   **H**
Tintern Abbey nr Chepstow Gwent NP6 6SF

Stone-built hotel whose front rooms look out on to the ruins of 800-year-old Tintern Abbey in the Wye Valley. Children under 16 stay free in parents' room. Banqueting/conference facilities for 90/80. 7 miles from Junction 22 of M4. Jarvis Hotels. *Rooms 24. Garden, coarse fishing, games room. Access, Amex, Diners, Visa.*

| TINTERN ABBEY | **Royal George** | 59% | £72 |

Tel 01291 689205   Fax 01291 689448   Map 9 D5   **H**
Tintern Abbey nr Chepstow Gwent NP6 6SF

The beautiful Wye Valley is the setting for Tony and Maureen Pearce's hotel in the village centre at the foot of a wooded hillside. The river is across the main road and the ruins of Tintern Abbey are just a short walk away. The hotel began life in 1598 as the Irons Master's cottage for the nearby mines and was converted into a coaching inn in the 17th century. There are hints of the building's previous lives in its present appearance and versatility: there's ample bar and lounge space (one lounge is stocked with board games) and a large function room. Some of the bedrooms have balconies overlooking the gardens. One child under 14 free in parents' room. *Rooms 19. Garden. Access, Amex, Diners, Visa.*

| TRELLECH | **The Village Green** | | £45 |

Tel 01600 860119   Map 9 D5   **RR**
Trellech nr Monmouth Gwent NP5 4PA

Bob and Jane Evans's once-derelict, 450-year-old village inn fashionably combines bistro-style food with more traditional restaurant concepts. The dividing line between bistro and à la carte is now narrowed to a large degree with main courses changed daily on large blackboard menus to complement popular starters such as smoked halibut with pickled samphire and spicy lamb sausage with mango sauce. Tuscan fish stew, joint of lamb with honey and rosemary, and salmon with leek and mushrooms in lattice pastry are considered specialities whilst desserts are of the chocolate bread-and-butter pudding and apple and shortbread pie variety. *Seats 70. Parties 12. Private Room 24. L 11.45-2 D 7-10. Closed D Sun, all Mon, 1 week Jan. Set Sun L £11.75. Access, Visa.*

Rooms   £45

An adjacent stable conversion houses two small bedroom suites with kitchenettes let on a self-catering or bed-and-breakfast basis. The rooms have TV but no phones, and en-suite WC/shower rooms only. Children under 10 accommodated free.

| WELSH HOOK | **Stone Hall** | | £60 |

Tel 01348 840212   Fax 01348 840815   Map 9 A5   **RR**
Welsh Hook Wolfscastle nr Haverfordwest Dyfed SA62 5NS

Hidden down country lanes 1½ miles off the A40 (signed from Wolfscastle), the restaurant's interior is as Welsh as one would hope to find at such an address as this: stone alcoves, exposed roof timbers, flagged floors, metre-thick walls and by the huge hooded range there are even bread ovens built into the original inglenook. The setting may be Welsh but Martine Watson's cooking is uncompromisingly French. A la carte starters might include snails in garlic butter, warm goat's cheese on a bed of salad and *queues de crevettes sautées au Ricard et petits oignons* before magret of duck with apples and cider, brochette of monkfish with bacon and olives, and fillet of beef with wild mushrooms and Madeira. Finish with nougat glacé, a gratin of fresh fruit in egg custard or *puits d'amour au chocolat chaud*. The no-choice, four-course table d'hote is particularly good value. Not a half bottle in sight on the wine list, but prices are so reasonable that it hardly matters. No children under 10 after 7pm. *Seats 34. Private Room 20. L by arrangement D 7-9.30. Closed 2 weeks Jan. Set D £15.50. Access, Amex, Diners, Visa.*

Rooms   £63

Residents enjoy use of their own lounge and five en-suite bedrooms (three doubles and two singles) which are immaculately kept. Children, made welcome overnight, are offered their own supper at 5.30pm. The resident cats are great favourites, so no dogs admitted!

WHITEBROOK   **Crown at Whitebrook**   **£65**

Tel 01600 860254   Fax 01600 860607   Map 14 A2   **RR**
Whitebrook nr Monmouth Gwent NP5 4TX

Deep in the steeply wooded Whitebrook Valley, the original inn has resurfaced as
a modern, white-painted rectangular building run since 1988 by Roger and Sandra Bates
as a restaurant with rooms offering a relaxed, informal atmosphere with high standards of
personal service. A comfortable lounge (which houses the reception desk and small
dispense bar) leads on to a cottagey, beamed dining-room with wheelback chairs and pink
and blue tablecloths. A fixed-price dinner menu offers a choice of seven or eight dishes at
each stage: parfait of foie gras; Welsh goat's cheese tart with tomato and basil; crab cakes
on saffron sauce; best end of lamb with herb crust and a spinach and laverbread mousse;
steamed salmon with white wine, cream and herb sauce; duck breast poached in cider
with peas and duck croutons; tarte au chocolat; trio of citrus desserts. Sandra makes
everything herself from the bread, gravad lax, ice creams and sorbets, to the stocks that
are at the heart of some excellent sauces, while Roger is the chatty host front of house.
Lunchtime brings a shorter, simpler prix-fixe plus a varied light lunch menu also served
in the lounge. The cheese list usually runs to about ten, mostly Welsh, offerings. Very fair
prices (two champagnes under £25, two more under £30) on a wine list that has its fair
share of top-notch bottles, including some very fine offerings from the New World.
Seats 32. Private Room 12. L 12-2 D 7-9.30. Closed L Mon, D Sun (except for residents),
25 & 26 Dec, 2 weeks Jan, 2 weeks Aug. Set L £14.95 Set D £24.95.
Access, Amex, Diners, Visa.

Rooms   **£80**

Twelve well-kept, modestly furnished bedrooms (some recently refurbished) with
compact en-suite bathrooms offer good overnight accommodation. All have direct-dial
phones, remote-control TV, radio-alarm, hairdryer and tea/coffee-making facilities. The
terrace makes a good spot for breakfast if the weather is kind.

We welcome bona fide complaints and recommendations on the
tear-out pages at the back of the book for reader's comments.
They are followed up by our professional team.

Your **Guarantee** of **Quality** and **Independence**

- ● Establishment inspections are anonymous
- ● Inspections are undertaken by qualified Egon Ronay's Guides inspectors
- ● The Guides are completely independent in their editorial selection
- ● The Guides do not accept advertising, hospitality or payment from listed establishments

Titles planned for 1996 include

Hotels & Restaurants ● Pubs & Inns ● Europe Ireland ● Just A Bite And Children Come Too ● Paris Oriental Restaurants

Channel Islands
& Isle of Man

Alderney

BRAYE	First & Last	£30

Tel 01481 823162 Map 13 F4 **R**
Braye Alderney

The only restaurant on the island to benefit from the sea view, with a panoramic dining room on the first floor. The blue decor is strongly marine and as you would expect in this location, fish is the order of the day, including, as available, lobster, crab, scallops and mussels. Bouillabaisse is something of a speciality. There are also plenty of steaks and omelettes, and a concise wine list. In the evening, red lanterns are lit for a more romantic atmosphere. No children after 9.30. *Seats 75. Parties 50. L 12-1.45 D 6.45-11. Set Sun L £9.50. Closed Oct-Mar, also Mon exc Bank Holidays. Access, Amex, Diners, Visa.*

ST ANNE	Hotel Chez André	63%	£83

Tel 01481 822777   Fax 01481 822962   Map 13 F4   **H**
Victoria Street St Anne Alderney

Dating originally from the 1790s, the Marks family's friendly hotel was converted to its present use in 1965. The homely lounge and breakfast conservatory adjacent to the restaurant are attractive features. En-suite bedrooms have trouser press, satellite TV, hairdryer and tea/coffee facilities. *Rooms 11. Closed Nov-end Feb. Access, Amex, Visa.*

ST ANNE	Georgian House	£45

Tel & Fax 01481 822471   Map 13 F4   **R**
Victoria Street St Anne Alderney

There are several nice touches which make the Georgian House stand out: one is a courtesy car between the house and the harbour (book it when you make your table reservation); another is The Garden Beyond, the peaceful, fragrant garden area complete with open air bar and grill, designed to take full advantage of the kind climate in summer, and a third is the friendly welcome from owners Elizabeth and Stephen Hope. Between the à la carte and blackboard menus the choice ranges from avocado with prawns, and Galia melon to tournedos Rossini and bacon-wrapped lamb stuffed with olives and grain mustard in a Marsala sauce. Local seafood is well represented although 24 hours notice is required for the lobster and crab. Bedroom accommodation – one single, one small double and a two room suite – has just reopened after refurbishment (not inspected). *Seats 48. Private Room 24. L 12-2.30 D 7.15-9.30. Closed D Tue. Set Sun L £8.75. Access, Amex, Diners, Visa.*

ST ANNE	Inchalla Hotel	64%	£73

Tel 01481 823220   Fax 01481 824045   Map 13 F4   **HR**
The Val St Anne Alderney

Set in its own secluded grounds with lovely views across the English Channel and to the bird sanctuary island of Burhou, Inchalla has been in the capable and attentive hands of Valerie Willis since 1982. A lounge/conservatory is the main day room; bedrooms are smart and well-equipped. There's a small car park. No dogs. *Rooms 9. Garden, mini-gym, sauna, spa bath. Closed 2 weeks Christmas. Access, Amex, Visa.*

Restaurant   **£55**

Lobster, crab and other seafood are the speciality of the restaurant, where a new chef took over just before we went to press. *Seats 30. L (Sun only) 1-2 D 7-8.30. Set Sun L £8.75 Set D £12.*

Consult the blue pages for summary tables and lists of
recommended establishments.

Guernsey

| CASTEL | La Grande Mare | 72% | £113 |

Tel 01481 56576 Fax 01481 56532   Map 13 E4   **H**
Vazon Bay Castel Guernsey GY5 7BD

Situated on Guernsey's west coast with seaward aspects over the broad sandy sweep of Vazon Bay and the English Channel beyond, La Grande Mare enjoys its own 100 acres of land, complete with 9-hole golf course. The pastel-washed building, in a style appealingly somewhere between a traditional Guernsey farmhouse and a Mediterranean villa and bedecked with balconies, is set around an outdoor pool and patio. Inside, public rooms are relaxed and welcoming: arched windows, limed oak furniture and exposed brickwork enhance the Continental feel created by rugs and soft upholstery. However, it is in the bedroom accommodation that La Grande Mare is particularly unusual and innovative, in that it ranges from rooms (some with four-posters) to studios, to luxury exclusive penthouse suites, to one- or two-bed apartments, to a villa for eight. All bathrooms are spacious, extensively equipped and meticulously maintained; all suites have facilities for fixing light snacks and all ten apartments have a fully fitted kitchen. As well as the self-catering facilities, there is a full 24hr room service and although bed and breakfast rates are available (and quoted in our guide price), half-board terms are preferred. *Rooms 34. Garden, croquet, outdoor swimming pool, splash pool, spa bath, golf (9), fishing. Access, Amex, Diners, Visa.*

| CASTEL | Hougue du Pommier | £74 |

Tel 01481 56531 Fax 01481 56260   Map 13 E4   **I**
Castel Guernsey

'Apple Tree Hill' is the meaning of the name, so it's no surprise to find that this lovely inn is set in an old orchard. Quiet bedrooms, which overlook the well-kept gardens, are comfortable, with remote-control colour TV and tea/coffee facilities. The solar heated swimming pool is sheltered by trees. Bar meals served all day. Parking for 50. *Rooms 38. Garden, outdoor swimming pool, sauna, solarium, golf (18), games room. Access, Amex, Diners, Visa.*

| L'ERÉE | Taste of India | £35 |

Tel 01481 64516   Map 13 E4   **R**
Sunset Cottage L'Erée Guernsey GY7 9LN

One of the very few Indian restaurants on the island, it is well located at the end of Rocquaine Bay near Lihou island right on the west coast. The menu is strong on tandoori and there's also a section called Exquisite Dishes, which are the restaurant specialities. Seafood dishes too are featured as in tandoori lobster and garlic salmon. Dishes are prepared with quality ingredients and a delicate mix of spices. There is also a branch in St Peter Port (Tel 01481 723730). *Seats 35. L 12-2 D 6-11. Set Sun L £9.95 Set D £15/£18. Closed L Mon (Apr-Oct), 25 Dec. Access, Amex, Diners, Visa.*

| FOREST | Mallard Hotel | 67% | £70 |

Tel 01481 64164 Fax 01481 65732   Map 13 E4   **H**
Forest Guernsey

Conveniently located near the airport (there's a courtesy bus between the two, or from hotel to harbour), this hotel offers good accommodation at kind prices. Public rooms are particularly large and the big attraction is of course the outdoor solar-heated swimming pool with plenty of sun beds and outdoor tables. Bedrooms are comfortable, with trouser press, hairdryer, colour TV and tea/coffee facilities. Rooms overlooking the swimming pool have balconies facing south. Rooms facing the back of the building are quieter. Perfect for families. Parking for 120 cars. The cinema now houses 4 screens and a new children's soft play area has a Disney theme throughout. *Rooms 47. Garden, outdoor swimming pool, keep-fit equipment, sauna, spa bath, sun beds, tennis, mini-golf course, pétanque, children's outdoor playground, young children's playroom, games room, 4-screen cinema. Closed 1 Dec-mid Mar. Access, Amex, Diners, Visa.*

PLEINMONT   Imperial Hotel   £56

Tel 01481 64044 Fax 01481 66139   Map 13 E4   **I**
Pleinmont Torteval Guernsey GY8 0PS

Attractive little hotel ideally located at the south end of Rocquaine Bay, also overlooking the harbour at Portelet. Bar, restaurant (restored to its all-wood design of 100 years ago) and most of the bedrooms benefit from a beautiful view of the bay. Four rooms have attractive balconies with patio furniture, all have clean and bright accommodation with tea/coffee facilities, colour TV and direct-dial telephone. Rooms with sea views attract a supplement. *Rooms 17. Garden, café (10.30am-11.45pm). Closed Nov-Mar. Access, Visa.*

ROCQUAINE BAY   Rocquaine Seafood Bistro   £50

Tel 01481 63149 Fax 01481 63989   Map 13 E4   **R**
Rocquaine Bay Guernsey

Seafood is the thing here, spanking fresh and displayed on ice for your selection at a friendly bistro overlooking the sea (try for a window table if your booking coincides with sunset). Decor is simple – green ceiling, whitewashed walls, a low room with big windows. Josef Tautscher is Austrian so that makes for a tri-lingual menu. There are a couple of steak dishes and a pasta concoction for vegetarians, but basically it's hard to resist the fish and shellfish – shiny turbot, local oysters, blushing crabs and lobsters. The fish is mostly grilled, often with garlic, or served meunière or with a creamy sauce of mushrooms or pink peppercorns. *Seats 60. L 12-2.15 D 7-10.30. Closed Oct-Feb. Access, Amex, Diners, Visa.*

ST MARTIN   Hotel Bon Port   66%   £100

Tel 01481 39249 Fax 01481 39596   Map 13 E4   **H**
Rue Gros Jean Moulin Huet Bay St Martin Guernsey GY4 6EW

The modern Bon Port has good views over two of the island's prettiest bays (Moulin Huet, often painted by Renoir, and Petit Port) and is quiet and comfortable. Bedrooms (including four suites) are well maintained and equipped – best ones have sea views and balconies. The Gate House cottage alongside the main building has one double and two single bedrooms and is let by the week on a self-catering basis. Recent additions are the health suite and the Atrium with plants and a fountain. No children under 14. No dogs. *Rooms 18. Garden, pitch and putt, boules, outdoor swimming pool, sauna, mini-gym. Access, Visa.*

ST MARTIN   St Margaret's Lodge   63%   £75

Tel 01481 35757 Fax 01481 37594   Map 13 E4   **H**
Forest Road St Martin Guernsey

Bright and friendly staff welcome you to St Margaret's Lodge, one of Guernsey's longest established tourist hotels. Not far from the airport and the south coast beaches, it offers comfortable and well-maintained public rooms and bedrooms (some reserved for non-smokers). There's a courtesy bus into St Peter Port, as well as the facilities on site. *Rooms 47. Garden, croquet, outdoor pool, sauna, solarium. Access, Amex, Diners, Visa.*

ST PETER PORT   Absolute End   £60

Tel 01481 723822 Fax 01481 729129   Map 13 E4   **R**
St George's Esplanade St Peter Port Guernsey GY1 2BG

Although the menu sounds traditional in style, the execution of the cooking here is definitely bang up to date, while both decor and service are equally crisp and professional. The restaurant is (relatively) far out at the north end of St Peter Port, but enjoys pretty views over the bay. Daily specials supplement the regular menu dishes: raw scallops are marinated in lime, ginger and dill. This is one of the best places in Guernsey to eat lobster, perhaps simply grilled; or some excellent sea bass – fresh and succulent and simply steamed with herbs. For pudding, try an unusual Austrian nut pudding: a light concoction of breadcrumbs, hazelnuts and chocolate shaped into a dome and steamed, served with vanilla ice-cream. *Seats 60. Parties 20. Private Room 22. L 12-2 D 7-10. Closed Sun & Jan. Set L £11. Access, Amex, Diners, Visa.*

ST PETER PORT   Braye Lodge   £75

Tel 01481 723787   Fax 01481 712876   Map 13 E4   **H**
Ruette Braye St Peter Port Guernsey

Sixteen bedrooms are en suite. The remainder, which presently share three bathrooms, are scheduled to have their own facilities added from January 1996, following which the hotel will be regraded. No dogs. *Rooms 26. Garden, outdoor swimming pool. Closed November. No credit cards.*

ST PETER PORT   Da Nello's   £50

Tel 01481 721552   Map 13 E4   **R**
46 Le Pollet St Peter Port Guernsey

Long-established, hugely popular Italian restaurant which succeeds in catering for several markets at the same time and yet doesn't disappoint any of them – local businessmen spending huge amounts on expenses, moderate-budget tourists, and by-passing light snackers. A big plus here is the friendly ambience generated by Nello himself. A good-value set dinner is offered as well as an extensive carte. Warm smoked scallop salad was offset by a wonderful balsamic vinaigrette; there's an excellent home-made minestrone. Pasta, such as penne with dolcelatte and broccoli, is served in chunky bowls, hand-made in Italy, while baked aubergine parmigiana is more traditionally served in terracotta bakeware. Straightforward puds like panna cotta, profiteroles, caffè affogato or zabaglione with strawberries, round off the meal. *Seats 66. L 12-2 D 6.30-10.30. Closed 25 & 26 Dec. Set L £7.75 Set D £12.50. Access, Amex, Visa.*

ST PETER PORT   Duke of Richmond   63%   £65

Tel 01481 726221   Fax 01481 728945   Map 13 E4   **H**
Cambridge Park St Peter Port Guernsey GY1 1UY

The hotel began life in 1790 as Grover's Hotel but was renamed after a regular visitor, the third Duke of Richmond, who was Master of Ordnance here from 1781-1795 and was instrumental in building the Martello watchtowers which give Guernsey's coastline such character. The hillside location provides excellent views from many of the bedrooms, some of which have balconies. Inland rooms are the cheapest, while top of the range is the penthouse suite. Conference/banqueting facilities for 240/220. Children under 12 free sharing parents' room. *Rooms 75. Terrace, outdoor swimming pool. Access, Amex, Diners, Visa.*

Set menu prices may not always include service or wine.

ST PETER PORT   La Frégate   64%   £95

Tel 01481 724624   Fax 01481 720443   Map 13 E4   **H**
Les Cotils St Peter Port Guernsey

Set in its own peaceful gardens above St Julian's Avenue, La Frégate is an 18th-century manor house providing high standards of comfort and service along with views of the harbour from most of the bedrooms. Some rooms have double-glazed patio doors opening on to private balconies. No children under 14. No dogs. *Rooms 13. Terrace. Access, Amex, Diners, Visa.*

ST PETER PORT   Le Nautique   £55

Tel 01481 721714   Fax 01481 721786   Map 13 E4   **R**
The Quay Steps St Peter Port Guernsey GY1 2LE

Long-established French restaurant standing on the seafront, overlooking the harbour and marina, with a reassuringly unchanged menu. Fish is the pick of the menu, as you might expect. Sole comes grilled, meunière or with a champagne and lobster sauce; lobster itself is offered grilled and flambéed with whisky, Thermidor or cold with mayonnaise and salad. Duck, lamb and steaks are also popular and there's a selection of three vegetarian dishes. Service is polished and efficient, booking essential. Smart dress is preferred. Smoking allowed in the bar and after 9 in the dining-room. No children under five or after 8.30pm. *Seats 68. Parties 14. Private Room 30. L 12-2 D 7-10. Closed Sun & 25Dec-1Jan. Access, Amex, Diners, Visa.*

St Peter Port   Old Government House   68%   £92

Tel 01481 724921   Fax 01481 724429   Map 13 E4   **H**
Ann's Place St Peter Port Guernsey GY1 4AZ

OGH, as it's affectionately known, offers traditional standards of decor and service, and the classically elegant entrance hall is a reminder of the days when it actually was the Governor's residence. Bedrooms and public rooms are well maintained. The Governor's Bar is cosy and intimate with its military memorabilia and the Centenary Bar, opened in 1958 to mark 100 years of the hotel's existence, features dancing to the hotel band Monday to Saturday in summer and weekends in winter. Best bedrooms are in a modern wing. Conference/banqueting facilities for 110. *Rooms 72. Garden, outdoor swimming pool, solarium, coffee shop 10am-8pm. Access, Amex, Diners, Visa.*

St Peter Port   St Pierre Park   71%   £135

Tel 01481 728282   Fax 01481 712041   Map 13 E4   **H**
Rohais St Peter Port Guernsey GY1 1FD

The St Pierre Park was built in 1983 on the edge of the main town, in 45 acres of parkland. All the bedrooms are well equipped, and several are suitable for family use (28 interconnect). Most impressive of all is the leisure complex, with its Tony Jacklin-designed 9-hole golf course, three outdoor tennis courts, a 25m indoor swimming pool and a fully-equipped health suite. Public rooms are airy and elegant. The lounge/bar and some bedrooms overlook the garden and ornamental lake. Banqueting/conferences for 360/400. Children under 12 stay free in their parents' room. *Rooms 135. Garden, croquet, golf course (9-hole), pitch & putt, putting, tennis, indoor swimming pool, gym, sauna, steam room, spa bath, solarium, beauty & hair salons, snooker, coffee shop (10am-10.30pm), gift & clothes shop, outdoor play area. Access, Amex, Diners, Visa.*

St Peter   Café du Moulin   £60

Tel 01481 65944   Fax 01481 66468   Map 13 E4   **R**
Rue de Quanteraine St Peter Guernsey

Not really a café, more a serious restaurant (though light meals and afternoon teas are also available) paying great attention to the smaller details: all canapés, breads, ices, sorbets and petits fours are home-made. The building's origins as a watermill create a pretty but not fussy atmosphere to the long, low dining room which opens on to a terrace. Gina Mann is the influence at front of house, while husband David is in charge of the kitchen, from where he turns out some of the best food on the island. A wide variety of dishes is on offer, though fish is naturally predominant, tackled here in some off-beat ways – a starter of Thai-style stuffed squid salad was both fragrant and piquant. Main courses, several listed on a daily-changing board, range from lamb's sweetbreads through Gressingham duck (crispy) to a delicious crépinette of seafood – prawns, scallops, monkfish and salmon bound by bacon into a sausage, thickly sliced and served on a tomato hollandaise – a triumph of flavours and textures. Boned wing of skate was spanking fresh and quite delicious. Accompanying vegetables, perfectly cooked, could include a little square of dauphinoise potatoes, Jerusalem artichokes, a curried purée of parsnip, carrot discs, cauliflower and broccoli. A well-judged lemon tart makes for a perfect finish, or ditherers can have the grand plat and thus also taste, for example, a perfect English trifle, chocolate millefeuille with orange, prune and armagnac ice cream, mixed berry and honey and melon sorbets. Self-catering accommodation is also available. *Seats 45. Parties 8. L 12.15-1.45 D 7.15-9.45. Set L £8.95/£10.95/£13.95 Set D £15.95 (not Sat, Aug & Sep). Closed D Sun & all Mon in winter. Access, Amex, Diners, Visa.*

St Saviour   Auberge du Val   £50

Tel 01481 63862   Fax 01481 64835   Map 13 E4   **R**
Sous L'Eglise St Saviour Guernsey

This unusual place combines a terraced herb garden, health suite, residential accommodation and a restaurant, serving inventive food in relaxed surroundings. Meals are taken at wooden tables, served by cheerful and efficient staff, and a blackboard lists daily specials which augment the printed menu. There's a new boldness to the cooking in

Guernsey, clearly demonstrated here and embracing Oriental and Pacific Rim influences. On a summer visit Thai scallop salad was full of taste sensations, tingly with chili and lemon grass. Crab samosas, stuffed with beansprouts and fine noodles but mostly lots of crab, were delicious. Another popular starter is porc Nabgatch – ground pork with garlic, cooked Chinese-style and served with rice noodles and crisp lettuce. Madagascan fishcakes used rösti for the potato element, but were still definitely fishy; spinach and carrot roulade was generously portioned and well balanced. The accompanying vegetables could be new potatoes, mangetout and spaghetti of carrots. Other main dishes could be guinea fowl with mushrooms or duck breast served pink with a port and green peppercorn sauce. Amongst the desserts, lemon tart was superb, intensely lemony; "hazelnutty" treacle tart also benefited from a tang of lemon to counteract the sweetness; and the iced chocolate terrine was of enormous proportions. Wines are all from the New World, so as to offer "the best value in quality, price and consistency" – and very fairly priced they are, too. *Seats 42. Parties 15. L 12-2 D 7-9.30. Closed Mon, also D Sun Nov-Apr. Access, Amex, Visa.*

Herm

HERM	White House	64%	£110*

Tel 01481 722159   Fax 01481 710066   Map 13 E4   **HR**
Herm

"Paradise is this close" says the White House's brochure, and indeed at this, the only hotel on the island, there is comfortable accommodation for those who want to escape the hurly-burly of mainland life. The hotel produces its own electricity and there are no televisions or telephones in the bedrooms; a small butane cooker is used to heat up the kettles. The best bedrooms have sea view and balcony. The hotel is self-contained with a succession of homely lounges, an elegant sea view restaurant and a pub with a Carvery dining room. Half-board terms only. Self-catering cottages and flats available. No dogs. *Rooms 38. Garden, croquet, tennis, outdoor swimming pool. Closed Oct-Mar. Access, Visa.*

Restaurant   £40

The White House has its own oyster farm so it will come as no surprise that the specialities on the set menu are largely seafood, though meat-eaters are also well catered for and vegetarians are not neglected. Try oysters or a warm mousseline of crab served on a prawn sauce, then perhaps honey-basted breast of duckling on a bed of stir-fried vegetables, or tournedos with wild mushrooms and a port wine sauce, and rich chocolate mousse with grapes on a duo of chocolate sauces to finish. The well-priced gourmet menu has choice of five courses and carries owner Michael Hester's personal recommendations for accompanying wines. Meals are served in an elegant dining room where smoking is not allowed. *Seats 118. Parties 14. L 12.30-2 D 7-9.30. Set Sun L £10.50/£15.50 (Sun £9.95). Set D £15.75/£16.75.*

Jersey

BOULEY BAY	Water's Edge Hotel	64%	£104

Tel 01534 862777   Fax 01534 863645   Map 13 F4   **H**
Les Charrières de Boulay Bouley Bay Trinity Jersey JE3 5AS

A unique location on the island, as it stands alone in Bouley Bay with a beautiful view, direct access to the pebble beach and outdoor swimming pool. Bar and dining rooms both overlook the sea. Bedrooms are comfortable the best ones have small balconies and sea views. Children up to 11 stay free in parents' room (meals charged as taken). Children's menu and early suppers available. Banqueting/conferences for 120/65. 24hr room service. *Rooms 51. Garden, outdoor swimming pool, sauna, sunbeds, coffee shop (9.30-5.30). Closed 10 Oct-mid Easter. Access, Amex, Diners, Visa.*

GOREY   Jersey Pottery Garden   ↑   £60

Tel 01534 851119   Fax 01534 856403   Map 13 F4   **R**
Gorey Village Gorey Jersey JE3 9EP

Colin Jones has been running the Garden Restaurant at the Jersey Pottery for an amazing 40 years. It's an attractive restaurant, set in a flowery conservatory with garden furniture, umbrellas, and climbing vines. The extensive menu offers any number of seafood dishes, some slightly more unusual such as cappucini, freshly picked crab meat with thin slices of smoked salmon in a brandy-flavoured Marie Rose sauce, or salmon Cameron – an escalope of salmon interleaved with home-made pasta. Beautiful fresh seafood salads and plateaux de fruits de mer using locally caught seafood are a speciality. A fish grill offers langoustines, brill, bass, salmon and scallops grilled with walnut oil and roast peppers. The next-door self-service café offers cold dishes (mainly seafood salads), pastries and afternoon teas. Children are very welcome in both restaurants. *Seats 250. Parties 24. Meals 12-4.30. Closed Sun, 1 week Christmas. Access, Amex, Diners, Visa.*

GOREY   Moorings Hotel   62%   £90

Tel 01534 853633   Fax 01534 857618   Map 13 F4   **H**
Gorey Pier Gorey Jersey JE3 6EW

A small, friendly, waterfront hotel tucked between Mont Orgueil Castle and Gorey Harbour, just a short distance from Grouville Bay. Two bars provide a choice for relaxing over a drink, and there's a lounge and roof garden. Bedrooms are furnished in simple style, with colour TV, radio, hairdryer, trouser press, direct-dial telephone and tea/coffee-making facilities. Banqueting/conferences for 60/30. No dogs. *Rooms 16. Access, Amex, Visa.*

GOREY   Old Court House Hotel   64%   £89

Tel 01534 854444   Fax 01534 853587   Map 13 F4   **H**
Gorey Village Grouville Jersey JE3 9FS

Parts of the Old Court House (specifically the restaurant) date back to the 15th century although the overall appearance is modern. Bedrooms and public areas are well equipped and maintained, making it popular for family holidays. New-wing bedrooms have balconies, but the pleasant older rooms are more spacious. *Rooms 58. Garden, outdoor swimming pool, sauna, solarium. Closed mid Oct-mid Apr. Access, Amex, Diners, Visa.*

GROUVILLE   Grouville Bay Hotel   62%   £80

Tel 01534 851004   Fax 01534 857416   Map 13 F4   **H**
Grouville Jersey JE3 9BB

Located right next to the Royal Jersey Golf course, the hotel has no golf concession but enjoys attractive views over the greens. In the other direction there are views of the 12th-century Mont Orgueil Castle. Bedrooms face either the golf course and the sea (with balconies), or the garden and the interior of the island. 40% are suitable for family use. Footpath to the nearby beach. Early suppers for children, plenty of high-chairs and baby-sitting are all available. Comfortable public rooms. *Rooms 56. Garden, croquet, outdoor swimming pool, children's swimming pool and playroom, games room. Closed mid Oct-Apr. Access, Amex, Diners, Visa.*

HAVRE DES PAS   Hotel de la Plage   66%   £70

Tel 01534 23474   Fax 01534 68642   Map 13 F4   **H**
Havre des Pas St Helier Jersey JE2 4UQ

On the outskirts of St Helier right on the seafront, this is a well-run modern hotel with picture windows to enhance the views. Day rooms are in various styles: subdued and modern in the split-level lounge-bar, tropical in the Caribbean Bar, bamboo in the sun lounge. The rate quoted is for an inland-view bedroom; sea-facing rooms, some with balconies, carry supplements. All have en-suite bathrooms with the usual electric gadgets and bathrobes. No dogs. *Rooms 78. Keep-fit facilities, sun beds, games room. Closed mid Oct-end Apr. Access, Amex, Diners, Visa.*

Many hotels offer reduced rates for weekend or out-of-season bookings. Always ask about special deals.

HAVRE DES PAS   Ommaroo Hotel   59%   £90

Tel 01534 23493   Fax 01534 59912   Map 13 F4   **H**
Havre des Pas St Helier Jersey JE2 4UQ

Traditional seaside hotel (popular with families), some of whose rooms have sea-facing balconies. Child-friendly. Relaxing lounges and bars. Banquets and conferences for up to 60. *Rooms 85. Garden. Access, Amex, Diners, Visa.*

PORTELET BAY   Portelet Hotel   66%   £104

Tel 01534 41204   Fax 01534 46625   Map 13 F4   **H**
Portelet Bay St Brelade Jersey JE3 8AU

The Portelet was built in the 30s and retains some Art Deco features, notably at the entrance. It also aims to observe the sentiments of that era in terms of courtesy and attention to detail. Most popular of the public rooms is the sun lounge overlooking the pool to St Brelade's Bay beyond. Elsewhere there's a quiet residents' lounge and a 70s-style cocktail bar. Many of the bedrooms have private balconies. Free early-morning tea or coffee and paper, mini-bus to town. Conference/banqueting for 140. No dogs. *Rooms 86. Garden, outdoor swimming pool, children's splash pool, tennis, putting, fishing, games room, snooker. Closed Oct-Apr. Access, Amex, Diners, Visa.*

ROZEL BAY   Chateau la Chaire   74%   £118

Tel 01534 863354   Fax 01534 865137   Map 13 F4   **HR**
Rozel Bay Jersey JE3 6AJ

Built in 1843 just above the charming harbour of Rozel Bay, the hotel has day rooms which retain the proportions and elegance of the last century, from the welcoming reception hall, with its large staircase, to the high-ceilinged rococo lounge and the intimate, oak-panelled dining room. There's an unusual suite on the ground floor which has a mezzanine level within it. Executive rooms on the first floor have comfortable sitting areas and jacuzzi bathtubs; some have balconies. Regular double bedrooms are much smaller, with the charming cosiness of lower ceilings under slanted roofs and small windows. Complimentary water, fruit basket and biscuits in all bedrooms. No children under 7. *Rooms 14. Garden. Access, Amex, Diners, Visa.*

Restaurant   £70

This year we were less enamoured with the quality of cooking than the customers who are actively encouraged to write in to the Guide with as much praise as they can muster (please stop!). Stick to the simple seafood dishes: mussel and safron soup, seared salmon or baked fillet of sea bass. The conservatory is non-smoking, and there are 40 seats outside on the terrace. Well-stocked wine list. *Seats 65. Parties 30. Private Rooms 16/30. L 12.30-2 D 7-10. Set L £11.75/£14.25 D £19.50/£25.*

ST AUBIN   Old Court House Inn   £80

Tel 01534 46433   Fax 01534 45103   Map 13 F4   **I**
St Aubin Harbour St Aubin Jersey

The Old Court House was actually more than simply that – the court house itself occupied the rear of the building while the front part was a merchant's house. The tall building overlooks the harbour, the best view of all being from the penthouse suite with its private sun terrace. All bedrooms are well furnished and equipped. A new bar area and conservatory have recently come on stream. *Rooms 10. Access, Amex, Diners, Visa.*

ST BRELADE   Atlantic Hotel   71%   £140

Tel 01534 44101   Fax 01534 44102   Map 13 F4   **H**
La Moye St Brelade Jersey JE3 8HE

The hotel sits amongst cultivated gardens with glorious views overlooking St Ouen's Bay on one side and La Moye golf course on the other. Bedrooms – all well maintained and equipped with all the usual extras – are priced according to their view. The Garden Studios on the ground floor are larger than the standard bedrooms, two suites are bigger again with their own terraces leading out into the garden. Another major feature is the Palm Club, a well-equipped health and leisure centre. Banqueting/conferences for 60. No dogs. *Rooms 50. Garden, indoor & outdoor swimming pools, mini-gym, sauna, spa bath, sun beds, tennis. Closed Jan & Feb. Access, Amex, Diners, Visa.*

ST BRELADE   Hotel Chateau Valeuse   65%   £84

Tel 01534 46281   Fax 01534 47110   Map 13 F4   **HR**
St Brelade Jersey JE3 8EE

Well-situated, on the south-facing St Brelade's Bay, the hotel is set back from the main road. Bedrooms (some with seaward balconies) are all simply and comfortably furnished. Impeccably maintained gardens surround the pool. No children under 5. *Rooms 33. Garden, outdoor swimming pool, putting. Closed mid Oct-late Mar. Access, Visa.*

Restaurant   £50

A carte (not Sundays) and set menus appeal to residents and day visitors alike. Lots of seafood prepared in classical ways, plus grills and flambés. *Seats 70. Parties 50. L 12.45-1.45 D 8-9. Closed D Sun. Set L £9 (Sun £11) Set D £14.50.*

ST BRELADE   La Place Hotel   67%   £110

Tel 01534 44261   Fax 01534 45164   Map 13 F4   **H**
Route du Coin La Haule St Brelade Jersey JE3 8BF

Just four miles from St Helier and seven minutes from the airport, La Place is nonetheless for those who like rural surroundings. It was once a farmhouse but is now much enlarged by modern extensions. The main public rooms are part of the original, 400-year-old building. There's a delightful open-air seating area in a south-facing courtyard, a bright bar with green bamboo furniture and two lounges, one of which has a black-beamed ceiling, a pink granite fireplace, antique furniture and polished brass ornaments. Bedrooms include seven around the pool. Children up to 12 stay free in parents' room. There's parking for 30 cars, and banqueting/conference facilities for 80/45. *Rooms 40. Garden, outdoor swimming pool, sauna. Access, Amex, Diners, Visa.*

ST BRELADE   Sea Crest   64%   £92

Tel 01534 46353   Fax 01534 47316   Map 13 F4   **HR**
Petit Port St Brelade Jersey JE3 8HH

Owners Julian and Martha Bernstein run this relaxing white-painted modern hotel, which overlooks a rocky bay at the south-west end of the island, with attention to detail that is apparent in personal touches throughout. Note their collection of modern art in the public rooms. Bedrooms, five with balconies, overlook the bay so guests can watch the often spectacular sunsets. No dogs. *Rooms 7. Garden, outdoor swimming pool, children's splash pool. Closed mid Jan-mid Feb. Access, Amex, Visa.*

Restaurant   £70

Set menus change every week, so that with the carte as well there's plenty of choice available in the pretty seaward-looking dining room. Good seafood is well handled in sensibly simple style – Breton fish soup with rouille, Dover or lemon sole either grilled or meunière, dressed local crab – or there is veal viennoise, duck with orange or apple sauce and stuffing plus steaks and a section of "dishes prepared at the table". French-only wine list at fair prices, eg a Chablis 1er cru under £20. Tables on the terrace for light meals in summer. *Seats 60. Parties 25. L 12.30-2 D 7.30-10. Closed all Mon, also D Sun in winter. Set L £11.50 Set D £19.50.*

ST BRELADE'S BAY   Hotel L'Horizon   72%   £170

Tel 01534 43101   Fax 01534 46269   Map 13 F4   **H**
St Brelade's Bay Jersey JE3 8EF

L'Horizon faces due south over the long stretch of St Brelade's Bay and so takes full advantage of sunny weather. Leisure facilities also shine here, with Club L'Horizon, a well-equipped centre for relaxing or keeping fit, and a 40ft motor yacht, Clipper L'Horizon, available for day charter. Public areas include a bar with picture windows and beach views, a drawing room, a library and three restaurants. Good-sized bedrooms, nearly all with sea views, have decent-quality furniture and well-equipped bathrooms. Banqueting/conference facilities for 240/150. No dogs. Parking for 125 cars. 24hr room service. *Rooms 106. Terrace, indoor swimming pool, mini-gym, sauna, steam room, spa bath, beauty and hair salons, brasserie (10am-10pm). Access, Amex, Diners, Visa.*

ST BRELADE'S BAY   St Brelade's Bay Hotel   70%   £140

Tel 01534 46141 Fax 01534 47278   Map 13 F4   **H**
St Brelade's Bay Jersey JE3 8EF

Family owned and run for five generations and set in seven acres of award-winning gardens, the St Brelade's Bay Hotel is a popular spot for family holidays, especially as there's a resident lifeguard at the two heated freshwater swimming pools. Although the exterior looks modern the interior has a timeless elegance with moulded ceilings and chandeliers, comfortable sofas and chairs and an abundance of fresh flowers. First - and second-floor rooms are traditional, while those on the third floor are more modern; all are attractively and tastefully decorated and furnished. Sea-view rooms have a balcony, while on the other side rooms overlook the gardens. Families are well catered for. *Rooms 72. Garden, croquet, tennis, pitch & putt, outdoor swimming pool, children's swimming pool, children's playground, keep-fit equipment, sauna, sun beds, snooker. Closed mid Oct-end Apr. Access, Visa.*

ST HELIER   Apollo Hotel   63%   £87

Tel 01534 25441 Fax 01534 22120   Map 13 F4   **H**
9 St Saviour's Road St Helier Jersey JE2 4LA

A modern two-storey hotel built round a courtyard. Public areas provide plenty of space to relax: there are two bars (one in pub style), a coffee shop serving snacks throughout the day, an indoor leisure centre and a sun-trap terrace. Bedrooms, some with balconies, include many suitable for family occupation. Children up to 5 stay free in parents' room. Parking for 60 cars. Banqueting facilities for 150. No dogs. *Rooms 85. Terrace, indoor swimming pool, gym, sauna, spa bath, solarium. Access, Amex, Diners, Visa.*

ST HELIER   Beaufort Hotel   60%   £93

Tel 01534 32471 Fax 01534 20371   Map 13 F4   **H**
Green Street St Helier Jersey

The cool marble reception area sets the scene at this friendly modern hotel in town. Free parking is a bonus; indoor leisure facilities and outdoor sun terrace are both popular. Relaxing day rooms, comfortable bedrooms; all have the usual gadgets. *Rooms 54. Terrace, indoor swimming pool, spa bath, games room (summer). Access, Amex, Diners, Visa.*

ST HELIER   La Capannina   £60

Tel 01534 34602 Fax 01534 77628   Map 13 F4   **R**
65 Halkett Place St Helier Jersey

Italian restaurant with a menu mostly written in French! The grills and flambés, pasta, fish and shellfish are supplemented by daily specials in their season – asparagus, scallops, plaice, spring lamb – and year-round, often including carpaccio and prosciutto. Extensive wine list. *Seats 90. Parties 18. Private Room 18. L 12-2 D 7-10. Closed Sun, Bank Holidays, 5 days Christmas. Access, Amex, Diners, Visa.*

ST HELIER   De Vere Grand   68%   £115

Tel 01534 22301 Fax 01534 37815   Map 13 F4   **HR**
Esplanade St Helier Jersey JE4 8WD

With its long gabled frontage, the De Vere Grand is a distinctive feature on the St Helier seafront – and the entrance is appropriately impressive, with ornate coloured pillars and a marble floor. The smart period-style bar and lounge have fine views and so do balconied front bedrooms, which attract a hefty surcharge. It's a busy hotel catering for both holiday and business visitors (conference/banqueting facilities for 180/280). Families are well provided for with free accommodation for under-14s in their parents' room, plus baby-sitting and children's meals also available. Good leisure facilities. *Rooms 115. Terrace, indoor swimming pool, keep-fit equipment, sauna, steam room, spa bath, sun bed, snooker. Access, Amex, Diners, Visa.*

Regency Room   £75

The elegant Regency Room, offering only a four-course table d'hote dinner, is the main hotel dining-room. Casserole of three fish in a cream and vegetable sauce, beef en croute and roast loin of pork from the trolley typify the main dishes. Separate vegetarian and vegan menu. *Seats 250. D only 7.30-9.30. Set D £19.50.*

See over

Victoria's   £75

A la carte as well as prix-fixe menus here where the dishes are a little more sophisticated
than in the Regency Room: millefeuille of lobster surrounded by dill weed and pink
peppercorn Chablis sauce, salade croquante with quail and lentils, supreme of chicken
à l'indienne, and several flambé dishes. Dancing to live music each evening. Alongside
France, only Italy is well represented on the wine list. Scant offerings from elsewhere,
though one Californian representative, a 1985 Opus One, is reasonably priced. *Seats 160.*
L 12.30-2.15 D 7-10. Set L £11.50/£15.50 (Sun £16.50) Set D £23.50. Closed D Sun.

St Helier	Hotel de France	£120

Tel 01534 38990   Fax 01534 614005   Map 13 F4   **H**
St Saviour's Road St Helier Jersey

A major refurbishment programme took place in time for the 1995 season which
included a smart new lay-out at the front of the hotel, the main drive being re-routed to
make way for Mediterranean-style gardens complete with palms. The reception hall has
also been enlarged and front-facing bedrooms redesigned to create an even more
comfortable ambience for guests. The hotel boasts its own multi-screen cinema as well as
Madisons, a nightspot. Banquets for up to 700 and theatre-style conferences for 800 are
further amenities along with a splendid Health and Fitness centre. Children under the age
of 11 are free in their parents' room. *Rooms 324. Garden, outdoor and indoor swimming
pool, gym, squash, sauna, spa bath, solarium, beauty & hair salon, games room, snooker,
news kiosk (8-12, 4-7). Access, Amex, Diners, Visa.*

St Helier	Pomme d'Or Hotel	65%	£100

Tel 01534 880110   Fax 01534 37781   Map 13 F4   **H**
The Esplanade St Helier Jersey JE2 3NF

An attractive location right on the harbour, overlooking the marina, adds to the appeal
here. Cool, refreshing decor is evident in air-conditioned public areas and comfortable
bedrooms. Children up to 12 stay free in parents' room; between 12 and 16 they are
accommodated free in their own room. Guests have use of the all-weather fun pool at
the Merton Hotel. Conference/banqueting facilities for 300. No dogs. *Rooms 147.
Coffee shop (7am-11pm). Access, Amex, Diners, Visa.*

Set menu prices may not always include service or wine.

St Ouen	The Lobster Pot	£70

Tel 01534 482888   Fax 01534 481574   Map 13 F4   **RR**
L'Etacq St Ouen Jersey JE3 2FB

A popular spot with tours and coaches where booking is recommended for weekends.
The location is attractive, overlooking St Ouen's Bay, and the original granite farmhouse
dates back to the 17th century. The fish and shellfish are landed about 200 yards away, so
it can't be much fresher nor more local! All manner of seafood is served in traditional
French style, as are the extensive meat and poultry options, but most people are here for
the lobsters, served grilled, à la nage, à la l'armoricaine, Newburg or Thermidor.
*Seats 90. Parties 8. Private Room 95. L 12.30-2 D 7.30-10. Set L £10.50 Set D £14.95.
Access, Amex, Diners, Visa.*

Rooms   £70

Thirteen large bedrooms have the usual amenities of TV, trouser press, hairdryer and
even a small bar area with tea and coffee facilities and a small refrigerator. The best rooms
naturally enjoy a sea view. Good for families. Parking for 65 cars. No dogs. Patio.

St Peter	Mermaid Hotel	64%	£92

Tel 01534 41255   Fax 01534 45826   Map 13 F4   **H**
Airport Road St Peter Jersey JE3 7BN

A modern hotel near the airport, standing in 18 acres of grounds overlooking a small
natural lake. Bedrooms have the expected facilities and though not large they benefit from
south-facing balconies with a lake view. The hotel is self-contained with restaurants, bar,

pub and impressive leisure facilities. No dogs. Children under 5 free in parents' room –
early suppers provided. *Rooms 68. Garden, croquet, tennis, golf (9-hole) outdoor & indoor
swimming pools, keep-fit equipment, sauna, spa bath, solarium. Access, Amex, Diners, Visa.*

ST SAVIOUR — Longueville Manor — 80% — £160

Tel 01534 25501   Fax 01534 31613   Map 13 F4   **HR**
St Saviour Jersey JE2 7SA

Built as a manor house in the 13th century, it is now
a grand hotel of international repute. Malcolm and
Ragnhild Lewis and Sue Dufty continue the long family
tradition of providing their guests with very high standards
of comfort and service. It is decorated throughout in
elegantly understated country-house style with deep-
cushioned settees and armchairs arranged in well-spaced
groups in the lounge which, in common with the other
public areas, also boasts beautiful flower arrangments, fine
paintings and period and antique furniture. Bedrooms, each
named after a different rose, are luxuriously appointed with
colourful chintzes used to create elaborate colourful drapes,
cushions and bedcovers. Space is not at a premium and
many rooms have sitting areas. Rooms overlooking the
rear have the added advantage of views over the
grounds. The view takes in the splendid heated outdoor swimming pool which in
summer is a sun-trap surrounded by well-appointed sun-loungers. Bathrooms are
magnificent, offering a fine selection of toiletries as well as large towels and cosseting
bathrobes. *Rooms 32. Garden, croquet, outdoor swimming pool, tennis.*
Access, Amex, Diners, Visa.

Restaurant   £90

The two dining-rooms cater for different moods, from the solemn atmosphere of the
13th-century carved-panelled oak room to the more relaxed armchairs of the light and
airy second room. Chef Andrew Baird has been in residence since 1971 and is
thoroughly at home, producing table d'hote, à la carte, dégustation and vegetarian menus
using some home-grown herbs and vegetables. The selection includes roast fillet of beef
with braised oxtail, creamed potatoes and red wine sauce, roast Gressingham duck with
glazed apricots and confit, and supreme of turbot with braised cabbage, morels and
a Madeira glaze. The tasting menu, served to complete tables only, is a balanced meal of
nine courses including coffee, and really displays Andrew's talents to the full, while the
carte is equally extensive. Impressive cheese trolley of farmhouse British and French
selections. A mostly French wine list offers standard names at quite high prices, though
there's a grande marque champagne under £30. Seating for 20 on the terrace. *Seats 65.
Parties 16. Private Room 20. L 12.30-2 D 7.30-9.30. Set L £16/18 (£17.50 Sun) Set D
£28.50/£50.*

ST SAVIOUR — Merton Hotel — 60% — £80

Tel 01534 24231   Fax 01534 68603   Map 13 F4   **H**
Belvedere Hill St Saviour Jersey JE2 7RP

Located right outside St Helier, on a sloped street off the A3, a spacious hotel whose
main feature is the amazing Aquadome complex of indoor and outdoor swimming pools.
Good for children, with a new creche/playroom and entertainment for them in the
evening. The most basic rooms have been converted into family suites and twins/doubles
with bunks. *Rooms 304. Garden, indoor and outdoor swimming pool, children's swimming
pool, squash, tennis, coffee shop (10.30-6.30), games room. Closed 1 Nov-31 Mar.
Access, Amex, Diners, Visa.*

We welcome bona fide complaints and recommendations on the
tear-out pages at the back of the book for reader's comments.
They are followed up by our professional team.

Sark

SARK	Aval du Creux Hotel	57%	£70

Tel 01481 832036   Fax 01481 832368   Map 13 E4   **HR**
Sark

Eight miles east of Guernsey is the island of Sark, a peaceful retreat with forty miles of coastline, bracing walks and no traffic. Peter and Cheryl Tonks' friendly little hotel, originally a farmhouse, is a good place for family holidays, with four of the bedrooms of a suitable size for families. Children up to 3 stay free in parents' room and early suppers are available. There are two lounges and a small bar hung with local pictures. Half-board terms preferred – we quote B&B rate. *Rooms 12. Garden, outdoor swimming pool, children's splash pool, boules. Closed Oct-Apr. Access, Amex, Diners, Visa.*

Restaurant   £55

As well as hotel residents and Sark visitors, folk from Guernsey have been known to make a day trip by boat to Sark, principally to have lunch at Aval du Creux and often for the lobsters. Seafood in general plays the leading role here, with local crab served hot in a shell with cheese glaze, as well as oysters, scallops and monkfish. On the lighter lunch menu, you'll find omelettes, pancakes and baguettes filled with seafood or the 'Aval bookmaker', with steak, ham, tomato, lettuce and mayonnaise. *Seats 40. L 12-2 D 7-9. Set L £4.95/£6.95 (Sun £8.95) Set D £15.95.*

SARK	Dixcart Hotel	64%	£70

Tel 01481 832015   Fax 01481 832164   Map 13 E4   **HR**
Sark GY9 OSD

Sark's longest established hotel was originally a 16th-century longhouse, the main dwelling in one of the 40 feudal Tenements which still warrant a seat in Sark's parliament. The absence of cars and continued existence of ancient ranks really makes a stay here seem like a step back in time though domestic comforts are modern. Homely lounge and bar for the occasional rainy day and fifty acres of land with private access to the Dixcart Bay beach. Children welcome if well behaved. Open all year. *Rooms 15. Garden. Access, Amex, Diners, Visa.*

Restaurant   £40

The restaurant's beautiful view over the sloping gardens is peaceful and relaxing. The table d'hote menu features plenty of local seafood (bream, brill, Herm oysters, Guernsey scallops, sole, sea bass), plus bacon-wrapped chicken stuffed with brie and served with white wine sauce and usually some Sark lamb. Simple steaks attract a supplement. *Seats 60. L 12-1.30 D 7-9.30. Set L £10.75 Set D £13.75.*

SARK	Hotel Petit Champ	61%	£72

Tel 01481 832046   Fax 01481 832469   Map 13 E4   **H**
Sark GY9 OSF

Splendid sea views are a feature at this small hotel, owned and run by Chris and Caroline Robins since 1991, in a quiet setting on carless Sark's west coast. Built as a private residence towards the end of the last century, the Petit Champ became a hotel in 1948. There's a tiny bar, leafy sun lounge and a quiet, homely sitting room. Bedrooms are best described as cosy, and are undisturbed by TVs (there's a small TV lounge) or telephones; some rooms have sliding patio doors. No children under seven. No dogs. Half-board terms preferred – we quote B&B rate. *Rooms 16. Garden, outdoor swimming pool, putting. Closed early Oct-Easter. Access, Amex, Diners, Visa.*

SARK	La Sablonnerie	66%	£70

Tel 01481 832061   Fax 01481 832408   Map 13 E4   **HR**
Sark

As there are no cars on the island, the hotel provides a vintage horse-drawn barouche to bring guests from the harbour to Little Sark, the southern part of the island connected by a narrow natural bridge with breathtaking views. The lovely beach of Grande Grève is just a short walk away. The hotel is a lesson in savoir vivre, and charming owner Elizabeth Perrée has been in charge since 1973. The heart of the hotel is the cosy bar with low ceiling, granite walls and blue velvet decor. The hotel is surrounded by beautifully kept gardens and its own farm which supplies fruit, vegetables and dairy products for the restaurant, mostly organic. The bright, comfortable bedrooms are individually decorated with simple pine furniture; about half of them are not ensuite; six are reserved for non-smokers. A lovely tea garden located a few yards from the main building is open all day for light meals and afternoon teas. *Rooms 22. Closed mid Oct-Easter. Garden, croquet, horses and carriages. Access, Amex, Visa.*

Restaurant   £55

The main dining-room has warm red decor, simple pine furniture and candle-light in the evening. Dinner begins with large plates of canapés in the bar, followed by perhaps oysters, or chili prawns, and progresses via soup or a sorbet to lobster, fillet of pork en croute or roast leg of lamb. Excellent salads are also available. *Seats 40. Parties 20. L 12-2.30 D 7-9.30. Set L from £10 Set D from £12.*

Many hotels offer reduced rates for weekend or out-of-season bookings. Always ask about special deals.

SARK	Stocks Hotel	61%	£70

Tel 01481 832001   Fax 01481 832130   Map 13 E4   **HR**
Sark GY9 0SD

Family-run, granite-built hotel lying in a quiet wooded valley overlooking Dixcart Bay, 20 minutes walk from the harbour. There's a homely atmosphere in the lounge, and comfortable, unfussy bedrooms are decorated with darkwood furniture and floral fabrics. No TVs in the rooms. *Rooms 24. Garden, outdoor swimming pool, Courtyard Bistro (10am-10pm). Closed Oct-Mar. Access, Amex, Diners, Visa.*

Cider Press Restaurant   £50

Both table d'hote (priced according to the number of courses taken) and à la carte menus are offered with local fish, shellfish and meat always featuring: lobster steamed with lemon butter sauce, scallops skewered on rosemary, rack of Sark lamb with sesame seed crust, polenta and brie tartlet with basil and tomatoes (there are always vegetarian options), warm coffee and walnut fudge pudding. Refreshingly, there's a good and inexpensive wine list. No children under eight (there's high tea for resident children from 5-7pm) but the Courtyard Bistro, which is open for coffee, lunch, cream teas and light evening meals, has a children's menu. *Seats 60. Parties 12. Private Room 12. L by arrangement D 7-9. Set D £10/£13/£16/£18.*

Isle of Man

BALLASALLA	Rosa's Place	£70

Tel 01624 822940   Fax 01624 822702   Map 4 A4   **R**
Main Road Ballasalla Isle of Man

Nothing other than the name has changed here. It was La Rosette. The menu continues to offer a good mix of fresh seafood which is plainly grilled or baked with garlic. Meat dishes include a varied selection of familiar and favourite classics while to finish there are some excellent hot as well as cold puddings. The restaurant is 5 minutes drive from the airport. *Seats 45. Parties 16. L 12-3 D 7-10. Closed 1st 2 weeks Jan. Set L from £9 Set D £22. Access, Amex, Visa.*

DOUGLAS — Palace Hotel — 65% — £95

Tel 01624 662662   Fax 01624 625535   Map 4 B4   **H**
Central Promenade Douglas Isle of Man

The excellent leisure complex, with its own bar/café, cinemas, night club and public casino provide plenty of entertainment for guests at the seafront Palace, one of the focal points of the island's night life. Other day rooms are smart and spacious, and bedrooms are quite well equipped; they range from singles through twins and doubles to sea view Executive rooms and sea view suites. Ample parking. Banqueting and conference facilities for 300+. Pleasant, helpful staff. Extensive refurbishment is planned to take place during winter 1995/96. No dogs. *Rooms 135. Indoor swimming pool, sauna, spa bath, solarium, beauty & hair salon, casinos, night club, cinemas, coffee shop (7am-10pm).* *Access, Amex, Diners, Visa.*

DOUGLAS — Sefton Hotel — 63% — £68

Tel 01624 626011   Fax 01624 676004   Map 4 B4   **H**
Harris Promenade Douglas Isle of Man

A turn-of-the-century seafront hotel with smart rooms behind its grand white frontage. The spacious interior is modern with just a hint of days gone by. There are good sea views from the lounge and the best bedrooms. Recent refurbishment means that there are now five family suites and 26 Executive rooms. Popular for weekend and special breaks (golf, rambling, bird-watching etc). There is a secret door leading to the adjacent Gaiety Theatre. Conference and banqueting facilities for 90/80. No dogs. Private car park. 24hr room service. *Rooms 79. Indoor swimming pool, gym, sauna, spa bath, steam room, sun beds, beauty salon, coffee shop (9.45am-11pm). 24 hour room service.* *Access, Amex, Diners, Visa.*

RAMSEY — Grand Island Hotel — 66% — £90

Tel 01624 812455   Fax 01624 815291   Map 4 B4   **H**
Bride Road Ramsey Isle of Man

One mile north of Ramsey on the Bride Road, the handsome white-painted hotel looks down past terraced lawns to Ramsey Bay. Originally a Georgian manor house, it has a traditional look and feel, and there are a few antiques among the furnishings. Bedrooms are done out prettily, with pinks and blues predominating. There are extensive conference facilities (for up to 300). Parking for 100. *Rooms 56. Garden, croquet, indoor swimming pool, sauna, spa bath, steam room, beauty & hair salon, putting, snooker. Access, Amex, Diners, Visa.*

RAMSEY — Harbour Bistro — £45

Tel 01624 814182   Map 4 B4   **R**
5 East Street Ramsey Isle of Man IM8 1DN

Informal eating in a friendly bistro near the quay. Seafood is quite a feature on the menu with fresh local supplies every day, and dishes available as starter or main course: the famous local queenie scallops cooked with Provençal sauce, with bacon, onion and black pepper or with creamed garlic sauce on a bed of spinach; fisherman's pie, poached or deep-fried plaice fillets, sautéed or deep-fried king prawns. Also plenty for meat-eaters (lots of ways with steak) and indulgent desserts – "to hell with the calorie count". Separate vegetarian menu. *Seats 50. L 12-2 D 6.30-10.30. Closed D Sun, 2 weeks Jan & 1 week Oct. Set L (Sun) £11. Access, Visa.*

N Ireland

AGHADOWEY   Greenhill House   £42

Tel 01265 868241   Map 22 C1   **PH**
24 Greenhill Road Aghadowey Coleraine Co Londonderry BT51 4EU

The Hegartys bought their pleasant Georgian farmhouse in 1969 because they wanted the
land and, although graciously framed by mature trees and lovely countryside views, it is
still very much the centre of a working farm. Elizabeth Hegarty greets arrivals at her guest
house with an afternoon tea in the drawing room that includes such an array of home-
made tea breads, cakes and biscuits that dinner plans may well waver. Rooms, including
two large family rooms, are unostentatious but individually decorated with colour co-
ordinated towels and linen; good planning makes them exceptionally comfortable and
there are many thoughtful touches - fresh flowers, fruit basket, chocolate mints,
tea/coffee-making facilities, hairdryer, bathrobe, proper clothes hangers, even a torch.
A 5-course set dinner is available (by arrangement) to residents (£26 for two) at 6.30pm,
except on Sundays; no wines are provided. *Rooms 6. Garden. Closed Nov-Feb. Access, Visa.*

ANNALONG   Glassdrumman Lodge   69%   £85

Tel 01396 768451   Fax 01396 767041   Map 22 D2   **HR**
85 Mill Road Annalong Co Down BT34 4RH

Situated just off the A2 coast road, with lovely views over the sea or back into the
Mournes, this former farmhouse now has luxurious bedrooms with fresh flowers, fruit,
mineral water and exceptionally well-appointed bathrooms. Service is a high priority,
including 24hr room service, overnight laundry and a secretarial service, and breakfast
a speciality - you can even go and choose your own newly-laid egg if you like. Beaches,
walking, climbing, and fishing available locally. No tariff reductions for children.
Rooms 10. Garden, tennis, riding. Access, Amex, Diners, Visa.

Restaurant   £60
♟

In the French-style restaurant good use is made of organically grown vegetables and
naturally reared beef and pork from the hotel farm and seafood from local ports.
Individual wines by the glass are chosen to go with each course of the daily-changing
menu (£12-£14 per person extra). No smoking in the dining-room. *Seats 40. Private
Room 20. L by reservation only to residents. D at 8. Set D £25.*

BALLYMENA   Galgorm Manor   71%   £105

Tel 01266 881001   Fax 01266 880080   Map 22 D1   **HR**
136 Fenaghy Road Ballymena Co Antrim BT42 1EA

Next to a natural weir on the River Maine, which runs through the 85 acres of grounds,
this Georgian manor has recently been acquired by new owners who have made a good
job of refurbishing the public areas with rich fabrics, warm colour schemes and
a scattering of antiques to create an unashamedly luxurious atmosphere. The `designer-
rustic' Gillies Bar in a converted outbuilding offers a change of mood. A couple of
Executive bedrooms are stylishly decorated and furnished with antiques but the
remainder, although spacious, comfortable and well equipped, do not quite manage to
match the style of the public areas; there are five suites. Bathrooms all have separate
shower cubicles in addition to the tub. There are also six self-catering cottages in the
grounds. 24hr room service. An equestrian centre to the rear of the house includes a
show-jumping course, eventing cross-country practice area, specially constructed gallops
and numerous rides through the estate. The splendid Great Hall conference (for up to
500) and banqueting (up to 450) centre (quite separate from the hotel) is most impressive,
with huge Waterford crystal chandeliers and quality decor to match. Considerably
reduced tariff at weekends (Fri-Sun). Located to the west of town half-way between
Galgorm and Cullybackey. *Rooms 23. Garden, riding, fishing. Access, Amex, Diners, Visa.*

Restaurant   £70
♛ ◎

A fine room with glittering chandeliers, elaborately draped curtains and Arcadian murals
depicting the four seasons. Chef Charles O'Neill offers a dinner menu that is priced by
choice of main course; starters might include game terrine, three styles of salmon and
chicken and lobster sausage while main courses encompass a good choice of meat (some
may be offered from a chargrill) and game as well as fish dishes. Cheese trolley is a popular
alternative to the half-dozen desserts. Shorter, fixed-price lunch menu. *Seats 73. Parties 24.
Private Rooms 14/60. L 12-2.30 D 7-9.30 (Sun 6 to 9). Set L £12.90/£16 (Sun £14.50).*

| BANGOR | **Back Street Café** | £45 |

Tel 01247 453990   Map 22 D2   **R**
14 Queen's Parade Bangor Co Down

A dark green, windowless, single-storey building with no name, down an alleyway called The Vennel off the marina waterfront. Don't be put off by the location, though, as inside it's friendly and appealing. Paintings by friends of young chef-patron Paul Arthers adorn the rough orange- and yellow-painted walls, while bentwood chairs sit around white-clothed tables on a quarry-tiled floor. The short menu, priced for two or three courses, offers generous portions of starters like confit of duck with black bean sauce, spiced venison meatballs with sautéed cabbage, thick soy sauce and poppy seeds or wild mushroom risotto to start, followed by rack of lamb with root vegetable purée and thyme jus, chargrilled loin of pork with salad and salsa verde, and beef sirloin on rösti potatoes with béarnaise sauce. Fish dishes are always a good bet with the day's selection – dependent on the market – written up on a blackboard. Just a few puds are offered like bread-and-butter pudding with butterscotch sauce and an excellent lemon tart or try the plated selection of four Irish cheeses. Good espresso coffee. Unlicensed (no corkage charge). *Seats 45. L by arrangement D 6.30-10. Set D £15.95/£17.95. Closed Sun & Mon, 26 Dec. Access, Visa.*

Set menu prices may not always include service or wine.

| BANGOR | **Clandeboye Lodge Hotel** | 61% | £87 |

Tel 01247 852500   Fax 01247 852772   Map 22 D2   **H**
10 Estate Road Clandeboye Bangor Co Down BT19 1UR

Just out of town to the west, this brand-new redbrick hotel joins a pre-existing conference (for up to 350) and banqueting (to 320) complex near the Blackwood Golf Centre, for which guests enjoy reduced green fees and priority booking. A few sofas in the rug-strewn, slate-floored lobby and a small cocktail bar area constitute the public areas. Good-sized bedrooms are both comfortable and practical with second phone point for fax or modem and good lightwood furniture offering plenty of desk space. Bathrooms, which come with huge bathsheets, all have showers over bathtubs. Room service operates in the evening and overnight until breakfast but not during the day. Electric room heaters are individually controllable, subject to an overriding time control at reception; best ask for it to be left on if it looks like being a cold night. Children under 12 stay free in parents' room. Significantly reduced tariff at weekends for one or two-night stays. A country-style pub is in a Victorian schoolhouse building in the hotel grounds. *Rooms 43. Golf, bikes, riding, sea fishing, scuba diving. Closed 3 days Christmas. Access, Amex, Diners, Visa.*

| BANGOR | **Marine Court Hotel** | 64% | £80 |

Tel 01247 451100   Fax 01247 451200   Map 22 D2   **H**
18-20 Quay Street Bangor Co Down BT20 5ED

A modern harbourside hotel that overlooks acres of public parking and the marina beyond; harbour views are restricted to public areas – notably the first-floor dining-room – but, although the outlook may be less than pleasing, room facilities are above average, with tea/coffee tray, hairdryer and trouser press as standard. Beds are comfortable, with orthopaedic mattresses and quality bedding and the functional fully-tiled bathrooms have plenty of shelf space and (except for the lighting) good attention to detail. 24hr room service, but only Continental breakfast is served in the rooms. Banqueting facilities for 300, conference facilities in four areas for 10-450 delegates. Limited free parking (29 spaces). No dogs. *Rooms 51. Indoor swimming pool, gym, solarium, steam room, whirlpool bath, sunbed, coffee shop (10am-10pm). Access, Visa.*

Many hotels offer reduced rates for weekend or out-of-season bookings. Always ask about special deals.

BANGOR   Shanks   ↑   £60

Tel 01247 853313   Map 22 D2   **R**
Blackwood Golf Centre 150 Crawfordsburn Road Bangor Co Down

One of Ulster's newest restaurants, Shanks shares a building with the brand-new, pay-as-you-play Blackwood Golf Centre just outside town. The centre itself is part of the Clandeboye Estate which provides venison, game and even their own Angus beef for chef Robbie Millar's shortish fixed-price dinner menus. Dishes such as rare beef salad with rocket, fried polenta and Roquefort, fresh prawn and cod chowder with truffle oil and chives, crispy duck confit with fresh foie gras, celeriac purée and wild mushroom butter, seared 'Whitehead scallops' with salsify, coriander butter and Chinese five spice, and estate venison with rösti potatoes and a port and peppercorn jus show Robbie's secure grasp of the modern idiom. The results on the plate demonstrate sound skills in the kitchen; these are exemplified by the selection of first-rate home-made breads that arrive with tapénade and houmus to keep you going while you look at the menu. Front of house, Robbie's wife Shirley marshals a smart, keen team who offer friendly, professional service. Clean-cut, modern decor features a strip-wood floor, contemporary prints on yellow walls, Conran-designed furniture and a window into the kitchen. From the short, wide-ranging wine list that offers plenty of choice at less than £20 a bottle, some half a dozen or so bottles are opened each evening and offered by the glass. The restaurant is open only for dinner but an upstairs bar offers a short snack menu at both lunch and dinner (closed D Sun & D Mon) plus sandwiches and soup all day. Toilets equipped for the disabled. *Seats 60. Parties 16. Private Room 36. L 12.30-2.30 D 7-10. Set D £18.95. Closed Sun & Mon, 25 & 26 Dec, 1 Jan. Access, Diners.*

BELFAST   Antica Roma   £65

Tel 01232 311121   Fax 01232 310787   Map 22 D2   **R**
67 Botanic Avenue Belfast Co Antrim BT7 1JL

Impressive decor based on ancient Rome - mosaic floor, classical murals, columns, distressed stucco - combines with more sophisticated Italian cooking at this fashionable restaurant in the university district. The evening à la carte includes the likes of wild mushrooms with crushed chili peppers, garlic and olive oil on toasted bread; gratinated oak-smoked crab claws in a light bisque sauce; boneless quails in Frascati, sage and ground pistachio and piccata of veal dipped in egg and herbs. Almond meringue filled with sweet mascarpone cheese and honey cream and (hot bananas in pastry garnished with a white chocolate mousse and coconut are typical desserts. Two good-value set menus each provide a choice of four main dishes. Particularly good Italian section on the wine list with some recherché offerings. *Seats 170. Private Room 70. L 12-3 D 6-11.30. Set L £9.95/£12.95. Closed L Sat & all Sun, 25 & 26 Dec. Access, Amex, Visa.*

BELFAST   Bengal Brasserie   £35

Tel 01232 640099   Map 22 D2   **R**
339 Ormeau Road Belfast Co Antrim BT7 3GL

About a mile south of the city centre, this Indian restaurant is situated in a modern shopping arcade. Sound Bengali cooking includes a list of daily blackboard specials such as scampi masala, tandoori duck and Indian river fish as well as a wide choice on the main menu with lamb and chicken dishes jostling for space beside prawns, lobster, crayfish and 'European dishes' (steaks with sauces, omelettes, chicken Kiev). Friendly, helpful staff. *Seats 46. L 12-1.45 D 5.30-11.15 (Sun to 10.15). Closed 25 Dec. Access, Diners, Visa.*

BELFAST   Dukes Hotel   67%   £98

Tel 01232 236666   Fax 01232 237177   Map 22 D2   **H**
65 University Street Belfast Co Antrim BT7 1HL

A Victorian facade covers a bright modern hotel in a residential area close to Queen's University and the Botanical Gardens. Black leather and chrome feature in the foyer seating. There are function facilities for up to 140 and a health club. Pastel decor and impressionist prints set the tone in the bedrooms, all double-glazed and some designated non-smoking. Comprehensive refurbishment of the bar, restaurant and function rooms took place in 1995. Children up to 16 stay free in parents' room. Much reduced weekend rates. *Rooms 21. Keep-fit equipment, sauna. Access, Amex, Diners, Visa.*

BELFAST	Europa Hotel	71%	£130

Tel 01232 327000 Fax 01232 327800   Map 22 D2   **H**
Great Victoria Street Belfast Co Antrim BT2 7AP

A 70s' high-rise, Belfast's best-known hotel has gained an impressive new facade as part of a total refurbishment following its acquisition by Hastings Hotels, the province's largest hotel group. Smart public areas cater for all moods, from an all-day brasserie and lively public bar on the ground floor (off the large lobby) to a more relaxed and comfortable split-level cocktail bar-cum-lounge on the first floor where a pianist plays nightly. For the really energetic a disco/night club operates four or five nights a week. Double-glazed bedrooms feature darkwood furniture and matching bedcovers and curtains in stylish floral fabrics. 24hr room service. There is concessionary parking at a nearby multi-storey for which friendly, efficient porters also offer a valet parking service (ask before checking out if you want the cost added to your hotel account). Extensive conference and function facilities (for up to 1200) include a new air-conditioned Eurobusiness centre with its own reception area and full secretarial services. Substantial weekend tariff reductions. *Rooms 184. Brasserie (6am-1.30am). Closed 25 & 26 Dec. Access, Amex, Diners, Visa.*

BELFAST	Manor House Cantonese Cuisine	£40

Tel 01232 238755   Map 22 D2   **R**
4 3-47 Donegall Pass Belfast Co Antrim BT7 1DQ

The main menu at this family-run Cantonese restaurant runs to more than 300 items, and there are others on the vegetarian and Peking-style set menus (book 3 days ahead for the vegetarian party menu). Sound cooking over the whole range, which adds fish head and duck's web to all the familiar favourites. *Seats 80. Private Room 50. Meals 12-11.30. Closed 25 & 26 Dec, 12 Jul. Set L from £5.50 Set D from £14.50. Access, Diners, Visa.*

BELFAST	Plaza Hotel	64%	£82

Tel 01232 333555 Fax 01232 232999   Map 22 D2   **H**
15 Brunswick Street Belfast Co Antrim BT2 7GE

Ultra-modern city-centre business hotel with well-equipped bedrooms, all with satellite TV, hairdryer and trouser press as standard, and five conference suites (capacity 70 theatre-style, 100 restaurant-style). There are 14 rooms reserved for non-smokers. Children up to 10 stay free in parents' room; four rooms have extra beds. No dogs. *Rooms 76. Access, Amex, Diners, Visa.*

BELFAST	Roscoff	★	£75

Tel 01232 331532 Fax 01232 312093   Map 22 D2   **R**
Lesley House Shaftesbury Square Belfast Co Antrim BT2 7DB

Still the Belfast restaurant in which to see and be seen, with sunny yellow walls and the recent removal of a room divider (originally intended to make a more private dining area - but it seems that nobody wanted to be behind it) opening up its modern interior. Given the cachet of a well-known chef (Paul and Jeanne Rankin have TV series and several books to their credit), slick service and quality cooking, the £21.50 fixed-price menu (three courses, coffee and petits fours) offers excellent value for money. With seven choices at each stage, the modern, weekly-changing menu offers something to suit most tastes: from the straightforward and familiar like warm salad of duck confit, sliced potatoes and green beans, rack of lamb with garlic and parsley crust, fillet of beef with leeks, shallots and red wine, dark chocolate truffle cake and tarte tatin to more adventurous options such as tagliatelle with sweetbreads, pancetta and fresh rosemary, roast haunch of venison with salsify and wild mushrooms, peppered monkfish with soy glaze and fresh coriander cream, and coconut crème brulée with fresh mango purée. As an alternative to the puds there's a good British/Irish cheese trolley. A bowl of olives and a selection of good home-baked breads give one something to nibble while looking at the menu. The shorter lunch menu is in similar style. New World wines are well represented on an interesting list that also offers half a dozen or so wines by the glass. *Seats 70. L 12.15-2.15 D 6.30-10.30. Set L £14.50 Set D £21.50. Closed L Sat, all Sun, 11 & 13 July, 25 & 26 Dec, 1 Jan. Access, Amex, Diners, Visa.*

BELFAST   Speranza   £40

Tel 01232 230213   Fax 01232 236752   Map 22 D2   **R**
16 Shaftesbury Square Belfast Co Antrim BT2 7DB

Large, bustling pizzeria/restaurant on two floors with red check tablecloths and rustic chalet-style decor. The menu offers a range of huge crisp-based pizzas and about a dozen pasta dishes plus a few chicken and other meat dishes. Attentive service from boys and girls smartly kitted out in bright red cummerbunds with matching bow ties. For children there are high-chairs and a special menu written on colouring mats (crayons supplied). In the same ownership as *Antica Roma* and *Villa Italia* (qv). *Seats 170. D only 5-11.30. Closed Sun, 3 days at Christmas & 11, 12 Jul. Access, Visa.*

BELFAST   Stormont Hotel   69%   £137

Tel 01232 658621   Fax 01232 480240   Map 22 D2   **H**
587 Upper Newtownards Road Stormont Belfast Co Antrim BT4 3LP

Way out of town on the Newtownards Road, opposite Stormont Castle, this modern hotel is always busy and bustling, having various function rooms in addition to the Confex Centre with its 10 purpose-built trade and exhibition rooms. Public areas centre around a sunken lounge (sometimes used as a conference 'break-out' area) off which is a cosy cocktail bar. A mezzanine lounge has huge glass windows overlooking the castle grounds. The majority of bedrooms have been completely refurbished in recent times and are spacious, comfortable and practical with good, well-lit work space and modern easy chairs. Good bathrooms feature marble tiling. All rooms are well equipped, with satellite TV etc. Smart, helpful staff offer attentive lounge service and there's a 24hr room-service menu. Good breakfasts are served in the informal all-day brasserie. *Rooms 106. Access, Amex, Diners, Visa.*

BELFAST   The Strand Restaurant   £35

Tel 01232 682266   Fax 01232 663189   Map 22 D2   **R**
12 Stranmillis Road Belfast Co Antrim BT9 5AA

Very much a neighbourhood restaurant, Anne Turkington's restaurant/wine bar has been packing them in since 1981 and its popularity shows no sign of waning. Decorated in a style somewhat reminiscent of Charles Rennie Mackintosh, with darkwood furniture and a strong colour theme in purples and greens, the layout seems to favour small parties at tables of four. The daytime menu is especially attractive to the budget-conscious. Some of the more adventurous dishes are occasionally less than totally successful, but the emphasis is on variety and good value, notably in an impressive selection of 'Complete Meals' (ie main dishes, including accompaniments) at just £3.95: spicy meatballs with grilled peppers and saffron rice and crispy onion rings, perhaps, or good, generous cod and chips. Vegetarian choices are strong - peanut patties, for example, are crunchy roasted burgers served with brown rice, lightly-curried fruit chutney and a black-eye bean casserole. There's a change of tone after 7pm when rather more sophisticated evening menus are offered. *Seats 55. Parties 12. Private Room 25. Meals Mon-Sat 12-11 (Sun 12-3, 5-10). Closed 25 & 26 Dec, 12 & 13 July. Access, Amex, Diners, Visa.*

BELFAST   Villa Italia   £45

Tel 01232 328356   Fax 01232 234978   Map 22 D2   **R**
39 University Road Belfast Co Antrim BT7 1ND

Sister restaurant to *Speranza* (see entry) but with a little less emphasis on pizzas and more on pasta and other Italian dishes. A shade more upmarket too, although still informal in style, with quieter background music and less rustic decor. Service is equally friendly and efficient. *Seats 180. D only 5-11.30. Closed 24-26 & 31 Dec, 12 July & Easter Sun & Mon. Access, Visa.*

Set menu prices may not always include service or wine.

BELFAST	The Warehouse	£45

Tel 01232 439690   Fax 01232 230514   Map 22 D2   **R**
35-39 Hill Street Belfast Co Antrim BT1 2LB

A popular and lively "bar with wine and restaurant", whose menus cover a fair range of tasty, straightforward dishes. From the evening table d'hote (available on both floors) could come leek and potato soup, beef and mixed pepper casserole, marinated herrings with Madeira, hot bread-and-butter pudding, chocolate biscuit cake and home-made ice creams. Similar à la carte selection in the restaurant at lunchtime, plus informal lunchtime menu and evening snack menu in the wine bar. Live music Fri and Sat nights. *Seats 90. Private Room 45. Wine bar open for drinks 11.30-11. Meals L 12-3 D 6-9. Closed D Mon, L Sat, all Sun, Bank Holidays, Easter Mon, 12 & 13 Jul, 25-27 Dec. Set D £13.95/£16.95. Access, Amex, Diners, Visa.*

BELFAST	Welcome Restaurant	£40

Tel 01232 381359   Fax 01232 664607   Map 22 D2   **R**
22 Stranmillis Road Belfast Co Antrim BT9 5AA

The entrance is topped by a pagoda roof, and inside dragons, screens and lanterns establish that this is indeed a Chinese restaurant. The menu runs to over 100 items, mainly familiar, popular dishes, and there are special menus for individuals and small parties. *Seats 60. Parties 20. Private Room 30. L 12-1.45 D 5-10.30. Closed 24-26 Dec. Set L £5 Set D from £12. Access, Amex, Diners, Visa.*

Many hotels offer reduced rates for weekend or out-of-season bookings. Always ask about special deals.

BELFAST	Wellington Park	59%	£90

Tel 01232 381111   Fax 01232 665410   Map 22 D2   **H**
21 Malone Road Belfast Co Antrim BT9 6RU

The locality and a thriving conference business (capacity 160 theatre-style) ensure a lively atmosphere here, but one of the three bars is kept exclusively for residents. Children up to 12 stay free in parents' room. Residents have free use of Queens University's sports centre, 5 minutes from the hotel. No dogs. *Rooms 50. Closed 25 Dec. Access, Amex, Diners, Visa.*

BELFAST AIRPORT	Aldergrove Airport Hotel	62%	£80

Tel 01849 422033   Fax 01849 423500   Map 22 D2   **H**
Belfast Airport Co Antrim BT29 4AB

The only hotel actually at the international airport, which is about 17 miles to the south of the city centre. Built three years ago as a Novotel it is now under local management but continues to offer good practical accommodation. All rooms have plenty of work space and, with families in mind, a sofa bed with additional truckle bed underneath; three rooms are equipped for disabled guests. Two children under 10 may stay free in their parents' room. Multi-channel TV includes flight information. 24hr room service. Banqueting/conference facilities for 180/250. Tariff reductions at weekends. *Rooms 108. Keep-fit equipment, sauna, outdoor children's play area. Access, Amex, Diners, Visa.*

BUSHMILLS	Bushmills Inn	58%	£78

Tel 01265 732339   Fax 01265 732048   Map 22 C1   **H**
25 Main Street Bushmills Co Antrim BT57 8QA

After the Giant's Causeway, the world's oldest distillery at Bushmills is the biggest attraction in the area (and well worth a visit; mid-week is most interesting); the Bushmills Inn also attracts year-round local support. The exterior, including a neat garden at the main (rear) entrance, creates a welcoming impression that extends into the hall, with its open fire and country antiques, and other public areas that encompass several bars and a large dining room. Bedrooms are quite modest, individually decorated and comfortably furnished; some family rooms are remarkable for their ingenious use of space. A beamed loft provides a splendid setting for private functions (up to 85 people) and the 'secret library' a unique venue for special occasions. *Rooms 11. Garden, fishing. Access, Visa.*

CARRICKFERGUS   Wind-Rose   £55

Tel 01960 364192   Fax 01960 351164   Map 22 D2   **R**
The Marina Carrickfergus Co Antrim BT38 8BE

Overlooking the marina, a well-appointed formal restaurant on the upper floor is approached by an exterior spiral staircase and has clear views across Belfast Lough (booking essential). A typical meal might be terrine of monkfish followed by cutlets of lamb and spinach soufflé with the house speciality crepe suzette to finish. The ground-floor wine bar below has a *pubby* atmosphere with a strongly nautical theme and provides simple bar food. *Seats 46. Open 12-12. Bar Food L 12-2.30 snacks 2.30-5 D 7-9. Closed Sun & Mon, 25 & 26 Dec. Access, Amex, Visa.*

COMBER   La Mon House   59%   £85

Tel 01232 448631   Fax 01232 448026   Map 22 D2   **H**
The Mills 41 Gransha Road Comber Co Down BT23 5RF

Public areas in this low-rise modern hotel include a bar featuring copper-topped tables, a small residents' lounge (which may be in private use), carvery restaurant and a fun bar with lots of entertainments including a Friday night disco. Practical bedrooms have simple fitted furniture; nine large rooms have balconies and there are eight small singles with shower only. Families will enjoy the country health club and outdoor areas. Banqueting facilities for 450, conferences up to 1100 theatre-style. Regular Saturday night dinner dances. In the countryside, 5 miles from Belfast city centre. No dogs. *Rooms 38. Garden, indoor swimming pool, gym, sauna, solarium, whirlpool bath, games room. Access, Amex, Visa.*

COMBER   The Refectory   £40

Tel & Fax 01247 870870   Map 22 D2   **R**
46 Mill Street Comber Co Down

Shallow stairs lead to a striking first-floor restaurant over a characterful old general store (complete with original green tiling). The main room is designed around the central stairs under an unusual atrium, with dashing window treatments and deep pumpkin rough-textured walls providing a warm background for otherwise simple decor – although the austerity of bare boards is offset by comfortably upholstered chairs, good linen and, perhaps, a dramatic arrangement of white lilies on the Victorian mantelpiece. This spacious, stylish room provides a fitting setting for the unobtrusive hospitality of Michael Thomas and his co-owner Stephen Jeffers. Stephen is a chef who cooks imaginatively yet keeps his feet firmly on the ground, transforming the best of local ingredients – game, lamb, wild salmon and organic vegetables – into wholesome, satisfying dishes that taste as good as they look. Short, daily à la carte lunch menus offer subtle soups and punchy salads alongside such delights as champ, beef sausages (from the local butcher) and onion gravy, all served on stylish plain white tableware. Dinner menus, including an à la carte that changes weekly, are wider ranging, typically tempting with starters like roulade of local game with a compote of blueberries or terrine of organic leek and monkfish with saffron dressing, then maybe rack of lamb with a herb crust or confit of duck leg with caramelised shallots followed, perhaps, by farmhouse cheeses or authentic renditions of classics like crème brulée or tarte au citron. *Seats 58. L 12.30-3 D 6.30-10. Set Sun L £12.95 Set D (Tue-Thu) £15.50. Closed L Tue-Wed, D Sun, all Mon, 1 week Christmas. Access, Visa.*

CRAWFORDSBURN   Old Inn   £85

Tel 01247 853255   Fax 01247 852775   Map 22 D2   **I**
15 Main Street Crawfordsburn Co Down BT19 1JH

Located off the main Belfast to Bangor road, this 16th-century inn is in a pretty village setting and is supposed to be the oldest in continuous use in all Ireland. Its location is conveniently close to Belfast and its City Airport. Oak beams, antiques and gas lighting emphasise the natural character of the building, an attractive venue for business people (conference facilities and banqueting for 90) and private guests alike. Individually decorated bedrooms vary in size and style, most have antiques, some four-posters and a few have private sitting rooms; all are non-smoking. Romantics and newly-weds should head for the honeymoon cottage. Free private car parking for overnight guests. No dogs. *Rooms 33. Garden. Closed 24-26 Dec. Access, Amex, Diners, Visa.*

DUNADRY   Dunadry Inn   64%   £100

Tel 01849 432474   Fax 01849 433389   Map 22 D2   **H**
2 Islandreagh Drive Dunadry Co Antrim BT41 2HA

Originally a paper mill founded early in the 18th century, later a linen mill, now a well-known riverside hotel 15 minutes from Belfast city centre and 10 from the airport. Best bedrooms are on the ground floor, with access to the gardens. Executive rooms feature computer points and fax machines. The Copper Bar under the main staircase is a popular spot for a drink and the lunchtime buffet. Extensive conference facilities. Children up to 5 stay free in parents' room. No dogs. *Rooms 67. Garden, croquet, crazy golf, game fishing, bicycles, indoor swimming pool, keep-fit equipment, spa bath, sauna, steam room, solarium. Closed 24-27 Dec. Access, Amex, Diners, Visa.*

DUNMURRY   Forte Posthouse Belfast   67%   £86

Tel 01232 612101   Fax 01232 626546   Map 22 D2   **H**
300 Kingsway Dunmurry Co Antrim BT17 9ES

This business-oriented hotel is a short drive from Belfast city centre and airport, and was until recently a Forte Crest. Accommodation includes Lady Crest rooms, non-smoking rooms and rooms designated as family-size. Children up to 16 stay free in parents' room. 24hr room service. Conference/meeting facilities for up to 450. Free parking for 200 cars. *Rooms 82. Keep-fit equipment, squash. Access, Amex, Diners, Visa.*

FIVEMILETOWN   Blessingbourne   £90

Tel 01365 521221   Map 22 C2   **PH**
Fivemiletown Co Tyrone

Built in 1874 in the Elizabethan style and immaculately maintained by its hospitable owners, Robert and Angela Lowry, Blessingbourne is a delightfully fairytale house of great character with mullioned windows, beautiful grounds that include a private lake and lovely views across the estate to the mountains beyond. Furnished in style and comfort with family antiques, the reception rooms are elegant yet relaxed and the four bedrooms (one with a four-poster bed) are very comfortably furnished and share two bathrooms. An unusual attraction is the Blessingbourne carriage and household museum, a collection which guests are free to browse around and is open to the public by arrangment (admission £1.50). Woodland walks are an added attraction. *Rooms 4. Garden, terrace, outdoor swimming pool, tennis, rowing, fishing. Closed Christmas week. No credit cards.*

GARVAGH   MacDuff's Restaurant   £50

Tel & Fax 01265 868433   Map 22 C1   **RR**
112 Killeague Road Garvagh nr Coleraine Co Londonderry BT51 4HH

A basement restaurant under a fine, immaculately kept Georgian house, MacDuff's is characterful, comfortable and convivial. There's a small separate reception area and it is run by staff who cope well under the busiest of circumstances. The generally relaxed atmosphere is carried through to a comforting ring of familiarity on Margaret Erwin's menu in starters like Stilton puffs with hot, sweet and sour sauce and twice-baked soufflé with summer salad – popular perennials kept on the menu by requests from regulars. Spicing is a feature, but traditional main courses like grilled wild local salmon with hollandaise are also given a further lift, as in a garnish of crispy dulse; local catches feature in a classic seafood symphony with halibut, fat prawns and mussels in a light wine sauce. Good desserts might include hazelnut meringue with raspberries (including a generous 'wee dram' of Drambuie in the cream) or simple Jamaican banana, split and grilled with rum and sugar. No children under 12. No smoking. On the A29 four miles north of Garvagh. *Seats 36. Parties 20. Private Room 14. D only 7-9.30. Closed Sun, Mon.& 3 days at Christmas. Access, Visa.*

Rooms   £60

Accommodation is available in five large, comfortably furnished en-suite rooms with lovely views over the gardens and surrounding countryside. No children under 12.

Set menu prices may not always include service or wine.

HELEN'S BAY   Deane's on the Square ↑   £75

Tel 01247 852841   Map 22 D2   **R**
7 Station Square Helen's Bay Co Down BT19 1TN

Built in 1863 in the style of a Scottish baronial castle, the first Marquis of Dufferin and Ava's own railway station is now the unlikely setting for some of the best food in Ireland – not least because it is still a fully operational station. This can be somewhat disconcerting on a first visit if you are shown straight to one of the tables for two in the long, narrow 'corridor' near the platform! However, the building is sympathetically converted, immaculately maintained inside and out and has an open kitchen and a great deal of atmosphere in all areas, including a small basement bar. Pleasingly understated table settings – white cloths, white china and simple modern cutlery and glasses - are complemented by comfortable chairs and, while there is no à la carte, Michael Deane offers a Tasting Menu and a choice of set menus. Typically, the two-course dinner menu offers a well-balanced and seriously tempting choice of six starters – fat, juicy golden brown roast scallops on a seed pancake bed, perhaps, topped off with crispy deep-fried julienne vegetables and surrounded by a light soya and balsamic vinegar dressing.
A similar range of main courses includes unusual combinations such as perfectly cooked roast fillet of beef served on a base of potato and haggis, surrounded by roast garlic, button onions and broccoli sprigs. This is all very typical of the house style: striking, layered dishes presented as carefully constructed little towers onto pools of imaginative and well-judged sauces. Ask for the separate vegetarian menu. Locals may be heard to grumble about steep price increases, as Deane's has become very fashionable of late; the dinner menu, for example, attracts supplements at every turn and side dishes are charged separately.. Service can be a little slow but thoughtful waiting staff do much to ease any delays. **Seats** 40. L Sun only 12.30-2.30 D 7-10. Set L £16.50 Set D £19/£23.75.
Closed D Sun & all Mon, 1 week July, 3 days Christmas & 2 weeks Jan.
Access, Amex, Diners, Visa.

Set menu prices may not always include service or wine.

HOLYWOOD   Culloden Hotel   72%   £157

Tel 01232 425223   Fax 01232 426777   Map 22 D2   **HR**
142 Bangor Road Craigavad Holywood Co Down BT18 0EX

Originally a palace of the Bishops of Down, this splendid 19th-century building in Scottish Baronial style stands in 12 acres of gardens overlooking Belfast Lough. Antiques, stained glass, fine plasterwork and paintings grace the day rooms. Good-sized, well-furnished bedrooms are mostly in an extension. There are two restaurants, an inn in the grounds, various function suites and a well-appointed health and fitness club. No dogs. A major refurbishment programme is underway and great improvements are promised by owners Hastings Hotels. **Rooms** 89. Garden, indoor swimming pool, keep-fit equipment, squash, sauna, spa bath, solarium, tennis, snooker, hairdresser, beauty salon. Closed 24-25 Dec. Access, Amex, Diners, Visa.

The Mitre Restaurant   £65

Comfortable and relaxing, with friendly, efficient service. The menu is quite extensive, ranging from traditional grills and classics such as scampi provençale or garlic snails to more contemporary creations like pan-fried monkfish with vegetable tagliatelle and a tomato/Pernod sauce. Sunday lunch always features a roast on the fixed-price menu. Separate vegetarian menu. There is also a grill bar in the complex, 'The Cultra Inn'. **Seats** 140. Private Room 40. L 12.30-2.30 D 7-9.45. Closed L Sat. Set L & D £17.

HOLYWOOD   Sullivans   £55

Tel & Fax 01232 421000   Map 22 D2   **R**
Sullivan Place Holywood Co Down BT18 9JF

Bright and cheerful with sunny yellow walls and colourfully upholstered chairs, Sullivans operates as a coffee shop during the day (Devon scones, pecan pie and lunchtime

savouries like venison terrine, salmon and leek quiche and soup) before turning into
a fully-fledged restaurant at night. After only a short time the accomplished cooking of
young chef-patron Simon Shaw (formerly at Roscoff in Belfast) has already gained such
a loyal following that booking is advisable at weekends. Dishes like a crispy duck confit
wth roast beetroot and truffle oil, grilled vegetables on sun-dried tomato bread, pigeon
breast with polenta come in portions substantial enough to satisfy local appetites. Desserts
range from pears poached in claret with ice cream to sweet ginger and apricot crème
brulée. There's a short à la carte in addition to the prix fixe. Unlicensed, but there are
wine merchants nearby. *Seats 40. L 10-2.30 D 6.30-10.30. Set D £19. Closed Sun, 1 week
July & 25 & 26 Dec. Access, Visa.*

KESH	Lough Erne Hotel	60%	£56

Tel 01365 631275   Fax 01365 631921   Map 22 C2   **H**
Main Street Kesh Co Fermanagh BT93 1TF

Located in the town centre but making the most of its position on the banks of the
Glendurragh River, this friendly family hotel offers homely accommodation in rooms
that tend to be on the small side but have all been recently modernised, with en-suite
bath/shower rooms, TV and tea/coffee facilities. The downstairs bar and function rooms
are particularly attractive, with direct access to a paved riverside walkway and garden.
Banqueting/conference for 200/250. Children welcome - cots, baby-listening/sitting,
high-chairs and early evening meals available. *Rooms 12. Garden, fishing. Closed 24 & 25
Dec. Access, Amex, Diners, Visa.*

LARNE	Magheramorne House	63%	£66

Tel 01574 279444   Fax 01574 260138   Map 22 D1   **H**
59 Shore Road Magheramorne Larne Co Antrim BT40 3HW

53 acres of woodland overlooking Larne Lough provide a fine setting for a late-Victorian
house which offers fresh, bright bedrooms, banqueting/conference facilities for up to 180
and free parking for 150 cars. Extensive Victorian gardens. No dogs. *Rooms 22. Garden.
Access, Amex, Diners, Visa.*

LONDONDERRY	Beech Hill House Hotel	59%	£85

Tel 01504 49279   Fax 01504 45366   Map 22 C1   **HR**
32 Ardmore Road Londonderry Co Londonderry BT47 3QP

Dating from 1726, Beech Hill is a substantial house set in 36 acres of mature parkland in
the rural hinterland south of the city; the hotel is signposted off the main A6 as you
approach Londonderry from the Belfast direction. Very much centred around its
restaurant and three function/meeting rooms (for up to 100) the only day room is
a comfortable bar/lounge with unusual 'cattle head' frieze under the ceiling. Attractive,
individually decorated bedrooms vary in shape and size and boast a variety of antique
pieces along with a well-lit desk or work space. Telephones are standard, as are remote-
control TVs (the latter with set-top ariels so reception is not always perfect). 13 of the
bathrooms have shower and WC only. No dogs. *Rooms 17. Garden, tennis.
Closed 24 & 25 Dec. Access, Amex, Visa.*

Ardmore Restaurant   £65

The dining-room is a former billiard room where green Regency-striped wallpaper, brass
'oil lamp' lights and views over the gardens set the scene for chef Noel McMeel's
generously-portioned, enthusiastic cooking. From the à la carte, start perhaps with
venison sausage on a 'spaghetti' of vegetables surrounded by juniper berry sauce or some
fresh local salmon on celeriac chips with potato rösti, a basil quenelle and tomato cream;
follow with a main dish like best end of lamb roasted with mustard and Provençal
breadcrumbs, a trio of chicken or stuffed roast tenderloin of pork with a rosemary and
garlic crust. A daily-changing fixed-price menu (you can mix and match) adds to the
choice with dishes like seafood sausage on vegetables with a tarragon sauce (an excellent
sausage but it actually came with a Meaux mustard sauce at a recent meal), confit of duck
with purée potatoes and pesto dressing, and sirloin of beef with a red wine and port jus.
There is also an interesting vegetarian menu with a good choice. As an alternative to
puds such as white chocolate and mint gateau with an orange jus or a traditional plum
pudding with brandy sauce try the plated selection of Irish cheeses that might come with
their own home-baked walnut bread and dried fruit. *Seats 40. Parties 8. L 12-2.30
D 7-9.30. Set L £13.95 Set D £18.95.*

LONDONDERRY   Everglades Hotel   59%   £80

Tel 01504 46722   Fax 01504 49200   Map 22 C1   **H**
Prehen Road Londonderry Co Londonderry BT47 2PA

South of the town on the banks of the River Foyle, this modern low-rise hotel is
a popular venue for conferences and banqueting (350/250) besides providing bright,
practical accommodation. Top of the bedroom range are two suites with jacuzzis and
turbo showers. Children up to 12 stay free in parents' room. *Rooms 52. Garden.
Closed 24 & 25 Dec. Access, Amex, Diners, Visa.*

NEWCASTLE   Slieve Donard Hotel   63%   £99

Tel 01396 723681   Fax 01396 724830   Map 22 D2   **H**
Downs Road Newcastle Co Down BT33 0AG

Imposing red-brick Victorian railway hotel facing the Irish Sea (next to the Royal
County Down Golf Club) with the Mountains of Mourne in the background, 'The
Slieve' caters mainly to conferences in winter and holidaymakers, tour groups and
weddings in the summer. A grand, galleried entrance hall sets the tone for public areas
which include a large elegant lounge with conservatory extension (sometimes used for
functions), cosy library sitting room and a bar named after Charlie Chaplin, who once
stayed here. Bedrooms vary in shape and size but share the same blue and peach colour
scheme, polycotton duvets and dark mahogany furniture. The only advertised room
service is breakfast, and that is not available for conference delegates. Good leisure centre.
Parking for 300 cars. *Rooms 117. Garden, indoor swimming pool, gym, solarium, steam
room, beauty salon, tennis, shop. Access, Amex, Diners, Visa.*

PORTAFERRY   Portaferry Hotel   63%   £85

Tel 01247 728231   Fax 01247 728999   Map 22 D2   **HR**
10 The Strand Portaferry Co Down BT22 1PE

Formed out of an 18th-century terrace on the seafront, where the ferry crosses the neck
of Strangford Lough, the Portaferry has been substantially remodelled over recent years to
create a delightful small hotel run with a winning combination of charm and
professionalism by John and Marie Herlihy. Public areas include a tweedy bar and several
tastefully decorated little lounges sporting pictures of the surrounding area by local artists.
Light, airy bedrooms come with lightwood furniture and matching floral bedcovers and
curtains, neat bathrooms with huge bath sheets. No dogs. *Rooms 14. Closed 24 & 25
Dec. Access, Amex, Diners, Visa.*

Restaurant   £65

The secret of Anne Truesdale's cooking is the use of the best local produce in dishes that
are essentially simple, although not without interest. Lamb from the Mountains of
Mourne and Ulster beef feature but it's seafood that takes pride of place with amazingly
plump scallops from the Lough (pan-fried with garlic and bacon perhaps or baked in
white wine and cheese), Murlough Bay mussels, prawns from Portavogie, Ardglass crab
(in filo pastry with tomato and basil sauce), goujons of monkfish (with fresh lime sauce),
salmon (wild Irish in season) and lobsters from their own tanks. Vegetables, often
organically grown, are well handled too. At lunchtime there is a fairly extensive bar menu
that is also served in the dining-room except on Sundays, when there is a fixed-price
menu that always features a traditional roast. *Seats 80. L 12.30-2.30 D 7-9. Set L (Sun
only) £12.95, Set D £17.50. Closed 24 & 25 Dec.*

PORTBALLINTRAE   Bayview Hotel   58%   £70

Tel 01265 731453   Fax 01265 732360   Map 22 C1   **H**
2 Bayhead Road Portballintrae nr Bushmills Co Antrim BT57 8RZ

Overlooking the tiny harbour and the bay, the long pebbledash hotel building stands half
a mile from the main A2 coastal route. Functions and conferences (up to 300) are quite
big business, but residents have their own sitting room, and there's also a convivial bar.
Bedrooms include one semi-suite with a small sitting-room area and generally have
modern bathrooms. Six cottages are a short distance from the hotel; these are let as self-
catering or as three-bedroom suites. *Rooms 16. Indoor swimming pool, sauna, solarium,
snooker. Access, Visa.*

| PORTRUSH | RAMORE | ★ | £55 |

Tel 01265 824313   Map 22 C1   **R**
The Harbour Portrush Co Antrim BT56 8BN

♕ 🍓 🗋

The sheer cosmopolitan buzz of this waterside restaurant, with its sleek, chic black-and-chrome decor, smoothly operating open kitchen flanked by huge baskets of freshly baked breads and serried ranks of highly professional staff, is apt to take the uninitiated by surprise. It's trendier than one might expect to find in Portrush town and a tribute to the remarkable style of chef George McAlpin and the family team that their bright, airy restaurant continues to attract flocks of enthusiastic diners from throughout Ireland and beyond. Local seafood still predominates, but a keen feeling for the mood of the moment imbues the cooking with unusual immediacy in starters like Dublin Bay prawns or fresh asparagus with egg-filled ravioli. The wide variety of modestly priced main dishes (escalopes of peppered fillet steak, confit of duck, rack of Irish lamb) includes a handful of interesting 'complete dishes' such as a local version of paella or garlic cream chicken - remarkable value at £7.50. Desserts are a speciality: there is always a hot soufflé on the list - perhaps hot fresh fruit and Grand Marnier - and daily blackboard specials like an excellent tangy lemon tart. Very good coffee, served with petits fours. **Seats** *85. D only 6.30-10.30 (lunchtime wine bar downstairs). Closed Sun & Mon, 24-26 Dec. Access, Visa.*

| TEMPLEPATRICK | Templeton Hotel | 66% | £100 |

Tel 01849 432984   Fax 01849 433406   Map 22 D2   **H**
882 Antrim Road Templepatrick Ballyclare Co Antrim BT39 0AH

An eye-catching modern hotel a mile from the M2 and handy for Belfast airport. Spacious bedrooms are equipped with the expected up-to-date amenities, and the four Executive rooms have additionally mini-bars and jacuzzis. Day rooms take various decorative themes - sleek black and gold for the cocktail bar, Scandinavian for the banqueting hall (catering for up to 350), echoes of medieval knights in the restaurant. New conference suite for up to 50 in a separate annexe. 24hr room service. Free parking for 165 cars. Weekend reductions. **Rooms** *20. Garden. Closed 25 & 26 Dec. Access, Amex, Diners, Visa.*

| TEMPO | Tempo Manor | | £100 |

Tel 01365 541450   Fax 01365 541202   Map 22 C2   **PH**
Tempo Co Fermanagh BT94 3FJ

An impressive Victorian manor house of considerable charm, set in 11 acres of lakes and gardens established in 1869 by the Langham family, Tempo is now in the capable young hands of John and Sarah Langham whose recent restoration, modernisation (including the installation of central heating) and redecoration is in keeping with the style of the house. Many original features and furniture, including three four-poster beds, have been retained and all of the spacious bedrooms have lovely views of the surrounding gardens and en-suite bathrooms - an ideal combination of the interesting old and convenient new. Reception rooms are impressive yet welcoming, with crackling log fires, and dinner is served in the beautiful dining room, overlooking the lake and garden. Non-residents may also book for dinner, which is served communally or at separate tables, as preferred. Banqueting for 300 (+ unlimited numbers in marquee, daytime only). Children welcome: under-5s may stay free in their parents' room. Woodland walks. **Rooms** *5. Garden, terrace, patio, croquet. Closed Christmas week. Access, Visa.*

We welcome bona fide complaints and recommendations on the tear-out pages at the back of the book for readers' comments. They are followed up by our professional team.

On the *Waterfront*

The human body is made up of over 90% water. Research shows that a 5% drop in bodily fluid can result in a 30% drop in performance.

Water intake is essential for maintaining hydration, lowering body temperature, removing cellular waste and reducing fatigue. Doctors suggest that you should drink between 2–3 litres of water each day.

Highly Recommended

...is Braebourne Spring's range of water coolers. They require no plumbing, only occupy the floorspace of just one telephone book, and provide a cooled, on tap supply of Natural Mineral Water that's bottled at its underground source in the Cotswolds.

For your Complimentary No Obligation Trial which includes machine delivery and 22.7 litres of water, call:

✆ 0181 291 9911

BRÆBOURNE *Spring*   *the cool mineral water people...*

Republic of Ireland

Egon Ronay's Jameson Guide to Ireland has replaced the Republic of Ireland section in this Guide. The new edition of the Ireland guide will be published in March 1996.

Your **Guarantee** of **Quality** and **Independence**

EGON
RONAY'S
GUIDES
1996

- Establishment inspections are anonymous
- Inspections are undertaken by qualified Egon Ronay's Guides inspectors
- The Guides are completely independent in their editorial selection
- The Guides do not accept advertising, hospitality or payment from listed establishments

The **Leading** Guides

Hotels & Restaurants ● Pubs & Inns ● Europe Ireland ● Just A Bite And Children Come Too ● Paris Oriental Restaurants

London by Postal District: Hotels

See How To Use This Guide, on Pages 14–15, for an explanation of our percentage rating system, room pricing and categories.

Location	Establishment	Tel. No.	Category	Room £	Hotel %	No. of Rooms	Conf Max	Banq Max	Disabled	In Swim	Out Swim	Tennis	Squash
E1	Tower Thistle	0171-481 2575	H	166	66%	803	180	230	◄				
E14	Britannia International	0171-712 0100	H	125	68%	442	600	450		◄			
N1	Great Northern Hotel	0171-837 5454	H	99	60%	89	100	80					
NW1	Dorset Square Hotel	0171-723 7874	HR	150	74%	37	8	45					
NW1	Kennedy Hotel	0171-387 4400	H	106	63%	360	100	60					
NW1	The Regent London	0171-631 8000	HR	245	87%	309	350	360		◄			
NW1	White House	0171-387 1200	H	132	71%	584	120	100	◄				
NW2	Holiday Inn Garden Court	0181-455 4777	H	92	60%	153	55						
NW3	Charles Bernard Hotel	0171-794 0101	H	65	60%	57		52					
NW3	Clive Hotel	0171-586 2233	H	70	60%	96	350	250	◄				
NW3	Forte Posthouse	0171-794 8121	H	75	65%	140	30	25					
NW3	Regent's Park Marriott	0171-722 7711	H	169	73%	303	400	280		◄			
NW3	Swiss Cottage Hotel	0171-722 2281	H	85	62%	81	50	70					
NW4	Hendon Hall	0181-203 3341	H	107	62%	50	350	250					

Location	Establishment	Tel. No.	Category	Room £	Hotel %	No. of Rooms	Conf Max	Band Max	Disabled	In Swim	Out Swim	Tennis	Squash
NW8	Hilton Internat. Regent's Park	0171-722 7722	H	150	73%	377	150	130					
SE3	Bardon Lodge	0181-853 4051	H	84	56%	60	40	55					
SE9	Yardley Court	0181-850 1850	B	46		9							
SE16	Scandic Crown Nelson Dock	0171-231 1001	H	129	69%	390	350	300					
SW1	The Berkeley	0171-235 6000	HR	332	89%	160	250	216		◄	◄	◄	
SW1	Cadogan Hotel	0171-235 7141	HR	170	74%	64	50	32		◄		◄	
SW1	The Chelsea	0171-235 4377	H	200	61%	225	150	100					
SW1	Collin House	0171-730 8031	B	56		13							
SW1	Dukes Hotel	0171-491 4840	H	213	80%	64	70	70				◄	
SW1	Durley House	0171-235 5537	PH	260		11							
SW1	Elizabeth Hotel	0171-828 6812	B	70		40	25	15					
SW1	Forte Crest Cavendish	0171-930 2111	H	176	71%	255	100	80					
SW1	The Goring	0171-396 9000	HR	179	81%	78	70	50					
SW1	Grosvenor Thistle Hotel	0171-834 9494	H	143	62%	366	200	110					
SW1	The Halkin	0171-333 1000	HR	262	86%	41	40	26					
SW1	Hyatt Carlton Tower	0171-235 1234	HR	295	87%	224	250	300					
SW1	Hyde Park Hotel	0171-235 2000	H	306	82%	185	250	275					
SW1	Knightsbridge Green Hotel	0171-584 6274	PH	129		25							
SW1	The Lanesborough	0171-259 5599	HR	334	89%	95	90	100					
SW1	The Lowndes Hotel	0171-823 1234	H	242	76%	78	25	22				◄	
SW1	Royal Court Hotel	0171-730 9191	H	154	63%	105	40	20					
SW1	Royal Horseguards Thistle	0171-839 3400	H	146	71%	377	300	400					

District	Hotel	Phone	Type								
SW1	Royal Westminster Thistle	0171-834 1821	H	151	71%	134	180	150			
SW1	Rubens Hotel	0171-834 6600	H	149	66%	180	75	140			
SW1	St James Court	0171-834 6655	HR	180	73%	471	250	200			
SW1	Scandic Crown Victoria	0171-834 8123	H	177	67%	210	180	180		◄	
SW1	Sheraton Belgravia	0171-235 6040	HR	259	75%	89	60	22		◄	
SW1	Sheraton Park Tower	0171-235 8050	HR	308	79%	295	70	150	◄		
SW1	The Stafford	0171-493 0111	H	223	74%	74	30	50			
SW1	Stakis St Ermin's	0171-222 7888	H	159	71%	290	200	200			
SW1	Tophams Ebury Court	0171-730 8147	HR	115	55%	42	30	28			
SW1	22 Jermyn Street	0171-734 2353	PH	230		18	10				
SW1	Wilbraham Hotel	0171-730 8296	H	94	55%	52					
SW1	Willett Hotel	0171-824 8415	B	92		19					
SW3	Basil Street Hotel	0171-581 3311	H	200	71%	93	75	65			
SW3	The Beaufort	0171-584 5252	PH	163		28	10				
SW3	Blair House Hotel	0171-581 2323	B	90		16					
SW3	The Capital	0171-589 5171	HR	257	85%	48	30	24			
SW3	The Draycott	0171-730 6466	PH	176		25					
SW3	Egerton House	0171-589 2412	PH	184		30	20	14			
SW3	The Fenja	0171-589 7333	PH	154		12	12				
SW3	Franklin Hotel	0171-584 5533	PH	170		40	14	14			
SW3	L'Hotel	0171-589 6286	HR	145		12					
SW3	Sydney House Hotel	0171-376 7711	PH	197		21	20	14			
SW5	Concord Hotel	0171-370 4151	B	60		40					
SW5	Hogarth Hotel	0171-370 6831	H	92	62%	86	50	45			
SW5	Kensington Court Hotel	0171-370 5151	B	75		35					
SW5	Hotel 167	0171-373 0672	B	75		19					
SW5	Swallow International Hotel	0171-973 1000	H	142	68%	416	150	150		◄	

Location	Establishment	Tel. No.	Category	Room £	Hotel %	No. of Rooms	Conf Max	Banq Max	Disabled	In Swim	Out Swim	Tennis	Squash
SW5	Terstan Hotel	0171-835 1900	B	52		48							
SW6	La Reserve	0171-385 8561	H	90	62%	40	10						
SW7	Adelphi Hotel	0171-373 7177	H	112	62%	68	80	60					
SW7	Aster House	0171-581 5888	B	94		12							
SW7	Blakes Hotel	0171-370 6701	HR	268	82%	51	20	20					
SW7	Embassy House Hotel	0171-584 7222	H	105	61%	69	35	70					
SW7	Forum Hotel	0171-370 5757	H	157	62%	911	400	330					
SW7	The Gloucester	0171-373 6030	HR	221	75%	548	400	400					
SW7	The Gore	0171-584 6601	H	166	65%	54	14						
SW7	Harrington Hall Hotel	0171-396 9696	H	142	72%	200	100	200					
SW7	Holiday Inn Kensington	0171-373 2222	H	187	68%	162	225	180					
SW7	Jurys Kensington Hotel	0171-589 6300	H	125	64%	170	80	30					
SW7	Kensington Manor	0171-370 7516	PH	94		14							
SW7	Norfolk Hotel	0171-589 8191	H	167	64%	96	24	24					
SW7	Number Sixteen	0171-589 5232	PH	130		36							
SW7	Pelham Hotel	0171-589 8288	HR	194	76%	41							
SW7	Periquito Queen's Gate	0171-370 6111	H	73		61							
SW7	Radisson Vanderbilt Hotel	0171-589 2424	H	139	62%	223	120	100					
SW7	Regency Hotel	0171-370 4595	H	166	69%	210	100	180					
SW7	Rembrandt Hotel	0171-589 8100	H	155	70%	195	250	200		◄			
SW7	Stuart Hotel	0171 373 1004	B	70		50							
SW10	Conrad International London	0171-823 3000	HR	285	86%	160	200	180		◄			

Postcode	Hotel	Phone	Type									
SW19	Cannizaro House	0181-879 1464	HR			160	76%	46	45	80		
W1	The Athenaeum	0171-499 3464	H			246	81%	156	55	40		
W1	Bentinck House Hotel	0171-935 9141	B			73		20				
W1	Berkshire Hotel	0171-629 7474	HR			231	72%	147	45	25		
W1	The Berners Hotel	0171-636 1629	H			162	73%	226	160	120		
W1	Britannia Inter-Continental	0171-629 9400	H			226	77%	318	110	85		
W1	Brown's Hotel	0171-493 6020	HR			256	76%	116	35	70		
W1	Chesterfield Hotel	0171-491 2622	H			210	74%	110	110	120		
W1	Churchill Inter-Continental	0171-486 5800	HR	◄		282	84%	448	350	240		
W1	Claridge's	0171-629 8860	HR			316	88%	190	250	210		
W1	The Clifton-Ford	0171-486 6600	H			210	73%	200	150	128		
W1	Concorde Hotel	0171-402 6169	B			87		27		22		
W1	The Connaught	0171-499 7070	HR			320	91%	90				
W1	Cumberland Hotel	0171-262 1234	H			155	69%	900	475	540	◄	
W1	The Dorchester	0171-589 4257	HR			298	91%	244	550	550		
W1	Durrants Hotel	0171-935 8131	H			118	65%	96	100	60		
W1	Forte Crest Regents Park	0171-388 2300	H			125	64%	317	650	360		
W1	47 Park Street	0171-491 7282	H			310	86%	52	30	20		
W1	Four Seasons Hotel	0171-499 0888	HR			331	89%	227	500	325		
W1	Grafton Hotel	0171-388 4131	H			160	63%	324	180	110		
W1	Green Park Hotel	0171-629 7522	H			164	67%	161	70	60		
W1	Grosvenor House	0171-499 6363	H		◄	272	83%	454	2400	1500		
W1	Holiday Inn Garden Court	0171-935 4442	H			148	56%	138	90	160		
W1	Holiday Inn Mayfair	0171-493 8282	H			172	72%	185	70	50		
W1	Hospitality Inn Piccadilly	0171-930 4033	H			139	62%	92	60	16		
W1	Inter-Continental London	0171-409 3131	HR			277	84%	460	1000	800	◄	
W1	The Langham Hilton	0171-636 1000	H			240	75%	379	320	240		

Location	Establishment	Tel. No.	Category	Room £	Hotel %	No. of Rooms	Conf Max	Band Max	Disabled	In Swim	Out Swim	Tennis	Squash
W1	London Hilton on Park Lane	0171-493 8000	H	250	75%	448	1200	1250	▲				
W1	London Marriott Hotel	0171-493 1232	H	266	77%	223	900	500					
W1	London Mews Hilton on Park Lane	0171-493 7222	H	207	68%	72	45	30	▲				
W1	Mandeville Hotel	0171-935 5599	H	135	62%	165							
W1	Marble Arch Marriott	0171-723 1277	H	189	68%	239	150	150		▲			
W1	May Fair Inter-Continental	0171-629 7777	HR	258	81%	287	290	320		▲			
W1	Le Meridien	0171-734 8000	HR	271	84%	266	260	250	▲	▲			▲
W1	Merryfield House	0171-935 8326	B	50		8							
W1	Montcalm Hotel	0171-402 4288	HR	234	76%	116	80	60					
W1	Mostyn Hotel	0171-935 2361	H	124	62%	122	150	130					
W1	The Park Lane Hotel	0171-499 6321	H	249	77%	307	500	600					
W1	Radisson SAS Portman Hotel	0171-208 6000	H	225	77%	279	400	440					
W1	Rathbone Hotel	0171-636 2001	H	162	69%	72	12	10					
W1	The Ritz	0171-493 8181	HR	249	86%	130	60	50					
W1	St George's Hotel	0171-580 0111	HR	166	67%	86	30	20					
W1	The Selfridge	0171-408 2080	HR	181	75%	295	280	280					
W1	Sherlock Holmes Hotel	0171-486 6161	H	121	66%	125	80	50					
W1	Washington Hotel	0171-499 7000	H	200	73%	173	90	60					
W1	The Westbury	0171-629 7755	H	191	77%	244	120	80					
W1	Abbey Court	0171-221 7518	PH	136		22		20					
W2	Columbia Hotel	0171-402 0021	B	60		103	200	140					

	Hotel	Telephone							
W2	Craven Gardens Hotel	0171-262 3167	B	66		43	40	18	
W2	Hospitality Inn Bayswater	0171-262 4461	H	113	62%	175	80	120	
W2	Jarvis London Embassy	0171-229 1212	H	138	68%	193			
W2	London Metropole Hotel	0171-402 4141	H	194	69%	742	1300	840	◀
W2	Mornington Hotel	0171-262 7361	H	89	63%	68	18		
W2	Parkwood Hotel	0171-402 2241	B	55		18			
W2	Pembridge Court Hotel	0171-229 9977	H	115	66%	20		60	
W2	Royal Lancaster Hotel	0171-262 6737	H	191		418	1400	1500	
W2	Stakis London Coburg	0171-221 221	H	103	60%	132	175	120	
W2	Whites Hotel	0171-262 2711	H	201	77%	54	20	20	
W6	Novotel	0181-741 1555	H	116	64%	635	900	750	◀
W8	Apollo Hotel	0171-835 1133	B	73		50	20	20	
W8	Atlas Hotel	0171-835 1155	B	73		50			
W8	Copthorne Tara	0171-937 7211	H	148	69%	825	500	360	◀
W8	Kensington Close Hotel	0171-937 8170	H	135	59%	530	180	140	
W8	Kensington Palace Thistle	0171-937 8121	H	127	62%	299	180	200	
W8	Kensington Park Thistle	0171-937 8080	H	165	67%	332	100	125	
W8	The Milestone	0171-917 1000	HR	275	78%	57	30	25	
W8	Royal Garden Hotel	0171-937 8000	H	0		398	900	600	
W9	Colonnade Hotel	0171-286 1052	H	90	63%	48			
W11	The Halcyon	0171-727 7288	HR	235	79%	43	18	12	
W11	London Kensington Hilton	0171-603 3355	H	165	67%	603	300	300	
W11	Portobello Hotel	0171-727 2777	H	120	60%	24			
W14	London Olympia Hilton	0171-603 3333	H	149	66%	405	500	350	
WC1	Bonnington in Bloomsbury	0171-242 2828	H	100	62%	215	250	130	◀
WC1	Euston Plaza Hotel	0171-383 4105	H	148	66%	150	130	72	
WC1	Forte Crest Bloomsbury	0171-837 1200	H	147	65%	284	700	650	

Location	Establishment	Tel. No.	Category	Room £	Hotel %	No. of Rooms	Conf Max	Banq Max	Disabled	In Swim	Out Swim	Tennis	Squash
WC1	Holiday Inn Kings Cross	0171-833 3900	H	165	68%	405	250	180		◄			◄
WC1	Kenilworth Hotel	0171-637 3477	H	172	63%	187	150	130					
WC1	The Marlborough	0171-636 5601	H	167	70%	169	275	200	◄				
WC1	The Montague	0171-637 1001	H	135	64%	109							
WC1	President Hotel	0171-837 8844	B	68		447	130	80					
WC1	Hotel Russell	0171-837 6470	H	146	68%	328	400	300					
WC2	Hampshire Hotel	0171-839 9399	HR	248	78%	124	100	80					
WC2	Howard Hotel	0171-836 3555	HR	267	81%	135	150	130					
WC2	Moat House	0171-836 6666	H	150	65%	153	100	100					
WC2	Mountbatten Hotel	0171-836 4300	HR	207	70%	127	100	80					
WC2	Royal Trafalgar Thistle	0171-930 4477	H	151	65%	108	100	108					
WC2	The Savoy	0171-836 4343	HR	303	91%	202	600	500		◄			
WC2	The Waldorf	0171-836 2400	HR	212	83%	292	400	420					

London: Lodge

Location	Establishment	Tel. No.	Map Ref	Motorway comments	Address
E5 (Beckton	Travel Inn	0171-511 3853	Map 11 B4		Winsor terrace, Beckton, A117

London by Postal District: Restaurants

See How To Use This Guide, on pages 14-15, for an explanation of our percentage rating system, room pricing and categories.
No-smoking denotes a ban on smoking throughout or a separate no-smoking room.

Location	Establishment	Tel. No.	Dinner for 2, £	Category	Stars	Seats	Parties	Private Rms	Sundays	No-Smoking	Open Air	Nat Cuisine	Seafood	Vegetarian	Dessert	Cheese	O/s Wine	New World	Italian Wine	Wines by glass
E1	Bloom's	0171-247 6001	40	R		144	40		All			Jewish								◄
E1	The Hothouse	0171-488 4797	50	R		150	20	yes	All											◄
E1	Namaste	0171-488 9242	35	R		125	45			yes		Indian								
E1	Shampan	0171-375 0475	40	R	↑	62	30		All			Indian								
E8	Faulkners	0171-254 6152	30	R		160			All				◄							
EC1	Alba	0171-588 1798	60	R		40	30	yes				Italian							◄	
EC1	Bubb's	0171-236 2435	75	R		75	18	yes				French								
EC1	Café du Marché	0171-608 1609	55	R		100	10	yes				Medit'r'n								◄
EC1	The Eagle	0171-837 1353	40	R	↑	55				yes		British								
EC1	The Hope & Sir Loin	0171-253 8525	40	R		30	16	yes				British								
EC1	Japanese Canteen	0171-833 3222	25	R		120	8	yes	All			Japanese								
EC1	Mange-2	0171-250 0035	70	R		80	20	yes				French								◄
EC1	Le Mesurier	0171-251 8117	65	R		20	25	yes				French								
EC1	The Peasant	0171-336 7726	50	R		80	30		L			Medit'r'n								◄
EC1	Quality Chop House	0171-837 5093	45	R		48	6		All			British								

Location	Establishment	Tel. No.	Dinner for 2, £	Category	Stars	Seats	Parties	Private Rms	Sundays	No-Smoking	Open Air	Nat Cuisine	Seafood	Vegetarian	Dessert	Cheese	O/s Wine	New World	Italian Wine	Wines by glass
EC1	Ravi Shankar	0171-833 5849	25	R								Indian								
EC1	St John	0171-251 0848	60	R		120	8	yes	D											▲
EC1	Stephen Bull's Bistro	0171-490 1750	60	R		120	25		All									▲		▲
EC2	Moshi Moshi Sushi	0171-247 3227	20	R		60						Japanese								
EC2	Sri Siam City	0171-628 5772	55	R		150	160					Thai								
EC2	Tatsuso	0171-638 5863	85	R	★	120	55	yes				Japanese		▲						
EC3	Hospitality Suite	0171-617 5042	75	R		30	8	yes				French								
EC3	Imperial City	0171-626 3437	55	R		180	60	yes				Chinese								
EC3	Luc's Restaurant	0171-621 0666	50	R		140						French								
EC3	Poons in the City	0171-626 0126	50	R		200	12	yes			yes	Chinese		▲						
EC3	Scoul	0171-480 5770	30	R		28						Korean								
EC4	Ginnan	0171-278 0008	50	R		72	20					Japanese								
EC4	Miyama	0171-489 1937	80	R		85	40	yes				Japanese								
EC4	Sweetings	0171-248 3062	60	R		65	8						▲							
EC4	Whittington's	0171-248 5855	70	R		52	18	yes												▲
N1	Anna's Place	0171-249 9379	50	R		42	12			yes		Swedish								
N1	Casale Franco	0171-226 8994	60	R		140	25	yes	All	yes		Italian								
N1	Euphorium	0171-704 6909	70	R	↑	40	8	yes			yes				▲	▲				
N1	Frederick's	0171-359 2888	65	R		130	20	yes			yes				▲	▲	▲	▲		▲
N1	Granita	0171-226 3222	50	R		60	25		All											
N1	Hodja Nasreddin	0171-226 7757	25	R		60	6	yes	All			Turkish								
N1	Mojees Restaurant	0171-226 0307	45	R		45	45													
N1	Nam Bistro	0171-354 0851	45	R		80	8	yes	All			Vietnamese								

Area	Restaurant	Telephone		Type						Cuisine							
N1	Pasha	0171-226 1454	35	R	80	20		All		Turkish							
N1	Satay Hut	0171-359 4090	30	R	95			D		S E Asian							
N1	Smargaon	0171-226 6499	50	R	60	30		All		Indian							
N1	Suruchi	0171-241 5213	30	R	34			L	yes	Indian							
N1	Tuk Tuk	0171-226 0837	30	R	40	40	yes			Thai							
N3	Rani	0181-349 4386	40	R	90	30	yes	All	yes	Indian							
N4	Chez Liline	0171-263 6550	45	R	50	20					▲						
N5	Iznik	0171-354 5697	45	R	54	6		L		Turkish		▲					
N8	Les Associés	0181-348 8944	60	R	38	20				French						▲	▲
N8	Florians	0181-348 8348	50	R	60	8		All	yes	Italian	▲						
N16	Istanbul Iskembecisi	0171-254 7291	30	R	80		yes	All		Turkish							
N16	Rasa	0171-249 0344	40	R	42	20		All		Indian		▲					
N16	Le Soir	0171-275 8781	35	R	46	10		D		French		▲					
N16	Yum Yum	0171-254 6751	45	R	120	40	yes	All		Thai		▲					
NW1	Asuka	0171-486 5026	70	R	40	24	yes			Japanese							
NW1	Belgo Noord	0171-267 0718	50	R	125	10		All		Belgian							
NW1	Big Night Out	0171-586 5768	55	R	65	8	yes	L	yes								▲
NW1	Camden Brasserie & Underground Café	0171-482 2114	55	R	100	19	yes			Medit'r'n							
NW1	Cheng-Du	0171-485 8058	60	R	70	82		All		Chinese							
NW1	China Jazz	0171-482 3940	70	R	110	90		All		Chinese							
NW1	Daphne	0171-267 7322	45	R	85	30				Greek				▲			
NW1	Dorset Square Hotel	0171-723 7874	65	HR	30												
NW1	Great Nepalese	0171-388 6737	60	R	48	34		All		Indian							
NW1	Hudson's	0171-935 3130	65	R	35	25	yes	All		British					▲		
NW1	The Regent London	0171-631 8000	95	HR	100	12	yes	All					▲				
NW1	Lemonia	0171-586 7454	40	R	140	14	yes	L		Greek							
NW1	Nontas	0171-387 4579	30	R	50	24			yes	Greek		▲					
NW1	Odette's	0171-586 5486	65	R	60	30	yes	L	yes	French		▲			▲	▲	
NW1	Otafuku	0171-482 2036	60	R	40				yes	Japanese							

Location	Establishment	Tel. No.	Dinner for 2, £	Category	Stars	Seats	Parties	Private Rms	Sundays	No-Smoking	Open Air	Nat Cuisine	Seafood	Vegetarian	Dessert	Cheese	O/s Wine	New World	Italian Wine	Wines by glass
NW1	Ravi Shankar	0171-388 6458	25	R		60		yes	All			Indian								
NW1	Singapore Garden	0171-723 8233	45	R					All			S E Asian								
NW1	Trattoria Lucca	0171-485 6864	45	R		60	24					Italian							◄	
NW2	Laurent	0171-794 3603	40	R		36	14					N African								
NW2	Quincy's	0171-794 8499	60	R		30	8	yes												
NW3	Benihana	0171-586 9508	75	R		112	10	yes	All	yes		Japanese								
NW3	Bradley's	0171-722 3457	65	R		45	8													
NW3	Caffe Graffitti	0171-431 7579	60	R		45	20	yes	All	yes		Italian		◄	◄			◄	◄	◄
NW3	Cucina	0171-435 7814	65	R		65			L			Italian				◄				◄
NW3	Green Boat	0171-722 8474	45	R		50	12		All			Chinese								
NW3	Green Cottage	0171-722 5305	40	R		95	16		All			Chinese								
NW3	Jinkichi	0171-794 6158	60	R		42	15		All			Japanese								
NW3	Qinggis	0171-586 4251	55	R		75	20	yes	All	yes		Chinese								
NW3	Wakaba	0171-586 7960	70	R		55						Japanese								
NW3	ZeNW3	0171-794 7863	45	R		140	15	yes	All			Chinese								
NW4	Kaifeng	0181-203 7888	80	R		70	18	yes	All	yes		Chinese								
NW5	Le Petit Prince	0171-267 0752	30	R		60	30	yes	L			Chinese								
NW6	Gung-Ho	0171-794 1444	50	R		105	14		All			Chinese								
NW6	Singapore Garden	0171-328 5314	45	R		100	12	yes	All			S E Asian								
NW6	Sushi Gen	0171-431 4031	50	R					All			Japanese								
NW6	Vijay	0171-328 1087	25	R		74	25		All			Indian								
NW7	Good Earth	0181-959 7011	55	R		90	80		All			Chinese								
NW7	Hee's	0181-959 7109	50	R		100	15	yes	All			Chinese								
NW8	Au Bois St Jean	0171-722 0400	70	R		85	12	yes	All	yes		French								◄

Area	Name	Phone		Type			Cards	Veg	Cuisine
NW8	L'Aventure	0171-624 6232	65	R	45	48	All	yes	French
NW8	Don Pepe	0171-262 3834	50	R	45	20	L		Spanish
NW8	Greek Valley	0171-624 3217	45	R	62	75	yes		Greek
NW8	Kashi-Noki	0171-586 0911	70	R	42	10			Japanese
NW10	Sabras	0181-459 0340	25	R	32	32	D		Indian
NW11	Bloom's	0181-455 1338	40	R	72	20	All		Jewish
NW11	Raffles	0181-458 9273	50	R	70	25	All		S E Asian
SE1	Bengal Clipper	0171-357 9001	70	R	170	35	All		Indian
SE1	Blue Print Café	0171-378 7031	60	R	86	15	L	yes	Indian
SE1	Butlers Wharf Chop-house	0171-403 3403	80	R	115	12	L	yes	British
SE1	Cantina del Ponte	0171-403 5403	65	R	95	20	L	yes	Italian
SE1	Mutiara	0171-277 0425	25	R	70				S E Asian
SE1	People's Palace	0171-928 9999	70	R	180	16			
SE1	Le Pont de la Tour	0171-403 8403	95	R ↑	105	9	All	yes	French
SE1	RSJ	0171-928 4554	65	R	90	10	All	yes	French
SE14	Thailand Restaurant	0181-691 4040	35	R	25	25			Thai
SE19	Luigi's	0181-670 1843	65	R	65	75	yes	yes	Italian
SE22	Sema	0181-693 3213	50	R	70	18	All	yes	Thai
SE5	Silver Lake	0171-701 9961	40	R	40	40	All		Chinese
SW1	Al Bustan	0171-235 8277	60	R	70	70	All	yes	Lebanese
SW1	The Atrium	0171-233 0032	60	R	155	142		yes	
SW1	The Berkeley	0171-235 6000	115	HR	65	14	All	yes	French
SW1	Cadogan Hotel	0171-235 7141	55	HR	40	14	All		
SW1	Café Fish	0171-930 3999	55	R ↑	94	25			
SW1	Le Caprice	0171-629 2239	70	R	70	8	All	yes	
SW1	Ebury Wine Bar	0171-730 5447	40	R	80	12	All		
SW1	Fifth Floor Restaurant	0171-235 5250	80	R	110	6		yes	
SW1	The Goring	0171-396 9000	95	HR	70	10	All	yes	British
SW1	Green's	0171-930 4566	75	R	65	6	L		British

Location	Establishment	Tel. No.	Dinner for 2, £	Category	Stars	Seats	Parties	Private Rms	Sundays	No-Smoking	Open Air	Nat Cuisine	Seafood	Vegetarian	Dessert	Cheese	O/s Wine	New World	Italian Wine	Wines by glass
SW1	The Grenadier	0171-235 3074	65	R		28	8		All		yes									
SW1	The Halkin	0171-333 1000	100	HR	★ ↑	45	10	yes	D			Italian			◄				◄	◄
SW1	Hunan	0171-730 5712	50	R		50	15	yes	D			Chinese								
SW1	Hyatt Carlton Tower	0171-235 1234	115	HR	↑	63	30	yes	All		yes	French					◄	◄	◄	
SW1	Hyatt Carlton Tower: Rib Room	0171-235 5411	110	R		84	10	yes	All		yes	British						◄	◄	
SW1	L'Incontro	0171-730 3663	100	R		55	20	yes				Italian					◄		◄	
SW1	Isohama	0171-834 2145	60	R		30	30		All			Japanese		◄						
SW1	Ken Lo's Memories of China	0171-730 7734	75	R		120	40	yes	D			Chinese								
SW1	Kundan	0171-834 3434	60	R		117	120	yes				Indian								
SW1	Kura	0171-581 1820	90	R		25	16		D			Japanese								
SW1	The Lanesborough	0171-259 5599	90	HR	★	106	12		All					◄		◄				
SW1	Marco Pierre White	0171-259 5380	175	R	★★★	50	12					French		◄	◄		◄	◄	◄	◄
SW1	Mijanou	0171-730 4099	85	R	↑	30	12	yes			yes	French			◄	◄	◄	◄	◄	◄
SW1	Mimmo d'Ischia	0171-730 5406	90	R		70	12	yes				Italian								
SW1	Mitsukoshi	0171-839 6714	100	R		56	12	yes				Japanese								
SW1	Motcomb's	0171-235 9170	60	R		70	10	yes	L			British								
SW1	Olivo	0171-730 2505	55	R		43	6					Italian	◄							
SW1	Overtons at St James's	0171-839 3774	80	R		52	8	yes			yes				◄	◄			◄	◄
SW1	Pomegranates	0171-828 6560	80	R		50	14	yes			yes					◄		◄		
SW1	La Poule Au Pot	0171-730 7763	55	R		65	16		All		yes	French								
SW1	Quaglino's	0171-930 6767	70	R		338	10	yes	L									◄		◄

	Restaurant	Telephone							Cuisine	Cards							
SW1	St James Court	0171-834 6655	90	HR	65	30		French									◄
SW1	Sale e Pepe	0171-235 0098	70	R	75	10		Italian			◄					◄	
SW1	Salloos	0171-235 4444	70	R	65	25		Indian									
SW1	Santini	0171-730 4094	100	R	55	25		Italian	D					◄		◄	
SW1	Shepherd's	0171-834 9552	60	R	75	10		British		yes				◄		◄	
SW1	Sheraton Belgravia	0171-235 6040	70	HR	55	18			D	yes	◄		◄				
SW1	Sheraton Park Tower	0171-235 8050	70	HR	80	25			All	yes							
SW1	Signor Sassi	0171-584 2277	60	R	80	15		Italian									
SW1	Simply Nico	0171-630 8061	65	R	45	10	★	French				◄◄	◄				
SW1	The Square	0171-839 8787	80	R	65	8	★ ↑		All	yes	◄	◄◄	◄			◄	◄
SW1	Suntory	0171-409 0201	120	R	101	15		Japanese		yes	◄						
SW1	Tate Gallery Rest.	0171-887 8877	55	R	100	16				yes			◄				
SW1	Tophams Ebury Court	0171-730 8147	50	HR	30	12		British		yes					◄		
SW1	Wilton's	0171-629 9955	110	R	100	16		British	All	yes	◄			◄		◄	
SW1	Zafferano	0171-235 5800	65	R	52	8		Italian									
SW3	Albero & Grana	0171-225 1048/9	70	R	150	40	↑	Spanish	D	yes	◄	◄	◄			◄	◄
SW3	Benihana	0171-376 7799	75	R	128	10		Japanese	All	yes	◄	◄	◄			◄	
SW3	Bibendum	0171-581 5817	120	R	72	8	★		All								
SW3	Bibendum Oyster Bar	0171-581 5817	70	R	45	6			All		◄						
SW3	Brasserie St Quentin	0171-581 5131	55	R	80	25		French	All	yes							
SW3	La Brasserie	0171-581 3089	60	R	130	30		French	All	yes			◄				
SW3	The Capital	0171-589 5171	120	HR	40	8	★★	British	All	yes	◄	◄	◄	◄		◄	◄
SW3	Charco's	0171-584 0765	65	R	70					yes							
SW3	Dan's	0171-352 2718	75	R	52	35	↑		L	yes							
SW3	Daphne's	0171-589 4257	85	R	120	6		Italian	All		◄					◄	
SW3	English Garden	0171-584 7272	75	R	70	20		British	All	yes							
SW3	English House	0171-584 3002	75	R	30	8		British	All	yes							
SW3	The Enterprise	0171-584 3148	55	R	35	12			All	yes							
SW3	Foxtrot Oscar	0171-352 7179	50	R	50	20			All	yes							
SW3	Fulham Road	0171-351 7823	80	R	80	8	↑		All	yes						◄	◄

Location	Establishment	Tel. No.	Dinner for 2, £	Category	Stars	Seats	Parties	Private Rms	Sundays	No-Smoking	Open Air	Nat Cuisine	Seafood	Vegetarian	Dessert	Cheese	O/s Wine	New World	Italian Wine	Wines by glass
SW3	La Giara	0171-591 0210	70	R		40	10					Italian							◄	
SW3	Good Earth	0171-584 3658	65	R		145	14	yes	All			Chinese								
SW3	Grill St Quentin	0171-581 8377	55	R		140	25	yes	All			French								◄
SW3	L'Hotel	0171-589 6286	40	HR		40	8													
SW3	Joe's Cafe	0171-225 2217	70	R		75	14		L	yes										
SW3	Khun Akorn	0171-225 2688	65	R		70	30		All			Thai								
SW3	Maroush II	0171-581 5434	70	R		90	10		All			Lebanese								
SW3	Monkeys	0171-352 4711	80	R		40	8	yes				British								
SW3	Poissonnerie de l'Avenue	0171-589 2457	95	R		100	10	yes		yes		French	◄							
SW3	S & P Patara	0171-581 8820	40	R		40						Thai								
SW3	S & P Restaurant	0171-351 5692	40	R		65	15		D			Thai								
SW3	Sambuca	0171-730 6571	70	R		75	12					Italian								
SW3	San Frediano	0171-584 8375	55	R		120	25			yes		Italian							◄	
SW3	San Lorenzo	0171-584 1074	100	R		150	10	yes				Italian							◄	
SW3	San Martino	0171-589 3833	60	R		130	42	yes	D	yes		Italian							◄	
SW3	Sandrini	0171-584 1724	70	R		80	12		All	yes		Italian							◄	
SW3	Scalini	0171-225 2301	70	R		100	18		All	yes		Italian							◄	
SW3	Le Suquet	0171-581 1785	70	R	★	70	10	yes	All	yes		French	◄							
SW3	La Tante Claire	0171-352 6045	140	R	★★★	43	10					French			◄		◄			
SW3	Thierry's	0171-352 3365	60	R		65	34	yes	All			French								
SW3	Turner's	0171-584 6711	100	R	†	50	50	yes	All								◄			
SW3	Waltons	0171-584 0204	100	R		90	12	yes	All			British				◄				

SW3	Zen Chelsea	0171-589 1781	80	R		85	14	yes	All			Chinese	
SW3	Ziani	0171-351 5297	65	R		50			All			Italian	
SW4	Grafton Français	0181-627 1048	65	R		64	5	yes		yes		French	
SW4	Newton's	0181-673 0977	55	R		70	30		All	yes	yes	French	
SW5	Lou Pescadou	0171-370 1057	50	R		69		yes	All	yes	yes	French	
SW5	Mr Wing	0171-370 4450	65	R		120	25	yes	All			Chinese	
SW5	Noor Jahan	0171-373 6522	40	R		60	25	yes	All			Indian	
SW5	La Primula	0171-370 5958	55	R		40	30	yes	All			Italian	
SW6	Blue Elephant	0171-385 6595	70	R		250	30	yes	All			Thai	
SW6	Bonjour Vietnam	0171-385 7603	45	R		100						Chinese	
SW6	De Cecco	0171-736 1145	40	R		92	12					Italian	
SW6	El Metro	0171-384 1264	45	R		60	20		All	yes		Spanish	
SW6	Mamta	0171-736 5914	30	R		40	20		All			Indian	
SW6	Nosh Brothers	0171-736 7311	65	R		60	55	yes					
SW6	Sushi Gen	0171-610 2120	50	R		50	15		All			Japanese	
SW6	Tandoori Lane	0171-371 0440	35	R		56	20	yes	All			Indian	
SW6	Tien Phat	0171-385 7147	30	R		60			All			Vietnamese	
SW7	Bangkok	0171-584 8529	40	R		60	12	yes				Thai	
SW7	Bistrot 190	0171-581 5666	50	R	†	55	10	yes	All	yes			
SW7	Blakes Hotel	0171-370 6701	150	HR	★	35	14	yes	All				
SW7	Bombay Brasserie	0171-370 4040	70	R	★	175	20	yes	All	yes		Indian	
SW7	La Bouchée	0171-589 1929	50	R		70			All	yes		French	
SW7	Café Lazeez	0171-581 9993	60	R		130		yes	All	yes		Indian	
SW7	Downstairs at 190	0171-581 5666	60	R	†	70	10	yes	All				
SW7	The Establishment	0171-589 7969	50	R									
SW7	Gilbert's	0171-589 8947	60	R		30	10			yes			
SW7	The Gloucester	0171-373 6030	60	HR		156	30		All				
SW7	Hilaire	0171-584 8993	85	R	★ †	60	30	yes					
SW7	Khan's of Kensington	0171-584 4114	45	R		60	25	yes	All	yes		Indian	
SW7	Khyber Pass	0171-589 7311	30	R		32			All			Indian	

Location	Establishment	Tel. No.	Dinner for 2, £	Category	Stars	Seats	Parties	Private Rms	Sundays	No-Smoking	Open Air	Nat Cuisine	Seafood	Vegetarian	Dessert	Cheese	O/s Wine	New World	Italian Wine	Wines by glass
SW7	Majlis	0171-584 3476	35	R		32	4		All			Indian								
SW7	Memories of India	0171-589 6450	40	R		50	20	yes	All		yes	Indian								
SW7	Ognisko Polskie	0171-589 4635	65	R		80	80	yes	All		yes	Polish								
SW7	Pelham Hotel	0171-589 8288	50	HR		30	15	yes	All		yes	British				◄				
SW7	Pun	0171-225 1609	50	R		70	20	yes	All	yes		Chinese								
SW7	Shaw's	0171-373 7774	70	R		44	10		All	yes								◄		
SW7	Shezan	0171-584 9316	70	R		100	10	yes	All			Indian								
SW7	Tui	0171-584 8359	45	R		56	12	yes	All			Thai								
SW8	Stepping Stone	0171-622 0555	55	R		54			L		yes			◄						◄
SW9	Twenty Trinity Gardens	0171-733 8838	45	R		54	25	yes	All	yes	yes	French						◄		◄
SW10	Aubergine	0171-352 3449	90	R	★★	40	6			yes		French			◄			◄		
SW10	The Canteen	0171-351 7330	75	R		135	12	yes	All		yes				◄			◄		
SW10	Chez Max	0171-835 0874	80	R	↑	60	8	yes		yes		French								
SW10	Chutney Mary	0171-351 3113	60	R	↑	110	16	yes	All		yes	Indian						◄		◄
SW10	Conrad International London	0171-823 3000	85	HR		50	14	yes			yes			◄				◄		◄
SW10	Formula Veneta	0171-352 7612	50	R		55	12	yes	L		yes	Italian							◄	
SW10	Il Goloso	0171-352 9827	50	R		50	20					Italian							◄	
SW10	Kartouche	0171-823 3515	60	R		78	10							◄				◄	◄	
SW10	Ken Lo's Memories of China	0171-352 4953	60	R		175	100	yes	All			Chinese								
SW10	Kingdom	0171-352 0206	50	R		80		yes	All			Chinese								

Area	Name	Phone		Type							Cuisine
SW10	Nikita's	0171-352 6326	70	R		58	40	yes	All	yes	Russian
SW11	Buchan's	0171-228 0888	59	R		70	50	yes	D	yes	British
SW11	The Green Room	0171-223 4618	50	R		40	25		D	yes	
SW11	Osteria Antica Bologna	0171-978 4771	45	R		75	30		All	yes	Italian
SW11	Phuket	0171-223 5924	60	R		60			All		Thai
SW11	Ransome's Dock	0171-223 1611	65	R		65	20	yes	L	yes	
SW13	Bangkok Garden	0181-392 9158	35	R		50			All		Thai
SW13	Riva	0181-748 0434	75	R		50	12		All	yes	Italian
SW13	Sonny's	0181-748 0393	65	R		100	12	yes	L		
SW14	Le Braconnier	0181-878 2853	60	R		30	20		L		French
SW14	Crowthers	0181-876 6372	65	R		32	32	yes			
SW15	Bangkok Symphonie	0181-789 4304	35	R		45		yes	All	yes	Thai
SW15	Dan Dan	0181-780 1953	50	R		60	40	yes	All	yes	Japanese
SW15	Del Buongustaio	0181-780 9361	60	R	↑	60	8		All		Italian
SW15	Enoteca	0181-785 4449	45	R		40	20	yes		yes	Italian
SW15	Royal China	0181-788 0907	60	R		70			All		Chinese
SW17	Chez Bruce	0181-672 0114	55	R		65		yes			
SW17	Oh'Boy Thai Rest	0181-947 9760	40	R		45	12	yes	All	yes	Thai
SW17	Sree Krishna	0181-672 4250	25	R		120	25	yes	All	yes	Indian
SW18	Le P'tit Normand	0181-871 0233	50	R		35	20	yes	All	yes	French
SW19	Cannizaro House	0181-879 1464	95	HR		36	10	yes		yes	Lebanese
W1	Al Hamra	0171-493 1954	55	R		75		yes	All	yes	Lebanese
W1	Alastair Little	0171-734 5183	85	R	★★	38	8	yes			
W1	Arirang Korean	0171-437 6633	50	R		40		yes			Korean
W1	Arisugawa	0171-636 8913	60	R		120	100	yes			Japanese
W1	Atelier	0171-287 2057	70	R		45	20	yes	D	yes	
W1	Au Jardin des Gourmets	0171-437 1816	75	R		150	10	yes		yes	French
W1	Baboon	0171-224 2992	70	R		65	16	yes			
W1	Bahn Thai	0171-437 8504	60	R		120	50	yes	All	yes	Thai
W1	Bentley's	0171-287 5025	80	R		90		yes		yes	British

Location	Establishment	Tel. No.	Dinner for 2, £	Category	Stars	Seats	Parties	Private Rms	Sundays	No-Smoking	Open Air	Nat Cuisine	Seafood	Vegetarian	Dessert	Cheese	O/s Wine	New World	Italian Wine	Wines by glass
W1	Berkshire Hotel	0171-629 7474	75	HR		38			D						◄					
W1	Bistrot Bruno	0171-734 4545	70	R	★	40	12					French								
W1	Brown's Hotel	0171-493 6020	85	HR		35	14	yes	All										◄	
W1	Café Royal Grill Room	0171-437 9090	135	R	★	45	8			yes		French			◄		◄	◄	◄	
W1	Caravan Serai	0171-935 1208	45	R		56	40	yes	All	yes	yes	Afghan								
W1	Chez Nico at Ninety Park Lane	0171-409 1290	150	R	★★★	70	10	yes	All			French			◄		◄	◄	◄	
W1	Chiang Mai	0171-437 7444	50	R		56		yes	D			Thai								
W1	Chuen Cheng Ku	0171-734 3281	35	R		450	12	yes	All			Chinese								
W1	Churchill Inter-Continental	0171-486 5800	80	HR		108	24	yes	All						◄		◄	◄	◄	◄
W1	Claridge's	0171-629 8860	130	HR		120	12	yes	All							◄	◄	◄	◄	◄
W1	Claridge's: The Causerie	0171-629 8860	85	R		45	8			yes						◄		◄		◄
W1	The Connaught	0171-499 7070	160	HR	★★	75	10	yes	All			French			◄	◄	◄		◄◄	
W1	Defune	0171-935 8311	80	R		15	8	yes				Japanese								
W1	dell'Ugo	0171-734 8300	40	R	↑	180	60	yes		yes	yes									◄
W1	Dorchester: Oriental Room	0171-629 8888	120	R	↑	51	16	yes				Chinese		◄						
W1	Dorchester: Terrace Restaurant	0171-629 8888	120	R	★★	81	14					French		◄	◄		◄	◄	◄	◄
W1	Dorchester: The Bar	0171-629 8888	70	R		59	8		All			Italian			◄				◄	◄
W1	The Dorchester	0171-589 4257	130	HR		81	12	yes	All			British				◄				

Area	Name	Phone		R/HR								Cuisine
W1	Dragon Inn	0171-494 0870	30	R		120	12		All			Chinese
W1	Dragon's Nest	0171-437 3119	45	R		130	40	yes	All			Chinese
W1	Efes Kebab House	0171-636 1953	40	R		50		yes				Turkish
W1	Elena's L'Etoile	0171-636 7189	80	R		82	18	yes		yes		French
W1	L'Escargot	0171-437 6828	100	R	↑	85	20	yes				French
W1	Est	0171-437 0666	40	R		41	26			yes		Italian
W1	Four Seasons Hotel	0171-499 0888	120	HR	★★	55	8		All			French
W1	Four Seasons Hotel Lanes Restaurant	0171-499 0888	80	R		75	10		All			
	French House Dining Room	0171-437 2477	50	R		30		yes				British
W1	Fuji	0171-734 0957	70	R		50			D	yes		Japanese
W1	Le Gavroche	0171-408 0881	160	R	★★★	60	10	yes				French
W1	Gay Hussar	0171-437 0973	60	R		60	12	yes				Hungarian
W1	Gopal's of Soho	0171-434 0840	50	R		50	20	yes	All			Indian
W1	Grahame's Seafare	0171-437 3788	45	R		86	86					
W1	Greenhouse	0171-499 3331	80	R	↑	90	12		All			British
W1	alistair Greig's Grill	0171-629 5613	60	R		60	20	yes				
W1	Harbour City	0171-439 7859	40	R		180	14	yes	All			Chinese
W1	Hardy's	0171-935 5929	50	R		80	20					
W1	Ho Ho	0171-493 1228	60	R		80	10	yes				Chinese
W1	Ikeda	0171-629 2730	110	R		30	8	yes				Japanese
W1	Ikkyu	0171-436 6169	50	R		45	30		D			Japanese
W1	Inter-Continental London	0171-409 3131	150	HR	★★↑	80	12		L			French
W1	Interlude de Chavot	0171-637 0222	80	R		54	10	yes				French
W1	Jade Garden	0171-437 5065	35	R		150	15	yes	All			Chinese
W1	Kaspia	0171-493 2612	70	R		60	20			yes		Russian
W1	Kaya	0171-437 6630	70	R		78	40			yes		Korean
W1	Lal Qila	0171-387 4570	40	R		70	30		D			Indian
W1	Langan's Bistro	0171-935 4531	65	R		34	8		All			

Location	Establishment	Tel. No.	Dinner for 2, £	Category	Stars	Seats	Parties	Private Rms	Sundays	No-Smoking	Open Air	Nat Cuisine	Seafood	Vegetarian	Dessert	Cheese	O/s Wine	New World	Italian Wine	Wines by glass
W1	Langan's Brasserie	0171-491 8822	85	R	†	220	12					British				◄				◄
W1	The Lexington	0171-434 3401	65	R		45	12	yes											◄	◄
W1	Lido	0171-437 4431	40	R		140	50		All			Chinese								
W1	Lindsay House	0171-439 0450	80	R		30	10	yes	All			British								
W1	Lok Ho Fook	0171-437 2001	35	R		100	40	yes	All			Chinese								
W1	London Chinatown	0171-437 3186	50	R		150	150	yes	All			Chinese								
W1	Maroush III	0171-724 5024	70	R		50			All			Lebanese								
W1	Masako	0171-935 1579	100	R		43	20	yes				Japanese				◄			◄	◄
W1	May Fair Inter-Continental	0171-629 7777	80	HR		65	20	yes	All			French					◄	◄		
W1	Le Meridien	0171-734 8000	135	HR	★	45	8					French			◄	◄	◄			
W1	Le Meridien: Terrace Garden Restnt	0171-734 8000	65	R		130	30		L											
W1	Ming	0171-734 2721	55	R	★	70	14	yes		yes	yes	Chinese								
W1	Miyama	0171-499 2443	75	R		67	30	yes	D			Japanese								
W1	Mon	0171-262 6528	70	R		96	8	yes	All			Japanese								◄
W1	Montcalm Hotel	0171-402 4288	80	HR		60	12			yes		Japanese								
W1	Le Muscadet	0171-935 2883	60	R		36	18					French								
W1	Nakamura	0171-935 2931	50	R		33	15	yes	D			Japanese								
W1	New Fook Lam Moon	0171-734 7615	50	R		80			All			Chinese								
W1	New Loon Fung	0171-437 6232	60	R		400	10	yes	All			Chinese								
W1	New World	0171-434 2508	35	R		600	200	yes	All			Chinese								
W1	Nico Central	0171-436 8846	60	R	★†	50	10	yes				French			◄					
W1	Nicole's	0171-499 8408	75	R		70	20		D			French							◄	◄

Area	Name	Phone	Seats	Type	Rating							Cuisine
W1	Ninjin	0171-388 4657	60	R			54	20				Japanese
W1	Nusa Dua	0171-437 3559	35	R			65	40	yes		yes	S E Asian
W1	O'Conor Don –											
W1	Ard Ri Dining Room	0171-935 9311	50	R			45					
W1	Odin's Restaurant	0171-935 7296	65	R			60	10	yes			
W1	Panda Si Chuen	0171-437 2069	50	R	★		63	18	yes			Chinese
W1	Pied à Terre	0171-636 1178	110	R	★★		36	10	yes			
W1	Ragam	0171-636 9098	35	R			36	40	yes	All	yes	Indian
W1	Rasa Sayang	0171-734 8720	40	R			180	180	yes	All		S E Asian
W1	La Reash	0171-439 1063	35	R			100			All	yes	N African
W1	Red Fort	0171-437 2115	70	R			130	12	yes	All		Indian
W1	The Ritz	0171-493 8181	120	HR	↑		110	30	yes	All	yes	British
W1	Saga	0171-408 2236	85	R			100	16	yes	All		Japanese
W1	St George's Hotel	0171-580 0111	70	HR			85	8	yes			
W1	St Moritz	0171-734 3324	55	R			50	12				Swiss
W1	Les Saveurs	0171-491 8919	120	R	★★★		50	16	yes		yes	French
W1	The Selfridge	0171-408 2080	65	HR			65					
W1	Shampers	0171-437 1692	50	R			80		yes			
W1	Shogun	0171-493 1877	90	R			60	20		D		Japanese
W1	Soho Soho	0171-494 3491	70	R	↑		60	8	yes		yes	
W1	Sri Siam	0171-434 3544	55	R			80	40		D		Thai
W1	Stephen Bull	0171-486 9696	80	R			55	14				
W1	Tamarind	0171-629 3561	60	R			80					Indian
W1	Topkapi	0171-486 1872	35	R			60	30		All		Turkish
W1	Villandry Dining Room	0171-224 3799	45	R			50	30	yes		yes	
W1	White Tower	0171-636 8141	70	R			75	8	yes			Greek
W1	Yumi	0171-935 8320	80	R			76	30	yes			Japanese
W1	Zen Central	0171-629 8089	95	R			70	12		All		Chinese
W1	Zen Garden	0171-493 1381	90	R			129			All		Chinese
W1	Zoe	0171-224 1122	65	R			150	30			yes	Chinese

Location	Establishment	Tel. No.	Dinner for 2, £	Category	Stars	Seats	Parties	Private Rms	Sundays	No-Smoking	Open Air	Nat Cuisine	Seafood	Vegetarian	Dessert	Cheese	O/s Wine	New World	Italian Wine	Wines by glass
W2	L'Accento Italiano	0171-243 2201	55	R	↑	65		yes	All		yes	Italian							◄	
W2	Al San Vincenzo	0171-262 9623	80	R	★	22	4					Italian							◄	
W2	Four Seasons	0171-229 4320	50	R		70	12		All			Chinese								
W2	Halepi	0171-262 1070	50	R		68	68		All			Greek								
W2	Hsing	0171-402 0904	50	R		60	14					Chinese								
W2	Kalamaras	0171-727 9122	40	R		88	30	yes			yes	Greek								
W2	Mandarin Kitchen	0171-727 9012	50	R		110	15		All			Chinese	◄							
W2	Maroush	0171-723 0773	70	R		90	20		All			Lebanese			◄					
W2	New Kam Tong	0171-229 6065	35	R		130	80		All			Chinese								
W2	Poons	0171-792 2884	55	R		100	30		All		yes	Chinese								
W2	Rasa Sayang	0171-229 8417	40	R		60	60		All		yes	S E Asian								
W2	Romantica Taverna	0171-727 7112	40	R		90	70	yes	All			Greek								
W2	Royal China	0171-221 2535	50	R		100	14	yes	All			Chinese								
W2	Standard	0171-727 4818	40	R		130	12	yes	All			Indian								
W2	Tawana Thai	0171-229 3785	40	R		50	10	yes	All			Thai								
W2	Thai Kitchen	0171-221 9984	50	R		40	30	yes				Thai								
W2	Veronica's	0171-229 5079	65	R		60	30	yes			yes	British		◄		◄				
W4	Chiang Mai	0181-995 5774	40	R		60	30					Thai								
W4	Christian's	0181-995 0382	60	R		42	18		L		yes	French			◄					
W4	La Dordogne	0181-747 1836	55	R		80		yes	D		yes	French								
W5	Charlotte's Place	0181-567 7541	50	R		40	18	yes												
W5	Momo	0181-997 0206	50	R		30	20					Japanese								
W5	Wine & Mousaka	0181-998 4373	40	R		90	50					Greek								

Area	Restaurant	Phone									Cuisine					
W5	Young's Rendezvous	0181-840 3060	40	R		100	110	yes	All		Chinese					◀
W6	The Brackenbury	0181-748 0107	55	R		55	8		L	yes	British					
W6	The Chiswick	0181-994 6887	55	R		70	14		L	yes						
W6	Los Molinos	0171-603 2229	35	R		80	45	yes		yes	Spanish					
W6	Mr Wong Wonderful House	0181-748 6887	40	R		200	25	yes	All		Chinese					
W6	Nanking	0181-748 7604	60	R		60	14	yes	All	yes	Chinese					
W6	River Café	0171-381 8824	80	R		100	10		L	yes	Italian		◀			◀
W6	Snows on the Green	0171-603 2142	70	R		70	8	yes	L							
W6	Sumos	0181-741 7916	35	R		40	40	yes			Japanese					
W8	Al Basha	0171-938 1794	70	R		140	40	yes	All		Lebanese					
W8	Arcadia	0171-937 4294	65	R		90		yes	D	yes	French		◀			◀
W8	The Ark	0171-229 4024	45	R		75	20	yes	L	yes						
W8	Boyd's	0171-727 5452	70	R		40								◀		◀
W8	Byblos	0171-603 4422	40	R		45	22		All		Lebanese			◀		
W8	Clarke's	0171-221 9225	90	R	★	90	12		All			◀	◀	◀	◀	
W8	Costa's Grill	0171-229 3794	25	R		50	25	yes		yes	Greek					
W8	L'Escargot Doré	0171-937 8508	85	R		50	20	yes		yes	French					
W8	Geales	0171-727 7969	30	R		100		yes		yes						◀
W8	Kensington Place	0171-727 3184	70	R	★	140	26	yes	All		British			◀		◀
W8	Launceston Place	0171-937 6912	65	R	↑	80			L	yes	British				◀	
W8	Malabar	0171-727 8800	40	R		56	16	yes	All	yes	Indian					
W8	The Milestone	0171-917 1000	80	HR		30	20									
W8	La Paesana	0171-229 4332	40	R		60	20	yes		yes	Italian		◀			
W8	Phoenicia	0171-937 0120	60	R		80	20		All		Lebanese					
W8	Shanghai	0171-938 2501	60	R		90					Chinese					
W8	Stratfords	0171-937 6388	70	R		50	10	yes		yes						◀
W8	Wodka	0171-937 6513	45	R		60	30	yes	D	yes	Polish					
W9	Supan	0181-969 9387	35	R		60	8				Thai					
W10	Brasserie du Marché aux Puces	0181-968 5828	50	R		40	14	yes		yes						

Location	Establishment	Tel. No.	Dinner for 2, £	Category	Stars	Seats	Parties	Private Rms	Sundays	No-Smoking	Open Air	Nat Cuisine	Seafood	Vegetarian	Dessert	Cheese	O/s Wine	New World	Italian Wine	Wines by glass
W10	Jimmy Beez	0181-964 9100	60	R		55	20	yes	All		yes				◄					
W10	Tabac	0181-960 2433	65	R		85	85	yes	L											
W11	L'Altro	0171-792 1066	60	R		45	20		L		yes	Italian	◄		◄				◄	
W11	Avenue West Eleven	0171-221 8144	65	R	↑	56	12	yes	All		yes			◄						
W11	Chez Moi	0171-603 8267	85	R		45	16					French						◄		
W11	The Halcyon	0171-727 7288	90	HR	★	50	8	yes	All		yes			◄	◄	◄				
W11	Hiroko	0171-603 5003	80	R		72	15		All			Japanese								
W11	Julie's	0171-229 8331	70	R		120	26	yes	All		yes				◄	◄				
W11	Leith's	0171-229 4481	115	R		70	16	yes	D			British		◄	◄	◄	◄	◄		◄
W11	Manzara	0171-727 3062	25	R		40	20		All		yes	Turkish								
W11	Mas Café	0171-243 0969	45	R		60	20		All									◄		
W11	192	0171-229 0482	75	R	↑	100	8	yes	All		yes				◄					◄
W11	Orsino	0171-221 3299	60	R		106	8	yes				Italian							◄	
W11	La Pomme d'Amour	0171-229 8532	50	R		62						French	◄							
W12	Adam's Café	0181-743 0572	30	R		60	36	yes				N African								
W12	Balzac Bistro	0181-743 5370	50	R		75	40	yes				French								
W12	Rajput	0181-740 9036	35	R		48	20					Indian								
W12	The Rotisserie	0181-743 3028	40	R		80	75		D									◄		
W13	Sigiri	0181-579 8000	30	R		65	24	yes	All			Sri Lankan								
W14	Chinon	0171-602 5968	65	R	★	30					yes				◄					
W14	Cibo	0171-371 6271	65	R		62	18		All		yes	Italian							◄	
W14	Russell's Bistro	0171-603 7645	50	R		80			All											
WC1	Chiaroscuro	0171-636 2731	65	R		59	12	yes			yes				◄					◄

WC1	Gonbei	0171-278 0619	45	R		34	8	yes				Japanese				◄
WC1	Museum Street Café	0171-405 3211	55	R	★	37	12	yes		yes		Italian			◄	◄
WC1	Poons	0171-580 1188	55	R		100	50		All			Chinese				
WC1	Wagamama	0171-323 9223	25	R		104				yes		Japanese				
WC2	Ajimura	0171-240 0178	60	R		60	6	yes				Japanese				
WC2	Alfred	0171-240 2566	60	R		67	10			yes		Japanese	◄	◄		
WC2	Belgo Centraal	0171-813 2233		R												
WC2	Bertorelli's	0171-836 3969	60	R		90	36					Italian		◄		
WC2	Bhatti	0171-831 0817	50	R		90	8	yes	All		yes	Indian				
WC2	China City	0171-734 3388	55	R		500	14	yes	All			Chinese	◄	◄	◄	
WC2	Christopher's	0171-240 4222	80	R		120	8	yes	L							
WC2	Emerald Garden	0171-437 5042	45	R		68		yes	All			Chinese				
WC2	L'Estaminet	0171-379 1432	60	R		60	12	yes				French				
WC2	Fung Shing	0171-437 1539	52	R	★	85			All			Chinese		◄		
WC2	Giovanni's	0171-240 2877	65	R		40	10					Italian				
WC2	Hampshire Hotel	0171-839 9399	75	HR		55	15	yes	All	yes					◄	
WC2	Hong Kong	0171-287 0324	40	R		200	18	yes	All			Chinese				
WC2	Howard Hotel	0171-836 3555	100	HR		93	10		All			French				
WC2	The Ivy	0171-836 4751	70	R	★	100	8	yes	All	yes			◄		◄	
WC2	Joe Allen	0171-836 0651	40	R		150	8	yes	All	yes		American			◄	
WC2	Joy King Lau	0171-437 1132	50	R		200	12	yes	All			Chinese				
WC2	Magno's Brasserie	0171-836 6077	70	R		60	18					French			◄	
WC2	Manzi's	0171-734 0224	70	R		110	20	yes	D				◄			
WC2	Mr Kong	0171-437 7341	45	R		115		yes	All			Chinese				
WC2	Mon Plaisir	0171-240 3757	50	R		95	20	yes				French				
WC2	Mountbatten Hotel	0171-836 4300	55	HR		75	12	yes							◄	
WC2	Neal Street Restaurant	0171-836 8368	100	R	★	60	12	yes								
WC2	Orso	0171-240 5269	65	R		100	10	yes	All			Italian				
WC2	Le Palais du Jardin	0171-379 5353	60	R		220	35	yes	All			French		◄		◄
WC2	Poons	0171-437 1528	30	R		110	14	yes	All			Chinese				◄

Location	Establishment	Tel. No.	Dinner for 2, £	Category	Stars	Seats	Parties	Private Rms	Sundays	No-Smoking	Open Air	Nat Cuisine	Seafood	Vegetarian	Dessert	Cheese	O/s Wine	New World	Italian Wine	Wines by glass
WC2	Poons	0171-437 4549	30	R		50	25		All			Chinese				◄				
WC2	Rules	0171-836 5314	60	R		140	10	yes	All			British								
WC2	Savoy: Upstairs at the Savoy	0171-836 4343	60	R		38	6													
WC2	The Savoy	0171-836 4343	130	HR	★	160	50	yes	All			French		◄	◄	◄	◄	◄	◄	◄
WC2	The Savoy: Grill Room	0171-836 4343	120	R	★	100	8					British				◄				◄
WC2	Sheekey's	0171-240 2565	65	R		90	12	yes			yes		◄							
WC2	Simpson's-in-the-Strand	0171-836 9112	75	R		240	12	yes	All			British				◄				
WC2	The Waldorf	0171-836 2400	90	HR		67	8		D		yes									
WC2	Westzenders	0171-497 0376	60	R		180	30		All			Chinese								

England by County: Hotels

See How To Use This Guide, on pages 14–15, for an explanation of our percentage rating system, room pricing and categories.
*15 mins Mway refers to hotels graded 70% or higher within 15 minutes of a motorway.

Avon

Location	Establishment	Tel. No.	Category	Room £	Hotel %	No. of Rooms	Conf Max	Bang Max	Beaut Slt	Disabled	In Swim	Out Swim	Tennis	Squash	Golf	Fishing	Riding	15 mins Mway*	Country House
Alveston	Alveston House Hotel	(01454) 415050	H	80	65%	30	85	75											
Alveston	Forte Posthouse	(01454) 412521	H	72	62%	74	100	120				◄							
Bath	Apsley House	(01225) 336966	H	55	67%	7	40												
Bath	Bath Spa Hotel	(01225) 444424	HR	176	87%	98	140	150			◄	◄	◄					◄	
Bath	Fountain House	(01225) 338622	PH	120		14													
Bath	Francis Hotel	(01225) 424257	H	112	67%	93	80	120											
Bath	Hilton National	(01225) 463411	H	126	67%	150	250	200			◄								
Bath	Lansdown Grove	(01225) 315891	H	85	65%	44	100	80		◄									
Bath	Priory Hotel	(01225) 331922	HR	155		21	70	75				◄						◄	
Bath	Queensberry Hotel	(01225) 447928	HR	133	75%	22	30												
Bath	Royal Crescent Hotel	(01225) 319090	HR	188	84%	46	75	80											
Bristol	Aztec Hotel	(01454) 201090	H	116	74%	109	240	200			◄	◄						◄	
Bristol	Berkeley Square Hotel	(0117) 9254000	H	106	69%	43	16	50						◄				◄	

Location	Establishment	Tel. No.	Category	Room £	Hotel %	No. of Rooms	Conf Max	Band Max	Beaut Sit	Disabled	In Swim	Out Swim	Tennis	Squash	Golf	Fishing	Riding	15 mins Mway*	Country House
Bristol	Bristol Marriott Hotel	(0117) 9294281	H	106	73%	289	600	500		◀	◀								
Bristol	Forte Crest	(0117) 9564242	H	112	67%	194	500	400			◀					◀			
Bristol	Grand Hotel	(0117) 9291645	H	113	62%	182	600	530											
Bristol	Hilton National Bristol	(0117) 9260041	H	100	69%	201	300	300			◀								
Bristol	Holiday Inn Crowne Plaza	(0117) 9255010	H	130	72%	128	200	180											
Bristol	Redwood Lodge Hotel	(01275) 393901	H	94	64%	108	250	250			◀	◀	◀	◀					
Bristol	Rodney Hotel	(0117) 9735422	H	74	59%	31													
Bristol	Stakis Bristol Hotel	(01454) 201144	H	117	61%	111	80	60			◀								
Bristol	Swallow Royal Hotel	(0117) 9255100	HR	120	76%	242	300	262			◀								
Bristol	Unicorn Hotel	(0117) 9230333	H	92	66%	187	320	300											
Chelwood	Chelwood House	(01761) 490730	HR	75	63%	10	30	45											
Dunkirk	Petty France Hotel	(01454) 238361	H	90	65%	20	25	75											
Freshford	Homewood Park	(01225) 723731	HR	135	78%	15	40	90	◀		◀	◀	◀					◀	
Hunstrete	Hunstrete House	(01761) 490490	HR	145	79%	23	50	30	◀			◀	◀					◀	
Monkton Combe	Combe Grove Manor	(01225) 834644	H	175	71%	40	100	80	◀		◀	◀	◀	◀					
Ston Easton	Ston Easton Park	(01761) 241631	HR	169	88%	21	20	24	◀				◀					◀	
Thornbury	Thornbury Castle	(01454) 281182	H	105	80%	18	20		◀				◀				◀		
Weston-super-Mare	Grand Atlantic	(01934) 626543	H	77	64%	76	250	250				◀							
Winterbourne	Jarvis Grange Hotel	(01454) 777333	H	100	68%	52	150	150			◀								

Bedfordshire

Location	Establishment	Tel. No.	Category	Room £	Hotel %	No. of Rooms	Conf Max	Band Max	Beaut Sit	Disabled	In Swim	Out Swim	Tennis	Squash	Golf	Fishing	Riding	15 mins Mway*	Country House
Apley Guise	Moore Place Hotel	(01908) 282000	H	90	70%	54	50	75											
Bedford	The Country Hotel	(01234) 799955	H	77	65%	100	450	400									◀		

Location	Hotel	Phone	Type		%			
Bedford	Woodlands Manor	(01234) 363281	H	85	72%	25	30	60
Dunstable	Old Palace Lodge	(01582) 662201	H	101	66%	50	40	35
Flitwick	Flitwick Manor	(01525) 712242	HR	125	73%	15	24	60
Luton	Chiltern Hotel	(01582) 575911	H	88	60%	91	350	250
Luton	Hotel Ibis	(01582) 424488	H	54	60%	98	100	50
Luton	Leaside Hotel	(01582) 417643	H	55	55%	12	30	50
Luton	Luton Gateway Hotel	(01582) 575955	H	76	57%	111	80	
Luton	Strathmore Thistle	(01582) 34199	H	110	63%	150	300	250
Woburn	Bedford Arms	(01525) 290441	H	100	68%	55	80	60
Woburn	Bell Inn	(01525) 290280	H	72	57%	27	36	45

Berkshire

Location	Hotel	Phone	Type		%			
Ascot	Berystede Hotel	(01344) 23311	H	136	67%	91	120	120
Ascot	Royal Berkshire	(01344) 23322	H	217	74%	63	70	70
Bracknell	Coppid Beech Hotel	(01334) 303333	HR	125	72%	205	375	200
Bracknell	Hilton National	(01344) 424801	H	116	69%	167	400	300
Bray-on-Thames	The Waterside Inn	(01628) 20691	RR	170		7	14	10
Elcot	Jarvis Elcot Park	(01488) 658100	H	112	67%	75	120	200
Hungerford	Jarvis Bear Hotel	(01488) 682512	H	96	60%	41	60	60
Hurley	Ye Olde Bell	(01628) 825881	H	114	65%	36	140	120
Kintbury	Dundas Arms	(01488) 658263	IR	65		5		20
Maidenhead	Fredrick's	(01628) 35934	HR	168	75%	37	100	140
Maidenhead	Holiday Inn	(01628) 23444	H	136	66%	189	400	400
Newbury	Chequers Hotel	(01635) 38000	H	102	66%	56	65	100
Newbury	Donnington Valley Hotel	(01635) 551199	H	108	74%	58	140	130
Newbury	Foley Lodge Hotel	(01635) 528770	H	115	71%	69	220	200
Newbury	Hilton National	(01635) 529000	H	108	69%	109	200	140

Location	Establishment	Tel. No.	Category	Room £	Hotel %	No. of Rooms	Conf Max	Band Max	Beaut Sit	Disabled	In Swim	Out Swim	Tennis	Squash	Golf	Fishing	Riding	15 mins Mway*	Country House
Newbury	Millwaters	(01635) 528838	H	78	67%	30	50	80		▲						▲			
Newbury	Regency Park Hotel	(01635) 871555	H	109	70%	50	160	120					▲				▲		
Newbury	Stakis Newbury Hotel	(01635) 247010	H	100	67%	112	100	80											
Pingewood	Kirtons Hotel & Country Club	(01734) 500885	H	100	60%	81	110	90			▲			▲			▲		
Reading	Forte Posthouse	(01734) 875485	H	75	64%	138	100	90											
Reading	Holiday Inn Reading	(01734) 391818	H	106	71%	111	200	180			▲						▲		
Reading	Ramada Hotel	(01734) 586222	H	117	68%	194	220	180			▲							▲	
Sindlesham	Reading Moat House	(01734) 499988	H	116	70%	96	80	200			▲					▲			
Slough	Copthorne Slough/Windsor	(01753) 516222	H	145	71%	217	250	230		▲	▲						▲	▲	
Slough	Courtyard by Marriott	(01753) 551551	H	92	60%	148	40				▲							▲	
Slough	Heathrow Marriott Hotel	(01753) 544244	H	154	73%	349	280	400			▲		▲				▲	▲	
Streatley-on-Thames	Swan Diplomat	(01491) 873737	HR	134	68%	46	90	980								▲			
Taplow	Cliveden	(01628) 668561	HR	266	92%	37	42	160	▲		▲	▲	▲	▲		▲	▲	▲	▲
Windsor	Castle Hotel	(01753) 851011	H	156	67%	104	190	300									▲	▲	
Windsor	Oakley Court	(01628) 74141	HR	183	78%	92	160	200	▲		▲				▲	▲	▲	▲	
Wokingham	Stakis St Anne's Manor	(01734) 772550	H	126	69%	130	300	300			▲							▲	
Woolton Hill	Hollington House Hotel	(01635) 255100	HR	130	83%	20	80	70	▲		▲	▲	▲				▲		▲

Buckinghamshire

Location	Establishment	Tel. No.	Category	Room £	Hotel %	No. of Rooms	Conf Max	Band Max	Beaut Sit	Disabled	In Swim	Out Swim	Tennis	Squash	Golf	Fishing	Riding	15 mins Mway*	Country House
Aston Clinton	The Bell Inn	(01296) 630252	HR	64	78%	21	250	220											
Aylesbury	Forte Posthouse	(01296) 393388	H	72	69%	94	100	80			▲							▲	
Aylesbury	Hartwell House	(01296) 747444	HR	176	86%	45	90	60	▲		▲	▲	▲			▲	▲		▲

Location	Hotel	Phone	Type		%			
Aylesbury	Holiday Inn Garden Court	(01296) 398839	H	49	58%	40	20	
Beaconsfield	Bellhouse Hotel	(01753) 887211	H	120	67%	136	450	300
Burnham	Burnham Beeches Hotel	(01628) 603333	H	122	68%	75	180	150
Burnham	Jarvis Grovefield Hotel	(01628) 603131	H	85	63%	40	170	120
Chenies	Bedford Arms	(01923) 283301	H	123	67%	10	25	65
Gerrards Cross	Bull Hotel	(01753) 885995	H	125	63%	95	200	160
High Wycombe	Forte Posthouse	(01494) 442100	H	75	65%	106	100	90
Marlow	Compleat Angler Hotel	(01628) 484444	HR	169	73%	62	120	120
Medmenham	Danesfield House	(01628) 891010	HR	145	77%	88	80	100
Milton Keynes	Forte Crest	(01908) 667722	H	117	68%	150	150	120
Milton Keynes	Friendly Hotel	(01908) 561666	H	87		88	150	100
Milton Keynes	Hilton National	(01908) 694433	H	111	64%	138	300	220
Old Amersham	Crown	(01494) 721541	H		64%	22	45	

Cambridgeshire

Location	Hotel	Phone	Type		%			
Cambridge	Arundel House	(01223) 367701	H	73	60%	105	50	100
Cambridge	Cambridge Lodge	(01223) 352833	H	70	58%	11	20	50
Cambridge	Cambridgeshire Moat House	(01954) 249988	H	97	63%	99	200	200
Cambridge	Forte Posthouse	(01223) 237000	H	75	67%	118	60	60
Cambridge	Garden House Moat House	(01223) 259988	H	153	69%	118	250	250
Cambridge	Gonville Hotel	(01223) 66611	H	87	62%	65	200	180
Cambridge	Holiday Inn	(01223) 464466	H	124	65%	199	150	100
Cambridge	Regent Hotel	(01223) 351470	HR	74	57%	25		
Cambridge	University Arms	(01223) 351241	H	115	65%	115	300	250
Duxford	Duxford Lodge	(01223) 836444	HR	88	65%	15	30	46
Ely	Lamb Hotel	(01353) 663574	H	70	57%	32	30	60
Huntingdon	Old Bridge Hotel	(01480) 452681	HR	95	68%	26	50	110

Location	Establishment	Tel. No.	Category	Room £	Hotel %	No. of Rooms	Conf Max	Band Max	Beaut Sit	Disabled	In Swim	Out Swim	Tennis	Squash	Golf	Fishing	Riding	15 mins Mway*	Country House
Peterborough	Butterfly Hotel	(01733) 64240	H	70	63%	70	80	50		▲									
Peterborough	Forte Posthouse	(01733) 240209	H	72	60%	90	50	40		▲	▲								
Peterborough	Peterborough Moat House	(01733) 260000	H	80	64%	125	400	400		▲	▲								
Peterborough	Swallow Hotel	(01733) 371111	H	105	69%	163	300	300		▲	▲								
Six Mile Bottom	Swynford Paddocks	(01638) 570234	H	107	74%	15	30	45					▲						
St Ives	Slepe Hall	(01480) 463122	H	62	61%	15	220	220											
Stilton	Bell Inn	(01733) 241066	IR	64		19	100	95											
Wansford-in-England	The Haycock	(01780) 782223	HR	98	70%	51	200	200								▲			

Cheshire

Location	Establishment	Tel. No.	Category	Room £	Hotel %	No. of Rooms	Conf Max	Band Max	Beaut Sit	Disabled	In Swim	Out Swim	Tennis	Squash	Golf	Fishing	Riding	15 mins Mway*	Country House
Alderley Edge	Alderley Edge Hotel	(01625) 583033	HR	117	72%	32	120	100									▲		
Alsager	Manor House	(01270) 884000	H	74	65%	57	200	150			▲								
Altrincham	Bowdon Hotel	0161-928 7121	H	79	65%	82	130	130											
Altrincham	Cresta Court	0161-927 7272	H	70	61%	138	300	300											
Altrincham	George & Dragon	0161-928 9933	H	46	60%	46	20	70											
Bramhall	Moat House	0161-439 8116	H	106	63%	65	110	90											
Broxton	Carden Park Hotel	(01829) 731000	H	120	71%	83	200	150			▲				▲		▲		
Bunbury	Wild Boar Hotel	(01829) 260309	H	75	67%	37	66	66											
Chester	Blossoms Hotel	(01244) 323186	H	97	63%	64	25												
Chester	Chester Grosvenor	(01244) 324024	HR	220	84%	86	250	220		▲								▲	
Chester	Crabwall Manor	(01244) 851666	H	125	76%	48	100	100		▲							▲	▲	
Chester	Forte Posthouse	(01244) 680111	H	72	62%	105	100	75			▲						▲		

Town	Hotel	Phone	Type					
Chester	Jarvis Abbots Well	(01244) 332121	H	89	62%	129	230	200
Chester	Moat House International	(01244) 322330	H	143	69%	152	500	400
Chester	Mollington Banastre	(01244) 851471	H	90	67%	64	300	280
Chester	Rowton Hall	(01244) 335262	H	88	64%	42	200	140
Handforth	Belfry Hotel	0161-437 0511	HR	88	69%	80	180	180
Knutsford	Brasserie Belle Epoque	(01565) 633060	RR	60		7	100	80
Knutsford	Cottons Hotel	(01565) 650333	H	114	65%	82	200	150
Macclesfield	Sutton Hall	(01260) 253211	I	85		10	30	60
Mottram St Andrew	De Vere Mottram Hall	(01625) 828135	H	140	70%	133	275	180
Nantwich	Rookery Hall	(01270) 610016	HR	150	80%	45	100	60
Northwich	Friendly Floatel	(01606) 44443	H	75	56%	60	80	70
Northwich	Hartford Hall	(01606) 75711	H	75	63%	20	40	100
Northwich	Nunsmere Hall	(01606) 889100	HR	147	77%	32	50	60
Parkgate	Ship Hotel	0151-336 3931	H	58	56%	26	50	40
Prestbury	Bridge Hotel	(01625) 829326	H	89	63%	23	100	100
Prestbury	White House Manor	(01625) 829376	HR	112		9	50	40
Puddington	Craxton Wood	0151-339 4717	HR	102	70%	14	40	50
Runcorn	Forte Posthouse	(01928) 714000	H	72	62%	135	500	450
Sandbach	Chimney House	(01270) 764141	H	80	62%	48	90	90
Stockport	Jarvis Alma Lodge	0161-483 4431	H	95	61%	52	250	220
Warrington	De Vere Lord Daresbury Hotel	(01925) 267331	H	105	67%	140	400	350
Warrington	Holiday Inn Garden Court	(01925) 838779	H	74	65%	99	12	
Wilmslow	Moat House	(01625) 529201	H	109	58%	125	300	300
Wilmslow	Stanneylands	(01625) 525225	HR	87	70%	32	90	100

Cleveland

Town	Hotel	Phone	Type					
Easington	Grinkle Park	(01287) 640515	H	80	70%	20	60	80

Location	Establishment	Tel. No.	Category	Room £	Hotel %	No. of Rooms	Conf Max	Bang Max	Beaut Sit	Disabled	In Swim	Out Swim	Tennis	Squash	Golf	Fishing	Riding	15 mins Mway*	Country House
Hartlepool	Grand Hotel	(01429) 266345	H	55	59%	47	200	180											
Middlesbrough	Hotel Baltimore	(01642) 224111	H	85	62%	31	16	100											
Middlesbrough	Hospitality Inn	(01642) 232000	H	98	59%	180	400	400											
Stockton-on-Tees	Swallow Hotel	(01642) 679721	H	96	67%	125	300	300			▲								
Thornaby-on-Tees	Forte Posthouse	(01642) 591213	H	72	60%	135	100	100											

Cornwall

Location	Establishment	Tel. No.	Category	Room £	Hotel %	No. of Rooms	Conf Max	Bang Max	Beaut Sit	Disabled	In Swim	Out Swim	Tennis	Squash	Golf	Fishing	Riding	15 mins Mway*	Country House
Calstock	Danescombe Valley Hotel	(01822) 832414	HR	120	72%	5	0	0	▲										
Camelford	Lanteglos Country House Hotel	(01840) 213551	H	96		9									▲				
Carlyon Bay	Carlyon Bay Hotel	(01726) 812304	H	132	68%	73	250	220	▲		▲	▲	▲		▲				
Carlyon Bay	Porth Avallen Hotel	(01726) 812802	H	83	60%	24	80	95	▲		▲								
Cawsand	Wringford Down	(01752) 822287	H	60		12					▲								
Constantine Bay	Treglos Hotel	(01841) 520727	H	102	65%	44	20	100			▲								
Falmouth	Falmouth Hotel	(01326) 312671	H	68	63%	73	300	200			▲								
Falmouth	Greenbank Hotel	(01326) 312440	H	105	69%	61	80	120											
Falmouth	Royal Duchy Hotel	(01326) 313042	H	119	66%	47					▲								
Falmouth	St Michael's Hotel	(01326) 312707	H	96	63%	66	250	200			▲								
Golant	Cormorant Hotel	(01726) 833426	H	84	63%	11		35	▲		▲								
Helford	Riverside	(01326) 231443	RR	75		6													
Helland Bridge	Tredethy Country Hotel	(01208) 841262	H	60	56%	11	60	50											
Lamorna Cove	Lamorna Cove Hotel	(01736) 731411	H	49	65%	12			▲		▲	▲							
Land's End	Land's End Hotel	(01736) 871844	H	75	64%	34	200	200	▲		▲	▲							
Liskeard	Well House	(01579) 342001	HR	105	74%	7		36	▲		▲	▲	▲						

Location	Hotel	Phone	Type					
Looe	Talland Bay Hotel	(01503) 72667	H	100	67%	21		
Mawgan Porth	Bedruthan Steps Hotel	(01637) 860555	H	97	65%	100	30	60
Mawnan Smith	Budock Vean Hotel	(01326) 250288	H	128	65%	54	80	130
Mawnan Smith	Meudon Hotel	(01326) 250541	H	170	69%	30	50	80
Mawnan Smith	Nansidwell	(01326) 250340	HR	123	70%	12		
Mousehole	Lobster Pot	(01736) 731251	H	70	57%	25		
Mullion	Polurrian Hotel	(01326) 240421	H	134	66%	39	100	120
Newlyn	Higher Faugan Country House Hotel	(01736) 62076	H	86	62%	12		
Newquay	Hotel Bristol	(01637) 875181	H	80	64%	74	250	265
Newquay	Hotel Riviera	(01637) 874251	H	83	63%	50	120	150
Padstow	St Petroc's House	(01841) 532700	HR	52		8		
Padstow	Seafood Restaurant	(01841) 532485	RR	98		10		
Penzance	Abbey Hotel	(01736) 66906	HR	85	67%	7		
Porth	Trevelgue Hotel	(01637) 872864	H	100	62%	70		
Portloe	Lugger Hotel	(01872) 501322	H	100	59%	19		
St Austell	Boscundle Manor	(01726) 813557	H	110	65%	10		
St Austell	White Hart	(01726) 72100	I	64		18	60	46
St Ives	Garrack Hotel	(01736) 796199	H	100	62%	18	25	50
St Martin's	St Martin's Hotel	(01720) 422092	HR	130	69%	24	100	60
St Mary's	Hotel Godolphin	(01720) 422316	H	92	58%	31		
St Mary's	Tregarthen's Hotel	(01720) 422540	H	126	60%	29	70	70
St Mawes	Idle Rocks Hotel	(01326) 270771	HR	118	66%	24	25	
St Mawes	Rising Sun	(01326) 270233	H	79	62%	11		
St Mawes	Hotel Tresanton	(01326) 270544	H	70	67%	21		
Tintagel	Trebrea Lodge	(01840) 770410	HR	64	66%	7		14
Tresco	Island Hotel	(01720) 422883	HR	186	67%	40	45	70

Cumbria

Location	Establishment	Tel. No.	Category	Room £	Hotel %	No. of Rooms	Conf Max	Band Max	Beaut Sit	Disabled	In Swim	Out Swim	Tennis	Squash	Golf	Fishing	Riding	15 mins Mway*	Country House
Truro	Alverton Manor	(01872) 76633	H	99	70%	34	200	120											
Veryan	Nare Hotel	(01872) 501279	HR	160	70%	35	50	90	▲		▲	▲	▲						
Alston	Lovelady Shield Country House Hotel	(01434) 381203	HR	98	68%	12	20	54	▲				▲						
Ambleside	Kirkstone Foot Hotel	(015394) 32232	H	108	65%	15				▲									
Ambleside	Nanny Brow	(015394) 32036	H	90	62%	18	30	20								▲			
Ambleside	Rothay Manor Hotel	(015394) 33605	HR	113	71%	18	24	32	▲	▲									
Ambleside	Wateredge Hotel	(015394) 32332	HR	98	63%	23													
Appleby-in-Westmorland	Appleby Manor Hotel	(017683) 51571	HR	98	66%	30	35			▲	▲								
Appleby-in-Westmorland	Tufton Arms	(017683) 51593	H	80	66%	21	120	120								▲			
Applethwaite	Underscar Manor	(017687) 75000	HR	150	74%	11	14	40	▲										
Bassenthwaite	Armathwaite Hall	(017687) 76551	H	100	65%	43	100	100	▲	▲	▲		▲			▲	▲		
Bassenthwaite Lake	Pheasant Inn	(017687) 76234	H	68	65%	20	35	55		▲									
Borrowdale	Borrowdale Hotel	(017687) 77224	H	98	60%	34	30	120	▲										
Borrowdale	Stakis Lodore Swiss Hotel	(017687) 77285	H	112	71%	70	80	80	▲		▲	▲	▲	▲					
Bowness-on-Windermere	Belsfield Hotel	(015394) 42448	H	113	62%	64	130	180		▲	▲		▲						
Bowness-on-Windermere	Gilpin Lodge	(015394) 88818	HR	110	71%	9	14	24											
Bowness-on-Windermere	Linthwaite House	(015394) 88600	HR	115	72%	18	22	45		▲						▲		▲	

Location	Hotel	Phone	Type		%				M1	M2	M3	M4	M5	M6	M7
Bowness-on-Windermere	Old England Hotel	(0153 94) 42444	H	127	65%	78	150	150		◀					
	Ivy House	(01768) 778338	H	60	66%	12									
Braithwaite	Farlam Hall	(016977) 46234	HR	184	75%	12	20	45						◀	
Brampton	Swallow Hilltop	(01228) 29255	H	90	59%	92	550	400	◀		◀				
Carlisle	Aynsome Manor	(015395) 36653	H	87	60%	12	0	32	◀						
Cartmel	Uplands	(01539) 536248	RR	136		5									
Cartmel	Sun Hotel	(015394) 41248	H		63%	11	50	70							
Coniston	Wild Boar Hotel	(015394) 45225	H	84	60%	36	40	100							
Crook	Crooklands Hotel	(015395) 67432	H	75	60%	30	130	120							
Crooklands	Crosby Lodge	(01228) 573618	HR	90	66%	11	20	50	◀						
Crosby-on-Eden	String of Horses Inn	(01228) 70297	I	68		14	20	60		◀					
Faugh	Michael's Nook	(015394) 35496	HR	210	79%	14	25	40	◀						◀
Grasmere	The Swan	(015394) 35551	H	108	65%	36	16								
Grasmere	White Moss House	(015394) 35295	HR	120	69%	6			◀			◀			
Grasmere	Wordsworth Hotel	(015394) 35592	HR	105	72%	37	130	100	◀		◀				
Grasmere	Grizedale Lodge	(015394) 36532	H	65	61%	9			◀	◀					
Grizedale	Woolpack Hotel	(01539) 723852	H	80	59%	54	150	120							
Kendal	Keswick Country House Hotel	(017687) 72020	H	80	60%	66	80	150			◀				
Keswick	Langdale Hotel	(015394) 37302	H	134	71%	65	90	90	◀		◀	◀	◀		
Langdale	Bridgefield House	(01229) 885239	HR	70	60%	5	20	24			◀				
Lowick Bridge	The Swan	(015395) 31681	H	88	61%	36	65	0							
Newby Bridge	North Lakes Hotel	(01768) 868111	H	108	71%	84	300	220						◀	
Penrith	Black Swan Inn	(015396) 23204	I	66		16	80	50				◀			
Ravenstonedale	Skinburness Hotel	(01697) 332332	H	63	67%	25	200	170	◀		◀				
Silloth-on-Solway	Mortal Man Inn	(015394) 33193	I	100		12									

Location	Establishment	Tel. No.	Category	Room £	Hotel %	No. of Rooms	Conf Max	Banq Max	Beaut Sit	Disabled	In Swim	Out Swim	Tennis	Squash	Golf	Fishing	Riding	15 mins Mway*	Country House
Ullswater	Leeming House	(017684) 86622	HR	142	75%	40	30	80	◄							◄		◄	
Ullswater	Old Church Hotel	(017684) 86204	HR	120	67%	9			◄							◄			
Ullswater	Rampsbeck Country House Hotel	(017684) 86442	HR	80	65%	21	20	60	◄							◄		◄	
Ullswater	Sharrow Bay	(017684) 86301	HR	260	82%	28	12		◄									◄	◄
Ulverston	Bay Horse Inn	(01229) 583972	RR	150		7		50											
Wetheral	The Crown	(01228) 561888	H	106	70%	51	175	150			◄							◄	
Windermere	Holbeck Ghyll	(015394) 32375	HR	130	72%	14	16	40						◄					
Windermere	Merewood Hotel	(015394) 46484	H	90	66%	20	40		◄										
Windermere	Miller Howe	(015394) 42536	H	150	70%	12	10												
Witherslack	Old Vicarage	(015395) 52381	HR	98	68%	14	12						◄						

Derbyshire

Location	Establishment	Tel. No.	Category	Room £	Hotel %	No. of Rooms	Conf Max	Banq Max	Beaut Sit	Disabled	In Swim	Out Swim	Tennis	Squash	Golf	Fishing	Riding	15 mins Mway*	Country House
Ashbourne	Ashbourne Lodge Hotel	(01335) 346666	H	78	66%	50	220	200			◄								
Ashbourne	Callow Hall	(01335) 343403	H	105	69%	16	45	30	◄										
Ashford-in-the-Water	Riverside Country House Hotel	(01629) 814275	HR	95	66%	15	25	30	◄		◄								◄
Bakewell	Hassop Hall	(01629) 640488	H	93	74%	13	60	120	◄				◄						
Baslow	Cavendish Hotel	(01246) 582311	HR	118	71%	23	25	50	◄							◄			
Baslow	Fischer's Baslow Hall	(01246) 583259	RR	120		6	40	40	◄										
Castle Donington	Donington Thistle	(01332) 850700	H	118	70%	110	220	200			◄						◄		
Chesterfield	Chesterfield Hotel	(01246) 271141	H	75	59%	73	150	240			◄								
Derby	European Inn	(01332) 292000	B	48		88	120												
Derby	Forte Posthouse	(01332) 514933	H	72	61%	62	60	50											

Location	Hotel	Phone	Type		%			
Derby	International Hotel	(01332) 369321	H	60	62%	62	70	200
Derby	Midland Hotel	(01332) 345894	H	92	65%	100	120	150
Dovedale	Izaak Walton Hotel	(01335) 350555	H	95	59%	33	60	100
Dovedale	Peveril of the Peak	(01335) 350333	H	102	60%	47	60	70
Grindleford	Maynard Arms	(01433) 630321	I	65		11	100	120
Hathersage	Hathersage Inn	(01433) 650259	I	62		15	12	
Hayfield	Bridge End Restaurant	(01663) 747321	RR	45		4	20	50
Matlock	Riber Hall	(01629) 582795	HR	98	71%	11	20	40
Matlock Bath	New Bath Hotel	(01629) 583275	H	97	63%	55	130	200
Morley	Breadsall Priory	(01332) 832235	H	111	69%	91	120	100
Newton Solney	Jarvis Newton Park	(01283) 703568	H	112	67%	50	120	100
Renishaw	Sitwell Arms	(01246) 435226	H	60	61%	30	180	160
Rowsley	Peacock Hotel	(01629) 733518	H	123	64%	14	20	24
South Normanton	Swallow Hotel	(01773) 812000	H	105	69%	161	200	250

Devon

Location	Hotel	Phone	Type		%			
Barnstaple	Imperial Hotel	(01271) 45861	H	112	60%	56	60	60
Barnstaple	Lynwood House	(01271) 43695	RR	61		5	60	60
Bigbury-on-Sea	Burgh Island Hotel	(01548) 810514	H	208	66%	14	150	100
Bishop's Tawton	Halmpstone Manor	(01271) 830321	HR	100	68%	5	12	20
Branscombe	Bulstone Hotel	(01297) 80446	H	50				
Branscombe	Masons Arms	(01297) 680300	H	54	64%	21	60	100
Brixham	Quayside Hotel	(01803) 855751	H	78	59%	30	30	20
Chagford	Gidleigh Park	(01647) 432367	HR	290	82%	15		24
Chagford	Great Tree Hotel	(01647) 432491	H	79	61%	12	20	40
Chagford	Mill End	(01647) 432282	H	85	63%	16		
Chittlehamholt	Highbullen	(01769) 540561	H	105	60%	39	20	

Location	Establishment	Tel. No.	Category	Room £	Hotel %	No. of Rooms	Conf Max	Bang Max	Beaut Sit	Disabled	In Swim	Out Swim	Tennis	Squash	Golf	Fishing	Riding	15 mins Mway*	Country House
Clawton	Court Barn Country House Hotel	(01409) 271219	H	69	61%	8	25	45					◄						
Dartmouth	Royal Castle Hotel	(01803) 833033	I	80		25	60	100											
Dartmouth	Stoke Lodge	(01803) 770523	H	74	60%	24	120	100			◄	◄	◄						
East Buckland	Lower Pitt	(01598) 760243	RR	60		3		16											
Exeter	Buckerell Lodge	(01392) 52451	HR	93	64%	54	60	130											
Exeter	Forte Crest	(01392) 412812	H	112	69%	110	160	120			◄								
Exeter	Rougemont Thistle Hotel	(01392) 54982	H	83	63%	90	300	208											
Exeter	Royal Clarence	(01392) 58464	H	117	71%	56	120	90									◄		
Exeter	St Olaves Court	(01392) 217736	HR	90	63%	17	70	80											
Exmouth	Imperial Hotel	(01395) 274761	H	102	60%	57	20	20			◄	◄	◄						
Gittisham	Combe House	(01404) 42756	H	97	73%	15	30	36	◄						◄				
Gulworthy	The Horn of Plenty	(01822) 832528	RR	108		7	18	12											
Hatherleigh	George Hotel	(01837) 810454	I	70		11	50	75				◄							
Hawkchurch	Fairwater Head Hotel	(01297) 678349	H	104	65%	21			◄										
Haytor	Bel Alp House	(01364) 661217	H	138	72%	9			◄										
Holbeton	Alston Hall	(01752) 830555	H	100	64%	20	72	100	◄		◄	◄	◄						
Hope Cove	Cottage Hotel	(01548) 561555	H	94	56%	35	50	90	◄										
Hope Cove	Lantern Lodge	(01548) 561280	H	74	59%	14			◄		◄								
Huntsham	Huntsham Court	(01398) 361365	HR	115	68%	14	25	120	◄				◄						
Kingsbridge	Buckland-Tout-Saints Hotel	(01548) 853055	H	150	73%	13	58	48	◄										
Lewdown	Lewtrenchard Manor	(01566) 783256	HR	98	73%	8	40	60	◄							◄		◄	
Lifton	Arundell Arms	(01566) 784666	HR	93	65%	29	100	80	◄						◄	◄			
Lympstone	River House	(01395) 265147	RR	87		4													

Location	Hotel	Phone	Type						F1	F2	F3	F4	F5	F6	F7	F8	F9	F10	F11	F12
Lynmouth	Rising Sun Hotel	(01598) 53223	I	89		16												▲		
Lynton	Lynton Cottage	(01598) 752342	H	78	65%	117	30	50											▲	
Moretonhampstead	Manor House Hotel	(01647) 440355	H	100	66%	70	150	200	▲									▲	▲	
Moretonhampstead	White Hart Hotel	(01647) 440406	I	63		20	80	90									▲	▲		
Newton Abbot	Passage House Hotel	(01626) 55515	H	75	65%	38	150	120						▲						
North Huish	Brookdale House	(01548) 821661	H	90	69%	8	40	45	▲											
Paignton	Palace Hotel	(01803) 555121	H	117	60%	52	50	90					▲	▲						
Paignton	Redcliffe Hotel	(01803) 526397	H	92	62%	60	160	210	▲				▲	▲						
Parkham	Penhaven Country House	(01237) 451388	H	100	64%	12	0	40				▲		▲			▲			
Plymouth	Copthorne Hotel	(01752) 224161	H	106	70%	135	75	80	▲		▲		▲							
Plymouth	Forte Posthouse	(01752) 662828	H	68	65%	106	120	100	▲		▲		▲		▲					
Plymouth	Jarvis Boringdon Hall	(01752) 344455	H	90	67%	40	120	110	▲		▲		▲	▲	▲		▲			
Plymouth	Moat House	(01752) 562866	H	123	70%	212	300	350	▲		▲		▲	▲						
Plymouth	Novotel	(01752) 221422	H	59	62%	100	240	160	▲		▲		▲				▲			
Poundsgate	Leusdon Lodge Hotel	(01364) 631304	HR	55	61%	7	10	18	▲		▲									
Salcombe	Marine Hotel	(01548) 844444	H	152	66%	51	75	120	▲		▲		▲	▲	▲					
Salcombe	Soar Mill Cove Hotel	(01548) 561566	HR	120	66%	16			▲		▲		▲	▲	▲	▲				
Salcombe	South Sands Hotel	(01548) 843741	H	94	60%	30			▲		▲		▲							
Salcombe	Tides Reach	(01548) 843466	H	124	71%	38			▲		▲		▲	▲	▲	▲				
Saunton	Saunton Sands	(01271) 890212	H	128	67%	96	175	100	▲		▲		▲	▲	▲	▲				
Sidmouth	Belmont Hotel	(01395) 512555	H	144	63%	51	40	120					▲							
Sidmouth	Fortfield Hotel	(01395) 512403	H	70	59%	55	100	120	▲				▲	▲						
Sidmouth	Hotel Riviera	(01395) 515201	H	112	66%	27	90	90			▲									
Sidmouth	Victoria Hotel	(01395) 512651	H	146	67%	62	200	120	▲		▲		▲	▲	▲	▲				
South Molton	Whitechapel Manor	(01769) 573377	HR	125	76%	10	28	36	▲				▲	▲	▲					▲
Teignmouth	Thomas Luny House	(01626) 772976	PH	60		4														

Location	Establishment	Tel. No.	Category	Room £	Hotel %	No. of Rooms	Conf Max	Banq Max	Beaut Sit	Disabled	In Swim	Out Swim	Tennis	Squash	Golf	Fishing	Riding	15 mins Mway*	Country House
Thurlestone	Thurlestone Hotel	(01548) 560382	H	140	69%	68	120	150	◄		◄	◄	◄	◄	◄		◄		
Torquay	Grand Hotel	(01803) 296677	H	105	68%	111	300	300			◄	◄	◄						
Torquay	Homers Hotel	(01803) 213456	H	60	64%	15	50	50											
Torquay	Imperial Hotel	(01803) 294301	H	120	83%	167	400	350			◄	◄	◄	◄					
Torquay	Livermead House Hotel	(01803) 294361	H	90	60%	65	300	250				◄	◄	◄					
Torquay	Livermead Cliff Hotel	(01803) 299666	H	76	60%	64	80	120				◄							
Torquay	Orestone Manor	(01803) 328098	H	90	58%	18	12	60				◄							
Torquay	Osborne Hotel	(01803) 213311	H	76	65%	23	80	100			◄	◄	◄	◄					
Torquay	Palace Hotel	(01803) 200200	H	120	68%	140	2000	550	◄		◄	◄	◄	◄	◄				
Tuckenhay	Floyd's Inn (Sometimes)	(01803) 732350	IR	125		3													
Whimple	Woodhayes Hotel	(01404) 822237	HR	90	75%	6		16	◄								◄	◄	
Wilmington	Home Farm	(01404) 831246	H	56	58%	13													
Woody Bay	Woody Bay Hotel	(01598) 763264	H	66	59%	15	20		◄										
Woolacombe	Woolacombe Bay Hotel	(01271) 870388	H	166	65%	61	200	200			◄	◄	◄	◄					
Yelverton	Moorland Links	(01822) 852245	H	85	65%	45	100	200											

Dorset

Location	Establishment	Tel. No.	Category	Room £	Hotel %	No. of Rooms	Conf Max	Banq Max	Beaut Sit	Disabled	In Swim	Out Swim	Tennis	Squash	Golf	Fishing	Riding	15 mins Mway*	Country House
Bournemouth	Carlton Hotel	(01202) 552011	H	120	76%	70	150	130			◄	◄							
Bournemouth	Chine Hotel	(01202) 396234	H	85	65%	96	150	160		◄	◄	◄							
Bournemouth	De Vere Royal Bath Hotel	(01202) 555555	HR	115	73%	131	350	450		◄	◄								
Bournemouth	Langtry Manor	(01202) 553887	H	99	62%	25	100	90											
Bournemouth	Norfolk Royale	(01202) 551521	H	138	70%	95	100	100		◄									
Bournemouth	Roundhouse Hotel	(01202) 553262	H	70	59%	98	100	100											

Location	Hotel	Phone	Type															
Bournemouth	Stakis Bournemouth Hotel	(01202) 557681	H	118	71%	110	200	250	▲					▲	▲			
Bournemouth	Swallow Highcliff Hotel	(01202) 557702	H	120	70%	157	350	220	▲				▲	▲	▲			
Charmouth	Fernhill Hotel	(01297) 560492	H	44														▲
Chedington	Chedington Court	(01935) 891265	HR	115	71%	10	20	30	▲								▲	
Chedington	Hazel Barton	(01935) 891613	PH	95		4	12											
Corfe Castle	Mortons House Hotel	(01929) 480988	H	80	62%	17	45	45		▲								
East Stoke	Kemps Country House Hotel	(01929) 462563	H	80	56%	15	70	120										
Evershot	Summer Lodge	(01935) 83424	HR	125	78%	17	20	20	▲				▲	▲				
Ferndown	Dormy Hotel	(01202) 872121	H	110	71%	130	250	300	▲			▲	▲	▲				
Gillingham	Stock Hill House	(01747) 823626	HR	180	76%	9	12	22	▲				▲					
Longham	Bridge House	(01202) 578828	H	60	61%	37	120	100				▲						
Lower Bockhampton	Yalbury Cottage	(01305) 262382	IR	58		8	8	30										
Lyme Regis	Alexandra Hotel	(01297) 442010	H	95	58%	27	50	80	▲	▲								
Milborne Port	The Old Vicarage	(01963) 251117	H	64	65%	8												
Mudeford	Avonmouth Hotel	(01202) 483434	H	107	59%	41	100	100	▲	▲			▲	▲				
Poole	Haven Hotel	(01202) 707333	HR	120	69%	96	160	160	▲	▲			▲	▲				
Poole	Mansion House	(01202) 685666	HR	110	74%	28	40	80			▲							
Poole	Quay Thistle Hotel	(01202) 666800	H	108	63%	68	65	50				▲						
Poole	Sandbanks Hotel	(01202) 707377	H	110	59%	107	120	200				▲						
Powerstock	Three Horseshoes Inn	(01308) 485328	RR	50		4												
Shaftesbury	Grosvenor Hotel	(01747) 852282	H	83	62%	35	150	120										
Shaftesbury	Royal Chase Hotel	(01747) 853355	H	70	60%	32	100	130		▲								
Sherborne	Eastbury Hotel	(01935) 813131	H	65	67%	15	100	80										
Sherborne	Sherborne Hotel	(01935) 813191	H	74	58%	59	100	75										
Studland Bay	Knoll House	(01929) 450450	H	146	63%	70			▲	▲	▲	▲	▲	▲	▲	▲		
Sturminster Newton	Plumber Manor	(01258) 472507	RR	115		16	25	50						▲		▲		
Wareham	Priory Hotel	(01929) 551666	HR	110	72%	19	20	40	▲									▲

Location	Establishment	Tel. No.	Category	Room £	Hotel %	No. of Rooms	Conf Max	Bang Max	Beaut Slt	Disabled	In Swim	Out Swim	Tennis	Squash	Golf	Fishing	Riding	15 mins Mway*	Country House
Wareham	Springfield Country Hotel	(01929) 552177	H	96	60%	32	200	160			◄	◄	◄	◄					
West Bexington	Manor Hotel	(01308) 897616	H	78	59%	13	50	65											
Winkton	Fisherman's Haunt Hotel	(01202) 484071	I	59		20		23	◄										
Durham																			
Barnard Castle	Jersey Farm Hotel	(01833) 638223	H	60	59%	20	150	200											
Blanchland	Lord Crewe Arms Hotel	(01434) 675251	I	80		18	24	24											
Chester-le-Street	Lumley Castle	0191-389 1111	H	110	69%	60	120	250		◄									
Coatham Mundeville	Hall Garth Hotel	(01325) 300400	HR	81	66%	41	300	250		◄	◄		◄		◄				
Darlington	Blackwell Grange	(01325) 380888	H	103	62%	99	250	250			◄								
Darlington	St George Thistle	(01325) 332631	H	80	56%	59	160	120											
Darlington	Swallow King's Head	(01325) 380222	H	95	57%	85	200	250		◄	◄								
Durham	Royal County Hotel	0191-386 6821	H	124	67%	150	150	120											
Greta Bridge	The Morritt Arms Hotel	(01833) 627232	I	70		17	200	250											
Middleton-in-Teesdale	Teesdale Hotel	(01833) 640264	I	61		10		45											
Neasham	Newbus Arms	(01325) 721071	H	70		15	120	80					◄	◄					
Romaldkirk	Rose and Crown	(01833) 650213	IR	75		12				◄									
Essex																			
Basildon	Forte Posthouse	(01268) 533955	H	72	59%	110	300	250											
Brentwood	Forte Posthouse	(01277) 260260	H	75	61%	115	120	120		◄	◄								
Brentwood	Mary Green Manor	(01277) 225252	H	118	65%	33	50	85											

Location	Hotel	Phone	Type		%			
Broxted	Whitehall	(01279) 850603	HR	105	69%	25	100	120
Coggeshall	White Hart Hotel	(01376) 561654	HR	82	69%	18	35	80
Colchester	Butterfly Hotel	(01206) 230900	H	62	61%	50	80	70
Colchester	Forte Posthouse	(01206) 767740	H	72	61%	110	50	100
Colchester	Red Lion Hotel	(01206) 577986	I	60	57%	24	35	30
Colchester	Rose & Crown	(01206) 866677	I	55		30	100	80
Dedham	Fountain House & Dedham Hall	(01206) 323027	RR	57		6		50
Dedham	Maison Talbooth	(01206) 322367	H	120	78%	10	20	32
Epping	Forte Posthouse	(01992) 573137	H	75	63%	79	100	85
Great Baddow	Pontlands Park	(01245) 476444	H	130	70%	17	40	200
Great Dunmow	Saracen's Head	(01371) 873901	H	97	58%	24	40	40
Great Dunmow	The Starr	(01371) 874321	RR	85		8	50	36
Harlow	Green Man	(01279) 442521	H	97	60%	55	60	60
Harlow	Moat House	(01279) 829988	H	84	68%	118	160	160
Harwich	Pier at Harwich	(01255) 241212	RR	63		6	50	90
Horndon-on-the-Hill	The Bell Inn & Hill House	(01375) 642463	IR	65	68%	14	36	36
Ingatestone	Heybridge Hotel	(01277) 355355	H	103	68%	22	600	500
Maldon	Blue Boar	(01621) 852681	H	92	59%	29	35	25
North Stifford	Stifford Moat House	(01708) 719988	H	93	61%	96	530	150
Old Harlow	Churchgate Manor	(01279) 420246	H	96	64%	85	130	170
Saffron Walden	Saffron Hotel	(01799) 522676	H	65	57%	17	80	80
Stanstead Airport	Hilton National	(01279) 680800	H	129	56%	237	300	200
Waltham Abbey	Swallow Hotel	(01992) 717170	H	115	66%	163	250	250
Woodford Bridge	Prince Regent Hotel	0181-505 9966	H	96	63%	51	400	300

Gloucestershire

Location	Hotel	Phone	Type		%			
Amberley	Amberley Inn	(01453) 872565	H	70	57%	14	30	40

Location	Establishment	Tel. No.	Category	Room £	Hotel %	No. of Rooms	Conf Max	Bang Max	Beaut Sit	Disabled	In Swim	Out Swim	Tennis	Squash	Golf	Fishing	Riding	15 mins Mway*	Country House
Ampney Crucis	Crown of Crucis	(01285) 851806	I	64		25	70	100											
Bibury	The Swan	(01285) 740695	HR	128	78%	18	12	80								◄			
Conf Maxlip	Kingshead House	(01452) 862299	RR	54		1		32											
Blockley	Crown Inn & Hotel	(01386) 700245	I	78		21	40	50											
Bourton-on-the-Water	Dial House	(01451) 822244	H	83	61%	10													
Charingworth	Charingworth Manor	(01386) 593555	HR	110	79%	24		36	◄									◄	
Cheltenham	Hotel de la Bere	(01242) 237771	H	82	64%	57	35	80					◄	◄					
Cheltenham	Cheltenham Park	(01242) 222021	H	114	68%	154	350	275			◄	◄	◄						
Cheltenham	Golden Valley Thistle	(01242) 232691	H	112	69%	124	220	300			◄		◄	◄					
Cheltenham	The Greenway	(01242) 862352	HR	110	80%	19	35	65	◄								◄	◄	
Cheltenham	On The Park	(01242) 518898	HR	101	76%	12		18											
Cheltenham	Queen's Hotel	(01242) 514724	H	120	69%	74	350	220											
Chipping Campden	Cotswold House	(01386) 840330	HR	95	70%	15	25	45											
Chipping Campden	Noel Arms	(01386) 840317	H	80	61%	26	40	70											
Chipping Campden	Seymour House	(01386) 840429	H	90	64%	16	40	55											
Cirencester	Jarvis Fleece Hotel	(01285) 658507	H	94	64%	30	35	60											
Cirencester	Stratton House	(01285) 651761	H	80	64%	41	120	150		◄									
Clearwell	Clearwell Castle	(01594) 832320	H	90	69%	14	250	120											
Clearwell	Wyndham Arms	(01594) 833666	I	61		17	50	40											
Corse Lawn	Corse Lawn House	(01452) 780771	HR	90	71%	19	40	60	◄		◄	◄	◄				◄		
Fairford	Bull Hotel	(01285) 712535	H	44	60%	20	80	80											
Gloucester	Forte Posthouse	(01452) 613311	H	72	66%	123	110	100			◄					◄			
Gloucester	Hatherley Manor	(01452) 730217	H	78	65%	56	300	250											

Location	Hotel	Phone	Type		%			
Gloucester	Hatton Court	(01452) 617412	H	95	72%	45	60	80
Lower Slaughter	Lower Slaughter Manor	(01451) 820456	HR	190	80%	14	24	30
Lower Swell	Old Farmhouse Hotel	(01451) 830232	I	66		14	8	20
Mickleton	Three Ways House	(01386) 438429	H	76	59%	41	130	75
Moreton-in-Marsh	Manor House	(01608) 650501	H	85	66%	39	90	90
Painswick	Painswick Hotel	(01452) 812160	H	98	70%	20	30	90
Puckrup	Puckrup Hall	(01684) 296200	H	98	75%	84	275	200
Stonehouse	Stonehouse Court	(01453) 825155	H	80	68%	36	150	150
Stow-on-the-Wold	Fosse Manor Hotel	(01451) 830354	H	98	60%	20	44	72
Stow-on-the-Wold	Grapevine Hotel	(01451) 830344	HR	108	68%	21	60	60
Stow-on-the-Wold	Unicorn Hotel	(01451) 830257	H	102	59%	20	20	
Stow-on-the-Wold	Wyck Hill House	(01451) 831936	HR	108	74%	31	50	70
Tetbury	Calcot Manor	(01666) 890391	HR	115	75%	20	60	60
Tetbury	The Close	(01666) 502272	H	95	72%	15	30	60
Tetbury	Snooty Fox Hotel	(01666) 502436	H	80	69%	12	20	20
Tewkesbury	Bell Hotel	(01684) 293293	H	75	57%	25	45	25
Tewkesbury	Royal Hop Pole Hotel	(01684) 293236	H	92	66%	29	12	
Tewkesbury	Tewkesbury Park	(01684) 295405	H	94	62%	78	50	150
Upper Slaughter	Lords of the Manor	(01451) 820243	HR	115	75%	27	45	60
Westonbirt	Hare & Hounds	(01666) 880233	H	80	59%	30	200	150

Greater Manchester

Location	Hotel	Phone	Type		%			
Bolton	Beaumont Hotel	(01204) 651511	H	71	58%	96	120	100
Bolton	Egerton House	(01204) 307171	H	104	63%	32	150	150
Bolton	Last Drop Village Hotel	(01204) 591131	H	105	68%	83	200	200
Bolton	Pack Horse Hotel	(01204) 27261	H	55	62%	72	375	230
Bury	Normandie Hotel	0161-764 3869	HR	83	64%	23	18	70

Location	Establishment	Tel. No.	Category	Room £	Hotel %	No. of Rooms	Conf Max	Bang Max	Beaut Sit	Disabled	In Swim	Out Swim	Tennis	Squash	Golf	Fishing	Riding	15 mins Mway*	Country House
Manchester	Britannia Hotel	0161-228 2288	H	123	66%	362	250	220			◄								
Manchester	Copthorne Hotel	0161-873 7321	H	134	70%	166	150	130		◄	◄							◄	
Manchester	Forte Posthouse	0161-998 7090	H	72	60%	190	150	100											
Manchester	Holiday Inn Crowne Plaza	0161-236 3333	H	158	73%	303	700	700			◄			◄				◄	
Manchester	Jarvis Piccadilly	0161-236 8414	H	144	73%	275	1000	700			◄							◄	
Manchester	Novotel	0161-799 3535	H	67	62%	119	220	200				◄							
Manchester	Portland Thistle	0161-228 3400	H	132	69%	205	300	250		◄	◄								
Manchester	Ramada Hotel	0161-835 2555	H	129	73%	200	450	330			◄							◄	
Manchester	Sachas Hotel	0161-228 1234	H	83	64%	223	650	650			◄								
Manchester	Victoria & Albert Hotel	0161-832 1188	HR	148	73%	132	350	210		◄									
Manchester	Woodlands	0161-336 4241	RR	60		3													
Manchester Airport	Etrop Grange	0161-499 0500	H	116	66%	41	85	85											
Manchester Airport	Forte Crest	0161-437 5811	H	120	65%	290	200	120			◄								
Manchester Airport	Four Seasons Hotel	0161-904 0301	H	121	68%	94	120	100											
Manchester Airport	Hilton International	0161-436 4404	H	159	71%	222	300	250		◄	◄							◄	
Manchester Airport	Moss Nook	0161-437 4778	RR	140		1													
Standish	Wigan Standish Moat House	(01257) 499988	H	90	63%	121	270	120		◄	◄								

Hampshire

Location	Establishment	Tel. No.	Category	Room £	Hotel %	No. of Rooms	Conf Max	Bang Max	Beaut Sit	Disabled	In Swim	Out Swim	Tennis	Squash	Golf	Fishing	Riding	15 mins Mway*	Country House
Alton	Grange Hotel	(01420) 86565	H	65	61%	29	80	116											
Alton	The Swan	(01420) 83777	H	77	58%	36	100	100											
Ampfield	Potters Heron Hotel	(01703) 266611	H	80	60%	54	140	120											
Andover	White Hart Hotel	(01264) 352266	I	65	60%	20	85	70											

Location	Name	Phone	Type					
Basingstoke	Audleys Wood	(01256) 817555	HR	128	75%	71	50	40
Basingstoke	Forte Posthouse	(01256) 468181	H	72	64%	84	180	180
Basingstoke	Hilton National	(01256) 460460	H	94	66%	141	150	130
Basingstoke	The Ringway	(01256) 20212	H	75	65%	135	150	100
Beaulieu	Montagu Arms	(01590) 612324	H	99	67%	24	30	100
Brockenhurst	Balmer Lawn Hotel	(01590) 623116	H	90	65%	55	100	100
Brockenhurst	Careys Manor	(01590) 623551	H	109	65%	79	100	130
Brockenhurst	Rhinefield House	(01590) 622922	H	110	68%	34	150	100
Buckler's Hard	Master Builder's House Hotel	(01590) 616253	I	85		23	60	60
Burley	Burley Manor	(01425) 403522	H	80	61%	30	90	60
Eastleigh	Forte Posthouse Southampton	(01703) 619700	H	72	66%	120	250	150
Fareham	Forte Posthouse	(01329) 844644	H	72	61%	126	140	100
Fareham	Red Lion	(01329) 822640	H	65	57%	43	100	100
Fareham	Solent Hotel	(01489) 880000	HR	108	75%	88	250	200
Farnborough	Forte Crest	(01252) 545051	H	130	66%	110	100	150
Havant	Bear Hotel	(01705) 486501	H	60	59%	42	120	100
Havant	Forte Posthouse	(01705) 465011	H	72	62%	92	140	120
Hurstbourne Tarrant	Esseborne Manor	(01264) 736444	HR	120	72%	12	12	
Lymington	Gordleton Mill	(01590) 682219	HR	92	67%	7	30	65
Lymington	Passford House	(01590) 682398	H	110	70%	55	120	120
Lymington	Stanwell House Hotel	(01590) 677123	H	85	65%	35	40	60
Lyndhurst	The Crown	(01703) 282922	H	93	65%	40	50	80
Lyndhurst	Lyndhurst Park	(01703) 283923	H	66	63%	59	500	300
Lyndhurst	Parkhill Hotel	(01703) 282944	HR	106	69%	20	60	120
Middle Wallop	Fifehead Manor	(01264) 781565	H	90	61%	16	30	42
Milford-on-Sea	South Lawn	(01590) 643911	H	84	66%	24	80	80
New Alresford	Hunters	(01962) 732468	RR	48		3	50	75

Location	Establishment	Tel. No.	Category	Room £	Hotel %	No. of Rooms	Conf Max	Bang Max	Beaut Sit	Disabled	In Swim	Out Swim	Tennis	Squash	Golf	Fishing	Riding	15 mins Mway*	Country House
New Milton	Chewton Glen	(01425) 275341	HR	214	89%	57	100	100	◀		◀	◀	◀		◀				
Odiham	George Hotel	(01256) 702081	I	75	63%	18	10	90											
Petersfield	Langrish House	(01730) 266941	H	55	63%	18	60	90											
Portsmouth	Forte Posthouse	(01705) 827651	H	72	65%	163	250	220			◀		◀						
Portsmouth	Hilton National	(01705) 219111	H	90	66%	118	230	200		◀	◀								
Portsmouth	Hospitality Inn	(01705) 731281	H	79	61%	115	300	250											
Portsmouth	Pendragon Hotel	(01705) 823201	H	49	59%	49	100	100											
Portsmouth	Portsmouth Marriott Hotel	(01705) 383151	H	105	73%	170	450	450			◀			◀			◀		
Romsey	White Horse Hotel	(01794) 512431	H	102	63%	33	40	90											
Rotherwick	Tylney Hall	(01256) 764881	HR	122	79%	91	100	100	◀		◀	◀	◀				◀		
Silchester	Romans Hotel	(01734) 700421	H	85	64%	25	60	45					◀						
Southampton	De Vere Grand Harbour	(01703) 633033	H	110	72%	172	500	400		◀	◀								
Southampton	Dolphin Hotel	(01703) 339955	H	77	60%	73	70	90											
Southampton	Forte Posthouse	(01703) 330777	H	72	58%	128	200	200			◀								
Southampton	Hilton National	(01703) 702700	H	96	68%	135	220	120		◀	◀								
Southampton	Novotel	(01703) 330550	H	65	62%	121	450	350		◀	◀								
Southampton	Polygon Hotel	(01703) 330055	H	71	65%	93	500	450		◀	◀								
Southampton	Southampton Park Hotel	(01703) 223467	H	68	64%	72	200	170			◀								
Stockbridge	Grosvenor Hotel	(01264) 810606	H	75	57%	25	80	70											
Stratfield Turgis	Wellington Arms	(01256) 882214	I	65	66%	35	50	70								◀			
Wickham	Old House Hotel	(01329) 833049	HR	87	66%	12	10	40											
Winchester	Forte Crest	(01962) 861611	H	114	69%	94	100	100											
Winchester	Hotel du Vin & Bistro	(01962) 841414	HR	75		13	30	40											

Hereford & Worcester

Location	Hotel	Phone	Type						
Winchester	Lainston House	(01962) 863588	H	145	75%	37	50	90
Winchester	Royal Hotel	(01962) 840840	H	97	68%	75	150	120
Winchester	Wykeham Arms	(01962) 853834	IR	75		7	10	0
Abberley	Elms Hotel	(01299) 896666	H	120	70%	25	60	80
Abbot's Salford	Salford Hall	(01386) 871300	H	105	66%	33	50	70
Brimfield	Poppies Restaurant	(01584) 711230	RR	60		3		
Broadway	Broadway Hotel	(01386) 852401	H	70	60%	20	20	
Broadway	Collin House	(01386) 858354	HR	87	65%	7		34
Broadway	Dormy House	(01386) 852711	HR	120	69%	49	200	140
Broadway	Lygon Arms	(01386) 852255	HR	195	80%	63	80	88
Bromsgrove	Grafton Manor	(01527) 579007	HR	125	70%	9	150	150
Bromsgrove	Jarvis Perry Hall	(01527) 579976	H	102	56%	58	70	90
Bromsgrove	Pine Lodge Hotel	(01527) 576600	H	97	64%	114	200	180
Bromsgrove	Stakis Hotel	0121-447 7888	H	120	69%	140	80	60
Buckland	Buckland Manor	(01386) 852626	HR	178	80%	14		
Chaddesley Corbett	Brockencote Hall	(01562) 777876	HR	110	75%	17	25	50
Droitwich Spa	Chateau Impney	(01905) 774411	H	150	70%	120	1250	400
Droitwich Spa	Raven Hotel	(01905) 772224	H	140	66%	72	150	250
Evesham	Evesham Hotel	(01386) 765566	HR	84	65%	40	12	15
Evesham	Riverside Hotel	(01386) 446200	HR	80	68%	7		
Eyton	Marsh Country Hotel	(01568) 613952	HR	110	65%	4		24
Harvington	The Mill at Harvington	(01386) 870688	HR	85	65%	15	30	40
Hereford	County Hotel Hereford	(01432) 354301	H	84	63%	60	300	250
Kidderminster	Stone Manor	(01562) 777555	H	73	65%	52	150	250
Kington	Penrhos Court	(01544) 230720	RR	70		19	100	70
Ledbury	The Feathers Hotel	(01531) 635266	I	85		11	100	120

Location	Establishment	Tel. No.	Category	Room £	Hotel %	No. of Rooms	Conf Max	Bang Max	Beaut Sit	Disabled	In Swim	Out Swim	Tennis	Squash	Golf	Fishing	Riding	15 mins Mway*	Country House
Ledbury	Hope End	(01531) 633613	HR	120	70%	9			▲									▲	
Malvern	Abbey Hotel	(01684) 892332	H	80	62%	107	350	300											
Malvern	Colwall Park Hotel	(01684) 540206	H	86	62%	20	120	100			▲								
Malvern	The Cottage in the Wood	(01684) 575859	HR	89	65%	20	14	12	▲										
Malvern	Foley Arms	(01684) 573397	H	92	61%	28	125	90											
Much Birch	Pilgrim Hotel	(01981) 540742	H	89	64%	20	45												
Ross-on-Wye	Chase Hotel	(01989) 763161	H	80	64%	39	300	300											
Ross-on-Wye	Pengethley Manor	(01989) 730211	H	100	67%	25	50	74		s		▲			▲				
Ross-on-Wye	Pheasants	(01989) 565751	RR	45		2													
Ruckhall	Ancient Camp Inn	(01981) 250449	I	48		5			▲							▲			
Stourport-on-Severn	County Hotel	(01299) 827733	H	86	62%	68	300	350				▲	▲	▲					
Weobley	Ye Olde Salutation Inn	(01544) 318443	I	55		4	12												
Worcester	Fownes Hotel	(01905) 613151	H	100	70%	61	120	120		▲								▲	
Worcester	Giffard Hotel	(01905) 726262	H	79	61%	103	150	150											

Hertfordshire

Location	Establishment	Tel. No.	Category	Room £	Hotel %	No. of Rooms	Conf Max	Bang Max	Beaut Sit	Disabled	In Swim	Out Swim	Tennis	Squash	Golf	Fishing	Riding	15 mins Mway*	Country House
Broxbourne	Cheshunt Marriott Hotel	(01992) 451245	H	85	66%	150	200	140			▲								
Dane End	Green End Park	(01920) 438344	H	95	62%	9	100	120											
Hadley Wood	West Lodge Park Hotel	0181-440 8311	HR	117	66%	45	80	63					▲						
Harpenden	Glen Eagle Hotel	(01582) 760271	H	91	63%	50	100	120											
Harpenden	Harpenden House Hotel	(01582) 764111	H	110	68%	53	150	120											
Hatfield Heath	Down Hall	(01279) 731441	H	134	71%	103	290	270	▲		▲		▲					▲	

Location	Hotel	Phone	Type		%			
Hemel Hempstead	Boxmoor Lodge	(01442) 230770	H	65	57%	18	25	64
Hemel Hempstead	Forte Posthouse	(01442) 251122	H	75	62%	146	60	55
Hertingfordbury	White Horse Hotel	(01992) 586791	H	107	63%	42	40	25
Letchworth	Broadway Toby Hotel	(01462) 480111	H	62	59%	35	180	180
Markyate	Hertfordshire Moat House	(01582) 840840	H	84	57%	89	300	300
South Mimms	Forte Posthouse	(01707) 643311	H	75	60%	120	200	120
St Albans	Noke Thistle	(01727) 854252	H	111	65%	111	70	70
St Albans	St Michael's Manor	(01727) 864444	H	96	63%	22	36	110
St Albans	Sopwell House	(01727) 864477	H	137	69%	92	400	300
Stanstead Abbots	Briggens House	(01279) 792416	H	115	70%	54	100	300
Stevenage	Forte Posthouse	(01438) 365444	H	72	58%	54	50	45
Stevenage	Novotel	(01438) 742299	H	68	60%	100	150	120
Thundridge	Hanbury Manor	(01920) 487722	HR	161	85%	96	140	100
Watford	Hilton National	(01923) 235881	H	115	64%	195	500	400
Watford	Jarvis International	0181-950 6211	H	118	67%	217	200	200
Welwyn	Clock Hotel	(01438) 716911	H	73	54%	95	200	275

Humberside

Location	Hotel	Phone	Type		%			
Beverley	Beverley Arms	(01482) 869241	H	88	62%	57	150	130
Bridlington	Expanse Hotel	(01262) 675347	H	65	60%	48	81	120
Cleethorpes	Kingsway Hotel	(01472) 601122	H	75	62%	50	15	24
Driffield	Bell Hotel	(01377) 256661	I	75		14	250	280
Grimsby	Forte Posthouse	(01472) 350295	H	72	64%	52	250	250
Hull	Forte Crest	(01482) 225221	H	115	69%	99	120	80
Hull	Forte Posthouse	(01482) 645212	H	70	62%	95	100	100
Tickton	Tickton Grange	(01964) 543666	H	75	62%	18	80	80
Walkington	Manor House	(01482) 881645	HR	97	72%	7	20	70

Location	Establishment	Tel. No.	Category	Room £	Hotel %	No. of Rooms	Conf Max	Bang Max	Beaut Sit	Disabled	In Swim	Out Swim	Tennis	Squash	Golf	Fishing	Riding	15 mins Mway*	Country House
Willerby	Grange Park	(01482) 656488	H	89	67%	101	550	500			▲								
Willerby	Willerby Manor	(01482) 652616	H	89	62%	34	500	400											
Winteringham	Winteringham Fields	(01724) 733096	RR	94		7													

Isle of Wight

Location	Establishment	Tel. No.	Category	Room £	Hotel %	No. of Rooms	Conf Max	Bang Max	Beaut Sit	Disabled	In Swim	Out Swim	Tennis	Squash	Golf	Fishing	Riding	15 mins Mway*	Country House
Bonchurch	Winterbourne Hotel	(01983) 852535	H	124	64%	14	35					▲							
Calbourne	Swainston Manor	(01983) 521121	H	76	66%	14	250	250			▲	▲			▲	▲			
Freshwater	Farringford Hotel	(01983) 752500	H	90	57%	40	30	120			▲	▲	▲		▲				
Seaview	Seaview Hotel	(01983) 612711	HR	60	62%	16	30	20								▲			
Shanklin	Cliff Tops Hotel	(01983) 863262	H	66	64%	88	240	200			▲	▲							
Shanklin	Hambledon Hotel	(01983) 862403	H	36		11													
Ventnor	Royal Hotel	(01983) 852186	H	66	60%	54	80	120	▲			▲							

Kent

Location	Establishment	Tel. No.	Category	Room £	Hotel %	No. of Rooms	Conf Max	Bang Max	Beaut Sit	Disabled	In Swim	Out Swim	Tennis	Squash	Golf	Fishing	Riding	15 mins Mway*	Country House
Ashford	Ashford International	(01233) 611444	H	102	71%	200	325	400	▲	▲	▲		▲						
Ashford	Eastwell Manor	(01233) 635751	HR	142	81%	23	70	65		▲									
Ashford	Forte Posthouse	(01233) 625790	H	75	66%	60	120	100		▲									
Ashford	Holiday Inn Garden Court	(01233) 713333	H	72	65%	104	30			▲									
Bearsted	Tudor Park Golf & Country Club	(01622) 734334	H	94	67%	117	275	216		▲	▲		▲		▲				
Bexley	Forte Posthouse	(01322) 526900	H	75	56%	103	80	60											
Bexleyheath	Swallow Hotel	0181-298 1000	H	98	71%	142	250	220			▲						▲		
Boughton Monchelsea	Tanyard Hotel	(01622) 744705	HR	90	63%	6	28		▲								▲		

Location	Hotel	Phone	Type												
Brands Hatch	Brands Hatch Thistle	(01474) 854900	H	▲						▲	98	70%	137	300	250
Bromley	Bromley Court	0181-464 5011	H								89	66%	118	150	200
Canterbury	Canterbury Hotel	(01227) 450551	H								55	58%	27	20	80
Canterbury	Chaucer Hotel	(01227) 464427	H						▲		103	61%	42	100	80
Canterbury	County Hotel	(01227) 766266	HR								100	69%	73	180	140
Canterbury	Ebury Hotel	(01227) 768433	H					▲			60	59%	15		
Canterbury	Falstaff Hotel	(01227) 462138	I								80		24	50	50
Canterbury	Howfield Manor	(01227) 738294	H				▲				85	68%	13	100	85
Chartham	Thruxted Oast	(01227) 730080	PH								75		3		
Cranbrook	Hartley Mount	(01580) 712230	H			▲					78	64%	6	40	60
Cranbrook	Kennel Holt Hotel	(01580) 712032	H				▲				118	66%	9	20	16
Dover	County Hotel	(01304) 509955	H					▲	▲		87	66%	79	150	120
Dover	Forte Posthouse	(01304) 821222	H					▲	▲		68	63%	67	65	50
Fawkham	Brandshatch Place	(01474) 872239	H		▲			▲			95	64%	40	100	100
Goudhurst	Star & Eagle Inn	(01580) 211512	I								45		11	25	60
Hawkhurst	Tudor Court	(01580) 752312	H		▲		▲				78	61%	18	70	60
Hollingbourne	Jarvis Great Danes	(01622) 631163	H	▲	▲		▲	▲			106	64%	126	600	320
Hythe	Hythe Imperial	(01303) 267441	H	▲	▲	▲	▲	▲	▲		108	71%	100	200	160
Hythe	Stade Court	(01303) 268263	H								83	62%	42	60	100
Lenham	Chilston Park	(01622) 859803	H	▲	▲		▲			▲	95	71%	38	100	100
Maidstone	Larkfield Priory	(01732) 846858	H								77	62%	52	70	65
Maidstone	Stakis Maidstone Hotel	(01622) 734322	H					▲	▲		113	67%	139	90	60
Rochester	Bridgewood Manor Hotel	(01634) 201333	H					▲	▲		105	68%	100	200	150
Rochester	Forte Posthouse	(01634) 687111	H					▲	▲		72	62%	105	110	85
Sevenoaks	Royal Oak	(01732) 451109	HR		▲						70	66%	39	35	85
Shorne	Inn on the Lake	(01474) 823333	H				▲	▲			70	61%	78	800	500
St Margaret's	Wallett's Court	(01304) 852424	HR								60	60%	10	20	45

Location	Establishment	Tel. No.	Category	Room £	Hotel %	No. of Rooms	Conf Max	Bang Max	Beaut Sit	Disabled	In Swim	Out Swim	Tennis	Squash	Golf	Fishing	Riding	15 mins Mway*	Country House
Tonbridge	Goldhill Mill	(01732) 851626	PH	70		3							◄						
Tonbridge	Rose & Crown	(01732) 357966	H	82	59%	48	120	80											
Tunbridge Wells	Royal Wells Inn	(01892) 511188	H	80	64%	19	100	100					◄						
Tunbridge Wells	Spa Hotel	(01892) 520331	HR	101	72%	76	300	240		◄	◄								
Wateringbury	Wateringbury Hotel	(01622) 812632	H	75	59%	40	80	64		◄									
Wrotham Heath	Forte Posthouse Maidstone Sevenoaks	(01732) 883311	H	75	67%	106	60	60			◄								

Lancashire

Location	Establishment	Tel. No.	Category	Room £	Hotel %	No. of Rooms	Conf Max	Bang Max	Beaut Sit	Disabled	In Swim	Out Swim	Tennis	Squash	Golf	Fishing	Riding	15 mins Mway*	Country House
Blackburn	Moat House	(01254) 264441	H	74	58%	98	350	350											
Blackpool	Imperial Hotel	(01253) 23971	H	114	64%	183	600	450			◄								
Blackpool	Pembroke Hotel	(01253) 23434	H	132	67%	274	900	650			◄								
Broughton	Broughton Park	(01772) 864087	HR	96	65%	98	200	220			◄		◄	◄					
Burnley	Oaks Hotel	(01282) 414141	H	89	63%	54	150	120			◄		◄	◄					
Chipping	Gibbon Bridge Hotel	(01995) 61456	H	70	65%	30	70	180		◄					◄	◄			
Clayton-le-Woods	Pines Hotel	(01772) 38551	H	55	65%	39	200	230											
Cowan Bridge	Cobwebs	(01524) 272141	RR	60		5	25												
Cowan Bridge	Hipping Hall	(01524) 271187	H	78	64%	7	20	20											
Lancaster	Forte Posthouse	(01524) 65999	H	72	69%	115	120	100			◄								
Langho	Northcote Manor	(01254) 240555	HR	85	67%	14	40	100											
Lytham	Clifton Arms	(01253) 739898	H	91	63%	44	200	200											
Lytham St Annes	Dalmeny Hotel	(01253) 712236	HR	81	60%	109	180	140			◄		◄	◄					
Mellor	Millstone Hotel	(01254) 813333	H	88		19	30	30											
Preston	Forte Posthouse	(01772) 259411	H	72	63%	121	120	100											

Location	Hotel	Phone						
Preston	Novotel	(01772) 313331	H	55	62%	98	180	130
Samlesbury	Swallow Trafalgar	(01772) 877351	H	95	60%	78	250	200
Samlesbury	Tickled Trout	(01772) 877671	H	112	63%	72	150	100
Standish	Kilhey Court	(01257) 472100	H	95	65%	62	180	180
Thornton-le-Fylde	River House	(01253) 883497	RR	80		5		40
Whitewell	Inn at Whitewell	(01200) 448222	I	60		11	250	170

Leicestershire

Location	Hotel	Phone						
Hambleton	Hambleton Hall	(01572) 756991	HR	152	84%	15	30	60
Hinckley	Hinckley Island Hotel	(01455) 631122	H	91	64%	270	400	350
Leicester	Belmont Hotel	(0116) 2544773	H	90	65%	65	130	120
Leicester	Forte Posthouse	(0116) 2630500	H	72	64%	165	85	80
Leicester	Holiday Inn	(0116) 2531161	H	119	72%	188	300	280
Leicester	Jarvis Grand Hotel	(0116) 2555599	H	106	66%	92	450	450
Leicester	Stakis Hotel	(0116) 2630066	H	118	69%	141	180	70
Lockington	Hilton National E Midlands Airport	(01509) 674000	H	113	69%	152	300	200
Loughborough	King's Head	(01509) 233222	H	99	58%	78	120	120
Loughborough	Quality Friendly Hotel	(01509) 211800	H	96	63%	94	225	180
Lutterworth	Denbigh Arms	(01455) 553537	H	65	66%	32	50	50
Market Harborough	Three Swans Hotel	(01858) 466644	H	77	65%	36	100	80
Melton Mowbray	George Hotel	(01664) 62112	H	45	57%	14	35	78
Oakham	Barnsdale Lodge Hotel	(01572) 724678	H	70	69%	29	300	300
Oakham	Whipper-In Hotel	(01572) 756971	HR	67	66%	24	75	60
Quorn	The Quorn Country Hotel	(01509) 415050	H	110	72%	19	120	108
Quorn	Quorn Grange	(01509) 412167	HR	102	67%	18	80	130
Rothley	Rothley Court	(0116) 2374141	H	102	67%	36	100	85

Location	Establishment	Tel. No.	Category	Room £	Hotel %	No. of Rooms	Conf Max	Bang Max	Beaut Sit	Disabled	In Swim	Out Swim	Tennis	Squash	Golf	Fishing	Riding	15 mins Mway*	Country House
Stapleford	Stapleford Park	(01572) 787522	HR	155	87%	43	200	170	◄			◄	◄			◄	◄		◄
Stretton	Ram Jam Inn	(01780) 410776	IR	61		7	30	48											
Uppingham	The Lake Isle	(01572) 822951	RR	66		12	10	44											

Lincolnshire

Location	Establishment	Tel. No.	Category	Room £	Hotel %	No. of Rooms	Conf Max	Bang Max	Beaut Sit	Disabled	In Swim	Out Swim	Tennis	Squash	Golf	Fishing	Riding	15 mins Mway*	Country House
Belton	Belton Woods Hotel	(01476) 593200	H	115	72%	136	275	240			◄			◄	◄				
Grantham	Swallow Hotel	(01476) 593000	H	98	67%	90	200	180			◄								
Lincoln	Courtyard by Marriott	(01522) 544244	H	78	65%	95	40	65											
Lincoln	D'Isney Place	(01522) 538881	PH	64		17													
Lincoln	Forte Posthouse	(01522) 520341	H	72	63%	70	90	70											
Lincoln	White Hart	(01522) 526222	H	117	69%	48	80	120											
Stamford	The George of Stamford	(01780) 55171	HR	105	72%	47	50	90											
Woodhall Spa	Dower House	(01526) 352588	H	58	62%	7	20	26											

Merseyside

Location	Establishment	Tel. No.	Category	Room £	Hotel %	No. of Rooms	Conf Max	Bang Max	Beaut Sit	Disabled	In Swim	Out Swim	Tennis	Squash	Golf	Fishing	Riding	15 mins Mway*	Country House
Birkenhead	Bowler Hat Hotel	0151-652 4931	H	85	65%	32	200	250											
Haydock	Forte Posthouse	(01942) 717878	H	64	65%	136	180	150			◄								
Haydock	Haydock Thistle	(01942) 272000	H	107	67%	139	300	200		◄	◄								
Liverpool	Atlantic Tower	0151-227 4444	H	106	65%	226	120	100											
Liverpool	Britannia Adelphi Hotel	0151-709 7200	H	105	68%	391	800	600			◄		◄						
Liverpool	Gladstone Hotel	0151-709 7050	H	90	60%	154	600	400											
Liverpool	Moat House	0151-709 0181	H	114	67%	251	450	300			◄								
Liverpool	St George's Hotel	0151-709 7090	H	81	58%	155	255	220											
Southport	New Bold Hotel	(01704) 532578	H	51	58%	23	100												
Southport	Prince of Wales Hotel	(01704) 536688	H	74	64%	102	400	300											

Middlesex

Location	Hotel	Phone						
Heathrow Airport	Excelsior Hotel	0181-759 6611	H	117	71%	827	750	500
Heathrow Airport	Forte Crest	0181-759 2323	H	117	68%	572	140	200
Heathrow Airport	Forte Posthouse (Ariel)	0181-759 2552	H	75	65%	186	50	
Heathrow Airport	Heathrow Hilton Hotel	0181-759 7755	HR	179	74%	400	300	240
Heathrow Airport	Holiday Inn Crowne Plaza	(01895) 445555	H	148	74%	374	200	150
Heathrow Airport	Jarvis International	0181-897 2121	H	85	67%	56	120	120
Heathrow Airport	Novotel	(01895) 431431	H	88	62%	178	250	150
Heathrow Airport	Park Hotel	0181-759 2400	H	113	61%	306	1000	1000
Heathrow Airport	Radisson Edwardian	0181-759 6311	H	210	76%	459	550	300
Heathrow Airport	Ramada Hotel Heathrow	0181-897 6363	H	135	66%	638	500	348
Heathrow Airport	Sheraton Skyline	0181-759 2535	H	204	73%	353	500	500
Heathrow Airport	Sheraton Heathrow Hotel	0181-759 2424	H	195	72%	431	50	120
Shepperton	Moat House	(01932) 241404	H	110	61%	183	300	300
Shepperton	Warren Lodge	(01932) 242972	I	85		50	18	90
Wembley	Hilton National	0181-902 8839	H	146	65%	306	350	350

Norfolk

Location	Hotel	Phone						
Barnham Broom	Barnham Broom Hotel	(01603) 759393	H	82	62%	52	150	200
Blakeney	Blakeney Hotel	(01263) 740797	H	124	64%	60	200	120
Blakeney	Manor Hotel	(01263) 740376	H	56	58%	37		
Burnham Market	Hoste Arms	(01328) 738257	I	92		21	30	70
Cawston	Grey Gables	(01603) 871259	RR	50		8	12	24
East Dereham	King's Head	(01362) 693842	I	55		17	70	45
Erpingham	The Ark	(01263) 761535	RR	95		3		36
Great Snoring	Old Rectory	(01328) 820597	H	87	61%	6		
Great Yarmouth	Carlton Hotel	(01493) 855234	H	79	67%	95	180	140

Location	Establishment	Tel. No.	Category	Room £	Hotel %	No. of Rooms	Conf Max	Banq Max	Beaut Sit	Disabled	In Swim	Out Swim	Tennis	Squash	Golf	Fishing	Riding	15 mins Mway*	Country House
Grimston	Congham Hall	(01485) 600250	HR	99	75%	14	25	50	▲			▲	▲					▲	
Hethersett	Park Farm	(01603) 810264	H	70	64%	37	120	100					▲						
King's Lynn	Butterfly Hotel	(01553) 771707	H	65	62%	50	40	30		▲									
King's Lynn	Duke's Head	(01553) 774996	H	87	60%	71	250	220											
King's Lynn	Knights Hill Hotel	(01553) 675566	H	89	62%	52	180	180			▲		▲						
Morston	Morston Hall	(01263) 741041	H	140	73%	6													
Norwich	Forte Posthouse	(01603) 56431	H	72	63%	116	100	65	▲										
Norwich	Friendly Hotel	(01603) 741161	H	77	60%	80	250	200		▲	▲								
Norwich	Hotel Nelson	(01603) 760260	H	87	65%	132	90	92		▲									
Norwich	Norwich Sport Village Hotel	(01603) 788898	H	69	63%	55	180	1500			▲	▲	▲	▲					
Norwich	Hotel Norwich	(01603) 787260	H	73	62%	107	350	300		▲	▲								
Norwich	Sprowston Manor	(01603) 410871	H	102	69%	94	120	90		▲	▲				▲				
Norwich Airport	Stakis Ambassador Hotel	(01603) 410544	H	82	65%	108	500	400											
Scole	Scole Inn	(01379) 740481	I	66		23	40	25											
Swaffham	Strattons Hotel	(01760) 723845	RR	78		7													
Thetford	The Bell	(01842) 754455	H	82	62%	47	80	60											
West Runton	The Links Country Park Hotel	(01263) 838383	H	120	62%	40	200	150		▲	▲		▲		▲				

Northamptonshire

Location	Establishment	Tel. No.	Category	Room £	Hotel %	No. of Rooms	Conf Max	Banq Max	Beaut Sit	Disabled	In Swim	Out Swim	Tennis	Squash	Golf	Fishing	Riding	15 mins Mway*	Country House
Castle Ashby	Falcon Hotel	(01604) 696200	I	75		16	40	40											
Corby	Rockingham Forest Hotel	(01536) 401348	H	65	60%	69	250	250											
Corby	Stakis Corby	(01536) 401020	H	89	67%	104	200	180		▲									

Location	Hotel	Phone	Type		%			
Crick	Forte Posthouse Northampton Rugby	(01788) 822101	H	72	64%	88	150	60
Daventry	Daventry Hotel	(01327) 301777	H	107	69%	138	600	320
Kettering	Kettering Park Hotel	(01536) 416666	H	105	71%	88	250	200
Northampton	Courtyard by Marriott	(01604) 22777	H	80	65%	104	40	0
Northampton	Moat House	(01604) 739988	H	112	63%	140	600	500
Northampton	Stakis Country Court	(01604) 700666	H	124	68%	139	300	220
Northampton	Swallow Hotel	(01604) 768700	H	102	72%	120	220	200
Northampton	Westone Hotel	(01604) 739955	H	95	59%	66	180	176
Oundle	Talbot Hotel	(01832) 273621	H	82	62%	39	120	100
Paulerspury	Vine House	(01327) 811267	RR	61		6	12	30
Weedon	Crossroads Hotel	(01327) 340354	H	49	55%	48	90	90

Northumberland

Location	Hotel	Phone	Type		%			
Alnwick	White Swan	(01665) 602109	H	74	58%	55	150	120
Bamburgh	Lord Crewe Arms	(01668) 214243	I	68		25	0	70
Belford	Blue Bell Hotel	(01668) 213543	H	88	63%	17	180	110
Berwick-upon-Tweed	Kings Arms	(01289) 307454	H	70	59%	36	200	120
Chollerford	George Hotel	(01434) 681611	H	110	59%	48	70	40
Corbridge	Angel Inn	(01434) 632119	I	54		5		50
Cornhill-on-Tweed	Tillmouth Park	(01890) 882255	H	95	68%	14	30	80
Hexham	Beaumont Hotel	(01434) 602331	H	80	62%	23	100	100
Langley-on-Tyne	Langley Castle	(01434) 688888	H	85	63%	16	160	120
Longhorsley	Linden Hall Hotel & Health Spa	(01670) 516611	H	125	75%	50	300	200
Powburn	Breamish Country House Hotel	(01665) 578266	H	116	67%	11	15	40
Seahouses	Olde Ship Hotel	(01665) 720200	I	68		16	20	0
Wylam	Laburnum House	(01661) 852185	RR	50		4	20	20

Nottinghamshire

Location	Establishment	Tel. No.	Category	Room £	Hotel %	No. of Rooms	Conf Max	Bang Max	Beaut Sit	Disabled	In Swim	Out Swim	Tennis	Squash	Golf	Fishing	Riding	15 mins Mway*	Country House
Barnby Moor	Ye Olde Bell	(01777) 705121	H	68	60%	55	250	250											
Langar	Langar Hall	(01949) 860559	HR	80	70%	12	20	20	▲										
Long Eaton	Sleep Inn	(0115) 9460000	B	50		101	75												
Nether Langwith	Goff's Restaurant	(01623) 744538	RR	50		2													
Newark	Grange Hotel	(01636) 703399	H	53	58%	15	20	30											
Nottingham	Forte Crest	(0115) 9470131	H	100	70%	130	600	500									▲		
Nottingham	Forte Posthouse	(0115) 9397800	H	72	61%	93	60	60											
Nottingham	Holiday Inn Garden Court	(0115) 9500600	H	80	65%	100	40	20		▲									
Nottingham	Nottingham Moat House	(0115) 9359988	H	99	59%	172	160	160											
Nottingham	Novotel	(0115) 9465111	H	58	62%	105	200	120		▲	▲								
Nottingham	Royal Moat House	(0115) 9414444	H	118	70%	201	600	500		▲		▲		▲			▲		
Nottingham	Rutland Square Hotel by the Castle	(0115) 9411114	H	78	63%	105	150	120											
Nottingham	Stakis Nottingham Hotel	(0115) 9419561	H	85	62%	167	200	150											
Nottingham	Strathdon Thistle	(0115) 9418501	H	110	66%	68	150	100											
Southwell	Saracen's Head	(01636) 812701	H	75	62%	27	120	120	s										

Oxfordshire

Location	Establishment	Tel. No.	Category	Room £	Hotel %	No. of Rooms	Conf Max	Bang Max	Beaut Sit	Disabled	In Swim	Out Swim	Tennis	Squash	Golf	Fishing	Riding	15 mins Mway*	Country House
Abingdon	Abingdon Lodge	(01235) 553456	H	94	61%	63	150	130											
Abingdon	Upper Reaches	(01235) 522311	H	112	62%	25	75	65											
Banbury	Banbury House Hotel	(01295) 259361	H	97	62%	48	70	120											
Banbury	Whately Hall	(01295) 263451	H	99	65%	74	120	90											
Burford	Bay Tree	(01993) 822791	H	110	67%	23	35	100											

Location	Hotel	Phone	Class	Price	Occ.	Rooms			Facilities
Burford	Lamb Inn	(01993) 823155	IR	86		16			
Chadlington	The Manor	(01608) 676711	HR	105	76%	7			▲
Charlbury	Bell Hotel	(01608) 810278	I	75		14	55	50	
Chipping Norton	Crown & Cushion	(01608) 642533	I	69		40	200	150	▲
Clanfield	The Plough at Clanfield	(01367) 810222	IR	85		6		20	
Dorchester-on-Thames	George Hotel	(01865) 340404	I	70		18	40	40	
Frilford Heath	Dog House Hotel	(01865) 390830	I	69		19	40	100	
Great Milton	Le Manoir aux Quat'Saisons	(01844) 278881	HR	195	86%	19	36	46	▲ ▲ ▲ ▲
Hailey	The Conf Max In Hand	(01993) 868321	I	50		16		30	
Henley-on-Thames	Red Lion	(01491) 572161	H	112	62%	26	60	70	
Horton-cum-Studley	Studley Priory	(01865) 351203	H	98	64%	19	45	55	▲ ▲
Kingham	Mill House Hotel	(01608) 658188	H	100	66%	23	50	50	▲
Middleton Stoney	Jersey Arms	(01869) 343234	I	80		16	12	50	
Milton Common	Belfry Hotel	(01844) 279381	H	93	60%	77	250	180	▲
Minster Lovell	Lovells at Windrush Farm	(01993) 779802	RR	95		2	0	20	▲
Minster Lovell	Old Swan	(01993) 774441	H	80	67%	57	50	50	▲ ▲ ▲
Moulsford-on-Thames	Beetle & Wedge	(01491) 651381	HR	95	71%	10	40	55	▲ ▲ ▲ ▲
North Stoke	Springs Hotel	(01491) 836687	H	155	70%	38	50	26	▲ ▲
Oxford	Bath Place Hotel	(01865) 791812	RR	105		10		40	
Oxford	Eastgate Hotel	(01865) 248244	H	122	61%	43	16		
Oxford	Moat House	(01865) 59933	H	135	62%	155	100	110	▲ ▲
Oxford	Old Parsonage	(01865) 310210	H	140	70%	30			▲
Oxford	The Randolph	(01865) 247481	H	143	68%	109	300	200	
Steeple Aston	Hopcrofts Holt Hotel	(01869) 340259	H	80	63%	88	200	250	
Stonor	Stonor Arms	(01491) 638345	RR	93		9	12	24	
Thame	Spread Eagle	(01844) 213661	H	90	65%	33	250	200	

Location	Establishment	Tel. No.	Category	Room £	Hotel %	No. of Rooms	Conf Max	Band Max	Beaut Sit	Disabled	In Swim	Out Swim	Tennis	Squash	Golf	Fishing	Riding	15 mins Mway*	Country House
Wallingford	George Hotel	(01491) 836665	H	72	60%	39	120	100											
Wallingford	Shillingford Bridge Hotel	(01865) 858567	H	95	61%	42	80	150				▲		▲		▲			
Wantage	Bear Hotel	(0123 57) 66366	H	65	58%	32	80	60											
Weston-on-the-Green	Weston Manor	(01869) 350621	H	105	61%	38	40	65				▲		▲					
Witney	Witney Lodge	(01993) 779777	H	96	62%	74	140	130		▲	▲								
Woodstock	Bear Hotel	(01993) 811511	HR	133	66%	44	70	30											
Woodstock	Feathers Hotel	(01993) 812291	HR	119	73%	17	30	60											
Wroxton St Mary	Wroxton House Hotel	(01295) 730777	H	95	66%	32	50	70											

Shropshire

Location	Establishment	Tel. No.	Category	Room £	Hotel %	No. of Rooms	Conf Max	Band Max	Beaut Sit	Disabled	In Swim	Out Swim	Tennis	Squash	Golf	Fishing	Riding	15 mins Mway*	Country House
All Stretton	Stretton Hall Hotel	(01694) 723224	H	79	59%	14	60	70								▲			
Alveley	Mill Hotel	(01746) 780437	H	120	72%	21	160	240											
Dorrington	Country Friends	(01743) 718707	RR	98	59%	3	20	50											
Hinstock	Goldstone Hall	(01630) 661202	HR	80	59%	8	60	220											
Ludlow	Dinham Hall	(01584) 876464	H	93	64%	12	28	24											
Ludlow	Feathers Hotel	(01584) 875261	H	98	70%	39	100	80		▲									
Norton	Hundred House Hotel	(01952) 730353	IR	69		10	25	30											
Oswestry	Wynnstay Hotel	(01691) 655261	H	93	66%	27	190	150			▲								
Shifnal	Park House	(01952) 460128	H	90	71%	54	200	200			▲					▲	▲		
Shrewsbury	Lion Hotel	(01743) 353107	H	82	62%	59	200	140											
Shrewsbury	Prince Rupert Hotel	(01743) 236000	H	85	64%	65	120	120											
Telford	Holiday Inn Telford/Ironbridge	(01952) 292500	H	109	68%	100	290	180			▲								
Telford	Madeley Court Hotel	(01952) 680068	H	98	67%	47	250	200											
Telford	Moat House	(01952) 291291	H	109	67%	148	450	400		▲	▲								

Location	Hotel	Telephone	Cat	Price	%	Rooms											
Telford	Telford Golf & Country Moat House	(01952) 429977	H	110	64%	86	240	240				▲			▲		
Weston-under-Redcastle	Hawkstone Park Hotel	(01939) 200611	H	65	61%	66	180	180				▲		▲			
Worfield	Old Vicarage	(01746) 716497	HR	90	67%	14	30	40								▲	
Somerset																	
Axbridge	The Oak House	(01934) 732444	I	51		9	25	44									
Beckington	Woolpack Inn	(01373) 831244	IR	65													
Castle Cary	Bond's	(01963) 350464	HR	64	63%	7		20									
Dulverton	Ashwick House	(01398) 323868	HR	95	68%	6											▲
Dulverton	Carnarvon Arms	(01398) 23302	H	80	60%	25	100	120			▲		▲	▲			
Dunster	Luttrell Arms	(01643) 821555	H	112	64%	27											
Hatch Beauchamp	Farthings Hotel	(01823) 480664	H	65	70%	8	25	40	▲								
Kilve	Meadow House	(01278) 741546	H	75	70%	10	20	24									▲
Lympsham	Batch Farm Country Hotel	(01934) 750371	H	54	56%	8	75	85			▲						
Middlecombe	Periton Park	(01643) 706885	HR	90	67%	8	24	50		▲							▲
Montacute	King's Arms Inn	(01935) 822513	I	69		13	30	30									
North Petherton	Walnut Tree Inn	(01278) 662255	H	68	65%	33	90	80							▲		
Porlock	Oaks Hotel	(01643) 862265	HR	80	65%	10											▲
Seavington St Mary	The Pheasant	(01460) 240502	H	88	69%	8											
Simonsbath	Simonsbath House	(01643) 83259	H	90	64%	7	35	35									
Somerton	Lynch Country House Hotel	(01458) 272316	H	55	69%	5											
Street	Bear Inn	(01458) 42021	H	62	63%	17	80	80						▲			
Taunton	Castle Hotel	(01823) 272671	HR	110	76%	35	100	90	▲								
Taunton	Forte Posthouse	(01823) 332222	H	72	66%	97	280	230									
Taunton	Porters	(01823) 256688	H														

Location	Establishment	Tel. No.	Category	Room £	Hotel %	No. of Rooms	Conf Max	Banq Max	Beaut Sit	Disabled	In Swim	Out Swim	Tennis	Squash	Golf	Fishing	Riding	15 mins Mway*	Country House
Williton	White House	(01984) 632306	RR	70		12				▲									
Winsford	Royal Oak Inn	(01643) 851455	I	90		14			▲							▲		·	
Wiveliscombe	Langley House	(01984) 623318	HR	85	66%	8	24	20											
Yeovil	Little Barwick House	(01935) 23902	RR	76		6	20	40											
Yeovil	The Manor	(01935) 231161	H	86	63%	41	60	70											

Staffordshire

Location	Establishment	Tel. No.	Category	Room £	Hotel %	No. of Rooms	Conf Max	Banq Max	Beaut Sit	Disabled	In Swim	Out Swim	Tennis	Squash	Golf	Fishing	Riding	15 mins Mway*	Country House
Burton-on-Trent	Riverside Inn	(01283) 511234	I	67		22	150	150							▲	▲			
Eccleshall	St George Hotel	(01785) 850300	I	70		10	65	65											
Hanchurch	Hanchurch Manor	(01782) 643030	PH			5	12								▲	▲	▲		
Lichfield	Jarvis George Hotel	(01543) 414822	H	92	59%	38	100	100											
Newcastle-under-Lyme	Clayton Lodge	(01782) 613093	H	97	60%	50	270	230											
Newcastle-under-Lyme	Forte Posthouse	(01782) 717171	H	72	60%	119	70	70			▲								
Rolleston-on-Dove	Brookhouse Hotel	(01283) 814188	H	85	62%	21	20	50											
Stafford	De Vere Tillington Hall	(01785) 53531	H	90	63%	90	200	174			▲		▲						
Stoke-on-Trent	Haydon House Hotel	(01782) 711311	H	62	65%	31	100	80											
Stoke-on-Trent	North Stafford Hotel	(01782) 744477	H	92	61%	69	450	600											
Stoke-on-Trent	Stakis Stoke-on-Trent	(01782) 202361	H	106	68%	127	300	200			▲								
Stoke-on-Trent	Stoke-on-Trent Moat House	(01782) 219000	H	107	70%	143	550	500			▲								
Stretton	Dovecliffe Hall	(01283) 531818	HR	95	68%	7	60	90											
Swinfen	Swinfen Hall	(01543) 481494	H	85	70%	20	200	160					▲			▲			
Tutbury	Ye Olde Dog & Partridge Inn	(01283) 813030	H	73		17	16												
Waterhouses	Old Beams	(01538) 308254	RR	80		5	20												

Suffolk

Location	Hotel	Phone	Type		%				
Aldeburgh	Brudenell Hotel	(01728) 452071	H	82	60%	47	50	50	◀
Aldeburgh	Uplands	(01728) 452420	H	60	60%	20	20	40	◀
Aldeburgh	Wentworth Hotel	(01728) 452312	H	86	68%	38	30	100	
Beccles	Waveney House	(01502) 712270	H	58	59%	13	90	95	◀
Brome	Oaksmere	(01379) 870326	H	75	67%	11	30	70	
Bury St Edmunds	Angel Hotel	(01284) 753926	H	85	66%	42	100	120	
Bury St Edmunds	Butterfly Hotel	(01284) 760884	H	66	62%	66	50	50	
Bury St Edmunds	Suffolk Hotel	(01284) 753995	H	82	59%	33	30	70	◀
Campsea Ashe	Old Rectory	(01728) 746524	RR	52		9		35	
Copdock	Ipswich Moat House	(01473) 209988	H	79	64%	73	500	350	◀
Felixstowe	Orwell Hotel	(01394) 309955	H	90	69%	58	200	200	
Framlingham	The Crown	(01728) 723521	H	97	62%	14	6		
Hintlesham	Hintlesham Hall	(01473) 652268	HR	153	82%	33	82	82	◀ ◀ ◀ ◀
Ipswich	Belstead Brook Manor Hotel	(01473) 684241	H	79	68%	76	60	65	
Ipswich	Constable Country Hotel	(01473) 690313	H	69	63%	112	140	100	◀
Ipswich	Marlborough Hotel	(01473) 257677	H	69	65%	22	60	72	
Ipswich	Novotel	(01473) 232400	H	67	61%	100	200	150	
Lavenham	Great House	(01787) 247431	RR	68		4		50	◀
Lavenham	The Swan	(01787) 247477	HR	128	71%	47	50	40	
Long Melford	Black Lion Hotel	(01787) 312356	H	70	65%	9	20	40	
Long Melford	Bull Hotel	(01787) 378494	H	102	65%	25	60	60	
Needham Market	Pipps Ford	(01449) 760208	H	55	60%	7	25	35	◀
Newmarket	Heath Court Hotel	(01638) 667171	H	70	62%	44	70	120	◀
Newmarket	White Hart	(01638) 663051	H	50	60%	23	120	90	
Southwold	The Crown	(01502) 722275	IR	69		12	45		
Southwold	The Swan	(01502) 722186	HR	91	65%	45	50	88	

Location	Establishment	Tel. No.	Category	Room £	Hotel %	No. of Rooms	Conf Max	Bang Max	Beaut Sit	Disabled	In Swim	Out Swim	Tennis	Squash	Golf	Fishing	Riding	15 mins Mway*	Country House
Sudbury	Mill Hotel	(01787) 375544	H	93	58%	56	70	78								◄			
Woodbridge	Seckford Hall	(01394) 385678	H	99	68%	32	100	100			◄				◄	◄			
Yoxford	Satis House	(01728) 668418	H	78	63%	7	40	28											
Surrey																			
Bagshot	Pennyhill Park	(01276) 471774	H	166	75%	76	60	80	◄				◄		◄	◄	◄	◄	
Bramley	Bramley Grange	(01483) 893434	H	108	64%	45	120	150		◄									
Camberley	Frimley Hall	(01276) 28321	H	115	68%	66	70	60											
Chiddingfold	Crown Inn	(01428) 682255	I	57		8													
Churt	Frensham Pond Hotel	(01252) 795161	H	88	62%	51	150	150			◄			◄					
Cobham	Hilton National	(01932) 864471	H	142	65%	152	300	250			◄		◄	◄					
Cobham	Woodlands Park	(01372) 843933	H	154	68%	58	350	270				◄	◄						
Croydon	Croydon Park	0181-680 9200	H	102	68%	212	300	250	◄		◄								
Croydon	Forte Posthouse	0181-688 5185	H	75	61%	83	250	200						◄					
Croydon	Hilton National	0181-680 3000	H	109	69%	168	400	350		◄	◄								
Croydon	Selsdon Park	0181-657 8811	H	109	68%	170	150	250	◄		◄	◄	◄		◄				
Dorking	White Horse	(01306) 881138	H	92	62%	68	60	100											
East Horsley	Jarvis Thatchers Hotel	(01483) 284291	H	108	62%	54	70	100											
Egham	Great Fosters	(01784) 433822	H	99	67%	44	100	220		◄		◄	◄						
Egham	Runnymede Hotel	(01784) 436171	H	145	74%	171	400	350			◄							◄	
Farnham	Bishop's Table Hotel	(01252) 710222	H	85	62%	18	36	200											
Farnham	Bush Hotel	(01252) 715237	H	87	62%	66	60	35											

Location	Hotel	Phone	Type		%			
Gatwick Airport	Chequers Thistle	(01293) 786992	H	107	63%	78	70	60
Gatwick Airport	Forte Posthouse Gatwick	(01293) 771621	H	72	63%	210	150	120
Gatwick Airport	Gatwick Moat House	(01293) 785599	H	93	62%	124	180	140
Gatwick Airport	Ramada Hotel Gatwick Airport	(01293) 820169	H	114	70%	255	180	150
Gatwick Airport	Scandic Crown Gatwick	(01293) 561186	H	109	64%		200	160
Godalming	Inn on the Lake	(01483) 415575	I	75		19	120	120
Guildford	The Angel	(01483) 64555	H	122	73%	21	80	40
Guildford	Forte Crest	(01483) 574444	H	130	68%	111	120	90
Haslemere	Lythe Hill Hotel	(01428) 651251	H	111	71%	40	60	130
Horley	Langshott Manor	(01293) 786680	HR	106	73%	7	12	20
Nutfield	Nutfield Priory	(01737) 822066	H	135	71%	52	100	100
Reigate	Bridge House	(01737) 246801	H	81	61%	40	70	240
Richmond	Petersham Hotel	0181-940 7471	HR	130	65%	54	50	30
Richmond	Richmond Gate Hotel	0181-940 0061	H	123	65%	64	70	70
Seale	Jarvis Hog's Back Hotel	(01252) 782345	H	112	64%	89	140	180
Sutton	Holiday Inn London Sutton	0181-770 1311	H	130	70%	116	220	250
Weybridge	Oatlands Park	(01932) 847242	H	128	69%	117	300	220
Weybridge	Ship Thistle	(01932) 848364	H	119	63%	39	150	125

East Sussex

Location	Hotel	Phone	Type		%			
Battle	Netherfield Place	(01424) 774455	HR	105	78%	14	40	75
Boreham Street	White Friars Hotel	(01323) 832355	H	75	57%	20	50	60
Brighton	Bedford Hotel	(01273) 329744	H	137	66%	129	450	350
Brighton	Brighton Metropole	(01273) 775432	H	174	70%	328	1800	1400
Brighton	Brighton Thistle Hotel	(01273) 206700	HR	160	77%	204	300	250
Brighton	Dove Hotel	(01273) 779222	H	65		8		

Location	Establishment	Tel. No.	Category	Room £	Hotel %	No. of Rooms	Conf Max	Bang Max	Beaut Slt	Disabled	In Swim	Out Swim	Tennis	Squash	Golf	Fishing	Riding	15 mins Mway*/Country House
Brighton	Grand Hotel	(01273) 321188	H	165	74%	200	850	730		▲	▲							
Brighton	Old Ship Hotel	(01273) 329001	H	80	65%	152	300	200										
Brighton	Topps Hotel	(01273) 729334	HR	79	69%	15												
Brighton (Hove)	Sackville Hotel	(01273) 736292	H	70	61%	45	40	80										
Brighton (Hove)	Whitehaven Hotel	(01273) 778355	H	70	56%	17	15	40										
Cooden	Cooden Beach Hotel	(01424) 842281	H	80	60%	41	160	160			▲							
Eastbourne	Cavendish Hotel	(01323) 410222	H	85	68%	112	220	350										
Eastbourne	Grand Hotel	(01323) 412345	HR	140	75%	164	400	400			▲	▲						
Eastbourne	Wish Tower Hotel	(01323) 722676	H	96	66%	65	100	120										
Hastings	Cinque Ports Hotel Periquito	(01424) 439222	H	59	66%	40	300	250										
Hastings	Royal Victoria Hotel	(01424) 445544	H	75	70%	50	100	130		▲								
Lewes	Shelleys Hotel	(01273) 472361	H	110	60%	19	50	60										
Rye	George Hotel	(01797) 222114	H	94	62%	22	80	100										
Rye	Mermaid Inn	(01797) 223065	H	117	60%	28		50										
Sedlescombe	Brickwall Hotel	(01424) 870253	H	62	56%	23		120				▲						
Uckfield	Horsted Place Sporting Est & Hotel	(01825) 750581	HR	136	79%	20	100	80	▲		▲	▲	▲	▲	▲			
Wych Cross	Ashdown Park Hotel	(01342) 824988	HR	115	78%	95	150	150			▲	▲	▲	▲	▲			

West Sussex

Location	Establishment	Tel. No.	Category	Room £	Hotel %	No. of Rooms	Conf Max	Bang Max	Beaut Slt	Disabled	In Swim	Out Swim	Tennis	Squash	Golf	Fishing	Riding	15 mins Mway*/Country House
Amberley	Amberley Castle	(01798) 831992	HR	130	81%	15	50	48	▲									▲
Arundel	Norfolk Arms	(01903) 882101	H	80	60%	34	100	100										
Ashington	Mill House Hotel	(01903) 892426	I	77		12	30	30										
Bognor Regis	Royal Norfolk	(01243) 826222	H	76	58%	51	120	120										
Bosham	Millstream Hotel	(01243) 573234	H	99	63%	29	45	102										
Chichester	Dolphin & Anchor	(01243) 785121	H	102	63%	49	40	180										

Location	Hotel	Phone	Type					
Climping	Bailiffscourt	(01903) 723511	HR	125	74%	27	50	85
Crawley	George Hotel	(01293) 524215	H	80	64%	81		100
Cuckfield	Ockenden Manor	(01444) 416111	HR	105	74%	22	50	70
East Grinstead	Gravetye Manor	(01342) 810567	HR	200	84%	18	12	20
East Grinstead	Woodbury House	(01342) 313657	H	85	61%	14	20	30
Findon	Findon Manor	(01903) 872733	H	70	58%	11	45	47
Gatwick Airport	Copthorne Effingham Park	(01342) 714994	H	128	72%	122	600	600
Gatwick Airport	Copthorne London Gatwick	(01342) 714971	H	118	69%	227	110	160
Gatwick Airport	Europa Gatwick	(01293) 886666	H	97	68%	211	150	130
Gatwick Airport	Forte Crest Gatwick	(01293) 567070	H	125	74%	468	280	280
Gatwick Airport	Hilton International	(01293) 518080	H	164	72%	550	500	360
Gatwick Airport	Holiday Inn Gatwick	(01293) 529991	H	102	68%	217	250	200
Goodwood	Goodwood Park	(01243) 775537	H	90	67%	88	120	120
Lower Beeding	Cisswood House Hotel	(01403) 891216	HR	92	70%	32	200	150
Lower Beeding	South Lodge	(01403) 891711	H	154	76%	39	85	80
Midhurst	Angel Hotel	(01730) 812421	IR	80		21	80	100
Midhurst	Spread Eagle	(01730) 816911	H	92	69%	41	60	110
Pulborough	Chequers Hotel	(01798) 872486	H	75	61%	11	20	50
Rusper	Ghyll Manor	(01293) 871571	H	101	65%	24	150	110
Storrington	Little Thakeham	(01903) 744416	HR	150	77%	9	12	80
Storrington	Manleys	(01903) 742331	RR	85		1		
Turners Hill	Alexander House	(01342) 714914	HR	150	79%	15	55	55
Walberton	Stakis Avisford Park Hotel	(01243) 551215	H	107	66%	127	350	300
West Chiltington	Roundabout Hotel	(01798) 813838	H	83	61%	23	60	55
Worthing	Beach Hotel	(01903) 234001	H	82	64%	81	200	200
Worthing	Chatsworth Hotel	(01903) 236103	H	90	57%	107	150	140

Tyne & Wear

Location	Establishment	Tel. No.	Category	Room £	Hotel %	No. of Rooms	Conf Max	Banq Max	Beaut Sit	Disabled	In Swim	Out Swim	Tennis	Squash	Golf	Fishing	Riding	15 mins Mway*	Country House
Gateshead	Jarvis Springfield Hotel	0191-477 4121	H	95	63%	60	120	100											
Gateshead	Newcastle Marriott Hotel	0191-493 2233	H	129	70%	150	450	330		▲	▲								
Gateshead	Swallow Hotel	0191-477 1105	H	95	60%	103	350	350			▲								
Newcastle-upon-Tyne	Copthorne Hotel	0191-222 0333	H	138	73%	156	200	150		▲	▲								
Newcastle-upon-Tyne	County Thistle	0191-232 2471	H	106	68%	115	130	170											
Newcastle-upon-Tyne	Europa Hotel	0191-262 8989	H	82	59%	147	400	300											
Newcastle-upon-Tyne	Forte Crest	0191-232 6191	H	101	61%	166	550	350											
Newcastle-upon-Tyne	Novotel	0191-214 0303	H	78	63%	126	250	160		▲	▲								
Newcastle-upon-Tyne	Swallow Hotel	0191-232 5025	H	90	63%	93	100	90											
Newcastle-upon-Tyne	Swallow Gosforth Park	0191-236 4111	H	120	73%	178	500	500			▲		▲	▲				▲	
Newcastle-upon-Tyne	Vermont Hotel	0191-233 1010	HR	134	72%	101	200	130											
Airport	Moat House	(01661) 824911	H	114	62%	100	400	350		▲	▲							▲	
Seaton Burn	Holiday Inn	0191-236 5432	H	128	70%	150	400	300		▲	▲								
Seaton Burn	Horton Grange	(01661) 860686	RR	80		9	20	30											
Sunderland	Swallow Hotel	0191-529 2041	H	105	70%	65	250	300			▲								
Washington	Forte Posthouse	0191-416 2264	H	72	59%	138	100	80						▲	▲				
Washington	Moat House	0191-417 2626	H	100	66%	106	200	180		▲	▲		▲	▲					

Warwickshire

Location	Establishment	Tel. No.	Category	Room £	Hotel %	No. of Rooms	Conf Max	Banq Max	Beaut Sit	Disabled	In Swim	Out Swim	Tennis	Squash	Golf	Fishing	Riding	15 mins Mway*	Country House
Alcester	Arrow Mill	(01789) 762419	I	72		18	100	120	▲							▲			
Ansty	Ansty Hall	(01203) 612222	H	100	70%	30	80	80											
Barford	Glebe Hotel	(01926) 624218	H	110	68%	41	130	120			▲							▲	

Location	Hotel	Phone	Type	Rooms	%			
Billesley	Billesley Manor	(01789) 400888	HR	168	75%	41	100	80
Bodymoor Heath	Marston Farm	(01827) 872133	H	95	65%	37	150	120
Brandon	Brandon Hall	(01203) 542571	H	92		60	90	120
Charlecote	Charlecote Pheasant	(01789) 470333	H	105	62%	67	120	120
Hockley Heath	Nuthurst Grange	(01564) 783972	HR	125	74%	15	100	90
Kenilworth	De Vere De Montfort	(01926) 55944	H	85	63%	96	300	230
Leamington Spa	Courtyard by Marriott	(01926) 425522	H	82	65%	94	50	40
Leamington Spa	Inchfield Hotel	(01926) 883777	H	78	63%	22	40	50
Leamington Spa	Mallory Court	(01926) 330214	HR	173	80%	10	16	50
Leamington Spa	Regent Hotel	(01926) 427231	HR	89	68%	80	100	200
Stratford-upon-Avon	Alveston Manor	(01789) 204581	H	125	67%	106	160	140
Stratford-upon-Avon	Dukes Hotel	(01789) 269300	H	70	65%	22		
Stratford-upon-Avon	Ettington Park	(01789) 450123	H	145	76%	48	75	48
Stratford-upon-Avon	Falcon Hotel	(01789) 279953	H	99	63%	73	200	130
Stratford-upon-Avon	Forte Posthouse	(01789) 266761	H	72	59%	60	150	100
Stratford-upon-Avon	Shakespeare Hotel	(01789) 294771	H	136	69%	62	90	90
Stratford-upon-Avon	Stratford House	(01789) 268288	H	85	62%	11	30	50
Stratford-upon-Avon	Stratford Moat House	(01789) 279988	H	144	66%	247	450	470
Stratford-upon-Avon	Welcombe Hotel	(01789) 295252	H	125	74%	75	150	150
Stratford-upon-Avon	White Swan	(01789) 297022	H	85	62%	37	45	15
Stratford-upon-Avon	Windmill Park	(01789) 731173	H	98	64%	103	360	350
Warwick	Hilton National	(01926) 499555	H	111	66%	181	400	450
Wishaw	The Belfry	(01675) 470301	H	150	73%	219	300	300

West Midlands

Location	Hotel	Phone	Type	Rooms	%			
Aldridge	Fairlawns	(01922) 55122	H	80	64%	35	80	82

Location	Establishment	Tel. No.	Category	Room £	Hotel %	No. of Rooms	Conf Max	Bang Max	Beaut Sit	Disabled	In Swim	Out Swim	Tennis	Squash	Golf	Fishing	Riding	15 mins Mway*	Country House
Berkswell	Nailcote Hall	(01203) 466174	H	115	67%	38	100	130					◀		◀				
Birmingham	Birmingham Metropole	0121-780 4242	H	195	72%	802	2000	1440			◀							◀	
Birmingham	Chamberlain Hotel	0121-627 0627	B	35		250	400	350											
Birmingham	Copthorne Hotel	0121-200 2727	H	136	70%	212	200	150		◀	◀							◀	
Birmingham	Forte Crest	0121-643 8171	H	111	66%	251	630	560						◀					
Birmingham	Forte Posthouse	0121-357 7444	H	72	60%	192	150	150											
Birmingham	Holiday Inn Crowne Plaza	0121-631 2000	H	128	72%	284	160	150		◀	◀							◀	
Birmingham	Hyatt Regency	0121-643 1234	HR	144	77%	319	240	240			◀							◀	
Birmingham	Midland Hotel	0121-643 2601	H			111	200	170											
Birmingham	Novotel	0121-643 2000	H	94	61%	148	250	150		◀									
Birmingham	Plough & Harrow	0121-454 4111	H	87	60%	44	70	80											
Birmingham	Royal Angus Thistle	0121-236 4211	H	107	65%	133	200	180											
Birmingham	Strathallan Thistle	0121-455 9777	H	108	63%	167	170	150											
Birmingham	Swallow Hotel	0121-452 1144	HR	145	77%	98	25	20			◀							◀	
Birmingham Airport	Forte Posthouse	0121-782 8141	H	72	61%	136	150	120											
Birmingham Airport	Novotel	0121-782 7000	H	84	65%	195	40	30		◀									
Brierley Hill	Copthorne Merry Hill Dudley	(01384) 482882	H	115	71%	138	250	190		◀	◀							◀	
Coventry	Chace Hotel	(01203) 303398	H	89	61%	67	100	80											
Coventry	Coventry Hill Hotel	(01203) 402151	H	81	60%	180	120	120											
Coventry	De Vere Hotel	(01203) 633733	H	95	69%	190	450	400											
Coventry	Forte Posthouse	(01203) 613261	H	72	66%	147	450	450			◀								
Coventry	Hilton National	(01203) 603000	H	111	72%	172	600	500		◀	◀							◀	
Coventry	Novotel	(01203) 365000	H	58	62%	98	200	120		◀		◀							
Meriden	Forest of Arden Hotel	(01676) 522335	H	127	70%	154	150	200		◀	◀		◀		◀	◀		◀	

Location	Hotel	Phone	Type													
Meriden	Manor Hotel	(01676) 522735	H	95	64%	74	275	250								
Solihull	Jarvis International Hotel	0121-711 2121	H	105	66%	127	200	180								◄
Solihull	Moat House	0121-623 9988	H	139	69%	115	200	160						◄		
Solihull	Regency Hotel	0121-745 6119	H	100	64%	112	150	150					◄	◄		
Solihull	St John's Swallow Hotel	0121-711 3000	H	95	63%	177	700	700					◄	◄		
Stourbridge	Talbot Hotel	(01384) 394350	H	50	59%	25	150	150								
Sutton Coldfield	Jarvis Penns Hall	0121-351 3111	H	115	66%	114	650	600			◄			◄		
Sutton Coldfield	Moor Hall	0121-308 3751	H	95	62%	75	300	250		◄				◄		
Sutton Coldfield	New Hall	0121-378 2442	HR	134	80%	60	40	40	◄	◄	◄	◄	◄	◄		
Walsall	Boundary Hotel	(01922) 33555	H	74	61%	94	45	25				◄	◄	◄		
Walsall	Friendly Hotel	(01922) 724444	H	85	60%	153	180	140				◄	◄	◄		
Walsall Wood	Baron's Court Hotel	(01543) 452020	H	74	62%	94	200	110					◄			
West Bromwich	Moat House	0121-609 9988	H	89	59%	171	180	140						◄		
Wolverhampton	Goldthorn Hotel	(01902) 29216	H	78	62%	92	150	132					◄			
Wolverhampton	Jarvis Mount Hotel	(01902) 752055	H	112	60%	56	100	140				◄				
Wolverhampton	Novotel	(01902) 871100	H	65	61%	132	120	120	◄	◄						

Wiltshire

Location	Hotel	Phone	Type													
Beanacre	Beechfield House	(01225) 703700	H	80	70%	24	50	50	◄	◄	◄	◄	◄			◄
Bradford-on-Avon	Woolley Grange	(01225) 864705	HR	140	75%	20	45	50	◄	◄	◄	◄				◄
Castle Combe	Castle Inn	(01249) 783030	I	55		7										
Castle Combe	Manor House	(01249) 782206	HR	140	80%	40	60	90	◄		◄	◄	◄	◄		◄
Chiseldon	Chiseldon House	(01793) 741010	HR	90	66%	21	65	80			◄	◄				
Colerne	Lucknam Park	(01225) 742777	HR	171	83%	42	100	80	◄		◄		◄			◄
Corsham	Methuen Arms	(01249) 714867	I	50		25	30	120								
Corsham	Rudloe Hall	(01225) 810555	H	80	64%	11	100	70								

Location	Establishment	Tel. No.	Category	Room £	Hotel %	No. of Rooms	Conf Max	Bang Max	Beaut Sit	Disabled	In Swim	Out Swim	Tennis	Squash	Golf	Fishing	Riding	15 mins Mway*	Country House
Hinton	Hinton Grange	(0117) 9372916	HR	105	62%	18	15	40			▲		▲			▲			
Lacock	At The Sign of The Angel	(01249) 730230	IR	75		6		20											
Malmesbury	Old Bell Hotel	(01666) 822344	H	70	65%	32	45	80											
Marlborough	Ivy House Hotel	(01672) 515333	H	68	61%	30	80	90											
Melksham	Toxique	(01225) 702129	RR	84		4		20											
Purton	Pear Tree	(01793) 772100	H	75	75%	18	70	50	▲								▲		
Salisbury	Rose & Crown	(01722) 327908	H	113	56%	29	90	40											
Salisbury	White Hart	(01722) 327476	H	112	63%	68	80	96											
Stanton St Quintin	Stanton Manor	(01666) 837552	HR	82	64%	10	30	60											
Swindon	Blunsdon House Hotel	(01793) 721701	H	93	69%	88	300	250			▲		▲	▲	▲				
Swindon	De Vere Hotel	(01793) 878785	H	115	69%	154	400	270			▲								
Swindon	Forte Posthouse	(01793) 524601	H	72	63%	98	80	80			▲								
Swindon	Hilton National	(01793) 881777	H	106	64%	150	350	300		▲		▲							
Swindon	Swindon Crest Hotel	(01793) 831333	H	96	62%	91	75	80											
Swindon	Swindon Marriott Hotel	(01793) 512121	H	115	71%	153	280	220			▲		▲	▲			▲		
Swindon	Wiltshire Hotel	(01793) 528282	H	79	62%	95	230	200											
Teffont Evias	Howard's House	(01722) 716392	HR	111	68%	9	25	40	▲										
Warminster	Bishopstrow House	(01985) 212312	HR	125	79%	30	60	65	▲	▲	▲	▲	▲	▲		▲			

North Yorkshire

Location	Establishment	Tel. No.	Category	Room £	Hotel %	No. of Rooms	Conf Max	Bang Max	Beaut Sit	Disabled	In Swim	Out Swim	Tennis	Squash	Golf	Fishing	Riding	15 mins Mway*	Country House
Askrigg	King's Arms Hotel	(01969) 650258	I	85		10	40	30											
Bilbrough	Bilbrough Manor	(01937) 834002	H	105	75%	15	50	50	▲										
Bolton Abbey	Devonshire Arms	(01756) 710441	H	130	74%	41	150	125		▲	▲		▲			▲			

Town	Hotel	Phone	Type		%					M1	M2	M3	M4	M5	M6	M7
Boroughbridge	The Crown	(01423) 322328	H	65	63%	42	150	150								
Crathorne	Crathorne Hall	(01642) 700398	H	125	72%	37	140	120		▲					▲	▲
Goathland	Mallyan Spout	(01947) 896486	H	65	61%	24	70	70								
Great Ayton	Ayton Hall	(01642) 723595	H	105	70%	9	100	60					▲	▲	▲	
Hackness	Hackness Grange	(01723) 882345	H	126	61%	28	20	70		▲	▲	▲				
Harome	Pheasant Hotel	(01439) 771241	H	117	68%	14										
Harrogate	The Crown	(01423) 567755	H	100	67%	121	450	300								
Harrogate	Hospitality Inn	(01423) 564601	H	96	61%	71	150	100								
Harrogate	Imperial Hotel	(01423) 565071	H	95	65%	85	200	160						▲		
Harrogate	Majestic Hotel	(01423) 568972	H	122	64%	156	500	800				▲	▲	▲		
Harrogate	Moat House	(01423) 500000	H	143	64%	214	400	250					▲			
Harrogate	Old Swan Hotel	(01423) 500055	HR	132	69%	136	300	400		▲						
Harrogate	St George Swallow Hotel	(01423) 561431	H	105	63%	93	150	150				▲				
Harrogate	Studley Hotel	(01423) 560425	H	98	64%	36	15									
Helmsley	Black Swan	(01439) 70466	H	120	69%	44	50	40								
Helmsley	Feversham Arms	(01439) 70766	H	70	66%	18	30	30					▲			
Hovingham	Worsley Arms Hotel	(01653) 628234	I	105		22	50	30			▲	▲	▲			
Jervaulx	Jervaulx Hall	(01677) 460235	H	125	70%	10		22		▲						
Knaresborough	Dower House	(01423) 863302	H	82	63%	32	70	100		▲						
Markington	Hob Green	(01423) 770031	H	90	70%	12	15	12								
Monk Fryston	Monk Fryston Hall	(01977) 682369	H	96	65%	28	50	80								
Newby Wiske	Solberge Hall	(01609) 779191	H	80	69%	25	120	100								
Nidd	Nidd Hall	(01423) 771598	H	120	76%	59	250	150		▲		▲	▲			
Pickering	The White Swan	(01751) 472288	I	76		13	12	36								
Reeth	Burgoyne Hotel	(01748) 884292	HR	60	66%	9		30				▲				
Ripley	Boar's Head Hotel	(01423) 771888	HR	90	66%	25		40					▲		▲	

Location	Establishment	Tel. No.	Category	Room £	Hotel %	No. of Rooms	Conf Max	Bang Max	Beaut Sit	Disabled	In Swim	Out Swim	Tennis	Squash	Golf	Fishing	Riding	15 mins Mway*	Country House
Ripon	Ripon Spa Hotel	(01765) 602172	H	97	62%	40	160	160											
Rosedale Abbey	Milburn Arms	(01751) 417312	H	74	60%	11	16	66											
Scalby	Wrea Head Country Hotel	(01723) 378211	H	99	65%	21	40	50	▲	▲									
Scarborough	The Crown	(01723) 373491	H	82	63%	78	200	160											
Skipton	Randell's Hotel	(01756) 700100	H	85	65%	76	420	320			▲			▲					
South Milford	Forte Posthouse Leeds/Selby	(01977) 682711	H	72	65%	105	120	100			▲		▲						
Staddlebridge	McCoy's	(01609) 882671	HR	99	70%	6	30	55											
Stokesley	Chapters	(01642) 711888	HR	60	65%	13	40	60											
Wath-in-Nidderdale	Sportsman's Arms	(01423) 711306	RR	58		7													
York	Dean Court Hotel	(01904) 625082	H	105	63%	41	50	74											
York	Forte Posthouse	(01904) 707921	H	72	65%	139	120	65											
York	Grange Hotel	(01904) 644744	HR	98	74%	30	60	80											
York	Jarvis Abbey Park Resort Hotel	(01904) 658301	H	96	57%	85	120	120											
York	Judges Lodging	(01904) 638733	H	95	64%	12	30	36											
York	Middlethorpe Hall	(01904) 641241	HR	141	79%	30	63	32	▲										
York	Mount Royale	(01904) 628856	H	85	66%	23	0	40				▲							
York	Novotel	(01904) 611660	H	89	62%	124	210	130		▲	▲								
York	Royal York Hotel	(01904) 653681	H	113	67%	145	280	250											
York	Stakis York	(01904) 648111	H	104	65%	128	150	150											
York	Swallow Hotel	(01904) 701000	H	110	64%	112	170	120		▲	▲								
York	York Viking Moat House	(01904) 659822	H	132	69%	187	300	300											

South Yorkshire

Location	Establishment	Tel. No.	Category	Room £	Hotel %	No. of Rooms	Conf Max	Bang Max
Barnsley	Ardsley Moat House	(01226) 289401	H	88	59%	73	400	320
Bawtry	The Crown	(01302) 710341	H	67	64%	57	150	150

Location	Hotel	Phone	Type						
Doncaster	Danum Swallow Hotel	(01302) 342261	H	90	64%	66	450	330	
Doncaster	Grand St Leger	(01302) 364111	H	80	64%	20	80	65	
Doncaster	Moat House	(01302) 310331	H	106	64%	100	400	350	◄
Rotherham	Carlton Park Hotel	(01709) 364902	H	90	69%	78	250	200	
Rotherham	Swallow Hotel	(01709) 830630	H	96	65%		300		◄
Sheffield	Charnwood Hotel	(0114) 2589411	H	90	64%	22	100	90	
Sheffield	Forte Posthouse	(0114) 2670067	H	72	65%	135	300	200	◄
Sheffield	Grosvenor House	(0114) 2720041	H	73	67%	103	385	270	
Sheffield	Holiday Inn Royal Victoria	(0114) 2768822	H	95	67%	100	450	300	
Sheffield	Moat House	(0114) 2829988	H	111	68%	95	500	300	◄
Sheffield	Novotel	(0114) 2781781	H	68	63%	144	200	150	◄
Sheffield	Swallow Hotel Sheffield	(0114) 2583811	H	98	64%	117	200	200	◄

West Yorkshire

Location	Hotel	Phone	Type						
Bingley	Bankfield Hotel	(01274) 567123	H	96	61%	103	300	260	
Bradford	Restaurant 19	(01274) 492559	RR	75		4		30	
Bradford	Novotel	(01274) 683683	H	55	60%	127	300	160	
Bradford	Stakis Bradford	(01274) 734734	H	97	61%	120	700	700	
Bradford	The Victoria	(01274) 728706	HR	99	67%	60	200	120	
Bramhope	Forte Posthouse	(0113) 2842911	H	86	66%	124	160	140	◄
Bramhope	Jarvis Parkway Hotel	(0113) 2672551	H	112	62%	105	300	220	◄
Brighouse	Forte Crest	(01484) 400400	H	116	68%	94	200	180	◄
Garforth	Hilton National	(0113) 2866556	H	90	61%	144	350	250	◄
Halifax	Holdsworth House	(01422) 240024	H	103	69%	40	150	100	
Haworth	Weavers	(01535) 643822	RR	70		4			
Huddersfield	George Hotel	(01484) 515444	H	89	62%	60	200	150	◄
Huddersfield	Hilton National	(01422) 375431	H	98	66%	118	400	350	◄

Location	Establishment	Tel. No.	Category	Room £	Hotel %	No. of Rooms	Conf Max	Band Max	Beaut Sit	Disabled	In Swim	Out Swim	Tennis	Squash	Golf	Fishing	Riding	15 mins Mway*	Country House
Ilkley	Rombalds Hotel	(01943) 603201	HR	84	61%	15	50	50											
Leeds	42 The Calls	(0113) 2440099	PH	140		41	55	50											
Leeds	Haley's Hotel	(0113) 2784446	HR	112	72%	22	30	25									▲		
Leeds	Hilton National	(0113) 2442000	H	114	69%	206	400	350		▲									
Leeds	Holiday Inn Crowne Plaza	(0113) 2442200	H	142	69%	125	200	150		▲	▲								
Leeds	Leeds Marriott Hotel	(0113) 2366366	H	100	74%	244	300	300			▲								
Leeds	Merrion Thistle Hotel	(0113) 2439191	H	107	65%	109	80	80											
Leeds	Oulton Hall Hotel	(0113) 2821000	H	115	75%	152	330	260	▲		▲			▲					
Leeds	Queen's Hotel	(0113) 2431323	H	106	68%	190	600	600											
Linton	Wood Hall	(01937) 587271	HR	98	76%	43	150	110	▲		▲					▲			
Otley	Chevin Lodge	(01943) 467818	H	92	64%	52	120	130	▲	▲	▲		▲			▲			
Wakefield	Cedar Court	(01924) 276310	H	92	59%	150	400	400											
Wakefield	Forte Posthouse	(01924) 276388	H	72	64%	99	150	140											
Wakefield	Swallow Hotel	(01924) 372111	H	89	59%	64	200	180											
Wentbridge	Wentbridge House	(01977) 620444	H	75	64%	13	120	130											

England by County: Lodges

See How To Use This Guide, on pages 14-15, for an explanation of our percentage rating system, room pricing and categories.

Location	Establishment	Tel. No.	Map Ref	Motorway comments	Address
Avon					
Beckington	Forte Travelodge	(01373) 830251	14 B3	A36	Beckington Nr Bath
Bristol	Forte Travelodge	(0117) 950 1530	13 F1	M5 J17/A4018	Cribbs Causeway Bristol
Gordano	Forte Travelodge	(01275) 373709	13 F1	M5 J19 Gordano Service Area	Gordano Nr Portbury
Sedgemoor	Forte Travelodge	(01934) 750831	13 E1	M5 N'bound J22 2m N	Welcome Break Sedgemoor Weston-super-Mare
Bedfordshire					
Hockliffe	Forte Travelodge	(01525) 211177	15 E1	A5	Watling Street Hockliffe Dunstable
Marston Moretaine	Forte Travelodge	(01234) 766755	15 E1	M1 J13/A421	Beancroft Road Marston Moretaine
Toddington	Granada Lodge (Luton)	(01525) 873881	15 E1	M1 J11/12	Toddington Service Area M1 Southbnd
					Toddington Nr Dunstable
Berkshire					
Membury	Forte Travelodge	(01488) 72336	14 C2	M4 J14/15	Membury Service Area Swindon
Reading	Forte Travelodge	(01734) 750618	15 D2	M4 J11/A33 S'bound	387 Basingstoke Road Reading
Reading	Granada Lodge	(01734) 566966	15 D2	M4 J11/12	Granada Reading Service Area Burghfield
Buckinghamshire					
Milton Keynes	Travel Inn	(01908) 663388	15 E1	M1 J14/H6	Secklow Gate West Central Milton Keynes
Newport Pagnell	Forte Travelodge	(01908) 610878	15 E1	M1 J14/15	Welcome Break Newport Pagnell

Location	Establishment	Tel. No.	Map Ref	Motorway comments	Address
Cambridgeshire					
Ely	Forte Travelodge	(01353) 668499	10 B2	A10/A142	Roundabout Witchford Road Ely
Fenstanton	Forte Travelodge	(01954) 230919	15 F1	A604	Eastbound Fenstanton Nr Cambridge
Lolworth	Forte Travelodge	(01954) 781335	15 F1	M11 J14/A604	Huntingdon Road Lolworth
Peterborough	Forte Travelodge	(01733) 231109	7 E4	A1 Alwalton	Great North Road Alwalton Village Nr Peterborough
Peterborough	Travel Inn	(01733) 235794	7 E4	A1/A605	Ham Lane Orton Meadows Peterborough
Swavesey	Forte Travelodge	(01954) 789113	15 F1	A604 8m NW Cambridge	Cambridge Road Swavesey Nr Cambridge
Cheshire					
Adlington	Forte Travelodge	(01625) 875292	6 B2	A523	London Road South Adlington Stockport
Burtonwood	Forte Travelodge	(01925) 710376	6 B2	M62 J7/9	Welcome Break Service Area Burtonwood
Childer Thornton	Travel Inn (Wirral South)	0151–339 8101	6 A2	M53/A41	New Chester Road Childer Thornton South Wirral
Crewe	Forte Travelodge	(01270) 883157	6 B3	M6 J16/A500	Barthomley Nr Crewe
Knutsford	Forte Travelodge	(01565) 652187	6 B2	M6 J19/A556	Chester Road Tabley Knutsford
Manchester Airport	Travel Inn	0161–499 1944	6 B2	M56 J5	Finney Lane Heald Green Nr Stockport
Preston Brook	Travel Inn (Runcorn)	(01928) 716829	6 B2	M56 J11 & 12/A56	Chester Road Preston Brook Nr Runcorn
Runcorn	Campanile Hotel	(01928) 581771	6 A2	M56 J12/A557	Lowlands Road Runcorn
Stockport	Travel Inn	0161–480 2968	6 B2	M63 J12/A6	Buxton Road Stockport
Warrington	Travel Inn	(01582) 482224	6 B2	M62 J9/A49	Winwick Road Warrington
Cleveland					
Sedgefield	Forte Travelodge	(01740) 623399	5 E3	A1(M) J60/A177 & A689	Roundabout Sedgefield Nr Stockton-on-Tees
Stockton-on-Tees	Travel Inn	(01642) 633354	5 E3	A66/A135	Yarm Road Stockton-on-Tees
Cornwall					
Saltash	Granada Lodge	(01752) 848408	12 C3	A38	By-Pass Saltash Nr Plymouth

Cumbria

| Penrith | Forte Travelodge | (01768) 66958 | 4 C3 | M6 J40 | Redhills | Penrith |
| Southwaite | Granada Lodge (Carlisle) | (0169 74) 73131 | 4 C3 | M6 J41/42 | Southwaite | Carlisle |

Derbyshire

| Alfreton | Forte Travelodge | (01773) 520040 | 7 D3 | M1 J28/A38 & A61 | Old Swanwick Colliery Road Alfreton |
| Chesterfield | Forte Travelodge | (01246) 455411 | 6 C2 | A61 Whittington | Brimington Road North Whittington Moor Chesterfield |

Devon

Exeter	Travel Inn	(01392) 875441	13 D2	M5 J30/A379/A38	398 Topsham Road Exeter
Plymouth	Campanile Hotel	(01752) 601087	12 C3	A38	Marsh Mills Longbridge Road Plymouth
Sampford Peverell	Forte Travelodge	(01884) 821087	13 E2	M5 J27	Sampford Peverell Service Area Nr Tiverton
Sourton	Forte Travelodge	(01837) 52124	13 D2	A30/A386	Sourton Cross Nr Okehampton
Whiddon Down	Forte Travelodge	(0800) 850 950	13 D2	A30	Whiddon Down Okehampton

Dorset

| Christchurch | Travel Inn | (01202) 485376 | 14 C4 | B3059 | Somerford Road Christchurch Bournemouth |
| Ferndown | Travel Inn | (01202) 874210 | 14 C4 | A348/A31 | Ringwood Road Tricketts Cross Ferndown |

Essex

Basildon	Campanile Hotel	(01268) 530810	11 B4	M25 J29/A127	Southend Arterial Road Pipps Hill Basildon
Basildon	Travel Inn	(01268) 522227	11 B4	M25 J29	Felmores East Mayne Basildon
Brentwood	Forte Travelodge	(01277) 810819	11 B4	M25 J29/A127	East Horndon Nr Brentwood
Chelmsford	Travel Inn	(01245) 464008	11 B4	A12/A130	Chelmsford Service Area Colchester Road Springfield Chelmsford
Gants Hill	Forte Travelodge	0181-550 4248	11 B4	A12	The Beehive Beehive Lane Ilford
Ilford	Travel Inn	0181-550 6451	11 B4	A12/M11 J3	Redbridge Lane East Ilford Ilford
Old Harlow	Travel Inn	(01279) 442545	11 B4	A414/A1184	Cambridge Road Old Harlow
Thurrock	Granada Lodge	(01708) 891111	11 B5	M25 J30/31	Dartford Crossing Thurrock

Location	Establishment	Tel. No.	Map Ref	Motorway comments	Address
Gloucestershire					
Cheltenham	Travel Inn	(01242) 233847	14 B1	M5 J10/A4019	Tewkesbury Road Uckington Cheltenham
Gloucester	Travel Inn	(01452) 862521	14 B1	A417	Witcombe Nr Gloucester
Gloucester	Travel Inn (Longford)	(01452) 523519	14 B1	A38	Tewkesbury Road Longford Gloucester
Lower Wick	Forte Travelodge	(01800) 850950	13 F1	M5 J13/14	Welcome Break Lower Wick Nr Dursley
Greater Manchester					
Ashton-upon-Mersey	Travel Inn (Manchester Sth)	0161-962 8113	6 B2	M63 J6/A6144(M)	Carrington Lane Ashton-upon-Mersey Nr Sale
Manchester	Granada Lodge	0161-655 3403	6 B2	M62 J18/19	Birch Manchester
Oldham	Travel Inn (Chadderton)	0161-681 1373	6 B2	A6104/663	The Broadway Chadderton Oldham
Hampshire					
Aldershot	Travel Inn	(01582) 414341	15 E3	A323	Wellington Avenue Aldershot
Alton	Forte Travelodge	(01420) 562659	15 D3	A31 Four Marks	Four Marks Winchester Road Alton
Barton Stacey	Forte Travelodge	(01264) 720260	15 D3	A303	Barton Stacey Nr Andover
Basingstoke	Forte Travelodge	(01256) 843566	15 D3	M3 J7/A30	Winchester Road Basingstoke
Basingstoke	Travel Inn	(01256) 811477	15 D3	M3 J6/B3400	Worting Road Basingstoke
Eastleigh	Forte Travelodge	(01703) 616813	15 D3	M3 J12/A335	Twyford Road Eastleigh Nr Southampton
Emsworth	Forte Travelodge	(01243) 370877	15 D4	A27	Emsworth Nr Havant
Fleet	Forte Travelodge	(01252) 815578	15 D3	M3 J4a/5 Westbound	Fleet Service Area Hartley Wintney Basingstoke
Southampton	Travel Inn	(01703) 732262	15 D4	A3057	Romsey Road Nursling Southampton
Sutton Scotney North	Forte Travelodge	(01962) 761016	15 D3	A34 Northbound	Sutton Scotney North Nr Winchester
Sutton Scotney South	Forte Travelodge	(01962) 760779	15 D3	A34 Southbound	Sutton Scotney South Nr Winchester
Hereford & Worcester					
Droitwich Spa	Forte Travelodge	(01527) 861545	14 B1	M5 J5/A38	Rashwood Hill Droitwich
Hartlebury	Forte Travelodge	(01299) 250553	14 B1	A449	Southbound Shorthill Nurseries Hartlebury

Hereford	Travel Inn	(01432) 274853	14 A1	A49/A4103	Holmer Road Holmer Nr Hereford
Redditch	Campanile Hotel	(01527) 510710	14 C1	M42 J3/A435 & A4032	Far Moor Lane Winyates Green Redditch

Hertfordshire

Baldock	Forte Travelodge	(01462) 835329	15 E1	A1 Southbound	Great North Road Hinxworth Nr Baldock
Hemel Hempstead	Travel Inn	(01442) 879149	15 E2	A41/M25 J20	Stoney Lane Bourne End Nr Hemel Hempstead
Rushden	Forte Travelodge	(01933) 57008	15 E1	A45 Eastbound	Saunders Lodge Rushden
South Mimms	Forte Travelodge	(01707) 665440	15 E2	M25 J23	South Mimms Service Area Bignells Corner South Mimms Nr Potters Bar
Stevenage	Travel Inn	(01438) 351318	15 E1	A1(M) J8/A602	Corey's Mill Lane Stevenage
Tring	Travel Inn	(01442) 824819	15 E2	A41	Tring Hill Tring

Humberside

Hull	Campanile Hotel	(01482) 525530	7 E1	A63 City Centre	Beverley Road Beverley Road Freetown Way Hull
Hull	Travel Inn	(01482) 645285	7 E1	A63	Ferriby Road Hessle Hull
South Cave	Forte Travelodge	(01430) 424455	7 E1	M62 J38/A63	Eastbound Beacon Services South Cave Hull

Kent

Ashford	Travel Inn	(01233) 712571	11 C5	A20/M20 J9	Maidstone Road Hothfield Common Ashford
Dartford	Campanile Hotel	(01322) 278925	11 B5	M25 J1a	Clipper Boulevard West Edisons Park Crossways Dartford
Dover	Travel Inn	(01304) 213339	11 D5	A20/B2011	Folkestone Road Dover
Folkestone	Travel Inn	(01303) 273620	11 C5	M20 J13	Cherry Garden Lane Folkestone
Gate	Forte Travelodge	(0800) 850950	11 C5	A2 Services	Dunkirk Nr Canterbury
Maidstone	Travel Inn	(01622) 752515	11 B5	M20 J5	London Road Maidstone
Wrotham Heath	Travel Inn (Sevenoaks)	(01732) 884214	11 B5	M26 J2a/A20	London Road Wrotham Heath Nr Sevenoaks

Lancashire

Burnley	Forte Travelodge	(01282) 416039	6 B1	M65 J10/A671 & A679	Cavalry Barracks Barracks Road Burnley

Location	Establishment	Tel. No.	Map Ref	Motorway comments	Address
Charnock Richard	Forte Travelodge	(01257) 791746	6 B1	M6 J27/28 N'bound	Welcome Break Mill Lane Charnock Richard
Preston	Travel Inn (Lea)	(01772) 720476	6 B1	A583	Blackpool Road Lea Preston
Leicestershire					
Leicester	Granada Lodge	(01530) 244237	7 D4	M1 J22/A50	Markfield Leicester
Leicester East	Travel Inn Leicester	(0116) 2394677	7 D4	M1 J21/A563/A47	Forest Park Hinckley Road Leicester Forest
Morcott	Forte Travelodge	(01572) 87719	7 E4	A47 E'bound	Glaston Road Morcott Nr Uppingham
Thrussington	Forte Travelodge	(01664) 424525	7 D3	A46 S'bound	Thrussington Green Acres Filling Stations
Lincolnshire					
Colsterworth	Forte Travelodge	(01476) 861181	7 E3	A1/A151	Southbound Colsterworth Nr Grantham
Colsterworth	Granada Lodge	(01476) 860686	7 E3	A1/A151	Colsterworth Grantham
Grantham	Forte Travelodge	(01476) 77500	7 E3	A1 Services	Grantham Service Area Gonerby Moor Grantham
Lincoln	Travel Inn	(01522) 525216	7 E2	B1131/B1188	Lincoln Road Canwick Hill Lincoln
Sleaford	Forte Travelodge	(01529) 414752	7 E3	A17/A15	Holdingham Sleaford
South Witham	Forte Travelodge	(01572) 767586	7 E3	A1 N'bound	New Fox South Witham Nr Colsterworth
Merseyside					
Bebington	Forte Travelodge	0151-327 2489	6 A2	M53 J5/A41 N'bound	Northbound Bebington New Chester Road Eastham Wirral
Bromborough	Travel Inn (Wirral)	0151-334 2917	6 A2	A41/M53 J5	High Street Bromborough Cross Wirral
Gayton	Travel Inn (Wirral Nth)	0151-342 1982	6 A2	M53 J4/A5137	Chester Road Gayton Wirral
Haydock	Forte Travelodge	(01942) 272055	6 B2	M6 J23/A580 W'bound	Piele Road Haydock St Helens
Liverpool	Campanile Hotel	0151-709 8104	6 A2	Queen's Dock	Chaloner Street Queen's Dock Liverpool
Liverpool	Travel Inn (W. Derby)	0151-228 4724	6 A2	A5058	Queens Drive West Derby Liverpool
Tarbock (Liverpool)	Travel Inn	0151-480 9614	6 A2	M62 (A5080)/M57	Wilson Road Tarbock Nr Liverpool

Middlesex

Hayes	Travel Inn (Heathrow)	0181-573 7479	15 E2	M4 J3/A4020	362 Uxbridge Road Hayes
Heathrow Airport	Granada Lodge (Heston)	0181-574 5875	15 E2	M4 J2/3	Heston
Kenton	Travel Inn	0181-907 1671	15 E2	A4006	Kenton Road Kenton

Norfolk

Acle	Forte Travelodge	(01493) 751970	10 D1	A47	Acle Bypass Acle
Long Sutton	Forte Travelodge	(01406) 362230	10 B1	A17	Wisbech Road Long Sutton Nr Spalding
Norwich	Forte Travelodge	(01603) 57549	10 C1	A11/A47	Interchange Norwich Southern By-Pass
Norwich					

Northamptonshire

Desborough	Forte Travelodge	(01536) 762034	7 D4	A6 S'bound/A14	Southbound Harborough Road Desborough
Kettering	Forte Travelodge	(0800) 850950	7 E4	A14	Kettering
Kettering	Travel Inn	(01563) 310082	7 E4	A14 J7	Rothwell Road Kettering
Northampton	Forte Travelodge	(01604) 758395	15 D1	M1 J15a/A45	Upton Way Northampton
Northampton	Travel Inn	(01604) 832340	15 D1	M1 J16/A45	Harpole Turn Weedon Road Harpole
Thrapston	Forte Travelodge	(01832) 735199	7 E4	A14	Lnk Road Thrapston By-Pass Thrapston
Towcester	Forte Travelodge	(01327) 359105	15 D1	A43 (M1 J15a)	East Towcester By-Pass Towcester

Nottinghamshire

Blyth	Forte Travelodge	(01909) 591775	7 D2	A1 S'bound	Blyth Nr Worksop
Blyth	Granada Lodge	(01909) 591836	7 D2	A1(M)/A614	Blyth Nr Worksop
Newark	Forte Travelodge	(01636) 703635	7 D3	A1 S'bound	North Muskham Newark
Nottingham	Travel Inn	(01582) 414341	7 D3	M1 J26/A610	Phoenix Park Babbington Nottingham
Retford	Forte Travelodge	(01777) 838091	7 D2	A1 N'bound	Markham Moor Nr Retford
Worksop	Forte Travelodge	(01909) 501528	7 D2	A57/A60	St Anne's Drive Dukeries Mill Worksop

Location	Establishment	Tel. No.	Map Ref	Motorway comments	Address
Oxfordshire					
Ardley	Granada Lodge	(01869) 346111	15 D1	M40 J10	Cherwell Valley Services Northampton Road Ardley Nr Bicester
Burford	Forte Travelodge	(01993) 822699	14 C2	A40	Berry Barn Burford
Oxford	Travel Inn	(01582) 414341	15 D2	A4142	Arlington Business Park Cowley Oxford
Thame	Forte Travelodge	(0800) 850 950	15 D2	M40 J7/8 A418	Thame
Wheatley	Forte Travelodge	(01865) 875705	15 D2	M40 J8/A418	London Road Wheatley Nr Oxford
Shropshire					
Ludlow	Forte Travelodge	(01584) 711695	6 B4	A49/A456 & B4362	Woofferton Ludlow
Oswestry	Forte Travelodge	(01691) 658178	8 D2	A5/A483	Mile End Service Area Oswestry
Shrewsbury	Forte Travelodge	(0800) 850950	6 A3	A5/A49	Bayston Hill Nr Shrewsbury
Telford	Forte Travelodge	(01952) 251244	6 B3	M54 J6/A5223/A442 & B5063	Admaston Road Shawbirch Crossroads Telford
Somerset					
Ilminster	Forte Travelodge	(01460) 53748	13 E2	A303	Southfield Roundabout Horton Cross Ilminster
Podimore	Forte Travelodge	(01935) 840074	13 F2	A303/A37	Podimore Nr Yeovil
Taunton	Travel Inn	(01823) 321112	13 E2	M5 J25	81 Bridgwater Road Taunton
Staffordshire					
Barton-under-Needwood	Forte Travelodge (N)	(01283) 716343	6 C3	A38 N'bound	Northbound Barton-under-Needwood
Barton-under-Needwood	Forte Travelodge (S)	(01283) 716784	6 C3	A38 S'bound	Southbound Barton-under-Needwood
Cannock	Travel Inn	(01543) 572721	6 C3	M6 J11 or J12/A5/A460	Watling Street Cannock
Rugeley	Forte Travelodge	(01889) 570096	6 C3	M6 J13/14 or J11 N'bound	A51/B5013 Western Springs Road Rugeley
Talke	Forte Travelodge (Stoke)	(01782) 777000	6 B3	M6 J16 A500/A34	Newcastle Road Talke Stoke-on-Trent
Tamworth	Granada Lodge	(01827) 260123	6 C4	M42 J10/A5	Tamworth
Tamworth	Travel Inn	(01827) 54414	6 C4	M42 J9/A446/A4091	Bitterscote Bonehill Road Tamworth
Uttoxeter	Forte Travelodge	(01889) 562043	6 C3	A50/B5030	Ashbourne Road Uttoxeter

Location	Establishment	Tel. No.	Map Ref	Motorway comments	Address
Suffolk					
Barton Mills	Forte Travelodge	(01638) 717675	10 B2	A11	Barton Mills Mildenhall
Beacon Hill	Forte Travelodge	(01449) 721640	10 C3	A14/A140	Needham Market Beacon Hill Nr Ipswich
Capel St Mary	Forte Travelodge	(0800) 850950	10 C3	A12	Capel St Mary Ipswich
Stowmarket	Forte Travelodge	(01449) 615347	10 C3	A14 W'bound	Stowmarket
Surrey					
Chessington	Travel Inn	(01372) 744060	15 E3	M25 J9/A243	Leatherhead Road Chessington
Croydon	Travel Inn	0181-686 2030	11 B5	M25 J7/M23/A23/A235	Coombe Road Croydon
Dorking	Forte Travelodge	(01306) 740361	15 E3	A25	Reigate Road Dorking
Guildford	Travel Inn	(01483) 304932	15 E3	A3/A25	Stoke Road . Guildford
Morden	Forte Travelodge	0181-640 8227	15 E2	A24	Epsom Road Morden
East Sussex					
Hellingly	Forte Travelodge	(01323) 844556	11 B6	A22	Boship Roundabout Hellingly Nr Hailsham
West Sussex					
Billingshurst	Forte Travelodge	(01403) 782711	11 A6	A29 N'bound	Five Oaks Billingshurst
Fontwell	Forte Travelodge	(01243) 543973	11 A6	A27/A29	Fontwell
Gatwick Airport	Forte Travelodge	(01293) 533441	15 E3	M23 J10	Church Road Lowfield Heath Crawley
Gatwick Airport	Travel Inn Crawley	(01293) 568158	15 E3	M23/North Terminal	North Terminal Longbridge Way Gatwick
Hickstead	Forte Travelodge	(01444) 881377	11 B6	A23	Hickstead
Horsham	Travel Inn	(01403) 250141	11 A6	M23 J11/A264	57 North Street Horsham
Rustington	Forte Travelodge	(01903) 733150	11 A6	A259	Worthing Road Rustington Littlehampton
Tyne & Wear					
Gateshead	Forte Travelodge	0191-438 3333	5 E2	A194(M)/A184	Leam Lane Wardley Whitemare Pool
Washington	Campanile Hotel	0191-416 5010	5 E2	A1(M)/A1231 & A195	Emerson Road Washington Nr Newcastle
Washington	Granada Lodge	0191-410 0076	5 E2	A1(M) S'bound/A195	Washington Nr Newcastle-

Location	Lodge	Phone	Map	Road	Address
Washington	Travel Inn (Sunderland)	0191-548 9384	5 E2	A1231/A19	Wessington Way Washington Nr Sunderland

Warwickshire

Location	Lodge	Phone	Map	Road	Address
Hockley Heath	Travel Inn (Solihull)	0121-744 2942	6 C4	M42 J4/A3400	Stratford Road Hockley Heath Shirley
Nuneaton	Travel Inn	(01203) 343584	6 C4	M6 J3/A444	Coventry Road Nuneaton
Nuneaton/Bedworth	Forte Travelodge	(01203) 382541	6 C4	M6 J3/A444	Bedworth Nuneaton Coventry
Nuneaton/Hinckley	Forte Travelodge	(01800) 850950	6 C4	M69 J1/A5	Yeoman St Nicholas Park Drive Nuneaton
Warwick	Forte Travelodge	(01926) 651681	14 C1	M40 J12 N'bound	Motorway Banbury Road Ashorne

West Midlands

Location	Lodge	Phone	Map	Road	Address
Birmingham	Campanile Hotel	0121-622 4925	6 C4	City Centre	Irving Street Lee Bank Birmingham
Birmingham	Granada Lodge	0121-550 3261	6 C4	M5 J3/4	Frankley Nr Birmingham
Birmingham	Travel Inn	0121-633 4820	6 C4	City Centre	20 Bridge Street Birmingham
Coventry	Travel Inn	(01203) 636585	6 C4	M6 J2/A46	Rugby Road Binley Woods Coventry
Coventry (North)	Campanile Hotel	(01203) 622311	6 C4	M6 J2/A4600	Wigston Road Walsgrave Coventry
Coventry (South)	Campanile Hotel	(01203) 639922	6 C4	A46/A45 & A423	Abbey Road Whitley Coventry
Dudley	Forte Travelodge	(01384) 481579	6 B4	A461	Dudley Road Dudley
Dunchurch	Forte Travelodge	(01788) 521528	7 D4	M45/A45 W'bound	London Road Thurlaston Dunchurch Hagley
Travel Inn		(01562) 883120	6 B4	M5 J3/A456 Birmingham Road	Hagley Nr Stourbridge
Oldbury	Forte Travelodge	0121-552 2967	6 C4	M5 J2/A4123 N'bound	Wolverhampton Road Oldbury Warly
Solihull	Travel Inn (Shirley)	0121-744 2942	6 C4	M42 J4/A34	Stratford Road Shirley Solihull
Sutton Coldfield	Forte Travelodge	0121-355 0017	6 C4	M6 J5 & J6	Boldmere Road Sutton Coldfield

Wiltshire

Location	Lodge	Phone	Map	Road	Address
Amesbury	Forte Travelodge	(01980) 624966	14 C3	A345/A303	Amesbury
Chippenham	Granada Lodge (Leigh Delamere)	(01666) 837097	14 B2	M4 J17/18	Leigh Delamere Chippenham
Warminster	Granada Lodge	(01985) 219639	14 B3	A36/A350	Warminster

Location	Establishment	Tel. No.	Map Ref	Motorway comments	Address
North Yorkshire					
Bilbrough	Travel Inn (York)	(01937) 835067	7 D1	A64	Bilbrough Colton Nr York
Scotch Corner	Forte Travelodge	(01748) 823768	5 D3	A1 N'bound	Scotch Corner Skeeby Nr Richmond
Skipton	Forte Travelodge	(01756) 798091	6 C1	A65/A59	Roundabout Gargrave Road Skipton
Tadcaster	Forte Travelodge	(01973) 531823	7 D1	A64 E'bound	Eastbound Tadcaster Nr York
South Yorkshire					
Barnsley	Forte Travelodge	(01226) 298799	6 C2	A633/A635	520 Doncaster Road Barnsley
Carcroft	Forte Travelodge	(01302) 330841	7 D2	A1 N'bound	Great North Road Carcroft Nr Doncaster
Doncaster	Campanile Hotel	(01302) 370770	7 D2	M18 J3/A1(M) J2	off A638Doncaster Leisure Park Bawtry
Doncaster					
Rotherham	Campanile Hotel	(01709) 700255	7 D2	M18 J1 past M1 J32	Lowton Way off Denby Way Hellaby
Industrial Estate	Rotherham				
Rotherham	Travel Inn	(01709) 543216	7 D2	A631/M18 J1 or M1 J33	Bawtry Road Rotherham
Sheffield	Forte Travelodge	(01142) 530935	6 C2	M1 J33/A630	340 Prince of Wales Road Sheffield
Sheffield	Travel Inn	(01582) 414341	6 C2	M1 J34/Sheffield Arena	Attercliffe Common Road Sheffield
West Yorkshire					
Ferrybridge	Granada Lodge	(01977) 670488	7 D1	M62 J33/A1	Ferrybridge Nr Pontefract
Hartshead Moor	Forte Travelodge	(01274) 851706	6 C1	M62 J25/26	Hartshead Moor Service Area Clifton Brighouse
Wakefield	Campanile Hotel	(01924) 201054	6 C1	M1 J39/A636	Monckton Road Wakefield
Wakefield	Granada Lodge	(01924) 830569	6 C1	M1 J38/39	Woolley Edge Wakefield
Wakefield	Travel Inn	(01924) 367901	6 C1	M1 J39/A636	Holmfield House Thornes Park Denby Dale Wakefield
Wentbridge	Forte Travelodge	(01977) 620711	7 D1	A1(M) J38/M62 J33	Barnsdale Bar Southbound Services Wentbridge

England by County: Restaurants

See How To Use This Guide, on pages 14-15, for an explanation of our percentage rating system, room pricing and categories.
No-smoking denotes a ban on smoking throughout or a separate no-smoking room.

Location	Establishment	Tel. No.	Dinner for 2, £	Category	Stars	Seats	Parties	Private Rms	Sundays	No-Smoking	Open Air	Nat Cuisine	Seafood	Vegetarian	Dessert	Cheese	O/s Wine	New World	Italian Wine	Wines by glass
Avon																				
Bath	Bath Spa Hotel	(01225) 444424	90	HR	↑	120	12	yes	All	yes	yes		◄	◄	◄	◄		◄	◄	◄
Bath	Clos du Roy	(01225) 444450	65	R		85	100		All	yes						◄		◄	◄	◄
Bath	Garlands	(01225) 442283	60	R		20	12	yes	All	yes		French								
Bath	Hole in the Wall	(01225) 425242	70	R	↑	70	18			yes								◄		◄
Bath	The New Moon	(01225) 444407	50	R		70			All	yes					◄			◄		◄
Bath	Priory Hotel	(01225) 331922	85	HR		60	12	yes	All	yes	yes					◄		◄		◄
Bath	Queensberry Hotel	(01225) 447928	55	HR		50	18	yes	All	yes	yes			◄	◄	◄	◄	◄		
Bath	Royal Crescent Hotel	(01225) 319090	95	HR	★↑	60	8	yes	All			British		◄			◄	◄		◄
Bristol	Blue Goose	(0117) 9420940	45	R		70	40					British					◄			
Bristol	Harveys Restaurant	(0117) 9275034	80	R		120	14	yes				British			◄	◄	◄	◄	◄	
Bristol	Howard's	(0117) 9262921	50	R		65	18	yes		yes						◄		◄		
Bristol	Hunt's	(0117) 9265580	65	R		40	10	yes						◄						
Bristol	Jameson's	(0117) 9276565	50	R		70	80	yes	L											
Bristol	Restaurant Lettonie	(0117) 9686456	80	R		24	24					French						◄		
Bristol	Markwicks	(0117) 9262658	65	R		28	8	yes								◄		◄	◄	

Location	Name	Phone		Type							Cuisine
Bristol	Michael's	(0117) 927 6190	60	R	55		yes	L			
Bristol	Rajdoot	(0117) 9268033	40	R	60	30		D			Indian
Bristol	Swallow Royal Hotel	(0117) 9255100	70	HR	60	8					
Chelwood	Chelwood House	(01761) 490730	50	HR	30	14	yes	All	yes		German
Freshford	Homewood Park	(01225) 723731	90	HR	60	26	yes	All	yes	yes	
Hunstrete	Hunstrete House	(01761) 490490	100	HR ↑	50	9	yes	All	yes	yes	
Ston Easton	Ston Easton Park	(01761) 241631	95	HR ↑	40	8	yes	All	yes	yes	

Bedfordshire

Location	Name	Phone		Type							Cuisine
Flitwick	Flitwick Manor	(01525) 712242	100	HR	40	8	yes	All	yes	yes	
Woburn	Paris House	(01525) 290692	90	R	44	21	yes	L	yes	yes	

Berkshire

Location	Name	Phone		Type							Cuisine
Ascot	Hyn's	(01344) 872583	50	R	90	12	yes	All			Chinese
Bracknell	Coppid Beech	(01334) 303333	70	HR	120	25	yes	All	yes		
Bray	Waterside Inn	(01628) 20691	130	RR	★★★ 75	10	yes	All	yes		French
Eton	Eton Wine Bar	(01753) 854921	55	R	100			All			
Goring	Leatherne Bottel	(01491) 872667	70	R ↑	50	6	yes	All	yes		
Highclere	The Yew Tree	(01635) 253360	50	R	60	24	yes	All			
Kintbury	Dundas Arms	(01488) 658263	65	IR	36	50		All	yes		
Maidenhead	Fredrick's	(01628) 35934	100	HR	60	20	yes	All			
Old Burghclere	Dew Pond	(01635) 278408	70	R	44	22	yes		yes		
Shinfield	L'Ortolan	(01734) 883783	140	R	★★★ 60	10	yes	L	yes		French
Streatley	Swan Diplomat	(01491) 873737	85	HR	75	75	yes	All			
Taplow	Cliveden	(01628) 668561	140	HR	65	12	yes	All	yes		
Taplow	Cliveden: Waldo's	(01628) 668561	120	R ★	26	4	yes	All	yes		
Windsor	Oakley Court	(01628) 74141	100	HR	70	12	yes	All			
Windsor	Oakley Court: Boaters	(01628) 74141	50	R	30	12			yes		
Woolton Hill	Hollington House	(01635) 255100	90	HR	50	22	yes	All	yes	yes	

Buckinghamshire

Location	Establishment	Tel. No.	Dinner for 2, £	Category	Stars	Seats	Parties	Private Rms	Sundays	No-Smoking	Open Air	Nat Cuisine	Seafood	Vegetarian	Dessert	Cheese	O/s Wine	New World	Italian Wine	Wines by glass
Aston Clinton	The Bell Inn	(01296) 630252	100	HR	↑	150	40	yes	All	yes	yes				◄	◄	◄	◄	◄	◄
Aylesbury	Hartwell House	(01296) 747444	100	HR		70	8	yes	All	yes	yes				◄	◄	◄	◄	◄	◄
Long Crendon	The Angel	(01844) 208268	50	R		70		yes		yes	yes		◄				◄	◄		◄
Marlow	Compleat Angler	(01628) 484444	125	HR		96	20	yes	All	yes							◄	◄		◄
Medmenham	Danesfield House	(01628) 891010	100	HR		4	10	yes	All	yes								◄		
Old Amersham	Gilbey's	(01494) 727242	55	R		50	8	yes		yes										◄

Cambridgeshire

Location	Establishment	Tel. No.	Dinner for 2, £	Category	Stars	Seats	Parties	Private Rms	Sundays	No-Smoking	Open Air	Nat Cuisine	Seafood	Vegetarian	Dessert	Cheese	O/s Wine	New World	Italian Wine	Wines by glass
Cambridge	Charlie Chan	(01223) 359336	45	R		160	100		All			Chinese								
Cambridge	Regent Hotel	(01223) 351470	35	HR		55						Italian							◄	
Cambridge	22 Chesterton Road	(01223) 351880	55	R		30	30	yes		yes	yes				◄					
Duxford	Duxford Lodge	(01223) 836444	50	HR		46	22	yes	All	yes	yes							◄		
Elton	Loch Fyne Oyster Bar	(01832) 280298	40	R		80			All	yes	yes		◄							
Ely	Old Fire Engine House	(01353) 662582	50	R		36	22	yes	L	yes	yes				◄					
Huntingdon	Old Bridge Hotel	(01480) 452681	80	HR		44	14	yes	All	yes	yes				◄	◄	◄	◄		◄
Keyston	Pheasant Inn	(01832) 710241	50	R	↑	100	12	yes	All	yes	yes				◄	◄	◄	◄		◄
Madingley	Three Horseshoes	(01954) 210221	65	R		94	10	yes	All	yes	yes									◄
Stilton	Bell Inn	(01733) 241066	45	IR		30	22	yes	All	yes				◄			◄	◄	◄	
Wansford	The Haycock	(01780) 782223	75	HR		90	12	yes	All	yes		British							◄	◄

Cheshire

Location	Establishment	Tel. No.	Dinner for 2, £	Category	Stars	Seats	Parties	Private Rms	Sundays	No-Smoking	Open Air	Nat Cuisine	Seafood	Vegetarian	Dessert	Cheese	O/s Wine	New World	Italian Wine	Wines by glass
Alderley Edge	Alderley Edge Hotel	(01625) 583033	90	HR		80	22	yes	All	yes	yes			◄	◄	◄	◄	◄	◄	
Altrincham	Francs	0161-941 1842	45	R		90	25	yes	L	yes	yes	French					◄			
Bollington	Mauro's	(01625) 573898	60	R		49	12					Italian						◄	◄	

Location	Restaurant	Phone		Type	★						Cuisine
Chester	Chester Grosvenor	(01244) 324024	110	HR	★	45	16	L			
Chester	Chester Grosvenor:										
	La Brasserie	(01244) 324024	50	R		100	20				
Handforth	Belfry Hotel	0161-437 0511	88	HR		120	30	All	yes		
Handforth	Handforth Chinese	(01625) 531670	45	R		80	18	D			Chinese
Knutsford	Brasserie Belle Epoque	(01565) 633060	60	RR		80	14		yes		
Nantwich	Churche's Mansion	(01270) 625933	70	R		50		L	yes	yes	
Nantwich	Rookery Hall	(01270) 610016	85	HR		30	8	All	yes	yes	
Northwich	Nunsmere Hall	(01606) 889100	70	HR		48	10	All	yes	yes	
Prestbury	White House Manor	(01625) 829376	65	HR		70	12		yes	yes	French
Puddington	Craxton Wood	0151-339 4717	70	HR		85	20		yes		
Wilmslow	Harry's	(01625) 528799		R		80	18	D	yes		
Wilmslow	Stanneylands	(01625) 525225	80	HR		80	15	L	yes		Chinese

Cornwall

Location	Restaurant	Phone		Type	★						
Calstock	Danescombe Valley	(01822) 832414	70	HR		12	8	D	yes		
Falmouth	The Pipe		50	R		45	8				
Falmouth	Seafood Bar	(01326) 315129	45	R		26	14	D	yes		
Helford	Riverside	(01326) 231443	80	RR		32	6	All			
Liskeard	Well House	(01579) 342001	65	HR		32	28	All		yes	
Mawnan Smith	Nansidwell	(01326) 250340	66	HR		45	18	All			
Mylor Bridge	Pandora Inn	(01326) 372678	50	R		46	52		yes	yes	
Padstow	St Petroc's House	(01841) 532700		HR		38					
Padstow	The Seafood Restaurant	(01841) 532485	80	RR	★ †	70	18				
Penzance	Abbey Hotel	(01736) 66906	60	HR		18	12	D			
Penzance	Harris's	(01736) 64408	70	R		40	12		yes		
Polperro	Kitchen at Polperro	(01503) 72780	55	R		24	4	D			
St Ives	Pig'n'Fish	(01736) 794204	45	R		30	12				
St Mawes	Idle Rocks Hotel	(01326) 270771	65	HR		65	20	All	yes	yes	

Location	Establishment	Tel. No.	Dinner for 2, £	Category	Stars	Seats	Parties	Private Rms	Sundays	No-Smoking	Open Air	Nat Cuisine	Seafood	Vegetarian	Dessert	Cheese	O/s Wine	New World	Italian Wine	Wines by glass
Tintagel	Trebrea Lodge	(01840) 770410	40	HR		14	12		D	yes							▲		▲		
Veryan	Nare Hotel	(01872) 501279	70	HR		70	12	yes	All			British					▲	▲	▲	▲	
Cumbria																				
Alston	Lovelady Shield	(01434) 381203	60	HR		40	10			yes							▲		▲		
Ambleside	Rothay Manor	(0153 94) 33605	70	HR		70	14	yes	L	yes							▲	▲	▲	▲	
Ambleside	Wateredge Hotel	(0153 94) 32332	80	HR		50	12		L	yes	yes										
Appleby-in-Westmorland	Appleby Manor	(0176 83) 51571	55	HR		70	30		All	yes		British					▲				
Applethwaite	Underscar Manor	(017687) 75000	65	HR		55	10	yes	All	yes	yes					▲	▲				
Bowness-on-Windermere	Gilpin Lodge	(015394) 88818	60	HR		45	24	yes	All	yes	yes			▲	▲	▲	▲	▲	▲	▲	▲
Bowness-on-Windermere	Linthwaite House	(015394) 88600	68	HR		48	22	yes	All	yes							▲		▲		
Brampton	Farlam Hall	(0169 77) 46234	60	HR		40	30		D								▲		▲		
Cartmel	Uplands	(01539) 536248	65	RR		30	12		All	yes											
Cockermouth	Quince & Medlar	(01900) 823579	30	R		26	14		D	yes				▲			▲				
Crosby-on-Eden	Crosby Lodge	(01228) 573618	65	HR		50	40	yes	All	yes							▲				
Grasmere	Michael's Nook	(015394) 35496	100	HR	★↑	32	10	yes	All	yes						▲	▲	▲	▲		
Grasmere	White Moss House	(015394) 35295	60	HR		20				yes							▲	▲	▲	▲	▲
Grasmere	Wordsworth Hotel	(0153 94) 35592	75	HR		65	12	yes	All	yes						▲	▲	▲	▲	▲	
Kendal	The Moon	(01539) 729254	35	R		38	22	yes	D	yes	yes			▲	▲					

Location	Name	Phone	Price	Type	Rating	Seats	Rooms	Meals	Cards	Lunch	Dinner	Cuisine
Lowick Bridge	Bridgefield House	(01229) 885239	60	HR		24	10		D		yes	
Melmerby	Village Bakery	(01768) 881515	30	R		45	8		L	yes	yes	
Ullswater	Leeming House	(0176 84) 86622	80	HR		80	10	yes	All	yes	yes	
Ullswater	Old Church Hotel	(0176 84) 86204	60	HR		24	6		D		yes	British
Ullswater	Rampsbeck	(0176 84) 86442	55	HR		40	12	yes	All	yes	yes	
Ullswater	Sharrow Bay	(017684) 86301	95	HR	★	65	10		All	yes	yes	British
Ulverston	Bay Horse Inn	(01229) 583972	65	RR		50	30	yes	All	yes	yes	British
Windermere	Holbeck Ghyll	(015394) 32375	55	HR		36	12	yes	D	yes	yes	
Windermere	Roger's Restaurant	(015394) 44954	55	R		22	12	yes	D			
Witherslack	Old Vicarage	(015395) 52381	60	HR		40	10	yes	D	yes	yes	

Derbyshire

Location	Name	Phone	Price	Type	Rating	Seats	Rooms	Meals	Cards	Lunch	Dinner	Cuisine
Ashford-in-the-Water	Riverside	(01629) 814275	75	HR		50	18	yes	All	yes	yes	
Baslow	Cavendish Hotel	(01246) 582311	75	HR		50	50	yes	All	yes		
Baslow	Fischer's Baslow Hall	(01246) 583259	95	RR	★★	40	17	yes	L	yes	yes	
Hayfield	Bridge End	(01663) 747321	65	RR		50	12	yes	L			
Matlock	Riber Hall	(01629) 582795	66	HR		50	24	yes	All	yes		
Ridgeway	Old Vicarage	(0114) 2475814	90	R	★★	50	12	yes	L		yes	

Devon

Location	Name	Phone	Price	Type	Rating	Seats	Rooms	Meals	Cards	Lunch	Dinner	Cuisine
Barnstaple	Lynwood House	(01271) 43695	70	RR		60	60	yes		yes	yes	
Bishop's Tawton	Halmpstone Manor	(01271) 830321	75	HR		24	16	yes		yes		
Braunton	Otters	(01271) 813633	50	R		40	14	yes				
Broadhembury	Drewe Arms	(01404) 841267	50	R		30	9		L		yes	
Chagford	Gidleigh Park	(01647) 432367	120	HR	★	40	8	yes	All	yes	yes	
Dartmouth	Carved Angel	(01803) 832465	110	R	★★	45	16	yes	L		yes	
East Buckland	Lower Pitt	(01598) 760243	50	RR		32	16	yes	L		yes	
Exeter	Buckerell Lodge	(01392) 52451	62	HR		60		yes		yes	yes	

Location	Establishment	Tel. No.	Dinner for 2, £	Category	Stars	Seats	Parties	Private Rms	Sundays	No-Smoking	Open Air	Nat Cuisine	Seafood	Vegetarian	Dessert	Cheese	O/s Wine	New World	Italian Wine	Wines by glass
Exeter	St Olaves Court	(01392) 217736	90	HR		45	24	yes			yes				◄			◄		◄
Gulworthy	The Horn of Plenty	(01822) 832528	100	RR	★	50	20	yes	All	yes	yes				◄	◄		◄		◄
Huntsham	Huntsham Court	(01398) 361365	75	HR		30	32	yes	D	yes										
Ide	Old Mill	(01392) 59480	55	R		40	22	yes												
Lewdown	Lewtrenchard Manor	(01566) 783256	75	HR		35	8	yes	All	yes	yes					◄		◄		◄
Lifton	Arundell Arms	(01566) 784666	75	HR		70		yes	All	yes	yes					◄		◄		◄
Lympstone	River House	(01395) 265147	80	RR		34	18	yes	All	yes	yes		◄							◄
Plymouth	Chez Nous	(01752) 266793	80	R		28						French			◄					
Poundsgate	Leusdon Lodge	(01364) 631304	90	HR		18	12			yes					◄	◄				
Salcombe	Soar Mill Cove	(01548) 561566	78	HR		40				yes	yes				◄	◄				◄
Salcombe	Spinnakers	(01548) 843408	50	R		60	14	yes	L	yes	yes		◄							
South Molton	Whitechapel Manor	(01769) 573377	80	HR		24	24	yes	All	yes						◄		◄		◄
Torquay	Table Restaurant	(01803) 324292	70	R	↑	20	20	yes	D	yes						◄		◄		
Tuckenhay	Floyd's Inn (Sometimes)	(01803) 732350	100	IR		26	6		L		yes					◄		◄		◄
Whimple	Woodhayes Hotel	(01404) 822237	65	HR		16	8		D			British								
Winkleigh	Pophams	(01837) 83767	30	R		10	10			yes										

Dorset

Location	Establishment	Tel. No.	Dinner for 2, £	Category	Stars	Seats	Parties	Private Rms	Sundays	No-Smoking	Open Air	Nat Cuisine	Seafood	Vegetarian	Dessert	Cheese	O/s Wine	New World	Italian Wine	Wines by glass
Bournemouth	De Vere Royal Bath	(01202) 555555	60	HR		300	12	yes	All											
Bournemouth	Ocean Palace	(01202) 559127	45	R		150		yes	All			Chinese								
Bridport	Riverside Restaurant	(01308) 422011	40	R		70	12		L	yes			◄							◄
Chedington	Chedington Court	(01935) 891265	65	HR		26	8	yes	D	yes						◄	◄	◄		
Christchurch	Splinters	(01202) 483454	55	R	↑	40	10	yes		yes		French				◄				

Town	Restaurant	Phone		Code							Cuisine
Dorchester	Mock Turtle	(01305) 264011	54	R	55	16					
Evershot	Summer Lodge	(01935) 83424	100	HR	50	20	yes	All	yes	yes	
Gillingham	Stock Hill House	(01747) 823626	80	HR ★†	30	12	yes	All	yes		
L.B'ampton Maiden	Yalbury Cottage	(01305) 262382	50	IR	26		yes	L			
Newton	Le Petit Canard	(01300) 320536	55	R	28	16					
Poole	Haven Hotel:										
Poole	La Roche	(01202) 707333	80	R	26	12	yes		yes		
Poole	Haven Hotel	(01202) 707333	55	HR	150	24	yes	All	yes		
Poole	Mansion House	(01202) 685666	65	HR	40	12	yes	L	yes		
Powerstock	Three Horseshoes	(01308) 485328	50	RR	60		yes	All	yes	yes	
Sturminster											
Newton	Plumber Manor	(01258) 472507	55	RR	60	40	yes	All	yes		
Wareham	Priory Hotel	(01929) 551666	75	HR	66	20	yes	All	yes	yes	
Weymouth	Perry's	(01305) 785799	60	R	54	50	yes	All	yes		
Wimborne	Les Bouviers	(01202) 889555	60	R	50	24	yes	L	yes		

Durham

Town	Restaurant	Phone		Code							Cuisine
Coatham											
Mundeville	Hall Garth Hotel	(01325) 300400	60	HR	80	12	yes	L	yes		
Darlington	Sardis	(01325) 461222	50	R	75	25	yes				Italian
Darlington	Victor's	(01325) 480818	55	R	30	30					
Romaldkirk	Rose and Crown	(01833) 650213	65	IR	24	12		L			

Essex

Town	Restaurant	Phone		Code							Cuisine
Broxted	Whitehall	(01279) 850603	80	HR	40	18	yes	All	yes		
Castle											
Hedingham	Rumbles Castle	(01787) 461490	55	R			yes		yes		
Coggeshall	White Hart	(01376) 561654	60	HR	70	20	yes	L	yes		Italian
Colchester	Warehouse Brasserie	(01206) 765656	50	R	90	30	yes	D	yes		

Location	Establishment	Tel. No.	Dinner for 2, £	Category	Stars	Seats	Parties	Private Rms	Sundays	No-Smoking	Open Air	Nat Cuisine	Seafood	Vegetarian	Dessert	Cheese	O/s Wine	New World	Italian Wine	Wines by glass
Dedham	Fountain House & Dedham Hall	(01206) 323027	50	RR		32	20	yes	L	yes							◄	◄	◄	
Dedham	Le Talbooth	(01206) 323150	100	R		85	16	yes	All	yes					◄		◄	◄		
Felsted	Rumbles	(01371) 820996	55	R		50	16	yes	L						◄	◄		◄		
Gt Dunmow	The Starr	(01371) 874321	80	RR		50	12	yes	L	yes							◄	◄		
Harwich	Pier at Harwich	(01255) 241212	70	RR		70	30	yes	All				◄				◄	◄		◄
High Ongar	Shoes Restaurant	(01277) 363350	60	R		60	12	yes									◄			
Horndon-on-the-Hill	The Bell	(01375) 673154	55	R		40	12	yes	L	yes										
Horndon-on-the-Hill	The Bell Inn	(01375) 642463	60	IR		30	12	yes		yes						◄	◄	◄		◄
Maldon	Francine's	(01621) 856605	50	R		24	10					French			◄					
Wethersfield	Dicken's	(01371) 850723	60	R		60	30	yes	L	yes								◄		

Gloucestershire

Location	Establishment	Tel. No.	Dinner for 2, £	Category	Stars	Seats	Parties	Private Rms	Sundays	No-Smoking	Open Air	Nat Cuisine	Seafood	Vegetarian	Dessert	Cheese	O/s Wine	New World	Italian Wine	Wines by glass
Bibury	The Swan	(01285) 740695	100	HR		65	10	yes	All	yes							◄	◄	◄	
Birdlip	Kingshead House	(01452) 862299	55	RR		34	12	yes	L	yes										◄
Charingworth	Charingworth Manor	(01386) 593555	80	HR		48	12	yes	All	yes						◄	◄	◄		◄
Cheltenham	Le Champignon Sauvage	(01242) 573449	75	R	★	30	30					French		◄						
Cheltenham	Epicurean	(01242) 222466	100	R		30	8	yes	L	yes					◄	◄	◄	◄		◄
Cheltenham	The Greenway	(01242) 862352	85	HR		50	12	yes	All	yes					◄	◄	◄	◄		◄
Cheltenham	On The Park	(01242) 518898	70	HR		32	12	yes		yes								◄		
Cheltenham	Staithes	(01242) 260666	50	R		30	24	yes		yes						◄				

Location	Restaurant	Telephone		Type							Cuisine								
Chipping Campden	Cotswold House	(01386) 840330	70	HR	40	14	yes	All	yes					◄	◄	◄	◄		◄
Cirencester	Tatyan's	(01285) 653529	45	R	50	20					Chinese								
Corse Lawn	Corse Lawn House	(01452) 780771	75	HR	50	60	yes	All	yes	yes		◄	◄	◄	◄	◄	◄		◄
Lower Slaughter	Lower Slaughter Manor	(01451) 820456	80	HR	26	8	yes	All	yes	yes			◄	◄	◄	◄	◄		
Moreton-in-Marsh	Annie's	(01608) 651981	60	R	30	12	yes	L	yes										
Moreton-in-Marsh	Marsh Goose	(01608) 652111	65	R	60	22	yes	L	yes						◄		◄		
Northleach	Old Woolhouse	(01451) 860366	90	R ★	18	18													
Northleach	Wickens	(01451) 860421	55	R	38	20			yes		British		◄	◄	◄	◄	◄		◄
Stow-on-the-Wold	Grapevine Hotel	(01451) 830344	50	HR	60	10	yes		yes	yes				◄					
Stow-on-the-Wold	Wyck Hill House	(01451) 831936	95	HR	70	8	yes	All	yes				◄	◄	◄	◄	◄		◄
Tetbury	Calcot Manor	(01666) 890391	65	HR	50		yes	All	yes	yes		◄		◄	◄	◄	◄		◄
Upper Slaughter	Lords of the Manor	(01451) 820243	90	HR	65	10	yes	All	yes	yes		◄	◄	◄	◄	◄	◄		◄

Greater Manchester

Location	Restaurant	Telephone		Type							Cuisine								
Bury	Normandie	0161-764 3869	80	HR ★	50	10										◄			
Manchester	Gaylord	0161-832 4866	50	R	92	14	yes	All	yes		Indian	◄	◄	◄	◄		◄		
Manchester	Market Restaurant	0161-834 3743	55	R	42	24	yes						◄		◄				
Manchester	Penang Village	0161-236 2650	45	R	60			All			S E Asian								
Manchester	Rajdoot	0161-834 2176	40	R	67	70		D			Indian					◄			
Manchester	Siam Orchid	0161-236 1388	60	R	50	20		All			Thai								
Manchester	Sonarga	0161-861 0334	45	R	64	70		D			Indian								
Manchester	That Café	0161-432 4672	45	R	80	50	yes	L											
Manchester	Victoria & Albert	0161-832 1188	75	HR	70	8	yes	All	yes	yes		◄		◄	◄	◄			◄

Location	Establishment	Tel. No.	Dinner for 2, £	Category	Stars	Seats	Parties	Private Rms	Sundays	No-Smoking	Open Air	Nat Cuisine	Seafood	Vegetarian	Dessert	Cheese	O/s Wine	New World	Italian Wine	Wines by glass
Manchester	Woodlands	0161-336 4241	70	RR		40	24	yes												
Manchester	Yang Sing	0161-236 2200	50	R	★	140	40	yes	All			Chinese								
Manchester Airport	Moss Nook	0161-437 4778	80	RR		65	10			yes										
West Didsbury	Lime Tree	0161-445 1217	45	R		80	35	yes	L	yes										

Hampshire

Location	Establishment	Tel. No.	Dinner for 2, £	Category	Stars	Seats	Parties	Private Rms	Sundays	No-Smoking	Open Air	Nat Cuisine	Seafood	Vegetarian	Dessert	Cheese	O/s Wine	New World	Italian Wine	Wines by glass
Basingstoke	Audleys Wood	(01256) 817555	80	HR		70	12	yes	All									◀		
Basingstoke	Hee's	(01256) 464410	40	R		80	85		D			Chinese								
Botley	Cobbett's	(01489) 782068	65	R		40	40	yes				French								
Brockenhurst	Le Poussin	(01590) 623063	75	R	★	24	10		L	yes	yes					◀				◀
Denmead	Barnard's	(01705) 257788	45	R		38	21	yes			yes									
Dunbridge	Mill Arms Inn	(01794) 340401	50	R		60		yes	All							◀				
Eversley	New Mill	(01734) 732277	80	R		80	80	yes	All		yes			◀		◀	◀	◀		◀
Fareham	Solent Hotel	(01489) 880000	55	HR		80	10	yes	All		yes						◀	◀		◀
Hurstbourne Tarrant	Esseborne Manor	(01264) 736444	80	HR		40	22		All				◀					◀		
Lymington	Gordleton Mill	(01590) 682219	105	HR	★	45	10	yes	All	yes	yes				◀		◀	◀		◀
Lyndhurst	Parkhill Hotel	(01703) 282944	70	HR		80	36	yes	All	yes	yes							◀		◀
Milford-on-Sea	Rocher's	(01590) 642340	65	R		30	30	yes	L		yes							◀		
New Alresford	Hunters	(01962) 732468	55	RR		30	12	yes	L		yes									
New Milton	Chewton Glen	(01425) 275341	100	HR	★	120	8	yes	All	yes	yes				◀	◀	◀	◀	◀	
Odiham	Blubeckers	(01256) 702953		R		160		yes		yes										
Romsey	Old Manor House	(01794) 517353	90	R	★	45	10	yes	L		yes						◀	◀	◀	

Location	Name	Phone		Type							Cuisine
Rotherwick	Tylney Hall	(01256) 764881	95	HR	100	8	yes	All	yes	yes	
Southampton	Kuti's	(01703) 221585	45	R	78	30	yes	All		yes	Indian
Southsea	Bistro Montparnasse	(01705) 816754	55	R	40	12	yes				
Stuckton	Three Lions	(01425) 652489	65	R	60	12	yes	L			
Wickham	Old House Hotel	(01329) 833049	75	HR	40	22	yes				French
Winchester	Hotel du Vin & Bistro	(01962) 841414	60	HR	45	12	yes				
Winchester	Old Chesil Rectory	(01962) 851555	50	R	55	14	yes		yes		
Winchester	Wykeham Arms	(01962) 853834	55	IR	90	8	yes		yes	yes	

Hereford & Worcester

Location	Name	Phone		Type							Cuisine
Brimfield	Poppies Restaurant	(01584) 711230	75	RR	40	6	yes		yes		
Broadway	Collin House	(01386) 858354	60	HR	24	243		All	yes	yes	British
Broadway	Dormy House	(01386) 852711	90	HR	85	18	yes	All			
Broadway	Hunters Lodge	(01386) 853247	65	R	40	40	yes	L			
Broadway	Lygon Arms	(01386) 852255	85	HR	120	20	yes	All	yes		
Bromsgrove	Grafton Manor	(01527) 579007	75	HR	40	14	yes	All	yes		
Buckland	Buckland Manor	(01386) 852626	95	HR	38	12	yes	All	yes	yes	
Chaddesley Corbett	Brockencote Hall	(01562) 777876	80	HR	75	10	yes	All	yes		French
Evesham	Evesham Hotel	(01386) 765566	60	HR	55	8	yes	All			
Evesham	Riverside Hotel	(01386) 446200	55	HR	45	8		L	yes		
Eyton	Marsh Country Hotel	(01568) 613952	60	HR	24	16	yes	All	yes		
Harvington	Mill at Harvington	(01386) 870688	60	HR	35	32	yes	All	yes	yes	
Kington	Penrhos Court	(01544) 230720	75	RR	70	48	yes		yes		
Ledbury	Hope End	(01531) 633613	70	HR	24	6	yes	D	yes		
Malvern	Anupam	(01684) 573814	40	R	54	40		All			Indian
Malvern	Cottage in the Wood	(01684) 575859	65	HR	50	14	yes	All	yes		
Malvern	Croque-en-Bouche	(01684) 565612	90	R ★	22	6	yes		yes		
Ross-on-Wye	Pheasants	(01989) 565751	70	RR	22				yes		
Worcester	Brown's	(01905) 26263	75	R	100	22		L	yes		

Location	Establishment	Tel. No.	Dinner for 2, £	Category	Stars	Seats	Parties	Private Rms	Sundays	No-Smoking	Open Air	Nat Cuisine	Seafood	Vegetarian	Dessert	Cheese	O/s Wine	New World	Italian Wine	Wines by glass
Hertfordshire																				
Hadley Wood	West Lodge Park	0181-440 8311	65	HR		85	10	yes	All	yes					◄	◄		◄		
Melbourn	Pink Geranium	(01763) 260215	105	R	↑	65	18	yes	All	yes					◄	◄		◄		◄
New Barnet	Mims Restaurant	0181-449 2974	75	R	↑	45	8		All							◄				
Thundridge	Hanbury Manor	(01920) 487722	130	HR		48	8	yes	L	yes							◄	◄		◄
Humberside																				
Hull	Ceruttis	(01482) 328501	60	R		40	12	yes					◄							
Walkington	Manor House	(01482) 881645	75	HR		60	24	yes								◄	◄	◄		
Winteringham	Winteringham Fields	(01724) 733096	115	RR	★★	28	8	yes		yes					◄	◄	◄	◄	◄	
Isle of Wight																				
Seaview	Seaview Hotel	(01983) 612711	50	HR		30	20	yes	L		yes		◄							
Shanklin																				
Old Village	The Cottage	(01983) 862504	60	R		32	10			yes	yes									
Isles of Scilly																				
St Martin's	St Martin's Hotel	(01720) 422092	60	HR		60	10	yes	D	yes	yes					◄				◄
Tresco	Island Hotel	(01720) 422883	95	HR		110	10	yes	All	yes								◄		
Kent																				
Ashford	Eastwell Manor	(01233) 635751	95	HR		65	12	yes	All	yes								◄		◄
Billingshurst	The Gables	(01403) 782571	55	R		50														

Town	Name	Phone	Seats	Type			Cards		Cuisine
Boughton Monchelsea	Tanyard Hotel	(01622) 744705	60	HR	28	16	yes	yes	
Canterbury	County Hotel	(01227) 766266	70	HR	50	8	yes	All	
Canterbury	River Kwai	(01227) 462090	40	R	70	30			Chinese
Edenbridge	Honours Mill	(01732) 866757	60	R	38	20	L		
Faversham	Read's	(01795) 535344	75	R	40		yes	yes	
Folkestone	Paul's	(01303) 259697	45	R	120	100	yes	All	yes
Folkestone	La Tavernetta	(01303) 254955	45	R	70	25		All	Italian
Herne Bay	L'Escargot	(01227) 372876	55	R	40	24	yes	All	French
Higham	The Knowle	(01474) 822262	68	R	2	22	yes	L	yes
Maidstone	Mandarin Chef	(01622) 755917	35	R	70	25	yes	All	yes Chinese
Sevenoaks	Royal Oak	(01732) 451109	65	HR	60	24	yes	All	yes
Sissinghurst	Rankins	(01580) 713964	65	R	30	20	L		
St Margaret's	Wallett's Court	(01304) 852424	60	HR	60	10	yes		yes
Tunbridge Wells	Cheevers	(01892) 545524	60	R	32	16			
Tunbridge Wells	Downstairs at Thackeray's	(01892) 537559	45	R	30	20	yes		
Tunbridge Wells	Spa Hotel	(01892) 520331	60	HR	80	60	yes	All	
Tunbridge Wells	Thackeray's House	(01892) 511921	90	R ★	50	24	yes	L	
Whitstable	Whitstable Oyster Fishery Co	(01227) 276856	45	R	130	28	yes	All	yes

Lancashire

Town	Name	Phone	Seats	Type			Cards		Cuisine
Blackpool	September Brasserie	(01253) 23282	65	R	40	28			
Broughton	Broughton Park	(01772) 864087	65	HR	110	8	yes	All	yes French
Clitheroe	Browns Bistro	(01200) 26928	55	R	66	12			
Cowan Bridge	Cobwebs	(01524) 272141	60	RR	25	25		yes	

Location	Establishment	Tel. No.	Dinner for 2, £	Category	Stars	Seats	Parties	Private Rms	Sundays	No-Smoking	Open Air	Nat Cuisine	Seafood	Vegetarian	Dessert	Cheese	O/s Wine	New World	Italian Wine	Wines by glass
Langho	Northcote Manor	(01254) 240555	90	HR	↑	80	12	yes	All	yes	yes				◄	◄		◄		
Longridge	Paul Heathcote's Restaurant	(01772) 784969	90	R	★★	55	18	yes	All	yes						◄		◄		◄
Lytham St Annes	Dalmeny Hotel	(01253) 712236	60	HR		40	10	yes		yes										
Preston	Heathcotes Brasserie	(01772) 252732	55	R		65	20													
Ramsbottom	Village Restaurant	(01706) 825070	45	R		40	8	yes	L	yes						◄		◄		◄
Scarisbrick	Master McGrath's	(01704) 880050	55	R		120	20									◄	◄			
Thornton-le-Fylde	River House	(01253) 883497	85	RR		40	30	yes	L							◄		◄		
Wrightington	High Moor	(01257) 252364	55	R		95	14										◄			◄

Leicestershire

Location	Establishment	Tel. No.	Dinner for 2, £	Category	Stars	Seats	Parties	Private Rms	Sundays	No-Smoking	Open Air	Nat Cuisine	Seafood	Vegetarian	Dessert	Cheese	O/s Wine	New World	Italian Wine	Wines by glass
Hambleton	Hambleton Hall	(01572) 756991	110	HR	★★	60	10	yes	All	yes	yes				◄	◄		◄	◄	
Leicester	Curry Pot	(0116) 2538256	45	R		55	20	yes				Indian								
Leicester	Man Ho	(0116) 2557700	40	R		68	14	yes	All	yes		Chinese								
Leicester	Rise of the Raj	(0116) 2553885	35	R		40	20	yes	All			Indian								
Leicester	Welford Place	(0116) 2470758	55	R		60	14	yes	All				◄			◄				
Oakham	Whipper-In Hotel	(01572) 756971	70	HR		50	30	yes	All	yes										
Quorn	Quorn Grange	(01509) 412167	65	HR		50	24	yes	All				◄					◄		
Stapleford	Stapleford Park	(01572) 787522	90	HR		70	8	yes	All	yes	yes					◄				◄
Stretton	Ram Jam Inn	(01780) 410776	40	IR		30	40	yes	All	yes	yes							◄		
Uppingham	The Lake Isle	(01572) 822951	65	RR		40	24	yes	L							◄	◄	◄		◄

Lincolnshire

Town	Restaurant	Phone		Code							Cuisine
Beckingham	Black Swan	(01636) 626474	55	R		35	28	yes	All	yes	
Gt Gonerby	Harry's Place	(01476) 61780	95	R	★	10	10			yes	
Lincoln	The Jew's House	(01522) 524851	60	R		28	30			yes	
Lincoln	Wig & Mitre	(01522) 535190	60	R		80			All	yes	
Stamford	The George	(01780) 55171	85	HR		67	12	yes	All	yes	
Stamford	Warunee's	(01780) 57291	35	R		45		yes		yes	Thai

Merseyside

Town	Restaurant	Phone		Code							Cuisine
Liverpool	La Grande Bouffe	0151-236 3375	50	R		60	16	yes			

Middlesex

Town	Restaurant	Phone		Code							Cuisine
Hampton Wick	Le Petit Max	0181-977 0236	65	R		35			All		
Heathrow Airport	Heathrow Hilton	0181-759 7755	60	HR		60			All		Chinese
Hounslow	Hee's	0181-577 3817	50	R		80			All		Chinese
Nth Harrow	Percy's Restaurant	0181-427 2021	70	R		70	10			yes	
Shepperton	Blubeckers	(01932) 243377		R							
Southall	Asian Tandoori Centre	0181-574 2597	15	R		84					Indian
Southall	Madhu's Brilliant	0181-574 1897	40	R		104	30		D		Indian
Twickenham	Hamiltons	0181-892 3949	50	R		50	16	yes	L		
Twickenham	McClement's Bistro	0181-744 9610	50	R		45	10	yes	All		

Norfolk

Town	Restaurant	Phone		Code							Cuisine
Burnham Market	Fishes	(01328) 738588	40	R		42	14				
Cawston	Grey Gables	(01603) 871259	56	RR		30	24	yes	D	yes	
Diss	Weavers	(01379) 642411	45	R		80	20	yes		yes	
Erpingham	The Ark	(01263) 761535	55	RR		36	12	yes	L	yes	

Location	Establishment	Tel. No.	Dinner for 2, £	Category	Stars	Seats	Parties	Private Rms	Sundays	No-Smoking	Open Air	Nat Cuisine	Seafood	Vegetarian	Dessert	Cheese	O/s Wine	New World	Italian Wine	Wines by glass
Gt Yarmouth	Seafood Restaurant	(01493) 856009	55	R		40	20						◄					◄		
Grimston	Congham Hall	(01485) 600250	70	HR		50	8	yes		yes	yes				◄	◄		◄		◄
Norwich	Adlard's	(01603) 633522	85	R	★	45	18		All	yes				◄	◄		◄	◄	◄	
Norwich	Brasted's	(01603) 625949	70	R	★	22	12													
Norwich	Greens Seafood Rest.	(01603) 623733	60	R		48	50						◄						◄	
Norwich	Marco's	(01603) 624044	80	R		22	12			yes		Italian								
Swaffham	Strattons Hotel	(01760) 23845	60	RR		20	14			yes				◄		◄				
Thetford	Martine's	(01842) 762000	55	R		30	10	yes		yes	yes			◄						
Wymondham	Number Twenty Four	(01953) 607750	45	R		65	40	yes		yes				◄		◄				

Northamptonshire

Location	Establishment	Tel. No.	Dinner for 2, £	Category	Stars	Seats	Parties	Private Rms	Sundays	No-Smoking	Open Air	Nat Cuisine	Seafood	Vegetarian	Dessert	Cheese	O/s Wine	New World	Italian Wine	Wines by glass
Horton	French Partridge	(01604) 870033	70	R		40	10			yes								◄		
Paulerspury	Vine House	(01327) 811267	55	RR		45	30	yes		yes										
Roade	Roadhouse Rest.	(01604) 863372	55	R		40	30		L											

Northumberland

Location	Establishment	Tel. No.	Dinner for 2, £	Category	Stars	Seats	Parties	Private Rms	Sundays	No-Smoking	Open Air	Nat Cuisine	Seafood	Vegetarian	Dessert	Cheese	O/s Wine	New World	Italian Wine	Wines by glass
Alnwick	John Blacknore's	(01665) 604465	60	R		28	8			yes						◄				
Berwick-upon-Tweed	Funnywayt'mekalivin	(01289) 308827	50	R		32	24	yes								◄				
Ponteland	Café 21	(01661) 820357	55	R	↑	34	12									◄				
Wylam	Laburnum House	(01661) 852185	65	RR		47	15		L							◄				◄

Nottinghamshire

Town	Restaurant	Phone	Seats	Type	Rating	No.					Cuisine
Langar	Langar Hall	(01949) 860559	70	HR		30	12	yes		yes	
Nether Langwith	Goff's Restaurant	(01623) 744538	65	RR		45	12	yes	L	yes	
Newark	Gannets Cafe-Bistrot	(01636) 702066	50	R		40				yes	
Nottingham	Higoi	(0115) 9423379	50	R		35	35				Japanese
Nottingham	Man Ho	(0115) 9474729	40	R		156	16	yes	All		Chinese
Nottingham	Ocean City	(0115) 9410041	40	R		250	12		All		Chinese
Nottingham	Sonny's	(0115) 9473041	60	R	↑	80	30		All		
Plumtree	Perkins Bar & Bistro	(0115) 9373695	50	R		73	24	yes		yes yes	

Oxfordshire

Town	Restaurant	Phone	Seats	Type	Rating	No.					Cuisine
Blewbury	Blewbury Inn	(01235) 850496	60	R		26			L	yes	
Burford	Lamb Inn	(01993) 823155	70	IR		50	12	yes	All	yes	
Chadlington	The Manor	(01608) 676711	60	HR		20	6	yes	D	yes	
Clanfield	The Plough	(01367) 810222	70	IR		40	20	yes	All	yes yes	
Great Milton	Le Manoir aux Quat'Saisons	(01844) 278881	195	HR	★★★110	10	yes	All	yes		French
Minster Lovell	Lovells at Windrush Farm	(01993) 779802	85	RR	★	18	10		All	yes	
Moulsford-on-Thames	Beetle & Wedge: The Boathouse	(01491) 651381	70	R	↑	60	16	yes	All	yes	
Moulsford-on-Thames	Beetle & Wedge	(01491) 651381	100	HR	★	30	10	yes	L	yes	
Oxford	Al-Shami	(01865) 310066	30	R		48	40	yes	All	yes	Lebanese
Oxford	Bath Place Hotel	(01865) 791812	80	RR		32	20		L	yes yes	
Oxford	Cherwell Boathouse	(01865) 52746	50	R		50	50		L	yes yes	
Oxford	Restaurant Elizabeth	(01865) 242230	75	R	↑	40	40	yes	All	yes	French
Oxford	15 North Parade	(01865) 513773	70	R		60	70	yes	L	yes yes	
Oxford	Ma Cuisine	(01865) 201316	55	R		30	10				

Location	Establishment	Tel. No.	Dinner for 2, £	Category	Stars	Seats	Parties	Private Rms	Sundays	No-Smoking	Open Air	Nat Cuisine	Seafood	Vegetarian	Dessert	Cheese	O/s Wine	New World	Italian Wine	Wines by glass
Stonor	Stonor Arms	(01491) 638345	80	RR		20	10	yes	L		yes						◄	◄		
Woodstock	Bear Hotel	(01993) 811511	60	HR		80	20	yes	All	yes						◄				
Woodstock	Feathers Hotel	(01993) 812291	75	HR		60	8	yes	All	yes	yes							◄		

Shropshire

Location	Establishment	Tel. No.	Dinner for 2, £	Category	Stars	Seats	Parties	Private Rms	Sundays	No-Smoking	Open Air	Nat Cuisine	Seafood	Vegetarian	Dessert	Cheese	O/s Wine	New World	Italian Wine	Wines by glass
Dorrington	Country Friends	(01743) 718707	65	RR		45	20			yes										
Hinstock	Goldstone Hall	(01630) 661202	60	HR		45										◄				
Ludlow	Merchant House	(01584) 875438	70	R	★↑	20		yes		yes							◄	◄		
Norton	Hundred House	(01952) 730353	65	IR		60	15	yes							◄	◄	◄			◄
Worfield	Old Vicarage	(01746) 716497	72	HR		50	16	yes	All	yes					◄	◄	◄	◄		◄

Somerset

Location	Establishment	Tel. No.	Dinner for 2, £	Category	Stars	Seats	Parties	Private Rms	Sundays	No-Smoking	Open Air	Nat Cuisine	Seafood	Vegetarian	Dessert	Cheese	O/s Wine	New World	Italian Wine	Wines by glass
Axbridge	Almshouse Bistro	(01934) 732493	35	R		32	32	yes		yes	yes									
Beckington	Woolpack Inn	(01373) 831244	65	IR		40		yes		yes	yes								◄
Castle Cary	Bond's	(01963) 350464	55	HR		20	10		D	yes	yes					◄				
Dulverton	Ashwick House	(01398) 323868	60	HR		35	18		All	yes	yes	British				◄				
Middlecombe	Periton Park	(01643) 706885	55	HR		24	18	yes												
Porlock	Oaks Hotel	(01643) 862265	45	HR		24	12		D	yes		British				◄		◄		
Shepton Mallet	Blostin's	(01749) 343648	50	R		32	30							◄						
Taunton	Castle Hotel	(01823) 272671	90	HR	★↑	80	8	yes	All						◄	◄				◄
Wells	Ritchers	(01749) 679085	55	R		14	24	yes	All		yes			◄	◄	◄	◄			
Williton	White House	(01984) 632306	70	RR		26	8		D	yes						◄	◄		◄
Wiveliscombe	Langley House	(01984) 623318	75	HR		20	8	yes	D	yes						◄	◄	◄		

Town	Name	Phone		Price		Seats			Meals			Cuisine
Yeovil	Little Barwick House	(01935) 23902	70	RR		40	8	yes			yes	

Staffordshire

Town	Name	Phone		Price		Seats			Meals			Cuisine
Penkridge	William Harding's	(01785) 712955	50	R		30	20		L			
Stretton	Dovecliffe Hall	(01283) 531818	65	HR		90	24	yes	L	yes		
Waterhouses	Old Beams	(01538) 308254	80	RR	★ ↑	40	20	yes	L	yes		

Suffolk

Town	Name	Phone		Price		Seats			Meals			Cuisine
Bury St Edmunds	Mortimer's Seafood Restaurant	(01284) 760623	45	R		72	12	yes		yes		
Campsea Ashe	Old Rectory	(01728) 746524	55	RR		36	18			yes		
Cavendish	Alfonso's	(01787) 280372	60	R		30	30		L	yes	yes	Italian
Fressingfield	Fox and Goose	(01379) 586247	65	R		50	20	yes	All	yes	yes	
Hintlesham	Hintlesham Hall	(01473) 652268		HR		120	10	yes	All	yes		
Ixworth	Theobald's	(01359) 231707	72	R		36	12		L			
Lavenham	Great House	(01787) 247431	45	RR		40	35	yes	L	yes		French
Lavenham	The Swan	(01787) 247477	75	HR		70	20	yes	All	yes		British
Long Melford	Chimneys	(01787) 379806	80	R		50	16		L			
Southwold	The Crown	(01502) 722275	50	IR		22	6	yes	All	yes	yes	
Southwold	The Swan	(01502) 722186	65	HR		86	12	yes	All	yes	yes	British
Stonham	Mr Underhill's	(01449) 711206	75	R	★	24	16	yes		yes	yes	
Sudbury	Mabey's Brasserie	(01787) 374298	55	R		50	8	yes		yes		

Surrey

Town	Name	Phone		Price		Seats			Meals			Cuisine
Camberley	Tithas	(01276) 65803	30	R		50	60		All			Indian
Chobham	Quails Restaurant	(01276) 858491	55	R		40	12		L			
Claygate	Les Alouettes	(01372) 464882	70	R		60			L			French
Cranleigh	La Barbe Encore	(01483) 273889	65	R		55	50		L			French
Dorking	Partners West Street	(01306) 882826	45	R		45	12	yes	L	yes		
Esher	Good Earth	(01372) 462489	85	R		85	28		All			Chinese

Location	Establishment	Tel. No.	Dinner for 2, £	Category	Stars	Seats	Parties	Private Rms	Sundays	No-Smoking	Open Air	Nat Cuisine	Seafood	Vegetarian	Dessert	Cheese	O/s Wine	New World	Italian Wine	Wines by glass
Farnham	Krug's Austrian Rest.	(01252) 723277	50	R		80	40	yes				Austrian								
Grayshott	Woods Place	(01428) 605555	58	R		36	16					Swedish								
Guildford	Mandarin	(01483) 572293	45	R		50	55		D			Chinese								
Haslemere	Fleur de Sel	(01428) 651462	70	R	★	50	10					French			◀					
Hersham	The Dining Room	(01932) 231686	55	R		90	12	yes	L	yes		British								
Horley	Langshott Manor	(01293) 786680	65	HR		14	6	yes	D	yes								◀		
Kew	Wine & Mousaka	0181-940 5696	35	R		50	50			yes		Greek								
Kingston-upon-Thames	Restaurant Gravier	0181-549 5557	70	R		40	45			yes		French	◀		◀					
Reigate	La Barbe	(01737) 241966	65	R		65	20					French								◀
Reigate	The Dining Room	(01737) 226650	65	R		50	12									◀				
Richmond	Burnt Chair	0181-940 9488	55	R		31														
Richmond	Petersham Hotel	0181-940 7471	65	HR		70	14	yes	All	yes				◀						
Richmond	Refectory	0181-940 6264		R																
Richmond	River Terrace	0181-332 2524	65	R		60	10	yes	L	yes										
Ripley	Michels'	(01483) 224777	90	R	★	50	12	yes	L	yes					◀	◀		◀		◀
Shere	Kinghams	(01483) 202168	60	R		44	25	yes	L	yes	yes							◀		
Surbiton	Chez Max	0181-399 2365	65	R		40	25					French								
Sutton	Heen's	0181-643 1221	50	R		70	50		All			Chinese								
Sutton	Partners Brasserie	0181-644 7743	50	R		32	12													
Tadworth	Gemini Restaurant	(01737) 812179	55	R		40	38		L			French				◀				
Weybridge	Casa Romana	(01932) 843470	70	R		90	25		All			Italian						◀		

East Sussex

Town	Restaurant	Phone	Type		N1	N2	N3	yes	Lic.	yes	Cuisine
Alfriston	Toucans Restaurant at Drusillas Zoo	(01323) 870656	R								
Battle	Netherfield Place	(01424) 774455	HR		70	50	14	yes	All	yes	
Brighting	Jack Fuller's	(01424) 838212	R		35	70	50	yes	L	yes	
Brighton	Black Chapati	(01273) 699011	R		45	30	10	yes	L	yes	Indian
Brighton	Brighton Thistle	(01273) 206700	HR		85	45	12				French
Brighton	China Garden	(01273) 325124	R		55	130		yes	All	yes	Chinese
Brighton	Langan's Bistro	(01273) 606933	R		70	45	10	yes	L		
Brighton	La Marinade	(01273) 600992	R		60	34	34	yes	L	yes	
Brighton	Topps Hotel	(01273) 729334	HR		50	20	6		D		
Brighton (Hove)	Quentin's	(01273) 822734	R		50	46	20	yes			
Eastbourne	Grand Hotel	(01323) 412345	HR		70	50	12	yes			
Hastings	Roser's Restaurant	(01424) 712218	R	★	65	30	8	yes			
Herstmonceux	Sundial	(01323) 832217	R		90	60	20	yes	L	yes	French
Jevington	Hungry Monk	(01323) 482178	R		60	44	7	yes	All	yes	
Rye	Landgate Bistro	(01797) 222829	R		60	30	10				
Uckfield	Horsted Place	(01825) 750581	HR		95	40	12	yes	All	yes	
Wych Cross	Ashdown Park	(01342) 824988	HR		80	150	10	yes	All	yes	

West Sussex

Town	Restaurant	Phone	Type		N1	N2	N3	yes	Lic.	yes	Cuisine
Amberley	Amberley Castle	(01798) 831992	HR		110	40	8	yes	All	yes	
Ashington	The Willows	(01903) 892575	R		55	30	15		L	yes	
Chichester	Comme Ca	(01243) 788724	R		55	80	28	yes	L	yes	French
Chichester	The Droveway	(01243) 528832	R		80	38	22	yes		yes	
Chilgrove	White Horse Inn	(01243) 535219	R		60	70	24	yes	L		
Climping	Bailiffscourt	(01903) 723511	HR		80	50	15	yes		yes	
Cuckfield	Murray's	(01444) 455826	R		66	32	12	yes		yes	
Cuckfield	Ockenden Manor	(01444) 416111	HR		80	45	8	yes		yes	

Location	Establishment	Tel. No.	Dinner for 2, £	Category	Stars	Seats	Parties	Private Rms	Sundays	No-Smoking	Open Air	Nat Cuisine	Seafood	Vegetarian	Dessert	Cheese	O/s Wine	New World	Italian Wine	Wines by glass
East Grinstead	Gravetye Manor	(01342) 810567	105	HR		42	8	yes	All	yes					◀	◀	◀	◀	◀	◀
Lower Beeding	Cisswood House	(01403) 891216	55	HR		60		yes	All						◀		◀	◀	◀	
Midhurst	Angel Hotel	(01730) 812421	60	IR		80	20	yes	All	yes						◀		◀		
Petworth	L'Amico	(01798) 343659	50	R		40	15	yes		yes		Italian							◀	
Pulborough	Stane Street Hollow	(01798) 872819	60	R		32	10	yes	L	yes										
Storrington	Little Thakeham	(01903) 744416	90	HR		30	24	yes	L	yes					◀					
Storrington	Manleys	(01903) 742331	102	RR		48	12	yes	L	yes					◀					
Storrington	The Old Forge	(01903) 743402	60	R		36		yes	L						◀	◀		◀		◀
Turners Hill	Alexander House	(01342) 714914	120	HR ↑		55	12	yes	All	yes	yes		◀		◀			◀		

Tyne & Wear

Location	Establishment	Tel. No.	Dinner for 2, £	Category	Stars	Seats	Parties	Private Rms	Sundays	No-Smoking	Open Air	Nat Cuisine	Seafood	Vegetarian	Dessert	Cheese	O/s Wine	New World	Italian Wine	Wines by glass
East Boldon	Forsters	0191-519 0929	65	R		28	30													
Newcastle-upon-Tyne	Blackgate	0191-261 7356	70	R		43	18	yes		yes	yes	British			◀	◀				
Newcastle-upon-Tyne	Courtney's	0191-232 5537	55	R		28	10	yes						◀						
Newcastle-upon-Tyne	Fisherman's Lodge	0191-281 3281	85	R		60	14	yes		yes	yes		◀	◀		◀				
Newcastle-upon-Tyne	King Neptune	0191-261 6657	45	R		120	18	yes	All			Chinese	◀							
Newcastle-upon-Tyne	21 Queen Street	0191-222 0755	95	R	★↑	50	12								◀			◀		
Newcastle-upon-Tyne	Vermont Hotel	0191-233 1010	80	HR		90	10								◀					

Location	Name	Phone		Type						Cuisine
Newcastle-upon-Tyne	Vermont Hotel: Brasserie	0191-233 1010	65	R	145					
Seaton Burn	Horton Grange	(01661) 860686	80	RR	30	15	yes		yes	

Warwickshire

Billesley	Billesley Manor	(01789) 400888	85	HR	80	8	yes	All	yes	
Hockley Heath	Nuthurst Grange	(01564) 783972	60	HR	50	14	yes	All	yes	yes
Kenilworth	Restaurant Bosquet	(01926) 852463	75	R	26	20				
Kenilworth	Simpson's	(01926) 864567	50	R	80	12	yes		yes	
Leamington Spa	Mallory Court	(01926) 330214	120	HR ★	50	22	yes	All		
Leamington Spa	Regent Hotel	(01926) 427231	65	HR	50	14				
Stratford-upon-Avon	Liaison	(01789) 293400	65	R	58	12	yes			
Stratford-upon-Avon	The Opposition	(01789) 269980	50	R	50	10		All	yes	

West Midlands

Birmingham	Adil Tandoori	0121-449 0335	30	R	80	30		All	yes	Indian
Birmingham	Chung Ying Garden	0121-666 6622	40	R	350	18	yes	All		Chinese
Birmingham	Chung Ying	0121-622 5669	40	R	220		yes	All		Chinese
Birmingham	Henry Wong	0121-427 9799	45	R	140	60	yes			Chinese
Birmingham	Henry's	0121-200 1136	45	R	140	50	yes			Chinese
Birmingham	Hyatt Regency	0121-643 1234	80	HR	75	16	yes		yes	
Birmingham	New Happy Gathering	0121-643 5247	35	R	90	100	yes	All		Chinese
Birmingham	Purple Rooms	0121-702 2193	35	R	30		yes	All		Indian
Birmingham	Rajdoot	0121-643 8805	40	R	74	30	yes	D		Indian
Birmingham	Shimla Pinks	0121-633 0366	50	R	180	40		D		Indian
Birmingham	Swallow Hotel: Langtry's	0121-452 1144	60	R	60				yes	
Birmingham	Swallow Hotel	0121-452 1144	96	HR	60	10	yes	All	yes	

Location	Establishment	Tel. No.	Dinner for 2, £	Category	Stars	Seats	Parties	Private Rms	Sundays	No-Smoking	Open Air	Nat Cuisine	Seafood	Vegetarian	Dessert	Cheese	O/s Wine	New World	Italian Wine	Wines by glass
Kinver	Berkley's Bistro	(01384) 873679	55	R		70	24	yes								▲				
Stourbridge	Bon Appetit	(01384) 375372	55	R		60	20									▲				
Sutton Coldfield	New Hall	0121-378 2442	95	HR		60	10	yes	All	yes	yes					▲		▲		▲

Wiltshire

Location	Establishment	Tel. No.	Dinner for 2, £	Category	Stars	Seats	Parties	Private Rms	Sundays	No-Smoking	Open Air	Nat Cuisine	Seafood	Vegetarian	Dessert	Cheese	O/s Wine	New World	Italian Wine	Wines by glass
Bradford-on-Avon	Woolley Grange	(01225) 864705	75	HR		50	40	yes	All	yes	yes				▲	▲	▲	▲	▲	▲
Castle Combe	Manor House	(01249) 782206	95	HR		75	8	yes	All	yes	yes					▲	▲	▲	▲	▲
Chiseldon	Chiseldon House	(01793) 741010	65	HR		48	10	yes	All					▲		▲			▲	
Colerne	Lucknam Park	(01225) 742777	100	HR		80	8	yes	All	yes						▲	▲			
Hirton	Hinton Grange	(0117) 9372916	50	HR		60	15	yes	All	yes										
Lacock	At The Sign of The Angel	(01249) 730230	70	IR		45	20	yes	L	yes						▲				
Melksham	Toxique	(01225) 702129	75	RR		30	20	yes	L	yes							▲	▲		▲
Rowde	George & Dragon	(01380) 723053	60	R		35	20			yes	yes		▲					▲		▲
Stanton St Quintin	Stanton Manor	(01666) 837552	50	HR		30	12	yes		yes				▲						
Teffont Evias	Howard's House	(01722) 716392	75	HR		35	28		All	yes	yes									▲
Warminster	Bishopstrow House	(01985) 212312	80	HR		65	8	yes	All	yes					▲	▲	▲	▲		▲

North Yorkshire

Location	Establishment	Tel. No.	Dinner for 2, £	Category	Stars	Seats	Parties	Private Rms	Sundays	No-Smoking	Open Air	Nat Cuisine	Seafood	Vegetarian	Dessert	Cheese	O/s Wine	New World	Italian Wine	Wines by glass
Harrogate	Café Fleur	(01423) 503034	45	R		56	14		D	yes		French								

Town	Restaurant	Phone		Type								Cuisine						
Harrogate	Drum & Monkey	(01423) 502650	45	R		50	8											◀
Harrogate	Miller's: The Bistro	(01423) 530708	60	R		40	14			yes								
Harrogate	Old Swan Hotel	(01423) 500055	70	HR		40	8	All	yes							◀		
Harrogate	Tannin Level	(01423) 560595	35	R		70	12		yes	yes			◀	◀	◀	◀		
Hetton	Angel Inn	(01756) 730263	70	R		54	10	L	yes	yes			◀	◀	◀	◀		
Low Laithe	Carters Knox Manor	(01423) 780607	35	R		80	12		yes									
Moulton	Black Bull	(01325) 377289	55	R		100	10	L	yes	yes								
Reeth	Burgoyne Hotel	(01748) 884292	55	HR		30		D	yes									◀
Ripley	Boar's Head Hotel	(01423) 771888	70	HR		40	14	All						◀	◀	◀		
Scarborough	Lanterna	(01723) 363616	45	R		36	10					Italian						
Staddlebridge	McCoy's	(01609) 882671	85	HR	★↑	50	12		yes							◀		
Stokesley	Chapters	(01642) 711888	40	HR		45	40	All		yes							◀	
Wath-in-Nidderdale	Sportsman's Arms	(01423) 711306	60	RR		50	8	All	yes	yes			◀	◀	◀			
York	Grange Hotel	(01904) 644744	60	HR		55	14	All	yes									
York	Melton's	(01904) 634341	50	R		42	30	L	yes				◀	◀				
York	Middlethorpe Hall	(01904) 641241	100	HR		60	8	All	yes				◀	◀	◀	◀		
York	19 Grape Lane	(01904) 636366	75	R		34	12		yes				◀	◀	◀	◀		

South Yorkshire

Barnsley	Armstrongs	(01226) 240113	55	R		60	16		yes									
Chapeltown	Greenhead House	(0114) 2469004	75	R		32	14			yes			◀		◀	◀		
Sheffield	Nirmal's	(0114) 2724054	40	R		80		D		yes		Indian					◀	

West Yorkshire

Bradford	Nawaab	(01274) 720371	30	R		120	30		yes			Indian	◀	◀	◀	◀		
Bradford	Restaurant 19	(01274) 492559	70	RR	★	36	14	D	yes			Indian	◀					
Bradford	The Victoria	(01274) 728706	50	HR		80												
Guiseley	Prachee	(01943) 872531	45	R		56	25	All				Indian						

Location	Establishment	Tel. No.	Dinner for 2, £	Category	Stars	Seats	Parties	Private Rms	Sundays	No-Smoking	Open Air	Nat Cuisine	Seafood	Vegetarian	Dessert	Cheese	O/s Wine	New World	Italian Wine	Wines by glass
Halifax	Design House	(01422) 383242	55	R		70														
Haworth	Weavers	(01535) 643822	50	RR		60	16	yes	L	yes		British				▲				▲
Ilkley	Box Tree	(01943) 608484	85	R	★	50	26	yes							▲		▲	▲	▲	▲
Ilkley	Rombalds Hotel	(01943) 603201	65	HR		35	8	yes	All	yes	yes	Italian				▲		▲		
Leeds	Adriano Flying Pizza	(0113) 2666501	30	R		150			All	yes	yes	Italian								
Leeds	Bibi's Italian	(0113) 2430905	50	R		160	40			yes	yes	Italian							▲	
Leeds	Brasserie Forty Four	(0113) 2343232	70	R	↑	112	60	yes		yes	yes									▲
Leeds	Dawat	(0113) 2872279	30	R		26	12		All			Indian								
Leeds	Haley's Hotel	(0113) 2784446	60	HR		45	12	yes								▲				
Leeds	Leodis Brasserie	(0113) 2421010	80	R		160	16	yes	All	yes		Vietnamese					▲			▲
Leeds	Maxi's Chinese	(0113) 2440552	40	R		300		yes	All			Chinese								
Leeds	New Asia	(0113) 2343612	35	R		60	60		All			Chinese								
Leeds	Olive Tree	(0113) 2569283	55	R		150		yes	L			Greek								
Leeds	Pool Court at 42	(0113) 2444242	80	R	★	38	8	yes		yes					▲		▲	▲		
Leeds	Rascasse	(0113) 2664411		R																
Leeds	Sang Sang	(0113) 2468664	50	R		90	30	yes				Chinese					▲	▲		
Leeds	Sous le Nez en Ville	(0113) 2440108	55	R		86	16	yes									▲			▲
Leeds	Thai Siam	(0113) 2451608	40	R		60			All			Thai					▲		▲	
Linton	Wood Hall	(01937) 587271	85	HR		70	12	yes	All	yes	yes		▲				▲		▲	▲

Scotland by County: Hotels

See How To Use This Guide, on pages 14-15, for an explanation of our percentage rating system, room pricing and categories.
*15 mins Mway refers to hotels graded 70% or higher within 15 minutes of a motorway.

Borders

Location	Establishment	Tel. No.	Category	Room £	Hotel %	No. of Rooms	Conf Max	Banq Max	Beaut Sit	Disabled	In Swim	Out Swim	Tennis	Squash	Golf	Fishing	Riding	15 mins Mway*	Country House
Dryburgh	Dryburgh Abbey Hotel	(01835) 822261	H	110	65%	26	200	120	◄		◄					◄			
Ettrickbridge	Ettrickshaws Hotel	(01750) 52229	H	70	62%	6	24		◄							◄			
Kelso	Ednam House	(01573) 224168	H	63	64%	32	240	180	◄							◄			
Kelso	Sunlaws House	(01573) 450331	H	140	72%	22	60	40	◄				◄			◄			
Melrose	Burts Hotel	(0189 682) 2285	I	74		21		50							◄				
Melrose	George & Abbotsford	(0189 682) 2308	H	70	56%	30	180	140											
Peebles	Cringletie House	(01721) 730233	HR	98	65%	13			◄				◄			◄			
Peebles	Park Hotel	(01721) 720451	H	106	62%	24	50	90											
Peebles	Peebles Hotel Hydro	(01721) 720602	H	103	70%	137	450	260	◄		◄		◄	◄			◄		
Peebles	Tontine Hotel	(01721) 720892	H	87	57%	35	90	90											
Selkirk	Philipburn House	(01750) 20747	H	97	60%	16	80	40				◄							
Tweedsmuir	Crook Inn	(01899) 880272	H	52	59%	8		50								◄			

Central

Location	Establishment	Tel. No.	Category	Room £	Hotel %	No. of Rooms	Conf Max	Bang Max	Beaut Slt	Disabled	In Swim	Out Swim	Tennis	Squash	Golf	Fishing	Riding	15 mins Mway*	Country House
Airth	Airth Castle	(01324) 831411	H	105	68%	75	400	280	◄				◄						
Bridge of Allan	Royal Hotel	(01786) 832284	H	70	59%	32	150	120											
Drymen	Buchanan Arms Hotel	(01360) 60588	H	114	62%	51	150	120						◄					
Dunblane	Cromlix House	(01786) 822125	HR	140	82%	14	40	40	◄		◄					◄		◄	
Dunblane	Stakis Dunblane	(01786) 822551	H	111	61%	214	500	400	◄		◄		◄						
Falkirk	Hotel Cladhan	(01324) 27421	H	69	60%	37	200	200											
Strathblane	Kirkhouse Inn	(01360) 770621	I	73		15	30	60								◄			

Dumfries & Galloway

Location	Establishment	Tel. No.	Category	Room £	Hotel %	No. of Rooms	Conf Max	Bang Max	Beaut Slt	Disabled	In Swim	Out Swim	Tennis	Squash	Golf	Fishing	Riding	15 mins Mway*	Country House
Annan	Warmanbie Hotel	(01461) 204015	H	74	59%	7	50	50								◄			
Auchencairn	Balcary Bay Hotel	(01556) 640217	HR	88	64%	17													
Auchencairn	Collin House	(01556) 640292	HR	78	68%	6		18											
Beattock	Auchen Castle	(0168 33) 407	H	76	64%	25	40	80	◄		◄					◄			
Canonbie	Riverside Inn	(0138 73) 71512	IR	72		6													
Gatehouse of Fleet	Cally Palace	(01557) 814341	H	135	69%	56	80		◄		◄		◄		◄	◄			
Gatehouse of Fleet	Murray Arms Inn	(01557) 814207	I	79		13	130	100											
Newton Stewart	Kirroughtree Hotel	(01671) 402141	HR	96	76%	17	30	20	◄				◄						
Port William	Corsemalzie House	(01988) 860254	H	86	61%	14	80	80	◄							◄			
Portpatrick	Knockinaam Lodge	(01776) 810471	HR	104	73%	10			◄							◄			
Rockcliffe	Baron's Craig	(01556) 630225	H	98	65%	22	20			◄									

Town	Hotel	Phone	Type		%			
Stranraer	North West Castle	(01776) 704413	H	70	68%	71	100	180

Fife

Town	Hotel	Phone	Type		%			
Dunfermline	King Malcolm Thistle	(01383) 722611	H	93	65%	48	130	120
Glenrothes	Balgeddie House	(01592) 742511	H	91	65%	18	70	70
Letham	Fernie Castle	(01337) 810381	H	70	60%	15	140	120
Markinch	Balbirnie House	(01592) 610066	HR	125	74%	30	150	120
North Queensferry	Queensferry Lodge	(01383) 410000	H	75	63%	32	200	200
Peat Inn	The Peat Inn	(01334) 840206	RR	135		8		24
St Andrews	Rufflets Country House	(01334) 472594	H	130	65%	25	40	80
St Andrews	Rusacks Hotel	(01334) 474321	H	138	74%	50	120	150
St Andrews	St Andrews Old Course Hotel	(01334) 474371	H	245	82%	125	300	220

Grampian

Town	Hotel	Phone	Type		%			
Aberdeen	Ardoe House	(01224) 867355	H	146	70%	71	300	200
Aberdeen	Caledonian Thistle	(01224) 640233	H	115	68%	78	40	26
Aberdeen	Copthorne Hotel	(01224) 630404	H	136	68%	89	220	180
Aberdeen	Holiday Inn Crowne Plaza	(01224) 713911	H	127	69%	144	500	400
Aberdeen	The Marcliffe at Pitfodels	(01224) 861000	HR	120	78%	42	600	400
Aberdeen	Stakis Aberdeen	(01224) 313377	H	128	63%	110	1000	800
Aberdeen Airport	Aberdeen Marriott Hotel	(01224) 770011	H	132	70%	154	400	350
Aberdeen Airport	Airport Skean Dhu Hotel	(01224) 725252	H	114	65%	148	500	420
Ballater	Craigendarroch Hotel	(013 97) 55858	H	125	74%	44	120	70
Ballater	Tullich Lodge	(013 97) 55406	HR	190	71%	10		
Banchory	Raemoir House	(01330) 824884	HR	95	71%	25	60	80
Banchory	Tor-na-Coille Hotel	(01330) 822242	H	69	66%	22	90	95
Chapel of Garioch	Pittodrie House	(01467) 681444	H	115	65%	27	150	130

Location	Establishment	Tel. No.	Category	Room £	Hotel %	No. of Rooms	Conf Max	Bang Max	Beaut Sit	Disabled	In Swim	Out Swim	Tennis	Squash	Golf	Fishing	Riding	15 mins Mway *	Country House
Craigellachie	Craigellachie Hotel	(01340) 881204	H	99	68%	30	40	50					◄						
Elgin	Mansion House	(01343) 548811	H	110	67%	23	250	200			◄								
Inverurie	Thainstone House Hotel	(01467) 621643	H	126	76%	48	350	220			◄					◄			
Kildrummy	Kildrummy Castle Hotel	(0197 55) 71288	H	130	70%	16	20	50	◄										
Maryculter	Maryculter House	(01224) 732124	H	115	65%	23	200	200	◄										
Newburgh	Udny Arms Hotel	(01358) 789444	H	85	60%	26	130	85											
Oldmeldrum	Meldrum House	(01651) 872294	H	95	65%	9	100	70	◄		◄				◄				
Peterhead	Waterside Inn	(01779) 471121	H	93	67%	110	200	245											
Rothes	Rothes Glen Hotel	(01340) 831254	H	90	65%	16	25												

Highland

Location	Establishment	Tel. No.	Category	Room £	Hotel %	No. of Rooms	Conf Max	Bang Max	Beaut Sit	Disabled	In Swim	Out Swim	Tennis	Squash	Golf	Fishing	Riding	15 mins Mway *	Country House
Achiltibuie	Summer Isles	(01854) 622282	HR	95	64%	12													
Advie	Tulchan Lodge	(01807) 510200	H	350	65%	9		22	◄				◄			◄			
Altnaharra	Altnaharra Hotel	(01549) 411222	H	113	60%	16	70	70	◄							◄			
Appin	Invercreran Country House Hotel	(01631) 730414	H	126	67%	9	60	20	◄										
Arisaig	Arisaig House	(01687) 450622	HR	160	75%	14	12	20											
Arisaig	Old Library Lodge & Restaurant	(01687) 450651	RR	62		6													
Aviemore	Aviemore Highlands Hotel	(01479) 810771	H	93	61%	102	120	100											
Aviemore	Stakis Aviemore Four Seasons	(01479) 810681	H			88	160	180			◄								
Aviemore	Stakis Coylumbridge Resort Hotel	(01479) 810661	H	103	62%	175	750	610			◄		◄						

Location	Hotel	Phone	Type					
Ballachulish	Ballachulish Hotel	(01855) 811606	H	82	60%	54	60	150
Ballachulish	Isles of Glencoe Hotel	(01855) 811602	H	92	59%	39	60	150
Beauly	Lovat Arms Hotel	(01463) 782313	H	74	59%	22	100	80
Contin	Craigdarroch Lodge	(01997) 421265	H	84	56%	13		
Cromarty	Royal Hotel	(01381) 600217	I	58		10	120	120
Drumnadrochit	Polmaily House	(01456) 450343	HR	90	66%	12	0	40
Dulnain Bridge	Auchendean Lodge	(01479) 851347	HR	69	62%	8		
Dulnain Bridge	Muckrach Lodge	(01479) 851257	H	82	59%	12	80	76
Duror	Stewart Hotel	(0163 174) 268	H	80	59%	19		
Fort William	The Factor's House	(01397) 705767	RR	110		5		24
Fort William	Inverlochy Castle	(01397) 702177	HR	276	90%	17		34
Fort William	Mercury Hotel	(01397) 703117	H	93	58%	86		
Gairloch	Creag Mor	(01445) 712068	H	80	66%	19	15	60
Garve	Inchbae Lodge	(01997) 455269	HR	60	57%	12	0	30
Glenelg	Glenelg Inn	(01599) 522273	IR	76		6		
Helmsdale	Navidale House	(01431) 821258	H	60	60%	15		65
Inverness	Bunchrew House	(01463) 234917	H	105	67%	11	90	90
Inverness	Caledonian Hotel	(01463) 235181	H	117	69%	106	300	240
Inverness	Culloden House	(01463) 790461	HR	175	73%	23	75	50
Inverness	Dunain Park	(01463) 230512	HR	130	69%	14		12
Inverness	Kingsmills Hotel	(01463) 237166	H	130	67%	84	60	80
Inverness	Mercury Hotel	(01463) 239666	H	115	62%	118	230	160
Kentallen of Appin	Ardsheal House	(01631) 740227	HR	160	64%	13	25	50
Kentallen of Appin	Holly Tree	(01631) 740292	H	90	65%	10	20	50
Kingussie	The Cross	(01540) 661166	RR	170		9		
Kinlochbervie	Kinlochbervie Hotel	(01971) 521275	H	84	64%	14		

Location	Establishment	Tel. No.	Category	Room £	Hotel %	No. of Rooms	Conf Max	Banq Max	Beaut Sit	Disabled	In Swim	Out Swim	Tennis	Squash	Golf	Fishing	Riding	15 mins Mway*	Country House
Kyle of Lochalsh	Lochalsh Hotel	(01599) 534202	H	85	63%	38	80	80								▲			
Lochinver	Inver Lodge Hotel	(01571) 844496	H	130	70%	20	80												
Muir-of-Ord	Dower House	(01463) 870090	RR	100		5		28											
Nairn	Clifton House Hotel	(01667) 453119	HR	96	70%	12	100	20											
Nairn	Golf View Hotel	(01667) 452301	H	112	67%	47	140	120			▲		▲						
Nairn	Newton Hotel	(01667) 53144	H	70	65%	44	60	100											
Onich	Allt-Nan-Ros Hotel	(01855) 821210	HR	95	63%	21	70	70	▲										
Onich	Lodge On The Loch Hotel	(01855) 821237	H	142	63%	22	60	55	▲	▲	▲								
Onich	Onich Hotel	(01855) 821214	H	80	61%	25			▲							▲			
Portree	Rosedale Hotel	(01478) 613131	H	70	56%	23													
Scarista	Scarista House	(01859) 550238	HR	89	67%	8		8	▲							▲			
Scourie	Eddrachilles Hotel	(01971) 502080	H	72	60%	11			▲							▲			
Scourie	Scourie Hotel	(01971) 502396	H	72	60%	20										▲			
Sceabost Bridge	Skeabost House	(01470) 532202	H	92	60%	26	60		▲						▲	▲			
Sleat	Kinloch Lodge	(01471) 833214	HR	130	67%	10			▲							▲			
Stornoway	Cabarfeidh Hotel	(01851) 702604	H	88	64%	47	400	330											
Strontian	Kilcamb Lodge	(01967) 402257	HR	135	68%	8			▲							▲			
Talladale	Loch Maree Hotel	(01445) 760288	I	80		30	50	50	▲							▲			
Uig	Uig Hotel	(01470) 542205	H	86	59%	17	12												
Ullapool	Altnaharrie Inn	(01854) 633230	HR	280	73%	8		18	▲								▲		
Ullapool	Ceilidh Place	(01854) 612103	IR	100		13	50	100											
Whitebridge	Knockie Lodge	(01456) 486276	HR	90	71%	10			▲							▲			

Lothian

Location	Hotel	Phone	Type		%			
Bonnyrigg	Dalhousie Castle	(01875) 820153	H	120	62%	25	120	100
Dirleton	Open Arms Hotel	(01620) 850241	H	119	67%	7	120	90
Edinburgh	The Balmoral Hotel	0131-556 2414	HR	167	83%	189	380	400
Edinburgh	Barnton Thistle	0131-339 1144	H	108	63%	50	150	120
Edinburgh	Braid Hills Hotel	0131-447 8888	H	95	61%	68	150	140
Edinburgh	Caledonian Hotel	0131-225 2433	HR	280	79%	236	400	220
Edinburgh	Capital Moat House	0131-334 3391	H	134	66%	111	300	300
Edinburgh	Carlton Highland	0131-556 7277	H	160	68%	197	350	250
Edinburgh	Channings	0131-315 2226	H	135	64%	48	35	18
Edinburgh	Forte Posthouse	0131-334 0390	H	75	62%	204	140	100
Edinburgh	George Inter-Continental	0131-225 1251	H	180	74%	195	200	150
Edinburgh	Greenside Hotel	(01315) 570022	PH	80		13		
Edinburgh	Hilton National	0131-332 2545	H	176	68%	143	125	90
Edinburgh	Holiday Inn Garden Court	0131-332 2442	H	95	65%	119	60	50
Edinburgh	Howard Hotel	0131-557 3500	H	180	74%	16	45	40
Edinburgh	King James Thistle Hotel	0131-556 0111	H	128	70%	147	250	250
Edinburgh	Malmaison Edinburgh	0131-555 6868	HR	90	65%	25	250	110
Edinburgh	Roxburghe Hotel	0131-225 3921	H	110	64%	75	275	250
Edinburgh	Royal Terrace Hotel	0131-557 3222	H	159	70%	93	80	60
Edinburgh	Scandic Crown Hotel	0131-557 9797	H	165	63%	238	220	150
Edinburgh	Sheraton Grand Hotel	0131-229 9131	H	231	79%	261	600	485
Edinburgh	Stakis Grosvenor Hotel	0131-226 6001	H	112	64%	136	500	500
Edinburgh	Swallow Royal Scot	0131-334 9191	H	125	65%	259	250	250
Gullane	Greywalls Hotel	(01620) 842144	HR	170	76%	22	30	50
Ingliston	Norton House	0131-333 1275	H	120	66%	47	250	160

Location	Establishment	Tel. No.	Category	Room £	Hotel %	No. of Rooms	Conf Max	Bang Max	Beaut Slt	Disabled	In Swim	Out Swim	Tennis	Squash	Golf	Fishing	Riding	15 mins Mway*	Country House
Kirknewton	Dalmahoy Hotel	0131-333 1845	HR	127	78%	151	180	120			◄		◄	◄	◄				
North Berwick	Marine Hotel	(01620) 892406	H	85	64%	83	300	250	◄			◄	◄						
North Middleton	Borthwick Castle Hotel	(01875) 820514	H	120	66%	10	50	50	◄										
South Queensferry	Forth Bridges Hotel	0131-461 9955	H	116	61%	108	250	250						◄					
Uphall	Houstoun House	(01506) 853831	H	133	69%	42	300	250											

Orkney

Location	Establishment	Tel. No.	Category	Room £	Hotel %	No. of Rooms	Conf Max	Bang Max	Beaut Slt	Disabled	In Swim	Out Swim	Tennis	Squash	Golf	Fishing	Riding	15 mins Mway*	Country House
Harray Loch	Merkister Hotel	(01856) 771366	H	66	59%	14	140	80	◄							◄			

Shetland

Location	Establishment	Tel. No.	Category	Room £	Hotel %	No. of Rooms	Conf Max	Bang Max	Beaut Slt	Disabled	In Swim	Out Swim	Tennis	Squash	Golf	Fishing	Riding	15 mins Mway*	Country House
Lerwick	Shetland Hotel	(01595) 5515	H	82	62%	64	225	180		◄									

Strathclyde

Location	Establishment	Tel. No.	Category	Room £	Hotel %	No. of Rooms	Conf Max	Bang Max	Beaut Slt	Disabled	In Swim	Out Swim	Tennis	Squash	Golf	Fishing	Riding	15 mins Mway*	Country House
Alexandria	Cameron House	(01389) 755565	HR	150	81%	68	300	240			◄		◄	◄	◄	◄			
Ardentinny	Ardentinny Hotel	(01369) 810209	H	86	62%	11	25	40	◄							◄			
Arduaine	Loch Melfort Hotel	(01852) 200233	H	93	65%	27	20	100	◄										
Ayr	Jarvis Caledonian Hotel	(01292) 269331	H	117	64%	114	175	200			◄								
Craignure	Isle of Mull Hotel	(01680) 812351	H	90	56%	87													
Crinan	Crinan Hotel	(01546) 830261	HR	115	69%	22	45	45	◄							◄			
Cumbernauld	Westerwood Hotel	(01236) 457171	HR	100	73%	49	220	170			◄				◄	◄	◄		
Dervaig	Druimard Country House	(01688) 400345	RR	85		6			◄								◄		
East Kilbride	Stakis Westpoint Hotel	(013552) 36300	H	115	74%	74	150	120		◄	◄			◄					

Location	Hotel	Phone	Type						
East Kilbride	Stuart Hotel	(0135 52) 21161	H	80	62%	39	200	150	
Eriska	Isle of Eriska	(01631) 720371	HR	165	75%	17	20	40	
Erskine	Forte Posthouse	0141-812 0123	H	72	62%	166	600	450	
Giffnock	Macdonald Thistle	0141-638 2225	H	87	64%	56	160	130	
Glasgow	Beardmore Hotel	0141-951 6000	H	110		168	170	50	
Glasgow	Copthorne Hotel	0141-332 6711	H	125	64%	140	100	80	
Glasgow	Devonshire Hotel	0141-339 7878	PH	137		14	50	35	
Glasgow	Forte Crest	0141-248 2656	H	120	74%	251	800	800	
Glasgow	Glasgow Moat House	0141-204 0733	H	144	69%	283	800	600	
Glasgow	Glasgow Marriott Hotel	0141-226 5577	H	100	73%	298	720	650	
Glasgow	Glasgow Hilton	0141-204 5555	HR	140	78%	319	1100	950	
Glasgow	Glasgow Thistle Hotel	0141-332 3311	H	141	67%	307	1500	1200	
Glasgow	Jurys Glasgow Hotel	0141-334 8161	H	92	59%	133	150	120	
Glasgow	Kelvin Park Lorne Hotel	0141-314 9955	H	93	63%	98	300	200	
Glasgow	Malmaison Hotel et Brasserie	0141-221 6400	HR	90	66%	21			
Glasgow	One Devonshire Gardens	0141-339 2001	HR	145	82%	27	50	50	
Glasgow	Stakis Grosvenor	0141-339 8811	H	116	66%	95	450	300	
Glasgow	Swallow Hotel	0141-427 3146	H	95	62%	117	300	220	
Glasgow	Tinto Firs Hotel	0141-637 2353	H	90	62%	28	200	130	
Glasgow	Town House	0141-332 3320	H	91	66%	34	180	130	
Glasgow Airport	Forte Crest	0141-887 1212	H	121	68%	307	450	450	
Glasgow Airport	Stakis Glasgow Airport	0141-886 4100	H	102	61%	141	1000	600	
Gourock	Stakis Gourock Hotel	(01475) 634671	H	102	64%	99	350	200	
Irvine	Hospitality Inn	(01294) 274272	H	118	68%	127	320	220	
Kilchrenan	Ardanaiseig	(01866) 833333	HR	142	74%	14	30	85	
Kilchrenan	Taychreggan Hotel	(01866) 833211	HR	80	66%	20	30	85	

Location	Establishment	Tel. No.	Category	Room £	Hotel %	No. of Rooms	Conf Max	Banq Max	Beaut Sit	Disabled	In Swim	Out Swim	Tennis	Squash	Golf	Fishing	Riding	15 mins Mway* Country House	Country House
Kilfinan	Kilfinan Hotel	(01700) 821201	IR	72		11	20	20								◀			
Kilmore	Glenfeochan House	(01631) 770273	HR	128	70%	3	10	10	◀							◀			
Kilwinning	Montgreenan Mansion House	(01294) 557733	H	92	70%	21	100	100	◀					◀	◀				
Langbank	Gleddoch House	(01475) 540711	H	140	68%	39	100	120	◀				◀		◀		◀		
Maybole	Ladyburn	(01655) 740585	HR	140	73%	8	20	20											
Milngavie	Black Bull Thistle	0141-956 2291	H	93	59%	27	100	100											
Oban	Alexandra Hotel	(01631) 562381	H	90	59%	60	120	120	◀	◀									
Oban	Columba Hotel	(01631) 562183	H	99	60%	48	300	250											
Oban	Knipoch Hotel	(01852) 316251	HR	130	72%	17	24	24	◀										
Port Appin	Airds Hotel	(01631) 730236	HR	266	75%	12			◀										
Port Appin	Pier House Hotel & Seadfood Rest'nt	(01631) 730302	IR	70		11													
Quothquan	Shieldhill	(01899) 20035	H	104	73%	11	25	40											
Skelmorlie	Manor Park	(01475) 520832	H	85	61%	23	150	130	◀										
Stewarton	Chapeltoun House	(01560) 482696	H	99	71%	8	80	55								◀			
Strachur	Creggans Inn	(01369) 860279	H	98	61%	21	50	85	◀						◀	◀			
Tarbert	Stonefield Castle	(01880) 820836	H	130	58%	33	200	150	◀			◀			◀	◀			
Tobermory	Tobermory Hotel	(01688) 302091	H	66	57%	17													
Troon	Marine Highland Hotel	(01292) 314444	H	146	67%	72	250	200		◀	◀		◀						
Troon	Piersland House	(01292) 314747	H	98	64%	23	110	150		◀	◀								
Turnberry	Turnberry Hotel	(01655) 331000	HR	210	84%	132	150	250	◀	◀	◀	◀	◀	◀	◀		◀		

Tayside

Location	Hotel	Phone	Type		%			
Aberfeldy	Farleyer House	(01887) 820332	HR	130	70%	11	25	35
Alyth	Drumnacree House	(01828) 632194	RR	65		6	0	50
Auchterarder	Auchterarder House	(01764) 663646	HR	130	75%	15	70	60
Auchterarder	Gleneagles Hotel	(01764) 662231	H	230	86%	234	360	240
Auchterhouse	Old Mansion House	(01382) 626366	HR	120	68%	6	20	20
Blairgowrie	Kinloch House	(01250) 884237	HR	152	70%	21	30	30
Callander	Roman Camp Hotel	(01877) 330003	HR	95	69%	14	50	47
Cleish	Nivingston House	(01577) 850216	H	95	65%	17	50	80
Crieff	Crieff Hydro	(01764) 655555	H	106	64%	239	350	250
Dundee	Angus Thistle	(01382) 226874	H	107	69%	58	500	400
Dundee	Invercarse Hotel	(01382) 669231	H	80	59%	35	200	280
Dunkeld	Kinnaird	(01796) 482440	HR	185	81%	9	25	25
Forfar	Royal Hotel	(01307) 62691	H	70	57%	19	220	160
Glamis	Castleton House	(01307) 840340	HR	90	71%	6		140
Glencarse	Newton House Hotel	(01738) 860250	H	90	58%	10	80	80
Kenmore	Kenmore Hotel	(01887) 830205	H	117	62%	39	80	70
Killiecrankie	Killiecrankie Hotel	(01796) 473220	H	145	64%	10		
Kinclaven by Stanley	Ballathie House	(01250) 883268	HR	155	74%	39	80	60
Kinross	Windlestrae Hotel	(01577) 863217	H	100	62%	46	250	200
Kirkmichael	Log Cabin Hotel	(01250) 881288	H	66	59%	13	30	90
Perth	Royal George Hotel	(01738) 624455	H	87	62%	42	100	80
Perth	Stakis City Mills Hotel	(01738) 628281	H	94	60%	76	130	150
Pitlochry	Green Park Hotel	(01796) 473248	H	90	58%	37		
Pitlochry	Pitlochry Hydro Hotel	(01796) 472666	H	106	64%	62	100	60
Scone	Murrayshall House	(01738) 551171	HR	125	72%	19	60	80
St Fillans	Four Seasons Hotel	(01764) 685333	HR	74	60%	18	90	100

THE INDEPENDENT

INDEPENDENT
ON SUNDAY

Your truly independent guides to life

Scotland by County: Lodges

See How To Use This Guide, on pages 14-15, for an explanation of our percentage rating system, room pricing and categories.

Location	Establishment	Tel. No.	Map Ref	Motorway comments	Address
Central					
Stirling	Granada Lodge	(01786) 815033	3 C5	M90/M80 J9	Stirling
Dumfries & Galloway					
Collin	Forte Travelodge	(0800) 850 950	4C2	A75	Annan Road Collin Nr Dumfries
Gretna Green	Forte Travelodge	(01461) 337566	4 C2	A74(M)	Trunk Road Gretna Green
Fife					
Glenrothes	Travel Inn	(01592) 773473	3 C5	M90 J3/A92	Beaufort Drive Bankhead Roundabout Glenrothes
Grampian					
Aberdeen	Travel Inn	(01224) 821217	3 D4	A92	Murcar Bridge of Don Aberdeen
Lothian					
Edinburgh	Forte Travelodge	0131-441 4296	3 C6	A720	E'bound Dreghorn Link City By-Pass
Edinburgh	Granada Lodge	0131-653 2427	3 C6	A1 Musselburgh	Musselburgh By-Pass Musselburgh Edinburgh
Edinburgh	Travel Inn	0131-661 3396	3 C6	A1	228 Willowbrae Road Edinburgh

Location	Establishment	Tel. No.	Map Ref	Motorway comments	Address
Strathclyde					
Abington	Forte Travelodge	(01864) 2782	4 B1	A74/M74 J13	Welcome Break Services Abington Biggar
Ayr (Monkton)	Travel Inn	(01582) 482224	4 A1	A77/A78	Kilmarnock Road Monkton Nr Ayr
Cumbernauld	Travel Inn	(01236) 725339	3 C5	A8011	4 South Muirhead Road Cumbernauld Nr Glasgow
Dumbarton	Forte Travelodge	(01389) 65202	3 B5	A82 W'bound	Milton Dumbarton
East Kilbride	Travel Inn	(01355) 222809	3 C6	M74 J5/A725/A726	Brunel Way The Murray East Kilbride
Glasgow	Granada Lodge	0141-420 3882	3 B6	M8 J20	25 Paisley Road Glasgow
Glasgow Airport	Travel Inn	0141-842 1563	3 B6	M8	Whitecart Road Glasgow Airport Paisley
Kilmarnock	Forte Travelodge	(01563) 73810	4 A1	A71/A76/A77	Bellfield Interchange Kilmarnock
Newhouse	Travel Inn (Motherwell)	(01698) 860277	3 C6	M74 J6/A723/M8 J6	Glasgow Road Newhouse Nr Motherwell
Tayside					
Dundee	Travel Inn	(01382) 203240	3 C5	A85/Dundee BR Station	Discovery Quay Riverside Drive Dundee
Dundee (Invergowrie)	Travel Inn (Dundee West)	(01382) 561115	3 C5	A90	Kingsway West Invergowrie Dundee
Kinross	Granada Lodge	(01577) 64646	3 C5	M90 J6	Kinross

Scotland by County: Restaurants

See How To Use This Guide, on pages 14–15, for an explanation of our percentage rating system, room pricing and categories.
No-smoking denotes a ban on smoking throughout or a separate no-smoking room.

Location	Establishment	Tel. No.	Dinner for 2, £	Category	Stars	Seats	Parties	Private Rms	Sundays	No-Smoking	Open Air	Nat Cuisine	Seafood	Vegetarian	Dessert	Cheese	O/s Wine	New World	Italian Wine	Wines by glass
Borders																				
Newtown																				
St Boswells	Le Provençale	(01835) 823284	40	R		40	18	yes		yes		French			◄			◄		
Peebles	Cringletie House	(01721) 730233	65	HR		56	12	yes	All									◄		
Central																				
Aberfoyle	Braval	(01877) 382711	75	R	↑	34	12		L						◄		◄			
Dunblane	Cromlix House	(01786) 822125	90	HR		40	8	yes	All	yes						◄				
Falkirk	Pierre's	(01324) 635843	50	R		40	14					French		◄						
Dumfries & Galloway																				
Auchencairn	Balcary Bay Hotel	(01556) 640217	60	HR		50	18							◄						
Auchencairn	Collin House	(01556) 640292	68	HR		16	9			yes					◄					
Canonbie	Riverside Inn	(0138 73) 71512	55	IR		24	6		D	yes	yes		◄		◄	◄				

Location	Establishment	Tel. No.	Dinner for 2, £	Category	Stars	Seats	Parties	Private Rms	Sundays	No-Smoking	Open Air	Nat Cuisine	Seafood	Vegetarian	Dessert	Cheese	O/s Wine	New World	Italian Wine	Wines by glass
Newton Stewart	Kirroughtree Hotel	(01671) 402141	65	HR		40	12	yes	All	yes						◄		◄		
Portpatrick	Knockinaam Lodge	(01776) 810471	80	HR		32	10		D	yes							◄	◄	◄	◄
Fife																				
Anstruther	Cellar	(01333) 310378	75	R		30	30			yes			◄			◄	◄	◄		
Cupar	Ostlers Close	(01334) 655574	60	R		28	12											◄		◄
Markinch	Balbirnie House	(01592) 610066	65	HR		100	10	yes	All	yes							◄	◄	◄	
Peat Inn	The Peat Inn	(01334) 840206	85	RR	★†	48	12	yes	All	yes					◄	◄	◄	◄		
St Andrews	Grange Inn	(01334) 472670	45	R		76	20	yes	yes	yes	yes			◄			◄			
Grampian																				
Aberdeen	Atlantis	(01224) 591403	65	R		50	25		All											
Aberdeen	Gerard's	(01224) 639500	70	R		70	50	yes		yes		French	◄	◄						
Aberdeen	Marcliffe at Pitfodels	(01224) 861000	90	HR		32	12	yes		yes						◄		◄		◄
Aberdeen	Silver Darling	(01224) 576229	65	R		35	30					French	◄							
Ballater	Tullich Lodge	(0133 97) 55406	60	HR		26	8		All	yes		British								
Banchory	Raemoir House	(01330) 824884	75	HR		70	16	yes	All	yes				◄				◄		◄
Drybridge	Old Monastery	(01542) 832660	55	R		45				yes								◄		◄
Highland																				
Achiltibuie	Summer Isles	(01854) 622282	75	HR		26	8		D	yes			◄			◄	◄			
Arisaig	Arisaig House	(01687) 450622	85	HR		36	10		All	yes yes			◄		◄	◄				

Town	Name	Phone		Code							Cuisine
Arisaig	Old Library Lodge	(01687) 450651	60	RR	28		12	All		yes	
Colbost	Three Chimneys	(01470) 511258	60	R	30				yes	yes	
Drumnadrochit	Polmaily House	(01456) 450343	45	HR	40	20	yes	D	yes	yes	
Dulnain Bridge	Auchendean Lodge	(01479) 851347	55	HR	18	18		D	yes		
Fort William	Crannog Seafood Restaurant	(01397) 705589	50	R	70		yes	All			
Fort William	The Factor's House	(01397) 705767	70	RR	24	8		D	yes		
Fort William	Inverlochy Castle	(01397) 702177	100	HR ★	34	8	yes	All	yes		
Garve	Inchbae Lodge	(01997) 455269	60	HR	30	8			yes	yes	
Glenelg	Glenelg Inn	(01599) 522273	55	IR	20	10		All	yes	yes	
Inverness	Culloden House	(01463) 790461	85	HR	50	18	yes	All	yes		
Inverness	Dunain Park	(01463) 230512	65	HR	45	12		D			
Kentallen of Appin	Ardsheal House	(01631) 740227	80	HR	45			All	yes	yes	
Kingussie	The Cross	(01540) 661166	70	RR	28	16		All	yes	yes	
Muir-of-Ord	Dower House	(01463) 870090	70	RR	28	26		All		yes	
Nairn	Clifton House Hotel	(01667) 453119	60	HR	35	30	yes	D			
Onich	Allt-Nan-Ros Hotel	(01855) 821210	55	HR	50	20		All	yes	yes	
Scarista	Scarista House	(01859) 550238	55	HR	16	8	yes	D	yes		
Sleat	Kinloch Lodge	(01471) 833214	75	HR	28	12		D	yes		
Spean Bridge	Old Station	(01397) 712535	45	R	30	10	yes	All			
Strontian	Kilcamb Lodge	(01967) 402257	70	HR	26				yes		
Ullapool	Altnaharrie Inn	(01854) 633230	150	HR	★★18	14		D			
Ullapool	Ceilidh Place	(01854) 612103	40	IR	50	26	yes	All	yes	yes	
Whitebridge	Knockie Lodge	(01456) 486276	70	HR	20	8			yes		

Lothian

Town	Name	Phone		Code							Cuisine
Edinburgh	Alp-Horn	0131-225 4787	45	R	66	12	yes	All	yes	yes	Swiss
Edinburgh	The Atrium	0131-228 8882	60	R ↑	70				yes		
Edinburgh	L'Auberge	0131-556 5888	75	R	65	20	yes	All			French
Edinburgh	The Balmoral: NB's	0131-556 2414	40	R	90	16		All			

Location	Establishment	Tel. No.	Dinner for 2, £	Category	Stars	Seats	Parties	Private Rms	Sundays	No-Smoking	Open Air	Nat Cuisine	Seafood	Vegetarian	Dessert	Cheese	O/s Wine	New World	Italian Wine	Wines by glass
Edinburgh	The Balmoral Hotel	0131-556 2414	110	HR	†	45	8		D					◄	◄	◄		◄		
Edinburgh	Caledonian Hotel	0131-225 2433	105	HR		60	10									◄		◄		
Edinburgh	Caledonian Hotel: Carriages	0131-225 2433	60	R		130	10													
Edinburgh	Denzlers 121	0131-554 3268	50	R		65	12					Swiss								
Edinburgh	Indian Cavalry Club	0131-228 3282	45	R		70	70	yes	All			Indian		◄						
Edinburgh	Kalpna	0131-667 9890	35	R		60	30	yes		yes		Indian		◄						
Edinburgh	Kelly's	0131-668 3847	60	R		34	22	yes								◄				◄
Edinburgh	Malmaison Edinburgh	0131-555 6868	60	HR		74		yes		yes										◄
Edinburgh	Le Marché Noir	0131-558 1608	60	R		35	45				yes	French								◄
Edinburgh	Martin's	0131-225 3106	75	R		28	10	yes		yes						◄	◄			
Edinburgh	Ristorante Raffaelli	0131-225 6060	45	R		60	20			yes		Italian			◄			◄	◄	
Edinburgh	Ristorante Tinelli	0131-652 1932	35	R		32	12					Italian			◄			◄	◄	
Edinburgh	Shamiana	0131-228 2265	40	R		36	22	yes	D	yes		Indian								
Edinburgh	Szechuan House	0131-229 4655	30	R		100	25	yes	D			Chinese								
Edinburgh	Vintners Room	0131-554 6767	55	R		60	16	yes		yes				◄						◄
Gullane	Greywalls Hotel	(01620) 842144	85	HR		50	12	yes	All	yes					◄	◄	◄	◄		
Gullane	La Potinière	(01620) 843214	75	R	★	30	12	yes	L	yes							◄	◄	◄	
Kirknewton	Dalmahoy Hotel	0131-333 1845	70	HR		120	20	yes	All	yes	yes					◄		◄		
Linlithgow	Champany Inn	(01506) 834532	100	R	★	50	16	yes		yes	yes				◄	◄	◄	◄	◄	
Linlithgow	Champany Inn Chop & Ale House	(01506) 834532	50	R		38	8		All		yes									◄

Strathclyde

Town	Restaurant	Phone	Seats	Type								Cuisine
Alexandria	Cameron House	(01389) 755565	80	HR		42	10	yes	All	yes		
Ayr	Fouters Bistro	(01292) 261391	50	R		38	18	yes	D	yes		
Ayr	The Stables	(01292) 283704	30	R		52			L	yes	yes	
Bearsden	Fifty Five BC	0141-942 7272	50	R		25	20		All		yes	
Cairndow	Loch Fyne Oyster Bar	(01499) 600236	50	R		80	50		All	yes	yes	
Crinan	Crinan Hotel: Westward Restaurant	(01546) 830261	70	R		45	12		D			
Crinan	Crinan Hotel	(01546) 830261	95	HR	★	20	20					
Cumbernauld	Westerwood Hotel	(01236) 457171	70	HR		75	8	yes	All	yes		
Dervaig	Druimard Country Hse	(01688) 400345	55	RR		30	12	yes		yes		
Dunoon	Chatters	(01369) 706402	50	R		35	30			yes		
Eriska	Isle of Eriska	(01631) 720371	85	HR		40	40		D			
Fairlie	Fins Restaurant	(01475) 568989	60	R		30			L			
Glasgow	Amber	0141-339 6121	40	R		60	30		All			Chinese
Glasgow	Ashoka West End	0141-339 0936	30	R		60	30	yes	D			Indian
Glasgow	Brasserie on West Regent Street	0141-248 3801	45	R		100	22	yes				
Glasgow	Buttery	0141-204 4639	75	R		50	12	yes				
Glasgow	Café Gandolfi	0141-332 6711	35	R		60	12		All			
Glasgow	D'Arcy's	0141-226 4309	40	R		72	16		All	yes		
Glasgow	Glasgow Hilton	0141-204 5555	95	HR		55	22	yes	D			
Glasgow	Loon Fung	0141-332 1240	45	R		190	30	yes	All			Chinese
Glasgow	Malmaison Hotel	0141-221 6400	60	HR		80						
Glasgow	Mata Hari	0141-332 9789	40	R		50				yes		S E Asian
Glasgow	One Devonshire Gardens	0141-339 2001	95	HR		50	8	yes	All			
Glasgow	La Parmigiana	0141-334 0686	50	R		60						Italian
Glasgow	Puppet Theatre	0141-339 8444	75	R	↑	65		yes	All			
Glasgow	Ristorante Caprese	0141-332 3070	35	R		60	70	yes				Italian
Glasgow	Roga	0141-248 4055	75	R		50	16	yes	D			
Glasgow	Two Fat Ladies	0141-339 1944	55	R		30	12	yes				

Location	Establishment	Tel. No.	Dinner for 2, £	Category	Stars	Seats	Parties	Private Rms	Sundays	No-Smoking	Open Air	Nat Cuisine	Seafood	Vegetarian	Dessert	Cheese	O/s Wine	New World	Italian Wine	Wines by glass
Glasgow	Ubiquitous Chip	0141-334 5007	75	R		140	60	yes	All		yes			▲		▲	▲	▲	▲	
Kilchrenan	Ardanaiseig	(01866) 833333	80	HR		30		yes	All							▲	▲	▲		▲
Kilchrenan	Taychreggan Hotel	(01866) 833211	70	HR		60	24	yes	All	yes	yes									
Kilfinan	Kilfinan Hotel	(01700) 821201	70	IR		22	10	yes	All	yes	yes									
Kilmore	Glenfeochan House	(01631) 770273	70	HR		10			D	yes						▲				
Maybole	Ladyburn	(01655) 740585	60	HR		25	22		D						▲					
Oban	Knipoch Hotel	(01852) 316251	80	HR		44	12	yes	D	yes						▲	▲	▲	▲	
Port Appin	Airds Hotel	(0163 173) 236	80	HR		34	8	yes	All								▲	▲		
Port Appin	Pier House Hotel	(01631) 730302	55	IR		40						British	▲							
Turnberry	Turnberry Hotel	(01655) 331000	130	HR		180	10	yes	All								▲			

Tayside

Location	Establishment	Tel. No.	Dinner for 2, £	Category	Stars	Seats	Parties	Private Rms	Sundays	No-Smoking	Open Air	Nat Cuisine	Seafood	Vegetarian	Dessert	Cheese	O/s Wine	New World	Italian Wine	Wines by glass
Aberfeldy	Farleyer House	(01887) 820332	75	HR		22	24	yes	D	yes	yes					▲		▲		▲
Alyth	Drummacree House	(01828) 632194	55	RR		30	22	yes		yes										
Auchterarder	Auchterarder House	(01764) 663646	90	HR		23	12	yes	All	yes							▲	▲		▲
Auchterhouse	Old Mansion House	(01382) 320366	75	HR		50	10	yes	All	yes	yes									
Blairgowrie	Kinloch House	(01250) 884237	75	HR		55	30	yes	All	yes	yes						▲	▲	▲	
Callander	Roman Camp Hotel	(01877) 330003	129	HR	↑	45	12	yes	All	yes				▲					▲	
Dunkeld	Kinnaird	(01796) 482440	90	HR		35	8	yes	All	yes					▲	▲	▲	▲		
Glamis	Castleton House	(01307) 840340	55	HR		28	7	yes	All				▲							
Kinclaven by Stanley	Ballathie House	(01250) 883268	70	HR		80	12	yes	All	yes							▲	▲		▲
Perth	Number Thirty Three	(01738) 633771	55	R		45	10													
Scone	Murrayshall House	(01738) 551171	60	HR		80	12	yes	All							▲				
St Fillans	Four Seasons Hotel	(01764) 685333	60	HR		55	20	yes	All	yes						▲				

Wales by County: Hotels

See How To Use This Guide, on pages 14–15, for an explanation of our percentage rating system, room pricing and categories.
*15 mins Mway refers to hotels graded 70% or higher within 15 minutes of a motorway.

Location	Establishment	Tel. No.	Category	Room £	Hotel %	No. of Rooms	Conf Max	Banq Max	Beaut Sit	Disabled	In Swim	Out Swim	Tennis	Squash	Golf	Fishing	Riding	15 mins Mway* Country House
Clwyd																		
Chirk	Starlings Castle	(01691) 718464	RR	58		10		50										
Colwyn Bay	Colwyn Bay Hotel	(01492) 516555	H	53	61%	43	200	180										
Ewloe	St David's Park Hotel	(01244) 520800	H	107	69%	121	325	220							◄			
Llanarmon Dyffryn Ceiriog	Hand Hotel	(01691) 600666	I	58		13	25	70								◄		
Llanarmon Dyffryn Ceiriog	West Arms Hotel	(01691) 600665	I	100		13	30	90	◄							◄		
Llandrillo	Tyddyn Llan	(01490) 440264	HR	88	66%	10	45	90	◄							◄		
Llangollen	Hand Hotel	(01978) 860303	H	68	55%	58	90	100		◄						◄		
Llangollen	Royal Hotel	(01978) 860202	H	82	59%	33	80	80								◄		
Northop	Soughton Hall	(01352) 840811	H	99	79%	14	40	150	◄				◄					
Rossett	Llyndir Hall	(01244) 571648	H	110	71%	38	130	90	◄		◄							
Ruthin	Ruthin Castle	(01824) 702664	H	85	62%	60	150	150	◄							◄		

Location	Establishment	Tel. No.	Category	Room £	Hotel %	No. of Rooms	Conf Max	Bang Max	Beaut Sit	Disabled	In Swim	Out Swim	Tennis	Squash	Golf	Fishing	Riding	15 mins Mway*	Country House
Dyfed																			
Aberystwyth	Conrah Country Hotel	(01970) 617941	H	93	63%	20	60	70	◄		◄								
Brechfa	Ty Mawr	(01267) 202332	RR	76		5	20	35											
Carmarthen	Ivy Bush Royal	(01267) 235111	H	75	59%	75	250	200											
Fishguard	Fishguard Bay Hotel	(01348) 873571	H	55	59%	62	80	300											
Gwbert-on-Sea	Cliff Hotel	(01239) 613241	H	59	60%	73	200	200	◄		◄	◄		◄	◄	◄			
Lamphey	Court Hotel	(01646) 672273	H	85	68%	32	100	80			◄								
Llandeilo	Cawdor Arms	(01558) 823500	H	70	65%	12	160	120											
Penally	Penally Abbey	(01834) 843033	HR	90	65%	12		46			◄								
St David's	St Non's Hotel	(01437) 720239	H	64	56%	24	180	120					◄						
St David's	Warpool Court	(01437) 720300	H	104	64%	25	40	120	◄		◄	◄			◄				
Welsh Hook	Stone Hall	(01348) 840212	RR	60		5	30	45											
Gwent																			
Abergavenny	Llanwenarth Arms Hotel	(01873) 810550	I	59		18		60		◄									
Chepstow	Castle View Hotel	(01291) 620349	I	61		13													
Chepstow	St Pierre Hotel	(01291) 625261	H	123	70%	141	220	220			◄		◄	◄	◄				
Llangybi	Cwrt Bleddyn Hotel	(01633) 450521	H	102	71%	36	200	160		◄	◄		◄	◄				◄	
Llanvihangel Gobion	Llansantffraed Court	(01873) 840678	H	75	66%	21	50	120											
Newport	Celtic Manor	(01633) 413000	H	120	75%	73	350	200			◄				◄			◄	
Newport	Hilton National	(01633) 412777	H	84	61%	119	500	300			◄								
Newport	Stakis Cardiff Newport	(01633) 413737	H	113	69%	141	80	60			◄								

Location	Hotel	Phone	Type						
Tintern Abbey	Beaufort Hotel	(01291) 689777	H	92	60%	24	80	90	◀
Tintern Abbey	Royal George	(01291) 689205	H	72	59%	19	80	120	◀
Trellech	Village Green	(01600) 860119	RR	45		2	30	36	
Whitebrook	Crown at Whitebrook	(01600) 860254	RR	65		12	30	30	

Gwynedd

Location	Hotel	Phone	Type						
Aberdovey	Penhelig Arms Hotel	(01654) 767215	IR	68		10			
Aberdovey	Plas Penhelig	(01654) 767676	H	80	62%	11	24	60	◀
Aberdovey	Trefeddian Hotel	(01654) 767213	H	70	60%	46	20	70	◀
Abersoch	Porth Tocyn Hotel	(01758) 713303	HR	94	69%	17			◀
Abersoch	Riverside Hotel	(01758) 712419	H	70	70%	12			◀
Beaumaris	Bulkeley Arms	(01248) 810415	H	67	59%	42	200	130	◀
Beddgelert	Royal Goat Hotel	(0176 686) 224	H	68	60%	34	120	100	◀
Betws-y-Coed	Royal Oak	(01690) 710219	H	74	59%	27	25	80	◀
Bontddu	Bontddu Hall	(01341) 430661	H	90	62%	20	30	90	◀
Capel Coch	Tre-Ysgawen Hall	(01248) 750750	HR	110	76%	20	150	120	◀
Conwy	Sychnant Pass Hotel	(01492) 596868	H	60	60%	13	40	40	◀
Holyhead	Trearddur Bay Hotel	(01407) 860301	H	98	65%	30	120	120	◀
Llandudno	Bodysgallen Hall	(01492) 584466	HR	140	77%	29	50	40	◀
Llandudno	Empire Hotel	(01492) 860555	H	70	70%	58	20		◀
Llandudno	St Tudno Hotel	(01492) 874411	HR	110	69%	21	25	60	◀
Llandudno	St George's Hotel	(01492) 877788	H	78	61%	87	290	260	◀
Llanrug	Seiont Manor	(01286) 673366	H	100	71%	28	100	90	◀
Llansanffraid Glan Conwy	Old Rectory	(01492) 580611	HR	84	73%	6			◀
Llanwnda	Stables Hotel	(01286) 830711	H	49	57%	14	40	80	◀

Location	Establishment	Tel. No.	Category	Room £	Hotel %	No. of Rooms	Conf Max	Banq Max	Beaut Sit	Disabled	In Swim	Out Swim	Tennis	Squash	Golf	Fishing	Riding	15 mins Mway*	Country House
Penmaenpool	George III Hotel	(01341) 422525	I	88		12		40	◄	◄						◄			
Portmeirion	Hotel Portmeirion	(01766) 770228	HR	132	74%	37	100	100	◄			◄	◄		◄				
Pwllheli	Plas Bodegroes	(01758) 612363	RR	140		8													
Talsarnau	Maes-y-Neuadd	(01766) 780200	HR	107	72%	16	40	50	◄	◄									
Talyllyn	Tynycornel Hotel	(01654) 782282	H	90	59%	15	60	70				◄				◄			

Powys

Location	Establishment	Tel. No.	Category	Room £	Hotel %	No. of Rooms	Conf Max	Banq Max	Beaut Sit	Disabled	In Swim	Out Swim	Tennis	Squash	Golf	Fishing	Riding	15 mins Mway*	Country House
Crickhowell	Bear Hotel	(01873) 810408	I	54		29	60	60											
Crickhowell	Gliffaes Country House	(01874) 730371	H	85	63%	22	16	80	◄				◄			◄			
Eglwysfach	Ynyshir Hall	(01654) 781209	HR	120	70%	8	25	25	◄	◄									
Llangammarch Wells	Lake Country House	(01591) 620457	HR	115	69%	19	80	80	◄	◄	◄		◄			◄			
Llanwyddyn	Lake Vyrnwy Hotel	(01691) 870692	HR	77	67%	35	120	120	◄				◄			◄			
Llyswen	Llangoed Hall	(01874) 754525	HR	155	81%	23	50	50	◄				◄			◄			
Machynlleth	Wynnstay Arms	(01654) 702941	H	53	60%	20	40	85											
Pant Mawr	Glansevern Arms	(01686) 440240	I	55		7			◄										
Presteigne	Radnorshire Arms	(01544) 267406	I	92		16	30	28											

Mid Glamorgan

Location	Establishment	Tel. No.	Category	Room £	Hotel %	No. of Rooms	Conf Max	Banq Max	Beaut Sit	Disabled	In Swim	Out Swim	Tennis	Squash	Golf	Fishing	Riding	15 mins Mway*	Country House
Abercynon	Llechwen Hall	(01443) 742050	I	70		11	60	80											
Coychurch	Coed-y-Mwstwr Hotel	(01656) 860621	H	140	70%	23	185	160				◄	◄				◄		
Merthyr Tydfil	Baverstock Hotel	(01685) 386221	H	55	57%	53	300	250											
Miskin	Miskin Manor	(01443) 224204	H	95	70%	32	180	120			◄		◄	◄			◄		

South Glamorgan

Location	Hotel	Phone	Type					
Barry	Mount Sorrel Hotel	(01446) 740069	H	90	59%	43	200	120
Cardiff	Angel Hotel	(01222) 232633	H	111	64%	91	300	280
Cardiff	Cardiff Marriott Hotel	(01222) 399944	H	116	68%	182	300	300
Cardiff	Cardiff International	(01222) 341441	H	103	67%	143	40	40
Cardiff	Copthorne Hotel	(01222) 599100	H	122	70%	135	300	200
Cardiff	Forte Posthouse Cardiff City	(01222) 388681	H	86	69%	155	180	180
Cardiff	Forte Posthouse Cardiff	(01222) 731212	H	72	63%	150	140	120
Cardiff	Moat House	(01222) 732520	H	94	70%	132	320	250
Cardiff	Park Hotel	(01222) 383471	H	116	70%	119	250	240
Porthkerry	Egerton Grey	(01446) 711666	H	85	68%	10	30	40

West Glamorgan

Location	Hotel	Phone	Type					
Gowerton	Cefn Goleu Park	(01792) 873099	HR	80	69%	4	12	30
Mumbles	Norton House	(01792) 404891	HR	65	65%	15	25	22
Reynoldston	Fairyhill	(01792) 390139	HR	85	65%	9	40	44
Swansea	Forte Posthouse	(01792) 651074	H	86	69%	66	230	230
Swansea	Hilton National	(01792) 310330	H	65	65%	118	180	120
Swansea	Langland Court Hotel	(01792) 361545	I	76		21	150	160
Swansea	Swansea Marriott Hotel	(01792) 642020	H	126	67%	117	250	180

Wales by County: Lodges

See How To Use This Guide, on pages 14–15, for an explanation of our percentage rating system, room pricing and categories.

Location	Establishment	Tel. No.	Map Ref	Motorway comments	Address
Clwyd					
Halkyn	Forte Travelodge	(01352) 780952	8 D1	A55 W'bound	Halkyn
Northop Hall	Forte Travelodge	(01244) 816473	8 D2	A55 E'bound	Northop Hall Mold
Wrexham	Forte Travelodge	(01978) 365705	8 D2	A483/A5152	Wrexham By-Pass Rhostyllen Wrexham
Wrexham	Travel Inn	(01978) 853214	8 D2	A483/B5445	Chester Road Gresford Nr Wrexham
Dyfed					
Cross Hands	Forte Travelodge	(01269) 845700	9 B5	A48 W'bound	Cross Hands Nr Llanelli
Gwent					
Newport (Magor)	Granada Lodge	(01633) 880111	9 D6	M4 J23	Magor Services Newport
Gwynedd					
Bangor	Forte Travelodge	(01248) 370345	8 B2	A5/A55	Llandegai Nr Bangor
Mid Glamorgan					
Bridgend	Travel Inn	(01656) 860133	9 C6	M4 J35	Pantruthyn Farm Pencoed Bridgend
Pencoed	Forte Travelodge	(01656) 864404	9 C6	M4 J35/A473	Old Mill Felindre Road Pencoed
Sarn Park	Forte Travelodge (Bridgend)	(01656) 659218	9 C6	M4 J36	Service Area Sarn Park Nr Bridgend

Location	Establishment	Tel. No.	Map Ref	Motorway comments	Address
South Glamorgan					
Cardiff	Campanile Hotel	(01222) 549044	9 D6	M4 J29/A48(M) Pentwyn	Caxton Place Pentwyn Cardiff
Cardiff	Forte Travelodge	(01222) 549564	9 D6	M4 J29/A48(M)	Circle Way East [Off A48(M)] Llanederyn
Cardiff	Travel Inn	(01633) 680070	9 D6	M4 J28/A48	Newport Road Castleton Nr Cardiff
West Glamorgan					
Port Talbot	Travel Inn	(01639) 813017	9 C6	M4 J41 (West) & J42 (East)	Baglan Road Port Talbot

Wales by County: Restaurants

See How To Use This Guide, on pages 14–15, for an explanation of our percentage rating system, room pricing and categories. No-smoking denotes a ban on smoking throughout or a separate no-smoking room.

Location	Establishment	Tel. No.	Dinner for 2, £	Category	Stars	Seats	Parties	Private Rms	Sundays	No-Smoking	Open Air	Nat Cuisine	Seafood	Vegetarian	Dessert	Cheese	O/s Wine	New World	Italian Wine	Wines by glass
Clwyd																				
Chirk	Starlings Castle	(01691) 718464	60	RR		65	25	yes	All							▲				
Colwyn Bay	Café Nicoise	(01492) 531555	45	R		32	10									▲		▲		▲
Llandrillo	Tyddyn Llan	(01490) 440264	60	HR		60	20	yes	All	yes		French				▲				
Dyfed																				
Brechfa	Ty Mawr	(01267) 202332	60	RR		35	12	yes	D	yes										
Penally	Penally Abbey	(01834) 843033	50	HR		46	6	yes	D											
Welsh Hook	stone Hall	(01348) 840212	63~	RR		34	45	yes	D											
Gwent																				
Abergavenny	Walnut Tree Inn	(01873) 852797	80	R	★	46					yes	Italian			▲	▲	▲	▲	▲	▲
Clydach	Drum & Monkey	(01873) 831980	50	R		50	14		All											
Trellech	Village Green	(01600) 860119	45	RR		70	12	yes	L	yes										
Whitebrook	Crown at Whitebrook	(01600) 860254	80	RR		32	24	yes	L	yes	yes						▲			

Location	Establishment	Tel. No.	Dinner for 2, £	Category	Stars	Seats	Parties	Private Rms	Sundays	No-Smoking	Open Air	Nat Cuisine	Seafood	Vegetarian	Dessert	Cheese	O/s Wine	New World	Italian Wine	Wines by glass
Gwynedd																				
Aberdovey	Penhelig Arms	(01654) 767215	55	IR		34	18	yes			yes					◄		◄		
Abersoch	Porth Tocyn	(01758) 713303	60	HR		50	20		All		yes					◄		◄		
Capel Coch	Tre-Ysgawen Hall	(01248) 750750	110	HR		64	12	yes	All							◄		◄		
Llanberis	Y Bistro	(01286) 871278	50	R		50	40	yes	D	yes		British						◄	◄	
Llandudno	Bodysgallen Hall	(01492) 584466	75	HR		60	12	yes	All	yes						◄	◄	◄		
Llandudno	St Tudno Hotel	(01492) 874411	70	HR		55	22	yes	All	yes						◄	◄	◄		
Llansanffraid																				
Glan Conwy	Old Rectory	(01492) 580611	70	HR		16	12		D	yes					◄	◄		◄		
Portmeirion	Hotel Portmeirion	(01766) 770228	65	HR		100	16	yes	All	yes						◄	◄	◄	◄	◄
Pwllheli	Plas Bodegroes	(01758) 612363	75	RR		35			D	yes					◄	◄	◄	◄		
Talsarnau	Maes-y-Neuadd	(01766) 780200	70	HR		50	12	yes	All	yes		British						◄		
Mid Glamorgan																				
Aberkenfig	New Garden	(01656) 724361	35	R		160			D			Chinese								
Powys																				
Eglwysfach	Ynyshir Hall	(01654) 781209	60	HR		40	16	yes	All	yes						◄		◄		◄
Llangammarch Wells	Lake Country House Hotel	(01591) 620457	65	HR		50	8		All	yes								◄		
Llanwyddyn	Lake Vyrnwy	(01691) 870692	65	HR		70	20	yes	yes	yes						◄				
Llyswen	Llangoed Hall	(01874) 754525	155	HR		40	8	yes	All	yes						◄	◄	◄	◄	◄

South Glamorgan

Barry	Bunbury's	(01446) 732075	50	R	32	36			
Cardiff	Armless Dragon	(01222) 382357	50	R	45	55			
Cardiff	La Brasserie	(01222) 372164	40	R	80	10			
Cardiff	Champers	(01222) 373363	40	R	180	70	D		
Cardiff	Le Monde	(01222) 387376	40	R	180	12	yes		

West Glamorgan

Gowerton	Cefn Goleu Park	(01792) 873099	60	HR	30	14	yes	L	yes French
Mumbles	Norton House	(01792) 404891	65	HR	30	12	yes	D	British
Reynoldston	Fairyhill	(01792) 390139	70	HR	68	24	yes	All	yes
Swansea	Number One	(01792) 456996	55	R	40	20			

Islands: Hotels

See How To Use This Guide, on pages 14–15, for an explanation of our percentage rating system, room pricing and categories.
*15 mins Mway refers to hotels graded 70% or higher within 15 minutes of a motorway.

Location	Establishment	Tel. No.	Category	Room £	Hotel %	No. of Rooms	Conf Max	Band Max	Beaut Sit	Disabled	In Swim	Out Swim	Tennis	Squash	Golf	Fishing	Riding	15 mins Mway*	Country House
Alderney																			
St Anne	Chez Andre	(01481) 822777	H	83	63%	11	50	70											
St Anne	Inchalla Hotel	(01481) 823220	HR	73	64%	9													
Guernsey																			
Castel	La Grande Mare Hotel	(01481) 56576	H	113	72%	34	30	75			◀				◀				
Castel	Hougue du Pommier	(01481) 56531	I	74		43	30	40			◀			◀					
Forest	Mallard Hotel	(01481) 64164	H	70	67%	47	80	120			◀	◀							
Pleinmont	Imperial Hotel	(01481) 64044	I	56		17													
St Martin	Hotel Bon Port	(01481) 39249	H	95	66%	14	25	60			◀			◀	◀	◀			
St Martin	St Margaret's Lodge	(01481) 35757	H	75	63%	47	80	140			◀								
St Peter Port	Braye Lodge	(01481) 723787	H	75		26	100	100			◀								
St Peter Port	Duke of Richmond	(01481) 726221	H	65	63%	75	240	220			◀								
St Peter Port	La Fregate	(01481) 724624	H	95	64%	13	0	50											

Location	Establishment	Tel. No.	Category	Room £	Hotel %	No. of Rooms	Conf Max	Bang Max	Beaut Sit	Disabled	In Swim	Out Swim	Tennis	Squash	Golf	Fishing	Riding	15 mins Mway*	Country House
St Peter Port	Old Government House	(01481) 724921	H	92	68%	72	110	110											
St Peter Port	St Pierre Park	(01481) 728282	H	135	71%	135	400	360		▲				▲					
Herm																			
Herm	White House	(01481) 722159	HR	110	64%	38	0	0			▲	▲							
Jersey																			
Bouley Bay	Water's Edge Hotel	(01534) 862777	H	104	64%	51	65	120			▲	▲							
Gorey	Moorings Hotel	(01534) 853633	H	90	62%	16	30	60											
Gorey	Old Court House Hotel	(01534) 854444	H	89	64%	58					▲								
Grouville	Grouville Bay Hotel	(01534) 851004	H	80	62%	56		150			▲	▲							
Havre des Pas	Hotel de la Plage	(01534) 23474	H	70	66%	78	20	15			▲								
Havre des Pas	Onmaroo Hotel	(01534) 23493	H	90	59%	85	60	60											
Portelet Bay	Portelet Hotel	(01534) 41204	H	104	66%	86	140	140			▲	▲			▲				
Rozel Bay	Chateau la Chaire	(01534) 863354	HR	118	74%	14	16	30	▲										
St Aubin	Old Court House Inn	(01534) 46433	I	80		9		30											
St Brelade	Atlantic Hotel	(01534) 44101	H	140	71%	50	60	60		▲	▲	▲							
St Brelade	Hotel Chateau Valeuse	(01534) 46281	HR	84	65%	33					▲								
St Brelade	La Place Hotel	(01534) 44261	H	110	67%	40	50	80			▲								
St Brelade	Sea Crest	(01534) 46353	HR	92	64%	7		70			▲								
St Brelade's Bay	Hotel L'Horizon	(01534) 43101	H	170	72%	107	150	240	▲	▲	▲								
St Brelade's Bay	St Brelade's Bay Hotel	(01534) 46141	H	140	70%	82						▲							

Location	Hotel	Phone	Type		%												
St Helier	Apollo Hotel	(01534) 25441	H	87	63%	85	120	150							◄	
St Helier	Beaufort Hotel	(01534) 32471	H	93	60%	54	70	40						◄	◄	
St Helier	De Vere Grand	(01534) 22301	HR	115	68%	115	180	280					◄	◄	◄	
St Helier	Hotel de France	(01534) 614000	H	120		324	800	700				◄	◄	◄	◄	
St Helier	Pomme d'Or Hotel	(01534) 880110	H	100	65%	147	300	250								
St Ouen	The Lobster Pot	(01534) 482888	RR	70		13	90	90								
St Peter	Mermaid Hotel	(01534) 41255	H	92	64%	68	80	80					◄	◄	◄	
St Saviour	Longueville Manor	(01534) 25501	HR	160	80%	32	30	65			◄	◄	◄	◄	◄	◄
St Saviour	Merton Hotel	(01534) 24231	H	80	60%	304	0	0				◄	◄	◄	◄	◄

Sark

Location	Hotel	Phone	Type		%												
Sark	Aval Du Creux	(01481) 832036	HR	70	57%	12		40					◄	◄		
Sark	Dixcart Hotel	(01481) 832015	HR	70	64%	15	15	80						◄		◄
Sark	Hotel Petit Champ	(01481) 832046	H	72	61%	16										
Sark	La Sablonnerie Hotel	(01481) 832061	HR	70	66%	22	0	40						◄		◄
Sark	Stocks Hotel	(01481) 832001	HR	70	61%	24	0	70					◄	◄		◄

Isle of Man

Location	Hotel	Phone	Type		%												
Douglas	Palace Hotel	(01624) 662662	H	95	65%	135	320	300							◄	
Douglas	Sefton Hotel	(01624) 626011	H	68	63%	79	80	90							◄	
Ramsey	Grand Island Hotel	(01624) 812455	H	90	66%	56	300	200	◄						◄	

Islands: Restaurants

See How To Use This Guide, on pages 14-15, for an explanation of our percentage rating system, room pricing and categories.
No-smoking denotes a ban on smoking throughout or a separate no-smoking room.

Location	Establishment	Tel. No.	Dinner for 2, £	Category	Stars	Seats	Parties	Private Rms	Sundays	No-Smoking	Open Air	Nat Cuisine	Seafood	Vegetarian	Dessert	Cheese	O/s Wine	New World	Italian Wine	Wines by glass
Alderney																				
Braye	First & Last	(01481) 823162	30	R		75	24		All											
St Anne	Georgian House	(01481) 822471	45	R		48	24	yes	All											
St Anne	Inchalla Hotel	(01481) 823220	55	HR		30	28		L	yes										
Guernsey																				
L'Eree	Taste of India	(01481) 64516	35	R		35		yes	All	yes	yes	Indian								
Rocquaine Bay	Rocquaine Seafood Bistro	(01481) 63149	50	R		40					yes		◄							
St Peter Port	Absolute End	(01481) 723822	60	R		60	20	yes					◄	◄						
St Peter Port	Da Nello's	(01481) 721552	50	R		66						Italian								
St Peter Port	Le Nautique	(01481) 721714	55	R		68	14	yes					◄							
St Peters	Café du Moulin	(01481) 65944	60	R		45	8			yes		French		◄	◄					
St Saviour	Auberge du Val	(01481) 63862	50	R		42	15			yes					◄			◄		

Herm

Location	Establishment	Tel. No.	Dinner for 2, £	Category	Stars	Seats	Parties	Private Rms	Sundays	No-Smoking	Open Air	Nat Cuisine	Seafood	Vegetarian	Dessert	Cheese	O/s Wine	New World	Italian Wine	Wines by glass
Herm	White House	(01481) 722159	40	HR		118	14		All	yes								◄		

Jersey

Location	Establishment	Tel. No.	Dinner for 2, £	Category	Stars	Seats	Parties	Private Rms	Sundays	No-Smoking	Open Air	Nat Cuisine	Seafood	Vegetarian	Dessert	Cheese	O/s Wine	New World	Italian Wine	Wines by glass
Gorey	Jersey Pottery Garden Restaurant	(01534) 851119	60	R	↑	250	24							◄							
Rozel Bay	Chateau la Chaire	(01534) 863354	70	HR		65	30	yes	All	yes	yes		◄							
St Brelade	Chateau Valeuse	(01534) 46281	50	HR		70			All											
St Brelade	Sea Crest	(01534) 46353	70	HR		60	25		All		yes		◄							
St Helier	La Capanna	(01534) 34602	60	R		90	18	yes				Italian								
St Helier	De Vere Grand	(01534) 22301	75	HR		160		yes	L										◄	
St Ouen	The Lobster Pot	(01534) 482888	70	RR		90	8	yes	All				◄							
St Saviour	Longueville Manor	(01534) 25501	90	HR		65	16	yes	All	yes	yes			◄	◄	◄				

Sark

Location	Establishment	Tel. No.	Dinner for 2, £	Category	Stars	Seats	Parties	Private Rms	Sundays	No-Smoking	Open Air	Nat Cuisine	Seafood	Vegetarian	Dessert	Cheese	O/s Wine	New World	Italian Wine	Wines by glass
Sark	Aval Du Creux	(01481) 832036	55	HR		40	15	yes	All		yes		◄							
Sark	Dixcart Hotel	(01481) 832015	40	HR		60	30		All											
Sark	La Sablonnerie	(01481) 832061	55	HR		40	12	yes	All							◄				
Sark	Stocks Hotel	(01481) 832001	50	HR		60	12	yes	All		yes									

Isle of Man

Location	Establishment	Tel. No.	Dinner for 2, £	Category	Stars	Seats	Parties	Private Rms	Sundays	No-Smoking	Open Air	Nat Cuisine	Seafood	Vegetarian	Dessert	Cheese	O/s Wine	New World	Italian Wine	Wines by glass
Ballasalla	Rosa's Place	(01624) 822702	70	R		45	16				yes									
Ramsey	Harbour Bistro	(01624) 814182	45	R		50	20		All											

N Ireland by County: Hotels

See How To Use This Guide, on pages 14-15, for an explanation of our percentage rating system, room pricing and categories.
*15 mins Mway refers to hotels graded 70% or higher within 15 minutes of a motorway.

Co Antrim

Location	Establishment	Tel. No.	Category	Room £	Hotel %	No. of Rooms	Conf Max	Bang Max	Beaut Sit	Disabled	In Swim	Out Swim	Tennis	Squash	Golf	Fishing	Riding	15 mins Mway*	Country House
Ballymena	Galgorm Manor	(01266) 881001	HR	105	71%	23	500	450	▲							▲	▲		
Belfast	Dukes Hotel	(01232) 236666	H	98	67%	21	130	140		▲									
Belfast	Europa Hotel	(01232) 327000	H	130	71%	184	1200	600											
Belfast	Plaza Hotel	(01232) 333555	H	82	64%	76	70	100											
Belfast	Stormont Hotel	(01232) 658621	H	137	69%	106	500	350		▲									
Belfast	Wellington Park	(01232) 381111	H	90	59%	50	180	120											
Belfast International Airport	Aldergrove Airport Hotel	(01849) 422033	H	80	62%	108	250	180											
Bushmills	Bushmills Inn	(01265) 732339	H	78	58%	11	85	85											
Dunadry	Dunadry Inn	(01849) 432474	H	100	64%	67	350	300			▲					▲			
Dunmurry	Forte Posthouse Belfast	(01232) 612101	H	86	67%	82	450	350						▲					
Larne	Magheramorne House	(01574) 279444	H	66	63%	22	180	180								▲			
Portballintrae	Bayview Hotel	(01265) 731453	H	70	58%	16	300	300		▲									
Templepatrick	Templeton Hotel	(01849) 432984	H	100	66%	20	400	350			▲								

Location	Establishment	Tel. No.	Category	Room £	Hotel %	No. of Rooms	Conf Max	Banq Max	Beaut Sit	Disabled	In Swim	Out Swim	Tennis	Squash	Golf	Fishing	Riding	15 mins Mway*	Country House
Co Down																			
Annalong	Glasdrumman Lodge	(01396) 768451	HR	85	69%	10	16	60					▲		▲		▲		
Bangor	Clandeboye Lodge Hotel	(01247) 852500	H	87	61%	43										▲			
Bangor	Marine Court Hotel	(01247) 451100	H	80	64%	51	450	300			▲								
Comber	La Mon House	(01232) 448631	H	85	59%	38	1100	450			▲								
Crawfordsburn	Old Inn	(01247) 853255	I	85		33	150	90											
Holywood	Culloden Hotel	(01232) 425223	HR	157	72%	89	500	300			▲		▲	▲					
Newcastle	Slieve Donard Hotel	(01396) 723681	H	99	63%	117	1000	440			▲		▲						
Portaferry	Portaferry Hotel	(01247) 728231	HR	85	63%	14	30	80											
Co Fermanagh																			
Kesh	Lough Erne Hotel	(01365) 631275	H	56	60%	12	250	200								▲			
Tempo	Tempo Manor	(01365) 541450	PH	100		5													
Co Londonderry																			
Aghadowey	Greenhill House	(01265) 868241	PH	42		6													
Garvagh	MacDuff's	(01265) 868433	RR			5													
Londonderry	Beech Hill House Hotel	(01504) 49279	HR	85	59%	17							▲						
Londonderry	Everglades Hotel	(01504) 46722	H	80	59%	52	350	250											
Co Tyrone																			
Fivemiletown	Blessingbourne	(01365) 521221	PH	90		4						▲	▲			▲			

N Ireland by County: Restaurants

See How To Use This Guide, on pages 14-15, for an explanation of our percentage rating system, room pricing and categories.
No-smoking denotes a ban on smoking throughout or a separate no-smoking room.

Co Antrim

Location	Establishment	Tel. No.	Dinner for 2, £	Category	Stars	Seats	Parties	Private Rms	Sundays	No-Smoking	Open Air	Nat Cuisine	Seafood	Vegetarian	Dessert	Cheese	O/s Wine	New World	Italian Wine	Wines by glass
Ballymena	Galgorm Manor	(01266) 881001	70	HR		73	24	yes	All											
Belfast	Antica Roma	(01232) 311121	65	R		170		yes				Italian								
Belfast	Bengal Brasserie	(01232) 640099	35	R		46		yes	D			Indian								
Belfast	Manor House Cantonese Cuisine	(01232) 238755	40	R		80		yes	All			Chinese								
Belfast	Roscoff	(01232) 331532	75	R	★	70									▲	▲	▲	▲		▲
Belfast	Speranza	(01232) 230213	40	R		170						Italian								
Belfast	Strand Restaurant	(01232) 682266	35	R		55	12	yes	All											
Belfast	Villa Italia	(01232) 328356	45	R		180			D			Italian		▲						
Belfast	The Warehouse	(01232) 439690	45	R		90		yes												▲
Belfast	Welcome Restaurant	(01232) 381359	40	R		60	20	yes	D			Chinese								
Carrickfergus	Wind-Rose	(01960) 364192	55	R		46														
Portrush	Ramore	(01265) 824313	55	R	★	85							▲		▲	▲				

Co Down

Location	Establishment	Tel. No.	Dinner for 2, £	Category	Stars	Seats	Parties	Private Rms	Sundays	No-Smoking	Open Air	Nat Cuisine	Seafood	Vegetarian	Dessert	Cheese	O/s Wine	New World	Italian Wine	Wines by glass
Annalong	Glasdrumman Lodge	(01396) 768451	60	HR		40		yes	D			French								▲
Bangor	Back Street Cafe	(01247) 453990	45	R																▲
Bangor	Shanks	(01247) 853313	60	R	↑	60	16	yes								▲				
Comber	The Refectory	(01247) 870870	40	R		58														
Helen's Bay	Deanes on the Square	(01247) 852841	75	R	↑	40			L					▲				▲		
Holywood	Culloden Hotel	(01232) 425223	65	HR		140	20	yes	All					▲						
Holywood	Sullivans	(01232) 421000	55	R		40							▲		▲					
Portaferry	Portaferry Hotel	(01247) 728231	62	HR		80			All											

Co Londonderry

Location	Establishment	Tel. No.	Dinner for 2, £	Category	Stars	Seats	Parties	Private Rms	Sundays	No-Smoking	Open Air	Nat Cuisine	Seafood	Vegetarian	Dessert	Cheese	O/s Wine	New World	Italian Wine	Wines by glass
Garvagh	MacDuff's	(01265) 868433	50	RR		36	36	yes					▲	▲	▲	▲				
Londonderry	Beech Hill	(01504) 49279	65	HR		40	8	yes	All					▲		▲				

Your **Guarantee** of **Quality** and **Independence**

- Establishment inspections are anonymous
- Inspections are undertaken by qualified Egon Ronay's Guides inspectors
- The Guides are completely independent in their editorial selection
- The Guides do not accept advertising, hospitality or payment from listed establishments

The **Leading** Guides

Hotels & Restaurants ● Pubs & Inns ● Europe
Ireland ● Just A Bite
And Children Come Too ● Paris
Oriental Restaurants

On the Waterfront

The human body is made up of over 90% water. Research shows that a 5% drop in bodily fluid can result in a 30% drop in performance.

Water intake is essential for maintaining hydration, lowering body temperature, removing cellular waste and reducing fatigue. Doctors suggest that you should drink between 2–3 litres of water each day.

Highly Recommended

...is Braebourne Spring's range of water coolers. They require no plumbing, only occupy the floorspace of just one telephone book, and provide a cooled, on tap supply of Natural Mineral Water that's bottled at its underground source in the Cotswolds.

For your Complimentary No Obligation Trial which includes machine delivery and 22.7 litres of water, call:

✆ 0181 291 9911

the cool mineral water people...

FOR THE WIDEST RANGE OF SERVICED APARTMENTS WORLDWIDE

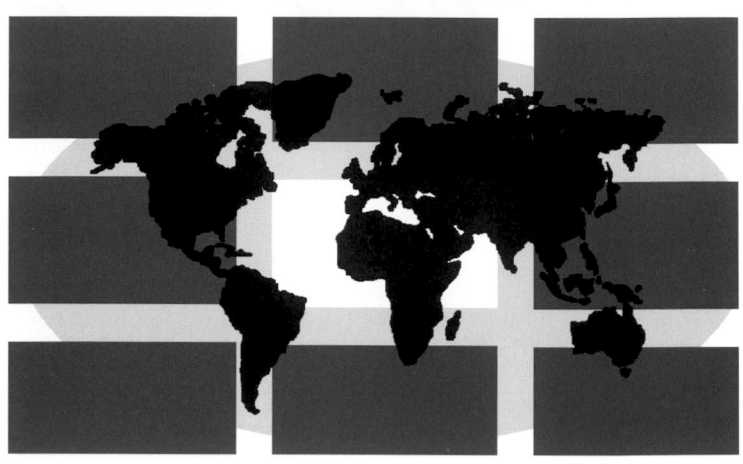

CALL THE SPECIALISTS

Serviced Apartments are the ideal alternative to hotel accommodation for holidays, business or as an interim housing solution.

Cost-effectively priced, all our apartments are serviced by maids, fully equipped and offer unrivalled luxury, space, privacy and security.

With over 25 international partners, The Apartment Service has unique representation in local markets who can help you choose the property that best suits your needs from the thousands of quality apartments throughout the World, from London to New York, from Paris to Sydney.

The Guide to Serviced Apartments containing details of over 3,000 apartments in Europe is available free of charge on request.

SERVICES APARTMENTS HAVE:-

- Lounges
- Kitchens
- Bathrooms
- Maid Service
- Baby Sitting Service
- Direct Dial Telephones

IDEAL FOR:-

- Holidays
- Training Courses
- Relocation
- Temporary Assignments
- Workbases
- Exhibitions
- Conference Presentations

Call today for more details of our
***FREE** service and our brochure.*

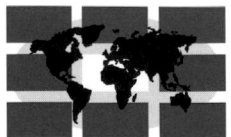

THE APARTMENT SERVICE

5-6 Francis Grove, Wimbledon, London SW19 4DT, UK.
Tel: 0181 944 1444   Fax: 0181 944 6744

*Call us toll free for our 96 page colour guide featuring
apartments in 28 European cities on request*

0800 243 163

THE INDEPENDENT

INDEPENDENT
ON SUNDAY

Your truly independent guides to life

Maps

2/3

4/5

6/7

8/9

22

14/15

10/11

16/21

12/13

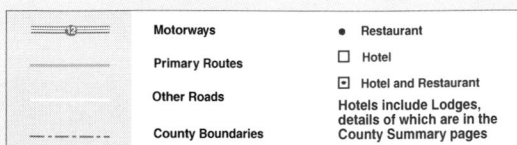

	Motorways	●	Restaurant
	Primary Routes	☐	Hotel
	Other Roads	⊡	Hotel and Restaurant
	County Boundaries		Hotels include Lodges, details of which are in the County Summary pages

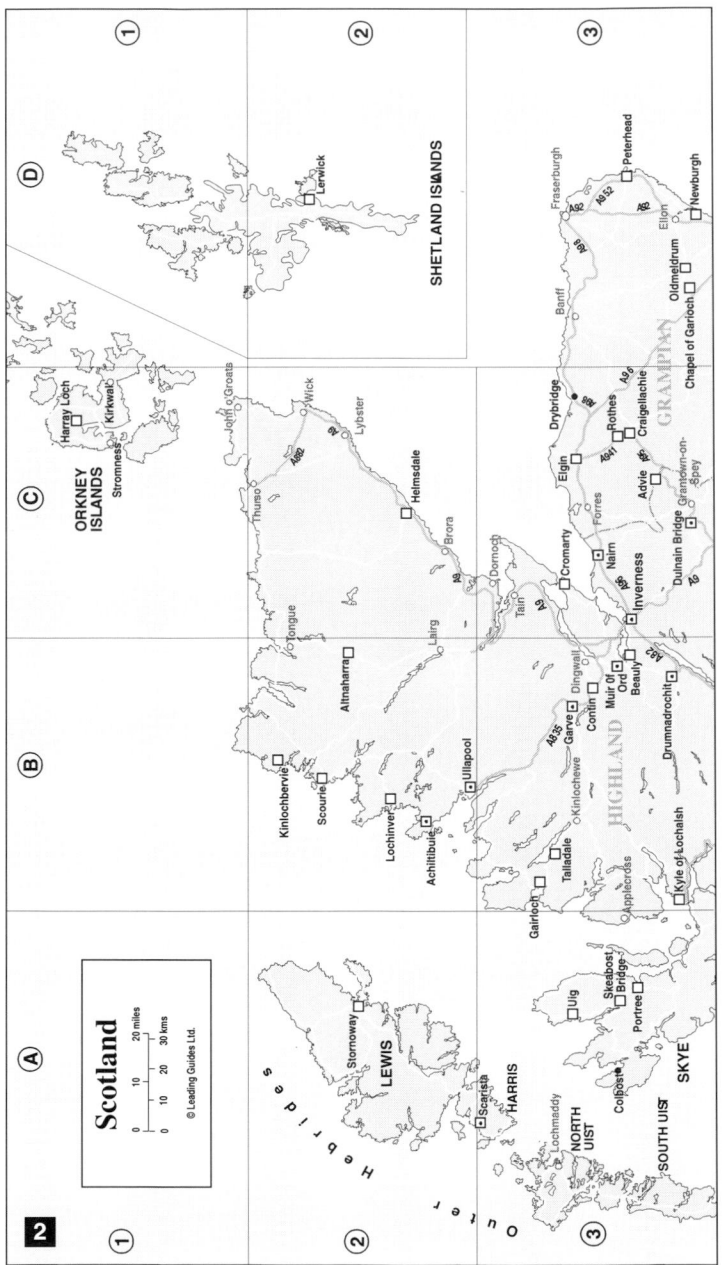

Scotland

0   10   20 miles
0   10   20   30 kms

© Leading Guides Ltd.

2

① ② ③ ④ ⑤

ORKNEY ISLANDS

Harray Loch
Kirkwall
Stromness

SHETLAND ISLANDS

Lerwick

GRAMPIAN

Peterhead
Fraserburgh
Newburgh
Elgin
Oldmeldrum
Banff
Chapel of Garioch
Drybridge
Rothes
Craigellachie
Elgin
Forres
Advie
Grantown-on-Spey
Dulnain Bridge
Nairn
Cromarty
Inverness

John o'Groats
Wick
Lybster
Helmsdale
Brora
Thurso
Dornoch
Tongue
Lairg
Tain
Altnaharra

HIGHLAND

Dingwall
Muir of Ord
Garve
Beauly
Contin
Drumnadrochit
Kinlochbervie
Scourie
Lochinver
Achiltibuie
Ullapool
Kinlochewe
Talladale
Applecross
Kyle of Lochalsh
Gairloch

Outer Hebrides

Stornoway
LEWIS
Scarista
HARRIS
Lochmaddy
NORTH UIST
Colbost
SOUTH UIST

Uig
Skeabost Bridge
Portree
SKYE

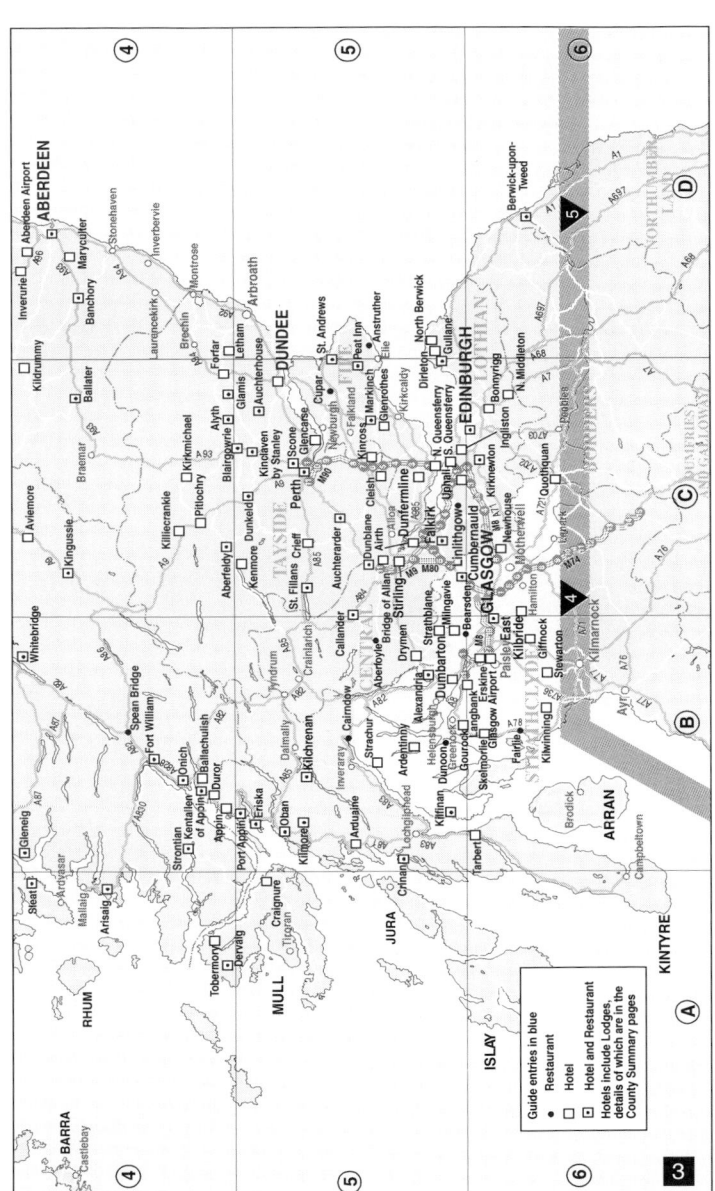

Guide entries in blue

• Restaurant
▫ Hotel
⬕ Hotel and Restaurant

Hotels include Lodges,
details of which are in the
County Summary pages

3

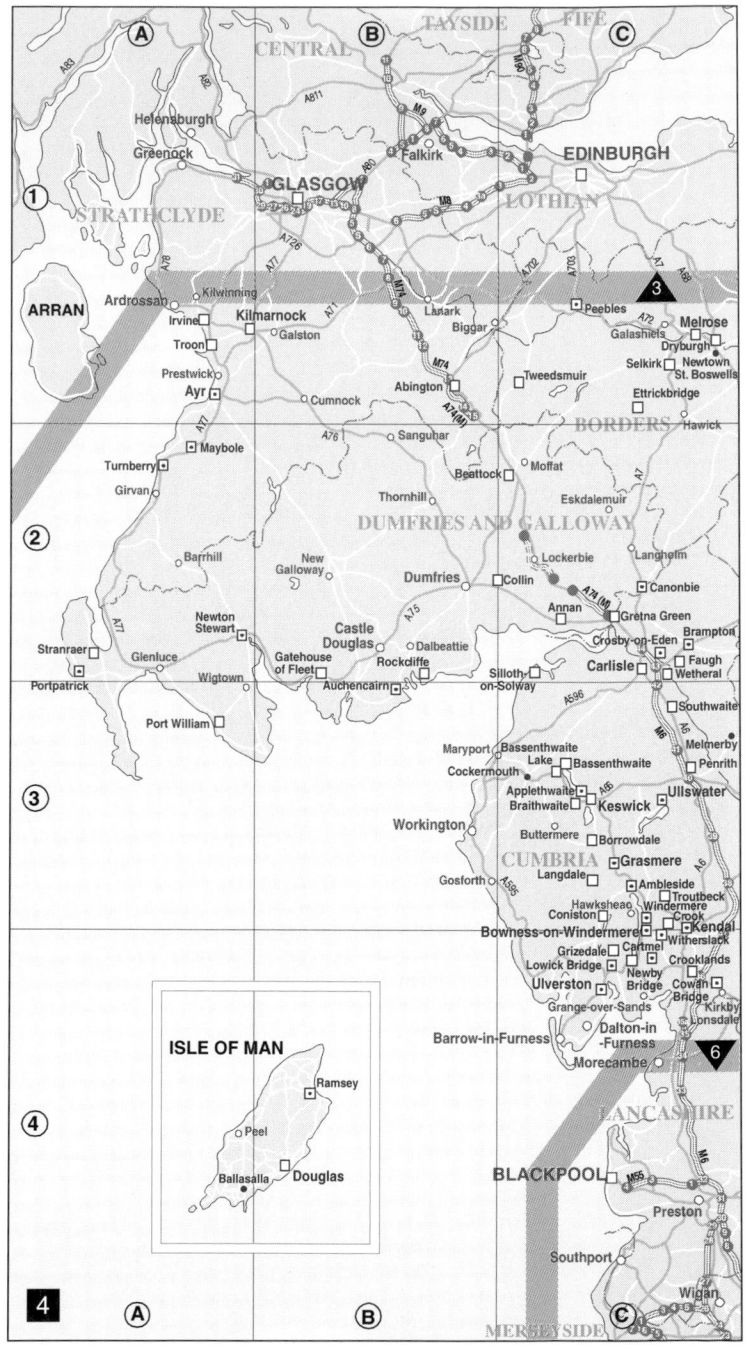

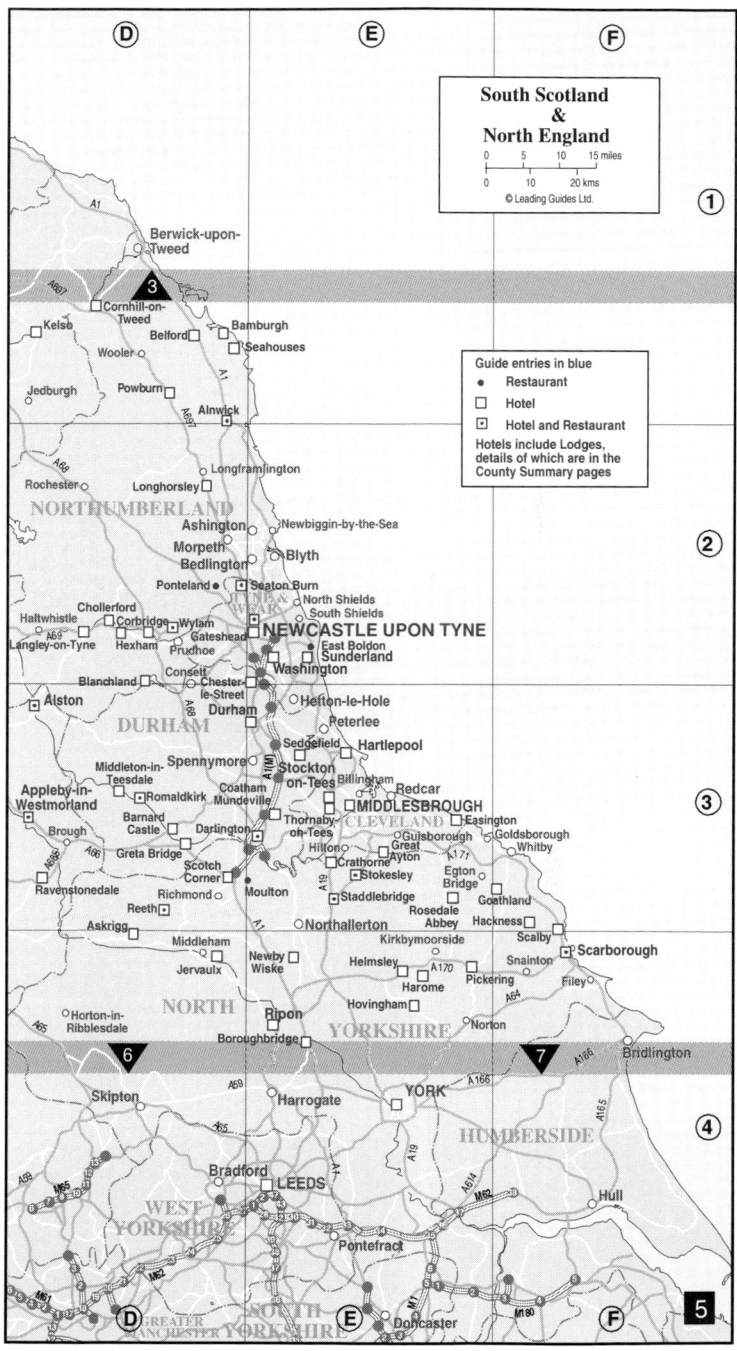

South Scotland
&
North England

0 5 10 15 miles

0 10 20 kms

© Leading Guides Ltd.

Guide entries in blue
- Restaurant
□ Hotel
⊡ Hotel and Restaurant

Hotels include Lodges,
details of which are in the
County Summary pages

Berwick-upon-Tweed

Cornhill-on-Tweed

Kelso

Belford

Bamburgh

Seahouses

Wooler

Jedburgh

Powburn

Alnwick

Rochester

Longframlington

Longhorsley

NORTHUMBERLAND

Ashington

Newbiggin-by-the-Sea

Morpeth

Bedlington

Blyth

Ponteland

Seaton Burn

North Shields

South Shields

Haltwhistle

Chollerford

Corbridge

Wylam

Langley-on-Tyne

Hexham

Gateshead

NEWCASTLE UPON TYNE

Prudhoe

East Boldon

Sunderland

Blanchland

Conset

Washington

Chester-le-Street

Durham

Hetton-le-Hole

Alston

DURHAM

Peterlee

Spennymoor

Sedgefield

Hartlepool

Middleton-in-Teesdale

Stockton-on-Tees

Billingham

Redcar

Appleby-in-Westmorland

Coatham Mundeville

Romaldkirk

MIDDLESBROUGH

Easington

Goldsborough

Brough

Barnard Castle

Darlington

Thornaby-on-Tees

CLEVELAND

Guisborough

Whitby

Greta Bridge

Hilton

Great Ayton

Egton Bridge

Goathland

Ravenstonedale

Scotch Corner

Crathorne

Stokesley

Hackness

Richmond

Moulton

Staddlebridge

Rosedale Abbey

Goathland

Reeth

Northallerton

Scalby

Askrigg

Middleham

Kirkbymoorside

Scarborough

Jervaulx

Newby Wiske

Helmsley

Snainton

Pickering

Filey

Horton-in-Ribblesdale

NORTH

Hovingham

Harome

A64

Ripon

YORKSHIRE

Norton

Boroughbridge

Bridlington

Skipton

Harrogate

YORK

HUMBERSIDE

Bradford

LEEDS

Hull

WEST YORKSHIRE

Pontefract

NORTH YORKSHIRE

Doncaster

GREATER MANCHESTER

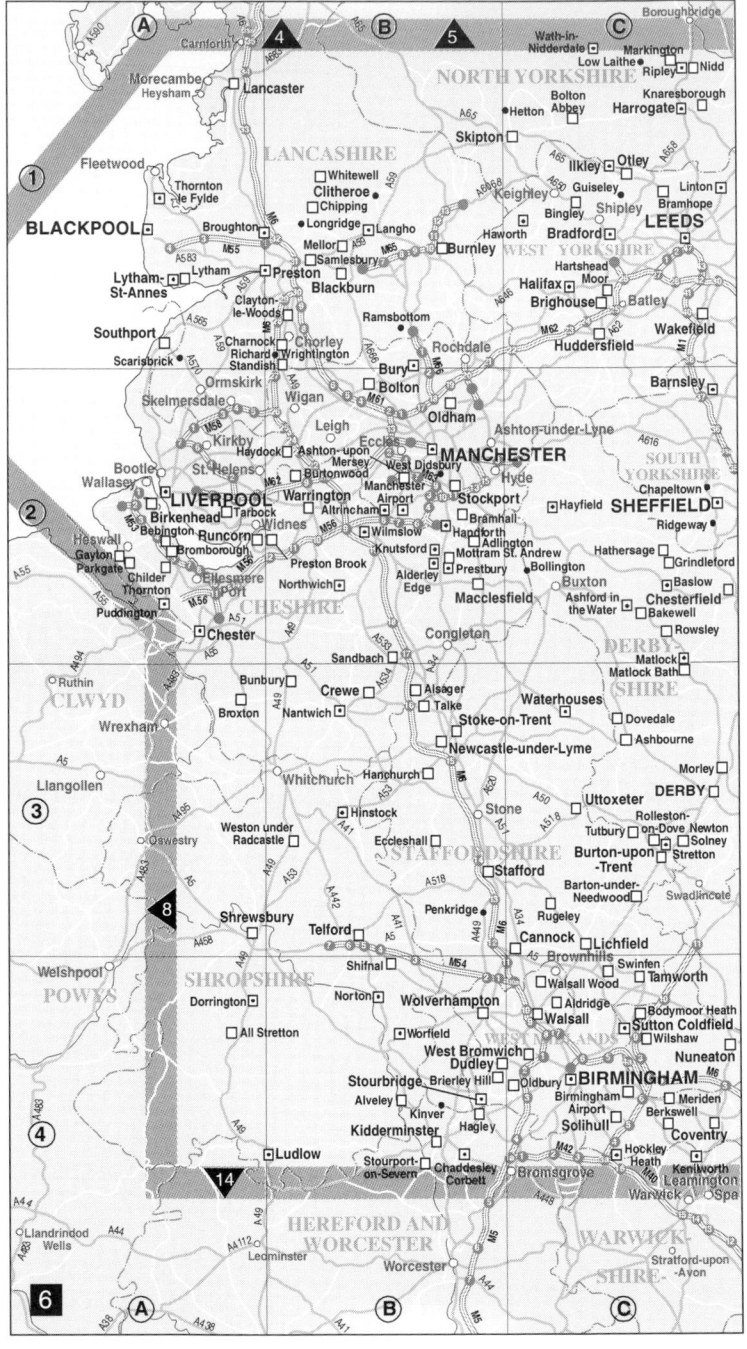

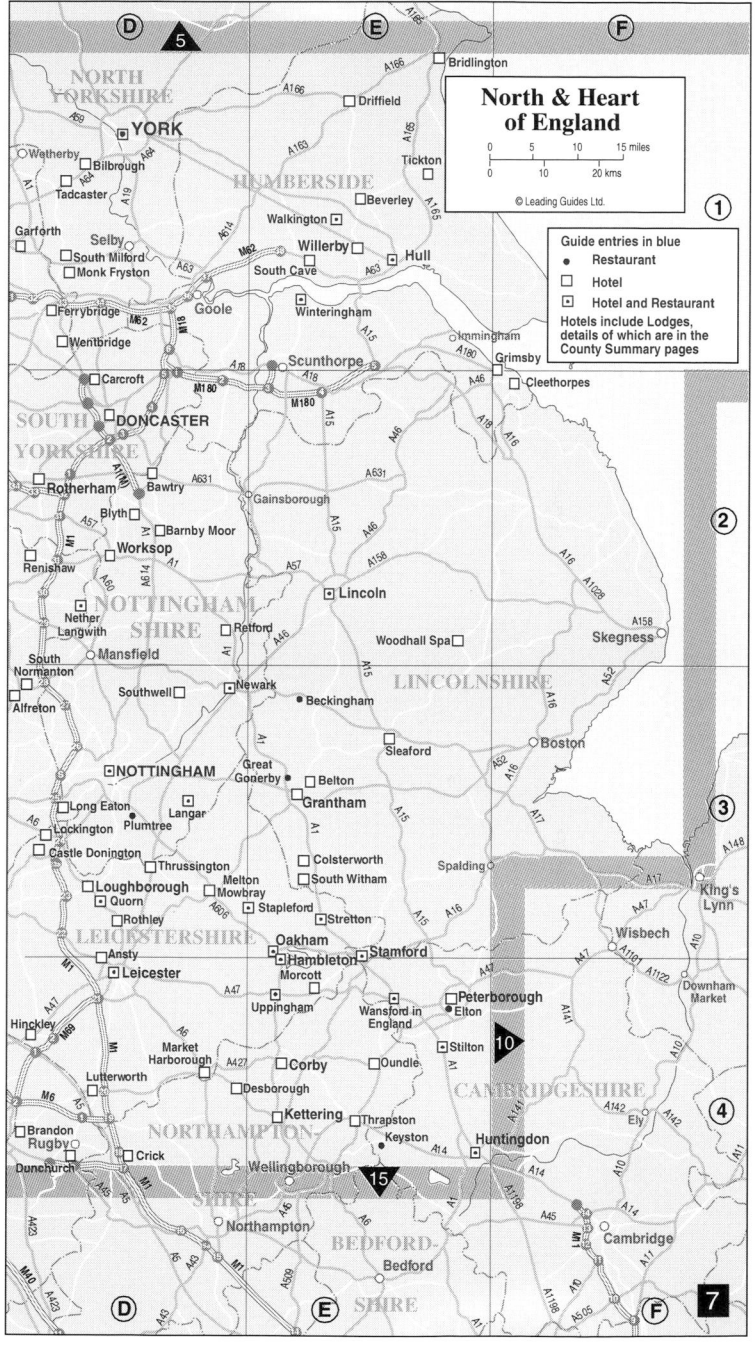

North & Heart
of England

0   5   10   15 miles
0   10   20 kms
© Leading Guides Ltd.

Guide entries in blue
●   Restaurant
□   Hotel
⊡   Hotel and Restaurant
Hotels include Lodges,
details of which are in the
County Summary pages

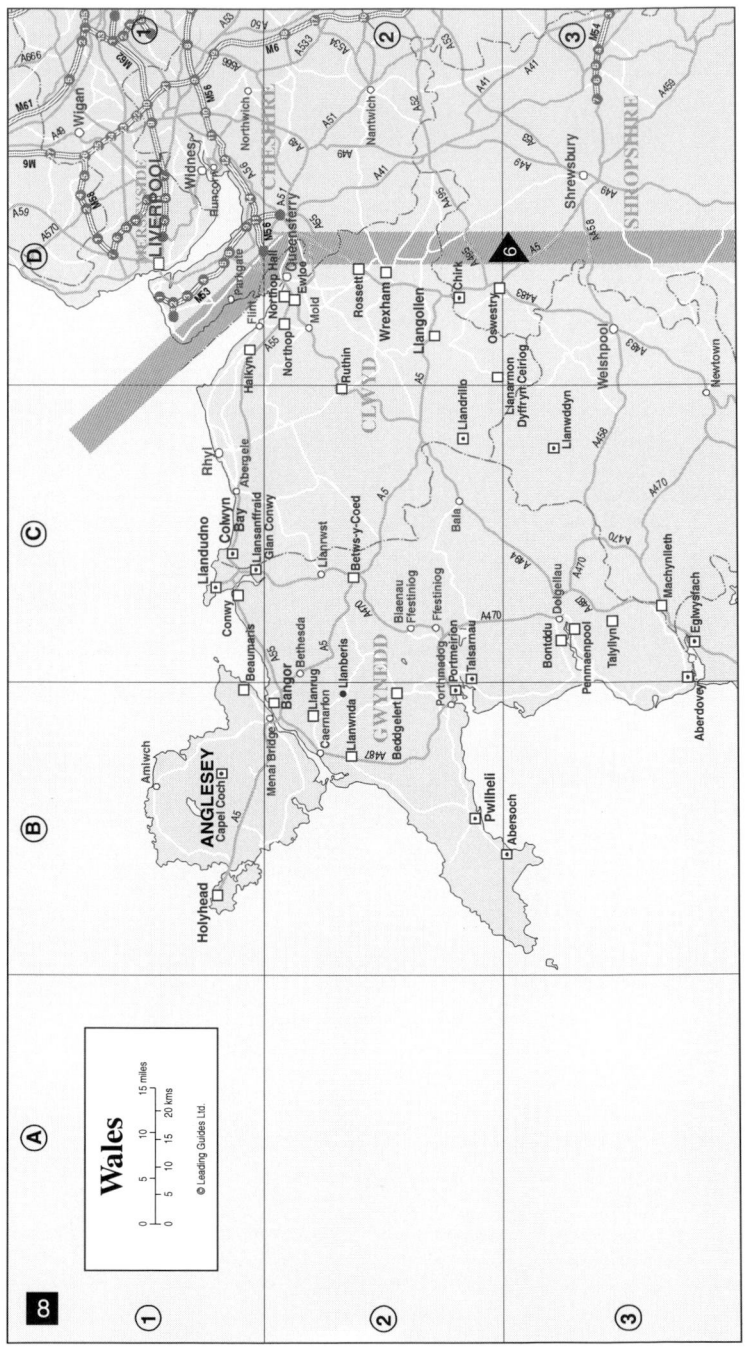

Wales

© Leading Guides Ltd

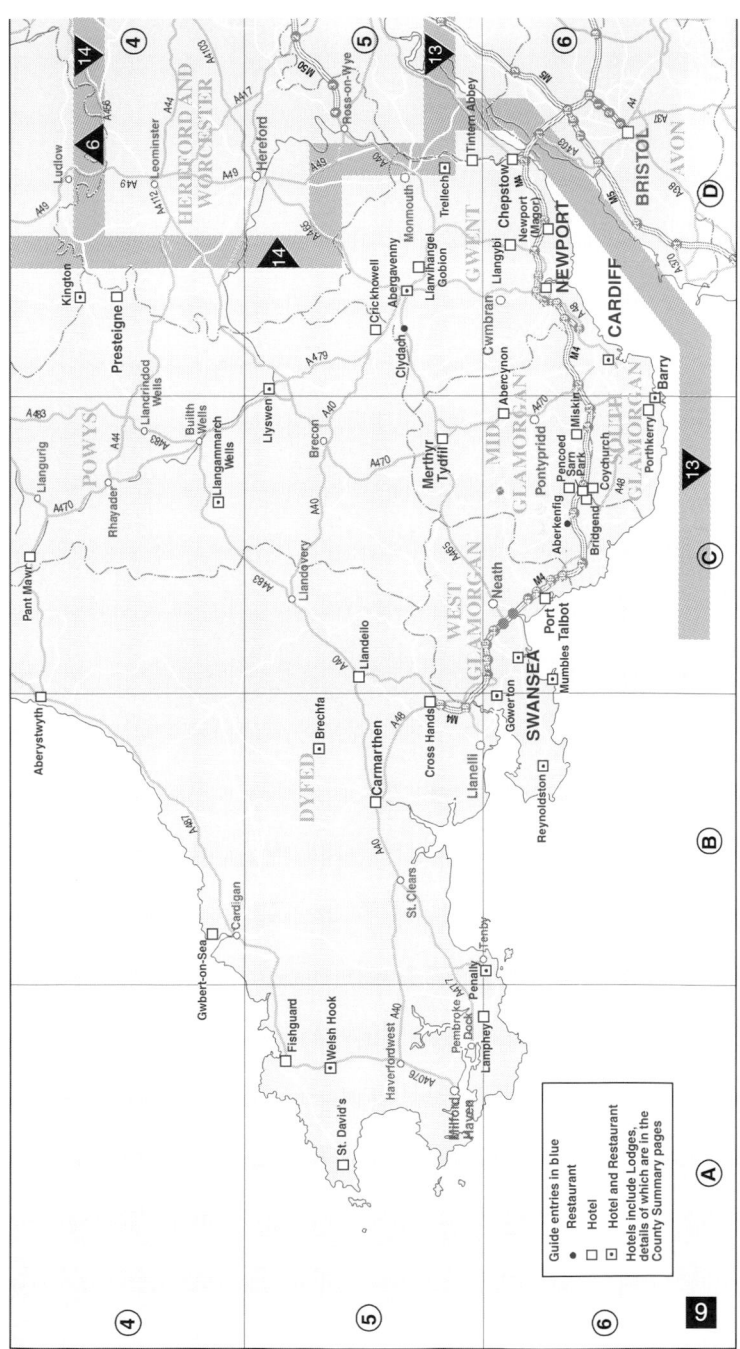

Guide entries in blue

● Restaurant

□ Hotel

⊡ Hotel and Restaurant

Hotels include Lodges,
details of which are in the
County Summary pages

9

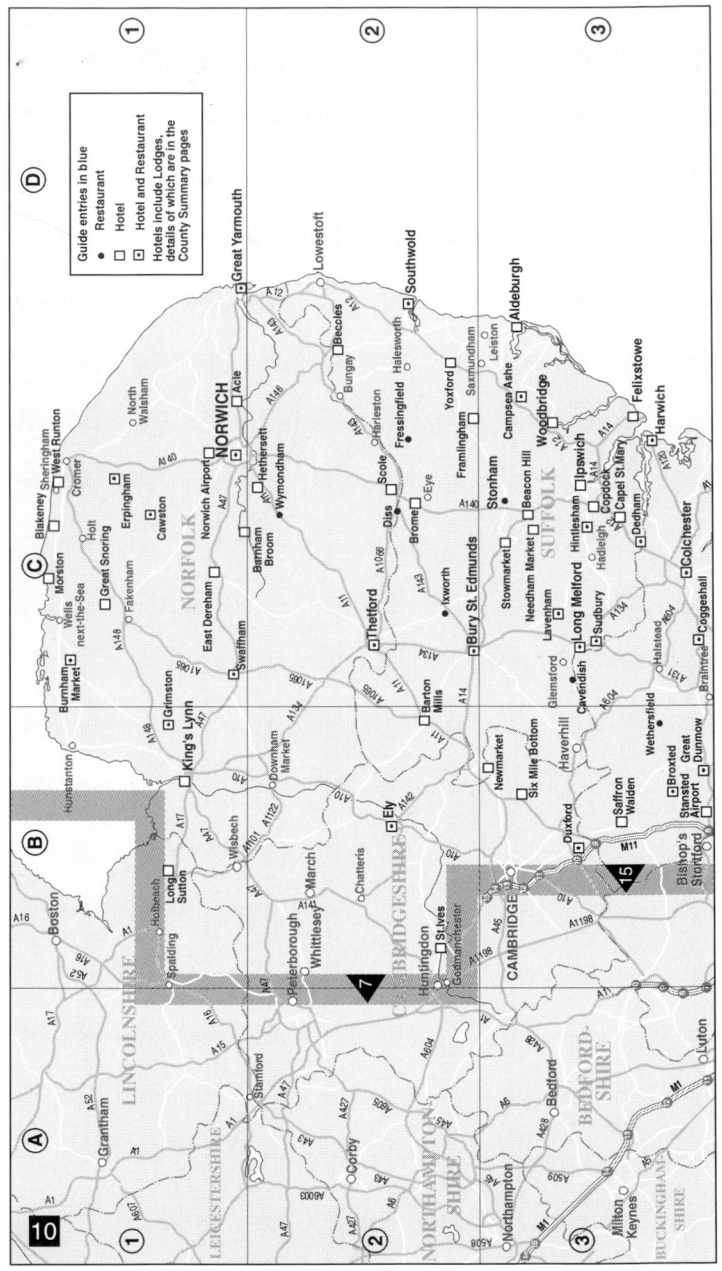

10

Guide entries in blue
- Restaurant
□ Hotel
⊡ Hotel and Restaurant

Hotels include Lodges, details of which are in the County Summary pages

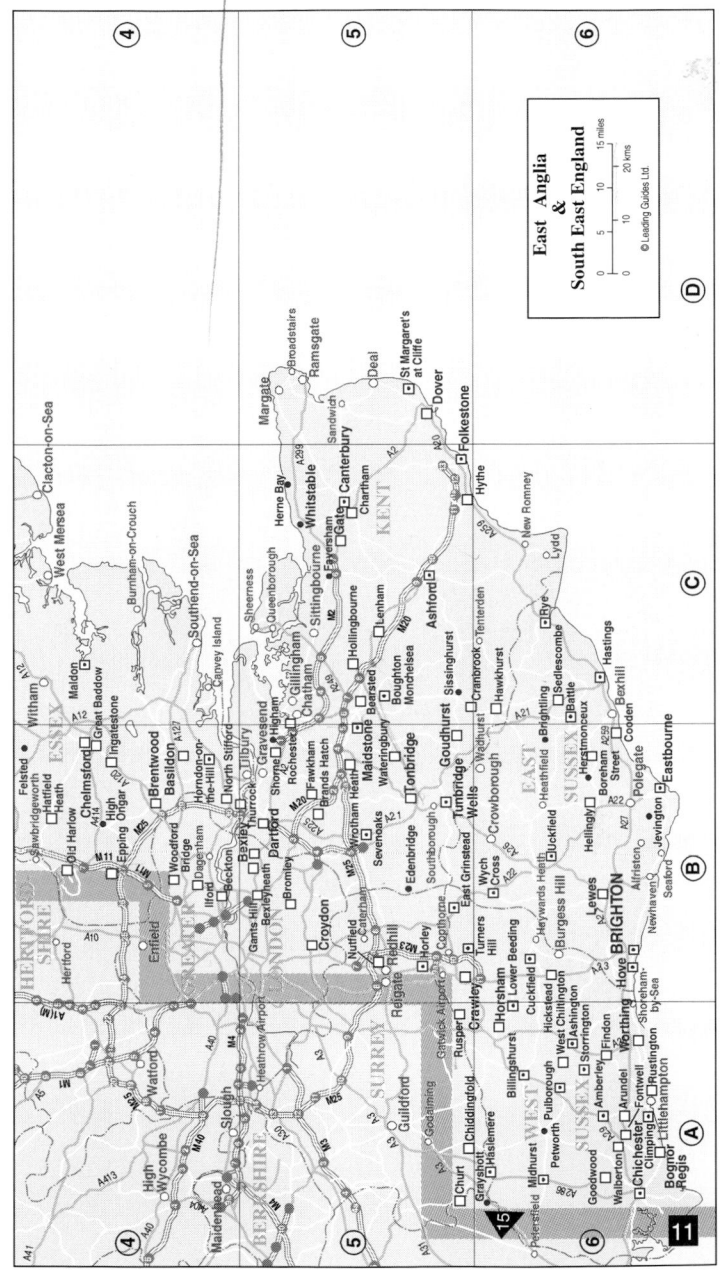

East Anglia
&
South East England

© Leading Guides Ltd

| 0 | 5 | 10 | 15 miles |
| 0 | 10 | 20 kms |

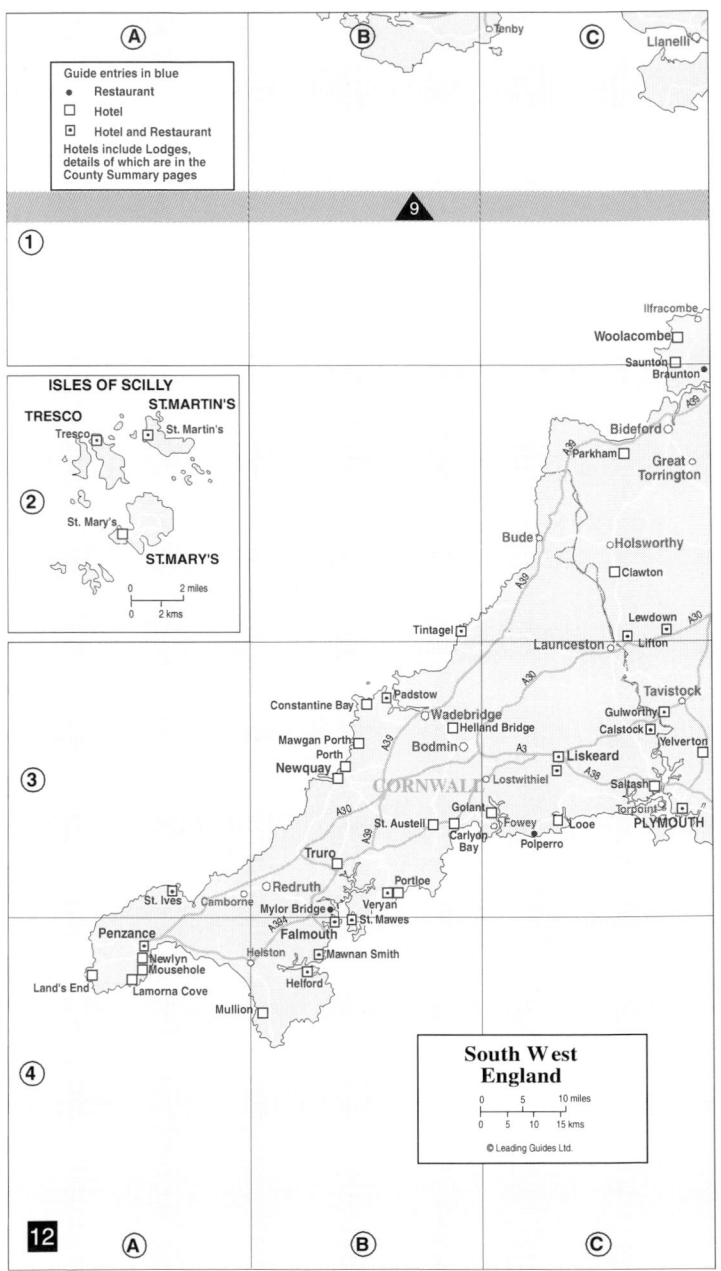

Guide entries in blue
• Restaurant
□ Hotel
⊡ Hotel and Restaurant
Hotels include Lodges,
details of which are in the
County Summary pages

Ⓐ
Ⓑ
Ⓒ

①
②
③
④

9

Tenby
Llanelli
Ilfracombe
Woolacombe
Saunton
Braunton
Bideford
Parkham
Great
Torrington
Bude
Holsworthy
Clawton
Lewdown
Tintagel
Launceston
Lifton
Tavistock
Padstow
Constantine Bay
Wadebridge
Gulworthy
Helland Bridge
Calstock
Mawgan Porth
Bodmin
Yelverton
Porth
Liskeard
Newquay
Saltash
CORNWALL
Lostwithiel
Torpoint
Golant
PLYMOUTH
St. Austell
Fowey
Looe
Carlyon
Bay
Polperro
Truro
Portloe
Redruth
Veryan
St. Ives
Camborne
Mylor Bridge
St. Mawes
Penzance
Falmouth
Helston
Mawnan Smith
Newlyn
Mousehole
Helford
Land's End
Lamorna Cove
Mullion

ISLES OF SCILLY
ST.MARTIN'S
TRESCO
TRESCO
St. Martin's
St. Mary's
ST.MARY'S
0   2 miles
0   2 kms

South West
England
0   5   10 miles
0   5   10   15 kms
© Leading Guides Ltd.

12
Ⓐ
Ⓑ
Ⓒ

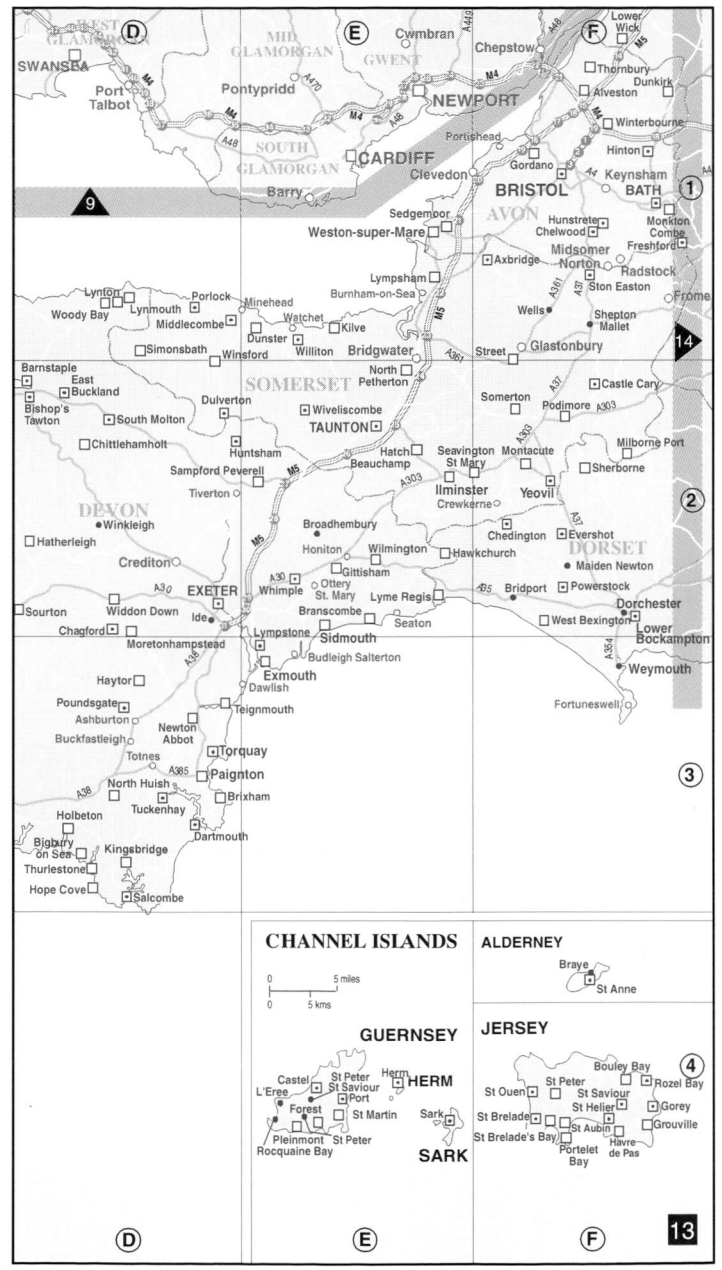

D **E** **F**

WEST GLAMORGAN
MID GLAMORGAN
GWENT

SWANSEA
Port Talbot
Cwmbran
Chepstow
Lower Wick
Thornbury
Dunkirk
Alveston

Pontypridd
NEWPORT
Winterbourne

Portishead
Hinton

SOUTH GLAMORGAN
CARDIFF
Clevedon
Gordano
Keynsham
BATH

Barry
BRISTOL
AVON
1

9
Sedgemoor
Weston-super-Mare
Hunstrete
Chelwood
Monkton Combe
Freshford

Axbridge
Midsomer Norton
Radstock
Ston Easton
Frome

Lynton
Porlock
Lympsham
Burnham-on-Sea
Wells
Shepton Mallet
14

Woody Bay
Lynmouth
Minehead
Middlecombe
Watchet
Kilve

Simonsbath
Dunster
Williton
Bridgwater
Street
Glastonbury

Barnstaple
Winsford
North Petherton
Castle Cary

East Buckland
SOMERSET
Somerton
Podimore
Milborne Port

Bishop's Tawton
Dulverton
Wiveliscombe
TAUNTON
Seavington
St Mary
Montacute
Sherborne

South Molton
Huntsham
Hatch Beauchamp
Ilminster
Yeovil

Chittlehamholt
Sampford Peverell
Crewkerne

DEVON
Tiverton
Broadhembury
Chedington
Evershot
DORSET

Winkleigh
Honiton
Wilmington
Hawkchurch
Maiden Newton

Hatherleigh
Crediton
Gittisham
Ottery St. Mary
Lyme Regis
Bridport
Powerstock
Dorchester

Sourton
EXETER
Whimple
Branscombe
Seaton
West Bexington
Lower Bockampton

Chagford
Widdon Down
Ide
Lympstone
Sidmouth

Moretonhampstead
Budleigh Salterton
Weymouth

Haytor
Exmouth
Dawlish
Fortuneswell

Poundsgate
Teignmouth

Ashburton
Newton Abbot

Buckfastleigh
Torquay

Totnes
Paignton

North Huish
Brixham

Holbeton
Tuckenhay
Dartmouth

Bigbury on Sea
Kingsbridge

Thurlestone
Hope Cove
Salcombe

3

CHANNEL ISLANDS

0 — 5 miles
0 — 5 kms

ALDERNEY

Braye
St Anne

GUERNSEY

JERSEY
4

Castel
St Peter
Herm
HERM
Bouley Bay
Rozel Bay

L'Eree
St Saviour
Port

St Ouen
St Peter
St Saviour

Forest
St Martin
St Helier
Gorey

Sark
St Brelade
St Aubin
Grouville

Pleinmont
St Peter
St Brelade's Bay
Portelet Bay
Havre de Pas

Rocquaine Bay
SARK

D **E** **F** **13**

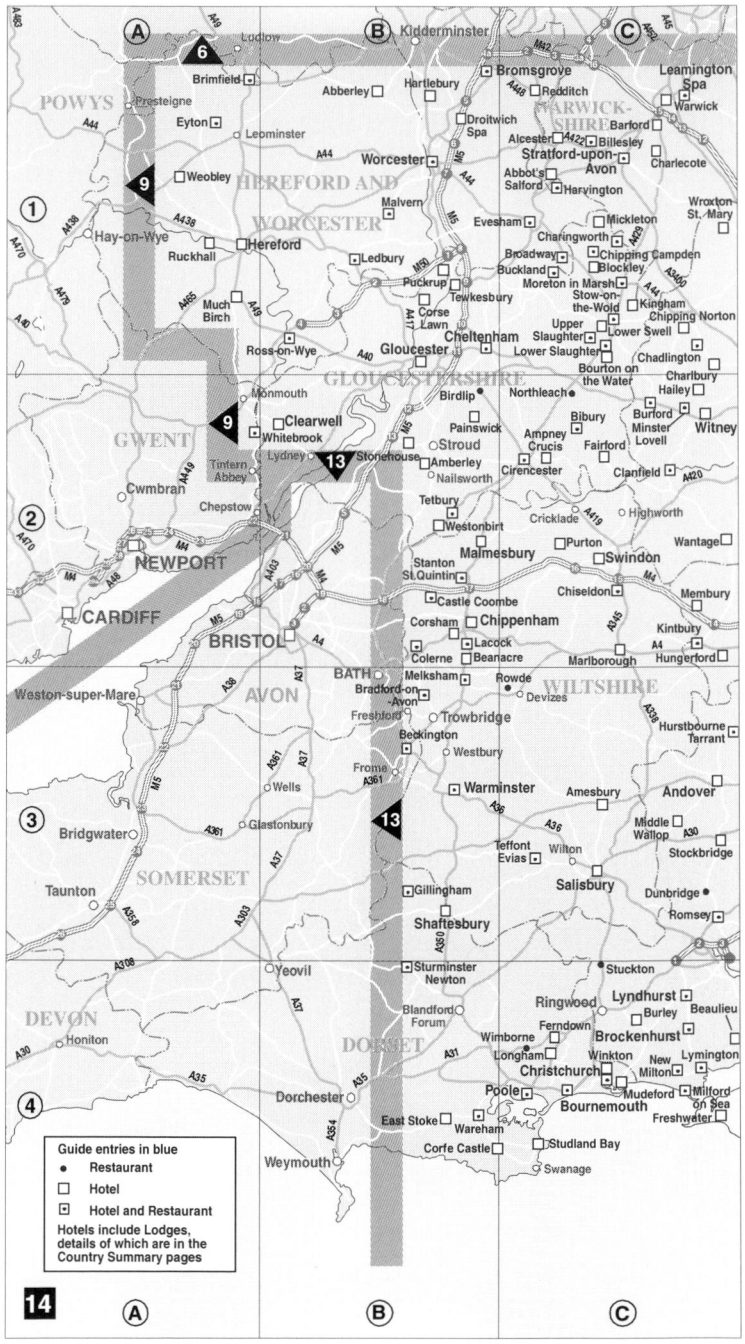

Guide entries in blue

- • Restaurant
- □ Hotel
- ⊡ Hotel and Restaurant

Hotels include Lodges,
details of which are in the
Country Summary pages

14

A   B   C

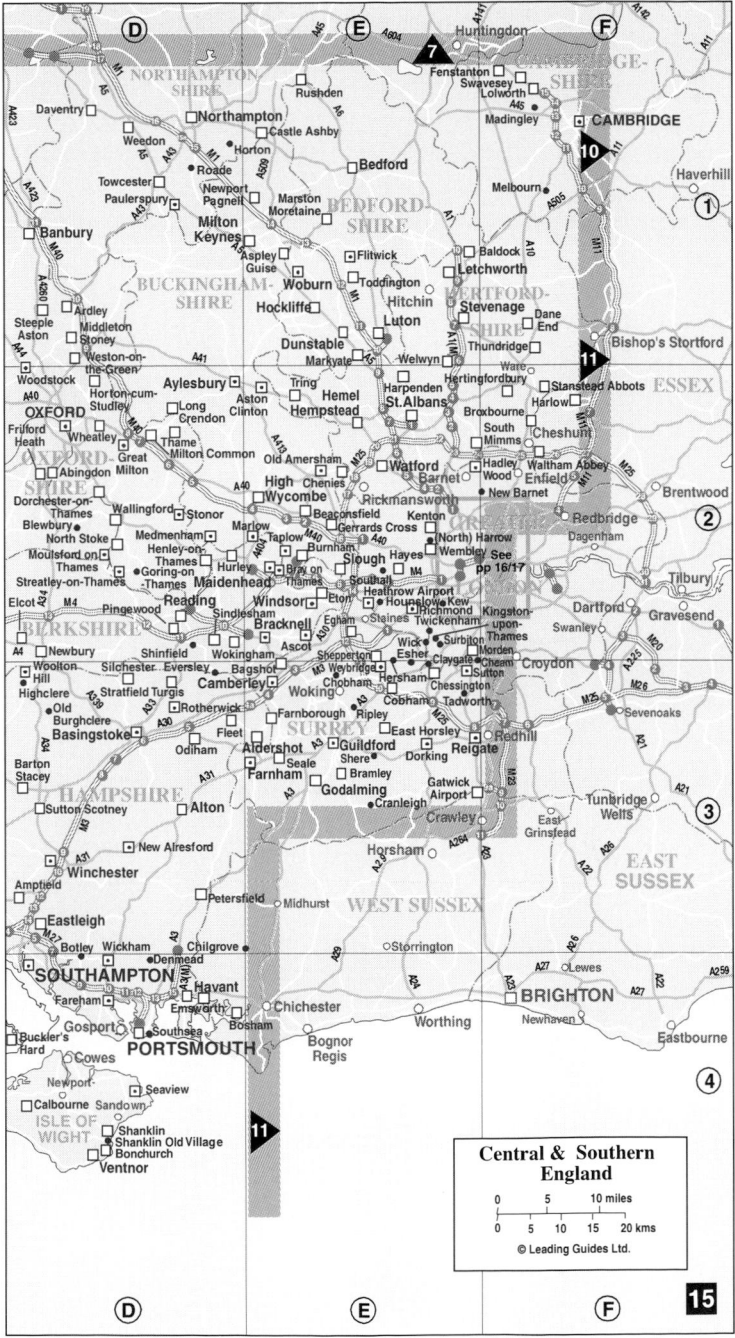

Central & Southern England

0   5   10 miles
0   5   10   15   20 kms

© Leading Guides Ltd.

15

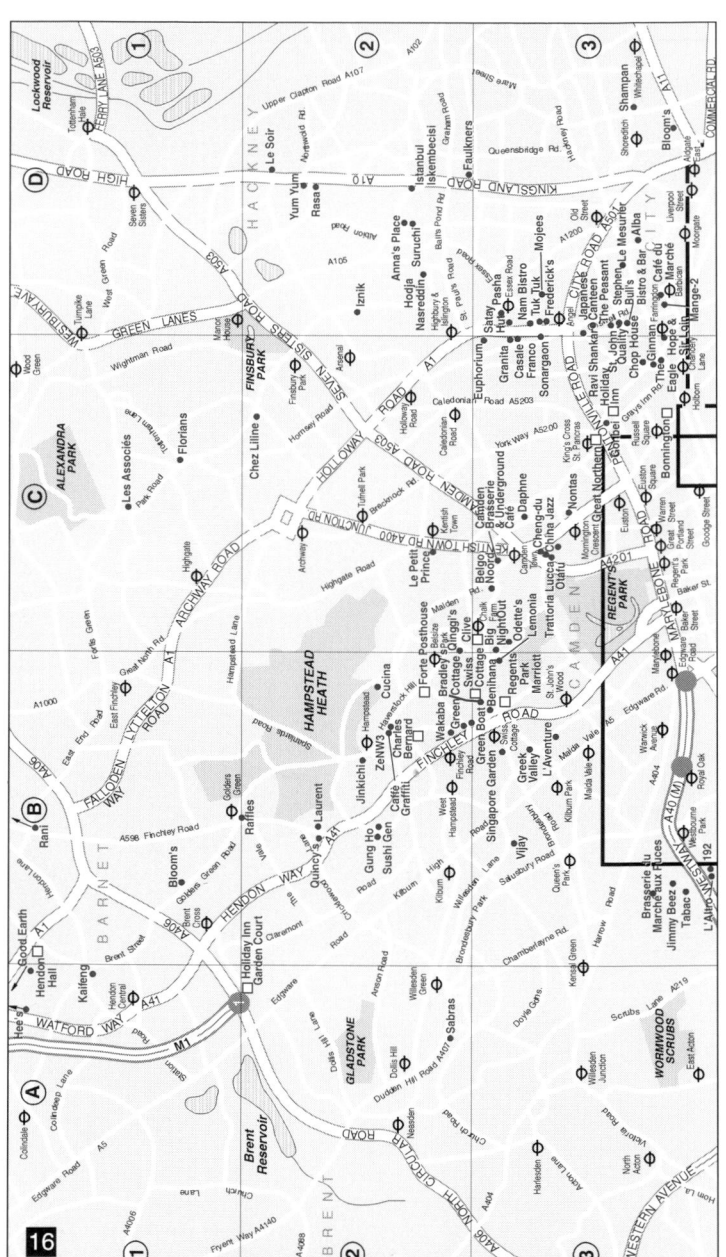

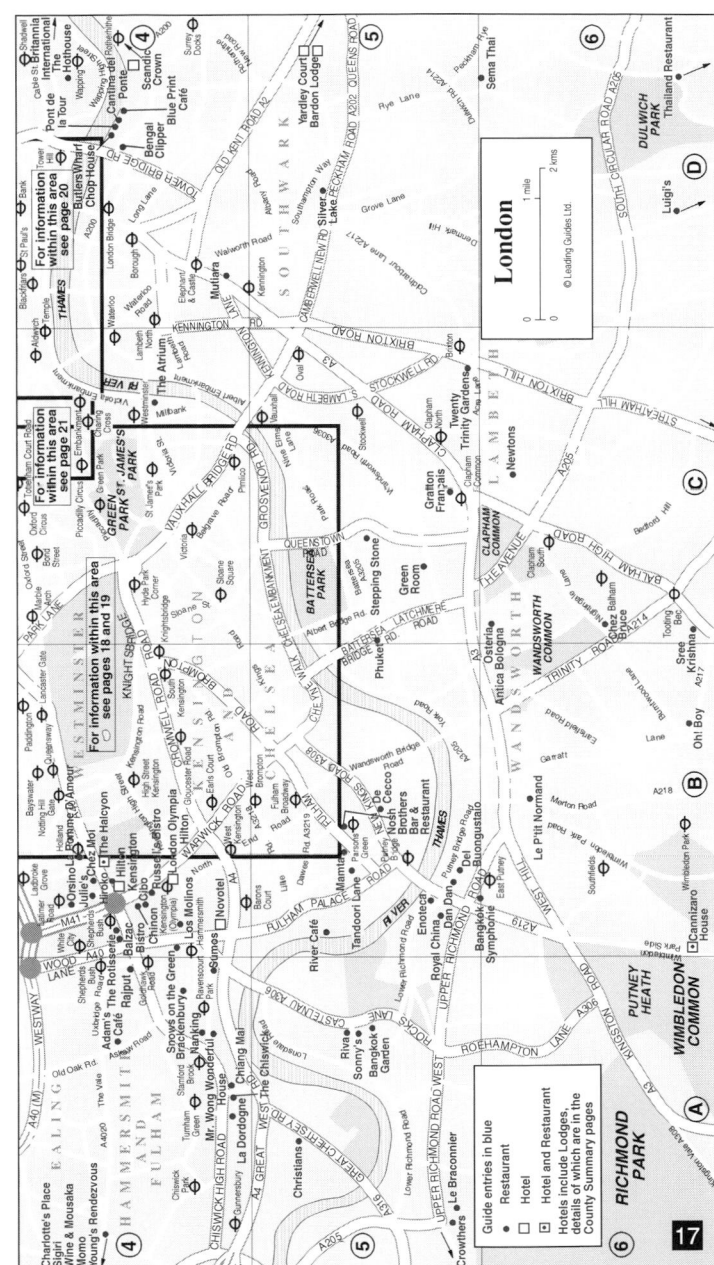

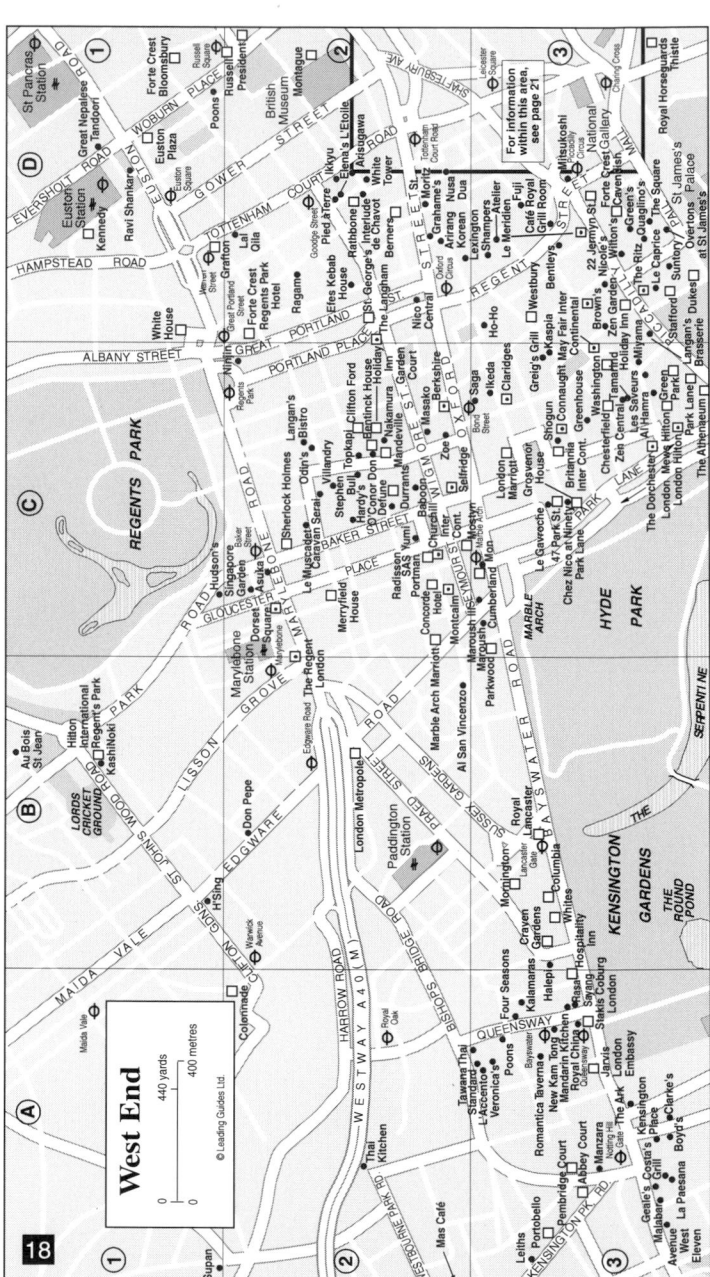

West End

0 440 yards
0 400 metres

© Leading Guides Ltd.

18

For information within this area, see page 21

REGENTS PARK

HYDE PARK

KENSINGTON

THE ROUND POND

KENSINGTON GARDENS

THE SERPENTINE

LORDS CRICKET GROUND

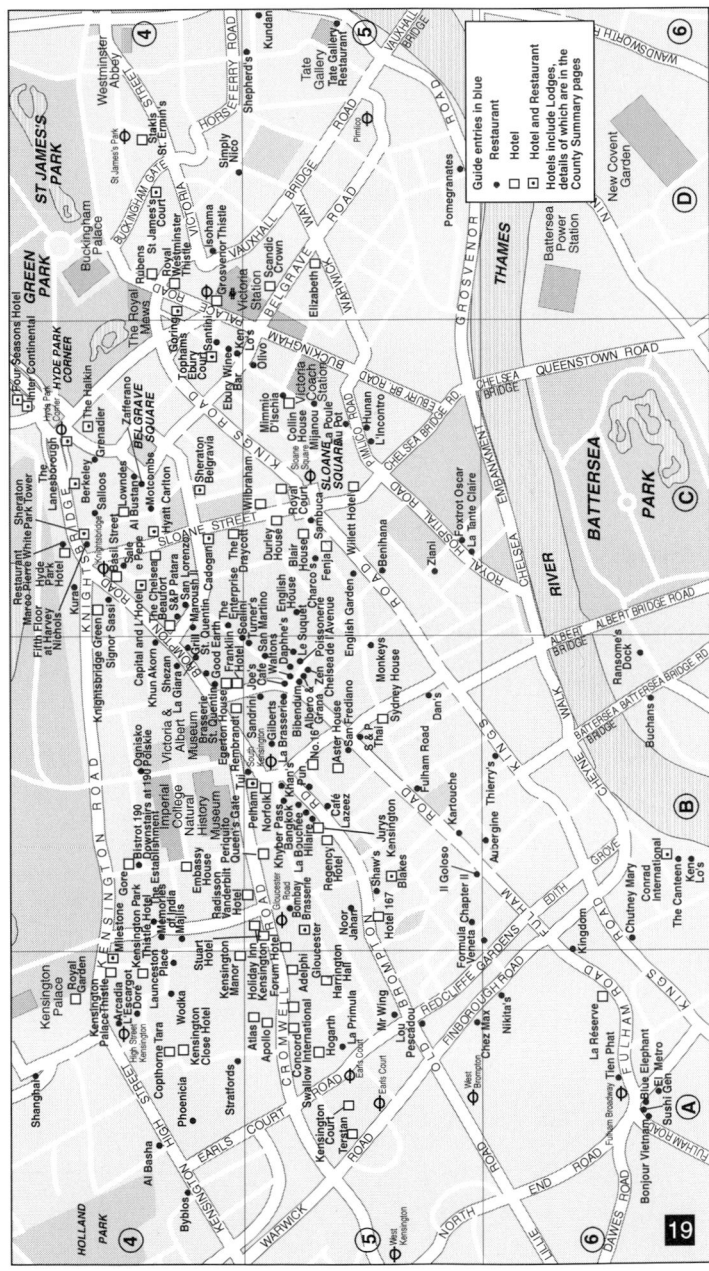

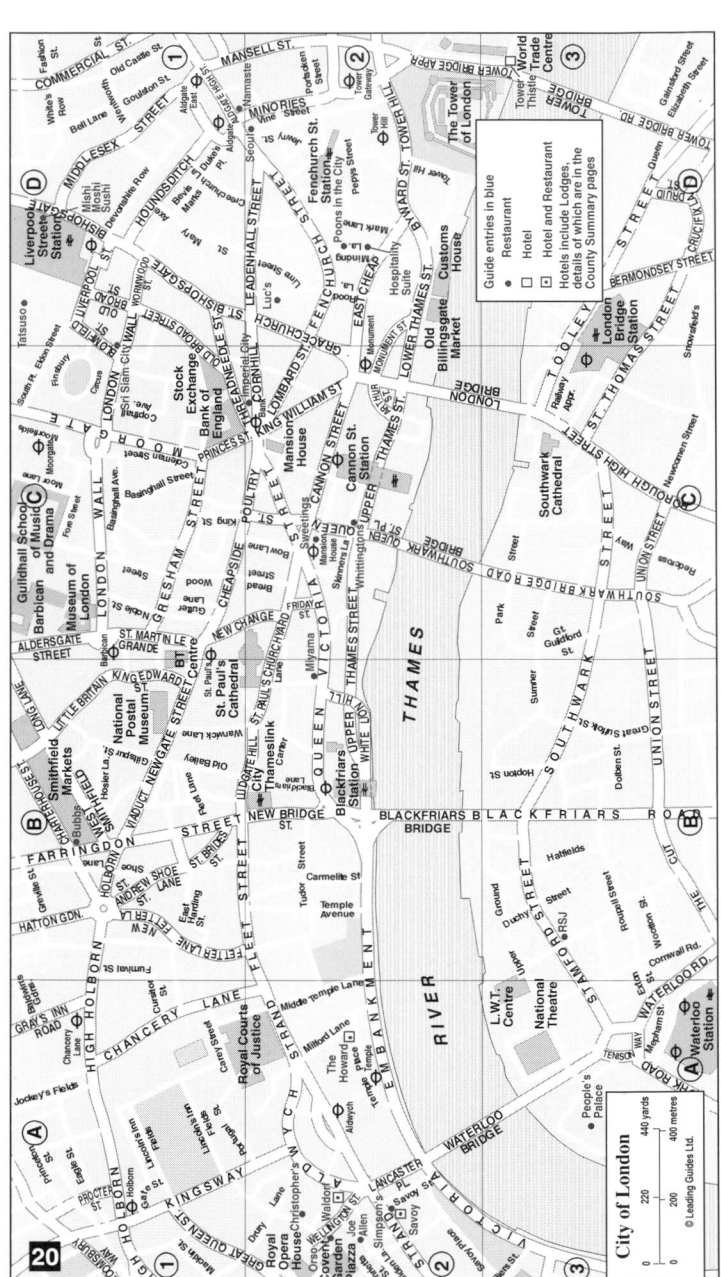

City of London

0   220   440 yards
0   200   400 metres

© Leading Guides Ltd.

Guide entries in blue

● Restaurant
□ Hotel
☒ Hotel and Restaurant

Hotels include Lodges, details of which are in the County Summary pages

20

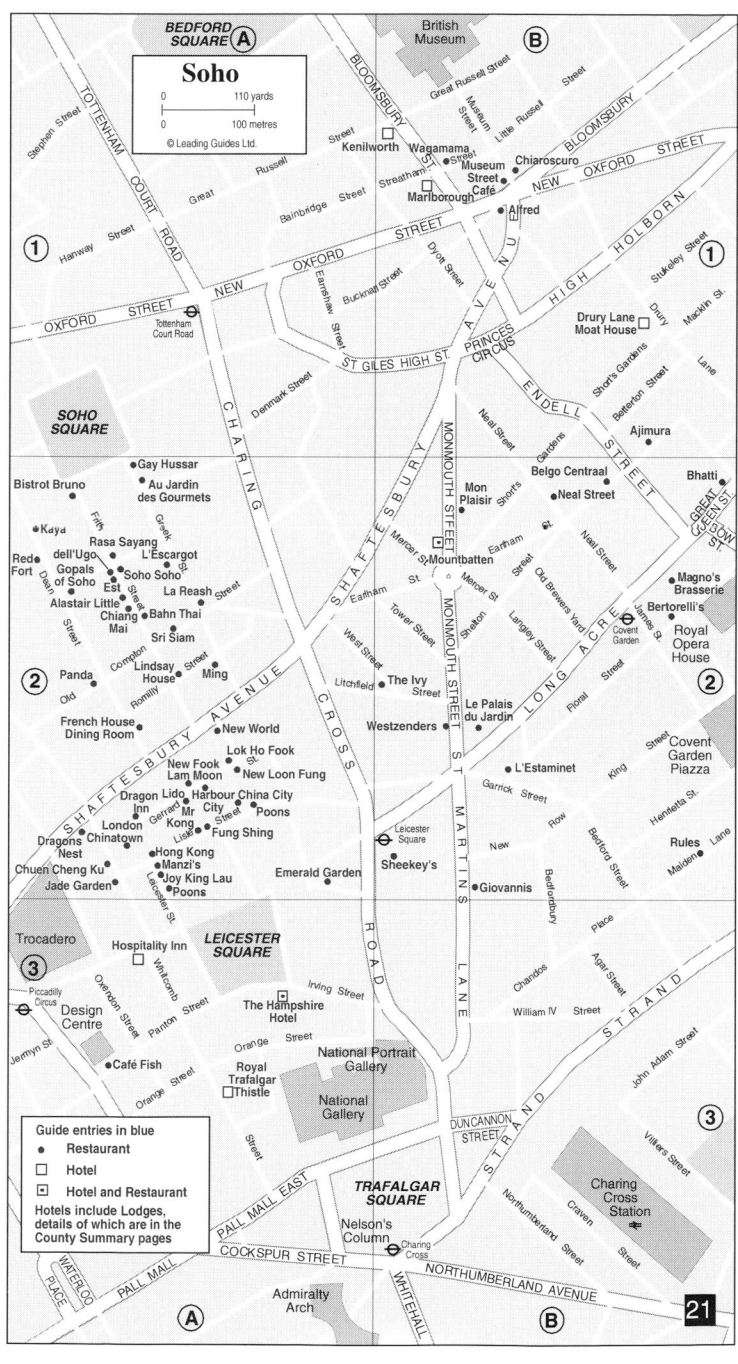

Soho

0   110 yards
0   100 metres
© Leading Guides Ltd.

BEDFORD SQUARE (A)

British Museum (B)

Tottenham Court Road

Stephen Street

Great Russell Street

Museum Street

Little Russel Street

BLOOMSBURY

Russell Street

Kenilworth

Wagamama
Museum Street Café
Marlborough
Streatham
Chiaroscuro
NEW OXFORD STREET

Bainbridge Street

Alfred

Hanway Street

OXFORD STREET

NEW OXFORD STREET

HIGH HOLBORN

Stukeley Street

Drury Lane

Mackin St.

(1)

OXFORD STREET
Tottenham Court Road

Bucknall Street

Earnshaw Street

Dyott Street

ST GILES HIGH ST.

PRINCES CIRCUS

Drury Lane Moat House

Short's Gardens

Betterton Street

Lane

SOHO SQUARE

Denmark Street

CHARING

SHAFTESBURY

ENDELL STREET

Neal Street

Gardens

Ajimura

Gay Hussar

Bistrot Bruno

Au Jardin des Gourmets

MONMOUTH STREET

Mon Plaisir

Belgo Centraal

Neal Street

Bhatti

GREAT QUEEN ST.

Kaya

Rasa Sayang

Red Fort

dell'Ugo

Gopals of Soho

L'Escargot

Soho Soho

Est

La Reash

Mercer St.

Mountbatten

Earlham

Old Brewers Yard

Magno's Brasserie

Bertorelli's

Alastair Little

Chiang Mai

Bahn Thai

Sri Siam

Mercer St.

Shelton

Langley Street

Covent Garden

Royal Opera House

Dean Street

Compton Street

Lindsay House

Ming

Tower Street

West Street

Floral

(2)

Panda

Old Compton

Romilly

Litchfield

The Ivy Street

Le Palais du Jardin

King

Covent Garden Piazza

French House Dining Room

New World

CHARING CROSS

Westzenders

ST MARTIN'S LANE

Garrick Street

Henrietta St.

New Fook

Lam Moon

Lok Ho Fook

New Loon Fung

L'Estaminet

Row

Bedford Street

Rules

Maiden

Dragon Lido

Gerrard

Harbour China City

Mr City

Poons

London Chinatown

Inn Kong

Lisle

Fung Shing

Leicester Square

New

Dragons Nest

Hong Kong

Manzi's

Chuen Cheng Ku

Joy King Lau

Jade Garden

Leicester St.

Poons

Emerald Garden

Sheekey's

Giovannis

Bedfordbury

Trocadero

Hospitality Inn

LEICESTER SQUARE

ROAD

Chandos

Agar Street

STRAND

(3)

Piccadilly Circus

Design Centre

Oxendon Street

Whitcomb Street

Panton Street

Irving Street

The Hampshire Hotel

William IV Street

John Adam Street

Jermyn St.

Café Fish

Orange Street

Royal Trafalgar Thistle

Orange Street

National Portrait Gallery

National Gallery

DUNCANNON STREET

STRAND

Villiers Street

Charing Cross Station

(3)

Guide entries in blue
● Restaurant
□ Hotel
⊡ Hotel and Restaurant

Hotels include Lodges, details of which are in the County Summary pages

WATERLOO PLACE

PALL MALL

PALL MALL EAST

COCKSPUR STREET

TRAFALGAR SQUARE

Nelson's Column

Charing Cross

NORTHUMBERLAND AVENUE

WHITEHALL

Northumberland Street

Craven Street

Admiralty Arch

(A)

(B)

21

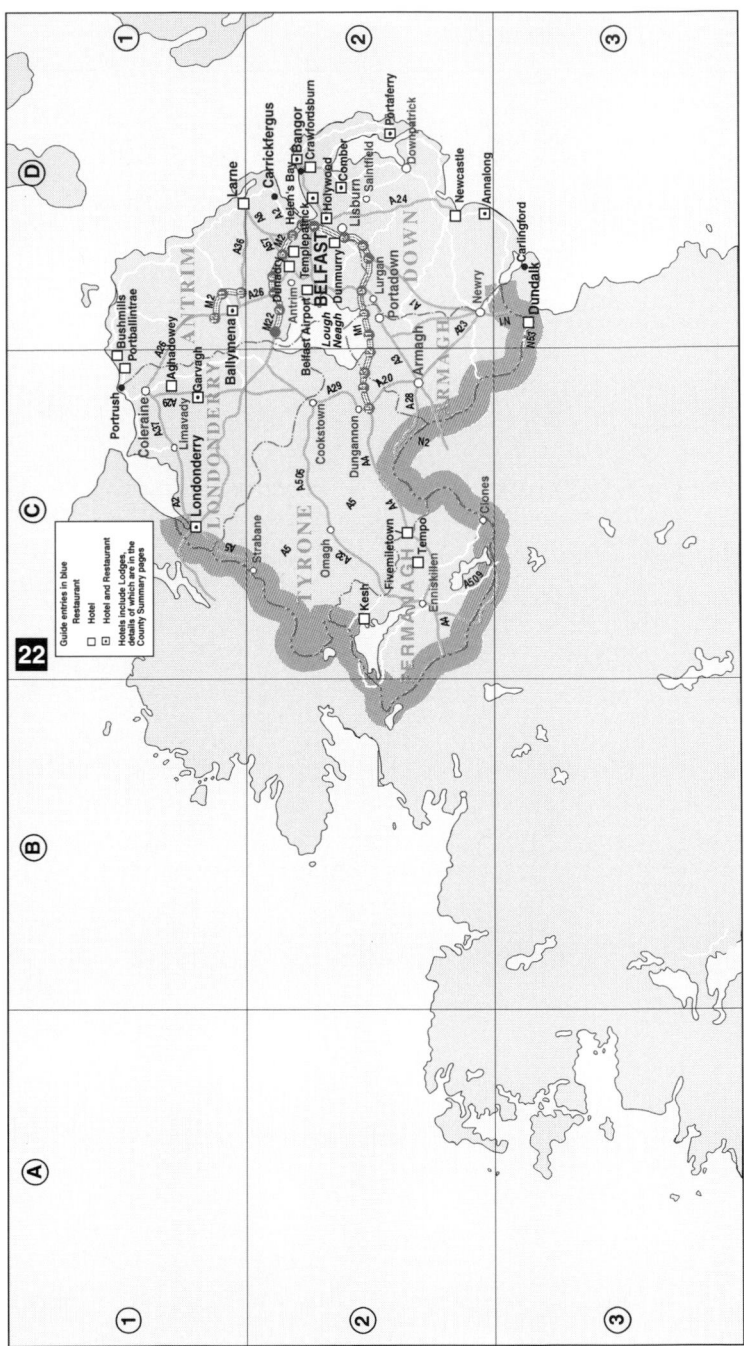

22

Guide entries in blue
□ Restaurant
□ Hotel
□ Hotel and Restaurant

Hotels include Lodges,
details of which are in the
County Summary pages

READERS' COMMENTS

Please use this sheet, and the continuation overleaf, to recommend hotels and restaurants of **really outstanding quality** and to comment on existing entries.

Complaints about any of the Guide's entries will be treated seriously and passed on to our inspectorate, but we would like to remind you always to take up your complaint with the management at the time.

We regret that owing to the volume of readers' communications received each year, we will be unable to acknowledge all these forms, but they will certainly be seriously considered.

Please post to:

Egon Ronay's Guides, 35 Tadema Road, London SW10 0PZ

Please use an up-to-date Guide. We publish annually. (H&R 1996)

Name and address of establishment   **Your recommendation or complaint**

Name and address of establishment   **Your recommendation or complaint**

Your Name (BLOCK LETTERS PLEASE)

Address

Telephone

READERS' COMMENTS

Please use this sheet, and the continuation overleaf, to recommend hotels and restaurants of **really outstanding quality** and to comment on existing entries.

Complaints about any of the Guide's entries will be treated seriously and passed on to our inspectorate, but we would like to remind you always to take up your complaint with the management at the time.

We regret that owing to the volume of readers' communications received each year, we will be unable to acknowledge all these forms, but they will certainly be seriously considered.

Please post to:

Egon Ronay's Guides, 35 Tadema Road, London SW10 0PZ

Please use an up-to-date Guide. We publish annually. (H&R 1996)

Name and address of establishment   **Your recommendation or complaint**

Name and address of establishment   **Your recommendation or complaint**

Your Name (BLOCK LETTERS PLEASE)

Address

Telephone

READERS' COMMENTS

Please use this sheet, and the continuation overleaf, to recommend hotels and restaurants of **really outstanding quality** and to comment on existing entries.

Complaints about any of the Guide's entries will be treated seriously and passed on to our inspectorate, but we would like to remind you always to take up your complaint with the management at the time.

We regret that owing to the volume of readers' communications received each year, we will be unable to acknowledge all these forms, but they will certainly be seriously considered.

Please post to:

Egon Ronay's Guides, 35 Tadema Road, London SW10 0PZ

Please use an up-to-date Guide. We publish annually. (H&R 1996)

Name and address of establishment   **Your recommendation or complaint**

Name and address of establishment   **Your recommendation or complaint**

_____   _____

_____   _____

_____   _____

_____   _____

_____   _____

_____   _____

_____   _____

_____   _____

_____   _____

_____   _____

_____   _____

_____   _____

_____   _____

_____   _____

_____   _____

_____   _____

_____   _____

_____   _____

_____   _____

Your Name (BLOCK LETTERS PLEASE)
_____

Address
_____

_____

Telephone
_____

READERS' COMMENTS

Please use this sheet, and the continuation overleaf, to recommend hotels and restaurants of **really outstanding quality** and to comment on existing entries.

Complaints about any of the Guide's entries will be treated seriously and passed on to our inspectorate, but we would like to remind you always to take up your complaint with the management at the time.

We regret that owing to the volume of readers' communications received each year, we will be unable to acknowledge all these forms, but they will certainly be seriously considered.

Please post to:

Egon Ronay's Guides, 35 Tadema Road, London SW10 0PZ

Please use an up-to-date Guide. We publish annually. (H&R 1996)

Name and address of establishment   **Your recommendation or complaint**

Name and address of establishment

Your recommendation or complaint

_____   _____

_____   _____

_____   _____

_____   _____

_____   _____

_____   _____

_____   _____

_____   _____

_____   _____

_____   _____

_____   _____

_____   _____

_____   _____

_____   _____

_____   _____

_____   _____

_____   _____

Your Name (BLOCK LETTERS PLEASE)
_____

Address
_____

_____

_____

Telephone
_____

Index